AMERICA ON WHEELS

Mid-Atlantic

DELAWARE, DISTRICT OF COLUMBIA, MARYLAND, NEW JERSEY, PENNSYLVANIA, VIRGINIA, AND WEST VIRGINIA

MACMILLAN • USA

Frommer's America on Wheels: Mid-Atlantic

Regional Editor: Tom Dove
Editorial Assistant: Pamela C Dove

Contributors: Matthew Bailey, Kathleen Bennett, Eugene Busnar, Jayne Clark, Lisa Dallyn, David DeKok, Pamela C Dove, Terry Fallon, Mary Ann Fusco, Carol Gallant, Ed Hitzel, Earlyne Leary, Thomas Lehman, Jacob List, Nancy List, Jennifer Loch, Shirley Longshore, Teresa A Lynch, Chris McCammon, Colleen Mogil, Andre Namenek, Catherine Namenek, Ellen Noel, Max Parrish, Kent Steinriede, Laura Troy, Nancy Wilkerson, Sharon Wilson

Inspections Coordinator: Laura Van Zee

Frommer's America on Wheels Staff
Project Director: Gretchen Henderson
Senior Editor: Christopher Hollander
Database Editor: Melissa Klurman
Assistant Editor: Marian Cole
Editorial Assistant: Tracy McNamara

Design by Michele Laseau
Driving the State maps for New Jersey and Pennsylvania by Raffaele DeGennaro

Macmillan Travel
A Simon & Schuster Macmillan Company
1633 Broadway
New York, NY 10019-6785

Find us online at **http://www.mgr.com/travel** or on America Online at keyword Frommer's.

MACMILLAN is a registered trademark of Macmillan, Inc.

Manufactured in the United States of America

ISSN: 1079-3585
ISBN: 0-02-861110-1

SPECIAL SALES
Bulk purchases (10+ copies) of Frommer's and selected Macmillan travel guides are available to corporations, organizations, mail-order catalogs, institutions, and charities at special discounts, and can be customized to suit individual needs. For more information write to Special Sales, Macmillan General Reference, 1633 Broadway, New York, NY 10019.

Contents

Introduction

America on Wheels introduces a brand-new lodgings rating system—one that factors in the latest trends in travel preferences, technologies, and amenities and is based on thorough inspections by experienced travel professionals. We rate establishments from one to five flags, plus a unique rating we call Ultra, a special award reserved for only a handful of outstanding properties in each category. Our restaurant selections represent the ethnic diversity of today's dining scene and are categorized with symbols according to their special features, ambience, and services available. In addition, the series provides in-depth sightseeing information, including driving tours and best-of-the-state highlights.

State Introductions

Coverage of each state in the *America on Wheels* series begins with background information that will help familiarize you with your destination. Included is a summary of the state's history and an overview of its geography, followed by practical tips that we hope you will find useful in planning your trip—what kind of weather to expect, what to pack, sources of information within the state, driving rules and regulations, and other essentials.

The "Best of the State" section provides you with a rundown of the top sights and attractions and the most popular festivals and special events around the state. It also includes information on spectator sports and an A-to-Z list of recreational activities available to you.

Driving Tours

The scenic driving tours included guide you along some of the most popular sightseeing routes. Every tour is keyed to a map and includes mileage information and precise directions, refreshment stops, and, for longer tours, recommended places to stay.

The Listings

The city-by-city listings of lodgings, dining establishments, and attractions together make up the bulk of the book. Cities are organized alphabetically within each state. You will find a brief description or "profile" for most cities, including a source to contact for additional information. Any listings will follow.

TYPES OF LODGINGS

Here's how we define the lodging categories used in *America on Wheels*.

Hotel

A hotel usually has three or more floors with elevators. It may or may not have parking, but if it does, entry to the guest rooms is likely to be through the lobby rather than directly from the parking lot. A range of lodgings is available (such as standard rooms, deluxe rooms, and suites), and a range of services is available (such as bellhops, room service, and a concierge). Many hotels have a restaurant or coffee shop open for breakfast, lunch, and dinner; they may have a cocktail lounge/bar. Recreational facilities may be available (such as a swimming pool, fitness center, and tennis courts).

Motel

A motel usually has one to three floors, and many of the guest rooms have doors facing the parking lot or outdoor corridors. A motel may only have a small, serviceable lobby and usually offers only limited services; the nearest restaurant may be down the street. A motel is most likely to be located alongside a highway or in a resort area.

Inn

An inn is a small-scale hotel or lodge, usually in an older building that may or may not have been designed for lodgings, and it is often located in scenic surroundings. An inn should have a warm, welcoming atmosphere, with a more homelike quality to its furnishings and facilities. The guest rooms may be individually decorated in a style appropriate to the inn's age and location, and the rooms may or may not have telephones, televisions, or private bathrooms. An inn usually has a lounge or sitting room for guests (with parlor games and perhaps a television) and a small dining room that may or may not be open to the public. Breakfast, however, is almost always served.

Lodge

A lodge is essentially a small hotel in a rural, remote, or mountainous location. The atmosphere, service, and furniture may be more casual than you'd find in a regular hotel, and there may not be televisions or telephones in every guest room. The facilities usually include a coffee shop or restaurant, bar or cocktail lounge, games room, and indoor or outdoor swimming pool or hot tub. In ski areas, the lounge usually has a fireplace and facilities for storing ski gear.

Resort

A resort usually has more extensive facilities and recreational activities than a hotel, and offers three meals a day. The atmosphere is generally more informal than at comparable hotels.

HOW THE LODGINGS ARE RATED

Every hotel, motel, resort, inn, and lodge rated in this series has been subjected to a thorough hands-on inspection by our team of accomplished travel professionals. We ask the kinds of questions that readers would ask if they could inspect the rooms in advance for themselves (How good is the sound-proofing? How firm is the bed? What condition are the room furnishings in?). Then all of the inspection reports are reviewed by regional editors who are experts on their territories. The top-rated properties are then rechecked by a special consultant who has been reviewing and critiquing luxury hotels around the world for almost 25 years. *Establishments are not charged to be included in our series.*

Our ratings are based on *average* guest rooms—not lavish suites or concierge floors—so they're not artificially high. Therefore, in some cases a hotel rated four flags may indeed have individual rooms or suites that might fall into the five-flag category; conversely, a four-flag hotel may have a few rooms in its lowest price range that might otherwise warrant three flags.

The detailed ratings vary by category of lodgings —for example, the criteria imposed on a hotel are more rigorous than those for a motel—and some features that are considered essential in, for example, a four-flag city hotel are relaxed for a resort that offers alternative attractions, sporting facilities, and/or beautiful and spacious grounds. Likewise, amenities such as telephones and televisions—essential in hotels and motels—are not required in inns, whose guests are often seeking peace and quiet. Instead, the criteria take into account such features as individually decorated rooms and complimentary afternoon tea.

There are, of course, several basic attributes that apply to all lodgings across the board: the cleanliness and maintenance of the building as a whole; the housekeeping in individual rooms; safety, both indoors and out; the quality and practicality of the furnishings; the quality and availability of the amenities; the caliber of the facilities; the extent and/or condition of the grounds; the ambience and cleanliness in the dining rooms; and the caliber and professionalism of the service in relation to the rates and types of lodging. Since the *America on Wheels* rating system is highly rigorous, just because a property has garnered only one flag does not mean it is inadequate or substandard.

WHAT THE INDIVIDUAL RATINGS MEAN

⬚ One Flag

These properties have met or surpassed the minimum requirements of cleanliness, safety, convenience, and amenities. The staff may be limited, but guests can generally expect a friendly, hospitable greeting. Rooms will have basic amenities, such as air conditioning or heating where appropriate, telephones, and televisions. The bathrooms may have only showers rather than tubs, and just one towel for each guest, but showers and towels must be clean. The one-flag properties are by no means places to avoid, since they can represent exceptional value.

⬚⬚ Two Flags

In addition to having all of the basic attributes of one-flag lodgings, these properties will have some extra amenities, such as bellhops to help with the luggage, ice buckets in each room, and better-quality furnishings. Some extra services may include availability of cribs and irons, and wake-up service.

⬚⬚⬚ Three Flags

These properties have all the basics noted above but also offer a more generous complement of amenities, such as firmer beds, larger desks, more drawer space, extra blankets and pillows, cable or satellite TV, alarm clock/radios, room service (although hours may be limited), and dry cleaning and/or laundry services.

≣≣≣≣ Four Flags

This is the realm of luxury, with refinements in amenities, furnishings, and service—such as larger rooms, more dependable soundproofing, two telephones per room, in-room movies, in-room safes, thick towels, hair dryers, twice-daily maid service, turndown service, concierge service, and 24-hour room service.

≣≣≣≣≣ Five Flags

These properties have everything the four-flag properties have, plus a more personal level of service and more sumptuous amenities, among them bathrobes, superior linens, and blackout drapes for lightproofing. Facilities normally include a business center and fitness center. Generally speaking, guests pay handsomely to stay in these properties.

◊ Ultra

This crème-de-la-crème rating is reserved for those rare hotels and resorts, possibly also motels and inns, that are truly outstanding in every or almost every department—places with a "grand hotel" presence, an almost flawless level of service, and a standard of dining equal to that of the finest restaurants.

UNRATED

In the few cases where an inspector was not able to make a detailed inspection, the property is listed as unrated. Also, in some cases where a property was in the process of changing owners or managers, or if the property was undergoing the kind of major renovations that made formal evaluation impossible, then, again, it is listed as unrated.

TYPES OF DINING

Restaurant

A restaurant serves complete meals and almost always offers seating.

Refreshment Stop

A refreshment stop serves drinks and/or snacks only (such as an ice cream parlor, bakery, or coffee bar) and may or may not have seating available.

HOW THE RESTAURANTS WERE EVALUATED

All of the restaurants reviewed in this series have been through the kind of thorough inspection described above for lodgings. Our inspectors have evaluated everything from freshness of ingredients to noise level and spacing of tables.

Unique to the *America on Wheels* series are the easy-to-read symbols that identify a restaurant's special features, its ambience, and special services. (See the inside front cover for the key to all symbols.) With them you can determine at a glance whether a place is a local favorite, offers exceptional value, or is "worth a splurge."

HOW TO READ THE LISTINGS

LODGINGS

Introductory Information

The rating is followed by the establishment's name, address, neighborhood (if applicable), telephone number(s), and fax number (if there is one). Where appropriate, location information is provided. In the resort listings, the acreage of the property is indicated. Also included are our inspector's comments, which provide some description and discuss any outstanding features or special information about the establishment. You can also find out whether an inn is unsuitable for children, and if so, up to what age.

Rooms

Specifics the number and type of accommodations available. If a hotel has an "executive level," this will be noted here. (This level, sometimes called a "concierge floor," is a special area of a hotel. Usually priced higher than standard rooms, accommodations at this level are often larger and have additional amenities and services such as daily newspaper delivery and nightly turndown service. Guests staying in these rooms often have access to a private lounge where complimentary breakfasts or snacks may be served.) Check-in/check-out times will also appear in this section, followed by information on the establishment's smoking policy ("No smoking" for properties that are entirely nonsmoking, and "Nonsmoking rms avail" for those that permit smoking in some areas but have rooms available for nonsmokers). This information may be followed by comments, if the inspector noted anything in particular about the guest rooms, such as their size, decor, furnishings, or window views.

Amenities

If the following amenities are available in the majority of the guest rooms, they are indicated by symbols (see inside front cover for key) or included in a list: telephone, alarm clock, coffeemaker, hair dryer, air conditioning, TV (including cable or satellite hook-up, free or pay movies), refrigerator, dataport (for fax/modem communication), VCR, CD/tape player, voice mail, in-room safe, and bathrobes. If some or all rooms have minibars, terraces, fireplaces, or whirlpools, that will be indicated here. Because travelers usually expect air conditioning, telephones, and televisions in their guest rooms, we specifically note when those amenities are not available. If any additional amenities are available in the majority of the guest rooms, or if amenities are outstanding in any way, the inspector's comments will provide some elaboration at the end of this section.

Services

If the following services are available, they are indicated by symbols (see inside front cover for key) or included in a list: room service (24-hour or limited), concierge, valet parking, airport transportation, dry cleaning/laundry, cribs available, pets allowed (call ahead before bringing your pet; an establishment that accepts pets may nevertheless place restrictions on the types or size of pets allowed, or may require a deposit and/or charge a fee), twice-daily maid service, car-rental desk, social director, masseur, children's program, babysitting (that is, the establishment can put you in touch with local babysitters and/or agencies), and afternoon tea and/or wine or sherry served. If the establishment offers any special services, or if the inspector has commented on the quality of services offered, that information will appear at the end of this section. Please note that there may be a fee for some services.

Facilities

If the following facilities are on the premises, they are indicated by symbols (see inside front cover for key) or included in a list: pool(s), bike rentals, boat rentals (may include canoes, kayaks, sailboats, powerboats, jet-skis, paddleboats), fishing, golf course (with number of holes), horseback riding, jogging path/parcourse (fitness trail), unlighted tennis courts (number available), lighted tennis courts (number available), waterskiing, windsurfing, fitness center, meeting facilities (and number of people this space can accommodate), business center, restaurant(s), bar(s), beach(es), lifeguard (for beach, not pool), basketball, volleyball, board surfing, games room, lawn games, racquetball, snorkeling, squash, spa, sauna, steam room, whirlpool, beauty salon, day-care center, playground, washer/dryer, and guest lounge (for inns only). If cross-country and downhill skiing facilities are located within 10 miles of the property, then that is indicated by symbols here as well. Our "Accessible for People With Disabilities" symbol appears where establishments claim to have guest rooms with such accessibility. If an establishment has additional facilities that are worth noting, or if the inspector has commented about the facilities, that information appears at the end of this section.

Rates

If the establishment's rates vary throughout the year, then the rates given are for the peak season. The rates listed are EP (no meals included), unless otherwise noted. We'll tell you if there is a charge for an extra person to stay in a room; if children stay free, and if so, up to what age; if there are minimum stay requirements; and if AP (three meals) and/or MAP (breakfast and dinner) rates are also available. The parking rates (if the establishment has parking) are followed by any comments the inspector has provided about rates.

If the establishment has a seasonal closing, this information will be stated. A list of credit cards accepted ends the listing.

DINING

Introductory Information

If a restaurant is a local favorite, an exceptional value (one with a high quality-to-price ratio for the area), or "worth a splurge" (more expensive by area standards, but well worth it), the appropriate symbol will appear at the beginning of the listing (see inside front cover for key to symbols). Then the establishment's name, address, neighborhood (if applicable), and telephone number are listed, followed by location information when appropriate. The type of cuisine appears in boldface type and is followed by our inspectors' comments on everything from decor and ambience to menu highlights.

The "FYI" Heading

"For your information," this section tells you the reservations policy ("recommended," "accepted," or "not accepted"), and whether there is live entertainment, a children's menu, or a dress code (jacket required or other policy). If the restaurant does not have a full bar, you can find out what the liquor policy is ("beer and wine only," "beer only," "wine only," "BYO," or "no liquor license"). This is also where you can check to see if there's a no-smoking policy for the entire restaurant (please note that smoking policies are in flux throughout the country; if smoking—or avoiding smokers—is important to you, it's a good idea to call ahead to verify the policy). If the restaurant is part of a group or chain, address and phone information will be provided for additional locations in the area. This section does not appear in Refreshment Stop listings.

Hours of Operation

Under the "Open" heading, "Peak" indicates that the hours listed are for high season only (dates in parentheses); otherwise, the hours listed apply year-round. If an establishment has a seasonal closing, that information will follow. It's a good idea to call ahead to confirm the hours of operation, especially in the off-season.

Prices

Prices given are for dinner main courses (unless otherwise noted). If a prix-fixe dinner is offered throughout dinner hours, that price is listed here, too. This section ends with a list of credit cards accepted. Refreshment Stop listings do not include prices.

Symbols

The symbols that fall at the end of many restaurant listings can help you find restaurants with the features that are important to you. If a restaurant has romantic ambience, historic ambience, outdoor dining, a fireplace, a view, delivery service, early-bird specials, valet parking, or is family-oriented, open 24 hours, or accessible to people with disabilities (meaning it has a level entrance or an access ramp, a doorway at least 36 inches wide, and restrooms that are on the same floor as the dining room, with doorways at least 36 inches wide and properly outfitted stalls), then these symbols will appear (see inside front cover for key to symbols).

ATTRACTIONS

Introductory Information

The name, street address, neighborhood (if located in a major city), and telephone number are followed by a brief rundown of the attraction's high points and key attributes so you can quickly determine if it's worth a full day of exploration or just a brief detour.

Hours of Operation & Admission

Service information includes hours of operation ("Peak" indicates that the hours listed are for high season only) and the cost of admission. The cost is

ABBREVIATIONS

A/C	air conditioning
AE	American Express (charge card)
AP	American Plan (rates include breakfast, lunch, and dinner)
avail	available
BB	Bed-and-Breakfast Plan (rates include full breakfast)
bkfst	breakfast
BYO	bring your own (beer or wine)
CC	credit cards
CI	check-in time
CO	check-out time
CP	Continental Plan (rates include continental breakfast)
ctr	center
D	double (indicates room rate for two people in one room (one or two beds))
DC	Diners Club (credit card)
DISC	Discover (credit card)
EC	EuroCard (credit card)
effic	efficiency (unit with cooking facilities)
ER	En Route (credit card)
info	information
int'l	international
JCB	Japanese Credit Bureau (credit card)
ltd	limited
MAP	Modified American Plan (rates include breakfast and dinner)
MC	MasterCard (credit card)
Mem Day	Memorial Day
mi	mile(s)
min	minimum
MM	mile marker
refrig	refrigerator
rms	rooms
S	single (indicates room rate for one person)
satel	satellite
stes	suites (rooms with separate living and sleeping areas)
svce	service
tel	telephone
V	Visa (credit card)
w/	with
wknds	weekends

indicated by one to four dollar signs (see inside front cover for key to symbols). It's a good idea to call ahead to confirm the hours.

SPECIAL INFORMATION

DISABLED TRAVELER INFORMATION

The Americans with Disabilities Act (ADA) of 1990 required that all public facilities and commercial establishments be made accessible to disabled persons by January 26, 1992. Any property opened after that date must be built in accordance with the ADA Accessible Guidelines. Note, however, that not all establishments have completed their renovations to conform with the law; be sure to call ahead to determine if your specific needs can be met.

TAXES

State and city taxes vary widely and are not included in the prices in this book. Always ask about the taxes when you are making your reservations. State sales tax is given under "Essentials" in the introduction to each state.

A DISCLAIMER

Readers are advised that prices fluctuate in the course of time, and travel information changes under the impact of the varied and volatile factors that affect the travel industry. The publisher cannot be held responsible for the experiences of readers while traveling. Readers are invited to send ideas, comments, and suggestions for future editions to: *America on Wheels,* Macmillan Travel, 1633 Broadway, New York, NY 10019-6785.

TOLL-FREE NUMBERS/WORLD WIDE WEB SITES

The following toll-free telephone numbers and URLs for World Wide Web sites were accurate at press time; *America on Wheels* cannot be held responsible for any number or address that has changed. The "TDD" numbers are answered by a telecommunications service for the deaf and hard-of-hearing. Be sure to dial "1" before each number.

LODGINGS

Best Western International, Inc
800/528-1234 North America
800/528-2222 TDD

Budgetel Inns
800/4-BUDGET Continental USA and Canada

Budget Host
800/BUD-HOST Continental USA

Clarion Hotels
800/CLARION Continental USA and Canada
800/228-3323 TDD
http://www.hotelchoice.com/cgi-bin/res/webres?clarion.html

Comfort Inns
800/228-5150 Continental USA and Canada
800/228-3323 TDD
http://www.hotelchoice.com/cgi-bin/res/webres?comfort.html

Courtyard by Marriott
800/321-2211 Continental USA and Canada
800/228-7014 TDD
http://www.marriott.com/lodging/courtyar.html

Days Inn
800/325-2525 Continental USA and Canada
800/325-3297 TDD
http://www.daysinn.com/daysinn.html

DoubleTree Hotels
800/222-TREE Continental USA and Canada
800/528-9898 TDD

Drury Inn
800/325-8300 Continental USA and Canada
800/325-0583 TDD

Econo Lodges
800/55-ECONO Continental USA and Canada
800/228-3323 TDD
http://www.hotelchoice.com/cgi-bin/res/webres?econo.html

Embassy Suites
800/362-2779 Continental USA and Canada
800/458-4708 TDD
http://www.embassy-suites.com

Exel Inns of America
800/356-8013 Continental USA and Canada

Fairfield Inn by Marriott
800/228-2800 Continental USA and Canada
800/228-7014 TDD
http://www.marriott.com/lodging/fairf.html

Fairmont Hotels
800/527-4727 Continental USA

Forte Hotels
800/225-5843 Continental USA and Canada

Four Seasons Hotels
800/332-3442 Continental USA
800/268-6282 Canada

Friendship Inns
800/453-4511 Continental USA
800/228-3323 TDD
http://www.hotelchoice.com/cgi-bin/res/
webres?friendship.html

Guest Quarters Suites
800/424-2900 Continental USA

Hampton Inn
800/HAMPTON Continental USA and Canada
800/451-IITDD TDD
http://www.hampton-inn.com

Hilton Hotels Corporation
800/HILTONS Continental USA and Canada
800/368-1133 TDD
http://www.hilton.com

Holiday Inn
800/HOLIDAY Continental USA and Canada
800/238-5544 TDD
http://www.holiday-inn.com

Howard Johnson
800/654-2000 Continental USA and Canada
800/654-8442 TDD
http://www.hojo.com/hojo.html

Hyatt Hotels and Resorts
800/228-9000 Continental USA and Canada
800/228-9548 TDD
http://www.hyatt.com

Inns of America
800/826-0778 Continental USA and Canada

Intercontinental Hotels
800/327-0200 Continental USA and Canada

ITT Sheraton
800/325-3535 Continental USA and Canada
800/325-1717 TDD

La Quinta Motor Inns, Inc
800/531-5900 Continental USA and Canada
800/426-3101 TDD

Loews Hotels
800/223-0888 Continental USA and Canada
http://www.loewshotels.com

Marriott Hotels
800/228-9290 Continental USA and Canada
800/228-7014 TDD
http://www.marriott.com/MainPage.html

Master Hosts Inns
800/251-1962 Continental USA and Canada

Meridien
800/543-4300 Continental USA and Canada

Omni Hotels
800/843-6664 Continental USA and Canada

Park Inns International
800/437-PARK Continental USA and Canada
http://www.p-inns.com/parkinn.html

Quality Inns
800/228-5151 Continental USA and Canada
800/228-3323 TDD
http://www.hotelchoice.com/cgi-bin/res/
webres?quality.html

Radisson Hotels International
800/333-3333 Continental USA and Canada

Ramada
800/2-RAMADA Continental USA and Canada
http://www.ramada.com/ramada.html

Red Carpet Inns
800/251-1962 Continental USA and Canada

Red Lion Hotels and Inns
800/547-8010 Continental USA and Canada

Red Roof Inns
800/843-7663 Continental USA and Canada
800/843-9999 TDD
http://www.redroof.com

Renaissance Hotels International
800/HOTELS-1 Continental USA and Canada
800/833-4747 TDD

Residence Inn by Marriott
800/331-3131 Continental USA and Canada
800/228-7014 TDD
http://www.marriott.com/lodging/resinn.html

Resinter
800/221-4542 Continental USA and Canada

Ritz-Carlton
800/241-3333 Continental USA and Canada

Rodeway Inns
800/228-2000 Continental USA and Canada
800/228-3323 TDD
http://www.hotelchoice.com/cgi-bin/res/
webres?rodeway.html

Scottish Inns
800/251-1962 Continental USA and Canada

Shilo Inns
800/222-2244 Continental USA and Canada

Signature Inns
800/822-5252 Continental USA and Canada

Super 8 Motels
800/800-8000 Continental USA and Canada
800/533-6634 TDD
http://www.super8motels.com/super8.html

Susse Chalet Motor Lodges & Inns
800/258-1980 Continental USA and Canada

Travelodge
800/255-3050 Continental USA and Canada

Vagabond Hotels Inc
800/522-1555 Continental USA and Canada

Westin Hotels and Resorts
800/228-3000 Continental USA and Canada
800/254-5440 TDD
http://www.westin.com

Wyndham Hotels and Resorts
800/822-4200 Continental USA and Canada

CAR RENTAL AGENCIES

Advantage Rent-A-Car
800/777-5500 Continental USA and Canada

Airways Rent A Car
800/952-9200 Continental USA

Alamo Rent A Car
800/327-9633 Continental USA and Canada
http://www.goalamo.com

Allstate Car Rental
800/634-6186 Continental USA and Canada

Avis
800/331-1212 Continental USA
800/TRY-AVIS Canada
800/331-2323 TDD
http://www.avis.com

Budget Rent A Car
800/527-0700 Continental USA and Canada
800/826-5510 TDD

Dollar Rent A Car
800/800-4000 Continental USA and Canada

Enterprise Rent-A-Car
800/325-8007 Continental USA and Canada

Hertz
800/654-3131 Continental USA and Canada
800/654-2280 TDD

National Car Rental
800/CAR-RENT Continental USA and Canada
800/328-6323 TDD
http://www.nationalcar.com

Payless Car Rental
800/PAYLESS Continental USA and Canada

Rent-A-Wreck
800/535-1391 Continental USA

Sears Rent A Car
800/527-0770 Continental USA and Canada

Thrifty Rent-A-Car
800/367-2277 Continental USA and Canada
800/358-5856 TDD

U-Save Auto Rental of America
800/272-USAV Continental USA and Canada

Value Rent-A-Car
800/327-2501 Continental USA and Canada
http://www.go-value.com

AIRLINES

American Airlines
800/433-7300 Continental USA and Western Canada
800/543-1586 TDD
http://www.americanair.com/aahome/aahome.html

Canadian Airlines International
800/426-7000 Continental USA and Canada
http://www.cdair.ca

Continental Airlines
800/525-0280 Continental USA
800/343-9195 TDD
http://www.flycontinental.com

Delta Air Lines
800/221-1212 Continental USA
800/831-4488 TDD
http://www.delta-air.com

Northwest Airlines
800/225-2525 Continental USA and Canada
http://www.nwa.com

Southwest Airlines
800/435-9792 Continental USA and Canada
http://iflyswa.com

Trans World Airlines
800/221-2000 Continental USA
http://www2.twa.com/TWA/Airlines/home/
home.html

United Airlines
800/241-6522 Continental USA and Canada
http://www.ual.com

USAir
800/428-4322 Continental USA and Canada
http://www.usair.com

TRAIN

Amtrak
800/USA-RAIL Continental USA
http://amtrak.com

BUS

Greyhound
800/231-2222 Continental USA
http://greyhound.com

The Top-Rated Lodgings

ULTRA

The Greenbrier, White Sulphur Springs, WV
The Inn at Little Washington, Washington, VA
Inn at Perry Cabin, St Michaels, MD

FIVE FLAGS

Four Seasons Hotel, Philadelphia, PA
The Hilton at Short Hills, Short Hills, NJ
Hotel du Pont, Wilmington, DE

FOUR FLAGS

The Abbey, Cape May, NJ
Adam's Mark Philadelphia, PA
Allenberry Inn, Boiling Springs, PA
ANA Hotel, Washington, DC
Annapolis Marriott Waterfront, Annapolis, MD
Atlantic Hotel, Berlin, MD
Bavarian Inn and Lodge, Shepherdstown, WV
Belle Grae Inn, Staunton, VA
The Bellevue Hotel, Philadelphia, PA
The Bernards Inn, Bernardsville, NJ
Bethesda Marriott Suites, Bethesda, MD
Bischwind, Wilkes-Barre, PA
Boardwalk Plaza, Rehoboth Beach, DE
Brunswick Hilton & Towers, East Brunswick, NJ
Caesar's Paradise Stream, Mount Pocono, PA
Caesar's Pocono Palace, Union Dale, PA
Camberley's Martha Washington Inn,
Abingdon, VA
The Capital Hilton, Washington, DC
The Carlton, Washington, DC
The Cavalier, Virginia Beach, VA
The Coconut Malorie, Ocean City, MD
Commonwealth Park Suites Hotel, Richmond, VA
Crescent Lodge, Cresco, PA
Cross Keys Inn, Baltimore, MD
DoubleTree Hotel Pittsburgh, PA
DoubleTree Inn at the Colonnade, Baltimore, MD
Eisenhower Inn & Conference Center,
Gettysburg, PA
Founders Inn & Conference Center,
Virginia Beach, VA
Four Seasons Hotel, Washington, DC

Glasbern, Fogelsville, PA
Georgetown Inn, Washington, DC
Glendorn, Bradford, PA
Grand Hyatt, Washington, DC
The Grand Summit Hotel, Summit, NJ
Harbor Court Hotel, Baltimore, MD
The Hay-Adams Hotel, Washington, DC
Hidden Valley Resort & Conference Center,
Hidden Valley, PA
Historic Inns of Annapolis, Annapolis, MD
The Homestead, Hot Springs, VA
The Hotel Hershey, Hershey, PA
Hotel Roanoke and Conference Center,
Roanoke, VA
Hotel Sofitel, Washington, DC
Hyatt Regency Baltimore, MD
Hyatt Regency Bethesda, Bethesda, MD
Hyatt Regency Reston, Reston, VA
Inn at Gristmill Square, Warm Springs, VA
The Jefferson, Washington, DC
The Jefferson Hotel, Richmond, VA
Keswick Inn, Keswick, VA
Lansdowne Conference Resort, Leesburg, VA
The Lighthouse Club, Ocean City, MD
Linden Row Inn, Richmond, VA
Loews Annapolis Hotel, Annapolis, MD
Loews L'Enfant Plaza Hotel, Washington, DC
The Madison, Washington, DC
Mainstay Inn, Cape May, NJ
The Manor at Taylor's Store, Bedford, VA
McLean Hilton at Tysons Corner, McLean, VA
Morrison-Clark Inn, Washington, DC

Morrison House, Alexandria, VA
Nemacolin Woodlands Resort, Farmington, PA
Norfolk Waterside Marriott, Norfolk, VA
Omni Hotel at Independence Park, Philadelphia, PA
Omni International Hotel, Norfolk, VA
Omni Shoreham Hotel, Washington, DC
The Oyster Point Hotel, Red Bank, NJ
Park Hyatt, Washington, DC
The Parsippany Hilton, Parsippany, NJ
Penn State Scanticon Conference Center Hotel, State College, PA
Philadelphia Marriott, PA
The Queen Victoria, Cape May, NJ
Radisson Lackawanna Station Hotel, Scranton, PA
Radisson Patrick Henry Hotel, Roanoke, VA
Renaissance Harborplace Hotel, Baltimore, MD
Renaissance Mayflower Hotel, Washington, DC
Red Fox Inn, Middleburg, VA
Richard Johnston Inn, Fredericksburg, VA
Rittenhouse Hotel, Philadelphia, PA
The Ritz-Carlton Pentagon City, Arlington, VA
The Ritz-Carlton Philadelphia, PA

The Ritz-Carlton Tysons Corner, McLean, VA
The Ritz-Carlton, Washington, DC
Sheraton Premiere at Tysons Corner, McLean, VA
The Tides Inn, Irvington, VA
The Tides Lodge, Irvington, VA
The Tidewater Inn, Easton, MD
Toftrees Hotel, Resort & Center, State College, PA
Trump Plaza Hotel & Casino, Atlantic City, NJ
Trump Taj Mahal Casino/Resort, Atlantic City, NJ
Virginia Beach Resort Hotel, VA
Washington Hilton and Towers, DC
The Watergate Hotel, Washington, DC
The Westin Hotel, Washington, DC
The Westin William Penn, Pittsburgh, PA
Willard Inter-Continental Washington, DC
The Williamsburg Inn, Williamsburg, VA
Willow Valley Resort & Conference Center, Lancaster, PA
Wintergreen Resort, Wintergreen, VA
Woodloch Pines, Hawley, PA
Wyndham Franklin Plaza Hotel, Philadelphia, PA

DELAWARE

First Among Many

Although it's the second smallest state, behind Rhode Island, Delaware has almost as much to offer today's traveler as it has nicknames.

Delaware is the "First State," because it was the first of the original 13 colonies to ratify the US Constitution in 1787. Since then it has taken precedence over all other states at official functions and in other matters of protocol. Earlier, in 1776, Delaware had also played a crucial role in the birth of the new nation when Caesar Rodney, one of its delegates to the Continental Congress, rode all night from Dover to Philadelphia to cast the tie-breaking vote in favor of the Declaration of Independence.

Thomas Jefferson, author of that document, once described Delaware as a jewel among the states. That later was turned into the "Diamond State." Indeed, what is most gemlike about it is its size vis-à-vis the brilliance of its attractions. Above all, there are the estates and museums created by the du Pont family. Admirers of American culture and collectors of the work of its talented craftsmen, the du Ponts built magnificent mansions to house family members amid their extensive collections. Most spectacular of these are Winterthur and Nemours (and Longwood Gardens in Pennsylvania), which nestle around Hagley in the rolling hills of the Brandywine Valley.

While the du Pont legacy is the crowning glory of a rich heritage of historical landmarks scattered throughout the state, Delaware also manages to crowd 28 miles of Atlantic Coast into its small space—almost one-third of its 96-mile length. The beach towns of Lewes, Rehoboth Beach, Dewey Beach, Bethany Beach, and Fenwick Island, some with and some without boardwalks, offer the full roster of summertime pleasures, from swimming and sunning to sandcastle contests and open-air band concerts. Inland from the beaches is the most rural part of the state, full of farmlands, fruit orchards, nature preserves, and some of Delaware's 11 state parks.

Frommer's #1

All of this is sometimes referred to as "Delmarvelous," a play on another name, one that applies to Delaware and two of its neighbors. The Delmarva Peninsula, a finger of land between the Chesapeake and Delaware Bays, is made up of part of Maryland and part of Virginia, but all of Delaware.

Other nicknames apply. During the Revolutionary War, roosters from a certain blue hen from Delaware won so many battlefield cockfights that the fiesty little enclave became known as the "Blue Hen State." (The nickname does *not* refer to the fact that poultry farming is big business in southern Delaware, which produces more than 180 million broiler chickens a year.) Of more recent derivation is the nickname, "Home of Tax-Free Shopping," which refers to the state's failure to impose a sales tax. That and beneficial tax treatment of corporations has made it a mecca for banks and large corporations. With more than half the Fortune 500 companies incorporated here, Delaware has earned another informal nickname: "Corporate Capital of the World."

From tax-free shopping to touring magnificent estates and museums to lying on its pristine Atlantic beaches, there is much to see and do in this delightful little state of many names.

Fun Facts

• Delaware's average altitude—approximately 60 feet above sea level—is the lowest of any state. The state's highest point, Ebright Road in New Castle County, is only 442 feet above sea level.

• Three of America's oldest churches—Old Swedes (1698) in Wilmington, Old Welsh Tract (1703) near Newark, and Barratt's Chapel (1780) in Frederica—are still in use in Delaware.

• Coin Beach was so named because 18th-century coins, believed to have washed ashore from a passenger ship that sank off the Delaware coast in 1785, have been found there.

• The DuPont Company, based in Delaware, first developed and manufactured nylon at its plant in Seaford, known as the "nylon capital of the world."

Dutchman Peter Minuit, in the employ of Sweden, established a fort where Wilmington now stands. He named the fort and the nearby river Christina, in honor of the Swedish queen, and the settlers in New Sweden set about building log cabins, probably the New World's first.

In 1655, Peter Stuyvesant asserted Dutch control over the area and established a fort several miles to the south of the Swedish one. When the English took over in 1664, they named the Dutch stronghold New Castle. The area, in turn, became part of the land grant ceded to William Penn by the English king in 1681, and New Castle eventually became Delaware's colonial capital.

The Mason-Dixon Line

Until 1776, Delaware existed as the three lower counties of Pennsylvania. The state's unusually neat southern and western borders are the handiwork of Charles Mason and Jeremiah Dixon, English surveyors hired from 1763 to 1768 to clear up a boundary dispute between Pennsylvania and Maryland. Not until much later did Mason and Dixon's Line come to delineate the boundary between slave and free states. (Delaware's northern border with Pennsylvania is also unique—a neat semicircle with a radius measuring 12 miles from the cupola of New Castle Court House.)

A Brief History

Going Dutch Delaware's written history goes back to 1609, when Henry Hudson, sailing under the Dutch flag, arrived at the broad bay between Cape Henlopen and Cape May. He and his contemporaries frequently plied these friendly waters, named later for an early Virginia governor, Lord De La Warr, who probably never saw his namesake.

Plentiful fish and a temperate climate attracted Dutch settlers as early as 1631, although this first colony, Zwaanendael (Valley of Swans), near Lewes, failed when the colonists were massacred by Native Americans in a misunderstanding over the theft of a piece of metal bearing a coat of arms.

Permanent settlement began in 1638 when

Migration Indentured servitude was the means by which many Presbyterian Scotch-Irish arrived in the 1700s. Irish Catholic immigrants increased rapidly during the potato famine of the 1840s. Many with skills sought jobs at the mills and factories springing up along the Brandywine River in northern Delaware.

Wilmington's ethnic populations were also growing. Italians, Poles, and other groups formed "little" areas of the city. In the 18th century, tobacco farmers of Anglo-Saxon heritage migrated with their slaves into rural Kent and Sussex Counties from Maryland's Eastern Shore. Their Methodism flourished; Barratt's Chapel in Frederica is known as the "cradle of Methodism in America." Amish, Jewish, and Italian farm communities sprang up during the early 20th century.

The Age of du Pont Among the immigrants was a Frenchman, Eleuthère Irenée du Pont de Nemours, who set up Hagley Mill, a black-powder (gun powder) factory along the fast-flowing waters of the Brandywine, in 1802. Du Pont and his family caught the wave of the approaching age of industrialism. Demand for cleared land created a wonderful market for quality explosives. So did timely wars.

By 1889 the company controlled more than 90 percent of the nation's gunpowder production. When Delaware passed easy laws of incorporation in 1899, E I du Pont de Nemours, Inc soon came into being. The company modernized, expanded, and diversified into the DuPont chemical company, which has given the world cellophane, acetate, rayon, Freon, Lucite, and its most famous manmade fiber, nylon.

The Chesapeake & Delaware Canal Already traversed by rivers, streams, and ponds, Delaware was cut in two in 1829 when the Chesapeake and Delaware Canal was built to join the Chesapeake Bay and the Delaware River and provided ocean-going vessels with a shortcut across the state. Many think the "Big Ditch" divided Delaware along philosophical as well as geographical lines. North of it are the urban and suburban workers and managers of New Castle County; downstate live the farmers of Kent and Sussex Counties. Historically, the two sections have opposed each other on virtually every issue—except Prohibition, which they both hated.

Modern Delaware Shipbuilding had been an important early industry, and today, ships from around the world still pass through the port of Wilmington, but since World War II, chemicals have been the state's largest industry. Down south, Sussex County chicken farmers have grown rich raising broilers to sell at home and abroad. Commercial development

of the beach areas in recent years has made them the fastest growing part of the state.

Despite its friendliness to industry and traditional conservatism (Delaware was the last state to abandon slavery, it delayed giving women the vote as long as possible, and in 1972 became the last state to abandon the whipping post as a form of punishment), the state does have a progressive streak. When Shell Oil tried to build a refinery in New Castle County in 1970, laws were passed prohibiting oil refiners and other types of industrial development along the shoreline. "To hell with Shell," said Governor Russell Peterson, a former DuPont scientist and executive—and instant hero to ecologists across the nation.

A Closer Look
GEOGRAPHY

Delaware measures only 96 miles from north to south and varies from 9 to 35 miles from east to west. The hilly piedmont terrain around Wilmington in the north is in marked contrast to most of the state, which tends to be flat with a marshy, sandy shoreline. The fall line where these two geographic divisions meet supported a variety of water-powered industries in the Brandywine Valley in early times.

The state's three counties more or less delineate its geographic regions. The rolling piedmont begins north of the Chesapeake and Delaware Canal in **New Castle County,** home of Wilmington and the Brandywine Valley. Dover, the state capital, and the rest of central Delaware lie in **Kent County.** Occupying the southern third of the state, **Sussex County** has a split personality. While farms and quiet towns dot the flat countryside inland, along the Atlantic Ocean sits the busy summertime playground known as the **Delaware Beaches.**

CLIMATE

Delaware enjoys a relatively mild climate, although temperatures along the coast can be 10°F cooler in

---

DRIVING DISTANCES

Wilmington

13 mi NE of Newark
29 mi SW of Philadelphia
48 mi N of Dover
70 mi NE of Baltimore
88 mi NW of Rehoboth Beach
108 mi NE of Washington

Dover

43 mi SE of Newark
43 mi NW of Rehoboth Beach
48 mi S of Wilmington
73 mi SE of Philadelphia
98 mi NE of Washington
99 mi E of Baltimore

Rehoboth Beach

43 mi SE of Dover
84 mi SE of Newark
88 mi SE of Wilmington
115 mi SE of Baltimore
116 mi S of Philadelphia
137 mi E of Washington

summer and 10°F warmer in winter than inland. Wintertime visitors may find snow or brisk northwesterly winds. However, it seldom freezes until late fall, and the long Indian summers of autumn are everybody's favorite time of year.

WHAT TO PACK

Dress comfortably for the season, but bear in mind that the plenitude of palatial mansions open for touring encourages dressing up a little bit. Evenings can be cool and breezy, even at the beach, and summertime can feel damp. State parks and wildlife refuges are infamously buggy from early spring on, so bring lightweight socks, scarves, and plenty of insect repellent.

TOURIST INFORMATION

Information, maps, and brochures are available at the Delaware Tourism Office, 99 Kings Hwy, PO Box 1401, Dover, DE 19903 (tel toll free 800/441-8846; fax 302/739-5749). International visitors may call or write the Delaware Council for International Visitors, PO Box 831, Wilmington DE 19899 (tel 302/656-9928).

The tourism office also maintains a World Wide Web page (http://www.state.de.us/tourism/intro.htm) with links to attractions, historic sites, scenic drives, transportation information, and more.

DRIVING RULES AND REGULATIONS

Speed limits are 55 mph on four-lane, divided, and limited-access highways; 50 mph on two-lane roads; 25 mph in business and residential districts; and 20 mph in school zones. Where posted limits differ from these, obey the signs. Seat belts are mandatory, and children under four must use approved child safety seats. Turning right on red is allowed after coming to a full stop.

You are legally drunk if your blood alcohol level is over 0.10. If you refuse to take a breathalyzer or sobriety test, you can be taken into custody.

RENTING A CAR

Check the yellow pages. The major companies present in Delaware include:

- **Alamo** (tel toll free 800/327-9633)
- **Avis** (tel 800/831-2847)
- **Bayshore Leasing and Rental** (tel 800/882-4738)
- **Budget** (tel 800/527-0700)
- **Enterprise** (tel 800/325-8007)
- **Hertz** (tel 800/654-3131)
- **Payless** (tel 800/729-5377)
- **Thrifty** (tel 800/367-2277)

AVG MONTHLY TEMPS (°F) & RAINFALL (IN)		
	Wilmington	Lewes
Jan	30/3.0	35/3.8
Feb	33/2.9	37/3.3
Mar	42/3.4	45/4.1
Apr	52/3.4	53/3.6
May	62/3.8	63/3.8
June	71/3.6	72/3.4
July	75/4.2	76/4.0
Aug	74/3.4	75/5.2
Sept	67/9.4	69/3.1
Oct	55/2.9	58/3.2
Nov	46/3.3	50/3.3
Dec	35/3.5	40/3.7

ESSENTIALS

Area Code: The entire state is in the **302** area code.

Emergencies: Call **911** for the police, fire department, or an ambulance anywhere in the state.

Liquor Laws: Beer, wine, and liquor are sold in liquor stores only, which are closed Sundays. Provided a bar serves food (most do), it can also serve alcohol on Sunday. You must be 21 to purchase alcoholic beverages.

Smoking: All food service establishments must maintain a nonsmoking section. Smoking is prohibited in libraries, theaters, auditoriums, and museums.

Taxes: There is no sales tax in Delaware, but there is an 8% hotel occupancy tax.

Time Zone: Delaware is in the Eastern time zone. Daylight saving time is in effect from the first Sunday in April through the last Sunday in October.

Best of the State

WHAT TO SEE AND DO

Below is a general overview of some of the top sights and attractions in Delaware. To find out more detailed information, look under "Attractions" under individual cities in the listings portion of this book.

Beaches Rehoboth inspired the first beauty contest ever, which was held there in 1880. Delaware's 25-mile string of ocean beaches is just as beautiful today. Rehoboth and Bethany are biblical names, reminders of early religious camp meetings along the coast. Serenity survives, at least in spots. Historic **Lewes** and nearby **Cape Henlopen** are spacious and peaceful. **Rehoboth Beach** is the most popular and the largest coastal town. Narrow, sandy **Dewey Beach** attracts young people with its nightspots and ubiquitous water views. Southernmost **Bethany Beach** and **Fenwick Island** are "quiet resorts," thanks to strict building codes.

Family Favorites   The state publishes an annual *Calendar of Events* that conveniently marks events of interest to children with a "C" and is an invaluable aid when planning activities for the family (see "Tourist Information" above). Unique in Delaware is the **Children's Museum** in Wilmington, which gears interactive exhibits to ages three and up: "Experience the ripple of a wave; investigate a human ear. . . ." Children also adore the restored jail cells in the basement of Wilmington's **Old Town Hall Museum.**

Cuisine   Look for steamed crabs and oysters on the halfshell along the coast; a variety of excellent ethnic foods around Wilmington; and Amish specialties such as fresh sausage and baked goods near Dover.

Historic Buildings & Sites   Some buildings have been saved by moving them into historic enclaves; architecturally rich **Willingtown Square** in Wilmington and the town of **Lewes** are examples of this preservation strategy. On the other hand, the historic structures of the 18th-century city of **New Castle** are architecturally diverse precisely because the town has not been "restored" (meaning all the way back to its beginnings as the colonial capital). Some entire towns, like the tiny sailing village of **Bethel,** are on the National Register. The Age of du Pont at its most gilded can be seen at **Nemours Mansion and Gardens,** near Wilmington, and at the elegantly restored **Hotel du Pont** in downtown Wilmington.

In addition to buildings, look for historic stone markers along the borders of the state. The **First Stone of the Transpeninsular Line,** on the grounds of the Fenwick Island Lighthouse, was the first stone marking the east-west boundary between Maryland and Pennsylvania's lower counties (which eventually became Delaware). Finished in 1751, the line was the forerunner of the Mason-Dixon Line.

Museums   If you only have time for two, see **Winterthur Museum and Gardens** and **Hagley Mu-**

seum, a short drive apart north of Wilmington. Winterthur's collection of 180-plus period rooms and the American antiques that decorate them is the best in the world. Hagley, an outdoor museum at the site of the first du Pont powder mill, offers a look at a 19th-century industrial village and at the first house inhabited by the du Ponts in America.

Delaware has many other fine museums large and small, with exhibits and special programs constantly bringing history to life. Shipbuilding, for instance, one of the state's most important early industries, is illustrated at the **Kalmar Nyckel Shipyard/Museum** and the **Maritime Center** in Wilmington, and at the **Zwaanendael Museum** in Lewes. Early shipbuilding tools and records can be seen at the **Lydia Ann B Cannon Museum** in Milton.

In a different vein, illustrators Howard Pyle and N C Wyeth, both native sons, are represented at the **Delaware Art Museum** in Wilmington. Other collections are in the **Delaware Center for the Contemporary Arts** in Wilmington and the **Sewell C Biggs Museum of American Art** in Dover.

Parks & Gardens   Chemists by trade, the du Ponts were closet botanists. Hundreds of beautifully landscaped acres at **Winterthur, Hagley,** and **Nemours** display splendid native and exotic plants, setting a high standard for other more modest but equally charming landscaped parks and gardens around the state.

Scenic Drives   Miles of blue stone fences line the rolling country roads in the Brandywine Valley (along DE 100 and DE 52 from Wilmington to US 1 in Pennsylvania). Elsewhere, charming historic towns and waterside fishing villages offer fresh steamed crabs and oysters on the halfshell (DE 9 from New Castle to Dover and DE 8 from the Maryland border to Little Creek). In the South, antique shops and flea markets, quiet restaurants, and fabulous wildlife areas beckon beach goers to wander off the beaten path along DE 1 from Dewey Beach south to Fenwick Island, DE 5 from Oak Orchard to DE 24, and DE 24 from Millsboro to Laurel.

Wildlife Refuges   The 15,000-acre **Bombay Hook National Wildlife Refuge** near Lewes offers auto tour routes, exploration via small boat or canoe, and nature trails leading to observation towers. The smaller **Prime Hook National Wildlife Refuge** near Milton has two trails, four boat ramps, two ponds, and seven miles of canoe trails.

EVENTS AND FESTIVALS

NORTHERN DELAWARE

- **St Patrick's Day Parade,** Wilmington. Sponsored by the Irish Culture Club of Delaware. Mid-March. Call 302/652-2970.
- **Wilmington Garden Day,** Wilmington. Guided bus tours of the top homes and gardens. May 1. Call 302/652-1966.
- **A Day in Old New Castle,** New Castle. The entire historic town opens to the public. Third Saturday in May. Call 302/322-5744.
- **Old Fashioned Ice Cream Festival,** Rockwood Museum, Wilmington. Bands, balloons, games, antiques, and crafts. First weekend after July 4. Call 302/761-4340.
- **Historic New Castle Antiques Show,** New Castle. See the best of the past. Last Sunday in August. Call 302/322-8411.
- **Hoots, Howls, and Haunts Halloween Carnival,** Wilmington. Ghosts and goblins at the Museum of Natural History. Late October. Call 302/658-9111.
- **Yuletide at Winterthur,** Winterthur. Tours and Victorian-style celebrations at Winterthur Museum and Gardens. Mid-November through December. Call 302/888-4600 or toll free 800/448-3883.

CENTRAL DELAWARE

- **Old Dover Days,** Dover. The capital's leading historic homes are open to the public, plus parades and maypole dancing. Late April. Call 302/734-1736.
- **Spring Tour of Historic Houses,** Odessa. Historic homes open for the season. Early May through July. Call 302/378-4069.
- **Tour DuPont,** Dover. The statewide bike race begins at Legislative Mall. Early May. Call 302/734-1736 or 302/773-0490.
- **Community Appreciation Days,** Dover Air Force Base. Historical Museum is focus for tours of the base. Third Saturdays, June through August. Call 302/677-3376.
- **Bluegrass Festival,** Harrington. Pickin' and fiddlin'. Third weekend in June. Call 302/492-1048.

DELAWARE BEACHES

- **Great Delaware Kite Festival,** Lewes. Demonstrations and competitions at Cape Henlopen State Park. Early April. Call 302/645-8073.
- **Ocean to Bay Bike-a-Thon,** Fenwick Island. Bike racing along the beach. Late April. Call 302/539-2100 or toll free 800/962-7873.
- **World Champion Weakfish Tournament,** Slaughter Beach. Who can catch the biggest. Early June. Call 302/422-3344.
- **Quiet Resorts Golf Classic,** Fenwick Island. Early June. Call 302/539-2100 or toll free 800/962-SURF.
- **Zwaanendael Heritage Garden Tour,** Lewes. One-day tour of historic houses and gardens. Fourth Saturday in June. Call 302/645-8073.
- **Fourth of July Celebration,** Bethany Beach. Partying and fireworks. Call 302/539-8011.
- **Sandcastle Contest,** Rehoboth Beach. Adults and children compete at Delaware Seashore State Park. Second weekend in July. Call 302/739-4702.
- **Rehoboth Art League Annual Members' Fine Arts Show,** Rehoboth Beach. Mid-August. Call 302/227-8408.
- **Boardwalk Arts Festival,** Bethany Beach. Judged show attracts artists and artisans from far and wide. Last Saturday in August. Call 302/539-2100 or toll free 800/962-7873.
- **Coast Day,** Lewes. Open house at the University of Delaware's College of Marine Studies. First Sunday in October. Call 302/645-4346.

SOUTHERN INLAND DELAWARE

- **Delmarva Hot-Air Balloon Festival,** Milton. Saturday of Memorial Day weekend. Call 302/684-1101.
- **The Laurel Watermelon Festival,** Laurel. Seed-spitting fun. August. Call 302/875-2277.
- **Nanticoke Indian Museum and Pow-Wow,** Millsboro. Celebration of Native American culture. Second weekend in September. Call 302/945-3400 or 302/945-7022.
- **Milton Holly Festival,** Milton. Red berries getting ready for Christmas. Second Saturday in December. Call 302/684-1101.
- **Farmer's Christmas,** Dover. Delaware Agricultural Museum and Village celebrates the season. Early December. Call 302/734-1618.

SPECTATOR SPORTS

Auto Racing Dover Downs International Speedway has NASCAR racing. Call 302/674-4600 for information, 302/734-RACE for tickets. **Delaware**

International Speedway, on US 13 at Delmar, has NHRA drag racing. Call 302/846-3968.

Baseball For information and tickets to see Wilmington's minor-league **Blue Rocks,** call 302/888-BLUE.

College Athletics For intercollegiate sports schedules, contact the **University of Delaware** (tel 302/UD1-HENS) and **Delaware State University** (tel 302/739-3553).

Horse Racing Delaware Park, southwest of Wilmington, at Stanton, has thoroughbred racing from mid-March to early November (tel 302/994-2521). Harness racing takes place at **Harrington Raceway,** one of the oldest pari-mutuel harness racing tracks in the United States, from September through November (tel 302/398-3551) and at **Dover Downs** (tel 302/674-4600 for information, 302/734-RACE for tickets) on winter weekends. Winterthur sponsors an amateur steeplechase in May (call 302/888-4600 or toll free 800/448-3883).

ACTIVITIES A TO Z

Bicycling Annual bike-a-thons and a bicycle rodeo, county bicycle touring clubs, and the state's excellent *Delaware Maps for Bicycle Users* series support this popular pastime. Commercial companies provide inn-to-inn biking tours. The Tour DuPont in May is among the world's top pro-cycling events.

Birdwatching Noting that the mud flats of the Delaware Bay at low tide are "a rich pudding stuffed with delicacies for birds with long, pointed bills," the Audubon Society recommends numerous Delaware locations. Waves of shorebirds traveling the **Atlantic Flyway** time their arrival in May to coincide with hordes of horseshoe crabs laying eggs; birdwatchers convene from far and wide to witness this special "crabfeast." For the latest information call the **Delaware Audubon Society** (tel 302/428-3959) or the **Delaware Birding Hotline** (tel 302/658-2747).

Boating So much water in Delaware, so little time to experience it all. The possibilities stretch from dolphin- and whale-watching expeditions and tall ship schooner cruises at Lewes to the Cape May–Lewes Ferry (a mini-cruise in itself) and the tiny Woodland Ferry, the state's last cable ferry, which began running across the Nanticoke River in 1793. Also consider windsurfing or sailing on the inland bays, or a sea kayak tour of the bays and wildlife

areas. For information about boating laws and regulations contact the **Delaware Recreation Office** (tel 302/739-4413) or the **Delaware Division of Parks and Recreation** (tel 302/739-4702).

Camping Some state parks offer camping facilities. For information on several excellent private camping facilities write the **Delaware Campground Association,** PO Box 156, Rehoboth Beach, DE 19971.

Fishing Accessible areas open for freshwater and non-tidal fishing provide trout and bass; crabbing and clamming in season. Saltwater fishing for weakfish, flounder, and blues is popular spring through early fall. Ocean-going charter boats at **Bowers Beach** offer a variety of services, while family-oriented head boats are reasonably priced.

For information on licensing, regulations, daily possession limits, and locations of approved areas, contact the **Division of Fish and Wildlife,** 89 Kings Hwy, PO Box 1401, Dover, DE 19903 (tel 302/739-4431). The **University of Delaware's Sea Grant Marine Advisory Service** in Lewes provides information on how to use Delaware's marine resources (tel 302/645-4346).

Golf The **Delcastle Golf Club,** 801 McKennan's Church Rd (tel 302/995-1990), located southwest of Wilmington near Delaware Park racetrack, offers an 18-hole championship course, pro shop, driving

---

SELECTED PARKS & RECREATION AREAS

- **Bombay Hook National Wildlife Refuge,** Rte 1, Box 147, Smyrna, DE 19977 (tel 302/653-9345)
- **Prime Hook National Wildlife Refuge,** Rte 3, Box 195, Milton, DE 19968 (tel 302/684-8419)
- **Bellevue State Park,** 800 Carr Rd, Wilmington, DE 19809 (tel 302/577-3390)
- **Brandywine Creek State Park,** PO Box 3782, Wilmington, DE 19807 (tel 302/577-3534)
- **Cape Henlopen State Park,** 42 Cape Henlopen Dr, Lewes, DE 19958 (tel 302/645-8983)
- **Fenwick Island State Park,** DE 1, Millville-Oceanview, DE 19970 (tel 302/539-9060)
- **Killens Pond State Park,** Rte 13, Felton, DE (tel 302/284-4526)
- **Trap Pond State Park,** County Rd 449, Laurel, DE 19956 (tel 302/875-5153)
- **White Clay Creek State Park,** DE 896, Newark, DE 19711 (tel 302/731-1310)

range, and miniature golf course. A par-71 course is located at the **Old Landing Golf Course,** 300 Old Landing Rd, Rehoboth Beach (tel 302/227-3131).

Hiking The **Delaware Department of Natural Resources and Environmental Control,** PO Box 1404, Dover, DE 19903 (tel 302/739-4403) publishes an excellent brochure called *Delaware Trails Guidebook: Hiking in the First State.*

Historic Trains Two lines, the **Queen Anne's** in Lewes (tel 302/644-1720) and the **Wilmington & Western** (tel 302/998-1930), offer train rides designed for tourists. Railroad artifacts are housed in a 1929 caboose museum by the Highball Signal near Delmar (tel 302/846-2645).

Hunting As a result of strict regulation, small game, deer, and waterfowl are plentiful in season. For information on licensing, regulations, daily possession limits, and locations of approved areas, write the **Division of Fish and Wildlife,** 89 Kings Hwy, PO Box 1401, Dover, DE 19903 (tel 302/739-4431).

Skating **Dover Skating Center** (tel 302/697-3218), **Skate World II** in Rehoboth (tel 302/645-0463), and **Christiana Skating Center** (tel 302/366-0473) are all for rollerskaters.

Tennis Indoor tennis courts are available at the **Dover Indoor Tennis Club** (tel 302/734-1404), which is open October–April and welcomes visitors.

COASTAL DELAWARE

Start	New Castle
Finish	Bethany Beach
Distance	130 miles
Time	1–3 days
Highlights	Historic towns and villages with restored 18th-century homes and other buildings; marshlands; wildlife preserves; Delaware's pleasant capital; splendid ocean beaches

This tour parallels the Delaware River through the southern two-thirds of the state. In the late 17th and early 18th centuries, this agricultural and fishing region was settled by colonists whose legacy endures in the many period homes still standing in quaint small towns, such as New Castle and Odessa. First, you'll follow DE 9, which skirts and sometimes crosses extensive marshlands; much of these wetlands are contained within wildlife preserves which give refuge to migrating birds. At Delaware's colonial-era capital in Dover, you'll pick up DE 1 and drive southeast to the oceanfront enclaves of Rehoboth Beach, Dewey Beach, Bethany Beach, and Fenwick Island, as well as to the dunes and unspoiled sands of Delaware Seashore State Park, which borders the Atlantic.

As you plan your trip, note that many of the key homes, museums, and buildings along this route are closed on Monday, and some are open only from April through October. For additional information on accommodations, restaurants, and attractions in the region covered by the tour, look under specific cities in the listings portion of this book.

DE 9, DE 141, and DE 273 converge 7 miles south of Wilmington, giving easy access to the first stop:

1. **New Castle,** a major seaport and Delaware's capital in English colonial times, and one of the country's best-preserved 18th-century villages. Indeed, New Castle seems suspended in time, for the town retains many of its early cobblestone streets, public buildings, and homes. It's the kind of place where you can still talk to a clerk through an open courthouse window. Maps for self-guided walking tours of the delightful historic district are available at the **New Castle Court House,** at 211 Delaware St (tel 302/323-4453), two blocks from the river. Built in 1722, this brick building's cupola marks the the center of the 12-mile arc that forms Delaware's

northern border with Pennsylvania. Other nearby attractions from the 1700s include **The Green,** between 2nd and 3rd Sts behind the Court House; the **Dutch House,** 32 E 3rd St facing The Green (tel 302/322-9168), now a museum with early-17th-century furnishings; the **Amstel House,** 4th and Delaware Sts (tel 302/322-2794), a fine example of Georgian architecture; and the Federal-style **George Read II House and Gardens** (tel 302/222-8411) on The Strand (a one-block cobblestone street near the river), the house has elaborately carved woodwork, relief plasterwork, and silver door hardware. The Court House and museums are all closed on Monday.

After taking a refreshment at the **David Finney Inn,** 216 Delaware St (tel 302/322-6367), the **Cellar Gourmet Restaurant,** 208 Delaware St (tel 302/323-0999), or the **Green Frog Tavern,** 114 Delaware St (tel 302/322-1844)—all of them facing or near the Court House—proceed away from the river on Delaware St, go straight through the traffic signal at River Plaza Shopping Center, and turn left onto DE 9. Drive south 9½ miles to:

2. **Delaware City,** the terminus of the Chesapeake and Delaware Canal until the cross-peninsula waterway was moved south to Reedy Point in 1927. Until then, ships docked at locks here and at Chesapeake City near the canal's western end. The old lock stands at the foot of Clinton St (turn left at the stoplight) along what is now the Delaware City Branch Canal. Across the lock stands the headquarters for **Fort Delaware State Park** (tel 302/834-7941), from which a passenger ferry leaves for the fort out on Pea Patch Island. Completed in 1859, this massive granite structure was used as a prison camp during the Civil War. The ferry runs Wednesday–Saturday, June 15 through Labor Day. Fares are $4.50 for adults, $3 for children under age 15. Call 302/834-7941 for details.

South of town, DE 9 first crosses the narrow old canal and then climbs the high-rise span over the modern waterway, giving an expansive view of this massive engineering project, the Delaware River, and the surrounding countryside and marshes. Two miles past the bridge you'll come to **Port Penn,** a small fishing village on a narrow peninsula of high ground extending into the marshes. At the right of the stop sign is an interpretive museum which is

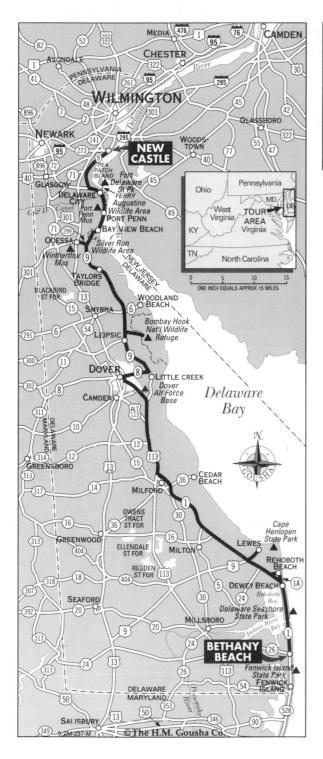

open Wednesday–Sunday afternoons during the summer. After Port Penn, DE 9 runs through the marshes of Augustine Wildlife Area until reaching a

Take a Break

You won't have another chance for refreshment for many miles, so walk across the park at the foot of Clinton St to the **Old Canal Restaurant and Inn** (tel 302/834-7442), which serves lunch Tuesday–Friday, 11:30am–2pm. If it's not open, try **Porto Pizza Place**, 88 Clinton St (tel 302/834-1261), for pizzas and deli sandwiches served in a simple, over-the-counter setting.

T-intersection. Turn right at the intersection and follow DE 299 north 1½ miles to:

3. **Odessa,** a small village on the high ground just beyond Appoquinimink Creek. This was a major grain shipping port in the early 1800s, but it now seems almost like a ghost town of 18th- and 19th-century homes. The **Wintherthur Museum** (tel 302/378-4069) administers a collection of these lovely houses, which are open March–December, Tuesday–Saturday 10am–4pm, Sunday 1–4pm. Tickets cost $7 for adults, $6 for seniors and students ages 12–16, $3 for children 5–11.

US 13 offers a shortcut from Odessa south to Dover, but this tour backtracks south on DE 299 until you pick up DE 9 again 1½ miles south of town. Continue south on DE 9 for 18 miles to Whitehall Neck Rd (DE 85), which goes to the left just south of the junction with Smyrna-Leipsic Rd. Turn left on Whitehall Neck Rd and drive east 2½ miles to the visitors center of:

4. **Bombay Hook National Wildlife Refuge** (tel 302/653-9345), a 23-square-mile expanse of saltmarsh and freshwater pools and one of the most important migratory stops on the Great Atlantic Flyway. More than 250 species of birds nest here, including great bald eagles, between November and June. Land-based wildlife also abounds. You can walk the nature trails, take a 12-mile driving tour, and climb the 30-foot-tall observation towers. The visitors center is open Monday–Friday 8am–4pm year-round, weekends 9am–5pm during fall and spring. The refuge itself is open daily from sunrise to sunset all year. Fees are $4 per vehicle, $2 for pedestrians and bicyclists.

Return to Smyrna-Leipsic Rd (DE 9), turn left, and drive 1½ miles south to the little riverside village of Leipsic.

After lunch, continue south another 6½ miles, turn right on DE 8, and drive east 4 miles into the heart of:

5. **Dover,** chartered in 1683 by William Penn and Delaware's capital since state leaders moved inland

Take a Break

Turn left on Market St in Leipsic to **Sambo's Tavern,** on Front St (tel 302/674-9724), overlooking the banks of the muddy Leipsic River. In true crab house fashion, you'll have newspapers for tablecloths and a roll of paper towels for napkins, which local residents consider absolutely necessary for cracking a mess of steamed crabs. Sambo's also serves sandwiches and fried seafood dishes, including terrific crab cakes. Platters cost $8–$18.

to avoid British naval attacks on New Castle in 1777. DE 8 brings you into town along Division St, the boundary between the Colonial and Victorian sections of Dover. Turn left at the second traffic signal after US 13 and follow State St south across The Green at the center of old Dover. On its east end stands the 1792-vintage **Delaware State House,** S State St (tel 302/739-4266), now a museum. Turn left on Water St and left again on Federal St to the **Delaware State Visitors Center,** 406 Federal St (tel 302/739-4266), beside the State House at the corner of Duke of York St. It's the best place to get information and maps, and to begin a self-guided walking tour of the historic district. Upstairs is the **Sewell C Biggs Museum of American Art,** with a large collection of American decorative arts. Downtown highlights include the 1910 **Supreme Court** on The Green; the 1933 **Legislative Hall** on Legislative Ave between William Penn and Duke of York Sts; several 19th-century stores in the Loockerman St commercial area; and the **State Museum Complex,** 316 S Governors Ave (tel 302/739-2630), which includes a 1790 Presbyterian Church and the Johnson Victrola Museum.

Located in central Delaware, Dover is a good place for an overnight stop. Several modern motels (such as **Sheraton Inn Dover, Comfort Inn of Dover,** and **Dover Budget Inn**) and numerous fast food and family-style restaurants sit along the Du Pont Hwy (US 13), the major commercial artery passing north-south through town.

From Dover, drive south on the combined US 113 and DE 1. **Dover Air Force Base** is 2 miles south of town; you can enter the main gate to visit its aviation museum (tel 302/677-3379). From there, keep going south and follow DE 1 when it branches off from US 113 at Milford. At 39 miles south of Dover Air Force Base, take Business US 9 to the left and drive north 2 miles into:

6. **Lewes,** northernmost of the Delaware beaches and an historic site in its own right. At the intersection of Business US 9 (Savannah Rd) and Kings Hwy stands the **Zaanendael Museum** (tel 302/645-9418), which commemorates the short-lived Dutch whaling colony established here in 1631. The **Chamber of Commerce Visitors Center** (tel 302/645-8073) is located in the early 1700s Fisher-Martin House behind the museum, on Kings Hwy. (Open year-round Monday–Friday 10am–4pm; also open Saturday 10am–2pm in the summer.) Here you can get a walking tour map and explore the surrounding historic district and its more than 50 houses dating back to the 17th and 18th centuries (some have been moved here from other sites). The local historical society maintains the **Lewes Historical Complex,** a group of old homes and a country store at Shipcarpenter and 3rd Sts. The Lewes and Rehoboth Canal runs east-west through Lewes, which is a major center for recreational boating. The town has a number of sightseeing cruises, including whale- and dolphin-watching expeditions. The **Queen Anne's Railroad,** a steam train, departs from its station at 730 Kings Hwy (tel 302/644-1720) for rides into the surrounding countryside.

Turn right at the Lewes Beach end of Savannah Rd for the ferry to Cape May, NJ, and the Atlantic beaches of **Cape Henlopen State Park** (tel 302/645-8983), where trails lead through sand dunes to the cape and the 80-foot Great Dune, the highest sand dune between Cape Hatteras and Cape Cod.

Take a Break

Lewes has plenty of dining spots, including a number of fast-food emporia on DE 1 between here and Rehoboth Beach. Among the better restaurants in the historic district are **Gilligan's,** 134 Market St (tel 302/645-7866), with seafood specialties; **Jerry's American Cafe,** 115 2nd St (tel 302/645-9733), serving old-time favorites such as chicken pot pie and crab cakes; and **La Rosa Negra,** 128 2nd St (tel 302/645-1980), featuring Italian entrees.

Backtrack to DE 1, turn left, drive south 4 miles, and take DE 1A to the left. This road dead-ends at the boardwalk of:

7. **Rehoboth Beach,** sometimes called the nation's Summer Capital because of its popularity with Washington, DC, residents who flock here to escape the real capital's summer heat and humidity. Two blocks from the beach, turn right on 2nd St, which becomes Bayard Ave (DE 1A), running south of

Rehoboth's sister resort, **Dewey Beach.** This stretch of sand lacks Rehoboth's charm but has the advantage of fronting both the ocean and Rehoboth Bay, a mecca for watersports enthusiasts.

DE 1 passes through Dewey Beach as its main thoroughfare. A mile south of town it enters:

8. **Delaware Seashore State Park** (tel 302/227-8800), a narrow seven miles of preserved beach and sand dunes separating the Atlantic from Rehoboth and Indian River Bays. The park has an ocean beach with a lifeguard, a bayside campground with RV hookups, and a full-service marina at Indian River Inlet, which lets fishing boats pass from the bay into the ocean for deep-sea fishing.

South of the park, DE 1 continues through a residential beach development until reaching the end of the tour at:

9. **Bethany Beach,** a quiet resort much favored by families who want to avoid the non-stop activity at Rehoboth and Dewey Beaches to the north and Ocean City, MD, to the south. Turn left at the stop light to reach Bethany's small commercial and boardwalk area.

South of town, the 2½-mile-long **Fenwick Island State Park** (tel 302/539-9060) separates Bethany from **Fenwick Island,** a beach resort extension of Ocean City just across the Maryland line. There you can see the 1859 **Fenwick Lighthouse,** which sits right on the state line. On its grounds is the First Stone of the Transpeninsular Line, which divides Maryland from Delaware.

From Ocean City, you can take the driving tour "Maryland's Eastern Shore" (see the Maryland chapter) in reverse.

Delaware Listings

Bear

Northern Delaware town, nearby to Delaware River and Lums Pond State Park.

ATTRACTION 📷

Lums Pond State Park
1068 Howell School Rd; tel 302/368-6989. Southwest of Wilmington off DE 71, Delaware's largest freshwater pond is the focus of this 1,757-acre park located on the north side of the Chesapeake and Delaware Canal. The 200-acre pond features a guarded swimming beach and rentals of sailboats, canoes, pedal boats, and rowboats. Anglers can try to catch largemouth bass, bluegill, crappie, catfish, and striped bass. The pond is also home to several beaver colonies and waterfowl. Camping, marina, hiking trails, picnic areas. **Open:** Daily 8am–sunset. **$$**

Bethany Beach

See also Fenwick Island, Rehoboth Beach

One of the "quiet resorts," located on a long sandy island off the coast of southern Delaware. Primarily residential and popular with families visiting nearby Delaware Seashore State Park. **Information:** Bethany Beach/Fenwick Island Chamber of Commerce, PO Box 1450, Bethany Beach, 19930 (tel 302/ 539-2100 or toll free 800/962-7873).

MOTELS 🏨

≣ Bethany Arms Motel and Apartments
5 Atlantic Ave, PO Box 1600, 19930; tel 302/539-9603. Exit DE 1 at DE 26. Located at the south end of the Bethany Beach boardwalk, with direct access to the beach and nearby shops, this property comprises several buildings, all in good repair. Building E, with large efficiencies right on the ocean, is the most attractive. **Rooms:** 52 rms and effic. CI 2pm/CO 11am. Middle-aged rooms are of several types, clean but not exciting. **Amenities:** 📞 A/C, cable TV, refrig. Some units w/terraces. Beach equipment rental. Friendly staff. **Services:** 🛎 Beach equipment rental available. **Facilities:** ⚒ 1 restau-
rant, 1 beach (ocean), lifeguard. **Rates:** Peak (June–Sept) $90–$100 S or D; $115–$130 effic. Extra person $5. Children under age 4 stay free. Min stay peak and wknds. Lower rates off-season. Parking: Outdoor, free. Closed Oct–Mar. MC, V.

≣≣ Harbor View Motel
Rte 1, Box 102, 19930; tel 302/539-0500; fax 302/ 539-5170. 3 mi N of Bethany Beach. At edge of Delaware Seashore Park, 1 mi S of Indian River Inlet. Built in the mid-1980s on the site of a fishing camp, this bayfront motel still appeals to those who trailer their boats here to enjoy the outdoors. **Rooms:** 60 rms and effic. CI 2pm/CO 11am. Nonsmoking rms avail. **Amenities:** 📞 A/C, cable TV. All units w/terraces. King-bed rooms have refrigerators. **Services:** 🛎 **Facilities:** ⚒ 🅿 1 restaurant (dinner only; see "Restaurants" below), 1 bar. Picnic tables and barbecue grills in backyard. Excellent fishing in area. Crabbing off bulkhead. Ocean beaches across highway via walkway. **Rates (CP):** Peak (June 30–Labor Day) $90–$100 S or D; $105–$115 effic. Extra person $10. Children under age 6 stay free. Min stay peak. Lower rates off-season. Parking: Outdoor, free. Closed Dec–Jan. AE, DISC, MC, V.

RESTAURANTS 🍽

Dream Café
Pennsylvania Ave and Campbell Place; tel 302/539-1588. 1 block N of Garfield Pkwy and 1 block W of Boardwalk, next to Post Office. **Cafe/Coffeehouse/Deli.** Works of local artists are hung gallery-style in this simple deli/cafe. Fare includes light, contemporary American selections, salads, quiche, vegetarian dishes, and fresh-baked breads. Espresso bar. Continental breakfast. Eat here or carry out an elegant alfresco lunch for the beach. **FYI:** Reservations not accepted. Children's menu. No liquor license. No smoking. Additional location: 26 Baltimore Ave, Rehoboth Beach (tel 266-2233). **Open:** Peak (Mem Day–Labor Day) daily 7am–10pm. Closed Thanksgiving–Easter. **Prices:** Lunch main courses $4–$7. AE, DISC, MC, V. 🎦

Harbor Lights Restaurant
In Harbor View Motel, Rte 1, Box 102; tel 302/539-3061. At the edge of Delaware Seashore Park. **American/Seafood.**

28

Simple rooms with wood-paneled walls, nautical prints, and hanging plants. A large upstairs bar has windows overlooking the bay. This is fishing country, so seafood dishes, including crab, are the mainstays. The wine list is extensive for such a menu. Separate room for smoking. **FYI:** Reservations accepted. Children's menu. **Open:** Daily 4:30–9:30pm. Closed Oct 31–Easter. **Prices:** Main courses $13–$21. AE, DISC, MC, V.

Holiday House Seafood Restaurant

Garfield Pkwy and the Boardwalk; tel 302/539-7298. Follow DE 1 to Garfield Pkwy; go east. **Seafood/Buffet.** Red is the predominant color in this semicasual seashore establishment with inlaid tables in mirrored rooms. Large windows afford views of the boardwalk and ocean. Most people come for the seafood buffet, but also available are some beef, chicken, and pasta entrees. Carryout available. **FYI:** Reservations accepted. Children's menu. **Open:** Peak (Mem Day–Labor Day) breakfast daily 8–11:30am; lunch daily 11:30am–2pm; dinner daily 5–9pm. Closed Thanksgiving–Easter. **Prices:** Main courses $9–$17. AE, DC, DISC, MC, V.

Centreville

See also Greenville

Northern suburb of Wilmington, nearby to Brandywine Creek State Park. **Information:** Greater Wilmington Convention & Visitors Bureau, 1300 Market St, Wilmington, 19801-1136 (tel 302/652-4088).

RESTAURANT

Buckley's Tavern

5812 Kennett Pike; tel 302/656-9776. Exit I-95 at Delaware Ave. **American.** Colonial decor, with good-quality wood tables and chairs in a rustic setting. Traditional American entrees with some regional and low-fat selections. Same menu in dining room, lounge, and rooftop deck. Light menu served after dining room closes. Good choice of international and domestic microbrewery beers. **FYI:** Reservations accepted. Children's menu. Dress code. No smoking. **Open:** Lunch Mon–Fri 11:30am–2:30pm, Sat 11:30am–3pm; dinner Mon–Wed 5:30–9:30pm, Thurs–Sat 5:30–10pm, Sun 5–9pm; brunch Sun 11am–3pm. **Prices:** Main courses $13–$19. AE, CB, DC, ER, MC, V.

Dewey Beach

Between the Atlantic Ocean and Rehoboth Bay, just south of Rehoboth Beach. Popular for sailing, boating, and windsurfing. **Information:** Rehoboth Beach/Dewey Beach Chamber of Commerce, PO Box 216, 501 Rehoboth Ave, Rehoboth Beach, 19971 (tel 302/227-2233 or toll free 800/441-1329).

MOTELS

Atlantic Oceanside

1700 DE 1, 19971; tel 302/227-8811 or toll free 800/422-0481. Standard highway motel that's clean, well-maintained, and close to the ocean. **Rooms:** 60 rms and effic. CI 3pm/CO 11am. Nonsmoking rms avail. Regularly refurbished units are neat and nicely decorated. Two dozen large townhouse-like cottages are in a separate building ½ block north on DE 1. **Amenities:** A/C, cable TV w/movies, refrig. Microwave. **Services:** Pets permitted off-season only. **Facilities:** 2 restaurants. Heated outdoor pool and sun deck are on the highway side of the premises. **Rates:** Peak (June–Aug) $59–$109 S or D; $64–$114 effic. Extra person $7. Children under age 15 stay free. Min stay peak and wknds. Lower rates off-season. Parking: Outdoor, free. Closed Nov–Mar. AE, DISC, MC, V.

The Bay Resort

126 Bellevue St, PO Box 461, 19971; tel 302/227-6400 or toll free 800/922-9240. Exit DE 1 at Bellevue St. Attractive and fresh, this simple motel has its own little bayfront lagoon and pier. The manager runs crabbing contests for the kids. **Rooms:** 64 effic. CI 3pm/CO 11am. Nonsmoking rms avail. Standard motel rooms are cheerful. King rooms have sleep sofas; bayfront rooms have splendid sunset views. **Amenities:** A/C, cable TV, refrig. All units w/terraces. **Services:** Car-rental desk, children's program. **Facilities:** 1 beach (cove/inlet), lifeguard, washer/dryer. Nearby boat rentals on the bay. Swimming is not especially good from the motel's beach. Good crabbing from the pier in summer. **Rates (CP):** Peak (Mem Day–Labor Day) $89–$139 effic. Extra person $10. Children under age 12 stay free. Min stay peak. Lower rates off-season. Parking: Outdoor, free. Closed Nov–Mar. DISC, MC, V.

Best Western Gold Leaf

1400 DE 1, 19971; tel 302/226-1100 or toll free 800/422-8566; fax 302/226-9785. This modern, well-maintained motel is convenient to both ocean beaches and bay water sports. **Rooms:** 75 rms. CI 2:30pm/CO 11am. Nonsmoking rms avail. Units are scrupulously clean. **Amenities:** A/C, cable TV w/movies, refrig, in-rm safe. All units w/terraces. **Services:** Babysitting. Many sports and social events can be arranged in conjunction with Ruddertowne, across the street. **Facilities:** Washer/dryer. Rooftop pool has nice view, and tennis courts are nearby. **Rates (CP):** Peak (June 15–Sept) $128–$198 S or D. Extra person $10. Children under age 12 stay free. Min stay peak and wknds. Lower rates off-season. Parking: Indoor, free. AE, CB, DC, DISC, ER, JCB, MC, V.

Dover

Located along the St Jones River in a rich farming and fruit-growing region, the state capital and Kent County seat is also a shipping center with diverse manufacturing interests. Home to Dover Air Force Base and many Georgian and Victorian home; horse-drawn buggies from the nearby Amish community are occasionally sighted. Historic and government buildings surround The Green, where delegates to Delaware's Constitutional Convention were the first to ratify the US Constitution. **Information:** Kent County Tourism Corp, PO Box 576, Dover, 19903 (tel 302/734-1736).

MOTELS 🛏

≣≣ Best Western Galaxy Inn
1700 E Lebanon Rd, 19901; tel 302/735-4700 or toll free 800/528-1234; fax 302/735-1604. A well-maintained highway motel close to Dover Air Force Base. **Rooms:** 64 rms. CI 2pm/CO 11am. Nonsmoking rms avail. Neat and clean. **Amenities:** 🛅 A/C, cable TV w/movies. Some units w/whirlpools. **Services:** 🚐 ⊍ Car-rental desk. **Facilities:** 🖼 ⅋ **Rates (CP):** $54–$69 S or D. Extra person $5. Children under age 12 stay free. Min stay special events. Parking: Outdoor, free. AE, DC, DISC, MC, V.

≣≣ Comfort Inn of Dover
222 S du Pont Hwy, 19901; tel 302/674-3300 or toll free 800/221-2222; fax 302/674-3300. On US 13 at Loockerman St, N of jct US 13/113. This quiet property is set back from the main highway and is convenient to both historic downtown and Dover Air Force Base. **Rooms:** 94 rms and effic. CI 2pm/CO noon. Nonsmoking rms avail. **Amenities:** 🛅 A/C, cable TV w/movies. **Services:** ⊍ **Facilities:** 🖼 ⅋ ⅋ 1 restaurant, 1 bar. Access to indoor pool, hot tub, and fitness center at Sheraton Inn and Conference Center Dover, about 2 miles north on US 13. **Rates (CP):** Peak (May–Labor Day) $60–$69 S or D; $75 effic. Extra person $5. Children under age 18 stay free. Lower rates off-season. Parking: Outdoor, free. Senior discounts avail. AE, DC, DISC, MC, V.

≣ Dover Budget Inn
1426 N du Pont Hwy, 19901; tel 302/734-4433; fax 302/734-4433. On US 13, ½ mi S of DE 1. As its name implies, this is a moderately priced highway motel, about 10 years old. **Rooms:** 69 rms and effic. CI 1pm/CO 11am. Nonsmoking rms avail. Standard rooms in good condition. **Amenities:** 🛅 A/C, satel TV w/movies. **Services:** ⊍ ⪦ **Facilities:** 🖼 Washer/dryer. **Rates:** Peak (June–Sept) $42–$45 S; $47–$50 D; $65–$75 effic. Extra person $5. Children under age 16 stay free. Lower rates off-season. Parking: Outdoor, free. AE, DC, DISC, MC, V.

≣≣≣ Sheraton Dover Hotel
1570 N du Pont Hwy, 19901; tel 302/678-8500 or toll free 800/325-3535; fax 302/678-9073. Exit 104 off DE 1. A large motel maintained to a high standard, near shopping malls and other stores in Dover's commercial and shopping area. Large public areas and extensive conference and meeting facilities. **Rooms:** 156 rms and stes. CI 3pm/CO noon. Nonsmoking rms avail. Attractive decor and good-quality furnishings. **Amenities:** 🛅 ⅋ A/C, satel TV w/movies. 1 unit w/terrace, some w/whirlpools. **Services:** ✕ ⊡ ⊍ Car-rental desk. **Facilities:** 🖼 ⅋ [2000] ⅋ 2 restaurants, 2 bars (w/entertainment), spa, whirlpool. **Rates:** $110 S; $120 D; $165 ste. Extra person $10. Children under age 17 stay free. Min stay special events. MAP rates avail. Parking: Outdoor, free. AE, DC, DISC, MC, V.

RESTAURANTS 🍽

Captain John's Restaurant
518 Bay Rd; tel 302/678-8166. Jct US 13/113. **American.** Five cheerful, bright dining rooms in casual family restaurant. Traditional beef, chicken, and seafood entrees are reasonably priced. Large salad bar. **FYI:** Reservations accepted. Children's menu. No liquor license. **Open:** Daily 6am–10pm. **Prices:** Main courses $5–$15; prix fixe $6–$11. MC, V. 🖾 ⅋

W T Smithers
140 S State St; tel 302/674-8875. Exit US 13 at Lockerman St; turn right onto State St. **New American/Seafood.** The dining rooms in this early 19th-century house are done in green and white and have bare wood floors. Wide range of American entrees with strong international influences. Extensive salad menu. **FYI:** Reservations accepted. Big band/rock. **Open:** Daily 11am–10pm. **Prices:** Main courses $10–$25. AE, DISC, MC, V. 🏛

ATTRACTIONS 🏛

Delaware State House
S State St; tel 302/739-4266. Built in 1792 and restored in 1976, this is the second-oldest state house in continuous use in America. The building contains a courtroom, a ceremonial governor's office, legislative chambers, and county offices. **Open:** Tues–Sat 10am–4:30pm, Sun 1:30–4:30pm. **Free**

Delaware State Museum Complex
316 S Governors Ave; tel 302/739-4266. Three museums are clustered here: the Meetinghouse Gallery I, formerly a Presbyterian church, built in 1790 and now the home of rotating exhibits highlighting life in Delaware; Meeting House Gallery II, a showcase for turn-of-the-century crafts; and the Johnson Victrola Museum, a tribute to Delaware-born Eldridge Reeves Johnson, inventor and founder of the Victor Talking Machine Company, known today as RCA. The Johnson Museum is designed as a 1920s Victrola dealer's store, with an extensive collection of talking machines and early recordings. **Open:** Tues–Sat 10am–3:30pm. **Free**

Delaware Agricultural Museum and Village
866 N du Pont Hwy; tel 302/734-1618. The main exhibit building houses over 10,000 artifacts and exhibitions on the poultry, dairy, and produce industries in Delaware. On the grounds behind the main building is a re-created 19th-century rural community, including a one-room schoolhouse,

a gristmill, a sawmill, a blacksmith shop, and a farmhouse. **Open:** Peak (Apr–Dec) Tues–Sat 10am–4pm, Sun 1–4pm. Reduced hours off-season. **$**

Dover Air Force Base
201 18th St (DE 113); tel 302/677-3379 or 677-5938. Dover's second-largest industry and the biggest airport facility on the East Coast, this base is also the home of the 436th Air Lift Wing and the giant C-5 Galaxy airplane, one of world's largest operational aircraft. Visitors can tour the base museum, which houses a collection of vintage aircraft and artifacts that reflect the history and evolution of both the base and the USAF. **Open:** Mon–Sat 9am–3pm. **Free**

Sewell C Biggs Museum of American Art
406 Federal St; tel 302/674-2111. Located in what was once the Kent County Building (circa 1858) on the second and third floors of what is now the Delaware State Visitors Center, this collection features paintings, silver, and furniture by American artists. **Open:** Wed–Sat 10am–4pm, Sun 1:30–4:30pm. **Free**

John Dickinson Plantation
Kitts-Hummock Rd; tel 302/739-3277. This was the boyhood home of John Dickinson, one of Delaware's foremost statesmen of the Revolutionary period. The house is an example of Delaware plantation architecture, built around 1740 and furnished with period antiques. **Open:** Peak (Mar–Dec) Tues–Sat 10am–3:30pm, Sun 1:30–4:30pm. Reduced hours off-season. **Free**

Killens Pond State Park
Killens Park Rd; tel 302/284-4526 or 284-3412 (campgrounds). Located 13 mi S of Dover. The highlight of this park is a 66-acre scenic mill pond, a popular spot for anglers who are rewarded with largemouth bass, catfish, carp, perch, crappie, bluegills, and pickerel. Canoes, rowboats, and pedal boats can be rented during the summer months. Other recreational opportunities in the 1,040-acre park include a water park (featuring two 35-ft water slides, water play structures, and a tot pool), hiking trails, an 18-hole disc golf course, playgrounds, and picnic areas. Modern and primitive campgrounds and cabin rentals are available. **Open:** Daily 8am–sunset. **$$**

Fenwick Island

This southernmost Delaware beach remains in a relatively wild state, and is the site of historic Fenwick Island Lighthouse. Located on the same barrier island as Ocean City, MD. **Information:** Bethany Beach/Fenwick Island Chamber of Commerce, PO Box 1450, Bethany Beach, 19930 (tel 302/539-2100 or toll free 800/962-7873).

MOTELS 🏨

≣ Atlantic Budget Inn Mason-Dixon
Ocean Hwy and DE 54, 19944; tel 302/539-7673 or toll free 800/432-8038. Straddling the Mason-Dixon Line, this older motel has been well maintained. **Rooms:** 48 rms and effic. CI 3pm/CO 11am. No smoking. Larger, nicer, and more expensive rooms are in the back section of the building. **Amenities:** 🛏 A/C, cable TV w/movies, refrig. Some units w/terraces. **Services:** 🛎 **Facilities:** 🏖 Public beaches with lifeguards are two blocks away across the highway. **Rates:** Peak (July–Labor Day) $85 S; $95 D; $100 effic. Extra person $8. Children under age 12 stay free. Min stay peak and wknds. Lower rates off-season. Parking: Outdoor, free. Closed Sept 30–Apr 15. AE, CB, DC, DISC, MC, V.

≣≣ Fenwick Islander
DE 1 and S Carolina Ave, 19944; tel 302/539-2333 or toll free 800/346-4520. 1 mi N of MD state line. The same families return each year to this simple, neatly kept motel. Adjacent to canal on the bay side of the island. **Rooms:** 62 rms. CI 2pm/CO 11am. Units are very basic, without cooking utensils or even coat hangers. **Amenities:** 🛏 A/C, cable TV. Some units w/terraces. Stoves and sinks. **Facilities:** 🏖 ᴅ Washer/dryer. Excellent ocean beach across the highway a block away. **Rates:** Peak (Apr–Oct) $95–$115 S or D. Extra person $10. Children under age 6 stay free. Min stay peak. Lower rates off-season. Parking: Outdoor, free. AE, DISC, MC, V.

≣≣ Fenwick Sea Charm
Oceanfront and Lighthouse Rd, 19944; tel 302/539-9613. From DE 1, turn toward beach on Lighthouse Rd. A collection of simple cottages and rooms by the sea. Decor is out of the 1960s, but everything is neat and attractive. **Rooms:** 47 rms and effic. CI 2pm/CO 10am. Seven units are basic motel rooms. All others have full kitchens and dinette tables. **Amenities:** 🛏 A/C, cable TV w/movies, refrig. No phone. All units w/terraces. **Facilities:** 🏖 ᴅ 1 beach (ocean), lifeguard. Excellent beach with lifeguards in summer. Barbecue grills at each building. Adjacent to miniature golf. **Rates:** Peak (June 22–Aug 24) $80 D; $110 effic. Extra person $10. Children under age 3 stay free. Min stay peak. Lower rates off-season. Parking: Outdoor, free. Closed Oct–Apr. DISC, MC, V.

≣ Sands Motel
DE 1, 19944; tel 302/539-7745. Families might otherwise pass this older motel by, but it is nicer inside than appearances from the highway would indicate. Renovation is needed, but the owner keeps the property clean. **Rooms:** 37 rms and effic. CI 2pm/CO 11am. Large rooms and apartments are decorated in 1960s browns with light wood-paneled walls. A variety of sizes from single rooms to two-bedroom apartments. **Amenities:** 🛏 A/C, cable TV w/movies, refrig. No phone. **Services:** 🛎 🐾 **Facilities:** 🏖 Excellent ocean beaches less than a block away, behind motel. **Rates:** Peak (June–Labor Day) $67–$87 S or D; $95 effic.

Extra person $7. Children under age 2 stay free. Min stay peak. Lower rates off-season. Parking: Outdoor, free. AE, DISC, MC, V.

RESTAURANTS

Harpoon Hanna's
DE 54 on the Bay; tel 302/539-3095. 1 mi W of DE 1. **American/Seafood.** Dark wood and high ceilings hung with plants surround the dark blue dining room of this nice seafood house on the water. Large windows and an outdoor deck look out on the boat canal. Menu is primarily fish and shellfish, with some beef, poultry, and pasta. **FYI:** Reservations not accepted. Rock. Children's menu. **Open:** Lunch daily 11am–4pm; dinner daily 4–9pm; brunch Sun 10am–3pm. **Prices:** Main courses $15–$35. AE, DISC, MC, V.

Libby's Restaurant
Ocean Hwy (DE 1) and Dagsboro St; tel 302/539-7379. **American.** Paneled walls with nautical prints characterize this family restaurant with booths in pink and gray. American family food is featured. Dinners include salad bar. Also at: Ocean Hwy, Bethany Beach (tel 302/539-4500). **FYI:** Reservations accepted. Children's menu. **Open:** Peak (Mem Day–Labor Day) Mon–Fri 8am–9pm, Sat–Sun 7am–9pm. Closed Dec 1–mid-Feb. **Prices:** Main courses $7–$20. AE, MC, V.

★ Tom and Terry's Seafood Restaurant
DE 54; tel 302/436-4161. 1½ mi W of DE 1. **Regional American/Seafood.** Guests can watch the sunset from large windows overlooking the bay and salt marshes at this very popular and often crowded seafood establishment. Tables have glass tops over lace cloths. The furniture is of light wood. The restaurant is an outgrowth of the adjacent seafood market, which still supplies the ingredients. Prime rib also available. **FYI:** Reservations not accepted. Children's menu. **Open:** Peak (May–Nov) lunch daily 11:30am–4pm; dinner daily 5–10pm. **Prices:** Main courses $16–$26. MC, V.

Uncle Raymond's Ocean Grill Restaurant and Bar
DE 1 and Atlantic Ave; tel 302/539-1388. **American/Seafood.** This traditional, casual, and unpretentious Eastern Shore–style seafood house has colonial tables and chairs and wood-paneled walls with old beer posters. The basic American seafood menu includes steamed crabs, served at picnic tables outside on a large deck or inside in the small dining room. Some items for landlubbers available. **FYI:** Reservations accepted. Children's menu. **Open:** Peak (Mem Day–Labor Day) daily 11am–1am. Closed Oct–Apr. **Prices:** Main courses $9–$18. MC, V.

Warren's Station
1406 Ocean Hwy (DE 1); tel 302/539-7156. At Indian St. **American.** There's an informal, family atmosphere in this white-and-blue room accented with knotty pine and paintings of beach scenes. Straightforward American family fare is the order of the day. **FYI:** Reservations not accepted. Children's menu. No liquor license. No smoking. **Open:** Peak (May–Sept) breakfast daily 8am–noon; lunch daily 11am–4pm; dinner daily 4–9pm. Closed Oct–Apr. **Prices:** Main courses $6–$15. MC, V.

ATTRACTIONS

Fenwick Island Lighthouse
DE 54. Built in 1859 on the Transpeninsular Line and still in operation today, this is one of the Delaware Shore's oldest landmarks. Its beams can be seen for 15 miles. **Open:** June–Aug, Wed 2–4pm. **Free**

Nanticoke Indian Museum
Jct DE 24/DE 5, Millsboro; tel 302/945-7022. Located on the Indian River, this former Native American schoolhouse contains artifacts and various historical displays on the lifestyle of the Nanticoke tribe. Each September about 500 tribe members convene for two days of ceremonial dancing, storytelling, crafts, and food. Visitors are welcome. **Open:** Peak (May–Sept) Tues–Fri 9am–4pm, Sat 10am–4pm, Sun noon–4pm. Reduced hours off-season. **$**

Fenwick Island State Park
DE 1; tel 302/539-9060. Just south of Bethany Beach, the park features 3 miles of seacoast beaches and dunes as well as 344 acres of parkland and open bayfront that's ideal for fishing, crabbing, and boating. Facilities include a boardwalk, showers, changing rooms, and a snack area. Birdwatchers will find rare seabirds, such as tern, piping plover, and black skimmer, nesting in protected areas. **Open:** Daily sunrise–sunset. **$$**

Fort Delaware State Park

Located on Pea Patch Island in the Delaware River; boats depart from Delaware City on the north side of the Chesapeake and Delaware Canal, off DE 9. Designated a National Historic Site, this Union fortress dates back to 1859, when it was built to protect the ports of Wilmington and Philadelphia. It also served as a prison for Confederate soldiers during the Civil War. A new living history program features costumed guides who conduct tours of the old fort and relate stories of Delaware's role in the Civil War. In addition, a 30-minute slide program details the fort's rich history, and two small museums feature artifacts and displays from the fort's past.

Pea Patch Island also features the largest wading bird nesting area on the East Coast. Visitors can view nine species of herons, egrets, and ibis from a scenic nature trail or an observation tower at the edge of the marsh area. Fort Delaware is open Apr–Sept, hours vary. Call the park office at 302/834-7941 for more details.

Frederica

This typical small Delaware town, once known as Johnny Cake Landing, is 10 miles south of Dover. **Information:** Kent County Tourism Corp, PO Box 576, Dover, 19903 (tel 302/734-1736).

ATTRACTION

Barratt's Chapel and Museum

6362 Bay Rd; tel 302/335-5544. Listed on the National Register of Historic Places and one of Delaware's most significant religious sites, the church is known as the "cradle of Methodism." An example of traditional Georgian architecture, it was erected in 1780. In 1784 Francis Asbury and Dr Thomas Coke, an emissary of John Wesley, met here and formulated plans for the organization of the Methodist Episcopal Church in America. A reconstructed 18th-century vestry has been added to the complex. **Open:** Sat–Sun 1:30–4:30pm. **Free**

Georgetown

Seat of Sussex County, with the center of town dominated by an 1839 Courthouse. Nearby to Redden and Ellendale State Forests. Noted as site of "Return Day," when winning and losing candidates and their supporters get together for post-election festivities. **Information:** Georgetown Chamber of Commerce, PO Box 1, Georgetown, 19947 (tel 302/856-1544).

ATTRACTION

Treasures of the Sea Exhibit

DE 18; tel 302/856-5700. Located just west of the town and west of DE 113 at the Delaware Technical and Community College, this display presents a collection of gold, silver, and other artifacts recovered from the 1622 shipwreck of the Spanish galleon *Nuestra Señora de Atocha*. **Open:** Mon–Tues 10am–4pm, Fri noon–4pm, Sat 9am–1pm. **$**

Greenville

See also Centreville

Just northwest of Wilmington and nearby to the Delaware River and the E M Hoops Reservoir. **Information:** Greater Wilmington Convention & Visitors Bureau, 1300 Market St, Wilmington, 19801-1136 (tel 302/652-4088).

RESTAURANT

Brandywine Brewing Company

In Greenville Center, 3801 Kennett Pike; tel 302/655-8000. I-95 at Delaware Ave N. **American/Burgers.** High wooden ceilings and exposed beams create a comfortable atmosphere at this popular brew pub. The place is popular for lunch, dinner, and evening gatherings of local folk, who come mostly for the ale. **FYI:** Reservations accepted. Folk. Children's menu. **Open:** Daily 11:30am–1am. **Prices:** Main courses $5–$17. AE, DISC, MC, V.

ATTRACTIONS

Delaware Museum of Natural History

DE 52; tel 302/652-7600. This museum houses over 100 exhibits and dioramas featuring birds, shells, and mammals as well as displays on the Great Barrier Reef, an African water hole, and Delaware's fauna. There is also a hands-on discovery room for young visitors, plus a continuous showing of nature films. **Open:** Mon–Sat 9:30am–4:30pm, Sun noon–5pm. **$$**

Brandywine Creek State Park

Adams Dam Rd; tel 302/577-3534. Originally a dairy farm owned by the du Pont family, this 1,000-acre park is bisected by the Brandywine Creek and is home to a variety of flora and wildlife, including deer and an active bluebird population; hawks can be seen migrating over the valley from mid-September to mid-November. The park incorporates 12 miles of hiking trails and Delaware's first two nature preserves—Tulip Tree Woods, a stand of 190-year-old tulip poplar, and Freshwater Marsh. **Open:** Daily 8am–sunset. **$$**

Lewes

Lewes was settled in 1631 by the Dutch, making it the state's oldest European settlement. Noted for its fishing industry and for the University of Delaware's College of Marine Studies. Southern terminal of the Cape May–Lewes Ferry that shuttles between New Jersey and Delaware; phone 302/645-6513 for information. **Information:** Lewes Chamber of Commerce and Visitors Bureau, PO Box 1, Lewes, 19958 (tel 302/645-8073).

MOTELS

The Beacon Motel

514 Savannah Rd, 19958; tel 302/645-4888 or toll free 800/735-4888. DE Business 9 exit off DE 1. This bright, spacious motel enjoys a nice location between the town and the beach. **Rooms:** 66 rms. CI 3pm/CO 11am. Nonsmoking rms avail. Standard-size rooms. **Amenities:** A/C, cable TV w/movies, refrig. All units w/terraces. **Services:** Babysitting. **Facilities:** Nice rooftop pool and two sun decks. **Rates:** Peak (July–Aug) $85–$115 S or D. Extra person $5. Children under age 12 stay free. Lower rates off-season. Parking: Outdoor, free. Closed Dec–Mar. AE, DISC, MC, V.

Cape Henlopen Motel

Savannah and Anglers Rds, PO Box 243, 19958; tel 302/645-2828 or toll free 800/447-3158. This roadside motel dates from 1960 but is a clean place to sleep. Anglers and outdoor-lovers should feel at home here, along with families on a tight budget. **Rooms:** 28 rms. CI 1pm/CO 11am. Nonsmoking rms avail. **Amenities:** 🛆 A/C, cable TV. **Services:** 🍽 **Facilities:** Washer/dryer. **Rates:** Peak (July–Aug) $60–$80 S; $65–$85 D. Extra person $5. Children under age 12 stay free. Min stay peak. Lower rates off-season. Parking: Outdoor, free. AE, DC, MC, V.

INNS

≡≡≡ The Inn at Canal Square

122 Market St, 19958; tel 302/645-8499 or toll free 800/222-7902; fax 302/645-7083. Savannah Rd exit off DE 1 to Front St. Modern yet traditional hostelry on the canal in town. Pleasant lobby. **Rooms:** 21 rms. CI 3pm/CO 11am. Nonsmoking rms avail. Units are attractive, with good-quality mahogany-finished furniture, nice fabrics, and framed prints. Separate two-story, two-bedroom houseboat with sun deck is permanently moored in marina. **Amenities:** 🛆 ⬙ 🍽 A/C, cable TV w/movies. Some units w/terraces, 1 w/fireplace. **Services:** 🍽 **Facilities:** 🔲 Guest lounge. **Rates (CP):** Peak (June–Sept) $125–$155 S or D. Extra person $15. Children under age 12 stay free. Min stay peak and wknds. Lower rates off-season. Parking: Indoor/outdoor, free. AE, DC, DISC, MC, V.

≡≡≡ The New Devon Inn

2nd and Market Sts, PO Box 516, 19958; tel 302/645-6466 or toll free 800/824-8754; fax 302/645-7196. Savannah Rd exit off DE 1 to 2nd St. On the National Register of Historic Places, this 1926 inn has been carefully updated with modern facilities while maintaining pedestal sinks and other historically accurate furnishings. Original pine floor throughout. Unsuitable for children under 12. **Rooms:** 26 rms and stes. CI 2pm/CO 11am. Nonsmoking rms avail. All rooms are individually decorated with period furniture. Sizes range from small to large, and there's one spacious suite. **Amenities:** 🛆 🍽 A/C. No TV. TVs on request. **Services:** 🔑 🍽 Twice-daily maid svce. **Facilities:** 🔲 ⬙ 1 restaurant, 1 bar, washer/dryer, guest lounge w/TV. An art gallery and several shops are downstairs. **Rates (CP):** Peak (June 14–Labor Day) $85–$130 S or D; $135–$170 ste. Extra person $20. Children under age 18 stay free. Min stay peak and wknds. Lower rates off-season. Parking: Outdoor, free. Bicycle-tour packages offered in conjunction with other historic inns. AE, CB, DC, DISC, MC, V.

RESTAURANTS 🍴

Gilligan's

134 Market St; tel 302/645-7866. Savannah Ave exit off DE 1. **New American/Seafood.** A waterfront room with views of the Lewes Canal enables guests to watch the boats go by; the grounded SS *Minnow* (hence the eatery's name) is visible from the street. Chef Larry Abrams, formerly of the Striped Bass in Philadelphia, produces an interesting array of dishes, including lamb (in season only) and a variety of pastas.

Seafood options include crab cakes, soft-shell crabs, tuna steak, and lemon-pepper shrimp. **FYI:** Reservations recommended. Children's menu. **Open:** Peak (Mem Day–Sept) daily 11am–midnight. Closed Nov–Mar. **Prices:** Main courses $13–$20. AE, DC, DISC, MC, V. 🍽 🖼

Jerry's American Café

115 2nd St; tel 302/645-9733. Off DE 1. **International/Seafood.** Informal but refined dining areas are decorated with interesting posters and local artwork. Several seafood specialties are augmented by meat and poultry prepared with an international flair. **FYI:** Reservations recommended. **Open:** Mon–Sat 11am–10pm. **Prices:** Main courses $9–$18. AE, MC, V. ⬙

Kupchick's Restaurant

3 E Bay Ave; tel 302/645-0420. Savannah St exit off DE 1. **American/Seafood.** An unpretentious building on the beach presents a simple, attractive formal dining room and an informal area by the bar. Both rooms serve traditional cuisine with an emphasis on beef and seafood. Some more interesting preparations are on the dining room menu. Everything is cooked fresh, and breads and desserts are made on premises. **FYI:** Reservations recommended. Jazz. Children's menu. **Open:** Peak (Mem Day–Sept) daily 4:30am–10pm. **Prices:** Main courses $6–$24. AE, CB, DC, DISC, MC, V. ⬛

★ La Rosa Negra

128 2nd St; tel 302/645-1980. Savannah St exit off DE 1. **Italian/Seafood.** Black and white decor with red accents and attractive table settings make a pleasant environment for Italian cuisine done in traditional and regionally specialized styles. Half-size portions available. **FYI:** Reservations recommended. **Open:** Lunch Mon–Sat 11:30am–2:30pm; dinner Mon–Sat 5–9:30pm. **Prices:** Main courses $7–$16. AE, MC, V. ⬛

ATTRACTIONS 📷

Zwaanendael Museum

Kings Hwy and Savannah Rd; tel 302/645-1148. Designed in memory of Lewes's first Dutch settlers, this museum was built to duplicate the town hall of Hoorn, Holland. The exhibits explore the rich and varied history of the area from the original colony to the present, including a display on the HMS *DeBraak*, an 18th-century ship that was sunk off the coast of Delaware and discovered in 1984. **Open:** Tues–Sat 10am–4:30pm, Sun 1:30–4:30pm. **Free**

Lewes Historical Complex

3rd and Shipcarpenter Sts; tel 302/645-7670. This cluster of buildings administered by the Lewes Historical Society includes an early plank house, a country store, and the Burton-Ingram House (circa 1789). This home, known for its fine collection of early American furniture, is constructed of hand-hewn timbers and cypress shingles; the cellar walls are made of stones and bricks once used as a ship's ballast. **Open:** Peak (July–Mar) Tues–Fri 10am–3pm, Sat 10am–12:30pm. Reduced hours off-season. **$$**

Cape Henlopen State Park

42 Cape Henlopen Dr; tel 302/645-8983. A 2,500-acre park bordered on one side by the Atlantic and on another by Delaware Bay, popular for swimming, tennis, picnicking, hiking, bayshore crabbing, and pier fishing. A refurbished World War II observation tower (115 steps) offers some of the best coastal views for miles. **Open:** Daily 8am–sunset. **$$**

Little Creek

This tiny town, northeast of Dover, is named for a nearby stream which leads to Delaware Bay. Bombay Hook Wildlife Refuge and the Little Creek Wildlife Area are also nearby.

RESTAURANT

★ Village Inn

DE 9; tel 302/734-3245. 3 mi E of Dover, exit US 13 at DE 9. **American/Seafood.** Large local clientele visits these rustic dining rooms with beamed ceilings and colonial-style furniture. Seafood, steaks, and prime rib. **FYI:** Reservations accepted. Children's menu. **Open:** Lunch Tues–Fri 11am–2pm, Sat 11am–3pm, Sun noon–3pm; dinner Tues–Fri 4:30–10pm, Sat 3–10pm, Sun noon–9pm. **Prices:** Main courses $13–$26. MC, V.

Newark

Small but lively city 14 miles southwest of Wilmington. Home to the University of Delaware and its scenic Old College, and nearby to White Clay Creek State Park. **Information:** Greater Wilmington Convention & Visitors Bureau, 1300 Market St, Wilmington, 19801-1136 (tel 302/652-4088).

HOTEL

Christiana Hilton Inn

100 Continental Dr, 19713; tel 302/454-1500 or toll free 800/445-8667; fax 302/366-0448. Exit 4B off I-95. Follow Churchman's Rd (DE 58) to Continental Dr. Well equipped for business travelers and for meetings, the hotel has attractively decorated public areas furnished traditionally. **Rooms:** 266 rms and stes. Executive level. CI 2pm/CO 11:30am. Nonsmoking rms avail. Good-quality traditional furniture. **Amenities:** A/C, cable TV w/movies. **Services:** **Facilities:** 2 restaurants (see "Restaurants" below), 2 bars, whirlpool. Well-regarded restaurant, English pub-style lounge. Pool, whirlpool, and gazebo in central courtyard. **Rates:** $77–$154 S or D; $190–$325 ste. Children under age 12 stay free. MAP rates avail. Parking: Outdoor, free. AE, DC, DISC, MC, V.

MOTEL

Fairfield Inn

65 Geoffrey Dr, 19713; tel 302/292-1500 or toll free 800/228-2800. Exit 4B off I-95. A Marriott-operated, budget-priced motel for business and highway travelers, this one is a neat, clean, and friendly place to stay. **Rooms:** 135 rms. CI 3pm/CO noon. Nonsmoking rms avail. Exceptionally clean. Energy-saving lights, heating, and cooling. **Amenities:** A/C, cable TV w/movies. **Services:** Babysitting. Fax and copying services. **Facilities:** **Rates (CP):** Peak (May–Sept) $47–$57 S or D. Extra person $3. Children under age 16 stay free. Lower rates off-season. Parking: Outdoor, free. Seniors discounts and "membership" plans avail. AE, DC, DISC, MC, V.

RESTAURANT

Ashley's

In Christiana Hilton Inn, 100 Continental Dr; tel 302/454-1500. Exit 4B off I-95 Follow DE 58 (Churchman's Rd) to Continental Dr, turn left. **American/Seafood.** With a large chandelier in the center and comfortable, upholstered chairs at the tables, this blue-and-peach room is upscale but casual. Veal, lamb, fish, and chicken are served in appropriate sauces, both à la carte and in three fixed-priced specials. Very good local and regional reputation. **FYI:** Reservations recommended. **Open:** Tues–Sat 6–10pm. **Prices:** Main courses $16–$32; prix fixe $22–$28. AE, CB, DC, DISC, ER, MC, V.

ATTRACTION

White Clay Creek State Park

425 Wedgewood Rd; tel 302/731-1310. Formerly Walter S Carpenter Jr State Park, this 1,600-acre expanse comprises the Carpenter Recreation Area, the White Clay Creek Preserve, and Possum Hill. The park features 16 miles of hiking trails, including one path to the granite markers used to sketch the Delaware-Pennsylvania state line. Anglers can fish for trout in White Clay Creek or for bass, bluegills, and crappie in Millstone and Cattail Ponds. Winter activities include cross-country skiing, ice skating, sledding, and shotgun deer hunting on a lottery system. Picnic area, disc golf, volleyball courts, primitive camping. **Open:** Daily 8am–sunset. **$$**

New Castle

With cobblestone streets dating from the Colonial era, New Castle has been described as The Undiscovered Jewel of the Eastern Seaboard. It was William Penn's first North American landing site, in 1682. Now the site of Wilmington's airport. **Information:** Historic New Castle Visitors Bureau, PO Box 465, New Castle, 19720 (tel 302/322-8411).

MOTELS 📥

▩▩▩ Ramada Inn New Castle

I-295 and US 13, PO Box 647, 19720; tel 302/658-8511 or toll free 800/272-6232; fax 302/658-3071. Exit I-295 at US 13 N. Hotel is 1 mi S of Delaware Memorial Bridge. Like many others of the chain, this motel offers nice public areas and pleasant, traditionally furnished rooms. **Rooms:** 131 rms. CI 2pm/CO noon. Nonsmoking rms avail. **Amenities:** 📻 📷 A/C, cable TV w/movies. Some units for long-term guests have refrigerators and coffeemakers available. **Services:** X 🚌 💺 💲 💷 Twice-daily maid svce, car-rental desk, babysitting. Can arrange tours to Brandywine Valley, New Castle, and Three Little Bakers Dinner Theater. **Facilities:** 💰 🛒 ♿ 1 restaurant, 1 bar (w/entertainment), games rm, lawn games, washer/dryer. Fitness center and golf courses nearby. **Rates:** $70–$76 S or D. Extra person $12. Children under age 12 stay free. Min stay special events. Parking: Outdoor, free. AARP, corporate, and other discounts avail. Weekend packages avail. AE, DC, DISC, MC, V.

▩ Rodeway Inn

111 S du Pont Hwy, 19720; tel 302/328-6246 or toll free 800/321-6246; fax 302/328-9493. On US 13 at DE 273; just S of Wilmington airport. Same owner has maintained this older motel well since 1976. Several detached buildings are spread over a large lawn with mature trees. **Rooms:** 40 rms. CI 1pm/CO noon. Nonsmoking rms avail. **Amenities:** 📻 A/C, cable TV w/movies. **Services:** 💷 ♿ **Facilities:** 1 restaurant (lunch and dinner only), 1 bar. **Rates:** Peak (May–Aug) $49–$59 S; $54–$64 D. Extra person $5. Children under age 18 stay free. Min stay special events. Lower rates off-season. Parking: Outdoor, free. AARP discount avail. AE, CB, DC, DISC, JCB, MC, V.

RESTAURANTS 🍽

Air Transport Command

143 N du Pont Hwy (US 13); tel 302/328-3527. DE 141 E exit off I-95. **American.** Dine here among sandbagged walls and World War II bric-a-brac, including trucks and jeeps. Large windows look onto runway of the airport (earphones at tables let guests listen to control tower). Music and photos from 1940s complete the mood. Hearty, simple fare with an emphasis on steak and prime rib. **FYI:** Reservations recommended. Big band/dancing. Children's menu. Dress code. **Open:** Lunch Mon–Sat 11am–3pm; dinner Sun–Thurs 3–10pm, Fri–Sat 3–11pm; brunch Sun 9:30am–3pm. **Prices:** Main courses $10–$23. AE, CB, DC, DISC, MC, V. 💺 🌄 📅 ♿

Lynnhaven Inn

154 N du Pont Hwy; tel 302/328-2041. **American/Seafood.** Colonial furnishings in large dining rooms decorated in attractive, muted colors. Beef and seafood in traditional American style have been served here by the same owners for more than 40 years, attesting to consistent quality. Popular in area as a pleasant place to take families or friends. **FYI:** Reservations accepted. Children's menu. **Open:** Lunch Mon–Fri 11:30am–3:30pm; dinner Mon–Thurs 3:30–9:30pm, Fri 3:30–10pm, Sat 4–10pm, Sun 1–9pm. **Prices:** Main courses $11–$26. AE, CB, DC, DISC, MC, V.

ATTRACTIONS 📷

Old Court House

211 Delaware St; tel 302/323-4453. One of the oldest-surviving courthouses in the United States, it once served as Delaware's colonial capitol. Its cupola is the center of the "12-mile circle," which creates the northern boundary between Delaware and Pennsylvania. The building's contents include portraits of men important to Delaware's early history, the original speaker's chair, and excavated artifacts. **Open:** Tues–Sat 10am–3:30pm, Sun 1:30–4:30pm. **Free**

George Read II House and Garden

42, the Strand; tel 302/322-8411. Built between 1791 and 1804, the house is a fine example of Federal architecture in a lovely garden setting. Features of the interior include elaborately carved woodwork, relief plasterwork, gilded fanlights, and silver door hardware. **Open:** Peak (Mar–Dec) Tues–Sat 10am–4pm, Sun noon–4pm. Reduced hours off-season. **$$**

Amstel House

4th and Delaware Sts; tel 302/322-2794. Dating back to the 1730s, this house is a model of 18th-century Georgian architecture. It was once the home of Nicholas Van Dyke, a state governor, and is furnished with antiques and decorative arts of the period. **Open:** Peak (Mar–Dec) Tues–Sat 11am–4pm, Sun 1–4pm. Reduced hours off-season. **$**

Dutch House

The Green; tel 302/322-9168. One of the oldest brick houses in Delaware, it has remained almost unchanged since its construction circa 1700. The furnishings, including a hutch table, a 16th-century Dutch Bible, and a courting bench, reflect the lifestyle of New Castle's early Dutch settlers. During seasonal celebrations, the dining table is set with authentic foods and decorations. **Open:** Peak (Mar–Dec) Tues–Sat 11am–4pm, Sun 1–4pm. Reduced hours off-season. **$**

Old Library Museum

40 E 3rd St; tel 302/322-2794. Built in 1892, this unique hexagonal building is now used by the New Castle Historical Society to house its exhibits. A representative of fanciful Victorian architecture, the building is attributed to noted Philadelphia architect Frank Furness. **Open:** Sat 11am–4pm, Sun 1–4pm. **Free**

Odessa

Known first as Appoquinimink, for the creek on which it lies, this small town was first settled by the Dutch in the 17th century. Its entire historic district is listed on the National Register of Historic Places.

ATTRACTION

Historic Houses of Odessa

2nd and Main Sts; tel 302/378-4069. In the 18th century, Odessa, north of Dover, prospered as a grain-shipping port. Today the town is a good example of a rural American adaptation of urban Georgian architecture; its historic houses are the centerpiece of the town. Administered by the Winterthur Museum in Wilmington, the structures include the Corbit-Sharp House, a three-story brick home dating back to 1774; the Wilson-Warner House, built in 1769; and the Brick Hotel Gallery, a federal-style building from 1822. **Open:** Mar–Dec, Tues–Sat 10am–4pm, Sun 1–4pm. $$$

Rehoboth Beach

See also Bethany Beach, Dewey Beach

Rehoboth has been called "The Nation's Summer Capital" due to its popularity with vacationing Washington, DC, residents. Boardwalk attractions and nightlife draw lots of visitors. **Information:** Rehoboth Beach/Dewey Beach Chamber of Commerce, PO Box 216, 501 Rehoboth Ave, Rehoboth Beach, 19971 (tel 302/227-2233 or toll free 800/441-1329).

HOTELS

Boardwalk Plaza

2 Olive Ave, at the Boardwalk, 19971; tel 302/227-7169 or toll free 800/332-3224; fax 302/227-0561. Exit 1A off DE 1 N on 1st St. It's back to 1890s style and grace at this Victorian-inspired resort, the top place to stay at the Delaware ocean beaches. A touch of humor and appropriate lobby music help set a turn-of-the-century tone. **Rooms:** 84 rms, stes, and effic. Executive level. CI 3pm/CO 11am. Nonsmoking rms avail. Authentic furnishings and decor throughout. **Amenities:** A/C, cable TV, dataport. Some units w/minibars, some w/terraces, some w/whirlpools. **Services:** Car-rental desk, masseur, children's program, babysitting. The staff is exceptionally helpful. Uniformed maids keep facilities spotless and attractive. **Facilities:** 1 restaurant, 1 bar, 1 beach (ocean), lifeguard, whirlpool, washer/dryer. The pool, with whirlpool jets, is closed to children in evening. **Rates:** Peak (June–Labor Day) $185–$225 S or D; $185–$345 ste; $200–$365 effic. Extra person $20. Children under age 6 stay free. Min stay peak. Lower rates off-season. Parking: Indoor/outdoor, free. AE, CB, DC, DISC, MC, V.

Henlopen Hotel

511 N Boardwalk, PO Box 16, 19971; tel 302/227-2551 or toll free 800/441-8450; fax 302/227-8147. Exit 1A off DE 1 N on 1st St. Nicely renovated, this older hotel is directly on the boardwalk and convenient to the center of town. Views are better than at many properties in this area, and the building is quiet. **Rooms:** 93 rms, stes, and effic. CI 3pm/CO 11am. Nonsmoking rms avail. Roomy mini-suite units have separate living and sleeping areas. **Amenities:** A/C, cable TV w/movies. All units w/terraces. **Services:** **Facilities:** 1 restaurant, 2 bars, 1 beach (ocean), lifeguard, playground. **Rates:** Peak (July–Labor Day) $140–$195 S or D; $160–$300 ste; $165 effic. Extra person $10. Children under age 18 stay free. Min stay peak and wknds. Lower rates off-season. MAP rates avail. Parking: Indoor, free. Closed Nov–Mar. AE, CB, DC, DISC, EC, ER, JCB, MC, V.

MOTELS

Admiral Motel

2 Baltimore Ave, 19971; tel 302/227-2103 or toll free 800/428-2424; fax 302/227-3620. Exit 1A off DE 1. While not on the beach, this comfortable motel is very close to the breakers, a block from downtown, and 60 feet from the boardwalk. **Rooms:** 73 rms and stes. CI 3pm/CO 11am. Nonsmoking rms avail. Upper-floor rooms have ocean views over rooftops. **Amenities:** A/C, cable TV w/movies, refrig. 1 unit w/whirlpool. **Services:** **Facilities:** 1 restaurant (bkfst and lunch only), whirlpool. Nice indoor pool with adjacent sun deck and outdoor spa. **Rates:** Peak (Mem Day–Labor Day) $84–$139 S or D; $124–$179 ste. Extra person $10. Children under age 11 stay free. Min stay peak. Lower rates off-season. Parking: Indoor/outdoor, free. AE, DISC, MC, V.

Atlantic Sands Hotel

101 N Boardwalk, 19971; tel 302/227-2511 or toll free 800/422-0600; fax 302/227-9476. Exit 1A off DE 1. An excellent location on the boardwalk is the attraction at this motel, whose lobby is more impressive than its rooms. **Rooms:** 114 rms and effic. CI 2:30pm/CO 11am. Nonsmoking rms avail. Deluxe rooms are somewhat larger than standard units. **Amenities:** A/C, cable TV w/movies, voice mail. Some units w/terraces, some w/whirlpools. Deluxe rooms have hair dryers, coffeemakers, and sink. **Services:** Babysitting. **Facilities:** 1 restaurant, 1 beach (ocean), whirlpool. Welcoming pool and rooftop sun deck overlook the ocean. Also hot tub and gas grills. **Rates:** Peak (July–Sept) $165–$250 S or D; $175–$195 effic. Extra person $10. Children under age 12 stay free. Min stay peak and wknds. Lower rates off-season. Parking: Outdoor, free. AE, DC, DISC, MC, V.

Brighton Suites

34 Wilmington Ave, 19971; tel 302/227-5780 or toll free 800/227-5788; fax 302/227-6815. Exit 1A off DE 1. A modern, attractive motel near the boardwalk and center of

town. Central hallways open to an attractive, multifloor atrium. Well planned for families. **Rooms:** 66 stes. CI 3pm/CO 11am. Nonsmoking rms avail. All rooms are suite-size, with sleep sofas suitable for children. Suites for guests with disabilities are equipped with Murphy beds. **Amenities:** 🛁 ⚱ 🍽 A/C, cable TV w/movies, refrig, in-rm safe. 2 TVs, wet bars. **Services:** 🍴 Children's program, babysitting. **Facilities:** 🏊 🚶 🅿️250 ⚿ Attractive, small indoor pool and large sun deck, whose roof and walls open in warm weather. Very good facilities for guests with disabilities, including ramp to pool. **Rates:** Peak (June 15–Sept 7) $179–$209 ste. Extra person $10. Children under age 16 stay free. Min stay wknds. Lower rates off-season. Parking: Indoor, free. AE, DC, DISC, MC, V.

🏨 Oceanus Motel

6 2nd St, PO Box 324, 19971; tel 302/227-8200 or toll free 800/852-5011. Exit 1A off DE 1. This neat mid-rise motel is arranged around an L-shaped outdoor pool on the street side. **Rooms:** 38 rms. CI 3pm/CO noon. Nonsmoking rms avail. Attractive, bright rooms are decorated in pastels. Small, basic bathrooms. All king rooms have sleep sofas. **Amenities:** 🛁 ⚱ A/C, cable TV w/movies, refrig. Microwaves in king rooms. **Services:** 🍴 Car-rental desk. **Facilities:** 🏊 Washer/dryer. **Rates (CP):** Peak (June–Aug) $119–$145 S or D. Extra person $10. Children under age 12 stay free. Min stay peak. Lower rates off-season. Parking: Outdoor, free. Closed Nov–Mar. DISC, MC, V.

🏨 Sandcastle Motel

123 2nd St, 19971; tel 302/227-0400 or toll free 800/372-2112. Exit 1A off DE 1. Turn left at first traffic light. This simple, well-kept motel, convenient to the center of town and just two blocks from the ocean, has a blue-gray color scheme and castle-like turrets. **Rooms:** 62 rms. CI 3pm/CO 11am. **Amenities:** 🛁 ⚱ 🍽 A/C, TV w/movies, refrig, in-rm safe. Some units w/terraces, 1 w/whirlpool. Wet bar in each room. **Services:** 🍴 Car-rental desk. **Facilities:** 🏊 🅿️30 ⚿ Sauna. Small indoor pool but large sun deck. Parking garage. **Rates:** Peak (Mem Day–Labor Day) $89–$125 S or D. Extra person $10. Children under age 11 stay free. Min stay special events. Lower rates off-season. Parking: Indoor, free. Closed Nov–Mar. AE, DISC, MC, V.

RESTAURANTS 🍴

Ann Marie's Italian and Seafood Restaurant

208 2nd St, at Wilmington Ave; tel 302/227-9902. Exit 1A off DE 1. Turn right at 2nd St. **Italian/Seafood.** Attractive, almost Victorian decor is found at this restaurant with both tables and booths. Formality varies from room to room; some have glass-covered tablecloths, others vinyl. Homemade Italian cuisine and American-style seafood are the mainstays. The Victorian-style Taylor's Seashore Restaurant adjacent is under the same management. **FYI:** Reservations recommended.

Children's menu. No smoking. **Open:** Peak (late May–Sept) Sun–Thurs 5–10pm, Fri–Sat 5–11pm. Closed Nov–Mar. **Prices:** Main courses $8–$19. AE, CB, DISC, MC, V. 🔲

Blue Moon

35 Baltimore Ave; tel 302/227-6515. Exit 1A off DE 1. **New American.** Floral prints and colorful artwork by local and international artists are the highlight at this establishment. Cuisine is "aggressively American" with international and ethnic influences. *Wine Spectator* Award of Excellence. **FYI:** Reservations recommended. Children's menu. **Open:** Peak (Apr–Oct) dinner daily 6–11pm; brunch Sun 11am–2pm. Closed Jan–Valentine's Day. **Prices:** Main courses $16–$26. AE, CB, DC, DISC, MC, V. 🖤 📷

Chez la Mer

210 2nd St; tel 302/227-6494. Exit 1A off DE 1. **Continental/Seafood.** Diners can choose a country French room, an informal front porch, or a rooftop deck at this old house. *Wine Spectator* Award–winning wine list complements a continental menu that stresses fresh seafood. All stocks, soups, salad dressings, and desserts are made on site. Chef will accommodate special dietary requirements. **FYI:** Reservations accepted. Dress code. **Open:** Peak (June–Aug) Sun–Thurs 5:30–10pm, Fri–Sat 5:30–10:30pm. Closed Dec–Mar. **Prices:** Main courses $16–$28. AE, DC, DISC, MC, V. 🖤 🏛 📷

The Club Potpourri Restaurant and Lounge

316 Rehoboth Ave; tel 302/227-4227. Exit 1A off DE 1, 1 block past State Rd. **Eclectic/Seafood.** Hanging lanterns, green plants, and wicker in the dining room, along with skylights and comfortable bar seating, make this a pleasant, popular spot. An eclectic, international collection of seafood, beef, and fowl is supplemented by a half-dozen dinner specials served 5–7pm. **FYI:** Reservations recommended. Jazz. Children's menu. **Open:** Daily 5–10pm. **Prices:** Main courses $10–$22. AE, DISC, MC, V. 🖤 🔲

Dream Café

26 Baltimore Ave; tel 302/226-2233. 1 block N of Rehoboth Ave, 1 block W of Boardwalk. **Cafe/Coffeehouse/Deli.** Simple wooden tables and chairs and a fine old Steinway upright piano punctuate this concrete-block basement opened to the light with greenhouse windows. Quiche, pastas, salads, brie, and other light, contemporary fare are featured, along with desserts and fresh-baked breads, croissants, and bagels. Herbal teas, espresso available. **FYI:** Reservations not accepted. Children's menu. No liquor license. No smoking. **Open:** Daily 7am–11pm. **Prices:** Lunch main courses $4–$7. AE, DISC, MC, V.

Grotto Pizza

36 Rehoboth Ave; tel 302/227-4571. Exit 1A off DE 1. **Italian/Pizza.** Two floors of dining rooms done in bright red and white come with comfortably padded chairs and a friendly staff. The place is best known for its pies, which are hand-tossed in a display kitchen so customers can watch, but

other Italian meals are also available. This original location has grown into a regional chain, with additional locations in Delaware and Pennsylvania. **FYI:** Reservations not accepted. Children's menu. **Open:** Peak (Mem Day–Labor Day) daily 11am–3am. **Prices:** Main courses $5–$6. AE, DISC, MC, V.

La La Land

22 Wilmington Ave; tel 302/227-3887. Exit DE 1 at Rehoboth Ave; turn right on 1st St, then left onto Wilmington Ave. **International.** New Age hits the beach here, with splashes of color and stars everywhere in a tasteful, playful combination. Bamboo surrounds an attractive patio. "International combinations" best describes the cuisine, such as southwestern-spiced mahimahi with corn salsa and guacamole. Excellent wine list. **FYI:** Reservations accepted. Dress code. **Open:** Peak (May–Sept) dinner daily 6–11:30pm; brunch Sun 11am–2pm. **Prices:** Main courses $18–$24. DISC, MC, V.

The Lamp Post Restaurant

DE 1 at DE 24; tel 302/645-9132. **American.** A split personality here: one dining room is set with tablecloths for dinner, while an informal room with hatch-cover tables is open for all meals. Menu features "take the family out to dinner" fare—meat, fish, and chicken in traditional American styles. **FYI:** Reservations not accepted. Children's menu. **Open:** Peak (Apr–Nov) daily 7am–10pm. **Prices:** Main courses $10–$22. AE, DISC, MC, V.

Obie's by the Sea

On the Boardwalk at Olive Ave; tel 302/227-6261. Exit 1A off DE 1. **Barbecue/Burgers/Seafood.** An informal, youthful place with high beamed ceilings and roll-up windows opening to the outdoors. A deck is adjacent to the boardwalk. Burgers, barbecue, and light seafood meals are aimed at beachgoers on the go. Menu is on the place mat. **FYI:** Reservations not accepted. Children's menu. **Open:** Peak (May–Columbus Day) daily 11:30am–1am. Closed Columbus Day–Apr. **Prices:** Main courses $10–$17. AE, DISC, MC, V.

Oscar's Seafood Restaurant and Bar

247 Rehoboth Ave, at Christian St; tel 302/227-0789. Exit DE 1 at Rehoboth Ave. **American/Seafood.** Formerly known as Cafe on the Green but still under the same family's management, this seafood house is light and casual, thanks to pastels, mirrors, green plants, and varnished oak tables. Seafood is primary draw, but some meat, poultry, and pasta too. **FYI:** Reservations accepted. Jazz. Children's menu. Dress code. **Open:** Peak (Mem Day–Labor Day) daily 4–11pm. Closed Nov–Feb. **Prices:** Main courses $15–$20. AE, MC, V.

Pierre's Pantry

1st St at Wilmington Ave; tel 302/227-7537. Exit 1A off DE 1. **Cafe/Deli.** This bright, street-front gourmet eatery with oak-and-glass tables offers a wide range of carryout snacks, including specialty sandwiches and soups, plus interesting light entrees featuring fresh ingredients. Also sells a variety of bagels and vegetarian items. **FYI:** Reservations not accepted. No liquor license. No smoking. **Open:** Peak (Mem Day–Labor Day) daily 7am–9pm. **Prices:** Main courses $6–$14. No CC.

★ Royal Treat

4 Wilmington Ave; tel 302/227-6277. Exit 1A off DE 1. **Ice cream/Breakfast.** This old house has a homey and friendly setting and is a popular place for breakfast, which, other than ice cream, is the only food served. Breakfast is along traditional American lines; the old-fashioned ice cream parlor dishes up real shakes and sundaes. **FYI:** Reservations not accepted. No liquor license. No smoking. **Open:** Peak (Mem Day–Labor Day) daily 8am–11:30pm. Closed Labor Day–Mother's Day. **Prices:** Lunch main courses $4–$7. No CC.

Sea Horse Restaurant

330 Rehoboth Ave, at State Rd; tel 302/227-7451. Exit 1B off DE 1. **American/Seafood.** A saltwater aquarium at the entrance, a big fireplace, and subdued mauve color scheme are accompanied by classical background music. Known for seafood, with fresh items depending on the daily catch. Some nonseafood dishes available. Friday night seafood buffet all year, but no brunch buffet in July and August. Dinner theater runs all year in a separate room (admission $23–$27). **FYI:** Reservations recommended. Cabaret. Children's menu. Dress code. **Open:** Peak (Mem Day–Labor Day) lunch daily 11:30am–4pm; dinner daily 4–10pm; brunch Sun 10am–2pm. **Prices:** Main courses $13–$22; prix fixe $19–$30. AE, DISC, MC, V.

Sidney's Side Street–A Restaurant and Blues Place

25 Christian St; tel 302/227-1339. Exit 1A off DE 1. Turn right at Christian St. **Cajun/Creole.** Pleasant, informal rooms in pastels with an impressive collection of glossy black-and-white movie stills. A "grazing" menu permits sampling smaller portions of several dishes or satisfies small appetites. Even a "flight tasting" wine sampler is available. Blues and jazz musicians perform beginning at 9:30pm nightly during summer, Thursday, Friday, and Saturday in the off-season. **FYI:** Reservations recommended. **Open:** Peak (Mem Day–Labor Day) dinner daily 5:30–10pm; brunch Sun 11am–2pm. **Prices:** Main courses $14–$20; prix fixe $30. AE, DC, DISC, MC, V.

Summer House Restaurant and Saloon

228 Rehoboth Ave; tel 302/227-3895. Exit 1A off DE 1. **American/Seafood.** Hanging ferns, green wallpaper, and bleached-oak tables give an air of informality to this establishment offering a selection of beef and seafood in classic styles. **FYI:** Reservations accepted. Dancing/rock. Children's menu. Dress code. **Open:** Peak (Apr 15–Oct) daily 5pm–2am. Closed Oct–Apr 15. **Prices:** Main courses $10–$22; prix fixe $6–$35. AE, CB, DC, DISC, MC, V.

ATTRACTIONS

Rehoboth Railroad Station Visitors Center
501 Rehoboth Ave; tel 302/227-2233. Erected in 1879 when there was regular train service to Rehoboth Beach, this station is an example of late Victorian style and ornamentation. Service came to an end in the late 1920s, and today this restored building serves as the visitors center for the chamber of commerce. **Open:** Peak (Mem Day–Labor Day) Mon–Fri 9am–5pm, Sat–Sun 10am–1pm. Reduced hours off-season. **Free**

Anna Hazzard Museum
17 Christian St; tel 302/226-1119. Named for a former owner and civic leader, this house is one of the original "tent" buildings erected during Rehoboth's camp-meeting era. This is a good place to gain a perspective on Rehoboth and its early days. **Open:** 1st and 3rd Sat of month, 1–4pm, or by appointment. **Free**

Delaware Seashore State Park
Inlet 850, DE 1; tel 302/227-2800. Located 2 mi S of Rehoboth Beach. Six-mile-long beachland offers both the crashing surf of the Atlantic and the gentle waters of Rehoboth Bay. Facilities include lifeguard-supervised swimming, surfing, and fishing. Full-service boat marina, bayshore campground. **Open:** Daily 8am–sunset. **$$**

Seaford

On the Nanticoke River, west of Georgetown. Known as the "Nylon Capital of the World," since the synthetic material was first produced at the DuPont plant here in 1939. **Information:** Greater Seaford Chamber of Commerce, PO Box 26, Seaford, 19973 (tel 302/629-9690).

ATTRACTION

Trapp Pond State Park
DE 13; tel 302/875-5153. Located 10 mi SE of Seaford. This 966-acre inland expanse is the northernmost natural stand of bald-cypress trees in the country. From a variety of hiking trails throughout the park, visitors can observe native animal species; flowering plants; and birds, including blue herons, owls, hummingbirds, warblers, bald eagles, and pileated woodpeckers. The Baldcypress Nature Center offers year-round cultural, historical, and recreational programs. Guarded beach, water sports, picnic and camping sites. **Open:** Daily 8am–sunset. **$$**

Smyrna

Located eight miles west of Delaware Bay and Bombay Hook Wildlife Refuge on the Smyrna River. This central Delaware town of some 5,000 residents offers a variety of architectural styles dating back to the Revolutionary era. **Information:** Smyrna/Clayton Chamber of Commerce, PO Box 126, Smyrna, 19977 (tel 302/653-9291).

RESTAURANT

Boon Docks Restaurant
Bayview Rd (Rd 82); tel 302/653-6962. Exit US 13 at DE 6 E. **Seafood/Steak.** Formerly a hunting lodge, this informal crab house is appropriately named, since it's off the beaten path. Rustic decor inside and a crab deck with picnic tables outside. Reasonably priced fish, shellfish, and beef in traditional Eastern Shore and Cajun styles. Bar offers drinks with names like Swampwater. **FYI:** Reservations not accepted. Country music/dancing. Children's menu. **Open:** Peak (Mar–Jan) Sun–Thurs 11am–9pm, Fri–Sat 11am–10pm. **Prices:** Main courses $10–$15. MC, V. 🍷🖼️🎁♿

ATTRACTION

Bombay Hook National Wildlife Refuge
DE 9; tel 302/653-9345 or 653-6872. Located 8 mi NE of Dover. 16,000-acre haven for wildlife, including over 250 species of migrating and resident birds. Created in 1937, it is one of the state's most important environmental resources and an essential link in the Great Atlantic Flyway. The site includes acres of salt marsh, swamp, freshwater pools, croplands, and woods, attracting such species as Canada and snow geese, great egrets, black-crowned night herons, and the bald eagle, which nests here from early December to mid-May; also found here are white-tailed deer, foxes, otters, opossums, woodchucks, and muskrats. Features of the refuge include auto-tour routes, walking paths, nature trails, and 30-foot observation towers. **Open:** Office: Mon–Fri 7:30am–4pm; refuge: daily sunrise–sunset. **$$**

Wilmington

See also Centreville, Greenville, Newark

The state's largest city and seat of Sussex County. Nearby to the rolling hills of the Brandywine Valley, and just across the Delaware River from New Jersey. First inbound deepwater port on the Delaware River, it annually handles 4.5 million tons of water-borne cargo. With a skyline that dominates northern Delaware, it is headquarters of DuPont Chemical and a major international financial center. Here was the site of the first Swedish settlement in the country, Fort Christina, in 1638. **Information:** Greater Wilmington Convention & Visitors Bureau, 1300 Market St, Wilmington, 19801-1136 (tel 302/652-4088).

HOTELS

▤▤▤ Brandywine Suites Hotel
707 N King St, 19801; tel 302/656-9300 or toll free 800/756-0070; fax 302/656-2459. Delaware Ave exit off I-95.

Downtown hotel is arranged around an atrium; public areas are tastefully furnished with antique reproductions. **Rooms:** 49 stes. CI 3pm/CO noon. Nonsmoking rms avail. **Amenities:** 🗄 🕐 🖵 🍷 A/C, cable TV, refrig. All units w/minibars. Wet bars. **Services:** ✗ 🆅🅿 ⌲ ⟲ ⟲ Van shuttle for local transportation. Very friendly and efficient staff. **Facilities:** ⛳ [150] & 1 restaurant, 1 bar. Health spa available nearby. **Rates (BB):** $79–$109 ste. Extra person $10. Children under age 16 stay free. MAP rates avail. Parking: Indoor, $8/day. AE, CB, DC, DISC, EC, ER, JCB, MC, V.

☰☰☰ Courtyard by Marriott Wilmington

1102 West St, 19801; tel 302/429-7600 or toll free 800/321-2211; fax 302/429-9167. Exit I-95 at Delaware Ave. A well-maintained downtown hotel with pleasing traditional decor and furnishings. **Rooms:** 125 rms. CI 3pm/CO noon. Nonsmoking rms avail. Quiet, spacious rooms. **Amenities:** 🗄 🕐 🖵 🍷 A/C, cable TV w/movies, refrig. Some rooms have microwaves. All rooms have iron and ironing board. **Services:** ✗ ⌲ ⌲ ⟲ ⟲ **Facilities:** ⛳ [30] & 1 restaurant (bkfst and dinner only), 1 bar, washer/dryer. **Rates:** Peak (Sept–June) $99 S; $104 D. Extra person $10. Children under age 12 stay free. Lower rates off-season. Parking: Indoor, $9/day. AARP and government discounts avail. AE, CB, DC, DISC, EC, ER, JCB, MC, V.

☰☰☰ Holiday Inn Downtown

700 King St, at Custom House Plaza, 19801; tel 302/655-0400 or toll free 800/465-4329; fax 302/655-5488. Delaware Ave exit off I-95 to 11th St. This downtown hotel has large public areas and extensive meeting and convention facilities. **Rooms:** 219 rms and stes. CI 3pm/CO noon. Nonsmoking rms avail. Comfortable rooms are traditionally furnished. **Amenities:** 🗄 🕐 🖵 🍷 A/C, cable TV w/movies. **Services:** ✗ ⌲ ⟲ Babysitting. **Facilities:** ⛳ [1200] 🖵 & 1 restaurant, 1 bar, games rm, whirlpool, beauty salon, washer/dryer. Attractive indoor pool area. **Rates:** $79–$109 S or D; $89 ste. Extra person $10. Children under age 19 stay free. Min stay special events. Parking: Indoor, $6/day. AE, CB, DC, DISC, EC, ER, JCB, MC, V.

☰☰☰☰☰ Hotel du Pont

11th and Market Sts, 19801 (Downtown); tel 302/594-3100 or toll free 800/441-9019; fax 302/656-2145. Exit 7 or 7A off I-95. An old-timer dating to 1913, now modernized and upgraded after recent 20-month shutdown and $40 million from EI du Pont de Nemours and Co, whose head offices share this 12-story Italian Renaissance–style structure. **Rooms:** 215 rms and stes. CI 3pm/CO 1pm. Nonsmoking rms avail. Recently enlarged rooms designed with input from frequent travelers; unusually efficient, in soothing colors of beige, peach, and mocha against mahogany cabinetry. His/her closets. Bathrooms of Spanish marble, with oversize tubs and separate showers. Sealed windows are a drawback for those desiring fresh air. **Amenities:** 🗄 🕐 🍷 A/C, satel TV w/movies, dataport, VCR, voice mail, in-rm safe, bathrobes. All units w/minibars, some w/whirlpools. Lots of extras

include bathroom slippers, dimmer switches, integrated TV/VCR in revolving cabinet for viewing from both bed and couch, voice mail in three languages. **Services:** 🍽 🗝 🆅🅿 ⌲ ⟲ Twice-daily maid svce, car-rental desk, babysitting. Afternoon tea in elegant lounge. Courtesy car for trips to nearby banks and offices. **Facilities:** ⛳ [1250] & 3 restaurants (see "Restaurants" below), 2 bars (1 w/entertainment), sauna. Special privileges at Du Pont Country Club. Fitness center, with top-of-the-line equipment and complimentary overnight laundering of gym clothes. Two of the top restaurants in Wilmington. **Rates:** $169–$385 S or D; $285–$385 ste. Extra person $25. Children under age 12 stay free. Parking: Outdoor, $9/day. AE, CB, DC, DISC, JCB, MC, V.

☰☰☰ Radisson Hotel Wilmington

4727 Concord Pike (US 202), 19803; tel 302/478-6000 or toll free 800/333-3333; fax 302/477-1492. Exit I-95 at US 202; hotel is 3 mi N. Formerly a Sheraton, this hotel offers very good conference facilities as well as comfortable guest rooms. Public areas are traditional, with mahogany furniture. **Rooms:** 154 rms and stes. CI 3pm/CO noon. Nonsmoking rms avail. Spacious and traditionally furnished. **Amenities:** 🗄 🕐 A/C, cable TV w/movies. **Services:** ✗ ⌲ ⌲ ⟲ Babysitting. Shuttle van available for local destinations, including Amtrak station. **Facilities:** ⛳ ⛳ [350] 1 restaurant, 1 bar, washer/dryer. Pool has privacy fence. Day care nearby for small fee. **Rates:** $119 S; $139 D; $165–$185 ste. Children under age 12 stay free. MAP rates avail. Parking: Outdoor, free. AE, CB, DC, DISC, ER, JCB, MC, V.

☰☰☰ Sheraton Suites Wilmington

422 Delaware Ave, 19801; tel 302/654-8300 or toll free 800/325-3535; fax 302/654-6036. Delaware Ave exit off I-95. A modern, classic hotel with marble floors at the entrance and subdued decor with an art-deco touch. **Rooms:** 230 stes. Executive level. CI 3pm/CO noon. Nonsmoking rms avail. **Amenities:** 🗄 🕐 🖵 🍷 A/C, cable TV w/movies, refrig. All units w/minibars. Units have wet bars; irons and ironing boards; TVs in living room, bedroom, and bathroom. **Services:** ✗ 🆅🅿 ⌲ ⌲ ⟲ ⟲ Twice-daily maid svce, babysitting. **Facilities:** ⛳ ⛳ [200] 🖵 & 1 restaurant, 1 bar (w/entertainment), washer/dryer. **Rates (MAP):** $165 ste. Extra person $10. Children under age 12 stay free. Parking: Indoor, $9/day. Weekend packages avail. AE, CB, DC, DISC, EC, ER, JCB, MC, V.

☰☰☰ Wilmington Hilton

630 Naamans Rd, 19703; tel 302/792-2700 or toll free 800/445-8667; fax 302/798-6182. At I-95. A comfortable highway hotel with attractive public areas, dining room, and lounge. Friendly staff contributes to informal atmosphere. **Rooms:** 193 rms. Executive level. CI 3pm/CO noon. Nonsmoking rms avail. Nicely furnished rooms are larger than average. **Amenities:** 🗄 🕐 A/C, satel TV w/movies, voice mail. **Services:** ✗ 🗝 ⌲ ⌲ ⟲ ⟲ Car-rental desk, babysitting. **Facilities:** ⛳ ⛳ [800] & 1 restaurant, 1 bar (w/entertainment), games rm, lawn games. Pretty pool area with privacy

fence and tables for light dining. **Rates:** $85–$159 S or D. Children under age 18 stay free. Lower rates off-season. MAP rates avail. Parking: Outdoor, free. AE, DISC, ER, MC, V.

MOTELS

≣≣≣ Best Western Brandywine Valley Inn

1807 Concord Pike (US 202), 19803; tel 302/656-9436 or toll free 800/537-7772; fax 302/656-8564. US 202 exit off I-95. An attractive property, built around a central courtyard. Well kept, with better-than-average furnishings and decor. Attractive lobby has piano, large windows, and high ceilings. **Rooms:** 95 rms, stes, and effic. CI 2pm/CO noon. Nonsmoking rms avail. Traditionally furnished. **Amenities:** 🛅 🖭 A/C, voice mail. About half the units have microwaves and refrigerators. **Services:** ✗ 🖂 🛏 🍽 Courtesy van to local area. **Facilities:** 🏊 ᕍ **Rates:** Peak (Apr–Oct) $68–$87 S; $74–$93 D; $90–$110 ste; $84–$90 effic. Extra person $5. Children under age 18 stay free. Min stay special events. Lower rates off-season. Parking: Outdoor, free. Many special getaway packages avail. AE, DC, DISC, MC, V.

≣ Tally Ho Motor Lodge

5209 Concord Pike (US 202), 19803; tel 302/478-0300 or toll free 800/445-0852; fax 302/478-2401. US 202 exit off I-95, 4½ mi N. A standard motel in reasonably good condition. Several restaurants and shops nearby. **Rooms:** 100 rms. CI 2pm/CO noon. Nonsmoking rms avail. Average rooms, with parking in front of each. **Amenities:** 🛅 A/C, cable TV w/movies. **Services:** 🚐 🍽 🍽 **Facilities:** 🖳 Washer/dryer. **Rates (CP):** Peak (Mar–Nov) $42 S; $48 D. Extra person $5. Children under age 12 stay free. Lower rates off-season. Parking: Outdoor, free. AE, DISC, MC, V.

RESTAURANTS 🍴

♥ Brandywine Room

In Hotel du Pont, 11th and Market Sts (Downtown); tel 302/594-3100. Exit 7 or 7A off I-95. **American.** More casual than the du Pont's Green Room, but just as serious about fresh ingredients and courteous service. The two connecting rooms date from the hotel's debut in 1913; one has high ceilings and wood paneling, one has cozy booths, and both are graced with Wyeth paintings. The menu features breaded oysters with black pepper and balsamic sauce; picatta of veal with lump crabmeat; saffron fettuccine with shrimp; and grilled porterhouse steak with garlic and wild-mushroom sauce. **FYI:** Reservations recommended. Dress code. No smoking. **Open:** Dinner Sun–Thurs 6–11pm. **Prices:** Main courses $16–$28. AE, CB, DC, DISC, MC, V. ♥ 🖭 VP ᕍ

☀ Columbus Inn

2216 Pennsylvania Ave; tel 302/571-1492. Exit I-95 at DE 52. **American.** The interior reflects the history of this building, which was the early 18th-century tollgate to the Kennett Pike. Decor includes a large collection of paintings by Frank Jefferies, noted local artist. Traditional and regional American cuisine is on tap, as is an award-winning wine list. **FYI:** Reservations recommended. Piano. Children's menu. Dress code. **Open:** Peak (Sept–May) lunch Mon–Fri 11:00am–5pm; dinner Mon–Thurs 5–11pm, Fri–Sat 5pm–midnight. **Prices:** Main courses $15–$22. AE, DC, DISC, MC, V. 🍽 🖭 VP ᕍ

Constantinou's House of Beef and Seafood

1616 Delaware Ave; tel 302/652-0653. Delaware Ave exit off I-95. **Seafood/Steak.** Dark-paneled rooms are furnished with antiques, chandeliers, moldings, and mirrors from various old hotels, theaters, and homes. Variety of fish and shellfish dishes; award-winning steaks are grilled in the dining room. **FYI:** Reservations recommended. Children's menu. Dress code. **Open:** Sun–Wed 11am–9:30pm, Thurs–Fri 11am–10:30pm, Sat 11am–11pm. **Prices:** Main courses $17–$40. AE, CB, DC, DISC, ER, MC, V. 🍽

Feby's Fishery

3701 Lancaster Pike; tel 302/998-9501. Exit I-95 at DE 141 N. **Seafood.** In an informal, nautical room with varnished wood tables, a racing powerboat hangs on the wall. Good local reputation for fresh seafood, which is prepared broiled, fried, or Italian-style, plus steaks. **FYI:** Reservations recommended. Children's menu. Dress code. **Open:** Lunch Mon–Fri 11am–4pm; dinner Mon–Thurs 4–9pm, Fri–Sat 4–10pm. **Prices:** Main courses $15–$20. AE, MC, V. 🖭 ᕍ

The Garden Restaurant and Tea Room

In the Winterthur Museum and Gardens, DE 52; tel 302/888-4826. 5 mi N of Wilmington Delaware Ave exit off I-95. **American.** Set in the park-like Winterthur estate, this open and airy space looks out on great natural beauty at all times of the year. A variety of light American entrees and an Oriental stir-fry are offered. Limited wine selection but excellent champagne. Appealing desserts. Elegant afternoon tea is popular. **FYI:** Reservations recommended. Dress code. No smoking. **Open:** Lunch Tues–Fri 11:30am–4:30pm, Sun 3–4:30pm; brunch Sun 10am–1:30pm. **Prices:** Lunch main courses $10–$15. AE, DISC, MC, V. 🖼 ᕍ

Govatos Restaurant and Homemade Candies

800 Market Street Mall; tel 302/652-4082. Delaware Ave exit off I-95, off 8th St. **American/Italian/Candies.** A variety of traditional American and Italian entrees is offered for lunch, plus an excellent assortment of candies, including nirvana-inducing chocolates. Adjacent Govatos Tavern has the same menu. **FYI:** Reservations accepted. Beer and wine only. No smoking. **Open:** Breakfast Mon–Sat 8–11am; lunch Mon–Sat 11am–3:30pm. **Prices:** Lunch main courses $5–$7. MC, V. 🍽 📷 ᕍ

♥ Green Room

In Hotel du Pont, 11th and Market Sts (Downtown); tel 302/594-3100. Exit 7 or 7A off I-95. **Continental/French.** Gracious old-time setting, polite and responsive service, first-rate cuisine. The handsome Edwardian room has a carved wood ceiling, a minstrel gallery, and wood-paneled walls hung with original paintings by regional artists. Specialties include lump crabmeat and shrimp mousse served with a champagne-mustard sauce; ginger-infused breast of squab with vegetable risotto; and grilled swordfish with a fennel sorrel sauce. **FYI:** Reservations recommended. Harp. Jacket required. No smoking. **Open:** Breakfast Mon–Fri 7–10:30am, Sat 7–11am; lunch Mon–Sat 11:30am–2pm; dinner Fri–Sat 6–10pm; brunch Sun 10am–3pm. **Prices:** Main courses $20–$29; prix fixe $29. AE, CB, DC, DISC, MC, V. ♥ ▼ VP &

Griglia Toscana

In the Rockford Shops, 1412 N Dupont St (West End); tel 302/654-8001. Exit 7 or 7B off I-95. **Italian.** Unpretentious and casual, located in a small shopping center near Trolley Square. Tuscan and other northern Italian specialties, including a variety of pastas. Meat and fish prepared on a grill visible from dining room. Pizzas baked in wood-fired oven. Noted Italian wine list. Toscana to Go in same shopping center (302/655-8600). **FYI:** Reservations recommended. Dress code. No smoking. **Open:** Lunch Mon–Fri 11:30am–2pm; dinner daily 5:30–10pm. **Prices:** Main courses $10–$21. AE, DC, DISC, MC, V. &

Kid Shelleen's

1801 W 14th St, at Scott St; tel 302/658-4600. DE 52 N exit off I-95, right at Pennsylvania Ave. **Regional American.** Western-movie decor sets the scene at this restaurant named after the character played by Lee Marvin in *Cat Ballou*. Exceptional mural in banquet room. The kitchen cranks out American dishes with a flair, some with California influence. A popular, busy place. **FYI:** Reservations accepted. Children's menu. Dress code. **Open:** Mon–Sat 11am–1am, Sun 10am–1am. **Prices:** Main courses $5–$15. AE, MC, V. ▲

Ristorante Carucci

In Wawaset Plaza, 504–506 Greenhill Ave; tel 302/654-2333. Exit 7 or 7B off I-95. Turn right on Delaware Ave; bear left on Pennsylvania Ave; turn left on Greenhill Ave. **Italian.** A fun restaurant, this simple, black-and-white room has splashes of colorful art, but nothing that distracts from the music provided by the opera-singing wait staff (some of whom have won competitions). Seafood, beef, and lamb grilled in northern Italian style, plus pasta dishes. The trio wine tasting is a great value. **FYI:** Reservations recommended. Piano/singer. Dress code. No smoking. **Open:** Lunch Mon–Fri 11:30am–2:30pm; dinner Mon–Sat 5:30pm–midnight. **Prices:** Main courses $15–$30. AE, DC, MC, V. &

Sal's Petite Marmite

603 N Lincoln St (Little Italy); tel 302/652-1200. Exit 7 or 7B off I-95. **French.** This French restaurant, incongruously located in Little Italy, is in an old building decorated in classic dark colors and furnished simply but comfortably. Winner of many awards for fine French cuisine. **FYI:** Reservations recommended. Dress code. **Open:** Lunch Mon–Fri 11:30am–2pm; dinner Mon–Sat 5–10pm. **Prices:** Main courses $15–$28. AE, CB, DC, DISC, MC, V. ♥ ▲

The Shipley Grill

913 Shipley St; tel 302/652-7797. Exit I-95 at Delaware Ave; turn right on Shipley St. **American/Seafood.** Dark paneling and well-worn traditional booths and tables are set with good linen and china in a comfortable, casual fashion. American-style steak and seafood are offered. Bar area adjacent to dining room is popular after-theater spot. **FYI:** Reservations recommended. Dress code. **Open:** Peak (Oct–Mar) lunch Mon–Fri 11am–3pm; dinner daily 5:30–10pm. **Prices:** Main courses $13–$22. AE, CB, DC, DISC, ER, MC, V.

The Silk Purse and Sow's Ear

1307 N Scott St; tel 302/654-7666. Exit 7 or 7B off I-95. **New American.** The Silk Purse downstairs is more formal than the whimsical Sow's Ear upstairs, which has mirrored walls and a tasteful, attractive decor. Light, creative treatment of fresh seafood, beef, and lamb in a fusion of continental and American styles. It's very easy to miss this inconspicuous building. **FYI:** Reservations accepted. Dress code. **Open:** Tues–Thurs 5:30–9:30pm, Fri–Sat 5:30–10pm. **Prices:** Main courses $14–$24. AE, MC, V. ♥ &

Temptations

In Trolley Square Shopping Center, Delaware Ave and Dupont St; tel 302/429-9162. Exit I-95 at Delaware Ave N; go 6 blocks. **Cafe/Ice cream.** A simple, old-fashioned interior in subdued reds and pinks has tables and a large ice cream bar. Sandwiches, salads, and other light lunches are also available. Also at: 2900 Concord Pike, at Brandywine Square, Wilmington (tel 302/478-9094). **FYI:** Reservations accepted. No liquor license. No smoking. **Open:** Peak (Apr–Sept) Mon–Thurs 10am–10pm, Fri–Sat 10am–11pm, Sun noon–5pm. **Prices:** Lunch main courses $4–$6. AE, MC, V. ▣

Terrace at Greenhill

At Ed Oliver Golf Course, 800 N Du Pont Rd (Greenville); tel 302/575-1990. Exit I-95 at Delaware Ave N. **Regional American.** Both the simple, green-and-pastel room and the outdoor terrace enjoy fine views of the golf course and of Wilmington, especially at night. Emphasis on regional seafood, but other American entrees available including rainbow trout amandine, blackened red snapper, and jambalaya. Good selection of beers from around the world. **FYI:** Reservations accepted. Children's menu. No smoking. **Open:** Lunch Mon–Sat 11:30am–2:30pm; dinner Mon–Thurs 5–9pm, Fri–Sat 5–10pm, Sun 4–9pm; brunch Sun 10am–3pm. **Prices:** Main courses $10–$14. AE, DC, MC, V. ▲ ▨ ▼ &

Tiffin

1210 N Market St; tel 302/571-1133. E of Delaware Ave exit off I-95. **New American/Californian.** Pastel decor, contemporary artworks, and wicker furniture make for a casual dining room. Light treatment of fish, shellfish, poultry, and meat entrees uses sauces with an international influence, as in breast of duck with raspberry vinaigrette. Pretty central courtyard. **FYI:** Reservations recommended. Piano. Dress code. **Open:** Lunch Mon–Fri 11:30am–2:30pm; dinner Mon–Thurs 5:30–10pm, Fri–Sat 5:30–11pm. **Prices:** Main courses $17–$22. AE, MC, V.

Waterworks Café

16th and French Sts; tel 302/652-6022. Delaware Ave S exit off I-95. **American/Continental.** Large windows in this century-old waterworks building overlook the Brandywine River downtown. Pleasant outdoor deck. Mostly American seafood and beef with continental sauces. **FYI:** Reservations recommended. Dress code. **Open:** Lunch Tues–Fri 11:30am–2:30pm; dinner Tues–Sat 5:30–9pm. **Prices:** Main courses $16–$27. AE, MC, V. 🍴 🏞

ATTRACTIONS 📷

Old Swedes Church

606 Church St; tel 302/652-5629. Erected in 1698, this is one of the oldest houses of worship in the United States. The church remains in its original form and is still regularly used for religious services. The churchyard predates the church by 60 years and was used as a burying ground for early settlers of Fort Christina and its community. A nearby reconstructed farmhouse depicts the everyday life of early Swedish settlers. **Open:** Mon, Wed, Fri, and Sat 1–4pm. **Free**

Willingtown Square

505 Market St Mall; tel 302/655-7161. These four stately 18th-century houses were moved from other parts of the city to this site in 1975–76; they now enclose a beautiful brick courtyard. Owned by the Historical Society, the houses are not open to the public. **Open:** Daily 24 hours.

Delaware Art Museum

2301 Kentmere Pkwy; tel 302/571-9590. Renowned for its collections of American art (from 1840 to the present), this museum is the home of the largest holding of works by Howard Pyle, the father of American illustration and founder of the Brandywine school of painting. Other outstanding examples of American sculpture, photography, and crafts—traditional and contemporary—are also on view, as is the largest display of English pre-Raphaelite art in the United States. **Open:** Tues–Sat 10am–5pm, Sun noon–5pm. $

Winterthur Museum and Gardens

DE 52; tel 302/888-4600 or toll free 800/448-3883. Located 6 mi NW of Wilmington. Named after a town in Switzerland, this nine-story mansion and country estate was once the country home of Henry Francis du Pont. Today it is the Brandywine Valley's star attraction, ranked as one of the world's premier collections of American antiques and decorative arts. Du Pont himself, a collector of furniture, made the initial acquisitions, and the collection grew over the years. The objects, which include Chippendale furniture, silver tankards by Paul Revere, and a dinner service made for George Washington, are displayed in over 180 period rooms.

The museum offers several types of guided tours, including a one-hour general overview tour and a two-hour in-depth decorative arts tour that requires reservations. Tours begin in a new pavilion known as the **Galleries,** featuring a 10-minute audiovisual program and a series of interactive exhibits that provide background about the mansion.

The meticulously landscaped 980-acre grounds are planted with a variety of native and exotic plants. Access to the gardens, which can be toured via self-guided walk or tram ride (Apr–Oct), is included in the admission fee. Special seasonal events, museum store, bookshop, restaurant. **Open:** Tues–Sat 9am–5pm, Sun noon–5pm. $$$

Hagley Museum

DE 141; tel 302/658-2400. This peaceful woodland setting directly on the Brandywine River is the spot that drew French émigré Eleuthère Irénée du Pont de Nemours to establish a black powder mill here in 1802. The first of the du Pont family developments in America, this mill was the forerunner of the large chemical companies developed by subsequent generations. Today the 240-acre outdoor museum re-creates the lifestyle and atmosphere of the original 19th-century mill village through a series of restored buildings, displays, replicas, demonstrations, working machines, and gardens. The highlight is a building called **Eleutherian Mills,** the first (1803) du Pont home in America, a Georgian-style residence furnished to reflect five generations of the du Ponts. **Open:** Peak (Mar 15–Dec) daily 9:30am–4:30pm. Reduced hours off-season. $$$

Nemours Mansion and Gardens

Rockland Rd; tel 302/651-6912. Built in 1909–10, the 300-acre estate of Alfred I du Pont was named after the family's ancestral home in north-central France. The 102-room Louis XVI–style château contains antique furnishings, Oriental rugs, tapestries, and paintings dating from the 15th century, as well as personal items—vintage automobiles, billiards equipment, and bowling alleys.

The gardens, which stretch almost 1/3 mile along the main promenade from the mansion, represent one of the finest examples of formal French-style gardens in America. Guided tours of the mansion and gardens (offered Tues–Sat at 9am, 11am, 1pm, and 3 pm; Sun at 11am, 1pm, and 3pm) take a minimum of two hours. Reservations are recommended; visitors must be over 16 years of age. **Open:** May–Nov. $$$

Rockwood Museum

610 Shipley Rd; tel 302/761-4340 or 571-7776. Inspired by an English country house, the rural Gothic mansion was designed in 1851 for Joseph Shipley, one of the city's early merchant bankers. The house itself is furnished with a blend of 17th-, 18th-, and 19th-century decorative arts from the United States, Britain, and continental Europe; the elaborate conservatory features a brilliant array of Victorian flora. Outbuildings include a porter's lodge, gardener's cottage, carriage house, and barn. Six acres of exotic foliage and landscaping complete the grounds. **Open:** Peak (Mar–Dec) Tues–Sun 11am–4pm. Reduced hours off-season. $$

Delaware History Museum

504 Market St; tel 302/655-7161. This new museum, housed in a restored 1940s F W Woolworth building, focuses on the state's agriculture, water-based industries, and corporate life. Recent exhibits have included "Delaware Goes to War" and "Distinctly Delaware," exploring the multicultural background of the state. **Open:** Tues–Fri noon–4pm, Sat 10am–4pm. **Free**

Delaware Center for the Contemporary Arts

103 E 16th St; tel 302/656-6466. The focus here is on contemporary painting, drawing, textiles, photography, and sculpture, by both national and local artists. Annual art auction in mid-April. **Open:** Tues–Fri 11am–5pm, Sat–Sun 1–5pm. **Free**

Kalmar Nyckel Foundation

1124 E 7th St; tel 302/429-7447. Set on the shores of the Christina River, this project aims to re-create the story of the first permanent European settlement in the Delaware Valley in 1638. It comprises a museum, a working 17th-century shipyard, and a full-scale working replica of the *Kalmar Nyckel,* the ship that first sailed to this area from Sweden. **Open:** Mon–Fri 10am–4:30pm. **$$**

Delaware Division of the Arts

Carvel State Office Bldg, 820 N French St; tel 302/577-3540. The umbrella arts organization for Delaware has in its headquarters building two galleries that showcase local arts and crafts exhibits. **Open:** Mon–Fri 8am–4:30pm. **Free**

Delaware Children's Museum

601 Market St; tel 302/658-0797. Designs and presents exhibits, programs, and events that promote learning by providing children with hands-on explorations in nature, creativity, and the global community. **Open:** Tues–Sat 10am–4pm. **$**

Grand Opera House

818 N Market St; tel 302/658-7897. Much of Wilmington's nightlife is centered around this impressive restored Victorian showplace. Built in 1871 as part of a Masonic temple, this 1,100-seat facility is one of the finest examples of cast-iron architecture in America and is listed on the National Register of Historic Places. The Opera House presents a diverse program of events ranging from classical music to pop, stand-up comedy, and dance; it also serves as home to the Delaware Symphony Orchestra and Opera Delaware. **Open:** Call for schedule. **$$$$**

Brandywine Zoo

1001 N Park Dr; tel 302/571-7747. On view in Delaware's only zoo are such exotica as monkeys, llamas, a giant sloth, a Siberian tiger, and South American species of pythons, parrots, and boas. **Open:** Daily 10am–4pm. **$**

Bellevue State Park

800 Carr Rd; tel 302/577-3390. Located on the northeast perimeter of the city, this 270-acre park was once the home of the William du Pont family. Recreational facilities include eight outdoor clay tennis courts; an equestrian facility with indoor and outdoor arenas; and a fishing pond stocked with bass, catfish, and sunfish. A bandshell hosts concerts and performances June–Aug. Picnic areas, garden paths, fitness trails. **Open:** Daily 8am–sunset. **$$**

DISTRICT OF COLUMBIA

The Spirit of America in Stone

Washington, DC—the capital of the United States and the governmental seat of the premiere global power—is also every American's hometown. Its site was selected in 1791 by George Washington, first president of a new nation embodying revolutionary ideals of freedom and democracy—ideals based on the political principles outlined by Thomas Jefferson in the Declaration of Independence. Its monuments, memorials, and major offices of government have always evoked the spirit in which this nation was founded. The White House is one of the world's few residences of a head of state that has always welcomed visitors ("I never forget," said Franklin Delano Roosevelt, "that I live in a house owned by all the American people").

At the Capitol, topped by a 19½–foot statue of Freedom, the public can sit in on the House of Representatives or the Senate in session. And few visitors will fail to be inspired by the serene classical dignity of the Supreme Court, its pledge etched in a frieze over a Corinthian-columned entrance: "Equal Justice Under Law." Equally moving are the walls of the Lincoln Memorial, inscribed with the stirring words of the visionary president. It is fitting that another freedom-loving American, Dr Martin Luther King Jr, chose the steps of Lincoln's shrine to proclaim "I have a dream." And the nation's most cherished documents—the Declaration of Independence, the Constitution, and the Bill of Rights—are on view in the National Archives. Washington is a federal showplace worthy of a great nation—a beautiful city of beaux-arts architecture, grand boulevards, grassy malls, monumental sculpture, and circular fountained plazas. But most importantly, it exemplifies what is finest about America.

Frommer'

#1

A Brief History

A City is Born In 1783, Congress proposed that a federal city be built to house the government of the newly independent United States of America. After some wrangling about its location, New Yorker Alexander Hamilton and Virginian Thomas Jefferson worked out a compromise: The South would pay off the North's Revolutionary War debts in exchange for northern support of a southern capital. President George Washington, an experienced surveyor, selected the city's site and hired French military engineer Pierre Charles L'Enfant to lay it out.

L'Enfant's design was inspired by Paris, with broad avenues radiating from squares and circles centered on monumental fountains and sculptures. The Mall was conceived as a ceremonial avenue of embassies and other important buildings with Pennsylvania Avenue as the city's main thoroughfare. L'Enfant was a genius, and his plan (which can be seen in the Library of Congress) was magnificent, but his arrogance and impatience with politics alienated city building commissioners. In 1792 he was fired.

Though much of L'Enfant's plan would languish for more than a century, a city slowly began to rise along the Potomac. The cornerstone of the "presidential palace" (later renamed the White House) was laid in 1792, that of the Capitol building (on a hill that L'Enfant had designated "a pedestal waiting for a monument") in 1793. By 1800 Congress was installed in the Capitol (though only its first wing was completed), and President John Adams and his wife had taken up residency in the executive mansion. Then came the War of 1812.

A City is Burned On August 24, 1814, the British fleet sailed into Chesapeake Bay, marched on the capital, and set fire to the fledgling city. Luckily, torrential rains that evening halted the flames, and a tornado, though causing some further damage the next day, daunted the British troops. Though many felt Washington was doomed (Congress came within nine votes of abandoning it as the American capital), an editorial in the *National Intelligencer* rallied municipal pride with the admonition that moving the capital would be tantamount to "kissing the rod an enemy has wielded." Thomas Jefferson donated his own books to replace the destroyed contents of the Library of Congress, and, in 1817, the charred walls of the executive mansion were painted white—transforming it ever after into the White House.

The city got a boost in 1829, when Englishman James Smithson died, leaving a bequest of half a million dollars "to found at Washington, under the name of the Smithsonian Institution, an establishment for the increase and diffusion of knowledge." The first Smithsonian building (today the "castle" housing its information center) was erected in 1849.

The Union Shall Go On The Civil War turned the capital into an armed camp. Churches were used as hospitals, parks became campgrounds, and attention turned from constructing federal buildings to constructing forts. But Lincoln insisted that, in spite of everything, work on the Capitol must continue. "If people see the Capitol going on, it is a sign we intend the Union shall go on," he said. When its giant dome was completed in 1863, a 35-star flag flew overhead, and a 35-gun salute honored all the states in the Union. After the war, President Ulysses S Grant appointed the flamboyant Alexander "Boss" Shepherd to the Board of Public Works and gave him free reign to make the city a showplace. Under his administration, 100 miles of streets— among them Pennsylvania Avenue—were paved and

Fun Facts

- In the early days of the federal government, ambassadors to Washington were provided with "hardship pay" in compensation for enduring the inconvenience of living there.
- Franklin Delano Roosevelt was the only president to be inaugurated in a ceremony held at the White House.
- Upon completion of his design for the city of Washington, French architect Pierre L'Enfant presented a $95,000 bill to the government for his services. Years later, Congress made a sole payment of $2,500 to him.
- No library in the world surpasses the Library of Congress in size. Its 2.85 million square feet of space and more than 575 miles of shelving house more than 101 million items.
- The presidential desk in the Oval Office, carved from the British ship *Resolute,* was presented by Queen Victoria to President Rutherford B Hayes.
- In 1835, President Andrew Jackson paid off the national debt. This would be the only time in the history of the United States that the federal books would be balanced.
- Herbert Hoover was the first US president to have a telephone on his desk.

lighted, sewers were installed, more than 50,000 trees were planted . . . and the city was saddled with over $20 million in debt.

The City Beautiful In 1900 Michigan Senator James McMillan, a retired railroad mogul with training in engineering and architecture, determined to realize L'Enfant's exalted vision for America's capital city. At his personal expense, he sent an illustrious committee—landscapist Frederick Law Olmsted, sculptor Augustus Saint-Gaudens, and noted architects Daniel Burnham and Charles McKim—to study the landscaping and architecture of Europe's great capitals. The famous words of Daniel Burnham best exemplify the committee's aims: "Make no little plans. They have no magic to stir men's blood, and probably themselves will not be realized. Make big plans, aim high in hope and work, remembering that a noble and logical diagram once recorded will never die, but long after we are gone will be a living thing, asserting itself with every growing consistency."

The committee's plans, all implemented along with L'Enfant's "noble and logical diagram," included the development of a complete park system, beautification of the Mall, the selection of sites for government buildings, and designs for the Lincoln and Jefferson Memorials, the Arlington Memorial Bridge, and a reflecting pool between the Lincoln Memorial and the Washington Monument. Several awe-inspiring buildings—the Library of Congress, the Corcoran Gallery, and Union Station (designed by Burnham)—were completed by the turn of the century. Under President William Howard Taft, the famous cherry trees (a gift from Japan) were planted in the Tidal Basin, and a National Commission of Fine Arts was created to advise on fountains, statues, and monuments. The city was further beautified during the 1930s Depression under FDR's Works Progress Administration.

Washington Today Washington in the 1990s is, architecturally and culturally, a city that all Americans can view with pride. It is a city that boasts the Smithsonian Institution, containing more than a dozen museums plus the National Zoo, and the John F Kennedy Center for the Performing Arts, a great cultural center; impressive governmental buildings and stirring monuments and memorials; and a host of delightful outdoor attractions. For the visitor, Washington offers an inimitable melange of big-city sophistication, natural beauty, political panache, and historical perspective.

A Closer Look
GEOGRAPHY

DRIVING DISTANCES
37 mi SW of Baltimore
106 mi NE of Richmond, VA
133 mi SW of Philadelphia
158 mi NW of Williamsburg, VA
221 mi SE of Pittsburgh
233 mi SW of New York
353 mi NE of Charleston, WV
381 mi NE of Charlotte, NC
429 mi SW of Boston
572 mi E of Indianapolis
608 mi NE of Atlanta
671 mi SE of Chicago
840 mi E of St Louis
1,057 mi NE of Miami

Situated on the northern bank of the Potomac River, Washington lies midway along the eastern seaboard of the United States, about 80 miles inland from the Atlantic Ocean. At its highest elevation, in northwest Washington, it rises 390 feet. Its lowest elevation is sea level, at the riverbank.

CLIMATE

Lushly planted with trees, flower gardens, and verdant grounds (including many areas designed by America's foremost landscape architect, Frederick Law Olmsted), Washington enjoys a beautiful spring and fall. It's a delight to stroll the city's streets, the C&O Canal, rustic parks, monument grounds, and the Arboretum during cherry blossom season or when fall foliage is at its peak. Temperatures are moderate to cold November through March, making winter a good season for indoor museum visiting—and the same might be said of the city's humid and sultry summers.

WHAT TO PACK

Let comfort be your guide. Few cities have more museums and sightseeing attractions, and you're going to be spending entire days walking around them. If your feet hurt, those days will not be pleasant. Pack your most comfortable shoes and clothing, keeping your wardrobe especially light in summer. You might, however, carry a sweater even in hot weather; interior spaces are often frigidly air conditioned. In winter, you'll need a hat, coat (a down jacket is lightest and easiest to pack and carry), and boots. And any season, a fold-up umbrella is a good idea.

Though you can find casual restaurants and clubs, Washingtonians do dress for dinner and shows. If your travel plans include dinner at an upscale restaurant, the theater, or a concert, jackets and ties are essential for men, and women will want to have at least one dressy outfit.

You don't need to pack a travel iron. Almost all hotels can provide irons at the front desk. Hair dryers are also usually available.

TOURIST INFORMATION

Before Leaving Home Contact the Washington, DC Convention and Visitors Association, 1212 New York Ave NW, Washington, DC 20005 (tel 202/789-7000), and request a free map, a calendar of events, and a booklet called *The Washington, DC Guide* that lists hotels, restaurants, shopping, sights, and more.

The Washington, DC *City Pages* maintains a World Wide Web page (http://dcpages.ari.net) with information on the arts, recreation, weather, and more. Other useful WWW pages are maintained by the Smithsonian Institution (http://www.si.edu) and the White House (http://www.whitehouse.gov).

Your senator and/or congressional representative can provide special passes for tours of the White House, the Capitol, the Kennedy Center, the FBI, and the Bureau of Engraving and Printing. These tours may be more comprehensive than regular tours, and, since they're for specific times, they guarantee admission (not always a sure thing in busy tourist seasons) and spare you the necessity of standing in long lines. Address requests to representatives to: US House of Representatives, Washington, DC 20515; and to senators to: US Senate, Washington, DC 20510. Write as far in advance as possible, since the ticket allotment for each site is limited, and be sure to include the exact dates of your trip. Note: Before writing, try calling your senator or congressperson's local office; in some states you can obtain passes by phone.

For a free copy of *Washington Weekends,* a brochure listing reduced weekend rates at dozens of Washington hotels, write or call the DC Committee to Promote Washington, PO Box 27489, Washington, DC 20038-7489 (tel 202/724-4091 or toll free 800/422-8644).

Upon Arrival Be sure to visit the Washington Visitor Information Center in the Willard Collection of Shops (next to but not in the Willard Inter-Continental Hotel) on Pennsylvania Ave NW between 14th and 15th Sts (tel 202/789-7038). Just a block from the White House, this facility provides a wide array of free maps and brochures, and its staff can answer all your questions. Hours are Monday through Saturday from 9am to 5pm.

DRIVING RULES AND REGULATIONS

In the District, the speed limit is 25 miles per hour, unless otherwise posted. The driver, all front-seat passengers, and rear-seat passengers under the age of 18 must wear seat belts. Children under four must ride in an approved child-restraint seat. Drunk-driving laws are strictly enforced, and the penalties are severe. Carrying open containers of alcohol in vehicles is unlawful. Read parking signs carefully; otherwise you may be ticketed and towed to one of the city's impoundment lots, where you will have to pay $75 to retrieve your vehicle.

RENTING A CAR

A car is absolutely unnecessary in Washington, DC, and because parking tends to be expensive (free street parking is almost nil), it's even something of an inconvenience (see "Public Transportation," below). You may, however, wish to rent one for excursions to nearby places of interest in Virginia (such as Mount Vernon, Potomac plantations, and Fredericksburg) or Annapolis in Maryland. All of the major car-rental firms are represented here. Their toll-free phone numbers are:
* **Alamo** (tel toll free 800/327-9633)
* **Avis** (tel 800/331-1212)
* **Budget** (tel 800/527-0700)
* **Hertz** (tel 800/654-3131)
* **National** (tel 800/227-7368)
* **Thrifty** (tel 800/367-2277)

PUBLIC TRANSPORTATION

Washington's Metrorail (subway) system is extensive, clean, efficient, and easy to use, with stops at or near almost every sightseeing attraction. The first time you enter a Metro station, go to the kiosk and ask for a free Metro System Pocket Guide, which contains a map of the system, explains how it works, and lists the closest stops to major points of interest. There's also a comprehensive bus network with routes throughout the District and beyond. Call 202/637-7000 for Metrorail or bus routing information.

In addition, it's easy to hail a taxi, anywhere, any time. Taxis charge by the zone (no meters here), and drivers are allowed to pick up as many passengers as they can comfortably fit; expect to share.

Two sightseeing-tram companies—Tourmobile (tel 202/544-5100) and Old Town Trolley (tel 301/985-3020)—provide reasonably priced and comfortable transport to all major attractions. Call for details.

ESSENTIALS

Area Code: 202

Emergencies: Call **911** for police, the fire department, or an ambulance.

Liquor Laws: The minimum drinking age is 21. Establishments can serve alcoholic beverages Monday through Thursday from 8am to 2am, Friday and Saturday from 8am to 2:30am, and Sunday from 10am to 2am. Liquor stores are closed on Sunday.

Smoking: There are nonsmoking sections in all Washington restaurants with a seating capacity of 50 or more, bar area excluded. Almost all hotels have nonsmoking rooms. Smoking is not permitted in retail establishments (except for restaurants within retail establishments, such as department-store or Union Station eateries).

Taxes: Sales tax in the District is 11%. Keep in mind that it will be added to your hotel rate, along with a $1.50 per room, per night occupancy tax.

Time Zone: Washington is in the Eastern time zone. Daylight saving time is observed from the first Sunday in April until the last Sunday in October.

Best of the City
WHAT TO SEE AND DO

Below is a general overview of some of the top sights and attractions in Washington. To find out more detailed information, look under "Attractions" in the listings portion of this book.

Architecture Washington's architecture ranges from Georgetown's quaint Federal-style homes to gorgeous neoclassical museums and government buildings. There are so many of the latter that the city has been dubbed "Athens on the Potomac." The three major houses of government form a splendid architectural triumvirate—the **White House,** designed by Dubliner James Hoban after the country estate of an Irish duke; the magnificent white-domed **Capitol,** along with the **Lincoln Memorial** and the **Washington Monument,** one of the city's most famous landmarks; and Cass Gilbert's Corinthian-marble **Supreme Court.**

Other neoclassical masterpieces include the circular colonnaded **Jefferson Memorial,** the **National Archives,** and the West Wing of the **National Gallery**—all designed by John Russell Pope; the Italian Renaissance–style Thomas Jefferson Building of the **Library of Congress,** one of the most beautiful buildings in America; and **Union Station**—a monument to the great age of rail travel modeled after Rome's Baths of Diocletian and Arch of Constantine. Also notable: The Victorian red sandstone "castle"—first home of the **Smithsonian** museum complex—and the **Renwick Gallery,** in the French Second Empire style. Both were designed by James Renwick.

Cuisine Washington is a great restaurant town. Many local chefs are in the vanguard of culinary trends, and in a city filled with foreign embassies there's plenty of good ethnic cuisine as well—everything from Spanish tapas to Indian tandoori. The city is especially known for its Ethiopian restaurants. In addition, fresh seafood comes in from Chesapeake Bay (look for crab cakes on many menus), and this being the South, cheese grits are also easy to come by.

Family Favorites Popular children's sights include the **National Air and Space Museum** (IMAX films, missiles, rockets), the **National Museum of Natural History** (a discovery room and dinosaurs), the **FBI** (gangster memorabilia and a sharpshooting demonstration), the **Capital Children's Museum** (hands-on exhibits for kids), the **House Where Lincoln Died,** and the **National Zoological Park.** You'll want to take in all the historic government sites—the White House, the Supreme Court, the Capitol, and the major monuments and memorials. Also inquire about special children's activities at museum information desks, and call the **Kennedy Center** (tel 202/467-4600 or toll free 800/444-1324) and the

National Theatre (tel 202/783-3370) for details about performances for kids.

Museums You won't see all of Washington's museums in one visit, and if you had several lifetimes, it wouldn't be long enough to view all of their contents. The **Smithsonian Institution** alone exhibits only 1% of its vast holdings at any given time, in more than 12 Washington museums. And that's not including the prestigious **National Gallery of Art,** equal in scope to New York's Metropolitan Museum or the Louvre in Paris; the exquisite **Phillips Collection,** conceived as "a museum of modern art and its sources"; the **National Geographic Society's Explorers Hall,** as fascinating as the magazine itself; collections of pre-Columbian and Byzantine art at **Dumbarton Oaks;** the **United States Holocaust Memorial Museum,** and many more.

Parks & Gardens **West Potomac Park,** with 1,300 cherry trees ringing the Tidal Basin, is the site of the Vietnam Memorial, the Lincoln and Jefferson Memorials, and the Reflecting Pool. **East Potomac Park** contains 1,800 additional cherry trees. You can hike or bike along the towpath of the 184-mile **C&O Canal** or—from mid-April to mid-October—take a mule-drawn boat ride on it. **Rock Creek Park,** in the center of town, is a 1,750-acre greenbelt—one of the biggest and finest city parks in the nation. The highlight of the **US National Arboretum**—444 hilly acres of rhododendrons and azaleas, dogwoods and day lilies, boxwoods and cherry trees (and much more)—is the exquisite National Bonsai Collection. And you can observe abundant bird life, flora, and fauna on the foot trails of **Theodore Roosevelt Island,** an 88-acre wilderness preserve.

Beautiful gardens include **Dumbarton Oaks,** with 10 acres of formal gardens; the **United States Botanic Garden**—a lovely oasis at the east end of the Mall; the Victorian **Enid A Haupt Garden** on the Mall, with its central magnolia-lined parterre, floral swags, and ribbon beds; and the **Hirshhorn Museum's** delightful tree-shaded sunken sculpture garden.

EVENTS AND FESTIVALS

Check the *Washington Post,* especially the Friday "Weekend" section, as well as the *City Paper,* a free weekly. Among the annual highlights:
- **Martin Luther King Jr's Birthday.** Speeches, readings, concerts, prayer vigils, and a wreath laying at the Lincoln Memorial to honor the civil rights leader. Third Monday in January. Call 202/789-7000 for details.
- **Chinese New Year Celebration.** A 10-day festival with traditional firecrackers, dragon dancers, and colorful street parades in Washington's small Chinatown at 7th and H Sts, NW. Late January or early to mid-February. Call 202/789-7000 or 202/724-4093.
- **Smithsonian Kite Festival.** Throngs of kite enthusiasts fly their original creations on the Washington Monument grounds and compete for prizes. Mid- or late March. Call 202/357-2700 for details.
- **Cherry Blossom Events.** The blossoming of the famous cherry trees is celebrated with a major parade, fireworks, fashion shows, concerts, a ball, and a marathon race. Late March or early April. Call 202/728-1135 for details.
- **White House Easter Egg Roll.** Hunting for eggs is the highlight for little kids (ages three to six), but there's plenty for everyone else—Easter bunnies, egg-decorating exhibitions, magic shows, military drill teams, clog dancers, clowns, and more. Easter Monday between 10am and 2pm (arrive early) on the White House South Lawn and the Ellipse. Call 202/456-2200 for details.
- **The Imagination Celebration.** A two-week festival of performing arts for young people at the Kennedy Center for the Performing Arts. Events are free or moderately priced. Mid-April. Call 202/467-4600 for details.
- **White House Gardens.** Special free tours between 2 and 5pm of these beautifully landscaped creations. Four days per year only, two in mid-April and two in mid-October. Call 202/456-2200 for details.
- **Memorial Day.** Ceremonies at the Tomb of the Unknowns in Arlington National Cemetery (call 202/475-0856 for details) and the Vietnam Veterans Memorial (call 202/619-7222 for details). In the evening, the National Symphony Orchestra performs a free concert at 8pm on the Capitol's West Lawn (call 202/619-7222 for details). Last Monday in May.
- **Smithsonian Festival of American Folklife.** Dozens of events on the Mall including music (everything from Appalachian fiddling to Native American dance), food, concerts, games, and crafts demonstrations. Early July. Call 202/357-2700 for details.

- **Independence Day.** A massive daytime parade down Constitution Avenue, baseball games, concerts, crafts exhibitions, and a reading of the Declaration of Independence in front of the National Archives (a Revolutionary War encampment is set up for the occasion); at night, a National Symphony Orchestra concert on the Capitol steps and a fabulous fireworks display over the Washington Monument. July 4. Call 202/789-7000 for details.
- **Tchaikovsky's 1812 Overture.** The US Army band performs this famous work, complete with roaring cannons, at the Sylvan Theatre on the Washington Monument grounds. August. Call 703/696-3718 for details.
- **National Frisbee Festival.** See world-class Frisbee champions and their disc-catching dogs on the Mall near the Air and Space Museum. First weekend in September. Call 301/645-5043 for details.
- **Washington National Cathedral Open House.** Stone carving, craft, carillon and organ demonstrations, as well as performances. Only time visitors can climb to the top of the central tower to see the carillon—a tremendous hike but a spectacular view. Late September or early October. Call 202/537-6200 for details.
- **Marine Corps Marathon.** A 26-mile race that begins at the Iwo Jima Memorial in Washington and passes some of Washington's major monuments. First Sunday in November. Call 703/690-3431 for details.
- **Veterans Day.** Ceremonies to honor the nation's war dead at the Tomb of the Unknowns in Arlington National Cemetery (call 202/475-0856 for details) and at the Vietnam Veterans Memorial (call 202/619-7222 for details). November 11.
- **National Tree Lighting.** The President lights the national Christmas tree to the accompaniment of choral and orchestral music, kicking off a two-week Pageant of Peace—a holiday celebration with seasonal music, caroling, and a Nativity scene. Early December. Call 202/619-7222 for details.
- **White House Candlelight Tours.** The President's holiday decorations open to view on three selected December evenings between 6 and 8pm. Call 202/456-2200 for dates and details.

SPECTATOR SPORTS

Baseball Pre-season major league exhibition games are held during the month of March at **Robert F Kennedy Memorial Stadium** (tel 202/547-9077 or 202/546-3337).

Basketball The NBA's **Washington Bullets** play home games at the 19,000-seat USAir Arena in Landover, MD (tel 301/350-3400). College teams competing in the NCAA's Division I include the formidable **Georgetown University Hoyas,** who play at USAir Arena, and the **George Washington University Colonials,** who play at the Smith Center on the GW campus (tel 202/994-8584) and also host the Red Auerbach Colonial Classic tournament held December 2–3.

Football Washington-area pro football fans are famously fanatic about their **Redskins,** who play their NFL home schedule at RFK Stadium (tel 202/547-9077 or 202/546-3337).

Hockey The NHL **Washington Capitals** play home games at USAir Arena in Landover, MD (tel 301/350-3400).

Soccer Fans can catch the **Washington Warthogs** of the CISL (an indoor league) at USAir Arena (tel 301/350-3400) from June through August.

ACTIVITIES A TO Z

Bicycling Both **Fletcher's Boat House** and **Thompson's Boat Center** (see "Boating" below) rent bikes, as does **Big Wheel Bikes** (tel 202/337-0254). The latter is right near the C&O Canal, a major cycling venue. Photo ID and a major credit card are required to rent bicycles. The *Washington Post's* Friday "Weekend" section lists cycling trips.

Boating Fletcher's Boat House, (tel 202/244-0461) is about 3.2 miles from Georgetown right on the C&O Canal. Open March to mid-November, daily from 7:30am to dusk, it rents canoes and rowboats and sells fishing licenses, bait, and tackle. **Thompson's Boat Center** (tel 202/333-4861 or 202/333-9543) rents canoes, sailboats, rowing shells, and rowboats. It's open mid-April through early October, daily from 8am to 5pm.

Camping There are camping areas with picnic tables and fire grills along the **C&O Canal** every five miles or so from Fletcher's Boat House to Cumberland, Maryland. Use is on a first-come, first-served basis. Call 301/739-4200 for details.

Fishing The Potomac River provides good fishing

from late February to November, but mid-March through June (spawning season) is peak. Perch and catfish are the most common catch, but during bass season a haul of 20 to 40 is not unusual. The Washington Channel offers good bass and carp fishing year-round. A fishing license is required. You can obtain one at **Fletcher's Boat House** (see above).

Golf Within the District, there are public golf courses in **Rock Creek Park** (tel 202/882-7332 or 202/723-9832) and **East Potomac Park** (tel 202/ 863-9007).

Hiking A favorite place to hike is the C&O Canal, offering 184 miles of scenic towpath. There are also 15 miles of hiking trails in Rock Creek Park (maps are available at park headquarters). If you prefer group hikes, contact the **Sierra Club** (tel 202/547-2326 or 202/547-5551) or check hiking club listings in the Friday "Weekend" section of the *Washington Post*.

Horseback Riding The **Rock Creek Park Horse** Center on Glover Rd NW (tel 202/362-0117) offers rental horses, for trail rides and instruction, as well as 14 miles of wooded bridle paths.

Ice Skating The **C&O Canal,** its banks dotted with cozy fires, is a delightful place to skate. Call 301/ 299-3613 for ice conditions.

Jogging There's a 1.5-mile Perrier Parcourse with 18 calisthenics stations in Rock Creek Park, beginning near the intersection of Cathedral Ave and Rock Creek Pkwy. The Mall is another peaceful and popular area to jog among "Hill staffers" and many others.

Tennis There are 144 outdoor public courts in the District at 45 locations. Court use is on a first-come, first-served basis. For a list of locations, call or write the **DC Department of Recreation,** 3149 16th St NW, Washington, DC 20010 (tel 202/673-7646). There are also courts in **Rock Creek Park** (tel 202/722-5949) and **East Potomac Park** (tel 202/ 554-5962).

District of Columbia Listings

Washington

In Maryland see also Bethesda, Chevy Chase, Silver Spring; In Virginia see also Alexandria, Arlington, Dulles Int'l Airport, Fairfax, Falls Church, McLean, Vienna

HOTELS 📠

≣ Allen Lee Hotel
2224 F St NW, 20037 (Foggy Bottom); tel 202/331-1224 or toll free 800/462-0186. Between 22nd and 23rd Sts. Looks more like an apartment building than a hotel. This older property shows signs of wear resulting from many guests. **Rooms:** 85 rms. CI open/CO noon. 35 rooms have private baths. **Amenities:** 📠 A/C, TV. **Rates:** $35–$45 S; $45–$56 D. Extra person $6. No CC.

≣≣≣ ANA Hotel
2401 M St NW, 20037 (Georgetown); tel 202/429-2400 or toll free 800/262-4683; fax 202/457-5010. Minutes from the Kennedy Center, this hotel has a tranquil setting, from the gracious lobby to the loggia and garden courtyard. **Rooms:** 415 rms and stes. Executive level. CI 3pm/CO 1pm. Nonsmoking rms avail. All rooms have sitting areas and an oversize desk. **Amenities:** 📠 ⚴ 🍴 A/C, cable TV w/movies, dataport, voice mail, in-rm safe, bathrobes. All units w/minibars, some w/terraces. Each room has three phones (two are speaker phones) with two lines and hold buttons. **Services:** 🍽 🔑 📺 🚗 📠 🛎 ⚴ Twice-daily maid svce, masseur, babysitting. Currency exchange. Complimentary shoe shine. **Facilities:** 🏋 🏊 650 🖥 ⚴ 2 restaurants, 2 bars (1 w/entertainment), spa, sauna, steam rm, whirlpool, beauty salon. Large fitness center has aerobics classes, tanning booths, lap pool, exercise rooms, health spa, juice bar, and lounge. **Rates:** Peak (Mar–May/Sept–Nov) $255–$285 S; $285–$315 D; $660–$1,595 ste. Extra person $30. Children under age 18 stay free. Lower rates off-season. Parking: Indoor, $19/day. Weekend packages include breakfast, parking. AE, CB, DC, DISC, JCB, MC, V.

≣≣ The Bellevue Hotel
15 E St NW, 20001 (Capitol Hill); tel 202/638-0900 or toll free 800/327-6667; fax 202/638-5132. Between New Jersey Ave and N Capitol St. Extremely elegant 70-year-old hotel, with Moorish touches throughout, including multiple arches, small leaded windows, and red marble columns. Lobby features a huge brass-and-crystal chandelier. **Rooms:** 137 rms and stes. CI 4pm/CO noon. Nonsmoking rms avail. Unfortunately the lobby's promise is not fulfilled in the rooms, which are functional and large but lack attention to detail. **Amenities:** 📠 A/C, cable TV w/movies, voice mail. **Services:** ✗ ⚴ 🛎 **Facilities:** 300 ⚴ 1 restaurant (bkfst only), 1 bar. **Rates (BB):** Peak (Mar–May/Sept–Nov) $79–$119 S; $89–$135 D; $250 ste. Extra person $15. Children under age 18 stay free. Lower rates off-season. Parking: Indoor, $8/day. Rates are extremely low given the hotel's location and free buffet breakfast. AE, DC, DISC, MC, V.

≣≣ Canterbury Hotel
1733 N St NW, 20036 (Dupont Circle); tel 202/393-3000 or toll free 800/424-2950; fax 202/785-9581. Built as apartments in 1901, this small European-style hotel offers intimacy and hospitality. **Rooms:** 99 rms. CI 2pm/CO noon. Nonsmoking rms avail. All units have kitchenettes. **Amenities:** 📠 ⚴ 🍴 A/C, cable TV w/movies. All units w/minibars. A few units have microwaves. **Services:** ✗ 📺 ⚴ 🛎 Twice-daily maid svce. **Facilities:** 30 ⚴ 1 restaurant, 1 bar. Guest privileges at nearby health club. **Rates (CP):** Peak (Sept–Nov/Mar–June) $195 S; $215 D. Extra person $20. Children under age 12 stay free. Lower rates off-season. Parking: Indoor, $15/day. AE, CB, DC, DISC, MC, V.

≣≣≣≣ The Capital Hilton
1001 16th Street, at K St, 20036; tel 202/393-1000 or toll free 800/HILTONS; fax 202/639-5784. A club-like atmosphere prevails in the cherrywood-paneled lobby with contemporary art and furniture. Convenient location in the heart of Washington's business district two blocks from the White House and two Metro stations. **Rooms:** 543 rms and stes. Executive level. CI 3pm/CO noon. Nonsmoking rms avail. The hotel originally had 800 rooms, but space was reallocated to create bigger units. Large marble baths with small TVs and phones. Deluxe tower rooms have extras, such as concierge lounge with bar. **Amenities:** 📠 ⚴ 🍴 A/C, cable TV w/movies, dataport, voice mail. All units w/minibars, some w/terraces. Irons and ironing boards. Toys available. **Services:** 🍽 🔑 📺 ⚴ 🛎 Twice-daily maid svce, babysitting. **Facilities:** 🏋

[1200] 🖥 ♿ 2 restaurants, 3 bars (1 w/entertainment), sauna, steam rm, beauty salon. Twigs dining room has garden-like ambience. **Rates:** Peak (Mar–June/Sept–Nov) $185–$230 S or D; $295–$1,100 ste. Extra person $25. Children under age 18 stay free. Lower rates off-season. Parking: Indoor, $22/day. AE, CB, DC, DISC, EC, ER, JCB, MC, V.

⊟⊟ Capitol Hill Suites
200 C St SE, at 2nd St, 20003 (Capitol Hill); tel 202/543-6000 or toll free 800/424-9165; fax 202/547-2608. One block to Library of Congress, US House of Representatives, and Capitol South Metro station. Popular with government workers and others on Congressional business. **Rooms:** 152 effic. CI 3pm/CO noon. Nonsmoking rms avail. Spacious suites with living areas are suited for long-term stays. **Amenities:** 📺 ♨ 📠 A/C, cable TV w/movies, refrig, dataport, voice mail. Kitchenettes have sink and two-burner stove. **Services:** ☞ 🅥🅟 ⌛ 🗝 Evening cocktails, morning newspaper and coffee. **Facilities:** [40] Washer/dryer. Complimentary passes to nearby health club. **Rates:** Peak (Mar–June/Sept–Nov) $129–$179 effic. Extra person $20. Children under age 18 stay free. Lower rates off-season. Parking: Indoor, $12/day. Weekend and long-term rates avail. AE, DC, DISC, MC, V.

⊟⊟⊟⊟ The Carlton
923 16th St NW, at K St, 20006; tel 202/879-6911 or toll free 800/562-5661; fax 202/638-4321. Many Washington and world notables have been through this spacious lobby, which has exquisite furnishings and decor and is the site of afternoon tea accompanied by a harpist. A definite European air is manifest in the 1926 building's Italian Renaissance exterior. **Rooms:** 193 rms and stes. CI 3pm/CO 1pm. Nonsmoking rms avail. **Amenities:** 📺 ♨ 🍴 A/C, cable TV w/movies, dataport, VCR, voice mail, in-rm safe, bathrobes. All units w/minibars, some w/whirlpools. Candies and bottled water. Fax machines in some rooms. **Services:** |◎| ☞ 🅥🅟 ⌛ 🗝 🚗 Twice-daily maid svce, children's program, babysitting. Complimentary cocktail-hour hors d'oeuvres in lounge bar. Free local calls. **Facilities:** 🖥 [300] ♿ 1 restaurant, 1 bar (w/entertainment), beauty salon. **Rates:** Peak (Mar–June/Sept–Nov) $260–$300 S or D; $500–$1,800 ste. Extra person $25. Children under age 18 stay free. Lower rates off-season. Parking: Indoor, $22/day. Various weekend and romance packages avail. AE, CB, DC, DISC, JCB, MC, V.

⊟⊟ The Carlyle Suites
1731 New Hampshire Ave NW, 20009 (Dupont Circle); tel 202/234-3200 or toll free 800/964-5377; fax 202/387-0085. Between R and S Sts. This historic art-deco building has a small lobby with black-and-white tiles, chrome, mirrors, and neon lighting. **Rooms:** 170 stes. CI 3pm/CO 1pm. Nonsmoking rms avail. Interesting architectural features such as alcoves and parquet floors. All units have fully equipped kitchenettes. **Amenities:** 📺 ♨ A/C, cable TV w/movies, refrig. Some units have dataports. **Services:** 🚐 ⌛ 🗝 🚗 Babysitting. **Facilities:** [100] ♿ 1 restaurant, 1 bar, games rm.

Free use of nearby health club. **Rates:** Peak (Apr–Aug) $69–$139 ste. Extra person $10. Children under age 18 stay free. Lower rates off-season. Parking: Outdoor, free. Long-term rates avail. AE, CB, DC, MC, V.

⊟⊟ The Center City Hotel
1201 13th St NW, 20005; tel 202/682-5300 or toll free 800/458-2817; fax 202/371-9624. At M St. Formerly a Best Western, this hotel now has new management, which has instituted cost-cutting measures such as eliminating cable TV from rooms. Nevertheless, premises remain well kept and in good order. Quality of the neighborhood might detract somewhat from a guest's visit. **Rooms:** 100 rms. CI 2pm/CO 11am. Nonsmoking rms avail. **Amenities:** 📺 ♨ 🍴 A/C, refrig, in-rm safe, bathrobes. No TV. 1 unit w/whirlpool. **Services:** |◎| ☞ ⌛ 🗝 🚗 Twice-daily maid svce, masseur. **Facilities:** 🏋 🖥 [750] 🖥 ♿ 1 restaurant (bkfst only), racquetball, squash, spa, sauna, steam rm, whirlpool. **Rates (CP):** Peak (Mar–Oct) $99–$109 S; $109–$119 D. Extra person $10. Children under age 16 stay free. Lower rates off-season. Parking: Outdoor, $9/day. AE, CB, DC, DISC, MC, V.

⊟⊟ Comfort Inn Downtown
500 H St NW, 20001 (Chinatown); tel 202/289-5959 or toll free 800/234-6423; fax 202/682-9152. Chain hotel in heart of Chinatown and its restaurants and shops. **Rooms:** 194 rms. CI 3pm/CO noon. Nonsmoking rms avail. **Amenities:** 📺 ♨ A/C, cable TV w/movies, dataport. Some units w/whirlpools. Fortune cookies in rooms. Video games available. **Services:** ⌛ 🗝 Car-rental desk. **Facilities:** 🖥 [100] ♿ 1 restaurant, sauna, washer/dryer. **Rates:** Peak (June–Aug) $69–$159 S or D. Extra person $10. Children under age 18 stay free. Lower rates off-season. Parking: Indoor, $12/day. AE, CB, DC, DISC, MC, V.

⊟⊟ Connecticut Avenue Days Inn
4400 Connecticut Ave NW, 20008; tel 202/244-5600 or toll free 800/966-3060; fax 202/244-6794. Between Yuma and Albermarle Sts. A chain property offering reasonable rates. Although removed from downtown, it has easy access to Washington attractions via nearby Van Ness Metro station. **Rooms:** 155 rms and stes. CI 2pm/CO noon. Nonsmoking rms avail. **Amenities:** 📺 ♨ 📠 A/C, cable TV, in-rm safe. **Services:** ⌛ 🗝 🚗 Babysitting. **Facilities:** [20] ♿ **Rates (CP):** Peak (Mar 15–Nov 15) $110 S; $120 D; $135 ste. Extra person $10. Children under age 18 stay free. Lower rates off-season. Parking: Indoor/outdoor, $5/day. Weekend rates avail. AE, DC, DISC, MC, V.

⊟⊟⊟ Courtyard by Marriott
1900 Connecticut Ave NW, 20009; tel 202/332-9300 or toll free 800/842-4211; fax 202/328-7039. At Leroy Place. Although this mid-rise hotel lacks the trademark courtyard of this business traveler–oriented chain, it does command a panoramic view of Washington from a hilltop perch. Intimate, club-like atmosphere prevails in lounge reserved for guests' use only. **Rooms:** 147 rms and stes. CI 3pm/CO

noon. Nonsmoking rms avail. Rooms lack sofas and easy chairs found in other members of this chain. **Amenities:** 🔒 📻 A/C, cable TV w/movies, voice mail, in-rm safe. Some units w/minibars. Long phone cords. **Services:** ✕ 🛆 🖶 🖏 Babysitting. Complimentary afternoon cookies and coffee. **Facilities:** 🏋 ⟦60⟧ ⅄ 1 restaurant (bkfst and dinner only), 1 bar, washer/dryer. **Rates:** Peak (Apr–June/Sept–Oct) $130–$175 S; $145–$190 D; $400–$650 ste. Extra person $15. Children under age 18 stay free. Lower rates off-season. Parking: Indoor, $10/day. AE, DC, DISC, MC, V.

≣≣ Days Inn Downtown

1201 K St NW, 20005; tel 202/842-1020 or toll free 800/562-3350; fax 202/289-0336. Convenient downtown location, two blocks from Metro station. Caters to tourists and tour groups. **Rooms:** 220 rms, stes, and effic. CI 2pm/CO 1pm. No smoking. **Amenities:** 🔒 A/C, satel TV w/movies, refrig, voice mail. **Services:** 🛆 🖶 🖏 **Facilities:** 🏋 💪 ⟦200⟧ 1 restaurant (bkfst and dinner only). **Rates:** Peak (Apr–Sept) $105–$115 S; $115–$125 D; $195 ste; $115–$125 effic. Extra person $10. Children under age 17 stay free. Lower rates off-season. Parking: Indoor, $8.50/day. Kids under 12 eat free. AE, CB, DC, DISC, ER, JCB, MC, V.

≣≣ DoubleTree Guest Suites

2500 Pennsylvania Ave NW, 20037; tel 202/333-8060 or toll free 800/222-TREE; fax 202/338-3818. An all-suites hotel convenient to Kennedy Center, downtown businesses, shops, restaurants. Outdoor landscaped patio has tables and chairs. **Rooms:** 123 stes. CI 3pm/CO noon. Nonsmoking rms avail. Units have fully equipped kitchens. All living rooms have sleep sofas. **Amenities:** 🔒 📻 📺 A/C, cable TV w/movies, refrig, dataport, voice mail. Units have dishwashers and microwaves. TVs in both living rooms and bedrooms. **Services:** ✕ 🆚 🚗 🛆 🖶 🖏 Babysitting. **Facilities:** ⟦10⟧ ⅄ Washer/dryer. Free membership in nearby health club. **Rates:** $99–$200 ste. Extra person $15. Children under age 18 stay free. Parking: Indoor, $15/day. Weekend packages avail. AE, CB, DC, DISC, MC, V.

≣≣≣ DoubleTree Hotel Park Terrace

1515 Rhode Island Ave NW, 20005; tel 202/232-7000 or toll free 800/222-TREE; fax 202/332-7152. Between 15th and 16th Sts NW. A modern downtown hotel with a European flair. Located 6 blocks north of the White House between Thomas and Scott Circles. **Rooms:** 219 rms and stes. CI 3pm/CO noon. Nonsmoking rms avail. **Amenities:** 🔒 📻 📺 A/C, cable TV w/movies. All units w/minibars. Suites have kitchenettes with small refrigerators, microwaves, ice makers. **Services:** 🍴 🆚 🛆 🖶 Babysitting. **Facilities:** 💪 ⟦175⟧ 🖥 ⅄ 1 restaurant, 1 bar, washer/dryer. Restaurant looks like large living room with chandelier, carved oak fireplace. **Rates:** $135–$165 S or D; $210 ste. Extra person $10. Children under age 18 stay free. Parking: Indoor, $12.50/day. AE, CB, DC, DISC, ER, MC, V.

≣≣ Dupont Plaza Hotel

1500 New Hampshire Ave NW, 20036 (Dupont Circle); tel 202/483-6000 or toll free 800/841-0003; fax 202/328-3265. Large lounge has panoramic view of the park in center of Dupont Circle. Convenient to restaurants, exclusive shops, Metro, Embassy Row. Caters to tour groups. **Rooms:** 314 rms and stes. CI 3pm/CO 1pm. Nonsmoking rms avail. **Amenities:** 🔒 📻 A/C, cable TV w/movies, refrig. **Services:** ✕ 🆚 🛆 🖶 Babysitting. **Facilities:** ⟦300⟧ ⅄ 1 restaurant, 1 bar. Guests get passes to YMCA health club. **Rates:** Peak (Apr–June/Sept–Nov 15) $165–$195 S; $185–$215 D; $395 ste. Extra person $20. Children under age 18 stay free. Lower rates off-season. Parking: Indoor, $13/day. AE, CB, DC, DISC, MC, V.

≣≣≣ Embassy Row Hotel

2015 Massachusetts Ave NW, 20036 (Dupont Circle); tel 202/265-1600 or toll free 800/424-2400; fax 202/328-7526. In the heart of Embassy Row, this hotel caters to corporate executives and diplomats. Lobby has wall murals, marble floors, recessed lighting, low ceilings. **Rooms:** 195 rms and stes. CI 4pm/CO noon. Nonsmoking rms avail. **Amenities:** 🔒 📻 A/C, cable TV w/movies, in-rm safe. Many rooms have refrigerators. **Services:** ✕ 🔑 🆚 🛆 🖶 Twice-daily maid svce, babysitting. Concierge will organize special tours and programs for children. **Facilities:** 🏋 💪 ⟦200⟧ ⅄ 1 restaurant, 1 bar. Access ramps for guests with disabilities are through parking garage. **Rates:** Peak (Apr–May/Sept–Oct) $145–$175 S; $165–$195 D; $350–$850 ste. Children under age 18 stay free. Lower rates off-season. Parking: Indoor, $12/day. AE, CB, DC, MC, V.

≣≣ Embassy Square Suites

2000 N St NW, 20036 (Dupont Circle); tel 202/659-9000 or toll free 800/424-2999; fax 202/429-9546. Two blocks from Dupont Circle and its Metro station, surrounded by shops and restaurants, this all-suites hotel is ideal for families and long-term stays. **Rooms:** 250 stes. CI 4pm/CO noon. Nonsmoking rms avail. **Amenities:** 🔒 📻 📺 A/C, cable TV w/movies, refrig. Some units w/terraces. Large, comfortable suites have full-size refrigerators, stoves, ovens, sinks, flatware. **Services:** 🛆 🖶 🖏 Babysitting. **Facilities:** 🏋 💪 ⟦100⟧ ⅄ Washer/dryer. **Rates (CP):** Peak (Mar–June/Sept–Nov) $119–$239 ste. Extra person $20. Children under age 18 stay free. Lower rates off-season. Parking: Indoor, $12/day. Long-term rates avail. AE, DC, DISC, MC, V.

≣≣ Embassy Suites

1250 22nd St NW, 20037; tel 202/857-3388 or toll free 800/362-2779; fax 202/293-3173. Between M and N Sts. Located in the West End neighborhood near Foggy Bottom, this nine-story building is constructed around an atrium with cascading waterfalls, lots of trees and plants, terra cotta tiles, wood benches, and wrought-iron tables and chairs. **Rooms:** 318 stes. CI 3pm/CO noon. Nonsmoking rms avail. All units have private bedroom and living room with fully equipped kitchen. **Amenities:** 🔒 📻 📺 A/C, cable TV w/movies, refrig, voice mail. 1 unit w/whirlpool. TVs in both rooms, irons and ironing boards. Toiletries on request. **Services:** ✗ 🗝 🖼 🗘 Babysitting. Complimentary evening reception. **Facilities:** 🏊 🍽 [225] 💻 ᕙ 1 restaurant, 1 bar, games rm, spa, sauna, whirlpool, washer/dryer. Moderately priced Italian restaurant on premises. **Rates (BB):** $169–$219 ste. Extra person $20. Children under age 18 stay free. Parking: Indoor, $14/day. AE, DC, DISC, MC, V.

≣≣ Embassy Suites Chevy Chase Pavilion
4300 Military Rd, 20015 (Friendship Heights); tel 202/362-9300 or toll free 800/EMBASSY; fax 202/686-3405. An all-suites hotel located in the Chevy Chase Pavilion, an upscale shopping and office complex at the Friendship Heights Metro station. Hotel opens to large atrium in center of the mall. **Rooms:** 198 stes. CI 3pm/CO noon. Nonsmoking rms avail. **Amenities:** 🛁 ⚖ 🖥 A/C, cable TV, refrig, VCR, voice mail. Full kitchens contain microwaves. **Services:** ✗ 🖼 🗘 Babysitting. Complimentary made-to-order breakfast, manager's reception every evening. **Facilities:** 🏊 🍽 [150] 💻 ᕙ 1 restaurant, 3 bars, spa, sauna, steam rm, whirlpool, beauty salon, washer/dryer. Full health club on top floor. **Rates (BB):** Peak (Mar–June/Sept–Nov) $180–$195 ste. Extra person $15. Children under age 16 stay free. Lower rates off-season. Parking: Indoor, $10/day. AE, CB, DC, DISC, JCB, MC, V.

≣≣≣≣ Four Seasons
2800 Pennsylvania Ave NW, at M St, 20007 (Georgetown); tel 202/342-0444 or toll free 800/332-3442; fax 202/944-2076. A tasteful and glamorous hostelry opened in 1979. Thousands of plants and large floral arrangements enhance the garden-like ambience of the lobby. Often attracts high-profile guests. **Rooms:** 196 rms and stes. CI 3pm/CO noon. Nonsmoking rms avail. Fairly small rooms, but smart and efficient. Some overlook the Chesapeake & Ohio (C&O) Canal, some face inner courtyard. **Amenities:** 🛁 ⚖ 🖥 A/C, cable TV w/movies, dataport, VCR, voice mail, in-rm safe, bathrobes. All units w/minibars. Phones have two lines. **Services:** 🍽 🗝 📞 🚗 🖼 🗘 🛎 Twice-daily maid svce, social director, masseur, children's program, babysitting. Complimentary early-morning coffee in lobby. Free limo to downtown offices. Portable phones, faxes, PCs, and pagers for rent. Overnight laundry. **Facilities:** 🏊 🍽 [800] 💻 ᕙ 1 restaurant (see "Restaurants" below), 2 bars (1 w/entertainment), spa, sauna, steam rm, whirlpool, beauty salon. Stunning three-story fitness center with vaulted ceiling and skylight and indoor lap pool. Massage rooms (with speaker phones). Private nightclub. **Rates:** $295–$340 S; $325–$370 D; $700–$2,125 ste. Extra person $30. Children under age 18 stay free. Parking: Indoor, $20/day. AE, CB, DC, MC, V.

≣≣≣ The Georgetown Dutch Inn
1075 Thomas Jefferson St NW, 20007 (Georgetown); tel 202/337-0900 or toll free 800/388-2410; fax 202/333-6526. Just below M St. A charming and elegant all-suites hotel situated amid Georgetown shops and a plethora of fine restaurants, which more than makes up for lack of on-premises dining room. **Rooms:** 47 stes. Executive level. CI 3pm/CO noon. Nonsmoking rms avail. Suites are elegantly decorated and furnished with federal-period reproductions. **Amenities:** 🛁 ⚖ A/C, cable TV w/movies, refrig, dataport. 1 unit w/terrace. **Services:** ✗ 🚗 🖼 🗘 Babysitting. **Facilities:** [60] **Rates (CP):** Peak (Mar 15–June 15/Sept 15–Nov 15) $110–$300 ste. Extra person $20. Children under age 17 stay free. Lower rates off-season. Parking: Indoor, free. AE, DC, MC, V.

≣≣≣≣ Georgetown Inn
1310 Wisconsin Ave NW, 20007 (Georgetown); tel 202/333-8900 or toll free 800/424-2979; fax 202/625-1744. A European-style hotel with definite Colonial-era accents. Lobby distinguished by a huge crystal chandelier. **Rooms:** 95 rms and stes. CI 3pm/CO noon. Nonsmoking rms avail. **Amenities:** 🛁 ⚖ A/C, cable TV. **Services:** ✗ 🅥🅟 🖼 🗘 **Facilities:** [100] 1 restaurant, 1 bar (w/entertainment). **Rates:** Peak (Aug–Nov) $129–$149 S; $149–$169 D; $209 ste. Extra person $20. Children under age 13 stay free. Lower rates off-season. Parking: Indoor, $15/day. AE, CB, DC, DISC, EC, ER, JCB, MC, V.

≣≣≣ Georgetown Suites
1111 30th St NW, 20007 (Georgetown); tel 202/298-7800 or toll free 800/348-7203; fax 202/333-5792. At M St. Located near the C&O Canal, this establishment's accommodations range from studios to two-bedroom town houses with separate entrance. **Rooms:** 136 stes and effic; 3 cottages/villas. CI 3pm/CO noon. Nonsmoking rms avail. All units have fully equipped kitchens and contemporary furnishings. **Amenities:** 🛁 ⚖ 🖥 🍴 A/C, cable TV, refrig, voice mail. Dishwashers and microwaves, irons and ironing boards. **Services:** 🖼 🗘 🛎 **Facilities:** 🍽 Washer/dryer. **Rates (CP):** $165–$180 ste; $150–$175 effic; $270 cottage/villa. Children under age 12 stay free. Parking: Indoor, $12/day. AE, CB, DC, MC, V.

≣≣≣ Georgetown University Conference Center
3800 Reservoir Rd NW, 20057 (Georgetown); tel 202/687-3200 or toll free 800/228-9290; fax 202/687-3297. One of the city's largest conference facilities, this comfortable hotel managed by the Marriott Corporation is hidden away on campus behind Georgetown University Hospital. **Rooms:** 146 rms and stes. CI 3:30pm/CO noon. Nonsmoking rms avail. **Amenities:** 🛁 ⚖ 🍴 A/C, cable TV w/movies, dataport, voice mail. Some units w/minibars. **Services:** ✗ 🅥🅟 🚗 🖼 🗘 Twice-daily maid svce, social director, babysitting. **Facilities:** 🏊 🎾 🌄⁴ 🍽 [1000] 💻 ᕙ 4 restaurants, 1 bar, spa, sauna, steam rm, beauty salon. Food service ranges from carryout pizza to formal dining room. University's bookstore is on premises. Exercise privileges at GU's Yates Field House. **Rates (CP):** Peak (Feb 15–June/Sept–Dec 15) $140–$165 S; $155–$185 D; $175–$225 ste. Extra person $15. Children under age 18 stay free. Lower rates off-season. Parking: Indoor, $12/day. AE, DC, DISC, MC, V.

≣≣ The Governor's House Hotel

1615 Rhode Island Ave, 20036; tel 202/296-2100 or toll free 800/821-4367; fax 202/331-0227. Intimate lobby, convenient downtown location. **Rooms:** 152 rms and stes. Executive level. CI 3pm/CO noon. Nonsmoking rms avail. Rooms were recently redone. **Amenities:** 🛅 ⚘ A/C, cable TV w/movies. **Services:** ✕ ☎ VP ⚲ Babysitting. **Facilities:** 🚪 ⚑150 1 restaurant, 1 bar (w/entertainment). Pleasant restaurant has exposed brick walls, lots of photographs and posters. Free use of adjoining health club with Olympic-size pool, racquetball courts, exercise equipment. **Rates:** $125–$145 S; $140–$160 D; $135–$165 ste. Extra person $15. Children under age 18 stay free. Parking: Indoor, $14/day. AE, CB, DC, DISC, MC, V.

≣≣≣ Grand Hyatt Washington

1000 H St NW, 20001; tel 202/582-1234 or toll free 800/233-1234; fax 202/637-4797. A refreshing, 12-story atrium with fountains, cascading waterfall, and walkways across a sparkling lagoon characterizes this large, group-oriented hotel across the street from the Convention Center. **Rooms:** 889 rms and stes. Executive level. CI 3pm/CO noon. Nonsmoking rms avail. Rooms have city or atrium views. **Amenities:** 🛅 ⚘ ⚑ A/C, cable TV w/movies, dataport, voice mail. Some units w/minibars, some w/whirlpools. **Services:** ✕ ☎ 🚗 ⚲ ⚲ Twice-daily maid svce, babysitting. **Facilities:** 🚪 ⚑ ⚑3000 ⚲ ⚲ 3 restaurants, 2 bars (w/entertainment), sauna, steam rm, whirlpool. Lounges range from quiet piano lounge to raucous sports bar. **Rates:** Peak (Apr–May/Sept–Oct) $234–$259 S or D; $475–$1700 ste. Extra person $25. Children under age 18 stay free. Lower rates off-season. Parking: Indoor, $12/day. AE, DC, DISC, MC, V.

≣≣ Guest Quarters Suite Hotel

801 New Hampshire Ave NW, 20037 (Foggy Bottom); tel 202/785-2000 or toll free 800/424-2900; fax 202/785-9485. Between H and I Sts. An all-suites hotel convenient to Kennedy Center, downtown businesses, shops, restaurants. **Rooms:** 101 stes. CI 3pm/CO noon. Nonsmoking rms avail. Units have fully equipped kitchens. All living rooms have sleep sofas. **Amenities:** 🛅 ⚘ ⚑ ⚑ A/C, cable TV w/movies, refrig. All units w/minibars. Units have dishwashers; some have microwaves, which are available for others on request. Some business units have computers. TVs in both living rooms and bedrooms. **Services:** ✕ VP ⚲ ⚲ ⚲ Babysitting. **Facilities:** 🚪 ⚑40 ⚲ Washer/dryer. Free membership in nearby health club. **Rates:** $210 ste. Extra person $15. Children under age 18 stay free. Parking: Indoor, $15/day. Weekend packages include breakfast. AE, CB, DC, DISC, MC, V.

≣≣≣ Hampshire Hotel

1310 New Hampshire Ave NW, 20036 (Dupont Circle); tel 202/296-7600 or toll free 800/296-7600; fax 202/293-2476. At N St. Behind an undistinguished glass-and-concrete facade, guests will discover 18th-century decor and numerous amenities in this former apartment building. **Rooms:** 82 rms and stes. CI 3pm/CO noon. Nonsmoking rms avail. Spacious units, most with kitchens. **Amenities:** 🛅 ⚘ ⚑ ⚑ A/C, cable TV, refrig, voice mail. Some units w/minibars, some w/terraces. On-line phone service for news, information, shopping, pizza delivery. **Services:** ✕ VP ⚲ ⚲ ⚲ Complimentary newspapers. **Facilities:** ⚑10 ⚲ ⚲ 1 restaurant, 1 bar, washer/dryer. Passes to nearby health club. **Rates:** $159–$189 S; $179–$199 D; $159–$199 ste. Extra person $20. Children under age 12 stay free. Parking: Indoor/outdoor, $10/day. AE, CB, DC, DISC, ER, JCB, MC.

≣ Harrington Hotel

11th and E Sts NW, 20004; tel 202/628-8140 or toll free 800/424-8532; fax 202/347-3924. An older but well-maintained hotel with small, dated rooms. **Rooms:** 265 rms and stes. CI 2pm/CO noon. Nonsmoking rms avail. Bare but clean rooms. **Amenities:** 🛅 A/C, cable TV, dataport. **Services:** ✕ ⚲ ⚲ **Facilities:** ⚑80 2 restaurants, 1 bar, washer/dryer. Cafeteria serves home-style meals. Bar provides sandwiches and salads. **Rates:** Peak (Apr–Oct) $70–$75 S; $74–$79 D; $105 ste. Extra person $5. Children under age 16 stay free. Lower rates off-season. Parking: Indoor, $5/day. AE, CB, DC, DISC, EC, ER, JCB, MC, V.

≣≣≣≣ The Hay-Adams Hotel

1 Lafayette Sq at 16th and H Sts NW, 20006; tel 202/638-6600 or toll free 800/424-5054; fax 202/638-2716. On Lafayette Square across from the White House, this exquisite Italian Renaissance hotel sits on the former site of homes belonging to John Hay and Henry Adams. Built in 1927, it has retained its original charm while offering all the amenities expected of a full-service luxury hotel. The lobby features fine English antiques, a 17th-century tapestry, and gilt moldings. **Rooms:** 143 rms and stes. CI 3pm/CO noon. Nonsmoking rms avail. Individually decorated rooms have high ceilings, carved moldings, and marble baths. **Amenities:** 🛅 ⚘ ⚑ A/C, cable TV w/movies, dataport, voice mail, in-rm safe, bathrobes. All units w/minibars, some w/terraces. **Services:** ⚲ ☎ VP 🚗 ⚲ ⚲ Twice-daily maid svce, babysitting. Full-time valet service. **Facilities:** ⚑100 ⚲ 2 restaurants, 1 bar (w/entertainment). **Rates:** $210–$360 S or D; $295–$2395 ste. Extra person $30. Children under age 16 stay free. Parking: Indoor, $20/day. AE, CB, DC, DISC, JCB, MC, V.

≣≣≣ Henley Park

926 Massachusetts Ave NW, at K St, 20001; tel 202/638-5200 or toll free 800/222-8474; fax 202/638-6740. A stately, elegant, European-style hotel built in 1918 as apartments. Near Convention Center, Metro. **Rooms:** 96 rms and stes. CI 3pm/CO noon. Nonsmoking rms avail. Distinctively decorated with antique furniture, silk grass cloth. **Amenities:** 🛅 ⚘ ⚑ A/C, cable TV w/movies, dataport, bathrobes. All units w/minibars. Selection of magazines in rooms. **Services:** ⚲ ☎ VP ⚲ ⚲ Twice-daily maid svce, babysitting. High tea served 4–6pm daily. **Facilities:** ⚑60 1 restaurant, 1 bar

(w/entertainment). **Rates:** $165–$215 S; $185–$235 D; $295–$675 ste. Extra person $10. Children under age 16 stay free. Parking: Outdoor, $15/day. AE, DC, DISC, MC, V.

Holiday Inn Capitol
550 C St SW, 20024; tel 202/479-4000 or toll free 800/HOLIDAY; fax 202/479-4353. South of the Mall, this hotel is convenient to the National Air and Space Museum and most other key capital sights. **Rooms:** 529 rms and stes. CI 3pm/CO noon. Nonsmoking rms avail. Modest rooms are comfortable and clean. **Amenities:** A/C, cable TV, voice mail. Some units w/minibars. **Services:** Babysitting. **Facilities:** 2 restaurants, 1 bar, spa, beauty salon, washer/dryer. Rooftop pool with landscaping, flowers. **Rates:** $160 S or D; $189–$219 ste. Children under age 18 stay free. Parking: Indoor, $10/day. AE, CB, DC, DISC, JCB, MC, V.

Holiday Inn Central
1501 Rhode Island Ave NW, at 15th St NW, 20005 (Dupont Circle); tel 202/483-2000 or toll free 800/248-0016; fax 202/797-1078. A modern hotel with convenient downtown location, comfortable lobby with overstuffed chairs. **Rooms:** 213 rms and stes. CI 3pm/CO noon. Nonsmoking rms avail. Pleasant and clean. **Amenities:** A/C, cable TV w/movies, dataport, voice mail. Some units w/minibars, some w/terraces. **Services:** Complimentary coffee in lobby, hors d'oeuvres in evening. **Facilities:** 1 restaurant, 1 bar, games rm, washer/dryer. Rooftop pool, pleasingly quaint restaurant. **Rates:** $129–$142 S or D; $150 ste. Extra person $13. Children under age 18 stay free. Parking: Indoor, $10/day. Senior and weekend rates avail. AE, CB, DC, DISC, JCB, MC, V.

Holiday Inn Franklin Square
1155 14th St NW, 20005; tel 202/737-1200 or toll free 800/HOLIDAY; fax 202/783-5733. An older property right on Thomas Circle. **Rooms:** 208 rms and stes. CI 3pm/CO noon. No smoking. **Amenities:** A/C, cable TV w/movies. **Services:** **Facilities:** 1 restaurant, 1 bar, washer/dryer. **Rates:** Peak (May–Oct) $135 S; $148 D; $180 ste. Extra person $13. Children under age 18 stay free. Lower rates off-season. Parking: Indoor/outdoor, $10/day. AE, CB, DC, DISC, JCB, MC, V.

Hotel Lombardy
2019 I St NW, 20006 (Foggy Bottom); tel 202/828-2600 or toll free 800/424-5486; fax 202/872-0503. Rich wood paneling greets guests in the lobby of this comfortable hotel, originally built as an apartment house. Old-fashioned, manually operated elevator and molding over room doors still remain. **Rooms:** 126 rms and stes. CI 3pm/CO noon. Nonsmoking rms avail. Most rooms and suites have kitchens. **Amenities:** A/C, cable TV w/movies, refrig, bathrobes. All units w/minibars. **Services:** Twice-daily maid svce, babysitting. **Facilities:** 1 restaurant, washer/dryer. **Rates:** $89–$130 S or D; $110–$150 ste. Extra person $10. Children under age 16 stay free. Parking: Indoor, $11.20/day. AE, DC, DISC, MC, V.

Hotel Sofitel
1914 Connecticut Ave NW, at Florida Ave, 20009 (Dupont Circle); tel 202/797-2000 or toll free 800/424-2464; fax 202/462-0944. Built in 1906 as an elegant apartment building on Embassy Row, this European-style hotel caters to discriminating travelers. Intimate lobby has gilt-framed paintings, ornate molding. **Rooms:** 145 rms and stes. CI 3pm/CO 1pm. Nonsmoking rms avail. Spacious rooms show unique architectural details from apartment days. **Amenities:** A/C, cable TV w/movies, dataport, voice mail, in-rm safe. All units w/minibars, 1 w/whirlpool. **Services:** Twice-daily maid svce, babysitting. European-schooled concierge and rest of multilingual staff pay much attention to detail. **Facilities:** 1 restaurant, 1 bar. **Rates:** Peak (Jan–May/Sept–Nov) $185–$205 S; $205–$225 D; $280–$550 ste. Extra person $25. Children under age 18 stay free. Lower rates off-season. Parking: Indoor, $15/day. AE, DC, MC, V.

Hotel Washington
15th St and Pennsylvania Ave NW, 20004; tel 202/638-5900 or toll free 800/424-9540; fax 202/638-1595. Recent improvements have added new appeal to this Washington institution within a block of the White House, the Mall, upscale shops, and the National Theater. **Rooms:** 344 rms and stes. CI 3pm/CO 1pm. Nonsmoking rms avail. Rooms have traditional mahogany furniture, marble baths, historical prints. **Amenities:** A/C, cable TV w/movies, voice mail. Some units w/minibars, some w/fireplaces. **Services:** Babysitting. **Facilities:** 2 restaurants, 2 bars, sauna. Rooftop Sky Terrace overlooking the White House and Mall is a favorite spot for cocktails. **Rates:** $159–$205 S; $174–$219 D; $426–$541 ste. Extra person $18. Children under age 14 stay free. Parking: Indoor, $16/day. AE, DC, DISC, MC, V.

Howard Johnson Premier Hotel
2601 Virginia Ave NW, 20037 (Foggy Bottom); tel 202/965-2700 or toll free 800/654-2000; fax 202/965-2700 ext 7910. It was from this hotel that the Democratic National Committee offices in the Watergate building across the street were bugged in 1972, leading to the infamous scandal that brought down the Nixon presidency. Within walking distance of the Kennedy Center and Potomac River. **Rooms:** 193 rms. CI 4pm/CO noon. Nonsmoking rms avail. Standard motel-style rooms. **Amenities:** A/C, TV, refrig, VCR. Some units w/terraces. **Services:** **Facilities:** 1 restaurant, games rm, washer/dryer. Family restaurant on premises. Use of Watergate Health Club across street for a fee. **Rates:** Peak (Apr–Aug) $89–$119 S or D. Extra person $5. Children under age 18 stay free. Lower rates off-season. Parking: Indoor, free. AE, CB, DC, DISC, JCB, MC, V.

☰☰ Howard Johnson's Hotel & Suites
1430 Rhode Island Ave NW, 20005 (Downtown); tel 202/
462-7777 or toll free 800/368-5690; fax 202/332-3519.
Between 14th St NW and Scott Circle. A moderately priced
hotel in close proximity to Convention Center and attractions. **Rooms:** 184 rms and stes. CI 4pm/CO 11am. Nonsmoking rms avail. Suites have full kitchens. **Amenities:** 🗝
A/C, cable TV. **Services:** ✕ VP 🛎 Babysitting. **Facilities:** 🏋
🗐 ♿ 1 restaurant, 1 bar, games rm, washer/dryer. **Rates:**
Peak (Mar–Nov) $109–$149 S; $119–$169 D; $149–$169
ste. Extra person $10. Children under age 16 stay free.
Lower rates off-season. Parking: Indoor, $9/day. AE, DC,
DISC, MC, V.

☰☰☰☰ The Jefferson
1200 16th St NW, at M St, 20036; tel 202/347-2200 or toll
free 800/368-5966; fax 202/331-7982. An unassuming exterior gives way to an ornate lobby with marble floor, numerous
Persian rugs, and chandeliers strung from arched ceilings—
all a mere prelude to the rest of this fine hotel, which has
been catering to famous journalists and literary figures since
1923. **Rooms:** 100 rms and stes. CI 3pm/CO 1pm. Nonsmoking rms avail. Each elegant room is individually decorated,
many featuring fine European antiques. **Amenities:** 🗝 ♨ 🍽
A/C, cable TV w/movies, dataport, VCR, CD/tape player,
bathrobes. All units w/minibars, 1 w/terrace, 1 w/fireplace, 1
w/whirlpool. Fax machines in all rooms. **Services:** 🎧 ☛ VP
🗐 🛎 🕭 Twice-daily maid svce, babysitting. Entire front-
office staff is trained in concierge duties. **Facilities:** 🗐 1
restaurant (*see* "Restaurants" below), 1 bar. The dining room
is one of Washington's finest places to eat. Adjoining health
club available for a nominal fee. **Rates:** $240–$280 S; $255–
$295 D; $340–$990 ste. Extra person $20. Children under
age 18 stay free. Parking: Indoor, $20/day. AE, CB, DC,
DISC, JCB, MC, V.

☰☰☰ JW Marriott Hotel
1331 Pennsylvania Ave NW, at E St, 20004 (Downtown); tel
202/393-2000 or toll free 800/228-9290; fax 202/626-6991.
Flagship of the Marriott chain, this large convention hotel
(adjacent to the National Theater and two blocks from the
Mall and the White House) has an attractive two-story lobby
with marble floors, comfortable seating, and crystal chandeliers. The facility opens to an enclosed shopping mall with
upscale shops and two food courts. **Rooms:** 772 rms and stes.
Executive level. CI 4pm/CO noon. Nonsmoking rms avail.
Rooms are richly appointed with dark wood furniture.
Amenities: 🗝 ♨ 🍽 A/C, cable TV w/movies, dataport, voice
mail. Some units w/terraces, 1 w/whirlpool. **Services:** 🎧 ☛
VP 🚗 🗐 🛎 🕭 Car-rental desk, masseur, babysitting.
Facilities: 🏋 🛎 🗐 ♿ 2 restaurants, 2 bars, games rm, spa,
sauna, steam rm, whirlpool. Food and beverage outlets range
from casual to elegant. **Rates:** Peak (Mar–June/Sept–Nov)
$199–$209 S or D; $575–$1,500 ste. Children under age 18
stay free. Lower rates off-season. Parking: Indoor, $16–$25/
day. AE, CB, DC, DISC, ER, JCB, MC, V.

☰☰ Lincoln Suites
1823 L St NW, 20036; tel 202/223-4320 or toll free 800/
424-2970; fax 202/223-8546. Small property in the heart of
downtown, near restaurants and shops. **Rooms:** 99 effic. CI
2pm/CO noon. Nonsmoking rms avail. Although dated,
rooms are spacious and comfortable, with sitting areas,
kitchenettes or wet bars. Although called suites, each unit is
one large room. **Amenities:** 🗝 ♨ ▣ 🍽 A/C, cable TV
w/movies, refrig, dataport, voice mail. In-room video games.
Services: ✕ 🗐 🛎 **Facilities:** 🗐 ♿ 2 restaurants, 2 bars.
Free use of nearby health club. **Rates:** Peak (Mar–June/Sept–
Nov) $109–$159 effic. Extra person $10. Children under age
16 stay free. Lower rates off-season. Weekend rates avail. AE,
CB, DC, DISC, MC, V.

☰☰☰☰ Loews L'Enfant Plaza Hotel
480 L'Enfant Plaza SW, 20024; tel 202/484-1000 or toll free
800/243-1166; fax 202/646-4456. Located among government office buildings near the Mall and Smithsonian Institution museums, this hotel caters to both business travelers and
families with children. Pets are definitely welcomed and
pampered, and 70% of pet fees go to the Humane Society.
Rooms: 370 rms and stes. CI 3pm/CO 1pm. Nonsmoking
rms avail. **Amenities:** 🗝 ♨ 🍽 A/C, cable TV w/movies,
dataport, VCR, voice mail, in-rm safe, bathrobes. All units
w/minibars, some w/terraces, 1 w/fireplace. **Services:** ✕ ☛
VP 🗐 🛎 🕭 Twice-daily maid svce, children's program,
babysitting. Pets allowed for additional fee. **Facilities:** 🏋 🛎
🗐 💻 ♿ 1 restaurant, 2 bars, games rm, beauty salon. Large
health club. Attractive rooftop pool with snack bar, umbrella
tables. **Rates:** $205–$225 S or D; $475–$700 ste. Extra
person $20. Children under age 16 stay free. Parking:
Indoor, $16/day. AE, CB, DC, DISC, MC, V.

☰☰☰☰ The Madison
15th and M Sts NW, 20005; tel 202/862-1600 or toll free
800/424-8577; fax 202/785-1255. One of Washington's
finest hotels is frequented by heads of state, royalty, and
other very important guests. Modern yet ornate public areas
are adorned with Louis XVI antiques. **Rooms:** 353 rms and
stes. Executive level. CI 3pm/CO 1pm. Nonsmoking rms
avail. Every room has Oriental rugs; some have works by well-
known artists. Quality of all furnishings is exquisite.
Amenities: 🗝 ♨ 🍽 A/C, cable TV w/movies, dataport, voice
mail, bathrobes. All units w/minibars, some w/terraces, some
w/whirlpools. Every guest provided fruit plate upon arrival.
Umbrellas in rooms. Heated towel racks. **Services:** 🎧 ☛ VP
🗐 🛎 🕭 Twice-daily maid svce, social director, masseur,
babysitting. Multilingual concierge staff. **Facilities:** 🛎 🗐
💻 ♿ 3 restaurants, 3 bars, spa, sauna, steam rm. **Rates:**
$235–$255 S or D; $395–$3,000 ste. Extra person $30.
Children under age 12 stay free. Parking: Indoor, $7–$14/
day. AE, DC, JCB, MC, V.

☰☰☰ Marriott at Metro Center
775 12th St NW, 20005; tel 202/737-2200 or toll free 800/
992-5891; fax 202/347-0860. Formerly a Holiday Inn

Crowne Plaza, this modern hotel recently switched to Marriott management. Convenient downtown location at Metro Center station, surrounded by shops, restaurants, businesses. **Rooms:** 456 rms and stes. Executive level. CI 4pm/CO noon. Nonsmoking rms avail. **Amenities:** 🛏 🖥 🍽 A/C, cable TV, refrig, voice mail. All units w/minibars, 1 w/whirlpool. **Services:** ✗ 📞 VP 🍷 🚗 Twice-daily maid svce, car-rental desk. **Facilities:** 🏊 🏋 550 💻 ♿ 1 restaurant, 1 bar, spa, sauna, steam rm, whirlpool. **Rates:** Peak (Sept–Thanksgiving) $199 S or D; $750 ste. Children under age 12 stay free. Lower rates off-season. Parking: Indoor, $12/day. AE, CB, DC, DISC, EC, ER, JCB, MC, V.

≣≣≣≣ Omni Shoreham Hotel
2500 Calvert St NW, at Connecticut Ave, 20008 (Woodley Park); tel 202/234-0700 or toll free 800/843-6664; fax 202/232-4140. A landmark built in 1930 on the edge of Rock Creek Park, this gracious and charming hotel has hosted inaugural balls for every president from Franklin D Roosevelt to Bill Clinton. Memorabilia exhibit in main lobby captures much of hotel's links to nation's history. **Rooms:** 770 rms and stes. CI 3pm/CO noon. Nonsmoking rms avail. **Amenities:** 🛏 🖥 🍽 A/C, cable TV w/movies. Some units w/terraces. Some rooms have dataports. **Services:** ✗ 📞 🚗 🍷 🚗 Social director, children's program, babysitting. Kids Concierge looks after the tots. **Facilities:** 🏊 🏌3 🏋 2500 💻 ♿ 1 restaurant, 2 bars (1 w/entertainment), lawn games, spa, sauna. Marquis Lounge is a popular local venue for political comedy. Gourmet shop sells carryout picnic fare. **Rates:** Peak (Mar–Apr/Sept–Oct) $209–$234 S; $234–$254 D; $400–$1,200 ste. Children under age 18 stay free. Lower rates off-season. Parking: Indoor/outdoor, $12/day. AE, CB, DC, DISC, JCB, MC, V.

≣≣≣≣ Park Hyatt
1201 24th St NW, at M St, 20037 (Georgetown); tel 202/789-1234 or toll free 800/922-7275; fax 202/457-8823. A European-style hotel with an emphasis on service. Traditional furniture and museum-quality art in public areas lend old-time ambience to a modern structure with contemporary charm. Just three blocks from Georgetown. **Rooms:** 223 rms and stes. Executive level. CI 3pm/CO noon. Nonsmoking rms avail. Large rooms all have sitting areas with sofas. **Amenities:** 🛏 🖥 🍽 A/C, cable TV w/movies, dataport, voice mail, bathrobes. All units w/minibars, some w/terraces, 1 w/fireplace, some w/whirlpools. Marble baths have brass fixtures, TVs with radios, porcelain canisters for toiletries. Two phone lines in each room. Suites have fax machines. **Services:** 🍽 📞 VP 🚗 🍷 🚗 Twice-daily maid svce, masseur, babysitting. High tea served (Thurs–Sun, 3–6pm), with palm reader on hand to tell guests' fortunes. **Facilities:** 🏊 🏋 400 💻 ♿ 1 restaurant, 2 bars (1 w/entertainment), spa, sauna, steam rm, whirlpool, beauty salon. The lounge features dancing to big bands on Saturday nights. **Rates:** Peak (Mar–June/Sept–Oct) $280–$305 S or D; $325–$2,100 ste.

Extra person $25. Children under age 18 stay free. Lower rates off-season. Parking: Indoor, $20/day. Weekend rates avail. AE, CB, DC, DISC, MC, V.

≣≣ Quality Hotel Downtown
1315 16th St NW, 20036; tel 202/232-8000 or toll free 800/228-5151; fax 202/667-9827. At Massachusetts Ave. An all-suites hotel conveniently located in the heart of downtown near Scott Circle. **Rooms:** 135 stes. Executive level. CI 2pm/CO 11am. Nonsmoking rms avail. **Amenities:** 🛏 🖥 🍽 A/C, cable TV w/movies, refrig, dataport, in-rm safe. **Services:** ✗ 🍷 🚗 **Facilities:** 50 💻 ♿ 1 restaurant, 1 bar, washer/dryer. **Rates:** Peak (Mar–June/Sept–Oct) $140–$160 ste. Extra person $12. Children under age 18 stay free. Lower rates off-season. Parking: Indoor, $10/day. AE, CB, DC, DISC, JCB, MC, V.

≣≣≣ Renaissance Washington, DC Hotel
999 9th St NW, at K St, 20001 (Downtown); tel 202/898-9000 or toll free 800/228-9898; fax 202/789-4213. A two-story atrium lobby highlights this modern establishment across the street from the Convention Center. Near Chinatown and numerous restaurants. **Rooms:** 800 rms and stes. Executive level. CI 3pm/CO noon. Nonsmoking rms avail. **Amenities:** 🖥 🍽 A/C, cable TV w/movies, dataport, voice mail. All units w/minibars, some w/terraces, some w/whirlpools. **Services:** 🍽 📞 VP 🍷 🚗 Babysitting. **Facilities:** 🏊 🏋 1000 ♿ 1 restaurant, 2 bars, sauna, steam rm, whirlpool. Health club free to Club Tower guests, small charge for others. **Rates:** Peak (Mar–June/Sept–Nov) $199 S; $219 D; $400–$2,000 ste. Extra person $20. Children under age 16 stay free. Lower rates off-season. Parking: Indoor, $15/day. AE, CB, DC, DISC, ER, JCB, MC, V.

≣≣≣≣ Rennaissance Mayflower Hotel
1127 Connecticut Ave NW, 20036; tel 202/347-3000 or toll free 800/HOTELS-1; fax 202/466-9082. Between L and M Sts. Home of presidential inaugural balls since the 1920s and regular lunch spot for the late FBI director J Edgar Hoover, this downtown landmark underwent a thorough renovation in the 1980s, which restored its ornate lobby and striking block-long promenade and brought its rooms up to luxury standards. **Rooms:** 660 rms and stes. CI 3pm/CO noon. Nonsmoking rms avail. Guest rooms are individually decorated and furnished with period reproductions. **Amenities:** 🛏 🖥 🍽 A/C, cable TV w/movies, dataport, bathrobes. Some units w/minibars, 1 w/terrace. Baths have TVs. **Services:** 🍽 📞 VP 🍷 🚗 Twice-daily maid svce, babysitting. **Facilities:** 🏋 1000 💻 1 restaurant, 1 bar. **Rates:** Peak (Mar–May/Sept–Oct) $300–$340 S or D; $575–$3,500 ste. Extra person $30. Children under age 18 stay free. Lower rates off-season. Parking: Indoor, $12/day. AE, CB, DC, DISC, JCB, MC, V.

≣≣≣≣ The Ritz-Carlton Washington
2100 Massachusetts Ave NW, at Q St, 20008 (Dupont Circle); tel 202/293-2100 or toll free 800/241-3333; fax 202/293-0641. An understated exterior gives way to rich Ritz-

Carlton elegance at this luxury hotel in the heart of Embassy Row. **Rooms:** 206 rms and stes. Executive level. CI 2pm/CO noon. Nonsmoking rms avail. Club Level rooms and suites on top two floors have goose-down beds. **Amenities:** 🛏 ⌂ ☎ A/C, cable TV w/movies, refrig, dataport, bathrobes. All units w/minibars, 1 w/whirlpool. Club Level units have VCRs with video library. **Services:** 🍽 ☎ VP 🏊 ⌣ Twice-daily maid svce, children's program, babysitting. Those staying on Club Level can take advantage of own concierge lounge with five daily food presentations, get complimentary use of fitness center. **Facilities:** 🛳 300 ♿ 1 restaurant, 2 bars (1 w/entertainment), spa, sauna. Jockey Club Restaurant is famous locally. **Rates:** $265–$375 S or D; $550–$2,100 ste. Children under age 18 stay free. Parking: Indoor, $20/day. AE, DC, JCB, MC, V.

≡≡ Savoy Suites Georgetown
2505 Wisconsin Ave NW, 20007; tel 202/337-9700 or toll free 800/944-5377; fax 202/337-3644. Just north of Calvert St. White brick building with mansard roof and imitation balconies, located north of Georgetown in a residential neighborhood with nearby shops and restaurants. **Rooms:** 150 stes and effic. CI 3pm/CO 1pm. Nonsmoking rms avail. Suites actually are one large room. **Amenities:** 🛏 A/C, satel TV w/movies, voice mail. Some units w/whirlpools. Rooms that don't have kitchenettes with microwaves have small refrigerators instead. **Services:** ✗ 🏊 ⌣ ⟳ Car-rental desk, babysitting. **Facilities:** 200 🖥 ♿ 1 restaurant, 1 bar, washer/dryer. **Rates:** $79–$139 ste; $79–$139 effic. Extra person $10. Children under age 18 stay free. Parking: Indoor, free. AE, DC, DISC, MC, V.

≡≡≡ State Plaza Hotel
2117 E St NW, 20037 (Foggy Bottom); tel 202/861-8200 or toll free 800/424-2859; fax 202/659-8601. Near the State Department, George Washington University, and the Kennedy Center. **Rooms:** 225 effic. CI 3pm/CO noon. Nonsmoking rms avail. Nicely appointed units range from studios to one-bedroom models with living and dining areas. **Amenities:** 🛏 ⌂ 📺 ☎ A/C, cable TV w/movies, refrig. All units w/minibars. **Services:** ✗ ☎ 🏊 ⌣ Twice-daily maid svce. **Facilities:** 🛳 100 ♿ 1 restaurant, 1 bar, washer/dryer. **Rates:** $165–$285 effic. Extra person $20. Children under age 16 stay free. Parking: Indoor, $12/day. Weekend rates avail. AE, CB, DC, DISC, MC, V.

≡≡≡≡ Washington Hilton and Towers
1919 Connecticut Ave NW, at T St, 20009 (Kalorama); tel 202/483-3000 or toll free 800/HILTONS; fax 202/265-8221. The largest hotel in Washington and one of its biggest convention and banquet venues this 10-story structure consists of two semicircles flaring from their meeting point at its public areas. Its perch atop a hill gives rooms at higher levels great views over the city. President Ronald Reagan was shot and wounded while leaving here in 1981. **Rooms:** 1,122 rms and stes. Executive level. CI 3pm/CO noon. Nonsmoking rms avail. Bright and cheerful. Cabana rooms have very high ceilings, garden views. **Amenities:** 🛏 ⌂ A/C, cable TV w/movies, dataport, voice mail. Some units w/minibars, some w/terraces. All rooms have irons and ironing boards. Tower units have fax machines. Cabana rooms have wet bars, coffeemakers and pool access. **Services:** ✗ ☎ 🏊 ⌣ ⟳ Car-rental desk, babysitting. **Facilities:** 🛳 🖥3 🛳 3500 🖥 ♿ 2 restaurants, 2 bars (1 w/entertainment), steam rm. **Rates:** $95–$185 S; $95–$205 D; $280–$1,500 ste. Extra person $20. Children under age 18 stay free. Parking: Indoor, $12/day. AE, CB, DC, DISC, EC, ER, JCB, MC, V.

≡≡≡ Washington Vista
1400 M St NW, 20005; tel 202/429-1700 or toll free 800/VISTA-DC; fax 202/785-0786. A soaring, 14-story atrium lobby with many live plants and fresh flower arrangements sets the tone at this modern hotel in the center of downtown. A huge lobby clock visible to all keeps track of every passing minute. **Rooms:** 400 rms and stes. Executive level. CI 3pm/CO noon. Nonsmoking rms avail. **Amenities:** 🛏 ⌂ ☎ A/C, cable TV w/movies, refrig, voice mail. All units w/minibars, some w/terraces, some w/whirlpools. Many rooms have balconies overlooking atrium. **Services:** 🍽 ☎ VP 🏊 ⌣ Twice-daily maid svce, babysitting. Executive floors have private lounge serving breakfast, snacks, drinks, and hors d'oeuvres. **Facilities:** 🛳 400 ♿ 2 restaurants, 2 bars. **Rates:** Peak (Mar–Jun/Sept–Nov) $190–$230 S; $215–$255 D; $390–$1,200 ste. Extra person $25. Children under age 18 stay free. Lower rates off-season. Parking: Indoor, $15/day. AE, CB, DC, DISC, EC, ER, JCB, MC, V.

≡≡≡≡ The Watergate Hotel
2650 Virginia Ave NW, 20037 (Foggy Bottom); tel 202/965-2300 or toll free 800/424-2736; fax 202/337-7915. An exquisite lobby with giant spotlighted flower arrangement, marble-tile floor, columns, and a grand piano is merely a prelude to one of Washington's finest hotels. Its location across Rock Creek Parkway from the Potomac River provides water views to many rooms and suites. The Watergate Office Building, site of the 1972 eavesdropping incident that led to President Richard Nixon's downfall, is next door. **Rooms:** 235 rms and stes. CI 3pm/CO noon. Nonsmoking rms avail. With decor by an interior designer, rooms have kitchenettes, two closets. **Amenities:** 🛏 ⌂ ☎ A/C, cable TV w/movies, refrig, dataport, voice mail, bathrobes. All units w/minibars, some w/terraces. All rooms have fold-out sofas and fax machines. Kitchen starter kit available on request. **Services:** 🍽 ☎ VP 🚐 🏊 ⌣ ⟳ Twice-daily maid svce, masseur, babysitting. Complimentary shoe shines, limousine transport within the District of Columbia. High tea served daily. Children's movies for rent at front desk. **Facilities:** 🛳 🛳 500 🖥 ♿ 3 restaurants, 2 bars (1 w/entertainment), spa, sauna, steam rm, whirlpool, beauty salon. **Rates:** Peak (Apr–June/Sept–Dec) $270–$395 S; $295–$420 D; $395–$1,885

ste. Extra person $N. Children under age 18 stay free. Lower rates off-season. Parking: Indoor, $18/day. AE, CB, DC, DISC, JCB, MC, V.

≣≣≣≣ The Westin Hotel

2350 M St NW, 20037 (Georgetown); tel 202/429-0100 or toll free 800/848-0016; fax 202/429-9759. Very understated elegance in lobby and rooms of this modern hotel convenient to Kennedy Center, downtown businesses, attractions. **Rooms:** 263 rms and stes. Executive level. CI 3pm/CO 1pm. Nonsmoking rms avail. **Amenities:** 🛅 🐵 🍴 A/C, cable TV w/movies, dataport. All units w/minibars, some w/terraces, some w/fireplaces, some w/whirlpools. Exquisite baths have sunken tubs, marble vanities, large mirrors. Fax machines. **Services:** 🍴 🛏 VP 🖼 🕭 Twice-daily maid svce, masseur, children's program, babysitting. Known for attentive, multilingual staff. **Facilities:** 🎣 🛎 🖳 🖥 2 restaurants, 1 bar. **Rates:** $175–$270 S; $195–$300 D; $550–$2,500 ste. Extra person $20. Children under age 16 stay free. Parking: Indoor, $15–18/day. AE, CB, DC, DISC, JCB, MC, V.

≣≣≣≣ Willard Inter-Continental Washington

1401 Pennsylvania Ave NW, 20004 (Downtown); tel 202/628-9100 or toll free 800/327-0200; fax 202/637-7326. This beaux-arts masterpiece has stood as a landmark at Pennsylvania Avenue and 14th St, two blocks from the White House and the Mall, since 1902. There has been a hotel on this corner since 1816 and a Willard Hotel since the 1850s. As such, it's steeped in national lore. The present building was closed from 1968 to 1986, when a complete renovation restored its grandeur. Today the Willard is an elegant luxury hotel worthy of the presidents and other famous notables who have graced its guest list. **Rooms:** 341 rms and stes. CI 3pm/CO noon. Nonsmoking rms avail. Gilt-framed French prints and Edwardian reproductions are part of the elegant luxury. **Amenities:** 🛅 🐵 🍴 A/C, cable TV w/movies, dataport, voice mail, bathrobes. All units w/minibars. Suites have two-line phones. **Services:** 🍴 🛏 🖼 🕭 🛎 Twice-daily maid svce, social director, babysitting. **Facilities:** 🛎 🖳 🖥 🖳 2 restaurants (see "Restaurants" below), 2 bars (1 w/entertainment). Excellent restaurants. Hotel opens to shopping arcade with upscale shops. **Rates:** Peak (Sept–July) $266–$350 S; $295–$380 D; $600–$2,500 ste. Extra person $30. Children under age 12 stay free. Lower rates off-season. Parking: Indoor, $20/day. AE, CB, DC, DISC, JCB, MC, V.

MOTELS

≣≣≣ Channel Inn

650 Water St SW, 20024 (Downtown); tel 202/554-2400 or toll free 800/368-5668; fax 202/368-1164. Between 7th St and Maine Ave. The city's only waterfront accommodations, convenient to Metro and Maine Avenue seafood restaurants. Lobby wall hangings and ship models make guests feel like old salts. **Rooms:** 100 rms and stes. CI 1pm/CO noon. Nonsmoking rms avail. Rooms facing the Potomac River offer views of numerous yachts docked in Washington Chan-

nel. Units on top floors have cathedral ceilings. **Amenities:** 🛅 🐵 A/C, cable TV w/movies. All units w/terraces. **Services:** ✕ 🖼 🕭 Twice-daily maid svce, car-rental desk, babysitting. Same-day laundry service except Sunday. **Facilities:** 🎣 🚲 🖳 🛎 1 restaurant, 1 bar. **Rates:** $110 S; $120 D; $180 ste. Extra person $10. Children under age 12 stay free. Parking: Indoor, free. AE, DC, DISC, MC, V.

≣≣ Days Inn Northeast

2700 New York Ave NE (US 50), 20002; tel 202/832-5800 or toll free 800/329-7466; fax 202/269-4317. A clean, well-kept motel on the northeastern outskirts of the District of Columbia. A good value. **Rooms:** 195 rms. CI 2pm/CO noon. Nonsmoking rms avail. **Amenities:** 🛅 A/C, cable TV w/movies. **Services:** ✕ 🕭 🛎 **Facilities:** 🎣 🖳 🛎 1 restaurant, 1 bar (w/entertainment), washer/dryer. **Rates:** Peak (Apr–Sept) $39–$56 S; $56–$72 D. Extra person $5. Children under age 13 stay free. Lower rates off-season. Parking: Outdoor, free. AE, CB, DC, DISC, JCB, MC, V.

INNS

≣≣ Adams Inn

1744 Lanier Place NW, 20009 (Adams-Morgan); tel 202/745-3600 or toll free 800/578-6807; fax 202/332-5867. Lovely turn-of-the-century homes with period furnishings and appealing decor in one of Washington's most interesting and diverse residential neighborhoods. **Rooms:** 24 rms (12 w/shared bath). CI 3pm/CO noon. No smoking. Each room individually decorated. Those without baths have in-room sinks. **Amenities:** 🛅 🐵 A/C. No TV. **Services:** 🕭 **Facilities:** Washer/dryer, guest lounge w/TV. Public phone in foyer. **Rates (CP):** $45 S w/shared bath, $60 S w/private bath; $55 D w/shared bath, $70 D w/private bath. Extra person $10. Children under age 2 stay free. Parking: Indoor/outdoor, $7/day. AE, CB, DC, DISC, MC, V.

≣≣ Capitol Hill Guest House

101 5th St NE, at A St, 20002 (Capitol Hill); tel 202/547-1050. Convenient to the US Capitol and Library of Congress, this is a well-kept Victorian-era row house. Neighborhood is exceptionally quiet with little traffic on nearby streets. Unsuitable for children under 8. **Rooms:** 10 rms (8 w/shared bath). CI 2pm/CO 11am. No smoking. **Amenities:** 🐵 A/C. No phone or TV. Rooms on top floor have ceiling fans. **Services:** Afternoon tea and wine/sherry served. **Facilities:** Guest lounge. **Rates (CP):** Peak (Mar–June/Sept–Nov) Extra person $15. Lower rates off-season. AE, DISC, MC, V.

≣≣ Embassy Inn

1627 16th St NW, 20009 (Dupont Circle); tel 202/234-7800 or toll free 800/423-9111; fax 202/234-3309. Constructed in 1922, this four-story federal-style building fits in among large town houses along 16th St, one of the capital's finest neighborhoods in the days before suburbs. Attractive lobby doubles as lounge for guests. No elevator in building. **Rooms:** 38 rms. CI 3pm/CO noon. Nonsmoking rms avail. Comfortable rooms furnished in federal style. **Amenities:** 🛅 🐵 A/C, cable TV w/movies. **Services:** ⬛ ⬛ Wine/sherry served. Complimentary newspapers and coffee. **Facilities:** Guest lounge. **Rates (CP):** Peak (Feb–June) $69–$130 S; $89–$130 D. Extra person $10. Children under age 18 stay free. Lower rates off-season. Higher rates for special events/hols. AE, DC, MC, V.

≣≣ The Kalorama Guest Houses

1854 Mintwood Place NW, 20009; tel 202/667-6369; fax 202/319-1262. Between 19th St and Columbia Rd, and at 2700 Cathedral Ave NW. Six late-19th-century row houses in the quiet residential neighborhoods of Kalorama Heights and Woodley Park have been converted into a modern inn, while retaining the charms of yesteryear. Unsuitable for children under 6. **Rooms:** 50 rms and stes (26 w/shared bath). CI 2pm/CO 11am. Nonsmoking rms avail. Each room individually decorated with brass bed and comforter. **Amenities:** ⬛ ⬛ A/C. No phone or TV. Some units w/terraces. **Services:** Wine/sherry served. Afternoon sherry served in the parlor. **Facilities:** ⬛ Washer/dryer, guest lounge w/TV. **Rates (CP):** Peak (Apr–June/Sept–Nov) $40–$75 S or D w/shared bath, $55–$95 S or D w/private bath; $90–$115 ste. Extra person $5. Children under age 12 stay free. Lower rates off-season. Higher rates for special events/hols. Parking: Indoor/outdoor, $7/day. AE, CB, DC, DISC, MC, V.

≣≣≣≣ Morrison-Clark Inn

Massachusetts Ave, at 11th St NW, 20001 (Franklin Square); tel 202/898-1200 or toll free 800/332-7898; fax 202/289-8576. Originally built in 1864 as two private homes, these Italianate houses connected by a third contemporary building and surrounding a courtyard are on the National Register of Historic Places. From 1923 to 1980 it served as a hostel for the Soldiers, Sailors, Marines and Airmen's Club. After extensive remodeling (lead by William Adair, the designer who renovated the White House), the inn re-opened in 1988. Public areas are Victorian in style, complete with Oriental antiques, original Pier mirrors, Italian Carrera marble fireplaces, and velvet-covered parlor chairs. Little touches, like old-fashioned phones and framed Shakespearean sonnets in the lobby and sitting room, add charm to the inn's elegance. **Rooms:** 54 rms and stes. CI 3pm/CO noon. Nonsmoking rms avail. Guest rooms have high ceilings, large windows, and armoires that house closet space and the entertainment center. Each room is individually decorated in one of three styles: French Country (with pine and birch furnishings), neoclassical (with recessed lighting and sunken beds), and Victorian (with ornate headboards, period antiques, and Victorian reproductions). Honeymoon suite has a very large private balcony. **Amenities:** ⬛ ⬛ ⬛ A/C, cable TV, refrig, dataport. All units w/minibars, some w/terraces. **Services:** ✗ ⬛ ⬛ ⬛ ⬛ Twice-daily maid svce, babysitting. **Facilities:** ⬛ ⬛ 1 restaurant (see "Restaurants" below). An elegant Victorian drawing room, the dining room is one of Washington's finest eateries. **Rates (CP):** $135 S; $155 D;

$160–$185 ste. Extra person $20. Children under age 16 stay free. Parking: Indoor, $12/day. AE, CB, DC, DISC, ER, MC, V.

≣≣≣ Normandy Inn

2118 Wyoming Ave NW, 20008 (Kalorama); tel 202/483-1350 or toll free 800/424-3729; fax 202/387-8241. A rather plain modern facade reminiscent of an economy motel masks a warm and hospitable small hotel with many inn features. **Rooms:** 75 rms. CI noon/CO noon. Nonsmoking rms avail. Comfortable, attractive rooms. **Amenities:** ⬛ ⬛ ⬛ ⬛ A/C, satel TV w/movies, refrig. **Services:** ⬛ ⬛ ⬛ ⬛ Continental breakfast available in parlor or room at reasonable price. Coffee and tea available all day with cookies set out at teatime. **Facilities:** ⬛ ⬛ Guest lounge. **Rates:** Peak (Mar–June/Sept–Nov) $94 S; $104 D. Children under age 12 stay free. Lower rates off-season. Parking: Indoor, $10/day. Weekend rates avail. AE, DC, DISC, MC, V.

≣≣ The Tabard Inn

1739 N St NW, 20036 (Dupont Circle); tel 202/785-1277; fax 202/785-6173. Cozy and warm, unhurried and tranquil, this establishment is in the heart of the Dupont Circle restaurant area. **Rooms:** 40 rms (13 w/shared bath). CI 2pm/CO 11am. Finished wood floors with large Oriental carpets. **Amenities:** ⬛ A/C. No TV. Ceiling fans, inoperable but attractive fireplaces. **Services:** ⬛ ⬛ **Facilities:** ⬛ 1 restaurant, 1 bar, guest lounge. **Rates (CP):** $59–$85 S w/shared bath, $99–$140 S w/private bath; $81–$97 D w/shared bath, $111–$152 D w/private bath. MC, V.

≣≣ Windsor Inn

1842 16th St NW, at T St, 20009 (Dupont Circle); tel 202/667-0300 or toll free 800/423-9111; fax 202/234-3309. Operated in conjunction with the Embassy Inn, this brick building on a residential portion of busy 16th St was a boardinghouse and inn from the 1920s to 1962. The present owners reopened it in 1985. Art-deco touches recapture the Roaring '20s spirit. There is no elevator nor off-street parking. **Rooms:** 46 rms and stes. CI 3pm/CO noon. Nonsmoking rms avail. Clean and comfortable rooms sport mahogany reproductions. **Amenities:** ⬛ ⬛ A/C, cable TV w/movies. **Services:** ⬛ ⬛ Wine/sherry served. **Facilities:** ⬛ Guest lounge. **Rates (CP):** Peak (Feb–June) $69–$130 S; $89–$130 D; $99–$150 ste. Extra person $10. Children under age 18 stay free. Lower rates off-season. Higher rates for special events/hols. AE, DC, MC, V.

≣≣ Windsor Park Hotel

2116 Kalorama Rd NW, 20008; tel 202/483-7700 or toll free 800/247-3064; fax 202/332-4547. Located in a residential neighborhood dotted with embassies, and within walking distance of Dupont Circle and Adams-Morgan restaurants and shops, this brick structure offers simple but comfortable accommodations. **Rooms:** 43 rms and stes. CI 2pm/CO 1pm. Nonsmoking rms avail. **Amenities:** ⬛ A/C, cable TV w/movies, refrig. **Services:** ⬛ ⬛ **Facilities:** ⬛ ⬛ **Rates**

(CP): Peak (Apr–June/Oct–Nov) $88 S; $98 D; $145 ste. Extra person $10. Children under age 12 stay free. Lower rates off-season. AE, CB, DC, DISC, MC, V.

RESTAURANTS ⑪

⑤ Adams Morgan Spaghetti Garden
2317 18th St NW (Adams-Morgan); tel 202/265-6665. Near Columbia Rd. **Italian.** An unpretentious, budget-priced eatery with red tile floor, small brick bar, and blue chairs and tables. Menu offers traditional Italian pastas and some meat and chicken dishes. **FYI:** Reservations accepted. Dress code. **Open:** Mon–Sat noon–midnight, Sun noon–11pm. **Prices:** Main courses $4–$11. AE, MC, V. 👥

Aditi Indian Cuisine
3299 M St NW (Georgetown); tel 202/625-6825. **Indian.** Contemporary decor with large mirror, plants, Indian wall hangings, and elegant stairwell to second-floor dining room. Brass chandelier in entrance. Cuisine ranging from samosas to vegetable curries to meat and chicken from the tandoor oven. Most notable choice is the sampler Aditi Dinner. **FYI:** Reservations recommended. **Open:** Lunch Mon–Sat 11:30am–2:30pm, Sun noon–2:30pm; dinner Sun–Thurs 5:30–10pm, Fri–Sat 5:30–10:30pm. **Prices:** Main courses $7–$14; prix fixe $14. AE, DC, DISC, MC, V. ♥

Alekos
1732 Connecticut Ave NW (Dupont Circle); tel 202/667-6211. Between R and S Sts. **Greek.** Corinthian columns support arches over stucco walls, which along with green plants are reflected in mirrors. Ceiling fans turn overhead. Specialties change from time to time; typical offerings include stuffed spring lamb and vegetables, broiled flounder, calf's liver, and broiled sea scallops, all prepared in the Greek fashion. **FYI:** Reservations accepted. **Open:** Mon–Fri 11am–11pm, Sat–Sun noon–11pm. **Prices:** Main courses $10–$16. AE, MC, V. ♥

★ America
In Union Station, 50 Massachusetts Ave NE (Capitol Hill); tel 202/682-9555. **Regional American.** Using the magnificent arches and curves of Union Station, and with wall murals depicting events in US history, this three-level restaurant lives up to its name. Solid wooden tables and chairs. A mix of cuisines is offered, from southwestern fajitas to New York Reuben sandwiches. Death by Chocolate cake is just that. **FYI:** Reservations recommended. **Open:** Daily 11:30am–midnight. **Prices:** Main courses $8–$18. AE, DC, DISC, MC, V. 🚢 ᕼ

The American Cafe
227 Massachusetts Ave NE (Capitol Hill); tel 202/547-8500. **Eclectic.** Member of a successful local chain, this one near the US Senate office buildings has exposed-brick and plaster walls, lots of plants, light woods, and mirrors to create a garden-like setting. Menu features light fare and full meals from various American regional and international cuisines.

Additional locations throughout the District of Columbia, Maryland, and northern Virginia. **FYI:** Reservations accepted. Children's menu. Dress code. Additional location: 8601 Westwood Center Dr, Tysons Corner (tel 703/848-9476). **Open:** Mon–Thurs 11am–11pm, Fri–Sat 11am–midnight, Sun 10am–10pm. **Prices:** Main courses $5–$13. AE, MC, V. 🚢 👥

The Art Gallery Grille
1712 I St NW; tel 202/298-6658. **Eclectic.** Contemporary decor is highlighted by neon lights. Menu offers salads, burgers, and a variety of cuisines including Tex-Mex, deli, and Middle Eastern. Bar open until 2am. **FYI:** Reservations accepted. Dancing. **Open:** Breakfast Mon–Fri 6–10:30am; lunch Mon–Fri 11am–3pm; dinner Mon–Fri 4:30–11pm. **Prices:** Main courses $13–$15. AE, CB, DC, DISC, MC, V. 🚢 🚗 ᕼ

★ Au Pied de Cochon
1335 Wisconsin Ave NW (Georgetown); tel 202/333-5440. Just below O St. **French.** This long-standing French restaurant in an old corner building with high ceilings has copper pots and photos on its brick walls, small marble tables, and, as you might expect in a place called the Pig's Foot, plenty of pig accents. French menu has some items with Basque influence. Open all day, but daily special begins at 4pm. Glassed sidewalk patio area. Adjoining shop sells French bread and pastries to carry out. **FYI:** Reservations not accepted. **Open:** Daily 24 hrs. **Prices:** Main courses $8–$12. AE, DISC, MC, V. ♥ 📋

★ Bistro Français
3124–28 M St NW (Georgetown); tel 202/338-3830. **French.** French decorative touches, and gold and dark-wood walls and ceilings, bring Parisian flair and elegance here. There's a wide range of traditional choices, from roast pigeon with truffle gravy to organic chicken with Dijon mustard sauce. Early-bird specials in effect 5–7pm and 10:30pm–1am. **FYI:** Reservations recommended. Dress code. **Open:** Sun–Thurs 11am–3am, Fri–Sat 11am–4am. **Prices:** Main courses $13–$19. AE, CB, DC, MC, V. ♥ 📋 VP

The Bombay Club
815 Connecticut Ave NW; tel 202/659-3727. **Indian.** One of the most refined and elegant Indian restaurants anywhere, this excellent establishment a block from the White House hearkens back to days of the Raj, with its slow-moving white ceiling fans, antiques, gold-framed pictures, cartoons, and magazine covers from the British Empire era. Gourmet Indian cuisine is nicely presented. Both vegetarian curries and tandoori meat dishes are perfectly seasoned. **FYI:** Reservations recommended. Piano. **Open:** Lunch Mon–Fri 11:30am–2:30pm; dinner Mon–Thurs 6–10:30pm, Fri–Sat 6–11pm, Sun 5:30–9pm; brunch Sun 11:30am–2:30pm. **Prices:** Main courses $8–$18. AE, DC, MC, V. ♥ VP ᕼ

★ **Bombay Palace**

2020 K St NW; tel 202/331-4200. **Indian.** Plush modern decor features recessed ceilings and lighting, upholstered chairs, and mirrors reflecting a collection of Indian art. Menu offers many meat and seafood dishes as well as vegetarian curries. Samplers are popular, as are weekend lunch buffets. **FYI:** Reservations recommended. Dress code. No smoking. **Open:** Lunch Mon–Fri 11:30am–2:30pm, Sat–Sun noon–2:30pm; dinner Sun–Thurs 5:30–10pm, Fri–Sat 5:30–10:30pm. **Prices:** Main courses $8–$20. AE, DC, MC, V. ⓥ 𝖵𝖯 ⓑ

Cafe at the Corcoran Gallery of Art

17th St NW; tel 202/638-1590. Between E St and New York Ave. **Cafe.** Soaring atrium over potted palms surrounded by Greek columns, classical busts, and a reproduction of the frieze from the Parthenon. Among the various sandwiches made with hearth-baked breads are the vegetable, turkey, and salmon; also available are soups, desserts, and a selection of coffees. **FYI:** Reservations recommended. Beer and wine only. No smoking. **Open:** Wed 11am–8pm, Thurs–Mon 11am–4pm. **Prices:** Main courses $6–$12. AE, CB, DC, DISC, MC, V. ⓥ ▪

Cafe Parma

1724 Connecticut Ave NW (Dupont Circle); tel 202/462-8771. **Italian.** The uncomplicated wooden tables and chairs are overshadowed by walls filled with family mementos, patriotic hangings, maps of Sicily. Specialties on an extensive menu include tortellini filled with veal, Sicilian linguine with shrimp and sun-dried tomatoes, and Naples rigatoni with chicken. Adjacent bar is owned by the same family, and serves the restaurant through a connecting door. **FYI:** Reservations not accepted. **Open:** Mon–Thurs 11:30am–midnight, Fri–Sat 11:30am–1am, Sun 11:30am–10:30pm. **Prices:** Main courses $9–$13; prix fixe $9. AE, MC, V. 👥

Center Café

In Union Station, 50 Massachusetts Ave NE (Capitol Hill); tel 202/682-0143. **Pizza/Seafood/Tex-Mex.** Among the shops under the majestic arching roof of Union Station, this diner is guarded by Roman centurion sculptures, part of the rail station's original decoration. The granite bar inside is impressive. Varied cuisines are offered, with emphasis on Tex-Mex. Cafe Pizzettes are wafer-thin pizzas with choice of toppings. **FYI:** Reservations not accepted. No smoking. **Open:** Breakfast Mon–Fri 8–11am; lunch Mon–Fri 11am–4pm, Sat–Sun 11:30am–4pm; dinner Sun–Thurs 4–10:30pm, Fri–Sat 4pm–midnight. **Prices:** Main courses $9–$15. AE, DC, DISC, MC, V. ▪ ▲ ⓑ

Charing Cross

3027 M St NW (Georgetown); tel 202/338-2141. **Italian.** Subdued lights and tastefully configured dark, varnished wood provide a sense of calm appropriate for enjoyable dining. Menu features the Italian mainstays of spaghetti, linguine, rigatoni, and lasagna, among others. Seafood and pasta dishes are complemented by poultry, veal, and sausage. **FYI:** Reservations accepted. **Open:** Mon–Fri 11am–2am, Sat 5pm–2am. **Prices:** Main courses $7–$14. AE, MC, V. ⓥ

★ **The Childe Harold**

1610 20th St NW (Dupont Circle); tel 202/483-6702. Between Q and R Sts. **Eclectic.** The three dining areas of this restaurant have their own distinct character. The main room is highlighted by dark wood, mirrors, flower arrangements, sconces with round shades, and portions of this old town home's original 1890s wallpaper still intact. The pub area is dominated by bare brick and, with three TVs, seems almost a sports bar. Outside dining reveals views of busy Connecticut Ave near the Dupont metro station. Main courses feature seafood, chicken, veal, and steak prepared a variety of ways. The Guards, 2915 M St NW in Georgetown (tel 202/965-2350), is a related establishment. **FYI:** Reservations accepted. **Open:** Mon–Thurs 11:30am–2am, Fri–Sat 11:30am–3am, Sun 10:30am–2am. **Prices:** Main courses $11–$17. AE, CB, DC, DISC, MC, V. ▲

★ **China Doll Gourmet**

627 H St NW (Chinatown); tel 202/289-4755. **Chinese/Thai.** Walnut-finished walls and bar, with mirrors and sconces along one side of the dining room. The chef's recommendations begin with roast duck Cantonese and include hot, thin slices of lamb with vegetables. A large number of Cantonese seafood dishes and a generous vegetarian menu add substance to the offerings. **FYI:** Reservations accepted. Children's menu. Dress code. **Open:** Sun–Thurs 11am–10pm, Fri–Sat 11am–midnight. **Prices:** Main courses $7–$25. AE, CB, DC, DISC, MC, V. 👥 ▼ ⓑ

⑤ **China Inn**

629–31 H St NW (Chinatown); tel 202/842-0910. **Chinese.** Oldest establishment on Chinatown's H St restaurant row, this landmark offers red-carpet dining on two levels, the upper reached via a winding staircase. Quiet atmosphere enhanced by paper paintings and framed Chinese prints. Some unusual dishes are served, such as fish dipped in boiling water with spices, but most items are standard Cantonese fare. Dim sum served daily 11am–3pm. **FYI:** Reservations recommended. **Open:** Sun–Thurs 11am–1am, Fri–Sat 11am–2pm. **Prices:** Main courses $14–$25; prix fixe $15–$25. AE, CB, DC, DISC, MC, V.

Churreria Madrid Restaurant

2505 Champlain St NW at Columbia Rd (Adams-Morgan); tel 202/483-4441. **Spanish.** Downstairs dining room has brick floors and white stucco walls hung with memorabilia of Spain and of the proprietors' families. Over 60 different ways to enjoy home-style Spanish cuisine, from paella to tripe. Churros, a funnel cake–like dessert, is a specialty. **FYI:** Reservations accepted. Dress code. **Open:** Tues–Sat 11am–10:30pm, Sun 11am–10pm. Closed Aug–Sept. **Prices:** Main courses $6–$14. AE, CB, DC, DISC, MC, V. 👥

★ Cities

2424 18th St NW (Adams-Morgan); tel 202/328-7194. **Eclectic.** Neon lights and a large dragon are parts of unusual and intriguing decor at this eclectic restaurant whose menu changes every year to reflect the cuisines of international cities. Italy was the featured country during 1996. **FYI:** Reservations recommended. **Open:** Mon–Thurs 6–11pm, Fri–Sat 6–11:30pm, Sun 11am–9:30pm. **Prices:** Main courses $13–$22. AE, DC, MC, V. &

★ City Lights of China

1731 Connecticut Ave NW (Dupont Circle); tel 202/265-6688. Between R and S Sts. **Chinese.** Sparse, minimal decorations here, where Chinese specialties include Peking duck, crispy fried shredded beef, and stir-fried tofu. Also on menu are cold and hot appetizers, soups, and numerous other pork, beef, lamb, chicken, duck, and seafood dishes. **FYI:** Reservations accepted. **Open:** Mon–Thurs 11:30am–10:30pm, Fri 11:30am–11pm, Sat noon–11pm, Sun noon–10:30pm. **Prices:** Main courses $7–$12. AE, DC, DISC, MC, V.

★ Clyde's

3236 M St NW (Georgetown); tel 202/333-9180. **Burgers/Seafood/Steak.** The original Clyde's, this Georgetown pub started a local chain back in 1963 and continues to be popular. Bar near entrance is more traditionally pub like, with checked tablecloths and walls hung with historic prints. Rear bar and dining rooms are a mix of French and contemporary, and plants create a garden-like feel in some areas. Pub staples, pastas, and regional favorites, such as soft-shell crabs. **FYI:** Reservations accepted. Children's menu. **Open:** Mon–Thurs 11:30am–2am, Fri 11:30am–3am, Sat 9am–3am, Sun 9am–2am. **Prices:** Main courses $9–$15. AE, DC, DISC, MC, V.

Ⓢ Copperfield's

In the Brawner Building, 888 17th St, NW, at I St; tel 202/293-2217. **New American.** The feel of an English country inn is fostered by copper tabletops, plaid wallpaper, antiques, and Tiffany lamps. Popular spot for breakfast. Lunch brings salads, burgers, sandwiches, and such full meals as Maryland crab cakes and chicken linguine. **FYI:** Reservations accepted. Dress code. **Open:** Breakfast Mon–Fri 7–10:30am; lunch Mon–Fri 11am–3:30pm. **Prices:** Lunch main courses $5–$7. AE, MC, V.

Dutch Mill Deli

639 Indiana Ave NW; tel 202/347-3665. Between 6th and 7th Sts. **Deli.** Simple hardwood tables, black upholstered stack chairs, and a tile floor are what you find in this establishment devoting little time to aesthetics. Regular deli fare only, such as bagels and lox, sandwiches of beef brisket, kosher salami. **FYI:** Reservations not accepted. Dress code. **Open:** Mon–Fri 7am–3pm. **Prices:** Lunch main courses $1–$6. AE, DC, DISC, MC, V.

Encore Café

In the Kennedy Center for the Performing Arts, New Hampshire Ave NW at Rock Creek Pkwy (Foggy Bottom); tel 202/416-8560. **New American/Cafeteria.** Grand views of the Potomac River make this cafeteria-style eatery atop the Kennedy Center a popular pre-theater stop. Contemporary furnishings add class, as do prime rib, crab cakes, lasagna, baked swordfish, and other entrees worthy of many restaurant menus. Shares chef and kitchen with the Roof Terrace Restaurant. **FYI:** Reservations not accepted. Children's menu. Beer and wine only. No smoking. **Open:** Daily 11am–8pm. **Prices:** Main courses $5–$13; prix fixe $7–$17. AE, CB, DC, DISC, MC, V.

★ Famous Luigi's

1132 19th St NW; tel 202/331-7574. Between L and M Sts. **Italian.** White paint, ceiling tiles and fans, checked tablecloths, and comfortable straw-bottom chairs produce a decidedly Italian environment in this upscale eatery. Diverse menu emphasizing pizza ranges from stuffed mushrooms to fettuccine and shrimp. **FYI:** Reservations not accepted. Dress code. **Open:** Mon–Sat 11am–2am, Sun noon–midnight. **Prices:** Main courses $6–$16. AE, DC, DISC, MC, V.

Food & Co

1200 New Hampshire Ave, at M St (Dupont Circle); tel 202/223-8070. **Cafe/Deli.** Colorfully packaged coffee beans and international deli goods add pizzazz to the varnished wood and red brick floor. Specializing in a variety of sandwiches, pâtés, quiches, and vegetarian dishes. Enticing pastries, cakes, and "old-fashioned" ice cream also available. **FYI:** Reservations not accepted. Dress code. Beer and wine only. **Open:** Mon–Fri 8am–9pm, Sat 9am–7pm, Sun 10am–5pm. **Prices:** Main courses $3–$9. AE, MC, V.

Food for Thought

1738 Connecticut Ave NW (Dupont Circle); tel 202/797-1095. Near S St. **Eclectic/Vegetarian.** The decor is modest, with minimal aesthetic emphasis. The long, hall-like room is oriented toward a stage. Of eight entrees offered, five are vegetarian: enchiladas, vegetables and brown rice, lasagna, grilled tofu, and sandwiches made with bean and sunflower patties. For those otherwise inclined, there are organically raised trout, charcoal-grilled beef with vegetables, and chicken wings. **FYI:** Reservations not accepted. Blues/country music/jazz. **Open:** Mon–Thurs 11:30am–12:30am, Fri 11:30am–2am, Sat noon–2am, Sun 4pm–12:30am. **Prices:** Main courses $7–$10. AE, CB, DC, DISC, MC, V.

The Gangplank on the Potomac

600 Water St SW; tel 202/554-5000. **American/Seafood.** The riverfront establishment actually is three restaurants in one, each with a different theme and menu. The dining room offers an upscale, pleasing decor and such daily specials as swordfish kabob. The bar provides a relaxed social atmosphere, sandwiches, and moderately priced specials, such as a vegetarian garden burger. A seasonal concrete patio serves salads, sandwiches, and limited entrees to be eaten in wide-

open spaces over the river. (Patio open only 4pm–1:30am during warm months.) **FYI:** Reservations recommended. Dress code. **Open:** Lunch Mon–Thurs 11:30am–2pm, Fri–Sat 11am–3pm; dinner Sun–Thurs 5:30–10pm, Fri–Sat 5:30–11pm; brunch Sun 11am–3pm. **Prices:** Main courses $16–$26. AE, DC, DISC, MC, V. 🌑 ⚘ ⛰ ⌄

✹ Garrett's Restaurant and Railroad Bar
3003 M St NW (Georgetown); tel 202/333-1033. **Eclectic.** The highlight is an upstairs atrium with glass ceiling above two brick walls. A trompe l'oeil mural forms a perfect reflection of the dining area, making it seem twice as large. Menu is topped by a 16-ounce chargrilled New York strip steak served with baked potato and vegetable. Other offerings include grilled salmon filet with butter sauce and baby-back ribs. **FYI:** Reservations recommended. Children's menu. Dress code. **Open:** Mon–Thurs 11:30am–2am, Fri 11:30am–3am, Sat noon–3am, Sun noon–2am. **Prices:** Main courses $6–$18. AE, DC, DISC, MC, V. 🖼 ⛰

HI Ribster's
800 Water St SW; tel 202/479-6857. **Regional American/ Barbecue.** Uncomplicated decor in this riverfront restaurant uses plain tables and booths, pictures and tapestries. Favorites on the place-mat menu are barbecued baby-back ribs, beef ribs, wet or dry Memphis-style spare ribs, and chicken. **FYI:** Reservations accepted. Children's menu. Dress code. **Open:** Mon–Fri 11am–10pm, Sat noon–11pm, Sun noon–10pm. **Prices:** Main courses $8–$16. AE, CB, DC, DISC, MC, V. ⚘ ⛰ &

Hogate's
800 Water St SW; tel 202/484-6300. **Seafood/Steak.** Highly varnished wooden tables with substantial upholstered captain's chairs are surrounded by maritime relics. In addition to hot and chilled appetizers like steamed clams and shucked oysters, menu emphasizes fried, broiled, and sautéed seafood platters. Lobster, shrimp, crab legs and cakes, clams, mussels, and fish all appear on the menu. **FYI:** Reservations accepted. Children's menu. Dress code. **Open:** Mon–Thurs 11am–10pm, Fri 11am–11pm, Sat noon–11pm, Sun 10:30am–10pm. **Prices:** Main courses $12–$29. AE, DC, DISC, MC, V. 🌑 ▮ ⚘ ⛰ &

✹ Houston's
1065 Wisconsin Ave NW (Georgetown); tel 202/338-7760. Located just below M St. **Burgers/Seafood/Steak.** Pleasing and unusual decor of finished dark wood, unfinished exposed beams, and ducts highlight this spot popular with the younger set. There are burgers with a variety of toppings, but fish, chicken, and beef dishes make this more than a burger palace. Wide selection of salads, including an eggless Caesar. **FYI:** Reservations not accepted. Dress code. **Open:** Mon–Thurs 5–11pm, Fri 5pm–midnight, Sat noon–midnight, Sun noon–11pm. **Prices:** Main courses $7–$24. AE, MC, V. 👥 &

✹ Hunan Chinatown
624 H St NW (Chinatown); tel 202/783-5858. **Chinese.** Subdued wall coverings and ceramic-tile floor emphasize the cubicle-like arrangement of half of this restaurant, while a prismatic mirror reflects the diners and bar across the room. Peking duck leads the list of recommended dishes, with additional specialties including orange beef, giant shrimp sautéed with vegetables, prawns with walnuts, and whole Hunan-style fish. **FYI:** Reservations accepted. **Open:** Sun–Thurs 11am–11pm, Fri–Sat 11am–midnight. **Prices:** Main courses $8–$25; prix fixe $15–$40. AE, DC, DISC, MC, V. 👥

✹ Iron Gate Restaurant
1734 N St NW (Dupont Circle); tel 202/737-1370. Between 17th and 18th Sts. **Mediterranean.** An extraordinary update of this 1890s stable has turned some of the old stalls into booths. Subdued lighting, dark woods, and a brick fireplace add to romantic atmosphere, with pleasant garden dining in good weather. From France and Spain to Morocco and Italy come the dishes on this varied, gourmet-quality menu. **FYI:** Reservations recommended. No smoking. **Open:** Mon–Fri 11:30am–10pm, Sat 5–10pm, Sun 5–9pm. **Prices:** Main courses $15–$20. AE, DC, DISC, MC, V. 🌑 ▮ ⚘ 🖼

✦ The Jefferson Restaurant
In The Jefferson, 1200 16th St NW at M St (Downtown); tel 202/347-2200. **New American.** Leather walls offset by indirect lighting and off-white moldings are strikingly done and supplemented by finished wood floors. Chef's most exciting creations include smoked lamb chops with lamb sausage, fresh corn griddle cakes and watermelon pickles, blueberry barbecued venison with sweet-potato salad, and confetti of vegetables and grilled tuna. **FYI:** Reservations recommended. Children's menu. Dress code. **Open:** Daily 6am–11pm. **Prices:** Main courses $18–$28; prix fixe $55–$75. AE, CB, DC, DISC, MC, V. 🌑 ▮ 🖼 VP &

Kelly's The Irish Times
14 F St NW (Capitol Hill); tel 202/543-5433. At N Capitol and Massachusetts Ave. **American/Irish.** Well-used bar is indicative of many toasts offered at this quintessential Irish pub, bedecked with appropriate memorabilia, flags, escutcheons, and photos of the old country. Standard pub fare, including half-pound burgers, is supplemented by the chef's apple and blueberry pies. Live Irish music Wednesday to Sunday evenings. The Dubliner Restaurant and Pub, 520 N Capitol St (202/737-3773), with an entrance next door on F St NW, is more upscale. **FYI:** Reservations accepted. Irish music. **Open:** Daily 11am–2am. **Prices:** Main courses $4–$12. AE, CB, DC, MC, V. &

Kolbeh
1645 Wisconsin Ave NW (Georgetown); tel 202/342-2000. Between Reservoir Rd and Q St. **Middle Eastern/Iranian.** Mirrored walls and ceiling and light woods provide a feeling of spaciousness in which to enjoy Middle Eastern cuisine with

an Iranian flair. Variety of lamb dishes offered. **FYI:** Reservations accepted. **Open:** Mon–Thurs 11:30am–10pm, Fri–Sun 11:30am–11pm. **Prices:** Main courses $8–$14. AE, MC, V.

Ⓢ Kozy Korner Restaurant
1253 20th St NW, at N St (Dupont Circle); tel 202/785-4314. **American/Greek/Italian.** Well-coordinated colors supplemented with Tiffany lamps, ceiling fans, and brass wall hangings seem incongruous alongside the budget-minded prices in this popular eatery. Noted for Italian and Greek specialties, including gyro and souvlaki sandwiches. Breakfast served all day. **FYI:** Reservations accepted. **Open:** Mon–Fri 7am–10pm, Sat 7am–3pm. **Prices:** Main courses $5–$9. AE, MC, V. 🖼️

★ Kramerbooks & Afterwords Cafe
1517 Connecticut Ave NW; tel 202/387-1462. Between Q St and Dupont Circle. **Eclectic.** The first combination bookstore/restaurant in Washington and still the most popular. The cafe portion has grown and now includes a solarium on the 19th St sidewalk behind the original bookstore. Menu offers a mix of international and American regional cuisine with some of the chef's own combinations, such as Thai jambalaya over fettuccine. **FYI:** Reservations not accepted. Blues/jazz. **Open:** Sun–Thurs 7:30am–1am, Fri–Sat 24 hrs. **Prices:** Main courses $9–$13. AE, DISC, MC, V. 🖼️

Le Lion d'Or
1150 Connecticut Ave NW (Dupont Circle); tel 202/296-7972. At M St. **French.** To step across the threshold of this fine establishment is to save the cost of traveling to Paris. An elegantly appointed dining room features huge chandeliers beneath cloth canopies, potted plants, copper cookware, and a variety of artistic paintings, lending an ambience suitable to one of America's finest restaurants. The talented owner/chef cooks such treats as Dover sole sautéed in artichokes, veal filet with shiitake mushrooms, and roast pigeon with mushrooms. Menu is in French with no translation. **FYI:** Reservations recommended. Jacket required. **Open:** Mon–Sat 6–10pm. Closed Aug. **Prices:** Main courses $24–$36. AE, DC, DISC, MC, V. 🖼️🖼️

The Lunch Garden
1015 18th St NW; tel 202/331-0860. Between K and L Sts. **Eclectic.** Bright, cheerful, clean establishment accented by green plants and gray and white tile floors. Sandwich menu includes hand-carved turkey, beef, and ham along with subs and platters served with bread and vegetables. **FYI:** Reservations not accepted. No liquor license. **Open:** Mon–Fri 7am–5pm. **Prices:** Main courses $4–$7. No CC. 🖼️

Marché Café and Bar
1810 K St NW; tel 202/293-3000. **Cafe/French.** A modern French bistro with mirrors, which add significantly to sense of spaciousness. Menu changes daily, includes French dishes with some Spanish and other cuisines. **FYI:** Reservations accepted. **Open:** Mon–Fri 11am–9pm. **Prices:** Main courses $6–$10. AE, CB, DC, MC, V. 🖼️

Mixtec
1792 Columbia Rd, at 18th St (Adams-Morgan); tel 202/332-1011. **Mexican.** Mexican cantina setting for authentic ethnic cuisine in one of Washington's most ethnically diverse and lively neighborhoods. Hand-painted wicker chairs, colorful hanging paper lanterns add festive air. Gaily painted tin ornaments hang on wall of larger dining room. Corn tortillas made on premises. **FYI:** Reservations not accepted. Beer and wine only. **Open:** Mon–Thurs 11am–10pm, Fri–Sun 11am–midnight. **Prices:** Main courses $6–$10. MC, V.

♣ Morrison-Clark Inn
Massachusetts Ave NW, at 11th St (Franklin Square); tel 202/289-8580. **New American/Southern.** Elegantly detailed Victorian decor in the dining room of this historic inn. Award-winning chef "does her own thing" in the kitchen. Examples are grilled halibut with roasted red-pepper aioli and eggplant flan, and smoked pork loin with honey mustard-herb sauce served with a grits soufflé. **FYI:** Reservations recommended. Jacket required. No smoking. **Open:** Lunch Mon–Fri 11am–2pm; dinner Sun–Thurs 6–9:30pm, Fri–Sat 6–10:30pm; brunch Sun 11:30am–2pm. **Prices:** Main courses $18–$28. AE, CB, DC, DISC, ER, MC, V. 🖼️🖼️🖼️🖼️🖼️

Morton's of Chicago
3251 Prospect St NW (Georgetown); tel 202/342-6258. **Seafood/Steak.** White stucco walls with carefully chosen hangings, Oriental runners, light wood floors, a varnished oak bar, and etched glass give class to this upscale steak house, a member of the Chicago-based chain. A 3-pound porterhouse tops the offerings, which range from aged filet mignon, prime rib, and chops to Maine lobsters and fresh fish. **FYI:** Reservations recommended. Dress code. **Open:** Mon–Sat 5:30–11pm, Sun 5–10pm. **Prices:** Main courses $19–$30. AE, DC, MC, V. 🖼️🖼️

National Gallery of Art Cafes
6th and Constitution Aves NW (Capitol Hill); tel 202/347-9401. **American/Cafe/International.** Four eateries grace the National Gallery. Stunning on all counts, the Cascade Espresso Bar, in the tunnel connecting the gallery's two wings, features a two-story waterfall, atrium with chrome ceiling, and marble-top tables. The cafeteria-style Café/Buffet is adjacent. The Garden Cafe, in the West Wing, sports much greenery and blooming flowers as well as an 11th-century bronze statute of Venus. The Terrace, in the East Wing, has light, contemporary wall decorations and outstanding views of greenery outside. Menus often are created based on the theme of current exhibits. **FYI:** Reservations accepted. Beer and wine only. No smoking. **Open:** Peak (Apr–Nov) Mon–Sat 11:30am–3pm, Sun noon–6:30pm. **Prices:** Lunch main courses $6–$11. AE, DC, DISC, MC, V. 🖼️🖼️🖼️🖼️🖼️

Nora: An Organic Restaurant
2132 Florida Ave NW at R St (Dupont Circle); tel 202/462-5143. **International/Organic.** A sense of quiet elegance and clubbiness pervades. Though quite diverse, the offerings have one thing in common: They are produced from additive-

free meat and organically grown produce. Recent examples have included veal and cashew curry with brown rice and apricot chutney; Chesapeake Bay soft-shell crabs with charred tomato sauce, corn pudding, and grilled squash; and veal scaloppine with tomatoes, thyme, roasted new potatoes, and French beans. **FYI:** Reservations recommended. No smoking. **Open:** Mon–Thurs 6–10pm, Fri–Sat 6–10:30pm. **Prices:** Main courses $19–$25. MC, V. ♥ ▮

✹ Old Ebbitt Grill

675 15th St NW (Downtown); tel 202/347-4801. Between F and G Sts. **American.** Located two blocks from the White House is the city's oldest saloon, founded in 1856. (Presidents Grant, Johnson, McKinley, Cleveland, Theodore Roosevelt, and Harding were patrons.) The existing facility is a plush reconstruction of the original tavern, with oak and marble floors, Persian rugs, etched-glass panels, and gas lighting; there are even animal trophies bagged by Teddy Roosevelt hanging from the walls. Menus change daily, but entrees might include roasted half-chicken (with lemon, herbs, and honey, and served with rice and fresh vegetables), or fettuccine tossed with spinach and walnuts in cream sauce. Lower-priced sandwiches and burgers are always available. Desserts include toll house pie à la mode. **FYI:** Reservations recommended. Dress code. **Open:** Mon–Fri 7:30am–1am, Sat 8am–1am, Sun 9:30am–1am. **Prices:** Main courses $9–$17. AE, DC, DISC, MC, V. ▮ VP ☕

✹ Old Europe Restaurant and Rathskeller

2434 Wisconsin Ave NW (Georgetown); tel 202/333-7600. **German.** For almost 50 years, this has been a premier retreat for lovers of German food and warm hospitality. The tranquil street-level dining room is complemented by a lively rathskeller downstairs; the menu is the same in both. The winter "game season" means there'll be hare, venison, duck, and boar on the menu; bratwurst, sauerbraten, and Wiener schnitzel are staples year-round. **FYI:** Reservations recommended. Dress code. **Open:** Lunch Mon–Sat 11:30am–3pm; dinner Mon–Thurs 5–9pm, Fri–Sat 5–10pm, Sun 4–9pm. **Prices:** Main courses $9–$11. AE, CB, DC, MC, V. ♥

♟✹ Palm Restaurant

1225 19th St NW (Dupont Circle); tel 202/293-9091. **American/Italian.** Known locally as the Palm. Walls here are covered with caricatures of longtime patrons, many of them famous politicians and news media personalities who hang out here for ample portions of seafood, poultry, steaks, chops, and pasta. Popular items are jumbo Nova Scotia lobster and thin, crispy fried potatoes and onion rings. **FYI:** Reservations recommended. Dress code. **Open:** Mon–Fri 11:45am–10pm, Sat 6–10:30pm, Sun 5:30–9:30pm. **Prices:** Main courses $14–$28. AE, DC, MC, V. VP

✹ Paolo's Ristorante

1303 Wisconsin Ave NW, at N St (Georgetown); tel 202/333-7353. **Italian.** Mirrored walls and subdued lighting contribute to the warm and cozy atmosphere. Menu includes pizza, pasta, and other traditional Italian favorites. Pizza served at the bar until last call. **FYI:** Reservations not accepted. **Open:** Sun–Thurs 11:30am–1:30am, Fri–Sat 11:30am–2:30am. **Prices:** Main courses $7–$17. AE, DC, DISC, MC, V.

Paru's

2010 S St NW; tel 202/483-5133. Located just east of Connecticut Ave. **Indian.** This storefront eatery with a carry-out counter and only eight tables might as well be in Madras, so authentic are its south Indian vegetarian selections, such as masala dosai, a rolled pancake filled with spicy potato curry. Paper plates and cups are de rigueur at this clean, bargain establishment. **FYI:** Reservations not accepted. No liquor license. **Open:** Mon–Sat 11:30am–8:30pm. **Prices:** Main courses $4–$9. No CC.

Patisserie Café Didier

3206 Grace St NW (Georgetown); tel 202/342-9083. Off Wisconsin Ave just below M St. **Cafe/Continental.** Pastels, white straw-back chairs, straw lamp shades, and a copse of real plants and flower arrangements are most restful and pleasing to the eye. Daily specials include various croissants, pastries, and scones. Other featured items include quiche, sandwiches, and salads. **FYI:** Reservations accepted. No liquor license. **Open:** Tues–Sat 8am–7pm, Sun 8am–5pm. **Prices:** Lunch main courses $6–$9. CB, DC, DISC, MC, V. ♥ ▦

✹ Peyote Café

2319 18th St NW (Adams-Morgan); tel 202/462-8330. Between Belmont and Kalorama Rds. **Southwestern/Tex-Mex.** Southwestern decor highlighted by neon signs, a jukebox, and a wood bar surrounded by high-back stools. Sharing space with Roxanne/On the Rox (see listing below), this is primarily a bar, although numerous interesting salads, sandwiches, and such Tex-Mex specialties as Ranchero Raphael's pizza with a grilled cornmeal crust are served. **FYI:** Reservations accepted. **Open:** Dinner Sun–Thurs 5–11pm, Fri–Sat 5pm–midnight; brunch Sat–Sun 11:30am–4pm. **Prices:** Main courses $6–$14. AE, DC, DISC, MC, V.

♟✹ Prime Rib

2020 K St NW (Foggy Bottom); tel 202/466-8811. **American/Seafood/Steak.** Art deco touches—black pillars, abundant flower arrangements and mirrors, striking art on the walls, and subdued lighting—establish an appropriate ambience for the Washington businesspeople and power brokers who practically call this place home. Aged prime rib roasted in its own juice is the main attraction, but steaks, lamb, pork, and lobster are also listed. Indulgent desserts. **FYI:** Reservations recommended. Piano. Jacket required. **Open:** Lunch Mon–Fri 11:30am–3pm; dinner Mon–Thurs 5–11pm, Fri–Sat 5–11:30pm. **Prices:** Main courses $15–$24. AE, DC, MC, V. ♥ VP

✦ Red Sage
605 14th St NW, at F St (Downtown); tel 202/638-4444. **New Southwestern.** An overall southwestern theme prevails in these three adjoining, architecturally creative restaurants, each with its own nuances. Adobe predominates in ceilings and walls, although the Chili Bar has a painted sky complete with clouds and lightning. The main dining room's largest area has a horse theme, with massive timbers supporting the ceiling above lighted, flower-filled alcoves. The Library provides more intimate dining, thanks to finished wood, high-quality table linens, and ash-colored chairs. Menu is fittingly southwestern, with cowboy rib-eye steaks and barbecued black beans heading the list. Also glazed quail, grilled swordfish, three varieties of chili. Price varies with dining area. **FYI:** Reservations recommended. Dress code. **Open:** Mon–Sat 11:30am–11:30pm, Sun 4:30–11:30pm. **Prices:** Main courses $5–$29. AE, CB, DC, DISC, MC, V. ▨ &

Red Sea
2463 18th St NW (Adams-Morgan); tel 202/483-5000. Located near Columbia Rd. **Ethiopian.** Red table linen and vinyl-upholstered chairs. Many posters of Ethiopia complement the Ethiopian dishes, including *lyb*, a spicy cheese, and some red-hot meat selections. Meals are served in traditional fashion on a round piece of steamed Ethiopian bread. Fingers are used to pick up food with pieces of bread resembling wet napkins. **FYI:** Reservations accepted. **Open:** Daily 11:30am–midnight. **Prices:** Main courses $6–$11. AE, DC, MC, V. 🚗

✦ Reeve's Restaurant and Bakery
1306 G St NW (Downtown); tel 202/628-6350. Between 13th and 14th Sts. **American.** Light woods, marble tile, and judicious use of mirrors provide a very pleasing atmosphere enhanced by rust-tone upholstered booths. Although regular restaurant fare such as burgers, pasta dishes, and salads are on the menu, the real highlights here are the desserts, like strawberry pie and strawberry shortcake. **FYI:** Reservations not accepted. Dress code. No liquor license. **Open:** Mon–Sat 7am–6pm. **Prices:** Lunch main courses $4–$7. MC, V. ▨ ♥ &

Refectory
Room S-112, 1st floor of US Capitol; tel 202/224-4870. **Diner.** There's nothing fancy about this fast-food diner under the US Senate chamber in the Capitol. Famous Senate bean soup is the only notable offering among a variety of sandwiches and simple main courses. Closing times depend on when the Senate adjourns for the day. **FYI:** Reservations not accepted. No liquor license. **Open:** Mon–Fri 8am–9pm. **Prices:** Main courses $5–$10. MC, V. ▨ &

Ristorante Tiberio
1915 K St NW; tel 202/452-1915. **Italian.** Many stucco arches and walls hung with contemporary art create a simple but elegant ambience in which to indulge in gourmet Italian cuisine. In addition to choosing from a variety of meat, fish, fowl, and pasta options, you are invited to ask for your favorite unlisted dish. **FYI:** Reservations recommended. Jacket required. **Open:** Lunch Mon–Fri 11:45am–2:30pm; dinner Mon–Sat 6–10:30pm. **Prices:** Main courses $20–$35. AE, DC, DISC, MC, V. ♥ ▨

♛ The River Club Restaurant
3223 K St NW; tel 202/333-8118. Wisconsin Ave at Potomac River. **Continental.** An updated example of a old-fashioned supper club, where a couple can click their heels in an art deco setting replete with fine dining, a dance floor, and live big-band or jazz music. The menu features items like Macadamia-crusted salmon fillet and veal rib chop Oscar. A place for a special evening with someone special. **FYI:** Reservations recommended. Big band/dancing/jazz/piano. Jacket required. **Open:** Wed–Thurs 6:30pm–2am, Fri–Sat 6:30pm–3am, Sun 6:30–11pm. **Prices:** Main courses $18–$28. AE, DC, DISC, MC, V. ♥ ▨

Roof Terrace Restaurant
In the Kennedy Center for the Performing Arts, New Hampshire Ave NW at Rock Creek Pkwy (Foggy Bottom); tel 202/416-8555. **Regional American.** Elegant chairs and linen beneath 18-foot ceilings are complemented by views of many Washington monuments from this restaurant atop the Kennedy Center. Menu features a regional variety, including mesquite-grilled salmon, smoked duck, crab cakes with herbs. Brunch served all year, but for dinner the restaurant is open only on performance nights. Adjoining Hors d'Oeuvres Lounge has marble-top tables for pre-theater drinks and snacks. **FYI:** Reservations recommended. Children's menu. Jacket required. No smoking. **Open:** Lunch daily 11am–3pm; dinner daily 5:30–9pm; brunch Sun 11:30am–3pm. **Prices:** Main courses $22–$27. AE, DC, MC, V. ♥ ▤ ▨ &

Roxanne/On the Rox
2319 18th St NW (Adams-Morgan); tel 202/462-8330. Between Belmont and Kalorama Rds. **Southwestern.** Sharing space with the Peyote Cafe, the main dining room's walls are hung with western paintings and southwestern mementos, including a longhorn skull. Upstairs, the Starlit Rooftop Terrace offers outdoor dining with a view. Southwestern cuisine is taken seriously. **FYI:** Reservations accepted. **Open:** Mon–Fri 5–11pm, Sat 11:30am–midnight, Sun 11:30am–11pm. **Prices:** Main courses $7–$14. AE, DC, DISC, MC, V. ♥ ▨

✦ Ruth's Chris Steak House
1801 Connecticut Ave NW; tel 202/797-0033. **Regional American/Steak.** Brick walls, dark exposed beams, low stucco ceilings, and lantern light bring rustic elegance to this Washington favorite. Cozy alcoves offer intimate seating, and a separate room has a brick fireplace and hearth. Corn-fed, carefully aged steaks are the mainstays, with lamb and veal chops, chicken, lobster, salmon, and tuna also put to the coals. **FYI:** Reservations recommended. **Open:** Daily 5–10:30pm. **Prices:** Main courses $16–$30. AE, MC, V. ♥ ▨ ▨ &

Sea Catch Restaurant and Raw Bar

1054 31st St NW (Georgetown); tel 202/337-8855. Located just below M St. **Seafood/Steak.** Two-centuries-old bricks and beams combine with contemporary light wood in this seafood emporium that cooks up live Maine lobsters, crab cakes, swordfish steak, and other morsels from the sea's harvest. **FYI:** Reservations recommended. Children's menu. **Open:** Lunch Mon–Sat noon–3pm; dinner Mon–Sat 5:30–10pm. **Prices:** Main courses $15–$20; prix fixe $20. AE, CB, DC, DISC, MC, V. ⊗ ▆ ⬟ 🎴 ⛰ ☑ VP

Seasons

In Four Seasons, 2800 Pennsylvania Ave NW, at M St (Georgetown); tel 202/342-0810. **Seafood.** Plush decor features bird prints, lacquered walls, leather banquettes, and stone floors. Specialties include smoked haddock in cream sauce flavored with malt whisky; loin of venison with root vegetables and bramble sauce; crispy Oriental sea bass with ginger sauce; and sugar-crusted baked rice pudding. Weekend brunch served in the Garden Terrace. **FYI:** Reservations recommended. Children's menu. Dress code. **Open:** Breakfast Mon–Fri 7–11am, Sat–Sun 8am–noon; lunch Mon–Fri noon–2:30pm; dinner daily 6:30–10:30pm; brunch Sat–Sun 10am–2:30pm. **Prices:** Main courses $16–$29. AE, CB, DC, MC, V. ⊗ VP ♿

1789

1226 36th St NW at Prospect St (Georgetown); tel 202/965-1789. **American.** Extra-dark woods and thematic wall hangings create an elegant country-inn ambience in this Federal-period town house named in honor of the year when Georgetown was incorporated. Offerings are pure Americana, from Maryland crab cakes to rack of lamb. Some dishes have an unusual flair, such as veal ravioli with sweetbreads. **FYI:** Reservations recommended. Jacket required. **Open:** Sun–Thurs 6–10pm, Fri–Sat 6–11pm. **Prices:** Main courses $18–$29. AE, CB, DC, DISC, MC, V. ⊗ ▆ ☑ VP

$ ★ Sherill's Bakery

233 Pennsylvania Ave SE (Capitol Hill); tel 202/544-2480. **American/Cafe.** This 1940s-vintage landmark eatery was immortalized in the Emmy-winning and Oscar-nominated documentary *Fine Food, Fine Pastries,* which spotlighted this family-owned and -operated enterprise. Pastries are made on premises. Other selections are plain American fare, such as home-style meatloaf and crab cakes. Popular for breakfast. **FYI:** Reservations not accepted. No liquor license. **Open:** Mon–Fri 6am–7pm, Sat–Sun 7am–7pm. **Prices:** Main courses $5–$10. No CC. 🎴

★ Sholl's Colonial Cafeteria

In Esplanade Mall, 1990 K St NW; tel 202/296-3065. **American/Cafeteria.** Washington's most popular and least expensive cafeteria is plain, with few decorative touches except plastic plants. A variety of fresh, plainly prepared foods are offered along the line. Roast beef and fried chicken are mainstays. **FYI:** Reservations not accepted. No liquor license. No smoking. **Open:** Breakfast Mon–Sat 7–10:30am, Sun 8:30–11am; lunch daily 11am–2:30pm; dinner Mon–Sat 4–8pm, Sun 2:30–6pm. **Prices:** Main courses $2–$5. No CC. 🎴

Sichuan Pavillion

In Int'l Sq Bldg, 1820 K St NW; tel 202/466-7790. **Chinese.** Pleasingly subdued wall colors are enhanced by Chinese art and decorative objects in this upscale restaurant. Wall-size screens separate private dining rooms from public areas. Spicy Szechuan cuisine is the prime offering, with crispy whole fish a house specialty. **FYI:** Reservations recommended. Dress code. **Open:** Mon–Fri 11am–10pm, Sat–Sun noon–10pm. **Prices:** Main courses $7–$20. AE, DC, DISC, MC, V. ⊗

South Buffet

In Dirksen Senate Office Building, 1st and C Sts NE (Capitol Hill); tel 202/224-4249. **Cafeteria.** Cloth tablecloths, historical photos of the Capitol area, and drinks delivered to the table add extra touches to this otherwise self-serve facility operated by the US Senate. Menu, consisting of basic choices, changes weekly. **FYI:** Reservations not accepted. Children's menu. No liquor license. **Open:** Mon–Fri 11:30am–2:30pm. **Prices:** Lunch main courses $8. MC, V. 🎴 ♿

Station Grill

In Union Station, 50 Massachusetts Ave NE (Capitol Hill); tel 202/898-4745. **American.** Dark colors from ceiling to the wooden chairs and subdued lighting seem to help quiet the multitude of sounds coming from the busy marble hallway outside. Good choices are roasted half chicken with spices, a crab-cake platter, char-grilled rib-eye in teriyaki sauce, open-face omelette with vegetables and cheese, London broil, and linguine. Various appetizers, soups, salads, burgers, and sandwiches round out the options. Two-hour validated parking in adjoining parking garage. **FYI:** Reservations not accepted. Children's menu. **Open:** Mon–Fri 8am–10pm, Sat 9am–10pm, Sun 9am–9pm. **Prices:** Main courses $5–$18. AE, MC, V. ⬟ 🎴

$ Szechuan Gallery Restaurant

617 H St NW (Chinatown); tel 202/898-1180. **Chinese.** Tufted leatherette booths, wood tables thickly laminated with clear plastic, nicely framed Oriental prints, and an attractive oak bar work together to give this establishment a bit more elegance than is sometimes found in Chinese restaurants. A mix of Szechuan and Taiwanese cuisines makes for spicy selections. **FYI:** Reservations recommended. **Open:** Sun–Thurs 11am–3am, Fri–Sat 11am–4am. **Prices:** Main courses $8–$25. AE, CB, DC, MC, V.

Tandoor Restaurant

3316 M St NW (Georgetown); tel 202/333-3376. **Indian.** Indian-style brass lights, teak, paintings, and tapestries set the tone for this ethnic restaurant featuring meat dishes from the tandoor oven and a selection of curries. Dining room in rear, known separately as Madurai, offers interesting vegetarian twists on traditional Indian cuisine. **FYI:** Reservations recommended. No smoking. **Open:** Lunch daily 11:30am–2:30pm; dinner Mon–Sat 5:30–10:30pm, Sun 5:30–10pm. **Prices:** Main courses $8–$12. AE, DC, DISC, MC, V. ♥ ⟨

★ Thai Taste
2606 Connecticut Ave NW (Woodley Park); tel 202/387-8876. Located just off Calvert St. **Thai.** Uncomplicated decor consists of a combination of tables and black booths lighted by antique art-deco electric sconces, but little in the way of ethnic identity. Fried beef or chicken in spicy red curry and coconut milk, soft-shell crabs sautéed with chili paste, and other Thai delights. **FYI:** Reservations recommended. Children's menu. Dress code. **Open:** Sun–Thurs 11:30am–10:30pm, Fri–Sat 11:30am–11pm. **Prices:** Main courses $6–$11. AE, DC, MC, V. 🚗

Timberlake's
1726 Connecticut Ave NW (Dupont Circle); tel 202/483-2266. Between R and S Sts. **Burgers/Seafood/Steak.** A varnished bar, overhead fans, and two TVs foster the sports-bar ambience in the front room of this restaurant. The back dining room with overhead skylights, growing plants, and modest wall hangings should make daytime dining pleasant. Menu changes every week, with a lobster special on Mondays and prime rib on Tuesday. Regular entrees include spinach fettuccine; trout sautéed with tomatoes, onions, olives, and lemon butter; steak au poivre; and a crab-cake platter. Sandwiches too. **FYI:** Reservations accepted. **Open:** Sun–Thurs 10:30am–midnight, Fri 11:30am–1am, Sat 10:30am–1am. **Prices:** Main courses $6–$15. AE, CB, DC, DISC, MC, V.

★ The Tombs
1226 36th St NW, at Prospect St (Georgetown); tel 202/337-6668. **Burgers/Pizza/Pub.** College memorabilia and a rathskeller atmosphere hint as to the clientele at this friendly institution near Georgetown University. A balanced choice of several types of salads, burgers, and sandwiches plus daily specials—two or three regular meals to keep Hoya students going between exams or basketball games. **FYI:** Reservations not accepted. **Open:** Mon–Fri 11:30am–1:30am, Sat 11am–2:30am, Sun 9:30am–1:30am. **Prices:** Main courses $7–$11. AE, CB, DC, DISC, MC, V. ♥

Trio Restaurant
1537 17th St NW at Q St (Dupont Circle); tel 202/232-6305. **American.** One of the last 1950s-style restaurants left in Washington, with red vinyl booths and modernistic chandeliers, with walls of rose and green. The regular menu is plain American fare—roast turkey with dressing, combination seafood platter, hot roast-beef sandwiches—but more interesting daily specials might include fresh Buffalo mozzarella cheese as an appetizer, grilled tuna with fresh field greens vinaigrette as main course. **FYI:** Reservations not accepted. Dress code. **Open:** Daily 7:30am–midnight. **Prices:** Main courses $5–$11. AE, DISC, MC, V. 🍴

✦ Uptown Bakers
3313 Connecticut Ave NW (Cleveland Park); tel 202/362-6262. Located just north of Macomb St. **Bakery.** Simple white plastic tables and chairs, and blue and white tile floors set the tone in this bakery specializing in a variety of breads, cakes, pies, pastries. A limited number of sandwiches at lunch. Bakeries are not required by DC law to have public rest rooms, and this one doesn't. **FYI:** Reservations not accepted. No liquor license. No smoking. Additional location: 3471 N Washington Blvd, Arlington (tel 703/527-6262). **Open:** Daily 7am–9pm. **Prices:** Main courses $4–$7. No CC. 👪

Vidalia
1990 M St NW (Dupont Circle); tel 202/659-1990. **Regional American.** Cozy, country-inn ambience is enhanced by smooth butterscotch-colored stucco walls and brass chandeliers. Inventive chef is well known for blending Southern ingredients, such as country ham, kale, and Vidalia onions, with Yankee fare to concoct adventurous dishes. Crab cakes with bell pepper, jicama slaw, and spicy Chesapeake Bay seasoned mayonnaise are a regular favorite. **FYI:** Reservations recommended. Dress code. **Open:** Lunch Mon–Fri 11:30am–2:30pm; dinner Mon–Sat 5:30–10:30pm. **Prices:** Main courses $17–$20. AE, CB, DC, DISC, MC, V. ♥ VP ⟨

★ Vie de France
In the Capitol Gallery Bldg, 600 Maryland Ave SW (L'Enfant Plaza); tel 202/554-7870. Off Independence Ave SW. **French.** An outgrowth of a fine local bakery of the same name, this cafe with sturdy oak tables (some with umbrellas), wicker-back chairs, and some booths has photos of France to set the mood for fine French soups, salads, and pastries, and sandwiches made with fresh croissants and crispy baguettes. Also at: 2nd floor of Esplanade Mall, 1990 K St NW (tel 202/659-0055). **FYI:** Reservations accepted. Children's menu. Dress code. **Open:** Mon–Fri 11am–9pm. **Prices:** Main courses $6–$11. AE, DC, MC, V. 👪 ⟨

⑤ ★ Vietnam Georgetown Restaurant
2934 M St NW, at 29th St (Georgetown); tel 202/337-4536. **Vietnamese.** Mirrors and white walls and tablecloths brighten up this small, 20-table restaurant. Still, it's an intimate room, and Vietnamese paintings add a sense of place. Outdoor dining on brick patio under huge shade tree is pleasant during warm weather. A pioneer Vietnamese restaurant in this area, which now has many, but still a fine bargain eatery. Buffet Mon–Fri, 11am–2pm. **FYI:** Reservations accepted. Dress code. No smoking. **Open:** Sun–Thurs 11am–11pm, Fri–Sat noon–midnight. **Prices:** Main courses $6–$9. CB, DC, MC, V. 🍴

The Willard Room
In the Willard Inter-Continental Hotel, 1401 Pennsylvania Ave NW (Downtown); tel 202/637-7440. **New American/French.** An elegant dining room with a sense of grandeur, where brass-and-crystal chandeliers hang from the ornate ceiling, double rows of massive green faux-marble columns

support the enormous finished oak beams that cross the dining room, and brocaded chairs surround the superbly decorated tables. Unique renditions of American and French entrees include grilled medallion of salmon on asparagus with puff pastry, and sautéed venison loin with vegetable strudel. **FYI:** Reservations recommended. Piano. Jacket required. **Open:** Breakfast Mon–Fri 7:30–10am; lunch Mon–Fri 11:30am–2pm; dinner daily 6–10pm. **Prices:** Main courses $17–$26. AE, DC, DISC, MC, V. ♥ ▇ VP ♿

The Wright Place

In the National Air and Space Museum, Independence Ave at 4th St SW; tel 202/371-8777. **Burgers/Cafe/Salads.** Contemporary light-wood chairs and granite-look tabletops surrounded by glass walls and ceilings supported by a modernistic arrangement of different size pipes. A view of Washington skies and the nearby Capitol could distract a diner from such specials as charbroiled beef cutlet, Brunswick stew, and vegetarian tamale pie, supplemented by a variety of sandwiches, soups, and vegetables. Menu changes seasonally. **FYI:** Reservations accepted. Dress code. Beer and wine only. **Open:** Daily 11:30am–3pm. **Prices:** Lunch main courses $8–$10. AE, DC, DISC, MC, V. ▇ ◰ ◱ ♿

⑤ Zed's Ethiopian Cuisine

3318 M St NW (Georgetown); tel 202/333-4710. **Ethiopian.** A minimally decorated but friendly establishment known not for its decor but as one of Washington's best and least expensive ethnic restaurants. House specialties include *bozena shuro* (a spicy beef stew with yellow split peas, cauliflower, beans, and carrots). Meals are served traditionally, on large pieces of Ethiopian bread. **FYI:** Reservations accepted. **Open:** Daily 11am–11pm. **Prices:** Main courses $6–$13. AE, DC, DISC, MC, V.

Zorba's Café

1612 20th St NW at Connecticut Ave (Dupont Circle); tel 202/387-8555. **Greek.** With simple decor, clean and uncluttered, this Greek fast-food restaurant offers high-quality food at low prices. Greek standards, such as moussaka and souvlaki, abound. A variety of daily specials includes potatoes marinated with oregano and other herbs, then baked and served with dolmades and pita. **FYI:** Reservations not accepted. Beer and wine only. **Open:** Mon–Sat 11am–11:30pm, Sun noon–10:30pm. **Prices:** Main courses $4–$7. MC, V. No CC. ◰ 🚗

ATTRACTIONS 📷

MONUMENTS

Jefferson Memorial

Washington; tel 202/426-6822. South of the Washington Monument, on Ohio Drive. A beautiful columned rotunda in the style of the Pantheon in Rome, the memorial was built on land reclaimed from the Potomac River now known as the Tidal Basin. Work began in 1939, and the memorial was opened to visitors in 1943.

Within the memorial is a 19-foot bronze statue of Jefferson standing on a 6-foot pedestal of black Minnesota granite. The sculpture is the work of Rudulph Evans, who was chosen from more than 100 artists in a nationwide competition. The interior walls bear engraved excerpts from Jefferson's many writings. The quotation inscribed on the rotunda's circular frieze reads: "I have sworn upon the altar of God eternal hostility against every form of tyranny over the mind of man."

Park rangers give short talks to visitors on request. **Open:** Daily 24 hours; staff on duty 8am–midnight. **Free**

Washington Monument

15th St and Constitution Ave NW (the Mall), Washington; tel 202/426-6839. Directly south of the White House, at 15th St and Constitution Ave NW, this stark 555-foot marble obelisk is the city's most visible landmark. The cornerstone was laid on July 4, 1848, but the breakout of the Civil War and funding problems brought construction to a halt until 1876, when President Grant approved federal monies to complete the project. Dedicated in 1885, the monument opened to the public in 1888.

A large elevator takes visitors to the top for a spectacular, 360° view. Guided "Down the Steps" tours are given, subject to staff availability, on weekends at 10am and 2pm (varies in summer), relating much about the monument's construction and about the 193 carved stones, including a piece of stone from the Parthenon, inserted into the interior walls. There is a snack bar near the entrance to the monument on 15th St. **Open:** Peak (Apr–Labor Day) daily 8am–midnight. Reduced hours off-season. **Free**

Lincoln Memorial

23rd St NW between Constitution and Independence Aves (the Mall), Washington; tel 202/426-6895. Located directly west of the Mall, in Potomac Park, this memorial attracts more than six million visitors each year. Designed by Henry Bacon in 1912 and dedicated in 1922, the temple-like memorial has 36 fluted Doric columns representing the states of the union at the time of Lincoln's death, plus 2 at the entrance. To the west, the Arlington Memorial Bridge over the Potomac recalls the reunion of North and South.

The memorial chamber, under 60-foot ceilings, has limestone walls inscribed with the Gettysburg Address and Lincoln's Second Inaugural Address. Two 60-foot murals by Jules Guerin on the north and south walls depict, allegorically, Lincoln's principles and achievements. Most powerful is Daniel Chester French's 19-foot-high seated statue of Lincoln in deep contemplation in the central chamber.

Information center and bookstore on lower lobby level. Ranger talks are given on request. **Open:** Daily 24 hours; staff on duty 8am–midnight. **Free**

Vietnam Veterans Memorial

Constitution Gardens (the Mall), Washington; tel 202/634-1568. The memorial is located across from the Lincoln Memorial, east of Henry Bacon Dr between 21st and 22nd Sts NW. It consists of 2 walls of polished black granite inscribed with the names of almost 60,000 Americans killed or missing in action between 1959 and 1975. The names are listed in chronological order, with the walls rising in height toward their midpoint at the height of the conflict, then receding again as the war drew to a close; directories at either end of the memorial help visitors to locate names.

In 1984 a life-size sculpture of three American soldiers in Vietnam by Frederick Hart was installed at the entrance plaza. Another sculpture, the **Vietnam Veterans Women's Memorial,** was added on Veterans Day in 1993. **Open:** Daily 24 hours; rangers on duty 8am–midnight. **Free**

United States Navy Memorial

701 Pennsylvania Ave NW, Washington; tel 202/737-2300 or toll free 800/821-8892. Authorized by Congress in 1980 to honor the men and women of the US Navy, this memorial is centered around a 100-foot-diameter circular plaza bearing a granite world map flanked by fountains and waterfalls salted with waters from the 7 seas. Exhibits include interactive video kiosks that provide a wealth of information about Navy ships, aircraft, and history; the Navy Memorial Log Room, with computerized record of past and present Navy personnel; and the Presidents Room, honoring six US presidents who served in the Navy and two who were secretaries of the Navy. The 30-minute film plays hourly throughout the day (additional fee charged). Guided tours are available from the front desk, subject to availability. **Open:** Mon–Sat 9:30am–5pm, Sun noon–5pm. **Free**

PUBLIC AND GOVERNMENT BUILDINGS

The White House

1600 Pennsylvania Ave NW (the Mall), Washington; tel 202/456-7041. Since the cornerstone was laid in 1792, the Executive Mansion has gone through considerable changes. Its numerous occupants often left their mark on it during their residence. Repairs and refurnishing were supervised by the Madison administration after the building was burned by the British in the War of 1812; the North and South porticoes were added in the 1820s (terms of James Monroe and John Quincy Adams); electricity was installed in 1891, during Benjamin Harrison's presidency; the West Wing, which includes the Oval Office, was added during Theodore Roosevelt's tenure; and in 1948 the interior of the building was completely gutted and replaced with a new framework of concrete and steel (the Truman family resided for four years at Blair House during the project).

Highlights of the tour include the East Room, scene of gala receptions and other dazzling events; the Green Room (named in the 19th century for its green upholstery), which was Thomas Jefferson's dining room and is today used as a sitting room; the oval Blue Room (where presidents and first ladies have officially received guests since the Jefferson administration), decorated in the French Empire style chosen by James Monroe in 1817; the Red Room, used as a reception room, usually for small dinners; and the State Dining Room, a superb setting for state dinners and luncheons.

More than a million people line up annually to see the White House. Tickets are *required* Memorial Day–Labor Day; they are distributed at the White House Visitor Center in the Department of Commerce building (1450 Pennsylvania Ave NW) beginning at 7:30am for that day only. Tickets are time stamped, so waiting in line should be brief.

Free tickets for a more intensive—and guided—"VIP" tour may be requested 6–8 weeks in advance from your congressperson or senator. These tours last 35–50 minutes and begin at 8:15, 8:30, and 8:45am; they are conducted by guides who provide explanatory commentary throughout the visit. **Open:** Tues–Sat 10am–noon. **Free**

United States Capitol

Entrance on E Capitol St and 1st St NW (Capitol Hill), Washington; tel 202/225-6827. As our most tangible national symbol since its first wing was completed in 1800, and the place where all our laws are debated, the Capitol is perhaps the most important edifice in the United States. For 134 years it housed not only both houses of Congress but also the Supreme Court and, for 97 years, the Library of Congress.

The Rotunda, 97 feet across under a 180-foot dome, is the hub of the Capitol; on its curved walls are eight immense oil paintings depicting events in American history, such as the reading of the Declaration of Independence and the surrender of Cornwallis at Yorktown. A trompe l'oeil frieze overhead illustrates events from Columbus's landing through the Wright brothers' flight at Kitty Hawk. There is also a life-size marble statue of Abraham Lincoln.

National Statuary Hall was originally the chamber of the House of Representatives, but was abandoned for that purpose because of its acoustics—guides demonstrate that a whisper can be heard clearly from across the room. In 1864 it became Statuary Hall, and each state was invited to donate two statues of native sons to the collection. Individuals represented here include Henry Clay, Ethan Allen, and Daniel Webster.

The **House and Senate chambers** can be viewed only during the congressional VIP tour (see below). The House of Representatives chamber, the largest legislative chamber in the world, is where Congress assembles to hear the president's annual State of the Union address.

Guided tours of the Capitol depart every 15 minutes between 9am and 3:45pm and last about 30 minutes. The congressional VIP tour begins at 8am. This tour is longer and includes a visit to either the House or Senate chamber, but it requires an advance ticket, obtained from your congressperson or senator. Passes to House and Senate sessions are also available from legislators, and some congressional committee meetings are open to the public. **Open:** Daily 9am–4:30pm. **Free**

Supreme Court of the United States

1 1st St NE (Capitol Hill), Washington; tel 202/479-3000. Located east of the Capitol between E Capitol St and Maryland Ave. Until 1935 the Supreme Court convened in the Capitol Building. The neoclassical marble building that houses the court today was considered rather grandiose by many when the design was first unveiled, but it does serve to reflect the power and dignity represented by the nation's highest tribunal.

The court is in session Monday–Wednesday from 10am–3pm (with a lunch-hour recess from noon–1pm) from the first Monday in October through late April, alternating (in approximately two-week intervals) between "sittings" to hear cases and deliver opinions and "recesses" for consideration of business before the court. From mid-May through early July, the public can attend brief sessons (about 15 minutes) at 10am on Monday, during which time the justices release orders and opinions. About 150 gallery seats are set aside each day for the general public—arrive at least an hour early.

When court is not in session, free lectures are given in the courtroom that discuss court procedure and the building's architecture. Lectures are given 9:30am–3:30pm every hour on the half hour. Afterward, visitors can explore the **Great Hall** and view a 20-minute film on the workings of the court. **Open:** Mon–Fri 9am–4:30pm. **Free**

Library of Congress

101 Independence Ave SE (Capitol Hill), Washington; tel 202/707-8000. This is the nation's library, established in 1800 "for the purchase of such books as may be necessary for the use of Congress," but over the years it has been expanded to serve all Americans. Today the collection includes more than 108 million items, ranging from books, audiotapes, and motion-picture reels to Stradivari violins, and it grows at the rate of 10 items per *minute*.

The ornate Italian Renaissance–style **Thomas Jefferson Building** (101 1st St SE), erected between 1888 and 1897, was designed to house the burgeoning collection in a setting that would rival the finest cultural institutions of Europe. There are elegant floor mosaics from Italy, over 100 murals, and allegorical paintings. Upon completion of an extensive restoration project, the Jefferson Building is scheduled to reopen to the public in April 1997. The James Madison Memorial Building provides additional exhibit and research space, while the John Adams Building contains a book depository and several reading rooms.

Tours leave Monday through Saturday at 11:30am and 1, 2:30, and 4pm from the Great Hall of the Jefferson Building. Free, same-day tickets for the tours are given out at the Information Desk on the first floor of the Jefferson Building, beginning at 11am. A 22-minute film about the Library is shown every half-hour (Mon–Fri 9am–9pm, Sat 9am–5:30pm) in LM-139 of the Madison Building. **Open:** Mon–Fri 8:30am–9pm, Sat 8:30am–6pm. **Free**

National Archives

Constitution Ave (between 7th and 9th Sts NW) (the Mall), Washington; tel 202/501-5000. Most famous as a center of genealogical research—Alex Haley began his work on *Roots* here—the archives are sometimes called "the nation's memory." The vast accumulation of information spans two centuries of census figures, military records, maps, charts, motion-picture films, and much more. (Anyone age 16 or over may apply for a research card by presenting a photo ID at Room 207.)

Housed in the Rotunda of the Exhibition Hall are the nation's three charter documents—the Declaration of Independence, the US Constitution, and the Bill of Rights—along with a 1297 version of the Magna Carta loaned to the archives by Texas billionaire Ross Perot. All are on view daily. The Circular Gallery houses major traveling exhibitions covering a variety of topics. Guided tours are given weekdays at 10:15am and 1:15pm by appointment only (phone 501-5205 for details). **Open:** Daily 10am–9pm. **Free**

Folger Shakespeare Library

201 E Capitol St SE (Capitol Hill), Washington; tel 202/544-7077. By 1930, when Henry Clay Folger and his wife, Emily, laid the cornerstone of a building designed to house their collection of printed Shakespearean works, they had amassed 93,000 books, 50,000 prints and engravings, and thousands of manuscripts. The facility today contains some 250,000 books and is an important research center for Shakespearean and Renaissance scholars. On display in the Great Hall are rotating exhibits from the permanent collection—costumes, playbills, musical instruments, and more.

The building's Georgian marble facade is decorated with nine bas-relief scenes from Shakespeare's plays. A statue of Puck stands in the west garden, and quotations from the Bard and from contemporaries like Ben Jonson adorn the exterior walls.

Free walk-in tours are given at 11am. The Elizabethan Theater, located at the end of the Great Hall, hosts concerts, readings, and Shakespeare-related events. **Open:** Mon–Sat 10am–4pm. **Free**

Department of the Treasury

Pennsylvania Ave at 15th St NW, Washington; tel 202/622-0896. A magnificent granite structure in the Greek Revival style, it was built over a period of 33 years. The impressive east front colonnade contains 30 columns that are 36 feet tall and carved from a single block of granite.

A 90-minute guided tour focuses on the history of the Treasury Department and on the architectural history of the building. The offices of Samuel P Chase, secretary of the treasury during the Civil War, and the suite of offices used by President Andrew Johnson following the assassination of Abraham Lincoln have been restored to their 1860s appearance. Portraits of former treasury secretaries are hung in gilded frames throughout various corridors. Also on the tour are the 1864 vault and the marble Cash Room, site of Ulysses S Grant's inaugural reception in 1869.

Tours (Sat at 10, 10:20, 10:40, and 11am) are by reservation only. Visitors must arrive 10 minutes before the scheduled tour time to check in and receive a building pass; visitors over the age of 16 must bring a form of photographic identification. **Free**

Bureau of Engraving and Printing
14th and C Sts SW (the Mall), Washington; tel 202/874-3188. A staff of about 2,000 works here around the clock, producing bills at the rate of 22.5 million a day. In addition to printing currency, the bureau is responsible for manufacturing postage stamps (more than 30 billion per year), treasury bonds, and even specialty items like White House invitations.

The 25-minute **self-guided tour** (with audiovisual aids and staff on hand to answer questions) begins with a short introductory film. Large windows allow visitors to view the various processes involved in making money. Exhibits include money no longer in use, counterfeit money, and an enlarged photo of a $100,000 bill designed for official transactions (since 1969, the largest denomination printed for general use has been $100). After the tour, you can visit the **Visitor Center,** which houses informative exhibits, videos, money-related electronic games, and a display of $1 million. Unique gifts, such as bags of shredded money, may be purchased here as well. **Open:** Mon–Fri 9am–2pm. **Free**

Federal Reserve Building
20th and C Sts (the Mall), Washington; tel 202/452-3149. Completed in 1937 and designed by noted Philadelphia architect Paul-Philippe Cret. Visitors may take a 45-minute guided tour through the building, during which they tour the halls of the Federal Reserve and its boardroom (when it is not in use), and are shown a film detailing the functions of the Federal Reserve. Also within the building is a permanent collection of 19th- and 20th-century American and European art, which may be viewed only by advance reservation. **Free**

Federal Bureau of Investigation
J Edgar Hoover FBI Building, E St NW, Washington; tel 202/324-3447. Over half a million annual visitors learn why crime doesn't pay by touring the headquarters of the FBI. Displays include weapons used by big-time gangsters, plus more than 400 photographs of felons who have made the Bureau's "10 Most Wanted List." Visitors can also see the DNA Lab; Firearms Unit; Metal Analysis Unit; and the Forfeiture and Seizure Unit, where there is a display of jewelry, furs, and other valuables confiscated from illegal narcotics operations. The one-hour tour ends with a sharpshooting demonstration given by an agent. To beat the crowds, arrive for the tour before 8:45am or write to a senator or congressperson for a scheduled reservation as far in advance as possible. **Open:** Mon–Fri 8:45am–4:15pm. **Free**

The Pentagon
Boundary Channel Dr N, Arlington, VA; tel 703/695-1776. This immense, five-sided building, the headquarters of the American military establishment, was built during the early years of World War II. It is the world's largest office building, with 6 million square feet of floor space accommodating 24,000 employees in a self-contained world that has its own bank and post office. Tours of the facility take about 60 minutes (no reservation necessary) and begin with an introductory film about the development of the Pentagon. Highlights include the **Commander-in-Chief's Corridor,** lined with portraits of past presidents, and the **Flag Corridor,** where historical and modern state and territorial flags are displayed.

The best way to get to the Pentagon from DC is via The Metro's Blue or Yellow line. By car, take I-395 to Boundary Channel Drive North Parking Exit. *Note:* Security here is no joke. A photo ID (a license or passport) must be presented upon admission, and all bags are searched. Tour guides walk backwards throughout the tour so they can better keep an eye on their charges, and there are no public eating facilities or rest rooms on site. **Open:** June–Aug, Mon–Fri 9:30am–3:30pm; Sept–May, Mon–Fri 9am–3pm. **Free**

Department of State Building
2201 C St NW, Washington; tel 202/647-3241. Even though the introductory lecture and tour discuss the functions performed by the State Department, this is primarily a fine arts tour of the department's Diplomatic Reception Rooms. These rooms, replete with 18th-century American furniture, paintings, and decorative art, are used by the secretary of state and other high government officials for formal, official government entertaining. Highlights of the tour are the desk at which the Treaty of Paris was signed in London, and an architectural tabletop desk believed to have belonged to Thomas Jefferson.

Reservations are required for this free tour and may be made up to 90 days in advance. It is wise to call 3–6 weeks prior to preferred tour date. Visitors must arrive 20 minutes prior to the scheduled tour time, and adults must submit a valid photo ID. **Free**

Martin Luther King Memorial Library
901 G St NW, Washington; tel 202/727-1111 or 727-0321. Dedicated in 1972, the new main library for the District of Columbia was designed by noted architect Mies van der Rohe. Among its special areas are the Library for the Blind and Physically Handicapped, a Black Studies Division, an AP Wire Service machine in the front lobby, three art galleries, and a local history section with a vast collection of photographs, clippings, and archives from the now-defunct *Washington Star* newspaper. **Open:** Mon and Wed–Thurs 10am–7pm, Tues 10am–9pm, Fri–Sat 10am–5:30pm, Sun 1–5pm. **Free**

National Academy of Sciences

2101 Constitution Ave, Washington; tel 202/334-2436. Located between 21st and 22nd Sts, directly across from the Vietnam Veterans Memorial; a 12-foot-tall statue of Albert Einstein stands on the front lawn. The National Academy of Sciences is a private organization that acts as an advisor to the federal government. The facility houses both art and science exhibits, which change every three months; open for self-guided tours. **Open:** Mon–Fri 9am–5pm. **Free**

Organization of American States

17th St NW and Constitution Ave, Washington; tel 202/458-3000. Founded in 1890, the OAS comprises 35 republics of the western hemisphere, including the United States. One of Washington's most beautiful buildings, the headquarters features many Mediterranean touches, such as terra-cotta–tiled roof, wrought-iron balconies, and arched doorways. The skylit garden patio contains palm trees and tropical plants surrounding a rose-colored fountain, as well as the Peace Tree planted by President Taft when the building was dedicated.

Flags of all member nations hang in the **Hall of Heroes,** and busts on marble pedestals of such heroes of the Americas as José Martí, Simón Bolívar, and George Washington line the walls. High-ranking dignitaries are received in the **Hall of the Americas,** adorned with glittering Tiffany chandeliers and 24 Corinthian columns supporting a 45-foot vaulted ceiling. Adjoining is the old **Council Room,** with bronze relief panels depicting the exploits of Cortés, Bolívar, Balboa, and others. Guided tours by appointment only, subject to staff availability. **Open:** Mon–Fri 9:30am–5pm. **Free**

Voice of America

330 Independence Ave NW (the Mall), Washington; tel 202/619-3919. Tour entrance on C Street, between 3rd and 4th Sts NW. On February 24, 1942, just 79 days after the United States' entry into World War II, the Voice of America began its first broadcast with the words "Here speaks a voice from America." Today, VOA radio broadcasts in 46 different languages and is heard by tens of millions of listeners around the world.

Tours of the facility last about 45 minutes and include a broadcast studio, the master control room, and the newsroom. Visitors may listen in on a live broadcast (if in progress) in whatever language VOA is broadcasting at the time. **Free**

Union Station

50 Massachusetts Ave NE, between 1st and 2nd Sts (Capitol Hill), Washington; tel 202/371-9441. When it opened in 1907, this was the largest train station in the world, elaborately finished with acres of white marble flooring, a half-million-dollars' worth of 22-karat gold leaf, rich Honduran mahogany, hand-stenciled ceilings, and stunning murals.

Today, after a $180 million restoration in the late 1980s, Union Station is again a transportation center, now augmented by shopping, dining, and entertainment opportunities. Three levels of retail shops, a nine-screen cinema com-plex, and a food court have been installed, along with an elliptical mahogany kiosk in the center of the Main Hall that houses a cafe and a visitor information center. **Open:** Shops Mon–Sat 10am–9pm, Sun noon–6pm. **Free**

Pavilion at the Old Post Office

1100 Pennsylvania Ave, Washington; tel 202/289-4224. One of the capital's most popular spots, the Pavilion is located in the former headquarters of the US Postal Service, built in 1899. The facility now houses dozens of specialty shops and eateries, daily live entertainment, and an indoor miniature-golf course. The Bell Clock Tower stands 315 feet tall and is the second-highest structure in DC. The tower's open-air observation deck offers unrivaled views of the city. **Open:** Peak (Mem Day–Labor Day) daily 10am–8pm. Reduced hours off-season. Observation Deck, daily 8am–10pm. **Free**

MUSEUMS

United States Holocaust Memorial Museum

100 Raoul Wallenberg Place SW (15th St SW) (the Mall), Washington; tel 202/488-0400. This museum, mandated by an act of Congress in 1980 and opened in 1993, is one of the capital's most popular attractions, despite its grim subject matter. Even the museum building itself was designed to be deliberately bleak and disturbing, with somber spaces and towers on the structure that recall the guard towers of Auschwitz.

Upon entering the museum's **permanent exhibition,** each visitor receives an ID card bearing the likeness of an actual person who experienced the Holocaust, then learns of that person's fate while retracing the chronology of more than a decade of Nazi persecution. (Most of the people whose lives are documented on these cards were dead by 1945.) Exhibits include a railroad freight car of the type used to transport Polish Jews from Warsaw to the Treblinka death camp, a segment of an actual Auschwitz barracks, concentration camp uniforms, photographs, diaries, documentary films, and mementos. The second floor includes accounts of the many non-Jews throughout Europe who helped protect Jews or assisted their escape.

Also in the museum are interactive videos, temporary exhibits, films, and lectures. Tickets (required for the permanent exhibition only) may be obtained for a fee in advance through Protix (tel toll free 800/400-9373); same day tickets are available from the museum box office, which opens at 9am daily in the summer, at 10am the rest of the year. All tickets are usually gone by noon. **Open:** Daily 10am–5:30pm. **Free**

National Gallery of Art

Between 3rd and 7th Sts NW (the Mall), Washington; tel 202/737-4215. The museum was a gift to the nation from Andrew W Mellon, who also contributed the nucleus of the collection, including 21 masterpieces from the Hermitage. It now houses one of the world's foremost collections of Western painting, sculpture, and graphic arts from the Middle Ages through the 20th century.

The original **West Building,** a neoclassic pink-marble structure designed by John Russell Pope, showcases works from the permanent collection. Galleries are devoted to Italians of the Renaissance and 17th and 18th centuries, including the only da Vinci outside Europe, *Ginerva De' Benci;* late-19th-century Americans, including Homer and Sargent; and Spaniards El Greco, Goya, and Velázquez. There are also 17th- and 18th-century prints, Chinese porcelains, small Renaissance bronzes, 16th-century Flemish tapestries, and 18th-century decorative arts.

The **East Building** is an asymmetrical trapezoid with glass walls and lofty tetrahedron skylights designed by I M Pei. It houses important traveling exhibitions but also contains a massive aluminum Alexander Calder mobile suspended from the skylight and an immense bronze sculpture by Henry Moore.

Audio tours and free guided highlight tours (phone for details) are highly recommended. Three restaurants, several shops. **Open:** Mon–Sat 10am–5pm, Sun 11am–6pm. **Free**

Phillips Collection

1600 21st St NW, at Q St (Dupont Circle), Washington; tel 202/387-2151 or 387-0961. Conceived as a "museum of modern art and its sources," this intimate establishment is the oldest museum of modern art in the country. The fully refurbished museum contains over 2,500 works of 19th- and 20th-century European and American painting and sculpture. Paintings include five van Goghs, seven Cézannes, and six O'Keeffes; there are also representative works by Klee, Rothko, Whistler, Ryder, and Matisse. Free tours are given on Wednesday and Saturday at 2pm. **Open:** Tues–Wed and Fri–Sat 10am–5pm, Thurs 10am–8:30pm, Sun noon–7pm. **$$$**

Corcoran Gallery of Art

500 17th St NW, between E St and New York Ave (the Mall), Washington; tel 202/638-3211 or 638-1439 (recorded info). The first art museum in Washington, and one of the first in the country, the Corcoran Gallery was housed from 1874 to 1896 in the red-brick and brownstone building that is now the Renwick Gallery (see under "Smithsonian Institution" below). When the collection outgrew its quarters it was transferred in 1897 to its present beaux-arts building, designed by Ernest Flagg.

The collection focuses chiefly on American art, from colonial portraiture to Hudson River landscape paintings to 20th-century modernism. European works include the recently restored 18th-century French Salon Doré, 16th-century Italian majolica, and an eclectic grouping of French, Dutch, and English paintings. Special exhibitions feature photography and international contemporary art.

Free 30-minute guided tours are given at 12:30pm (and at 7:30pm on Thurs). Museum shop; restaurant. **Open:** Mon, Wed, and Fri–Sun 10am–5pm, Thurs 10am–9pm. **$**

National Geographic Society's Explorers Hall

17th and M Sts NW (Dupont Circle), Washington; tel 202/857-7588. The National Geographic Society was formed in 1888 to further "the increase and diffusion of geographic knowledge." At Explorers Hall, the Society's headquarters, a seven-minute video introduces visitors to the worldwide activities of the National Geographic Society.

There are dozens of fascinating displays, most in the form of interactive video exhibits. In **Geographica,** on the north side of the hall, guests can touch a "tornado," learn how caves are formed, and study the origins of humankind. **Earth Station One** is an interactive amphitheater that simulates an orbital flight.

Among the numerous artifacts on display are pieces of equipment from Adm Robert E Perry's 1909 expedition to the North Pole; a scale model of the diving saucer in which Jacques Cousteau descended to 25,000 feet; and an egg from Madagascar's extinct 1,000-pound flightless species known as the "elephant bird." A 3.9-billion-year-old moon rock is displayed in the small planetarium, and excerpts of National Geographic TV specials are screened in the Television Room. On-premises shop sells all National Geographic publications, plus maps, games, and videos. **Open:** Mon–Sat 9am–5pm, Sun 10am–5pm. **Free**

National Building Museum

401 F St NW, Washington; tel 202/272-2448. Created by Congress in 1980, this museum celebrates American achievements in building. The permanent exhibit "Washington: Symbol and City" examines the forces that molded the nation's capital. A hands-on, interactive exhibit, it is designed to be experienced by the blind. Temporary exhibitions explore how buildings influence our lives and invites visitors to think about how and why we build.

Guided tours (offered daily at 12:30pm, and at 1:30pm on weekends) explore the NBM's home—the landmark **Pension Building** (1881–1887). The building's Great Hall, scene of gala inaugural balls, contains eight of the largest Corinthian columns in the world. A permanent exhibit on the construction of the building and its subsequent history is located on the second floor. Educational programs, special events. Museum shop. **Open:** Mon–Sat 10am–4pm, Sun noon–4pm. **Free**

Capital Children's Museum

800 3rd St NE (at H Street) (Capitol Hill), Washington; tel 202/675-4125. Hands-on exhibits allow children to explore, play games, and learn about a variety of subjects, from communications and history to physical science and animation. Included are a replica of a 30,000-year-old cave, an interactive TV studio, a maze with optical illusions, and a

Mexican pyramid. Inquire about ongoing workshops, demonstrations, and theater presentations for children. **Open:** Tues–Sun 10am–5pm. **$$$**

National Portrait Gallery

8th and F Sts NW, Washington; tel 202/357-2700. Persons who have made "significant contributions to the history, development, and culture of the United States" are represented here, in paintings, sculpture, photographs, and other forms of portraiture.

In addition to the **Hall of Presidents** (on the second floor), notable exhibits include Gilbert Stuart's famed "Lansdowne" portrait of George Washington, a portrait of Mary Cassatt by Degas, 19th-century silhouettes by French-born artist August Edouart, Jo Davidson's sculpture portraits, and a self-portrait by John Singleton Copley. On the mezzanine, the Civil War is documented in portraiture. The magnificent **Great Hall,** on the third floor, served as a Civil War hospital and was used by Abraham and Mary Lincoln to receive guests at his second inaugural ball.

Tours are given daily, usually 10am–3pm (call 357-2920 for tour information). **Open:** Daily 10am–5:30pm. **Free**

DAR Museum

1776 D St NW (the Mall), Washington; tel 202/879-3241. Preserved here is a collection of early American art and artifacts that includes Chinese export porcelain, English pottery, needlework samplers, quilts, period furnishings, and silver. Among the many notable painters represented are John Singleton Copley, Rembrandt Peale, Jacob Eichholtz, Ralph E W Earl, and John Wolleston.

Four floors are occupied by 33 rooms furnished as if they were in 18th- and 19th-century homes. Exhibits from the Americana Collection of documents, wills, correspondence, and other period papers are displayed on the second floor. The "Children's Attic" is filled with 19th-century toys, dolls, and children's furnishings; "Touch of Independence" has hands-on exhibits of everyday colonial items. Also on the premises is the **Children's American Revolution Museum,** featuring items and exhibits illustrating the Revolutionary era. Free guided tours are offered 10am–2:30pm on weekdays or 1–5pm on Sunday; period rooms and "Touch of Independence" are accessible only by tour. **Open:** Mon–Fri 8:30am–4pm, Sun 1–5pm. **Free**

B'nai B'rith Klutznick National Jewish Museum

1640 Rhode Island Ave NW (Dupont Circle), Washington; tel 202/857-6583. Housed in the international headquarters of B'nai B'rith, this museum documents 3,000 years of Jewish culture and history. The permanent collections consist of ceremonial and folk-art objects reflecting the life and festival cycles of Jewish tradition, as well as works by important contemporary Jewish artists. A small sculpture garden is filled with bronzes of Biblical figures by artist Philip Ratner. Museum shop offers a rich variety of books, handcrafted ceremonial objects, jewelry, and children's toys. Guided tours available upon request. **Open:** Sun–Fri 10am–5pm. **Free**

Department of the Interior Museum

1849 C St NW (the Mall), Washington; tel 202/208-4743. Once nicknamed "the Department of Everything Else," the Interior Department originally had a mix of many executive-branch responsibilities. Today, it includes the Bureau of Land Management, Bureau of Indian Affairs, National Park Service, US Geological Survey, Bureau of Reclamation, and the US Fish and Wildlife Service. Exhibits include geological samples, Indian pottery and basketry, and a diorama of Hoover Dam, as well as a diorama of a mine explosion that led to the creation of the Bureau of Mines in 1910. The building itself is architecturally significant, and contains numerous murals and sculptures, mostly added during the New Deal era of President Franklin D Roosevelt. (These may be viewed via guided tour; advance reservation only.) **Open:** Mon–Fri 8am–5pm. **Free**

Washington Navy Yard

9th and M Sts SE, Washington; tel 202/433-4882 or 433-3534. Encompasses three military museums and a US Navy destroyer. Exhibits in the **Navy Museum** include 14-foot-long model ships, undersea vehicles *Alvin* and *Triste,* working sub periscopes, a space capsule that kids can climb in, and, at the dock, a decommissioned destroyer to tour. The **Marine Corps Historical Museum** is less hands-on, featuring exhibit cases and Marine Corps mementos. The **Navy Art Gallery** is a small museum with paintings of naval actions created by combat artists. **Open:** Mon–Fri 9am–4pm, Sat–Sun 10am–5pm. **Free**

National Museum of Women in the Arts

1250 New York Ave NW (at 13th St), Washington; tel 202/783-5000. Founders Wilhelmina and Wallace Holladay donated the core of the permanent collection—more than 2,000 works by 500 women spanning the 16th through the 20th centuries. Housed in a landmark 1907 building designed as a Masonic temple, the collection includes works by Barbara Hepworth, Georgia O'Keeffe, Nancy Graves, and many others. **Open:** Mon–Sat 10am–5pm, Sun noon–5pm. **$**

Hillwood Museum and Gardens

4155 Linnean Ave NW, Washington; tel 202/688-8500. Hillwood was the Washington estate of cereal heiress, art collector, and philanthropist Marjorie Merriweather Post (1887–1973). The mansion contains her collection of fine and decorative arts, including dinner plates commissioned by Catherine the Great, Easter eggs by Carl Fabergé, 18th-century French tapestries, and chalices and icons from imperial Russia. The Russian collection is considered to be the most representative outside Russia. The gardens and auxiliary buildings may be visited without a guide, though guided tours are available without a reservation.

The **Dacha,** a one-room adaptation of a Russian country house, displays Russian objects. The **Native American Building** (1983) features a part of Mrs Post's collection of Native American objects. The **Hillwood Gardens** include a formal French parterre surrounding a pool with charming statuary.

The Japanese garden features enchanting quiet pools and a stream. Also here are a rose garden, a greenhouse, and a cutting garden. Museum shop; cafe. **Open:** Mar–Jan, Tues–Sat 9am–5pm. **$$$**

National Museum of Health and Medicine

Bldg 54, Walter Reed Army Medical Center, Washington; tel 202/782-2200. Established more than a century ago as the Army Medical Museum, it contains diverse collections that illustrate the critical connection between history and medical technology. Exhibits include one of the largest microscope exhibits anywhere in the world, a hands-on computerized cadaver used by medical students to practice surgical techniques, medicinal leeches, and the bullet that killed Abraham Lincoln. **Open:** Daily 10am–5:30pm. **Free**

Textile Museum

2320 S St NW, Washington; tel 202/667-0441. In 1896 George Hewitt Myers made the first acquisition in what would become one of the world's greatest collections of rugs and textiles. His wide-ranging collection, specializing in handwoven pieces, includes Islamic, Tibetan, Chinese, Caucasian, Turkish, and Navajo rugs. Among the textiles are Peruvian tunics, Chinese silks, Mexican serapes, Navajo blankets, and Egyptian tapestries. The collection totals roughly 14,000 textiles and 1,400 rugs and spans a period from 3500 BC to the present.

Guided tours are given September–May, every Wednesday, Saturday, and Sunday at 2pm. The gift shop offers an extensive collection of books on carpets and textiles, as well as such items as pillows, scarves, and ties. **Open:** Mon–Sat 10am–5pm, Sun 1–5pm. **Free**

National Aquarium

14th St and Constitution Ave NW (the Mall), Washington; tel 202/482-2825 (recorded info). Located in the Department of Commerce Building. The oldest aquarium in the United States, this facility was established in 1873 by the Federal Fish and Wildlife Commission for "the artificial propagation of desirable fishes." Today some 1,700 specimens, representing over 200 varieties of fish, amphibians, and reptiles, are on public view. A touch tank allows visitors to examine such marine creatures as sea urchins, starfish, and snails. **Open:** Daily 9am–5pm. **$**

National Museum of American Jewish Military History

1811 R Street NW, Washington; tel 202/265-6280. Operating under the auspices of the Jewish War Veterans of the USA, this museum documents and preserves the contributions of Jewish Americans who served in the armed forces. Featured are changing exhibits covering various topics relating to Jewish American soldiers from World War I through the Gulf War. Guided tours by appointment. **Open:** Mon–Fri 9am–5pm. Open some Sundays; call ahead for dates and times. **Free**

SMITHSONIAN INSTITUTION

Smithsonian Institution–The Castle

1000 Jefferson Dr SW (the Mall), Washington; tel 202/357-2700. The Smithsonian Institution evolved out of an endowment by James Smithson, an English scientist who had never been to America. In 1829 he bequeathed his entire fortune to the US government. Congress created a independent trust to carry out Smithson's will in 1846, and the Smithsonian Institution became a reality. The collection now amounts to more than 140 million objects from all over the world.

The Smithsonian is composed of 14 museums; 9 buildings are located between the Washington Monument and the Capitol on the Mall. Other buildings devoted to specialized exhibits are within walking distance of the Mall, and farther out, the National Zoological Park and the Anacostia Museum are also Smithsonian responsibilities.

The Smithsonian's **information center** is appropriately housed in the **Castle,** the original Victorian red-sandstone Smithsonian building. The Center provides a 20-minute video overview of the Institution. Interactive videos offer comprehensive information about the Smithsonian and all other capital attractions and transportation; brochures and parking maps are available here. A stop at the center is highly recommended, especially for first-time visitors to the Smithsonian. Most of the museums are within easy walking distance of the facility.

Dial-a-Museum (tel 202/357-2020, or 633-9126 for Spanish-language info) provides recorded information about daily goings-on at all Smithsonian museums. **Open:** Daily 9am–5:30pm. **Free**

National Air and Space Museum

Independence Ave and 7th St SW (the Mall), Washington; tel 202/357-2700. The National Air and Space Museum preserves artifacts from every era in the development of manned flight, from Kitty Hawk to Tranquility Base. There are 23 galleries, each filled with fascinating exhibits and enhanced by interactive computers and slide and video shows.

Highlights of the first floor include famous airplanes (like the *Spirit of St Louis*) and spacecraft (such as the *Apollo 11* Command Module); a moon rock that people can actually touch; numerous historical exhibits; and rockets, spacecraft, and lunar exploration vehicles. Also on view is the *Enola Gay,* the plane that dropped the atomic bomb on Hiroshima.

Occupying the second floor are a walk-through mock-up of the *Skylab* orbital workshop, plus galleries focusing on such topics as the solar system, US manned space flight, and military aviation during the two world wars. Seven exhibit areas are taken up by "Beyond the Limits: Flight Enters the Computer Age," illustrating applications of computer technology to air and space travel. Another major exhibit, "Where Next, Columbus?" looks at some possibilities for the next 500 years of exploration, featuring a fiber optic scale model of the solar system, a simulated Martian terrain, a small theater showing three short films, and much more.

Not to be missed are the IMAX films, shown in the **Samuel P Langley Theater** on the first floor. The museum's state-of-the-art **Albert Einstein Planetarium** is on the second floor; tickets for both the films and the planetarium should be purchased in advance (tel 202/357-1686).

Free 1½-hour highlight tours are given daily at 10:15am and 1pm. Recorded tours, narrated by astronauts, are also available for rental. A cafeteria and restaurant are available to the public, and the museum shop sells everything from model kits to freeze-dried astronaut ice cream. **Open:** Daily 10am–5:30pm. **Free**

Hirshhorn Museum and Sculpture Garden

Independence Ave and 7th St SW (the Mall), Washington; tel 202/357-2700. Set on massive sculptured piers 14 feet above the ground, the museum's contemporary cylindrical concrete-and-granite building shelters a plaza courtyard where 75 sculptures are displayed. Inside the museum, the permanent collection is displayed on the second and third floors; sculpture is exhibited in the inner galleries, which have floor-to-ceiling windows, and paintings and drawings are installed in the outer galleries. Across the street is a tree-shaded sunken sculpture garden providing additional exhibit space.

Among the best-known pieces in the collection are Rodin's *The Burghers of Calais* and four bas-reliefs by Matisse known as *The Backs*. Free guided tours are given several times a day. A guided "touch tour" for the visually impaired covers 35 sculptures within the museum. For details, inquire at the information desk on the plaza level. **Open:** Daily 10am–5:30pm. **Free**

Arthur M Sackler Gallery

1050 Independence Ave SW (the Mall), Washington; tel 202/357-2700. Opened in 1987, this museum of Asian art showcases major traveling exhibitions from around the world. Exhibition areas are entirely underground, with entrance provided through an above-ground pavilion in the garden behind the "Castle." The permanent collection includes Chinese bronzes from the Shang (1700–1028 BC) through the Han (206 BC–AD 220) dynasties; Chinese jade figures spanning the millennia from 3000 BC to the 20th century; Chinese paintings and lacquerware (from the 10th to the 20th centuries); ancient Near Eastern works in silver, gold, bronze, and clay; and stone and bronze sculptures from South and Southeast Asia.

The gallery shop offers a wide array of books on Asian art, reproductions, and gifts. Inquire at the information desk about temporary exhibits, highlight tours, and special programs. **Open:** Daily 10am–5:30pm. **Free**

National Museum of African Art

950 Independence Ave SW (the Mall), Washington; tel 202/357-2700. This is the only national art museum in the United States devoted to research in, and the collection and exhibi-

tion of, African art. Founded in 1964 and part of the Smithsonian since 1979, the museum was moved to its present location on the Mall in 1987.

The permanent collection of over 7,000 objects (shown in rotating exhibits) features the art of the vast sub-Saharan regions, with works from the western part of Sudan and the Guinea Coast particularly well represented. Highlights of the permanent collection include a display of Royal Benin art from Nigeria and the Eliot Elisofon Photographic Archives, with more than 300,000 photographic prints and transparencies on African arts and culture. (The archives and the Warren M Robbins Library are open to the public only by appointment.)

Special programs include events, children's programs, films, lectures, storytelling, guided tours, and demonstrations; inquire at the information desk. **Open:** Daily 10am–5:30pm. **Free**

Enid A Haupt Garden

10th St and Independence Ave SW (the Mall), Washington; tel 202/357-2700. Tranquil oasis with central parterre and 1870s cast-iron furnishings, elaborate flower beds and borders, plant-filled turn-of-the-century urns, and lush baskets hung from 19th-century–style lampposts. **Open:** Peak (Mem Day–Labor Day) daily 7am–8pm. Reduced hours off-season. **Free**

Freer Gallery of Art

Jefferson Dr and 12th St SW (the Mall), Washington; tel 202/357-2700. Opened in 1923, the gallery contains Asian art and American works from the 19th and early 20th centuries. The Asian collection includes Chinese and Japanese sculpture, painting, lacquerware, metalwork, and ceramics; early Christian illuminated manuscripts; Japanese screens and woodblock prints; Chinese jades and bronzes; Korean ceramics; Near Eastern manuscripts, metalwork, and miniatures; ancient Near East metalware; and Indian sculpture, manuscripts, and paintings.

Among the American works are over 1,200 pieces by Whistler, including the famous **Peacock Room.** Originally a dining room designed for a London mansion, the room features a painting by Whistler, who also adorned the walls with paintings of golden peacocks. Other American painters represented in the collection are Childe Hassam, Thomas Wilmer Dewing, and John Singer Sargent.

An underground exhibition space connects the Freer to the neighboring Sackler Gallery (see above). The **Meyer Auditorium** presents free chamber music concerts, dance performances, and other programs. Museum shop. **Open:** Daily 10am–5:30pm. **Free**

Arts and Industries Building

900 Jefferson Dr SW (the Mall), Washington; tel 202/357-2700. Completed in 1881 as the first National Museum, this red-brick and sandstone structure was the scene of President Garfield's inaugural ball. Since 1976 it has housed exhibits from the 1876 United States International Exposi-

tion in Philadelphia—a celebration of the nation's 100th birthday that featured the latest advances in technology. The Exposition was re-created here in 1976 for the Bicentennial.

The entrance floor is like a turn-of-the-century mall with displays of Victorian furnishings, fashions, clocks, tools, photographic equipment, and medicines. Areas off the central rotunda contain such machinery as steam and gas engines and printing presses, plus a display of weaponry and vehicles, including a steam locomotive.

An area called the Experimental Gallery, in the building's south hall, features interactive exhibits covering topics from race relations to the history of graphic arts. The Discovery Theater hosts a variety of programs (call 202/357-1500 for details and ticket info). A Victorian-themed shop sells books, jams and jellies, china, reproduction antique dolls, and more. **Open:** Daily 10am–5:30pm. **Free**

National Museum of American Art

8th and G Sts NW, Washington; tel 202/357-2700. The National Museum of American Art owns some 37,500 works representing of our national art history. A rotating sampling of about 1,000 of these works are on display at any given time. The museum is housed in the palatial 19th-century Old Patent Office Building, which it shares with the National Portrait Gallery (see above).

Twentieth-century art occupies the most exalted setting: the third-floor **Lincoln Gallery,** with vaulted ceilings and marble columns. Mid- to late 19th-century artists are on the second floor, as is the **Hiram Powers Gallery,** housing the contents of the 19th-century neoclassic sculptor's Florence studio. The first floor features 19th- and 20th-century folk art and Western art.

Special exhibitions are presented throughout the year. Free tours are given at noon on weekdays and at 2pm on Sat and Sun. Courtyard cafeteria; museum shop. **Open:** Daily 10am–5:30pm. **Free**

Renwick Gallery of the National Museum of American Art

Pennsylvania Ave and 17th St NW, Washington; tel 202/357-2700. A department of the National Museum of American Art, the Renwick is housed in a historic mid-1800s landmark building of the French Second Empire style. It is a national showcase for American creativity in crafts. The rich and diverse display of objects here includes both changing exhibitions of contemporary works and pieces dating from the 19th and 20th centuries that are part of the museum's permanent collection. The museum shop offers books on crafts and decorative arts, as well as crafts items, many for children. **Open:** Daily 10am–5:30pm. **Free**

National Museum of American History

Constitution Ave and 14th St NW (the Mall), Washington; tel 202/357-2700. Dealing with "everyday life in the American past," this museum preserves bits and pieces from each stage of America's transformation from upstart colony to global superpower.

Exhibits on the first floor (enter on Constitution Avenue) explore the development of farm machines, power machinery, transportation, timekeeping, phonographs, and typewriters. Here, too, is the Palm Court, with re-creations of turn-of-the-century buildings, including an entire post office that was brought here from Headsville, West Virginia.

Entering from the Mall, visitors find themselves on the second floor facing the original Star-Spangled Banner that inspired Francis Scott Key to write the US national anthem in 1814. Also here is a fascinating demonstration of a Foucault pendulum, a copy of the original model exhibited in Paris in 1851.

A vast collection of ship models, uniforms, weapons, and other things military is found on the third floor. Major exhibits focus on the experiences of GIs in World War II and the postwar world as well as the internment of Japanese-Americans during that war. Other areas include money and medals, textiles, printing and graphic arts, and ceramics.

Inquire at the information desk about highlight tours. Hands-on activities for children are featured at the Demonstration Center. Shops, bookstore; cafeteria. **Open:** Daily 10am–5:30pm. **Free**

National Museum of Natural History

Constitution Ave and 12th St NW (the Mall), Washington; tel 202/357-2700. (*Note: Due to renovation projects currently underway at the museum, certain exhibit areas may be relocated within the building or temporarily closed.*)

Within the museum are more than 120 million artifacts and specimens, ranging from one of the largest African elephants ever bagged by a hunter to the legendary Hope Diamond, the single most popular display in the museum.

On the **Mall level** are exhibits illustrating 3.5 billion years of evolution, with fossils ranging from stromatolites to dinosaur bones, including many ancient land and sea creatures. The World of Mammals and Life in the Sea are also here, the latter featuring a living coral reef in a 3,000-gallon tank.

The **second floor** features the Hall of Gems, with the Hope Diamond, the 182-carat Star of Bombay sapphire once owned by Mary Pickford, a rare red diamond (one of five in the world), and a pair of Marie Antoinette's earrings. Also here are the **O Orkin Insect Zoo,** an exhibit with living insects; and the **Naturalist Center,** a resource center for the study of the natural sciences. On display are skeletons that range from the tiny to the gigantic, plus exhibits illustrating the origins of Western cultures.

Free highlight tours are given daily at 10:30am and 1:30pm, but a self-guided audio tour provides the most comprehensive commentary on exhibits (available in the Rotunda for a nominal fee). A **Discovery Room,** filled with creative hands-on activities and games for children, is on the first floor, as is a popular exhibit dealing with Native American cultures. Changing exhibits are featured throughout the year. Cafeteria, several shops. **Open:** Daily 10am–5:30pm. **Free**

National Postal Museum

2 Massachusetts Ave NE, at 1st St (Capitol Hill), Washington; tel 202/357-2700. Created to house and display the Smithsonian's national philatelic and postal history collection of more than 16 million objects, this museum also documents America's postal history from 1673 (about 170 years before the advent of stamps, envelopes, and mailboxes) to the present.

In the central gallery, three early mail planes are suspended from a 90-foot atrium ceiling. The exhibit also contains a railway mail car, a 1851 mail/passenger coach, and a Ford Model-A mail truck. Another exhibit illustrates how mail served to bind families together in the developing nation. It includes correspondence from a Revolutionary War soldier to his wife, from immigrants to their families back home, and from pioneers during America's westward expansion. The Civil War section includes the story of Henry "Box" Brown, a Southern slave who had himself mailed to a Pennsylvania abolitionist in 1856.

There is a vast philatelic research library on the premises; also a stamp store and museum shop. **Open:** Daily 10am–5:30pm. **Free**

Anacostia Museum

1901 Fort Place SE, Washington; tel 202/287-3382 or 357-2700. This unique Smithsonian establishment was created in 1967 as a neighborhood museum. Its major focus is the history and cultural interests of the predominantly black Anacostia community. Over the years it has expanded to include every aspect of black history, art, and culture, both American and worldwide. The collection includes more than 5,000 items, ranging from videotapes and sheet music to historical documents and works of art. The museum also produces a varying number of shows each year, and offers a comprehensive schedule of free educational programs. Call for an events calendar (which always includes children's activities) or pick one up at the museum. **Open:** Daily 10am–5pm. **Free**

HISTORIC HOMES

Frederick Douglass National Historic Site (Cedar Hill)

1411 W Street SE, Washington; tel 202/426-5961. Born a slave in 1818, Frederick Douglass fled north in 1838 and became a leading figure in the abolitionist movement. An orator, diplomat, and essayist, he lectured widely, founded and published his own newspaper, met with Abraham Lincoln to protest treatment of black soldiers during the Civil War, and eventually held government posts as US marshal of the District of Columbia and consul general to Haiti, among others.

In 1877, Douglass bought Cedar Hill, the handsome Victorian house high on a hill overlooking the Anacostia River, where he lived and worked until his death in 1895. The 21-room house, whitewashed brick with green shutters and Doric columns supporting the front porch, contains many of the original furnishings and personal memorabilia of the Douglass family. Among them are photographs (in the entrance foyer) of abolitionist John Brown, a close friend. **Open:** Peak (mid-Apr–mid-Oct) daily 9am–4pm. Reduced hours off-season. **Free**

The House Where Lincoln Died (Petersen House)

516 10th St NW, Washington; tel 202/426-6830 or 426-6924 (tour info). Furnished in period style, the house looks much as it did on the night the president was carried here after the shooting at Ford's Theatre, across the street. The room where Lincoln died on the morning of April 15, 1865, contains a bed of the same design as the original. **Open:** Daily 9am–5pm. **Free**

Woodrow Wilson House

2340 S Street NW (Dupont Circle), Washington; tel 202/387-4062. Washington's only presidential museum, this fashionable Georgian Revival townhouse, located just off Embassy Row, is where President Wilson lived after leaving office in 1921. After Wilson's death in 1924, his wife, Edith, continued to live in the house, carefully preserving its mementos and furnishings. On her death in 1961, she bequeathed the house and its contents to the National Trust for Historic Preservation. Each room today offers a glimpse into the life—personal and public—of the 28th president. The museum contains a 7,000-item collection of the Wilsons' personal artifacts. Guided tours are available. **Open:** Tues–Sun 10am–4pm. **$$**

Heurich House Museum

1307 New Hampshire Ave NW (Dupont Circle), Washington; tel 202/785-2068. A five-story, 31-room late-Victorian manison built in 1894 by well-known German brewer Christian Heurich. It is furnished with elaborate Victorian pieces, most of which are original to the Heurich family. A garden of the late Victorian style was created by the Smithsonian Horticultural Society. The mansion now houses the Historical Society of Washington, DC, as well as the society's Library of Washington History, a research library focusing on the city's social history. The entire mansion may be viewed only on a guided tour; the garden and library are open to the public during business hours. **Open:** Wed–Sat 10am–4pm. **$**

Decatur House

748 Jackson Place, Washington; tel 202/842-0920. This three-story Federal-style brick townhouse (1818–19) was designed by noted architect Benjamin Latrobe. His client was Commodore Stephen Decatur, the naval hero famous for his victories in the War of 1812. The first floor is furnished in the style of Decatur's occupancy, with period furnishings and mementos of his life and naval exploits. The second floor is Victorian in decor, reflecting the period of residence by Gen Edward Fitzgerald Beale. The house's architecture and design are explained on 30-minute guided tours given daily on the hour and half hour. Period Christmas decorations are

featured in December, and the house hosts an annual craft fair in November. **Open:** Tues–Fri 10am–3pm, Sat–Sun noon–4pm. **$$**

The Octagon

1799 New York Ave NW, at 18th St between E and F Sts, Washington; tel 202/638-3221. One of the first town houses built in Washington, the Octagon was designed in 1798 for Col John Tayloe III, a Virginia planter, breeder of racehorses, and friend of George Washington. Steeped in history, the building was a prominent social center in the early 1800s. When the White House was burned in 1812, James and Dolley Madison moved into the Octagon; it was here that Madison signed the Treaty of Ghent in 1815, establishing peace with Great Britain.

The circular Treaty Room, on the second floor, contains the table on which Madison signed the treaty and the box in which it arrived from Britain. Below the magnificent oval staircase, an ongoing archeological dig is underway. Tours of the house are available daily. **Open:** Tues–Fri 10am–4pm, Sat–Sun noon–4pm. **$**

Tudor Place

1644 31st St NW (Georgetown), Washington; tel 202/965-0400. The builder of Tudor Place, Thomas Peter, was the son of a successful Scottish tobacco merchant. His wife, Martha Parke Custis, was a granddaughter of Martha Washington. The large neoclassical house, surrounded by extensive gardens, was designed by William Thornton, architect of the US Capitol; it was completed in 1816. Since Mrs Peter was one of George Washington's heirs, the house still contains many relics from Mount Vernon. The Peter family continued to live here until 1984 and the house is filled with original furniture, silver, porcelain and glass, portraits and photographs, textiles, books, and manuscripts, giving visitors a rare insight into American cultural history.

The gardens of Tudor Place retain the expanse of green lawns, parterres, and woodland developed by the Peters in the federal period. Guided tours of the house are given Tues–Fri; special tours of the garden are conducted during the summer (phone for details). **Open:** Tues–Sat 10am–4pm. **$$$**

Dumbarton Oaks

1703 32nd St NW (Georgetown), Washington; tel 202/339-6400 or 339-6401. This 19th-century Georgetown mansion was the residence of Robert Wood Bliss and his wife, Mildred. In 1940 the Blisses turned over the estate, their extensive Byzantine collection, a library of works on Byzantine civilization, and 16 acres (including 10 acres of formal gardens) to Harvard University. Twenty years later they also donated their collection of pre-Columbian art and Mrs Bliss's library of rare books on landscape gardening.

Today the 16-acre estate is a research center for studies in Byzantine and pre-Columbian art and archeology, as well as landscape architecture. The Byzantine collection is one of the world's finest, with illuminated manuscripts, a 4th-century sarcophagus, and a 13th-century icon of St Peter. The collection of pre-Columbian art features jade and serpentine figures from the Olmec civilization (an ancient Mexican culture dating back some 3,000 years), Mayan relief panels, and textiles from 900 BC to the Spanish Conquest.

The historic **Music Room,** furnished in French, Italian, and Spanish antiques, was the setting for the 1944 Dumbarton Oaks Conferences that led to the founding of the United Nations. On display are pieces of sculpture, paintings, and tapestries, including El Greco's *The Visitation*. The formal gardens contain an orangery and a rose garden. **Open:** Peak (Apr–Oct) daily 2–6pm. Reduced hours off-season. **$**

Meridian International Center

1624 and 1630 Crescent Place NW, Washington; tel 202/939-5552. The Meridian International Center is a nonprofit institution dedicated to the promotion of international understanding through the exchange of people, ideas, and arts. Founded in 1960, the center hosts cultural programs, rotating art exhibitions, concerts, lectures, and other events. Meridian's three-acre site takes up an entire city block, and comprises two historic mansions designed by John Russell Pope: the White-Meyer Mansion (1912), a red-brick Georgian-style home; and the Meridian House (1921), executed in the 18th-century French renaissance style. **Meridian Hill Park,** located across from the center, encompasses just over one city block. **$**

The Society of the Cincinnati Museum at Anderson House

2118 Massachusetts Ave NW (Dupont Circle), Washington; tel 202/785-2040. This historic house/museum is located in a preserved turn-of-the-century Embassy Row mansion. It features rotating exhibits from a permanent collection that includes portraiture by early American artists; 18th-century paintings; 17th-century tapestries; Asian and European decorative arts; and collections of books, medals, and swords, as well as silver, glass, and china. A free concert series is offered to the public one Saturday each month at 1:30pm (Oct–May), the US Air Force Chamber Players also offer free concerts, twice a month from Oct–May (phone for schedule and further details). **Open:** Tues–Sat 1–4pm. **Free**

CHURCHES

Washington National Cathedral

Massachusetts and Wisconsin Aves, Washington; tel 202/537-6200. Pierre L'Enfant's 1791 plan for the capital city included "a great church for national purposes," but possibly because of early America's fear of mingling church and state, more than a century elapsed before the foundation for the National Cathedral was laid. The sixth-largest cathedral in the world, it was completed with the placement of a final stone atop a pinnacle on the west front towers on September 29, 1990—83 years from the day of its inception.

English Gothic in style, complete with flying buttresses and 101 gargoyles, the cathedral is built in the shape of a cross, its nave 10 stories high from its marble floor to the vaulting. Its 20th-century origins are evident in such details as the Space Window, a stained-glass window containing a moon rock brought back by the crew of *Apollo 11*. The landscaped grounds contain two gardens, five schools (including the College of Preachers), and a greenhouse. President Woodrow Wilson and his wife are buried here, as are Helen Keller and her teacher, Anne Sullivan.

Tours leave continually from the west end of the nave Mon–Sat from 10am–3:15pm and Sun from 12:30–2:45pm. Allow time to visit the observation gallery, where 70 windows provide panoramic views. There is a large gift shop on the premises. **Open:** Daily 10am–4:30pm. **Free**

St John's Church

16th and H Sts, Washington; tel 202/347-8766. Every president of the United States since James Madison has worshiped at the Episcopal church across Lafayette Square from the White House. The Greek Revival building, with a dome and colonnaded portico entrance, was designed by Benjamin Latrobe. The **Parish House** served as the residence of British Minister Lord Ashburton during US-British negotiations in 1842 to settle the Canadian boundary dispute. Guided tours of the church are offered every first and fifth Sunday of the month after the 11am service. Organ recitals are given Wednesday at 12:10pm, except July–Sept and during Lent. **Open:** Daily 9am–3pm. **Free**

Basilica of the National Shrine of the Immaculate Conception

4th St and Michigan Ave NE, Washington; tel 202/526-8300. The National Shrine is the largest Roman Catholic church in the United States and among the largest churches in the world. Construction of the basilica dates to 1920, when the cornerstone was laid. The **Crypt Church,** which recalls the catacombs of ancient Rome, has been in continuous use since 1926. The Great Upper Church was dedicated in 1959, but additional chapels are still being added, each reflecting the religious heritage brought to America by generations of immigrants.

Guided tours (offered Mon–Sat 9–11am and 1–3pm, Sun 1:30–4pm) last one hour and require no reservation. The basilica also offers a summer recital series (phone for details). **Open:** Peak (Apr–Oct) daily 7am–7pm. Reduced hours off-season. **Free**

Franciscan Monastery

1400 Quincy St NE, Washington; tel 202/526-8300. Located within the church and on the grounds is what is known as "the Holy Land of America"—a collection of replicas of the principal shrines and chapels found in the Holy Land. The main shrine is a replica of the Holy Sepulcher, the tomb of Jesus Christ. Other replicas include the Grotto of Lourdes in southern France, the Grotto of Gethsemane, the Chapel of the Ascension on Mount Olivet, and the Nativity Grotto in Bethlehem. The crypt of the church contains replicas of the Catacombs of Rome and has fine copies of early Christian art and inscriptions. Guided tours conducted by the friars. **Free**

PARKS AND GARDENS

National Zoological Park

Connecticut Ave NW, Washington; tel 202/673-4800 or 673-4717. Established in 1889, the National Zoo is home to more than 4,000 animals of some 500 species, many rare and/or endangered. Animals live in large, open enclosures designed to simulate their natural habitats. The zoo's star resident is Hsing-Hsing, a giant panda donated by the People's Republic of China. He is most regularly seen at feeding time (11am and 3pm).

Special exhibits include the **Invertebrate Exhibit,** the only one of its kind in the country, which teaches about starfish, sponges, giant crabs, anemones, insects, and other spineless creatures; the **Reptile Discovery Center,** which offers a closer look at reptiles and amphibians; and **Amazonia,** an immense glass-domed building housing plants, fish, and animals of the Amazon River region. (Special exhibit hours and days of operation vary; phone ahead.)

An audiotape tour is available. Snack bars, restaurant; picnicking permitted. Gift shops; stroller rentals. **Open:** Peak (May–Aug) daily 8am–8pm. Reduced hours off-season. **Free**

United States National Arboretum

3501 New York Ave NE, Washington; tel 202/245-2726. A research and educational center for all kinds of landscape plants, the National Arboretum's 9½ miles of paved roads meander through 444 hilly acres of rhododendrons, azaleas, magnolias, hollies, peonies, and a great deal more. A different species of plant life is in bloom at almost every time of year; in autumn the arboretum is ablaze with the reds and oranges of changing leaves.

The **National Bonsai and Penjing Museum,** a Bicentennial gift from Japan, is a collection of 53 miniature trees, some more than 3 centuries old. The area also includes a Japanese garden. The arboretum's **acropolis** was created with 22 of the original columns from the US Capitol, which were removed a few decades ago when they were deemed too fragile to support the building's new marble construction. The **National Bird Garden** features berrying shrubs that attract a variety of species of birds. The **New American Garden,** opened in 1990, is a collection of ornamental grasses and perennials along brick walkways with carefully placed teak benches. The **American Friendship Garden** also features an extensive array of perennials and bulb plants.

Frequent tours, lectures, and workshops are offered. A guidebook is available in the gift shop. **Open:** Daily 8am–5pm. **Free**

United States Botanic Garden

100 Maryland Ave SW (the Mall), Washington; tel 202/225-7099. Originally conceived by Washington, Jefferson, and Madison and opened in 1820, the Botanic Garden is a lovely oasis—a series of connected glass-and-stone buildings and greenhouses that has been described as a "living museum under glass." The park contains a rose garden, a large year-round collection of orchids, and other themed areas, with

tropical, subtropical, and desert plants, and featuring a Dinosaur Garden of cycads, mosses, and liverworts that existed in the Jurassic era. The complex also includes **Bartholdi Park,** which centers on a splendid cast-iron fountain created by Frédéric-Auguste Bartholdi, designer of the Statue of Liberty. Special shows, lectures, and classes (phone ahead). **Open:** Daily 9am–5pm. **Free**

Kenilworth Aquatic Gardens

Anacostia Ave and Douglas St NE, Washington; tel 202/426-6905. Located directly across the Anacostia River from the National Arboretum. This 12-acre haven is the only national park site devoted to water plants. The gardens today are a showcase for wetland plants, as well as such animals as turtles, snakes, and frogs and 40 different species of migratory birds. Water lilies, lotuses, and other water plants bloom from mid-May until the first frost. A mile-long river trail may be followed through the gardens' 77-acre marshland to the Potomac River. Visits to the gardens should begin at the visitors center. Guided tours available on weekends in the summer. **Open:** Daily 7am–5pm. **Free**

Rock Creek Park

5000 Glover Rd NW, Washington; tel 202/282-1063 or 426-6828 (Nature Center). It is common to spot deer and other wildlife in this 1,700-acre urban oasis. Park facilities include extensive hiking trails, historic sites, the Carter Baron Amphitheater, tennis center, horse stable, and an 18-hole golf course. An 11-mile paved bicycle path stretches north from the Lincoln Memorial through the park into Maryland. On weekends and holidays a large section of the park is closed to vehicular traffic.

Places of interest include **Pierce Mill** (an original 19th-century gristmill), the **Old Stone House** (the oldest-surviving structure in the District of Columbia), and the remains of four Civil War forts. The **Rock Creek Nature Center** features native wildlife displays, a planetarium, auditorium, nature trails, and public programs. **Open:** Park, daily; headquarters Mon–Fri 7:45am–4:15pm; Nature Center Wed–Sun 9am–5pm. **Free**

THEATERS AND OTHER VENUES

John F Kennedy Center for the Performing Arts

New Hampshire Ave NW at Rock Creek Pkwy (Foggy Bottom), Washington; tel 202/467-4600 or toll free 800/444-1324. Set on 17 acres overlooking the Potomac, this striking $73 million facility contains an opera house, a concert hall, two stage theaters, and a film theater. The best way to see the Kennedy Center—including areas not available to the public—is on a free 50-minute guided tour, given daily between 10am and 1pm. Tours depart from a small waiting area on Level A, one level below the main floor.

The tour first visits the **Hall of Nations,** where flags of all countries recognized by the United States are displayed. Throughout the center are numerous gifts from more than 40 nations, including all the marble used in the building (3,700 tons), donated by Italy. Gifts of other nations include 18 crystal chandeliers from Sweden, tapestries by Henri Matisse from France, an alabaster vase dating from 2600 BC from Egypt, and a Barbara Hepworth sculpture from England. Stops on the tour include the Grand Foyer, Israeli Lounge, African Room, Opera House, Hall of States, and Performing Arts Library. **Open:** Daily 10am–midnight. **Free**

Ford's Theatre

511 10th St NW, between E and F Sts, Washington; tel 202/347-4833 or 426-6924 (tour info). On April 14, 1865, President Lincoln was part of the audience at Ford's Theater, one of Washington's most popular playhouses, for a performance of the comedy *Our American Cousin*. Everyone was laughing at a line of dialogue when Lincoln was shot by actor John Wilkes Booth. The president was carried across the street, to the home of William Petersen, where he died the next morning. Ordered closed by Secretary of War Edwin Stanton, the theater was used for many years afterward by the War Department. In 1893, 22 clerks were killed when 3 floors of the building collapsed. The building remained in disuse until the 1960s, when it was remodeled and restored to its appearance on the night of the tragedy. Today it is once again the setting for theatrical performances.

Except during rehearsals or matinee performances (phone ahead), visitors can see the theater and retrace Booth's movements on the night of the shooting. Free 15-minute talks are given throughout the day on the assassination and the history of the theater. Located in the basement, the **Lincoln Museum** contains, among other items, the Derringer pistol used by Booth, the clothes worn by Lincoln the night he was shot, and the killer's diary outlining his rationalization for the deed. **Open:** Daily 9am–5pm. **Free**

National Theatre

1321 Pennsylvania Ave NW, Washington; tel 202/628-6161 or toll free 800/447-7400. The luxurious, federal-style National Theatre (circa 1835), elegantly renovated in 1983 for $6.5 million, is the oldest continuously operating theater in Washington and the third-oldest in the nation. The National is also the closest thing Washington has to a Broadway-style playhouse. Managed by New York's Shubert Organization, the National presents star-studded hits—often pre- or post-Broadway—all year round. Call for schedule information. **$$$$**

Arena Stage

6th St and Maine Ave SW, Washington; tel 202/488-3300. Now in its fifth decade, Arena Stage is the home of one the longest-standing acting ensembles in the nation. Several works nurtured here have moved to Broadway, and many graduates—among them *LA Law's* Jill Eikenberry and Michael Tucker, Ned Beatty, James Earl Jones, and Jane Alexander—have gone on to commercial stardom.

Arena's subscription-season productions (there are eight annually) are presented on two stages—the Fichandler (a theater-in-the-round), and the smaller, fan-shaped Kreeger.

In addition, Arena houses the Old Vat, a space used for new play readings and productions. Call for schedule information. **$$$$**

Warner Theatre
1299 Pennsylvania Ave NW, Washington; tel 202/783-4000. Opened in 1924 as the Earle Theatre (a movie/vaudeville palace) and restored to its original appearance in 1992 at a cost of $10 million, this stunning neoclassical-style theater now hosts a variety of Broadway productions, comedy, dance, film, and music concerts. Everything is plush and magnificent, from the glittering crystal chandeliers to the gold-tasseled swagged-velvet draperies and the gold-leafed grand lobby. **$$$$**

Source Theatre Company
1835 14th St NW, Washington; tel 202/462-1073. Source presents top local artists in a year-round schedule of dramatic and comedy plays by new and established playwrights; each July a four-week showcase of new plays, the Washington Theatre Festival, presents 50 new works to Washington audiences. **$$$$**

Shakespeare Theatre
450 7th St NW, Washington; tel 202/393-2700. A core ensemble of actors are regularly joined by such distinguished guest artists as Tom Hulce, Kelly McGillis, and Richard Thomas. Five productions are featured each season: four at the company's downtown home and one, outdoors and free of charge, at Carter Barron Amphitheater in Rock Creek Park. **Open:** Sept–June. Call for performance schedule. **$$$$**

Robert F Kennedy Memorial Stadium/DC Armory
E Capitol St between 19th and 20th Sts NE, Washington; tel 202/547-9077 or 546-3337. The 55,000-seat stadium is the home of the NFL's Washington Redskins. Events at RFK (and at the 10,000-seat DC Armory complex) include wrestling, nationally televised boxing, roller derby, the circus, soccer games, concerts, and rodeos. **$$$$**

Arlington National Cemetery
Arlington National Bridge at Jefferson Davis Hwy, Arlington, VA; tel 703/602-8052. One of America's most famous national shrines, this cemetery honors many national heroes and more than 230,000 war dead, veterans, and dependents. Five-star Gen John J Pershing is buried here, as are President William Howard Taft and Supreme Court Justice Thurgood Marshall.

The **gravesite of John Fitzgerald Kennedy,** 35th US president, has a low crescent wall embracing a marble terrace inscribed with some of the most famous JFK quotations. Senator Robert Kennedy's gravesite is nearby, marked by a simple white cross. Nearby is the well-known **Marine Corps Memorial,** depicting the raising of the American flag on Iwo Jima. A tribute to Marines who died in all wars, this is one of the largest statues ever cast in bronze. The 49-bell **Netherlands Carillon,** a gift from the people of the Netherlands, is located close to the Iwo Jima statue. Concerts are given on Saturdays from April through September (phone 703/285-2598 for schedule).

The **Tomb of the Unknowns,** containing the unidentified remains of soldiers from both World Wars through the Vietnam War, is located here. Soldiers stand guard at the tomb 24 hours a day; changing of the guard is performed every 30 minutes from April–September (hourly the rest of the year).

Arlington House (tel 703/557-0613), located within the cemetery grounds, was for 30 years the residence of Gen Robert E Lee and his family. Hosts in costume give an orientation talk and answer questions; visitors may take self-guided tours of the house and the small museum next door. (Apr–Sept, daily 9:30am–6pm; Oct–Mar, daily 9:30am–4:30pm; closed some hols).

Near Arlington House is the **grave of Pierre Charles L'Enfant,** overlooking a fine view of Washington, DC, the city he designed. **Free**

Theodore Roosevelt Island
George Washington Memorial Parkway, Washington; tel 703/285-2598. A serene 88-acre wilderness preserve, Theodore Roosevelt Island is a memorial to the 26th president, in recognition of his contributions to conservation. In the northern center of the island, overlooking an oval terrace encircled by a water-filled moat, stands a 17-foot bronze statue of Roosevelt. From the terrace rise four 21-foot granite tablets inscribed with the tenets of his philosophy.

The island was inhabited as far back as the 1600s by Native Americans. Today the complex ecosystem incorporates swamp, marsh, and upland forest, creating a habitat for abundant bird life as well as rabbits, chipmunks, great owls, fox, muskrat, turtles, and groundhogs. There are 2½ miles of foot trails winding throughout the preserve. Picnicking is permitted on the grounds near the memorial.

To get to the island, take the George Washington Memorial Parkway exit north from the Theodore Roosevelt Bridge. The parking area is accessible only from the northbound lane; from there, a pedestrian bridge connects the island with the Virginia shore. **Open:** Daily 7:30am–sunset. **Free**

MARYLAND

A Miniature America

Marylanders like to boast that their state is "America in miniature."

Its Atlantic Coast has long beaches shared by both a pristine national seashore and a bustling resort, making it seem a little like Florida during summer. Its flat eastern farmlands are as rich as any of the Midwest. As an inland waterway, its great Chesapeake Bay rivals the Great Lakes. Its rolling hill country has more thoroughbred horses per square mile than Kentucky. And although not nearly as high as the Rockies, its western mountains offer their own scenic beauty.

Here you will find something to do all year long, from summertime vacationing on the 10-mile beach at Ocean City to wintertime skiing down the slopes of the Alleghenies. The Chesapeake Bay offers countless opportunities for fishing, boating, and other water sports. As one of the 13 original colonies, the state has historic sites to explore and historic buildings to visit. Annapolis alone has more than 1,500 18th-century houses, churches, and public buildings, and elsewhere are towns whose streetscapes exhibit a medley of architectural styles from Federal and Georgian and Greek Revival to Queen Anne and Victorian. Visitors to Maryland can also catch a vintage steam train traveling a scenic mountain route or hike the towpath of a vintage canal.

The state also offers more up-to-date and urban entertainments in its largest city. Baltimore's Inner Harbor, once a ramshackle assemblage of warehouses, factories, and urban neglect, has been revitalized with Harborplace, a waterfront complex of restaurants, food markets, boutiques, and nightspots. Here also is the spectacular National Aquarium to be visited, while out on the water is every type of craft, offering lunch cruises, dinner cruises, and moonlight sails.

Nearby, Baltimore has a revitalized business district, modern buildings and plazas, art museums, theaters, a symphony orchestra, and an opera house. It also has the Cab Calloway Jazz Institute, which houses the

STATE STATS

CAPITAL
Annapolis

AREA
9,837 square miles

BORDERS
Pennsylvania, Delaware, Virginia, West Virginia, District of Columbia, and the Atlantic Ocean.

POPULATION
4,781,468 (1990)

ENTERED UNION
April 28, 1788 (7th state)

NICKNAMES
Old Line State, Free State

STATE FLOWER
Black-eyed Susan

STATE BIRD
Baltimore oriole

FAMOUS NATIVES
Russell Baker, Frederick Douglass, Thurgood Marshall, Francis Scott Key, Babe Ruth

Maryland native's memorabilia as part of its collection of Maryland jazz history, and the Eubie Blake National Museum and Cultural Center, which does the same for the ragtime great.

Marylanders love their music, and festivals are dedicated to country and western, bluegrass, rock 'n' roll, Irish folk, blues, and more. Accompanying these are festivals celebrating the Delmarva chicken-producing industry, Maryland wine, and Maryland seafood—fishing tournaments, oyster-shucking contests, crab races, crab-picking competitions, and crab cook-offs.

Luckily for motorists, all this bounty comes in a relatively compact package—just 200 miles from end to end. So that wherever you are when the mood strikes, you'll get there while the food's still hot and the music is still playing.

A Brief History

In Search of Freedom The Algonquins and other Native American tribes had been living along the Chesapeake Bay and the inland rivers feeding it long before the tiny ships *Ark* and *Dove* brought Maryland's first colonists in 1634. Having been granted land by Lord Baltimore, whose Calvert family owned the colony, that band of 140 mostly Catholic settlers came in search of religious tolerance they had not enjoyed in Protestant England. They founded a town named St Mary's City and quickly enacted laws guaranteeing religious freedom. Their colony became known as Maryland, which after independence took an appropriate nickname, the "Free State."

A group of Puritans arrived in 1649 and established Annapolis, which grew into a center of commerce, trade, and learning. It became the colonial capital in 1649 and still is Maryland's seat of government. In 1722, other settlers named their new town Baltimore, which would come to dwarf Annapolis in size and importance.

After Independence From November 1783 to August 1784, Annapolis served as the first peacetime capital of the United States and was the scene of meetings of the Continental Congress. Maryland ratified the new US Constitution in April 1788, and

Fun Facts

• Maryland became known as the "Old Line State" after George Washington praised the colony's "troops of the line," who led the way in many Revolutionary War encounters.

• The British colony of Maryland was named for Queen Henrietta Maria, the wife of King Charles I.

• The majestic Chesapeake Bay, Maryland's most prominent feature, provides the state with more than 3,000 miles of coastline.

• In southern Maryland, tobacco was once so prized it was used as legal tender.

• The official state dog is the Chesapeake Bay retriever, a breed that originated in Maryland in the early 19th century.

became a hub of transportation during the country's early years. The major seaport at Baltimore was linked to the frontier at Cumberland, in the state's western panhandle, by the first National Pike; the nation's first passenger railroad was opened between Baltimore and Ellicott City; and the Chesapeake & Ohio Canal along the Maryland side of the Potomac River was completed as far west as Cumberland.

Oh, Say Can You See Maryland was a major battleground during the War of 1812, as British troops followed the Potomac River to Washington, where they burned the Capitol and White House. In 1814, they laid siege to Fort McHenry in Baltimore Harbor. It was during the rockets' red glare of that bombardment that Marylander Francis Scott Key composed the words to "The Star-Spangled Banner."

Civil War Despite its "Free State" nickname, Maryland was a slave state at the outbreak of the Civil War, and President Abraham Lincoln sent Union troops to put down a riot and virtually occupy Baltimore early in that conflict. The state saw its only major action on September 17, 1862, at the Battle of Antietam, the bloodiest single day of the war.

Modern Maryland Transportation and industry grew after the Civil War, and they continue to make Maryland a prosperous state strategically located between North and South. In 1952, the 4.3-mile-long William Preston Lane Jr Bridge spanning the Chesapeake Bay was built at Annapolis, joining the eastern counties to the rest of the state by road and making possible resort development at Ocean City. Once down on its heels, Baltimore has made a remarkable comeback in the past two decades, with its Inner Harbor and the surrounding area a showplace of urban revitalization.

A Closer Look

GEOGRAPHY

Situated midway along the Atlantic seaboard, Maryland is a mix of flat coastal plain, rolling hills, and mountains reaching as high as 3,300 feet above sea level. The state's geometrically perfect eastern and northern borders with Delaware and Pennsylvania are the results of a survey by Charles Mason and Jeremiah Dixon between 1763 and 1768; hence, the Mason-Dixon Line. The Potomac River forms most of its twisting southern border.

Maryland's most distinguishing geographical feature is the **Chesapeake Bay,** which it shares with Virginia to the south. The world's largest estuary, this magnificent body of inland water and its winding tributaries give the state some 4,000 miles of waterfront property and provide a home to some 3,000 species of plants and animals, including Canada geese, bald eagles, whistling swans, and ospreys. It also is a treasure trove of seafood, harvested by a hearty gang known as watermen.

Maryland's **Eastern Shore** lies on the Delmarva Peninsula between the Chesapeake and the Atlantic Ocean. This relatively flat land was settled in the early 1600s, and historic towns like Oxford, St Michaels, Princess Anne, and Chestertown still boast homes dating from the colonial period. Most people derive their livings from the bay and the land, including those employed by Perdue, Inc of Salisbury, one of the nation's largest poultry producers. On the Atlantic coast—or "down the ocean"—sits the lively beach resort of Ocean City, frequented in summertime by droves of inland residents. South of Ocean City beckons the enchanting, undeveloped paradise of Assateague Island National Seashore. And on the Bay side is Crisfield, so-called "Seafood Capital of the World."

Southern Maryland consists of the state's other peninsula, formed by the Chesapeake Bay and Potomac River. It was here

at St Mary's that Maryland was founded in 1634. The area still is Maryland's prime tobacco-growing region, although it is increasingly a bedroom community for the huge Washington, DC, metropolitan area to its northwest.

The rolling hills of **Central Maryland** make up the heart of the state and are home to Baltimore, one of the nation's major seaports. The 45-mile strip between Baltimore and Washington has become one large metropolitan area, swallowing in-between towns like Laurel. Such Maryland suburbs as Bethesda, Chevy Chase, Silver Spring, College Park, Rockville, and Gaithersburg are very much under the spell of Washington. North and west of Baltimore, however, are the pastures of horse and dairy farms. And Annapolis, the state capital on the Chesapeake, still retains the historical ambience of its colonial beginnings.

From Frederick to Frostburg, **Western Maryland** consists of foothills rising to the ridges of the Allegheny Mountains. An old Native American footpath through this region became the National Pike, America's first official highway. Known today as US 40, it still follows the old trail through the mountains. In the far western panhandle sits Deep Creek Lake, a year-round resort area.

CLIMATE

The best times to visit are during the warm days and cool evenings of spring and autumn. Summers can be uncomfortably hot and humid. Unpredictable winters can be bitterly cold or relatively moderate, with freezing weather and snow more common in the mountains than in the rest of the state.

WHAT TO PACK

Outdoor summertime activities will require shorts and light-

DRIVING DISTANCES

Annapolis

30 mi SE of Baltimore
31 mi E of Washington, DC
77 mi SE of Frederick
117 mi NW of Ocean City
145 mi NE of Richmond, VA
171 mi SE of Cumberland
225 mi SW of New York, NY
416 mi NE of Charleston, WV

Baltimore

30 mi N of Annapolis
39 mi NE of Washington, DC
47 mi SE of Frederick
147 mi SE of Cumberland
147 mi SE of Ocean City
153 mi NE of Richmond, VA
211 mi SW of New York, NY
386 mi NE of Charleston, WV

Cumberland

94 mi NW of Frederick
141 mi NW of Baltimore
141 mi NW of Washington, DC
169 mi NW of Annapolis
245 mi NE of Charleston, WV
263 mi SW of Philadelphia, PA
286 mi NW of Ocean City
332 mi SW of New York, NY

Ocean City

117 mi SE of Annapolis
144 mi S of Philadelphia, PA
147 mi SE of Baltimore
148 mi SE of Washington, DC
194 mi SE of Frederick
250 mi SW of New York, NY
262 mi NE of Richmond, VA
286 mi SE of Cumberland

weight shirts, blouses, and dresses. Bring a jacket or wrap for cool spring and autumn evenings, and even summer ones in the mountains. Winter requires moderately heavy coats, hats, boots, and gloves. A few restaurants require men to wear jackets and ties; others insist on "smart casual" attire—no cut-off jeans, tank tops, skimpy halters, or bare feet. Pack at least one respectable outfit for evening wear.

Comfortable walking shoes, a hat, sunglasses, and a folding umbrella will always come in handy. Bring sunscreen and insect repellent during the summer months, especially for visits to the Eastern Shore.

TOURIST INFORMATION

The **Maryland Office of Tourism Development,** 9th Floor, 217 E Redwood St, Baltimore, MD 21202 (tel 410/767-3400, or toll free 800/543-1036), provides free copies of its annual *Destination Maryland,* which contains a complete list of attractions, activities, accommodations, state parks, and campgrounds throughout the state. Ask for separate booklets describing family travel opportunities and listing fairs, festivals, and special events. The office also maintains a World Wide Web page (http://www.mdisfun.org/mdisfun).

Most cities and towns have visitor information offices or chambers of commerce that provide details about their locales. Largest is the **Baltimore Area Visitors Center,** 300 W Pratt St, Baltimore, MD 21202 (tel 410/837-4636, or toll free 800/282-6632).

DRIVING RULES AND REGULATIONS

Although you would never guess it by the way Marylanders drive, the speed limit is 55 mph (*not* 65 mph) on all interstate highways. Many other rural highways have a 50 mph limit. In-town speed limits vary.

Drivers and all front-seat passengers must wear seat belts. Children under 4 or less than 40 pounds must ride in an approved safety seat; those under 10 or more than 40 pounds must wear seat belts or ride in an approved safety seat. Police strictly enforce drunk-driving laws.

RENTING A CAR

Rental cars are widely available in Maryland's metropolitan areas. It pays to shop around, since promotional deals, weekend rates, age requirements, and group discounts vary. The major companies in Maryland include:

- **Alamo** (tel toll free 800/327-9633)
- **Avis** (tel 800/831-2847)
- **Budget** (tel 800/527-0700)
- **Hertz** (tel 800/654-3131)
- **National** (tel 800/227-7368)
  - **Thrifty** (tel 800/367-2277)

AVG MONTHLY TEMPS (°F) & RAINFALL (IN)		
	Cumberland	Baltimore
Jan	30/2.4	35/3.1
Feb	33/2.3	37/3.2
Mar	43/3.1	47/3.6
Apr	54/3.2	57/3.2
May	63/3.7	67/4.1
June	71/3.3	76/3.3
July	75/3.8	80/3.7
Aug	74/3.3	79/4.3
Sept	67/3.1	72/3.5
Oct	55/2.8	60/3.0
Nov	45/2.8	50/3.6
Dec	35/2.6	39/3.8

ESSENTIALS

Area Code: The area code for Baltimore, Annapolis, and the Eastern Shore is **410**; for southern and western Maryland and the suburbs of Washington, DC, **301.**

Emergencies: Call **911** for the police, fire department, or an ambulance from anywhere within Maryland.

Liquor Laws: Privately owned package stores sell beer, wine, and liquors, which are not available at grocery and convenience stores in Maryland. The legal drinking age is 21.

Smoking: The state of Maryland prohibits smoking in many public areas, including bars and restaurants. Smoking areas are sometimes available; if in doubt, call ahead.

Taxes: The state sales tax is 5%. Many localities also impose hotel taxes.

Time Zone: All of Maryland is in the Eastern time zone. Daylight saving time is observed from the first Sunday in April until the last Sunday in October.

Best of the State

Below is a general overview of some of the top sights and attractions in Maryland. To find out more detailed information, look under "Attractions" under individual cities in the listings portion of this book.

WHAT TO SEE AND DO

Battlefields With one exception, Maryland escaped most of the heavy fighting during both the American Revolution and the Civil War. That one exception was the Battle of Antietam, near Sharpsburg, when Union troops met the advancing Confederates on September 17, 1862. It was the single bloodiest day of the war, with a combined casualty list of 23,110 men killed or wounded. The battlefield is now the **Antietam National Battlefield.**

Historic Buildings & Sites It seems that the streets of every Maryland town are lined with historic homes and commercial buildings. But **Annapolis** excels in this respect, with the largest concentration of 18th-century buildings in America, including the oldest US state capitol in continuous use. Architecture buffs will also find the Eastern Shore rich in towns with historic districts, including **Easton,** which has some forty 18th- and 19th-century buildings, **Salisbury,** and **Chestertown.** In Western Maryland, **Frederick** has a 33-block district of well-preserved 18th- and 19th-century mansions and town houses.

The state also has a number of historic sites of national importance, beginning with **Antietam National Battlefield,** at Sharpsburg, near Frederick. Two more frequently visited sites are the 1797-vintage **USS Frigate** *Constellation,* the oldest warship of the US Navy, and **Fort McHenry National Monument and Historic Shrine,** where Francis Scott Key wrote "The Star-Spangled Banner" during the War of 1812. Both are in Baltimore Harbor.

Historic Trains Railroad buffs will find plenty of interest in Maryland, home of the nation's first passenger train. Old engines and other equipment are displayed in the **Baltimore and Ohio (B&O) Railroad Museum** in Baltimore and the **B&O Railroad Station Museum** in Ellicott City. The **Western Maryland Scenic Railroad** operates a vintage steam train through the lovely mountain valley between Cumberland and Frostburg.

Museums In addition to those dedicated to railroads, Maryland has many other museums devoted to a wide variety of subjects. Baltimore leads the way with the **Baltimore Maritime Museum, Streetcar Museum, Baltimore Museum of Art,** the **Great Blacks in Wax Museum,** and the **American Indian Cultural Center and Museum.** At Ocean City, the **Delmarva Shipwreck and Historical Museum** houses relics of shipwrecks and a collection of Native American artifacts.

Beaches Ocean City's 10-mile-long beach is bordered by boardwalk, hotels, resorts, condominiums, restaurants, and amusement parks. A few miles south, the preserved expanse of **Assateague Island National Seashore** offers 30 miles of undisturbed sand and surf.

Cuisine H L Mencken once described the Chesapeake Bay as a "great protein factory." He meant the enormous amount of crabs, oysters, clams, and fish harvested from the Bay each year, which in turn means great seafood eating in Maryland. Tops on the list is the blue crab, served steamed and sprinkled with spice. Most local residents will gladly demonstrate how to "crack" these hard-shelled morsels. You also can order the soft-shell version or enjoy the meat in crab cakes, one of Maryland's characteristic dishes. And with all that poultry on the Eastern Shore, try some Southern-style fried chicken.

Family Favorites A water-oriented recreational facility with land-based carnival rides, **Adventure World** at Largo is the state's only theme park. Nevertheless, families will find much to keep them occupied in Maryland. Children usually enjoy the **Baltimore Zoo,** the **Catoctin Mountain Zoological Park** in Thurmont, and **Plumpton Park Zoo** in Rising Sun. The National Aquarium in Baltimore's Inner Harbor offers 5,000 sea mammals, fish, birds, and reptiles, plus a jungle display with exotic tropical birds and animals. The **Maryland Science Center** in Baltimore has hands-on educational exhibits for everyone. Other suggestions include traditional family vacations at places such as **Ocean City** and **Deep Creek Lake,** or looking for wild ponies on **Assateague Island.**

EVENTS AND FESTIVALS

THE EASTERN SHORE

- **North American Wildlife Craft Show,** Ocean City. Leading artists and carvers offer their works for sale. Mid-January. Call toll free 800/OC-OCEAN.
- **Chestertown Tea Party Festival,** Chestertown. Re-enacts local 1774 protest against British tea tax. Parade, art show, music, entertainment. Third weekend in May. Call 410/778-0416.

- **Queen Anne's County Waterman's Festival,** Kent Narrows. Celebrates seafood gatherers' unique way of life with food, entertainment, workboat contests. Wells Cove Public Landing. First weekend in June. Call 410/827-4810.
- **Bay Country Music Festival,** Centreville. Outdoor bluegrass, country, rock 'n' roll in 4-H Park. Second Saturday in June. Call 410/827-4810.
- **Canal Day,** Chesapeake City. Carriage and boat rides, music, artisans, crab feast celebrate the Chesapeake and Delaware Canal. Last Saturday in June. Call 410/392-7922 or 410/885-3112.
- **National Hard Crab Derby and Fair,** Crisfield. Crab picking, cooking, and racing, plus pageants and parades. Annual event since 1947. Somers Cove Marina. Labor Day weekend. Call 410/968-2682.
- **Olde Princess Anne Days,** Princess Anne. Only chance to tour 18th- and 19th-century homes, with costumed guides. Start at Teackle Mansion. First weekend in October. Call 410/651-2986 or toll free 800/521-9189.
- **Waterfowl Festival,** Easton. Major show of wildlife paintings and carvings, including antique decoys. Food and crafts for sale. Second weekend in November. Call 410/822-4567.

SOUTHERN MARYLAND

- **Maryland Day Weekend,** St Mary's. Historic town opens to celebrate founding of Maryland there in 1634. Weekend nearest March 25. Call 301/862-0990 or toll free 800/762-1634.
- **Governor's Cup Yacht Race,** St Mary's. Largest overnight yacht race on East Coast leaves waterfront at St Mary's College. First weekend in August. Call 301/862-0380.
- **Historic Pageant and Blessing of the Fleet,** St Clement's Island. Boat ride from Colton's Point to historic island, hayride to festivities, food, blessing of workboats. First weekend in October. Call 301/769-2222.
- **St Mary's County Oyster Festival,** Leonardtown. National oyster-shucking and cooking contests, seafood, entertainment, and children's games. Third weekend in October. Call 301/863-5015.

CENTRAL MARYLAND

- **Annapolis Heritage Antiques Show,** Annapolis. Dealers offer 18th- and 19th-century furnishings, works of art. National Guard Armory. Mid- to late January. Call 410/222-1919.
- **Babe Ruth's Birthday Party,** Baltimore. Celebrate the anniversary of The Bambino's birth in 1895. Babe Ruth Museum. February 6. Call 410/727-1539.
- **St Patrick's Day,** Baltimore. City's large Irish community celebrates with parade, 3-mile run, lots of green. Call 410/837-4636 or toll free 800/282-6632.
- **Annapolis Spring Boat Show,** Annapolis. Region's largest features sailboats and powerboats. City Dock. Third weekend in April. Call 410/268-8828.
- **Annapolis Waterfront Festival,** Annapolis. Arts and crafts, flotillas of tall ships, boat races, music. City Dock. Last weekend in April. Call 410/269-0661 or 410/268-8890.
- **Preakness Festival,** Baltimore. Week-long celebrations culminate in the Preakness Stakes, second jewel of thoroughbred racing's Triple Crown. Pimlico Race Course. Week before third Saturday in May. Call 410/837-3030 for festivities, 410/542-9400 for Preakness tickets.
- **Maryland Seafood Festival,** Annapolis. Sample the bounty of the Bay at Sandy Point State Park. Second weekend in September. Call 410/268-7682.
- **New Market Days,** New Market. Maryland's antique capital goes all out, with food, crafts, entertainment, and all 30 shops open. Last weekend in September. Call 301/865-3926.
- **United States Sailboat Show,** Annapolis. Hundreds of "rag haulers" and their accessories displayed in tents at City Dock. First weekend in October. Call 410/268-8828.
- **United States Power Boat Show,** Annapolis. "Stink pots" and their accessories move into same City Dock tents used by sailboat show. Second weekend in October. Call 410/268-8828.
- **State House by Candlelight,** Annapolis. Maryland's historic capitol is decorated for Christmas. First weekend in December. Call 410/974-3400.

WESTERN MARYLAND

- **Winterfest Weekend,** Deep Creek Lake. Wisp Ski Resort hosts ski races, parties, frigid golf tournament. First weekend in March. Call 301/387-4911.
- **National Pike Festival,** Washington County. Conestoga wagon train travels US 40, the original National Pike, accompanied by arts and crafts, old-fashioned entertainment. Third weekend in

May. Call 301/791-3130 or toll free 800/228-STAY.

- **Fort Frederick Rendezvous,** Big Pool. Re-enactment of life during the French and Indian Wars of the 1750s. Fort Frederick State Park. Last weekend in May. Call 301/842-2155.
- **McHenry Highland Festival,** McHenry. Traditional gathering of the clans, with bagpipes, dances, sheep dogs. Garret County Fairgrounds. First Saturday in June. Call 301/334-1948.
- **Heritage Days Festival,** Cumberland. Tours of historic homes and buildings, arts and crafts, entertainment, children's program. Call 301/759-4400 or toll free 800/872-4650.
- **Chesapeake and Ohio Canal Boat Festival,** Cumberland. Canal boats on display, Civil War re-enactments, music, food, arts and crafts. North Branch of C&O National Historical Park. Second weekend in July. Call 301/777-5905 or toll free 800/508-4748.
- **Rocky Gap Country/Bluegrass Music Festival,** Cumberland. Nationally known entertainers, Baltimore Symphony Orchestra, local musicians, workshops, arts and crafts. Rocky Gap State Park. First weekend in August. Call 301/724-2511 or toll free 800/424-2511.
- **Maryland Railfest,** Cumberland. Three-day festival of railroad history, rides on Western Maryland Scenic Railroad. Late October. Call 301/759-4400 or toll free 800/TRAIN-50.
- **Antietam National Battlefield Memorial Illumination,** Sharpsburg. Lighting of 23,110 luminaries provides haunting memorial to dead and wounded of the Civil War battle. First Saturday in December. Call 301/842-2722.

SPECTATOR SPORTS

Baseball The American League **Baltimore Orioles** play in the modern yet classic Oriole Park at Camden Yards, 333 W Camden St, Baltimore (tel 410/685-8900). Inquire early, since the "O's" usually pack this beautiful, Inner Harbor ballpark. Old-time fans will enjoy visiting Babe Ruth's Birthplace, now a baseball museum within walking distance of Camden Yards at 216 Emory St.

Popular minor league teams include the **Bowie Baysox** (tel 301/805-6000), the **Frederick Keys** (tel 301/662-0013), and the **Hagerstown Suns** (tel 301/791-6266).

Basketball The NBA **Washington Bullets** play most of their games at USAir Arena in Landover, on Central Ave just off I-95 east of Washington, DC, but they appear a few times each season at the Baltimore Arena. Call 301/350-3400 for schedules and tickets.

College Athletics The University of Maryland **Terrapins** play their Atlantic Coast Conference games at Cole Field House in College Park. For information call 301/314-7070.

Football Baltimore's entry into the Canadian Football League, **Baltimore CFL,** plays its home games at Memorial Stadium, on 33rd St at Ellerslie Ave. Call 410/554-1040 for schedules and tickets.

Golf The world's top PGA pros tee off during the first week of June in the **Kemper Open** at the Tournament Player's Club at Avenel, near I-495 in Potomac. Call 301/469-3737 for dates and tickets.

Horse Racing **Pimlico Race Course** at Hayward and Winner Aves in Baltimore (tel 410/542-9400) has daily racing and hosts the Preakness Stakes on the third Saturday in May. **Laurel Race Course,** at MD 98 and Race Track Rd in Laurel, is another thoroughbred racing venue (tel 301/725-0400, or toll free 800/638-1859). **Rosecroft Raceway** in Fort Washington (tel 301/567-4000) features harness racing.

Ice Hockey The NHL **Washington Capitals** face off at USAir Arena in Landover (tel 410/350-3400). The minor league **Baltimore Skipjacks** play in the Baltimore Arena, 201 W Baltimore St (tel 410/347-2010).

ACTIVITIES A TO Z

Bicycling Maryland has several areas ideal for bike riding, beginning with the 184-mile towpath of the **C&O Canal National Historical Park,** which follows the Potomac River from Washington, DC, to Cumberland. The 13-mile **Baltimore-Annapolis Trail** runs north from US 50 and MD 2 just outside Annapolis. Several flat rural roads on the Eastern Shore have wide paved shoulders to accommodate bikes, such as MD 20 between Chestertown and Rock Hall, and MD 333 between Easton and Oxford.

For information about trails throughout the state, call the Maryland State Highway Administration's bicycling hotline, Monday–Friday 8:15am–

4:15pm (tel 410/333-1663). The Geography Department of the University of Maryland–Baltimore County (tel 410/455-2002) publishes a guide to biking and hiking trails in the Baltimore-Annapolis area. Commercial companies offer inn-to-inn touring and camping.

Spectators can watch the pros race through Maryland on the annual **Tour DuPont** in early May. Downtown Hagerstown is the finish line for the Maryland portion of this 1,000-mile race that begins in Wilmington, Delaware. For information call 301/791-3080.

Birdwatching　The Eastern Shore is a prime area for watching birds, especially in **Blackwater National Wildlife Refuge** south of Cambridge and in **Assateague Island National Seashore,** which adjoins the Chincoteague National Wildlife Refuge just below the Virginia line. For information, contact the Audubon Naturalist Society for the Middle Atlantic States, 8940 Jones Mill Rd, Chevy Chase, MD (tel 301/652-9188).

Boating　The Chesapeake Bay and its many tributaries are a draw for pleasure craft of all types. Every waterfront town and village has at least one marina, many of which rent or charter power boats and sailboats. The Maryland Office of Tourism Development's *Destination Maryland* has a complete town-by-town list (see "Tourist Information," above). Annapolis, one of the world's major sailing centers, has three excellent schools where both children and adults can learn to sail.

The state's slow-moving coastal rivers and creeks offer gentle going for canoeists and kayakers, and its swift-flowing mountain streams pose challenges. A number of outfitters provide boats and guides, especially in the towns along the Potomac River.

Several scenic cruises operate in Baltimore, Annapolis, and Ocean City. Water taxis, useful for sightseeing, scoot around Baltimore's Inner Harbor, and day cruises leave Crisfield for Virginia's unusual Tangier Island.

Camping　The state is well equipped for campers, whether they pitch a tent along the Appalachian Trail or hook up the RV near a big city. Twenty-two of Maryland's 44 state parks have camping facilities, and there are more than 30 private campgrounds. For a complete list, request a copy of the Maryland Office of Tourism Development's *Destination Maryland* (see "Tourist Information," above).

Fishing　With the deep sea off its Atlantic Ocean beaches, the saltwater expanse of the Chesapeake Bay, and hundreds of freshwater streams and lakes, it's difficult to go anywhere in the state that isn't a few minutes drive from someone's favorite fishing hole. The Maryland Office of Tourism Development's *Destination Maryland* has a chart showing when and where to try your luck (see "Tourism Information," above). Separate freshwater and Chesapeake Bay licenses are required of both Marylanders and visitors alike, including a special stamp for striped bass (or "rockfish"). For information, contact the **Fish, Heritage and Wildlife Service,** E-1, Maryland Department of Natural Resources, 580 Taylor Ave, Annapolis, MD 21401 (tel 410/974-3211).

Golf　Duffers can play almost year-round on Maryland's numerous public and private golf courses. Most famous is Potomac's Tournament Player's Club at Avenel, home of the annual Kemper Open. Most hotels and resorts can arrange a tee time at a local course. The Maryland Office of Tourism Development's *Destination Maryland* lists all courses county-by-county.

Guided Excursions　Several guided tours are available in Baltimore and Annapolis, but one unusual excursion is the **John Wilkes Booth Escape Route Bus Tour,** which retraces the steps of Abraham Lincoln's assassin into southern Maryland. The bus leaves the Surratt House Museum in Clinton several times a year. Reservations are essential (tel 301/868-1121).

Hiking　Numerous trails include the state's 37 miles of the **Appalachian Trail** and the 184-mile-long towpath of the C&O Canal National Historic Park along the Potomac River. The 29-mile **Catoctin Trail** links 3 state parks and Cunningham Falls. For the Baltimore-Annapolis area, ask for a copy of the University of Maryland–Baltimore County Geography Department's guide to local hiking and biking trails (tel 410/455-2002).

Horseback Riding　Maryland has a plethora of stables, especially in the horse country that runs from north of Baltimore through the rolling hills of central Maryland. Hotels and local tourist offices can help arrange riding.

Hunting　In addition to its famous ducks and Canada geese in the Atlantic Flyway on the Eastern Shore,

SELECTED PARKS & RECREATION AREAS

• **Assateague Island National Seashore,** 7206 National Seashore Lane, Berlin, MD 21811 (tel 410/641-1441)
• **C&O Canal National Historical Park,** Box 4, Sharpsburg, MD 21782 (tel 301/299-3613)
• **Eastern Neck National Wildlife Refuge,** Rte 2, Box 225, Rock Hall, MD 21661 (tel 410/639-7056)
• **Patuxent National Wildlife Refuge,** Rte 197, Laurel, MD 20708 (tel 301/498-0342)
• **Catoctin Mountain Park,** 6602 Foxville Rd, Thurmont, MD 21788 (tel 301/663-9388)
• **Deep Creek Lake State Park,** Rte 2, Box 69-C, Swanton, MD 21561 (tel 301/387-5563)
• **Greenbelt Park,** 6565 Greenbelt Rd, Greenbelt, MD 20770 (tel 301/344-3948)
• **Gunpowder Falls State Park,** 10815 Harford Rd, PO Box 5032, Glen Arm, MD 21057 (tel 410/592-2897)
• **Herrington Manor State Park,** 222 Herrington Lane, Oakland, MD 21550 (tel 301/334-9180)
• **Patapsco Valley State Park,** 8020 Baltimore National Pike, Ellicott City, MD 21043-3499 (tel 410/461-5005)
• **Pocomoke River State Forest and Park,** 3461 Worcester Hwy, Snow Hill, MD 21863 (tel 410/632-2566)
• **Sandy Point State Park,** 1100 E College Pkwy, Annapolis, MD 21401 (tel 410/974-2149)
• **Tuckahoe State Park,** 13070 Crouse Mill Rd, Queen Anne, MD 21657 (tel 410/634-2810)

Maryland offers grouse, whitetail deer, and even wild turkeys to be hunted. The state has thousands of acres of public hunting lands, state forests, and parks. For information about licenses, seasons, and bag limits, contact the **Wildlife Division, Maryland Department of Natural Resources,** 580 Taylor Ave, Annapolis, MD 21401 (tel 410/974-3195).

Shopping Most Maryland towns have at least one antiques shop, and **Baltimore's Antique Row** has more than 75 shops along the 700 and 800 blocks of Howard Street just northwest of the Inner Harbor. Another antiquer's paradise is New Market, on US 40 east of Frederick.

A number of outlet malls dot the state, with major shopping along US 50 near both ends of the Chesapeake Bay Bridge.

Skiing Maryland's one downhill ski facility is **Wisp Resort** in Deep Creek Lake (tel 301/387-5581), which has 4 miles of slopes and trails, a 610-foot drop, and snowmaking equipment. Many state parks, especially those in western Maryland, have cross-country trails.

Tennis The temperate climate makes tennis a popular outdoor sport most of the year in Maryland, which has a host of public and private courts. Some of the larger hotels and resorts have their own facilities for guests, and most others can point you to nearby courts.

Water Sports Fronted by the Atlantic Ocean and backed by Assawoman and Isle of Wight Bays, the narrow but long resort town of Ocean City offers a host of water sports, especially windsurfing and parasailing.

Driving the State

Start	Easton
Finish	Ocean City
Distance	170 miles
Time	2–3 days
Highlights	17th- and 18th-century towns and villages; scenic expanses of forests, farmland, and marshes; winding waterways; wildlife refuges; a ferry ride; fabulous seafood; pounding surf at a major beach resort

This tour follows US 50 (the so-called Ocean Gateway) across the low, waterway-laced Delmarva Peninsula, which Marylanders call their Eastern Shore. You'll detour from this major highway to visit lovely waterfront towns like St Michaels and Oxford, two of the state's oldest municipalities, and wildlife refuges set aside for the waterfowl that make this area famous among birdwatchers, photographers, woodcarvers, and hunters. You'll also have many opportunities to sample the succulent Chesapeake seafood harvested by the area's hearty Watermen. While most stops are in colonial-era towns and villages, you'll end up in a far different world: The high-rise condominiums of Ocean City, a bustling and very modern summertime beach resort.

For additional information on accommodations, restaurants, and attractions in the region covered by the tour, look under specific cities in the listings portion of this book.

US 50 can be congested with weekend beach traffic from Memorial Day to Labor Day. The worst driving times are Friday nights and Saturday mornings eastbound, Sunday evenings westbound. Plan accordingly.

US 50 crosses the Chesapeake Bay east of Annapolis. From the Bay Bridge, it's 26 miles to:

1. **Easton,** a peaceful little community (pop 8,500) facing the center of the bay yet sheltered by the coves of the Miles and Red Avon Rivers. William Penn once preached at the **Third Haven Meeting House,** built in 1692 at 405 S Washington St (tel 410/822-0293), ½ mile south of the **Talbot County Court House.** There has been a court house at this Washington St site between Dover and Federal Sts since 1711 (the present one was finished in 1974). Many other Easton homes and commercial buildings are also from the Federal period. The **Historical Society Museum,** 25 S Washington St (tel 410/822-0773), and the nearby James and Joseph Neall Houses (both restored residences of Quaker cabinetmaker brothers), focus on Easton's past.

They are open Tuesday–Saturday from 10am–4pm, Sunday 1–4pm. A host of upscale shops around the Court House attest to Talbot's being one of the wealthiest counties on the Eastern Shore.

Consider spending at least one night in this area. In Easton, the charming **Tidewater Inn** may be found at Dover and Harrison Sts, and there are comfortable chain motels, such as **Holiday Inn Express** and **Days Inn,** on the US 50 commercial strip east of town. You can also bunk down in St Michaels or Oxford, the next stops on this tour. This area is a very popular weekend retreat, so advance reservations are strongly advised. For refreshment, nearly every fast food chain has an outlet along US 50 in Easton, and there are fine seafood restaurants in both St Michaels and Oxford.

From downtown Easton, take Bay St (MD 33) west for 6½ miles to a delightful view of the Miles River from atop the Oak Creek Bridge. From there it's 2½ miles to the trendy shops along Talbot St, the main thoroughfare of charming:

2. **St Michaels,** an important Miles River shipbuilding port from the late 1600s until the 1830s, when its shipwrights worked on the small Chesapeake Bay bugeye and skipjack sailboats. Turn right on Mill St to visit the excellent **Chesapeake Bay Maritime Museum** (tel 410/745-2916), where examples of these and other local vessels are on display. From there, you can take a self-guided walking tour around the harbor and have lunch at the rustic **Crab Claw** (tel 410/745-2900) seafood restaurant or another waterside eatery. Other sights include the **Cannonball House** on Mulberry St, which received its name during the War of 1812, when St Michaels's residents blacked out the town and hung lanterns in the trees to fool an attacking British fleet into overshooting their houses. Their ruse worked, except for one shot which hit the chimney on Cannonball House.

From St Michaels, backtrack 3 miles east on MD 33, turn right on MD 329, and follow the signs south 4½ miles to the 9-car **Oxford-Bellevue Ferry** (tel 410/745-9023), which shuttles across the Tred Avon River until 9pm from June through Labor Day, until sunset from March to May and from September to mid-December. Fares are $4.50 for car and driver, 50¢ for each passenger. (The ferry doesn't operate from mid-December to March, so during that time return to Easton on MD 33, turn right on the Easton Pkwy (MD 322), and right again

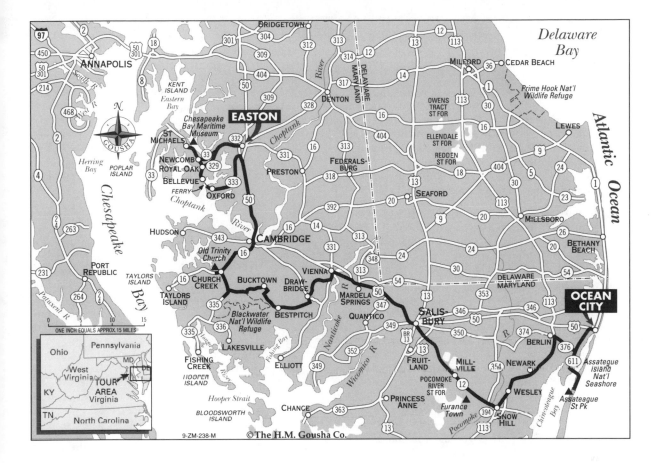

on MD 333 to reach the next stop.) While riding the ferry for 20 minutes, grab a free brochure with a map of:

3. **Oxford,** a serene little town on a narrow peninsula formed by the Tred Avon River and Town Creek. There was a Colonial settlement here as early as 1673. The historic 1710 **Robert Morris Inn** stands opposite the ferry landing at the corner of Morris St and The Strand, which skirts the river. Find a place to park, explore this gem of a town on foot, and enjoy the seafood at one of the restaurants on Town Creek.

Take a Break

The **Trappe Station Country Store,** at the junction of MD 333 and Almshouse Rd (tel 410/822-9338), isn't a country store any more but a fine little deli where you can chow down on country-style breakfasts, sandwiches, burgers, and fresh salads, which are priced $3–$5.

Take Morris St (MD 333) out of town and drive 4 miles east to Trappe Station.

From behind the store, follow Almshouse Rd east 2½ miles through the countryside to the second stop sign. Turn right there on US 50 (it isn't marked) and drive 8 miles east to the broad Choptank River. On the other side lies:

4. **Cambridge.** The second-largest town on Maryland's Eastern Shore, it lacks the charm of St Michaels and Oxford. Turn right on Maryland Ave to reach Cambridge Creek, the town's harbor; beyond that are the **Dorchester County Courthouse** and **Christ Church,** opposite each other on High St. Turn right on High St to observe a number of nearby 17th- and 18th-century homes. There's a riverside park and marina at the end of High St. The small **Brannock Maritime Museum** is at Talbot Ave and Tubman St (tel 410/228-1245), 8 blocks west of the court house, but it's open only Saturday 10am–4pm and Sunday 1–4pm. East of US 50, on Greenway Dr via Maryland Ave, you will find the Dorchester County Historical Society's **Meredith**

House (built circa 1760) and adjacent **Neild Museum,** which feature maritime, industrial, and farming exhibits in a Georgian-style residence. They are open Tuesday–Saturday 9am–5pm (tel 410/228-7953).

From Maryland Ave, go 1 mile east on US 50, turn right on MD 16, and drive 7 miles west to the whitewashed community of Church Creek. Keep going through the MD 335 intersection for exactly 1 mile for a look at **Old Trinity Church.** Built in the 1670s, this is one of America's oldest Episcopal churches. Backtrack to MD 335, turn right, and follow the signs 5 miles south to:

5. **Blackwater National Wildlife Refuge** (tel 410/228-2677), on the edge of south Dorchester County's Everglades-like marshlands. This former muskrat fur farm is a major stop for Canada geese and other migratory birds along the Atlantic Flyway. The visitor center on Key Wallace Dr has interpretive displays, maps of the refuge, and rest rooms. The sanctuary has a driving loop, a tower overlook, and hiking trails, which are open year-round daily from dawn to dusk. Admission is $3 per vehicle or motorbike, $1 for pedestrians and bicyclists.

At this point, you could backtrack to Cambridge and US 50. Instead, take the scenic route along unnumbered county roads for 25 miles to Vienna. (Drive carefully through these marshes, forests, and farmlands, and watch out for right-angle curves.) From the refuge, turn right and go about 2½ miles east on Key Wallace Dr to a T-intersection. Turn left on Maple Dam Rd (which returns to Cambridge), and drive only ³⁄₁₀ of a mile north then bear right onto Greenbriar Rd. Follow it east about 2½ miles to a T-intersection with Bestpitch Ferry Rd, turn right, and continue east about 13 miles (crossing a one-lane wooden bridge along the way) to another T-intersection at Drawbridge. Turn right on narrow but paved Steele's Neck Rd and drive east 4.8 miles to its T-intersection with Vienna-Henry's Crossroads Rd. Turn left and drive 2 miles north to the town of Vienna, known primarily for its electric power plant on the Nanticoke River. To reach US 50, turn left on Race St, then right on Gay St (MD 331), where you will find one of those combination gasoline station–food marts, our first chance at refreshment since Cambridge.

Get on US 50 east and drive 17 miles for an overnight stop.

On the upper reaches of the Wicomico River, **Salisbury** is the Eastern Shore's largest city, chief commercial center, and home of the Perdue chicken empire, one of whose processing plants you'll pass on your way into town. Although Ocean City is only 30 miles east, Salisbury is a centrally located place to spend a night before your last sidetrip off US 50. Several modern and comfortable chain motels (such as **Sheraton Salisbury Inn, Comfort Inn,** and **Hampton Inn),** as well as most of the town's shopping centers and restaurants, are 3 miles north of US 50 on Salisbury Blvd (US 13).

While you're here, you can visit the 12-acre open-air **Salisbury Zoo,** 755 S Park Dr (tel 410/548-3188), and the **Ward Museum of Wildfowl Art,** 909 Schumaker Dr (tel 410/860-BIRD), the largest of its kind in the world, featuring antique decoys, contemporary carvings, and paintings. Both attractions are on the east side of town.

From Salisbury, take MD 12 south. If you are traveling between April and the end of October, then right 13½ miles south of Salisbury onto Furnace Rd. Drive 1 mile west, where in a forest on the left you will find:

6. **Furnace Town** (tel 410/632-2032), a restored early 19th-century company town built around the ruins of the Nassawango Iron Works' 45-foot-tall chimney. Exhibits explain how the furnace extracted iron from limonite deposits (known as bog ore) from the surrounding swamps. The Nature Conservancy maintains a one-mile nature trail through the cypress swamp behind the chimney. The town is open April–October, daily 11am–5pm. Admission is $3 adults, $1.50 children under 18.

Back at MD 12, continue south 4 miles to:

7. **Snow Hill,** once an important port on the Pocomoke River and today an attractive waterfront town with more than 100 buildings dating back a century or more. You will want to see the small but impressive collection of historic clothes and artifacts at the **Julia A Purnell Museum** on Market St (tel 410/632-0515). Open April–October, Monday–Friday 10am–4pm, weekends 1–4pm. **All Hallows Episcopal Church,** at Market and Church Sts, was built around 1750. The **Mount Zion One-Room School Museum,** at Church and Ironside Sts, looks exactly as it did in 1900 (open Thursday–Sunday 1–4pm). The winding, jungle-like Pocomoke River is a favor-

---

Take a Break

The **Snow Hill Inn Restaurant,** 104 E Market St (tel 410/632-2102), a bed-and-breakfast in a restored 1790s vintage house, offers a charming setting for dining in this colonial-era town. Specialties are fresh seafood and lamb chops. Lunch items run $3–$8; main courses at dinner are priced $10–$15. The inn has three guest rooms upstairs.

ite spot for canoeing, especially between Snow Hill and Shad Landing, in the swamps of Pocomoke State Forest downstream. **Pocomoke River Canoe Company** (tel 410/632-3971), near the bridge, rents boats and equipment from April through November. During the summer *Tillie the Tug* makes hour-long excursions on the river from its dock at Strugis Park on River St. Fares are $6.

From downtown, take Market St (MD 394) east to US 113, then follow it north 14 miles to Berlin. Turn right there on MD 376, go 4 miles east to MD 611, turn right and drive 5 miles south to:

8. **Assateague Island National Seashore** (tel 410/641-2120), Maryland's share of this unspoiled, 37-mile-long barrier island. Here you can see the wild ponies made famous at Chincoteague, across the border in Virginia, and enjoy what seems like endless miles of undeveloped surf beach. The seashore and adjoining state park have camping, visitor centers, hiking trails, and public beach facilities. Both are open from 8am to dusk and charge admission fees.

From Assateague, backtrack north on MD 611 for 8 miles, turn east on US 50, and cross Isle of Wight Bay into:

9. **Ocean City,** whose high-rise condominiums and hotels stand in stark contrast to the pristine beach we just left behind. A small fishing village was established in 1875 on this skinny barrier island, with the Atlantic on one side and Assawoman and Isle of Wight Bays on the other. Now Ocean City is a major summertime vacation destination with a multitude of amusements, excellent fishing and water sports (everything from jet skiing and parasailing to sailboating and windsurfing), a host of fine seafood restaurants, and accommodations ranging from small motels to large convention resorts.

From Ocean City, you can drive north across the state line to Bethany Beach and take the driving tour "Coastal Delaware" (see the Delaware chapter) in reverse.

Driving the State

Start	Frederick
Finish	Deep Creek Lake
Distance	175 miles
Time	2–4 days
Highlights	Valleys dotted with horse and dairy farms; mountain panoramas; historic towns and villages; a restored fort; a major Civil War battlefield; the C&O Canal National Historical Park; a cavern with unusual stalagmites and stalactites; year-round fun at a mountain lake

This tour follows the routes of the National Pike and the National Road, both built soon after the founding of the United States to further the young nation's westward expansion. Today this drive is known as US 40, although stretches of it now merge with I-70 and I-68. These modern highways still follow ancient Native American footpaths through Western Maryland's rolling valleys and across the region's heavily forested mountain ridges. Near Hancock, the tour skirts the Potomac River and its adjacent C&O Canal. These two famous waterways run a parallel course a few miles to the south. With a centuries-old route and bountiful natural beauty surrounding you, your drive will be both a historic and scenic tour de force.

For additional information on accommodations, restaurants, and attractions in the region covered by the tour, look under specific cities in the listings portion of this book.

I-70 and US 15 intersect in the Middletown Valley at the first stop:

1. **Frederick,** whose photogenic historic district is studded with well-preserved 18th- and early 19th-century buildings which recall its founding in 1745 by German and English settlers. Among them are the **Roger Brooke Taney House** and **Francis Scott Key Museum,** both located at 123 S Bentz St (tel 301/663-8687). Taney was the US Supreme Court Justice who swore in Abraham Lincoln and five other US presidents. His law partner, Francis Scott Key, wrote the words to "The Star Spangled Banner" during the War of 1812. The museum is open April–October, Saturday–Sunday 10am–4pm. The flag also was the focus of events in 1862 at the **Barbara Fritchie House and Museum,** 154 W Patrick St (tel 301/698-0630), where the Unionist Mrs Fritchie, then in her 90s, refused Confederate Gen Stonewall Jackson's order to lower her Stars

and Stripes. That inspired John Greenleaf Whittier to pen his famous line: "Shoot if you must this old grey head, but spare your country's flag." Information and organized tours of these and other attractions in the area are available at the **Frederick Tourism Council,** 19 E Church St (tel 301/663-8687), just south of Patrick St.

Follow W Patrick St (Alternate US 40) west out of Frederick. This is the Old National Pike, which after Middletown Valley begins to climb South Mountain. At the top of Turner's Gap, turn right and drive 1 mile to:

2. **Washington Monument State Park** (tel 301/791-4767), where a stone tower was constructed in 1827 as the country's first memorial to George Washington. On a clear day, you can see parts of Maryland, Virginia, and West Virginia from the tower. The Appalachian Trail winds through the park, which has picnic and camping facilities. It's open Fri–Mon, 8am–sunset.

Take a Break

Atop Turner's Gap, opposite the Washington Monument State Park turn-off, stands the **Old South Mountain Inn** (tel 301/371-5400 from the Frederick side of the mountain, or 301/431-6155 from the Hagerstown side). Built in 1799 during stagecoach days, this charming inn offers early American ambience and a variety of cuisines, all excellently prepared. Portraits of early US presidents in the cozy lounge are balanced at the entrance by photos of many modern politicos who have dined here. Dinner main courses cost $15–$25. Closed Monday.

From South Mountain, you should descend into Hagerstown Valley, which is known as the Shenandoah Valley down in Virginia. After 3 miles you'll arrive in **Boonsboro,** a small town founded in 1744 not by Daniel Boone but by his reputed relatives, brothers George and William Boone. There take a left on Potomac St and follow MD 34 south 2 miles to:

3. **Crystal Grottoes Caverns** (tel 301/432-6336), which were discovered in 1920 during excavation of a rock quarry. Unusual stalactites and stalagmites can be seen during 30-minute guided tours. Open April–October, daily 9am–6pm; November–

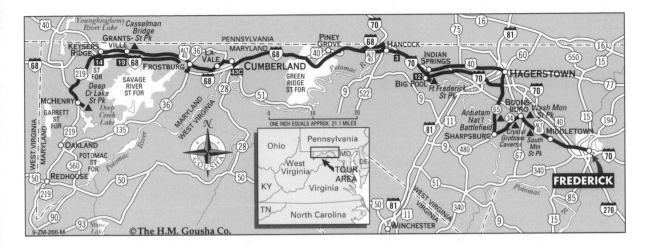

March, weekends 11am–4pm. Admission is $7 adults, $3.50 children 11 and under.

From the caverns, keep going south 4 miles through the rolling fields along MD 34 to the little village of:

4. **Sharpsburg,** where the road actually goes through **Antietam National Cemetery.** Here lie some of the more than 23,000 men who were killed and wounded on September 17, 1862, the single bloodiest day of the Civil War. Turn right on MD 65 and follow the signs to **Antietam National Battlefield** (tel 301/432-5124), where Union troops stopped Gen Robert E Lee's first attempt to invade the North (his next try ended at Gettysburg a year later). Lee's failure at Antietam caused Great Britain to delay recognizing the Confederate government, thereby changing the course of the war. President Abraham Lincoln issued his preliminary Emancipation Proclamation a few days later. The battlefield is open daily from sunrise to sunset. The visitors center has historical exhibits and shows an audiovisual program every half-hour; it is open Memorial Day–Labor Day 8:30am–6pm; the rest of the year 8:30am–5pm. Admission to the visitors center is $2 per person, $4 per family.

From the battlefield, drive 12 miles north on MD 65 into downtown:

5. **Hagerstown,** noted for its Early American stone buildings. Worth seeing is the **Jonathan Hager House and Museum** (tel 301/739-8393), on Key St in the City Park (from MD 65, turn left on Wilson Blvd, right on Virginia Ave, and follow the signs). The house was the fort-like home of Jonathan Hager, a German who settled here in 1739 and later founded the village which took his name. Today, period furnishings and artifacts are on display. **Zion Reformed Church,** at Potomac and Church Sts, dates back to 1744 and is the city's oldest building. The **Miller House,** 135 W Washington St (tel 301/797-8782), a Federal-period townhouse, is home to the **Valley Store Museum** (which displays period furnishings and Civil War memorabilia) as well as the Washington County Historical Society. The **Maryland Theater,** near the Public Square, has been restored to its 1915 neoclassical grandeur. For maps and more information, drop by the **Washington County Convention and Visitors Bureau,** 1826 Dual Hwy (tel 301/791-3130, or 797-8800 for recorded information).

Hagerstown is the last sizable city we will visit in western Maryland and, although it lacks the charm of Frederick, its motels and restaurants offer a good place to stay and dine before we head into the mountains.

From Hagerstown, US 40 follows W Franklin St and resumes its westward trek along the Old National Pike. If you take this scenic route, go 15 miles west to **Indian Springs.** If you opt for the faster I-70, drive 20 miles to exit 12 for **Big Pool.** In either case, turn left on MD 56 at Indian Springs or at exit 12, and drive 1 mile east to:

6. **Fort Frederick State Park** (tel 301/842-2155), home of an impressive fort built in 1756 during the French and Indian Wars. Settlers huddled inside its thick stone walls during a Native American uprising in 1763, British prisoners of war lived here during the American Revolution, and it was a Union outpost during a brief Civil War skirmish. Costumed guides are on hand from May through October to explain the fort and its interior buildings, which have been restored to their 1758 appearance. The park is open daily 8am–sunset. The visitors center is open Memorial Day–Labor Day 8am–4pm; September–October, open weekends

only. The C&O Canal runs through the park, which has picnicking and primitive camping facilities.

From the fort, backtrack on MD 56 and take I-70 west at Big Pool. The Interstate, the C&O Canal, and the CSX Railroad all run along the Potomac River for the next 10 miles to exit 3 and:

7. **Hancock,** an important early 19th-century way-station on both the National Pike and the C&O Canal. Stop at the **C&O Canal National Historical Park visitor center** (tel 301/722-8226), on the right as you drive into town on Main St (Alternate US 40); the center has exhibits on the canal's history. Then drive along the canal by turning left on Pennsylvania Ave. There are remnants of lock, dams, and lock houses along the way. The area also has a towpath, a nearly level trail for walkers and bicyclists.

Take a Break

Hancock is still an important transportation center, for this is where I-70 turns north into Pennsylvania, and I-68 begins. We will take I-68, a relatively new highway with scant service facilities, for the next 38 miles, so gas up and take a refreshment break in Hancock.

Since 1946, Hancock residents have been eating at the **Park-N-Dine,** 189 Main St (tel 301/678-5242), where they can overlook the C&O Canal while waiting for American and Italian fare. Main courses cost $4–$7.

The Old National Pike (known as both Alternate US 40 and MD 144) laboriously climbs four Allegheny Mountains west of Hancock. Take this much slower route if you have plenty of time. If not, get on I-68 at Hancock and drive west 38 miles to exit 43C in downtown:

8. **Cumberland,** which in the 1800s was the "Gateway to the American West." The C&O Canal reached Cumberland in 1850, and the town was the beginning point of the National Road. Cumberland later was an important stop on the Chesapeake and Ohio Railroad, which also followed the Potomac River westward. From exit 43C, turn left on Harrison St and drive straight into the parking lot of the **Allegany County Visitor Center** (tel 301/777-5905) in the old railroad station, which also houses a small **C&O Canal museum** and the ticket office of the **Western Maryland Scenic Railroad** (tel 301/759-4400). If you can stay overnight, be sure to take this 34-mile round-trip vintage steam train ride between Cumberland and Frostburg. The scenic mountain valley route includes the Cumberland

Narrows, Helmstetter's Horseshoe Curve, various tunnels, and panoramic vistas.

In Cumberland, you will want to stroll around the Washington St **Historic District** on the western side of town, with the 1851 **Emmanuel Episcopal Church** at 16 Washington St, as well as many 18th-century homes featuring elaborate stained-glass windows, graceful cupolas, and sloping mansard roofs. You can also view the exterior of **George Washington's Headquarters** during the French and Indian War; this log cabin is located in Riverside Park on Greene St at the junction of Wills Creek and the Potomac River.

As the primary commercial center of far western Maryland, Cumberland has good motels, such as **Holiday Inn,** and the charming **Inn at Walnut Bottom.**

From downtown Cumberland, follow Henderson Ave and Alternate US 40 for 5 miles west through the Narrows, an appropriately named gorge through Wills Mountain. On the other side, you'll drive into:

9. **La Vale,** where on the left next to Cooper Tires you will see Maryland's last **Toll Gate House** left from the National Road. Although federal money was used to build the road, the US Government ceded it to the states, which immediately levied tolls. Built about 1833, the small brick building charged 12 cents for each horse and rider, 6 cents for each score of sheep or hogs. It's open weekends 1:30–4:30pm, but you can look in the windows anytime.

Keep going west on Alternate US 40 for 5 more miles to:

10. **Frostburg,** where Mesach Frost built a log cabin for his bride when they got married in 1812. When stagecoaches began running along the new National Road, the Frosts turned their home into an inn named Highland Hall. Later it became the Frost Mansion, a summer retreat for the rich and famous. Get your bearings and information at the **Allegany County Visitor Center** (tel 301/777-5905) in the old Palace Theater on Main St (Alternate US 40). The refurbished railroad depot contains a casual restaurant, and the **Thrasher Carriage Collection,** 19 Depot St (tel 301/689-3380), is next door (turn right at the Exxon Station at the beginning of the hilltop business district). The collection, stored in a renovated warehouse, features late 19th- and early 20th-century horse-drawn carriages, formal closed vehicles, milk wagons, open sleighs, funeral wagons, dogcarts, and more. **Failinger's Gunther Hotel,** on Main St in the center of town, is a grand 1897 four-story landmark offering rooms individually furnished in the Victorian style.

From Frostburg, continue west 17 miles on I-68 or Alternate US 40 to:

11. **Grantsville,** an Amish and Mennonite town which became another stagecoach stop on the National Road. A mile before the village is **Casselman**

Take a Break

Adjoining Casselman Bridge State Park is **Penn Alps,** US 40 (tel 301/895-5985), originally a stagecoach stop built in 1818 and now a nonprofit restaurant and crafts shop marketing the works of more than 2,000 regional artisans (watch some of them at work in Spruce Forest Artisan Village, on the Penn Alps grounds). You will have to ask to see the original log cabin, which now is a private dining room in the center of the complex. The restaurant offers standard American fare and Pennsylvania Dutch–style meals. Main courses cost $8–$11.

If you don't dine at Penn Alps, drive a mile into Grantsville to the **Casselman Restaurant and Motel** (tel 301/895-5266), a Federal-style house built in 1824 as another stagecoach way-station. From the front porch, the central hallway leads past living rooms furnished with antiques. The dining room's bill of fare includes grilled ham, fried chicken, baked fish, and that local delicacy, breaded beef brains. Main courses cost $7–$9.

Bridge State Park, where you can still see the single-span structure that carried the National Road and US 40 over the Casselman River from 1812 until 1933. In a setting more like medieval England than western Maryland, this old stone bridge provides an excellent photo opportunity.

From Grantsville, continue west 6 miles on I-68 or Alternate US 40 to Keyser's Ridge (exit 14). Here you'll leave the National Road, turn left on US 219, and drive 15 miles south to:

12. **Deep Creek Lake,** a man-made body of water surrounded by a major resort area offering a multitude of sporting activities year-round, including wintertime skiing at **Wisp Resort** on Marsh Hill Rd. Turn left before the bridge for **Deep Creek Lake State Park,** or keep going across the bridge and get your bearings at a lakeside information office (tel 301/387-6171), which is open mid-May to mid-October, Sunday–Thursday, 10am–6pm; Friday–Saturday until 8pm. You can easily spend a week in the area exploring the lake and the mountains, which include Backbone Ridge, the highest point in Maryland at 3,360 feet. Several other state parks and lakes are within short drives. The town of Oakland, 10 miles south on US 219, was a favorite summer retreat of US presidents and other notables in Victorian times.

From Deep Creek Lake, you can take US 219 south 34 miles into Canaan Valley and follow the driving tour "New River Gorge to the Highlands" (see the West Virginia chapter) in reverse.

Maryland Listings

Aberdeen

Located northeast of Baltimore, near Chesapeake Bay and the Susquehanna River. Home of Aberdeen Proving Grounds, the US Army's ammunition and weapons test facility.

HOTELS 🏨

☰☰☰ Four Points Hospitality Way

980 Hospitality Way, 21001; tel 410/273-6300 or toll free 800/346-3612; fax 410/575-7195. Exit 85 off I-95. A clean, pleasant place to stay. **Rooms:** 136 rms and stes. Executive level. CI 2pm/CO 11am. Nonsmoking rms avail. **Amenities:** 🛎 🕭 A/C, cable TV w/movies, refrig. Some units w/minibars. **Services:** ✗ ⊠ ⇦ ⇦ Secretarial services include fax, photocopying, overnight mail. **Facilities:** 🔥 ⬛ ⬛ ⬛ ⬛ 1 restaurant, 2 bars (1 w/entertainment), racquetball, sauna, whirlpool, washer/dryer. Free use of adjacent health club. **Rates:** Peak (May–Aug) $99–$109 S; $99–$119 D; $154–$164 ste. Extra person $10. Children under age 18 stay free. Lower rates off-season. Parking: Outdoor, free. AE, CB, DC, DISC, EC, MC, V.

☰☰ Holiday Inn Chesapeake House

1007 Beards Hill Rd, 21001; tel 410/272-8100 or toll free 800/HOLIDAY; fax 410/272-1714. Exit 85 off I-95. Acceptable, basic accommodations suitable for family or business travel. **Rooms:** 122 rms, stes, and effic. Executive level. CI 2pm/CO noon. Nonsmoking rms avail. **Amenities:** 🛎 🕭 A/C, cable TV w/movies. Some units w/terraces. **Services:** ✗ ⊠ ⇦ ⇦ Children's program. **Facilities:** 🔥 ⬛ 🕭 1 restaurant, 1 bar, whirlpool, washer/dryer. Indoor pool has pleasant garden and sunning area adjacent. **Rates:** Peak (May–Sept) $94 S or D; $125 ste; $99 effic. Extra person $10. Children under age 18 stay free. Lower rates off-season. Parking: Outdoor, free. AE, CB, DC, DISC, MC, V.

Annapolis

Founded in 1650 on the Severn River, a tributary of Chesapeake Bay, Annapolis just finished a year-long celebration of its 300th anniversary as the Maryland state capital. The self-proclaimed sailing capital of the country, it is the site of the US Naval Academy and a harbor area brimming with opportunities for water tours and seafood, souvenirs and galleries. **Information:** Greater Annapolis Chamber of Commerce, One Annapolis St, Annapolis, 21401 (tel 410/268-7676).

HOTELS 🏨

☰☰☰☰ Annapolis Marriott Waterfront

80 Compromise St, 21401; tel 410/268-7555 or toll free 800/336-0072; fax 410/269-5864. Exit US 50 at Rowe Blvd. Within easy walking distance of the historic district and marinas, this full-service waterfront hotel has outstanding views of Annapolis harbor and the Severn River. **Rooms:** 150 rms and stes. CI 4pm/CO 11am. No smoking. **Amenities:** 🛎 🕭 🥂 A/C, cable TV w/movies, refrig, bathrobes. Some units w/terraces, some w/whirlpools. Irons and ironing boards in all rooms. **Services:** ✗ ⊡ VP 🚗 ⊠ ⇦ Babysitting. **Facilities:** 🕭 ⬛ 🕭 1 restaurant, 1 bar (w/entertainment). **Rates:** Peak (Apr–Oct) $154–$220 S or D; $325 ste. Min stay special events. Lower rates off-season. MAP rates avail. Parking: Indoor/outdoor, $10/day. AE, CB, DC, DISC, MC, V.

☰☰☰ Courtyard by Marriott

2559 Riva Rd, 21401 (Parole); tel 410/266-1555 or toll free 800/321-2211; fax 410/266-6376. Exit 22 off US 50. Turn right on Riva Rd, go ½ mile. A nicely landscaped, attractive hotel arranged around a central courtyard. **Rooms:** 149 rms and stes. CI 3pm/CO noon. No smoking. **Amenities:** 🛎 🕭 🖬 A/C, cable TV w/movies, refrig. All units w/minibars, all w/terraces. Hot water dispenser. **Services:** 🚗 ⊠ ⇦ Car-rental desk, babysitting. **Facilities:** 🕭 ⬛ ⬛ 🕭 1 restaurant, 1 bar, spa, whirlpool, washer/dryer. Restaurant serves breakfast and lunch only. Very nice pool area with solarium. **Rates:** Peak (May–Oct) $79–$99 S; $89–$109 D; $119 ste. Extra person $10. Min stay special events. Lower rates off-season. Parking: Outdoor, free. Rates vary with advance reservation. AE, DC, DISC, MC, V.

☰☰☰☰ Loews Annapolis Hotel

126 West St, 21401 (West Annapolis); tel 410/263-7777 or toll free 800/526-2593; fax 410/268-7777. Exit US 50/301 at Rowe Blvd. This modern, full-service hotel is a few blocks

from the center of historic Annapolis. **Rooms:** 217 rms and stes. Executive level. CI 3pm/CO noon. Nonsmoking rms avail. Top two floors have luxury rooms, with higher level of services and concierge-directed lounge. **Amenities:** 🛅 🗄 🖭 🗞 A/C, cable TV w/movies, refrig. All units w/minibars, some w/terraces. Irons and ironing boards in all rooms. **Services:** ✗ ☎ 📼 🚐 🗲 🗘 🗑 Car-rental desk, babysitting. Van services to areas within the city. 24-hour security guard and cameras. **Facilities:** 🖳 🏧 🖳 ⅙ 1 restaurant (*see* "Restaurants" below), 1 bar (w/entertainment), games rm, beauty salon. Extensive meeting facilities include a lovely atrium area. Aerobics, racquetball, tanning salon, masseurs, swimming at nearby facilities for an additional fee. **Rates:** $135–$155 S; $145–$165 D; $175–$300 ste. Extra person $15. Children under age 18 stay free. Min stay special events. Parking: Indoor/outdoor, $7–$10/day. Children under 5 dine free. AE, CB, DC, DISC, JCB, MC, V.

⧉⧉⧉ Wyndham Garden Hotel

173 Jennifer Rd, 21401; tel 410/266-3131 or toll free 800/351-9209. Exit 23 off US 50. Across from Annapolis Mall. An attractive, comfortable hotel conveniently located adjacent to a shopping mall and restaurants. **Rooms:** 197 rms and stes. CI 4pm/CO noon. No smoking. **Amenities:** 🛅 🗄 A/C, satel TV w/movies. **Services:** ✗ 📼 🚐 🗲 🗘 Babysitting. **Facilities:** 🏧 🖳 🏧 🖳 ⅙ 1 restaurant, 1 bar (w/entertainment), spa, sauna, whirlpool. Extensive meeting-room space in several areas, totaling 8,500 square feet, has flexible floor plan for groups of various sizes. Business center is well equipped. **Rates:** Peak (Apr–Nov) $69–$129 S; $79–$149 D; $125 ste. Extra person $10. Children under age 16 stay free. Lower rates off-season. AP rates avail. Parking: Outdoor, free. AE, CB, DC, DISC, MC, V.

MOTELS

⧉⧉⧉ Annapolis Holiday Inn

210 Holiday Court, 21401; tel 410/224-3150 or toll free 800/465-4329; fax 410/224-3413. Exit 22 off US 50. The largest lodging in Annapolis enjoys a suburban location near shopping centers and restaurants. **Rooms:** 220 rms and stes. CI 4pm/CO noon. Nonsmoking rms avail. Half have king beds, half have two doubles. A bridal suite and a three-bedroom suite are also available. **Amenities:** 🛅 🗄 A/C, cable TV w/movies, dataport. **Services:** ✗ 🚐 🗲 🗘 🗑 **Facilities:** 🏧 🖳 ⅙ 1 restaurant, 1 bar, volleyball, washer/dryer. Golf, swimming, and tennis are nearby. **Rates:** Peak (May–Oct) $89–$119 S; $99–$129 D; $135–$175 ste. Extra person $10. Children under age 19 stay free. Min stay special events. Lower rates off-season. Parking: Outdoor, free. AE, CB, DC, DISC, JCB, MC, V.

⧉⧉ Comfort Inn

76 Old Mill Bottom Rd N, 21401; tel 410/757-8500 or toll free 800/228-5150; fax 410/757-4409. Exit 28 off US 50/301; follow Bay Dale Dr to Old Mill Bottom Rd N. A well-maintained chain motel convenient to downtown Annapolis

and the US Naval Academy, although other nearby establishments have more extensive facilities. **Rooms:** 60 rms. CI 2pm/CO 11am. Nonsmoking rms avail. Rooms are attractively decorated and very clean. **Amenities:** 🛅 🗞 A/C, cable TV w/movies. Some units w/whirlpools. Some rooms have large mirrors. **Services:** 🗘 **Facilities:** 🏧 ⅙ Washer/dryer. **Rates (CP):** Peak (Apr–mid Nov) $70–$120 S; $80–$130 D. Extra person $8. Children under age 18 stay free. Min stay special events. Lower rates off-season. Parking: Outdoor, free. AE, CB, DC, DISC, ER, JCB.

INNS

⧉⧉⧉ Gibson's Lodgings

110 Prince George St, 21401; tel 410/268-5555; fax 410/268-2775. These three historic houses adjacent to the US Naval Academy have a central courtyard. Public rooms are exceptionally attractive. **Rooms:** 21 rms and stes (14 w/shared bath). CI 2pm/CO 11am. No smoking. Professionally decorated and comfortable rooms come in a variety of sizes. **Amenities:** 🗄 A/C. No phone or TV. 1 unit w/terrace. **Services:** 🚐 Wine/sherry served. Large breakfasts, served in the pleasant courtyard, feature home-baked breads. **Facilities:** 🏧 ⅙ Guest lounge w/TV. **Rates (BB):** $58–$98 D w/shared bath, $98–$125 D w/private bath; $110–$125 ste. Extra person $10. Min stay special events. Parking: Outdoor, free. AE, MC, V.

⧉⧉⧉⧉ Historic Inns of Annapolis

16 Church Circle, 21401; tel 410/263-2641 or toll free 800/847-8882; fax 410/268-3813. These four historic properties—the Maryland Inn, Governor Calvert House, State House Inn, and Robert Johnson House—combine great historic charm with modern amenities. All are centrally located in the historic district and close to the waterfront. **Rooms:** 137 rms and stes. CI 3pm/CO noon. Each comfortable room is different, but all have antique furnishings. **Amenities:** 🛅 A/C, cable TV. 1 unit w/terrace, some w/whirlpools. **Services:** ✗ 📼 🚐 🗲 🗘 Twice-daily maid svce, car-rental desk, babysitting. Management is especially helpful with information and arrangements in Annapolis. **Facilities:** 🏧 ⅙ 1 restaurant, 2 bars (1 w/entertainment). Guests may use nearby Marriott Athletic Club for free. **Rates:** Peak (Apr–Oct) Children under age 18 stay free. Lower rates off-season. Parking: Indoor, $10/day. AE, CB, ER, JCB, MC.

⧉⧉ Scotlaur Inn

165 Main St, 21401; tel 410/268-5665. A separate entrance leads to these quiet rooms above Chick and Ruth's Delly. Unsuitable for children under 10. **Rooms:** 10 rms. CI 2pm/CO 11am. No smoking. Although not sumptuous, these "real Annapolis" rooms are comfortable and were tastefully decorated by the same person who did several historic buildings in town. **Amenities:** 🛅 A/C, TV. **Services:** 🗘 **Facilities:** 1 restaurant (*see* "Restaurants" below). A municipal parking garage is behind the building. The deli downstairs serves full meals 24 hours a day. **Rates (BB):** $55–$70 S; $60–$75 D.

Extra person $5. Min stay special events. Higher rates for special events/hols. Parking: Indoor/outdoor, $8/day. MC, V.

RESTAURANTS 🍴

Armadillo's
132 Dock St; tel 410/268-6680. Exit US 50/301 at Rowe Blvd; turn right at Calvert St, go around Church Circle, turn right on Duke of Gloucester and left on Green St; proceed to City Dock. **American/Southwestern.** California meets Maryland in this pleasant, relaxed establishment, whose colonial brick and timber interior is decorated with southwestern art. In keeping with the theme, a variety of fajitas, quesadillas, and other Mexican-American favorites are complemented by a few traditional American beef and seafood dishes. Sunday brunch also has a southwestern orientation. Popular with regular local clientele and tourists alike. **FYI:** Reservations not accepted. Big band/blues/rock. **Open:** Lunch daily 11am–5pm; dinner daily 5pm–midnight; brunch Sun 8:30am–noon. **Prices:** Main courses $10–$17. AE, DISC, MC, V. 🍸 🖼️

Buddy's Crabs and Ribs
100 Main St; tel 410/626-1100. Rowe Blvd exit off US 50/301. **Regional American/Barbecue/Seafood.** With a bright, airy dining room and windows overlooking City Dock, this large establishment is more elegant than most traditional Chesapeake Bay crab houses but is still informal. Steamed blue crabs and barbecued ribs are featured, but other traditional main courses, sandwiches, and light fare are also available. Buffet specials at lunch and dinner. Validated parking. **FYI:** Reservations not accepted. Children's menu. **Open:** Mon–Thurs 11am–11pm, Fri–Sat 11am–midnight, Sun 8:30am–11pm. **Prices:** Main courses $9–$16. AE, CB, DC, DISC, MC, V. 🛥️ 🖼️ 👥 🚗 🔲 ♿

Cafe Normandie
185 Main St; tel 410/263-3382. Exit US 50/301 at Rowe Blvd. **French.** Stucco and oak walls with simple, comfortable seating in booths and small areas that make for easy conversation. Enjoys area reputation as a very good country-French restaurant with a wide selection of wines and interesting daily specials. Competent, Parisian-born owner/chef and friendly staff make French cuisine "user friendly." **FYI:** Reservations recommended. Children's menu. No smoking. **Open:** Breakfast daily 8am–noon; lunch daily 11am–4:45pm; dinner Sun–Thurs 5–10pm, Fri–Sat 5–10:30pm. **Prices:** Main courses $9–$15. AE, MC, V. 🔲 🔲

🌱 Carrol's Creek Restaurant
410 Severn Ave; tel 410/263-8102. Exit US 50/301 at Rowe Blvd. **American/Seafood.** Set among the yachts at a pier in Eastport, the restaurant has big windows with splendid views of Annapolis harbor and the US Naval Academy. On Wednesday night you can watch sailboats departing Annapolis Yacht Club to race. Varnished-wood interior complements the scene. Fresh seafood predominates in specialty dishes. Meat,

fowl, and pasta also offered. Gourmet carryout shop on premises. **FYI:** Reservations recommended. No smoking. **Open:** Lunch Mon–Sat 11:30am–4pm; dinner Mon–Sat 5–10pm, Sun 3–9pm; brunch Sun 10am–2pm. **Prices:** Main courses $13–$24; prix fixe $22. AE, DC, DISC, MC, V. 🛥️ 🖼️ ♿

★ Chick and Ruth's Delly
In Scotlaur Inn, 165 Main St; tel 410/269-6737. Exit US 50/301 at Rowe Blvd; turn right on Calvert St, go around Church Circle, turn right on Duke of Gloucester, left on Green St and left on Main St. **Deli/Jewish.** A New York deli in the heart of Maryland, this bustling, friendly place is one of the last remnants of what Annapolis was like before gentrification began two decades ago. The walls are covered with interesting political and historic photos accumulated over years by owners of this popular meeting spot near the state capitol. Sandwiches are named for local and state politicos. Breakfast available 24 hours. Dinner specials vary. **FYI:** Reservations not accepted. Children's menu. Beer and wine only. No smoking. **Open:** Daily 24 hrs. Closed Dec 25–Jan 2. **Prices:** Main courses $6–$10. No CC. 👥 🍴

The Corinthian
In Loews Annapolis Hotel, 126 West St; tel 410/263-7777. Exit US 50/301 at Rowe Blvd. **New American.** Traditionally furnished with comfortable upholstered chairs, this light and elegant hotel dining room is one of the finest restaurants in town. American seafood, beef, lamb, pork, and fowl are given a contemporary touch. **FYI:** Reservations recommended. Children's menu. **Open:** Breakfast Mon–Sun 6:30–11am; lunch Mon–Sat 11am–2pm; dinner daily 5–10pm; brunch Sun 11am–2pm. **Prices:** Main courses $19–$24; prix fixe $26. AE, CB, DC, DISC, MC, V. 🌱 🅥🅟 ♿

Harry Browne's
66 State Circle (State Circle); tel 410/263-4332. Exit US 50/301 at Rowe Blvd. **Continental.** Opposite the Maryland statehouse, this tasteful, elegant establishment features custom serving plates and wine-colored, upholstered chairs. Classical background music. Menu small but interesting, with nice treatment of beef, lamb, seafood, and pasta. Wine list is extensive and the staff knowledgeable. **FYI:** Reservations recommended. Guitar/piano. No smoking. **Open:** Mon–Thurs 4:30–10pm, Fri–Sat 4:30–11pm, Sun 4:30–9pm. **Prices:** Main courses $16–$18. MC, V. 🌱 🛥️ 🅥🅟 ♿

★ Little Campus Inn
61–63 Maryland Ave; tel 410/263-9250. Exit US 50/301 at Rowe Blvd. **American.** Operated by the same family since 1924 and a traditional gathering place for legislators, students, and neighborhood residents. Photos accent brick and wood walls. Moderately priced entrees are traditional American fare with an occasional excursion into regional foods. **FYI:** Reservations accepted. Children's menu. No smoking.

Open: Lunch Mon–Sat 11am–3pm; dinner Mon–Sat 5–10:30pm. **Prices:** Main courses $10–$15. AE, DISC, MC, V.

Middleton Tavern
2 Market Space and Randall St (City Dock); tel 410/263-3323. Exit US 50/301 at Rowe Blvd. **American/Eclectic.** A historic tavern in use since Revolutionary times, the brick and wood rooms are decorated with nautical and outdoor items and attract the sailing crowd as well as landlubber locals and tourists. A varied American menu covers southwestern, seafood, and beef. No guaranteed reservations, but call ahead for preferred seating. Very busy in summer and autumn. **FYI:** Reservations not accepted. Blues/guitar/rock. Children's menu. Dress code. **Open:** Daily 11:30am–midnight. **Prices:** Main courses $14–$18. AE, DC, DISC, MC, V.

♣ **Northwoods Restaurant**
609 Melvin Ave (West Annapolis); tel 410/268-2609. Exit US 50/301 at Rowe Blvd; turn left onto Melvin Ave, go 1 block. **Continental.** Considered by many to be the finest restaurant of its kind in the Annapolis area. Dining room is tasteful and quiet, decorated in pastels. An attractive, fenced deck offers outdoor dining in spring and fall. Fresh ingredients and skillful preparation of seafood, beef, fowl, and pasta. Excellent appetizers. **FYI:** Reservations recommended. Dress code. No smoking. **Open:** Mon–Sat 5:30–10pm, Sun 5–9pm. **Prices:** Main courses $18–$22; prix fixe $24. AE, CB, DC, DISC, MC, V.

O'Leary's Seafood Restaurant
310 3rd St; tel 410/263-0884. Rowe Blvd exit off US 50/301. **Seafood.** Light wood beams in an open, bright room with large windows looking out on marinas but not the water. A changing selection of fresh fish, posted daily on a chalkboard, may be mesquite grilled, sautéed, poached, baked, blackened, or served in a sautéed medley. **FYI:** Reservations recommended. Children's menu. No smoking. **Open:** Mon–Thurs 5:30–10pm, Fri–Sat 5–11pm, Sun 5–10pm. **Prices:** Main courses $14–$22. AE, DC, MC, V.

Red Hot & Blue
200 Old Mill Bottom Rd; tel 410/626-7427. Exit 28 (Bay Dale Dr) off US 50/301. **Barbecue.** The menu claims to have "The best bar-b'que you'll ever have in a building that hasn't already been condemned." A blues theme carries through in the decor, with music on the speakers and posters on the red walls of the windmill-topped building. Memphis-style, slow-smoked pulled pork and excellent ribs (served wet or dry) are the biggest sellers. **FYI:** Reservations not accepted. Children's menu. Additional location: 677 Main St, Laurel (tel 301/953-1943). **Open:** Sun–Thurs 11am–10pm, Fri–Sat 11am–11pm. **Prices:** Main courses $5–$12. AE, MC, V.

Reynolds Tavern
7 Church Circle at Franklin St; tel 410/626-0380. Exit US 50/301 at Rowe Blvd; turn right at College Ave, then proceed to Church Circle. **Regional American.** The National Trust for Historic Preservation owns this faithfully restored 18th-century inn furnished with antiques. American entrees have creative sauces enhanced by fresh herbs grown on the premises. A charming, intimate bar offers darts in an adjoining room; limited lodging is available upstairs. **FYI:** Reservations recommended. Guitar. Dress code. **Open:** Peak (Mem Day–Oct) lunch Mon–Fri 11:30am–2pm, Sat 11:30am–4pm; dinner Mon–Thurs 6–9pm, Fri–Sat 6–10pm, Sun 5:30–8:30pm; brunch Sun 11am–2pm. **Prices:** Main courses $13–$24; prix fixe $20. AE, MC, V.

Riordan's Saloon and Restaurant
26 Market Space; tel 410/263-5449. Exit US 50/301 at Rowe Blvd; turn right on Calvert St, go around Church Circle, turn right on Duke of Gloucester, and left on Green St; proceed to City Dock. **American/Seafood.** Owned by former NBA basketball star Mike Riordan, this pub is adorned with dark wood, brass and antique wall mirrors, and Tiffany-style lamps. Upstairs windows overlook the harbor. A variety of fresh seafood and beef main courses are supplemented by moderately priced lunch and dinner specials. Classic saloon fare. **FYI:** Reservations recommended. Children's menu. Dress code. **Open:** Daily 11am–2am. **Prices:** Main courses $11–$17. AE, DC, DISC, MC, V.

Saigon Palace
In West Annapolis Shopping Center, 609 B Taylor Ave; tel 410/268-4463. **Vietnamese.** A simple room in a very ordinary strip mall, but the food is exceptional and authentic. Diners may choose from a wide range of beef, seafood, and noodle dishes (served mild, medium, or spicy). Piping hot tea, wine, and imported beer are available to wash it all down. **FYI:** Reservations recommended. **Open:** Mon–Thurs 11am–10pm, Sun 5–9pm, Fri–Sat 11am–11pm. **Prices:** Main courses $9–$18. AE, MC, V.

Treaty of Paris Restaurant
16 Church Circle, at Duke of Gloucester St; tel 410/263-2641. Exit US 50/301 at Rowe Blvd; turn right at College Ave, proceed to Church Circle. **New American.** Situated downstairs in an 18th-century building, this dining room is authentic and comfortable. Fresh preparation and style of American foods stressed. Meals can be made from extensive appetizer listings. Light fare offered in tavern. Desserts are made in-house. Free valet parking at night. Jazz offered in the King of France Tavern five nights a week. **FYI:** Reservations recommended. Jazz. Jacket required. **Open:** Breakfast Mon–Fri 7–10:45am, Sat 8–10:45am, Sun 8–9am; lunch daily 11:30am–2:30pm; dinner Mon–Thurs 6–10pm, Fri–Sat 6–11pm, Sun 5:30–9:30pm; brunch Sun 10am–2pm. **Prices:** Main courses $18–$27; prix fixe $20–$25. AE, DC, MC, V.

ATTRACTIONS 📷

Maryland State House
State Circle; tel 410/974-3400. Built in 1772, this is the oldest US state capitol in continuous legislative use and was the setting for the ratification of the Treaty of Paris, which ended the Revolutionary War. The building's dome, the largest of its kind constructed entirely of wood, is made of cypress beams and is held together by wooden pegs. Exhibits depict life in Annapolis during colonial times. **Open:** Daily 9am–5pm. **Free**

US Naval Academy
King George and Randall Sts; tel 410/263-6933. Founded in 1845, the US Navy's undergraduate professional college—and a National Historic Site—is spread over 30 acres along the Severn River. Visitors can explore the grounds and tour the chapel and crypt of John Paul Jones as well as the Preble Hall Museum, which exhibits nautical relics, paintings, ship models, and other historic items relating to the navy's role in wars, global exploration, and space. **Open:** Daily 9am–5pm. **Free**

Historic Annapolis Foundation Museum Store & Welcome Center
77 Main St; tel 410/268-5576. Distinctive reproductions, pottery, jewelry, hand-blown glassware, books, among other products reflecting the architectural, social, cultural, and maritime histtory of Annapolis. Two different guided walking tours start here. **Open:** Mon–Sat 10am–5pm, Sun noon–5pm. **Free**

William Paca House and Garden
186 Prince George St; tel 410/263-5553. Built in 1763, this was the home of William Paca, a signer of the Declaration of Independence and a governor of Maryland during the Revolutionary period. The five-part Georgian residence overlooks a two-acre pleasure garden (with a Chinese Chippendale bridge), five terraces, a fish-shaped pond, and a wilderness garden. **Open:** Peak (Mar–Dec) Mon–Sat 10am–4pm, Sun noon–4pm. Reduced hours off-season. **$$$**

Hammond-Harwood House
19 Maryland Ave; tel 410/269-1714. This 1774 house is one of the finest examples of Georgian architecture in the United States, famous for its center doorway of tall Ionic columns. The interior is a showcase of decorative ornamentation and wood carvings. **Open:** Mon–Sat 10am–4pm, Sun noon–4pm. **$$**

Banneker-Douglass Museum
84 Franklin St; tel 410/974-2893. Named after two former local residents, Benjamin Banneker and Frederick Douglass, the museum presents arts and crafts, exhibits, lectures, and films, all designed to portray the historical life and cultural experiences of African Americans in Maryland. **Open:** Tues–Fri 10am–3pm, Sat noon–4pm. **Free**

Charles Carroll House
107 Duke of Gloucester St; tel 410/269-1737. Built in 1721 and enlarged in 1770, it is the birthplace and dwelling of Charles Carroll of Carrollton, the only Roman Catholic to sign the Declaration of Independence. Visitors can tour the house, the 18th-century terraced boxwood gardens, and the 19th-century wine cellar. **Open:** Fri noon–4pm, Sat 10am–2pm. **$$**

Baltimore

See also Baltimore-Washington Int'l Airport, Pikesville, Towson

Founded in 1729, Baltimore's rich industrial and maritime history is complemented by a growing emphasis on tourism and commerce, with historic roots evident in its neighborhoods and museums. Harborplace draws five million visitors a year to its shops, restaurants, amphitheater, and the National Aquarium. Fort McHenry, whose brave defense in the War of 1812 inspired Francis Scott Key to write "The Star-Spangled Banner," is also located here. **Information:** Baltimore Area Convention and Visitors Bureau, 100 Light St, 12th fl, Baltimore, 21202 (tel 410/659-7300 or toll free 800/343-3468).

PUBLIC TRANSPORTATION
Baltimore's **Mass Transit Administration (MTA)** operates a 27-mile system of above-ground rail lines, a subway connecting the downtown area with the northwest suburbs, and a network of buses. The base fare for each is $1.25. For more information, call the MTA at 410/539-5000 or toll free 800/543-9809.

HOTELS 🏨

☰☰☰ Baltimore Marriott Inner Harbor
110 S Eutaw St, at Lombard St, 21202 (Inner Harbor); tel 410/962-0202 or toll free 800/228-9290. Exit I-95 at I-395 S, turn left on Lombard St. Across street from Oriole Park at Camden Yards and one block from the Convention Center, this well-kept hotel has attractive rooms and public spaces. **Rooms:** 525 rms and stes. Executive level. CI 4pm/CO noon. Nonsmoking rms avail. **Amenities:** 🛁 🌣 🍴 A/C, cable TV w/movies, dataport, voice mail. Some units w/whirlpools. **Services:** ✕ ⌨ 🚗 🖼 ⇄ 🐕 Car-rental desk, masseur, babysitting. Friendly, accommodating staff. **Facilities:** 🏋 🍽 📞 🖥 ♿ 1 restaurant, 1 bar (w/entertainment), sauna, whirlpool. **Rates:** Peak (Mar–Nov) $186 S; $201 D; $179–$450 ste. Extra person $20. Children under age 17 stay free. Min stay special events. Lower rates off-season. Parking: Indoor, $8/day. AE, CB, DC, DISC, JCB, MC, V.

☰☰☰ Brookshire Inner Harbor Suite Hotel
120 E Lombard St, 21202 (Inner Harbor); tel 410/625-1300 or toll free 800/647-0013; fax 410/625-0912. An all-suites hotel conveniently located one block from waterfront.

Rooms: 90 stes. Executive level. CI 3pm/CO noon. Nonsmoking rms avail. Two-room suites are sizable, with kitchenettes and snack bars. Units facing Lombard St have water views but get more street noise than others. **Amenities:** ☎ ⓧ 🖵 A/C, cable TV, refrig. All units w/minibars. **Services:** ✗ VP 🚐 🛇 ⌣ Twice-daily maid svce, babysitting. **Facilities:** 🔲 135 ⚹ 1 restaurant (bkfst and dinner only), 1 bar. Rooftop restaurant. Guests can use complete health club five blocks away. **Rates:** $165–$218 ste. Extra person $20. Children under age 18 stay free. Parking: Indoor, $10/day. AARP discounts avail. AE, CB, DC, DISC, JCB, MC, V.

UNRATED Clarion Hotel

612 Cathedral St, 21202 (Mount Vernon); tel 410/727-7101 or toll free 800/CLARION; fax 410/789-3312. Exit I-95 at I-395; follow Howard St to Monument St, turn right, then right on Cathedral St. A classic, European-style hotel with marble staircase from the lobby and Baccarat crystal chandelier. Quiet and elegant. **Rooms:** 104 rms and stes. CI 3pm/CO noon. Nonsmoking rms avail. **Amenities:** ☎ ⓧ 🖵 ⌱ A/C, cable TV w/movies, refrig. All units w/minibars, some w/whirlpools. Private Reserve rooms have bathrobes, irons, and ironing boards. Some have wet bars. **Services:** ✗ ⚷ VP 🚐 🛇 ⌣ Car-rental desk, babysitting. Van to local attractions. Complimentary newspapers. **Facilities:** 🔲 150 🖳 ⚹ 1 restaurant. Reading room. Use of local health club. **Rates:** $119–$149 S or D; $129–$159 ste. Extra person $20. Children under age 18 stay free. MAP rates avail. Parking: Indoor, $10/day. AE, CB, DC, DISC, EC, ER, JCB, MC, V.

⊨⊨⊨⊨ Cross Keys Inn

5100 Falls Rd, 21210 (Village of Cross Keys); tel 410/532-6900 or toll free 800/532-KEYS; fax 410/532-2403. Exit 10A off I-83. Go east on Northern Pkwy, then south on Falls Rd for ½ mi. Wonderful, resort-like accommodations and facilities in a huge complex, including a large shopping court and garden plaza. **Rooms:** 148 rms and stes. CI 3pm/CO 11am. No smoking. Lovely, elegant, and spacious rooms. Top-floor units have cathedral ceilings. **Amenities:** ☎ ⓧ 🖵 A/C, cable TV w/movies. Some units w/terraces. **Services:** ✗ 🛇 ⌣ Shuttle bus, newspapers. Business services including typing. **Facilities:** 🔲 🛀 200 🖳 ⚹ 1 restaurant, 1 bar, sauna, whirlpool. Gorgeous pool surrounded by an intimate garden. **Rates:** $85–$150 S or D; $150–$425 ste. Extra person $10. Children under age 16 stay free. Min stay special events. MAP rates avail. Parking: Indoor/outdoor, free. AE, CB, DC, MC, V.

⊨⊨⊨ Days Inn Inner Harbor

100 Hopkins Place at Lombard St, 21202 (Inner Harbor); tel 410/576-1000 or toll free 800/329-7466; fax 410/576-9437. Exit I-95 at I-395. One of the better hotels in this chain, this one is convenient to Oriole Park at Camden Yards and the Convention Center. **Rooms:** 250 rms and stes. Executive level. CI 3pm/CO noon. Nonsmoking rms avail. Suites are actually large rooms with alcoves. **Amenities:** ☎ ⓧ A/C, cable TV w/movies, voice mail, in-rm safe. Some rooms and all

suites have refrigerators. **Services:** ✗ ⚷ 🚐 🛇 ⌣ ⌣ Babysitting. **Facilities:** 🔲 100 ⚹ 1 restaurant, 1 bar, washer/dryer. Nice pool courtyard with adjacent terrace restaurant. Guest privileges at nearby health club. Parking in adjacent garage. **Rates:** Peak (Mar–Oct) $105 S; $115 D; $125 ste. Extra person $10. Children under age 16 stay free. Min stay special events. Lower rates off-season. Parking: Indoor, $8/day. AE, CB, DC, DISC, ER, JCB, MC, V.

⊨⊨⊨⊨ DoubleTree Inn at the Colonnade

4 W University Pkwy, 21218; tel 410/235-5400 or toll free 800/222-TREE; fax 410/235-5572. Just west of Charles St. Entry to rotunda-like lobby is actually through a colonnade at this very elegant, European-style hotel with classical Roman decor. Adjacent to Johns Hopkins University's Homewood Campus. **Rooms:** 125 rms and stes. CI 3pm/CO noon. Nonsmoking rms avail. Spacious and comfortable. **Amenities:** ☎ ⓧ A/C, cable TV, voice mail, bathrobes. Some units w/terraces, some w/whirlpools. **Services:** ✗ VP 🛇 ⌣ ⌣ Masseur. **Facilities:** 🔲 🛀 410 ⚹ 1 restaurant, 1 bar, whirlpool, beauty salon. Pool has domed glass roof, Italian marble, Tivoli lights. Polo Grill is award-winning restaurant. **Rates:** Peak (Apr–June/Sept–Nov) $119–$159 S or D; $225 ste. Extra person $15. Children under age 18 stay free. Min stay special events. Lower rates off-season. Parking: Indoor, $7–$9/day. AE, CB, DC, DISC, EC, ER, JCB, MC, V.

⊨⊨⊨⊨ Harbor Court Hotel

550 Light St, 21202 (Inner Harbor); tel 410/234-0550 or toll free 800/824-0076; fax 410/659-5925. Exit 53 off I-95. Turn right on Conway St, then right on Light St; go 1½ blocks. A modern rendition of a classic hotel. Public spaces are quietly refined, with oil paintings, Oriental carpets, and marble floors. Well maintained and attractively decorated. **Rooms:** 203 rms and stes. CI 3pm/CO noon. No smoking. **Amenities:** ☎ ⓧ ⌱ A/C, satel TV w/movies, refrig, bathrobes. All units w/minibars. **Services:** ⟦⟧ ⚷ VP 🚐 🛇 ⌣ Twice-daily maid svce, car-rental desk, masseur, babysitting. Friendly, helpful staff. **Facilities:** 🔲 🏌 🏐 🛀 200 🖳 ⚹ 2 restaurants (see "Restaurants" below), 1 bar (w/entertainment), racquetball, spa, sauna, whirlpool, beauty salon. Exceptional fitness center, with tanning, massage, and many machines. Lovely rooftop gardens and tennis court. **Rates:** $160–$220 S or D; $300–$650 ste. Extra person $15. Children under age 18 stay free. MAP rates avail. Parking: Indoor, $10–$12/day. Weekend family rates avail. AE, CB, DC, DISC, MC, V.

⊨⊨⊨ Holiday Inn Inner Harbor

301 W Lombard St, 21201 (Inner Harbor); tel 410/685-3500 or toll free 800/465-4329; fax 410/727-6169. Exit I-95 at I-395; turn left onto Lombard St. A $6.5 million renovation in 1993 brought this downtown hotel up to date. **Rooms:** 375 rms. CI 3pm/CO noon. Nonsmoking rms avail. Rooms are attractive and in good condition. **Amenities:** ☎ ⓧ A/C, satel TV w/movies, dataport. Some units w/terraces, 1 w/whirlpool. **Services:** ✗ 🛇 ⌣ ⌣ Babysitting. **Facilities:** 🔲

[icons] [550] & 1 restaurant, 1 bar, sauna, washer/dryer. **Rates:** Peak (Mar–Nov) $125 S or D. Children under age 18 stay free. Min stay special events. Lower rates off-season. Parking: Indoor/outdoor, $5/day. AE, CB, DC, DISC, MC, V.

Hyatt Regency Baltimore

300 Light St, 21202 (Inner Harbor); tel 410/528-1234 or toll free 800/233-1234; fax 410/685-3362. Exit 53 off I-95, at Pratt St. A large hotel catering to conventioneers and other business travelers as well as families and tourists, this building has expansive public areas and dramatic skylights. **Rooms:** 487 rms and stes. Executive level. CI 3pm/CO noon. Nonsmoking rms avail. Standard, pleasant rooms. Views from most, either of city or harbor. **Amenities:** [icons] A/C, cable TV w/movies, refrig, dataport, voice mail. All units w/minibars. **Services:** [icons] Masseur, children's program, babysitting. **Facilities:** [icons] 2 restaurants (see "Restaurants" below), 3 bars (2 w/entertainment), basketball, spa, sauna, whirlpool. Rooftop restaurant has excellent harbor view, as does nicely landscaped rooftop pool. Large fitness center opens onto rooftop tennis courts. **Rates:** Peak (Mar–Nov) $155–$210 S; $180–$235 D; $300–$450 ste. Extra person $25. Children under age 21 stay free. Min stay wknds and special events. Lower rates off-season. Parking: Indoor, $10/day. AE, CB, DC, DISC, MC, V.

Omni Inner Harbor Hotel

101 W Fayette St, at Baltimore St, 21201; tel 410/752-1100 or toll free 800/843-6664; fax 410/625-3805. Exit I-95 at I-395. This large, modern, high-rise hotel in the heart of the business district was refurbished in 1994. Popular for conventions. **Rooms:** 703 rms, stes, and effic. Executive level. CI 3pm/CO noon. Nonsmoking rms avail. **Amenities:** [icons] A/C, cable TV w/movies, refrig. Some units w/minibars, some w/whirlpools. Club floor rooms have bathrobes. **Services:** [icons] Car-rental desk, babysitting. Attentive, helpful staff. **Facilities:** [icons] 2 restaurants, 1 bar (w/entertainment), games rm. Health club across street has racquetball, sauna, aerobics, lap pool. **Rates:** Peak (Mar 15–June 14/July 15–Nov 15) $150 S; $175 D; $260 ste; $310 effic. Extra person $20. Children under age 18 stay free. Min stay special events. Lower rates off-season. MAP rates avail. Parking: Indoor, $9–$14/day. AE, CB, DC, DISC, MC, V.

Radisson Plaza Lord Baltimore

20 W Baltimore St, 21202 (Inner Harbor); tel 410/539-8400 or toll free 800/333-3333; fax 410/625-1060. Exit I-95 at I-395; go 3 blocks to Baltimore St; turn right. The Lord Baltimore is a grand old hotel built in 1928, with high, decorated ceilings in the lobby, massive stairway rails, brass trim. Pianist often performs in main lobby. **Rooms:** 419 rms, stes, and effic. Executive level. CI 3pm/CO noon. Nonsmoking rms avail. Rooms vary in size. Some are rather small. **Amenities:** [icons] A/C, cable TV w/movies, dataport, voice mail. Some units w/whirlpools. **Services:** [icons] Car-rental desk, masseur, babysitting. Good service.

Facilities: [icons] [800] & 1 restaurant, 1 bar (w/entertainment), spa, sauna, whirlpool, washer/dryer. The lounge has jazz. Deli, gift shop. **Rates:** Peak (Apr–Thanksgiving) $139–$159 S; $159–$179 D; $250–$300 ste; $600–$800 effic. Extra person $15. Children under age 18 stay free. Min stay special events. Lower rates off-season. MAP rates avail. Parking: Indoor, $12/day. AE, CB, DC, DISC, EC, ER, JCB, MC, V.

Renaissance Harborplace Hotel

202 E Pratt St, 21202 (Inner Harbor); tel 410/547-1200 or toll free 800/468-3571; fax 410/783-9676. Exit 53 off I-95. Follow I-95 to Pratt St, turn right, then left on South St. The largest hotel on scenic Inner Harbor, this is a comfortable, modern hotel with traditional charm and service. **Rooms:** 622 rms and stes. Executive level. CI 3pm/CO noon. Nonsmoking rms avail. Some rooms have harbor views. **Amenities:** [icons] A/C, cable TV w/movies, refrig, dataport. All units w/minibars, some w/whirlpools. **Services:** [icons] Car-rental desk, babysitting. Wake up includes newspaper and coffee or tea. USAir ticket office in hotel. **Facilities:** [icons] [1400] & 1 restaurant, 2 bars (1 w/entertainment), spa, sauna, whirlpool. Pretty rooftop courtyard adjacent to pool and fitness center. Gallery shopping arcade within building. Arrangement with nearby athletic club for racquetball, squash, etc. **Rates:** Peak (Apr–Nov) $165–$250 S or D; $300–$1,200 ste. Extra person $20. Children under age 18 stay free. Min stay special events. Lower rates off-season. Parking: Indoor, $10/day. AE, CB, DC, DISC, JCB, MC, V.

Sheraton Inner Harbor

300 S Charles St, 21202; tel 410/962-8300 or toll free 800/325-3535; fax 410/962-8211. Exit 53 off I-95, at Conway St. This large hotel is the official Baltimore Orioles headquarters. Central to Baltimore attractions, including Camden Yards ballpark. Skywalks lead to Inner Harbor, Convention Center. **Rooms:** 337 rms and stes. Executive level. CI 3pm/CO noon. Nonsmoking rms avail. **Amenities:** [icons] A/C, cable TV w/movies, refrig, dataport, voice mail, bathrobes. All units w/minibars. Nintendo games, irons and ironing boards. **Services:** [icons] Car-rental desk, babysitting. **Facilities:** [icons] [1000] & 1 restaurant, 2 bars (1 w/entertainment), games rm, spa, sauna. **Rates:** Peak (Apr–Nov) $155–$170 S or D; $275–$575 ste. Extra person $15. Children under age 18 stay free. Lower rates off-season. Parking: Indoor, $10/day. AE, CB, DC, DISC, EC, ER, MC, V.

The Tremont Hotel

8 E Pleasant St, 21202 (Mount Vernon); tel 410/576-1200 or toll free 800/873-6668; fax 410/244-1154. Off I-95, follow I-395 to Conway St, turn right, then left on Charles St and right on Pleasant St. Lots of repeat business due to comfortable accommodations, helpful staff, and a quiet location. **Rooms:** 60 rms and effic. CI 3pm/CO noon. Nonsmoking rms avail. Spacious, quiet units are converted apartments

with full kitchens. **Amenities:** ▨ ⏾ ▣ A/C, cable TV w/movies, refrig. TV in both living room and bedroom. **Services:** ✗ VP 🚍 ⬛ ↵ ⬗ Car-rental desk, babysitting. Highly personalized service. **Facilities:** 🔲 1 restaurant, 1 bar. Access to pool, fitness center at both Tremont Plaza Hotel and, for a fee, major fitness center nearby. **Rates:** Peak (Apr–June/Sept–Nov) $135 S or D; $105 effic. Extra person $20. Children under age 16 stay free. Lower rates off-season. Parking: Outdoor, $8.50/day. AE, DC, DISC, MC, V.

☰☰☰ Tremont Plaza Hotel

222 St Paul Place, at Saratoga St, 21202; tel 410/727-2222 or toll free 800/873-6668; fax 410/244-1154. Exit I-95 at I-395 N. Formerly an apartment building, this hotel is narrow but quite tall, so upper floors are very quiet. **Rooms:** 230 effic. CI 3pm/CO noon. Nonsmoking rms avail. Units, all with full kitchens, are very spacious, quiet, and comfortable for extended stays. **Amenities:** ▨ ⏾ ▣ A/C, cable TV w/movies, refrig. **Services:** ✗ VP 🚍 ⬛ ↵ ⬗ Car-rental desk, babysitting. High standard of service. **Facilities:** 🔲 🍴 🔲 ♿ 1 restaurant, 1 bar, games rm, sauna, washer/dryer. Popular deli in hotel. Lounge decorated with photos of celebrities who have stayed here. Access to fitness center one block away for a fee. **Rates:** Peak (Apr–June/Sept–Nov) $115 effic. Extra person $20. Children under age 16 stay free. Lower rates off-season. Parking: Indoor, $8.50/day. AE, DISC, MC, V.

MOTELS

☰☰☰ Best Western Baltimore East

5625 O'Donnell St, 21224; tel 410/633-9500 or toll free 800/528-1234; fax 410/633-4314. Exit 57 off I-95. Completely renovated in 1994. Attractive motel adjacent to Peter Pan/Trailways bus terminal. **Rooms:** 173 rms. Executive level. CI 3pm/CO noon. Nonsmoking rms avail. Pleasant, bright, spacious. **Amenities:** ▨ ⏾ A/C, cable TV w/movies. Some units w/whirlpools. **Services:** ✗ 🚍 ⬛ ↵ Babysitting. **Facilities:** 🔲 🍴 🔲 🖥 ♿ 1 restaurant, 2 bars (1 w/entertainment), games rm, spa, sauna, whirlpool, washer/dryer. Indoor pool. Dinner theater with Hawaiian show. Country-and-western lounge with line dancing and band. **Rates:** $79–$129 S or D. Extra person $10. Children under age 18 stay free. MAP rates avail. Parking: Outdoor, free. AE, DC, DISC, MC, V.

☰☰☰ Biltmore Suites

205 W Madison St, 21201 (Mount Vernon); tel 410/728-6550 or toll free 800/868-5064; fax 410/728-5829. Between Park and Howard Sts. This lovely brick motel on a quiet, tree-lined side street has provided comfortable accommodations since 1890. Separating the two main buildings, a charming courtyard sports willow trees, small bubbling pond, wrought-iron tables and chairs. Common areas and rooms are sprinkled with antiques and decorated in rose and cream. Overlooking Madison St through double-hung windows, lobby displays etched-glass doors and intricate woodwork on

stairway. **Rooms:** 24 rms, stes, and effic. CI 2pm/CO 11am. Nonsmoking rms avail. Most sizable units are apartment-like, with sitting rooms and kitchenettes. Wooden armoires double as TV cabinets and closets. **Amenities:** ▨ ⏾ ▣ A/C, cable TV, refrig. Some units w/terraces. **Services:** ✗ 🔑 🚍 ⬛ ↵ ⬗ Evening wine-and-cheese receptions in lobby. Staff members are extremely warm and helpful. **Facilities:** 🔲 🖥 ♿ Main building is not readily accessible to guests with disabilities, but other facilities are available to them. **Rates (CP):** Peak (Mar–Sept) $90–$115 S or D; $115–$125 ste; $95–$115 effic. Extra person $10. Children under age 18 stay free. Min stay. Lower rates off-season. Parking: Indoor, $2.50/day. AE, CB, DC, DISC, MC, V.

☰☰ Holiday Inn Security/Belmont

1800 Belmont Ave, 21244; tel 410/265-1400 or toll free 800/465-4329; fax 410/281-9569. 12 mi W of Inner Harbor. Exit 17 off I-695. An older, well-maintained motel convenient to the Baltimore Beltway and a large shopping mall. Popular for family reunions. **Rooms:** 136 rms. CI 2pm/CO noon. Nonsmoking rms avail. **Amenities:** ▨ ⏾ A/C, satel TV w/movies. **Services:** ✗ ⬛ ↵ ⬗ **Facilities:** 🔲 🔲 ♿ 1 restaurant, 1 bar, washer/dryer. **Rates:** $69–$75 S or D. Children under age 12 stay free. MAP rates avail. Parking: Outdoor, free. Group rates. AE, CB, DC, DISC, MC, V.

INNS

☰☰☰ Admiral Fell Inn

888 S Broadway, 21202 (Fells Point); tel 410/522-7377 or toll free 800/292-4667; fax 410/522-0707. With completion of its 1994 restoration, this lovely inn in historic Fells Point district should be more popular than ever. It has a quiet, comfortable, friendly atmosphere and Queen Anne reproduction furnishings. **Rooms:** 50 rms and stes. CI 3pm/CO noon. Nonsmoking rms avail. Rooms vary in shape and size, but all have period furnishings and modern conveniences. Most have canopy beds. **Amenities:** ▨ A/C, cable TV. 1 unit w/fireplace, some w/whirlpools. **Services:** VP ⬛ ↵ ⬗ Car-rental desk, afternoon tea served. Pets only within guidelines. Van service to athletic club. **Facilities:** 🔲 ♿ 3 restaurants, 2 bars, guest lounge. **Rates (CP):** $175–$185 D; $265 ste. Extra person $15. Children under age 16 stay free. MAP rates avail. Parking: Outdoor, free. AE, DC, MC, V.

☰☰☰ The Inn at Henderson's Wharf

1000 Fell St, 23231 (Fells Point); tel 410/522-7777 or toll free 800/522-2088; fax 410/522-7087. Only the exterior walls are old, but this traditionally furnished, modern, comfortable inn is faithful to its heritage in mood. Outstanding decor in public areas. **Rooms:** 38 rms. CI 3pm/CO noon. Nonsmoking rms avail. Bright and spacious rooms, with nice views of the Inner Harbor or beautiful, well-tended central courtyard. **Amenities:** ▨ ⏾ A/C, satel TV w/movies. **Services:** ✗ 🚍 ⬛ ↵ Car-rental desk, masseur, babysitting, afternoon tea served. Very accommodating staff will provide concierge-level services. **Facilities:** 🍴 🔲 ♿ Washer/dryer, guest lounge. Marina with slips available for guests. **Rates (BB):** Peak (Apr–Nov) $175 D. Extra person $15. Children under age 18 stay free. Min stay special events. Lower rates off-season. Higher rates for special events/hols. MAP rates avail. Parking: Outdoor, free. AE, CB, DC, MC, V.

RESTAURANTS 🍽️

Berry and Elliot's

In Hyatt Regency Baltimore, 300 Light St (Inner Harbor); tel 410/605-2835. Across from Light St Pavilion. **Regional American/Seafood.** All tables enjoy views of the Inner Harbor from windows running the entire length of this restaurant atop the high-rise Hyatt Regency Baltimore. Award-winning cuisine features salmon, swordfish, sautéed rockfish, and cream of crab soup. **FYI:** Reservations accepted. DJ. **Open:** Lunch Mon–Fri 11:30am–2pm; dinner daily 5:30–10pm. **Prices:** Main courses $19–$27. AE, CB, DC, DISC, MC, V. ❤️ 🖼️ &

✹ Bertha's

734 S Broadway (Fells Point); tel 410/327-5795. **British/Seafood.** Name comes from an antique stained-glass window, now hanging on the wall. Wooden decor has rustic look. Fun place to eat. Well known in Baltimore for mussels. Afternoon high tea, served Monday to Saturday, requires reservations. Bar stays open until 2 am. **FYI:** Reservations not accepted. Jazz. No smoking. **Open:** Sun–Thurs 11:30am–11pm, Fri–Sat 11:30am–midnight. **Prices:** Main courses $11–$20. MC, V. 🍴 📷

♟ The Brass Elephant

924 N Charles St (Mount Vernon); tel 410/547-8480. Between Read and Eager Sts. **Regional American/Italian.** Tables are scattered throughout the front parlor and dining room of this grand 1861 row house. Fireplaces no longer work, but mantels were carved by Rhinehardt and Meislehm. Historic ambience enhanced by leaded-glass windows, wooden staircase leading to second-floor lounge. Specializes in fine northern Italian cuisine, all freshly prepared. Excellent wine list. Smoking permitted in rear room only. **FYI:** Reservations recommended. No smoking. **Open:** Lunch Mon–Fri 11:30am–2pm; dinner Mon–Thurs 5:30–9:30pm, Fri–Sat 5:30–11pm, Sun 5–9pm. **Prices:** Main courses $15–$22; prix fixe $20. AE, DC, DISC, MC, V. ❤️ 🍴 🔽

✹ Burke's Café

36 Light St, at Lombard St (Inner Harbor); tel 410/752-4189. **Seafood/Steak.** Pub known for its rustic decor, brick walls, and large, scrumptious onion rings. Also daily specials, wide range of sandwiches, seafood, and sizzling steaks. Food service available at bar. **FYI:** Reservations accepted. Comedy. Children's menu. **Open:** Daily 7am–2am. **Prices:** Main courses $8–$20. AE, MC, V. 🍴 🚗

The Chart House

601 E Pratt St (Inner Harbor); tel 410/539-6616. Next to National Aquarium. **Seafood/Steak.** Comfortable decor, al-

though the dining rooms may be noisy depending upon the kid-to-adult ratio. Menu offers other favorites, but seafood is house specialty. **FYI:** Reservations recommended. Children's menu. No smoking. **Open:** Peak (Mem Day–Labor Day) lunch daily 11:30am–2:30pm; dinner Mon–Fri 5–10pm, Sat 4–11pm, Sun 4–9:30pm. **Prices:** Main courses $15–$25. AE, DC, DISC, MC, V. 🍷 🖼️ &

✹ Chiapparelli's

237 S High St (Little Italy); tel 410/837-0309. **Italian.** One of Baltimore's most popular eateries for half a century, it has a red brick interior hung with pictures of Italian street scenes. Large menu has nearly 50 main courses, including lobster fra diavolo, shrimp parmigiana, and steak Italiana. Large house salad is locally famous. **FYI:** Reservations recommended. Children's menu. **Open:** Sun–Tues 11am–10pm, Wed–Thurs 11am–11pm, Fri–Sat 11am–midnight. **Prices:** Main courses $9–$22. AE, CB, DC, DISC, MC, V. &

Da Mimmo

217 S High St (Little Italy); tel 410/727-6876. **Italian.** Bar on main floor features many pictures of famous patrons, including President Clinton. Italian fare ranges from popular pastas to some truly extraordinary dishes, including lobster pizzaiola, butterflied veal chops, and the Mimmo seafood special. **FYI:** Reservations recommended. Piano. **Open:** Mon–Thurs 11:30am–11:30pm, Fri–Sat 11:30am–1am, Sun 2–11:30pm. **Prices:** Main courses $10–$25. AE, DC, MC, V. 🅥🅟

Foster's Restaurant and Raw Bar

606 S Broadway (Fells Point); tel 410/558-3600. **Seafood.** Part of this high-quality establishment is casual and features an oyster raw bar. Other dining area is more romantic, with fancier table settings. Italian and southwestern seafood dishes are produced, but kitchen is best known for local delicacies, such as rock fish (striped bass) and Maryland-style crab cakes. **FYI:** Reservations recommended. Dress code. **Open:** Daily 11:30am–11:30pm. **Prices:** Main courses $9–$18. AE, CB, DC, DISC, MC, V. ❤️ 📷

♟ Hampton's

In Harbor Court Hotel, 550 Light St (Inner Harbor); tel 410/234-0550. Across from Science Center. **New American/Continental.** Edwardian elegance characterizes one of Baltimore's finest restaurants, in one of its very best hotels. Gourmet cuisine ranges from Dover sole and rack of lamb to seared duck. Service lives up to the restaurant's fine reputation. **FYI:** Reservations recommended. Jacket required. No smoking. **Open:** Dinner Tues–Thurs 5:30–9:30pm, Fri–Sat 5:30–11pm, Sun 5:30–9:30pm; brunch Sun 10:30am–2:30pm. **Prices:** Main courses $24–$34; prix fixe $45–$55. AE, CB, DC, DISC, MC, V. ❤️ 🅥🅟 &

Haussner's

3244 Eastern Ave (Highlandtown); tel 410/327-8365. Exit 59 off I-95, 2 mi W. **German/Seafood.** Just about every square inch of this restaurant is covered with art, providing a feast for the eyes. For the palate, the food is always excellent, with a focus on hearty German cuisine including seafood items. The bakery products alone make this worth a visit. **FYI:** Reservations not accepted. Dress code. No smoking. **Open:** Tues–Sat 11am–10pm. **Prices:** Main courses $8–$30. AE, DC, DISC, MC, V. &

★ Louie's Bookstore Café
518 N Charles St (Mount Vernon); tel 410/962-1224. Between Centre and Franklin Sts. **Eclectic.** The front of this establishment really is a bookstore, but in the rear are a long bar and ice cream parlor tables and chairs. Seating is on main floor, in a loft, and, in good weather, outside in a small garden. Highlights here, however, are musicians from the Peabody Conservatory and artists from the Maryland Institute of Art; both schools also supply waiters, bartenders, and much of the clientele, bestowing bohemian flair. A friendly, laid-back, comfortable place that prides itself on providing a showcase for young talent. **FYI:** Reservations recommended. Guitar/harp/jazz/piano. **Open:** Mon 11:30am–midnight, Tues–Thurs 11:30am–1am, Fri–Sat 11:30am–1:30am, Sun 10:30am–midnight. **Prices:** Main courses $6–$15. AE, MC, V. ≜ &

Obrycki's
1727 E Pratt St (Fells Point); tel 410/732-6399. **Seafood.** Brick arches, wood beams, brass chandeliers, wall sconces, and Shaker chairs exude Baltimore history. Highlight is seafood, especially steamed crabs. A city institution for more than 50 years. **FYI:** Reservations not accepted. Children's menu. **Open:** Mon–Sat noon–11pm, Sun noon–9:30pm. Closed Jan–Feb. **Prices:** Main courses $14–$26. AE, CB, DC, DISC, MC, V. ▄ VP &

The Orchid
419 N Charles St (Mount Vernon); tel 410/837-0080. Between Centre and Mulberry Sts. **French/Asian.** In the first and second floors of a row house, this intimate restaurant has an Oriental flair, with screens and drawings scattered throughout the dining rooms. Food reflects the theme—lamb chops under Thai curry sauce, Malaysian-style chicken breast, and Singapore shrimp and scallops—but French influence is also felt. Co-owners/chefs use only fresh ingredients. After-theater menu available Friday and Saturday 10–11:30pm. **FYI:** Reservations recommended. **Open:** Lunch Tues–Fri 11:30am–2:30pm; dinner Tues–Thurs 5–10:30pm, Fri–Sat 5–11:30pm, Sun 4–9:30pm. **Prices:** Main courses $9–$23; prix fixe $20. AE, DC, DISC, MC, V. ♥

Paolo's Ristorante
In Harborplace Light Street Pavilion, 301 Light St (Inner Harbor); tel 410/539-7060. **Californian/Italian.** An open kitchen with wood-burning oven is a big draw at this modishly decorated restaurant in the Harbor Place shopping complex. Best known for pizza. **FYI:** Reservations not accepted. Children's menu. Additional locations: 1 W Pennsylvania Ave, Towson (tel 321-7000); 1801 Rockville Pike, Rockville (tel

301/984-2211). **Open:** Mon–Fri 11am–1:30am, Sat–Sun 10:30am–1:30am. **Prices:** Main courses $8–$17. AE, CB, DC, DISC, MC, V. ♥ ≜ ⊞ &

The Pavilion at the Walters
600 N Charles St (Mount Vernon); tel 410/727-2233. Between Centre and Monument Sts. **Regional American.** At the site of the original garden of the Hackerman House, an 1850s mansion and now the Walters Art Gallery's Museum of Asian Art. Descend a grand, curving double staircase, within which sits a fountain with bronze *Boy and Panther Cub* by noted American sculptor Malvina Hoffmann, to the pristine classicism of a white-walled dining room. Seating is scattered among towering pillars and skylights, which flood the room in daylight, create dramatic shadows at night. Salads, sandwiches, pastas, and light main courses. **FYI:** Reservations recommended. No smoking. **Open:.** Lunch Tues–Sun 11:30am–3:30pm. **Prices:** Main courses $6–$12. AE, MC, V. ♥ ▄ &

Phillips Harborplace
In Harborplace Light Street Pavilion, 301 Light St (Inner Harbor); tel 800/782-2722. **Regional American/Seafood.** Hanging Tiffany-style lamps and lots of wood and brass set the mood at this seafood emporium. Maryland crab is the specialty, but raw bar is also popular. Carryout counter in the mall area. **FYI:** Reservations not accepted. Singalong. Children's menu. **Open:** Sun–Thurs 11am–11pm, Fri–Sat 11am–midnight. **Prices:** Main courses $11–$25. AE, CB, DC, DISC, MC, V. ≜ ⊞ &

Prime Rib
1101 N Calvert St, at E Chase St (Mount Vernon); tel 410/539-1804. **American.** In a row house on a steep side street behind a high-rise apartment building, this New York–style restaurant has had consistently excellent food and service for more than 25 years. Unassuming entrance leads to rather dark, quietly elegant room where fresh flower arrangements, ebony piano, mirrors, and small table lights set a mellow, romantic ambience. Main offerings are prime cuts of aged beef, lightly seasoned to enhance the natural flavors. **FYI:** Reservations recommended. Piano. Dress code. **Open:** Mon–Sat 5pm–midnight, Sun 4–11pm. **Prices:** Main courses $20–$27. AE, CB, DC, DISC, MC, V. ♥ &

★ Restaurante Tio Pepe
10 E Franklin St (Downtown); tel 410/539-4675. Between St Paul and Charles Sts. **Spanish.** Several steps lead from street level to this large restaurant with six dining rooms (three of them small and private). Decor, music, and staff uniforms are strictly Spanish, and specialties hail from Alhambra, Madrid, Seville, and other parts of Iberia. Signature dishes include beef with sherry sauce and mushrooms, filet of sole with bananas and hollandaise sauce, and Spanish prawns flavored with brandy. **FYI:** Reservations recommended. Jacket required. **Open:** Lunch Mon–Fri 11:30am–2:30pm; dinner

Mon–Thurs 5–10:30pm, Fri–Sat 5–11:30pm, Sun 4–10:30pm. **Prices:** Main courses $15–$26. AE, DC, DISC, MC, V. 🍷 VP &

★ Sabatino's

901 Fawn St, at High St (Little Italy); tel 410/727-9414. **Italian.** Wonderful Italian aromas greet patrons at the small entry, which opens to several dining rooms on three levels, making this large establishment seem smaller. Red brick walls and low ceilings make basement area feel grotto-like, while upstairs rooms are lighter, airier. Extensive traditional Italian menu; all sauces, pastas, salad dressings, and breads prepared on premises. Minimum $7.50 per person. Patrons with disabilities should call ahead to reserve tables on the main level. **FYI:** Reservations recommended. Dress code. **Open:** Daily noon–3am. **Prices:** Main courses $9–$30. AE, CB, DC, DISC, MC, V.

★ Tony Cheng's Szechuan Restaurant

801 N Charles St, at Madison St (Mount Vernon); tel 410/539-6666. **Chinese.** The two main dining rooms in the large brick row house retain their original plasterwork, although walls are painted dark burgundy with light rose and gray trim. Double-hung, floor-to-ceiling windows add light for lunch, historic touch at night. Large selection of spicy Szechuan dishes is augmented by mild Cantonese fare. **FYI:** Reservations recommended. Dress code. **Open:** Daily 11am–10:30pm. **Prices:** Main courses $9–$32. AE, DC, MC, V. 🍴 🚗

Water Street Exchange

110 Water St (Inner Harbor); tel 410/332-4060. Just off Light St. **Burgers/Cajun/Tex-Mex.** High ceilings, exposed brick, wall sconces, mirrors, and highly polished oak wainscoting set a formal tone for this pub's main dining room, which is one flight below a large, casual bar. In addition to pub-style burgers, sandwiches, and salads, there's a mix of Cajun, Tex-Mex, pasta, and seafood. Bar is popular spot on weekend evenings, when crowds of young people often spill out onto a front brick patio. **FYI:** Reservations accepted. **Open:** Mon–Wed 11:30am–10pm, Thurs 11:30am–midnight, Fri–Sat 11:30am–2am. **Prices:** Main courses $5–$18. AE, CB, DC, DISC, MC, V. 🍽 &

★ Woman's Industrial Exchange

333 N Charles St, at E Pleasant St (Downtown); tel 410/685-4388. **American/Tea Room.** Located in an early 19th-century row house, this plain but very clean tearoom harkens back to 1881, when it opened as a means for needy women to earn money. An elderly doorman ushers guests into front parlor filled with handmade quilts, crocheted work, and baked goods for sale. Tearoom in rear offers home-style breakfasts and unpretentious lunch platters served by friendly, veteran waitresses. Basement room has "quick lunch" counter (the only place where smoking's allowed) for sandwiches. **FYI:** Reservations accepted. No liquor license. No smoking. **Open:** Mon–Fri 7am–2pm. **Prices:** MC, V. 🍴 🍷 🎦

ATTRACTIONS 🏛

TOP ATTRACTIONS

National Aquarium
501 E Pratt St (Inner Harbor); tel 410/576-3800. This spectacular five-level glass-and-steel structure stretches over Piers 3 and 4 of the Inner Harbor. It contains more than 5,000 specimens of mammals, fish, rare birds, reptiles, and amphibians. All the creatures are on view in settings that re-create their natural habitats, which include a South American rain forest, an Atlantic coral reef, and an open-ocean tank. The **Marine Mammal Pavilion** houses Atlantic bottlenose dolphins in a 1.2-million-gallon complex of 4 pools surrounded by the world's largest acrylic windows and a 1,300-seat amphitheater. In addition, there are nature films, an aquatic education resource center, and an animal care and research complex. **Open:** Peak (July–Aug) Sun–Thurs 9am–6pm, Fri–Sat 9am–8pm. Reduced hours off-season. $$$$

US Frigate *Constellation*
Pier 1, off Pratt St (Inner Harbor); tel 410/539-1797. Continuously afloat longer than any other ship in the world, the *Constellation* was launched from Baltimore in 1797. It was the first boat the US Navy put to sea and the first to defeat an enemy man-of-war. **Open:** Peak (mid-June–Labor Day) daily 10am–8pm. Reduced hours off-season. $$

Harborplace
Light and Pratt Sts (Inner Harbor); tel 410/332-4191. This historic area, positioned right on the waterfront, has been designed to duplicate the look of an early steamship pier headquarters. It is made up of two pavilions named after the streets they occupy—the Light Street Pavilion and the Pratt Street Pavilion. The contemporary, bright, and airy complex of restaurants, food markets, curiosity shops, and trendy boutiques has made this the centerpiece of Baltimore's revitalization. **Open:** Mon–Sat 10am–10pm, Sun noon–6pm.

Maryland Science Center
601 Light St (Inner Harbor); tel 410/685-5225. Situated on the edge of the Inner Harbor, the science center features hundreds of hands-on activities, live demonstrations, and displays ranging from a simulated space station control center to experiments revealing the properties of sight, sound, magnetism, light, and mechanics. Admission includes all exhibits, an IMAX film presentation, and Davis Planetarium shows. **Open:** Mon–Fri 10am–5pm, Sat–Sun 10am–6pm. $$$

Christopher Columbus Center of Marine Research and Exploration
Piers 5 and 6, off Pratt St (Inner Harbor); tel 410/547-8727. Slated to open in the winter of 1996–97, this $160 million attraction promises to be a world-class center for marine

research as well as a tourist draw to Baltimore's waterfront. The center will include four major units—research centers for marine biotechnology and nautical archeology, plus a lecture hall and a public exhibition center with hands-on exhibits. Operating hours were not available at press time; call for current information. **$$$**

Top of the World

401 E Pratt St (Inner Harbor); tel 410/837-4515. This observatory on the 27th floor of the World Trade Center, the world's tallest pentagonal building, offers a sweeping overview of the whole harbor and the city. In addition, hands-on displays, exhibits, and multimedia presentations explore Baltimore's history. **Open:** Peak (Labor Day–Mem Day) Mon–Sat 10am–4:30pm, Sun noon–5:30pm. Reduced hours off-season. **$**

Baltimore Zoo

Greenspring Ave, Druid Hill Park; tel 410/396-7102. This natural expanse comprises 180 acres of grassy slopes, tree-topped hills, and mountain caves providing an agreeable habitat to more than 1,200 animals, birds, and reptiles from seven continents, including rhinos, zebras, gazelles, bears, chimpanzees, and black-footed penguins. There is also an eight-acre interactive children's zoo. **Open:** Daily 10am–4pm. **$$$**

MUSEUMS

Baltimore Maritime Museum

Pier 3, off Pratt St (Inner Harbor); tel 410/396-5528. This outdoor complex is the home of the US Coast Guard cutter *Taney,* the last ship still afloat that fought in Pearl Harbor; the submarine USS *Torsh,* which sank the last enemy ship in World War II; and the lightship *Chesapeake,* a floating lighthouse built in 1930. The vessels are moored to the dock and are open to visitors. **Open:** Mon–Fri 9am–5pm, Sat–Sun 9:30am–7pm. **$$**

Baltimore and Ohio (B&O) Railroad Museum

901 W Pratt St; tel 410/752-2490. Often called a railroad university, this museum has hundreds of exhibits—from double-decker stagecoaches on iron wheels and early diesels to steam locomotives and the 1830 Mount Clare Station, the nation's first passenger and freight station. Also on display is the 1844 roundhouse with the original B&O tracks and turntable. **Open:** Daily 10am–5pm. **$$$**

Baltimore Museum of Industry

1415 Key Hwy; tel 410/727-4808. Housed in the 1865 Baltimore oyster cannery, this museum illustrates the industrial history of the city through a series of 19th-century workshop settings—from a machine shop and a print shop to a clothing factory and cannery works. **Open:** Wed 7–9pm, Thurs–Fri and Sun noon–5pm, Sat 10am–5pm. **$$**

Baltimore City Life Museums

33 S Front St (Inner Harbor); tel 410/396-3523. A collection of nine museums and historic sites, seven of which are clustered together on "museum row." The **Morton K Blaustein City Life Exhibition Center** contains family-oriented exhibits such as "What Makes Baltimore *Bawlamer?*" and "Nipper's Neighborhood." **Nickelodeon Theatre** offers short films on Baltimore history. **Carroll Mansion** is the former winter home of Charles Carroll of Carrollton, the longest-surviving signer of the Declaration of Independence. The **Center for Urban Archaeology** contains an exhibit explaining how archeologists uncover the city's past. The **1840 House,** once the home of a middle-class wheelwright and his family, has living-history programs with costumed interpreters. The **Shot Tower** is a 215-foot, 19th-century "factory in a smokestack" with a sound and light show describing how buckshot was once made there.

Brewers' Park, site of the city's largest Revolutionary War–era brewery, has a self-guided archeological walking tour that ends at a modern-day microbrewery. All the above sites may be visited for one all-inclusive price. **Open:** Peak (Apr–Oct) Tues–Sat 10am–5pm, Sun noon–5pm. Reduced hours off-season. **$$$**

Maryland Historical Society

201 W Monument St (Mount Vernon); tel 410/685-3750. Houses many of the city's great treasures, such as the original "Star-Spangled Banner" manuscript; silver tureens from America's largest 19th-century silver collection; and maps, prints, relics, and artifacts, all depicting Maryland long ago. **Open:** Tues–Fri 10am–5pm, Sat 9am–5pm, Sun 1–5pm. **$$**

Great Blacks in Wax Museum

1601–3 E North Ave (Mount Vernon); tel 410/563-3404. The nation's first and only wax museum dedicated to famous African-American heroes and historical legends. The people portrayed include inventors, pilots, religious and educational leaders, and scientists. **Open:** Peak (Jan 15–Oct 15) Tues–Sat 9am–6pm, Sun noon–6pm. Reduced hours off-season. **$$$**

Eubie Blake National Museum & Cultural Center

34 Market Place; tel 410/625-3113. Located in the heart of the city, this center, dedicated to Baltimore-born ragtime great James Hubert "Eubie" Blake, displays items from his life such as his piano and original sheet music. There is also a gallery with changing exhibits of current interest by local artists. **Open:** Mon–Fri 8:30am–4:30pm. **Free**

Babe Ruth Birthplace & Museum/Baltimore Orioles Museum

216 Emory St; tel 410/727-1539. The restored house and adjoining museum contain personal mementos of George Herman "Babe" Ruth, otherwise known as the "Sultan of Swat." The exhibits, which focus on the Baltimore Orioles and Maryland baseball as well as the great Babe, include such touchable items as hats, bats, and gloves; there's also an audiovisual presentation on the Babe and World Series film highlights. **Open:** Peak (Apr–Oct) daily 10am–5pm (until 7pm on Orioles game days). Reduced hours off-season. **$$**

Lacrosse Hall of Fame Museum

113 W University Pkwy (Mount Vernon); tel 410/235-6882. This unique museum presents 350 years in the history of lacrosse, America's oldest sport and a particular favorite in Maryland. The displays include rare photographs and photomurals of men and women at play, art, vintage equipment and uniforms, sculptures, trophies, and other memorabilia. **Open:** Peak (Mar–May) Mon–Fri 9am–5pm, Sat 10am–3pm. Reduced hours off-season. **$**

Baltimore Museum of Art

10 Art Museum Dr (Mount Vernon); tel 410/396-7100. The largest museum in Maryland, with over 100,000 artworks, most notably the Cone Collection of 20th-century art with works by Matisse, Picasso, and Cézanne. Also featured are the arts of Africa, Asia, and Oceania, plus two outdoor sculpture gardens. **Open:** Wed–Fri 10am–4pm, Sat–Sun 11am–6pm. **$$$**

Walters Art Gallery

600 N Charles St (Mount Vernon); tel 410/547-9000. Designed in an Italianate palazzo style, the museum has more than 30,000 works of art spanning 5,000 years. The collection includes Asian, Egyptian, Greek, Roman, Byzantine, medieval, renaissance, baroque, romantic, impressionist, and art nouveau works. **Open:** Tues–Sun 11am–5pm. **$$**

HISTORIC SITES AND MONUMENTS

Fort McHenry National Monument and Historic Shrine

E Fort Ave (Inner Harbor); tel 410/962-4299. The birthplace of the American national anthem, written by Francis Scott Key during the 1814 Battle of Baltimore. Fort McHenry was an active military base until 1925, when it was designated a national park. To assist visitors in touring the fort, there are historical and military exhibits, explanatory maps, and a 15-minute film shown every half-hour. **Open:** Peak (mid-June–Labor Day) daily 8am–8pm. Reduced hours off-season. **$**

Star-Spangled Banner Flag House and 1812 Museum

844 E Pratt St (Inner Harbor); tel 410/837-1793. The restored home of Mary Pickersgill, the seamstress who created the 30-by-42-foot red, white, and blue Fort McHenry flag that inspired Francis Scott Key to compose "The Star-Spangled Banner." The federal-style house (1793) is full of period furnishings and a collection of early American art. **Open:** Tues–Sat 10am–4pm. **$$**

H L Mencken House

1524 Hollins St (Mount Vernon); tel 410/396-7997. One of the City Life museums, this stately 19th-century row house was the home of the influential and caustic writer and editor Henry Louis Mencken, the "Sage of Baltimore." The house has been restored to include many of Mencken's original furnishings and belongings. **Open:** Sat 10am–5pm, Sun noon–5pm. **$**

Edgar Allan Poe House

203 N Amity St (Mount Vernon); tel 410/396-7932. This tiny house, where the great poet and short-story writer Edgar Allan Poe lived from 1832 to 1835, contains Poe memorabilia plus period furniture, changing exhibits, and a video presentation of leading Poe works. **Open:** Call for hours. **$**

Basilica of the National Shrine of the Assumption of the Blessed Virgin Mary

Cathedral and Mulberry Sts (Mount Vernon); tel 410/727-3564. The Mother Church of Roman Catholicism in the United States, this 1806 basilica was the first metropolitan cathedral in the country and is considered one of the finest examples of neoclassical architecture in the world. Designed by Benjamin Latrobe (architect of the US Capitol building). Daily masses; guided tours available every Sunday or by appointment. **Open:** Mon–Fri 7am–5pm, Sat–Sun 7am–6:30pm. **Free**

Old St Paul's Church

Charles and Saratoga Sts (Mount Vernon); tel 410/685-3404. Opened in 1856, this church is part of a parish dating back to 1692 and is the mother church for the city of Baltimore. Designed by Richard Upjohn in basilica style, it is noted for its Tiffany windows and inlaid mosaic work. **Open:** Mon–Fri 11:30am–1pm, Sun 7:45am–12:30pm. **Free**

Holocaust Memorial

Corner of Water, Gay, and Lombard Sts (Inner Harbor); tel 410/752-2630. Nestled in the heart of downtown, this open-air memorial center and sculpture stand as a stark reminder of the six million Jews murdered by the Nazis in Europe between 1933 and 1945. **Open:** Daily 24 hours. **Free**

THEATERS AND CONCERT HALLS

Pier Six Concert Pavilion

Pier 6, off Pratt St (Inner Harbor); tel 410/837-4636. A 4,300-seat concert pavilion in the format of a six-point open-air aluminum tent. It presents music's top names in live concerts from May through September. **Open:** Call for schedule. **$$$$**

Peabody Conservatory of Music

1 E Mount Vernon Place (Mount Vernon); tel 410/659-8124. A division of Johns Hopkins University, it is America's oldest school of music, dating back to 1866. From September through May there are more than 60 events open to the public, featuring the Peabody Symphony Orchestra and student performers. **Open:** Call for schedule. **$$$**

Lyric Opera House

1404 W Mount Royal Ave; tel 410/685-0692. A replica of Germany's Leipzig music hall, this impressive facility is home to the Baltimore Opera Company, which performs classic operas during an October-to-May season. **Open:** Call for schedule. **$$$$**

Joseph Meyerhoff Symphony Hall

1212 Cathedral St; tel 410/783-8000. Famed for its acoustics, this 2,450-seat hall is the home of the Baltimore Symphony Orchestra; it also presents visiting classical, pop, and jazz artists. **Open:** Call for schedule. $$$$

SPORTS VENUES

Baltimore Memorial Stadium

1000 E 33rd St; tel 410/396-7111. Professional football is back in Baltimore after a ten-year absence with the arrival of the NFL's Baltimore Ravens. The team will play at this stadium, the old home of the Baltimore Colts, for at least the 1996–97 and 1997–98 seasons. A new stadium is due to be built near Oriole Park in the Camden Yards area. For team information, call toll free 888/9-RAVENS or call 888/919-9797 to order tickets $$$$

Pimlico Race Course

Park Heights and Belvedere Aves; tel 410/542-9400. Located about five miles from the Inner Harbor on the city's northwest side, this is Maryland's oldest thoroughbred track and the site of the annual Preakness Stakes. Also on the grounds is the **National Jockey's Hall of Fame**, open 9–11am during the racing season, free of charge. **Open:** Two meets per year. Call for schedule. $

Oriole Park at Camden Yards

333 W Camden St (Inner Harbor); tel 410/685-9800. Situated between two 19th-century landmarks—the Baltimore & Ohio Railroad Warehouse and Camden Station—this is the Baltimore Orioles new "old-fashioned ballpark," fashioned after big-league parks from the early 1900s such as Ebbets Field in Brooklyn, Fenway Park in Boston, and Wrigley Field in Chicago. The style is obtained through the use of steel, rather than concrete trusses, an arched brick facade, a sun roof over the upper deck, an asymmetrical playing field, and natural grass turf. Go to a game or take a behind-the-scenes tour given weekdays when the Orioles are not playing. **Open:** Call for schedule. $$$$

Baltimore Arena

201 W Baltimore St; tel 410/347-2090. This facility, with a seating capacity of 16,000, plays host to a changing program of entertainment and sports events. Featured on the schedule are concerts, circuses, ice shows, indoor lacrosse, and soccer and hockey matches. **Open:** Call for schedule. $$$$

MUSEUMS

Peale Museum

225 Holliday St (Mount Vernon); tel 410/396-1149. Built in 1814 by American portrait painter Rembrandt Peale, the oldest museum building in the United States was also Baltimore's first city hall. A member of the City Life Museums, it houses a collection of historical photographs, prints, and paintings of Baltimore and the Peale family. **Open:** Peak (Apr–Oct) Sat 10am–5pm, Sun noon–5pm. Reduced hours off-season. $

Baltimore-Washington Int'l Airport

HOTELS 🏨

≣≣≣ BWI Airport Marriott Hotel

1743 W Nursery Rd, Linthicum, 21240; tel 410/859-8300 or toll free 800/228-9290; fax 410/691-4555. 10 mi S of Baltimore. Exit I-95 at I-295. Modern design and spacious, bright public areas in pastels make this a very attractive hotel. **Rooms:** 310 rms and stes. Executive level. CI 3pm/CO noon. Nonsmoking rms avail. **Amenities:** 🛏 🕹 A/C, cable TV w/movies, dataport, voice mail. Concierge-level units have shoe polishers, bathrobes, scales, hair dryers. Irons and ironing boards in all rooms. **Services:** ✕ 🔑 🚗 ◺ ↵ Masseur. Friendly, accommodating staff. **Facilities:** 🛗 🎿 🐾 🏊 ⛳ 💻 ♿ 1 restaurant, 2 bars, whirlpool, washer/dryer. Dramatic, lovely pool with waterfall and high windows. Excellent fitness, games, massage facilities. **Rates:** $129–$145 S; $139–$155 D; $250–$350 ste. Extra person $10. Children under age 18 stay free. Parking: Outdoor, free. Weekend rates include breakfast. AE, CB, DC, DISC, EC, JCB, MC, V.

≣≣≣ Sheraton International Hotel BWI Airport

7032 Elm Rd, Baltimore, 21240; tel 410/859-3300 or toll free 800/638-5858; fax 410/859-0565. Exit 1A off I-95. Turn left at Elm Rd. Closest hotel to BWI Airport terminal; well-situated for either business or pleasure travelers. No elevator. **Rooms:** 196 rms and stes. Executive level. CI 3pm/CO noon. Nonsmoking rms avail. **Amenities:** 🛏 🕹 📺 A/C, cable TV w/movies, voice mail. Shaving mirrors and hair dryers in executive rooms. **Services:** 🍽 🚗 ◺ ↵ 🐾 Car-rental desk, babysitting. Airport arrivals and departures displayed on video screens in lobby. **Facilities:** 🛗 🐾 ⛳ ♿ 1 restaurant, 2 bars (1 w/entertainment). Large pool set in a well-kept courtyard. Well-regarded restaurant. **Rates (CP):** $109–$130 S or D; $139–$189 ste. Extra person $10. Children under age 18 stay free. MAP rates avail. Parking: Outdoor, free. AE, DC, DISC, MC, V.

MOTELS

≣≣≣ Comfort Inn Airport

6921 Baltimore-Annapolis Blvd, 21225; tel 410/789-9100 or toll free 800/221-2222; fax 410/355-2854. Exit 6A off I-695; follow MD 170 ¼ mile. A convenient, modern motel near the Baltimore Beltway and within walking distance of local light-rail system for trips into downtown Baltimore. **Rooms:** 200 rms and stes. CI 3pm/CO 11am. Nonsmoking rms avail. Standard motel rooms. **Amenities:** 🛏 🕹 A/C, cable TV w/movies. 1 unit w/whirlpool. Closed captioning for TVs. **Services:** 🚗 🐾 ◺ ↵ Babysitting. Shuttle to Amtrak station. **Facilities:** 🐾 ⛳ ♿ 1 restaurant, 1 bar, games rm, spa, sauna, whirlpool, washer/dryer. **Rates (BB):** Peak (Apr–June/Sept–Nov) $69–$79 S; $69–$86 D; $225 ste. Extra person $8. Children under age 17 stay free. Lower rates off-season. Parking: Outdoor, free. AE, CB, DC, DISC, ER, JCB, MC, V.

≣≣≣ Holiday Inn BWI

890 Elkridge Landing Rd, Linthicum, 21090; tel 410/859-8400 or toll free 800/465-4329; fax 410/684-6778. 10 mi S of Baltimore. Basic and attractive chain motel. **Rooms:** 259 rms and stes. CI 3pm/CO noon. Nonsmoking rms avail. King rooms are substantially larger than standard. **Amenities:** 🛢 🕭 🔳 A/C, cable TV w/movies, dataport. **Services:** ✗ 🚗 🖼 🖅 🖅 Babysitting. **Facilities:** � 🖳 🖮 ⌷450⌷ 🖢 1 restaurant, 1 bar, washer/dryer. **Rates:** $79–$119 S or D; $190 ste. Children under age 19 stay free. Parking: Outdoor, free. Children eat free. Priority Club rates include continental breakfast. AE, CB, DC, DISC, JCB, MC, V.

≣≣ Holiday Inn Glen Burnie South

6600 Ritchie Hwy, Glen Burnie, 21061; tel 410/761-8300 or toll free 800/465-4329; fax 410/760-4966. Exit 3B off I-695. An older motel, this property has been maintained well. Sits across street from Maryland Motor Vehicles Administration headquarters. Close to several shopping malls. **Rooms:** 100 rms. CI 3pm/CO noon. Nonsmoking rms avail. **Amenities:** 🛢 🕭 A/C, cable TV w/movies, dataport. **Services:** ✗ 🖼 🖅 🖅 **Facilities:** � ⌷50⌷ 🖢 1 restaurant, 1 bar. Free access to Bally's Health Spa nearby. **Rates:** Peak (Mar–Oct) $55–$75 S or D. Extra person $10. Children under age 18 stay free. Lower rates off-season. Parking: Outdoor, free. AE, CB, DC, DISC, MC, V.

≣≣ Ramada Hotel BWI Airport

7253 Parkway Dr, Hanover, 21076; tel 410/712-4300 or toll free 800/272-6232; fax 410/712-0921. 15 mi S of Baltimore. Exit 43E off I-95. Follow MD 100 to US 1; follow US 1 to Dorsey Rd, turn left, then left onto Parkway Dr. Maintenance of this motel has slipped a bit, but accommodations are adequate and the location—close to Amtrak and the airport—is good for business travelers. **Rooms:** 132 rms. CI 3pm/CO noon. No smoking. **Amenities:** 🛢 🕭 A/C, satel TV w/movies. All units w/terraces. Balconies are small. TVs have closed captioning. **Services:** ✗ 🚗 🖼 🖅 Babysitting. **Facilities:** � 🖳 🖮 ⌷150⌷ 🖢 1 restaurant, 1 bar (w/entertainment), games rm, washer/dryer. Game room has billiard table. Free access to nearby health club with Olympic-size pool. **Rates:** Peak (Apr–Aug) $98 S; $108 D. Extra person $5. Children under age 16 stay free. Lower rates off-season. MAP rates avail. Parking: Outdoor, free. AE, CB, DC, DISC, EC, ER, JCB, MC, V.

Berlin

Small town west of Ocean City on the Eastern Shore, with a quaint, Victorian-style commercial district.

INN 🏨

≣≣≣≣ Atlantic Hotel

2 N Main St, 21811; tel 410/641-3589; fax 410/641-4928. A beautiful Victorian-era hotel, carefully restored and furnished throughout with high-quality antiques. Enclosed and open porches for sitting. **Rooms:** 17 rms and effic. CI 3pm/CO 11am. No smoking. Accurate in period style, very lovely rooms range from large to quite small. **Amenities:** 🛢 🕭 A/C. No TV. **Services:** 🖅 **Facilities:** ⌷20⌷ 2 restaurants (*see* "Restaurants" below), 1 bar (w/entertainment), guest lounge. **Rates (CP):** Peak (June–Oct) $65–$135 D; $150 effic. Extra person $20. Children under age 12 stay free. Min stay wknds. Lower rates off-season. Parking: Outdoor, free. AE, MC, V.

RESTAURANT 🍴

Atlantic Hotel Restaurant

In Atlantic Hotel, 2 N Main St; tel 410/641-3589. Exit US 50 at Main St. **Regional American.** A Victorian landmark that evokes *Age of Innocence* luxury, with period antiques throughout. A short but varied menu is marked by interesting sauces, while the extensive wine list reflects the manager's interest in American vintages. **FYI:** Reservations recommended. Piano. Dress code. No smoking. **Open:** Lunch Mon–Sat 11:30am–9pm; dinner daily 6–9pm; brunch Sun 11am–2pm. **Prices:** Main courses $19–$29. AE, MC, V. ♥ 🍴 🖢

Bethesda

See also Chevy Chase

A residential and commercial center northwest of Washington, DC. Home to the National Institutes of Health, Bethesda Naval Hospital, and the National Library of Medicine. **Information:** Greater Bethesda–Chevy Chase Chamber of Commerce, 7910 Woodmont Ave #1204, Bethesda, 20814 (tel 301/652-4900).

HOTELS 🏨

≣≣ American Inn of Bethesda

8130 Wisconsin Ave (MD 355), 20814; tel 301/656-9300 or toll free 800/323-7081; fax 301/656-2907. Exit 34 off I-495. Go south on Wisconsin Ave. A clean and comfortable, if not esthetically appealing, hotel. Convenient to shops, restaurants, and Metro. Property has considerably more potential than has been realized. **Rooms:** 76 rms. CI 3pm/CO 12:30pm. Nonsmoking rms avail. **Amenities:** 🛢 🕭 A/C, cable TV w/movies, refrig. **Services:** 🖼 🖅 Babysitting. **Facilities:** � ⌷50⌷ 🖢 2 restaurants (lunch and dinner only), 1 bar, washer/dryer. Reasonably priced Latin American restaurant on premises. **Rates (CP):** Peak (Jan–June/Sept–Nov) $90 S; $100 D. Children under age 18 stay free. Lower rates off-season. Parking: Indoor/outdoor, free. Weekend rates; corporate, government, and family discounts avail. AE, CB, DC, DISC, MC, V.

Bethesda Marriott Hotel

5151 Pooks Hill Rd, 20814; tel 301/897-9400 or toll free 800/228-9290; fax 301/897-0192. Exit 34 off I-495. A fine suburban hotel in a private residential setting yet adjacent to the Capital Beltway (I-495). Frequented by groups, tourists, and business travelers. **Rooms:** 407 rms and stes. Executive level. CI 4pm/CO noon. Nonsmoking rms avail. **Amenities:** A/C, cable TV w/movies, voice mail. Some units w/terraces. Irons and ironing boards in all rooms. Weekday morning newspaper delivered to rooms. **Services:** Babysitting. Morning coffee available in lobby. **Facilities:** 3 restaurants, 1 bar, games rm, sauna, whirlpool, washer/dryer. **Rates:** Peak (Mar–June/Sept–Dec) $160–$180 S or D; $275 ste. Children under age 18 stay free. Lower rates off-season. Parking: Outdoor, free. AE, CB, DC, DISC, MC, V.

Bethesda Marriott Suites

6711 Democracy Blvd, at Fernwood Rd, 20817; tel 301/897-5600 or toll free 800/228-9290; fax 301/530-1427. Exit 36 off I-495. A modern, all-suites hotel in a nicely landscaped office park containing the corporate headquarters of Marriott Hotels; two-story lobby has large windows, skylights, ficus trees, bar. **Rooms:** 274 stes. CI 4pm/CO 1pm. Nonsmoking rms avail. Most units have sofa beds. All have desk, sinks, dressing area in bath. Attractively furnished. **Amenities:** A/C, satel TV w/movies, refrig, dataport, voice mail. Some units w/terraces. Large TVs, irons and ironing boards. **Services:** Twice-daily maid svce, babysitting. Complimentary morning newspaper and grocery delivery. **Facilities:** 1 restaurant, 1 bar, spa, whirlpool, washer/dryer. **Rates:** Peak (Apr–June/Oct–Dec) $130–$160 ste. Children under age 18 stay free. Lower rates off-season. Parking: Indoor, free. AE, CB, DC, DISC, MC, V.

Bethesda Ramada Hotel & Conference Center

8400 Wisconsin Ave, 20814; tel 301/654-1000 or toll free 800/331-5252; fax 301/654-0751. This contemporary hotel exhibits considerable exterior appeal; however, neither services, room decor, nor amenities realize the full potential of the building or its location two blocks from National Institutes of Health and its Metro station. **Rooms:** 160 rms and stes. CI 3pm/CO 1pm. No smoking. **Amenities:** A/C, cable TV w/movies. Some units w/terraces. **Services:** Car-rental desk. **Facilities:** 1 restaurant, 1 bar (w/entertainment), washer/dryer. Olympic-size pool. **Rates:** Peak (Feb–Apr/Sept–Oct) $79 S or D; $150 ste. Extra person $10. Children under age 10 stay free. Lower rates off-season. Parking: Outdoor, free. AE, DC, DISC, MC, V.

Holiday Inn

8120 Wisconsin Ave (MD 355), 20814; tel 301/652-2000 or toll free 800/631-5954. Exit 34 off I-495. A moderately priced hotel surrounded by numerous restaurants, night spots, and exclusive shops. **Rooms:** 270 rms and stes. Executive level. CI 4pm/CO noon. Nonsmoking rms avail. **Amenities:** A/C, cable TV w/movies, dataport, voice mail. Some units w/minibars, some w/terraces. **Services:** Complimentary shuttle service to Bethesda Naval Medical Center/National Institutes of Health Metro station. Pets cannot be left unattended in rooms. **Facilities:** 2 restaurants, 2 bars (1 w/entertainment), games rm. Comedy club entertainment Wednesday to Saturday evenings. **Rates:** $129–$249 S or D; $149 ste. Extra person $10. Children under age 18 stay free. Parking: Indoor, $6/day. AE, CB, DC, DISC, MC, V.

Hyatt Regency Bethesda

1 Bethesda Metro Ctr, 20814; tel 301/657-1234 or toll free 800/233-1234; fax 301/657-6453. On Wisconsin Ave at Old Georgetown Rd. A contemporary hotel in downtown Bethesda at Metro station plaza. Atrium lobby. **Rooms:** 381 rms and stes. Executive level. CI 3pm/CO noon. Nonsmoking rms avail. Attractive and comfortable rooms have luxurious marble baths with attractive floral wallpaper and well-lighted three-way mirrors. **Amenities:** A/C, cable TV w/movies, dataport, voice mail. Some units w/minibars, some w/terraces. **Services:** Twice-daily maid svce, social director, children's program, babysitting. Complimentary newspaper. **Facilities:** 1 restaurant, 1 bar, sauna, whirlpool, playground. Rooftop health club. **Rates:** $175–$200 S or D; $350–$475 ste. Extra person $25. Children under age 16 stay free. Parking: Indoor, $10/day. AE, CB, DC, DISC, EC, ER, JCB, MC, V.

Marriott Residence Inn

7335 Wisconsin Ave, 20814; tel 301/718-0200 or toll free 800/331-3131; fax 301/718-0679. A home away from home; attractive for long-term stays. **Rooms:** 187 effic. CI 3pm/CO noon. Nonsmoking rms avail. **Amenities:** A/C, cable TV w/movies, refrig, dataport, voice mail. Some units w/terraces. Microwaves. First-nighters kit includes coffee and popcorn. **Services:** Babysitting. **Facilities:** Games rm, sauna, washer/dryer. **Rates (CP):** Peak (Mar–July/Sept–Nov) $89–$169 effic. Children under age 18 stay free. Min stay peak. Lower rates off-season. Parking: Indoor, $10/day. Charge for extra persons applies only when additional beds are required. AE, CB, DC, DISC, MC, V.

RESTAURANTS

Andalucia de Bethesda

4931 Elm St; tel 301/907-0052. 2 blocks off Wisconsin Ave between Arlington Rd and Woodmont Ave. **Spanish.** Old-world charm defines the mood here, from the Spanish paintings, antique-style brass lamps, and Mediterranean lace curtains, to the formally dressed waiters. The menu lists a variety of fresh seafood, poultry, and meat prepared Andalucian-style, and there's an extensive wine selection.

FYI: Reservations recommended. Guitar. No smoking. **Open:** Lunch Mon–Fri 11:30am–2:30pm; dinner Mon–Thurs 5:30–10pm, Fri–Sat 5:30–10:30pm, Sun 5–9:30pm. **Prices:** Main courses $14–$22. AE, CB, DC, DISC, MC, V. ♥

Ⓢ Armadilla Grill
8011 Woodmont Ave; tel 301/907-9637. At Cordell Ave. **Southwestern.** Native American spirit dolls grace the entry to this "casual restaurant in the Santa Fe tradition." Desert colors and Native American accents, such as Navajo and Hopi rugs, add proper ambience for eating southwestern fare. All cooking is done over a wood fire. **FYI:** Reservations recommended. Children's menu. No smoking. **Open:** Sun–Thurs 5–10pm, Fri–Sat 5–11pm. **Prices:** Main courses $8–$17. DC, MC, V. ♥ 🎦

The Athenian Plaka
7833 Woodmont Ave; tel 301/986-1337. **Greek.** Gold trim, white archways, and murals of Greece adorn the walls, while Greek music adds to the Mediterranean atmosphere. Favorites from the old country such as roast lamb, kabobs, and Greek-style seafood. Outdoor tables available in fair weather. **FYI:** Reservations accepted. **Open:** Sun–Thurs 11am–10pm, Fri–Sat 11am–11pm. **Prices:** Main courses $8.50–$14.95. AE, CB, DC, DISC, MC, V. ♥ 🏛 VP ♿

Bacchus
7945 Norfolk Ave; tel 301/657-1722. Between St Elmo and Fairmont Aves. **Mediterranean.** Middle Eastern atmosphere begins at entry, continues through stone courtyard with tables and into dining room with magnificent chandelier and regional decor. Extensive appetizers include hummus, baba ghanouj, kibbeh, and other Lebanese favorites. Main courses continue the theme: kabobs, rice dishes with lamb, beef, chicken. **FYI:** Reservations recommended. **Open:** Lunch Mon–Fri noon–2pm; dinner Sun–Thurs 6–10pm, Fri–Sat 6–10:30pm. **Prices:** Main courses $13–$15. AE, MC, V. ♥ VP

Bangkok Garden
4906 St Elmo Ave; tel 301/951-0670. Between Old Georgetown Rd and Norfolk Ave. **Thai.** A multitude of Siamese artifacts and souvenirs sets tone for Thai cuisine ranging from mild shrimp curry with coconut milk and peanut sauce to spicy soft-shell crabs or whole fish in chili and garlic. An intriguing specialty is whole pineapple stuffed with fried rice. **FYI:** Reservations recommended. Dress code. **Open:** Mon–Thurs 11am–10:30pm, Fri–Sat 11am–11pm, Sun 3–10pm. **Prices:** Main courses $6–$18. AE, MC, V.

Café Bethesda
5027 Wilson Lane; tel 301/657-3383. **New American/French.** Intimate dining is enhanced by stark white tablecloths, wicker chairs, and French paintings gracing the walls of this small, bright restaurant. **FYI:** Reservations recommended. Dress code. Beer and wine only. No smoking. **Open:** Lunch Mon–Fri 11:30am–2pm; dinner daily 5pm–close; brunch Sun 10am–2pm. **Prices:** Main courses $14–$25; prix fixe $12. AE, MC, V. ♥ ▼

★ Cottonwood Cafe
4844 Cordell Ave; tel 301/656-4844. Between Norfolk and Woodmont Aves. **Southwestern.** Warm desert colors, adobe-like walls, Navajo rugs give a sense of region and an artistic touch to this two-level restaurant that cooks up mesquite-grilled chicken, steak, fresh fish, and other southwestern favorites. **FYI:** Reservations recommended. **Open:** Lunch Mon–Sat 11:30am–2:30pm; dinner Sun–Thurs 5:30–10pm, Fri–Sat 5:30–11pm. **Prices:** Main courses $12–$20. AE, DC, MC, V. VP ♿

Foong Lin Restaurant
7710 Norfolk Ave; tel 301/656-3427. At Fairmont Ave. **Chinese.** A storefront restaurant with the usual decor of hanging baskets and Oriental paintings and screens. A mix of Cantonese, Szechuan, Hunan, and Mongolian cuisines. Low-fat items offered. **FYI:** Reservations recommended. Dress code. No smoking. **Open:** Mon–Thurs 11am–10:30pm, Fri–Sat 11am–11pm, Sun noon–10pm. **Prices:** Main courses $8–$14. AE, MC, V. VP ♿

♟ La Miche
7905 Norfolk Ave; tel 301/986-0707. At St Elmo Ave. **French.** Baskets hanging from exposed beams contribute to a warm ambience that matches the country-style French cuisine, ranging from veal kidneys in mustard sauce to roast rack of lamb. **FYI:** Reservations recommended. Dress code. **Open:** Lunch Tues–Fri 11:30am–2:30pm; dinner Mon–Sat 6–9:45pm, Sun 5:30–8:30pm. **Prices:** Main courses $15–$24. AE, CB, DC, MC, V. ♥ VP ♿

Parioli
4800 Elm St; tel 301/951-8600. Just off Wisconsin Ave. **Italian.** Winding wrought-iron stairs lead to bright dining area with gold-framed Italian paintings, textured stone walls, and black chairs contrasting with white tablecloths. Italian fare such as *bucatini* (thick pasta with bacon in a red chili-tomato sauce). **FYI:** Reservations recommended. Jazz/Opera. Dress code. No smoking. **Open:** Lunch Mon–Fri 11:30am–2:30pm; dinner Sun–Thurs 5:30–10pm, Fri–Sat 5:30–11pm. **Prices:** Main courses $11–$13. AE, DC, MC, V. ♥ 🏛 ▼ VP ♿

★ Rio Grande Cafe
4919 Fairmont Ave; tel 301/656-2981. Between Old Georgetown Rd and Norfolk Ave. **Tex-Mex.** One of George Bush's favorite taco haunts when he lived at 1600 Pennsylvania Ave, this popular eatery looks like a southwestern roadhouse, with billboard-style advertisements painted on adobe-like walls, straightback wooden chairs, and exposed metal rafters. Tacos, enchiladas, burritos, fajitas, and other regular fare are augmented with mesquite-grilled frogs' legs, quail, chicken, or beef. **FYI:** Reservations not accepted. Dress code. **Open:** Mon–Thurs 11:30am–11pm, Fri–Sat 11:30am–11:30pm, Sun 11:30am–10:30pm. **Prices:** Main courses $7–$14. AE, CB, DC, DISC, MC, V. ♿

⑤ St Elmo's Café
7820 Norfolk Ave; tel 301/657-1607. At St Elmo Ave. **French.** Large windows slide open to a sidewalk dining area at this cafe-style eatery, making it a pleasant spot for lunch. **FYI:** Reservations recommended. Dress code. **Open:** Lunch Mon–Fri 11:30am–3pm; dinner Mon–Thurs 5–10pm, Fri–Sat 5–11pm, Sun 5–9pm. **Prices:** Main courses $13–$22; prix fixe $13. AE, CB, DC, MC, V. ♥ ⚓ ▼ VP

★ Tako Grill
7756 Wisconsin Ave; tel 301/652-7030. Exit I-495 at Wisconsin Ave. **Japanese.** Downtown restaurant with peaked, blond wood ceiling. Each black enamel table is topped with a sake vase containing a lone orchid. Sushi bar serves traditional Japanese selections, while menu offers cooked items including soft-shell crabs. **FYI:** Reservations not accepted. Dress code. Beer and wine only. No smoking. **Open:** Lunch Mon–Fri 11:30am–2pm; dinner Mon–Thurs 5:30–9:45pm, Fri–Sat 5:30–10:15pm. **Prices:** Main courses $9–$16. AE, MC, V. ⅙

Terramar
7800 Wisconsin Ave; tel 301/654-0888. Exit I-495 at Wisconsin Ave, go south. **Latin American.** A sunny dining room with whitewashed walls, archways, fountain. Bar has red-tile roof-like canopy. Indoor courtyard. Nicaraguan fare includes seafood and beef dishes on seasonal menu. Nicaraguan entertainment Friday and Saturday. Smoking in bar only. **FYI:** Reservations recommended. Children's menu. No smoking. **Open:** Lunch Tues–Fri 11:30am–2:30pm; dinner Tues–Thurs 5–10pm, Fri–Sat 5–11pm, Sun 5–9pm. **Prices:** Main courses $11–$20. AE, DC, DISC, MC, V. ♥

★ Tragara
4935 Cordell Ave; tel 301/951-4935. Between Old Georgetown Rd and Norfolk Ave. **Italian.** Art-deco curves and a burgundy-and-pink color scheme set off this elegantly simple establishment, one of the area's most popular upscale Italian restaurants. A window lets guests glimpse talented chef at work on gourmet northern Italian dishes such as swordfish with currants, pine nuts, and basil. Specials offered on seasonal basis. **FYI:** Reservations recommended. Children's menu. Jacket required. No smoking. **Open:** Lunch Mon–Fri 11:30am–2:30pm; dinner Mon–Thurs 5:30–10pm, Fri–Sat 5:30–10:30pm, Sun 5–9pm. **Prices:** Main courses $16–$27. AE, CB, DC, MC, V. ♥ VP ⅙

★ Volare Ristorante Italiano
4926 St Elmo Ave; tel 301/907-7503. Between Old Georgetown Rd and Norfolk Ave. **Italian.** Two small dining rooms are festooned with potted and hanging plants, creating a garden-like atmosphere in a narrow storefront setting. Italian opera on sound system complements the traditional Italian menu, which is augmented by nightly specials. **FYI:** Reservations recommended. Dress code. No smoking. **Open:** Lunch Tues–Fri 11am–2pm; dinner Sun–Sat 5–10:30pm. **Prices:** Main courses $10–$18. AE, CB, DC, DISC, MC, V. VP ⅙

ATTRACTION 🖼

Clara Barton National Historic Site
5801 Oxford Rd; tel 301/492-6245. Once the headquarters for the American Red Cross, today it displays furniture and other possessions once belonging to the woman who founded the organization in 1881. Guided tours are offered hourly. **Open:** Daily 10am–5pm. **Free**

Bowie

Huge, Levitt-built bedroom community between Washington, DC, and Annapolis. Once the site of Belair Farms, "The Cradle of American Thououghbred Racing." **Information:** Bowie Chamber of Commerce, 6770 Race Track Rd, Bowie, 20715 (tel 301/263-0920).

HOTEL 🏨

≣≣≣ Comfort Inn Hotel & Conference Center
Harbor Way, PO Box 730, 20718; tel 301/464-0089 or toll free 800/228-5150; fax 301/805-5563. Jct US 50/US 301. Housed in a six-story building, this business-minded hotel is convenient to the light industrial parks of the area. **Rooms:** 110 rms and stes. CI 3pm/CO 11am. Nonsmoking rms avail. Sizable rooms. **Amenities:** 🖥 ⅙ A/C, satel TV. Some units w/whirlpools. **Services:** 🛎 **Facilities:** 🏊 300 ⅙ 1 restaurant (lunch and dinner only), 1 bar, washer/dryer. The Orioles farm team play at Prince George's Stadium across the street. Restaurant is locally famous for its lunch buffet. **Rates (CP):** Peak (Apr–Oct) $69–$155 S; $74–$159 D; $155–$159 ste. Extra person $5. Children under age 18 stay free. Min stay special events. Lower rates off-season. Parking: Outdoor, free. AE, CB, DC, DISC, MC, V.

MOTELS

≣≣ Econo Lodge
Harbor Way, PO Box 730, 20718; tel 301/464-2200 or toll free 800/55-ECONO; fax 301/805-5563. Jct US 50/US 301. This older property at the highway junction has been recently redecorated, and the furniture is new. **Rooms:** 80 rms. CI 3pm/CO 11am. Nonsmoking rms avail. **Amenities:** 🖥 ⅙ A/C, satel TV. **Services:** 🛎 🛏 **Facilities:** 🏊 ⅙ Access to pool at adjacent Comfort Inn. **Rates:** Peak (Apr–Oct) $53–$78 S or D. Extra person $5. Children under age 18 stay free. Lower rates off-season. Parking: Outdoor, free. AE, CB, DC, DISC, MC, V.

≣≣ Rips Country Village Motel
US 301, PO Box 1469, 20717; tel 301/805-5900 or toll free 800/359-RIPS; fax 301/262-0900. 1 mi S of US 50. Before the rolling farmland northeast of DC was turned into one of Maryland's largest incorporated cities, this roadside motel was here. It's still in excellent condition, and has a prime location on two major routes. **Rooms:** 40 rms. CI 1pm/CO 11am. Nonsmoking rms avail. Spacious and tastefully deco-

rated. Family suites have two rooms with three double beds. **Amenities:** 🛏 A/C, TV. **Services:** 🛎 🍽 **Facilities:** 🏊 1 restaurant, 1 bar, playground. **Rates:** Peak (Apr–Oct) $50 S; $58–$68 D. Extra person $6. Children under age 12 stay free. Lower rates off-season. Parking: Outdoor, free. AE, CB, DC, DISC, MC, V.

Cambridge

Seat of Dorchester County, located on the Choptank River. Once a thriving port and ship-building center (and still the state's second-largest port city), today it's a major center for seafood packaging and tourism. **Information:** Dorcester County Chamber of Commerce, 203 Sunburst Hwy, Cambridge, 21613 (tel 410/228-3575).

ATTRACTIONS 📷

Old Trinity Church
MD 16; tel 410/228-3583. Eight miles southwest of Cambridge is this landmark church built circa 1685 and meticulously restored in recent years. It is one of the oldest Episcopal churches in active use in the United States. **Open:** Peak (Apr–Oct) Mon, Wed, and Fri–Sat 10am–4pm; Sun 1–4pm. Reduced hours off-season. **Free**

Dorchester Heritage Museum
1904 Horn Point Rd; tel 410/228-1899. Housed in an airplane hangar on the old du Pont estate, now a part of the University of Maryland. Exhibits highlight local history and heritage with displays on aviation, archeology, and maritime industries. **Open:** Apr–Oct, Sat–Sun 1–4:30pm. Open by appointment in off-season. **Free**

Meredith House
902 Greenway Dr; tel 410/228-7953. The Georgian-style residence, circa 1760, includes the Governor's Room honoring past leaders of Maryland who are associated with Dorchester county, plus an antique doll collection. The adjacent Neild Museum contains exhibits on local maritime and industrial development and on farm life, as well as an original 1831 McCormick reaper. Other attractions on the property are an herb garden, a meat house, and an 18th-century stable. **Open:** Apr–Dec, Thurs–Sat 10am–3pm or by appointment. **Free**

Blackwater National Wildlife Refuge
Key Wallace Dr; tel 410/228-2677. Located 12 mi SE of Cambridge, this 21,000-acre site of rich tidal marsh, freshwater ponds, and woodlands serves as a resting and feeding area for migrant and wintering wildfowl, including huge flocks of Canadian geese and ducks. The grounds are also the home of three endangered species: the bald eagle, the Delmarva fox squirrel, and the migrant peregrine falcon. Visitors center, wildlife trail, five-mile wildlife drive, hiking and biking paths. **Open:** Daily sunrise–sunset. **$**

Chesapeake City

This tiny burg on the northern end of the Eastern Shore was once a busy canal boat center. Now its streets are lined with B&Bs, specialty shops, and restaurants.

RESTAURANTS 🍽

Bayard House Restaurant
11 Bohemia Ave; tel 410/885-5040. On MD 213 at C&D Canal. **New American.** This historic building dating to the late 18th century is furnished with authentic Hitchcock and spindle-back chairs and fine needlepoint hangings. Lower level and outdoor deck overlook Chesapeake and Delaware Canal. Menu features light, creative treatment of American dishes, with an emphasis on seafood. **FYI:** Reservations recommended. Dress code. No smoking. **Open:** Lunch Mon–Sat 11:30am–3pm, Sun noon–2:30pm; dinner Mon–Thurs 5–9pm, Fri–Sat 5–10pm, Sun 4–9pm. **Prices:** Main courses $16–$19. AE, DISC, MC, V. 🍴 🏔 🖼 ♿

Schaefer's Canal House
208 Bank St; tel 410/885-2200. On MD 213 at C&D Canal. **Regional American/Seafood.** Spacious wood-beamed rooms with cathedral ceilings overlook busy Chesapeake and Delaware Canal. Chesapeake Bay pilots board passing ships here; home ports and destinations are announced to guests. Traditional and regional American entrees feature such Eastern Shore favorites as crab cakes and oysters. This special-occasion restaurant accepts no reservations on Saturday during summer months, when a reggae band plays on outdoor patio. **FYI:** Reservations accepted. Reggae. Dress code. No smoking. **Open:** Breakfast daily 8–11am; lunch daily 11am–4pm; dinner Mon–Sat 4–10pm, Sun noon–9pm. **Prices:** Main courses $18–$25. AE, MC, V. 🏔 🖼 ♿

ATTRACTION 📷

C&D Canal Museum
815 Bethel Rd; tel 410/885-5622. Located on the waterfront at 2nd St. A series of exhibits depicts the history and operation of the 160-year-old canal that connects the Chesapeake and Delaware Bays. **Open:** Peak (Apr–Oct) Mon–Sat 8:15am–4:15pm, Sun 10am–6pm. Reduced hours off-season. **Free**

Chestertown

Located on the Chester River just north of Kent Island. Charming, historic town with a roguish history connected to its harbor. Seat of Kent County. **Information:** Kent County Chamber of Commerce, 400 S Cross St, PO Box 146, Chestertown, 21620 (tel 410/778-0416).

MOTEL

≡≡≡ Great Oak Lodge

22170 Great Oak Landing Rd, 21620; tel 410/778-2100 or toll free 800/526-3464; fax 410/778-3977. 70 acres. This older but adequately maintained waterfront motel is next to a popular pleasure-boating harbor. **Rooms:** 28 rms. CI 2pm/CO 11am. Standard motel rooms, some with excellent views of Fairlee Creek. **Amenities:** 🛏 ⚬ A/C, satel TV w/movies. **Services:** ✗ ⤶ Twice-daily maid svce, babysitting. Yacht brokerage, ship's store, boat repairs. **Facilities:** 🎣 🚴 ⚠ ▶9 🐚1 ⌕120 1 restaurant, 4 bars (2 w/entertainment), 1 beach (cove/inlet), games rm, lawn games, whirlpool, washer/dryer. Large restaurant is on the water, has nice view. Marina. Beach suitable for small boats, not swimming. **Rates:** Peak (Apr–Jan) $85–$130 S or D. Extra person $15. Children under age 12 stay free. Min stay wknds and special events. Lower rates off-season. MAP rates avail. Parking: Outdoor, free. AE, DISC, MC, V.

INN

≡≡≡ Imperial Hotel

208 High St, 21620; tel 410/778-5000; fax 410/778-9662. This beautiful turn-of-the-century inn is like a time capsule in the center of this historic and picturesque riverfront town. **Rooms:** 13 rms. CI 3pm/CO 11am. Nonsmoking rms avail. Faithfully furnished with antiques in excellent condition. **Amenities:** 🛏 📺 A/C, cable TV. 1 unit w/terrace. **Services:** ✗ ⤶ Masseur. **Facilities:** ⌕15 ♿ 1 restaurant (see "Restaurants" below), 1 bar (w/entertainment), washer/dryer, guest lounge w/TV. Fine restaurant done in same late-Victorian decor. Swimming available at nearby Washington College. **Rates (CP):** $95–$125 D. Extra person $35. Children under age 8 stay free. Min stay special events. Parking: Outdoor, free. AE, DC, DISC, MC, V.

RESTAURANT

Imperial Hotel Restaurant

In Imperial Hotel, 208 High St; tel 410/778-5000. Cross St exit off MD 213. **Regional American/Seafood.** The authentic late-Victorian dining room in the restored 1903 hotel offers award-winning wine list and cuisine oriented toward American seafood and regional dishes. Extensive list of aperitifs, brandies, and cognacs, plus a variety of coffees. **FYI:** Reservations recommended. Jazz. Dress code. No smoking. **Open:** Lunch Tues–Sat 11:45am–2pm; dinner Tues–Sat 5:30–9:30pm; brunch Sun 11:30am–3pm. **Prices:** Main courses $14–$22; prix fixe $80. AE, DISC, MC, V. ■ 🗹 ♿

ATTRACTION

St Paul's Church

7579 Sandy Bottom Rd; tel 410/778-1540. Erected in 1713, this is one of the oldest continually used churches in Mary-land. Among the notables buried in the church's oak tree–shaded graveyard is actress Tallulah Bankhead. **Open:** Daily 9am–5pm. **Free**

Chevy Chase

See also Bethesda

This prosperous suburb northwest of Washington, DC, is a major economic and business center. The Audubon Naturalist Society, a 40-acre nature sanctuary and education center, draws tourists. **Information:** Greater Bethesda–Chevy Chase Chamber of Commerce, 7910 Woodmont Ave #1204, Bethesda, 20814 (tel 301/652-4900).

RESTAURANT

La Ferme

7101 Brookville Rd (Brookville); tel 301/986-5255. From Chevy Chase Circle, go east on Western Ave, turn left onto Brookville Rd; ½ mile to restaurant. **French.** Tucked away in an affluent residential neighborhood, this former barn has been expertly decorated in a French country style. High peaked ceiling adds spaciousness. Patio for outdoor dining when weather permits. Traditional French cuisine includes variety of fish selections plus various meats, all excellently prepared by co-owner/chef. **FYI:** Reservations recommended. Dress code. **Open:** Lunch Tues–Fri noon–2pm; dinner Tues–Sat 6–10pm, Sun 5–9pm. **Prices:** Main courses $18–$22. AE, CB, DC, MC, V. 🍽 ♿

College Park

This northeastern suburb of Washington, DC, is home to the University of Maryland. **Information:** Baltimore–Washington Corridor Chamber of Commerce, 7901 Sandy Spring Rd, #501, Laurel, 20707 (tel 301/725-4000).

MOTELS

≡≡≡ Best Western Maryland Inn & Fundome

8601 Baltimore Blvd, 20740; tel 301/474-2800 or toll free 800/528-1234; fax 301/474-0714. Exit 25B off I-495. Follow US 1 S for ¾ mile. A well-kept older property convenient to the University of Maryland. Outdoor courtyard, enclosed atrium. **Rooms:** 118 rms. CI 2pm/CO noon. Nonsmoking rms avail. Standard rooms, some on pool atrium and some exterior. New furniture and carpeting installed in 1996. **Amenities:** 🛏 ⚬ A/C, cable TV w/movies, dataport, voice mail. Some units w/terraces. **Services:** ✗ 🚐 🖨 ⤶ Free shuttle to Metro station. **Facilities:** 🎣 🏊 ⌕250 ♿ 1 restaurant, 1 bar, games rm, sauna, steam rm, whirlpool. Putting green, shuffleboard, billiard table, very attractive pool and whirlpool in atrium. **Rates:** Peak (Mar 15–Nov 24) $59–$89

S; $64–$99 D. Extra person $5. Children under age 12 stay free. Lower rates off-season. Parking: Outdoor, free. AE, CB, DC, DISC, MC, V.

Days Inn College Park

9137 Baltimore Blvd, 20740; tel 301/345-5000 or toll free 800/329-7466; fax 301/345-4577. Exit 25 off I-495. Follow US 1 S for ½ mile. A middle-aged motel in average condition, kept clean and neat. **Rooms:** 68 rms. CI 1pm/CO noon. No smoking. Standard motel-type rooms. **Amenities:** ☎ A/C, cable TV w/movies. **Services:** 🚐 🖨 ↵ Car-rental desk. **Facilities:** 🍴 1 restaurant (*see* "Restaurants" below), 1 bar. Well-regarded Korean restaurant on premises. Large pool. **Rates:** $48–$60 S or D. Extra person $5. Children under age 12 stay free. Parking: Outdoor, free. AE, CB, DC, DISC, MC, V.

Holiday Inn

10000 Baltimore Blvd, 20740; tel 301/345-6700 or toll free 800/872-5564; fax 301/441-4923. 5 mi N of Washington; exit 25 off I-495. The attractive, welcoming lobby of this motel is exceptionally large, but it has comfortable furniture and several cozy areas for small groups. **Rooms:** 221 rms and stes. Executive level. CI 3pm/CO 1pm. Nonsmoking rms avail. All units recently redecorated. **Amenities:** ☎ 🕹 🖨 🍷 A/C, cable TV w/movies, dataport, voice mail. **Services:** ✗ 🖨 ↵ Children's program. Courtesy van to Metro station. **Facilities:** 🍴 🏋 🔲 💻 & 1 restaurant, 1 bar, games rm, sauna, whirlpool, washer/dryer. Family-style steak restaurant on premises. Nice indoor pool and exercise room. **Rates:** $89 S or D; $150–$350 ste. Children under age 18 stay free. Parking: Outdoor, free. AE, CB, DC, DISC, JCB, MC, V.

Quality Inn

7200 Baltimore Blvd, 20740; tel 310/864-5820 or toll free 800/221-2222; fax 301/927-8634. 2 mi N of Washington. Exit 25B off I-495. Left on US 1; follow US 1 S for 3 miles. Convenient to the University of Maryland and just three blocks from College Park Metro station, this motel is good for events at the college and for long-term stays. **Rooms:** 154 rms and effic. CI 3pm/CO noon. No smoking. Recently refurnished and in good condition. **Amenities:** ☎ 🕹 A/C, cable TV. Some units w/terraces. **Services:** 🖨 ↵ Car-rental desk, babysitting. **Facilities:** 🍴 & 1 restaurant, washer/dryer. Laundry. Guests receive complimentary use of sauna, whirlpool, and exercise equipment across the street. **Rates (CP):** Peak (Sept–Nov/Mar–June) $49–$54 S; $54–$59 D; $59 effic. Extra person $5. Children under age 18 stay free. Lower rates off-season. MAP rates avail. Parking: Outdoor, free. Long-term rates avail. AE, DC, DISC, ER, JCB, MC, V.

Royal Pine Inn

9113 Baltimore Blvd, 20740; tel 301/345-4900 or toll free 800/660-5162; fax 301/345-3017. 3 mi N of Washington. Exit 25 off I-495. Follow US 1 S for ½ mile. This older motel has seen regular maintenance but could use some sprucing up with new carpets and paint. Still it is an adequate, basic facility in a convenient location. **Rooms:** 114 rms and stes. CI noon/CO noon. No smoking. Larger than average rooms; some are family-size. **Amenities:** ☎ A/C, cable TV w/movies. **Services:** 🚐 🖨 ↵ Car-rental desk. Tours of Washington, DC, pick up at lobby. **Facilities:** 🍴 & **Rates (CP):** Peak (May–Sept) $72 S; $82 D; $82 ste. Extra person $5. Children under age 18 stay free. Lower rates off-season. Parking: Outdoor, free. AE, DC, DISC, MC, V.

RESTAURANTS 🍴

★ Ledo Restaurant

In Adelphi Plaza, 2420 University Blvd, Hyattsville; tel 301/422-8122/8622. University Blvd near University of Maryland. **American/Italian.** This cozy place, with its Tiffany-style lamps and ceiling fans, has been a favorite of the college crowd for 40 years. The menu offers a variety of American and Italian dishes, prepared with fresh ingredients. Pizza is very popular. **FYI:** Reservations accepted. Children's menu. No smoking. **Open:** Mon–Thurs 9am–11pm, Fri–Sat 9am–midnight, Sun 9am–10pm. **Prices:** Main courses $6–$12. MC, V. 👪 🍷

Yijo

In Days Inn College Park, 9137 Baltimore Blvd; tel 301/345-6500. 4 mi N of Washington DC. Exit 25 off I-495. Go south on US 1 for ½ mile. **Korean.** Two simple rooms off the lobby of a motel. Neat but unpretentious. Extensive Korean menu, authentic and reasonably priced. Friendly, accommodating service. **FYI:** Reservations recommended. **Open:** Lunch daily 11:30am–2pm; dinner daily 2–10:30pm. **Prices:** Main courses $8–$14. AE, DISC, MC, V.

Columbia

A planned community created in 1966 by architect James Rouse, also known for his renovation of Boston's Faneuil Hall Marketplace, Baltimore Harborplace, and Norfolk Waterside. **Information:** Howard County Chamber of Commerce, 5560 Sterrett Pl #105, Columbia, 21044 (tel 410/730-4111).

HOTEL 🏨

Columbia Inn Hotel & Conference Center

10207 Wincopin Circle, 21044; tel 410/730-3900 or toll free 800/638-2817; fax 410/730-1290. I-95 to MD 175 W. Beautifully set on the lake in Columbia, this hotel caters to corporate travelers on weekdays and offers many special packages to pleasure travelers on weekends. Located across street from major shopping mall. **Rooms:** 289 rms and stes. CI 3pm/CO noon. Nonsmoking rms avail. Many rooms provide excellent views. **Amenities:** ☎ 🕹 A/C, satel TV w/movies. **Services:** ✗ 🚐 🖨 ↵ 🍸 Car-rental desk, babysitting. Tours of Washington, Baltimore, other nearby sights arranged. **Facilities:** 🍴 ⛰ 🏊 🎾 🏊 & 1 restaurant, 1 bar, washer/dryer. Restaurant has very nice lake view, well-regarded Sunday brunch. Guest passes to seven nearby swim, golf, and fitness clubs. **Rates (CP):** Peak (Mar–Nov) $127 S; $137 D; $250–$300 ste. Extra person $15. Children under age 18 stay free. Lower rates off-season. Parking: Indoor/outdoor, free. AE, CB, DC, DISC, MC, V.

MOTEL

≡≡≡ Columbia Hilton Inn

5485 Twin Knolls Rd, 21045; tel 410/997-1060 or toll free 800/235-0653; fax 410/997-0169. Exit 41 off I-95, follow MD 175 W. Modern motel with a dramatic atrium and attractive public areas. **Rooms:** 152 rms and stes. CI 3pm/CO noon. Nonsmoking rms avail. **Amenities:** A/C, satel TV w/movies. Some units w/minibars. Wet bars, microwaves in suites. **Services:** Car-rental desk, babysitting. Van to Columbia businesses and shopping. **Facilities:** 1 restaurant, 1 bar, spa, sauna, whirlpool. Very nice indoor pool in a bright, airy space. **Rates:** $99–$149 S or D; $235 ste. Extra person $10. Children under age 18 stay free. Parking: Outdoor, free. AE, DC, DISC, MC, V.

RESTAURANTS

⑤ Cover to Cover Café

In Owen Brown Village Center, 7284 Cradlerock Way; tel 410/381-9200. MD 32 W exit off I-95, turn right on Broken Land Pkwy, right on Candlerock Way, left into Owen Brown Center. **New American/Cafe.** Unique, inexpensive, appealing, and informal. The room, in a bookstore, has simple decor and bentwood furniture. A sidewalk cafe is open during fine weather. French-American cafe-style dishes with some southwestern influence. Entertainment is folk or light rock, including guitar, piano, or dulcimer. **FYI:** Reservations accepted. Children's menu. No smoking. **Open:** Mon–Wed 11am–9pm, Thurs 11am–10pm, Fri–Sat 11am–11pm, Sun 10am–9pm. **Prices:** Main courses $7–$14. AE, DC, DISC, MC, V.

The Kings Contrivance Restaurant

10150 Shaker Dr; tel 410/995-0500. MD 32 W exit off I-95, ½ mile N on Shaker Dr. **American.** In a 19th-century house, quiet and distinctive dining rooms are decorated and furnished in Federal style. Entrees feature meat, fish, and pasta selections. **FYI:** Reservations recommended. **Open:** Lunch Mon–Fri 11:30am–2pm; dinner Mon–Sat 5:30–9pm, Sun 4–8pm. **Prices:** Main courses $15–$26; prix fixe $16. AE, DISC, MC, V.

Crisfield

Called the "Crab Capital of the World." Many residents of this small Eastern Shore town make their living pulling crabs, fish, and oysters from Chesapeake Bay. **Information:** Crisfield Area Chamber of Commerce, PO Box 292, Crisfield, 21817 (tel 410/968-2500).

MOTELS

≡ Pines Motel

N Somerset Ave, PO Box 106, 21817; tel 410/968-0900. Exit US 13 at MD 413. This simple, basic motel with clean, neat rooms is located in a residential neighborhood. **Rooms:** 40 rms and effic. CI noon/CO 11am. Nonsmoking rms avail. Efficiency units are in a newer section. **Amenities:** A/C, cable TV, refrig. No phone. **Facilities:** Picnic tables and barbecue grill. **Rates:** Peak (July–Aug) $60–$70 S or D; $75–$85 effic. Extra person $5. Min stay special events. Lower rates off-season. Parking: Outdoor, free. No CC.

≡≡ Somers Cove Motel

707 RR Norris Dr, PO Box 387, 21817; tel 410/968-1900 or toll free 800/827-6637. MD 413 off US 13. A basic but good place to stay, this motel next to the municipal marina attracts boating and fishing enthusiasts. The exterior is ready for some refinishing. **Rooms:** 40 rms and effic. CI 11am/CO 11am. Rooms are standard and adequate, recently repainted. No pictures on the walls. **Amenities:** A/C, cable TV w/movies. Some units w/terraces. Private balconies have some views of the marina. **Services:** Car-rental desk. **Facilities:** **Rates:** Peak (Mem Day–Labor Day) $55–$75 S or D; $85 effic. Extra person $5. Min stay special events. Lower rates off-season. MAP rates avail. Parking: Outdoor, free. MC, V.

RESTAURANTS

Captain's Galley

1021 W Main St; tel 410/968-3313. Exit US 13 at MD 413. **Seafood.** Large windows look onto the water from this paneled room with nautical bric-a-brac and wood-grained formica tables. Crabmeat, and especially some of the best crab cakes available anywhere, built this restaurant's reputation. The delicate seasoning is sold to take home. Discounts for seniors over 60. **FYI:** Reservations recommended. Children's menu. **Open:** Peak (Mem Day–Sept) breakfast daily 8am–noon; lunch Sun–Thurs 11am–9pm, Fri–Sat 11am–10pm; dinner Sun–Thurs 11am–9pm, Fri–Sat 11am–10pm. **Prices:** Main courses $8–$20. MC, V.

Watermen's Inn

9th and Main Sts (Town Center); tel 410/968-2119. MD 413 exit off US 13. **American/Seafood.** Works by local artists are displayed in this informal, country-style establishment. Noise from adjacent local bar does not intrude on dining room. Known for crab and shellfish, but beef and fish are also featured, many in creative sauces. **FYI:** Reservations recommended. Children's menu. **Open:** Peak (Mem Day–Labor Day) breakfast Fri–Sat 8–11am, Sun 8am–noon; lunch Tues–Sun 11:30am–5pm; dinner Tues–Sat 5–10pm, Sun 5–9pm. **Prices:** Main courses $8–$20. AE, DISC, MC, V.

ATTRACTIONS 📷

J Millard Tawes Museum

39th St on the Somers Cove Marina; tel 410/968-2501. Founded in 1982 to honor a Crisfield-born former governor of Maryland, this museum features exhibits that provide background about the history of the town and the development of the city's seafood industry. **Open:** May–Sept, daily 9am–4:30pm. **$**

Teackle Mansion

Mansion St, Princess Anne; tel 410/651-3020. Built in 1801–1803 and patterned after a Scottish manor house, this was the residence of Littleton Dennis Teackle, an associate of Thomas Jefferson and one of the principal transoceanic shipping magnates of the 18th century. With two entrances, one fronting the Manokin River and one facing the town, the grand house measures nearly 200 feet in length and is symmetrically balanced throughout. The interior includes elaborate plaster ceilings, mirrored windows, a seven-foot fireplace and beehive oven, American Chippendale furniture, Della Robbia (fruit-designed) ceilings, a Tudor-Gothic pipe organ, an 1806 silk world map, and a 1712 family Bible. **Open:** Wed 1–3pm, Sat 11am–3pm, Sun 2–4pm. **$**

Smith Island

Tangier Sound; tel 410/968-2500. Smith Islanders are the direct descendants of British colonists who first settled the island in the early 1700s. Because of their isolation from the mainland, they speak to this day with a distinct accent, said to be a holdover from Elizabethan times. Today the island is a world apart—there are no sidewalks, beaches, convenience stores, boat rentals, movie theaters, liquor stores, bars, fast-food chains, boutiques, laundromats, or taxi cabs. Passenger ferries to the island depart year-round from Crisfield's city dock daily at noon. The ferry fee includes round-trip transportation, sightseeing on the island, and a family-style lunch at one of the local homes or guesthouses. **$$$$**

Cumberland

A railway, manufacturing, and coal mining center on the banks of the Potomac. As a natural gateway through the Appalachian Mountains to the Ohio Valley, it became an important portal to the West during the 19th century. Today, it is best known as the northern terminus of the C&O Canal. **Information:** Allegany County Chamber of Commerce, Bell Tower Bldg, Cumberland, 21502 (tel 301/722-2820).

HOTELS 🏨

≣≣≣ Best Western Braddock Motor Inn

1268 National Hwy, La Vale, 21502; tel 301/729-3300 or toll free 800/296-6006; fax 301/729-3300. Exit 39 off I-68. Wraparound sun deck and adjoining glassed-in pool form one entrance to this attractive facility. Landscaping and walkway corridors with large floor-to-ceiling windows lend an air of quality. **Rooms:** 108 rms and stes. CI 2pm/CO 11am. Nonsmoking rms avail. Rooms have the standard integrated decor of a chain, but some offer a larger area for sitting and oak furnishings in fine shape, including large desks. 11 suites with pull-out sofas. **Amenities:** 🛁 A/C, cable TV. Some units w/whirlpools. Suites have 2 phones. Refrigerators, coffee-makers, microwaves, and VCRs for rent. **Services:** ✕ 🚐 ⚆ 🛎 Babysitting. **Facilities:** 🔓 🛏 🍴 ⚓ 1 restaurant, 1 bar, games rm, sauna, whirlpool. Miniature golf and bowling across the highway. **Rates:** $48–$58 S; $54–$65 D; $85–$105 ste. Extra person $6. Children under age 18 stay free. Parking: Outdoor, free. Anniversary, Getaway packages avail. AE, CB, DC, DISC, MC, V.

≣≣ Holiday Inn

100 S George St, 21502; tel 301/724-8800 or toll free 800/HOLIDAY; fax 301/724-4001. Exit 43C off I-68. Convenient downtown location for this nicely maintained facility, 25 miles from skiing. **Rooms:** 130 rms and stes. CI 2pm/CO noon. Nonsmoking rms avail. Integrated decor. King or 2-bedded rooms, some with pull-out sofas; 1 room for the disabled available. **Amenities:** 🛁 ⚆ A/C, cable TV, voice mail. **Services:** ✕ 🚐 ⚆ 🛎 🐾 Twice-daily maid svce. Friendly staff. Safe-deposit boxes available. **Facilities:** 🔓 🍴 ⚓ 1 restaurant (*see* "Restaurants" below), 1 bar (w/entertainment). Use of facilities at local YMCA. **Rates:** Peak (May–Sept) $79 S or D; $159 ste. Children under age 18 stay free. Lower rates off-season. Parking: Outdoor, free. Children eat free. Ski, golf, and bike packages. Weekly and monthly rates avail. AE, CB, DC, DISC, JCB, MC, V.

INN

≣≣≣ Inn at Walnut Bottom

120 Greene St, 21502; tel 301/777-0003 or toll free 800/286-9718; fax 301/777-8288. A gracious 19th-century inn in two small buildings near historic area of Cumberland and the C&O Canal towpath. Complete with oak bannister and floors, antiques, chandeliers, and comfy wicker-furniture parlor with games and parakeets. **Rooms:** 12 rms and stes (4 w/shared bath). CI 3pm/CO 11am. No smoking. All uniquely decorated in antique and period reproduction furniture. Rooms accommodate two people in twin beds, a queen bed, or a full bed, and some have a day bed for a third person, for extra charge; two-family suites available. **Amenities:** 🛁 ⚆ A/C, cable TV, bathrobes. **Services:** ✕ 🛎 Parlor offers tea and coffee. Trays delivered for breakfast if guest is checking out before restaurant opens. Lunches packed on request. Dinners brought to room if necessary. **Facilities:** ⚓ 1 restaurant (*see* "Restaurants" below), 1 bar, guest lounge. Communal refrigerator. Small gift shop sells local wares. **Rates (BB):** $75 D w/shared bath, $95 D w/private bath; $105 ste. Extra person $15. Children under age 5 stay free. Min stay wknds. Parking: Outdoor, free. MAP available for groups. Special packages avail for skiing, horseback riding, canoeing, bicycling, theater, golf. AE, DISC, MC, V.

RESTAURANTS 🍴

Harrigan's
In Holiday Inn, 100 S George St; tel 301/724-8800. Exit 43C off I-68. **American.** Quiet dining in low-ceilinged room decorated with framed paintings of the area and impressionist murals. Floor-to-ceiling windows along one side and white-banistered area add lightness to the solid mahogany chairs and tables. Steaks a specialty, and all-you-can-eat dinners available some nights. **FYI:** Reservations recommended. Big band/comedy/piano/singer. Children's menu. No smoking. **Open:** Daily 76am–10pm. **Prices:** Main courses $5–$21. AE, DISC, MC, V. 👥 ❤ ♿

★ Mason's Barn
I-86 at exit 46; tel 301/722-6155. **American.** This family-operated restaurant is in an antiques-adorned barn with loft. A favorite of locals and travelers for 40 years, it serves up down-home country cooking the likes of burgers and sandwiches, "bread bowl" soups, and slow-roasted prime rib. **FYI:** Reservations recommended. Children's menu. No smoking. **Open:** Breakfast Mon–Fri 6–11am, Sat–Sun 6am–1pm; lunch daily 11am–4pm; dinner Mon–Sat 4pm–close, Sun 1pm–close. **Prices:** Main courses $8–$15. AE, CB, DC, DISC, MC, V. 👥

★ Oxford House
In Inn at Walnut Bottom, 118 Greene St; tel 301/777-7101. Exit 43A off I-68. **New American/Continental/Seafood.** Located in a 19th-century inn, this dining room presents traditional country-inn food in an intimate low-ceilinged room with oak chairs and large tables. Specialties are fresh filleted salmon, crab, and homemade desserts. **FYI:** Reservations accepted. No smoking. **Open:** Lunch Mon–Fri 11am–2:30pm; dinner Mon–Thurs 5–9:00pm, Fri–Sat 5–9:30pm. **Prices:** Main courses $11–$19. AE, DC, DISC, MC, V. 🏛

★ Pennywhistle's
25 N Centre St; tel 301/724-6626. Exit 43C off I-68. **Cafe.** Sparkling bright, this fresh American-style downtown cafe, with overhead grape arbor, has placed plexiglass between the tables, fostering privacy. Flowered vinyl tablecloths and cut flowers add to attractive atmosphere. Specialties include chicken salad and the "Pennywhistle" vegetable soup and salad. Vegetarian fare available. **FYI:** Reservations not accepted. Beer and wine only. No smoking. **Open:** Mon–Sat 8am–5pm. **Prices:** Lunch main courses $5–$6. MC, V. 🍰 ♿

ATTRACTIONS 🏛

George Washington's Headquarters
Riverside Park, Greene St; tel 301/777-5905. The log cabin, believed to be the only remaining section of the original Fort Cumberland, was used by Washington as his official quarters during the French and Indian War. The cabin interior is not accessible, but there is a viewing window and a tape-recorded description activated by a push button. **Open:** Daily 24 hours. **Free**

History House
218 Washington St; tel 301/777-8678. This restored 18-room dwelling contains such antique furnishings as a Victorian courting couch and an 1840 square grand piano. Other features include an early 19th-century brick-walled garden and a basement kitchen with authentic cooking utensils, a fireplace, a coal stove, dishes, and pottery. **Open:** Peak (May–Oct) Tues–Sat 11am–4pm, Sun 1:30–4pm. Reduced hours off-season. **$**

Emmanuel Episcopal Church
16 Washington St; tel 301/777-3364. Built on the foundations of Fort Cumberland, where George Washington began his military career, this parish dates back to 1803. The church, which contains original Tiffany stained-glass windows and a scale model of Fort Cumberland, is open to the public only during services: Thursday at 10:30am and Sunday at 8 and 10am. **Free**

Toll Gate House
La Vale exit off MD 40A; tel 301/729-4938. Built in 1836, this historic toll gate house is the last of its kind in Maryland. When the country's first national road was built, federal funds were used to finance it; ownership was then turned over to the states, which built toll gate houses to collect tolls from travelers. **Open:** Peak (June–Aug) Fri–Sun 1:30–4:30pm. Reduced hours off-season. Closed Nov–Apr. **Free**

Western Maryland Scenic Railroad
13 Canal St; tel 301/759-4400. A vintage steam train that makes a 34-mile round-trip excursion between Cumberland and Frostburg. The trip follows a scenic mountain valley route through the Cumberland Narrows, Helmstetter's Horseshoe Curve, various tunnels, many panoramic vistas, and a 1,300-foot elevation change between the two destinations. The trip takes 3 hours, including a 1½-hour layover in Frostburg for local sightseeing. **Open:** Call for schedule. **$$$$**

C&O Canal Boat Replica
North Branch exit off MD 51; tel 301/729-3136. A full-scale boat modeled after the ones that used to move along the 184-mile canal between Georgetown and Cumberland. It features a captain's cabin with furnishings from the 1828–1924 canal era, a hay house where feed was stored for the mules, and an on-board mule stable. A restored log-cabin lock house is located nearby. **Open:** June–Aug, Sat–Sun 1–4pm. **Free**

C&O Canal National Historical Park
Canal St; tel 301/722-8226. The C&O Canal came to this area in 1850, after 184 miles of ditch and towpath had been constructed. Today it is maintained by the National Park Service, and the canal has evolved as Cumberland's tourism focal point. Start a visit at the Canal Visitor Center, in the Western Maryland Station Center at track level, to see the background exhibits on the canal's history. There are remnants here of locks, dams, and lock houses. **Open:** Tues–Sun 9am–5pm. **Free**

Rocky Gap State Park

MD 1, Flinstone; tel 301/777-2138. This park features a 243-acre lake with 3 full-service beaches. Popular activities include fishing, swimming, hiking, and biking. There's also a 278-unit campsite. **Open:** Daily sunrise–sunset. **$**

Easton

See also St Michaels

Business and cultural center of Maryland's Eastern Shore. The town dates back to the 17th century and boasts Third Haven Friends Meeting House (1682), the oldest frame building in America still in continuous use. **Information:** Talbot County Conference and Visitors Bureau, PO Box 1366, Easton, 21601 (tel 410/822-4606).

HOTEL 🏨

▆▆▆▆ The Tidewater Inn

101 E Dover St, at Harrison St, 21601; tel 410/822-1300 or toll free 800/237-8775; fax 410/820-8847. Exit US 50 at Dover St. This lovely historic building has been meticulously renovated and furnished with antique reproductions. It is beautifully maintained. One-year advance reservations necessary for Waterfowl Festival. **Rooms:** 114 rms and stes. CI 3pm/CO noon. Nonsmoking rms avail. Rooms are spacious and charming, with fine furnishings. Since building is historic, bathrooms are small. **Amenities:** 🔒 🐾 A/C, cable TV, dataport. 1 unit w/minibar. VCRs available. **Services:** ✕ ☎ 🆅🅿 🚐 △ ◁ ⬠ Twice-daily maid svce, car-rental desk, masseur, babysitting. Complimentary van to golf, boating, and nearby towns of Oxford and St Michaels. Staff is very accommodating. **Facilities:** 🈺 🎱 💻 ⚿ 2 restaurants (*see* "Restaurants" below), 2 bars (w/entertainment). Attractive courtyard pool. Kennel in basement. Nearby fitness club. **Rates:** Peak (Sept–Nov 15/May–July) $96–$160 S; $104–$170 D; $225–$375 ste. Extra person $10. Children under age 12 stay free. Min stay peak. Lower rates off-season. AP and MAP rates avail. Parking: Outdoor, free. AE, DC, MC, V.

MOTELS

▆▆ Days Inn

7018 Ocean Gateway (US 50), PO Box 968, 21601; tel 410/822-4600 or toll free 800/329-7466; fax 410/820-9723. Set back from the main road in a shady setting, this motel is a favorite with families. **Rooms:** 80 rms and stes. CI 3pm/CO 11am. Nonsmoking rms avail. **Amenities:** 🔒 A/C, cable TV. Two suites have refrigerators. **Services:** ◁ ⬠ Car-rental desk. **Facilities:** 🈺 ⚿ **Rates (CP):** Peak (Apr 1–Dec 1) $73 S; $78 D; $84–$90 ste. Extra person $8. Children under age 18 stay free. Min stay special events. Lower rates off-season. Parking: Outdoor, free. AE, CB, DC, DISC, MC, V.

▆▆ Holiday Inn Express

8561 Ocean Gateway, 21601; tel 410/819-6500 or toll free 800/HOLIDAY; fax 410/819-6505. On US 50, ½ mi N of Goldsborough St. Built in 1995, this motel has pleasant green decor throughout; the large, modern lobby has a nice breakfast area. Just the thing for an overnight stop. **Rooms:** 73 rms. CI 3pm/CO 11am. Nonsmoking rms avail. Better than average furniture and soft goods, with professionally coordinated decor. **Amenities:** 🔒 🐾 A/C, cable TV w/movies, dataport. **Services:** ◁ **Facilities:** 🈺 🛎 � ⚿ Indoor pool, in an atrium with a whirlpool, is large enough for lap swimming. Small fitness room. **Rates (CP):** Peak (Apr 15–Nov 30) $69–$89 S; $79–$99 D. Children under age 19 stay free. Lower rates off-season. Parking: Outdoor, free. Rates higher during annual Waterfowl Festival. AE, CB, DC, DISC, EC, JCB, MC, V.

RESTAURANTS 🍽

Hunter's Tavern

In The Tidewater Inn, 101 E Dover St, at Harrison St; tel 410/822-1300. Dover St exit off US 50. **Regional American.** This postwar building looks like it has been here since colonial times. Inside, the sporty dining room is filled with decoys and antiques, and a clientele that ranges from Washington power figures to hunters and recreational fishermen. Regional meat and seafood entrees dominate the menu. **FYI:** Reservations recommended. Guitar/jazz/piano. Children's menu. **Open:** Daily 6:30am–11pm. **Prices:** Main courses $12–$23. AE, DC, MC, V. 🍴 🅅 🆅🅿 ⚿

Legal Spirits

42 E Dover St; tel 410/820-0033. Exit US 50 at Dover St. **New American/Seafood.** Situated in a historic building adjacent to the restored Avalon Theater, this tasteful, comfortable, and popular restaurant is attractively done in appropriate style, with 1930s gangster memorabilia on the walls of one room and a stained-glass window in the other. Local favorites include wild mushroom stroganoff and shrimp and mussel stir fry. **FYI:** Reservations recommended. Children's menu. **Open:** Mon–Thurs 11:30am–10pm, Fri–Sat 11:30am–11pm. **Prices:** Main courses $10–$19. AE, DC, DISC, MC, V. 🍴 ⚿

Peach Blossoms

14 N Washington St; tel 410/822-5220. Exit US 50 at Dover St; turn right onto Washington St. **New American.** Contemporary art and mirrors give an appearance of space to this long and narrow but bright modern dining room. Dinner selections include molasses-glazed duck with green-chili cornbread stuffing. **FYI:** Reservations recommended. Children's menu. No smoking. **Open:** Lunch Wed–Fri 11:30am–2pm; dinner Wed–Sat 6–9pm. **Prices:** Main courses $16–$20. MC, V. ♥ 🅅 ⚿

ATTRACTIONS

Historical Society of Talbot County
25 S Washington St; tel 410/822-0773. This society maintains eight historic buildings, five of which are open to the public. A focal point of the historic district, the buildings include an 1850s commercial building, the headquarters of the society and site of a modern museum with changing exhibits; the 1795 Joseph Neall House and the 1810 James Neall House, both restored homes of Quaker cabinetmaker brothers; the partially restored 1670 Wenlocke Christison House, known locally as "The Ending of Controversie" House; and the 1810 Tharpe House, which now serves as a museum shop and library. The buildings surround a federal-style garden, also open to visitors. **Open:** Tues–Sat 10am–4pm, Sun 1–4pm. **$$**

Third Haven Friends Meeting House
405 S Washington St; tel 410/822-0293. Believed to be the oldest frame building dedicated to religious meetings in the United States and the oldest-known building in Maryland, the pine-and-oak structure has been used continuously since the late 17th century. **Open:** Daily 9am–5pm. **Free**

Academy of the Arts
106 South St; tel 410/822-0455 or 822-ARTS (recorded info). Regional arts center in newly renovated 24,000-square-foot 19th-century building. Programs include over 280 arts and educational progarms annually: art exhibitions, concerts, classes, lectures, docent-led tours. **Open:** Mon–Tues and Thurs–Sat 10am–4pm, Wed 10am–9pm. **$**

Orrell's Biscuits
14124 Old Wye Mill Rd; tel 410/822-2065. A family enterprise producing a unique biscuit that has been a tradition for over 300 years. In their kitchen-turned-bakery, the Orrell family produces hundreds of biscuits every day using an original recipe. The Orrells and their staff literally "beat" these doughy treats, and then shape each one by hand into the size of a walnut, producing a crusty biscuit with a soft center. Visitors are welcome to watch the baking process, sample the results, and purchase at the source. **Open:** Tues–Thurs, call for schedule. **Free**

Wye Mill
MD 662; tel 410/827-6909. This mill, dating from the 17th century, is the earliest industrial-commercial building in continuous use in the state. Visitors today can see the mill in operation and sample some of the flour, whole wheat, or cornmeal.

Nearby is the **Wye Oak**, the largest white oak in the United States and Maryland's official state tree. It is 37 feet in circumference, 95 feet high, and over 400 years old. **Open:** Apr–Nov, Sat–Sun 11am–4pm, and by appointment. **Free**

Ellicott City

Founded in 1772, with historic district offering offbeat fashions, specialty gifts, and hard-to-find books. Seat of Howard County.

HOTEL

Turf Valley Hotel & Country Club
2700 Turf Valley Rd, 21042; tel 410/465-1500 or toll free 800/666-TURF; fax 410/465-8280. Exit 83 off I-70. Said to be one of the finest golf resorts on the East Coast, this modern hotel is set on a lovely course. In fine condition, the property is continually being improved and enlarged. Lovely landscaping throughout. **Rooms:** 173 rms and stes. CI 3pm/CO noon. Nonsmoking rms avail. Pretty decor and large sliding doors give nice views of rolling hills. **Amenities:** A/C, cable TV w/movies. All units w/terraces. **Services:** Car-rental desk, babysitting. Informal but courteous staff. **Facilities:** 2 restaurants, 3 bars (2 w/entertainment), lawn games. Lighted driving range and putting green. Large pool and lounging area. Softball, volleyball, basketball. **Rates:** Peak (Apr–Nov) $95 S; $110 D; $130–$415 ste. Extra person $10. Children under age 12 stay free. Lower rates off-season. MAP rates avail. Parking: Outdoor, free. AE, CB, DC, DISC, MC, V.

RESTAURANTS

★ Crab Shanty
3410 Plumtree Dr; tel 410/465-9660. Exit I-70 at US 29 S; go 1 mile to US 40, turn right. **Regional American/Seafood.** Mixed in with a Chesapeake Bay motif in this elegant but casual crab house are antique leaded-glass windows, wooden spindles, and carved brackets from Victorian homes; solid oak beams from an old barn; and the sled in which Bing Crosby rode in the movie *White Christmas*. Seafood specialties are cooked to order using fresh ingredients, in both traditional Maryland and French styles. Carryout available. **FYI:** Reservations not accepted. Children's menu. Dress code. **Open:** Lunch Mon–Fri 11:30am–2:30pm; dinner Mon–Thurs 5–10pm, Fri–Sat 5–11pm, Sun 2–9pm. **Prices:** Main courses $9–$24. AE, DC, MC, V.

Il Giardino Ristorante
In Golden Triangle Shopping Center, 8809 Baltimore Nat'l Pike; tel 410/461-1122. Follow I-70 to US 29 S to US 40 E. **Italian.** Large greenhouse window on one end sets the tone for this dining room decorated in pale greens with white wainscoting. Aroma greets guests, announces traditional and reasonably priced Italian fare, with daily pasta and seafood specials. **FYI:** Reservations recommended. Children's menu. Dress code. No smoking. **Open:** Mon–Thurs 5–10pm, Fri–Sat 5–11pm, Sun 4–9pm. **Prices:** Main courses $8–$18. AE, DC, MC, V.

Tersiguel's French-Country Restaurant
8293 Main St; tel 410/465-4004. Follow US 29 to US 40 E; turn right at light, then left onto Main St. **French.** Dining rooms in this highly regarded establishment are furnished simply and with photos and mementos of Brittany. A wide range of fish, shellfish, grilled meats, and French specialties. Extensive wine list includes interesting regional country choices. Prix-fixe specials for both lunch and dinner. **FYI:** Reservations recommended. Dress code. No smoking. **Open:** Lunch daily 11:30am–2:30pm; dinner Sun–Thurs 5–9pm, Fri–Sat 5–10pm. **Prices:** Main courses $15–$23; prix fixe $28. AE, DC, MC, V. 🐾 🏋

ATTRACTION 📷

B&O Railroad Museum
2711 Maryland Ave; tel 410/461-1944. This is where the first terminus of the first railroad in the United States was located. Today it is a registered National Historic Landmark and houses a full-size B&O caboose, railroad displays, and other memorabilia. **Open:** Mon and Wed–Sat 11am–4pm, Sun noon–5pm. $

Frederick

Famous for its 33-block stretch of historic homes and mansions, over a dozen churches, museums, and historic sites from 18th and 19th century. Ardent Unionist Barbara Fritchie lived here and was immortalized by John Greenleaf Whittier's poem. Seat of Frederick County. **Information:** Tourism Council of Frederick County, 19 E Church St, Frederick, 21701 (tel 301/663-8687).

HOTELS 🏨

Hampton Inn
5311 Buckeystown Pike, 21701; tel 301/698-2500 or toll free 800/426-7866; fax 301/695-8735. Exit 31B off I-270. A step up from the usual chain-hotel look. Large lobby with nice touches: aquarium, free popcorn, tables with chairs. An outdoor pavilion with a small pond and arched bridge. **Rooms:** 160 rms, stes, and effic. CI 3pm/CO noon. Nonsmoking rms avail. Some rooms have waterbeds, some have kitchenettes. Ask for quieter rooms away from the highway. **Amenities:** 🍽 👜 A/C, cable TV w/movies. Video games, refrigerators, microwaves, and hair dryers available. **Services:** 🖼 🍴 🛎 Free local calls. Local and Washington, DC tour services available. **Facilities:** 🏋 🚼 50 👜 1 restaurant (lunch and dinner only), 1 bar (w/entertainment). Catch-and-release fishing in pond. Bar just off lobby is separately owned and operated. Fitness center has stair-stepper, Universal weights. **Rates (CP):** Peak (Mar–Oct) $75 S or D; $125 ste; $75 effic. Children under age 18 stay free. Lower rates off-season. Parking: Outdoor, free. AE, DC, DISC, MC, V.

Holiday Inn
5400 Holiday Dr, 21703; tel 301/694-7500 or toll free 800/HOLIDAY; fax 301/694-0589. Exit 31A off I-70. A nicely decorated facility near shopping mall and restaurants. **Rooms:** 154 rms and stes. Executive level. CI 3pm/CO noon. Nonsmoking rms avail. Rooms have rich wood furnishings, which set them apart from the standard hotel room. Suites have separate sitting area; six rooms are equipped for guests with disabilities. **Amenities:** 🍽 👜 A/C, cable TV, dataport. Some units w/terraces. 40 rooms have refrigerators; 40 have microwaves. King Executives have VCRs. **Services:** ✕ 🖼 🍴 🛎 Twice-daily maid svce, social director. **Facilities:** 🏋 🚼 750 👜 2 restaurants, 1 bar (w/entertainment), volleyball, spa, sauna, whirlpool, playground, washer/dryer. Holidome has pool with skylight and umbrella tables, greenery, and sauna. Miniature golf. Courtyard restaurant and entertainment in lounge/bar four nights a week. **Rates:** Peak (Mar–Sept) $95–$105 S or D; $250 ste. Extra person $10. Children under age 12 stay free. Lower rates off-season. Parking: Outdoor, free. $15 extra for King Executives. Special weekend rates avail. AE, CB, DC, DISC, MC, V.

MOTEL

Comfort Inn
420 Prospect Blvd, 21701; tel 301/695-6200 or toll free 800/228-5150; fax 301/695-7895. Jefferson St exit off US 15 N or off I-270. Clean and attractive, with added practical touches. It's far enough off the highway to feel suburban while still being convenient to the interstate. Within walking distance of shopping centers, and a few miles from the main square of Frederick. **Rooms:** 119 rms. CI 3pm/CO noon. Nonsmoking rms avail. **Amenities:** 🍽 👜 A/C, cable TV w/movies. Refrigerators, safes, and VCRs available. **Services:** 🍴 🛎 24-hour coffee in lobby. Passes for Charles Town, West Virginia, racetrack (25 miles). **Facilities:** 🏋 60 👜 Playground, washer/dryer. Truck parking. Picnic area. **Rates (CP):** Peak (Apr–Oct) $63–$78 S or D. Extra person $5. Children under age 18 stay free. Min stay special events. Lower rates off-season. Parking: Outdoor, free. AE, CB, DC, DISC, JCB, MC, V.

RESTAURANTS 🍴

$ ★ Brown Pelican
5 E Church St (Historic District); tel 301/695-5833. Exit I-70 at exit 54, or I-270 at exit 31A. **Continental/Seafood.** Just off the main square in the historic district, the Brown Pelican is in the basement of an early-18th-century building. Dark-beamed ceiling, comfortably wide bar, and waterfowl paintings. Voted best restaurant in Frederick three years running by local newspaper and magazine. Best picks are catch of the day, veal, or duck. **FYI:** Reservations recommended. **Open:** Lunch Mon–Fri 11:30am–3pm; dinner Mon–Thurs 5–9:30pm, Fri–Sun 5–10pm. **Prices:** Main courses $12–$17. AE, CB, DC, MC, V. 🐾 🏋

★ The Province Restaurant

129 N Market St (Historic District); tel 301/663-1441. Exit 31 off I-270. **American.** Handmade cane chairs from New England, antique pieces, and brick walls decorated with locally stitched quilts give this dining room a distinctive personality. A view of the herb garden out back create an atmosphere that is both historic and folksy. The desserts are superb. The prix-fixe menu is available only Tuesday to Thursday. **FYI:** Reservations recommended. No smoking. **Open:** Lunch Mon–Fri 11:30am–3pm; dinner Tues–Thurs 5:30–9pm, Fri–Sat 5:30–10pm, Sun 4–8pm; brunch Sat 11:30am–3pm, Sun 11am–2:30pm. **Prices:** Main courses $13–$18. AE, CB, DC, DISC, MC, V. ■

The Province Too

12 E Patrick St (Historic District); tel 301/663-3315. **Deli/ Vegetarian.** Squeaky wood floors, round oak tables with soda-fountain chairs, and chefs creating pastries before diners' eyes all make for a fun little spot for specialty desserts, homemade soups, and some 20 sandwiches (including vegetarian versions). One of the few downtown restaurants open for breakfast on Sundays. **FYI:** Reservations not accepted. No liquor license. No smoking. **Open:** Mon–Fri 7am–5pm, Sat 9am–4pm, Sun 8am–3pm. **Prices:** Lunch main courses $4–$5. AE, DISC, MC, V. ▦ ♿

★ Red Horse Restaurant

996 W Patrick St; tel 301/663-3030. Located at jct US 40/15. **Seafood/Steak.** Busy and crowded, this popular restaurant presents a western theme, with wagon-wheel lights, beamed barn ceilings, and large-portion steaks. Nightly entertainment in downstairs bar, including dance area. **FYI:** Reservations recommended. Country music/dancing. Children's menu. Dress code. **Open:** Lunch Mon–Fri 11:30am–3pm; dinner Mon–Sat 4:30–10:30pm, Sun 4–9pm. **Prices:** Main courses $14–$29. AE, CB, DC, DISC, MC, V. ◉ ▦ ▽ ♿

♣ Tauraso's

In Everdy Square, 6 East St; tel 301/663-6600. Exit I-70 at Patrick St. **Regional American/Italian/Seafood.** Located in the artsy area of town in what was once called Shab Row, the restaurant boasts a unique decor that includes open ceilings with exposed steam pipes painted bright red and a large brick-walled, split-level bar area sporting the same red pipes and old oak furnishings. The dining room has an elegant ambience, thanks to black marble tables, chandelier lighting, and a view of the patio dining area. Local reputation for fine food, especially seafood. Recipient of the *Wine Spectator* Award of Excellence. **FYI:** Reservations recommended. Children's menu. No smoking. **Open:** Daily 11am–10pm, Sun–Thurs 11am–10pm, Fri–Sat 11am–11pm. **Prices:** Main courses $8–$24. AE, CB, DC, MC, V. ◉ ⬛ ▦ ♿

ATTRACTIONS ▣

Antietam National Battlefield

MD 65; tel 301/432-5124. Located 10 mi NW of Frederick, on the site of the single bloodiest day of the Civil War. More than 23,000 men were killed or wounded here when Union forces met and stopped the first Southern invasion of the North on September 17, 1862. A visitor center at the battlefield has historical exhibits and shows an 18-minute audiovisual program every half-hour. **Open:** Peak (Jun–Aug) 8:30am–6pm. Reduced hours off-season. **$**

Frederick County Historical Society Museum

24 E Church St; tel 302/663-1188. Exhibits here focus on local historical figures, such as Roger B Taney, chief justice of the US Supreme Court and author of the infamous *Dred Scott* decision, and Francis Scott Key, author of "The Star-Spangled Banner." There is also a genealogical library and a formal garden on the premises. **Open:** Mon–Sat 10am–4pm, Sun 1–4pm. **$**

Schifferstadt

1110 Rosemont Ave; tel 301/663-3885. Built in 1756, this is the oldest standing house in Frederick as well as one of America's finest examples of German colonial architecture. Unusual original features include an enclosed staircase, a vaulted cellar and chimney, and a five-plate cast-iron stove. **Open:** Apr–mid-Dec, Tues–Sat 10am–4pm, Sun noon–4pm. **$**

National Shrine of St Elizabeth Ann Seton

333 S Seton Ave; tel 301/447-6606. The home of the United States' first native-born canonized saint. The complex includes the Stone House, where Mother Seton established her religious community in 1809, and the White House, where she began the first parochial school in America. Visitors center offers 15-minute video orientation; self-guided tours available. **Open:** Peak (Apr–Oct) daily 10am–4:30pm. Reduced hours off-season. **Free**

Lily Pons Water Garden

6800 Lilypons Rd; tel 301/874-5133. Named after famed opera singer Lily Pons, who visited here in 1936, the site is one of the largest suppliers of ornamental fish and aquatic plants in the world and houses acres of water lilies and goldfish ponds. The lilies are at their blooming peak in July. **Open:** Peak (Mar–Oct) daily 9:30am–5:30pm. Reduced hours off-season. **Free**

Rose Hill Manor Children's Museum

1611 N Market St; tel 301/694-1650. This hands-on museum, in a 1790s Georgian mansion that was the home of Maryland's first governor, is designed to let children experience early American life: combing unspun wool, throwing a shuttle on the loom, and adding a few stitches to a quilt. Costumed guides conduct walking tours. **Open:** Peak (Apr–Oct) Mon–Sat 10am–4pm, Sun 1–4pm. Reduced hours off-season. Closed Jan–Feb. **$**

Crystal Grottoes Caverns

MD 34; tel 301/432-6336. Located 15 mi NW of Frederick. Maryland's only commercial underground caverns, with formations created by millions of years of chemical and mineral action. Today, nature's work can be seen in the corridors of limestone lined with jeweled stalactites and stalagmites. Guided tours available. **Open:** Daily 10am–5pm. **$$$**

Barbara Fritchie House and Museum

154 W Patrick St; tel 301/698-0630. At the age of 95, Barbara Fritchie bravely waved the Stars and Stripes in the path of Confederate soldiers and was immortalized in a poem by John Greenleaf Whittier as the "bravest of all in Fredericktown." A visit to the house includes a video presentation of her life and times; a collection of mementos including quilts and linens; and period clothing and furniture. **Open:** Peak (Apr–Sept) Mon and Thurs–Sat 10am–4pm, Sun 1–4pm. Reduced hours off-season. **$**

Frostburg

West of Cumberland in the Allegheny Mountains, Frostburg is home to Frostburg State University. Nearby to Savage River State Forest.

HOTELS 🏨

🏨 Comfort Inn

MD 36 N at Frostburg Industrial Park, 21532; tel 301/689-2050 or toll free 800/221-2222; fax 301/689-2050. Exit 34 off I-68. A skylight and small atrium area in lobby add to the mood at this sparkling-clean facility. **Rooms:** 100 rms and stes. CI 4pm/CO 11am. Nonsmoking rms avail. Integrated decor. eight king rooms, two honeymoon suites, two family suites. **Amenities:** 🛎 A/C, cable TV. Some units w/terraces, some w/whirlpools. Microwaves available. **Services:** 🍽 🛏 Coffee/tea bar area in lobby 24 hours. **Facilities:** 🛎 🏌️ 🏊 Landscaped outdoor seating area with stone picnic tables. Cooperative arrangement with nearby country club for use of pool, golf course. **Rates (CP):** Peak (May–Oct) $62–$72 S; $68–$78 D; $94–$137 ste. Extra person $5. Children under age 18 stay free. Lower rates off-season. Parking: Outdoor, free. AE, DC, DISC, MC, V.

🏨 Failinger's Hotel Gunter

11 W Main St, 21532; tel 301/689-6511. Exit 34 off I-68. Aptly described as offering turn-of-the-century charm, this fine old downtown hotel (circa 1896) has been lovingly restored. A massive oak stairway greets guests, hallways display old gilt-framed photos and lantern wall sconces, and the huge lobby with ornate candelabra is comfortable for residents of the facility as well as guests. Family-owned and -operated. **Rooms:** 17 rms. CI 1pm/CO 11am. No smoking. Charming, individually decorated rooms have nice touches, such as canopy beds, antique vanity sitting table, claw-foot tub. Floral splashes on curtains and bedspreads, or lighter feel courtesy of filmy white curtains and canopies. **Amenities:** 🛎 A/C, cable TV w/movies. Refrigerator and microwave available. **Services:** 🍽 **Facilities:** 🛎 🍴 1 bar. Museum in basement includes replica of an underground coal mine, the

original jail where prisoners were once kept when being transported over the Old Trail Rd. **Rates (CP):** $50 S; $55–$60 D. Extra person $5. Children under age 15 stay free. Parking: Outdoor, free. Long-term rates avail. AE, DC, DISC, MC, V.

RESTAURANTS 🍽

🏆 Au Petit Paris Restaurant Français

86 E Main St; tel 301/689-8946. Exit 34 off I-68. **French.** The rich and colorful ambience of Paris prevails, starting with a Montmartre-style alleyway leading to the restaurant. Of three dining areas, one is 100 years old. Throughout are unique and interesting accents, such as the wall-size terracotta wine rack, kiosk replica, chandeliers, and old lace curtains. Lounge area has plush chairs and working fireplace. This family-owned and -operated restaurant offers a variety of fine French dishes, with specialties of seafood, beef, and veal. **FYI:** Reservations recommended. Dress code. **Open:** Tues–Sat 6–9:30pm. **Prices:** Main courses $11–$30. AE, CB, DC, DISC, MC, V. ❤ 🖼 ♿

⭐ Giuseppe's

11 Bowery St; tel 301/689-2220. Exit 34 off I-68. **Italian/Seafood/Steak.** This intimate Italian restaurant in a restored 1890s building offers casual dining on two levels, with a bar on each floor. Favorites include veal dishes and cappellini with a hearty marinara sauce. **FYI:** Reservations accepted. Children's menu. No smoking. **Open:** Sun 3–9pm, Mon–Thurs 4:30–11pm, Fri–Sat 3–11pm. **Prices:** Main courses $8–$17. AE, DISC, MC, V. 🖼

ATTRACTION 🏛

Thrasher Carriage Museum

19 Depot St; tel 301/689-3380. The museum displays an extensive collection of late 19th- and early 20th-century horse-drawn carriages: formal closed vehicles, milk wagons, open sleighs, funeral wagons, dogcarts, phaetons, and runabouts. **Open:** Peak (May–Sept) daily 11am–4pm. Reduced hours off-season. **$**

Gaithersburg

City of some 30,000 people, northwest of Washington, DC. A thriving business, commercial, and residential center, and home of the National Bureau of Standards. **Information:** Greater Gaithersburg Chamber of Commerce, 9 Park Ave, Gaithersburg, 20877 (tel 301/840-1400).

HOTELS 🏨

🏨 Comfort Inn at Shady Grove

16216 Frederick Rd, 20877; tel 301/330-0023 or toll free 800/228-5150; fax 301/258-1950. Exit 8 off I-270. A modern, clean hotel convenient to restaurants, shops, and Metro station. **Rooms:** 127 rms. Executive level. CI 2pm/CO 11am.

Nonsmoking rms avail. Simple rooms have neutral decor. **Amenities:** 📺 🛁 📱 A/C, cable TV w/movies. **Services:** 🖨 🛎 🐕 Babysitting. Complimentary shuttle to Metro station and nearby businesses, shops. Manager's reception weekly. **Facilities:** 🏋 🏊 🛏 60 ♿ Washer/dryer. Two restaurants within walking distance give discounts. **Rates (CP):** Peak (Mar–Nov) $69 S; $79 D. Extra person $10. Children under age 18 stay free. Lower rates off-season. Parking: Outdoor, free. AE, CB, DC, DISC, MC, V.

☰☰☰ Courtyard by Marriott

805 Russell Ave, 20879; tel 301/670-0008 or toll free 800/336-6880; fax 301/948-4538. Exit I-270 at MD 124 E; follow Montgomery Village Ave. Member of a chain of comfortable hotels catering to business travelers. Surrounded by landscaped office park. **Rooms:** 203 rms and stes. CI 3pm/CO 1pm. Nonsmoking rms avail. Decorated in pastels. King-bed rooms have sofas. **Amenities:** 📺 🛁 📱 A/C, cable TV w/movies, dataport. 1 unit w/minibar, some w/terraces, 1 w/whirlpool. All rooms have hot-water taps for tea and instant coffee. Phones have on-line service with information about tourist attractions, items of local interest, stock quotes, business news, reservations service. **Services:** ✕ 🚗 🖨 🛎 Babysitting. Complimentary shuttle locally and to Metro station. **Facilities:** 🏋 🏊1 🛏 40 ♿ 1 restaurant (bkfst and dinner only), 1 bar, spa, steam rm, whirlpool, washer/dryer. Nicely landscaped outdoor pool. Restaurant serves breakfast (daily) and dinner (Mon–Thurs). **Rates:** Peak (Feb–Mar) $79–$99 S; $89–$109 D; $250 ste. Extra person $10. Children under age 16 stay free. Lower rates off-season. Parking: Outdoor, free. AE, DC, MC, V.

☰☰☰ Gaithersburg Hilton

620 Perry Pkwy, 20877; tel 301/977-8900 or toll free 800/599-5111; fax 301/869-8597. Exit I-270 at MD 124 E. This modern hotel has an attractive lobby with marble floors, indirect lighting, comfortable hunter-green furniture, and large floral arrangements. **Rooms:** 301 rms and stes. Executive level. CI 3pm/CO noon. Nonsmoking rms avail. Handsome decor includes colorful spreads, nice artwork. Furniture a bit worn. **Amenities:** 📺 🛁 A/C, cable TV w/movies. Some units w/terraces. Iron and ironing board in all rooms. **Services:** ✕ 🚗 🖨 🛎 🐕 Twice-daily maid svce, car-rental desk, social director. **Facilities:** 🏋 🛏 600 ♿ 1 restaurant, 1 bar, whirlpool, washer/dryer. Attractive indoor-outdoor pool. **Rates (CP):** $64–$115 S or D; $300 ste. Children under age 21 stay free. Parking: Outdoor, free. AE, CB, DC, DISC, MC, V.

☰☰ Holiday Inn

2 Montgomery Village Ave, 20879; tel 301/948-8900 or toll free 800/465-4329; fax 301/258-1940. Exit 11 off I-270. Quiet suburban hotel convenient to shopping mall. **Rooms:** 303 rms, stes, and effic. CI 3pm/CO noon. Nonsmoking rms avail. **Amenities:** 📺 🛁 📱 🍴 A/C, cable TV w/movies, dataport. Some units w/terraces. **Services:** ✕ 🚗 🖨 🛎 🐕 Car-rental desk. Complimentary shuttle to Metro or nearby

stores. **Facilities:** 🏋 🛏 800 ♿ 1 restaurant, 1 bar, games rm, spa, sauna, whirlpool, washer/dryer. Nicely done indoor pool opens to outdoor table area with restaurant and bar service. **Rates:** Peak (Apr–June) $54–$109 S; $64–$119 D; $250–$350 ste; $114 effic. Extra person $10. Children under age 12 stay free. Lower rates off-season. Parking: Outdoor, free. AE, CB, DC, DISC, ER, JCB, MC, V.

MOTEL

☰ Econo Lodge

18715 N Frederick Ave, 20879; tel 301/963-3840 or toll free 800/424-4777; fax 301/948-7443. Exit 11A off I-270 S. Set at the crest of a high hill, this chalet-style motel has dark peaked wooden eaves and shutters, beamed lobby with attractive sitting area. A few miles from Metro station. **Rooms:** 97 rms and effic. CI 3pm/CO noon. Nonsmoking rms avail. Blond wood furniture, pastel paintings, and spreads brighten basic rooms. **Amenities:** 📺 🛁 A/C, satel TV w/movies. **Services:** 🚗 🛎 🐕 Free local calls. Games available at front desk. **Facilities:** 🛏 70 ♿ Games rm, washer/dryer. Snack bar with 24-hour coffee and tea. Sports facilities next door. **Rates:** Peak (Apr–Nov) $39–$58 S; $42–$65 D; $46–$69 effic. Extra person $6. Children under age 16 stay free. Lower rates off-season. Parking: Outdoor, free. AE, CB, DC, DISC, ER, JCB, MC, V.

RESTAURANTS 🍴

Hunan Palace

9011 Gaither Rd; tel 301/977-8600. Exit 8 off I-270. Follow Shady Grove Rd east to Gaither Rd, turn left. **Chinese.** Blond wood tables and booths, Oriental paintings make for simple but pleasing decor. More than 100 main courses feature Taiwanese cooking, which is a bit spicier than Cantonese. One of the best bargains in area. **FYI:** Reservations not accepted. **Open:** Daily 11:30am–10pm. **Prices:** Main courses $9–$20. AE, MC, V.

Ichiban

637 N Frederick Ave; tel 301/670-0560. Exit 11 off I-270N. Go north on Frederick Ave. **Japanese/Korean.** Small rock-garden entry with bonsai trees, lattice-work windows, wood booths and tables, and subdued lighting provide the proper setting for a mix of Asian cuisines. Some dishes cooked at table. Separate sushi bar. Weekday "lunchbox" specials. **FYI:** Reservations accepted. Karaoke. **Open:** Mon–Thurs 11:30am–10pm, Fri–Sat 11:30am–11pm, Sun 12:30–10pm. **Prices:** Main courses $10–$25. AE, DC, DISC, MC, V. ♿

Thai Sa-Mai

8369 Snouffer School Rd; tel 301/963-1800. Exit 8 off I-270. **Thai/Vegetarian.** There are only a dozen tables in this intimate dining room done in gray and aqua. Fresh flowers and soda fountain–style chairs grace each table. Paintings of Thailand, carved temple peaks in bar area set tone for noodle dishes and southern Thai curries. Each dish prepared individually. Extensive menu features many vegetarian dishes. **FYI:**

Reservations recommended. Beer and wine only. No smoking. **Open:** Lunch Tues–Fri 11am–3pm; dinner Sat 4–10:30pm, Sun 5–9pm, Tues–Thurs 5–9:30pm, Fri 5–10:30pm. **Prices:** Main courses $7–$8. DISC, MC, V. ♿

Grantsville

Small town northwest of Frostburg. Home of the Spruce Village Forest, an artisan area dedicated to showcasing the work of some 2,000 artists.

RESTAURANT 🍴

★ Penn Alps Restaurant and Craft Shop
US Alt 40; tel 301/895-5985. Exit 22 off I-68W. **Regional American.** Housed in the last remaining log tavern on the first National Rd, this restaurant is part of the Spruce Forest Artisan Village. The restaurant offers a gift shop in its open-beamed lobby, complete with rocking chairs and old lantern lights. Oak tables and floor, country curtains add to the sense of place. Alpine Room has floor-to-ceiling windows and plank walls. Another small dining area is in the 1813 Old Stagecoach Building. Specialties include unique breads, Pennsylvania Dutch fries, Mennonite sausage, and dried corn. **FYI:** Reservations accepted. Children's menu. No liquor license. No smoking. **Open:** Peak (Mem Day–Oct) Mon–Sat 7am–8pm, Sun 7am–3pm. **Prices:** Main courses $8–$14. DISC, MC, V. 🍴♿

ATTRACTION 🏛

Yoder's Country Market
MD 669; tel 301/895-5148. Started as a Mennonite family farm enterprise in 1932, this has grown from a one-room butcher shop to an extensive specialty market offering Amish, Mennonite, and Pennsylvania Dutch food and craft items. **Open:** Mon–Sat 8am–6pm. **Free**

Grasonville

Bay-side town located at the mouth of the Chester River. Nearby is Kent Narrows, a popular boating area.

MOTELS 🏨

≣≣≣ Comfort Inn Kent Narrows
3101 Main St, 21638; tel 410/827-6767 or toll free 800/828-3361; fax 410/827-8626. Exit 42 off US 50/301. This handsome new motel sits at Kent Narrows, a popular and growing boating center, where work and pleasure craft seem to be everywhere. Outlet shopping nearby. **Rooms:** 87 rms, stes, and effic. CI 3pm/CO 11am. Nonsmoking rms avail. Some rooms have water views; others face the highway. **Amenities:** 🛏 ♨ 📺 A/C, cable TV, refrig. Some units w/whirlpools. Microwaves in each unit. **Services:** 🖨 ↩ **Facilities:** 🏋 ⚽ 🏊 ♿ Lawn games, sauna, whirlpool,

washer/dryer. Restaurants and bars are adjacent. Nearby fishing, bike and boat rentals, parasailing. **Rates (CP):** Peak (May–Nov) $89–$128 S; $94–$128 D; $135–$195 ste; $135–$195 effic. Extra person $6. Children under age 18 stay free. Lower rates off-season. Parking: Outdoor, free. Senior discounts avail. AE, CB, DC, DISC, EC, ER, JCB, MC, V.

≣≣ Grasonville/Kent Island Sleep Inn
101 VFW Ave, 21638; tel 410/827-5555 or toll free 800/627-5337; fax 410/827-8801. 1 mi E of Kent Narrows, exit 43B or 44A off US 50/301. A nearly new building where the rooms and lobby are much more attractive than one expects from a standard-looking highway motel. Near Kent Narrows boating center and outlet malls. **Rooms:** 51 rms and stes. CI 3pm/CO 11am. No smoking. **Amenities:** 🛏 ♨ A/C, cable TV w/movies. Some units w/whirlpools. Deluxe rooms have refrigerators, VCRs, and attractive whirlpool-tub combinations. **Services:** ↩ Car-rental desk. **Facilities:** 🏋 🏊 ♿ **Rates (CP):** Peak (June–Oct) $60–$90 S or D; $99–$149 ste. Extra person $6. Children under age 18 stay free. Min stay special events. Lower rates off-season. Parking: Outdoor, free. Many special plans, including golf packages, avail. AE, CB, DC, DISC, ER, JCB, MC, V.

RESTAURANTS 🍴

$ Anglers
3015 Kent Narrows Way S; tel 410/827-6717. Exit 41 or 42 off US 50/301; follow MD 18 past Kent Narrows Bridge. **American/Seafood.** A friendly mix of local watermen and the well-to-do makes this simple, clapboard building a legend in the area. The late entertainer Jackie Gleason used to stop in to shoot pool. Apparently a charmed place, too, since one owner won $10 million in the lottery. Basic American fare is offered at low prices. Popular for breakfast and daily dinner specials. **FYI:** Reservations not accepted. **Open:** Sun–Thurs 7am–10:30pm, Fri–Sat 7am–midnight. **Prices:** Main courses $5–$7. DISC, MC, V. ♿

Annie's Paramount Steak House
500 Kent Narrows Way N; tel 410/827-7103. Exit 42 off US 50/301. **American/Seafood/Steak.** Attractive woods and ceiling fans highlight this comfortable establishment overlooking Kent Narrows and its marinas. Although known primarily for steaks and prime rib, it's also strong on seafood. **FYI:** Reservations accepted. Piano. Children's menu. Dress code. **Open:** Lunch Mon–Sat 11am–4pm; dinner Mon–Thurs noon–10:30pm, Fri–Sat noon–11:30pm; brunch Sun 9am–2pm. **Prices:** Main courses $11–$25. AE, DC, MC, V. 🖼♿

★ Fisherman's Inn, Crab Deck & Seafood Market
Main St, Box 118; tel 410/827-8807. Exit 42 off US 50/301. **American/Seafood.** This large room with big windows on its water side is decorated with ship models, duck-stamp prints, and antique oyster plates. Traditional Eastern Shore seafood is the mainstay. Directly on Kent Narrows, the Crab Deck cooks up steamed crabs and other Chesapeake fare. Bands

perform on weekends. **FYI:** Reservations not accepted. Big band/country music/dancing/rock. Children's menu. Dress code. **Open:** Daily 11am–10pm. **Prices:** Main courses $10–$19. AE, DISC, MC, V. 🍴 🏞 👥 ⚬

Harris Crab House

433 N Kent Narrows Way; tel 410/827-9500. Exit 42 off US 50/301. Turn right at stop sign, then right into restaurant. **Seafood.** This classic waterfront crab house has a large, simple room with long tables covered with brown wrapping paper. Both expansive windows and a large rooftop deck overlook Kent Narrows. Since the place is an outgrowth of a seafood-packing house, its primary business is shellfish. **FYI:** Reservations not accepted. Dress code. **Open:** Peak (May–Oct) daily 11am–11pm. **Prices:** Main courses $12–$18. MC, V. 🍴 🏞 ⚬

The Narrows Restaurant

3023 Kent Narrows Way S; tel 410/827-8113. Exit 42 off US 50/301. **New American/Seafood.** A fair-weather sun room and open deck augment this bright, waterfront dining room with skylights and windows looking out on Kent Narrows. Seafood, beef, and chicken are prepared in a light style and served with interesting sauces. **FYI:** Reservations accepted. Children's menu. Dress code. **Open:** Lunch Mon–Sat 11am–4pm; dinner Mon–Sat 4–9pm, Sun 11am–9pm; brunch Sun 11am–2pm. **Prices:** Main courses $12–$25. AE, DC, DISC, MC, V. ♥ 🍴 🏞 ⚬

Greenbelt

ATTRACTION 🏛

NASA/Goddard Space Flight Visitor Center

Exit 22A off I-95; tel 301/286-8981. Established in 1959, this was NASA's first major scientific laboratory devoted entirely to the exploration of space. Visitor center tours include special working areas that show satellite control, spacecraft construction, and communication operations. Exhibits housed inside the center offer such interactive experiences as piloting a personal manned maneuvering unit to retrieve a satellite in space and controlling a spacecraft by steering a gyro-chair. Picnic area, gift shop. **Open:** Daily 9am–4pm. **Free**

Hagerstown

Organized circa 1740 as a trading center for frontier settlements, Hagerstown later became an important railroad center. Today, it is the seat of Washington County and has about 40,000 residents. **Information:** Hagerstown–Washington County Chamber of Commerce, 111 W Washington St, Hagerstown, 21740 (tel 301/739-2015).

HOTELS 🏨

≡≡≡ Best Western Venice Inn

431 Dual Hwy, 21740; tel 301/733-0830 or toll free 800/2-VENICE; fax 301/733-4978. Exit 6A off I-81, or exit 32B off I-70. A full-service hotel with inviting, split-level lobby. Convenient to major thoroughfare but set back from traffic on huge lot. **Rooms:** 218 rms, stes, and effic. Executive level. CI 2pm/CO noon. Nonsmoking rms avail. Efficiencies have full kitchens. Rooms for guests with disabilities on each floor. **Amenities:** 🛁 ⚬ A/C, cable TV w/movies, dataport. Some units w/whirlpools. One executive suite with bar. **Services:** ✕ 🚗 📠 🍴 🛎 Car-rental desk. **Facilities:** 🛗 🏊 ⚬ 1 restaurant, 1 bar (w/entertainment), games rm, beauty salon, washer/dryer. Liquor store with wine cellar. Six-lane, Olympic-size pool. Golf course across the street and skiing within 16 miles. **Rates:** Peak (Sept–Nov) $52–$58 S or D; $85–$135 ste; $85–$135 effic. Extra person $5. Lower rates off-season. Parking: Outdoor, free. Special weekend packages, with meals, avail. AE, DISC, MC, V.

≡≡ Ramada Inn Convention Center

901 Dual Hwy, 21740; tel 301/733-5100 or toll free 800/272-6232; fax 301/733-9192. Exit 6B off I-81, or exit 32B off I-70. An air of faded elegance predominates. Lobby offers elegant touches like old marble fireplaces. **Rooms:** 210 rms and stes. CI 3pm/CO 11am. Nonsmoking rms avail. Rooms, some poolside, are acceptable. **Amenities:** 🛁 ⚬ 🖥 A/C, cable TV, refrig, voice mail. Some units w/terraces, some w/fireplaces, some w/whirlpools. **Services:** ✕ 🚗 📠 🍴 **Facilities:** 🛗 🏊 🏊 ⚬ 1 restaurant, 1 bar, games rm, spa, sauna, steam rm, whirlpool. Volleyball court. Atrium with swimming pool and running track. **Rates:** $62–$72 S or D; $95–$200 ste. Extra person $10. Children under age 18 stay free. Parking: Outdoor, free. AE, CB, DC, DISC, MC, V.

≡≡ Sheraton Inn Hagerstown Conference Center

1910 Dual Hwy, 21740; tel 301/790-3010 or toll free 800/325-3535; fax 301/733-4559. Exit 6B off I-81, or exit 32B off I-70. Spacious lobby, including palace-size gilt-framed mirror, lends air of elegance to this property. **Rooms:** 108 rms and stes. Executive level. CI 2pm/CO noon. Nonsmoking rms avail. Honeymoon and executive suites available. **Amenities:** 🛁 ⚬ A/C, cable TV, dataport. Some units w/whirlpools. Executive suites have dataports. **Services:** ✕ 🚗 📠 🍴 🛎 Babysitting. Professional staff is informed and courteous. **Facilities:** 🛗 🏊 🏊 ⚬ 1 restaurant, 1 bar (w/entertainment), spa, sauna, steam rm, whirlpool. **Rates (CP):** Peak (May–Oct) $60–$76 S or D; $75–$125 ste. Extra person $4. Children under age 17 stay free. Lower rates off-season. Parking: Outdoor, free. AE, CB, DC, DISC, MC, V.

≡ Wellesley Inn

1101 Dual Hwy, 21740; tel 301/733-2700 or toll free 800/444-8888; fax 301/791-2106. Exit 6A off I-81, or exit 32B off I-70. This small, intimate, and charming hotel has a cozy lobby with a sitting area and fireplace. **Rooms:** 84 rms and stes. CI 2pm/CO 11am. Nonsmoking rms avail. Rooms, though on the small side, are attractively decorated and inviting. **Amenities:** 🔒 📺 A/C, cable TV. Some rooms have refrigerators. **Services:** 🖼 🍴 🍷 **Facilities:** 🚹 Cooperative arrangement with restaurant across the street for room service until 10pm. **Rates (CP):** Peak (May–Sept) $42–$50 S; $49–$56 D; $66 ste. Extra person $5. Children under age 18 stay free. Lower rates off-season. Parking: Outdoor, free. Ski packages avail. AE, DC, DISC, MC, V.

RESTAURANTS 🍴

★ Cafe Matisse
15 W Washington St; tel 301/791-2414. 1 block W of main square. **Regional American/International.** A small eatery with a striking decor: the simplicity of white tablecloths and white walls is offset by colorful Matisse prints on the walls. The menu would suit just about any taste, with specialties ranging from vegetarian sandwiches to pasta with spicy Italian sausage to Chinese chicken-and-peanut salad. **FYI:** Reservations accepted. BYO. **Open:** Lunch Mon–Sat 11:30am–2:30pm; dinner Fri–Sat 5:30–8:30pm. **Prices:** Main courses $9–$14. No CC.

Twilight's Gourmet Deli & Restorante
45 S Potomac St; tel 301/791-6070. 1 block S of Washington St. **Italian.** An appealing spot, just off the main square downtown, where brick-and-stone walls and lots of greenery set a casual tone. The menu is northern Italian, with paella and Shrimp Basilica being particular standouts. Upstairs, a deli counter sells gourmet items with an Italian focus. **FYI:** Reservations recommended. Dress code. **Open:** Lunch Mon–Sat 11:30am–2:30pm; dinner Mon–Sat 4:30–10pm. **Prices:** Main courses $9–$18. AE, MC, V. ❤ 📧 🚹

ATTRACTIONS 📷

Washington County Museum of Fine Arts
91 Key St; tel 301/739-5727. The ten galleries here offer changing exhibits of 19th- and 20th-century American art. On Sunday the museum offers diverse musical programs in its concert hall. **Open:** Tues–Sat 10am–5pm, Sun 1–5pm. **Free**

Jonathan Hager House and Museum
110 Key St; tel 301/739-8393. The home of the city's founder is situated on the northern edge of City Park. The 3½-story structure was built in 1739 by Hager himself and is styled in the German tradition, with a large chimney at its center and 22-inch-thick walls. It has been completely restored and outfitted with authentic period furnishings. Next door is the Hager Museum, a collection of hundreds of farm implements, coins, household items, clothing, and other artifacts from the Hagerstown area. **Open:** Apr–Dec, Tues–Sat 10am–4pm, Sun 2–5pm. **$**

Mansion House Art Center
135 W Washington St; tel 301/797-8782. Built in 1818, this museum features a collection of dolls, clocks, and furniture from the federal period. There are exhibits on the C&O Canal and the Civil War, as well as a re-creation of a turn-of-the-century general store. **Open:** Wed–Fri 1–4pm, Sat 2–5pm. **$**

Hagerstown Roundhouse Museum
300 S Burhans Blvd; tel 301/739-4665. Depicts the history of the seven railroads that passed through the city, including the Western Maryland Railroad, making Hagerstown the "Hub City." **Open:** Fri–Sun 1–5pm. **$**

Ziem Vineyards
MD 63; tel 301/223-8352. This eight-acre winery is set in a farmland complex that includes a 200-year-old stone house, a spring house, and a bank barn. It produces all of its wines (5 whites and 10 reds) from grape to bottle. Visitors are welcome to tour the facilities, taste the wines, and buy the product at the source. **Open:** Thurs–Sun 1–6pm. **Free**

Hagerstown City Park
Virginia Ave; tel 301/739-4673. Among the nation's most beautiful natural city parks is this 50-acre oasis centered around an artificial lake that is home to hundreds of ducks, swans, and geese. Facilities include tennis courts, softball fields, wooded picnic areas, flower gardens, and an open-air band shell. **Open:** Daily sunrise–sunset. **Free**

Fort Frederick State Park
11100 Fort Frederick Rd; tel 301/842-2155. Built in 1756, the fort served as Maryland's frontier defense during the French and Indian War. Today the stone wall and two barracks have been restored to their original appearance and house exhibits on the history of the fort. Activities in the park include hiking, picnicking, fishing, boating, and primitive camping. Pets prohibited. **Open:** Peak (Apr–Oct) daily sunrise–sunset. Reduced hours off-season. **Free**

Hanover

See Baltimore-Washington Int'l Airport

Havre de Grace

North of Baltimore at the mouth of the Susquehanna River and the Chesapeake Bay. Features wooden promenade winding from the old lighthouse to the city park, providing visitors view of the bay.

ATTRACTIONS 📷

Havre de Grace Maritime Museum
100 Lafayette St; tel 410/939-4800. This museum displays artifacts, memorabilia, and photographs representing the time when Havre de Grace was a major hub for water-related

commerce and recreational activities on the Upper Chesapeake Bay. In addition, there are educational programs and displays on local maritime history, as well as an annual classic boat show every June. **Open:** May–Sept, Sat–Sun 1–5pm. **Free**

Steppingstone Museum

461 Quaker Bottom Rd; tel 410/939-2299. Located on what was once a working Harford County farm, this living history museum is dedicated to preserving and demonstrating the rural arts and crafts of the late 1800s and early 1900s. The main farmhouse is furnished with turn-of-the-century pieces, including a kitchen with a woodburning stove and an ice box. Other historic buildings include a blacksmith shop, woodworking shop, dairy, potter's shed, canning house, and carriage barn. There are 10 sites in all. **Open:** May–Oct, Sat–Sun 1–5pm. **$**

Concord Point Lighthouse

Lafayette St; tel 410/939-1498. Built in 1827, it is the oldest continually operated lighthouse in the state of Maryland. Its construction coincided with the opening of the Chesapeake and Delaware Canal linking the Chesapeake and Delaware Bays. Today the lighthouse is the most photographed and painted structure in the city and is the starting point of the self-guided Havre de Grace tour available at the visitors center. **Open:** April–Oct, Sat–Sun 1–5pm. **Free**

La Plata

Small town and regional shopping center south of Washington, DC, incorporated in 1888. Seat of Charles County. **Information:** Charles County Chamber of Commerce, 6360 Crain Hwy, La Plata, 20646 (tel 301/932-6500).

MOTEL 🏨

▤▤ Best Western La Plata Inn

6900 Crain Hwy (US 301), 20646; tel 301/934-4900 or toll free 800/528-1234; fax 301/934-5389. An attractive, modern roadside motel of brick and stucco, it appears more like a low-rise office building or apartment complex. Clean and comfortable throughout. **Rooms:** 74 rms and stes. CI 2pm/CO 11am. Nonsmoking rms avail. L-shaped suites have living area with bay windows, sofas. **Amenities:** 🛜 🐴 A/C, cable TV w/movies, refrig. Microwaves. Wet bars, 2 TVs in suites. **Services:** 🐶 🐾 Pet fee. **Facilities:** 🔥 🏊 🚻 Washer/dryer. Small pool in rear surrounded by wooden fence. **Rates (CP):** $55 S; $57 D; $77 ste. Extra person $5. Children under age 16 stay free. Parking: Outdoor, free. AE, CB, DC, DISC, MC, V.

ATTRACTION 🏛️

Smallwood State Park

MD 225; tel 301/743-7613. This 630-acre recreational area includes the restored home of Revolutionary War hero Gen William Smallwood. Also located on the grounds are Sweden Point Marina and Mattawoman Natural Area. Picnicking, hiking, and boat rentals. **Open:** Daily sunrise–sunset. **$**

Laurel

On the Patuxent River north of Greenbelt, this busy commercial center is home to Laurel Race Track. **Information:** Baltimore–Washington Corridor Chamber of Commerce, 7901 Sandy Spring Rd, #501, Laurel, 20707 (tel 301/725-4000).

MOTELS 🏨

▤▤▤ Best Western Maryland Inn

15101 Sweitzer Lane, 20707; tel 301/776-5300 or toll free 800/200-0333; fax 301/604-3667. Exit I-95 at MD 198 W. A better-than-average chain motel with excellent entertainment facilities for families with children. **Rooms:** 205 rms and stes. Executive level. CI 3pm/CO noon. No smoking. Executive-level units have king beds. Some first-floor rooms have both exterior and atrium access. **Amenities:** 🛜 🐴 A/C, satel TV w/movies, voice mail. Executive-level units have hair dryers, coffeemakers. **Services:** ✕ 🏊 🐶 Babysitting. **Facilities:** 🔥 🚻 🏊 🏊 1 restaurant, 1 bar, games rm, spa, sauna, whirlpool, washer/dryer. Putting green, pool, shuffleboard, billiard table, and video games in atrium. **Rates (BB):** $75 S or D; $85–$91 ste. Extra person $6. Children under age 18 stay free. Parking: Outdoor, free. AE, CB, DC, DISC, MC, V.

▤▤ Comfort Suites

14402 Laurel Place, 20707; tel 301/206-2600 or toll free 800/628-7760; fax 301/725-0056. Exit 33A off I-95. Follow MD 198 E to US 1 S, turn left; go 1 mile to Mulberry St, turn right. A recent, attractive motel adjacent to several shopping centers and near Fort Meade and a pretty park with lake. **Rooms:** 119 rms and stes. CI 2pm/CO noon. No smoking. Most are large hotel rooms with a sitting area and not true suites, but all are attractively decorated and comfortable. **Amenities:** 🛜 🐴 🚹 A/C, cable TV w/movies, refrig. Microwaves in most rooms. **Services:** 🚐 🏊 🐶 🐾 Car-rental desk. Van transportation. Very accommodating and competent staff. **Facilities:** 🔥 🏊 🚹 🚻 🏊 🏊 Games rm, lawn games, spa, whirlpool, playground, washer/dryer. Golf course ¾ mile away. Jogging trail adjacent to motel. Some local restaurants give 20% discount. **Rates (CP):** $78–$125 S or D; $59 ste. Extra person $10. Children under age 18 stay free. Parking: Outdoor, free. AE, DC, DISC, ER, MC, V.

▤▤ Holiday Inn

3400 Fort Meade Rd, 20724; tel 301/498-0900 or toll free 800/HOLIDAY. ½ mi from exit MD 198 off MD 295. An older but well-kept highway motel convenient to Laurel Race Track and the Baltimore-Washington Pkwy (US 1). **Rooms:** 120 rms. CI 1pm/CO 11am. Nonsmoking rms avail. Standard rooms have new carpets and wallpaper. **Amenities:** 🛜 🐴 A/C, cable TV w/movies, dataport. **Services:** ✕ 🖼 🎧 **Facilities:** 🔏 🖥 300 🔥 1 restaurant, 1 bar, washer/dryer. Pleasant pool and sun-deck area, small fitness room; 18-hole golf course and driving range within 2 miles. **Rates:** Peak (June–Aug) $69 S; $75 D. Extra person $6. Children under age 18 stay free. Lower rates off-season. Parking: Outdoor, free. AE, CB, DC, DISC, EC, ER, JCB, MC, V.

RESTAURANT 🍴

★ Bay & Surf Seafood Restaurant
14411 Baltimore Ave (US 1); tel 301/776-7021. **Seafood.** The gray, weathered clapboard facade is easy to spot, and the nautical interior—complete with lobster traps and an aquarium—reminds you that this is a seafood place. It has been a local favorite for 30 years. The cream of crab soup is an award-winning way to start your meal; prime rib is also recommended. **FYI:** Reservations accepted. Children's menu. Dress code. No smoking. **Open:** Mon–Thurs 11am–9pm, Fri–Sat 11am–10pm, Sun 11am–10:30pm. **Prices:** Main courses $20–$30. AE, DISC, MC, V. 🔥

Leonardtown

Located in southern Maryland in the Potomac Tidewater area. Founded in 1690, it features Drum Point Lighthouse (circa 1883), one of only three remaining screwpile lights on Chesapeake Bay.

ATTRACTIONS 🏛

Calvert Marine Museum
MD 2; tel 410/326-2042. Nestled on the shore of the Patuxent River near the Chesapeake Bay, this museum focuses on life above, below, and on Maryland's waters. In the Fossils of the Calvert Cliffs exhibit, visitors view fossil shark teeth, crocodile jaws, and whale skulls collected from the Calvert Cliffs, and stand beneath the open jaws of the extinct giant great white shark. Also, the museum has created a living salt marsh with blue crabs, fiddler crabs, and green-backed heron.

Outdoor attractions include cruises around Solomons Harbor on the *Wm B Tennison,* the oldest Coast Guard–licensed passenger vessel on the Chesapeake. On the shore is the **Drum Point Lighthouse.** South of the main museum is the **J C Lore Oyster House,** which displays tools and gear used by local watermen to harvest fish, crabs, oysters, and eels. **Open:** Daily 10am–5pm. **$$**

Sotterley Plantation
MD 245; tel 301/373-2280. Set on a working colonial plantation along the Patuxent River, the mansion contains period furnishings, a Chinese Chippendale staircase, and other handcarved woodwork. On the grounds are a formal garden, a smoke house, a spinning cottage, a custom house, slave quarters, an 18th-century necessary house, and a tobacco farming museum. **Open:** June–Oct, Tues–Sat 11am–4pm. **$$**

Potomac River Museum
Bayview Rd; tel 301/769-2222. This museum traces the history of the area and life along the Potomac River through archeological exhibits. The building also houses an 1890 country store and an 1840 little red schoolhouse. **Open:** Mon–Fri 9am–5pm, Sat–Sun noon–4pm. **$**

McHenry

See also Oakland

Small community north of Oakland in western Maryland. Nearby Deep Creek Lake, the state's largest, draws in visitors with skiing, golfing, and water sports.

MOTELS 🏨

▣▣ Innlet Motor Lodge
Deep Creek Dr, PO Box 178, 21541; tel 301/387-5596. Exit 14A off I-68. Follow US 219 S to McHenry. This small and friendly motel offers sparkling rooms that open onto a rail porch and a rolling green lawn with ducks. **Rooms:** 20 rms. CI 2pm/CO 11am. All rooms overlook Deep Creek Lake and Wisp Ski Resort; one room for the disabled available. Rooms offer integrated decor, excellent mattresses. Sink separate from bathroom area. **Amenities:** 📺 A/C, cable TV w/movies. All units w/terraces, some w/fireplaces. **Services:** 🎧 🐾 Well-behaved pets allowed. Logs and duck food for sale at desk. **Facilities:** 🎿 🏖 🔥 1 beach (lake shore). Boat dock, picnic tables. **Rates:** Peak (June 29–Oct 31/Dec 24–Mar 15) $45–$68 S; $65–$78 D. Extra person $5. Children under age 12 stay free. Min stay wknds. Lower rates off-season. Parking: Outdoor, free. AE, DISC, MC, V.

▣ Point View Inn
US 219, PO Box 100, 21541; tel 301/387-5555. Exit 14A off I-68. Drive 16 miles south on US 219. Rustic building, largely stone, set by Deep Creek Lake. **Rooms:** 24 rms. CI 2pm/CO 11am. Country theme throughout, including such special touches as rocking chairs. All individually decorated with antique reproductions and country furnishings, and all afford view of Deep Creek Lake. Rooms could be fresher. **Amenities:** 📺 Cable TV w/movies. No A/C. All units w/terraces, some w/fireplaces. Some rooms have clock radios, VCRs. **Services:** 🎧 Masseur. **Facilities:** 🎿 🏖 100 1 restaurant, 2 bars (1 w/entertainment), 1 beach (lake shore), beauty salon. Public porch. Outdoor dining available at adjoining restaurant. **Rates:** $59–$75 S or D. Extra person $10. Children under age 12 stay free. Parking: Outdoor, free. AE, DISC, MC, V.

RESORT

≣≣≣ Wisp Resort Hotel

Marsh Hill Rd, Star Rte 2, PO Box 35, 21541; tel 301/387-5581 or toll free 800/462-9477; fax 301/387-4127. Exit 14A off I-68. 90 acres. This ski and golf resort set by Deep Creek Lake has a hospitable staff and nice views of a duck pond and Deep Creek in front, mountain trails in rear. **Rooms:** 168 rms and stes. CI 5pm/CO 11am. Nonsmoking rms avail. Comfortable rooms; two VIP suites consist of two rooms and full kitchen, dining room; 100 minisuites, some with queen-size beds and separate master bedroom, some with two doubles; three rooms for guests with disabilities. All standard rooms have a pull-out sofa. **Amenities:** 🛢 ⚷ A/C, cable TV w/movies, refrig. Some units w/fireplaces. **Services:** ⚲ **Facilities:** 🛍 ♠️ ▶18 ♨️ 🐟 🎱 💻 ⚹ 2 restaurants (see "Restaurants" below), 1 bar, games rm, lawn games, whirlpool. Olympic-size pool with adjoining hot tub. Miniature golf, ice skating, 30 miles of trails. Pizza snack bar. **Rates:** Peak (Dec 26–Mar 7) $75–$145 S or D; $150 ste. Children under age 6 stay free. Lower rates off-season. Parking: Outdoor, free. Ski and golf packages avail. AE, DC, DISC, MC, V.

RESTAURANT 🍴

Bavarian Room

In the Wisp Resort Hotel, Marsh Hill Rd; tel 301/387-4911. Exit 14A off I-68. **Seafood/Steak.** Located on the lower level of the McHenry House at this ski resort, the Bavarian Room offers rathskeller decor, including red-checked tablecloths, half-timbered walls, and a fireplace. Soup and salad bar. Intimate dining on seafood, pasta, and signature steaks, such as 20-ounce porterhouse. **FYI:** Reservations not accepted. No smoking. **Open:** Sun–Thurs 5–10pm, Fri–Sat 5–10:30pm. **Prices:** Main courses $9–$18. AE, DC, DISC, MC, V. ❤️ 🖼️

Oakland

See also McHenry

In mountainous western Maryland, this old town is the gateway to Swallow Falls, Maryland's highest waterfall. Seat of Garrett County. **Information:** Garret County Chamber of Commerce, 200 S 3rd St, Oakland, 21550 (tel 301/334-1948).

MOTEL 🏨

≣≣≣ Alpine Village Inn

Glendale Rd (Rte 4), PO Box 5200, 21550; tel 301/387-5534 or toll free 800/343-5253; fax 301/387-4119. Exit 14A off I-68. Chalet-style lodge and cabins offering lakefront view, bubbling spring in wooded setting, and rustic decor. Extended lobby area has intimate sections (1 with fireplace) with stone walls, games, large tables. **Rooms:** 29 rms and effic. CI 4pm/CO 11am. Nonsmoking rms avail. Open-beam ceilings and brick-and-wood walls create a warm mood. Of 29 lodge rooms, 9 have kitchenette. Some studio apartments off main lobby and some rooms on sun-deck level. **Amenities:** 🛢 A/C, cable TV w/movies. All units w/terraces, some w/fireplaces. **Services:** ⚲ **Facilities:** 🛍 ♠️ 🐟 ⚹ 1 beach (lake shore), playground, washer/dryer. Picnic tables and grill overlook lake. Free boat docking. **Rates (CP):** Peak (Mem Day–Labor Day) $66–$72 S or D; $77–$89 effic. Extra person $5. Min stay peak and wknds. Lower rates off-season. Parking: Outdoor, free. High-season rates prevail on all weekends, holidays, festivals, deer season, and Christmas and New Year's weeks; two- and three-bedroom chalets have minimum-stay requirements. AE, DC, DISC, MC, V.

RESTAURANTS 🍴

The Four Seasons

In Will O' the Wisp, US 219; tel 301/387-5503 ext 2201. Exit 14A off I-68. **Continental.** This elegant stone and wood dining area, complete with a chandelier hanging from the high ceiling, overlooks Deep Creek Lake. All dinners include soup or salad, vegetable or bread, and dessert. One of few restaurants in area to welcome reservations. Specialties include chicken Romano, Flounder Four Seasons. **FYI:** Reservations accepted. Children's menu. Dress code. **Open:** Breakfast daily 7–11:30am; lunch daily 11:30am–2pm; dinner daily 5–9:30pm. **Prices:** Main courses $12–$19. AE, CB, DC, DISC, MC, V. 🖼️

$ ★ Silver Tree Inn Restaurant

Glendale Rd; tel 301/387-4040. Exit 14A off I-68. Follow US 219 to Glendale Rd. **Italian/Seafood/Steak.** Set in the woods adjacent to Deep Creek Lake and the Alpine Inn. The 1890s decor is dominated by two huge stone-hearth fireplaces and log walls providing a warm and rustic dining atmosphere. A separate windowed section overlooks the lake. Adjacent building on the water, accessible by boat, has raw bar and entertainment. Favorites include lasagna, crab imperial, and prime rib. **FYI:** Reservations not accepted. **Open:** Sun 4–10pm, Mon–Thurs 5–10pm, Fri–Sat 5–11pm. **Prices:** Main courses $8–$36. AE, CB, DC, DISC, MC, V. 🖼️ 🖼️

$ Uno Restaurant & Bar

US 219; tel 301/387-4866. **Burgers/Pizza.** A classy step up from a pizzeria, it offers a range of foods and a view of Deep Creek Lake from many tables and booths. Open-beamed ceilings, massive stone fireplace in center, funky neon-light accents, and framed movie posters add to the fun. Best are pastas, Chicago-style deep-dish pizza, orange roughy, Delmonico steaks. **FYI:** Reservations not accepted. Children's menu. No smoking. **Open:** Mon–Thurs 11am–midnight, Fri–Sat 11am–1am, Sun 11am–11pm. **Prices:** Main courses $5–$11. AE, DC, DISC, MC, V. 🖼️ 🖼️ 🖼️ ⚹

ATTRACTIONS

Wisp Four Seasons Resort

Marsh Hill Rd, Deep Creek Lake; tel 301/387-4911. Maryland's largest ski area features an elevation of 3,080 feet and a vertical rise of 610 feet. The 23 major ski runs on 80 acres of terrain offer night skiing as well as daytime runs. In summer, the resort welcomes visitors to its 18-hole championship golf course. **Open:** Year-round. Call for hours. **$$$$**

Deep Creek Lake State Park

898 State Park Rd, Swanton; tel 301/387-5563. This recreation area features a 365-foot sandy beach on the shore of Maryland's largest freshwater lake. Guarded swimming area, boating, picnicking, and camping. **Open:** Apr–Oct, daily sunrise–sunset. **$**

Ocean City

First incorporated in 1880, Ocean City is today a sprawling, bustling resort city on the state's famous Eastern Shore. **Information:** Ocean City Convention and Visitors Bureau, 4001 Coastal Hwy, PO Box 116, Ocean City, 21842 (tel 410/289-8181).

HOTELS

Carousel Hotel and Resort

11700 Coastal Hwy, at 118th St, 21842; tel 410/524-1000 or toll free 800/641-0011; fax 410/524-7766. Exit US 50 at MD 90. Once the showplace in this part of Ocean City, this large resort hotel is beginning to show its age. Nevertheless, it's right on an excellent stretch of beach, and sports an exceptional atrium. Popular with groups year-round. **Rooms:** 265 rms, stes, and effic. CI 4pm/CO 11am. Nonsmoking rms avail. Rooms are either oceanfront, ocean view, street side, or facing an ice-skating rink. Those on street and rink sides are noisier than others. **Amenities:** A/C, cable TV w/movies, voice mail. All units w/terraces, some w/whirlpools. **Services:** Car-rental desk, social director, children's program, babysitting. Bellhops, concierge, and social director during high season only. **Facilities:** 1 restaurant, 2 bars (1 w/entertainment), 1 beach (ocean), lifeguard, volleyball, games rm, spa, sauna, whirlpool. Indoor ice-skating rink. Attractive indoor pool. **Rates:** Peak (June–Aug) $89–$209 S or D; $169–$229 ste; $189–$289 effic. Extra person $10. Children under age 18 stay free. Min stay wknds. Lower rates off-season. AP and MAP rates avail. Parking: Outdoor, free. AE, CB, DC, DISC, MC, V.

The Coconut Malorie

201 60th St, in the Bay, 21842; tel 410/723-6100 or toll free 800/767-6060; fax 410/524-9327. Exit US 50 at MD 90. This luxury hotel on the bay side of Ocean City has an entrance of white marble. **Rooms:** 85 stes. Executive level. CI 4pm/CO noon. Nonsmoking rms avail. Bright and airy rooms are decorated in elegant island style—off-whites, dark or light wood, high-quality Haitian art, tile floors. **Amenities:** A/C, cable TV w/movies, refrig. All units w/terraces, all w/whirlpools. Luxury rooms have tables set with linen, good grade of china, and stainless cutlery. **Services:** Twice-daily maid svce, car-rental desk, masseur, babysitting. Arrangements for van transportation to and use of a health club, beach, and other facilities are made through hotel. **Facilities:** 2 restaurants (lunch and dinner only; *see* "Restaurants" below), 3 bars (1 w/entertainment). All water sports are nearby. Beautiful library and gallery of Haitian art are in the Tower Room. **Rates:** Peak (June–Sept) $159–$219 ste. Extra person $15. Children under age 6 stay free. Min stay peak. Lower rates off-season. AP and MAP rates avail. Parking: Indoor/outdoor, free. AE, CB, DC, MC, V.

Dunes Manor Hotel

28th St, 21842; tel 410/289-1100 or toll free 800/523-2888; fax 410/289-4905. At Oceanfront. A Victorian-style resort hotel with reproduction furniture and attractive balconies overlooking the ocean. Very pretty lobby and public rooms. **Rooms:** 170 rms and stes. CI 3pm/CO 11am. Nonsmoking rms avail. **Amenities:** A/C, cable TV w/movies, refrig. All units w/terraces. Microwave. **Services:** Complimentary afternoon tea daily. **Facilities:** 1 restaurant, 1 bar (w/entertainment), 1 beach (ocean), lifeguard, spa, whirlpool. Nearby golf, fishing, and water sports. **Rates:** Peak (June 24–Sept 25) $149–$199 S or D; $245–$285 ste. Extra person $10. Children under age 17 stay free. Min stay peak. Lower rates off-season. Parking: Indoor/outdoor, free. AE, CB, DC, DISC, MC, V.

Princess Royale Oceanfront Hotel

Oceanfront at 91st St, 21842; tel 410/524-7777 or toll free 800/476-9253; fax 410/524-7787. Exit US 50 at MD 90. A dramatic, modern, oceanfront resort hotel with extensive facilities. **Rooms:** 340 effic. CI 4pm/CO 11am. Nonsmoking rms avail. All units have fully equipped kitchens, separate sitting rooms. Atrium rooms overlook a dramatic pool area and have ocean view through a high glass wall. **Amenities:** A/C, refrig, in-rm safe. All units w/terraces, some w/whirlpools. All have 2 TVs. "Green" timers automatically shut off lights after guests leave units. **Services:** Masseur, children's program, babysitting. **Facilities:** 1 restaurant, 4 bars (1 w/entertainment), 1 beach (ocean), lifeguard, games rm, spa, sauna, steam rm, whirlpool, beauty salon, washer/dryer. Miniature golf. **Rates:** Peak (July–Aug) $179–$400 effic. Extra person $15. Children under age 12 stay free. Min stay peak. Lower rates off-season. MAP rates avail. Parking: Indoor, free. AE, CB, DC, DISC, MC, V.

Sheraton Fontainebleau Hotel

10100 Ocean Hwy, at 101st St, 21842; tel 410/524-3535 or toll free 800/638-2100; fax 410/524-3834. Exit 50 at MD 90. This large oceanfront hotel is conveniently located on the Gold Coast near shopping. It is self-contained and enjoyable year-round. **Rooms:** 250 rms, stes, and effic. CI 3pm/CO 11am. Nonsmoking rms avail. **Amenities:** 🅰 ⬡ ⬛ A/C, cable TV w/movies, refrig, dataport, voice mail. All units w/terraces. **Services:** ✗ ⬛ VP ⬛ ⬛ ⬡ ⬡ Twice-daily maid svce, car-rental desk, babysitting. **Facilities:** ⬛ ⬛ 1500 ⬛ ⬛ 1 restaurant, 3 bars (1 w/entertainment), 1 beach (ocean), lifeguard, games rm, spa, sauna, steam rm, whirlpool, beauty salon. **Rates:** Peak (Mem Day–Labor Day) $159–$235 S or D; $305 ste; $305 effic. Extra person $15. Children under age 18 stay free. Min stay peak and special events. Lower rates off-season. MAP rates avail. Parking: Outdoor, free. Condos rent by week only ($1,500–$1,900/wk). AE, CB, DC, DISC, EC, ER, MC, V.

MOTELS

⬛⬛⬛ Best Western Flagship Oceanfront
2600 Baltimore Ave, at 26th St, 21842; tel 410/289-3384 or toll free 800/638-2106, 800/429-3147 in MD. Exit US 50 at Baltimore Ave and go north to 26th St. A good, well-kept oceanfront motel, with better-than-average facilities for this area. **Rooms:** 93 rms and effic. CI 3pm/CO 11am. Nonsmoking rms avail. All rooms have an ocean view, though some are limited; six are directly on the oceanfront. All rooms have two double beds. Attractive decor. **Amenities:** 🅰 ⬡ ⬛ ⬛ ⬡ A/C, cable TV w/movies, refrig, VCR. All units w/terraces. **Services:** ⬡ Children's program, babysitting **Facilities:** ⬛ 🚲 ⬛ ⬛ 1 restaurant (dinner only), 1 bar (w/entertainment), 1 beach (ocean), lifeguard, games rm, spa, sauna, whirlpool, playground, washer/dryer. Restaurant offers all-you-can-eat buffets. **Rates:** Peak (June 24–Aug 27) $159 S or D; $169–$179 effic. Extra person $7. Children under age 4 stay free. Min stay. Lower rates off-season. MAP rates avail. Parking: Outdoor, free. AE, CB, DC, DISC, MC, V.

⬛⬛ Best Western Sea Bay Inn
6007 Coastal Hwy, 21842; tel 410/524-6100 or toll free 800/888-2229; fax 410/524-6100. Exit US 50 at MD 90. A chain motel on the bay side of Ocean City, with easy access to sports facilities and the ocean. **Rooms:** 92 rms. CI 3pm/CO 11am. Nonsmoking rms avail. **Amenities:** 🅰 A/C, cable TV w/movies, refrig. All units w/terraces. Some have coffeemakers. All have wet bar, microwave. **Services:** ⬛ ⬛ ⬡ Car-rental desk, babysitting. **Facilities:** ⬛ 100 ⬛ 1 restaurant, games rm, washer/dryer. Adjacent to lighted public tennis courts. Guests get 50% discount at nearby fitness center. **Rates:** Peak (May–Oct) $84–$119 S or D. Extra person $15. Children under age 18 stay free. Min stay peak. Lower rates off-season. AP and MAP rates avail. Parking: Outdoor, free. Golf packages avail. AE, CB, DC, DISC, EC, ER, JCB, MC, V.

⬛⬛ Brighton Suites
12500 Coastal Hwy, at 125th St, 21842; tel 410/250-7600 or toll free 800/546-0042; fax 410/250-7603. MD 90 to left on Coastal Hwy to 125th St. On the highway one block from the ocean, this stucco motel lacks views but has good, clean accommodations and is well maintained. Shopping malls

across Ocean Hwy. **Rooms:** 57 stes. CI 3pm/CO 11am. Nonsmoking rms avail. Rooms for guests with disabilities have Murphy beds to give more open floor space during the day. **Amenities:** 🅰 ⬡ ⬛ A/C, cable TV w/movies, refrig, in-rm safe. Some units w/terraces. Microwaves, stoves. **Services:** ⬡ Babysitting. Fax service available. **Facilities:** ⬛ ⬛ 200 ⬛ Bike rentals and other sports available nearby. Playground, fishing piers across street at Northside Park. **Rates:** Peak (May–Oct) $154–$194 ste. Extra person $5–$10. Children under age 17 stay free. Min stay peak and wknds. Lower rates off-season. Parking: Outdoor, free. Closed Nov–Feb. AE, CB, DC, DISC, MC, V.

⬛⬛⬛ Castle in the Sand Hotel
Oceanfront at 37th St, PO Box 190, 21842; tel 410/289-6846 or toll free 800/552-7263; fax 410/289-9446. Exit US 50 at Baltimore Ave; turn right on Coastal Hwy; then right on 37th St. Spread over an entire block, several buildings include detached cottages, oceanfront and street-side rooms and suites. Friendly management. **Rooms:** 176 rms and effic. CI 3pm/CO 11am. Nonsmoking rms avail. Some units are oceanside; others are bayside. Most have cooking facilities. Pleasant decor. **Amenities:** 🅰 ⬛ A/C, cable TV w/movies, refrig. Some units w/terraces. **Services:** ✗ ⬛ ⬡ Social director, children's program, babysitting. Beach-equipped wheelchair available. **Facilities:** ⬛ 150 ⬛ 1 restaurant, 2 bars (w/entertainment), 1 beach (ocean), lifeguard, games rm, lawn games, washer/dryer. Large sun deck. Very large pool with diving board. **Rates:** Peak (June 4–Labor Day) $159 S or D; $179 effic. Extra person $7. Children under age 11 stay free. Min stay peak. Lower rates off-season. MAP rates avail. Parking: Outdoor, free. Cottages/villas rent by week only ($605–$1,035/wk). AE, DISC, MC, V.

⬛⬛ Comfort Inn Boardwalk
5th St and Oceanfront, 21842; tel 410/289-5155 or toll free 800/282-5155. Exit US 50 at Baltimore Ave and go north to 5th St. An oceanfront chain motel with nicely decorated rooms and hallways and a convenient location near the south end of the boardwalk. **Rooms:** 84 effic. CI 3pm/CO 11am. Nonsmoking rms avail. Attractively decorated efficiencies. Some are oceanfront; others overlook parking lot or have partial ocean views. **Amenities:** 🅰 ⬛ A/C, cable TV w/movies, refrig. All units w/terraces. **Services:** ⬡ Babysitting. **Facilities:** ⬛ ⬛ 1 beach (ocean), lifeguard. An attractive, kidney-shaped indoor pool. **Rates (CP):** Peak (June 24–Aug 21) $135–$189 effic. Extra person $10. Children under age 12 stay free. Min stay peak. Lower rates off-season. Parking: Outdoor, free. Closed Dec–Jan. AE, CB, DC, DISC, MC, V.

⬛⬛⬛ Comfort Inn Gold Coast
11201 Coastal Hwy, at 112th St, 21842; tel 410/524-3000 or toll free 800/221-2222; fax 410/524-8255. Exit US 50 at MD 90. A well-kept, better-than-average motel on Sinepuxent Bay, two blocks from ocean, and next to a shopping center. **Rooms:** 202 rms. CI 3pm/CO 11am. Nonsmoking rms avail. **Amenities:** 🅰 A/C, cable TV w/movies, refrig, dataport.

Some units w/whirlpools. Each room has sink and microwave. **Services:** ⟲ Very hospitable, competent staff. **Facilities:** 🔒 🛏 ⅙ 1 restaurant, 1 bar (w/entertainment), whirlpool, washer/dryer. **Rates:** Peak (June–Aug) $85–$145 S or D. Extra person $10. Children under age 18 stay free. Min stay peak. Lower rates off-season. Parking: Outdoor, free. Golf packages avail. AE, DC, DISC, MC, V.

☰☰☰ Days Inn Bayside
4201 Coastal Hwy, 21842; tel 410/289-6488 or toll free 800/329-7466; fax 410/289-1617. Exit US 50 at MD 90. This facility is set up especially well for conventioneers, rather than for beach-goers, although the oceanfront is not far away. Adjacent to convention center, restaurants, and stores. **Rooms:** 162 rms. CI 4pm/CO 11am. Nonsmoking rms avail. Wide variety of room views: some of the bay, some of the distant ocean. **Amenities:** 🔒 🛏 A/C, cable TV w/movies. All units w/terraces. **Services:** ⟲ ⟲ Car-rental desk, children's program. **Facilities:** 🔒 🛏 ⅙ Games rm, washer/dryer. Public tennis and basketball courts as well as public beach nearby. Miniature golf next door. **Rates (CP):** Peak (June–Aug) $75–$210 S or D. Extra person $10. Children under age 18 stay free. Min stay peak and wknds. Lower rates off-season. MAP rates avail. Parking: Outdoor, free. AE, DC, DISC, MC, V.

☰☰ Fenwick Inn
13801 Coastal Hwy, at 138th St, 21842; tel 410/250-1100 or toll free 800/492-1873; fax 410/250-0087. Exit US 50 at MD 90. A modern, glass-and-concrete motel on the bay side of the highway, near the northern end of Ocean City. **Rooms:** 201 rms, stes, and effic. CI 3pm/CO 11am. Nonsmoking rms avail. Suites are better furnished and equipped with two baths, walk-in closets. **Amenities:** 🔒 🛏 A/C, cable TV, refrig. Suites have stoves. **Services:** ✕ ⟲ ⟲ **Facilities:** 🔒 🛏 ⅙ 1 restaurant, 1 bar (w/entertainment), games rm, whirlpool. Rooftop restaurant with view. **Rates:** Peak (July–Aug) $119–$169 S or D; $250–$325 ste; $139–$169 effic. Extra person $10. Children under age 18 stay free. Min stay wknds. Lower rates off-season. MAP rates avail. Parking: Outdoor, free. Golf packages avail. AE, DC, DISC, MC, V.

☰☰ Georgia Belle Hotel
12004 Coastal Hwy, at 120th St, 21842; tel 410/250-4000 or toll free 800/542-4444; fax 410/250-9014. Exit US 50 at MD 90. A stucco-and-concrete motel close to the beach. Clean and basic. **Rooms:** 98 rms and stes; 1 cottage/villa. CI 2pm/CO 11am. Nonsmoking rms avail. Large, simple rooms. Some have ocean view across parking lot; some can see ocean from side. **Amenities:** 🔒 A/C, cable TV w/movies. All units w/terraces. Microwaves and refrigerators available for a fee. **Services:** ✕ Car-rental desk, babysitting. **Facilities:** 🔒 🛏 ⅙ 1 restaurant. Passes available to nearby fitness and health center. **Rates:** Peak (July–Aug) $99–$199 S or D; $119–$299 ste; $299 cottage/villa. Extra person $6. Children under age

12 stay free. Min stay peak. Lower rates off-season. AP and MAP rates avail. Parking: Outdoor, free. Golf and other packages avail. AE, DISC, MC, V.

☰☰☰ Holiday Inn Oceanfront
6600 Coastal Hwy, at 67th St, 21842; tel 410/524-1600 or toll free 800/638-2106; fax 410/524-1135. Exit US 50 at MD 90. A large resort motel with extensive indoor facilities. **Rooms:** 216 effic. CI 3pm/CO 11am. Nonsmoking rms avail. Fairly large rooms. Separate sitting area with its own sofa bed can be partitioned off. **Amenities:** 🔒 🛏 🍽 A/C, satel TV w/movies, refrig, dataport. All units w/terraces. **Services:** ✕ 🛥 ⟲ Children's program. **Facilities:** 🔒 🎾 🛝 🛏 ⅙ 1 restaurant (*see* "Restaurants" below), 2 bars, 1 beach (ocean), lifeguard, games rm, sauna, whirlpool, washer/dryer. Attractive outdoor pool/bar/tennis court area. Tanning rooms. Very large game room with pool table and video games. **Rates:** Peak (June–Aug) $189–$229 effic. Extra person $9. Children under age 19 stay free. Min stay peak. Lower rates off-season. AP and MAP rates avail. Parking: Outdoor, free. Golf packages avail. AE, CB, DC, DISC, ER, JCB, MC, V.

☰☰☰ Howard Johnson Hotel on the Boardwalk
1109 Atlantic Ave, 21842; tel 410/289-7251 or toll free 800/926-1122; fax 410/289-3435. Exit US 50 at Baltimore Ave. Right on the boardwalk and beach, this motel has all the facilities of a standard oceanfront resort. **Rooms:** 90 rms. CI 3pm/CO 11am. Nonsmoking rms avail. Rooms range in size but are furnished similarly. **Amenities:** 🔒 A/C, cable TV w/movies, in-rm safe. All units w/terraces. Amenities vary somewhat from room to room. Some have hair dryers and refrigerators. **Services:** ✕ ⟲ **Facilities:** 🔒 🚲 🛏 ⅙ 1 restaurant, 1 bar, 1 beach (ocean), lifeguard, board surfing. **Rates (CP):** Peak (June 10–Sept 4) $125–$175 S or D. Extra person $5. Children under age 12 stay free. Min stay peak and wknds. Lower rates off-season. Parking: Indoor, free. Premium for oceanfront rooms. MC, V.

☰☰☰ Quality Inn Beachfront
Oceanfront at 33rd St, PO Box 910, 21842; tel 410/289-1234 or toll free 800/221-2222. Exit US 50 at Baltimore Ave N; turn right at 33rd St. A nearly new chain motel with attractive decor throughout. **Rooms:** 75 effic. CI 3pm/CO 11am. Nonsmoking rms avail. All are oceanfront or ocean view. **Amenities:** 🔒 🛏 A/C, cable TV w/movies, refrig, VCR. All units w/terraces. **Services:** ✕ ⟲ **Facilities:** 🔒 🛏 ⅙ 1 restaurant (bkfst only), 1 beach (ocean), lifeguard, games rm, sauna, steam rm, whirlpool, washer/dryer. A very attractive indoor pool and spa in an atrium. **Rates:** Peak (July 15–Aug 28) $180–$200 effic. Extra person $10. Min stay peak. Lower rates off-season. Parking: Indoor, free. AE, DC, DISC, MC, V.

☰☰☰ Quality Inn Boardwalk
1601 Boardwalk, at 17th St, 21842; tel 410/289-4401 or toll free 800/638-2106; fax 410/289-8620. Exit US 50 at Baltimore Ave; go north to 17th St. A well-maintained, middle-

aged oceanfront motel with an excellent location on the boardwalk. Good choice for families. **Rooms:** 179 effic. Executive level. CI 3pm/CO 11am. Nonsmoking rms avail. Furnishings are better than average. All but 20 rooms are oceanfront. **Amenities:** 🏨 ☙ 🍴 A/C, satel TV w/movies. Some units w/terraces. Most units have stove, microwave, and refrigerator. **Services:** 🛎 Video cameras available for a fee. **Facilities:** 🏊 ⛱ ♿ 1 restaurant, 1 beach (ocean), lifeguard, games rm, spa, sauna, steam rm, whirlpool, washer/dryer. Tanning room. **Rates:** Peak (June 26–Labor Day) $199 effic. Extra person $7. Children under age 6 stay free. Min stay peak. Lower rates off-season. Parking: Outdoor, free. Attractive packages for those over 50. AE, DISC, MC, V.

☰☰☰ Quality Inn Oceanfront

5400 Coastal Hwy, at 54th St, 21842; tel 410/524-7200 or toll free 800/837-3586; fax 410/723-0018. MD 90 exit off US 50. North of the boardwalk, this oceanfront resort motel is built around an attractive atrium with pools, ponds, spas, tropical plants, and, especially interesting for children, parrots and other birds. **Rooms:** 130 effic. CI 3pm/CO 11am. Nonsmoking rms avail. All units are attractively decorated in beach-theme pastels. **Amenities:** 🏨 ☙ 🍴 A/C, cable TV w/movies, refrig. All units w/terraces. Microwaves. **Services:** ✗ 🛎 **Facilities:** 🏊 ⚓¹ ⛱ ♿ 1 restaurant, 1 bar, 1 beach (ocean), lifeguard, games rm, spa, sauna, whirlpool, playground, washer/dryer. **Rates:** Peak (June 28–Aug 25) $179–$234 effic. Extra person $5. Children under age 6 stay free. Min stay wknds. Lower rates off-season. MAP rates avail. Parking: Outdoor, free. Closed Dec 15–25. AE, CB, DC, DISC, ER, JCB, MC, V.

☰☰ Ramada Limited Oceanfront

Oceanfront at 32nd St, PO Box 160, 21842; tel 410/289-6444 or toll free 800/638-2106; fax 410/289-0108. Exit US 50 at Baltimore Ave; go north, then right at 32nd St. Formerly the Stardust Oceanfront, this well-kept but basic motel is located on the ocean in a pleasant area behind the dunes. **Rooms:** 76 effic. CI 3pm/CO 11am. Nonsmoking rms avail. Some are oceanfront; others have ocean views. **Amenities:** 🏨 ☙ 📺 🍴 A/C, cable TV w/movies, refrig. Some units w/terraces. **Services:** 🛎 Maid replaces towels each afternoon after swimming time. **Facilities:** 🏊 ♻ 1 beach (ocean), lifeguard, lawn games, washer/dryer. Volleyball on private beach area. **Rates (CP):** Peak (July 1–Aug 27) $164–$173 effic. Extra person $7. Children under age 3 stay free. Min stay peak. Lower rates off-season. Parking: Outdoor, free. Favorable weekly rates. AE, DISC, MC, V.

☰☰ Talbot Inn

311 Talbot St, PO Box 548, 21842; tel 410/289-9125 or toll free 800/659-7703; fax 410/289-6792. Off US 50. A basic but exceptionally well-maintained property with efficiency units. Located near fishing and watersports center of Ocean City. **Rooms:** 34 effic. CI 2pm/CO 11am. Very clean and neat. **Amenities:** 🏨 A/C, cable TV, refrig. Microwaves.

Facilities: 🏊 ♿ Parasailing available. **Rates:** Peak (June 10–Sept 5) $83–$90 effic. Extra person $4. Children under age 2 stay free. Min stay peak and wknds. Lower rates off-season. Parking: Outdoor, free. MC, V.

INN

☰☰☰☰ The Lighthouse Club

56th St, in the Bay, 21842; tel 410/524-5400 or toll free 800/767-6060; fax 410/524-9327. Exit US 50 at MD 90. 3¼ acres. Styled as a large lighthouse, this building is situated among the natural marshes of Sinepuxent Bay. Hallways are adorned with nautical prints. Unsuitable for children under 12. **Rooms:** 23 stes. CI 4pm/CO noon. Large rooms are very light and airy, outfitted with elegant island-style furniture including four-poster beds. Some closets have doors; some do not. **Amenities:** 🏨 📺 🍴 A/C, cable TV w/movies, refrig, bathrobes. All units w/terraces, some w/fireplaces, some w/whirlpools. China and good-quality glassware in rooms. **Services:** ✗ 🗝 VP 🚐 🚗 🛎 Twice-daily maid svce, car-rental desk, masseur, babysitting. **Facilities:** 🏊 ⛴ 2 restaurants (see "Restaurants" below), 3 bars (1 w/entertainment). Guests enjoy all facilities at Coconut Malorie hotel and at nearby health club. **Rates (CP):** Peak (June–Sept) $159–$249 ste. Extra person $15. Children under age 6 stay free. Min stay peak. Lower rates off-season. AP and MAP rates avail. Parking: Outdoor, free. AE, CB, DC, MC, V.

RESTAURANTS 🍴

The Bayside Skillet/The Crepe and Omelette Place

77th St and Coastal Hwy; tel 410/524-7950. MD 90 exit off US 50. **American/Seafood.** A pretty dining room, done in light wood, pink, and white, with large windows and a central skylight. Also has outdoor dining on the deck overlooking the bay. Crepes and omelettes are specialties, with a few soups and other light dishes. Dinner (in season only) is primarily seafood. A favorite place for light fare. **FYI:** Reservations not accepted. Children's menu. Beer and wine only. **Open:** Peak (June–Aug) daily 24 hrs. **Prices:** Main courses $8–$20. MC, V. ⚓ 🏔 🍴 ♿

Bonfire

71st and Coastal Hwy; tel 410/524-7171. Jct US 50/MD 90. **Seafood/Steak.** A large establishment with several warm, semiformal dining rooms. The very large oval bar is comfortable. All-you-can-eat seafood and prime rib buffet is popular. **FYI:** Reservations recommended. Dancing/rock. Children's menu. **Open:** Peak (May–Oct) daily 4am–10pm. Closed Christmas week. **Prices:** Main courses $10–$25. AE, DC, MC, V. 👪 🍸

Captain Bill Bunting's Angler

312 Talbot St; tel 410/289-7424. Follow US 50 to Philadelphia Ave, turn right, go 1 block to Talbot St, turn right. **American/Seafood.** An outdoor deck and excellent views of the boat harbor more than make up for the simple decor of this traditional seafood restaurant, family-owned since 1938.

Fresh seafood predominates, but other American fare is offered. Each dinner includes complimentary cruise aboard a party boat. **FYI:** Reservations recommended. Rock. Children's menu. No smoking. **Open:** Peak (May–Sept) daily 5am–11pm. Closed Oct–Apr. **Prices:** Main courses $10–$20. AE, MC, V. ⚓ ⛰ ▾ VP ♿

Dumser's Dairyland Restaurant

12305 Coastal Hwy, at 123rd St; tel 410/250-5543. Jct US 50/MD 90. **American/Cafe.** A bright, traditional cafe/ice cream parlor with old-fashioned ceiling fans and drop lights, white wooden booths, and pastel walls. Standard American breakfast and lunch plus *real* ice cream shakes, sodas, and floats. Ice cream and baked goods made on premises; 1940s musical memorabilia on walls. Four other locations in Ocean City. **FYI:** Reservations not accepted. Children's menu. No liquor license. No smoking. **Open:** Peak (June–Sept) daily 7am–1am. **Prices:** Main courses $6–$16. MC, V. 👶 ♿

Fager's Island

In The Coconut Malorie, 60th St on the Bay; tel 410/524-5500. Jct US 50/MD 90. **American/Seafood.** Attractive rooms in blue with large windows on Sinepuxent Bay. Nice sunset views. Bar is less formal than dining room, which has dark woods, green linen, and wood chairs. Mostly seafood with various specialty sauces for dinner. Seafood raw bar. Fresh breads. Wine list contains regional descriptions and maps. **FYI:** Reservations recommended. Rock. Children's menu. **Open:** Peak (June–Sept) daily 11am–11pm. **Prices:** Main courses $17–$25. AE, DC, MC, V. ⛰ ▾ ♿

Hanna's Marina Deck

306 Dorchester St; tel 410/289-4411. **American/Seafood.** Fresh seafood, breads, and muffins are signatures of this simple restaurant with wooden deck floor and large windows looking out on the boat harbor. Some beef, veal, and poultry are offered. **FYI:** Reservations accepted. Children's menu. Dress code. **Open:** Peak (Apr–Oct) lunch Mon–Sat 11:30am–4pm; dinner Mon–Sat 4–11pm, Sun 3–11pm; brunch Sun 11am–3pm. Closed mid-Oct–Mar. **Prices:** Main courses $8–$23. AE, DISC, MC, V. ⚓ ⛰ ▾ VP

Harrison's Harbor Watch

Boardwalk S overlooking inlet; tel 410/289-5121. Exit US 50 at Baltimore Ave. **Seafood.** Casual, with booths and tile-topped tables overlooking Ocean City Inlet. Fresh seafood is kept refrigerated throughout shipping, storage, and preparation. Some pasta, meat, and fowl dishes. Efficient, computerized order system. **FYI:** Reservations recommended. Children's menu. **Open:** Peak (Mid-May–mid-Oct) lunch daily 11:30am–10pm; dinner daily 4:30–10pm. **Prices:** Main courses $16–$25. AE, CB, DC, DISC, MC, V. ⛰ ▾ ♿

Higgins' Crab House

31st St and Coastal Hwy; tel 410/289-2581. Baltimore Ave exit off US 50, N to 31st St. **Seafood.** A classic Maryland crab house with wood paneling and tables covered with rolls of brown paper. The bar is for service, not lingering. Fresh steamed hard crabs are the specialty, but other seafood dishes are available, plus barbecued ribs and a few other meat and chicken offerings. **FYI:** Reservations accepted. Children's menu. Additional location: MD 33 and Pea Neck Rd, St Michaels (tel 745-5056). **Open:** Peak (May–Sept) daily 2:30–10pm. Closed Dec–Jan. **Prices:** Main courses $12–$20. AE, DC, DISC, MC, V. ▾

The Hobbit Restaurant and Bar

81st St and the Bay; tel 410/524-8100. Jct US 50/MD 90. **Cafe/Continental.** Attractive dining rooms in mauve and gray, with large windows overlooking a saltwater marsh and Sinepuxent Bay. Cafe menu with excellent selection of salads and other light fare in addition to dinner menu. **FYI:** Reservations recommended. Children's menu. **Open:** Daily 11am–midnight. **Prices:** Main courses $16–$23. AE, DISC, MC, V. ⛰ ▾ ♿

⑤ Paul Revere Smorgasbord

2nd St and Boardwalk; tel 410/524-1776. Exit US 50 at Baltimore Ave. **American/Seafood.** Brick and rough-hewn wood walls, bare wood tables, and colonial decor in this large restaurant that often serves 2,000 diners a day in peak summer season. Straightforward, American-style food. Price (reduced for children) covers all-you-can-eat meal, with large salad and dessert bars. **FYI:** Reservations not accepted. Children's menu. Beer and wine only. **Open:** Peak (June–Sept) daily 3:30–9pm. Closed Oct–Mar. **Prices:** Prix fixe $10. MC, V. 👶 ▾ ♿

★ Phillips Crab House

2004 Philadelphia Ave, at 20th St; tel 410/289-6821. Exit US 50 at Baltimore Ave; go north to 20th St. **Seafood.** Dark wood paneling and inlaid tables covered with white butcher paper. Tiffany-style lamps in most dining rooms, along with stained-glass windows. Downstairs has an à la carte menu, while upstairs is an all-you-can-eat buffet. Crab and seafood dominate in both. The 13 dining rooms and 6 kitchens, including 2 display-cooking areas upstairs, make this one of the largest restaurants in Maryland. **FYI:** Reservations not accepted. Children's menu. **Open:** Peak (June–Sept) daily noon–10pm. Closed Nov–Easter. **Prices:** Main courses $13–$26. AE, DC, DISC, MC, V. ▾ ♿

Reflections

In Holiday Inn Oceanfront, 6600 Coastal Hwy; tel 410/524-5252. MD 90 exit off US 50. **New American/French.** Brick walls, statuary, and attractive furnishings make for a classical setting at this award-winning establishment. Affiliated with the *Chaine des Rotisseurs,* chef is highly qualified and well recognized. Menu changes daily, according to availability of fresh items. Specialty is tableside cooking. Exceptional wine list. **FYI:** Reservations recommended. Children's menu. Dress code. **Open:** Breakfast daily 6:30–11:30am; lunch daily 11:30am–2pm; dinner daily 5–10pm. **Prices:** Main courses $15–$26. AE, DC, DISC, MC, V. ♥ ▾ ♿

Windows on the Bay
In Ocean City Health Club, 6103 Sea Bay Dr; tel 410/723-DINE. At jct US 50/MD 90 off 61st St. **International.** A very attractive second-floor dining room decorated simply and in excellent taste. Comfortable seating and fine views of Sinepuxent Bay. A wide range of American, French, Italian, and German dishes prepared by chef with very good reputation. Breads baked on premises. **FYI:** Reservations recommended. Piano. Children's menu. Dress code. **Open:** Daily 5am–9pm. **Prices:** Main courses $9–$19. AE, DC, MC, V. ♥ ▲ ▼

ATTRACTIONS 📷

Ocean City Life-Saving Station Museum
813 S Atlantic Ave; tel 410/289-4991. Perched on the southern tip of the boardwalk, this small museum is housed in a building that dates from 1891. Displays include rare artifacts of the region; dollhouse models depicting Ocean City in its early years; a pictorial history of the significant hurricanes and storms that have hit the mid-Atlantic coast; saltwater aquariums with indigenous sea life; and a unique collection of sand from around the world. **Open:** Peak (June–Sept) daily 11am–10pm. Reduced hours off-season. $

Ocean City Wax Museum
Boardwalk (at Wicomico St); tel 410/289-7766. Some of the over 150 lifelike figures here are in settings enhanced by animation, high-tech lighting, and sound effects. The cast of characters ranges from such Hollywood greats as Charlie Chaplin and Marilyn Monroe to such music stars as Elvis Presley, Michael Jackson, and Dolly Parton. In addition, there are scenes from classic movies and fairy tales, as well as great moments of history from the California gold rush to man's first walk on the moon. **Open:** Peak (Mem Day–Labor Day) 10am–midnight. Reduced hours off-season. $$

Trimper's Park
Boardwalk between S Division and S 1st Sts; tel 410/289-8617. This amusement park, established in 1887, has over 100 rides and attractions including an 1890 Boomerang roller coaster and a 1902 merry-go-round with hand-carved animals. **Open:** Peak (May–Sept) daily 1pm–midnight. Reduced hours off-season. $

Jolly Roger Park
30th St and Coastal Hwy; tel 410/289-3477. Home to Ocean City's largest roller coaster, as well as miniature-golf courses, a petting zoo, water slides, and magic shows. Each attraction is priced individually. **Open:** Mem Day–Labor Day, daily 2pm–midnight.

Frontier Town and Rodeo
MD 1; tel 410/289-7877. Set on 38 acres of woodland, this park features an 1860s replica of a western town, rodeos, cowboy and dance-hall shows, stagecoach rides, riverboats, and a steam train. Children can also ride the trails, pan for gold, or visit a petting zoo. Free shuttle bus between park and downtown Ocean City. **Open:** Mid-June–Labor Day, daily 10am–6pm. $$$

Assateague State Park
MD 611; tel 410/641-2120. Situated on an island 10 miles south of Ocean City, the park is famous for the bands of wild ponies that roam the land. Although they are a thrill to see, visitors are warned to keep a safe distance; these animals can kick and bite, and it is illegal to feed or touch them. The park has 2 miles of ocean frontage, with a white-sand beach and dunes up to 14 feet high. Visitors can swim, surf, fish, and picnic, and there are over 300 campsites. **Open:** Apr–Oct, daily 8am–sunset. $

Oxford

Settled in 1635, this small village at the mouth of the Tred Avon River is noted for its harbor and historic district. **Information:** Talbot County Conference and Visitors Bureau, PO Box 1366, Easton, 21601 (tel 410/822-4606).

INNS 🛏

≣≣ Oxford Inn
510 S Morris St, PO Box 627, 21654; tel 410/226-5220. MD 333 S to Morris St. This handsome old clapboard building is at the edge of town, within walking distance of the harbor and historic district. The wide front porch is used for outdoor dining and watching the boats and cars pass by. **Rooms:** 11 rms and stes (2 w/shared bath). CI 2pm/CO 11am. No smoking. Armoires substitute for closets. **Amenities:** 🛁 A/C. No phone or TV. **Services:** Masseur, babysitting, wine/sherry served. **Facilities:** 🎿 ●2 [30] Playground, guest lounge w/TV. Public tennis courts across street. Public beach nearby. Bicycle rentals available in town. **Rates (CP):** Peak (Apr–Nov) $80–$105 D w/shared bath, $100–$140 D w/private bath; $165–$210 ste. Extra person $10. Children under age 6 stay free. Min stay peak. Lower rates off-season. Parking: Outdoor, free. DISC, MC, V.

≣≣≣ Robert Morris Inn
314 N Morris St and the Strand, PO Box 70, 21654; tel 410/226-5111; fax 410/226-5744. MD 333 S to ferry dock in town. Beautiful historic inn that was originally the home of Robert Morris, "financier of the Revolution." Decorated and furnished in an authentic manner. Unsuitable for children under 10. **Rooms:** 35 rms, stes, and effic. CI 3pm/CO noon. No smoking. Decor varies, but all rooms are furnished with antiques and reproductions. **Amenities:** 🛁 A/C. No phone or TV. Some units w/terraces. Rooms in the Sandaway House (1875) have private porches overlooking the Tred Avon River. **Services:** Car-rental desk. **Facilities:** [20] 🛁 1 restaurant (see "Restaurants" below), 1 beach (cove/inlet), guest lounge w/TV. Nice beach for swimming except during late-summer jellyfish season. **Rates:** Peak (Apr–Nov) $90–$220 S

or D; $130–$190 ste; $160–$190 effic. Min stay wknds. Lower rates off-season. Parking: Outdoor, free. When the restaurant is closed (mid-January to mid-March), rooms are available only on weekends. AE, MC, V.

RESTAURANTS 🍽

★ Pier St Restaurant
104 W Pier St; tel 410/226-5171. Off MD 333 S. **Regional American/Seafood.** A traditional Maryland crab house and still part of a seafood-packing business, this pleasant, windowed dining room opens to a deck beside the Tred Avon River. Locals come here for spectacular river views and seafood, especially crab cakes made from fresh local crabmeat. Prime rib, chicken, and steak are also available. **FYI:** Reservations accepted. Children's menu. No smoking. **Open:** Daily 11:30am–9:30pm. Closed Nov–Mar. **Prices:** Main courses $10–$17. MC, V. 🛥 🏞

Robert Morris Inn
314 N Morris St; tel 410/226-5111. MD 333 S to ferry dock in town. **Regional American/Seafood.** Located in the family home of Robert Morris, a financier of the American Revolution, this historic inn and tavern has old wood paneling in some rooms, wallpaper in others, reproduction period chairs in all. Famous for crab cakes but has a good variety of other seafood and meat entrees as well. **FYI:** Reservations not accepted. Children's menu. Dress code. No smoking. **Open:** Breakfast Wed–Mon 8–11am; lunch Wed–Mon noon–3pm; dinner daily 6–9pm. Closed Jan–Mar. **Prices:** Main courses $14–$30. AE, MC, V. ♥ 🏺 ♿

Pikesville

This city of some 25,000 is a busy center of commerce and a bedroom community for the Baltimore metro area.

HOTELS 🏨

🏨🏨 Comfort Inn Northwest
10 Wooded Way, 21208; tel 410/484-7700 or toll free 800/ 732-2458; fax 410/653-1516. Exit 20 off I-695. This is a very acceptable, comfortable place to stay, convenient to the Baltimore Beltway (I-695). **Rooms:** 179 rms, stes, and effic. CI 3pm/CO 11am. No smoking. Clean rooms have simple but coordinated decor. **Amenities:** 🏠 🍸 A/C, cable TV w/movies. Some units w/terraces. **Services:** 🛎 🛏 🍽 **Facilities:** 🏋 125 ♿ 1 restaurant, playground, washer/dryer. **Rates (CP):** Peak (May–Aug) $59–$69 S; $69–$79 D; $89 ste; $89 effic. Lower rates off-season. Parking: Outdoor, free. AE, CB, DC, DISC, ER, JCB, MC, V.

🏨🏨🏨 Pikesville Hilton Inn
1726 Reisterstown Rd, 21208; tel 410/653-1100 or toll free 800/445-8667; fax 410/484-4138. Exit 20 off I-695. A polished, elegant hotel with resort-like facilities and ambience, beautiful lobby. **Rooms:** 171 rms and stes. Executive

level. CI 3pm/CO noon. No smoking. Nice, well-furnished rooms. **Amenities:** 🏠 🍸 A/C, cable TV w/movies. Some units w/terraces. **Services:** ✕ 🛎 🛏 🍽 Car-rental desk, masseur. **Facilities:** 🏋 🏊 ♿ 800 💻 ♿ 1 restaurant, 1 bar (w/entertainment), spa, sauna, whirlpool, beauty salon. Lovely pool surrounded by flowers, trees, good patio furniture. **Rates (CP):** Peak (May–Oct) $99–$150 S or D; $300 ste. Extra person $10. Children under age 12 stay free. Lower rates off-season. Parking: Indoor/outdoor, free. AE, CB, DC, DISC, EC, ER, JCB, MC, V.

RESTAURANT 🍽

Puffin's
1000 Reisterstown Rd; tel 410/486-8811. Exit 20 off I-695. **Californian.** The atmosphere is a cross between a simple local restaurant and an art gallery, with paintings, sculpture, textiles, jewelry, and other artworks on display and for sale virtually everywhere. Color scheme is black and white. Healthy food here, with no red meat and no dairy products used in preparation. Vegetarians and those with dietary restrictions will feel right at home. **FYI:** Reservations recommended. No smoking. **Open:** Lunch Mon–Sat noon–2:30pm; dinner Mon–Thurs 5:30–9:30pm, Fri–Sat 5:30–10:30pm, Sun 5–8:30pm. **Prices:** Main courses $8–$20. AE, DISC, MC, V. 👨‍👩‍👧 ♿

Pocomoke City

South of Salisbury on the Pocomoke River on the Eastern Shore. Pocomoke City is a gateway for both Pocomoke State Forest and Shad Landing State Park.

MOTELS 🏨

🏨🏨 Days Inn Pocomoke
1540 Ocean Hwy (US 13), 21851; tel 410/957-3000 or toll free 800/329-7466; fax 410/957-3147. This standard chain motel is in average condition. **Rooms:** 87 rms. CI 3pm/CO 11am. Nonsmoking rms avail. **Amenities:** 🏠 A/C, cable TV. All rooms have steam baths. **Services:** ✕ 🛏 🍽 🍸 **Facilities:** 🏋 150 ♿ 1 restaurant, 1 bar. **Rates:** Peak (June–Sept) $63–$68 S or D. Extra person $6. Children under age 18 stay free. Lower rates off-season. Parking: Outdoor, free. Senior and other discounts avail. AE, DC, DISC, MC, V.

🏨🏨 Quality Inn
825 Ocean Hwy (US 13), PO Box 480, 21851; tel 410/ 957-1300 or toll free 800/221-2222; fax 410/957-9329. This middle-aged motel is in good if not superior condition. **Rooms:** 64 rms. CI 1pm/CO 11am. Nonsmoking rms avail. **Amenities:** 🏠 A/C, cable TV. Some units w/whirlpools. Deluxe rooms have refrigerators. **Services:** 🛏 🍽 🍸 Car-rental desk, babysitting. Complimentary newspapers. **Facilities:** 🏋 20 1 restaurant, 1 bar. Picnic tables and grills on a wooded lawn. **Rates (CP):** Peak (June 15–Labor Day)

$65–$88 S or D. Extra person $5. Children under age 18 stay free. Lower rates off-season. Parking: Outdoor, free. Senior discounts avail. AE, CB, DC, ER, JCB, MC, V.

Potomac

See Rockville

Rockville

Half an hour northwest of Washington, DC, this city of some 50,000 is a popular home base for capital workers. Nearby Potomac, a well-heeled suburb between Rockville and Washington, DC, is noted for its expensive residential areas.

HOTELS 🏨

▤▤▤ Clarion Hotel

1251 W Montgomery Ave, 20850; tel 301/424-4940 or toll free 800/366-1251; fax 301/424-1047. Exit 6B off I-270. Popular with business travelers. **Rooms:** 162 rms and stes. CI 3pm/CO noon. No smoking. **Amenities:** 🛎 A/C, cable TV w/movies, voice mail. **Services:** ✕ ☛ 🚗 🛄 ⇦ ⇦ Car-rental desk. Complimentary van service to Metro, local businesses. **Facilities:** 🔦 🛁 🖳 🖥 ⅙ 1 restaurant, 1 bar, games rm. 24-hour business center. **Rates:** $74 S; $78 D; $89 ste. Extra person $10. Children under age 18 stay free. Parking: Outdoor, free. Weekend rates avail. AE, DC, DISC, JCB, MC, V.

▤▤▤ Courtyard by Marriott

2500 Research Blvd, 20850; tel 301/670-6700 or toll free 800/321-2211; fax 301/670-9023. Exit 8 off I-270. Drive west on Shady Grove Rd, turn left on Research Blvd. Attractive lobby with skylights, pastel colors, lots of brass and plants, fireplace. Beautiful landscaped gardens and gazebo in center courtyard. **Rooms:** 157 rms and stes. CI 3pm/CO 1pm. No smoking. All units have desks. **Amenities:** 🛎 🜊 🝐 A/C, cable TV w/movies. Some units w/minibars, some w/terraces. Long phone cords, hot-water tap for tea and instant coffee. Some units have patio or balcony overlooking courtyard. Special phone with on-line information, reservations service, shopping. **Services:** ✕ 🛄 ⇦ **Facilities:** 🔦 🛁 🖳 🖥 ⅙ 1 restaurant (bkfst and dinner only), 1 bar, whirlpool, washer/dryer. **Rates:** $54–$99 S or D; $89–$119 ste. Children under age 18 stay free. Parking: Outdoor, free. AE, DC, DISC, JCB, MC, V.

▤▤▤ DoubleTree

1750 Rockville Pike (MD 355), 20852; tel 301/468-1100 or toll free 800/638-5963; fax 301/468-0308. Exit I-270 at Montrose Rd; go east 1¾ mile to Rockville Pike, turn left; go ¾ mile. A seven-story atrium lobby with putting green, gazebo restaurant, and bar highlights this suburban hotel. **Rooms:** 315 rms and stes. Executive level. CI 3pm/CO noon.

No smoking. **Amenities:** 🛎 🜊 🝐 A/C, cable TV w/movies, voice mail. Some units w/terraces, some w/whirlpools. **Services:** ✕ ☛ 🆅🅿 🚗 🛄 ⇦ Car-rental desk, masseur, children's program. **Facilities:** 🔦 🛁 🖳 🖥 ⅙ 2 restaurants, 2 bars (1 w/entertainment), games rm, spa, sauna, whirlpool, beauty salon. Free use of extensive health club with six racquetball courts, Nautilus, weights, aerobics classes. Studebaker's nightclub popular with local singles. **Rates:** $89–$129 S or D; $225 ste. Extra person $10. Children under age 19 stay free. Parking: Indoor/outdoor, $3–$5/day. AE, DC, DISC, JCB, MC, V.

▤▤▤ Ramada Inn at Congressional Park

1775 Rockville Pike (MD 355), 20852; tel 301/881-2300 or toll free 800/255-1775; fax 301/881-9047. Exit I-270 at Montrose Rd; go east to Rockville Pike, turn left. Special emphasis on business travelers at this suburban hotel directly across from Metro station. **Rooms:** 160 rms and stes. Executive level. CI 2pm/CO noon. No smoking. Executive level has oversize recliners, large desks. **Amenities:** 🛎 🜊 🝐 A/C, cable TV w/movies. Some units w/minibars. Small refrigerators in executive-level rooms. **Services:** ✕ 🚗 🛄 ⇦ ⇦ **Facilities:** 🖳 ⅙ 1 restaurant. **Rates:** $69–$105 S or D; $150 ste. Extra person $8. Children under age 18 stay free. Parking: Outdoor, free. AE, CB, DC, DISC, EC, JCB, MC, V.

▤▤▤ Woodfin Suites

1380 Piccard Dr, 20850; tel 301/590-9880 or toll free 800/237-8811; fax 301/590-9614. Exit 8 off I-270. 1 mi W of MD 355. Elegant, all-suites facility in landscaped office park. The three-tiered lobby features grand piano, ornate fireplace with hearth, floor-to-roof windows. **Rooms:** 203 stes. CI 4pm/CO noon. No smoking. All units have completely stocked kitchens and open to courtyards. Most units have sitting area and separate bedroom; some have two bedrooms. **Amenities:** 🛎 🜊 🝐 A/C, cable TV w/movies, refrig, VCR, CD/tape player, in-rm safe. Some units w/fireplaces. Irons and ironing boards in all units. **Services:** 🛄 ⇦ ⇦ Free van service within five-mile radius includes Metro station. Complimentary newspapers. Daily coffee service. Pet fee $5 daily plus $50 deposit. **Facilities:** 🔦 🛁 🖳 🖥 ⅙ 1 restaurant, 1 bar, whirlpool, washer/dryer. Full 24-hour business center with computers, printers, typewriters, fax, copier. **Rates (CP):** $127 ste. Extra person $15. Children under age 12 stay free. Parking: Outdoor, free. AE, CB, DC, DISC, ER, JCB, MC, V.

RESTAURANTS 🍴

Benjarong

In Wintergreen Plaza, 855-C Rockville Pike; tel 301/424-5533. Exit 6 off I-270. Follow Montgomery Ave east to Rockville Pike; turn right. **Thai.** Peaceful Oriental decor: Thai ceramic pieces, vases, huge carved elephant, and Buddha. Window display of brass works, mirrors also add sense of place. Excellent selection of Thai dishes, including curries and hot-pepper selections. Fish dishes are especially recommended, and soft-shell crabs are available year-round. Large portions. **FYI:** Reservations recommended. **Open:** Mon–Thurs 11:30am–9:30pm, Fri–Sat 11:30am–10:30pm, Sun 5–9:30pm. **Prices:** Main courses $7–$11. AE, CB, DC, DISC, MC, V. &

Bombay Bistro
98 W Montgomery Ave; tel 301/762-8798. Exit 6A off I-270. Follow MD 28 to Rockville Pike (Md 355) west; turn right on Washington St, then left on W Montgomery Ave. **Indian.** Outside it's a one-story brick business building tucked away on a side street, but it's a bit of India inside, thanks to slow-turning ceiling fans, hanging plants, Indian fabrics on wall, bamboo curtains and chairs. A blend of south Indian vegetarian curry dishes, such as *masala dosai,* and meat and chicken kabobs from a tandoor oven. **FYI:** Reservations not accepted. Beer and wine only. **Open:** Lunch Mon–Fri 11am–2:30pm, Sat–Sun noon–3pm; dinner Sun–Thurs 5–9:30pm, Fri–Sat 5–10pm. **Prices:** Main courses $6–$10. MC, V.

Four Rivers
184 Rollins Ave, at Jefferson St; tel 301/230-2900. Exit 4A off I-270. Follow Montrose Rd to Jefferson St, turn left. **Chinese.** Housed in an unpretentious one-story brick building, but don't let the exterior fool you. Inside, red booths, pink tablecloths, and Oriental paintings set a festive mood. The food, prepared by Chef Chiang, is a hit among area diplomats, who flock here for the Imperial specialties and other spicy Szechuan cuisine. **FYI:** Reservations recommended. No smoking. **Open:** Mon–Thurs 11:30am–10:30pm, Sat–Sun 11:30am–3pm. **Prices:** Main courses $8–$15; prix fixe $10–$20. DISC, MC, V. &

Il Pizzico
15209 Frederick Rd; tel 301/309-0610. Exit 6A off I-270. **Italian.** An intimate trattoria with simple tile floors, stucco-like walls, salmon-colored tablecloths, and fresh-cut flowers. The chef has been cited by *Washingtonian* magazine for his fine Italian cuisine. **FYI:** Reservations not accepted. Beer and wine only. No smoking. **Open:** Lunch Mon–Fri 11am–2:30pm; dinner Mon–Thurs 5–9:30pm, Fri–Sat 5–10pm. Closed Dec 23–Jan 3. **Prices:** Main courses $8–$13. AE, MC, V. ♥&

Kashmir Palace
855-A Rockville Pike (MD 355); tel 301/251-1152. Exit 6 off I-270. Follow Montgomery Ave (MD 28) east to Rockville Pike, turn right. **Indian.** Richly and elegantly decorated with Indian folk art, gold, and brass; quiet Indian music is a soothing background. Choose from a wide selection of northern Indian and Pakistani dishes. Meats are grilled in a traditional tandoor oven. Popular Sunday buffet noon–3pm. **FYI:** Reservations accepted. **Open:** Lunch daily 11:30am–2:30pm; dinner daily 5:30–10:30pm. **Prices:** Main courses $7–$12. AE, MC, V. &

♣ Old Angler's Inn
10801 MacArthur Blvd, Potomac; tel 301/365-2425. Exit 41 off I-495. **New American.** This 1860s structure on 10 acres near the C&O Canal has an elegant country decor, with lace curtains, floral wallpaper, wooden floors. Cozy lounge/bar area has upholstered sofas around a fireplace. Calling on a variety of cuisines, chef is known for creative daily specials using fresh and sometimes exotic ingredients. Berries are picked on the grounds, seafood is smoked in-house. Jackets are requested for men in the dining room; more casual dress appropriate for stone patio under huge trees. Dining room is nonsmoking on Friday and Saturday. **FYI:** Reservations recommended. Dress code. **Open:** Lunch Tues–Sat noon–2:30pm; dinner Tues–Sat 6–10:30pm, Sun 5:30–9:30pm; brunch Sun noon–2:30pm. **Prices:** Main courses $21–$29; prix fixe $55. AE, CB, DC, MC, V. ♥ ▇ ⛴ 🖼

St Mary's City

This historic town on St Mary's River in southern Maryland was settled in 1634 and was the state's first capital. **Information:** St Mary's County Chamber of Commerce, 6260 Waldorf Leonardstown Rd, Mechanicsville, 20659 (tel 301/884-5555).

ATTRACTIONS 🧳

Historic St Mary's City
MD 5; tel 301/862-0990. Maryland's first capital has been transformed into an 800-acre outdoor history museum. Attractions include a replica of the square-rigged *Maryland Dove,* one of the two ships that brought the first settlers and supplies from England; the reconstructed 1676 State House; the Godiah Spray Tobacco Plantation; and a visitor center that houses an archeology exhibit. **Open:** Wed–Sun 10am–5pm. Outdoor exhibits open Apr–Nov only. **$$$**

Point Lookout State Park
MD 5; tel 301/872-5688. This 580-acre peninsula at the confluence of the Chesapeake Bay and the Potomac River is the location of Fort Lincoln, an earthen building constructed by Confederate prisoners, as well as two monuments honoring the 3,364 Confederate soldiers that died in prison camps here. The visitor's center contains a Civil War museum, open weekends May–Sept. The park has an extensive beach, swimming, fishing, picnicking, hiking trails, and playgrounds. **Open:** Daily sunrise–sunset.

St Michaels

Colorful bay-side village on the banks of the Miles River. Home to the Chesapeake Bay Maritime Museum and an important 19th-century shipyard. **Information:** Talbot County Conference and Visitors Bureau, PO Box 1366, Easton, 21601 (tel 410/822-4606).

HOTEL 🏨

▤ ▤ ▤ St Michaels Harbour Inn and Marina

101 N Harbor Rd, 21663; tel 410/745-9001 or toll free 800/955-9001; fax 410/745-9150. This modern waterfront hotel has splendid views of St Michaels harbor and the Maritime Museum docks. **Rooms:** 46 rms and stes. CI 4pm/CO noon. Nonsmoking rms avail. All rooms have queen or king beds. **Amenities:** 🛎 ⏲ 🖥 A/C, cable TV w/movies, refrig. Some units w/terraces. Most rooms are suites with sink, refrigerator, and counter but no cooking facilities. **Services:** ✕ 🚐 🗗 Babysitting. **Facilities:** 🛟 🚲 ⛰ ▢ 🚤 🏊50 🔽 1 restaurant, 2 bars (1 w/entertainment), whirlpool, washer/dryer. **Rates:** Peak (May 27–Oct 9) $159–$229 S or D; $229–$409 ste. Extra person $12. Children under age 18 stay free. Min stay peak and wknds. Lower rates off-season. Parking: Outdoor, free. Special theme weekends, such as wine tasting, during off-season. AE, CB, DC, DISC, MC, V.

MOTEL

▤ ▤ Best Western St Michaels Motor Inn

1228 S Talbot St, 21663; tel 410/745-3333 or toll free 800/528-1234; fax 410/745-2906. MD 322 exit off US 50; 9 mi W on MD 33. Highway motel. A modern alternative to the historic accommodations in the center of St Michaels. **Rooms:** 93 rms. CI 3pm/CO 11am. Nonsmoking rms avail. Pleasant, standard motel rooms. **Amenities:** 🛎 A/C, TV. Some units w/terraces. **Services:** 🗗 **Facilities:** 🏊2 🏊250 🔽 Large lawn area. **Rates (CP):** Peak (Apr–Nov) $62–$82 S; $68–$90 D. Extra person $8. Children under age 18 stay free. Lower rates off-season. Parking: Outdoor, free. Less expensive than most in the area. AE, CB, DC, DISC, MC, V.

INNS

◈ Inn at Perry Cabin

308 Watkins Lane, 21663; tel 410/745-2200 or toll free 800/722-2949; fax 410/745-3348. 9 mi W of Easton. 25 acres. An imposing two-story white clapboard manor, owned by British industrialist Sir Bernard Ashley. Location on Maryland's Eastern Shore is surrounded by extensive lawns and endless miles of river. Unsuitable for children under 10. **Rooms:** 41 rms and stes. CI 3pm/CO noon. Nonsmoking rms avail. All different rooms, some new and shipshape, some old and tilty as an old inn should be. Filled with antiques and period objects; decorated stem to stern with Laura Ashley fabrics and stocked with Laura Ashley toiletries. **Amenities:** 🛎 ⏲ A/C, cable TV w/movies, bathrobes. Some units w/terraces, some w/whirlpools. Mineral water and fresh fruit in every room. **Services:** ✕ 🆅🅿 🗗 Twice-daily maid svce, babysitting, afternoon tea served. Coffee and tea at any time. Pampering, butler-style service. **Facilities:** 🛟 🚲 ⛰ 🚤 🏊40 🔽 1 restaurant (see "Restaurants" below), 1 bar, games rm, lawn games, sauna, steam rm, guest lounge. More recreational facilities than usual in an inn of this size, including classic launches for trips on the river, indoor pool, billiard room.

Double wooden deck chairs on the lawns. Delightful restaurant with fireplaces and view of river. **Rates (CP):** Peak (Apr–Dec) $195–$375 D; $435–$575 ste. Extra person $15. Min stay special events. Lower rates off-season. Parking: Outdoor, free. Rates are the highest in the area but not out of sight given the setting, amenities, and service. Guest are advised to make dinner reservations when they reserve rooms, especially on weekends. AE, CB, DC, MC, V.

▤ ▤ ▤ Wades Point Inn on the Bay

Wades Point Rd, PO Box 7, 21663; tel 410/745-2500. 120 acres. A stay at this Victorian inn is like a visit to grandmother's. Many wide porches beckon for reading, conversing, or relaxing. A new adjacent building has more modern comforts. Unsuitable for children under 1. **Rooms:** 23 rms and effic (7 w/shared bath). CI 2pm/CO 11am. No smoking. Rooms vary from small, 1890s-style with shared bath, to large rooms on the bay. **Amenities:** No A/C, phone, or TV. Some units w/terraces. Some rooms have air conditioning. **Services:** 🗗 Babysitting, afternoon tea served. **Facilities:** ▢ 🏊 🏊30 🔽 Lawn games, guest lounge w/TV. Large bayfront grounds are suitable for fishing, crabbing, or launching a small boat. Beach frontage is along a bulkhead. **Rates (CP):** $84–$140 D w/shared bath, $140–$180 D w/private bath; $185 effic. Extra person $10. Children under age 12 stay free. Min stay wknds. Parking: Outdoor, free. Closed Jan–Feb. MC, V.

RESORT

▤ ▤ ▤ Harbourtowne Golf Resort

MD 33 at Martingham Dr, PO Box 126, 21663; tel 410/745-9066 or toll free 800/446-9066; fax 410/820-9142. 153 acres. This attractive waterfront golf resort adjacent to the historic town of St Michaels has outstanding public areas. **Rooms:** 111 rms and stes. CI 3pm/CO 11am. Nonsmoking rms avail. All rooms have water views. **Amenities:** 🛎 ⏲ 🖥 A/C, cable TV w/movies. All units w/terraces, some w/fireplaces. **Services:** 🚐 ⛱ 🗗 🏌 Babysitting. **Facilities:** 🛟 🚲 ⛰ ▢ ⛳18 🏊 🎾2 🚤 🏊350 🔽 2 restaurants, 2 bars (1 w/entertainment), 1 beach (cove/inlet), games rm, lawn games. Pete Dye–designed golf course is in excellent condition. Beach is protected, on shallow water. Horseback riding and other activities can be arranged nearby. **Rates (CP):** Peak (May–Sept) $100–$150 S; $110–$155 D; $155–$250 ste. Extra person $10. Children under age 18 stay free. Min stay wknds. Lower rates off-season. AP and MAP rates avail. Parking: Outdoor, free. Golf packages avail. AE, DISC, MC, V.

RESTAURANTS 🍴

Crab Claw

Navy Point, by Maritime Museum; tel 410/745-2900. MD 33 W exit off US 50; right on Mill St. **Seafood.** A St Michaels tradition, this two-story, large-windowed building on the harbor has casual dining on the dock during good weather, or inside, where exposed dark wood beams, red-checked table-cloths, and captain's chairs add to the nautical ambience. Seafood here is famous, especially steamed hard crabs and crab cakes. Said to be St Michaels' only restaurant still under original ownership. **FYI:** Reservations recommended. Children's menu. No smoking. **Open:** Daily 11am–10pm. Closed Jan–Feb. **Prices:** Main courses $12–$19. No CC. 🦀 🏞 &

Higgins' Crab House

1218 S Talbot St; tel 410/745-5151. MD 33 W exit off US 50; 9 mi W. **American/Seafood.** Nautical decor creates an Eastern Shore feeling at this restaurant that grew out of a still-active seafood-packing business. Reasonably priced seafood is cooked in traditional style. Some nonseafood dishes offered. **FYI:** Reservations recommended. Dress code. No smoking. **Open:** Peak (Apr–Dec) Sun–Thurs 11am–9pm, Fri–Sat 11am–10pm. **Prices:** Main courses $10–$16. AE, DISC, MC, V. 🍴 👪 💟 &

🍷 Inn at Perry Cabin

In the Inn at Perry Cabin, 308 Watkins Lane; tel 410/745-2200. US 322 to MD 33. **Continental.** The refined setting, excellent cuisine, and good value justify the lengthy drive to get here. The country inn decor features floor-to-ceiling mullioned windows that overlook lawns and private docks. A terrace is used for cocktails and after-dinner coffee. Summer specialties include duck spring roll with plum chutney; noisettes of lamb with gâteau of eggplant and potato puree; medallions of swordfish, red snapper, and salmon on spinach pasta; and white chocolate crème brûlée with kirsch-flavored cherries. Guests can finish their evening with a game of billiards. Five-course prix fixe dinner. **FYI:** Reservations recommended. No smoking. **Open:** Breakfast daily 8–10:30am; lunch daily 12:30–2:30pm; dinner daily 6–9:30pm. **Prices:** Prix fixe $57. AE, CB, DC, MC, V. 💟 🍴 &

Morsels

205 N Talbot St; tel 410/745-2911. From US 50, follow MD 33 W. **New American/Californian.** Fresh and innovative preparations with a touch of French and California influence. **FYI:** Reservations accepted. Children's menu. No smoking. **Open:** Peak (May–Dec) lunch daily 11am–3pm; dinner Sun–Thurs 5:30–9pm, Fri–Sat 5:30–10pm. **Prices:** Main courses $13–$20. MC, V.

St Michaels Crab House Restaurant

305 Mulberry St; tel 410/745-3737. MD 33 W exit off US 50. **Regional American/Seafood.** The bricks and exposed beams of this converted packing house add authenticity to a lovely location and view. Primarily a crab house, it serves up many other traditional Maryland-style seafood choices and a few beef and chicken selections. **FYI:** Reservations recommended. Children's menu. No smoking. **Open:** Sun–Thurs 11am–10pm, Fri–Sat 11am–11pm. Closed Jan–Feb. **Prices:** Main courses $10–$18. DISC, MC, V. 🦀 🏞 👪

Town Dock Restaurant

125 Mulberry St; tel 410/745-5577. MD 33 W exit off US 50; right on Mulberry St. **International/Seafood.** Attractive pastels, large windows, and ceiling fans augment some of the finest harbor views of any St Michaels restaurant. Diners enjoy the panoramas from an inside dining room, enclosed porch, or deck. Known for seafood with an international touch. **FYI:** Reservations recommended. Children's menu. No smoking. **Open:** Peak (Apr–Dec) lunch daily 11am–4pm; dinner Sun–Thurs 4–9pm, Fri–Sat 4–10pm; brunch Sun 11am–2pm. **Prices:** Main courses $13–$25. AE, DC, DISC, MC, V. 🦀 🏞 💟

208 Talbot

208 N Talbot St; tel 410/745-3838. From US 50, follow MD 33 W for 9 miles. **New American.** Country, colonial, and wicker furnishings enhance the brick walls and beamed ceilings. Entrees are innovative and attractively presented. Excellent local and regional reputation for fine dining. **FYI:** Reservations recommended. No smoking. **Open:** Peak (Mar–Dec) lunch Tues–Fri noon–2pm; dinner Tues–Sat 5–10pm, Sun 5–9pm; brunch Sun 11am–2pm. Closed Presidents' Day–mid-Mar. **Prices:** Main courses $18–$25. DISC, MC, V.

ATTRACTIONS 🏛

Chesapeake Bay Maritime Museum

Mill St; tel 410/745-2916. Dedicated to the preservation of maritime history, this waterside museum consists of 9 buildings on 18 acres of land. Some of the highlights are an authentic 116-year-old Chesapeake Bay lighthouse, a comprehensive bay-craft collection, a working boat yard, and an extensive waterfowl decoy collection. **Open:** Peak (June–Sept) daily 9am–6pm. Reduced hours off-season. **$$$**

St Mary's Square Museum

409 St Mary's Square; tel 410/745-9561. Located in the historic St Mary's Square in the center of town, the main building (1800) was originally part of a gristmill. The adjacent "Teetotum" building displays exhibits significant to local history and culture. **Open:** May–Oct, Sat–Sun 10am–4pm. **Free**

Salisbury

Located on the Eastern Shore, Salisbury is an important agricultural center and the state's leading producer of chickens. Home of the North American Wildfowl Art Museum. Seat of Wicomico County. Whitehaven, southwest of Salisbury on the Wicomico River, offers bay activities. **Information:** Salisbury Area Chamber of Commerce, 300 E Main St, PO Box 510, Salisbury, 21803 (tel 410/749-0144).

HOTEL 🏨

≣≣≣ Sheraton Inn Salisbury

300 S Salisbury Blvd, 21801; tel 410/546-4400 or toll free 800/325-3535; fax 410/546-2528. On US 13 Business, ¾ mi S of US 50. A downtown hotel adjacent to municipal River-walk Park. Underwent some renovation and upgrading in 1994. **Rooms:** 156 rms. CI 3pm/CO noon. Nonsmoking rms avail. Spacious rooms, all the same size, but some have king beds. **Amenities:** 🔟 🍷 A/C, cable TV w/movies. 1 unit w/terrace. Wet bars in some rooms. **Services:** ✗ 🚐 🖼 🍴 **Facilities:** 🛗 ⛳ 🎱 👤 1 restaurant, 1 bar, games rm. **Rates:** Peak (May–Sept) $85–$110 S or D. Extra person $20. Children under age 18 stay free. Min stay special events. Lower rates off-season. MAP rates avail. Parking: Outdoor, free. AE, DC, DISC, MC, V.

MOTELS

≣≣ Comfort Inn Salisbury

2701 N Salisbury Blvd, 21801; tel 410/543-4666 or toll free 800/221-2222; fax 410/749-2639. On US 13, 3 mi N of US 50. An attractive, well-maintained motel of recent vintage. **Rooms:** 96 rms. CI 3pm/CO 11am. Nonsmoking rms avail. Large and nicely furnished rooms. **Amenities:** 🔟 A/C, cable TV w/movies, refrig. Some units w/whirlpools. **Services:** 🖼 🍴 👐 **Facilities:** 🎱 👤 1 restaurant (lunch and dinner only), lawn games. Guests may use pool at Holiday Inn next door. **Rates (CP):** Peak (Mem Day–Labor Day) $54–$75 S or D; $85–$125 ste. Extra person $6. Children under age 18 stay free. Lower rates off-season. Parking: Outdoor, free. Special rates for persons over 50. AE, CB, DC, DISC, JCB, MC, V.

≣≣≣ Holiday Inn Salisbury

2625 N Salisbury Blvd, 21801; tel 410/742-7194 or toll free 800/465-4329; fax 410/742-5194. A large motel typical of this chain, it's well maintained and has full facilities. **Rooms:** 123 rms. CI 3pm/CO 11am. Nonsmoking rms avail. **Amenities:** 🔟 🍷 📺 A/C, cable TV w/movies. Closed-captioned TV. **Services:** ✗ 🖼 🍴 👐 **Facilities:** 🛗 🎱 👤 1 restaurant (bkfst and dinner only), 1 bar, washer/dryer. Large, attractive pool in courtyard. **Rates:** Peak (Apr–Sept) $55–$99 S; $67–$107 D. Extra person $8. Children under age 18 stay free. Lower rates off-season. MAP rates avail. Parking: Outdoor, free. Children under 13 eat free. AE, CB, DC, DISC, JCB, MC, V.

RESTAURANTS 🍴

English's Family Restaurant

735 S Salisbury Blvd; tel 410/742-8182. On Business US 13, 1 mi S of US 50. **Regional American/Seafood.** A classic railroad car–style diner front is reminiscent of the 1930s. Dining room adjoins. Basic American family fare, with regional items such as crab cakes. **FYI:** Reservations accepted. Children's menu. **Open:** Sun–Thurs 6am–9pm, Fri–Sat 6am–10pm. **Prices:** Main courses $6–$12. DISC, MC, V. 🍽️ 👤

Webster's 1801

1801 N Salisbury Blvd; tel 410/742-8000. On Business US 13, 1 mi S of shopping mall. **American/Steak.** An informal but attractive steak house with an especially nice lounge and outdoor deck. Beef predominates, plus a short selection of other traditional American entrees. **FYI:** Reservations accepted. Big band/dancing. Children's menu. **Open:** Mon–Thurs 4–9pm, Fri–Sat 4–10pm. **Prices:** Main courses $6–$20. AE, CB, DC, DISC, MC, V. 🅿️ 💳 👤

ATTRACTIONS 🏛️

Ward Museum of Wildfowl Art

909 S Schumaker Dr; tel 410/742-4988. In this area known for its waterfowl population, this museum is a key attraction, the largest of its kind in the world. It is a prime showcase for displays of antique decoys and contemporary carvings, as well as paintings and works on paper. Interpretive galleries help visitors trace the development of the art form from hunters' tools to sculpture. **Open:** Mon–Sat 10am–5pm, Sun noon–5pm. **$$**

Poplar Hill Mansion

117 Elizabeth St; tel 410/749-1776. The Federal-style mansion, built circa 1799, features second-story Palladian windows, two bull's-eye windows, cornice moldings, and a fanlight over the fluted-pilaster front doorway. Also on display are collections of period furniture and original fireplaces and mantels. **Open:** Sun 1–4pm. Also open by appointment (admission charged). **Free**

Pemberton Hall

Pemberton Dr off MD 349; tel 410/742-1741. Listed on the National Register of Historic Places, this 1741 gambrel-roofed brick house is one of Maryland's oldest. It is surrounded by a park with nature trails, a picnic area, and a pond. **Open:** May–Oct, Sun 2–4pm and by appointment. **Free**

Salisbury Zoological Park

755 S Park Dr; tel 410/548-3188. A 12-acre open-air zoo in the heart of City Park. It houses more than 200 mammals, birds, and reptiles in naturalistic habitats among shade trees and exotic plants. Major exhibits include spectacled bears, monkeys, jaguars, bison, bald eagles, river otters, and waterfowl, all native to North, Central, and South America. **Open:** Peak (June–Aug) daily 8am–7:30pm. Reduced hours off-season. **Free**

Maryland Lady

505B W Main St; tel 410/543-2466. An 85-foot Victorian-style riverboat offering narrated cruises. The route takes in a variety of sights—from the Salisbury skyline and historic river homes to tugboats, barges, and wildlife and waterfowl in natural habitats. Lunch and dinner cruises are offered; reservations are required at least 48 hours in advance. **Open:** Mar–Dec, daily. Call for schedule. **$$$$**

Silver Spring

A city of some 80,000, immediately north of Washington, DC. Popular stop for business travelers. Close to Northwest Branch Park and Paint Branch Park. **Information:** Greater Silver Spring Chamber of Commerce, 8601 Georgia Ave #203, Silver Spring, 20910 (tel 301/565-3777).

HOTELS

Courtyard by Marriott Silver Spring

12521 Prosperity Dr, at Cherry Hill Rd, 20904 (White Oak); tel 301/680-8500 or toll free 800/321-2211; fax 301/680-9232. 4½ mi N of I-495 via US 29. A typical member of this comfortable chain, with a landscaped courtyard with gazebo for sitting. Attractive lobby has fireplace set among glass panels looking to courtyard. Located in office park. **Rooms:** 146 rms and stes. CI 3pm/CO noon. Nonsmoking rms avail. King rooms have sofas; all have large desks. **Amenities:** A/C, cable TV w/movies, dataport, voice mail. Some units w/terraces. Hot-water tap for tea and coffee, long phone cords. **Services:** Babysitting. Morning newspapers at door. **Facilities:** 1 restaurant, 1 bar, whirlpool, washer/dryer. **Rates:** $92 S; $102 D; $117–$127 ste. Children under age 12 stay free. Parking: Outdoor, free. AE, CB, DC, DISC, MC, V.

Quality Hotel

8727 Colesville Rd, 20910 (Downtown); tel 301/589-5200 or toll free 800/376-7666; fax 301/588-1841. Exit 30B off I-495. Go south on Colesville Rd for ½ mile; between Fenton and Spring Sts. A 14-story downtown hotel within walking distance of Metro station, shopping mall, restaurants, movies. Marble-floored lobby is attractive but not easily accessible for guests with disabilities. **Rooms:** 256 rms and stes. CI 3pm/CO noon. Nonsmoking rms avail. Above-average dark wood furniture lends touch of elegance. King-bed rooms have easy chairs. **Amenities:** A/C, cable TV w/movies. Some units w/terraces. **Services:** Facilities: 3 restaurants, 1 bar (w/entertainment), sauna. Indoor pool on ninth floor open weekday evenings, all day on weekends. Cafe-style restaurant open for breakfast and lunch; Italian eatery serves dinner. **Rates (BB):** $94–$104 S or D; $105–$125 ste. Extra person $10. Children under age 12 stay free. Parking: Indoor, free. AE, CB, DC, DISC, MC, V.

RESTAURANT

Crisfield Seafood Restaurant

In Lee Plaza, 8606 Colesville Rd at Georgia Ave (Downtown); tel 301/588-1572. Exit 30B off I-495. Follow Colesville Rd south for ½ mile. **Seafood.** Named for the Eastern Shore town known as the "Seafood Capital of the World," this longtime family establishment moved to these modern quarters a few years ago, when urban redevelopment caused its funky, industrial-area home of many decades to be torn down. Adorned with tile floors and wall accents, plain white tables and booths, Chesapeake-area paintings. Popular with locals in search of fresh Maryland-style seafood. Free parking in rear after 4pm. **FYI:** Reservations recommended. Children's menu. **Open:** Mon–Thurs 11:30am–10pm, Fri 11:30am–11pm, Sat 4–11pm, Sun 4–10pm. **Prices:** Main courses $9–$25; prix fixe $22. AE, CB, DC, MC, V.

Stevensville

See also Grasonville

Located on the northern end of Kent Island, in the center of Chesapeake Bay. Four area marinas and an abundance of water sports make the area a popular vacation destination. **Information:** Queen Anne's County Chamber of Commerce, 102 E Main St #104B, Stevensville, 21666 (tel 410/643-8530).

INN

Kent Manor Inn

500 Kent Manor Dr, PO Box 291, 21666; tel 410/643-5757; fax 410/643-8315. 226 acres. A truly beautiful country inn that sits on what originally was a private estate on Thompson Creek. The building dates from the early 19th century and has been carefully restored. Unsuitable for children under 8. **Rooms:** 24 rms and stes. CI 3pm/CO 11am. No smoking. Rooms are in excellent condition and furnished in period style. **Amenities:** A/C, TV. All units w/terraces, some w/fireplaces. **Services:** Babysitting. **Facilities:** 1 restaurant, 1 bar, lawn games, guest lounge w/TV. A well-regarded restaurant downstairs specializes in seafood, beef, and veal. A pier and waterfront along the creek permit fishing, crabbing, and small-boat recreation. **Rates (BB):** $109–$149 D; $170 ste. Extra person $8. Children under age 18 stay free. Parking: Outdoor, free. AE, DC, DISC, MC, V.

RESTAURANT

Café Sophie

401 Love Point Rd; tel 410/643-8811. MD 18 exit off US 50/301. **French.** This former country store with blue, white, and a touch of red recalls the small-town restaurants of France. The owner/chef, a former opera singer and weaver for Coco Chanel, made Jackie Kennedy's inaugural gown. Menu varies according to her preferences, but all selections are prepared in provincial French style from fresh ingredients. **FYI:** Reservations recommended. Dress code. Beer and wine only. No smoking. **Open:** Lunch Wed–Sun noon–3pm; dinner Fri–Sat 6:30–9:30pm. **Prices:** Main courses $6–$17; prix fixe $40. No CC.

Taneytown

Small town northwest of Westminister, named for the Taney family who settled the area in 1660s. The fine 19th-century homes here offer visitors a view into the past.

INN 🏨

≣≣≣ **Antrim 1844**
30 Trevanion Rd, 21787; tel 410/756-6812 or toll free 800/858-1844; fax 410/756-2744. 24 acres. Lovely and charming, this 1844 inn offers a sense of tranquil elegance. While ordinary in some respects—the porch is nondescript, the grounds not grand—it does feature impressive antique furnishings and unusual decorating themes. Unsuitable for children under 6. **Rooms:** 9 rms and stes; 5 cottages/villas. CI 3pm/CO noon. No smoking. A converted barn, icehouse, and plantation overseer's house serve as suites. The icehouse has an 18th-century vanity with original hand-painted sink in bath area. Featherbeds, antiques are highlights. **Amenities:** A/C. No phone or TV. Some units w/minibars, some w/terraces, some w/fireplaces, some w/whirlpools. **Services:** ✗ 🆅🅿 ⚖ 🍷 Babysitting, afternoon tea and wine/sherry served. Country buffet tray outside the door each morning, hors d'oeuvres in living room in evening, gourmet picnic baskets fixed for lunch on request. **Facilities:** 🔥 🚴 🧗 🛶 🐦¹ 🎱 🖥 ⚖ 1 restaurant, 1 bar (w/entertainment), lawn games, guest lounge. Pool is painted black and retains heat. Outdoor area, including croquet and garden, popular for private parties. **Rates (CP):** $150–$300 D; $200 cottage/villa. Extra person $50. Min stay wknds. Parking: Outdoor, free. AE, DISC, MC, V.

Thurmont

Located in the Catoctin Mountain Valley, with many outdoor recreation areas nearby as well as presidential retreat Camp David.

INN 🏨

≣≣≣ **Cozy Country Inn**
103 Frederick Rd, 21788; tel 301/271-4301; fax 301/271-4301. MD 806 exit off US 15. 2 acres. This inn in the foothills of the Catoctin Mountains has a character all its own. Behind the pale pink exterior is decor with a Camp David/presidential emphasis. Right on the highway, you're in the "Cozy Historic Village" which publishes its own newspaper and includes crafts, collectibles, and Cal Ripken memorabilia. Family-owned and -operated since 1929. **Rooms:** 16 rms, stes, and effic; 5 cottages/villas. CI 3pm/CO noon. Nonsmoking rms avail. Charming rooms styled to recall presidents, dignitaries, or newspeople who've visited Camp David or Cozy Inn. For example, the Roosevelt Room has hangings from Hyde Park, a model of FDR's bed, and an oversize bath. Executive, Premium, and Traditional Rooms available, some with waterbed, towel warmer, whirlpool, kitchenette. **Amenities:** 🔥 🕐 📺 🍷 A/C, cable TV w/movies. Some units w/fireplaces, some w/whirlpools. Many have refrigerators; some have pants pressers, wet bars, VCRs. **Services:** ✗ 🆒 **Facilities:** 🍽₃₂₅ 1 restaurant (see "Restaurants" below), 1 bar, guest lounge w/TV. Golf course nearby. **Rates (CP):** $42–$92 S; $45–$64 D; $76 ste; $45 effic; $45–$64 cottage/villa. Extra person $5. Children under age 12 stay free. Parking: Outdoor, free. Weekend rates higher. AE, MC, V.

RESTAURANT 🍴

★ **Cozy Restaurant**
In the Cozy Country Inn, 103 Frederick Rd; tel 301/271-7373. **American.** This one-of-a-kind eatery has been owned and operated by the same family since 1929 and since it's on the route to Camp David, you never know who you might see here. Decor ranges from a brick-laid Victorian "street" to a spacious dining room with huge windows and a wall mural; one dark-timbered hallway displays presidential memorabilia. The menu ranges from country food to finer fare; the 75-item buffet is especially popular and the desserts are notable. **FYI:** Reservations recommended. Children's menu. **Open:** Peak (Apr 11–Jan 9) Mon–Thurs 11am–8:45pm, Fri 11am–9:15pm, Sat 8am–9:15pm, Sun 8am–8:45pm. **Prices:** Main courses $8–$16. AE, MC, V. 🔥 🖼 📷 ✔ ⚖

ATTRACTIONS 📷

Catoctin Zoo Park
13019 Catoctin Furnace Rd; tel 301/271-7488. This is a wildlife, breeding, and petting zoo in a 30-acre woodland setting. It is home to more than 500 animals, including big cats, monkeys, bears, and farmyard pets. **Open:** Peak (May–Aug) daily 9am–6pm. Reduced hours off-season. **$$$**

Catoctin Mountain Park
MD 77 off MD 15; tel 301/663-9388. Located 3 mi W of Thurmont. Adjacent to Camp David, the presidential retreat, lies this 5,769-acre park administered by the National Park Service. Facilities include hiking trails, fishing, cross-country skiing, camping, and cabin rentals. **Open:** Daily 10am–4:30pm. **Free**

Tilghman

This historic bayside village, located on Tilghman Island in the central Chesapeake Bay region, remains a busy seafaring port. Site of Knapps Narrows, and a good place to see America's last fleet of working sailing vessels, the skipjacks. **Information:** Talbot County Conference and Visitors Bureau, PO Box 1366, Easton, 21601 (tel 410/822-4606).

RESTAURANTS ⑪

Bay Hundred Restaurant
MD 33, at Knapps Narrows; tel 410/886-2622. 15 mi W of St Michaels; exit 322 off US 50. **International/Seafood.** Guests watch the workboats in Knapps Narrows from this open, airy eatery whose porch dining area is decorated in quiet good taste. Regional seafood dishes are interspersed with southwestern, Cajun, and Thai entrees. **FYI:** Reservations recommended. No smoking. **Open:** Peak (Mar–Dec) lunch daily 11:30am–4:30pm; dinner daily 5:30–9:30pm. **Prices:** Main courses $13–$18. AE, CB, DC, DISC, MC, V. ⚓ 🏞

★ Harrison's Chesapeake House
MD 33; tel 410/886-2121. 1 mi past Knapps Narrows. **American/Seafood.** One of the oldest restaurants on the Chesapeake, this old building with paneled walls looks out over the water. The waiting room and porch are Eastern Shore friendly and comfortable. Family-style service from a menu emphasizing seafood but with a selection of landlubber entrees. **FYI:** Reservations accepted. Country music. Children's menu. No smoking. **Open:** Breakfast daily 6–11am; lunch daily 11am–5pm; dinner daily noon–10pm. **Prices:** Main courses $10–$18. CB, DC, DISC, MC, V. ⚓ 🏞 👨‍👩‍👧

Towson

City of 50,000 residents, convenient to all Baltimore attractions and nearby to Loch Raven Reservoir and Gunpowder Falls State Park. Seat of Baltimore County. **Information:** Baltimore Area Convention and Visitors Bureau, 100 Light St, 12th fl, Baltimore, 21202 (tel 410/659-7300 or toll free 800/343-3468).

HOTEL 🏨

⬕⬕⬕ Sheraton Baltimore North Hotel
903 Dulaney Valley Rd, 21204; tel 410/321-7400 or toll free 800/433-7619; fax 410/296-9534. Exit 27A off I-695. A great place for business conferences, with facilities geared to the business traveler. Well-kept grounds. Skywalk leads to region's largest shopping mall. **Rooms:** 283 rms and stes. Executive level. CI 3pm/CO noon. Nonsmoking rms avail. Quiet rooms, with lots of desk space. **Amenities:** 🛁 ⚡ 📺 🍴 A/C, cable TV w/movies, refrig, dataport, voice mail. Some units w/minibars. **Services:** ✗ 🔑 VP 🚗 🛄 ⏲ Babysitting. **Facilities:** 🏋 🏊 800 💻 ♿ 1 restaurant, 2 bars (1 w/entertainment), spa, sauna, whirlpool, washer/dryer. **Rates:** $152 S or D; $350 ste. Extra person $12. Children under age 18 stay free. Min stay special events. Parking: Indoor, free. AE, DC, DISC, MC, V.

RESTAURANTS ⑪

Café Troia
In the Penthouse Condominiums, 28 W Allegheny Ave; tel 410/337-0133. Exit 27A off I-695. **Italian.** Elegant pastels, high ceilings, and attractive print fabrics create a pleasant atmosphere in both dining areas and bar of this informal establishment offering good, authentic Italian fare and fine wines. Bar serves appetizers and desserts from main menu, excellent breads, and Belgian chocolates. **FYI:** Reservations recommended. No smoking. **Open:** Lunch Tues–Fri 11am–3pm; dinner Mon–Thurs 5–10pm, Fri–Sat 5–11pm. **Prices:** Main courses $10–$22. DC, MC, V. 💗 ♿

★ Gibby's
In Padonia Plaza, 22 W Padonia Rd, Cockeysville; tel 410/560-0703. Exit 17 off I-83. **Seafood.** Whimsical pictures of fish and Chesapeake Bay scenes give this place a cheerful, comfortable atmosphere. Seafood is flown in from the restaurant's own processing plant in Florida. Be prepared to wait in line. **FYI:** Reservations accepted. Children's menu. No smoking. **Open:** Mon–Sat 11am–2am, Sun noon–2am. **Prices:** Main courses $12–$25. AE, DC, DISC, MC, V. 👨‍👩‍👧 ♿

Hersh's Orchard Inn
1528 E Joppa Rd; tel 410/823-0384. Exit 29B off I-695. **American/Seafood.** Formal but cozy, with tapestry-like patterned fabric and dark woods. Entrance has photos of famous patrons from worlds of sports and entertainment. Emphasis on seafood and other fine American selections. Extensive wine list. Service from uniformed staff is very good. **FYI:** Reservations recommended. Piano. Dress code. **Open:** Mon–Thurs 11:30am–10pm, Fri–Sat 11:30am–11pm, Sun noon–9pm. **Prices:** Main courses $16–$28. AE, MC, V. 💗 VP

Waldorf

Southeast of Washington, DC. John Wilkes Booth sought medical attention here following his assassination of President Lincoln.

HOTEL 🏨

⬕⬕⬕ Holiday Inn Waldorf
1 St Patrick's Dr, 20603; tel 301/645-8200 or toll free 800/HOLIDAY; fax 301/843-7945. At Crain Hwy (US 301). A pleasant, three-story brick building set off from busy US 301 by a lawn dotted with pine trees. Grounds are well landscaped, including trees to break up parking lot. Attractive lobby has polished brick floor, early American furnishings. Convenient to shopping centers, mall, restaurants. **Rooms:** 192 rms and effic. CI 3pm/CO 11am. Nonsmoking rms avail. Units on front have view of lawn. **Amenities:** 🛁 ⚡ 📺 A/C, cable TV w/movies. 1 unit w/minibar. **Services:** ✗ 🛄 ⏲ 🐕 **Facilities:** 🏋 🏊 250 ♿ 1 restaurant, 1 bar (w/entertainment), beauty salon, washer/dryer. Large pool with ample concrete deck for sunning. **Rates (CP):** $62–$65 S; $68–$75 D; $70–$87 effic. Extra person $6. Children under age 18 stay free. Parking: Outdoor, free. AE, CB, DC, DISC, JCB, MC, V.

MOTELS

▤▤ Econo Lodge Waldorf

US 301 at Acton Lane, 20601; tel 301/645-0022 or toll free 800/55-ECONO; fax 301/645-0058. A clean and comfortable chain motel. Brick building located among shopping centers, discount stores, restaurants. **Rooms:** 89 rms. CI noon/CO 11am. Nonsmoking rms avail. **Amenities:** 🛏 🕐 A/C, cable TV w/movies. Some units w/whirlpools. Half of rooms have refrigerators and microwaves. Two large suites have whirlpool in living room. **Services:** 🛎 🖐 **Facilities:** 🔲 Games rm, washer/dryer. **Rates (CP):** Peak (Apr–Oct) $52–$135 S or D. Extra person $5. Children under age 12 stay free. Lower rates off-season. Parking: Outdoor, free. $15 pet fee. AE, DC, DISC, MC, V.

▤▤ HoJo Inn by Howard Johnson

3125 Crain Hwy (US 301), at MD 228, 20602; tel 301/932-5090 or toll free 800/826-4504; fax 301/932-5090. At MD 228. This older, low-slung motel has been immaculately maintained and improved over the years. Spotlessly clean throughout. Convenient to shopping centers, malls, restaurants. **Rooms:** 110 rms and effic. Executive level. CI 3pm/CO 11am. Nonsmoking rms avail. Standard rooms have bright wood furniture, light color schemes. Some have been turned into executive rooms with sofas, better-quality dark furniture, desks. **Amenities:** 🛏 A/C, cable TV w/movies, refrig, in-rm safe. Executive rooms have coffeemakers. **Services:** ✗ 🖼 🛎 🖐 Babysitting. $10 pet fee. **Facilities:** 🖼 🔲 ⅙ 1 restaurant (lunch and dinner only). Small pool surrounded by concrete deck and wooden fence to screen from parking lot. Free use of nearby fitness center. **Rates (CP):** Peak (Mar–Oct) $43–$45 S; $44–$50 D; $45–$50 effic. Extra person $2. Children under age 18 stay free. Lower rates off-season. Parking: Outdoor, free. Weekend rates, romantic getaway packages avail. AE, CB, DC, DISC, MC, V.

ATTRACTION 🏛

Dr Samuel A Mudd House

Tel 301/645-6870 or 934-8464. US 301 to MD 5, then left on MD 205; after 4 miles, turn right onto Poplar Hill Rd, then right onto Dr Samuel Mudd Rd; the house is 4/10 mile from there. Situated on 10 acres of family farmland. John Wilkes Booth went to Dr Mudd to have his broken leg set after he fatally shot President Lincoln in 1865. Tours of the home and its period furnishings are often conducted by members of the Mudd family. **Open:** Apr–Nov, Wed 11am–3pm, Sat–Sun noon–4pm. **$**

Whitehaven

This tiny Eastern Shore village is one terminus of an equally tiny cable-drawn ferry across the Wicomico River.

RESTAURANT 🍴

The Red Roost

Clara Rd; tel 410/546-5443. Exit US 50 at MD 349; go 6½ miles to MD 352, then 8 miles to Clara Rd; turn left. **Regional American/Seafood.** The name is appropriate, since this unusual eatery is in a converted chicken house, with rustic bare wood walls and ceilings, plain wooden furniture, and tables covered with brown paper. Known for massive all-you-can-eat seafood, fried chicken, and rib specials. Popular with bus tours drawn by a sing-along, party atmosphere. **FYI:** Reservations not accepted. Karaoke/piano/singer. Children's menu. **Open:** Peak (May–Labor Day) Mon–Fri 5:30–10pm, Sat 4:30–10pm, Sun 4–9pm. Closed Nov–mid-Mar. **Prices:** Main courses $7–$22. AE, DISC, MC, V. 🅿

NEW JERSEY
A Garden of Delights

STATE STATS

CAPITAL

Trenton

AREA

7,419 square miles

BORDERS

New York, Pennsylvania,
Delaware, and the
Atlantic Ocean

POPULATION

7,748,600

ENTERED UNION

December 18, 1787
(3rd state)

NICKNAME

Garden State

STATE FLOWER

Violet

STATE BIRD

Eastern goldfinch

FAMOUS NATIVES

Count Basie, Aaron Burr,
Jack Nicholson,
Frank Sinatra,
Zebulon Pike

To many motorists, New Jersey is merely a turnpike between New York and Philadelphia. Indeed, the Garden State has been a conduit between the two great cities since America's first stagecoach line ran across it in colonial times. In 1911, then-Gov Woodrow Wilson said, "We have always been inconvenienced by New York on the one hand and Philadelphia on the other."

This popular image of throughways bordered by suburban sprawl and factories is misleading, however, for modern motorists who get off the superhighways will find much to see and do here. Beyond the exits lie small towns that hearken back to New Jersey's colonial days; beach resorts that are some of America's oldest summertime playgrounds; a lovely stretch of horse country in the rolling foothills of the Appalachian Mountains; and the mysterious Pine Barrens, which have changed little since George Washington's Continental Army passed through.

Washington spent a fourth of the Revolutionary War in New Jersey—including two winters at Morristown that were colder than the one at Valley Forge—and he won three of his most important victories here (at Trenton, Princeton, and Monmouth). Another American success at Red Bank helped convince France to enter the war on Washington's side, which gave him the men and ships he needed to secure his new nation's independence.

Much of America's economic history also is on display in our most industrialized state. Steamboats, railroads, submarines, pistols, and the telegraph all were developed here. Thomas A Edison of West Orange invented the light bulb and many other devices which have given comfort and convenience to modern life.

New Jersey offers a surprisingly wide array of outdoor activities for today's visitors, from swimming, boating, and fishing along 127 miles of Atlantic shoreline to shooting the rapids of the Delaware Water Gap. Hiking trails run along the coast, through the Pine Barrens, and atop the mountains. Indeed, this small but remarkably diverse state has everything from skiing to scuba diving, from snorkeling to sky diving, from horseback riding to hot air balloons. New Jersey is a fine place to drive through, and an even better place to hike, ride, or fly.

A Brief History

First to Freedom He is best remembered for giving his name to the narrows leading to New York Harbor, but in 1524, Giovanni de Verrazano became the first European to lay eyes on what is now New Jersey. Thanks to Henry Hudson, however, the land became a Dutch colony from 1609 until Holland ceded it to Great Britain in 1664. Charles II promptly gave it to his brother James, the Duke of York, who turned the western half over to Baron John Berkeley, the eastern half to Sir George Carteret. A former governor of the Isle of Jersey, Carteret convinced the Duke of York to call it all New Jersey.

West Jersey was settled by Quakers, who under William Penn bought their half from Berkeley in 1676. They also purchased Carteret's half six years later, but East Jersey became the home of Puritans from New England and Long Island. In 1702, the Quakers ceded both halves back to the king, who consolidated them under a single royal governor.

The colony prospered during the first half of the 18th century. Farmers supplied the needs of New York and Philadelphia, thus giving rise to New Jersey's nickname: The Garden State. America's first stagecoach line crossed New Jersey to link the two growing cities. Iron was discovered in the Kittatinny Mountains and in the otherwise desolate Pine Barrens. And New Jersey assumed a leading intellectual role with the founding of what are today Princeton and Rutgers Universities, making it the only colony with two institutions of higher learning.

British trade restrictions caused growing sentiment for independence during the 1760s and early 1770s. Citizens of Greenwich staged their own "Tea Party" to protest the tax on their favorite beverage. The provincial congress sent delegates to the first Continental Congress in 1774, and two years later it declared New Jersey to be free of England two days before the Declaration of Independence was proclaimed at Philadelphia.

Crossing to Victory With the outbreak of the Revolutionary War, George Washington tried to bottle up the British forces under Lord Cornwallis in New York by building a series of forts on the New Jersey side of the Hudson River. In November 1776, however, Cornwallis captured Fort Lee, forcing Washington to retreat into Pennsylvania and prompting Newark pamphleteer Thomas Paine to write of "the times that try men's souls." Washington didn't stay in Pennsylvania long, for on Christmas night of 1776, he and 2,400 soldiers slipped across the ice-strewn Delaware River and surprised a Hessian garrison stationed at Trenton. Cornwallis marched down from New York and almost caught the rebels at Trenton, but Washington moved instead on a smaller British force at Princeton, where on January 3, 1777, he won his second victory in a week.

Washington then retired for the first of his two winter encampments at Morristown. There he was protected by the mountains and supplied with munitions by the nearby iron mines and forges. The Morristown winter of 1779–80 was the worst of the century; supplies were so short then that his soldiers "ate every kind of horse food but hay," Washington wrote.

New Jersey escaped further action until October 22, 1777, when nine-year-old Jonas Cattell ran nine miles to warn the Americans at Fort Mercer in Red Bank that a force of Hessians were on their way. With time to prepare, the revolutionaries won the important victory that encouraged France to enter the war on the colonies' side. The Hessians returned in a month to capture the Red Bank fort, but the seeds of Washington's great victory of 1781 at Yorktown had been already been sown.

New Jersey's last action was the war's longest and

Fun Facts

• Through a loophole in the law, New Jersey became the first state to grant suffrage to women. The law was rescinded in 1807 when male legislators discovered that the votes of women were becoming decisive in close elections.

• New Jersey was home to the nation's first commercial brewery, the world's first boardwalk, and the world's first drive-in movie theater.

• More people live in New Jersey per square mile than any other state.

• The first organized baseball game was played on June 19, 1846, in Hoboken. The New York Nine beat the New York Knickerbockers 23–1.

bloodiest, but Washington rallied his forces to win the Battle of Monmouth in June 1778. Local woman Mary Ludwig Hays won her place in history as "Mary Pitcher" by carrying water to the Americans during the conflict. When the 100°F summer heat felled her husband, Mrs Hays took his place loading cannon.

The Mother of Invention With its independence won, New Jersey set out on the course that has made it America's most industrialized state. In 1791, Alexander Hamilton founded Paterson, the country's first planned industrial community. It soon became a leader in textiles and silk production. In the 19th century, Paterson saw the invention of Samuel Colt's famous revolver. The world's first operational steamboat began running between Trenton and Philadelphia, and John Stevens put another in service between Hoboken and New York. The machinery for the *Savannah,* the first steamship to cross the Atlantic, was forged at Morristown. To prove the worth of railroads, John Stevens built the country's first "steam waggon" here. The first successful submarine was built at Elizabeth. Samuel F B Morse and Alfred Vail demonstrated their newfangled telegraph at Speedwell in 1838, thus changing communications forever. And the greatest inventor of them all, Thomas Alva Edison, produced the light bulb, phonograph, Dictaphone, and a host of other modern devices at his West Orange laboratory.

With lenient incorporation laws, the state became the home of so many monopolies during the late 19th and early 20th centuries that muckraking author Lincoln Stephens called it "The Mother of Trusts." Woodrow Wilson was elected governor on a reform platform in 1910, but after he moved on to the White House four years later, the state legislature reversed course and gutted most of the antitrust laws he had pushed through it. (Most of New Jersey's modern tycoons are people who made their fortunes across the rivers but who lived here, such as the late publisher Malcolm Forbes Sr and his son, unsuccessful 1996 Republican presidential aspirant Steve Forbes.)

In the early 20th century, Fort Lee became the world's first movie capital. (As is only fitting, since Thomas Edison had invented the movie camera in his West Orange lab.) The studios moved to Hollywood in the 1920s, but not before the Palisades provided the dramatic backdrop for *The Perils of Pauline* and other serial cliffhangers.

Modern Suburban Mecca With the opening of bridges across the Hudson and Delaware Rivers in the 1930s, the New Jersey towns opposite New York and Philadelphia quickly became bedroom communities. New Jersey's farms continue to produce food for the two great metropolises, and its malls and outlet stores draw thousands of city shoppers every weekend due to the lack of a statewide sales tax on clothing and shoes. New York's football teams—the NFL's Jets and Giants—even play in New Jersey, at the Meadowlands.

Today, New Jersey produces a great variety of commodities: pharmaceuticals, chemicals, textiles, clothing, machinery, transportation equipment, metal and rubber products, leather, glass, and refined oil. It also has some of the most-traveled highways in the country. But off the beaten path lie seaside boardwalks, mountain wineries, posh shopping malls, historic battlefields, and many more delights just waiting to be discovered.

A Closer Look
GEOGRAPHY

New Jersey actually is a peninsula. To the north, it shares a 50-mile land boundary with New York, but the rest of the state is surrounded by the Hudson River, New York Bay, the Atlantic Ocean, Delaware Bay, and the Delaware River.

DRIVING DISTANCES

Trenton

126 mi NW of Atlantic City
52 mi SW of Newark
65 mi SW of New York, NY
32 mi NE of Philadelphia, PA
345 mi E of Pittsburgh, PA
276 mi NE of Richmond, VA
170 mi NE of Washington, DC

Atlantic City

129 mi S of Newark
142 mi S of New York, NY
63 mi SE of Philadelphia, PA
386 mi SE of Pittsburgh, PA
293 mi NE of Richmond, VA
126 mi SE of Trenton
187 mi NE of Washington, DC

Newark

129 mi N of Atlantic City
13 mi SW of New York, NY
84 mi NE of Philadelphia, PA
403 mi NE of Pittsburgh, PA
333 mi NE of Richmond, VA
52 mi NE of Trenton
227 mi NE of Washington, DC

From the east, the state begins with 127 miles of Atlantic beaches, many of them on skinny barrier islands separating the sea from shallow back bays and marshes. Then comes the northern end of the great coastal plain which stretches from Texas almost to New York City. New Jersey's southern three-fifths sits on this flat plain, including the unique Pine Barrens, a 1,000-square-mile area of sparsely inhabited forests and marshes. Then come a line of hills, stretching from northeast to southwest, which actually are terminal moraines laid down by glaciers during the last Ice Age. These give way to a rolling Piedmont, which yields to the Appalachian Mountains in the northwestern corner of the state.

Skylands is what they call the picturesque mountainous region in the northwest corner of the state. Highlights here include High Point, the state's tallest peak at 1,803 feet, and Lake Hopatcong, its largest lake. Spanning the Delaware River's dramatic gorge, the beautiful Delaware Water Gap National Recreation Area offers hiking, biking, tubing, and horseback riding. During winter, three ski areas run down the slopes of these mountains. This is horse country, too, with the United States Equestrian Team headquartered at Gladstone.

To the east of the mountains, the highly developed Gateway region commands views from the palisades across the Hudson River to New York City's dramatic skyline. You can ride ferries from Liberty State Park in Jersey City across New York Harbor to the Statue of Liberty and to Ellis Island, where so many immigrants first set foot on American soil. Nearby you can visit Newark, New Jersey's largest city and home to one of its finest museums.

While New York City exerts its inevitable influence on northeastern New Jersey, so does Philadelphia on the Delaware River region to the southwest. Across the river from "Philly" sits Camden, home of the Walt Whitman House and Cultural Museum, the soup company's unique Campbell Museum, and the New Jersey State Aquarium. Upriver is Trenton, with the nation's second oldest state capitol building still in use. Washington made his famous surprise crossing of the Delaware a few miles upriver of

Trenton, at Titusville. Just off US 1 to the north stands stately Princeton with its famous Ivy League university and 1777 battlefield. Heading southeast on US 30, the rolling hills give way to the flat coastal plains and fishing, canoeing, and horseback riding in the vast and pristine Pine Barrens.

All roads east eventually end at the Jersey Shore. Long a popular summertime playground for New Yorkers, the northern section is famous for Gateway National Recreation Area, at the mouth of New York Harbor, and Asbury Park, the beach town that launched the careers of rock-and-rollers Bruce Springsteen and Southside Johnny. Beginning at Point Pleasant, the state's long chain of barrier islands and back bays runs south past Barnegat and Little Egg Inlets to Atlantic City, the state's most popular single destination. The southern shore area—often called South Jersey—is best known for Cape May and its town full of Victorian houses, many of them now used as B&Bs.

AVG MONTHLY TEMPS (°F) & RAINFALL (IN)		
	Atlantic City	Newark
Jan	31/3.5	31/3.4
Feb	33/3.1	33/3.0
Mar	42/3.6	42/3.9
Apr	50/3.6	52/3.8
May	60/3.3	63/4.1
June	69/2.6	73/3.2
July	75/3.8	78/4.5
Aug	73/4.1	76/3.9
Sept	66/2.9	69/3.6
Oct	53/2.8	56/3.1
Nov	46/3.6	47/3.9
Dec	36/3.3	36/3.5

CLIMATE

New Jersey has four distinct seasons. Temperatures are influenced by altitude, decreasing about 5°F or more year-round from Atlantic City on the coast to Newton in the mountains. Best times to sightsee are during the warm days and cool evenings of spring and autumn. Unpredictable winters can be bitterly cold or relatively moderate, with freezing weather and snow more likely in the mountains than in the rest of the state. Summers can be uncomfortably hot and humid, but the beaches enjoy more temperate weather in both summer and winter because of the Atlantic Ocean.

WHAT TO PACK

Summertime outdoor activities will require shorts and lightweight shirts, blouses, and dresses. A jacket or wrap will come in handy on cool spring and autumn evenings, and even on summer ones in the mountains. Hats, boots, heavy coats, and gloves are necessary in winter. Jackets and ties are required of men in some restaurants, although most at the beaches require "smart casual" attire. Bring or buy sunscreen and insect repellent during the summer months, especially along the shore.

TOURIST INFORMATION

Contact the **Division of Travel and Tourism,** CN 826, Trenton, NJ 08625-0826 (tel toll free 800/ JERSEY-7), for free copies of *New Jersey Travel Guide, New Jersey Cultural & Historical Guide,* and *New Jersey Outdoor Guide,* as well as the semi-annual *New Jersey Calendar of Events.* The state Office of Telecommunications and Information Systems maintains a World Wide Web page (http:// www.state.nj.us) with general information about New Jersey and its attractions.

To find out how to obtain tourist information for individual cities and parks in New Jersey, look under specific cities in the listings section of this book.

DRIVING RULES & REGULATIONS

The maximum statewide speed limit is 55 mph on interstates. Driver and all front-seat passengers must wear seat belts, and children under age five must ride in an approved safety seat. Motorcyclists must wear helmets. Drunk-driving laws are strictly enforced, and the penalties are severe. Radar detectors are legal in New Jersey. There are no self-service gasoline stations in New Jersey since motorists are not allowed to pump their own fuel.

RENTING A CAR

The following rental agencies have offices in New Jersey. Before you leave, check with your insurance company to see if you are insured while driving a rental car. Most companies provide this service; if not, the agencies can sell you insurance.

- **Alamo** (tel toll free 800/327-9633)
- **Avis** (tel 800/831-2847)
- **Budget** (tel 800/527-0700)
- **Hertz** (tel 800/654-3131)
- **National** (tel 800/227-7368)
- **Thrifty** (tel 800/367-2277)

ESSENTIALS

Area Codes: Northern New Jersey (from Newark west to the Pennsylvania state line) is in area code **201.** Central New Jersey is in area code **908,** while Trenton, Atlantic City, and the rest of southern New Jersey are in area code **609.**

Emergencies: Call **911** for police, fire, or ambulance from anywhere within New Jersey.

Liquor Laws: The statewide legal drinking age is 21, and proof of age (including a photo) may be required of any young adult who seeks to purchase alcoholic beverages.

Road Info: Call 201/648-7011 to find out about road conditions in northern New Jersey; for the central and southern regions, call 609/866-4980. The following numbers provide information on specific roads: 908/247-0900 (New Jersey Turnpike), 908/PARK-WAY (Garden State Parkway), 609/ 965-6060 (Atlantic City Expressway).

Smoking: Most New Jersey restaurants have no-smoking sections, and hotels and motels offer at least some rooms exclusively for nonsmokers.

Taxes: The statewide sales tax is 6% on all items except clothing and shoes. Localities can charge up to 6% on lodging; Atlantic City, however, is allowed to impose a 9% tax on hotel rooms and 3% on alcoholic beverages.

Time Zone: All of New Jersey is in the Eastern time zone and observes daylight saving time from April through October.

Best of the State

WHAT TO SEE AND DO

Below is a general overview of some of the top sights and attractions in New Jersey. To find out more detailed information, look under "Attractions" under individual cities in the listings portion of this book.

Natural Wonders Mother Nature has been diverse in the bounty she has bestowed on New Jersey. Along the coast are Sandy Hook, on the southern flank of New York Harbor, and the long string of Atlantic barrier islands that protect shallow back bays. Many marshes exist where the bays meet the low mainland.

On the coastal plain, more than 1 million acres of the Pine Barrens have been preserved in Wharton, Bass River, Green Bank, Penn, and Lebanon State

Forests. So pristine is this area that it's considered an international environmental treasure. Sand dunes alternate with cranberry bogs and dense woods of pine, cedar, and oak. The dry, sandy soil won't tolerate most crops; hence, the area has always been sparsely inhabited by humans. Deer, foxes, raccoons, and other small animals abound, however, and the area supports an enormous variety of wildflowers, including 20 species of orchids.

Forming the western boundary of the state, the Delaware River shrinks from a broad, marsh-bordered bay in the south to the dramatic gorge known as the Delaware Water Gap at New Jersey's northwestern corner. The gap cuts through the Appalachian Mountains not far from High Point, the state's tallest peak. Ice Age glaciers scoured these mountains, forming hundreds of clearwater lakes, including Lake Hopatcong, New Jersey's largest.

Wildlife Most of the state's inland parks abound in deer and small mammals such as foxes, raccoons, and squirrels, but the highlight in New Jersey are the multitudes of wildfowl which migrate along the coast in spring and fall. See "Bird Watching," below, for the best places to observe them.

Historic Areas, Sites & Monuments New Jersey has a number of sites recalling the Revolutionary War. Prime among them is **Morristown National Historical Park,** where Gen George Washington and his army spent two winters. This 1,600-acre area was designated in 1933 as the nation's first national historical park, and visitors can tour Washington's headquarters and the Ford Mansion where he lived. On the Hudson River opposite New York City, **Fort Lee Historic Park** marks the spot where Washington ordered a fort built in 1776 to keep the British from sailing up the river; the Redcoats captured it instead, forcing the rebels to retreat into Pennsylvania. **Washington Crossing State Park** at Titusville marks the spot of the general's surprise crossing of the Delaware River on Christmas night in 1776. He and his men advanced on Trenton, where they attacked British forces, including Hessian mercenaries living in what is now the **Old Barracks Museum,** still standing from the French and Indian Wars of the 1750s.

Other historic attractions hearken back to the state's leading role in the development of industry and commerce. Established by Alexander Hamilton, **Paterson** was America's first planned industrial town and played a major role in the industrialization of the new nation. Its **Great Falls Historic District** preserves a number of early factories, including the Old Gun Mill that made Samuel Colt's name synonymous with the revolver. **Wheaton Village** is a restored 19th-century glass-making community at Millville in southern New Jersey. Founded in the 1740s as an iron-making center, **Waterloo Village** near Stanhope no longer has forges, but costumed guides take visitors through its restored homes and shops. In the Pine Barrens, restored iron-making **Batsto Village** has a gristmill and sawmill if not the original furnaces. But New Jersey's greatest shrine to industry is the **Edison National Historic Site** in West Orange, the laboratory where the great inventor created a host of other useful machines.

Museums New Jersey's multitudinous museums contain everything from Tibetan artifacts to tureens used to serve Campbell's Soup. Among the best, the seven-building **Newark Museum** includes the Shaeffer Collection of ancient glass, the Tibetan Collection, a sculpture garden, a Fire Museum, and the adjacent Ballantine House, the opulent Victorian home of the brewing family. **Montclair Art Museum** has a collection of American art, including a Native American Gallery and works by two noted native sons, landscape painter George Inness and sculptor Thomas Ball. The **Art Museum of Princeton University** has an outstanding collection of Chinese art. In Trenton, the state's **Museum of Natural History** has dinosaur bones, while the **New Jersey State Museum** displays American art and has a planetarium and children's theater. Camden is home to both the **Walt Whitman House** and the **Campbell Museum,** in which the soup company displays its collection of elegant tureens, bowls, platters, and silver gathered from throughout the world. In Flemington, the **Great American Wonder Railroad Museum** has the world's largest model railroad exhibition. And the **Trash Museum** in Lyndhurst is anything but a joke: it's a hands-on demonstration of the importance of recycling.

Battlefields Visitors can follow the Revolutionary War action at **Fort Lee Historic Park** on the Hudson River, in Trenton at **Old Barracks Museum,** at **Princeton Battlefield State Park** near the university, at **Monmouth Battlefield State Park** in Freehold, and at **Red Bank Battlefield,** on a bluff overlooking the Delaware River.

Beaches The state's beaches run the gamut from the gambling oasis of Atlantic City to Ocean City (founded as a straight-laced Christian summer resort in 1879 and still devoid of liquor licenses), from carnival-style boardwalks and amusements piers to the pristine beauty of **Island Beach State Park.** Asbury Park was also established as a temperance retreat, but its modern blue-collar bars have given rise to rock-and-rollers such as Bruce Springsteen. Long Branch, another historic resort, was the summer home of Presidents Ulysses S Grant, Rutherford B Hayes, James A Garfield, Chester A Arthur, Benjamin Harrison, William McKinley, and Woodrow Wilson. North of Cape May, the Wildwoods have the safest beaches in the state, with the surf pounding as much as 1,000 feet offshore.

Family Favorites Families will find much to do in New Jersey, from quiet beach retreats to amusement parks packed with fun. Even Atlantic City has plenty to keep the kids busy, from riding "rolling chairs" along the famous boardwalk to soaring on a Ferris wheel above one of the piers.

Inland, **Six Flags Great Adventure** at Jackson is one of America's largest theme parks. Kids of all ages will get their thrills on the American Scream Machine, the Viper, and Batman the Ride; there's also a drive-through big-game park. At **Wild West City** near Netcong, kids can watch the Pony Express ride into town, watch gunslingers fight it out on the streets, and see what it was like to be held up while riding a Old West stagecoach. In the mountains, **Vernon Valley/Great Gorge** turns from a winter ski resort to a summertime theme park with water slides, bungee jumping, raft rides, and white-water tubing.

Shopping With no sales tax on clothing and shoes, New Jersey's many outlet malls are meccas for serious shoppers. The **Secaucus Shopping Outlet/ Harmon Cove Outlet Center** in Secaucus is one of the nation's largest outlet complexes, and the **Princeton Forrestal Center** has another 35 shops. Antiquers can browse Mullica Hill's famous Antique Row, while bargain hunters can spend days poking through the 1,000 flea market vendors at the outdoor **Meadowlands Marketplace,** in East Rutherford's Meadowlands Sports Complex.

EVENTS AND FESTIVALS

JANUARY

- **Polar Bear Kite Fly,** Belmar. Arctic blasts help participants fly kites on the beach. First Saturday in January. Call 908/787-4945.
- **Winter Activities,** Morristown. Washington's army may have shivered at Morristown, but Fosterfields Living Historic Farm shows how to stay busy (and warm): ice-cutting on a pond, making maple sugar, woodcutting, cooking on wood stoves. Every Saturday in January and February. Call 201/326-7645.

FEBRUARY

- **Sail Expo,** Atlantic City. The nation's largest collection of new sailboats and equipment, at the Convention Center. First week in February. Call 609/449-7130.
- **Atlantic City Classic Car Auction,** Flea Market and Antique Show, Atlantic City. The Convention Center hosts the nation's largest indoor auto auction, with hundreds of antique cars on display and for sale. Third weekend in February. Call 609/449-7130.

MARCH

- **New Jersey Flower & Garden Show,** Somerset. Considered the state's "Harbinger of Spring," do-it-yourself demonstrations take place among landscaped gardens and floral designs. First 10 days in March. Call 908/919-7660.

APRIL

- **Shad Festival,** Lambertville. Shad migrating up the Delaware River provide excuse for judged arts and crafts, live music, food stalls, charity poster auction. Last weekend in April. Call 609/397-0055.

MAY

- **Tour of Somerville,** Somerville. Called the "Kentucky Derby of Bicycling," America's oldest bike race attracts top national competitors. Memorial Day weekend. Call 908/725-0461.

JUNE

- **Heritage Days,** Trenton. Two-day festival in Mill Hill Park with ethnic food, crafts, children's activities, and four stages with jazz, salsa, gospel, blues, folk, Dixieland music. First weekend in June. Call 609/695-7107.
- **New Jersey Seafood Festival,** Belmar. Entertainment, craft fair, educational exhibits, and children's activities accompany samples of Jersey's finest fish. Second weekend in June. Call 908/681-2900.

- **IBM/United States Equestrian Team Festival of Champions,** Gladstone. The nation's best riders and horses compete in Olympic disciplines of dressage and show-jumping, plus world-championship endurance and combined driving events. Last weekend in June. Call 908/234-1251.

JULY

- **Return to Beaver Creek Pow-Wow,** Matarazzo Farms, Belvidere. One of the major Native American events on the East Coast features dancing, music, educational seminars, traditional food and crafts. Third weekend in July. Call 908/475-3872.

AUGUST

- **New Jersey State Fair,** Garden State Park, Cherry Hill. Rides, nationally known entertainers, vendors, food stalls, trade shows and exhibits spotlight the state's accomplishments and attractions. First week in August. Call 609/646-3340.

SEPTEMBER

- **Miss American Pageant,** Atlantic City. The grandmother of all beauty pageants features a boardwalk parade of international contestants. Public can attend the preliminaries. Second weekend in September. Call 609/345-7571.
- **Super Fifties Weekend,** Ocean City. The Ocean City Music Pier features more than 600 hot-rod cars, entertainment, dances, games, and contests, all from the 1950s. First weekend in September. Call toll free 800/BEACHNJ.
- **Garden State Wine Grower's Fall Festival,** Waterloo Village, Stanhope. New Jersey's finest wines are available for tasting amid music and food. Amateur vintners have their own competition. Second weekend in September. Call 908/475-3671.

OCTOBER

- **Victorian Week,** Cape May. The Victorian resort's bygone charm and elegance come back to life during historic house tours, fashion shows, arts and crafts workshops, an evening of Victorian vaudeville, antique shows. Columbus Day weekend. Call 609/884-5404.
- **Chatsworth Cranberry Festival,** Chatsworth. New Jersey's cranberry harvest is celebrated with bog tours, flower and antique car show, authentic Pine Barren entertainment, and home decorating, photo, recipe, storytelling, quilting, and priz-

es for the biggest (and smallest) berry. Third weekend in October. Call 609/859-9701.

NOVEMBER

- **Grand Christmas Exhibition,** Millville. The 18th-century glass-making town of Wheaton Village is decorated for the holidays, each year with a different theme. Thanksgiving to early January. Call 609/825-6800.

DECEMBER

- **George Washington Crossing the Delaware,** Titusville. Landing at Washington Crossing State Park, Revolutionary War soldiers re-enact the general's surprise river crossing on Christmas 1776. Christmas Day. Call 609/737-0623.

SPECTATOR SPORTS

Auto Racing Fans can watch cars speed around **Atco Raceway** (tel 609/768-2167); **Central Jersey Speedway** in New Egypt (tel 908/758-1800); **Flemington Speedway** (tel 908/782-2413); **Raceway Park** in Englishtown (tel 908/446-6331); and **Wall Stadium** (tel 908/681-6400).

Baseball Two minor league baseball teams play in New Jersey. The **New Jersey Cardinals,** Class A affiliate of the St Louis Cardinals, are based at Skylands Park in Sussex County (tel 201/702-2656). The **Trenton Thunder,** Class AA affiliate of the Boston Red Sox, play at Mercer County Waterfront Park in Trenton (tel 609/989-6654).

Basketball The **New Jersey Nets** of the NBA play in Continental Airlines Arena at the Meadowlands Sports Complex in East Rutherford. Call 201/935-3900 for ticket information.

College Athletics The state's two leading universities have active programs of intercollegiate athletics: **Princeton University** (tel 609/258-3538 for ticket information) and **Rutgers University** (tel 908/445-2766).

Football The NFL's **New York Giants** and **New York Jets** both play their home games at Giants Stadium in the Meadowlands Sports Complex, East Rutherford. Call 201/935-8222 for Giants ticket information, 516/538-7200 for the Jets.

Hockey The **New Jersey Devils** of the NHL play in Continental Airlines Arena in the Meadowlands Sports Complex, East Rutherford. Call 201/935-3900 for ticket information.

Horse Racing New Jersey's love of things equestrian extends from stables to pari-mutuel race tracks. You can see the ponies gallop at **Atlantic City Race Course** in McKee City (tel 609/641-2190), **Freehold Raceway** in Freehold (tel 908/462-2190), **Garden State Park** in Cherry Hill (tel 609/488-8400), **Meadowlands Race Track** in East Rutherford (tel 201/935-8500), and **Monmouth Park Race Track** in Oceanport (tel 908/222-5100). Each August, the **Meadowlands Race Track** hosts the Hambletonian, the nation's top harness race.

ACTIVITIES A TO Z

Ballooning New Jersey literally is a hotbed of hot air ballooning, with operators drifting aloft from Piscataway, Pittstown, Phillipsburg, White House Station, Southhampton, Mount Laurel, Bedminster, Blairstown, and Neptune. Annual highlights include the **Quick Chek New Jersey Festival of Ballooning** at Solbert Airport in Readington on the last weekend in July (tel 201/529-0464) and the **Magic of Alexandria Balloon Festival** in Pittstown on the first weekend in August (tel 908/735-0870).

Bicycling America's oldest bike race, the **Tour of Somerville,** attracts top national racers. Many of state parks and forests have trails which bicyclists can use for less strenuous peddling. Among them, the trail in Delaware & Raritan Canal State Park covers 72 miles between New Brunswick to Bordentown on the Delaware River. The Batona Trail runs for 50 miles through Wharton and Lebanon State Forests in the Pine Barrens wilderness. Bikers already can use parts of the New Jersey Coastal Heritage Trail, which eventually will be 275 miles long (see "Hiking," below). In the mountains, Kittatinny Valley State Park has a 26-mile multiple use trail.

Bird Watching New Jersey's coastal marshes are on the main Atlantic Flyway for migrating birds. Among the best places to see them are in the two branches of the Edwin B Forsythe National Wildlife Refuge at Oceanville and Barnegat. More may be observed at the Wetlands Institute in Stone Harbor, a beach resort which also has one of the nation's few heron sanctuaries. Another good spot is the **Cape May Bird Observatory** (tel 609/884-2626), which sponsors a weekend of bird watching in mid-May. To the west of Cape May, the shores of Delaware Bay offer many species of birds, some of them rare.

Camping Twenty New Jersey state parks and forests have camping facilities, including High Point and Jenny Jump state parks in the mountains and Wharton, Bass River, and Lebanon State Forests in the Pine Barrens. The **Delaware Water Gap National Recreation Area** (tel 717/588-2451) also has campgrounds, and there are scores of private campgrounds and RV parks throughout the state.

Canoeing & Kayaking New Jersey's many bays, rivers, lakes, and canals make for fine canoeing and kayaking. The best known whitewater is in the **Delaware Water Gap National Recreation Area** (tel 717/588-2451), which has canoeing, rafting, kayaking, and tubing, depending on how fast the river is running. You can canoe or kayak through the winding waterways of the Pine Barrens from Vincentown, Green Bank, Birmingham, New Gretna, and Chatsworth, all of which have rentals. At the shore, you take a back-bay kayak tour at Island Beach State Park, the state's longest stretch of undeveloped ocean beach. Around on the Delaware Bay side, canoeist and kayakers can explore the wild and scenic Maurice River. The Delaware & Raritan Canal State Park includes 72 miles of the waterway, from New Brunswick to the Delaware River above Trenton.

Fishing New Jersey's long coastline, miles of back bays, and 1,400 miles of trout streams abound with both saltwater and freshwater fish. No licenses are required for deep-sea or surf fishing, but you must have them to take shellfish or for freshwater fishing. Contact the **New Jersey Division of Fish, Game & Wildlife,** CN 400, Trenton, NJ 08625 (tel 609/292-2965) for information.

Golf Golfers need not look far for a place to play, since New Jersey has more than 150 courses, some of championship caliber. For information about courses in Atlantic City and Cape May, call toll free 800/GOLF-222. Students of the game can review its storied past at Golf House (tel 908/234-2300), a restored Georgian mansion in Far Hills where the sport's ancient lore and traditions are displayed.

Hiking A 25-mile leg of the Appalachian Trail runs along the Kittatinny Ridge in northwestern New Jersey. Begun in 1988, the New Jersey Coastal Heritage Trail eventually will be a 275-mile route running along the Atlantic coast, around Cape May, and up the Delaware Bay shoreline. At present three areas—Sandy Hook, Cape May, and Delsea—have visitor centers, but trail information is available at

SELECTED PARKS & RECREATION AREAS

- **Delaware Water Gap National Recreation Area,** River Rd, Bushkill, PA 18324 (tel 717/588-2451)
- **Gateway National Recreation Area,** PO Box 530, Highlands, NJ 07732 (tel 908/872-0115)
- **Morristown National Historical Park,** Washington Place, Morristown, NJ 07960 (tel 201/543-4030)
- **Edwin B Forsythe National Wildlife Refuge,** Great Neck Rd, US 9, Oceanville, NJ 08231 (tel 609/562-1665)
- **Barnegat Lighthouse State Park,** Box 167, Broadway, Barnegat Light, NJ 08006 (tel 908/494-2016)
- **Bass River State Forest,** Stage Rd (PO Box 118), New Gretna, NJ 08224 (tel 609/296-1114)
- **Cape May Point State Park,** Box 107, Cape May Point, NJ 08212 (tel 609/884-2159)
- **Delaware & Raritan Canal State Park,** RD 1, Box 8, Belle Meade, NJ 08502 (tel 908/873-3050)
- **High Point State Park,** RR 4, Box 287, NJ 23, Sussex, NJ 07461 (tel 201/875-4800)
- **Hopatcong State Park,** Box M519, Lakeside Blvd, Landing, NJ 07850 (tel 201/398-7010)
- **Island Beach State Park,** NJ 35, Seaside Park, NJ 08752 (tel 908/793-0506)
- **Jenny Jump State Forest,** Box 150, State Park Rd, Hope, NJ 07844 (tel 908/459-4366)
- **Liberty State Park,** Morris Pesin Dr, Jersey City, NJ 07305 (tel 021/915-3400)
- **Monmouth Battlefield State Park,** RD 1, NJ 33, Freehold, NJ 07723 (tel 908/462-9616)
- **Mount Mitchell Overlook State Park,** Scenic Dr, Atlantic Highlands, NJ 07738 (tel 908/842-4000)
- **Princeton Battlefield State Park,** Mercer St, Princeton, NJ 08540 (tel 609/737-0623)
- **Seven Presidents Oceanfront State Park,** Ocean and Joline Aves, Long Branch, NJ 07738 (tel 908/842-4000)
- **Washington Crossing State Park,** 355 Washington Crossing–Pennington Rd, Titusville, NJ 08560 (tel 609/737-0623)
- **Wharton State Forest,** Batsto, RD 4, Rte 542, Hammonton, NJ 08037 (tel 609/561-0024)

most local tourist information offices. Access to the trail is marked by blue, green, and tan signs. For information, contact the **New Jersey Coastal Trail Office,** PO Box 118, Mauricetown, NJ 08329 (tel 609/785-0676). The Batona Trail runs for 50 miles through the Pine Barrens wilderness, including historic Batsto Village and the Lebanon, Wharton, and Bass River State Forests.

Hunting Deer, waterfowl, and other game abound in New Jersey's wildlife areas. The **New Jersey Division of Fish, Game & Wildlife,** CN 400, Trenton, NJ 08625 (tel 609/292-2965), publishes guidebooks and maps. Visiting hunters must provide a license or hunter education certificate from another state before being issued a New Jersey hunting license. Those wishing to hunt waterfowl must also buy a state stamp in addition to a Federal Duck Stamp.

Skiing Northwestern New Jersey has three downhill ski areas: **Hidden Valley Ski and Tennis Resort** (tel 201/764-6161) and **Vernon Valley/Great Gorge Ski Area** (tel 201/827-2000), both near Vernon; and **Craigmeur Ski Area** at Newfoundland (tel 201/697-4500). In addition, many state parks have cross-country ski trails for wintertime enjoyment. **High Point State Park** (tel 201/875-4800) even has a cross-country ski center.

Scuba Diving & Snorkeling Sunken wrecks provide dive sites off New Jersey's Atlantic beaches, and there are dive operators waiting to take you out to them. For a complete list, send a check or money order for $2 for a copy of *Scuba & Skin Diving in New Jersey* to the **New Jersey Department of Community Affairs,** Division of Community Resources, CN 814, Trenton, NJ 08625 (tel 609/984-6654).

Sky Diving You can take a flying leap with **Skydive Sussex** in Sussex (tel 201/702-7000) and **Skydive East** in Pittstown (tel 908/735-5119).

Water Sports New Jersey's beach resort towns offer a host of watersports, from body surfing in the breakers to windsurfing on the back bays. Many communities even have "beachwheels" programs which provide Surf Chairs in which disabled visitors can be pushed across the sand and into the shallow surf near shore.

Whale Watching Whale- and dolphin-watching cruises are popular along New Jersey's shore. Boats venturing forth during the summer months include the *Big Flamingo* from Wildwood Crest, *Miss Barnegat Light* from Long Beach Island, *North Star* and *Evening Star* from Ocean City, Prince Cruise Lines from Sea Isle City, and TNT Hydrolines from Atlantic Highlands.

Driving the State

Start	Princeton
Finish	Finesville
Distance	70 miles
Time	1–2 days
Highlights	Historic homes, Revolutionary War sites, recreational areas, living history farm museums, vineyards, antique shops

This driving tour follows in the footsteps of George Washington's troops, the Continental Congress (which met in Princeton in 1783), and the Quakers who settled this section of New Jersey in the 19th century. Following in Washington's steps would not have been easy: The Continental Army moved across the state of New Jersey four times during the Revolutionary War. Besides that, Washington's men had to endure two bitter winters in encampments, and they fought battles along the Delaware Valley as well as across the state. The Quakers settled in west-central New Jersey, farming the land that is now the rolling horse country east of the Delaware River. Apart from suburban developments around Princeton and Trenton, the area is still largely rural in character.

We begin this tour in Princeton and then swing over to the Delaware River for a visit to the historic Washington Crossing State Park. Next we drive upstream along the riverside through the Delaware & Raritan Canal State Park and continue farther north through a series of interesting river towns.

For additional information on lodgings, dining, and attractions in the region covered by this tour, look under specific cities in the listings portion of this chapter.

1. **Princeton** has had several concurrent lives, beginning with its founding by Quakers in 1696 and continuing more than three centuries later as a mecca for research and educational institutions like world-famous Princeton University (the fourth-oldest university in the country) and the Educational Testing Service. In recent decades it has also attracted many high-tech laboratories and corporate headquarters, but most of this recent growth has occurred east of town along US 1. The area around the university remains just as attractive as it was fifty years ago, with many small shops along Nassau St and Palmer Square.

The College of New Jersey was founded here in 1756 and renamed **Princeton University** in 1896. The architecture of the campus, reminiscent of Cambridge University in England, is predominately collegiate Gothic in style. Newer buildings are more varied architecturally; the Woodrow Wilson School of International Affairs, with its reflecting pool, is especially stunning.

Nassau Hall, the central building of the university for the first 50 years of its existence, was used as a barracks and a hospital during the Revolutionary War. The Continental Congress met in the hall in 1783; now it is the administrative center of the university. Also worth visiting are the 1928 Gothic Chapel, with its beautiful stained-glass windows, and the newly expanded Firestone Library. One of Princeton's most illustrious professors, Albert Einstein, lived at 112 Mercer St for the last 20 years of his life while working at the school's Institute for Advanced Study. (At Einstein's request the building has not been turned into a museum; the building still belongs to the Institute and is used as a private residence.)

For a guided tour of the Princeton campus, contact the Orange Key Guide Service in Maclean House (tel 609/258-3603) at 73 Nassau St.

Morven (tel 609/683-4495), at 55 Stockton St, was the residence of Richard Stockton, a signer of the Declaration of Independence. Dating from 1755, the house has an interesting history and archaeologists have uncovered artifacts in recent digs. Rooms in the house are furnished in 18th-century style; free lectures are given on Sundays. Call for information and an appointment to visit. A monument just east of the house (where Stockton, Mercer, and Nassau Sts meet) commemorates Washington's victory in the Battle of Princeton on January 3, 1777.

Bainbridge House (tel 609/921-6748), at 158 Nassau St, is the home of the Historical Society of Princeton. This 1766 house was the birthplace of William Bainbridge, commander of the USS *Constitution* during the War of 1812. Visitors can tour the museum in the house and obtain information on Princeton and nearby Revolutionary War sites.

Princeton Battlefield State Park (tel 609/921-0074) is located 1.4 miles south of the Battle Monument at 500 Mercer Rd. The Thomas Clarke house, built by a Quaker farmer about 1770, is on the grounds. Gen Hugh Mercer was injured in the battle and died in the house.

Those who want to visit more Revolutionary War sites can take a 6.7-mile side trip in the other direction. From the center of town, head east on

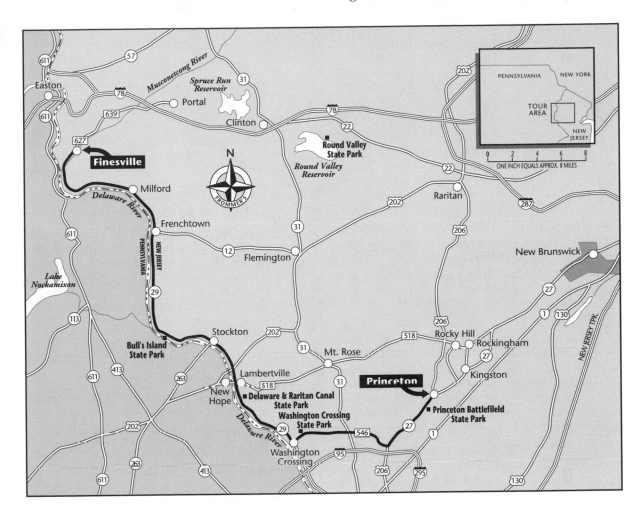

Nassau St (NJ 27) to Kingston, then take a left on River Road (also known as County Rd 604) 2.8 miles into Rocky Hill. Then turn right to Washington St east, which leads into the Georgetown and Franklin Tpk (County Rd 518) and on to Rockingham. **Rockingham State Historic Site** (tel 609/921-8835) was the last wartime headquarters of General Washington and home to Martha and George in 1783. The **Berrien Mansion** has been restored with period furnishings but is suffering from the quarry blasting nearby so will be moved within four or five years.

The next stop on the drive is along the Delaware River, just 14.9 miles away. From the center of Princeton take Stockton St southwest, turn right on Elm Rd and left on Rosedale Rd. At a T-junction turn left onto Carter Rd (NJ 569), and right on Cold Soil Rd, which leads into Blackwell Rd. Turn right on Federal City Rd which veers to the left and

Take a Break

Princeton has a multitude of places for a meal. **Lahiere's,** Witherspoon St just off Nassau St (tel 609/921-2798), is noted for its French cuisine. The **Peacock Inn,** 20 Bayard Lane (tel 609/924-1707), offers meals and lodging in a 1775 house. Dinner entrees at either restaurant cost $18–$26.

continues, becoming Delaware Ave. Follow signs at NJ 31 to County Rd 546 (Pennington Rd) and continue west to:

2. **Washington Crossing State Park,** 355 Washington Crossing–Pennington Rd (tel 609/737-0623). This park includes the site where Washington and the Continental Army landed after crossing the Dela-

ware on Christmas night in 1776. The visitor center has exhibits focusing on the events of that desperate winter. The human toll of the campaign is illustrated by the memorial markers that line the length of Continental Lane. **The Ferry House** (tel 609/737-2512), located at the south end of the Lane, is a Dutch farmhouse with taproom, bedroom, and kitchen, all decorated with period furnishings. Living history demonstrations, including those on early American music, foods, and textiles, are held on weekends. Those who are there on December 25 will see the annual re-enactment of the crossing of the Delaware, while summer visitors can enjoy the open-air theater, picnicking, and hiking. (Free admission. Parking is $3 on weekends and holidays from Memorial Day to Labor Day.)

From Washington Crossing, head north along the river on NJ 29 for 8 miles to the next stop:

3. **Lambertville.** Dating from 1705, this town has an abundance of Victorian and Federal-style houses painted in all the colors of the rainbow. Art galleries and antique shops line the main streets. The nearby **Delaware & Raritan Canal State Park** provides a fine place to walk, run, and cycle along the towpath. The Lambertville section of the canal hosts the two-day Shad Festival on the last full weekend in April.

The **Holcombe-Jimison Farmstead** on NJ 29 just north of Lambertville, is the place to see farm equipment, a farm kitchen, a country doctor's office, and other 19th-century buildings. The first section of the main house dates from 1733, and in fact, George Washington stayed here in July 1777 and June 1778 prior to the Battles of Germantown and Monmouth. Homestead Farm Market stands in a red barn next door.

Howell Living History Farm (tel 609/737-3299) is located just south of Lambertville, 1.6 miles off NJ 29. To reach it turn away from the river on Valley Rd, drive by the Belle Mountain Ski Area, and continue to turn left on Woodens Lane to the entrance. Lots of animals live on the 126 acres of

this working farm, where a variety of activities, from hayrides to corn planting, are offered.

If you have the time for an overnight stop, Lambertville has some places you should consider. **Chimney Hill Farm B & B,** 207 Goat Hill Rd (tel 609/397-1516), offers tastefully furnished rooms in a country-estate setting. Canopied four-poster beds, fireplaces, and antiques make this home very attractive. **The Inn at Lambertville Station,** 11 Bridge St (tel 609/397-4400), offers river-view rooms with antique furnishings. Rooms at both inns are moderately priced.

From Lambertville, continue north on NJ 29 for about 12 miles to the next stop:

4. **Prallsville Mills,** 7 miles south of Stockton along the Daniel Bray Hwy (NJ 29) (tel 609/397-2000). The mill has nine buildings dating from 1796 to the early 20th century. Visitors will see a linseed-oil mill, sawmill, and gristmill. (At the moment, the facilities are not open to the public except for special events, but people are free to wander around the grounds.)

Take a Break

The **Stockton Inn,** on Main St in Stockton (tel 609/397-1250), was built in 1796 as a private residence and converted into an inn in 1832. (According to legend, this hostelry was the inspiration for Richard Rodgers' lyrics for "There's a Small Hotel with a Wishing Well.") Lunch and dinner are offered in the intimate dining room, where entrees cost $14–$28.

From Stockton, continue north on NJ 29 for a little over 3 miles to the next stop:

5. **Bull's Island** (tel 609/397-2949), a recreation area offering canoeing, camping, fishing, hiking, and biking. The old towpath along the Delaware & Raritan Canal runs through the area. The path, covered with stone dust and cinders, is a popular route for hikers, joggers, and mountain bikers. Bull's Island has one of the few nesting sites in New Jersey for northern parula warblers, cerulean warblers, yellow-throated warblers and acadian flycatchers; a Natural Area trail is the place for bird watchers.

Continue north on NJ 29 to the next stop:

6. **Frenchtown,** which has had ferry service across the Delaware for the last 250 years. Townspeople assumed that a French-speaking Swiss aristocrat, who arrived in town while escaping a French order for

Take a Break

Also in Lambertville is **DeAnna's** (tel 609/397-8957), located at 18 S Main St, where regional Italian cuisine is a specialty. Dinner entrees are $9–$15. **The Ferry House** (tel 609/297-9222), which stands at 21 Ferry St, offers eclectic cuisine in an 1855 building. Dinner entrees are $18–$26.

his arrest, was French. It was thought (mistakenly, as it turned out) that he was an escaped hero of the French Revolution, so the town was named in his honor. Today Frenchtown has a number of shops, including the **Blue Fish,** located in a 1856 mill on County Rd 29; **Arcadia,** on Bridge St, with its collection of folk art; and a gallery named **Beyond the Looking Glass,** also on Bridge St.

Take a Break

There's been a hotel on the site of **The French-town Inn,** 7 Bridge St (tel 908/996-3300), since 1805. The dining room of today's inn serves a very innovative menu, and each dish is beautifully presented. Dinner entrees cost $19–$26, and a prix-fixe menu is available on Saturday evenings.

Head along NJ 29 north for 3.6 miles, or take the scenic route along Harrison Street and County Rd 619, to:

7. **Milford,** home of the first modern brew pub in New Jersey using traditional brewing methods. The de-

cor at **The Ship Inn,** 61 Bridge St (tel 908/995-7007), is English: mugs over the bar, models of three-masted ships, photographs of ships, and British hand pumps for the beer.

About four miles north of town, on Adamic Hill Rd, the Volendam Windmill makes for a dramatic sight in the middle of the New Jersey woods. The windmill's arms extend for 68 feet tip to tip. From the Volendam Windmill, continue on Adamic Hill Rd for a pretty winding drive through the country. After 1.2 miles turn right on Alfalfa Hill's cork-screw curves (still named Adamic Hill Rd) to Mount Joy Rd, where you will turn left. Then turn right on County Rd 627 to the village of Finesville. In another 0.6 mile you will come to the next and last stop:

8. **Alba Vineyard,** 269 Rte 627, Finesville (tel 908/995-7800). The Vineyard is open all year for tastings and tours as well as purchase of wine to take home.

If you want to go to I-78 westbound, take County Rd 518 to NJ 639, then NJ 173E to signs for exit 6. Heading eastbound on I-78 is easier on County Rd 639 and NJ 173E, to exit 7.

New Jersey Listings

Absecon

MOTEL 🏨

⊨⊨ Fairfield Inn by Marriott
405 E Absecon Blvd, 08201; tel 609/646-5000 or toll free 800/228-2800; fax 609/383-8744. On US 30 about 5 mi W of Atlantic City. The largest Fairfield Inn in the country is on a hill overlooking a bay and the Atlantic City skyline. It was last renovated in late 1995. **Rooms:** 200 rms and stes. CI 4pm/CO 11am. Nonsmoking rms avail. Lodgenet (pay-per-view movies and video games) in all rooms. **Amenities:** 🛭 ⚬ A/C, cable TV w/movies. Some units w/whirlpools. **Services:** 🚗 ⚬ ⚬ Babysitting. **Facilities:** ⚬ 🔲 ⚬ **Rates (CP):** Peak (June–Sept) $40–$110 S or D; $70–$150 ste. Extra person $10. Children under age 18 stay free. Lower rates off-season. Parking: Outdoor, free. AE, CB, DC, DISC, MC, V.

RESORT

⊨⊨⊨ Marriott's Seaview Resort
401 S New York Rd, 08201; tel 609/652-1800 or toll free 800/932-8000; fax 609/652-2307. On NJ 9. Elegant and spacious public areas, a friendly staff, and two outstanding golf courses are the focal points of this property. **Rooms:** 300 rms and stes. CI 4pm/CO 12:30pm. Nonsmoking rms avail. **Amenities:** 🛭 ⚬ ⚬ A/C, cable TV w/movies, dataport, voice mail. Some units w/terraces. **Services:** ✕ ⚬ ⚬ 🚗 ⚬ ⚬ ⚬ Twice-daily maid svce, masseur, children's program, babysitting. Accommodating front-desk staff will provide many extras on request. **Facilities:** ⚬ ▶36 ⚬ ⚬4 ⚬ ⚬ 🔲 ⚬ ⚬ 2 restaurants, 2 bars, volleyball, games rm, spa, sauna, steam rm, whirlpool, playground, washer/dryer. Teleconferencing capability. **Rates:** Peak (Apr–Oct) $240 S or D; $225–$695 ste. Children under age 18 stay free. Lower rates off-season. MAP rates avail. Parking: Outdoor, free. AE, DC, DISC, MC, V.

RESTAURANTS 🍽

♣ The Fislio
500 W White Horse Pike; tel 609/965-3303. On US 30, 9 mi W of Atlantic City. **Italian.** Italian family recipes served in an atmosphere of candlelight and white linens. Locals suggest the homemade lemon-pepper pasta sautéed with mushrooms, sundried tomatoes, and artichoke hearts, or the lobster ravioli. **FYI:** Reservations recommended. Dress code. **Open:** Sun–Thurs 4–9:30pm, Fri–Sat 4–10:30pm. **Prices:** Main courses $13–$29; prix fixe $20. AE. ♥ ⚬

⑤ Mama Mia
In Cedar Square Shopping Ctr, 2087 S Shore Rd, Seaville; tel 609/624-9322. Exit 25 off Garden State Pkwy, 5 mi S on US 9. **Italian.** A restaurant in a shopping mall, designed like an Italian plaza. The owner allows creativity, resulting in dishes like osso buco Bertina (gnocchi in rose sauce) and cozze chiocce Toscane (New Zealand mussels and bay scallops topped with sautéed broccoli rabe and spinach in a creamy honey–Dijon mustard sauce). **FYI:** Reservations recommended. Dress code. BYO. **Open:** Peak (June–Aug) Sun–Thurs 10am–10pm, Fri–Sat 10am–11pm. **Prices:** Main courses $11–$23. AE, MC, V. ⚬

♣ Ram's Head Inn
9 W White Horse Pike; tel 609/652-1700. On US 30, 6 mi W of Atlantic City. **American/Continental.** Locals call this the area's most beautiful restaurant, with skylights, wood beams, fireplaces, and a garden filled with greenery. Menu specialties include rack of lamb for two, grilled veal chop, and grilled salmon fillet with champagne-and-leek sauce. The 24-page wine list lists over 300 selections. **FYI:** Reservations recommended. Guitar/piano. Children's menu. Jacket required. **Open:** Lunch Mon–Fri noon–3pm; dinner Mon–Fri 5–9:30pm, Sat 5–10pm, Sun 3:30–9:30pm. **Prices:** Main courses $15–$26; prix fixe $15–$20. AE, CB, DC, DISC, MC, V. ♥ ⚬ ⚬ ⚬ ⚬

Asbury Park

See also Eatontown, Tinton Falls

A resort town noted for its excellent beach and, in more recent years, as the launching pad for rocker Bruce Springsteen's career. **Information:** Greater Asbury Park Chamber of Commerce, 100 Lake Ave, PO Box 649, Asbury Park, 07712 (tel 908/775-7676).

HOTEL

≣≣≣ The Berkeley-Carteret Hotel

1401 Ocean Ave, 07712; tel 908/776-6700; fax 908/776-9546. NJ 35 to Sunset Ave to Ocean Ave. A spacious, old-fashioned property with a spa atmosphere. **Rooms:** 245 rms and stes. Executive level. CI 3pm/CO noon. Nonsmoking rms avail. Exceptionally large rooms, many with ocean views. **Amenities:** A/C, TV, in-rm safe. Some units w/whirlpools. **Services:** Babysitting. **Facilities:** 1 restaurant, 1 beach (ocean), lifeguard, spa, playground. Spa offers individualized steam and purification therapies. **Rates (CP):** Peak (May 25–Sept 10) $95 S or D; $120–$160 ste. Extra person $10. Children under age 18 stay free. Lower rates off-season. Parking: Outdoor, free. AE, CB, DC, DISC, MC, V.

RESTAURANT

★ Jimmy's

1405 Asbury Ave; tel 908/774-5051. NJ 35 to Asbury Ave. **Italian/Seafood.** Meunière-style sole, veal chops, and chicken scarpariello with sausage, garlic, and white wine draw lots of couples to this popular spot near the beach. Extensive wine list. **FYI:** Reservations recommended. **Open:** Mon–Thurs noon–10pm, Fri noon–11pm, Sat–Sun 1–11pm. **Prices:** Main courses $11–$24. AE, DC, MC, V. ♥ 🎦 &

ATTRACTION

Monmouth Park

175 Oceanport Ave, Oceanport; tel 908/222-5100. Located 5 mi S of Red Bank. Built in 1946, this is a popular venue for thoroughbred flat and turf racing. **Open:** June–Sept, Mon–Sat; post time 1:30pm. $$

Atlantic City

See also Absecon, Mays Landing, Somers Point

Famed for its four-mile-long boardwalk (built in 1870), "AC" is also known for landmark hotels and casinos, the annual Miss America pageant, and saltwater taffy. Its streets served as the model for the popular Monopoly board game. **Information:** Atlantic City Convention & Visitors Authority, 2314 Pacific Ave, Atlantic City, 08401 (tel 609/348-7100).

HOTELS

UNRATED Bally's Grand Casino Resort

Boston at Pacific Ave, 08401; tel 609/347-7111 or toll free 800/257-8677. Large rooms and elegant public spaces are the trademarks of this casino, built as The Golden Nugget and subsequently bought by Bally. Peregrine falcons nesting on the roof lend their name to one of the five restaurants. **Rooms:** 509 rms and stes. CI 4pm/CO noon. Nonsmoking rms avail. **Amenities:** A/C, cable TV w/movies, dataport, voice mail, in-rm safe. Some units w/whirlpools. **Services:** Masseur, children's program, babysitting. **Facilities:** 5 restaurants (see "Restaurants" below), 2 bars (1 w/entertainment), 1 beach (ocean), lifeguard, games rm, spa, sauna, steam rm, whirlpool, beauty salon. **Rates:** Peak (June–Aug) $220 S or D; $315–$950 ste. Extra person $20. Children under age 18 stay free. Lower rates off-season. MAP rates avail. Parking: Indoor/outdoor, $2/day. AE, CB, DC, DISC, MC, V.

UNRATED Bally's Park Place Casino Resort

Park Place and Boardwalk, 08401; tel 609/340-2000 or toll free 800/225-5977. This hotel is a luxurious mix of the new and the historic, with a new 50-story tower added beside the venerable, and completely remodeled, Dennis Hotel. **Rooms:** 1,265 rms and stes. CI 4pm/CO noon. Nonsmoking rms avail. Upper-floor rooms have wonderful views. **Amenities:** A/C, cable TV w/movies, voice mail. Some units w/whirlpools. Some suites have fully equipped office centers. **Services:** Masseur, babysitting. **Facilities:** 9 restaurants (see "Restaurants" below), 1 bar (w/entertainment), 1 beach (ocean), lifeguard, racquetball, spa, sauna, steam rm, whirlpool, beauty salon. **Rates:** Peak (June–Sept) $125–$215 S or D; $375–$2,500 ste. Children under age 16 stay free. Lower rates off-season. Parking: Indoor/outdoor, $2/day. AE, CB, DC, DISC, MC, V.

≣≣≣ Claridge Casino Hotel

Park Place and Boardwalk, 08401; tel 609/340-3400 or toll free 800/257-8585. US 30 to Martin Luther King Blvd to Boardwalk. Modeled after the Empire State Building, this hotel from Atlantic City's grand old days has been completely modernized. **Rooms:** 506 rms and stes. Executive level. CI 4pm/CO noon. Nonsmoking rms avail. **Amenities:** A/C, satel TV w/movies, refrig, voice mail. Some units w/terraces, some w/whirlpools. **Services:** Twice-daily maid svce, masseur, babysitting. **Facilities:** 5 restaurants (see "Restaurants" below), 4 bars, 1 beach (ocean), lifeguard, spa, sauna, steam rm, whirlpool, beauty salon. Three-level casino with 65 game tables and 1,400 slot machines. **Rates:** $80–$165 S or D; $160–$480 ste. Children under age 18 stay free. Parking: Indoor/outdoor, $2/day. AE, CB, DC, DISC, MC, V.

≣≣≣ Harrah's Atlantic City

777 Harrah's Blvd, 08401; tel 609/441-5000 or toll free 800/2-HARRAHS. Brigantine Blvd to Harrah's Blvd. Appropriate to its location near the marina, this quiet, airy hotel has a nautical theme. **Rooms:** 760 rms and stes. Executive level. CI 4pm/CO noon. Nonsmoking rms avail. Units in atrium tower are all impressive suites. **Amenities:** A/C, cable TV w/movies, voice mail. Some units w/minibars, some w/whirlpools. **Services:** Twice-daily maid svce, masseur, babysitting. Early check-in of bags. Complimentary coffee. **Facilities:** 7 restaurants (see "Restaurants" below), 2 bars (1 w/entertainment), games rm, spa, sauna, steam rm, whirlpool, beauty salon, day-care ctr.

Casino (65,000 square feet) with 105 game tables and nearly 2,000 slot machines. Miniature-golf course. Charter boats available by prior arrangement. **Rates:** Peak (Apr–Sept) $59–$159 S or D; $79–$189 ste. Extra person $10. Children under age 12 stay free. Lower rates off-season. Parking: Indoor, $2/day. AE, CB, DC, DISC, MC, V.

🍽🍽 Holiday Inn Boardwalk

Chelsea Ave and Boardwalk, 08401; tel 609/348-2200 or toll free 800/HOLIDAY; fax 609/345-5110. A standard facility for this chain, whose chief attractions are the views from the upper floors and a fine location on the Boardwalk. **Rooms:** 220 rms and stes. CI 3pm/CO 11am. Nonsmoking rms avail. **Amenities:** 🛏 📺 🍴 A/C, cable TV, refrig. **Services:** ✕ 🆅🅿 🚐 🛎 **Facilities:** 🏊 🏋 325 🚹 1 restaurant, 1 bar, 1 beach (ocean), lifeguard. Indoor pool at adjacent property available in winter. **Rates:** Peak (June–Sept) $117–$169 S or D; $188–$288 ste. Extra person $15. Children under age 12 stay free. Lower rates off-season. MAP rates avail. Parking: Indoor, free. AE, CB, DC, DISC, MC, V.

🍽🍽🍽 Merv Griffin's Resorts Casino Hotel

1133 Boardwalk, 08401; tel 609/344-6000 or toll free 800/336-MERV; fax 609/340-7684. At North Carolina Ave. When the former landmark Haddon Hall Hotel became Atlantic City's first casino, it took on a flamboyant, bright atmosphere. This Atlantic City pioneer holds a prime boardwalk location adjacent to the Steel Pier. **Rooms:** 662 rms and stes. CI 4pm/CO noon. Nonsmoking rms avail. Units range from mini-suites to "super-suites." **Amenities:** 🛏 A/C, cable TV w/movies, voice mail, in-rm safe. Some units w/minibars, some w/terraces, some w/whirlpools. Guests get a box of "Mervaroons" at check-in time. **Services:** 🍽 🆓 🆅🅿 🛎 🛎 Twice-daily maid svce, social director, masseur, babysitting. **Facilities:** 🏊 🏋 🏋 1100 🚹 7 restaurants (see "Restaurants" below), 3 bars, 1 beach (ocean), lifeguard, games rm, squash, spa, sauna, steam rm, whirlpool, beauty salon. Casino with 1,700 slot machines and 110 game tables. **Rates:** Peak (May–Sept) $50–$150 S or D; $150–$400 ste. Extra person $10. Children under age 16 stay free. Lower rates off-season. Parking: Indoor/outdoor, $2/day. AE, CB, DC, DISC, MC, V.

🍽🍽🍽 The Sands Hotel & Casino

Indiana Ave and Brighton Park, 08404; tel 609/441-4000 or toll free 800/AC-SANDS; fax 609/441-4180. US 30 to Indiana Ave. This casino hotel faces Brighton Park and is connected to the boardwalk by a weatherproof "people mover" moving sidewalk. Bright decor. **Rooms:** 535 rms and stes. Executive level. CI 3pm/CO noon. Nonsmoking rms avail. **Amenities:** 🛏 🍴 A/C, cable TV w/movies, voice mail, bathrobes. Some units w/minibars, some w/whirlpools. VCRs available on request. **Services:** 🍽 🆓 🆅🅿 🚐 🛎 🛎 Twice-daily maid svce, masseur, babysitting. Front desk can arrange boating and tennis nearby. **Facilities:** 🏋 🚹 7 restaurants (see "Restaurants" below), 1 bar (w/entertainment), spa, sauna, steam rm, whirlpool. Casino with 91 game tables and 1,500

slot machines. **Rates:** Peak (May–Sept) $109–$229 S or D; $229–$459 ste. Children under age 12 stay free. Lower rates off-season. Parking: Indoor/outdoor, $2/day. AE, CB, DC, MC, V.

🍽🍽 Sheraton Atlantic City West

6821 Black Horse Pike, Egg Harbor Township, 08234; tel 609/272-0200 or toll free 800/44-ROOMS. 1 mi E of Garden State Pkwy. 18 acres. Nice facility with a six-story atrium surrounded by attractive, two-room suites. **Rooms:** 213 rms and stes. Executive level. CI 4pm/CO noon. Nonsmoking rms avail. **Amenities:** 🛏 🍴 📺 🍴 A/C, cable TV w/movies, dataport. Some units w/terraces, some w/whirlpools. Nintendo. **Services:** ✕ 🆓 🚐 🛎 🛎 Babysitting. Shuttle service to casinos. **Facilities:** 🏊 🏌 9 🏋 🏋 1000 🚹 1 restaurant, 1 bar (w/entertainment). **Rates:** Peak (June–Oct) $65–$149 S or D; $75–$179 ste. Extra person $15. Children under age 17 stay free. Lower rates off-season. Parking: Outdoor, free. AE, CB, DC, DISC, JCB, MC, V.

🍽🍽🍽 Showboat Casino Hotel

Delaware Ave and Boardwalk, 08401; tel 609/343-4000 or toll free 800/621-0200. US 30 to Delaware Ave. Dixieland bands and wrought-iron railings set a New Orleans motif. **Rooms:** 800 rms and stes. Executive level. CI 2pm/CO 11am. Nonsmoking rms avail. Most rooms have views of the beach and the boardwalk. **Amenities:** 🛏 🍴 A/C, cable TV w/movies. Some units w/terraces, some w/whirlpools. **Services:** 🍽 🆓 🆅🅿 🚐 🛎 🛎 Masseur, babysitting. **Facilities:** 🏊 🏋 🏋 2000 🚹 9 restaurants (see "Restaurants" below), 2 bars, 1 beach (ocean), lifeguard, games rm, spa, sauna, steam rm, whirlpool, beauty salon. Casino has 80 gaming tables (blackjack, craps, roulette, baccarat) and 1,700 slot machines. **Rates:** $122–$182 S or D; $252–$476 ste. Parking: Indoor/outdoor, free. AE, CB, DC, MC, V.

🍽🍽🍽🍽 Trump Plaza Hotel & Casino

Boardwalk at Mississippi Ave, 08401; tel 609/441-6000 or toll free 800/677-7378; fax 609/441-7881. Atlantic City Expwy to end. Donald Trump's boardwalk centerpiece is in a state of apparently constant renovation and expansion. **Rooms:** 895 rms and stes. Executive level. CI 4pm/CO noon. Nonsmoking rms avail. Best views in the city from upper floors. **Amenities:** 🛏 🍴 A/C, cable TV w/movies, VCR, voice mail. Some units w/terraces, some w/whirlpools. Multilingual information on closed-circuit television. **Services:** 🍽 🆓 🆅🅿 🚐 🛎 🛎 Twice-daily maid svce, masseur, babysitting. **Facilities:** 🏊 🏌 4 🏋 🏋 5000 🚹 7 restaurants (see "Restaurants" below), 2 bars, 1 beach (ocean), lifeguard, games rm, spa, sauna, steam rm, whirlpool, beauty salon. Second-floor casino with 95 game tables and over 1,700 slot machines. **Rates:** Peak (May–Sept) $120–$230 S or D; $250 ste. Extra person $10. Children under age 17 stay free. Min stay special events. Lower rates off-season. Parking: Indoor, $2/day. AE, CB, DC, DISC, MC, V.

MOTEL

≣≣ Best Western Bayside Resort

8029 Black Horse Pike, 08232; tel 609/641-3546 or toll free 800/999-9466; fax 609/641-4329. Jct NJ 322/40. A completely renovated motel with pleasant rooms and a complete tennis facility. **Rooms:** 110 rms. CI 3pm/CO 11am. Nonsmoking rms avail. **Amenities:** 🛍 A/C, cable TV w/movies. **Services:** ✕ 🚐 Babysitting. **Facilities:** 🔧 📶 🏊 200 🔧 1 restaurant, 1 bar, spa, day-care ctr, washer/dryer. **Rates:** Peak (Mem Day–Labor Day) $50–$125 S or D. Extra person $10. Children under age 17 stay free. Lower rates off-season. Parking: Outdoor, free. AE, DC, DISC, MC, V.

RESORTS

≣≣≣ Tropworld Casino & Entertainment Resort

Brighton and Boardwalk, 08401; tel 609/340-4000 or toll free 800/843-8767; fax 609/340-4266. This sprawling, modern casino hotel was built around the steel of the former Ambassador Hotel, a landmark of old Atlantic City. **Rooms:** 1,624 rms and stes. CI 4pm/CO noon. Nonsmoking rms avail. **Amenities:** 🛍 A/C, cable TV w/movies. Some units w/whirlpools. **Services:** 🍽 🖥 VP 🚐 🏊 🔧 Masseur. **Facilities:** 🔧 📶 1900 🔧 7 restaurants (see "Restaurants" below), 1 bar (w/entertainment), 1 beach (ocean), lifeguard, spa, sauna, steam rm, whirlpool, beauty salon. Rooftop lounge with an impressive view of the city. **Rates:** Peak (Mem Day–Labor Day) $105–$195 S or D; $175 ste. Extra person $10. Children under age 12 stay free. Lower rates off-season. MAP rates avail. Parking: Indoor, $2/day. Suites avail Mon–Thurs only. AE, MC, V.

≣≣≣ Trump's Castle Casino Resort

1 Castle Blvd, 08401; tel 609/441-2000 or toll free 800/777-8477. Brigantine Blvd to Castle Blvd. 14½ acres. This marble-and-brass showpiece on the marina impresses with sheer size and opulence, from massive chandeliers to first-class restaurants. **Rooms:** 728 rms and stes. Executive level. CI 4pm/CO noon. Nonsmoking rms avail. Top floors have spectacular views of city and ocean. **Amenities:** 🛍 🖥 🔧 A/C, cable TV w/movies, refrig. Some units w/whirlpools. **Services:** 🍽 🖥 VP 🏊 🔧 Twice-daily maid svce, masseur, babysitting. **Facilities:** 🔧 📶 5 🔧 3400 🔧 8 restaurants (see "Restaurants" below), 2 bars (1 w/entertainment), basketball, games rm, spa, sauna, steam rm, whirlpool, beauty salon. 70,000-square-foot casino with 88 gaming tables and 1,800 slot machines. **Rates:** Peak (May–Sept) $74–$110 S or D; $250–$420 ste. Extra person $15. Children under age 12 stay free. Min stay wknds. Lower rates off-season. Parking: Indoor, $2/day. AE, CB, DC, DISC, MC, V.

≣≣≣≣ Trump Taj Mahal Casino/Resort

1000 Boardwalk, 08401; tel 609/449-1000 or toll free 800/825-8786. At Virginia Ave. 17 acres. "Spare no expense" truly describes this opulent, 51-story hotel. The public spaces include $14 million worth of crystal chandeliers; uniforms and costumes worn by the staff account for another $4 million. The lobby practically drips with Italian marble and sports nine, two-ton stone elephants. **Rooms:** 1,250 rms and stes. Executive level. CI 4pm/CO noon. Nonsmoking rms avail. Top floors have fine views. **Amenities:** 🛍 🔧 A/C, voice mail, in-rm safe. Some units w/whirlpools. **Services:** 🍽 🖥 VP 🚐 🏊 🔧 Masseur, babysitting. **Facilities:** 🔧 📶 🔧 🔧 🔧 9 restaurants, 3 bars (1 w/entertainment), 1 beach (ocean), lifeguard, games rm, spa, sauna, steam rm, whirlpool, beauty salon. Claims to be the world's largest casino; at 120,000 square feet, it's twice as large as most others in town and has 157 gaming tables and nearly 3,000 slot machines. **Rates:** Peak (May–Sept) $100–$175 S or D; $275–$400 ste. Extra person $30. Children under age 18 stay free. Min stay wknds. Lower rates off-season. Parking: Indoor/outdoor, $2/day. AE, CB, DC, DISC, MC, V.

RESTAURANTS 🍴

Andreotti's

In Harrah's Atlantic City, 777 Harrah's Blvd; tel 609/441-5576. Brigantine Blvd to Harrah's Blvd. **Italian.** Corinthian columns surround this grand casino dining room. Menu features zuppa di pesce, veal mignon with eggplant, and angel-hair pasta with sea scallops and baby shrimp. **FYI:** Reservations recommended. Guitar. Dress code. **Open:** Peak (Mem Day–Labor Day) Fri–Tues 5:30–11pm. Closed one week in Dec. **Prices:** Main courses $11–$30. AE, CB, DC, DISC, MC, V. ♥ VP 🔧

♟ Casa di Napoli

In Showboat Casino Hotel, Delaware Ave and Boardwalk; tel 609/343-4000. US 30 to Delaware Ave to Boardwalk. **Italian.** The menu of this colorful room provides a culinary trip through Italy. Red snapper in tomato sauce; Italian sausage sautéed with olives, broccoli, and hot pepper; and broiled veal chop with mushrooms are among the top choices. **FYI:** Reservations recommended. Violin. Dress code. **Open:** Peak (June–Sept) Wed–Sun 5:30–11:30pm. **Prices:** Main courses $12–$24; prix fixe $35. AE, CB, DC, DISC, MC, V. VP 🔧

Castle Steak House

In Trump's Castle, 1 Castle Blvd; tel 609/441-8342. Brigantine Blvd to Castle Blvd. **Seafood/Steak.** Photographs and sculptures by famed Western artist Frederic Remington set the ambience at this "beefy" steakhouse. The menu emphasizes prime rib, porterhouse, and New York strip, but there are seafood selections, too. **FYI:** Reservations recommended. **Open:** Peak (Mem Day–Labor Day) Mon–Tues 6–10pm, Sat 6–11pm, Sun 5–9pm. **Prices:** Main courses $18–$35. AE, CB, DC, DISC, MC, V. ♥ VP

Chef Vola's

111 S Albion Place; tel 609/345-2022. From Atlantic City Expwy; right on Pacific, left on Albion. **Italian/Steak.** This tiny restaurant is in the basement of a house so exclusive that you'll probably be asked the name of the person who sent you. Tell them your friend in the travel business recommend-

ed the sirloin, orange roughy, or red snapper with Caribbean banana sauce. Space is cramped but no one seems to care. **FYI:** Reservations recommended. Dress code. BYO. **Open:** Peak (June–Sept) Tues–Sun 6–10pm. **Prices:** Main courses $14–$20. No CC. ●

Fortune's

In Trump Plaza, Boardwalk and Mississippi Ave; tel 609/441-6000. **Chinese.** An elegant, painstakingly decorated Chinese restaurant overlooking the Boardwalk. Specialties include Mongolian lamb stir-fry, Fortune's seafood combination, and Cantonese-style cashew chicken. Diners can pick their own lobster from tank in dining room. **FYI:** Reservations recommended. **Open:** Peak (May–Oct) Fri–Mon 6–11pm. **Prices:** Main courses $16–$32. AE, DC, DISC, MC, V. VP &

Gary's Little Rock Cafe

5212–14 Atlantic Ave, Ventnor; tel 609/823-2233. From Black Horse Pike, right on Atlantic Ave. **New American.** A striking decor of black and white with touches of pink, white lights, and mirrors sets the mood for this whimsical restaurant. The osso buco Navone is "one of those entrees you remember for weeks afterward," according to a local critic. Prix fixe dinner and Sunday brunch are available seasonally; a sushi bar is available on some nights. **FYI:** Reservations recommended. Dress code. No liquor license. **Open:** Peak (June–Aug) lunch Mon–Fri 11am–3pm; dinner Sun–Thurs 4–9pm, Fri–Sat 4–10pm. Closed Jan. **Prices:** Main courses $14–$22. AE, MC, V. ● &

Il Verdi

In Tropworld Casino & Entertainment Resort, Boardwalk and Brighton Ave; tel 609/340-4070. **Italian.** Cozy and romantic, with low lights and elegant table settings. Menu includes homemade sausage in Bolognese cream sauce, pan-fried T-bone steaks, and red snapper filet. **FYI:** Reservations recommended. Dress code. **Open:** Peak (Mem Day–Labor Day) Wed–Sun 6–11pm. Closed one week in Dec. **Prices:** Main courses $20–$39. AE, MC, V. ● VP &

★ Knife & Fork Inn

Atlantic and Pacific Aves; tel 609/344-1133. **Regional American.** Awards and accolades hang everywhere in the bar of this landmark eatery, where the bouillabaisse, lobster thermidor, and fried zucchini are locally famous. **FYI:** Reservations recommended. **Open:** Peak (Mem Day–Thanksgiving) Tues–Sun 6–10pm. **Prices:** Main courses $18–$37. AE, DC, DISC, MC, V.

Le Palais

In Merv Griffin's Resorts Casino Hotel, 1133 Boardwalk; tel 609/340-6400. At North Carolina Ave. **French.** Lots of red velvet and crystal chandeliers set a luxurious tone here. Kitchen specialties include breast of Muscovy duckling Bigarde, filet mignon Red River, and sauté of shellfish Olga. Excellent service. **FYI:** Reservations recommended. Piano/

singer. Dress code. **Open:** Wed–Sat 6pm–midnight, Sun 10am–2pm. **Prices:** Main courses $20–$39. AE, CB, DC, DISC, MC, V. ● VP &

Martino's

In Claridge Casino Hotel, Park Place and Boardwalk; tel 609/340-3400. US 30 to Martin Luther King Blvd to Boardwalk. **Italian.** Hotel guests and locals come to this charming spot to enjoy a harpist along with their lobster bisque, lobster tail simmered in marinara sauce, or saltimbocca Romana. **FYI:** Reservations recommended. Harp. Dress code. **Open:** Wed–Sun 5–11pm. **Prices:** Main courses $9–$36. AE, CB, DC, DISC, MC, V. VP &

♣ Medici

In Sands Hotel & Casino, Indiana Ave and Brighton Park; tel 609/441-4259. US 30 to Indiana Ave. **Italian.** Both decor and menu aim to re-create the feel of an intimate Florentine trattoria. Entrees include marinated swordfish filet in Barolo wine and porcini mushroom sauce, and zuppe di pesce. Vegetarian and low-fat selections available. **FYI:** Reservations recommended. Dress code. **Open:** Peak (Mem Day–Labor Day) Fri–Tues 6pm–midnight. **Prices:** Main courses $15–$35. AE, CB, DC, MC, V. ● VP &

⑤ Peking Duck House

2801 Atlantic Ave at Iowa Ave; tel 609/348-1313. US 40 to N on Atlantic Ave. **Chinese.** Atlantic City's only non-casino gourmet Chinese restaurant specializes in Peking duck (carved at the table), lobster tail Cantonese supreme, lamb (or beef) in Thai-style peanut sauce, and steak kumquat. **FYI:** Reservations recommended. **Open:** Mon–Thurs noon–11pm, Fri–Sat noon–midnight, Sun 2–11pm. **Prices:** Main courses $10–$19; prix fixe $13–$19. AE, CB, DC, MC, V. ● &

Peregrines'

In Bally's Grand Casino Resort, Boardwalk and Boston Ave; tel 609/340-7870. **New American.** An elegant eatery named for the family of rare falcons who live on the roof of this building. Menu focuses on the inventive, with highlights such as duck with pastrami on potato pancakes with pear chutney, and filet of buffalo with polenta lasagna and grilled wild mushrooms. **FYI:** Reservations recommended. **Open:** Peak (June–Aug) Thurs–Sun 6–11pm. **Prices:** Main courses $28–$45; prix fixe $60–$90. AE, CB, DC, DISC, MC, V. VP &

Prime Place

In Bally's Park Place, Park Place and Boardwalk; tel 609/340-2000. **Steak.** Diners flock here to sit at the famous Monopoly intersection and enjoy porterhouse, sirloin, prime rib, or filet mignon au poivre. A massive salad bar sprawls under its own stained-glass rotunda. **FYI:** Reservations recommended. Dress code. **Open:** Fri–Tues 6–11pm. **Prices:** Main courses $18–$25. AE, CB, DC, DISC, MC, V. VP &

★ White House

2301 Arctic Ave; tel 609/345-1564. **Cafe/Deli.** Celebrities from the Beatles to Frank Sinatra have chomped submarine sandwiches here, and management has the photos to prove it. Locals claim this place sets the standard for Italian, cheesesteak, and turkey subs in AC. **FYI:** Reservations not accepted. No liquor license. **Open:** Fri–Sat 10am–midnight, Sun–Thurs 10am–11pm. **Prices:** Lunch main courses $4–$6. No CC. 🎥

ATTRACTIONS 📷

Convention Hall
2301 Boardwalk; tel 609/348-7000. Home of the Miss America Pageant and the world's largest pipe organ, this hall has also been the site of huge rock concerts, professional ice hockey and basketball games, top boxing matches, and flower, dog, boat, and horse shows. The Convention Hall is located at the colonnaded arc of Kennedy Plaza, the site of a bronze bust of John F Kennedy which was dedicated in 1964. **Open:** Call for schedule. **$$$$**

Lucy, the Margate Elephant
Decatur and Atlantic Aves, Margate; tel 609/823-6473. Built in 1881 as a promotion by James V Lafferty to stimulate real estate sales in the area, Lucy is a visual as well as a historical landmark, standing as tall as a 6-story building, constructed from nearly 1 million pieces of wood, and weighing 90 tons. She has been designated a National Historic Landmark and reflects the ornate craftsmanship of the Victorian era in which she was built. Visitors can climb the stairs in Lucy's back leg to the *howdah* (basket) on her back to view the surrounding land. Antique photos and elephant memorabilia are also on display. **Open:** Peak (mid-June–Labor Day) daily 10am–8:30pm. Reduced hours off-season. Closed Nov–Mar. **$**

Marine Mammal Stranding Center
3625 Brigantine Blvd, Brigantine; tel 609/266-0538. Located 5 mi NE of Atlantic City. Since it opened in 1978, the center has responded to more than 1,000 calls to rescue stranded whales, dolphins, seals, and sea turtles that have washed ashore on New Jersey beaches. Visitors may observe the animals, who are brought back here for rehabilitation and eventual release. **Open:** Peak (Mem Day–Labor Day) daily 11am–5pm. Reduced hours off-season. **$**

Augusta

This small town in the NW region of the state is close to Culvers Lake and Lake Kemah, as well as the Bear Swamp Wildlife Management Area.

ATTRACTION 📷

Skylands Park
94 Champion Place; tel 201/579-7500. Located in rural Sussex County at the junction of NJ 206N, NJ 15, and NJ 565. The Class AA New Jersey Cardinals play baseball here; the stadium itself seats 4,340 and is loved for its old-fashioned baseball park feel. Ticket-holders may bring picnic blankets or beach chairs to use on two grassy knolls adjacent to the infield. **Open:** Mid-June–August, call for schedule. **$$$**

Avalon

Located in the southern portion of the Jersey Shore. Guests may take a walk along the town boardwalk or along one of its beaches. Close to Marmora Coastal Wetlands Area. **Information:** Avalon Chamber of Commerce, 30th and Ocean Dr, Avalon, 08202 (tel 609/967-3936).

MOTEL 🏨

🏊🏊 Golden Inn Hotel & Conference Center
Oceanfront at 78th St, 08202; tel 609/368-5155; fax 609/368-6112. Stone Harbor exit off Garden State Pkwy to Dune Dr right to 78th St. This beachfront complex abuts the dunes in a quiet residential neighborhood. Business conferences keep the facility busy in the off-season. **Rooms:** 160 rms and stes. CI 3pm/CO 11am. **Amenities:** 🛏 ⚒ 📺 🍷 A/C, cable TV w/movies, refrig, dataport. All units w/terraces, some w/whirlpools. **Services:** ✕ 🔑 🖥 🎵 Children's program, babysitting. **Facilities:** 🏋 🏊 ⚿ 2 restaurants, 1 bar (w/entertainment), 1 beach (ocean), lifeguard, washer/dryer. **Rates:** Peak (June–Sept) $159–$309 S or D; $290–$309 ste. Extra person $15. Children under age 15 stay free. Min stay peak. Lower rates off-season. Parking: Indoor/outdoor, free. MC, V.

Barnegat Light

See Long Beach Island

Belvidere

Established in 1845, Belvidere sits on the Delaware River in the NW region of the state. It is the site of a noted winery and home of the Country Gate Playhouse, featuring a year-round schedule of Broadway shows. Seat of Warren County.

ATTRACTION 📷

Shippen Manor
8 Belvidere Ave, Oxford; tel 908/453-4381. This three-story Georgian manor, built circa 1754, now serves as the Warren County Museum. Tours of the restored mansion are conducted by costumed docents who often participate in authentic food preparation in the open-fire kitchen or dress up as members of the Civil War–era New Jersey Militia. The remains of a colonial iron furnace are also on the grounds. **Open:** First and second Sun of each month, 1–4pm. **Free**

Bernardsville

Located west of Newark, this 18th-century town was formerly called Veal Town (for the Veal Town Tavern, a favorite of Revolutionary War soldiers). The Scherman/Hoffman Wildlife Sanctuary is located here.

INN ▥

▤▤▤▤ The Bernards Inn

27 Mine Brook Rd, 07924; tel 908/766-0002; fax 908/766-4604. On US 202 across from train station. This 1907 stone and stucco structure was completely restored in 1987. Railings of polished brass lead up to a richly decorated lobby with a fireplace and fresh flowers. Unsuitable for children under 12. **Rooms:** 21 rms and stes. CI 2pm/CO 11am. Rooms feature an antique armoire and individual decor. Original oil paintings decorate the walls. **Amenities:** ▥ ▨ A/C, cable TV, dataport, bathrobes. Some units w/minibars. Complimentary daily newspaper. **Services:** ✗ ▨ ▱ Twice-daily maid svce. Personalized service, including preferred lunch and dinner reservations. **Facilities:** ▣ ▯ 1 restaurant (see "Restaurants" below), 1 bar (w/entertainment). **Rates (CP):** $99 S; $145–$155 D; $165–$185 ste. Higher rates for special events/hols. Parking: Outdoor, free. Corporate rates and special packages avail. AE, DC, MC, V.

RESTAURANT ▥

♣ Restaurant

In The Bernards Inn, 27 Mine Brook Rd; tel 908/766-0002. Across from Bernardsville train station. **New American/French.** Rich hues of forest green and eggshell, complemented by mahogany and polished brass, set a refined tone at this turn-of-the-century restaurant. The kitchen specializes in progressive American cuisine with a French touch: grilled eggplant and Montrachet cheese on a champagne roll, grilled Atlantic salmon with pinot noir sauce, grilled magret of duck. The wine list includes over 100 labels. **FYI:** Reservations recommended. Jazz/piano. Jacket required. **Open:** Lunch Mon–Sat 11:30am–3pm; dinner Mon–Thurs 5:30–10pm, Fri–Sat 5:30–11pm. **Prices:** Main courses $21–$28. AE, CB, DC, MC, V. ▰

ATTRACTION ▥

Great Swamp National Wildlife Refuge

Off Pleasant Plains Rd, Basking Ridge; tel 201/425-1222. Located 2 mi E of Bernardsville. This 7,000-acre swamp (comprised of swamp woodland, hardwood ridges, cattail marsh, and grassland) hosts more than 220 species of birds during the course of the year. White-tailed deer, river otter, muskrat, red fox, opposum, raccoon, and a variety of fish, reptiles, and amphibians also call the refuge home, including the endangered bog turtle and blue-spotted salamander. The best times for visitors to observe wildlife are early morning and late afternoon. **Open:** Daily 8am–sunset. **Free**

Blackwood

This town of some 5,000, located in the SW region of the state, is near to Chews Landing.

MOTEL ▥

▤▤ HoJo Inn Blackwood

832 N Black Horse Pike, 08012; tel 609/228-4040 or toll free 800/446-4656; fax 609/227-7544. Blackwood exit off NJ 42. Humble roadside motel consisting of several two-story buildings grouped around a swimming pool. **Rooms:** 100 rms and stes. CI 2pm/CO noon. Nonsmoking rms avail. First-floor rooms have sliding glass doors; second-floor rooms have balconies with chairs. All units face the pool. **Amenities:** ▥ A/C, cable TV. Some units w/terraces, some w/whirlpools. **Services:** ▨ ▱ ▱ **Facilities:** ▣ ▣ ▱ Whirlpool, washer/dryer. **Rates (CP):** Peak (Apr–Sept) $42–$59 S or D; $105–$125 ste. Extra person $7. Children under age 16 stay free. Lower rates off-season. Parking: Outdoor, free. AE, DC, DISC, MC, V.

Bordentown

Settled in 1682, just south of Trenton on the Delaware River, Bordentown is the western terminus of the Old Delaware and Raritan Canal. Home of the Clara Barton School (built in 1739), now a Red Cross Memorial. **Information:** Greater Bordentown Chamber of Commerce, PO Box 65, Bordentown, 08505 (tel 609/298-7774).

MOTELS ▥

▤▤ Best Western Inn Bordentown

US 206 and Dunn's Mill Rd, 08505; tel 609/298-6100 or toll free 800/528-1234; fax 609/291-9757. Exit 7 off NJ Tpk. The lobby and pool are inside a circular building fronted with glass bricks to let the sun shine in; the rooms themselves are in more prosaic two-story buildings. **Rooms:** 101 rms. CI 2pm/CO noon. Nonsmoking rms avail. Thick carpeting. **Amenities:** ▥ ▯ A/C, cable TV w/movies, refrig. Video games. **Services:** ▨ ▱ ▱ **Facilities:** ▣ ▣ ▱ ▣ ▱ 1 restaurant (dinner only), 1 bar, volleyball, spa, sauna, steam rm, whirlpool. Barbecue pits, picnic tables. **Rates (CP):** Peak (May–Sept) $80–$110 S; $85–$150 D. Extra person $10. Children under age 16 stay free. Min stay special events. Lower rates off-season. Parking: Outdoor, free. AE, CB, DC, DISC, ER, MC, V.

▤▤ Days Inn Bordentown

1073 US 206, 08505; tel 609/298-6100 or toll free 800/329-7466; fax 609/298-7509. Exit 7 off NJ Tpk. The lobby, with its restaurant and bar, is detached from the main building, and the entire property faces the highway. **Rooms:** 130 rms. CI 2pm/CO 11am. Nonsmoking rms avail. **Amenities:** ▥ A/C, cable TV, refrig. **Services:** ✗ ▨ ▱ ▱

Facilities: 🛗 🚪 ⅙ 1 restaurant (bkfst and dinner only), 1 bar (w/entertainment), games rm, washer/dryer. **Rates:** Peak (Mem Day–Labor Day) $75–$85 S; $85–$95 D. Extra person $10. Children under age 12 stay free. Lower rates off-season. Parking: Outdoor, free. AE, CB, DC, DISC, JCB, MC, V.

Bridgeport

Located in the SW region of the state near the Delaware River, it is the home of Bridgeport Speedway and is near to Logan Pond Wildlife Management Area.

HOTEL 🏨

🏳🏳🏳 Holiday Inn Bridgeport

Center Square Rd, PO Box 304, 08014; tel 609/467-3322 or toll free 800/942-4429; fax 609/467-3031. Exit 10 off I-295. Exceptionally pretty lobby and public areas distinguish this conference hotel located in an industrial complex right off the interstate. **Rooms:** 149 rms and stes. Executive level. CI 3pm/CO noon. Nonsmoking rms avail. East side rooms have views of the woods; west side units face the interstate. **Amenities:** 🛁 🔥 📺 🍴 A/C, satel TV w/movies, dataport, voice mail. Some units w/terraces, some w/whirlpools. **Services:** ✕ 🔑 🚗 🛏 ⤶ Car-rental desk. **Facilities:** 🛗 📹 🏊 🖥 ⅙ 1 restaurant, 1 bar (w/entertainment), basketball, volleyball, games rm, spa, whirlpool, washer/dryer. **Rates:** $89–$99 S or D; $135–$175 ste. MAP rates avail. Parking: Outdoor, free. AE, CB, DC, DISC, JCB, MC, V.

Bridgeton

Settled in 1829, Bridgeton boasts a 1,100-acre zoo and the state's largest historic district, with more than 2,200 homes and public buildings from the colonial, federal, and Victorian periods. Seat of Cumberland County. **Information:** Bridgeton Area Chamber of Commerce, PO Box 100, Bridgeton, 08302 (tel 609/455-1312).

ATTRACTIONS 🏛

New Sweden Farmstead/Museum

Bridgeton City Park; tel 609/455-9785. Commemorates pioneer Swedish and Finnish settlements in this area. The farmstead has seven re-creations of log structures, including a blacksmith shop, a storehouse, a threshing barn, a stable, and a period residence, all outfitted with antique furnishings and farm equipment of Swedish-Finnish origin. **Open:** Apr–Sept, call for tour information. **$**

Nail Mill Museum

1 Mayor Aitken Dr, Bridgeton City Park; tel 609/455-4100. Built in 1815, this building served as the office for the old Cumberland Nail & Iron Works, the principal industry in town from 1815 to 1899. Many of the exhibits relate to the nail factory, but there are also displays about other early industries in Bridgeton, notably glass and pottery. **Open:** Mar–Dec, Tues–Sun 10:30am–3:30pm. **Free**

Brigantine

See Atlantic City

Burlington

Best known as the birthplace of James Fenimore Cooper, the town features a historic district dating from 1677. It was here that Benjamin Franklin learned the printing trade and printed the first colonial money in 1726. **Information:** Greater Burlington Chamber of Commerce, PO Box 67, Burlington, 08016 (tel 609/387-0335).

RESTAURANT 🍴

Cafe Gallery

219 High St; tel 609/386-6150. Exit 47B off I-295, follow NJ 541 to the Delaware River. **Continental/French.** This Federal-era building, part of the town's riverfront renaissance, is both an art gallery and a restaurant. It overlooks the Delaware River and food is served beside the fountain on the patio during the pleasant months. Escargots, stuffed mushrooms, shrimp thermidor, and filet mignon are superior. **FYI:** Reservations recommended. **Open:** Lunch Mon–Sat 11:30am–4pm; dinner Sun–Thurs 5–10pm, Fri–Sat 5–11pm; brunch Sun 11:30am–3pm. **Prices:** Main courses $14–$22. AE, CB, DC, MC, V. 🍷 🏞 ⅙

Camden

See also Mount Laurel

A city of some 90,000 on the Delaware River directly opposite Philadelphia, Camden was settled in 1681. It is a commercial and manufacturing center (the headquarters of Campbell Soup Company is here), and was the final home and burial site of poet Walt Whitman.

REFRESHMENT STOP ☕

Giumarello's

512 Station Ave, Haddon Heights; tel 609/547-9393. Exit 29 off I-295. **Cafe/Italian.** Foccacia bread is the specialty of this fine Italian bakery tucked away on a small shopping street. The bread can be topped with tomato and onion, spinach and pine nuts, or other garnishes. There's also an assortment of cakes and *pasterios,* as well as chocolate-covered pretzels and cappuccino. **Open:** Tues–Wed 7am–8pm, Thurs 7am–9pm, Fri–Sat 7am–9:30pm, Sun 7am–4pm. Closed July 3–July 10. No CC. 🅿 ⅙

ATTRACTIONS 🖼

Thomas H Kean New Jersey State Aquarium

1 Riverside Dr; tel 609/365-3300. The main attraction here is the 76,000-gallon tank, the second-largest indoor aquarium in the country. Specators sit on the amphitheater-style seating around the tank, which contains sharks, rockfish, a shipwreck, and a mock-up of the underwater Hudson canyon off the Jersey coast. (Three times a day, a diver answers visitors' questions through a "scuba phone.") Also located on the first floor is an open-air New Jersey beach setting, complete with shorebirds, a pine barrens stream, and salt marsh. The second floor features "Dangers of the Deep," with more than 30 sharks in residence. There are touch tanks on both floors, and a 170,000-gallon tank housing nine Atlantic seals is located outside. **Open:** Daily 9:30am–5:30pm. **$$$$**

Walt Whitman House

330 Mickle Blvd; tel 609/964-5383. The great American poet Walt Whitman bought this house in 1884, when he was 54. It was the first and last house he ever owned, and he died here in 1892. On display are manuscripts, personal items, documents, and photographs chronicling Whitman's long career. **Open:** Wed–Sat 9am–noon and 1–4:30pm, Sun 1–4pm. **Free**

Cape May

See also Stone Harbor, Wildwood

One of the nation's oldest seaside resorts, featuring more than 250 Victorian buildings and numerous B&Bs. Attractions include Sunset Beach, Cape May Point Lighthouse, and the Cape May Bird Observatory. The Cape May–Lewes (DE) ferry connects New Jersey's southernmost point with the Delmarva Peninsula, phone 800/64-FERRY for information. The nearby historic village of Cold Springs features a recreation of a 19th-century farming community. **Information:** Cape May County Dept of Tourism, PO Box 365, Cape May Courthouse, 08210 (tel 609/886-0901).

HOTELS 🏨

≣ Chalfonte Hotel

301 Howard St, PO Box 475, 08204; tel 609/884-8409; fax 609/884-4588. From Garden State Pkwy, left on Madison, right on Columbia to Howard. This 120-year-old spot is one of the oldest hostelries in Cape May. The place is supposedly haunted by ghosts, and many families return generation after generation to bestow affection, if not paint, on the old building. **Rooms:** 80 rms; 2 cottages/villas. CI 2pm/CO 11am. No smoking. **Amenities:** No A/C, phone, or TV. **Services:** 🛎 🖾 🍴 Children's program, babysitting. **Facilities:** ⌐70⌐ 1 restaurant (bkfst and dinner only), 2 bars (1 w/entertainment), playground. Oft-praised dining room serves Southern cuisine. Children's dining room for age six and under. **Rates (MAP):** $60–$120 S; $133–$170 D; $133–

$300 cottage/villa. Extra person $25. Children under age 2 stay free. Min stay wknds. AP and MAP rates avail. Closed Oct 25–May 25. MC, V.

≣ The Grand Hotel of Cape May

1045 Beach Dr, 08204; tel 609/884-5611 or toll free 800/257-8550. Garden State Pkwy to right on Madison to Beach. Not so grand as the name, this beachfront hotel could use some refurbishing and a decorator's touch. **Rooms:** 220 rms, stes, and effic. Executive level. CI 2pm/CO 11am. Adequate but nondescript. **Amenities:** 🛅 A/C, cable TV, refrig. Some units w/terraces. **Services:** 🛎 🖾 🍴 Babysitting. Fax service available. **Facilities:** ⌐⌐ ⌐700⌐ 🖥 ⅙ 1 restaurant, 1 bar (w/entertainment), 1 beach (ocean), lifeguard, games rm, spa, sauna, whirlpool, beauty salon, washer/dryer. **Rates:** Peak (May–Oct) $110–$135 S or D; $210–$290 ste; $125–$165 effic. Extra person $10. Children under age 2 stay free. Min stay wknds. Lower rates off-season. Parking: Indoor/outdoor, free. Minimum stay sometimes required. Closed Dec 24–Dec 26. AE, DC, MC, V.

MOTELS

≣≣ La Mer Motor Inn

1317 Beach Ave, 08204; tel 609/884-9000; fax 609/884-5004. From Garden State Pkwy, left on Madison, left on Beach. Pleasant motel right across the street from the beach. **Rooms:** 67 rms. CI 2pm/CO 11am. **Amenities:** 🛅 ⅙ 🍴 A/C, cable TV, refrig. All units w/terraces. **Services:** 🍴 Babysitting. **Facilities:** ⌐⌐ 1 restaurant (dinner only; *see* "Restaurants" below), 1 beach (ocean), lifeguard, playground, washer/dryer. **Rates:** Peak (July–Aug) $115–$129 S; $126–$155 D. Extra person $15. Children under age 2 stay free. Min stay wknds. Lower rates off-season. Parking: Outdoor, free. $10 extra for children over age 2. Closed Nov–Apr. AE, CB, DC, DISC, MC, V.

≣≣ Montreal Inn

Beach and Madison Aves, 08204; tel 609/884-7011 or toll free 800/525-7011; fax 609/884-4559. From Garden State Pkwy, left on Madison, right on Beach Ave. This cozy, comfortable motel is popular with families due to its array of recreational facilities. **Rooms:** 70 rms, stes, and effic. CI 2pm/CO 11am. Nonsmoking rms avail. **Amenities:** 🛅 🖵 🍴 A/C, cable TV w/movies, refrig. All units w/terraces. Efficiencies have two TVs. **Services:** ✕ 🖾 🛎 🖾 🍴 Masseur, babysitting. **Facilities:** ⌐⌐ 🏌 ⌐30⌐ 1 restaurant, 1 bar, 1 beach (ocean), lifeguard, games rm, sauna, whirlpool, washer/dryer. Miniature golf, shuffleboard, barbecue grills, beach access. **Rates:** Peak (June–Aug) $59–$87 S; $85–$120 D; $85–$120 ste; $99–$143 effic. Extra person $6–$8. Lower rates off-season. Parking: Outdoor, free. Closed Dec–Feb. AE, DISC, MC, V.

≣≣ Periwinkle Inn

1039 Beach Ave, 08204; tel 609/884-9200. Garden State Pkwy to Madison, left to Beach, then right. Oddly pleasant architectural flourishes attract the eye to this otherwise standard motel across from the beach. **Rooms:** 50 rms, stes, and effic. CI 3pm/CO 11am. **Amenities:** ☎ ⚲ A/C, cable TV w/movies, refrig, voice mail. All units w/terraces. **Services:** ⚬ Babysitting. **Facilities:** ⚲ ⚬ **Rates:** Peak (June–Sept) $111–$136 S or D; $140–$235 ste; $140–$235 effic. Extra person $15. Children under age 1 stay free. Min stay peak. Lower rates off-season. Parking: Outdoor, free. Closed Oct 20–Apr 5. No CC.

INNS

☰☰☰☰ The Abbey

34 Gurney St at Columbia Ave, 08204; tel 609/884-4506; fax 609/884-2379. Garden State Pkwy to left on Madison, right on Columbia. Built in 1869 by a coal tycoon, this aqua-colored Victorian has been beautifully restored by owners Jay and Marianne Schatz but it still has a very old-fashioned air. The rooms also have distinct, pleasant personalities. Unsuitable for children under 12. **Rooms:** 14 rms and stes; 1 cottage/villa. CI 2pm/CO 11am. No smoking. Original 1869 showers, clawfoot bathtubs, stenciled-glass windows, and pullchain toilets. **Amenities:** ⚲ A/C, refrig, bathrobes. No phone or TV. **Services:** ☎ Babysitting, afternoon tea served. Breakfast is buffet style in summer. Tours and tea at 4pm on Mon, Wed, and Fri. **Facilities:** ⟮15⟯ Guest lounge. Grand piano in parlor. **Rates (BB):** Peak (June–Sept) $90–$185 D; $110–$185 ste. Min stay wknds. Lower rates off-season. Parking: Outdoor, free. Extended-stay discounts avail. Closed Jan–Mar. DISC, MC, V.

☰☰ Angel of the Sea

5 Trenton Ave, 08204; tel 609/884-3369 or toll free 800/848-3369, fax 609/884-3331. From Garden State Pkwy, right on Madison, left on Beach Dr, left on Trenton. Angels are everywhere—in paintings, sculptures, and even music boxes—in these two pink-and-white Victorian buildings connected by a common porch. Unsuitable for children under 7. **Rooms:** 27 rms. CI 2pm/CO 11am. No smoking. **Amenities:** ☎ ⚲ Cable TV. No A/C. Some units w/terraces. **Services:** ☎ Afternoon tea and wine/sherry served. **Facilities:** ⟮12⟯ Guest lounge w/TV. The owners have published a cookbook. **Rates (BB):** Peak (May–Oct) $95–$285 S or D. Extra person $50. Min stay wknds and special events. Lower rates off-season. Parking: Outdoor, free. MC, V.

☰☰☰ Carroll Villa Hotel

19 Jackson St, 08204; tel 609/884-9619; fax 609/884-0264. Straight at end of Garden State Pkwy, left on Jackson. This was the first of the Cape May Victorian houses to be remodeled with all the modern amenities. **Rooms:** 22 rms. CI 2pm/CO 11am. No smoking. Antique furnishings lend an air of authenticity. **Amenities:** ☎ ⚲ A/C, dataport, bathrobes. No TV. 1 unit w/terrace. **Services:** ⚬ Babysitting. **Facilities:** ⟮50⟯ 1 restaurant (see "Restaurants" below), guest lounge w/TV. Small private garden. **Rates (BB):** Peak (Mem Day–Labor Day) $90–$125 S; $100–$135 D. Extra person $20.

Children under age 3 stay free. Min stay wknds. Lower rates off-season. Higher rates for special events/hols. MAP rates avail. Parking: Outdoor, free. MC, V.

☰☰☰ Colvmns by the Sea

1513 Beach Dr, 08204; tel 609/884-2228. From Garden State Pkwy, left on Madison, left on Beach Dr. The inventor of calamine lotion spread some of his fortune on this Italian Renaissance mansion in 1905. The property is now a delightful inn, with large public areas and rooms decorated with Victorian furnishings. **Rooms:** 11 rms and stes. CI 2pm/CO 11am. No smoking. Most rooms have ocean views. **Amenities:** Cable TV, refrig, bathrobes. No A/C or phone. TVs in rooms on request. **Services:** ☎ ⚲ Twice-daily maid svce, afternoon tea and wine/sherry served. **Facilities:** ⟮35⟯ 1 beach (ocean), lifeguard, washer/dryer, guest lounge w/TV. Ocean-front sitting rooms on each floor. Complimentary Sunday brunch at nearby Peter Shields restaurant. **Rates (BB):** Peak (May–Sept) $130–$215 S; $140–$225 D; $225 ste. Extra person $40. Children under age 18 stay free. Min stay. Lower rates off-season. Parking: Outdoor, free. MC, V.

☰☰☰☰ Mainstay Inn

635 Columbia Ave, 08204; tel 609/884-8690. From Garden State Pkwy, left on Madison, right on Columbia. A barrage of media praise makes it essential to reserve a room well in advance at this wonderfully restored inn. Unsuitable for children under 12. **Rooms:** 16 rms and stes. CI 2pm/CO 11am. No smoking. Rooms are authentically appointed and furnished in fine antiques, and are named after famous Cape May guests. **Amenities:** ⚲ A/C. No phone or TV. Some units w/terraces, some w/fireplaces, some w/whirlpools. **Services:** ☎ Babysitting, afternoon tea served. Full breakfast in spring and fall; continental breakfast in summer. **Facilities:** ⟮14⟯ ⚬ Lawn games, guest lounge. **Rates (CP):** Peak (June–Sept) $140–$200 S; $140–$250 D; $195–$250 ste. Extra person $35. Min stay peak and wknds. Lower rates off-season. Parking: Outdoor, free. No CC.

☰☰☰☰ The Queen Victoria

102 Ocean St, 08204; tel 609/884-8702. From Garden State Pkwy, right on Ocean St. One of the town's most popular hostelries, this bed-and-breakfast complex has three pristine buildings, including a cottage. **Rooms:** 23 rms and stes; 3 cottages/villas. CI 2pm/CO 11am. No smoking. Some rooms have ceiling fans. **Amenities:** ⚲ A/C, cable TV, refrig. No phone. Some units w/terraces, some w/fireplaces, some w/whirlpools. **Services:** ✗ ☎ ⚲ ⚬ Twice-daily maid svce, masseur, babysitting, afternoon tea and wine/sherry served. Complimentary beach towels and chairs. **Facilities:** ⟮15⟯ Washer/dryer, guest lounge w/TV. **Rates (BB):** $65–$155 S; $115–$250 ste. Extra person $20. Min stay. Higher rates for special events/hols. MC, V.

☰☰☰ Virginia Hotel

25 Jackson St, 08204; tel 609/884-5700 or toll free 800/732-4236; fax 609/884-1236. Straight at end of Garden

State Pkwy, left on Jackson. This 1879 Victorian inn elicits superlatives from its guests, many of whom return each year. **Rooms:** 24 rms. CI 3pm/CO noon. Comfortable, modern rooms. Proprietors claim to have the "best mattresses in Cape May." **Amenities:** 🛏 🐾 A/C, cable TV w/movies, dataport, VCR, bathrobes. Some units w/terraces. **Services:** ✗ ☛ VP 🛎 Twice-daily maid svce. **Facilities:** 🍽 💻 1 restaurant (dinner only; *see* "Restaurants" below), 1 bar (w/entertainment), guest lounge. **Rates (CP):** Peak (June–Sept) $86–$260 S or D. Extra person $20. Children under age 12 stay free. Min stay wknds. Lower rates off-season. Higher rates for special events/hols. AP and MAP rates avail. Parking: Outdoor, free. Three-night minimum if stay includes a Saturday. Closed Jan. AE, CB, DC, DISC, MC, V.

RESTAURANTS 🍴

⑤ Bradbury's
In The Doctor's Inn, 2 N Main St, Cape May Court House; tel 609/463-9330. On US 9. **New American/Continental.** This neglected mansion was meticulously restored and now has individual dining rooms and a growing reputation. Lamb ragoût (with roasted peppers, goat cheese, and intense raspberry lamb essence) and Rising Sun Flounder (with shrimp, wontons, and crab cakes) are exemplary. **FYI:** Reservations recommended. Piano. Dress code. BYO. No smoking. **Open:** Peak (June–Aug) lunch Mon–Fri 11am–2:30pm; dinner Wed–Sat 5–10pm; brunch Sun 11am–2pm. **Prices:** Main courses $17–$29. AE, MC, V. 💙 🍽 ♿

♣ The Ebbitt Room
In the Virginia Hotel, 25 Jackson St; tel 609/884-5700. Off Garden State Pkwy. **New American/Regional American.** Grilled salmon, bourbon-glazed country-style chicken, and boneless loin of venison get rave reviews from local residents. **FYI:** Reservations recommended. Piano. Dress code. No smoking. **Open:** Daily 5–10pm. Closed Jan. **Prices:** Main courses $18–$26. AE, CB, DC, DISC, MC, V. 🍽 VP

410 Bank Street
410 Bank St; tel 609/884-2127. **Seafood/Louisiana French.** One of the reasons Cape May is known as a dining town, this popular, innovative restaurant wins awards on a regular basis for items such as swordfish with champagne, crabmeat served in cream sauce, and blackened, home-smoked Black Angus prime rib. Edible flowers grown by the chef's wife add color to the plate. The inside dining room has paper tablecloths for scribbling. **FYI:** Reservations recommended. Children's menu. BYO. **Open:** Peak (June–Aug) daily 5pm–midnight. Closed Oct 21–Apr. **Prices:** Main courses $19–$26. AE, CB, DC, DISC, MC, V. 💙 🍴 ♥

Frescos
412 Bank St; tel 609/884-0366. **Italian.** The decor is simple and the food at this family-owned eatery has received many accolades. Items include filet mignon in spicy Chianti demiglacé, fettuccine with shrimp and scallops in fresh tomato-cream sauce, and slow-braised osso buco. The garlic bread is exceptional. **FYI:** Reservations recommended. Children's menu. Dress code. BYO. **Open:** Peak (June–Aug) daily 5pm–midnight. Closed Dec–Apr. **Prices:** Main courses $14–$22. AE, CB, DC, DISC, MC, V. 💙 ♥

The Mad Batter Restaurant
In the Carroll Villa Hotel, 19 Jackson St; tel 609/884-9619. Straight at end of Garden State Pkwy, left on Jackson St. **New American/Eclectic.** One of the pioneers of the Cape May dining renaissance. Oriental lamb dumplings, eggplant ravioli, and clam chowder (some say the area's best) star on the changeable menu. **FYI:** Reservations recommended. Children's menu. BYO. No smoking. **Open:** Breakfast daily 8am–2:30pm; dinner Mon–Thurs 5:30–10pm, Fri–Sat 5:30–11pm; brunch Sun 8am–2:30pm. Closed Jan. **Prices:** Main courses $15–$23. DISC, MC, V. 🍴 🍴

♣ Maureen
Beach and Decatur Sts; tel 609/884-3774. Garden State Pkwy to right on Jackson, right on Beach. **International.** The ocean and promenade stretch out below the porch. Adventuresome entree choices include tuna crusted with nori, ginger, and wasabi, and covered in a shiitake mushroom and jasmine tea sauce; and lobster, shrimp, and crab with fresh basil and plum tomatoes. Maureen herself greets the guests. **FYI:** Reservations recommended. Dress code. No smoking. **Open:** Peak (July–Aug) Tues–Sun 5–10pm. Closed Nov–Mar. **Prices:** Main courses $18–$26. AE, DC, DISC, MC, V. 💙

Merion Inn
106 Decatur St; tel 609/884-8363. From Garden State Pkwy, left on Jackson, left on Beach, left on Decatur. **Seafood.** This is the oldest continuously operated restaurant in town, but what is more impressive is that the quality of the food has remained consistently high. Classics include steak or seafood with various toppings; spices, and sauces (such as crab imperial or smoked salmon and asparagus on fettuccine). Dining on the porch is especially pleasant. **FYI:** Reservations accepted. Children's menu. Dress code. **Open:** Peak (July–Sept) lunch daily noon–2:30pm; dinner daily 5–10pm. Closed Jan–Mar. **Prices:** Main courses $13–$32; prix fixe $14. AE, DC, DISC, MC, V. 💙 🍴 ♥

Peter Shields Restaurant
1301 Beach Dr; tel 609/884-6491. **Continental/French.** This talented chef provided the cuisine for several local restaurants before setting up his own place. Favored main courses include pecan-encrusted rack of lamb, Maryland crab cakes, and a smoked fish duo. **FYI:** Reservations recommended. Guitar/piano. Jacket required. BYO. **Open:** Peak (Apr–Oct) dinner daily 5–11pm; brunch Sun 10am–2pm. **Prices:** Main courses $18–$25. AE, CB, DC, DISC, MC, V. 💙

♣ Washington Inn
801 Washington St; tel 609/884-5697. Garden State Pkwy, left on Madison, right on Washington. **Regional American/Seafood.** A cellar of some 8,500 wines plus a reputation for excellent food make this one of the most impressive opera-

tions in the region. Gardens, porches, and soft music complement the dining. Flounder Jefferson, veal chop, and fresh Atlantic salmon are top entree choices. **FYI:** Reservations recommended. Children's menu. Dress code. **Open:** Peak (May–Oct) daily 5–10pm. Closed Jan–Feb 15. **Prices:** Main courses $18–$25; prix fixe $35–$55. AE, CB, DC, DISC, MC, V. ● �C

Waters Edge

In La Mer Motor Inn, Beach Dr and Pittsburgh Ave; tel 609/884-1717. From Garden State Pkwy, left on Madison, left on Beach. **Regional American/Eclectic.** This kitchen is on the cutting edge of dining, serving dishes such as grilled breast of duck marinated in Szechuan sauce, and sautéed Hudson Valley fois gras. The bar stocks a remarkable collection of single malt scotches, beers, and vodkas. Caviar-by-the-ounce is also available, and the ocean views are free. **FYI:** Reservations recommended. Children's menu. Dress code. No smoking. **Open:** Peak (July–Aug) daily 4–11pm. Closed Jan–Feb 10. **Prices:** Main courses $16–$24. AE, CB, DC, DISC, MC, V. ● ▲ ㅎ

ATTRACTIONS 🖾

Historic Cold Spring Village

720 US 9; tel 609/898-2300. A living history re-creation of a southern Jersey farm community. Although it never existed as a real village, all the buildings here—craft shops, country store, restaurant—are genuine period structures that were moved here from their original sites. Events at Cold Spring Village include sheepshearing demonstrations, square dancing, and a harvest festival with corn grinding, open-hearth cooking, and bread making. **Open:** Peak (June–Labor Day) daily. Reduced hours off-season. Closed Oct–May.

The Emlen Physick Estate

1048 Washington St; tel 609/884-5404 or toll free 800/275-4278. Designed by Frank Furness, a famous Philadelphia architect, in 1879. The exterior of the house features elaborate chimneys, dormers, and elaborate trim. The 18-room interior is no less stunning; highlights include a dining room table set for a Victorian dinner, the personal belongings of a Victorian gentleman, and the quarters of the servants who worked in the home. **Open:** Peak (Mar–Dec) daily. Reduced hours off-season. $$$

Cape May Point State Park

Lighthouse Ave; tel 609/884-2159. The park features 300 acres of freshwater marshland, woodland, and beaches where visitors can picnic, fish, or hike. During spring and fall migration periods, bird-watchers can spot songbirds, waterfowl, shorebirds, and birds of prey. A self-guided nature tour gives visitors the opportunity to look at all species of birds, plants, reptiles, amphibians, and wildflowers. (Coded markers along the trail correspond with the tour booklet, which is available at the visitors center).

Visitors driving into the park on Lighthouse Ave will pass the **Cape May lighthouse,** built in 1859 and still in operation.

The lighthouse is open daily during the summer to allow guests to climb upstairs to the gallery and see the panoramic view (additional fee charged). **Open:** Daily sunrise–sunset. Free

Cape May Court House

See Cape May

Chatham

Settled in 1749, Chatham is located 10 miles west of Newark on the Passaic River. **Information:** Chatham Area Chamber of Commerce, PO Box 231, Chatham, 07928 (tel 201/635-2444).

RESTAURANTS 🍴

★ Fresh Fields Cafe

In Hickory Square Mall, 641 Shunpike Rd; tel 201/337-4072. At LaFayette Ave. **New American.** Naive paintings of single vegetables surround a compact dining room at this tiny shopfront cafe. The imaginative menu emphasizes fresh ingredients, and includes paillards of lamb and fresh catch-of-the-day. **FYI:** Reservations not accepted. No liquor license. No smoking. **Open:** Lunch Tues–Fri noon–2pm; dinner Tues–Sun 5:30–9pm. **Prices:** Main courses $17–$23. MC, V.

The Townsquare Inn

In Townsquare Mall, 6 Roosevelt Ave; tel 201/701-0303. Off Main St. **New American.** Bright and contemporary decor, centered around a large fireplace. Creative main dishes—like pan-seared, poached, or roasted fish of the day—are prepared with the freshest ingredients and served alongside an unusual array of vegetables. There's a killer dessert cart too. **FYI:** Reservations recommended. Jazz/piano. Jacket required. No smoking. **Open:** Lunch Mon–Sat noon–2pm; dinner Mon–Sat 6–9:30pm. **Prices:** Main courses $20–$27. AE, MC, V. ● ▣ ㅎ

Cherry Hill

An eastern suburb of Camden, with easy access to Atlantic City and Philadelphia. Site of Scarborough Covered Bridge, one of only two covered bridges remaining in the state. **Information:** Greater Cherry Hill Chamber of Commerce, 1060 Kings Hwy N, Cherry Hill, 08034 (tel 609/667-1600).

HOTELS 🏨

🗏 🗏 🗏 Holiday Inn Cherry Hill

NJ 70 and Sayer Ave, 08002; tel 609/663-5300 or toll free 800/465-4329; fax 609/663-5300 ext 7731. A six-story building right across from Garden State Park. Fine for an overnight stay but if you're looking for a secluded location, look elsewhere. **Rooms:** 185 rms. CI 3pm/CO noon. Non-smoking rms avail. Most rooms are nonsmoking; rooms facing west overlook train tracks. **Amenities:** 🛅 🐾 🖭 A/C, satel TV w/movies, dataport. **Services:** ✗ 🖾 🗘 🐾 Car-rental desk. **Facilities:** 🛱 🍴 🖾 ⅚ 2 restaurants, 1 bar (w/entertainment), spa, sauna, steam rm, washer/dryer. Fitness center with TVs. Pool is small, but is said to be the only indoor one in town. **Rates:** $89–$97 S or D. Children under age 19 stay free. Parking: Outdoor, free. AE, CB, DC, DISC, JCB, MC, V.

≣≣≣ Marriott Residence Inn Cherry Hill
1821 Old Cuthbert Rd, 08034; tel 609/429-6111 or toll free 800/331-3131; fax 609/429-0345. Exit 34A (NJ 70) off I-295. The buildings resemble a condominium complex, and the clientele is primarily business people who are in the area on extended assignments. **Rooms:** 96 effic. Executive level. CI 3pm/CO noon. Nonsmoking rms avail. **Amenities:** 🛅 🐾 🖭 A/C, cable TV w/movies, refrig, dataport. Some units w/terraces, some w/fireplaces. Videotape library in the lobby. **Services:** 🍴 🖾 🗘 🐾 Car-rental desk, babysitting. **Facilities:** 🛱 🍴 🖾 ⅚ Basketball, spa, whirlpool, playground, washer/dryer. Full access to tennis and health club next door. Sand volleyball court. **Rates (CP):** $75–$160 effic. Children under age 18 stay free. Parking: Outdoor, free. AE, CB, DC, DISC, JCB, MC, V.

RESTAURANT 🍴

Caffé Aldo Lamberti
2011 NJ 70 W; tel 609/663-1747. Exit 34B off I-295/Exit 4 off NJ Tpk. **Italian/Seafood.** Off the busy suburban main drag, this dining room feels like an Italian garden, filled with trees and greenery and exquisitely set marble tables. The menu is more contemporary than traditional, albeit with a few of the classic dishes. Homemade pastas, fresh seafood, and organic chicken selections are popular main courses; the large wine list focuses on Californian and Italian labels. **FYI:** Reservations recommended. Jazz. **Open:** Daily 11am–11:30pm. **Prices:** Main courses $11–$19. AE, CB, DC, DISC, MC, V. 🌑 🖤 🆅🅿 ⅚

Cliffside Park

This Hudson River town is named for its location on the Palisades, the cliffs lining the west bank of the river.

REFRESHMENT STOP 🗗

★ Bertolotti
738 Anderson Ave; tel 201/941-9298. About 2 mi off Fort Lee Rd/Main St. **Desserts.** Espresso and cappuccino complemented by specialty cheesecakes, gelati, sorbets, spumoni,

tortoni, tartufi, and chocolate-dipped cannoli. Low-fat ice creams and fat-free sorbets, too. **Open:** Peak (June–Aug) Sun–Thurs 11am–11pm, Fri–Sat 11am–1am. No CC.

Clifton

This city of some 72,000 residents is a center for high-tech industries, including medical research, aerospace, and telecommunications. **Information:** North Jersey Chamber of Commerce, 1033 Rte 46 E, PO Box 110, Clifton, 07011 (tel 201/470-9300).

HOTEL 🏨

UNRATED Howard Johnson Lodge
680 NJ 3 W, 07014; tel 201/471-3800 or toll free 800/654-2000; fax 201/471-2128. Housed in a relatively new, Spanish stucco–style building in a mixed industrial and residential area, this hotel caters to both families and business travelers. **Rooms:** 116 rms and stes. CI 2pm/CO 11am. Nonsmoking rms avail. **Amenities:** 🛅 🐾 A/C, cable TV w/movies. Some units w/terraces. Complimentary morning newspaper. **Services:** 🖾 🗘 Car-rental desk, masseur. **Facilities:** 🛱 🖾 ⅚ 1 restaurant, 1 bar. **Rates (CP):** $79–$89 S or D; $105–$110 ste. Extra person $10. Children under age 12 stay free. Min stay special events. Parking: Outdoor, free. Extended-stay rates avail. AE, CB, DC, DISC, MC, V.

East Brunswick

Located on the Raritan River, this township of some 45,000 was founded in 1860. Nearby to Farrington Lake and Pigeon Swamp State Park.

HOTEL 🏨

≣≣≣≣ Brunswick Hilton & Towers
3 Tower Center Blvd, 08816; tel 908/828-2000 or toll free 800/HILTONS; fax 908/828-6958. Exit 9 off NJ Tpk to NJ 18 N to Tower Center Blvd. A luxurious lobby, a restaurant with a five-star chef, a health spa, and a sports bar comprise the public areas of this large hotel. The rooms are less dramatic. **Rooms:** 405 rms and stes. Executive level. CI 4pm/CO noon. Nonsmoking rms avail. **Amenities:** 🛅 🐾 🖭 A/C, cable TV w/movies, refrig, dataport, voice mail, bathrobes. All units w/minibars, some w/whirlpools. Nice touches include shaving/makeup mirrors and washlines. **Services:** 🍴 🗝 🆅🅿 🚐 🖾 🗘 Car-rental desk, masseur, children's program, babysitting. **Facilities:** 🛱 🏊 🍴 🖾 💻 ⅚ 1 restaurant, 3 bars, games rm, spa, sauna, whirlpool. **Rates:** Peak (Mar 5–June) $120–$180 S; $140–$200 D; $270–$875 ste. Extra person $15. Children under age 12 stay free. Lower rates off-season. MAP rates avail. Parking: Outdoor, free. AE, CB, DC, DISC, MC, V.

MOTEL

≣≣ Ramada Inn

195 NJ 185, 08816; tel 908/828-6900 or toll free 800/
272-6252; fax 908/937-4838. Exit 9 off NJ Tpk to NJ 18 S. A
basic chain motel with a convenient location. **Rooms:** 136
rms. CI 3pm/CO noon. Nonsmoking rms avail. **Amenities:** 🛅
🛁 📺 A/C, cable TV w/movies, refrig. **Services:** ✕ VP 🖎 🖘
Facilities: 🔧 🖳 250 🕭 1 restaurant, 1 bar, washer/dryer.
Small exercise room. Outdoor pool abuts the highway. **Rates:**
Peak (May–Aug) $125 S; $135 D. Extra person $10. Children
under age 18 stay free. Min stay. Lower rates off-season. AP
rates avail. Parking: Outdoor, free. AE, MC, V.

East Rutherford

See also Secaucus

North of Newark and just west of Manhattan, East Rutherford offers year-round entertainment for this densely populated area at its Meadowlands Sports Complex, which includes the Meadowlands Racetrack, Giants Stadium, and
Continental Airlines Arena. Home of the NFL's Giants and
Jets, the NBA's Nets, the NHL's Devils, as well as collegiate
sporting events, concerts, and performances. **Information:**
East Brunswick Chamber of Commerce, 24 Brunswick Woods
Dr, PO Box 56, East Brunswick, 08816 (tel 908/257-3009).

HOTELS 🏨

≣≣ Days Inn Meadowlands

850 NJ 120 S, 07073; tel 201/507-5222 or toll free 800/
DAYS-INN; fax 201/507-0744. NJ 3 to NJ 17 N to NJ 120 S
(Patterson Plank Rd E). Renovation of this property was
interrupted in 1996, pending a change in ownership, leaving
the carpeting new but bedspreads worn. **Rooms:** 139 rms. CI
3pm/CO noon. Nonsmoking rms avail. Windows on fourth
and fifth floors do not open. **Amenities:** 🛅 A/C, cable TV.
Some rooms have dataports, coffeemakers, and hair dryers;
refrigerators available on request. Free daily newspaper
delivered to room. **Services:** 🖎 🖘 🥤 **Facilities:** 🖳 55 🕭
1 restaurant (bkfst and dinner only), 1 bar. Coffee shop
occupies most of the lobby. **Rates:** $70 S; $75 D. Extra
person $10. Children under age 16 stay free. Min stay special
events. Parking: Outdoor, free. AE, CB, DC, DISC, MC, V.

≣≣≣ Sheraton Meadowlands Hotel

2 Meadowlands Plaza, 07073; tel 201/896-0500 or toll free
800/325-3535; fax 201/896-9696. Sheraton Plaza Dr exit off
NJ 3 E. This quiet, elegant hotel has an airy lobby and an
efficient, personable staff. **Rooms:** 425 rms and stes. Executive level. CI 3pm/CO 1pm. Nonsmoking rms avail.
Amenities: 🛅 🛁 📺 🍽 A/C, cable TV w/movies, dataport,
voice mail. All units w/minibars. VCRs and refrigerators
available on request. **Services:** ✕ VP 🚐 🖎 🖘 🥤 Babysitting. Poolside food service. **Facilities:** 🔧 🖳 1300 🖥 🕭 1

restaurant, 2 bars, games rm, spa, sauna, whirlpool. Glass-
enclosed pool with sundeck and views of the Manhattan
skyline. **Rates:** Peak (Sept–Dec) $135 S or D; $250–$500 ste.
Extra person $20. Children under age 17 stay free. Min stay
special events. Lower rates off-season. Parking: Outdoor,
free. AE, CB, DC, DISC, EC, ER, JCB, MC, V.

RESTAURANT 🍽

★ Park & Orchard

240 Hackensack St; tel 201/939-9292. NJ 17 S to right on
Union Ave, right on Hackensack St. **Eclectic.** Specialties at
this quaint bistro include grilled seafood, vegetarian entrees,
and stir-fry dishes, and bread baked daily on the premises.
The wine list is the largest in the state, with 1,850 selections.
FYI: Reservations accepted. **Open:** Mon 5–10pm, Tues–Fri
noon–10pm, Sat–Sun 2–9pm. Closed week of July 4. **Prices:**
Main courses $7–$21. AE, CB, DC, DISC, MC, V. 🕭

ATTRACTION 🏛

Meadowlands Sports Complex

50 NJ 120; tel 201/935-3900. A multiple-building entertainment complex featuring the 76,900-seat **Giants Stadium,** the
20,000-seat **Continental Airlines Arena,** and the **Meadowlands Racetrack,** which can accommodate 35,000 people.
Giants Stadium is home of the Jets and Giants of the NFL, as
well as the Metrostars major league soccer team. The stadium
is also used for concerts and other major events.

    Continental Airlines Arena is the home court of the New
Jersey Nets as well as the home ice of the New Jersey Devils.
Roller-hockey, tennis, the circus, concerts, and other events
are also held here. The **Meadowlands Racetrack** (tel 201/
935-8500) is the scene of both thoroughbred and harness
racing, live and simulcast, throughout the year. **Open:** Call
for schedule. $$$$

Eatontown

This borough five miles NW of Asbury Park was settled in
1670. It is nearby to Swimming River Recreational Area and
Fort Monmouth. **Information:** Eastern Monmouth Area
Chamber of Commerce, 170 Broad St, Red Bank, 07701 (tel
908/741-0055).

HOTEL 🏨

≣≣≣ Sheraton Eatontown Hotel

NJ 35 at Industrial Way E, 07724; tel 908/542-6500 or toll
free 800/325-3535; fax 908/542-6607. Exit 105 off Garden
State Pkwy to NJ 35 S. The rooms and public areas at this
hotel are well kept and spacious. **Rooms:** 208 rms and stes.
Executive level. CI 3pm/CO noon. Nonsmoking rms avail.
Amenities: 🛅 🛁 📺 A/C, cable TV w/movies, dataport, voice
mail. Refrigerators available on request. **Services:** ✕ 🗝 🚐
🖎 🖘 Car-rental desk, social director. **Facilities:** 🔧 🖳 500

🖳 ⅋ 2 restaurants, 2 bars (1 w/entertainment), games rm, spa, whirlpool. **Rates:** Peak (May–Sept) $114–$134 S or D; $200–$250 ste. Extra person $10. Children under age 12 stay free. Lower rates off-season. Parking: Outdoor, free. AE, CB, DC, DISC, EC, ER, MC, V.

MOTEL

🗏🗏 Crystal Motor Lodge
170 Main St, 07724; tel 908/542-4900 or toll free 800/562-5290; fax 908/542-1718. NJ 35 S to right on Main St. This simple motel has clean rooms, a nice outdoor pool and a playground, and is convenient to the beaches and a shopping mall. **Rooms:** 77 rms. CI 10am/CO noon. Nonsmoking rms avail. **Amenities:** 🛅 ⅛ 🖭 A/C, cable TV w/movies, refrig, VCR. Some units w/terraces. **Services:** ⌑ 🐕 Babysitting. **Facilities:** 🔔 Playground. **Rates:** Peak (May–Aug) $62 S; $68–$74 D. Extra person $5. Children under age 2 stay free. Lower rates off-season. Parking: Outdoor, free. AE, CB, DC, DISC, MC, V.

Edison

Thomas Edison once lived in this township on the Raritan River, east of New Brunswick, and the town is named for him. **Information:** Edison Chamber of Commerce, PO Box 2103, Edison, 08818 (tel 908/494-0300).

HOTEL 🏨

🗏🗏🗏 Clarion Hotel & Conference Center
2055 Lincoln Hwy, 08817; tel 908/287-3500 or toll free 800/331-6756; fax 908/287-8190. Exit 10 off NJ Tpk to I-287 N to NJ 27 S. An attractive, upscale hotel with beautiful public areas and well-kept rooms. **Rooms:** 169 rms and stes. Executive level. CI 2pm/CO noon. Nonsmoking rms avail. Rooms are larger than average. **Amenities:** 🛅 ⅛ 🖭 🕮 A/C, cable TV w/movies, refrig, dataport. Some units w/terraces. **Services:** ✗ 🗨 ⚠ ⌑ **Facilities:** 🏋 🎱 🛢 🖳 ⅋ 1 restaurant, 1 bar (w/entertainment), spa. **Rates (CP):** $109–$119 S or D; $175–$225 ste. Extra person $10. Children under age 18 stay free. Parking: Outdoor, free. AE, CB, DC, DISC, EC, ER, MC, V.

RESTAURANTS 🍴

Constantine's
1012 Amboy Ave; tel 908/225-0540. Garden State Pkwy to Amboy Ave exit. **French/Health/Spa.** The chef at this cozy spot specializes in classic French and northern Italian cuisine, but is happy to accommodate special dietary needs and personal favorites. **FYI:** Reservations recommended. BYO. **Open:** Lunch Mon–Fri 11:30am–3pm; dinner Mon–Sat 5–10:30pm. **Prices:** Main courses $15–$26. AE, MC, V. ♥

Ⓢ Moghul
1665-195 Oaktree Center; tel 908/549-5050. Exit 131A off Garden State Pkwy, 4th light make left on Oaktree Rd, left 1st light. **Indian.** A large, lovely, well-lighted room with flowers and Indian decor, where the specialty is the cuisine of northern India. Lamb chops and chicken from the tandoor oven are popular, as is the weekday lunch buffet. **FYI:** Reservations recommended. BYO. Additional location: 1670A Oaktree Rd (tel 549-6222). **Open:** Lunch Tues–Sun noon–3pm; dinner Tues–Thurs 5:30–10:30pm, Fri–Sat 5:30–11pm, Sun 5:30–10:30pm; brunch Sat–Sun noon–3pm. **Prices:** Main courses $9–$17; prix fixe $17. AE, DISC, MC, V. ♥ ⅋

Egg Harbor Township
See Atlantic City

Elizabeth
See also Newark, Newark Int'l Airport, Union

Known as Elizabethtown until 1740, it was once the capital of East Jersey. Today it is the county seat of Union County and is largely an industrial city of factories and plants. **Information:** Union County Chamber of Commerce, 135 Jefferson Ave, PO Box 300, Elizabeth, 07207 (tel 908/352-0900).

HOTELS 🏨

🗏🗏🗏 Holiday Inn Jetport
1000 Spring St, 07201; tel 908/355-1700 or toll free 800/HOLIDAY; fax 908/355-0294. At US 1/9 Airport Service Rd. An older building with a recently spruced-up lobby. Convenient connections to air and rail services. **Rooms:** 392 rms and stes. Executive level. CI 3pm/CO noon. Nonsmoking rms avail. **Amenities:** 🛅 ⅛ A/C, cable TV w/movies, voice mail. Complimentary hors d'oeuvres in lounge from 5–7pm. **Services:** 🚐 ⚠ ⌑ Car-rental desk, babysitting. Free shuttle to Newark airport and Penn Station. **Facilities:** 🏋 🎱 🛢 ⅋ 1 restaurant, 1 bar, spa, sauna, whirlpool, washer/dryer. **Rates:** $84–$99 S or D; $109–$140 ste. Children under age 18 stay free. Parking: Outdoor, free. AE, CB, DC, DISC, MC, V.

🗏🗏🗏 Newark Airport Hilton
1170 Spring St, 07201; tel 908/351-3900 or toll free 800/HILTONS; fax 908/351-9556. US 1/9, Airport Service Rd. Recently renovated hotel with cozy rooms and efficient service. The beautiful lobby boasts a brass staircase and monumental flower arrangements. **Rooms:** 374 rms and stes. CI 3pm/CO noon. Nonsmoking rms avail. **Amenities:** 🛅 ⅛ 🖭 🕮 A/C, cable TV w/movies, dataport, voice mail. Some units w/whirlpools. Pay-per-view movies. **Services:** 🍽 📼 🚐 ⚠ ⌑ Masseur. Complimentary shuttle to airport and Newark's

Penn Station. **Facilities:** 🛗 🖥 🖵 👤 ⚙ 1 restaurant, 1 bar, spa, sauna, steam rm, whirlpool, washer/dryer. **Rates:** $145–$180 S or D; $245–$500 ste. Extra person $10. Children under age 18 stay free. Parking: Indoor, free. Weekend rates avail. AE, CB, DC, DISC, MC, V.

Englewood

Settled in the mid-18th century on the Hudson River, Englewood is now a city of some 25,000 people. Home of the John Harms Center for the Arts. **Information:** Englewood Chamber of Commerce, 2-10 N Van Brunt St, Englewood, 07631 (tel 201/567-2381).

HOTEL 🏨

≣≣≣ Radisson Hotel Englewood

401 Van Brant St, 07631; tel 201/871-2020 or toll free 800/333-3333; fax 201/871-7116. Van Brant/Englewood exit off NJ 4. This nearly new hotel in an industrial park is geared to business travelers but is also close to sports and shopping. The rooms are standard but the public spaces are elegant and inviting. **Rooms:** 194 rms and stes. Executive level. CI 3pm/CO noon. Nonsmoking rms avail. **Amenities:** 🛏 ⚙ A/C, cable TV w/movies, voice mail. 1 unit w/whirlpool. Dataports in some rooms. Free newspapers, including foreign editions. **Services:** ✕ 🗝 🚗 🖼 🖙 Car-rental desk. Multilingual staff. Complimentary morning coffee and evening cocktails. **Facilities:** 🛗 🖥 🖵 👤 ⚙ 1 restaurant, 1 bar, washer/dryer. **Rates:** $139–$149 S; $149–$159 D; $250 ste. Extra person $10. Children under age 21 stay free. Min stay special events. Parking: Outdoor, free. Corporate rates avail. AE, CB, DC, DISC, MC, V.

RESTAURANT 🍽

Jamie's

574 US 9 W, Englewood Cliffs; tel 201/568-4244. US 80, I-95, or NJ 4 E to last exit before GW Bridge then left onto US 9 W. **American.** The warm paisley-and-oak interior is reminiscent of a hunting lodge and the atmosphere is clublike, with notably fine service. The lunch crowd is filled with corporate types who come for the $16 prix fixe lunch which includes salad, entree, dessert, and coffee. Other specialties are salmon, swordfish, rack of veal, and lamb. **FYI:** Reservations recommended. Dress code. **Open:** Lunch Mon–Fri noon–3pm; dinner Mon–Thurs 5–10pm, Fri 5–11pm, Sat 6–11pm, Sun 4–9pm. **Prices:** Main courses $17–$26. AE, CB, DC, MC, V. 🆅🅿 ⚙

Fairfield

In the state's NE region, this town dates from the 18th century and is close to Lake Hiawatha and Lake Valhalla. **Information:** West Essex Chamber of Commerce, 3 Fairfield Ave, West Caldwell, 07006 (tel 201/226-5500).

HOTEL 🏨

≣≣≣ Radisson Hotel & Suites

690 US 46 E, 07004; tel 201/227-9200 or toll free 800/333-3333; fax 201/227-4308. ¼ mi past Passaic Ave. Pleasant appointments, good facilities, and easy access from major highways are the hallmarks of this suburban hotel. The staff is professional and courteous. **Rooms:** 204 rms, stes, and effic. Executive level. CI 3pm/CO noon. Nonsmoking rms avail. **Amenities:** 🛏 ⚙ 🖥 A/C, cable TV w/movies, voice mail. Some units w/whirlpools. Free daily newspapers. Complimentary hors d'oeuvres and cocktails at daily happy hour. Presidential Suites have dataports and whirlpools. **Services:** ✕ 🖼 🖙 🖘 Twice-daily maid svce. **Facilities:** 🛗 🖥 🖵 ⚙ 1 restaurant, 1 bar (w/entertainment), basketball, sauna, washer/dryer. **Rates:** $125–$145 S or D; $245–$335 ste; $135–$155 effic. Extra person $10. Children under age 12 stay free. Parking: Outdoor, free. Extended-stay rates and weekend packages avail. AE, DC, DISC, JCB, MC, V.

Flemington

Flemington gained fame in 1935 when its courthouse became the scene of the Hauptman Trial for the kidnapping of Charles A Lindbergh Jr. The town also features one of the most picturesque shopping communities in the state, offering a quality shopping outlet complex with early American architecture and landscaping. Several noted wineries are located in the area.

MOTEL 🏨

UNRATED The Bel-Air Inn & Conference Center

250 US 202 at NJ 31, 08822; tel 908/782-7472; fax 908/782-1975. Slightly run-down two-story building. Scheduled to become a Ramada Inn. **Rooms:** 104 rms and stes. CI 3pm/CO noon. Nonsmoking rms avail. **Amenities:** 🛏 ⚙ A/C, cable TV. **Services:** 🖙 **Facilities:** 🛗 **Rates:** $76 S or D; $85–$110 ste. Children under age 12 stay free. Parking: Outdoor, free. AE, MC, V.

Fort Lee

Located on the west bank of the Hudson River opposite Manhattan, it is the site of Fort Lee Historic Park, dating back to the American Revolution. **Information:** Greater Fort Lee Chamber of Commerce, 2357 Lemoine Ave, Fort Lee, 07024 (tel 201/944-7575).

HOTEL 🛏

≡≡≡ Fort Lee Hilton

2117 NJ 4 E, 07024; tel 201/461-9000 or toll free 800/
367-8533; fax 201/585-9807. ½ mi from GW Bridge; Fort
Lee/Palisades Pkwy exit off NJ 4E. Polished marble, brass,
glass, traditional furnishings, and a Japanese-style water
garden grace the lobby of this business hotel. **Rooms:** 235
rms and stes. Executive level. CI 3pm/CO noon. Nonsmoking
rms avail. **Amenities:** 🛜 🍸 A/C, cable TV w/movies, voice
mail. Some units w/whirlpools. **Services:** ✕ 🗝 🖎 🛎 Babysitting. Multilingual staff speaks Japanese, Korean, Chinese,
Italian, Spanish, Russian. Free van service to local companies.
Facilities: 🛐 🏋 🔄 🖳 🛠 2 restaurants (*see* "Restaurants"
below), 2 bars (w/entertainment), sauna, whirlpool. **Rates:**
Peak (Mar–Oct) $125–$155 S; $137–$167 D; $350–$750
ste. Extra person $12. Children under age 18 stay free. Min
stay special events. Lower rates off-season. MAP rates avail.
Parking: Indoor/outdoor, free. AE, CB, DC, DISC, JCB, MC,
V.

MOTEL

≡≡ Days Inn of Fort Lee

2339 NJ 4 E, 07024; tel 201/944-5000 or toll free 800/
DAYS-INN; fax 201/944-0623. Between Jones Rd and Fort
Lee exits, ½ mi W of GW Bridge. A traditionally furnished,
standard motel with a very friendly staff. **Rooms:** 175 rms. CI
noon/CO noon. Nonsmoking rms avail. Furnishings are a bit
tired. **Amenities:** 🛜 🍸 A/C, satel TV w/movies. Dataports in
some rooms. **Services:** ✕ 🖎 🛎 **Facilities:** 🛐 🔄 🛠 1
restaurant (bkfst and lunch only), 1 bar. **Rates:** $71–$85 S;
$81–$85 D. Extra person $10. Children under age 18 stay
free. Parking: Outdoor, free. AE, CB, DC, DISC, EC, JCB,
MC, V.

RESTAURANTS 🍽

Archer's Ristorante

1310 Palisade Ave; tel 201/224-5652. **Italian.** A very elegant
establishment serving a variety of pastas (all cooked to order),
seafood, and chateaubriand. **FYI:** Reservations recommended. Dancing. Dress code. **Open:** Lunch Mon–Fri noon–3pm;
dinner Mon–Fri 5–11pm, Sat 5pm–midnight, Sun 2–10pm.
Prices: Main courses $13–$27. AE, CB, DC, MC, V. 🖤 VP

Caffé Milano

In Fort Lee Hilton, 2117 NJ 4 E; tel 201/461-9000 ext 7240.
Palisades Pkwy exit off NJ 4 E. **Italian.** Modern design and
oversize paintings of scenes from commedia dell'arte give a
dramatic feel to this small restaurant. The kitchen produces a
range of high quality Italian specialties. An array of fine wines
is also available. **FYI:** Reservations recommended. Guitar/
piano/singer. Dress code. **Open:** Breakfast daily 6:30–11am;
lunch daily 11am–3pm; dinner Mon–Sat 5–11pm, Sun 5–
10:30pm; brunch Sun noon–3pm. **Prices:** Main courses $13–
$22. AE, DC, DISC, MC, V. 🛠

Sugi

In Fort Lee Hilton, 2117 NJ 4 E; tel 201/461-8038. Palisades
Pkwy exit off NJ 4 E. **Japanese.** The name means "cedar" in
Japanese, and that is the material of the authentic furnishings. Put on the slippers and dine in tatami-floored rooms,
served by waitresses in traditional Japanese garb. A chef's
special Japanese traditional dinner is $45–$75. **FYI:** Reservations accepted. Dress code. **Open:** Lunch Mon–Fri noon–
2:30pm; dinner Mon–Sat 5–10:30pm. **Prices:** Main courses
$13–$95; prix fixe $18–$39. AE, DC, DISC, MC, V. 🛠

Yea Jeon

1616 Palisade Ave; tel 201/944-0505. I-95 N to exit 70A; stay
on Fort Lee Rd/Main St through Leonia and Fort Lee, right
on Palisade Ave. **Japanese/Korean.** Climb 20 steps to the
level above the parking lot and eat Korean or Japanese
food—anytime, any day—at this restaurant near the George
Washington Bridge. Specialties include marinated steak and
shortribs, assorted pan-fried and deep-fried entrees, and rich
stews. **FYI:** Reservations recommended. **Open:** Daily 24 hrs.
Prices: Main courses $9–$17. AE, CB, DC, DISC, MC, V. 🕐
VP

Gateway National Recreation Area

RESTAURANTS 🍽

★ Barnacle Bill's

1 First St, Rumson; tel 908/747-8396. Garden State Pkwy
exit 109 to River Rd. **Burgers/Seafood.** A neighborhood
hangout with very attractive views of the Navesink River.
Burgers, swordfish, and the baked seafood combo are among
the most popular entree options. **FYI:** Reservations not
accepted. **Open:** Dinner Sun–Sat 5–11:30pm; brunch Sun
11:30am–3pm. **Prices:** Main courses $5–$23. AE, MC, V. 🖤
📷 🖼 🛠

Doris & Ed's Seafood

348 Shore Dr, Highlands; tel 908/872-1565. **New Ameri-
can/Seafood.** A pretty candlelit dining room offering waterfront views and an extensive menu. Typical entrees might
include grilled tuna on wasabi mayonnaise with ginger-
scallion sauce, and sautéed red snapper with fresh rock
shrimp and plum tomatoes. **FYI:** Reservations recommended.
Children's menu. No smoking. **Open:** Closed Jan–Feb.
Prices: Main courses $19–$26. AE, CB, DC, MC, V. 🖤 🖼 🛠

✿ Fromagerie

26 Ridge Rd, Rumson; tel 908/842-8088. River Rd E to end,
left on Ridge Rd. **French.** Local reviewers call this classic
French restaurant one of Monmouth County's best. Filet
mignon, Dover sole, and sautéed Long Island duck are
popular, and the surroundings are quietly romantic. **FYI:**
Reservations recommended. Jacket required. **Open:** Peak
(Mem Day–Labor Day) lunch Mon–Fri 11:30am–2:30pm;

dinner Sun 4–9:30pm, Mon–Thurs 5–9:30pm, Fri–Sat 5–11:30pm. **Prices:** Main courses $22–$35. AE, DC, MC, V. ♥ 🛋 VP

Harry's Lobster House

1124 Ocean Ave, Sea Bright (Oceanfront); tel 908/842-0205. NJ 36 to Ocean Ave. **Continental/Seafood.** The family is still turning out exceptional lobster bisque, caesar salad, lobster and filet mignon as they have done for 40 years. The fireplace is cozy in winter, the ceiling fans and outdoor deck are refreshing in summer, and the oceanside location is nice at any season. **FYI:** Reservations recommended. **Open:** Peak (May 15–Sept 15) daily 5:30–11pm. **Prices:** Main courses $18–$20. AE, DC, MC, V. ♥ ⚓ 🛋 ⬧

ATTRACTION 📷

Gateway National Recreation Area

NJ 36, Highlands; tel 908/872-0115. Consisting of a hodge-podge of rescued, undeveloped tracts situated at or near the entrance to New York Harbor, Gateway is administered by the National Park Service and is comprised of the Sandy Hook unit in New Jersey and three units in New York.

Sandy Hook is 6½ miles long and three-quarters of a mile wide at its widest point. The park offers swimming (with lifeguards in summer), nature trails, and picnicking. There are seven different parking areas and beach sections. Also located here is Sandy Hook Lighthouse (circa 1764), one of the oldest in the nation. **Open:** Mem Day–Labor Day, daily sunrise–sunset. **$**

Hackensack

North of Jersey City on the Hackensack River, Hackensack was settled by the Dutch in 1639 and was the site of several engagements during the Revolutionary War. Now a commercial and industrial center, and seat of Bergen County. **Information:** Hackensack Chamber of Commerce, 190 Main St #305, Hackensack, 07601 (tel 201/489-3700).

HOTEL 🏨

≣≣≣ Best Western Oritani

414 Hackensack Ave, 07601; tel 201/488-8900 or toll free 800/528-1234; fax 201/488-5456. Hackensack Ave exit off NJ 4E. Across the parking lot from an upscale shopping mall and a 24-hour supermarket. Popular with business travelers, it's about 15 minutes from the George Washington Bridge. **Rooms:** 127 rms and effic. CI 2pm/CO noon. Nonsmoking rms avail. **Amenities:** 🛁 🍽 A/C, cable TV. Some units w/whirlpools. **Services:** 🛎 🛗 Babysitting. **Facilities:** 🛗 🖥 🚐 ⬧ 1 restaurant (lunch and dinner only), sauna. **Rates (CP):** $82 S or D; $82 effic. Children under age 21 stay free. Parking: Outdoor, free. Weekend rates avail. AE, CB, DC, DISC, MC, V.

RESTAURANTS 🍴

★ Capri Mia

70 Hackensack Ave; tel 201/489-0743. NJ 4 E to Hackensack Ave exit; restaurant is ¼ mi on left. **Italian.** Despite the ramshackle exterior, the inside of this eatery is very neat and inviting. The menu features cassoulets and a variety of dishes served *en croûte*. Desserts are made on the premises, including bread pudding, crème brûlée, cappuccino ice cream cake, and flavored cheesecake. **FYI:** Reservations not accepted. Dress code. **Open:** Lunch Mon–Fri 11:45am–2:30pm; dinner Mon–Thurs 5–9:30pm, Fri–Sat 5–10:30pm. **Prices:** Main courses $11–$21. AE, MC, V. ⬧

♥ Stony Hill Inn

231 Polifly Rd; tel 201/342-4085. US 80 E to exit 64B. **Italian.** This exquisitely restored Dutch Colonial manor home dates from 1810 and is listed on the National Register of Historic Places. Dining is in a variety of rooms: the Pipe Room was once servants' quarters, bouquets of herbs hang from the rafters of the Herb Room, and music and dancing are available Thurs–Sat in the Garden Room. Daily specials enlarge the northern Italian menu. **FYI:** Reservations recommended. Dancing. Jacket required. **Open:** Lunch Mon–Sat 11:30am–3:30pm; dinner Mon–Thurs 5–10:30pm, Fri–Sat 5–11:30pm, Sun 3–10:30pm. **Prices:** Main courses $15–$29. AE, CB, DC, DISC, MC, V. ♥ 🍺 VP ⬧

Hamilton Township

Just east of Trenton and site of the Sayen Park Botanical Gardens, offering rare collection of rhododendrons.

ATTRACTION 📷

Kuser Farm Mansion and Park

390 Newkirk Ave, Hamilton; tel 609/890-3630. This was the country home of prominent businessman Fred Kuser and his family. Kuser is well-known for his role in helping William Fox start the Fox Film Corporation (later to become 20th Century-Fox). Visitors can see the Kuser theater in the grand dining room, with its 18-foot curved Cinema-Scope screen and separate projection room. The 22-acre grounds, known as Kuser Park, feature two picnic areas, lawn bowling, a children's playground, clay tennis courts, and a bandstand-sized gazebo. Special events include summer concerts, Victorian craft classes, and a Victorian Christmas open house. Self-guided walking tours and guided mansion tours available. **Open:** Peak (May–Nov) Thurs–Sun 11am–3pm. Reduced hours off-season. Closed Dec–Jan. **Free**

Hammonton

Located 27 miles SE of Camden, Hammonton is near Wharton State Forest and the Batsonia Trail, a 50-mile wilderness hiking trail, as well as the Hammonton Lake Natural Area and Batsto Village. **Information:** Greater Hammonton Chamber of Commerce, 231 Fairview Ave, PO Box 554, Hammonton, 08037 (tel 609/561-9080).

ATTRACTION 🏛

Batsto Historic Site
NJ 542; tel 609/561-3262. Located in Wharton State Forest. Batsto was founded in 1766 by industrialist Charles Read, who built the Batsto Iron Works near the mouth of the Batsto River. Today, visitors can explore what life was like for the residents of the town. Buildings open for touring include a milk house; a stable and carriage house; a stone barn (circa 1830); blacksmith and wheelwright shops; general store and post office (circa 1852); as well as the iron furnace, gristmill, and glassworks which provided employment for the area's residents. **Open:** Daily 9am–4pm. $

Hasbrouck Heights

This borough of some 12,000, just minutes from Manhattan, was founded in 1685 and named for a Dutch colonist. Home of Felegian College.

HOTEL 🏨

UNRATED Crowne Plaza Hasbrouck Heights
650 Terrace Ave, 07604; tel 201/288-6100 or toll free 800/ TEAM-ONE; fax 201/288-4717. US 80 W local lanes to exit 64B, at end of ramp make left onto Terrace. Near major highways and about 20 minutes from Manhattan and the Meadowlands Sports Complex. Unrated due to ongoing major renovations. **Rooms:** 355 rms and stes. Executive level. CI 3pm/CO noon. Nonsmoking rms avail. New rooms have very attractive decor, with new furniture and bathroom counters. **Amenities:** 🛏 🐕 ☎ 🍷 A/C, satel TV w/movies, dataport, voice mail. Suites include kitchenette with microwave and refrigerator. **Services:** ✕ 🖼 🍷 Babysitting. **Facilities:** 🏋 🏌 800 💻 🚴 1 restaurant, 1 bar (w/entertainment). **Rates:** $129 S; $144 D; $175–$400 ste. Extra person $15. Children under age 18 stay free. Parking: Outdoor, free. AE, CB, DC, DISC, MC, V.

Hazlet

Hazlet is SE of Perth Amboy and is the home of the PNC Bank Arts Center (formerly known as the Garden State Arts Center), site of a popular summer concert series.

MOTELS 🏨

📼📼 Ramada Inn
2870 NJ 35, 07730; tel 908/264-2400 or toll free 800/2-RAMADA; fax 908/739-9735. Exit 117 off Garden State Pkwy to NJ 35 S (approx 2 mi). There are some nice facilities

at this chain motel, but it could use some maintenance. **Rooms:** 120 rms and stes. CI 3pm/CO noon. Nonsmoking rms avail. Standard, typical rooms. **Amenities:** 🛏 🐕 A/C, cable TV w/movies, dataport. **Services:** ✕ 🚐 🖼 🍷 🛎 Babysitting. **Facilities:** 🏋 🏌 500 1 bar (w/entertainment), spa, sauna, whirlpool, washer/dryer. **Rates (BB):** Peak (May 20–Sept 6) $82–$99 S; $82–$110 D; $150 ste. Extra person $10. Children under age 17 stay free. Lower rates off-season. Parking: Outdoor, free. AE, CB, DC, DISC, JCB, MC, V.

📼 Wellesley Inn
3215 NJ 35N, 07730; tel 908/888-2800 or toll free 800/ 444-8888; fax 908/888-2902. Exit 117 off Garden State Pkwy to NJ 35 S. The rooms and facilities are clean and well maintained, making this a good bet for an overnight stop. **Rooms:** 89 rms and stes. CI 2pm/CO 11am. Nonsmoking rms avail. **Amenities:** 🛏 🐕 ☎ A/C, cable TV, refrig. **Services:** 🍷 🛎 **Facilities:** 12 Washer/dryer. **Rates (CP):** Peak (May–Aug) $60–$65 S; $66–$75 D; $175 ste. Extra person $10. Children under age 21 stay free. Lower rates off-season. Parking: Outdoor, free. AE, DC, DISC, MC, V.

ATTRACTION 🏛

PNC Bank Arts Center
Exit 116 off Garden State Pkwy, Holmdel; tel 908/442-9200. Located 10 mi W of Red Bank. Set on a hillside in a 400-acre park, this 5,300-seat amphitheater offers a summertime program of evening open-air pop, rock, and classical concerts, musicals, ballets, and ethnic heritage festivals. **Open:** June–Sept, call for schedule. $$$$

Hoboken

Two miles north of Jersey City on the Hudson River, Hoboken is heavily industrialized and a bedroom community of New York City. In the 1980s, it became a haven for artists who converted empty warehouses into studios. Site of the Stevens Institute of Technology.

PUBLIC TRANSPORTATION

PATH (Port Authority Trans-Hudson) trains connect Hoboken to Newark, Jersey City, and New York City. Trains run 24 hours and fare is $1. For more information, call PATH at toll free 800/234-PATH.

RESTAURANTS 🍴

★ Amanda's
908 Washington St; tel 201/798-0101. 5 blocks from 14th St. **New American.** This intimate place (only 48 seats) can get very busy on weekends, and the bar area near the entrance gets very crowded as diners wait for their chance to try the exceptional food. Possibilities include creamy polenta with tomato Provençal and three-cheese sauce, and mixed grill of salmon, shrimp, and scallops with aioli. **FYI:** Reservations

recommended. **Open:** Dinner Tues–Thurs 5–10pm, Fri–Sat 5–11pm, Sun 5–9pm; brunch Sat–Sun 11am–3pm. **Prices:** Main courses $14–$21. AE, MC, V. ⬛

Baja
104 14th St; tel 201/653-0610. **Mexican.** A cramped, funky Mexican restaurant where enchiladas, tacos, burritos, quesadillas, and grilled entrees are cranked out in full view of the dining area. The bar stays open about half an hour after the kitchen closes. **FYI:** Reservations recommended. **Open:** Mon–Thurs 5–10:30pm, Fri–Sat noon–11:30pm, Sun noon–10pm. **Prices:** Main courses $8–$15. AE, DC, MC, V. VP &

Frankie & Johnnie's on the Waterfront
163 14th St; tel 201/659-6202. **Italian/Steak.** A mixed crowd comes to this bistro-style steak house for the live jazz and piano music (Tues–Sat) as well as for a variety of grilled fish dishes and pasta. **FYI:** Reservations recommended. Jazz/piano. **Open:** Sun–Thurs 5–11pm, Fri–Sat 5pm–midnight. **Prices:** Main courses $15–$24. AE, CB, DC, DISC, MC, V. VP &

La Scala
159 14th St; tel 201/963-0884. **Italian.** The decor is casually elegant, and entrees carry operatic names (Norma, Bohème, Puccini) in keeping with the theme of the place. Popular dishes include various types of *schiacciata* (a flavored Tuscan flatbread) and pasta. **FYI:** Reservations recommended. Opera. Dress code. BYO. No smoking. **Open:** Tues–Thurs 5–10:30pm, Fri–Sat 5–11pm, Sun 4–10:30pm. Closed two weeks mid-Aug. **Prices:** Main courses $9–$29. AE, CB, DC, DISC, MC, V. &

★ Maxwell's
1039 Washington St; tel 201/798-0406. At 11th St. **Eclectic.** Music—with bands ranging from alternative to zydeco—is the draw to this tavern-style restaurant once favored by city dock workers and now popular with Manhattan scenesters who otherwise wouldn't be caught dead in New Jersey. The tiny back room hosts all the up-and-coming bands, while Tuesday brings poetry readings. The food tends toward burgers and bar munchies; there are also plans to add a microbrewery. **FYI:** Reservations accepted. Blues/folk/rock. **Open:** Dinner Tues–Sun 5pm–midnight; brunch Sun 11am–4pm. **Prices:** Main courses $7–$15. AE, CB, DISC, MC, V.

Ristorante Gerrino
96 River St; tel 201/656-7731. At First St. **Italian.** Reservations are essential for rooftop dining (and spectacular views of Manhattan) from May through October. The menu focuses on pasta, veal, steak, and grilled seafood. Dress is casual yet neat, and there's validated parking at the garage one block north. **FYI:** Reservations accepted. DJ. Dress code. **Open:** Mon–Fri 11:30am–11pm, Sat 5–11pm. **Prices:** Main courses $11–$20. AE, DC, DISC, MC, V. ▦ &

Ho-Ho-Kus

RESTAURANT ⟨⟩
Claude's Ho-Ho-Kus Inn
E Franklin Tpk; tel 201/445-4115. At Maple Ave. **Continental/French.** Each of the three main dining rooms in this Colonial landmark features a fireplace; three more private dining rooms are upstairs. Award-winning cuisine. **FYI:** Reservations recommended. Jacket required. **Open:** Lunch Tues–Fri noon–2:30pm; dinner Tues–Fri 5–11pm, Sat 5pm–midnight, Sun 3–9pm; brunch Sun noon–2pm. **Prices:** Main courses $23–$29. AE, MC, V. ♥ ⬛ ▣ ⬛ VP

Hope

This small town was settled in 1769 by the Moravians. The historic district features a gristmill, church, and cemetery.

INN ⟨⟩
▤▤▤ The Inn at Millrace Pond
NJ 519, PO Box 359, 07844; tel 908/459-4884 or toll free 800/7-INNHOPE; fax 908/459-5276. Exit 11 off I-80. 23 acres. Housed in an 18th-century gristmill and surrounded by a quaint Moravian village, this inn offers a relaxed pace and individual attention from the staff. **Rooms:** 17 rms. CI 3pm/CO noon. Shaker-style furniture, wide-board floors, and braided rugs add to the authenticity and warmth. **Amenities:** ▦ ♨ A/C, satel TV, dataport. 1 unit w/fireplace, some w/whirlpools. **Services:** ✗ ▨ Babysitting. **Facilities:** ▣ ●1 ▣ 1 restaurant (dinner only; *see* "Restaurants" below), 1 bar, guest lounge. **Rates (CP):** $85–$165 D. Extra person $15. Children under age 3 stay free. Min stay special events. Parking: Outdoor, free. Corporate rates and golf packages avail. AE, DC, MC, V.

RESTAURANT ⟨⟩
♣ The Inn at Millrace Pond
NJ 519; tel 908/459-4884. **Eclectic.** This painstakingly decorated 1769 gristmill has wide-board floors and colonial furnishings in a warm, upscale atmosphere. Chef Jack Rudewick creates an eclectic assortment of traditional American dishes prepared with European, Asian, and regional influences. **FYI:** Reservations recommended. Dress code. No smoking. **Open:** Mon–Thurs 5–9pm, Fri–Sat 5–9:30pm, Sun noon–7:30pm. **Prices:** Main courses $18–$23. AE, DC, MC, V. ⬛ &

Iselin

Near to Edison State Park and the Raritan Bay. Iselin is home to the Garden for the Blind, a sensory garden with descriptions in braille.

HOTEL 🏨

≣≣≣ Woodbridge Hilton Hotel

120 Wood Ave S, 08830; tel 908/494-6200 or toll free 800/
HILTONS; fax 908/603-7777. Exit 131A off Garden State
Pkwy (Metro Park), follow bend. This hotel has been well
maintained since it opened about 10 years ago. **Rooms:** 200
rms. CI 3pm/CO noon. Nonsmoking rms avail. Large rooms.
Amenities: 🛏 🖥 ⚒ A/C, cable TV w/movies, dataport, VCR,
voice mail. **Services:** ✕ ⊶ ⌷ ⌐ Twice-daily maid svce, car-
rental desk, social director, babysitting. Aerobics classes.
Facilities: 🛉 🏋 🟥 🖵 ⚒ 3 restaurants, 3 bars (2 w/enter-
tainment), games rm, racquetball, spa, sauna, steam rm,
whirlpool. **Rates (BB):** $74–$119 S or D. Parking: Outdoor,
free. Weekend rates avail. AE, CB, DC, DISC, EC, MC, V.

Jackson

Named for President Andrew Jackson, it lies SE of Camden
and adjacent to Wharton State Forest. Home of Six Flags
Great Adventure, the state's largest theme park.

ATTRACTION 🏛

Six Flags Great Adventure

NJ 537; tel 908/928-2000. One of the largest entertainment
complexes in the Northeast, with more than 100 rides, shows,
and attractions. The Great American Scream Machine (a
huge, looping roller coaster), Shockwave (a looping, stand-up
roller coaster), and Batman the Ride are just a few of the
high-speed rides in the park; new rides in 1996 included the
Skull Mountain indoor roller coaster. Shows include everything from trained dolphins and sea lions to a water stunt
spectacular based on the **Lethal Weapon** movies, while the
drive-through **Wild Safari Animal Park** features more than
2,000 animals situated on 350 acres. **Open:** Peak (Mem Day–
Labor Day) daily. Reduced hours off-season. **$$$$**

Jersey City

On the Hudson River opposite Manhattan and connected to
it by the Holland Tunnel, Jersey City (population 230,000) is
a major seaport and industrial center in its own right. Home
to Liberty State Park, with ferries to Ellis Island and the
Statue of Liberty. **Information:** Hudson County Chamber of
Commerce, 574 Summit Ave #404, Jersey City, 07306 (tel
201/653-7400).

PUBLIC TRANSPORTATION

PATH (Port Authority Trans-Hudson) trains connect Jersey
City to Hoboken, Newark, and New York City. Trains run 24
hours and fare is $1. For more information, call PATH at toll
free 800/234-PATH.

HOTEL 🏨

≣≣ Quality Inn

180 12th St, 07302; tel 201/653-0300 or toll free 800/
228-5151; fax 201/659-1963. Exit 140 off NJ Tpk extension.
This clean and comfortable hotel is right on the Holland
Tunnel approach plaza, so it's great for convenience but not
so great for noise. **Rooms:** 150 rms. CI 11am/CO 11am.
Nonsmoking rms avail. Some rooms were recently refur-
bished. **Amenities:** 🛏 A/C, cable TV. Some units w/terraces.
Services: ✕ 🟥 ⌐ **Facilities:** 🛉 🟥 1 restaurant, 1 bar.
Rates: Peak (June–Aug) $70–$80 S; $75–$85 D. Extra
person $5. Children under age 17 stay free. Lower rates off-
season. Parking: Outdoor, free. AARP discounts avail. AE,
CB, DC, DISC, JCB, MC, V.

RESTAURANTS 🍴

Casa Dante

737 Newark Ave; tel 201/795-2750. Between JFK Blvd and
Summit Ave. **Italian.** Very elegant yet comfortable dining
room with etched glass, elegant prints, and deep-upholstered
barrel chairs. The pan-Italian cuisine includes lightly battered
veal franchese, African lobsters, and chicken Sorrentina with
prosciutto, mushrooms, and eggplant. The homemade rum
cake is a favorite dessert. **FYI:** Reservations recommended.
Dress code. **Open:** Mon–Sat 11am–11pm. Closed last 2
weeks of Aug. **Prices:** Main courses $12–$26. AE, CB, DC,
DISC, MC, V. 🅥 🆅🅿

★ Laico's

67 Terhune Ave; tel 201/434-4115. Between Spring St and
Fowler off JFK Blvd. **Italian.** This casual, family-run eatery
serves massive quantities of fresh pasta, antipasto, chicken,
and veal to a grateful neighborhood clientele. Combination
plates (with shrimp, chicken, and veal parmigiana or
franchese) also available. Finish with a dessert of homemade
tiramisù. **FYI:** Reservations not accepted. Dress code. **Open:**
Mon–Fri 11:30am–10pm, Sat noon–11pm, Sun 1:30–10pm.
Closed 1 week in Aug. **Prices:** Main courses $7–$20. No CC.
🎦

ATTRACTIONS 🏛

Liberty Science Center

251 Phillip St; tel 201/200-1000. Located in Liberty State
Park (see below), the science center offers 250 hands-on
science exhibits. The four-story main building is divided into
theme sections exploring environment, health, and invention.
The environment section offers visitors the opportunity to
hold and examine insects such as the four-inch-long hissing
Madagascar cockroach. The senses are tested in the health
area as guests crawl through a 100-foot-long "touch tunnel."
On the invention floor, visitors can explore the "take apart
table" where the inner workings of machines such as microwaves, copiers, and computers can be investigated. An 11-
ton, 110-foot geodesic dome houses one of the world's

largest Omnimax theaters, where feature films are shown on an 88-foot screen with realistic surround sound. **Open:** Peak (Apr–Labor Day) daily 9:30am–5:30pm. Reduced hours off-season. $$$

Liberty State Park
Exit 14B off NJ Turnpike; tel 201/915-3400. Open water-front park and recreation area overlooking the New York Harbor. The park is located less than 2,000 feet from the Statue of Liberty; visitors can catch the ferry here for visits to either the statue or Ellis Island. Other attractions include playgrounds, picnic areas, nature trails, boating, and fishing. Ethnic festivals in fall; summer music series. **Open:** Daily 7am–8pm. **Free**

Jersey City Museum
472 Jersey Ave; tel 201/547-4514. Established in 1901, the museum is located on the top floor of the 100-year-old public library in the historic Van Vorst Park neighborhood. The museum presents exhibitions from its permanent collection of 19th- and 20th-century painting and prints. **Open:** Tues and Thurs–Sat 10:30am–5pm, Wed 10:30am–8pm. **Free**

Lambertville

Founded in 1732, on the Delaware River NW of Trenton. It was the site of the first post office, opened shortly after the War of 1812. Numerous art galleries and antique shops draw visitors today. **Information:** Lambertville Area Chamber of Commerce, 4 S Union St, Lambertville, 08530 (tel 609/397-0055).

INN 🏨

☰☰☰ The Inn at Lambertville Station
11 Bridge St, 08530; tel 609/397-4400 or toll free 800/524-1091; fax 609/397-9744. Off US 29. This antique-looking riverfront inn, with its large marble fireplace, vaulted ceiling, and Victorian chandeliers, was actually built in 1985. **Rooms:** 45 rms and stes. CI 2pm/CO noon. Nonsmoking rms avail. Large, with decor from great cities around the world. Fine views of Delaware River. **Amenities:** 🏧 A/C, cable TV. Some units w/fireplaces. **Services:** ⛄ 🍽 Babysitting. Fax, copy, audiovisual, and computer rental services. **Facilities:** 🛗 1 restaurant, 1 bar (w/entertainment). Convenient to boating, cross-country skiing, tubing, antiquing, horseback riding, ballooning. Jogging trail along the Delaware Canal. Dramatic conference/banquet room is suspended over the river in a glass enclosure. **Rates (CP):** Extra person $15. Children under age 2 stay free. MAP rates avail. Parking: Outdoor, free. AE, CB, DC, MC, V.

RESTAURANT 🍴

Lambertville Station Restaurant & Bar
In Lambertville Station; tel 609/397-8300. **Regional American.** The beautiful, daylight-filled dining areas of this meticu-

lously restored 1867 railroad station on the banks of the Delaware are furnished with Victorian antiques. (The architect was Thomas Ustick Walter, who also designed the dome of the US Capitol.) Hearty menu specials include buffalo and rack of lamb. Outdoor tables and a bar are on a deck overlooking a babbling creek. **FYI:** Reservations accepted. Jazz. Children's menu. **Open:** Lunch Mon–Sat 11:30am–3pm; dinner Sun–Thurs 4–9:30pm, Fri–Sat 4–11pm; brunch Sun 10:30am–3pm. **Prices:** Main courses $10–$25. AE, MC, V. 🍴🚤♿

Lawrenceville

Just north of Trenton, it is the site of 56 historic homes. Rider College is located here.

MOTEL 🏨

☰☰ Howard Johnson Lodge
2995 Brunswick Pike, 08648; tel 609/896-1100 or toll free 800/446-4656; fax 609/895-1325. On US 1, ½ mi S of I-295. Well-kept highway motel; good for an overnight stop. **Rooms:** 104 rms and stes. Executive level. CI 3pm/CO noon. Nonsmoking rms avail. Modern-looking Formica furnishings. **Amenities:** 🏧 ⚬ A/C, satel TV w/movies, dataport. Some units w/terraces. **Services:** ⛄ 🍽 ⚬ **Facilities:** 🛗 🏊 ♿ 1 restaurant, 1 bar, games rm. **Rates (CP):** Peak (May 15–Sept 6) $70 S; $80 D; $125 ste. Extra person $10. Children under age 12 stay free. Lower rates off-season. Parking: Outdoor, free. AE, CB, DC, DISC, MC, V.

RESTAURANT 🍴

Acacia
2637 Main St; tel 609/895-9885. Exit 7B off I-295 and I-95. **New American.** The former post office of the village is now a restaurant, and the windows of the light, comfortable dining room face the Lawrenceville prep school across the street. The menu changes seasonally but often features items like seared tuna encrusted with shallots and sesame and poppy seeds, then served on spinach and potato cakes. There is a daily vegetarian special as well. **FYI:** Reservations recommended. BYO. No smoking. **Open:** Lunch Mon–Fri noon–2:30pm; dinner Mon–Thurs 6–9:30pm, Fri 6–10pm, Sat 5:30–10pm, Sun 5–9pm. **Prices:** Main courses $19–$20. AE, DISC, MC, V. ♥♿

Ledgewood

Northern New Jersey town nearby to the Hopacang and Lake Musconetcong State Parks as well as Berkshire Valley and the Black River Wildlife Management Area. **Information:** Roxbury Area Chamber of Commerce, 187 E Main St, PO Box 436, Ledgewood, 07852 (tel 201/927-5622).

MOTEL 🛏

UNRATED Days Inn
1691 US 46, 07852; tel 201/347-5100 or toll free 800/DAYS-INN; fax 201/263-3094. US 46 W exit off I-80. This older building needs maintenance and the decor is tired, but it's a sufficient stop for travelers looking for basic lodging. **Rooms:** 98 rms. CI 4pm/CO noon. Nonsmoking rms avail. **Amenities:** 🛏 ⚲ A/C, cable TV w/movies, VCR. Videos available. **Services:** ✗ 🖳 ↺ Fax service available. **Facilities:** 🛗 ⚊1 🖳 200 ⚹ 1 restaurant, 1 bar. **Rates (CP):** $59–$85 S; $67–$89 D. Extra person $8. Children under age 12 stay free. Min stay special events. Parking: Outdoor, free. Senior, corporate, and military rates avail. AE, CB, DC, DISC, JCB, MC, V.

Long Beach Island

ATTRACTION 🏛

Barnegat Lighthouse
Broadway and the Bay, Barnegat Light; tel 609/494-2016. This historic lighthouse has stood on the northern tip of Long Beach island since 1858. In its prime, its light flashed every ten seconds at each point on the compass to warn ocean vessels away from the "graveyard of the Atlantic." In 1927 a lightship anchored off Barnegat took over the lighthouse's work. Today, the historic lighthouse serves as a museum and affords magnificent views to visitors willing to walk up the 217 steps to the observation platform. **Open:** Peak (Mem Day–Labor Day) daily. Reduced hours off-season. Closed Nov–Apr. $

Madison

West of Newark, this town of 16,000 was named for President James Madison and is the site of Drew University and the Playwright's Theater of New Jersey. **Information:** Madison Chamber of Commerce, PO Box 152, Madison, 07940 (tel 201/377-7830).

RESTAURANT 🍴

Il Mondo Vecchio
72 Main St; tel 201/301-0024. At Central Ave. **Italian.** Arriving guests are greeted by an inviting display of antipasti and a homey interior with 19th-century brick, oak paneling, and a pressed-tin ceiling. The chef's menu relies heavily on family recipes brought over from Italy. **FYI:** Reservations recommended. Dress code. BYO. **Open:** Lunch Mon–Fri noon–2:30pm; dinner Mon–Thurs 5:30–9:30pm, Fri–Sat 5:30–10:30pm. **Prices:** Main courses $18–$25. AE, MC, V. ♥ 🍽

ATTRACTION 🏛

Museum of Early Trades and Crafts
Main St and Green Village Rd; tel 201/377-2982. Victorian-era displays housed in the Romanesque Revival–style James Library (circa 1899) include tools once used by craftsmen—cabinetmakers, hornsmiths, ironworkers, cobblers, opticians, surveyors—and by homemakers to cook and bake, make candles, concoct medicines, spin wool, stencil wall decorations, and sew clothes. Other exhibits include a reconstructed schoolroom adapted from the Madison Academy (1809–1881) and a full-size Colonial kitchen. **Open:** Tues–Sat 10am–4pm, Sun 2–5pm. $

Mahwah

Outdoor activities draw visitors to this city of some 18,000 people on the New York state border. Campgaw Mountain Ski Center, the Campgaw Mountain Reservation, and the Ranapoo River are all nearby.

HOTELS 🛏

≣≣≣ Courtyard by Marriott
140 NJ 17 S, 07430; tel 201/529-5200 or toll free 800/205-6521; fax 201/529-1991. 1 mi S of I-287. With an attractive indoor heated pool and spa as well as the chain's typical landscaped courtyard, this is a comfortable and well-located hotel. **Rooms:** 146 rms and stes. Executive level. CI 3pm/CO 1pm. Nonsmoking rms avail. **Amenities:** 🛏 ⚲ 📺 A/C, cable TV w/movies, dataport, voice mail. All units w/terraces. **Services:** ✗ 🖳 ↺ Babysitting. **Facilities:** 🛗 50 ⚹ 1 restaurant (bkfst only), 1 bar, whirlpool, washer/dryer. **Rates:** Peak (Apr 15–Dec 15) $59–$89 S; $64–$99 D; $110–$120 ste. Children under age 18 stay free. Lower rates off-season. Parking: Outdoor, free. AE, DC, DISC, MC, V.

≣≣≣ Sheraton Crossroads Hotel & Towers
Crossroads Corporate Center, 07495; tel 201/529-1660 or toll free 800/325-3535; fax 201/529-4709. Mountainside Ave exit off NJ 17. This eight-year-old hotel, just ½ mile from the New York state line and set back from the highway in an office park, has an elaborate lobby with a waterfall and attractive outdoor landscaping. **Rooms:** 225 rms and stes. Executive level. CI 3pm/CO noon. Nonsmoking rms avail. Rooms are standard but comfortable. **Amenities:** 🛏 ⚲ 📺 🍷 A/C, cable TV w/movies. All units w/minibars, some w/whirlpools. Free newspaper. Dataports in some rooms. Refrigerators on request. **Services:** ✗ 🖬 🚗 🖳 ↺ ⊙ Car-rental desk. Evening cocktails and concierge service (weekdays only). **Facilities:** 🛗 ⚹ 📷 📺 🖳 1000 🖥 ⚹ 2 restaurants, 2 bars (1 w/entertainment), spa, sauna. **Rates:** $149 S; $159 D; $265–$750 ste. Extra person $10. Children under age 10 stay free. Parking: Indoor/outdoor, free. AE, CB, DC, DISC, EC, ER, JCB, MC, V.

Margate

See Atlantic City

Marlton

This community of 10,000, located SE of Camden, is near Taunton Lake.

RESTAURANT 🍴

Mrs London's Cafe
In Meadows Edge Market Place, 515 NJ 73 E; tel 609/983-7744. **New American/Continental.** Although surrounded by suburban asphalt, the dining room here is like a Victorian parlor, complete with striped wallpaper, faux finishes, and prints. The menu changes several times a year, but crab cakes, paella, grilled tuna, filet mignon, and baked oysters make regular appearances. **FYI:** Reservations recommended. BYO. **Open:** Lunch Tues–Sat 11:30am–2:30pm; dinner Tues–Sun 5–10pm. Closed Jan 1–10. **Prices:** Main courses $18–$27. AE, MC, V. ⬤ ▣ ⅋

Mays Landing

The seat of Atlantic County, sitting on the Great Egg Harbor River. Home of Atlantic Community College and near Lake Lanape.

RESTAURANTS 🍴

⑤ ✱ Huntzinger's American Food & Drink
6489 Harding Hwy; tel 609/625-4447. 2 mi W of town on US 40. **New American/American.** A family member is always cooking in this chef-owned restaurant, using fresh ingredients in items such as osso buco, crab cakes, and roasted rib eye. **FYI:** Reservations recommended. Children's menu. **Open:** Tues–Thurs 7am–10pm, Fri–Sat 7am–11pm, Sun 7am–10pm. **Prices:** Main courses $10–$17. AE, DISC, MC, V. ⬤ ▦ ▣ ⅋

✱ Joe Italiano's Maplewood II
6126 Black Horse Pike; tel 609/625-1181. On US 322, 4 mi W of Atlantic City Race Course. **Italian/Seafood.** The decor is plain, but the food is freshly prepared and portions are ample. Most popular entrees are mussels in red sauce, shrimp with broccoli, and USDA prime steak. **FYI:** Reservations not accepted. Children's menu. Additional locations: 47 White Horse Pike, Hammonton (tel 561-9621); 594 White Horse Pike, Atco (tel 768-5202). **Open:** Mon–Fri 11:30am–11pm, Sat–Sun 1–11pm. **Prices:** Main courses $11–$25. AE, CB, DC, DISC, MC, V. ▦ ⅋

Medford

Village on the western edge of the Pine Barrens, an area of vast forests and state parks, lakes, cranberry bogs, and ghost towns of the industrial era. Founded in 1750, Medford is now a city of 20,000 residents, but it retains its historic flavor with Victorian clapboard houses and craft shops.

RESTAURANTS 🍴

♛ Beau Rivage
128 Taunton Blvd; tel 609/983-1999. ¼ mi S of jct Tuckerton Rd. **Continental/French.** Stained glass–bordered windows look out on a lake and a pleasant garden at this old-school French restaurant in the New Jersey countryside. Beef Wellington, rack of lamb, escargots, poached salmon, and filet of sole meunière are menu highlights; the wine cellar has more than 500 bottles, with California cabernets and chardonnays and Bordeaux reds and port wines predominating. **FYI:** Reservations recommended. Jacket required. **Open:** Lunch Mon–Fri 11:30am–2:30pm; dinner Mon–Sat 5:30–9:30pm, Sun 4–8pm. Closed last two weeks of Aug. **Prices:** Main courses $16–$23. AE, CB, DC, MC, V. ⬤

Braddock's Tavern
39 S Main St; tel 609/654-1604. **Continental.** The present clapboard structure dates from 1844, but food has been served at this site since 1823. History is preserved with 19th-century portraits and antique plates along the walls. The menu also tends toward the classic, with crab cakes, escargots florentine, onion soup, veal normande, and steak au poivre. Colonial game pie, stuffed with rabbit, duck, and beef, is a local favorite. **FYI:** Reservations recommended. **Open:** Lunch Mon–Fri 11:30am–2:30pm; dinner Mon–Fri 5:30–10pm, Sat 5–10pm, Sun 4–9pm; brunch Sun 11am–2:30pm. **Prices:** Main courses $17–$25. AE, CB, DC, DISC, MC, V. ♟ ⅋

Milford

Located on the Delaware River and named for an old mill located at a ford across the river. Home of New Jersey's only Dutch-style grain-grinding windmill.

RESTAURANT 🍴

The Ship Inn
61 Bridge St; tel 908/995-0188. 2 blocks from Upper Black Eddy/Milford Bridge on Delaware River. **British/Irish.** The state's first brew pub in over 50 years produces a variety of ales, malt whiskey, and hard cider. Traditional fish and chips, shepherd's pie, and other British and Irish favorites are available in the dining room, where musicians entertain on weekends. **FYI:** Reservations accepted. Piano/singer. Dress code. **Open:** Mon–Thurs 11:30am–9pm, Fri–Sat 11:30am–10pm. **Prices:** Main courses $10–$20. AE, MC, V. ♟

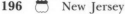

ATTRACTION 📷

Volendam Windmill Museum
231 Adamic Hill Rd; tel 908/995-4365. The seven-story mill stands 60 feet high and features sail arms that are 68 feet from tip to tip. It was built almost in its entirety by Paul and Mary Jorgensen to demonstrate an authentic model of the centuries-old wind-driven mill used for grinding raw grain into flour. **Open:** May–Sept, Sat–Sun noon–4:30pm (weather permitting). $

Millburn

Home of the renowned Paper Mill Playhouse, which hosts the New Jersey Ballet, theater, concerts. **Information:** Millburn–Short Hills Chamber of Commerce, 56 Main St, PO Box 651, Millburn, 07041 (tel 201/379-1198).

RESTAURANTS 🍴

FM Kirby Carriage House
In Paper Mill Playhouse, Brookside Dr; tel 201/379-2420. Exit 50B off NJ 24/I-78 to right to left on Millburn, right on Old Short Hills Rd to right on Brookside. **New American.** This charming riverside spot shares a courtyard with the Paper Mill Playhouse, and is decorated in antique copper, brass, and tapestry chairs. The three-course prix fixe dinner offers pasta cassoulet, confit pork, risotto, mahimahi, medallions of beef, and braised rabbit. Some of the staff may be temperamental. **FYI:** Reservations recommended. Dress code. **Open:** Lunch Thurs 11:30am–noon, Sat–Sun 12:30am–1pm; dinner Wed–Sun 5:30–6pm. **Prices:** Prix fixe $35. AE, DISC, MC, V. 🍷 🍺 🚢 🖼 🏔 VP ♿

⭐ 40 Main St
40 Main St; tel 201/376-4444. Between Essex St and Millburn Ave. **New American.** This cozy dining room, with stark white walls and dried-flower sconces, is a popular hangout for the cast and patrons of nearby Paper Mill Playhouse. The menu changes daily, but regularly lists roasted red snapper, lamb Gorgonzola, or beef tenderloin with garlic whipped potatoes. The upstart sibling next door, Cafe Main, has lunch and lighter fare. **FYI:** Reservations recommended. Dress code. No smoking. **Open:** Tues–Thurs 5:30–9pm, Fri–Sat 5:30–11pm, Sun 11am–9pm. **Prices:** Main courses $15–$25. AE, MC, V.

ATTRACTION 📷

Paper Mill Playhouse
Brookside Dr; tel 201/376-4343. Located on the site of a 1790 red-brick papermill, this is New Jersey's official state theater. Classics and full-scale Broadway productions are performed here, as well as children's programs and regular appearances by the New Jersey Ballet and the New Jersey Symphony. Paintings are displayed in the old mill part of the playhouse. **Open:** Call for schedule. $$$$

Millville

On the Maurice River in northern New Jersey, this city of some 26,000 is near to High Point State Park (named for the state's highest point). **Information:** Millville Chamber of Commerce, 13 S High St, PO Box 831, Millville, 08332 (tel 609/825-2600).

ATTRACTION 📷

Wheaton Village
1501 Glasstown Rd; tel 609/825-6800. Located 10 mi E of Bridgeton. The village features the T C Wheaton Glass Factory, where visitors can watch artists transform hot molten glass into bottles, bowls, and paperweights. Also on the grounds are the Gallery of American Craft (which has displays of pottery and glass made by the Village's artists-in-residence), a general store, the Centre Grove Schoolhouse (circa 1876), and the 1863 C P Huntington Train, which takes visitors on a scenic ride through the pinelands. Seasonal events, craft demonstrations. **Open:** Peak (Apr–Dec) daily 10am–5pm. Reduced hours off-season. $$$

Montclair

Six miles NW of Newark, Montclair is home to Montclair State College and the Montclair Art Museum, one of the oldest fine-arts museums in the state. **Information:** Montclair Chamber of Commerce, 50 Church St, Montclair, 07042 (tel 201/744-7660).

RESTAURANT 🍴

Hudson Place
98 Walnut St; tel 201/746-0789. Between Valley and Grove Sts. **New American/Soul/Southern.** What this spot lacks in decor is made up for by the warm personality of owner Rosa Hudson. The kitchen doles out massive portions of homey favorites like fried chicken with pecan-honey sauce, and ribs in Rosa's secret sauce. Daily fish specials. **FYI:** Reservations accepted. Dress code. BYO. No smoking. **Open:** Lunch Wed–Fri noon–2pm; dinner Tues–Thurs 5–9pm, Fri–Sat 5–10pm, Sun 4–9pm. **Prices:** Main courses $15–$22. No CC.

ATTRACTION 📷

The Montclair Art Museum
3 S Mountain Ave; tel 201/746-5555. Housed in a Greek Revival–style building, the museum's collections comprise over 11,000 works of American and Native American art from the mid-18th-century to the present. Highlights of the collection include works by Mary Cassatt, John Singleton Copley, Mark Rothko, and Edward Hopper. Children's art workshops, Native American craft demonstrations, gallery

talks, an independent film festival, and classical music concerts are also offered periodically. **Open:** Tues 11am–5pm, Thurs and Sun 1–5pm, Fri–Sat 11am–5pm. **$$**

Montvale

The name of this small borough on the New York border reflects the topography of the area. Home of Alphonsus College, and close to Lake Tappan.

MOTEL 🖼

⬰⬰ Ramada Inn

100 Chestnut Ridge Rd, 07645; tel 201/391-7700 or toll free 800/272-6232; fax 201/391-6648. Exit 172 off Garden State Pkwy, left off ramp, left at Chestnut Ridge Rd. Draws more corporate groups than individual travelers, who might criticize the lax housekeeping. **Rooms:** 167 rms and stes. CI 2pm/CO noon. Nonsmoking rms avail. Suites available on monthly basis. **Amenities:** 🖥 🅰 A/C, cable TV. Some units w/terraces. Refrigerators on request. **Services:** 🖼 🗘 **Facilities:** 🖼 🖼 🖼 🅰 2 restaurants, 1 bar (w/entertainment), sauna. **Rates:** $65–$85 S or D; $90 ste. Extra person $8. Children under age 2 stay free. Parking: Outdoor, free. AE, DC, DISC, MC, V.

RESTAURANT 🍽

Aldo & Gianni

In A & P Shopping Plaza, 108 Chestnut Ridge Rd; tel 201/391-6866. Exit 172 off Garden State Pkwy; left on Grand St, right on Chestnut Ridge Rd. **Italian.** The dining room of this restaurant in a strip mall is neat and modern in style. Dinner specialties include a carpaccio appetizer, linguini alla genovese, and Tuscan-style shrimp. **FYI:** Reservations recommended. **Open:** Lunch Mon–Fri 11:45am–2:30pm; dinner Mon–Fri 5–9:30pm, Sat 5–10pm. **Prices:** Main courses $11–$21. AE, CB, DC, MC, V. 🅰

Morristown

See also Parsippany, Rockaway

This populous business and residential city played an important role in Washington's Revolutionary War campaigns. The Rabbinical College of America, the world's largest campus for study of Hasidic Judaism, is located here. **Information:** Morris County Chamber of Commerce, 101 Park Ave, Morristown, 07960 (tel 201/539-3882).

HOTELS 🖼

⬰⬰⬰ Best Western Morristown Inn

270 South St, 07960; tel 201/540-1700 or toll free 800/688-4646; fax 201/267-0241. At jct I-287. Three-story, white-brick structure with colonial decor; red, white, and blue color scheme; antique furnishings. Very friendly staff. **Rooms:** 60 rms and effic. CI 3pm/CO noon. Nonsmoking rms avail. **Amenities:** 🖥 🅰 🖥 A/C, satel TV w/movies, dataport. Some units w/minibars. VCRs available. **Services:** ✕ 🚐 🖼 🗘 Car-rental desk, babysitting. **Facilities:** 🖼 🅰 1 restaurant, sauna. **Rates:** $89–$99 S; $99–$109 D; $99–$109 effic. Extra person $10. Children under age 12 stay free. Parking: Outdoor, free. Extended-stay and corporate rates avail. AE, CB, DC, DISC, JCB, MC, V.

UNRATED Headquarters Plaza Hotel

3 Headquarters Plaza, 07960; tel 201/898-9100 or toll free 800/225-1941; fax 201/292-0112. A business-oriented hotel in a complex housing corporate offices, a shopping mall, and a movie theater. The art deco lobby is richly decorated, with marble floors and tables, tapestry-upholstered chairs and couches, and mirrored columns. **Rooms:** 264 rms and stes. Executive level. CI 3pm/CO 1pm. Nonsmoking rms avail. **Amenities:** 🖥 🅰 🍽 A/C, cable TV w/movies, dataport. Some units w/whirlpools. Complimentary morning newspaper. **Services:** ✕ 🖛 VP 🚐 🖼 🗘 Babysitting. Translation services and currency exchange available. **Facilities:** 🖼 🖥 🅰 2 restaurants, 1 bar, spa, day-care ctr. Free use of adjacent health and racquetball club, with Olympic-style pool, saunas, whirlpools, steam rooms, massage therapy, fitness and nutritional guidance. One restaurant is casual, the other more formal. **Rates (CP):** $145–$175 S or D; $330–$465 ste. Children under age 12 stay free. Min stay special events. Parking: Indoor, free. Corporate rates avail. AE, DC, MC, V.

RESTAURANT 🍽

♟ The Grand Cafe

42 Washington St; tel 201/540-9444. Just off the green. **Continental/French.** Light oak paneling, salmon-colored walls, brass fixtures, and candlelit tables adorned with fresh flowers create a warm ambience in this French-style bistro. The menu focuses on traditional French and nouvelle American dishes, some with a dash of Oriental and Middle Eastern influence. Over 300 French and California wines are available, and the service is excellent. **FYI:** Reservations recommended. Jacket required. No smoking. **Open:** Mon–Thurs 11:45am–9pm, Fri 11:45am–10pm, Sat 6–10pm. **Prices:** Main courses $19–$29. AE, DC, MC, V.

ATTRACTIONS 🖼

Morristown National Historical Park

Washington Place; tel 201/539-2085. The park encompasses four separate units: Washington's Headquarters, Fort Nonsense, Jockey Hollow, and the New Jersey Brigade Area. Washington's Headquarters and Fort Nonsense are located in Morristown itself, while Jockey Hollow and the New Jersey Brigade area are located 5–7 miles south.

In early December of 1779, Mrs Jacob Ford Jr offered her home to General and Mrs Washington. The home, now a museum, was used as **Washington's Headquarters** in 1779–

80. Guided tours of the building, which houses historical exhibits about the area, leave from the adjacent museum building. A 20-minute orientation film is available.

Jockey Hollow is a 1,200-acre area which was used during the winter of 1779–80 as the encampment site of the 10,000-soldier Continental Army. Today, visitors can view the 18th-century farm and several reconstructed soldier huts. Volunteers in period dress present living history interpretations about farm and soldier life; there's also a 3-mile driving tour road and 23 miles of hiking trails.

Fort Nonsense (so named because legend says the fort had only been built to keep the troops occupied) and the New Jersey Brigade Area are not staffed, but feature hiking trails and interpretive signs to guide visitors.

For more information contact the National Park Service, Morristown National Historical Park, Washington Place, Morristown, NJ 07960. **Open:** Daily 9am–5pm. **$**

Acorn Hall

68 Morris Ave; tel 201/267-3465. This Italianate Victorian mansion, built in 1853, now serves as the headquarters of the Morris County Historical Society. The interior features carved marble fireplaces, trompe l'oeil details on walls and ceilings, a rococo revival parlor, and original 1860s furnishings, while the gardens are planted with flowers and shrubs typical of 19th-century landscapes. Guided tours available. **Open:** Mar–Dec, Thurs 11am–3pm, Sun 1:30–4pm. **$**

Morris Museum

6 Normandy Heights Rd; tel 201/538-0454. Collections in fine arts, anthropology, geology, decorative arts, history, and natural science grace this local museum. The live animal gallery, dinosaurs, and model trains are favorites of children, and the museum presents a wide array of performing arts (including plays and concerts) at the 312-seat **Bickford Theatre**. **Open:** Mon–Sat 10am–5pm, Sun 1–5pm. **$$**

Mountainside

Named for its location in wooded hills. Outdoor activities are available at the Trailside Nature and Science Center and the Watchung Reservation.

RESTAURANTS ▯▯▯

Raagini

1085 US 22 E; tel 908/789-9777. 2 mi E of jct NJ 28. **Indian.** Housed in an attractive stucco building with large arched windows, this dining room is filled with Asian artwork, tapestries, and a display of Indian musical instruments. The menu offers vindaloo, for those who like it hot, along with more subtle dishes like passandas and the chef's special (fish in a delicate cream sauce). Authentic offerings from the tandoor over include tikkas and masalas. **FYI:** Reservations

accepted. Dress code. **Open:** Lunch Tues–Sun 11:30am–2:30pm; dinner Sun–Thurs 5–10pm, Fri–Sat 5–11pm. **Prices:** Main courses $13–$26. AE, DC, DISC, MC, V.

Spanish Tavern

1239 US 22 E; tel 908/232-2171. 1 mi E of jct NJ 28. **Spanish.** Mediterranean fixtures accent the warm dark wood of this rambling roadhouse. Chicken with garlic or green sauce, veal with brandy and almonds, and a variety of paellas anchor the menu. Fideva (shellfish over green pasta) is especially noteworthy. **FYI:** Reservations recommended. Dress code. **Open:** Mon–Fri 11:30am–10pm, Sat 3–10:30pm, Sun noon–10pm. **Prices:** Main courses $15–$24. AE, CB, DC, DISC, MC, V. ♥ VP

Mount Arlington

Located west of Paterson on the shore of Lake Hopatcong, the state's largest lake.

MOTEL ▥

▤▤▤ Sheraton Inn Mount Arlington

15 Howard Blvd, 07856; tel 201/770-2000 or toll free 800/325-3535; fax 201/770-2000 x615. Exit 30 off I-80. In a quiet setting close to I-80, this well-maintained property caters to business travelers visiting the International Trade Center and major corporations in Morris County. Ample parking. **Rooms:** 124 rms, stes, and effic. CI 1pm/CO noon. Nonsmoking rms avail. Tastefully decorated and impeccably clean. **Amenities:** ▯ ☖ A/C, satel TV w/movies. **Services:** ✕ ▨ ☖ **Facilities:** ▯ ▯ ▯ ☖ 1 restaurant (see "Restaurants" below), 1 bar (w/entertainment), washer/dryer. **Rates:** $80–$118 S or D; $140–$160 ste; $118 effic. Min stay special events. Parking: Outdoor, free. AE, DC, DISC, MC, V.

RESTAURANT ▯▯▯

Sports Authority Restaurant & Lounge

In Sheraton Inn Mount Arlington, 15 Howard Blvd; tel 201/398-9393. **Continental.** The lighting is dim and the forest-green decor is unremarkable, but the continental fare is well regarded. Broiled salmon, broiled sirloin, stuffed breast of chicken, and fettuccine Alfredo are popular, as is the all-you-can-eat Sunday brunch buffet. **FYI:** Reservations accepted. **Open:** Mon–Fri 6:30am–10pm, Sat–Sun 7am–10pm. **Prices:** Main courses $10–$20. AE, CB, DC, DISC, MC, V. ☖

Mount Holly

In the state's Delaware River region, Mount Holly was settled in 1676 and named for a hill covered with holly trees. Seat of Burlington County.

MOTELS 🏨

UNRATED **Best Western Motor Inn Mount Holly**
2020 NJ 541, PO Box 2020, 08060; tel 609/261-3800 or toll free 800/528-1234; fax 609/267-0958. Exit 5 off NJ Tpk. A busy facility right off the turnpike. **Rooms:** 62 rms. CI noon/CO 11am. Nonsmoking rms avail. **Amenities:** 🏧 ⓐ A/C, cable TV. **Services:** ⌕ ⌂ **Facilities:** 🎱 🎬 ♿ **Rates:** $47–$55 S; $52–$65 D. Extra person $8. Children under age 14 stay free. Parking: Outdoor, free. AE, CB, DC, DISC, MC, V.

⊟⊟ **Howard Johnson Lodge**
Mount Holly Rd, PO Box 73, 08060; tel 609/267-6550 or toll free 800/446-4656; fax 609/267-2575. Exit 5 off NJ Tpk. A basic roadside motel, with rooms clustered in several one- and two-story buildings. **Rooms:** 138 rms and stes. Executive level. CI 2pm/CO noon. Nonsmoking rms avail. Rooms are in good condition; most face the parking lot. **Amenities:** 🏧 A/C, satel TV. Some units w/whirlpools. **Services:** ✗ ⌕ ⌂ Car-rental desk, babysitting. **Facilities:** 🏛 🎬 ♿ 1 restaurant, 1 bar, games rm, whirlpool, playground. **Rates (CP):** Peak (Mem Day–Labor Day) $58–$86 S; $60–$84 D. Extra person $7. Children under age 18 stay free. Lower rates off-season. Parking: Outdoor, free. AE, CB, DC, DISC, JCB, MC, V.

Mount Laurel

Township of some 30,000 east of Camden. Rancocas Woods Village offers a unique shopping experience in a woodland setting.

HOTELS 🏨

⊟⊟⊟ **Clarion Hotel of Mount Laurel**
915 NJ 73, 08054; tel 609/234-7300 or toll free 800/252-7466; fax 609/866-9401. Exit 4 off NJ Tpk; exit 36A off I-295. Business-oriented hotel with extensive facilities and a beautiful lobby with a marble floor and large chandeliers. **Rooms:** 283 rms and stes. Executive level. CI 3pm/CO 11am. Nonsmoking rms avail. Some rooms face the pool. **Amenities:** 🏧 ⓐ A/C, cable TV w/movies. Some units w/terraces. **Services:** ⦿ 🍽 ⌧ ⌂ Car-rental desk. **Facilities:** 🏛 ●2 🎬 🎬 ♿ 1 restaurant, 1 bar, games rm, beauty salon, washer/dryer. **Rates:** $59–$89 S or D; $150–$200 ste. Children under age 4 stay free. Parking: Outdoor, free. AE, CB, DC, DISC, MC, V.

⊟⊟⊟ **Courtyard by Marriott**
1000 Century Pkwy, 08054; tel 609/273-4400 or toll free 800/321-2211; fax 609/273-2889. From NJ Tpk exit 4 take NJ 73 N; from I-295 take exit 36A. A gazebo is the focal point of the courtyard of this group of attractive buildings, and the lobby has marble floors and a restaurant. **Rooms:** 151 rms and stes. CI 3pm/CO noon. Nonsmoking rms avail. Solid, dark-wood furniture. **Amenities:** 🏧 ⓐ 📺 A/C, satel TV w/movies, dataport. Some units w/terraces. **Services:** ✗ ⌧

⌂ Babysitting. **Facilities:** 🏛 🎬 🎬 ♿ 1 restaurant (bkfst and dinner only), 1 bar, whirlpool, washer/dryer. **Rates:** $79–$105 S; $89–$150 D; $110–$130 ste. Extra person $10. Parking: Outdoor, free. AE, CB, DC, DISC, ER, MC, V.

⊟⊟⊟ **DoubleTree Guest Suites**
515 Fellowship Rd, 08054; tel 609/778-8999 or toll free 800/879-5562; fax 609/778-9720. Exit 36A off I-295; exit 4 off NJ Tpk. Shelves of books, fresh flowers, and a fireplace set a pleasant mood. The marble-floored lobby provides a welcoming entrance. **Rooms:** 129 stes. CI 2pm/CO 11am. Nonsmoking rms avail. **Amenities:** 🏧 ⓐ 📺 A/C, satel TV, refrig, dataport, VCR, CD/tape player, voice mail. Some units w/terraces. All units have VCRs and wet bars. **Services:** ✗ ⌧ ⌂ Babysitting. **Facilities:** 🏛 🎬 🎬 ♿ 1 restaurant, 1 bar (w/entertainment), whirlpool. Pool is in a pretty atrium, detached from the lobby. **Rates (BB):** $110–$137 ste. Extra person $15. Children under age 5 stay free. Parking: Outdoor, free. AE, DC, DISC, MC, V.

Netcong

See Stanhope

Newark

See also Rockaway, Westfield

The state's largest city (population 275,000), Newark is located on the Passaic River in Newark Bay. It is an important manufacturing center and commercial port, but offers many cultural activities as well, including the New Jersey Ballet, the New Jersey Opera and Symphony Orchestra, and several museums. **Information:** Chamber of Commerce for Metro Newark, One Newark Center, 22nd fl, Newark, 07102 (tel 201/242-6237).

PUBLIC TRANSPORTATION
PATH (Port Authority Trans-Hudson) trains connect Newark to Hoboken, Jersey City, and New York City. Trains run 24 hours and fare is $1. For more information, call PATH at toll free 800/234-PATH.

HOTEL 🏨

UNRATED **Hilton Gateway**
Raymond Blvd, 07102; tel 201/622-5000 or toll free 800/HILTONS; fax 201/622-2644. In Gateway business and shopping complex. Part of a large shopping/office center in the heart of town, convenient to Newark's Penn Station and the Ironbound District. Under new management since 1996. **Rooms:** 253 rms and stes. Executive level. CI 4pm/CO 11am. Nonsmoking rms avail. **Amenities:** 🏧 ⓐ A/C, cable TV w/movies, dataport, voice mail. Some units w/whirlpools. **Services:** ⦿ 🍽 VP 🚗 ⌧ ⌂ Masseur. **Facilities:** 🏛 🎬 🎬 💻

&. 2 restaurants, 2 bars, spa, whirlpool. **Rates:** $139–$159 S or D; $215–$299 ste. Parking: Indoor, free. Weekend rates include continental breakfast. AE, CB, DC, DISC, MC, V.

RESTAURANTS 🍴

Fornos of Spain
47 Ferry St; tel 201/589-4767. Between McWhorter and Union Sts. **Spanish.** A classy eatery with three distinctive dining rooms, including a skylit Garden Room with wraparound murals and a dark wood-and-brass lounge. Paella heads the long menu, which includes chicken in garlic, stuffed lobster tails, and veal cutlet in white wine. On Fridays and Saturdays, some dishes must be ordered for two. **FYI:** Reservations recommended. Dress code. No smoking. **Open:** Mon–Thurs 11:30am–10:30pm, Fri–Sat 11:30am–11pm, Sun noon–10:30pm. **Prices:** Main courses $13–$27. AE, MC, V. ❤

★ Seabra's Marisqueira
87 Madison St; tel 201/465-1250. Between Ferry and Lafayette Sts. **Portuguese.** *Marisqueira* is Portuguese for "seafood." The lively entrance is centered on a large counter area with stacks of "live tanks," and a blue-and-white-tiled hall leads to a pretty dining room with long communal tables. The Frutos do Mar Platter has enough clams casino, stuffed oysters, garlic shrimp, fish kebob, mussels, and lobster for the whole family. **FYI:** Reservations not accepted. Children's menu. **Open:** Sun–Thurs noon–midnight, Fri–Sat noon–1am. **Prices:** Main courses $8–$27. AE, MC, V. 👥

ATTRACTIONS 🏛

Newark Museum
49 Washington St; tel 201/596-6550. The permanent collection here features American, Oriental, and Greek and Roman paintings; there's also an unusual collection of Tibetan artifacts and artwork. The restored Victorian Ballantine House (ca 1885), a national historic landmark, is accessed through the museum, and contains two floors of period rooms with original furnishings and decorative arts galleries. Planetarium, fire museum, sculpture garden. **Open:** Mon and Fri–Sat 9am–5:30pm, Tues–Thurs 9am–8:30pm. **Free**

Cathedral of the Sacred Heart
89 Ridge St, at Clifton and Park Aves; tel 201/484-4600. This French Gothic cathedral covers an area of 40,000 square feet and is topped with a great copper spire which soars to 260 feet. The interior of the church features Italian Cararra marble; handcrafted bronze doors and bells cast in Italy; more than 200 stained-glass windows by German artisan Franz Zettler; and marble, granite, and limestone carvings and statues. Pope John Paul II celebrated mass here during his October 1995 tour of America. Donation requested. **Open:** Wed–Sun noon–5pm.

Newark Symphony Hall
1020 Broad St; tel 201/643-8009. This restored 1925 landmark theater, in the heart of the city, is the home of the New Jersey State Opera as well as the New Jersey Symphony Orchestra. Performances also include concerts, dance groups, and plays. **Open:** Call for schedule. $$$$

Newark Int'l Airport

See also Elizabeth

HOTELS 🏨

🏨🏨 Days Inn Newark Airport
450 US 1 S, Newark, 07114; tel 201/242-0900 or toll free 800/325-2525; fax 201/242-8480. Exit 14 off NJ Tpk. A simple yet cheerful hotel handy to the airport. **Rooms:** 191 rms and stes. CI 3pm/CO noon. Nonsmoking rms avail. Serviceable, standard rooms. **Amenities:** 🛁 ⚙ A/C, cable TV w/movies. **Services:** ✕ 🚐 🖼 ↵ 24-hour airport shuttle. **Facilities:** 🔟 &. 1 restaurant, 1 bar. **Rates:** $59–$79 S; $64–$84 D; $99–$125 ste. Extra person $5. Children under age 12 stay free. Parking: Outdoor, free. Weekend rates and senior discounts avail. AE, CB, DC, DISC, MC, V.

🏨🏨🏨 Holiday Inn North
160 Frontage Rd, Newark, 07114; tel 201/589-1000 or toll free 800/HOLIDAY; fax 201/589-2799. Exit 14 off NJ Tpk. Notable mostly for its airport location. **Rooms:** 234 rms. CI 4pm/CO noon. Nonsmoking rms avail. **Amenities:** 🛁 ⚙ A/C, cable TV w/movies, dataport, voice mail. Some units w/whirlpools. **Services:** ✕ 🚐 🖼 ↵ Car-rental desk. **Facilities:** 🔢 ◗2 🛒 📶 &. 1 restaurant, 1 bar (w/entertainment). **Rates:** $99–$109 S or D. Extra person $10. Children under age 16 stay free. Parking: Outdoor, free. Day rates and weekend packages avail. AE, DC, DISC, MC, V.

🏨🏨🏨 Newark Airport Marriott
Newark Int'l Airport, Newark, 07114; tel 201/623-0006 or toll free 800/882-1037; fax 201/623-7618. Exit 14 off NJ Tpk. This well-appointed corporate mecca is surprisingly calm, given its location at the airport entrance. Relaxing public areas. **Rooms:** 590 rms and stes. Executive level. CI 4pm/CO noon. Nonsmoking rms avail. Rooms have runway views. **Amenities:** 🛁 ⚙ 🍴 A/C, cable TV w/movies, voice mail. Complimentary newspaper and coffee. **Services:** 🛎 🔑 VP 🚐 🖼 ↵ Car-rental desk, masseur, babysitting. Multilingual staff. **Facilities:** 🔢 📶 💻 &. 3 restaurants, 2 bars (1 w/entertainment), games rm, spa, sauna, whirlpool. **Rates:** $159–$179 S or D; $450 ste. Parking: Outdoor, free. Weekend rates avail. Rates allow up to five people per room. AE, CB, DC, DISC, JCB, MC, V.

🏨🏨🏨 Radisson Hotel Newark Airport
128 Frontage Rd, Newark, 07114; tel 201/690-5500 or toll free 800/333-3333; fax 201/465-7195. Exit 14 off NJ Tpk. A dramatic, nine-story atrium rises over the plant-filled lobby

and pool area. **Rooms:** 503 rms and stes. Executive level. CI 4pm/CO noon. Nonsmoking rms avail. Oversized rooms with lots of light; some have balconies into the atrium. **Amenities:** 🏧 🕹 A/C, cable TV w/movies, dataport, voice mail. Some units w/terraces. Complimentary coffee and newspaper. Irons and ironing boards in all rooms. **Services:** ✗ 🚐 🖼 🛎 Car-rental desk. Afternoon hors d'oeuvres. **Facilities:** 🔓 🛝 ▱₁₀₀₀ 🖳 ⟐ 2 restaurants, 2 bars, games rm, spa, whirlpool. Lovely sunken-garden lounge. **Rates:** $155 S or D; $395–$495 ste. Parking: Outdoor, free. Weekend rates avail. AE, CB, DC, DISC, MC, V.

MOTEL

📼📼📼 Courtyard by Marriott
US 1/9 at I-78, Newark, 07114; tel 201/643-8500 or toll free 800/321-2211; fax 201/648-0662. Exit 14 off NJ Tpk. A bright, pretty property with a lounge, a fireplace, and a relaxing interior garden. **Rooms:** 146 rms and stes. CI 4pm/CO noon. Nonsmoking rms avail. Well-appointed rooms have separate vanity area and a separate seating area in the main room. **Amenities:** 🏧 🕹 🖥 A/C, cable TV w/movies, dataport, voice mail. Some units w/terraces. Irons and ironing boards in all rooms. **Services:** ✗ 🚐 🖼 ⟐ Complimentary daily paper and coffee in lounge. Friendly staff. **Facilities:** 🔓 🛝 ▱₈₀ ⟐ 1 restaurant, 1 bar, spa, whirlpool, washer/dryer. **Rates:** $79–$109 S or D; $125–$135 ste. Extra person $10. Parking: Outdoor, free. Weekend and extended-stay rates avail. AE, DC, DISC, MC, V.

New Brunswick

See also Somerville

Located on the Raritan River, this city is home to the beautiful main campus of Rutgers University (founded in 1776). Other cultural resources include the George Street Playhouse, the American Repertory Ballet, and the Cross Roads Theater, one of the country's premier African-American theater groups. The city's Old Market section offers a variety of shops, boutiques, and restaurants.

HOTEL 🏨

📼📼📼 Hyatt Regency New Brunswick
2 Albany St, 08901; tel 908/873-1234 or toll free 800/233-1234; fax 908/873-1382. Exit 9 off NJ Tpk to NJ 18 N to NJ 27 S. A spacious and attractive hotel, built in 1984 and well-kept since then. **Rooms:** 286 rms and stes. Executive level. CI 3pm/CO noon. Nonsmoking rms avail. **Amenities:** 🏧 🕹 🖥 🍷 A/C, cable TV w/movies, refrig, dataport, voice mail. Some units w/terraces. **Services:** ✗ 🗝 🖼 ⟐ Social director, children's program, babysitting. **Facilities:** 🔓 🏀 ▱₂ 🛝 ▱₈₀₀ 🖳 ⟐ 1 restaurant, 2 bars (1 w/entertainment), basketball, spa, sauna, whirlpool, washer/dryer. Sports bar. Nice indoor pool with health spa. **Rates:** Peak (Mar–Dec)

$140 S; $160 D; $150–$460 ste. Extra person $15. Children under age 18 stay free. Lower rates off-season. Parking: Indoor, $6/day. AE, CB, DC, DISC, JCB, MC, V.

RESTAURANTS 🍽

The Frog and the Peach
29 Dennis St; tel 908/846-3216. NJ 18 S to NJ 27 S 1 block to right at Dennis St. **New American.** A stained-glass canopy hangs under the high ceiling of this converted 19th-century factory. The menu is just as creative as the decor, with choices like snapper in saffron sauce and tenderloin of lamb. **FYI:** Reservations recommended. No smoking. **Open:** Lunch Mon–Fri 11:30am–2:30pm; dinner Mon–Sat 5:30–10:30pm, Sun 4:30–9:30pm. **Prices:** Main courses $19–$30. AE, CB, DC, DISC, MC, V. ♥ 🍴 ⟐

★ La Fontana
120 Albany St; tel 908/249-7500. Exit 9 off Tpk to NJ 18 N to NJ 27 S. **Italian.** The cuisine here reflects all regions of Italy, ranging from oven-roasted sea bass to filet mignon with Alaskan king-crab meat. A six-course tasting menu and a healthy-heart menu are available. The wine list includes over 500 selections. **FYI:** Reservations recommended. Jacket required. **Open:** Lunch Mon–Fri noon–2:30pm; dinner Mon–Thurs 5–10pm, Fri–Sat 5–11pm. **Prices:** Main courses $23–$28. AE, MC, V. ♥ VP ⟐

⑤ Stage Left: An American Cafe
5 Livingston Ave; tel 908/828-4444. NJ 18 N 2 mi from New St exit 3rd light make right on Livingston Ave. **New American/Eclectic.** Praised for excellent food at moderate prices, this spot has a jazzy, semi-bohemian ambience. The menu changes seasonally, and there's live jazz every Sunday. **FYI:** Reservations recommended. Jazz. **Open:** Tues–Thurs 5–11pm, Fri 11:45am–1am, Sat 5pm–1am, Sun 4–10pm. **Prices:** Main courses $15–$20. AE, CB, DC, MC, V. ♥ 🍴 ⟐

Zia Grill
19 Dennis St; tel 908/249-1551. NJ 18 S to NJ 27 S; go 1 block to right on Dennis St. **Southwestern.** Grilled smoked rib eye steak and paella are favorites in this charming, two-level dining spot. Regional artwork imparts a feel of the Southwest. **FYI:** Reservations accepted. Blues. **Open:** Lunch Mon–Fri 11:30am–2:30pm; dinner Mon–Sat 5:30–10:30pm, Sun 4–9pm. **Prices:** Main courses $17–$25. AE, DC, MC, V. ▣ ⟐

New Providence

Founded in 1889, New Providence features a substantial historic district and is adjacent to the Passaic River and the Great Swamp National Wildlife Refuge. **Information:** Suburban Chamber of Commerce, 360 Springfield Ave, PO Box 824, Summit, 07902 (tel 908/522-1700).

MOTEL 🏨

🏨🏨 Best Western Murray Hill Inn

535 Central Ave, 07974; tel 908/665-9200 or toll free 800/688-7474; fax 908/665-9562. At South St. A convenient motel with a bright "California-inspired" lobby and newly refurbished rooms. **Rooms:** 76 rms, stes, and effic. CI 2pm/CO noon. Nonsmoking rms avail. **Amenities:** 🛏 ⌚ A/C, cable TV w/movies, dataport. Some units w/whirlpools. **Services:** ✕ 🖼 🍸 **Facilities:** 🛁 120 1 restaurant, sauna, washer/dryer. **Rates:** $79–$99 S or D; $125–$150 ste; $115 effic. Extra person $10. Children under age 12 stay free. AP and MAP rates avail. Parking: Outdoor, free. Weekend and extended-stay rates avail. AE, CB, DC, DISC, MC, V.

RESTAURANT 🍴

★ Joe's Mexican Cantina

24 South St; tel 908/464-4360. Between Livingston and Central Aves. **Mexican.** Upon arrival, guests wend through a maze of intimate dining areas ablaze with color, handpainted tile, ochre-washed walls hung with serapes, and a series of small oil paintings. Joe adds his personal touch to all the standard South of the Border favorites, as well as whole red snapper, marinated pork loin, and combination platters. **FYI:** Reservations accepted. Dress code. BYO. Additional location: 125 Washington Valley Rd, Warren (tel 563-0480). **Open:** Sun–Thurs 11:30am–10pm, Fri–Sat 11:30am–10:30pm. **Prices:** Main courses $9–$20. AE, MC, V.

Ocean City

Family resort perched between Great Egg Harbor and the Atlantic Ocean. The town features long white beaches and a fun-filled boardwalk. Special events, such as the Doo-Dah Parade and Nights in Venice Boat Parade, are held during summer months. **Information:** Ocean City Tourism Development Commission, PO Box 916, Ocean City, 08226 (tel 609/399-6344 or toll free 800/BEACH-NJ).

HOTELS 🏨

🏨🏨 Port-O-Call Hotel

1510 Boardwalk, 08226; tel 609/399-8812 or toll free 800/334-4546; fax 609/399-0387. Wesley Ave between 15th and 16th Sts. A landmark on the beach and boardwalk for more than two decades, this friendly place has a relaxing pool and deck. **Rooms:** 99 rms; 1 cottage/villa. Executive level. CI 2:30pm/CO 11am. Nonsmoking rms avail. **Amenities:** 🛏 ⌚ 📺 A/C, cable TV w/movies, refrig. All units w/terraces, 1 w/fireplace, 1 w/whirlpool. Fresh flowers in each room. **Services:** ✕ 🚐 🖼 🍸 Twice-daily maid svce, babysitting. **Facilities:** 🛁 🛁 190 ⚹ 1 restaurant, 1 beach (ocean), lifeguard, sauna, beauty salon, washer/dryer. **Rates:** Peak

(June–Sept) $170–$230 S or D. Extra person $15. Children under age 12 stay free. Min stay wknds. Lower rates off-season. Parking: Outdoor, free. AE, CB, DC, MC, V.

🏨🏨 Watson's Regency Suites

9th St and Ocean Ave, PO Box 331, 08226; tel 609/398-4300 or toll free 800/445-9944; fax 609/398-0197. Pleasant family-style hotel. The beach and boardwalk are a block away. **Rooms:** 79 stes and effic. CI 4pm/CO 11am. Nonsmoking rms avail. **Amenities:** 🛏 ⌚ 📺 A/C, cable TV w/movies, refrig, VCR. Some units w/terraces. All the suites are brightly decorated, and all have full kitchens and ceramic-tile bathrooms. **Services:** 🚐 🍸 Babysitting. **Facilities:** 🛁 50 ⚹ Sauna, whirlpool, washer/dryer. **Rates:** Peak (June–Sept) $259 ste; $259 effic. Children under age 18 stay free. Min stay wknds. Lower rates off-season. Parking: Outdoor, free. Rates based on four people to a room. AE, MC, V.

MOTEL

🏨 Impala Motel

1001 Ocean Ave at 10th St, 08226; tel 609/399-7500; fax 609/398-4379. It's a short walk to the boardwalk and the beach from this pleasant motel in the heart of town. **Rooms:** 109 rms and effic. CI 2:30pm/CO 11am. Nonsmoking rms avail. Rooms are clean and neat. **Amenities:** 🛏 A/C, cable TV w/movies, refrig. All units w/terraces. **Services:** ✕ 🍸 Babysitting. **Facilities:** 🛁 1 restaurant, washer/dryer. **Rates:** Peak (June–Sept) $58–$124 S or D; $80–$165 effic. Extra person $10. Children under age 16 stay free. Min stay peak. Lower rates off-season. Parking: Outdoor, free. AE, DC, MC, V.

RESTAURANTS 🍴

★ Cousins

104 Asbury Ave; tel 609/399-9462. From 9th St, left on Asbury. **Continental/Italian.** The talented chef at this fun eatery recommends shrimp and crabmeat scampi, veal Alfredo, veal Diablo, and the Cousins Special. **FYI:** Reservations recommended. Children's menu. No liquor license. No smoking. **Open:** Peak (July–Aug) daily 4–10pm. Closed Jan–Mar. **Prices:** Main courses $10–$20. DISC, MC, V. 👪 💟

Culinary Garden

841 Central Ave; tel 609/399-3713. 9th St and Asbury Ave. **New American.** The dinner menu includes classic favorites like sautéed chicken saltimbocca, chicken and broccoli Dijon, and jumbo lump crab imperial. **FYI:** Reservations recommended. Children's menu. No liquor license. **Open:** Peak (July–Aug) breakfast daily 8–11am; lunch daily 11am–2pm; dinner daily 5–10pm. Closed Dec–Mar. **Prices:** Main courses $10–$20. AE, DISC, MC, V. 💟

ATTRACTION 🎭

Ocean City Historical Museum

1735 Simpson Ave at 17th St; tel 609/399-1801. While walking on the beach in Ocean City, visitors may notice the remains of a ship right on the coast. This is the *Sindia*, a ship that ran aground and sank in 1901 on a return trip to New York from Kobe, Japan. Relics from the *Sindia,* as well as ship models and old photos, are on display in this museum. Other exhibits include natural history displays of seashells and mounted birds, and re-created Victorian period rooms including a dining room, bedroom, and kitchen. **Open:** Peak (June–Aug) Mon–Fri 10am–4pm, Sat 1–4pm. Reduced hours off-season. **Free**

Palisades Interstate Park

An 81,000-acre system of wilderness areas stretching along the banks of the Hudson River, including parts of Bergen County, in New Jersey and Rockland, Orange, Ulster, and Sullivan Counties in New York. Major areas in New York State include Harriman and Bear Mountain State Parks, both of which offer hiking and biking trails, swimming, fishing, playing fields, and picnic areas. The 2,500-acre New Jersey section includes the Alpine and Englewood-Bloomers Areas and Ross Dock (all of which offer boating, fishing, hiking, and picnicking), and Fort Lee Historic Park. A visitors center, located on Palisades Interstate Parkway at exit 17, sells train and road maps, books, and guides. For more information on the New Jersey section of the park, contact Palisades Interstate Park Commission, PO Box 155, Alpine 07620 (tel 201/768-1360).

Paramus

Home of New Jersey Children's Museum and Van Saun Park Zoo, featuring an 1860 farmyard and walk-through aviary. Its biggest attraction, however, is its shopping malls. **Information:** Paramus Chamber of Commerce, 80 E Ridgewood Ave, PO Box 325, Paramus, 07653 (tel 201/261-4600).

MOTELS 📻

🚬🚬 Holiday Inn
50 NJ 17 N, 07652; tel 201/843-5400 or toll free 800/465-4329; fax 201/712-0434. At NJ 4 interchange. On a heavily trafficked shopping highway, just minutes from some of New Jersey's best malls and eight miles from the George Washington Bridge. The lobby is small but pleasant, with plenty of comfortable seating. **Rooms:** 78 rms and stes. CI noon/CO noon. Nonsmoking rms avail. **Amenities:** 📻 🗄 🍴 A/C, cable TV w/movies, in-rm safe. **Services:** ✗ 🖎 🖵 **Facilities:** 📻 🛌 🎱 ⚐ 1 restaurant. **Rates:** $70 S or D; $125 ste. Children under age 19 stay free. Parking: Outdoor, free. B&B package avail. AE, CB, DC, DISC, JCB, MC, V.

🚬🚬🚬 Radisson Inn Paramus
601 From Rd, 07652; tel 201/262-6900 or toll free 800/333-3333; fax 201/262-4955. Midland Ave exit off NJ 17N, then left. The lobby decor is a bit odd, but the location is great for hard-core shoppers heading for the Paramus Mall.

Rooms: 120 rms. CI 3pm/CO noon. Nonsmoking rms avail. **Amenities:** 📻 🗄 🖵 🍴 A/C, cable TV w/movies, voice mail. Refrigerators on request. King rooms have two phones and a dataport. **Services:** ✗ 🖎 🖵 🐾 Twice-daily maid svce. Free van service to local business offices. **Facilities:** 📻 🏊 ⚐ 1 restaurant, 1 bar (w/entertainment), volleyball, washer/dryer. Full-service restaurant has jazz on weekends and a pleasant lounge with a pool table. **Rates:** $125 S or D. Extra person $10. Children under age 12 stay free. AP and MAP rates avail. Parking: Outdoor, free. AE, CB, DC, DISC, JCB, MC, V.

Park Ridge

A borough of some 8,000 residents, located on the New York state border. Minutes from the Hudson River, and close to Lake Tappan.

HOTEL 🏨

🚬🚬🚬 Park Ridge Marriott
300 Brae Blvd, 07656; tel 201/307-0800 or toll free 800/882-1038; fax 201/307-0859. Exit 172 off Garden State Pkwy N. Set in a corporate park, with a large atrium lobby. Caters mostly to business travelers. **Rooms:** 289 rms. Executive level. CI 4pm/CO noon. Nonsmoking rms avail. **Amenities:** 📻 🗄 🍴 A/C, satel TV w/movies, dataport, voice mail. Some units w/terraces. Refrigerators available. **Services:** ✗ 🖎 🖵 🐾 Babysitting. **Facilities:** 📻 🛌 🏊 ⚐ 2 restaurants, 2 bars (1 w/entertainment), basketball, volleyball, spa, sauna, whirlpool, washer/dryer. **Rates:** $75–$119 S or D. Children under age 18 stay free. Parking: Outdoor, free. AE, CB, DC, DISC, JCB, MC, V.

RESTAURANT 🍴

Esty Street
86 Spring Valley Rd; tel 201/307-1515. Exit 172 off Garden State Pkwy N, right off exit, right at second light. **New American.** Award-winning cuisine in a warm, wood-paneled room. The varied menu—focusing on fish and pasta dishes for the health-conscious—makes it popular with the corporate lunch crowd. **FYI:** Reservations recommended. **Open:** Lunch Mon–Fri 11:30am–2:30pm; dinner Mon–Thurs 5:30–9pm, Fri–Sat 5:30–10pm. **Prices:** Main courses $17–$27. AE, DC, MC, V.

Parsippany

Six miles NE of Morristown, Parsippany is the home of the Craftsmen Farm Museum, once the home of Gustav Stickley, maker of arts and crafts furniture. Near to Lake Hiawatha.

HOTELS 🏨

≡≡≡ Embassy Suites

909 Parsippany Blvd, 07054; tel 201/334-1440 or toll free 800/EMBASSY; fax 201/402-1188. Off US 46. All the suites of this meticulously landscaped modern building face an open, five-story tropical atrium. Catering mainly to business travelers, the hotel is close to several major corporations. **Rooms:** 274 stes. Executive level. CI 3pm/CO noon. Nonsmoking rms avail. All units have sofa beds. **Amenities:** 🛎 ♨ 🔳 ⌀ A/C, cable TV w/movies, refrig, dataport, voice mail. Microwaves. **Services:** ✗ 🚐 ⊠ ⇦ Car-rental desk, babysitting. Complimentary reception each evening. **Facilities:** 🔂 🛏 200 💻 ⑇ 1 restaurant (lunch and dinner only; *see* "Restaurants" below), 1 bar, volleyball, games rm, spa, sauna, whirlpool, playground, washer/dryer. Exceptional fitness facility. **Rates (BB):** $104–$184 ste. Extra person $25. Children under age 12 stay free. Parking: Outdoor, free. AE, CB, DC, DISC, JCB, MC, V.

≡≡≡≡ The Parsippany Hilton

One Hilton Court, 07054; tel 201/267-7373 or toll free 800/HILTONS; fax 201/984-6853. NJ 10 W off Campus Dr. Neat landscaping surrounds this well-run business hotel. The lobby is spacious and attractive. **Rooms:** 508 rms and stes. CI 3pm/CO 11am. Nonsmoking rms avail. **Amenities:** 🛎 ♨ ⌀ A/C, cable TV w/movies, dataport, voice mail. Feather or foam pillows on request. **Services:** ✗ 🚐 ⊠ ⇦ Twice-daily maid svce, car-rental desk. User-programmable wake-up service. **Facilities:** 🔂 🚲 🏋 🏊 🛏 💻 ⑇ 2 restaurants (*see* "Restaurants" below), 1 bar (w/entertainment), basketball, whirlpool, washer/dryer. **Rates:** $72–$145 S or D; $275 ste. Extra person $20. Children under age 9 stay free. Parking: Outdoor, free. AE, CB, DC, DISC, JCB, MC, V.

UNRATED Sheraton Tara Hotel

199 Smith Rd, 07054; tel 201/515-2000 or toll free 800/THE-TARA; fax 201/515-3180. At jct I-80/I-287. Housed in a castle-like building in an impeccably maintained wooded area; there's even a serene lake. Hard to believe Newark International Airport and New York City are just half an hour away. **Rooms:** 383 rms and stes. Executive level. CI 3pm/CO noon. No smoking. **Amenities:** 🛎 ♨ 🔳 ⌀ A/C, cable TV w/movies, dataport, voice mail. Some units w/whirlpools. **Services:** ✗ ▣ 🚐 ⊠ ⇦ Masseur, babysitting. Scheduled shuttle service to airport. **Facilities:** 🔂 🛏 1200 💻 ⑇ 2 restaurants, 1 bar (w/entertainment), racquetball, spa, sauna, steam rm, whirlpool. Entire facility is nonsmoking. **Rates:** Peak (Sept–Nov 17) $160 S; $170 D; $270 ste. Extra person $10. Children under age 12 stay free. Lower rates off-season. Parking: Outdoor, free. Corporate and extended-stay rates avail. AE, CB, DC, DISC, JCB, MC, V.

MOTELS

UNRATED Days Inn Parsippany

3159 US 46, 07054; tel 201/335-0200 or toll free 800/DAYS-INN; fax 201/263-3094. ¼ mi W of jct I-287/US 202. These older buildings are showing some wear, but business travelers will appreciate the location. **Rooms:** 120 rms and stes. CI 1pm/CO noon. Nonsmoking rms avail. Rooms were refurbished in 1995. **Amenities:** 🛎 ♨ A/C, cable TV, dataport. Some units w/terraces, some w/whirlpools. Irons, microwaves, refrigerators available on request. **Services:** ✗ ⊠ ⇦ ⇦ Twice-daily maid svce. Same-day dry cleaning and laundry (weekdays only). **Facilities:** 🔂 150 💻 ⑇ 1 restaurant (lunch and dinner only), 1 bar. **Rates (CP):** $64 S; $69 D; $125 ste. Extra person $5. Children under age 15 stay free. Parking: Outdoor, free. AE, CB, DC, DISC, JCB, MC, V.

≡≡ Hampton Inn

3535 US 46 at Cherry Hill Rd, 07054; tel 201/263-0095 or toll free 800/HAMPTON; fax 201/263-6133. Exit 42 off I-80. A modern motel, close to major highways, restaurants, businesses, and shopping centers. **Rooms:** 100 rms and effic. CI 3pm/CO noon. Nonsmoking rms avail. Simple, tastefully decorated rooms. **Amenities:** 🛎 ♨ A/C, satel TV w/movies. Some units w/whirlpools. Free daily newspapers and in-room movies. **Services:** ✗ ⊠ ⇦ Pleasant, helpful staff. Free local calls. **Facilities:** 🛏 50 ⑇ 1 restaurant (lunch and dinner only), 1 bar, sauna, whirlpool. **Rates (CP):** $65–$89 S or D; $75–$125 effic. Extra person $10. Children under age 12 stay free. Parking: Outdoor, free. Weekend, holiday, and extended-stay packages avail. AE, MC, V.

RESTAURANTS 🍴

Caffe Sport

In Embassy Suites, 909 Parsippany Blvd; tel 201/334-1440. Off US 46. **Continental/Italian.** Northern Italian and continental cuisine served in an attractive 190-seat dining room. The grill and patio are open for warm-weather dining. **FYI:** Reservations recommended. Children's menu. Dress code. **Open:** Daily 11am–11pm. **Prices:** Main courses $7–$25. AE, CB, DC, DISC, MC, V. �&

Livingston's Chophouse Restaurant

In The Parsippany Hilton, One Hilton Court; tel 201/267-7373. NJ 10 W off Campus Dr. **American/Continental.** Classic, continental variations on beef, seafood, and chicken are served in this oak-paneled, colonial-style room. Very impressive wine list. **FYI:** Reservations recommended. Dress code. No smoking. **Open:** Daily 5–11pm. **Prices:** Main courses $13–$22. AE, CB, DC, DISC, MC, V. 🖼&

Villa Domenico

258 US 46 W; tel 201/808-9866. **Italian.** Owner/chef Domenico Parotta prepares the homemade Italian entrees, and desserts are either made on the premises or imported from Italy. There's a keyboard musician or a guitarist on Wednesdays, and dancing on Fridays and Saturdays. **FYI:**

Reservations recommended. Dress code. **Open:** Lunch Mon–Fri 11am–3pm; dinner Mon–Thurs 5–10pm, Fri–Sat 5–11pm, Sun 2–9pm. **Prices:** Main courses $11–$18. AE, CB, DC, MC, V. &

Paterson

See also Saddle Brook

Founded in 1791 as an industrial settlement on the banks of the Passaic River, Paterson continues today as a manufacturing and industrial center. Near to Packansack Lake and Passaic Falls, as well as Lamberth Castle and the Garret Mountain Reservation. **Information:** Greater Paterson Chamber of Commerce, 100 Hamilton Plaza #1201, Paterson, 07505 (tel 201/881-7300).

RESTAURANT 🍴

★ Eastside Restaurant

730 Broadway; tel 201/523-6424. At E 33rd St. **Diner/Soul/Southern.** Chefs Gary and Larry serve up classic soul food at this basic shopfront cafe and lunch counter. Favorites are fried whiting, smothered pork chops, ribs, and fried chicken, with piles of collard greens, yams, and mashed potatoes. Regulars line up on Thursdays for the meat loaf and chitlins. Sweet potato pie is available for dessert. **FYI:** Reservations not accepted. No liquor license. **Open:** Tues–Thurs 6am–9pm, Fri–Sat 6am–11pm, Sun 6am–6pm. **Prices:** Main courses $5–$9. No CC.

ATTRACTION 🏛

Great Falls on Passaic River

72 McBride Ave; tel 201/279-9587. Visitors center located across from the falls gives tours and information about America's first planned industrial city (1791), conceived by Alexander Hamilton and made famous by William Carlos Williams. The 77-foot-high falls for which the city was named cascade across an area of 280 feet. The Great Falls Hydroelectric Station (circa 1914) is open for tours Wednesday 10am–2pm. **Open:** Daily sunrise–sunset. **Free**

Plainfield

HOTEL 🏨

🏨🏨 Holiday Inn

4701 Stelton Rd, South Plainfield, 07080; tel 908/753-5500 or toll free 800/HOLIDAY; fax 908/753-5500. Durham Ave exit off I-78. Right in New Jersey's corporate and strip-mall heartland, this property is convenient to major highways. **Rooms:** 173 rms and stes. Executive level. CI 1pm/CO 1pm. Nonsmoking rms avail. **Amenities:** 🔧 ₫ A/C, cable TV w/movies, dataport, voice mail. Nintendo, Nordic Track delivered to room on request. **Services:** ✗ ⊠ ↲ **Facilities:** ⚿

🔌 📺 🖥 & 1 restaurant, 1 bar, spa, sauna, whirlpool, washer/dryer. **Rates:** $99–$104 S or D; $198 ste. Children under age 18 stay free. Parking: Outdoor, free. Weekend and AARP rates avail. AE, CB, DC, DISC, MC, V.

Princeton

Home of Princeton University, founded in 1746 as the College of New Jersey. Other cultural and historical highlights include the Princeton Art Museum, the Bainbridge Home, Princeton Battlefield, and Morven, home of the New Jersey Historical Society. **Information:** Princeton Area Convention & Visitors Bureau, 179 Nassau St, Princeton, 08540 (tel 609/683-1760).

HOTELS 🏨

🏨🏨🏨 Hyatt Regency Princeton

102 Carnegie Center, 08540-6293; tel 609/987-1234 or toll free 800/233-1234; fax 609/987-2584. Located a mile from campus in a 500-acre office park. A large atrium houses guest reception and (a few steps down) the hotel's restaurant and bar. **Rooms:** 348 rms and stes. Executive level. CI 3pm/CO noon. Nonsmoking rms avail. Spacious rooms; some balconies overlook the atrium. **Amenities:** 🔧 ₫ 🖥 🍴 A/C, cable TV w/movies, dataport, voice mail. Some units w/terraces, 1 w/fireplace, 1 w/whirlpool. **Services:** ✗ 🕿 📹 🚗 ⊠ ↲ Car-rental desk, children's program, babysitting. Courtesy shuttle to University, corporate parks, and attractions. Extensive business services, including secretarial services and equipment rentals. **Facilities:** ⚿ 🏊 🍷2 🔌 📺 🖥 1 restaurant, 1 bar (w/entertainment), sauna, whirlpool. **Rates:** $135–$164 S or D; $325–$675 ste. Children under age 18 stay free. Parking: Outdoor, free. AE, CB, DC, DISC, MC, V.

🏨🏨🏨 Marriott Princeton Forrestal Village

201 Village Blvd, 08540; tel 609/452-7900 or toll free 800/MARRIOTT; fax 609/452-1223. In Forrestal Village on US 1. Located at Princeton's Forrestal Village, a popular outlet shopping center with more than 40 shops (including Oneida, Bass, and Geoffrey Beene) as well as restaurants and a food court. **Rooms:** 294 rms and stes. Executive level. CI 3pm/CO 11am. Nonsmoking rms avail. Rooms are spacious and attractive. **Amenities:** 🔧 ₫ 🍴 A/C, cable TV w/movies, dataport, voice mail. Some units w/terraces. **Services:** ✗ 🕿 🚗 ⊠ ↲ Car-rental desk, children's program. **Facilities:** ⚿ 🍷2 🔌 📺 🖥 & 2 restaurants, 1 bar (w/entertainment), volleyball, sauna, whirlpool, washer/dryer. Golf nearby. **Rates:** $99–$154 S or D; $400–$700 ste. Extra person $15. Children under age 18 stay free. Parking: Outdoor, free. AE, CB, DC, DISC, ER, JCB, MC, V.

UNRATED Nassau Inn

10 Palmer Square, 08542; tel 609/921-7500 or toll free 800/8-NASSAU; fax 609/921-9385. Located in the heart of downtown, this establishment has served as an inn for more

than 200 years. Guest reception is at the side entrance, in the new part of the building, but the original entrance still serves as a comfortable sitting area for guests, with its hardwood floors, Oriental rugs, exposed beam ceiling, huge fireplace, and grand piano. Book far in advance for university events. **Rooms:** 215 rms and stes. CI 3pm/CO noon. Nonsmoking rms avail. Rooms are individually decorated, and vary in size, shape, and amount of light. **Amenities:** 🔋 ⚕ A/C, cable TV w/movies, voice mail. **Services:** ✗ 🚐 ⊠ ⤶ **Facilities:** 🔲 3 restaurants, 1 bar (w/entertainment). Dining choices include the elegant Palmer's Restaurant, the Greenhouse (overlooking Palmer Square), and the Tap Room (for food and drinks in a casual, historic atmosphere). **Rates:** $165 S; $185 D; $290 ste. Min stay special events. Parking: Indoor, $11/day. AE, MC, V.

≡≡ Novotel Princeton

100 Independence Way, 08540; tel 609/520-1200 or toll free 800/NOVOTEL; fax 609/520-0594. On US 1. Located two miles from Princeton University. Small, plain lobby, but front desk is well staffed. Clocks tell guests the current time in Los Angeles, Princeton, and Paris. **Rooms:** 180 rms. CI 3pm/CO 1pm. Nonsmoking rms avail. **Amenities:** 🔋 ⚕ ⛾ A/C, cable TV w/movies, dataport. All units w/minibars. **Services:** ✗ 🗝 ⊠ ⤶ ⤶ Car-rental desk. Free local transportation (within 10 miles) 7am to 7pm. Complimentary newspapers and coffee in lobby. Complimentary breakfast for kids sharing parents' room. **Facilities:** 🛋 🍴 🔲 ⚷ 1 restaurant, whirlpool, washer/dryer. **Rates:** $79–$99 S or D. Children under age 16 stay free. Parking: Outdoor, free. AE, CB, DC, DISC, ER, MC, V.

≡≡ Palmer Inn Best Western

3499 US 1 S, 08540; tel 609/452-2500 or toll free 800/688-0500; fax 609/452-1371. Located near Princeton's MarketFair mall, this hotel offers basic, comfortable accommodations in a convenient location. **Rooms:** 103 rms. CI 2pm/CO 11am. Nonsmoking rms avail. **Amenities:** 🔋 ⚕ A/C, cable TV w/movies, voice mail. Some units w/minibars, some w/terraces. **Services:** ⊠ Car-rental desk. Complimentary local transportation (within a five-mile radius). **Facilities:** 🛋 🍴 🔲 1 restaurant, 1 bar, sauna, whirlpool. The pool is located in an attractive garden courtyard. Charlie Brown's restaurant offers basic American fare. **Rates:** $80–$106 S or D. Extra person $10. Children under age 16 stay free. Parking: Outdoor, free. AE, CB, DC, DISC, MC, V.

INN

≡≡≡ Peacock Inn

20 Bayard Lane, 08540; tel 609/924-1707; fax 609/924-0788. Built as a private home in 1775, the colonial building was moved here from its original location on Princeton's main street and opened as an inn in 1912. The street is somewhat busy, but the inn is set far enough back to prevent noise problems. Great in-town location, convenient to university, shopping, and dining. **Rooms:** 17 rms (7 w/shared bath).

CI 3pm/CO noon. Nonsmoking rms avail. Rooms are individually decorated. **Amenities:** 🔋 ⚕ A/C, cable TV. **Services:** ⤶ ⤶ Friendly, helpful staff will provide information about the area. **Facilities:** 1 restaurant (see "Restaurants" below), 1 bar. A fine French restaurant (Le Plumet Royal) occupies much of the inn's first floor. **Rates (CP):** $100–$135 S or D w/shared bath, $100–$135 S or D w/private bath. Extra person $10. Higher rates for special events/hols. Parking: Outdoor, free. AE, MC, V.

RESTAURANTS 🍴

Alchemist & Barrister

28 Witherspoon St; tel 609/924-5555. **American.** The menu features classic dishes prepared in modern style, such as grilled filet mignon with southwestern polenta fries, roasted corn and black beans, and a tomatillo and chipolte sauce; and grilled fillet of salmon with lemongrass, shiitake mushrooms, and rice noodles. **FYI:** Reservations recommended. Dress code. No smoking. **Open:** Lunch Mon–Sat 11:30am–2:30pm; dinner Mon–Thurs 5:30–10pm, Fri–Sat 5:30–10:30pm, Sun 5–10pm; brunch Sun 11:30am–3pm. **Prices:** Main courses $16–$25. MC, V.

Lahiere's

11 Witherspoon St; tel 609/921-2798. **French.** A Princeton institution (opened in 1919), located just across the street from the university's gates. Menu features specialties such as porcini-dusted fillet of halibut in a light vegetable stew, and thyme-grilled sirloin of beef with roasted garlic potatoes and wilted chard. Features a fine wine list. **FYI:** Reservations recommended. Dress code. No smoking. **Open:** Lunch Mon–Sat 11:30am–2:30pm; dinner Mon–Sat 5:30–10pm. **Prices:** Main courses $16–$27. AE, MC, V.

♣ Le Plumet Royal

In the Peacock Inn, 20 Bayard Lane; tel 609/924-1707. **French.** Attractive dining room in 1775 inn located off Princeton's main street. Menu changes seasonally and may include appetizers such as warmed duck leg confit accompanied by toasted pasta tossed with wild mushrooms and roasted peppers, or grilled shrimp layered between fresh corn relish and potato wafers and set on a black bean compote. Entrees may include roasted beef tenderloin complemented with Forme d' Amberte cheese and a basil demiglacé, accompanied by a bed of gratin potatoes and fresh vegetables. The inn has its own pastry chef; desserts are creative and delicious. **FYI:** Reservations recommended. Dress code. No smoking. **Open:** Lunch daily 11:30am–2:30pm; dinner daily 5:30–9:30pm. **Prices:** Main courses $20–$43. AE, MC, V. 📷

Quilty's

18 Witherspoon St; tel 609/683-4771. Off Nassau St. **French bistro.** Owned and operated by two young men, Quilty's has a modern feel. The menu changes seasonally; recent appetizers included a stilton and endive salad with raspberry-apple vinaigrette and country pâté with tapenade and croutons.

Entrees include such favorites as pan-seared salmon with cucumbers, tomatoes, and a champagne-dill sauce, and boursin and steak au poivre with a cognac, mustard, and cream sauce. Pastries are all made in-house. Servers are knowledgeable and attentive. **FYI:** Reservations recommended. No smoking. **Open:** Tues–Fri 11:30am–close, Sat 5pm–close, Sun 11am–close. **Prices:** Main courses $18–$23. AE, DC, MC, V. ♥

Triumph Brewing Company

138 Nassau St; tel 609/924-7855. **New American.** The soaring space provides seating on three levels; steel brewing tanks are visible through glass behind the bar. The menu offers an enticing selection of eclectic fare, but quality can be hit or miss. Popular appetizers include grilled artichoke and tomato quesadillas, and jerk chicken wings served with pear slices and mango salsa. Entree selections include fish (beer battered, of course) and chips with malt vinegar, and leg of lamb braised in stout beer with garlic, tomatoes, and fresh herbs. Six varieties of beer are brewed on the premises (tours offered on Saturdays at 1 and 3pm). **FYI:** Reservations accepted. No smoking. **Open: Prices:** Main courses $11–$18. AE, DC, DISC, MC, V. ♿

ATTRACTIONS 🏛

Princeton Battlefield State Park

500 Mercer Rd; tel 609/921-0074. This park commemorates a major turning point in the American Revolution: the Battle of Princeton, fought on January 3, 1777, in which Gen George Washington led his forces to victory over the much-better-prepared Redcoats. Located in the park is the Thomas Clarke House (500 Mercer St), built in 1770 by Clarke, a Quaker farmer. The house was used as an interim hospital during the Battle of Princeton, and today the home is furnished with Revolution-era pieces. Visitors can tour the home, carriage shed, and smokehouse, and see demonstrations of late-18th-century crafts performed by living history interpreters. Interior photography is not permitted. **Open:** Daily sunrise–sunset. **Free**

Rockingham Historic Site

108 County Rd 518; tel 609/921-8835. Gen George Washington was at Rockingham when he received the news that the Treaty of Paris had been signed. It was also here that he wrote his farewell address to the troops on November 2, 1783. Built circa 1710, the mansion has been preserved as it was during the months that George and Martha Washington resided here: rooms are decorated in 18th-century style, the dining room table is set, the parlor tea table is ready to receive visitors, the General's desk is laid out with quills and a whale-oil lamp. **Open:** Wed–Sat 10am–noon and 1–4pm, Sun 1–4pm. **Free**

Princeton University

Maclean House; tel 609/258-3603. Originally chartered in 1746 as the College of New Jersey, the school was first located in Elizabeth, then in Newark, and was finally relocated to Princeton in 1756. In 1896, it officially became known as Princeton University. Highlights of the Ivy League campus include Nassau Hall, where the state's first legislature met in 1776; the University Library, which holds more than five million books and journals; the University Chapel (circa 1928), modeled after the chapel of King's College, Cambridge; and the Art Museum, whose entrance is marked by the Picasso sculpture *Head of a Woman*. (Eighteen other sculptures, including works by Moore, Noguchi, and Calder, are scattered throughout the campus.) Guided tours, led by student Orange Key guides, leave from the Maclean House. **Open:** Mon–Sat 9am–5pm, Sun 1–5pm. **Free**

The Art Museum at Princeton University

McCormick Hall; tel 609/258-3788. Among the highlights of this museum's permanent collection are pre-Columbian art (with examples of works by the Maya); Roman mosaics from Princeton's excavations in Antioch; medieval European sculpture and stained glass; and a collection of 20th-century works by such modern masters as Pablo Picasso, Jasper Johns, and Jacques Lipchitz. **Open:** Tues–Sat 10am–5pm, Sun 1–5pm. **Free**

Bainbridge House

158 Nassau St; tel 609/921-6748. Built in 1766, this is one of the oldest surviving buildings in Princeton and one of the area's best preserved examples of mid-Georgian architecture. Nearly 70 percent of the original interior woodwork remains, including original paneled walls and flooring. Today the home serves as the headquarters of the Princeton Historical Society. On display are more than 40,000 artifacts, manuscripts, photographs, artworks, and articles of clothing dating from the 17th century to the present. Guided tours of Princeton begin here every Sunday at 2pm. **Open:** Peak (Mar–Dec) Tues–Sun noon–4pm. Reduced hours off-season. **Free**

Morven

55 Stockton Rd; tel 609/683-4495. Originally built in 1759 by Richard Stockton, a signer of the Declaration of Independence. This national historic landmark was used as a headquarters during the Revolutionary War and was the official residence for five of New Jersey's governors. The house, now administered by the New Jersey State Museum, is decorated with period furnishings and contains portraits of its famous residents. **Open:** Wed and Sat 10am–2pm. **$$**

McCarter Theatre Center for the Performing Arts

91 University Place; tel 609/683-8000. Since it opened its doors in 1930, this theater has hosted the premieres of such auspicious plays as Thornton Wilder's *Our Town*, Philip Barry's *Without Love* (starring Katherine Hepburn), and William Inge's *Bus Stop*. Today, the theater presents a wide variety of theater, dance, and music performances throughout the year. **Open:** Sept–June. Call for schedule.

Red Bank

See also Hazlet

Gateway to the Sandy Hook unit of Gateway National Recreation Area. This six-mile peninsula offers long stretches of beaches and dune trails. Historic sites include Fort Hancock, constructed in 1890 for the defense of New York; and the Sandy Hook Lighthouse (built in 1764), the nation's oldest continuously operating beacon. **Information:** Eastern Monmouth Area Chamber of Commerce, 170 Broad St, Red Bank, 07701 (tel 908/741-0055).

HOTELS 🏨

🏳🏳 Courtyard by Marriott

245 Half Mile Rd, 07701; tel 908/530-5552 or toll free 800/321-2211; fax 908/530-5756. Exit 109 off Garden State Pkwy. Caters mostly to business travelers and long-term guests. **Rooms:** 146 rms and stes. CI 4pm/CO noon. Nonsmoking rms avail. **Amenities:** 🛁 ⚙ A/C, cable TV w/movies, refrig, dataport, voice mail, bathrobes. Some units w/terraces. **Services:** 🚐 🖼 🍴 **Facilities:** 🏊 💪 🅿️ 💻 ⚙ 1 restaurant (bkfst only), 1 bar, spa, whirlpool, washer/dryer. **Rates:** Peak (May–Sept) $95 S; $105 D; $125–$135 ste. Extra person $10. Children under age 2 stay free. Min stay wknds. Lower rates off-season. Parking: Outdoor, free. AE, CB, DC, DISC, MC, V.

🏳🏳🏳 The Oyster Point Hotel

146 Bodman Place, 07701; tel 908/530-8200 or toll free 800/345-3484; fax 908/747-1875. NJ 35 S to left after Cooper's Bridge onto Bodman Place. Every room of this lovely waterfront property has a water view and high quality furnishings. While there is no pool, there's an outdoor hot tub. **Rooms:** 58 rms and stes. CI 3pm/CO 11am. Nonsmoking rms avail. **Amenities:** 🛁 ⚙ 📺 🍴 A/C, cable TV w/movies, dataport, voice mail. Some units w/terraces, some w/whirlpools. **Services:** ✕ 🔑 🆅🅿️ 🚐 🖼 🍴 Babysitting. Turndown service available. **Facilities:** ⚓ 💪 🏊 ⚙ 1 restaurant, 1 bar (w/entertainment), spa. Small health club has a panoramic water view. **Rates:** $120 S or D; $170–$550 ste. Extra person $10. Children under age 12 stay free. Parking: Outdoor, free. AE, CB, DC, DISC, EC, ER, MC, V.

RESTAURANTS 🍽️

The Garden Restaurant

7 E Front St; tel 908/530-8681. NJ 35 S left on W Front St. **Vegetarian.** Vegetable tempura, curries, and other inventive vegan (egg-, dairy-, and meat-free) cuisine is the focus at this homey eatery. **FYI:** Reservations not accepted. Children's menu. BYO. No smoking. **Open:** Lunch Mon–Fri 11:30am–2:30pm; dinner Mon–Thurs 5:30–9pm, Fri–Sat 5:30–10pm. **Prices:** Main courses $8–$13. No CC. 🆅🅿️ ⚙

🍷 Little Kraut

115 Oakland St; tel 908/842-4830. NJ 35 into Red Bank; bear left at train tracks, then right on Oakland St. **Continental/German.** The decor is subtle, with fine linens, flowers, plants, and gaslights at each table. Stained-glass windows separate the bar from the dining room. The extensive menu includes an enticing variety of meat and seafood prepared with continental style. **FYI:** Reservations accepted. Children's menu. No smoking. **Open:** Lunch Mon–Fri 11:30am–4pm; dinner Mon–Thurs 5–10pm, Fri 5–11pm, Sat 5–11pm, Sun 3–9pm. **Prices:** Main courses $9–$19; prix fixe $26. AE, MC, V. ❤️ 🍴 ⚙

Rockaway

Small town, NW of Newark, named for the Rockaway River. Berkshire Valley Wildlife Management Area is nearby.

MOTEL 🏨

🏳🏳 Howard Johnson Lodge

14 Green Pond Rd, 07866; tel 201/625-1200 or toll free 800/I-GO-HOJO. Exit 37 off I-80. This older building is clean and pleasant, and is near restaurants and the I-80 interchange. **Rooms:** 64 rms. CI noon/CO noon. Nonsmoking rms avail. **Amenities:** 🛁 ⚙ A/C, satel TV w/movies. Free daily newspaper. Microwaves and refrigerators on request. **Services:** ✕ 🖼 🍴 Complimentary weekly pizza party for guests. **Facilities:** 🏊 1 restaurant, 1 bar, games rm. **Rates (CP):** $68–$125 S or D. Extra person $10. Children under age 12 stay free. Min stay special events. Parking: Outdoor, free. AE, MC, V.

ATTRACTION 🏛️

Craigmeur Ski Area

1175 Green Pond Rd; tel 201/697-4500. Located 8 mi N of Morristown in the Copperas Mountains. A small ski area conceived with the beginner and novice skier in mind. There are four trails and four lifts, with a vertical of 250 feet. Large ski school; snowmaking; night skiing; rentals. **Open:** Dec–Mar, Tues–Sun 8:30am–10pm. $$$$

Saddle Brook

Largely residential community, 3 miles east of Paterson. **Information:** Saddle Brook Chamber of Commerce, PO Box 819, Saddle Brook, 07662 (tel 201/587-2909).

HOTEL 🏨

🏳🏳 Howard Johnson Plaza Hotel

129 Pehle Ave E, 07662; tel 201/845-7800 or toll free 800/I-GO-HOJO; fax 201/845-7061. Exit 159 off Garden State Pkwy, bear right then turn right at stop sign. This suburban hotel caters primarily to clients doing business nearby. The

staff is friendly and professional. **Rooms:** 141 rms. Executive level. CI 3pm/CO noon. Nonsmoking rms avail. Heavily used rooms could use some maintenance. **Amenities:** 🔒 ♨ A/C, cable TV. All units w/terraces, some w/whirlpools. Coffeemakers, dataports, and refrigerators in executive-level rooms. **Services:** ✗ 🚗 🗺 🛎 **Facilities:** 🛗 📷 250 ♿ 1 restaurant, 1 bar (w/entertainment), whirlpool. **Rates:** Peak (Mar–June/Sept–Nov) $98 S; $108 D. Extra person $10. Children under age 16 stay free. Lower rates off-season. Parking: Outdoor, free. AE, CB, DC, DISC, JCB, MC, V.

MOTEL

🏢🏢 Holiday Inn & Conference Center
50 Kenney Place, 07662; tel 201/843-0600 or toll free 800/HOLIDAY; fax 201/843-2822. Exit 62 off I-80. Located in a rather bleak landscape of highway turnoffs and railroad tracks. Sufficient for quick stays. **Rooms:** 144 rms and stes. CI 3pm/CO noon. Nonsmoking rms avail. Noise from passing trains is loud in some rooms. **Amenities:** 🔒 ♨ 📺 🍷 A/C, satel TV w/movies, dataport. Refrigerators on request. Complimentary newspapers. **Services:** ✗ 🗝 🗺 🛎 Twice-daily maid svce. Dry-cleaning and laundry service (weekdays only). **Facilities:** 🛗 📷 400 ♿ 1 restaurant, 1 bar (w/entertainment). Comedy club; restaurant with live jazz on weekends. Complimentary passes to local fitness club. **Rates:** $110 S or D; $150 ste. Extra person $10. Children under age 12 stay free. MAP rates avail. Parking: Outdoor, free. AE, CB, DC, DISC, JCB, MC, V.

Salem

The historic seat of Salem County, near to the Salem and Delaware Rivers. Offers 60 18th-century buildings and the 500-year old Salem Oak. **Information:** Greater Salem Chamber of Commerce, 104 Market St, Salem, 08079 (tel 609/935-1415).

ATTRACTION 🏛

Fort Mott State Park
Fort Mott Rd; tel 609/935-3218. Located 8 mi W of Salem, on the Delaware River. Originally built in 1872–76 as part of the federal government's plan for the defense of American harbors against foreign attack, the fort was manned by Army artillery units until 1922. Today, visitors to the park can picnic, go fishing or crabbing, and explore the historic buildings on the grounds. **Open:** Peak (Mem Day–Labor Day) daily 8am–7pm. Reduced hours off-season. **Free**

Sandy Hook

See Gateway National Recreation Area

Scotch Plains

Settled in 1689 by Scottish immigrants. Today, it is site of Terry Lou Zoo, a small family-owned zoo with a variety of animals and tropical birds.

RESTAURANT 🍽

🍷★ Stage House Inn
366 Park Ave; tel 908/322-4224. At E Front St. **Eclectic.** Built in 1690, this building became a tavern when owner Colon Recompense Stanbery needed a meeting place for officers in the Revolutionary War. (The original oak beams, wide plank floors, and stencilled walls remain.) The menu, which changes seasonally, tends toward contemporary treatment of traditional dishes like leg of lamb, roasted guinea hen, saddle of rabbit, and Maine scallops. Tasting menu also available. **FYI:** Reservations recommended. Dress code. **Open:** Lunch Tues–Fri 11:30am–2:30pm; dinner Tues–Sun 5:30–10pm. **Prices:** Main courses $22–$29; prix fixe $65. AE, MC, V. ♥ 🍴

Secaucus

See also East Rutherford

On the Hackensack River opposite Manhattan, this town of some 15,000 residents is widely known for the Secaucus Outlet Center, one of the top sites in the country for bargain hunters.

HOTELS 🏨

🏢🏢 Courtyard by Marriott Meadowlands
455 Harmon Meadow Blvd, 07094; tel 201/617-8888 or toll free 800/321-2211; fax 201/319-0035. Exit 16 E off NJ Tpk. Standard chain hotel, near shopping and entertainment. Giants Stadium is just down the road, and midtown Manhattan is three miles away. **Rooms:** 165 rms. CI 3pm/CO noon. Nonsmoking rms avail. Most rooms are nonsmoking. **Amenities:** 🔒 ♨ 📺 A/C, satel TV w/movies, dataport, voice mail. Refrigerators and hairdryers available on request. **Services:** ✗ 🗺 Bellmen and doorman on weekdays only. **Facilities:** 📷 100 ♿ 1 restaurant (bkfst only), 1 bar. Free passes to local fitness club. Restaurant serves breakfast and catered business luncheons only. **Rates:** $110 S; $120 D. Children under age 18 stay free. Min stay special events. Parking: Indoor/outdoor, free. Weekend packages avail. AE, DC, DISC, JCB, MC, V.

🏢🏢🏢 Embassy Suites
455 Plaza Dr, 07094; tel 201/864-7300 or toll free 800/EMBASSY; fax 201/864-5391. Exit 16 E off NJ Tpk. A family-friendly hotel located in a shopping center. Atrium-style lobby has lots of seating and a big-screen TV. Pleasant staff. **Rooms:** 261 rms and stes. CI 3pm/CO noon. Nonsmoking rms avail. **Amenities:** 🔒 ♨ 📺 🍷 A/C, satel TV w/movies,

refrig, dataport, voice mail. All units have two TVs, microwave, wet bar, and dining table. **Services:** ✗ 🚐 📠 ⬭ ⬭ Transportation to Teterboro airport (free) and other local destinations (for a fee). **Facilities:** 🔲 ⬭ 📺 💻 ♿ 1 restaurant (lunch and dinner only), 1 bar (w/entertainment), games rm, sauna, whirlpool, washer/dryer. **Rates (BB):** $109 S or D; $179 ste. Extra person $25. Children under age 12 stay free. Min stay special events. Parking: Indoor/outdoor, free. AE, CB, DC, DISC, EC, JCB, MC, V.

UNRATED Holiday Inn

300 Plaza Dr, 07094; tel 201/348-2000 or toll free 800/465-4329; fax 201/348-6035. Exit 16 E off NJ Tpk. A basic, well-located Holiday Inn. Fine for a brief stay. Unrated due to ongoing major renovations. **Rooms:** 160 rms and stes. Executive level. CI 3pm/CO noon. Nonsmoking rms avail. **Amenities:** 📺 ⬭ 🖥 A/C, satel TV w/movies, dataport, voice mail. **Services:** ✗ 🗝 VP 📠 ⬭ ⬭ Car-rental desk, babysitting. **Facilities:** ⬭ 📺 ♿ 1 restaurant, 1 bar (w/entertainment), basketball, washer/dryer. **Rates:** $109 S or D; $150–$175 ste. Extra person $10. Children under age 12 stay free. Min stay special events. Parking: Indoor/outdoor, free. AE, CB, DC, DISC, EC, JCB, MC, V.

≡≡≡ Meadowlands Hilton

Two Harmon Plaza, 07094; tel 201/348-6900 or toll free 800/HILTONS; fax 201/348-4436. NJ 3 E to left on Meadowland Pkwy, then right at light onto Harmon Plaza. This hotel offers value for the money, given its handy location and good condition. It's in a quiet spot, yet near major highways and local attractions. **Rooms:** 296 rms and stes. Executive level. CI 3pm/CO noon. Nonsmoking rms avail. **Amenities:** 📺 ⬭ 🖥 🍽 A/C, satel TV w/movies, dataport, voice mail. **Services:** ✗ VP 🚐 📠 ⬭ Babysitting. **Facilities:** 🔲 ⬭ 1000 ♿ 1 restaurant, 1 bar, sauna, whirlpool, washer/dryer. Upscale coffee shop overlooks Hackensack River. **Rates:** $89–$150 S or D; $150–$350 ste. Extra person $10. Children under age 12 stay free. Min stay special events. Parking: Indoor/outdoor, free. AE, CB, DC, DISC, ER, MC, V.

Short Hills

This small Passaic River community is the home of Cora Hartshorn Arboretum and Bird Sanctuary. **Information:** Millburn–Short Hills Chamber of Commerce, 56 Main St, PO Box 651, Millburn, 07041 (tel 201/379-1198).

HOTEL 🏨

≡≡≡≡≡ The Hilton at Short Hills

41 John F Kennedy Pkwy, 07078; tel 201/379-0100 or toll free 800/HILTONS in the US, 800/268-9275 in Canada; fax 201/379-6870. Exit 24 off I-78 (The Mall at Short Hills). Surrounded by upscale shopping and corporate headquarters, this hotel harbors a level of service and opulence one would expect for the area. **Rooms:** 300 rms and stes.

Executive level. CI 3pm/CO noon. Nonsmoking rms avail. Oversized rooms have carved hardwood furniture and marble baths. **Amenities:** 📺 ⬭ 🍽 A/C, cable TV w/movies, dataport, VCR, CD/tape player, voice mail, bathrobes. Some units w/minibars, 1 w/whirlpool. Complimentary morning coffee, shoeshine, and newspaper. **Services:** 🍽 🗝 VP 🚐 📠 ⬭ Twice-daily maid svce, car-rental desk, masseur, babysitting. **Facilities:** 🔲 ⬭ 700 💻 ♿ 2 restaurants (see "Restaurants" below), 2 bars (1 w/entertainment), spa, sauna, steam rm, whirlpool, beauty salon. Complimentary full European-style spa; lagoon pool with bar and massage cabanas. **Rates:** $215–$265 S or D; $300–$335 ste. Extra person $20. Children under age 18 stay free. Parking: Indoor, free. Weekend rates avail. AE, CB, DC, DISC, MC, V.

RESTAURANT 🍽

♥ The Dining Room

In The Hilton at Short Hills, 41 JFK Pkwy; tel 201/379-0100. Exit 24 off I-78. **Continental.** Mahogany paneling, brass fixtures, crystal chandeliers, and English sporting prints produce a sophisticated, clublike atmosphere. Classic continental fare includes marinated venison, baked salmon and tuna strudel, seafood cioppino, and roulade of pheasant fois gras. **FYI:** Reservations recommended. Harp. Jacket required. **Open:** Sun–Fri 6–10pm, Sat 6–10:30pm. **Prices:** Prix fixe $58–$135. AE, CB, DC, DISC, MC, V. VP ♿

Somerset

This community on the Raritan River is the home of Colonial Park Arboretum and the Meadows Foundation, which features historic homes and a nature trail.

HOTELS 🏨

≡≡ Madison Suites Hotel

25 Cedar Grove Lane, 08873; tel 908/563-1000; fax 908/563-0352. Exit 6 off I-287. Caters to business travelers due to its location in a mixed residential and industrial area. **Rooms:** 83 rms and stes. CI 3pm/CO noon. Nonsmoking rms avail. Furniture is somewhat dated but in good condition. Suites have two floors, with a living room downstairs and bedroom upstairs. **Amenities:** 📺 ⬭ 🖥 🍽 A/C, cable TV w/movies, refrig. Suites have two phones and a microwave. **Services:** ✗ 🚐 📠 ⬭ VCRs and movies available for rent. **Facilities:** 65 ♿ 1 restaurant (bkfst only), 1 bar. Complimentary use of nearby fitness center. **Rates (CP):** $65–$87 S or D; $85–$107 ste. Extra person $10. Children under age 16 stay free. Parking: Outdoor, free. AE, CB, DC, MC, V.

UNRATED Somerset Marriott

110 Davidson Ave, 08873; tel 908/560-0500 or toll free 800/238-3198; fax 908/560-3669. Exit 6 off I-287. Careful maintenance, clean grounds, and ample parking mark this 1970s-style mid-rise building convenient to major corporate

offices. **Rooms:** 434 rms and stes. Executive level. CI 3pm/CO 11am. Nonsmoking rms avail. **Amenities:** 📺 ⏱ A/C, cable TV w/movies, dataport, voice mail. Some units w/minibars, some w/terraces. **Services:** ✕ 🔑 🚐 🖨 🍴 Car-rental desk. **Facilities:** 🏊 🏊2 🛥 800 🖥 ⅙ 1 restaurant, 1 bar, basketball, spa, sauna, beauty salon, washer/dryer. **Rates:** $79–$139 S or D; $275 ste. Children under age 12 stay free. Parking: Outdoor, free. AE, DC, DISC, JCB, MC, V.

Somers Point

On the Great Egg Harbor, 10 miles SW of Atlantic City, Somers Point is the home of the Southern Jersey Regional Theater.

LODGE 🏨

🏨🏨 Residence Inn by Marriott at Greate Bay

900 Mays Landing Rd, 08244; tel 609/927-6400 or toll free 800/331-3131; fax 609/926-0145. 1 mi W of Somers Point Circle. Extended-stay guests are the primary clientele for this attractive facility. **Rooms:** 119 rms and stes. Executive level. CI 3pm/CO 11am. Nonsmoking rms avail. Full kitchens and sofa beds in each unit. **Amenities:** 📺 ⏱ 🖨 A/C, cable TV w/movies, refrig, dataport. Some units w/terraces, some w/fireplaces. **Services:** 🚐 🖨 🍴 🐾 Babysitting. Small pets allowed with $50 cleaning fee. **Facilities:** 🏊 ▶18 🛥 200 ⅙ 1 restaurant (bkfst only), basketball, volleyball, washer/dryer. **Rates (CP):** Peak (June 14–Sept 14) $89–$145 S or D; $89–$195 ste. Extra person $10. Children under age 16 stay free. Min stay peak. Lower rates off-season. Parking: Outdoor, free. AE, DC, DISC, JCB, MC, V.

Somerville

Somerset County seat, located 10 miles NW of New Brunswick. Home of the US Bicycling Hall of Fame and the Duke Farm and Gardens. **Information:** Somerset County Chamber of Commerce, 64 W End Ave, PO Box 833, Somerville, 08876 (tel 908/725-1552).

RESTAURANT 🍴

Filippo's Autentica Cucina Italiana

132 E Main St; tel 908/218-0110. Near courthouse. **Italian.** This former pizza parlor has evolved into an elegant bistro serving homemade regional dishes like veal medallions, veal scaloppine, and grilled swordfish. Only the freshest ingredients are used—nothing comes from a can. **FYI:** Reservations accepted. Piano/singer. Dress code. BYO. No smoking. **Open:** Lunch Mon–Fri noon–3pm; dinner Mon–Thurs 5–10pm, Fri–Sat 5–11pm. **Prices:** Main courses $14–$22. DISC, MC, V. ⅙

Spring Lake

South of Long Branch, this beautiful coastal town offers charming Victorian inns and seaside hotels.

INNS 🏨

🏨🏨🏨 Normandy Inn

21 Tuttle Ave, 07762; tel 908/449-7172; fax 908/449-1070. Exit 98 off Garden State Pkwy. The guest rooms of this lovely Victorian-style B&B are all individually decorated with beautiful antiques. Children are welcomed. **Rooms:** 19 rms and stes. CI 2pm/CO 11am. No smoking. **Amenities:** 📺 ⏱ A/C, cable TV. 1 unit w/terrace, some w/fireplaces, some w/whirlpools. Breakfast made to order. **Services:** 🔑 Afternoon tea served. Free beach passes. **Facilities:** 🚲 35 1 beach (ocean), lifeguard, guest lounge w/TV. Tennis, golf nearby. **Rates (BB):** Peak (May 30–Sept) $85–$161 S; $114–$171 D; $245–$270 ste. Extra person $10. Min stay peak. Lower rates off-season. Parking: Outdoor, free. AE, CB, DC, DISC, MC, V.

🏨🏨🏨 Sea Crest by the Sea

19 Tuttle Ave, 07762; tel 908/449-9031 or toll free 800/803-9031; fax 908/974-0403. Exit 98 off Garden State Pkwy to NJ 34 S, right on NJ 524 E. Fine antiques, friendly atmosphere, and great location (half a block from the ocean) make this 1885 Queen Anne–style B&B a romantic getaway destination. Unsuitable for children under 18. **Rooms:** 12 rms and stes. CI 2pm/CO 11am. No smoking. Most rooms have water views. Suites have separate sitting rooms. **Amenities:** 📺 🍴 A/C, cable TV w/movies, refrig, VCR, bathrobes. Some units w/terraces, some w/fireplaces, 1 w/whirlpool. **Services:** Afternoon tea served. Free beach passes. **Facilities:** 🚲 12 1 beach (ocean), lifeguard, guest lounge w/TV. **Rates (BB):** Peak (May 15–Sept) $139–$249 D; $239–$249 ste. Min stay wknds. Lower rates off-season. Parking: Outdoor, free. AE, MC, V.

RESTAURANT 🍴

Old Mill Inn

Old Mill Rd, Spring Lake Heights; tel 908/449-1800. NJ 138 E to N Bedford Rd, make right 2 mi. **Regional American/Steak.** The large room overlooks the lake, and hanging plants and flowers accent each table at this venue for well-known entertainers. Prime rib tops the dining room playbill. **FYI:** Reservations recommended. Big band/jazz/piano. Children's menu. **Open:** Mon–Thurs 11:30am–10pm, Fri–Sat 11:30am–11pm, Sun 11am–10pm. **Prices:** Main courses $20–$35. AE, CB, DC, MC, V. ♥ 🖼 💌 ⅙

Stanhope

Adjacent to Lake Hopatcong, the state's largest lake. Waterloo Village, a restored 18th-century village of colonial craft shops and homes, is also here.

INN

The Whistling Swan Inn

110 Main St, 07874; tel 201/347-6369; fax 201/347-3391. 1½ acres. Guests often read their morning papers on the wicker-furnished, stone-pillared front porch of this Victorian home, an indication of the homelike atmosphere. Unsuitable for children under 12. **Rooms:** 10 rms. CI 1pm/CO 11am. No smoking. Each room has a unique theme (Art Deco, the Forties, Age of Swing, Oriental Antique). **Amenities:** A/C, dataport, bathrobes. No TV. **Services:** Car-rental desk, afternoon tea and wine/sherry served. **Facilities:** Washer/dryer, guest lounge w/TV. Video library. **Rates (BB):** $85 S; $95 D. Extra person $20. Min stay special events. Higher rates for special events/hols. Parking: Outdoor, free. AE, DISC, MC, V.

RESTAURANT

$ Cattleman's Steakhouse

136 NJ 46 W, Netcong; tel 201/347-2132. **American.** Wooden fence railings, red-checkered tablecloths, and sturdy tables and chairs lend a ranch-like atmosphere to the dining and bar areas. Generous portions and reasonable prices for standard beef, chicken, and seafood entrees make this a popular choice for families and large groups. **FYI:** Reservations accepted. **Open:** Tues–Thurs 11:30am–11pm, Fri 11:30am–midnight, Sat 4pm–midnight. **Prices:** Main courses $7–$13. AE, MC, V.

ATTRACTIONS

Village of Waterloo

525 Waterloo Rd; tel 201/347-0900. Originally known as Andover Forge when it was settled by iron-mining entrepreneurs in the 18th century, the Forge was so well known for the quality of its work that the Continental Army seized it in 1778, so that it could make armaments. Prosperity came with the opening of the Morris Canal in 1831 and the construction of a railroad in 1847; most of the village's elegant Victorian homes date from the last half of the 19th century. More than 25 mansions, industrial sites, gardens, taverns, and craft shops are open for tours; living history and craft demonstrations are given and a self-guided walking tour map is available. A summertime music festival is held at the concert tent. **Open:** Mid-Apr–mid-Dec, Wed–Sun 10am–6pm. $$$

Wild West City

US 206, Netcong; tel 201/347-8900. A live action re-creation of an Old West town. Activities include stagecoach and pony rides, miniature frontier railroad ride, "Golden Nugget" saloon with live stage shows and refreshments, and children's petting zoo. Picnic area. **Open:** Peak (mid-June–Labor Day) daily 10:30am–6pm. Reduced hours off-season. Closed mid-Oct–Apr. $$$

Stone Harbor

A small community in the Cape May area. Highlights include the Wetlands Institute and the Stone Harbor Bird Sanctuary.

ATTRACTIONS

Wetlands Institute

1075 Stone Harbor Blvd; tel 609/368-1211. Set on a 6,000-acre tract of coastal wetlands. Scientific research here has included studies of local fishes and birds and pollution in the marine environment. A hands-on area for children features animals, games, and microscopes. Inside there are also saltwater aquariums and a gallery with arts-and-crafts exhibits. On the grounds are nature trails, a marsh walk, and an observation tower popular with bird-watchers. **Open:** Peak (mid-May–mid-Oct) Mon–Sat 9:30am–4:30pm, Sun 10am–4pm. Reduced hours off-season. $$

Stone Harbor Bird Sanctuary

3rd Ave and 114th St; tel 609/368-5102. This 21-acre sanctuary provides ample feeding grounds for some 7 species of heron and the glossy ibis, attracted here by the thickets of holly, cedar, sassafras, and bayberry. Some of the other migratory species that have been seen here include loons, grebes, scoters, and snowy egrets. **Open:** Daily 24 hours. **Free**

Summit

Named for its location in the Watchung Mountains, this city of some 20,000 is a gateway to nearby Great Swamp National Wildlife Refuge. **Information:** Suburban Chamber of Commerce, 360 Springfield Ave, PO Box 824, Summit, 07902 (tel 908/522-1700).

HOTEL

The Grand Summit Hotel

570 Springfield Ave, 07901; tel 908/273-3000 or toll free 800/346-0773; fax 908/273-4228. Summit Ave exit off NJ 24/124 W. The vaulted ceilings in the lobby of this landmark Tudor mansion are of rare chestnut, and the gardens and public areas are gracious. Even the resident ghost is purported to be friendly. **Rooms:** 146 rms and stes. CI 4pm/CO noon. Nonsmoking rms avail. Rooms are uniquely decorated and standards of furnishings vary. **Amenities:** A/C, cable TV w/movies, dataport, voice mail. Some units w/terraces, some w/fireplaces, some w/whirlpools. Complimentary morning coffee and newspaper. Irons and ironing boards in all rooms. **Services:** Twice-daily maid svce, masseur. Afternoon tea. Chocolate chip cookies served at turndown. **Facilities:** 1 restaurant, 1 bar

(w/entertainment), washer/dryer. Small gym. **Rates (BB):** $145–$155 S or D; $175–$300 ste. Extra person $15. Children under age 12 stay free. Parking: Outdoor, free. Weekend and honeymoon packages avail. AE, CB, DC, DISC, MC, V.

Sussex

Northern New Jersey town near two noted ski areas, the Annandale Stokes Forest, and the Appalachian Trail. **Information:** Sussex County Chamber of Commerce, 120 Hampton House Rd, Newton, 07860 (tel 201/579-1811).

ATTRACTIONS

High Point State Park
180 NJ 23; tel 201/875-4800. This 14,056-acre park is named after New Jersey's highest mountain, High Point, which stands 1,803 feet above sea level. Recreational activities available in the park include swimming, fishing, and boating in natural spring–fed Lake Marcia; hiking a portion of the Appalachian Trail (which passes through the park), or the other 14 miles of marked trails; and picnicking and camping. **Open:** Peak (Mem Day–Labor Day) daily 8am–8pm. Reduced hours off-season. **$$**

Space Farms Zoo & Museum
218 NJ 519, Beemerville; tel 201/875-5800. A 100-acre complex with more than 500 animals, birds, and reptiles including bears, elk, wolves, lions, coyotes, and tigers. Also on the grounds is a museum featuring antique cars, wagons, carriages (including Teddy Roosevelt's maple-burl carriage), and farm implements. Playground, picnic area, miniature golf also available. **Open:** May–Oct, daily 9am–5pm. **$$$**

Teaneck

A bedroom community of 38,000, minutes from Manhattan. Home of the American Stage Company.

HOTEL

⊨⊨⊨ Marriott at Glenpointe
100 Frank W Burr Blvd, 07666; tel 201/836-0600 or toll free 800/992-7752; fax 201/836-0638. Exit 70B off I-95 N. This modern and well-kept hotel—convenient to both New York City and suburban malls—is a popular site for weddings and corporate functions. The lobby features a soaring atrium, polished marble, and interior landscaping. **Rooms:** 341 rms and stes. Executive level. CI 4pm/CO noon. Nonsmoking rms avail. **Amenities:** 🛁 🍷 A/C, satel TV w/movies, dataport, voice mail. Some units w/whirlpools. Irons and ironing boards in all rooms; some rooms have refrigerators. **Services:** ✕ ⊞ 🚗 ⌷ Car-rental desk, masseur, babysitting. **Facilities:** ⬜ 🏋 🏊 🖥 ❧ 1 restaurant, 1 bar, spa, sauna, whirlpool. Nearby Overpeck Park offers tennis, horse stables,

picnicking, and a walking/jogging track. **Rates:** $145 S; $160 D; $450–$650 ste. Children under age 21 stay free. Min stay special events. MAP rates avail. Parking: Indoor/outdoor, free. Weekend packages avail. AE, CB, DC, DISC, JCB, MC, V.

RESTAURANT

★ Avanti Restaurant & Night Club
In Glenpointe Complex, 400 Frank Burr Blvd; tel 201/836-3222. Exit 70B off I-95. **New American/Italian.** With a simple, pleasant decor, this is a popular place on weekends, when a club atmosphere prevails. The menu lists straightforward American and Italian favorites, and the portions are generous. **FYI:** Reservations recommended. Dancing. **Open:** Lunch Mon–Fri noon–3pm; dinner Mon–Thurs 5–10pm, Fri 5–11pm, Sat 6–11pm. **Prices:** Main courses $16–$23. AE, DC, DISC, MC, V. 🅥🅟 ♿

Tenafly

HOTEL

⊨⊨⊨ The Clinton Inn Hotel
145 Dean Dr, 07670; tel 201/871-3200 or toll free 800/34-THE-INN; fax 201/871-3435. The personal service and quiet, genteel air of this hotel is especially refreshing given its urban location. **Rooms:** 112 rms and stes. Executive level. CI 2:30pm/CO 11am. Nonsmoking rms avail. Rooms are comfortable and well tended, but the furnishings could use some improvement. **Amenities:** 🛁 🍷 A/C, cable TV w/movies, dataport, VCR, voice mail. Refrigerators on request. **Services:** ✕ 🚗 🛎 ⌷ Twice-daily maid svce. **Facilities:** 🏀 🚺 🖥 ♿ 1 restaurant (see "Restaurants" below), 1 bar, basketball. Stylish, Tuscan-style bistro on premises. **Rates:** $115 S; $125 D; $180–$275 ste. Extra person $10. Children under age 12 stay free. Parking: Indoor/outdoor, free. AE, DC, MC, V.

RESTAURANTS

Christino's
In The Clinton Inn Hotel, 145 Dean Dr; tel 201/567-4800. **Italian/Mediterranean.** Dramatic and often food-oriented artwork—a 6-foot asparagus sculpture, a 25-foot mural of a field of sunflowers, and a pomegranate-and-eggplant bas-relief behind the bar—fills this attractive dining room. Pastas, steaks, chops, and distinctive desserts are among the kitchen's specialties. A light bar menu is available from 3–5pm. **FYI:** Reservations recommended. **Open:** Breakfast Mon–Fri 6:30–11:30am, Sat–Sun 7am–3pm; lunch Sun–Sat 11:30am–3pm; dinner Sun–Thurs 5–10pm, Fri–Sat 5–11pm; brunch Sun 11:30am–3pm. **Prices:** Main courses $13–$28. AE, CB, DC, MC, V. 🅥🅟 ♿

Villa Cortina
18 Piermont Rd; tel 201/567-6477. Exit 71 off I-95. **Italian.** The proprietors of this casual, country-Italian restaurant serve specialties from their home region of Friuli, in northern Italy. Menu highlights include *casonsei* (ravioli stuffed with seafood) and *frico* (an appetizer of montasio cheese sautéed with onions and potatoes). **FYI:** Reservations recommended. **Open:** Mon–Fri noon–10pm, Sat–Sun 5–11pm. **Prices:** Main courses $13–$20. AE, CB, DC, MC, V. 🗨 ♿

Tinton Falls

Named for the falls in the Swimming River, this town of 13,000 is minutes from Asbury Park and the Atlantic Ocean.

HOTELS 🏨

≡≡ Courtyard by Marriott
600 Hope Rd, 07724; tel 908/389-2100 or toll free 800/321-2211; fax 908/389-1727. Exit 105 off Garden State Pkwy to NJ 36 E. The beaches are a five-minute ride away from this neat, inn-like facility. **Rooms:** 120 rms and stes. CI 4pm/CO noon. Nonsmoking rms avail. Rooms are somewhat small but very well maintained. **Amenities:** 🛁 🛎 📺 A/C, cable TV w/movies, refrig, dataport, voice mail. **Services:** 🚗 🛄 🛎 Babysitting. **Facilities:** 🏋 🏊 ⛳45 ♿ 1 restaurant (bkfst only), washer/dryer. **Rates:** Peak (May 30–Sept) $49–$95 S; $49–$105 D; $110–$120 ste. Extra person $10. Children under age 12 stay free. Lower rates off-season. Parking: Outdoor, free. AE, DC, DISC, MC, V.

≡≡≡ Holiday Inn at Tinton Falls
700 Hope Rd, 07724; tel 908/544-9300 or toll free 800/2-JERSEY; fax 908/544-9370. Exit 105 off Garden State Pkwy to right on Hope Rd. Extra-large rooms, an attractive lobby, and a modern health club with a sauna are the main attractions at this well-kept hotel. **Rooms:** 171 rms. CI 3pm/CO noon. Nonsmoking rms avail. Three "suites" are just large standard rooms (without separate living area). **Amenities:** 🛁 🛎 📺 A/C, cable TV w/movies, refrig, dataport. **Services:** ✗ 🚗 🛄 🛎 Babysitting. **Facilities:** 🏋 🏊 ⛳250 ♿ 1 restaurant, 1 bar (w/entertainment), sauna, washer/dryer. **Rates:** Peak (May 15–Sept 15) $109 S; $119–$129 D. Extra person $10. Children under age 18 stay free. Min stay wknds. Lower rates off-season. Parking: Outdoor, free. AE, CB, DC, DISC, EC, ER, MC, V.

Totowa

Formed in 1898, Totowa was named for a Native American term meaning "between a river and a mountain." **Information:** North Jersey Chamber of Commerce, 1033 Rte 46 E, PO Box 110, Clifton, 07011 (tel 201/470-9300).

HOTEL 🏨

≡≡ Holiday Inn Totowa
1 US 46 W, 07512; tel 201/785-9000 or toll free 800/HOLIDAY; fax 201/785-3031. Exit 154 S or exit 153B N off Garden State Pkwy. A warm welcome and clean, comfortable rooms offset a rather unfortunate industrial-park location. **Rooms:** 155 rms and stes. CI 2pm/CO noon. Nonsmoking rms avail. **Amenities:** 🛁 🛎 A/C, cable TV w/movies, dataport. 1 unit w/whirlpool. **Services:** ✗ 🛄 🛎 Car-rental desk. Half-price entry to cinema and tennis complex nearby. **Facilities:** 🏋 🏊 ⛳200 1 restaurant, 1 bar (w/entertainment), spa, washer/dryer. **Rates:** $93 S or D; $200 ste. Extra person $6. Children under age 19 stay free. Parking: Indoor/outdoor, free. Weekend rates avail. AE, CB, DC, DISC, MC, V.

Trenton

Trenton was first settled by Quakers in 1670. A century later, it was the scene of a Revolutionary War battle in which Washington's army captured some 900 Hessians; it also boasts the second-oldest capitol (built circa 1790) in continuous use in the country. Today, Trenton is a commercial center (best known for its porcelain and rubber) and cultural mecca, with institutions such as the New Jersey State Museum and Trenton State College. **Information:** Mercer County Chamber of Commerce, 214 W State St, Trenton, 08608 (tel 609/393-4143).

RESTAURANTS 🍴

★ Joe's Tomato Pies
548–550 S Clinton Ave; tel 609/393-3945. Butler and Baird. **Italian/Pizza.** The family business has been pizzas since 1910, and the walls carry snapshots of customers and family members. Local polls put it at the top for its classic pies, antipasto, cannoli, sandwiches, seafood, and pasta. **FYI:** Reservations recommended. BYO. No smoking. **Open:** Lunch Tues–Fri 11am–2:30pm; dinner Tues–Fri 4–10pm, Sat 4–10pm, Sun 4–9pm. **Prices:** Main courses $4–$8. No CC. 👥

La Gondola Ristorante
762 Roebling Ave; tel 609/392-0600. At Anderson St. **Italian.** Located in Trenton's "Little Italy," this trattoria has a grotto ambience, and opera drifts from the sound system. As one would expect, the food is traditional Italian served in whopping portions. **FYI:** Reservations recommended. **Open:** Lunch Mon–Fri 11:30am–2:30pm; dinner Mon–Thurs 4:30–10pm, Fri–Sat 4:30–11pm. **Prices:** Main courses $13–$20. AE, CB, DC, DISC, MC, V. ◉

ATTRACTIONS 🏛

Washington Crossing State Park
NJ 29, Titusville; tel 609/737-0623. Located 8 mi NW of Trenton. This 840-acre park along the Delaware River commemorates the site where Gen George Washington and his

troops pulled in their boats after their historic Christmas 1776 crossing of the Delaware. Attractions include the Ferry House (a restored Colonial inn), an arboretum, an amphitheater, nature trails, and bird-watching areas. In addition, the visitors center houses a unique collection of Revolutionary period items, ranging from weapons and uniforms to coins, documents, eating utensils, medical equipment, and games (see **Washington Crossing, PA,** for more information). **Open:** Peak (Mem Day–Labor Day) daily 8am–8pm. **$**

William Trent House
15 Market St; tel 609/989-3027. This Georgian mansion was built as a summer home between 1716 and 1719 by William Trent, a wealthy Philadelphia merchant trader. Restored to its original appearance, the house is furnished with pewter dishes, hand-woven linen, a Chippendale wardrobe, and Colonial kitchen implements. Guided tours available. **Open:** Daily 12:30–4pm. **$**

New Jersey State House
125 W State St; tel 609/633-2709. Built in 1792, this is the second-oldest state house in continuous use in the United States. The governor's wing (circa 1872) and legislative quarters have been restored to their turn-of-the-century appearance. Reservations required for guided tours. **Open:** Tues–Wed and Fri 9am–4pm. **Free**

New Jersey State Museum
205 W State St; tel 609/292-6464 or 292-6308. Includes American art of the 19th- and 20th-century, plus Native American artifacts, dinosaur fossils, and decorative arts and furniture. Planetarium and children's theater. **Open:** Tues–Sat 9am–4:45pm, Sun noon–5pm. **Free**

Union

Established in 1808, this township north of Elizabeth is home to Kean College and Wilkens Theater. **Information:** Union Township Chamber of Commerce, 355 Chestnut St, Union, 07083 (tel 908/688-2777).

RESTAURANT 🍴

★ Cafe Z
In Ideal Professional Park, 2333 Morris Ave; tel 908/686-4321. At Rahway Ave. **Italian.** Urban decor and rap music help bring the outdoors indoors at this unique cafe, where a "sidewalk" winds among tables, graffiti-covered walls, and a chain-link fence. The pan-Italian menu offers antipasti and a dozen homemade pastas; the house specialty is seafood marinara over linguini. **FYI:** Reservations accepted. Dress code. BYO. **Open:** Lunch Mon–Fri 11:30am–3pm; dinner Mon–Thurs 5–10pm, Fri–Sat 5–11pm, Sun 4–9pm. **Prices:** Main courses $10–$17. AE, DC, MC, V.

Ventnor

See Atlantic City

Vernon

Site of the Hidden Valley Ski Area and Vernon Valley Action Park, with its self-operating rides.

ATTRACTIONS 🏛

Action Park
NJ 94; tel 201/827-2000. More than 75 wild and wet rides, shows, and attractions draw visitors to this family-style park in the North Jersey mountains. The emphasis here is on "hands-on" amusements: miniature race-car driving, water slides, bungee jumping, speed boats, a children's water park, and other mostly low-tech rides. One exception is the new Space Shot, which blasts passengers 200 feet into the air in just seconds. **Open:** Peak (mid-June–Labor Day) daily 10am–8pm. Reduced hours off-season. Closed Labor Day–Mem Day. **$$$$**

Vernon Valley/Great Gorge
NJ 94; tel 201/827-2000. Notable ski area featuring 52 trails on 3 mountains, with a network of 17 lifts and tows with a 17,500 people per hour capacity. Summit elevation is 1,480 feet with a vertical of 1,040 feet (by far the highest in New Jersey) and a base elevation of 440 feet. Trail breakdown (30% beginner, 40% intermediate, 30% expert) offers something for everyone. Night skiing, ski school, and *Twisted World* snowboard park also available. For the latest information on snow conditions, call 201/827-3900. **Open:** Late Nov–mid-Apr, Mon–Thurs 9am–10pm, Fri–Sun 8:30am–11pm. **$$$$**

Hidden Valley Ski Area
Breakneck Rd; tel 201/764-6161 or 764-4200. A popular ski area featuring 12 slopes, 3 lifts, a summit elevation of 1,400 feet, and a vertical drop of 610 feet. The terrain is evenly divided (beginner 10%, intermediate 40%, expert 50%), so that everyone can find a slope matched to their level of skill. Snowboarding; ski school also available. For the latest information on snow conditions, call 201/764-4200. **Open:** Dec–Mar, call for schedule. **$$$$**

Warren

Named for Revolutionary War Gen Joseph Warren, this township is near to Washington Rock State Park, with its noted scenic overlook.

HOTEL 🏨

≡≡≡ Somerset Hills Hotel
200 Liberty Corner Rd, 07059; tel 908/647-6700 or toll free 800/688-0700; fax 908/647-8053. Exit 33 off I-78. This

imposing neo-Georgian building, set gracefully amid hills and corporate headquarters, has elegant public areas. **Rooms:** 111 rms, stes, and effic. CI 3pm/CO noon. Nonsmoking rms avail. Spacious rooms. **Amenities:** 🛏 👁 A/C, cable TV w/movies, dataport, voice mail. Some units w/minibars, some w/terraces, some w/whirlpools. Nintendo available. **Services:** ✗ 🖛 ⬜ ⌂ Complimentary shuttle to nearby companies. **Facilities:** 🔓 🏋 🟨350 2 restaurants (*see* "Restaurants" below), 1 bar (w/entertainment), spa. Privileges at local racquet club and YMCA. **Rates:** $155 S; $165 D; $260–$320 ste; $180–$190 effic. Extra person $10. Children under age 16 stay free. Parking: Outdoor, free. Honeymoon and weekend packages avail. AE, DC, MC, V.

RESTAURANT 🍽

Christine's

In Somerset Hills Hotel, 200 Liberty Corner Rd; tel 908/647-6700. Exit 33 off I-78. **Mediterranean.** Jackets are preferred in this sparkling room off the main hotel lobby. Dramatic lighting sets off the soft colors and fresh flowers. The fresh pasta is served with inspired sauces like crabmeat and arugula, or Morrocan olive. Seafood specialties, frog legs in garlic, prosciutto-stuffed chicken, and aged beef are all popular. **FYI:** Reservations recommended. Piano. Dress code. **Open:** Lunch Mon–Fri 11:30am–3pm; dinner Mon–Thurs 5–10pm, Sat–Fri 5–11pm; brunch Sun 10:30am–3pm. **Prices:** Main courses $15–$25. AE, CB, DC, DISC, MC, V. 💟 ♿

Wayne

Site of Dey Mansion, once used as George Washington's headquarters during the Revolutionary War. **Information:** Tri-County Chamber of Commerce, 2055 Hamburg Turnpike, Wayne, 07470 (tel 201/831-7788).

MOTEL 🏨

🚩 Holiday Inn

334 US 46 E, 07470; tel 201/256-7000 or toll free 800/292-6483; fax 201/890-5406. The exterior of this two-story brick structure needs some work, but the rooms are clean and in decent repair. Sufficient for a quick stop. **Rooms:** 139 rms. CI noon/CO noon. Nonsmoking rms avail. Sturdy, simple furnishings and mismatched decor. **Amenities:** 🛏 👁 A/C, satel TV. **Services:** ✗ ⬜ ⌂ ⏱ Manager's cocktail reception every Wednesday. **Facilities:** 🔓 🏋 🟨300 1 restaurant, 1 bar (w/entertainment), games rm. Bus parking. Complimentary access to adjacent health spa. Golf driving range next door. **Rates (CP):** $75–$85 S or D. Children under age 19 stay free. Min stay special events. Parking: Outdoor, free. AE, CB, DC, DISC, JCB, MC, V.

Weehawken

Across the Hudson River from New York City. Weehawken was the site of the infamous 1804 duel between Vice President Aaron Burr and Alexander Hamilton, in which Hamilton was killed. Homeport of the *Spirit of New Jersey,* which offers cruises around New York.

RESTAURANT 🍽

♣ Arthur's Landing

In Port Imperial Ferry Landing, Pershing Circle; tel 201/867-0777. **American.** Spectacular views of the New York skyline are the big draws at this waterfront eatery with a waterborne connection to the ferry to Manhattan. Seafood and rack of lamb are popular entrees; a tasting menu includes a salad, appetizer, two entrees, and dessert for $55 per person. There's outdoor dining in summer, and the restaurant validates the ferry fare for lunch and brunch. **FYI:** Reservations recommended. Piano. Children's menu. Dress code. **Open:** Lunch Mon–Sat noon–3pm; dinner Sun–Thurs 5–9:30pm, Fri–Sat 5–10:30pm; brunch Sun 11:30am–2:30pm. **Prices:** Main courses $19–$30; prix fixe $40. AE, DISC, MC, V. 🍴 🖼 💟 VP ♿

West Atlantic City

See Atlantic City

West Caldwell

Small borough located SW of Paterson. **Information:** West Essex Chamber of Commerce, 3 Fairfield Ave, West Caldwell, 07006 (tel 201/226-5500).

RESTAURANT 🍽

★ Italianissimo

In Broadway Square Mall, 40 Clinton Rd; tel 201/228-4824. At Passaic Ave. **Italian.** Half of this deli's open space is given over to cafe tables and a small espresso bar, while the other half consists of a stunning dining room put together by an opera set designer from Rome. Tuscan specialties are led by risotto paniscia and rigatoni pancetta, and there are all manner of fish in light sauces. Chicken, veal, homemade pastas, and brick-oven pizza complete the assortment. **FYI:** Reservations recommended. BYO. Additional location: 555 Passaic Ave (tel 882-8889). **Open:** Mon–Thurs 11:30am–10:30pm, Fri–Sat 11am–11pm, Sun 4–9pm. **Prices:** Main courses $9–$17. AE, DISC, MC, V. 🖼

Westfield

A largely residential town SW of Newark. Home to Cory House Museum, built circa 1740. **Information:** Westfield Area Chamber of Commerce, 111 Quimby St, PO Box 81, Westfield, 07091 (tel 908/233-3021).

RESTAURANT 🍴

Ken Marcotte

115 Elm St; tel 908/233-2309. Between Orchard and E Broad Sts. **New American.** High ceilings, etched glass, and art deco fittings give this former bank an air of gentility. The husband-and-wife team who own and operate the place turn out thoughtful dishes like quail and tuna from the wood-burning grill, and there's lots of game and organic vegetables. Homemade ice cream is available for dessert. **FYI:** Reservations recommended. Dress code. **Open:** Lunch Tues–Fri 11:30am–2pm; dinner Mon–Thurs 5:30–9pm, Fri–Sat 5:30–10pm, Sun 4:30–8:30pm. **Prices:** Main courses $18–$24. AE, DC, MC, V. 💟

West Orange

The Thomas A Edison Historic Site pays tribute to the town's most famous resident, and includes the inventor's home, laboratory, and library.

RESTAURANTS 🍴

Dali

540 Valley Rd; tel 201/736-9869. Between Northfield and South Orange Aves. **Spanish.** The hot-pink stucco exterior is in stark contrast to the subdued and understated dining room. Seafood specialties include lobsters, shrimp, and monkfish in a variety of sauces. Chicken in garlic is the biggest seller, but paella (served in massive portions) is also worth checking out. **FYI:** Reservations recommended. Dress code. **Open:** Tues–Thurs 11:30am–9pm, Fri–Sat 11:30am–10:30pm, Sun 4–9pm. **Prices:** Main courses $13–$24. AE, MC, V.

✸ Empress Garden

In Essex Green Shopping Center, 136 Prospect Ave; tel 201/736-9699. Exit 8 off I-280. **Chinese.** A truly exceptional Cantonese restaurant hidden away in a suburban shopping mall. The menu offers traditional Chinese-American dishes plus those usually not seen outside of Chinatown: miniature woks brought to table with braised bean curd and assorted seafood, *wor ba* (sizzling rice piled with chicken and seafood), and chicken Soong in lettuce wraps. Dim sum served on weekends until 3pm. **FYI:** Reservations accepted. Dress code. **Open:** Mon–Thurs 11:30am–10pm, Fri–Sat 11:30am–11pm, Sun 10am–10pm. **Prices:** Main courses $9–$30. AE, MC, V.

♣ The Manor

111 Prospect Ave; tel 201/325-1400. Exit 8B off I-280. **Eclectic.** A regal dining room housed in a magnificent Georgian estate and surrounded by English-style gardens and artisan studios. Silver service dining features roast breast of duck, grilled filet mignon, and free-range chicken, all served with vegetables grown on the premises. Seafood buffet available Tuesday–Saturday. **FYI:** Reservations recommended. Jacket required. **Open:** Lunch Tues–Fri noon–2:30pm; dinner Tue–Sat 6–9:30pm, Sun 4–7:30pm. **Prices:** Main courses $16–$29. AE, CB, DC, MC, V. 💟 ⬛ 🖼 VP ♿

ATTRACTIONS 🖼

Edison National Historic Site

Main St and Lakeside Ave; tel 201/736-5050. Inventor, manufacturer, and businessman Thomas Alva Edison lived here for 44 years. Out of his West Orange laboratories came the motion picture camera, vastly improved phonographs, sound recordings, silent and sound movies, and the nickel-iron alkaline electric storage battery. The museum contains the largest single body of Edison-related material in the world. Using the site's resources, a visitor can trace the invention process from the first idea jotted down in a laboratory notebook, through the research and development steps, and the finished mass-produced product. A replica of the world's first structure designed as a motion picture studio, the "Black Maria," is also part of the site. Guided tours available. **Open:** Daily 9am–5pm. $

Turtle Back Zoo

560 Northfield Ave; tel 201/731-5800. This 15-acre zoo is home to a wide variety of animals including deer, llama, penguins, seals, yak, bison, owls, bald eagles, and a herd of wild sheep. In addition, visitors can see a pack of wolves in a new naturalistic setting known as the "wolf woods." Free train rides through the South Mountain Reservation are also available. **Open:** Mon–Sat 10am–5pm, Sun 10:30am–6pm. $$

Wildwood

Located on the South Jersey Shore, Wildwood (and the neighboring resort of Wildwood Crest) features five miles of wide beaches and three miles of boardwalk, with rides and a carnival-like atmosphere. **Information:** Greater Wildwood Chamber of Commerce, PO Box 823, Wildwood, 08260 (tel 609/729-4000).

HOTEL 🏨

🏨🏨 Adventurer Motor Inn

5401 Ocean Ave, Wildwood Crest, 08260; tel 609/729-1200 or toll free 800/232-7873. Ocean Ave S to Morning Glory. This six-story hotel on the beach has standard rooms plus two- and three-bedroom efficiencies, which rent quickly in summer. **Rooms:** 120 rms, stes, and effic. CI 2pm/CO 11am.

Average size, decor and amenities. Large efficiency suites accommodate up to eight people. **Amenities:** 🛅 A/C, cable TV, refrig. All units w/terraces. **Services:** ✗ VP 🛏 Babysitting. **Facilities:** 🛋 300 🛴 1 restaurant, 1 beach (ocean), lifeguard, games rm, washer/dryer. **Rates:** Peak (July 12–Aug 24) $56–$130 S or D; $311 ste; $145–$189 effic. Extra person $12. Children under age 3 stay free. Min stay wknds. Lower rates off-season. Parking: Indoor/outdoor, free. Closed Oct 15–Apr 3. AE, MC, V.

MOTELS

🖿🖿 Aqua Beach Resort
5501 Ocean Ave, Wildwood Crest, 08260; tel 609/522-6507 or toll free 800/247-4776; fax 609/522-8535. Ocean Ave to Morning Glory Rd. A family-friendly beachfront motel. **Rooms:** 123 rms, stes, and effic; 8 cottages/villas. Executive level. CI 3pm/CO 11am. Nonsmokers may request aerated rooms. **Amenities:** 🛅 🖃 A/C, cable TV w/movies, refrig, dataport. All units w/terraces, some w/whirlpools. **Services:** 🛏 Social director, children's program, babysitting. Fax service available. **Facilities:** 🛋 35 1 restaurant (bkfst and lunch only), 1 beach (ocean), lifeguard, games rm, whirlpool, washer/dryer. Free barbecues (Tuesdays and Thursdays, in season). **Rates:** Peak (July–Aug) $120 S or D; $152–$241 ste; $133–$150 effic; $155–$176 cottage/villa. Extra person $10. Children under age 3 stay free. Min stay peak. Lower rates off-season. Parking: Outdoor, free. Off-season packages avail. Closed Oct 20–Mar 20. DISC, MC, V.

🖿 Attache Resort Motel
Heather Rd and Beach, Wildwood Crest, 08260; tel 609/522-0241. Ocean Ave to Heather Rd. Standard-issue beachfront motel. **Rooms:** 42 rms and effic. CI 2pm/CO 11am. **Amenities:** 🛅 🖃 A/C, cable TV. All units w/terraces. Most rooms have stoves and refrigerators. **Services:** 🛏 Babysitting. **Facilities:** 🛋 1 beach (ocean), lifeguard, games rm, washer/dryer. A sundeck overlooks the beach. **Rates:** Peak (July–Aug) $125–$170 S or D; $145–$205 effic. Min stay peak. Lower rates off-season. Parking: Outdoor, free. Some rates include up to four people. Spring and fall packages avail. Closed Nov–Apr. AE, MC, V.

🖿🖿 Days Inn
4610 Ocean Ave, PO Box 38, 08260; tel 609/522-0331 or toll free 800/DAYS-INN; fax 609/522-2018. From Wildwood exit S on Garden State Pkwy, right on Ocean. A simple but welcoming motel popular with families. The beach is adjacent, and a city park is across the street. **Rooms:** 36 stes and effic. CI 2pm/CO 11am. Nonsmoking rms avail. **Amenities:** 🛅 A/C, cable TV, refrig. All units w/terraces. **Services:** 🛏 Babysitting. **Facilities:** 🛋 🛴 1 beach (ocean), lifeguard, games rm, washer/dryer. Shuffleboard in the city park. **Rates:** Peak (July–Aug) $155–$170 ste; $155–$170 effic. Extra person $5–$10. Children under age 12 stay free. Min stay peak. Lower rates off-season. Parking: Outdoor, free. Closed Oct 23–Apr 5. AE, CB, DC, DISC, MC, V.

🖿🖿 Pan American Hotel
5901 Ocean Ave, Wildwood Crest, 08260; tel 609/522-6936; fax 609/522-6937. Ocean Ave to Crocus Rd. Popular with active families due to the abundance of recreational activities in the area. **Rooms:** 78 rms, stes, and effic. CI 2pm/CO 11am. Some rooms overlook the pool deck and/or the beach. **Amenities:** 🛅 A/C, cable TV, refrig. All units w/terraces. **Services:** ✗ 🖂 🛏 Twice-daily maid svce, social director, children's program, babysitting. **Facilities:** 🛋 75 1 restaurant, 1 beach (ocean), lifeguard, volleyball, games rm, sauna, day-care ctr, washer/dryer. **Rates:** Peak (June 30–Sept 3) $150–$154 S or D; $178–$185 ste; $160–$165 effic. Extra person $12. Children under age 3 stay free. Lower rates off-season. Parking: Indoor/outdoor, free. Rates include up to four people per room. Closed Oct 12–May 1. MC, V.

🖿 Sea-N-Sun Motel
3909 Ocean Ave, 08260; tel 609/522-2826. Spicer Ave to Ocean Ave. Lots of families have been returning to this motel for years. If you want one of the four beachfront efficiencies you should reserve far in advance. **Rooms:** 21 rms and effic. CI 2pm/CO 11am. Very clean, simple rooms. **Amenities:** 🛅 🖃 A/C, cable TV, refrig, in-rm safe. Some units w/terraces. Microwaves. **Services:** 🛏 **Facilities:** 🛋 🛴 1 beach (ocean), lifeguard, whirlpool. **Rates:** Peak (July–Aug) $88 S or D; $120 effic. Extra person $12. Children under age 2 stay free. Min stay wknds. Lower rates off-season. Parking: Outdoor, free. Closed Nov–Mar. AE, DISC, MC, V.

ATTRACTIONS 📷

Morey's Piers
On the Boardwalk; tel 609/522-3900. Two seaside amusement piers featuring more than 60 rides, including roller coasters, children's rides, Ferris wheels, and a log flume. Raging Waters (at two locations) features high-speed water slides, wave pools, and lazy river and inner-tube rides. Wild Wheels is a daredevil's paradise with jet skis, car races, batting cages, bungee jumping, and helicopter rides. Separate admission fees for each park. **Open:** Piers, daily 11am–midnight. Water park, daily 9am–7pm. **$$$$**

Ocean Discovery Center
6006 Park Blvd, Wildwood Crest; tel 609/898-0999 or toll free 800/942-5373. Nonprofit educational organization with exhibits about the local marine environment. Dolphin and whale watching excursions are offered; phone ahead for details. **Open:** May–Dec, daily 9am–4pm. **$$$**

Woodbridge

Settled in 1665 by the Puritans. Now best known as the home of Woodbridge Center, with over 230 specialty stores. **Information:** Woodbridge Convention & Visitors Bureau, 52 Main St, Woodbridge, 07095 (tel 908/636-4040).

MOTEL 🛏

≣≣ The Landmark Inn

US 1/9, 07095; tel 908/636-2700; fax 900/855-7623. Exit 130 off Garden State Pkwy. A simple motel with exceptional banquet facilities and a courteous staff. The last full renovation was 20 years ago, and the hallways need brightening up. **Rooms:** 116 rms, stes, and effic. CI noon/CO noon. Nonsmoking rms avail. Bridal suite available. **Amenities:** 📞 A/C, cable TV w/movies, VCR. Some units w/minibars, some w/terraces. **Services:** ✗ VP 🛎 Twice-daily maid svce. **Facilities:** 🎣 1000 1 restaurant, 1 bar (w/entertainment), washer/dryer. **Rates (MAP):** $58 S; $66 D; $100 ste; $75–$150 effic. Extra person $6. Children under age 6 stay free. Parking: Outdoor, free. AE, CB, DC, DISC, MC, V.

Wyckoff

North of Paterson and close to Campgaw Mountain Reservation, Wyckoff is the site of a noted environmental center. **Information:** Wyckoff Chamber of Commerce, PO Box 2, Wyckoff, 07481 (tel 201/891-3616).

RESTAURANT 🍴

Aldo's

393 Franklin Ave; tel 201/891-2618. At Wyckoff Ave. **Italian.** Friendly neighborhood restaurant, where the booths and tables are bathed in a soft pink glow. Specialties include shrimp stuffed with crabmeat béchamel and chicken alla Aldo. The adjacent cafe (with party room, outdoor terrace, and enclosed patio) serves a variety of desserts. **FYI:** Reservations recommended. BYO. Additional location: 56 NJ 46 E, Rockaway (tel 586-3006). **Open:** Lunch Mon–Sat noon–3pm; dinner Mon–Sat 5–10pm, Sun 1–9pm. **Prices:** Main courses $12–$16. AE. 🍰 ♿

PENNSYLVANIA
Cradle of the Nation

STATE STATS

CAPITAL

Harrisburg

AREA

45,888 square miles

BORDERS

New York, New Jersey,
Delaware, Maryland,
West Virginia, Ohio,
Lake Erie

POPULATION

12,010,000

ENTERED UNION

December 12, 1787 (2nd state)

NICKNAME

Keystone State

STATE FLOWER

Mountain laurel

STATE BIRD

Ruffed grouse

FAMOUS NATIVES

Louisa May Alcott,
Alexander Calder,
Robert Fulton, Betsy Ross,
Andy Warhol

Centrally located as the "Keystone" of the 13 colonies, Pennsylvania was indeed a key site in the founding of the United States. The Founding Fathers met in Philadelphia to officially declare their colonies free of England on July 4, 1776. In the following years, Pennsylvania's iron ore and rich farms supplied George Washington's Continental Army with the bullets, cannon, and food they need to turn back the Redcoats. When the Articles of Confederation (adopted in York in 1777) proved unworkable, the Founders met again in Philadelphia and wrote the United States Constitution in 1787.

While Philadelphia has at least as many historic sites as any other American city, the Keystone State has much more to offer today's visitors than meeting halls and museums. There are the horse-drawn wagons and unique barns of the Pennsylvania Dutch country, the covered bridges of Bucks County, the rolling valleys of the Susquehanna River, theme parks and farm visits for families, and a cultural renaissance blooming in Pittsburgh, the city built by steel.

Industry has played an important role in Pennsylvania since iron ore was discovered here in 1684. Pennsylvanians built the nation's first steamship and railroad locomotive and drilled its first oil well. Allentown, Scranton, Wilkes-Barre, and Altoona mined the coal which fired the Industrial Revolution.

Yet despite the coal mines, oil wells, and steel mills which created some of America's biggest fortunes, Pennsylvania also has the wildest and least populated land in the eastern United States. From the Poconos to the Laurel Highlands, it beckons lovers of the great outdoors with mountains, streams, lakes, white-water rivers, and ski slopes. In Pennsylvania, you can walk in the footsteps of Benjamin Franklin and Thomas Jefferson, or make your own along thousands of miles of trails set aside for hikers, bicyclists, and horseback riders. Indeed, this largest of the mid-Atlantic states has something for just about everyone.

A Brief History

Haven for Immigrants Ironically, it was the Swedes who first settled this land upon which so much American history was played out. Established in 1643, their little colony on Tinicum Island in the Delaware River was taken over by the Dutch in 1655 and subsequently ceded to England in 1664. But what we know as Pennsylvania really began in 1681, when King Charles II of England settled a debt by making the largest private land grant in America to a young Quaker named William Penn.

Imprisoned in England for his beliefs, Penn set out to establish a colony named Pennsylvania ("Penn's Woods"), dedicated to religious freedom. He built Philadelphia (from the Greek for "city of brotherly love") on a peninsula between the Delaware and Schuylkill Rivers. Not only were Penn's religious ideas revolutionary for the 17th century, so was his new city: its wide streets were laid out in a grid to prevent the fires and plagues which often ravaged unplanned English towns. Although he stayed in America only from 1682 to 1684 and again from 1699 to 1701, Penn's Charter of Privileges set up a colonial government whose guarantees of freedom helped lay the groundwork for the founding of an independent United States 75 years after his final departure.

Philadelphia became the preeminent American city during the early 1700s, and the colony grew steadily as Quakers from England and Wales were joined by Scotch-Irish and German immigrants. Many of the Germans belonged to the Amish, Mennonite, Moravian, Dunker, and Schwenkfelder sects; a mispronunciation of *Deutsch* (the word for "German") caused them to be called the Pennsylvania Dutch.

French, Indians & the Way West Penn was fair and scrupulous in his dealings with Native Americans, and the colony's frontier remained calm until the 1750s, when the French extended their claims to western Pennsylvania. In 1753, a 21-year-old major in the Virginia militia named George Washington went to Fort LeBoeuf near Lake Erie to warn the French to stop fortifying the area. He was rebuffed, but returned the next spring with a fighting force. Besieged by a larger contingent of French troops and their Native American allies, Washington quickly built Fort Necessity. The ensuing battle was the first significant engagement of the French and Indian War, known in Europe as the Seven Years' War.

Key conflicts were fought over Fort Duquesne at the confluence of the Allegheny, Monongahela, and Ohio Rivers. In 1758, a colonial army under Gen John Forbes hacked a wagon-width trail to the fort, which the French promptly burned and abandoned. Forbes rebuilt the structure and named it Fort Pitt. (The town that grew up around the new fort was called Pittsburgh.) After the French relinquished their claims to North America in 1763, the trail Forbes built became the key highway west. Despite a bloody Indian uprising known as Pontiac's Rebellion, pioneers by the thousands crossed through Pittsburgh on their way to the Ohio Valley. Most rode in Conestoga wagons developed by the Pennsylvania Dutch in Lancaster, and many carried Kentucky rifles, another Lancaster product.

Revolution & Independence With resentment growing over British taxes and trade policies, the First Continental Congress met in Philadelphia in 1774. It vented the American colonists' grievances against the crown and adopted a Declaration of Rights. The battles at Lexington and Concord were old news by the time the Second Continental Congress assembled in 1775 to debate not just rights but independence. Pennsylvanians were split over the question: Scotch-Irish settlers on the frontier were all for independence, but many Quakers were against taking up arms at all and some Germans living on isolated farms didn't care one way or the other. With Benjamin Franklin in the lead, the Pennsylvania delegation narrowly voted in favor of

Fun Facts

- The Philadelphia Zoological Gardens, which opened in 1874, was the first zoo in the United States.
- Benjamin Franklin acted as Philadelphia's first postmaster, organized its first fire department, and established the state's first university and public hospital.
- The Liberty Bell didn't get its name until 1839, when it was used in an antislavery pamphlet as a symbol of freedom for black slaves.
- The biggest chocolate factory in the world is the Hershey Factory in Hershey, Pennsylvania.
- Ardmore, Pennsylvania, was home to the world's first suburban shopping mall. The Suburban Square Mall was built in 1928 and included two department stores, 17 small shops, and a movie theater.

the Declaration of Independence, for which the Liberty Bell rang on July 4, 1776.

Pennsylvania played a major role in the ensuing Revolutionary War. Iron ore had been discovered here in 1684, and the state's 50 forges were major suppliers of armaments to Gen George Washington's Continental Army. The British in New York forced that army across New Jersey and into Pennsylvania in October 1776, but Washington won his first victory by slipping across the Delaware River on Christmas night and surprising a British garrison at Trenton, New Jersey.

As the de facto national capital, Philadelphia became the British army's target in September 1777, when they landed in Maryland and moved north toward the city. Washington suffered a major defeat when he tried to stop them at Brandywine Creek. A few days later he attacked again at Germantown; although he lost in a fog, his tactics were impressive enough to help convince the French to enter the war on America's side.

The British marched unopposed into Philadelphia and spent the ensuing winter there while Washington and his troops nearly froze at Valley Forge, just west of the city. Although some 2,000 underclothed and under-fed patriot troops died of disease or starvation, Prussian drillmaster Baron Friedrich von Stueben whipped the rest into a fighting force. With France's entry into the war the next summer, the British evacuated Philadelphia and headed overland to New York. The rejuvenated Continental Army overtook them at Monmouth, New Jersey, in the war's bloodiest and fiercest battle.

During the British occupation of Philadelphia, the Continental Congress met in York, where in 1777 it created the first national government by adopting the Articles of Confederation. The system proved unwieldy, however, and in 1787 a special convention met in Philadelphia and wrote the United States Constitution. Philadelphia served as the national capital from 1790 until 1800, when the federal government moved to its new quarters in Washington, DC.

Coal, Oil & Gettysburg The new state grew and prospered during the 19th century. Roads, canals, and railroads pushed into the north and west, where coal, iron, and lumber provided riches. A man named E L Drake struck oil near Titusville in 1859, setting off history's first oil boom.

Pennsylvania had emancipated all its slaves in 1781, and when the Civil War broke out in 1861, the state was strongly on the side of the Union. Just as it had done for Washington's army, the state became an arsenal for Abraham Lincoln's. Pennsylvania saw only two battles in that conflict, but one of them ultimately determined the war's outcome. In June 1863, the Army of Northern Virginia under Gen Robert E Lee invaded south-central Pennsylvania, hoping to cut the Union's supply lines and win a major victory that would convince Lincoln to end the war. In early July, the Yankees defeated Lee in the war's bloodiest battle at Gettysburg, a key road junction. Although he escaped to Virginia and fought on for almost two more years, it was the beginning of Lee's road to Appomattox. The state saw one more Civil War episode when a Rebel raiding party crossed the border and burned the town of Chambersburg in 1864.

After the war, Pennsylvania took its place at the forefront of the Industrial Revolution. With the help of Henry Clay Frick and J P Morgan, Andrew Carnegie produced two-thirds of the nation's steel in Pittsburgh's mills. Other industries flourished, and Rockefeller's Standard Oil became one of the country's richest corporations. Their influence is still felt today, as Pennsylvania continues as one of America's industrial leaders.

Key to the Future Today, Pennsylvania is the fifth most populous state in the country. With many of its factories shut down and its coal mines aban-

---

DRIVING DISTANCES

Philadelphia

442 mi SE of Cleveland, OH
105 mi E of Harrisburg
106 mi SW of New York, NY
313 mi E of Pittsburgh
244 mi NE of Richmond, VA
138 mi NE of Washington, DC

Pittsburgh

129 mi SE of Cleveland, OH
208 mi W of Harrisburg
403 mi SW of New York, NY
313 mi W of Philadelphia
353 mi NE of Richmond, VA
247 mi NE of Washington, DC

Harrisburg

337 mi SE of Cleveland, OH
403 mi SW of New York, NY
105 mi W of Philadelphia
208 mi E of Pittsburgh
221 mi N of Richmond, VA
115 mi N of Washington, DC

doned, Pennsylvania is increasingly turning to tourism as a major source of revenue. Industry is no longer the economic mainstay that it once was, but the ski resorts of the Poconos and the burgeoning arts scenes in Philadelphia and Pittsburgh are pointing the way toward a bright future for the state.

A Closer Look

GEOGRAPHY

The great arc of the Appalachian Mountains sweep across the state from Maryland northwestward to New Jersey. To the south and east, the foothills surrender to a strip of flat coastal plain around Philadelphia. To the north and west, the Allegheny Plateau drops from its highest point in the Laurel Highlands near Maryland to a flat plain bordering Lake Erie. Cutting north-south, the Susquehanna and Delaware Rivers flow toward the Atlantic Ocean. Near the western edge of the state, the Monongahela and Allegheny Rivers join at Pittsburgh to form the Ohio, which eventually meets the mighty Mississippi.

AVG MONTHLY TEMPS (°F) & RAINFALL (IN)		
	Philadelphia	Pittsburgh
Jan	30/2.3	26/2.5
Feb	33/2.8	29/2.4
Mar	42/3.5	39/3.4
Apr	52/3.6	47/3.2
May	63/3.8	60/3.6
June	72/3.7	68/3.7
July	76/4.3	72/3.8
Aug	76/3.8	71/3.2
Sept	68/3.4	64/3.0
Oct	56/2.6	52/2.4
Nov	46/3.3	42/2.9
Dec	36/3.4	31/2.9

Philadelphia and its countryside, in the southeast corner of the state, are the entry to Pennsylvania for many visitors. The city is filled with historic buildings in which the likes of George Washington, Benjamin Franklin, and Thomas Jefferson created the United States. To the north of the city, picturesque **Bucks County** has artists, boutiques, covered bridges, and the spot where George Washington's army slipped across the Delaware River on Christmas Night 1776. West of Philadelphia, descendants of early Amish settlers still use horse-drawn carriages to move about the rolling hills of the **Pennsylvania Dutch Country.** Today's visitors will find Hershey and its amusement park, Gettysburg and its turning-point Civil War battlefield, Harrisburg with its Italian Renaissance–style state capitol, and Reading with its multitudes of outlet shops.

In the northeast corner of the state, New Yorkers know the resorts in the **Pocono Mountains** for their honeymoon suites equipped with heart-shaped hot tubs and champagne-glass whirlpools. The region is also home to downhill skiing resorts, canoeing and kayaking in the Delaware Water Gap National Recreation Area, white-water rafting through the Lehigh River Gorge, and coal mining around the industrial cities of Scranton, Wilkes-Barre, and Pottsville.

In the center of the state, riverfront towns like Williamsport, Lock Haven, Selinsgrove, and Lewisburg sit among the hills, farmland, and covered bridges of the **Susquehanna River Valley.** North and west of the river lies the great wilderness of the **Allegheny National Forest** region, one of the wildest and least populated areas in the eastern United States. Thousands of these pristine acres are protected in the national forest and several state forests, including Pennsylvania's version of the Grand Canyon, Pine Creek Gorge.

The hills drop in the northwest corner of the state to the flat plains near **Lake Erie,** where Commodore Oliver Hazard Perry's won an important War of 1812 victory. Moored in Erie, his USS *Niagara* now serves as Pennsylvania's modern flagship. On a peninsula forming Erie's harbor, Presque Isle State Park is an urban haven for wildlife and birds. Fishing and boating are big sports on the lake during summer, ice fishing and skating in winter.

Anchoring western Pennsylvania, the city of **Pittsburgh** has changed vastly from its often-hazy days as the "City of Steel." Today it has a host of museums, historic sites, and beautiful views from atop Mount Washington. In contrast to flat Philadelphia, its streets form a maze up narrow valleys. South of Pittsburgh, the rugged mountains of the **Laurel Highlands and Southern Alleghenies** are reminiscent of nearby West Virginia, with skiing resorts and white-water rafting down the Youghiogheny, Cheat, and Russell Fork Rivers.

CLIMATE

The lowlands and hills of Pennsylvania have the same four-season climate as the other mid-Atlantic states: pleasant and flowery springs, warm and colorful falls, hot and humid summers, and usually (but not always) mild winters. The mountains, on the other hand, see short, cool summers and harsh, snowy winters.

WHAT TO PACK

Outside the cities, Pennsylvanians emphasize outdoor recreation, so you can pack accordingly. Bring shorts for summer, heavy coats and mittens for winter, sweaters for fall, and rainwear for spring. You'll appreciate long pants and jackets in the mountains and forests—even in summer. Dress outfits will come in handy at some restaurants in Philadelphia and Pittsburgh.

TOURIST INFORMATION

For a free copy of the *Pennsylvania Visitors Guide,* write or call the **Office of Travel and Tourism,** Forum Building, Rm 453, Harrisburg, PA 17120 (tel 717/787-5453 or toll free 800/VISIT-PA). The state maintains a World Wide Web page (http://www.state.pa.us) with general information about Pennsylvania and its attractions. To find out how to obtain tourist information for individual cities and parks in Pennsylvania, look under specific cities in the listings section of this book.

DRIVING RULES AND REGULATIONS

The speed limit is 65 mph on 1,400 miles of rural interstate, 55 mph in urban areas. Driver and all front-seat passengers must wear seat belts, and children under age four must ride in an approved safety seat. Drunk-driving laws are strictly enforced, and the penalties are severe.

RENTING A CAR

The following rental agencies have offices in Pennsylvania. Before you leave, check with your insurance company to see if you are insured while driving a rental car. Most insurers provide this service; if not, the agencies can sell you insurance.

- **Alamo** (tel toll free 800/327-9633)
- **Avis** (tel 800/831-2847)
- **Budget** (tel 800/527-0700)
- **Hertz** (tel 800/654-3131)
- **National** (tel 800/227-7368)
- **Thrifty** (tel 800/367-2277)

ESSENTIALS

Area Codes: Philadelphia and its inner suburbs are in area code **215.** The outer ring around Philadelphia, from Allentown through Reading, is in area code **610.** Central Pennsylvania, including Harrisburg and the Pennsylvania Dutch Country, are in area code **717.** Pittsburgh and the southwestern corner of the state are in area code **412,** while the rest of western Pennsylvania is in area code **814.**

Emergencies: Call **911** for police, fire, or ambulance from anywhere within Pennsylvania. Call toll free 800/932-0586 for State Police emergency road service; motorists with cellular phones can dial *11.

Liquor Laws: The statewide legal drinking age is 21. Beer can be purchased in package outlets or taverns but not in grocery stores. Wine and liquor are available at 670 state-owned Wine and Spirits Shoppes (tel toll free 800/932-0586 for the nearest location).

Road Info: Call toll free 800/331-3414 from within Pennsylvania or 717/939-9871 from outside the state for information about highway and weather conditions.

Smoking: Smoking is not restricted by state law, but most restaurants have nonsmoking sections, and all but a few hotels and motels set aside rooms for nonsmoking guests.

Taxes: The sales tax is 6% in all counties except Philadelphia and Allegheny (Pittsburgh), where it is 7%. Clothing is tax-exempt statewide. Local jurisdictions may levy up to 6% lodging tax.

Time Zone: All of Pennsylvania is in the Eastern time zone. Daylight saving time is observed from the first Sunday in April until the last Sunday in October.

Best of the State

WHAT TO SEE AND DO

Below is a general overview of some of the top sights in Pennsylvania. To find out more detailed information, look under "Attractions" under individual cities in the listings portion of this book.

Parks & Natural Wonders   Rivers have cut several gorges through the Appalachian Mountains, providing some of Pennsylvania's most dramatic scenery in the process. Along the state's eastern boundary with New Jersey, the Delaware River chiseled its famous gorge, now preserved in the **Delaware Water Gap National Recreation Area.** The river then turns to the northwest, forming Pennsylvania's boundary with New York and becoming officially known as the **Upper Delaware Scenic and Recreational River.** The Delaware and Hudson Canal actually crosses the river at Lackawaxen via the Delaware Aqueduct, the oldest wire suspension bridge in America.

In north central Pennsylvania, **Pine Creek Gorge** runs for some 50 miles through the Allegheny Plateau south of Wellsboro. At times 1,000 feet deep, it is known as the "Grand Canyon of Pennsylvania." The surrounding wilderness area sports several state parks and forests with numerous hiking and riding trails.

One of Pennsylvania's great outdoor treasures is the **Allegheny National Forest,** whose 516,000 acres make up the largest woods in the state. This wonderland has something for everyone in every season: hiking, snowmobiling, cross-country skiing, boating, fishing, canoeing, mountain biking, camping, and spectacular colors when the trees change in autumn.

The state has a number of caverns to explore. **Penn's Cave,** near Centre Hall, is America's only all-water cavern, and visitors take boat rides to see colorful limestone formations such as the "Statue of Liberty" and "Niagara Falls." **Indian Caverns** near Spruce Creek contains Native American artifacts, and **Lincoln Caverns** near Huntingdon is known for its crystal rock formations. One of the five rooms at **Lost River Caverns,** near Hellerton, is so big that it is used for weddings and baptisms.

Historic Areas, Sites & Monuments   The state abounds with sites that played leading roles in American history. At the top of the list is **Independence National Historical Park,** in downtown Philadelphia. Its 40 sites include **Independence Hall,** in which the Continental Congress issued the Declaration of Independence in 1776. Delegates met there again in 1787 to draft the US Constitution. Nearby stands the **Betsy Ross House,** where in 1776 the famous seamstress stitched together the first American flag with 13 stars and 13 stripes.

Washington Crossing Historic Park marks the spot where Gen George Washington led the Continental Army across the Delaware River on Christmas 1776 to surprise a British garrison at Trenton, New Jersey. **Valley Forge National Historical Park** preserves the area where Washington's men suffered through the bitter winter of 1777–78. Washington's headquarters and fortifications have been rebuilt, and there's a museum with some 3,000 artifacts recovered from the encampment.

In Pittsburgh, Point State Park is home of the **Fort Pitt Museum,** with a reconstruction of the blockhouse built by British forces (including a company under then-Col George Washington) after the French abandoned the site in 1758 during the French and Indian War. In Erie, the rebuilt brig **USS** *Niagara* was the flagship of Commodore Perry, who led a small American fleet to victory in the Battle of Lake Erie in 1813, thus halting British advances southward during the War of 1812. Now Presque Isle State Park, Erie's peninsula was Perry's home port.

Museums   An entire vacation could be spent exploring the many fine museums in the City of Brotherly Love, starting with the **Philadelphia Museum of Art,** America's third-largest art museum and one of its best. Part of the country's first art school, the **Museum of American Art of the Pennsylvania Academy of Fine Arts** has a collection of more than 6,000 works dating back to Gilbert Stuart and the Peale family. The **Barnes Foundation** is crammed with 1,000 French masterpieces, including 180 by Renoir and 80 by Cézanne, and the **Rodin Museum** houses the largest collection of this master's works outside Paris. The **Norman Rockwell Museum** houses hundreds of his *Saturday Evening Post* covers and other works.

Pittsburgh boasts the **Carnegie Museum of Art,** which houses a collection of 19th- and 20th-century European and American masterpieces and unique architectural casts; the **Frick Art Museum,** holder of many Flemish, French, and Italian paintings and decorative arts; and the **Andy Warhol Museum,** the largest museum in the country to focus on the works of a single artist. Pittsburgh's **Carnegie Museum of Natural History** has dinosaur bones, an African wildlife exhibit, and minerals and gems; and the **Carnegie Science Center** has a host of educational exhibits for adults and children alike.

The **State Museum of Pennsylvania** at Harrisburg traces all aspects of the state's history from the beginning of time to the present. A special feature for Civil War buffs is "The Battle of Gettysburg: Pickett's Charge," one of the world's largest paintings. Smaller museums around the state appeal to diverse interests. Occupying a restored 19th-century gristmill, the **Brandywine River Museum** at Chadds Ford has a large collection of paintings by the Wyeth family. Clock lovers can observe 8,000 timepieces dating back to the 17th century at the **Watch and Clock Museum of the National Association of Watch and Clock Collectors** in Columbia. The 66-acre **Pennsylvania Military Museum** at Boalsburg commemorates the state's soldiers from the Revolutionary War through Operation Desert Storm. The early history of the petroleum industry is depicted at the **Drake Well Museum** near Titusville, site of the world's first successful oil well. And the **Jimmy Stewart Museum** stores many of the actor's mementos in Indiana, his hometown.

Literary Shrines   Several sites recall the careers of Pennsylvania residents who made their mark in the world of letters. The **Pearl S Buck House** in Dublin has the famous novelist's Nobel and Pulitzer Prizes on display. In addition to a collection of 20th-century paintings, the **James A Michener Art Museum,** at Doylestown in Bucks County, displays his desk, typewriter, and a manuscript from a lengthy Michener tome. In Lackawaxen on the Upper Delaware River, the **Zane Grey Museum** occupies the house where he began writing his western novels. It isn't furnished today, but the famous author of horror stories spent two years at what is now the **Edgar Allan Poe National Historical Site** in Philadelphia. Philadelphia's **Rosenbach Museum and Library** houses the manuscript of James Joyce's *Ulysses* and first editions of Herman Melville.

Battlefields   Fighting in three of America's wars and one rebellion took place on Pennsylvania soil. Major battles from those conflicts are marked by several commemorative parks.

Fort Necessity National Battlefield, on US 40 east of Uniontown, contains a reconstruction of the fort that Maj George Washington built in 1754, when his British colonial force came up against a much larger continent of French and Indians. On September 11, 1777, the British defeated the Continental Army at what is now **Brandywine Battlefield Park** near Chadds Ford, leaving Philadelphia defenseless. With the British warmly ensconced in the city, Washington's army spent the following winter freezing at Valley Forge.

Bushy Run Battlefield near Jeannette marks the spot where a detachment of 500 British Colonial troops ambushed and routed a force of Native Americans during Pontiac's Rebellion in 1763.

One of America's most visited battlefields, **Gettysburg National Military Park** marks the pivotal Civil War conflict in which Union forces defeated the Army of Northern Virginia under Gen Robert E Lee in July 1863, thus ending Lee's advance into Pennsylvania and turning the tide against the Confederacy.

Family Favorites   In Langhorne, Big Bird, Cookie Monster, and other "Sesame Street" characters walk around **Sesame Place,** a theme park with inner tubes, splash pools, and other water activities. Among the entertainments are a re-created *Sesame Street* studio set and Tweedlebug Land, where adults and kids alike will feel as small as the residents of Bert and Ernie's flower box. If your brood doesn't watch *Sesame Street,* they might find familiar faces at **Idlewild Park** in Ligonier, home of Mr Rogers' Neighborhood of Make-Believe.

In Hershey, the aroma of chocolate will alert the youngsters they are nearing **Hersheypark,** a 90-acre amusement park with more than 50 rides and amusements, including four roller coasters, several water-related adventures, and areas with German, English, and Pennsylvania Dutch themes. When they've had their fun there, take them to **Hershey's Chocolate World,** where they learn how the sweet stuff is produced, or to the **Hershey Museum** for a look at the history of both the chocolate company and south-central Pennsylvania.

Families can spend days in Philadelphia's many museums. **Please Touch Museum** was the country's first designed specifically for kids under eight years of age. Housed in converted factories, it has a host of hands-on educational and cultural experiences for children. The city's **Franklin Institute Science Museum** is another fascinating as well as educational experience, with many hands-on exhibits geared to children. And kids love the huge *Tyrannosaurus rex* and other dinosaur bones displayed at the **Academy of Natural Sciences,** and the Egyptian mummies at the **University of Pennsylvania Museum of Archaeology and Anthropology.**

If they miss the dinosaurs in Philadelphia, the kids can see them at the **Carnegie Museum of Natural**

History in Pittsburgh. They can also learn about nature at the **Carnegie Science Center,** which has hands-on exhibits aimed at children. And the **Pittsburgh Children's Museum** uses interactive exhibits to teach about a variety of physical and social phenomena.

Working farms throughout the state can provide city kids a taste of modern rural life—they can even help with the chores. For a copy of *The Pennsylvania Farm Vacation Directory,* write the Department of Agriculture, Attn: Farm Vacations, 2301 N Cameron St, Harrisburg, PA 17110-9408.

Shopping Shoppers know Pennsylvania for its numerous outlet malls selling name-brand merchandise at discount prices. In fact, **Reading** started the whole phenomenon of outlet shopping in the 1960s, when its factories and mills opened their own shops to get rid of excess merchandise. Today Reading has more than 300 manufacturers' stores and bills itself as the "Outlet Capital of the World." **Franklin Mills,** outside Philadelphia, is the world's largest outlet mall, with 200 stores under one roof. In the Pennsylvania Dutch Country, **Lancaster** has more than 120 stores in its Factory Outlet Village. In the Poconos, The Crossings in **Tannersville** has 65 outlet shops, while the Pocono Outlet Complex in **Stroudsburg** has another 31. **York** boasts several factory outlet centers near the intersection of I-83 and US 30. **Georgian Place,** a hour's drive east of Pittsburgh, has more than 50 outlets. Antique, art, and craft lovers congregate on weekends at the shops in New Hope and other towns in **Bucks County** north of Philadelphia.

Gardens More than 11,000 types of plants grow in the Brandywine Valley's world-famous **Longwood Gardens,** the former home of industrialist Pierre S du Pont. One of the nation's finest formal gardens, these 1,050 acres sport fountains, conservatories, heated greenhouses full of flowers, two lakes, and an outdoor theater with performances during the summer months.

Wineries Pennsylvania vintners have been producing wine for two centuries, and today 50 wineries are spread across the state. For a list, write to the Pennsylvania Wine Association, 103 S Duke St, Lancaster, PA 17602.

EVENTS AND FESTIVALS

PHILADELPHIA REGION AND THE POCONOS

- **Mummer's Parade,** Philadelphia. World-famous parade attracts 30,000 costumed Mummers, string bands, comics. January 1. Call 215/636-1666.
- **Music Festival and Cherry Blossom Time,** Wilkes-Barre. Three days of blossoms, music, food, and fun. Early May. Call 717/823-3264.
- **Mayfair Festival of the Arts,** Allentown. Free performances, arts and crafts, children's art activities at Lehigh County's premier event. Last weekend in May. Call 610/437-6900.
- **Willow Grove Air Show,** Horsham. Extraordinary aerial acrobatics, US Navy's steel band, and static naval displays at Willow Grove Naval Air Station. Mid-June. Call 215/443-1776.
- **La Festa Italiana,** Scranton. Spotlights Italian food, culture, music, entertainment. Labor Day weekend. Call 717/344-7411 or 717/346-6384.
- **Celtic Classic Highland Games & Festival,** Bethlehem. Weekend of Irish, Scottish, and Welsh culture, games, and music. Last weekend in September. Call 610/868-9599.
- **Mellon PSFS/Channel 6 Thanksgiving Day Parade,** Philadelphia. The nation's oldest "Turkey Day" parade features floats, balloons, clowns, bands. Thanksgiving Day. Call 215/581-4529.

PENNSYLVANIA DUTCH COUNTRY

- **Pennsylvania Renaissance Faire,** Manheim. Mount Hope Estate and Winery hosts a rollicking re-creation of 16th-century English country fair. Weekends August to October. Call 717/665-7021.
- **Gettysburg Civil War Heritage Days,** Gettysburg. Reenactment of Civil War battle, collectors show, book fair, lectures, concerts. First week in July. Call 717/334-6274.
- **Kutztown Pennsylvania German Festival,** Kutztown. Authentic crafts, quilts, entertainment, food celebrate Pennsylvania Dutch culture. Late June to early July. Call 610/375-4085 or toll free 800/963-8824.
- **Hershey Museum Christkindlmarkt,** Hershey. Authentic foods, live entertainment highlight traditional German holiday festival. First weekend in December. Call 717/534-3439 or 717/534-3432.

SUSQUEHANNA VALLEY

- **Central Pennsylvania Festival of the Arts,** State College. Penn State University hosts performances, films, nationally known sidewalk sales and exhibits. Second weekend in July. Call 814/237-3682.

- **Little League Baseball World Series,** Williamsport. Teams from around the world compete in Little League's crowning event. Third week in August. Call 717/326-1921.
- **Bloomsburg Fair,** Bloomsburg. Top entertainers perform at largest agricultural fair in the Eastern United States. Last week in September. Call 717/784-4949 or 717/784-5728.

NORTHWESTERN PENNSYLVANIA

- **Groundhog Day,** Punxsutawney. If famous furry forecaster "Punxsutawney Phil" sees his shadow when he emerges from his burrow, there'll be six more weeks of winter. February 2. Call 814/938-7700 or toll free 800/752-7445.
- **Grove City Strawberry Days,** Grove City. Strawberry fields yield treats, accompanied by artists and artisans, music, classic cars. First weekend in June. Call 412/458-6410 or 412/458-8000.
- **Applefest,** Franklin. Arts, crafts, quilting, 5K race, antique cars, entertainment. First weekend in October. Call 814/432-5823.

PITTSBURGH REGION

- **Hartwood Music & Dance Festival,** Pittsburgh. Outdoor concerts and dance performances by local, national, internationally acclaimed groups. Mid-June to late August. Call 412/767-9200.
- **National Pike Festival,** Washington. Wagon trains, arts and crafts, entertainment, down-home food celebrate the nation's first federal highway. Third weekend in May. Call toll free 800/531-4114.
- **Three Rivers Arts Festival,** Pittsburgh. Point State Park is bedecked with paintings, sculpture, photography, alive with children's activities, video and music performances. Second and third weeks in June. Call 412/481-7040.
- **Pittsburgh Vintage Grand Prix,** Pittsburgh. Ancient models compete in nation's premier vintage automobile race. Third weekend in July. Call 412/471-7847.
- **Allegheny Rib Cook-Off,** Washington. National contestants vie in best barbecue contest, others enjoy antiques, crafts, music by national and local bands, pig racing. Labor Day weekend. Call 412/678-1727.
- **Covered Bridge Festival,** Washington and Greene Counties. Covered bridges in picturesque countryside, arts and crafts, entertainment, traditional food. Third weekend in September. Call toll free 800/531-4114.

LAUREL HIGHLANDS/SOUTHERN ALLEGHENIES

- **Pennsylvania Maple Festival,** Myersdale. Syrup making, crafts, entertainment, children's activities, hot air balloon rides, carnival, parades, car shows celebrate rising of the sap. Last two weekends in April. Call 814/634-0213.
- **Johnstown Folkfest,** Johnstown. Traditional music by international performers, ethnic foods, historic church tours. Labor Day weekend. Call 814/539-1889.
- **Fall Foliage Festival,** Bedford. Antique cars, wagon train parades, 350 craftspersons, barbecues, scarecrow making, quilting, apple cider, 5K run. First two weekends in October. Call 814/623-1771 or toll free 800/765-3331.

SPECTATOR SPORTS

Auto Racing   Speed cars zoom around the track at **Pocono International Raceway** in Long Pond (tel 717/646-2300 or toll free 800/RACEWAY), home of the annual UAW-GM Teamwork 500 in June and the Miller Genuine Draft 500 in July. Races on the NASCAR Winston Cup circuit take place at **Jennerstown Speedway** in Jennerstown (tel 814/629-6677).

Baseball   Both ends of Pennsylvania boast a National League team: The **Philadelphia Phillies** play in Veterans Stadium (tel 215/463-1000), while the **Pittsburgh Pirates** call Three Rivers Stadium home (tel 412/323-5000). You don't have to be in the big city to see good baseball, however, for the state has six minor league clubs: **Erie Seawolves** (tel 814/456-1300), **Harrisburg Senators** (tel 717/231-4444), **Johnstown Steal** (tel 814/536-TEAM), **Reading Phillies** (tel 610/375-8469), **Scranton/Wilkes-Barre Red Barons** (tel 717/969-2255), and **Williamsport Cubs** (tel 717/326-3389). At the opposite end of the spectrum, the **Little League World Series** is held every summer at Williamsport, home of the Little League Baseball Museum (tel 717/326-3607).

Basketball   The **Philadelphia 76ers** of the NBA play their home games at the CoreStates Spectrum (tel 215/339-7676).

College Athletics   Rivaling the professional teams in popularity, the **Penn State University Nittany Lions** (tel 814/863-1000 or toll free 800/863-5533) from State College are always powerful on the gridiron and on the basketball court. In the Philadelphia area, fans cheer on the **Villanova University**

Wildcats (tel 610/519-4140) and **Temple University Owls** (tel 215/204-5040); in the western part of the state, the **University of Pittsburgh Panthers** (tel 412/648-8300) are the leading college team.

Football   The National Football League has two professional teams in Pennsylvania. The **Pittsburgh Steelers,** who play at Three Rivers Stadium (tel 412/323-1200), recently lost a Super Bowl to the Dallas Cowboys. Some observers think the **Philadelphia Eagles,** whose home is Veterans Stadium (tel 215/463-5500), are on their way to the big game.

Hockey   Two National Hockey League teams call Pennsylvania home: the **Philadelphia Flyers,** who play at the CoreStates Spectrum (tel 215/464-4500), and the **Pittsburgh Penguins,** who call the Pittsburgh Civic Arena home (tel 412/642-1300). Minor league teams include the **Hershey Bears** of the American Hockey League (tel 717/534-3911); and the **Erie Panthers** (tel 814/452-4857) and **Johnstown Chief** (tel toll free 800/CHF-TIXX), both members of the East Coast Hockey League.

ACTIVITIES A TO Z

Ballooning   Among the state's operators, **Windswept Hot Air Balloon Adventures** (tel 412/238-2555) soars over the scenic Ligonier Valley in the Laurel Highlands of southwestern Pennsylvania. **United States Hot Air Balloon Co** (tel toll free 800/76-FLY-US) offers a bird's-eye view of Valley Forge.

Bicycling   Bicyclists will find thousands of rural roads, trails, and a growing system of rails-to-trails conversions in Pennsylvania. Urban bikers can ride the route in Philadelphia's Fairmount Park, the world's largest municipal park, and along Erie's Seaway Trail. These and other options are described in the free *Bicycling Directory of Pennsylvania,* available from the state's Department of Transportation, Room G-123, Transportation & Safety Building, Harrisburg, PA 17120. Information about biking in the state parks is available from the **Bureau of State Parks** (tel 717/783-4356). National and international competitions are held at the Lehigh County Velodrome, at Trexlertown near Allentown, one of the country's few outdoor bicycle race tracks.

Bird Watching   The state abounds with birds of all feathers, including red-tailed hawks, meadowlarks, red-winged black birds, and many waterfowl including great blue herons. The best place to catch some

20,000 hawks, eagles, and falcons is at Hawk Mountain Sanctuary in Berks County. Waterfowl can be seen best at Middle Creek and Pymatuning Wildlife Management Areas and at Presque Isle State Park in Erie. For more information, contact the Mid-Atlantic regional office of the **National Audubon Society** (tel 717/763-4985).

Camping   There are campgrounds literally all over Pennsylvania, with more than 7,000 sites in 55 state parks. The **Bureau of State Parks** (tel 717/783-4356) distributes brochures specifically dealing with camping (see "Tourist Information," above). For a detailed directory of private campgrounds, contact the **Pennsylvania Campground Owners Association,** PO Box 5, New Tripoli, PA 18066-0005 (tel 610/767-5026). For information about the state's 395 RV parks, contact the **Pennsylvania Recreational Vehicle & Camping Association,** PO Box 248, New Cumberland, PA 17070 (tel toll free 800/732-2226).

Canoeing & Kayaking   Visitors will find ample opportunities for canoeing and kayaking on the state's rivers, from the Delaware and Lehigh in the east to the Allegheny, Clarion, Youghiogheny, Cheat, and Russell Fork in the west. Rentals are available along the Delaware River in Marshalls Creek, Matamoras, Minisink Hills, and Dingmans Bridge. Jim Thorpe, White Haven, and Albrightsville are launching points for trips down the Lehigh River Gorge. Ohiopyle and its nearby Ohiopyle State Park are bases from which to explore the wild Youghiogheny, Cheat, and Russell Fork Rivers in the southwestern Laurel Highlands. More information is available from the **Pennsylvania Scenic Rivers Program,** PO Box 1467, Harrisburg, PA 17120 (tel 717/787-6816).

Fishing   The state's 5,000 miles of stocked trout streams and thousands of acres of lakes and ponds abound with 25 game species, including trout, bass, walleye, pike, bluegill, perch, crappie, and muskie. You can even go ice fishing during the winter months when the lakes and ponds are frozen over. Licenses are available in sporting goods stores throughout the state. For information about the best places to fish and the licenses required, contact the **Fish and Boat Commission,** PO Box 67000, Harrisburg, PA 17106-7000 (tel 717/657-4518).

Golf   As would be expected of the home of Arnold Palmer (who grew up in Latrobe), Pennsylvania is a golfer's delight, with hundreds of public courses throughout the state. *The Pennsylvania Golf Course Guide* gives details about private courses. For a free copy, send a stamped, self-addressed envelope to **Pennsylvania Golf Course Owners Association,** Dept 10, 121 Narragansett Dr, McKeesport, PA 15135.

Hiking The Appalachian Trail follows the mountain ridges across Pennsylvania from the Maryland line in the Laurel Highlands to the Delaware Water Gap boundary with New Jersey. State parks and forests have hundreds of miles of hiking trails, many of them blazed with markings on rocks or trees. In addition, some 8,000 acres of the Allegheny National Forest wilderness are reserved for hiking, including five campgrounds that can only be reached on foot. Contact the **Bureau of State Parks** (tel 717/783-4356) for information about state lands (see "Tourist Information," above). For the trails in Allegheny National Forest, contact the **National Forest Service,** PO Box 847, Warren, PA 16365 (tel 814/723-5150).

Horseback Riding Equestrians will find plenty of places to ride in Pennsylvania, which has hundreds of miles of trails in its state parks, state forests, and the Allegheny National Forest. The 130-mile Horse-Shoe Trail runs from Valley Forge to the Appalachians; for a guidebook, contact the Horse-Shoe Trail Club, Warwick County Park, RD 2, Pottstown, PA 19464 (tel 215/469-9461).

Hunting Pennsylvania has one of the nation's largest populations of white-tailed deer, and hunters can also look for black bears, wild turkeys, ruffed grouse, squirrels, cottontail rabbits, ring-necked pheasants, and waterfowl. Many of Pennsylvania's state game lands, state parks, and the Allegheny National Forest are open for hunting and trapping on a seasonal basis. For information, contact the **Pennsylvania Game Commission,** Dept MS, 2001 Elmerton Ave, Harrisburg, PA 17110-9797 (tel 717/783-7507).

Skiing Pennsylvania has 28 downhill ski areas scattered throughout its mountains, from the Poconos to the Alleghenies. Denton Hill, Blue Knob, and Laurel Mountain State Parks all have downhill slopes. They and 69 other state parks and the Allegheny National Forest have cross-country ski trails. You can actually ski downhill in the city of Pittsburgh at Boyce Park, which has four tows. The **Pennsylvania Bureau of Forestry,** PO Box 8552, Harrisburg, PA 17105-8552 (tel 717/783-7941), publishes maps for cross-country ski trails.

SELECTED PARKS & RECREATION AREAS

- **Allegheny National Forest,** 222 Liberty St, Warren, PA 16365 (tel 814/723-5150)
- **Delaware Water Gap National Recreation Area,** River Rd, Bushkill, PA 18324 (tel 717/588-2451)
- **Blue Knob State Park,** RR 1, Box 449, Imler, PA 16655 (tel 814/276-3576)
- **Bucktail State Park,** RR 1, Box 1-A, Emporium, PA 15834 (tel 814/486-3365)
- **Colton Point State Park,** RR 6, Box 199, Wellsboro, PA 16901 (tel 717/724-3061)
- **Delaware Canal State Park,** RR 1, Box 615-A, Upper Black Eddy, PA 18972 (tel 610/982-5560)
- **Denton Hill State Park,** RR 1, Box 136, Galeton, PA 16922 (tel 814/435-5010)
- **Elk State Park,** PO Box A, Johnsonburg, PA 15845 (tel 814/965-2646)
- **Hickory Run State Park,** RR 2, Box 81, Whitehaven, PA 18661 (tel 717/443-0400)
- **Laurel Mountain State Park,** PO Box 50, Rector, PA 15677 (tel 412/238-6623)
- **Lehigh Gorge State Park,** RR 2, Box 81, Whitehaven, PA 18661 (tel 717/443-0400)
- **Leonard Harrison State Park,** RR 6, Box 199, Wellsboro, PA 16901 (tel 717/724-3061)
- **McConnell's Mill State Park,** RR 2, Box 16, Portersville, PA 16051 (tel 412/368-8091)
- **Moraine State Park,** 225 Pleasant Valley Rd, Portersville, PA 16051 (tel 412/368-8811)
- **Nockamixon State Park,** 1542 Mountain View Dr, Quakertown, PA 18951 (tel 215/529-7300)
- **Ohiopyle State Park,** PO Box 105, Ohiopyle, PA 15470 (tel 412/329-8591)
- **Point State Park,** 101 Commonwealth Place, Pittsburgh, PA 15222 (tel 412/471-0235)
- **Presque Isle State Park,** PO Box 8510, Erie, PA (tel 814/871-4251)
- **Promised Land State Park,** RR 1, Box 96, Greentown, PA 18426 (tel 717/676-3428)
- **Ralph Stover State Park,** 6011 State Park Rd, Pipersville, PA 18947 (tel 610/982-5560)
- **Ricketts Glen State Park,** RR 2, Box 130, Benton, PA 17814-8900 (tel 717/477-5675)
- **Worlds End State Park,** PO Box 62, Forksville, PA 18616-0062 (tel 717/924-3287)

Snowmobiling Some 2,800 miles of trails in state parks and forests and another 360 miles in the Allegheny National Forest are open for snowmobiling from approximately November 15 until April 1. All snowmobiles must be registered in Pennsylvania, but you can bring your own if your state accepts Pennsylvania's registration. For more information about state lands, including a Snowmobile Trail Directory and maps, contact the Snowmobile/ATV Unit of the **Pennsylvania Department of Conservation and Natural Resources,** PO Box 8553, Harrisburg, PA 17105-8553 (tel 717/ 783-1364).

White-Water Rafting The Delaware and Lehigh Rivers in the east and the Youghiogheny, Cheat, and Russell Fork Rivers in the west offer some of the best rafting in the mid-Atlantic region. Operators are based along the Delaware in Marshalls Creek, Matamoras, Minisink Hills, and Dingmans Bridge. Jim Thorpe, White Haven, and Albrightsville are launching points for trips down the Lehigh River Gorge. In the Laurel Highlands, the Youghiogheny River runs through lovely Ohiopyle State Park; it and the nearby town of Ohiopyle are bases from which to explore this wild and scenic waterway.

Wildlife Viewing Almost 300 state game lands (covering more than 1.3 million acres) are home to the likes of elk, groundhogs, squirrels, chipmunks, wild turkeys, and white-tailed deer. The **Pennsylvania Game Commission** (tel 717/783-7507) publishes *Pennsylvania Wildlife: A Viewers Guide,* a paperback book which gives full details about 93 of the best places in the state for wildlife viewing. To get a copy, send a check or money order for $12.95 to the Pennsylvania Game Commission, Department MS, 2001 Elmerton Ave, Harrisburg, PA 17110-9797. State game lands maps cost 50¢.

Driving the State

Start	Longwood Gardens (near Kennett Square)
Finish	Historic Yellow Springs (near Chester Springs)
Distance	Approximately 43 miles
Time	1–2 days
Highlights	Historic homes; battlefield; wineries; garden; art museum; sculptural furniture studio; 18th- and 19th-century villages

Over 300 years ago William Penn founded Chester County, now one of two Pennsylvania counties in the Brandywine Valley. In the following decades, immigrant families from all over Europe moved in, bringing their old-world traditions with them. Cabins, taverns, and houses were built of logs, stone, and brick; some of them still stand and can be viewed on this tour. The architecture reflects familiar English and German styles such as medieval leaded-glass windows, raised hearths, and herb gardens.

By 1777 the men of the Brandywine Valley were involved in the Revolutionary War, including Gen Anthony Wayne, who grew up in the area. The Brandywine Battlefield was the site of a crushing defeat for the Continental Army, and two houses that remain on the property served as headquarters for George Washington and the Marquis de Lafayette. Historic Yellow Springs village pulls these strands of colonial life together with mineral springs, the site of a hospital during the War, and Washington's post-battle headquarters.

The Brandywine Valley is as rich in culture as it is in history. Howard Pyle, a painter and illustrator of adventure tales, established an art school here in the late 19th century. Some of his students, including N C Wyeth, Frank Schoonover, and Harvey Dunn, eventually became known as the Brandywine school of painters. The prolific Wyeths still live and paint there. The Brandywine River Museum is a tribute to them and to other area artists.

Whenever possible we suggest routes on minor roads through the beautiful countryside, which is otherwise obscured by commercial development along highways. Depending on your starting point, you may begin this tour from either end.

For additional information on lodgings, dining, and attractions in the region covered by the tour, look under specific cities in the listings portion of this chapter.

1. **Longwood Gardens** (tel 610/388-1000) is located east of Kennett Square near the junction of US 1 and PA 52. William Penn sold this piece of land to the Peirce family in 1700. By 1798, Joshua and Samuel Peirce began to collect specimens for a private arboretum. Pierre S du Pont bought the property in 1906 and continued to develop the horticultural garden. Today, visitors can savor the colors and the fragrance of both indoor and outdoor gardens. Four acres of massive bronze and glass conservatories guarantee splashes of color throughout the year. Outdoors, a topiary garden of closely pruned trees surrounds a 37-foot sundial, and a Fountain Garden spews up illuminated jets of water. There's also an open-air theater with performances during the summer.

    The Brandywine Valley Tourist Office Center (tel 610/388-2900), located at the entrance to Longwood Gardens, is a good place to stop for detailed information, including current hours for the valley's many attractions.

Take a Break

The **Terrace Restaurant at Longwood Gardens** (tel 610/388-6771) offers a full-service dining room with a seasonal regional menu; crab cakes and mushroom dishes are among the specialties. Afternoon tea is also available. Entrees are $12–$20.

Drive east on US 1 to Chadds Ford, noting the sign for Delaware Museums on the right at PA 52 if you plan to dip into that part of the valley after this tour. (Those planning such an extension might want to begin this tour at the other end.) There are a number of 18th-century stone houses along US 1, and antiques shops sell all sorts of furnishings and collectibles. In 2.8 miles you will come to the next stop:

2. **Chadds Ford,** site of an old Native American trail that forded the Brandywine Creek. The town is named after John Chad, a Quaker immigrant who purchased the land from William Penn.

    Visitors can watch grapes being crushed at the **Chaddsford Winery,** (tel 610/388-6221) located on US 1 in an 18th-century barn. The wine is fermented, barrel-aged, and bottled on site; after

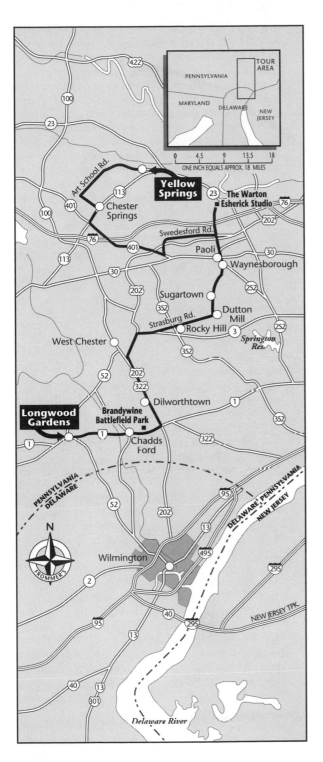

tours, visitors may have a taste and enjoy the atmosphere in the beautifully restored barn.

Continue to the next driveway or walk along the path from the winery to visit the **Barns-Brinton House** (tel 610/388-7376). This brick building has handsome Flemish-bond brickwork and gables with patterns. Built in 1714, the structure served as a home for the William Barns family as well as a tavern and inn for travelers from 1722 until 1731. In 1753 James Brinton bought the house, and it stayed in the Brinton family for the next 100 years. The cage bar has been restored, which gives the tavern an authentic atmosphere. Guides in Colonial dress discuss tavern life.

The **Brandywine River Museum** (tel 610/388-2700) is located on US 1 two miles from the winery and just west of PA 100, near the center of the tiny village of Chadds Ford. The museum is housed in the 1864 Hoffman's Gristmill, which was restored in 1968. Inside, natural light falls on many of the paintings and white plaster walls add to the feeling of spaciousness in interiors that open themselves to the bucolic riverside. The museum features the work of three generations of the Wyeth family: N C, his son Andrew, and his grandson Jamie. The Andrew Wyeth Gallery houses the world's largest collection of his work. Jamie has an affinity for pigs and visitors like to look for his painting of "Den-Den." There's also a section of trompe l'oeil work.

For more Wyeth memorabilia head north on PA 100 to the **Christian C Sanderson Museum** (tel 610/696-3234), which is across US 1 from the Brandywine River Museum. Chris Sanderson, a friend of the family, saved all the sketches and paintings the Wyeths gave him over the years, and supplemented the collection with memorabilia from all over the world. His guest book was signed by members of the Wyeth family many times, and Jamie left a sketch of Den-Den. There is no admission charge but donations are appreciated.

The **John Chad House** (tel 610/388-7376) stands a little bit further along PA 100 from the Christian Sanderson Museum. John Chad, for whom the town was named, built the bluestone home in about 1725, married Elizabeth Richardson in 1729, then opened a tavern and began a ferrying service across the Brandywine. Although he died in 1760, Elizabeth lived there through the Brandywine Battle, when she could probably have witnessed the action from her attic window. Today, living-history interpreters bake Colonial breads in her beehive oven and make traditional crafts in her parlor.

The **Chadds Ford Historical Society** (tel 610/388-7376) stands directly across the road from the

John Chad House. The Society is housed in an attractive barn-style building and contains displays and information on Chadds Ford.

A side trip of six miles north brings you to **Baldwin's Book Barn** (tel 610/696-0816), located at 865 Lenape Road on PA 100, where you can lose yourself for some time with rare books, maps, and out-of-print books.

From the John Chad House return to US 1 and head east to the **Brandywine Battlefield Park** (tel 610/459-3342), which sprawls for 50 acres along the north side of US 1, just ¾ miles east of PA 100. The Visitors Center offers orientation exhibits and an audiovisual presentation about the battle, which dealt a crushing blow to the American cause. Two restored houses are on the grounds: The Ring house and the Gilpin house. Benjamin Ring offered his home as Gen George Washington's headquarters. Unfortunately the British army destroyed the house after the battle, but it has been reconstructed and furnished with period pieces. The British also plundered the house of Gideon Gilpin, who had turned the house over to the Marquis de Lafayette. (After the war Gilpin filed a claim for his loss, including 10 cows, 50 pounds of bacon, 4000 fence rails, and a clock.)

Take a Break

Chadds Ford Inn (tel 610/388-7361), located at the junction of PA 100 and US 1, offers lunch, dinner, and Sunday brunch in a 1736 building. Brandywine decor gives atmosphere to the dining rooms. Dinner entrees are $15–$25. **Pace One Restaurant and Country Inn** (tel 610/459-3702), located on the Concord-Thornton and Glens Mills Rd, offers imaginative cuisine (for lunch, dinner, and Sunday brunch) in a 1740s stone barn. The inn upstairs has six guest rooms. Dinner entrees are $15–$27.

If you're looking to spend the night, the Chadds Ford area has some lovely inns. **Sweetwater Farm** (tel 610/459-4711), 50 Sweetwater Rd, offers seven guest rooms in an elegant 18-century fieldstone mansion. (Five guest cottages are also available.) The late Princess Grace of Monaco was aunt to one of the owners, Grace LeVine, and family pictures are on display. **Fairville Inn** (tel 610/388-5900), located south of town on PA 52 between US 1 and the Delaware Museums, offers 15 guest rooms in an 1820s house.

From Chadds Ford head east on US 1 and north on US 202 to signs for the:

3. **Brinton 1704 House** (tel 610/399-0913 or 302/478-2853), located on Oakland Rd just west of US 202 in Dilworthtown. William and Ann Brinton fled England because of religious persecution against Quakers in 1684. This unusually fine stone house was built in 1704 and still displays 27 leaded casement windows, many of them large; the bedrooms also have closets, which were often lacking in Colonial homes. It is easy to imagine Ann Brinton filling her bake oven in the large kitchen below and tending the herbs in the garden outside her door.

For a scenic and bucolic drive through rolling horse and estate country to Waynesborough, head north on US 202, and take the West Chester Bypass which starts three miles from Brinton Bridge Rd. Then take the exit for PA 3E (signed Newtown Square) and look for a left turn onto Strasburg Rd. Cross PA 352 at Rocky Hill, continue to Dutton Mill, then turn left onto Sugartown Rd for a short distance. Turn right onto Spring, which will become Jaffrey, cross Warren and turn left onto Grubb to Waynesborough Rd. There turn right and drive one mile to the next stop:

4. **Waynesborough,** at 2049 Waynesborough Rd (tel/610/647-1779). This stone home was built in 1715 with two original rooms: a keeping room downstairs and a lodging chamber upstairs. In 1724 Gen Anthony Wayne's grandfather bought the house. The center of the mansion was added in the 1730s and in 1792 Anthony Wayne built the east wing. The mansion was the core of a large plantation on more than 1,000 acres of land. Anthony Wayne became a Revolutionary War hero, retired here after the war, then came out of retirement in 1792 when President Washington asked him to return as Major General and Commander-in-Chief of the Legions of America.

Come out of the driveway and turn right onto Waynesborough Rd to South Valley Rd, turn right, cross Rte 30 in Paoli, now on North Valley Rd. Go over the railroad tracks and down the mountainside to a dead end on Swedesford Rd. Head right on Swedesford Rd and take an immediate left onto North Valley, crossing Yellow Springs Road under the Pennsylvania Tpk (I-76). The first fork on the left will take you to the next stop:

5. **The Wharton Esherick Studio** (tel 610/644-5822), located ⅒ miles down Horseshoe Trail. The studio itself is a visual marvel, with its strikingly carved and sculptured furniture and decorative pieces. Esherick studied painting in Philadelphia and in 1913 moved to this old stone farmhouse. He began carving frames for his paintings and woodcuts,

sculpting in wood, and making his own furniture. The shapes and textures provide more than the eye can follow in this studio of many angles and curves. Reservations must be made in advance, so be sure to call ahead.

Head back on Horseshoe Trail, Diamond Rock Rd, and North Valley Rd, crossing Yellow Springs Rd, to Swedesford Rd; there turn right and drive 5 miles to Conestoga Rd (PA 401). Turn right onto PA 401 for about 6 miles to PA 113N, turn right again and continue to Yellow Springs Rd on the left which dead ends at Art School Rd. There turn right to get to the next and last stop on the tour:

6. **Historic Yellow Springs** (tel 610/827-7414). Since 1722 people have been traveling to "take the waters" here. Gen George Washington ordered a hospital built on the site, and it was used for the sick and injured from Valley Forge during the Revolutionary War. Later, as a health spa, the three springs were in use until 1860. Iron Spring, now under a gazebo, is named for the yellow, iron-rich water which patients drank and bathed in. Jenny Lind may have used the sulphur spring and also slept in the stone farmhouse on the grounds.

To return to the Chadds Ford area the fast way take Rte 100 to US 202 back to US 1, a distance of 20 miles.

Pennsylvania Listings

Allentown

See also Easton

A diverse industrial city on the Lehigh River, Allentown is a center of truck manufacturing. It also offers cultural opportunities such as the Pennsylvania Stage Company and Allentown Art Museum, as well as vineyards and historic sites. **Information:** Allentown–Lehigh County Chamber of Commerce, 462 Walnut St, Allentown, 18102 (tel 610/437-9661).

HOTELS 🏨

≣≣≣ **Allentown Hilton**
904 Hamilton Mall, 18101 (Downtown); tel 610/433-2221 or toll free 800/999-7784; fax 610/433-6455. 7th St exit off US 22 W/15th St exit off US 22 E. A business travelers' hotel which often hosts corporate groups. Spacious lobby and quality amenities. **Rooms:** 224 rms and stes. CI 3pm/CO 11am. Nonsmoking rms avail. **Amenities:** 🛎 🍸 🖥 🍷 A/C, cable TV w/movies, voice mail. **Services:** ✕ 🚐 🖼 🛏 **Facilities:** 🎱 🛳 🏊 🖥 ঌ 1 restaurant, 1 bar, games rm, sauna. **Rates:** $90–$126 S; $100–$136 D; $150 ste. Extra person $10. Children under age 18 stay free. Parking: Indoor/outdoor, $5.75/day. AE, CB, DC, DISC, EC, ER, JCB, MC, V.

UNRATED **Clarion Hotel Allentown**
549 Hamilton St, 18101 (Downtown); tel 610/434-6101 or toll free 800/CLARION; fax 610/434-6828. 7th St exit off I-78. Catering to corporate and government travelers and located near the Federal Building. Stately lobby with large windows. **Rooms:** 81 rms, stes, and effic. CI 3pm/CO noon. Nonsmoking rms avail. **Amenities:** 🛎 🍸 🖥 🍷 A/C, cable TV. Some units w/minibars, some w/whirlpools. Some rooms have dataports, refrigerators. **Services:** ✕ 🚐 🖼 🛏 **Facilities:** 🏊 ঌ 1 restaurant, 1 bar. Guests have access to nearby racquetball courts. **Rates:** $79–$109 S or D; $109–$149 ste; $350–$400 effic. Extra person $10. Children under age 18 stay free. Parking: Outdoor, free. AE, CB, DC, DISC, EC, ER, JCB, MC, V.

≣≣≣ **Sheraton Inn Jetport**
3400 Airport Rd, 18103 (Lehigh Valley); tel 610/266-1000 or toll free 800/383-1100; fax 610/266-1888. N Airport Rd exit off PA 22. This full-service hotel is a comfortable choice for families or business travelers. **Rooms:** 147 rms and stes. CI 3pm/CO noon. Nonsmoking rms avail. Effective soundproofing cuts jet noise. Only some of the rooms have windows that open. **Amenities:** 🛎 🍸 🖥 🍷 A/C, cable TV w/movies, dataport, voice mail. **Services:** ✕ 🚐 🖼 🛏 🚗 Twice-daily maid svce, car-rental desk. Complimentary evening hors d'oeuvres. **Facilities:** 🎱 🛳 🏊 ঌ 1 restaurant, 1 bar (w/entertainment), sauna, whirlpool, playground. Dramatic, glass-enclosed pool is suitable for lap swimming. Stairstepper, treadmill, and exercise cycle for workouts. **Rates:** $97–$130 S; $107–$130 D; $117–$130 ste. Extra person $10. Children under age 12 stay free. MAP rates avail. Parking: Outdoor, free. AE, CB, DC, DISC, EC, ER, MC, V.

MOTELS

≣≣≣ **Allentown Comfort Suites**
3712 Hamilton Blvd, 18103; tel 610/437-9100 or toll free 800/228-5150; fax 610/437-0221. An upscale stop for the corporate traveler; also popular with families due its location across the street from Dorney Park. The expansive atrium lobby has foliage, a fountain, leather furniture, and contemporary art. **Rooms:** 122 stes. CI 3pm/CO noon. Nonsmoking rms avail. Large rooms, with sofa beds. **Amenities:** 🛎 🍸 A/C, cable TV w/movies, refrig, VCR, voice mail. Some units w/whirlpools. Microwaves. In-house TV channel. **Services:** ✕ 🚐 🖼 🛏 Office services available. **Facilities:** 🛳 🏊 ঌ 1 restaurant, 1 bar (w/entertainment). Walking track on grounds. **Rates (CP):** Peak (June–Oct) $94–$109 ste. Extra person $10. Children under age 18 stay free. Lower rates off-season. Parking: Outdoor, free. Comfort Lovers package includes champagne, chocolate, and a whirlpool room. AE, CB, DC, DISC, JCB, MC, V.

≣≣ **Days Inn Conference Center**
1151 Bulldog Dr, 18104; tel 610/395-3731 or toll free 800/DAYS-INN; fax 610/395-9899. US 22 and PA 309. A large business motel, with a bright, pleasant, spacious lobby. **Rooms:** 282 rms and stes. CI 4pm/CO noon. Nonsmoking rms avail. **Amenities:** 🛎 🍸 A/C, cable TV, in-rm safe. Some units w/terraces. Refrigerators available. **Services:** 🚐 🛏 🚗 Twice-daily maid svce. Free local calls. Express checkout for

Premier Business Club members. Two complimentary cocktails every evening. **Facilities:** ⛽ 🖼 ♿ 1 restaurant, 1 bar, volleyball, games rm, washer/dryer. Access to 24-hour fitness club across street. **Rates:** Peak (July–Sept 7) $55–$75 S; $61–$81 D; $99 ste. Extra person $6. Children under age 12 stay free. Lower rates off-season. Parking: Outdoor, free. Ski and Dorney Park packages avail. AE, CB, DC, DISC, JCB, MC, V.

UNRATED **Ramada Inn Whitehall**
1500 MacArthur Rd, Whitehall, 18052; tel 610/439-1037 or toll free 800/228-2828; fax 610/770-1425. PA 145 exit off US 222. This clean, comfortable hotel caters to corporate travelers. The public areas are attractive, with a water fountain at the entrance and a small, art deco–style lobby. **Rooms:** 122 rms and stes. CI 3pm/CO noon. Nonsmoking rms avail. **Amenities:** 📺 A/C, cable TV, dataport. Some units w/terraces. Refrigerators available on request. **Services:** ✕ 🚐 🖼 🍽 Car-rental desk. **Facilities:** ⛽ 🖼 ♿ 1 restaurant, 2 bars (w/entertainment), volleyball, games rm. **Rates (CP):** Peak (May–Sept) $70–$100 S or D; $130 ste. Extra person $6. Children under age 17 stay free. Min stay special events. Lower rates off-season. Parking: Outdoor, free. Special packages (including murder-mystery and Dorney Park) avail. AE, CB, DC, DISC, MC, V.

RESTAURANTS 🍴

Ambassador Restaurant
3750 Hamilton Blvd; tel 610/432-2025. Exit 16 off I-78; across from Dorney Park. **Mediterranean.** Lovely, hospitable Mediterranean surroundings, accented with plants and ceramic tile, recommended for couples or for an intimate gathering with friends. Extensive wine list. **FYI:** Reservations accepted. Children's menu. **Open:** Mon–Sat 11:30am–10pm. **Prices:** Main courses $13–$16. AE, CB, DC, DISC, ER, MC, V. ❤ ♿

★ The Brass Rail Restaurant
3015 Lehigh St; tel 610/797-1927. Exit 18 off I-78. **American/Italian.** This family-style restaurant is a long-time favorite with locals, who will tell you that the famous Allentown steak sandwich originated here. **FYI:** Reservations not accepted. Children's menu. Additional location: 1137 Hamilton St (tel 434-9383). **Open:** Daily 7am–midnight. **Prices:** Main courses $6–$13. AE, DISC, MC, V. 🖼 ♿

Finley's American Restaurant
3400 Lehigh St; tel 610/965-8447. 1½ mi E of Lehigh St exit off I-78. **American.** A family-style place, with friendly waitresses and quick service. The kitchen is well known for its ribs. **FYI:** Reservations not accepted. Children's menu. **Open:** Sun–Thurs 11am–10pm, Fri–Sat 11am–11pm. **Prices:** Main courses $6–$13. AE, DC, DISC, MC, V. 🖼 ♿

ATTRACTIONS 🏛

Dorney Park and Wildwater Kingdom
3700 Hamilton Blvd; tel 610/395-3724. A massive amusement complex with over 100 rides, including Hercules (a giant wooden roller coaster) and the White Water Landing water plunge. (A train shuttles visitors back and forth between the two parks). Dorney Park has kiddie rides and a miniature-golf course, among its other attractions; Wildwater Kingdom has many other activities, such as white-water rafting and water slides. Picnicking and live shows also available. **Open:** Peak (Mem Day–Labor Day) daily 10am, closing times vary. **$$$$**

Trout Hall
414 Walnut St; tel 610/435-4664. Trout Hall was built in 1770 as a summer home for James Allen—son of the founder of Allentown—and is considered the city's oldest surviving home. At first the home was a refuge from Philadelphia's summer heat and epidemics, but during the American Revolution it became the family's year-round political haven as well. (Allen chose neutrality in the war.) Interiors feature period rooms with Georgian furnishings and a local history museum. **Open:** Tues–Sat noon–3pm, Sun 1–4pm. **Free**

Lehigh County Museum
501 Hamilton St; tel 610/435-4664. The county's Old Courthouse, constructed between 1814 and 1817, is home to both the Lehigh County Museum and the Lehigh County Historical Society. Permanent and visiting exhibitions at the museum take in geology, Native American culture, agriculture, the rise of industry, and the role of immigrants. **Open:** Mon–Fri 9am–4pm, Sat 10am–4pm, Sun 1–4pm. **Free**

Haines Mill Museum
Haines Mill and Dorney Park Rd; tel 610/435-4664. The Haines Mill was built before the American Revolution and continued to serve Pennsylvania German farmers, bakeries, and flour wholesalers until 1956, when national competition put the family-run operation out of business. The water-driven gristmill was gutted by fire in 1908, but it has been reconstructed and is once again operational and open to visitors. **Open:** Sat–Sun 1–4pm. **Free**

Museum of Indian Culture
2825 Fish Hatchery Rd; tel 610/797-2121. Operated by the Lenni Lenape Historical Society. The Lenni Lenape, or Delaware Indians, settled and farmed parts of the eastern United States 1,000 years before the first European settlers. The museum features exhibitions of tribal crafts and storytelling, and holds outdoor events, including the corn festivals, three times a year. **Open:** Wed–Sun noon–3pm. **$**

Frank Buchman House
117 N 11th St; tel 610/435-4664. Lutheran pastor Frank Buchman moved to this Victorian rowhouse with his Pennsylvania German parents in 1893. The interior is furnished with

late Victorian antiques. (Buchman would later found Moral Re-Armament, a movement dedicated to peace and international understanding.) **Open:** Sat–Sun 1–4pm. **Free**

Liberty Bell Shrine

Hamilton Mall at Church St; tel 610/435-4232. During the American Revolution, the Liberty Bell was kept in Allentown for safety. At Zion's Reformed Church, the site where the bell was hidden in 1777, there is now a shrine to the symbol of freedom, including a full-size replica of the bell and a 46-foot mural depicting the bell's journey to Allentown. **Open:** Mon–Sat noon–4pm. **Free**

Altoona

A railroad center and industrial city in the Allegheny Mountains. Popular tourist area offering railroading attractions and amusement parks. **Information:** Altoona–Blair County Convention & Visitors Bureau, Logan County Mall, Altoona, 16602 (tel 814/943-4183 or toll free 800/84-ALTOONA).

MOTELS 🏨

≣≣ Days Inn

3306 Pleasant Valley Blvd, 16602; tel 814/944-9661 or toll free 800/329-7466; fax 814/944-9557. Frankstown Rd exit off US 220 to W on Frankstown Rd, right on Pleasant Valley Blvd, ¼ mi on left. This meticulously maintained motel is on the major shopping strip, close to downtown and area attractions. Fireplace in lobby adds to cozy atmosphere. **Rooms:** 111 rms. CI noon/CO noon. Nonsmoking rms avail. Single rooms have sofa beds. **Amenities:** 📺⚒💻 🍽A/C, cable TV w/movies, refrig, dataport. Microwaves. **Services:** ▲♻ Babysitting. **Facilities:** ⚖⨯🍽 🚼 Whirlpool, washer/dryer. **Rates:** $55 S; $60 D. Extra person $5. Children under age 12 stay free. Min stay special events. Parking: Outdoor, free. AE, CB, DC, DISC, JCB, MC, V.

≣≣≣ Holiday Inn

2915 Pleasant Valley Blvd, 16602; tel 814/944-4581 or toll free 800/465-4329; fax 814/943-4996. Frankstown Rd exit off US 220 to W on Frankstown Rd, right on Pleasant Valley Blvd, ½ mi on right. A standard Holiday Inn, adjacent to the main shopping district and with easy access to downtown. **Rooms:** 140 rms and stes. Executive level. CI 2pm/CO noon. Nonsmoking rms avail. Some rooms have mountain and valley views. **Amenities:** 📺⚒💻 A/C, cable TV w/movies, dataport, in-rm safe. Some units w/whirlpools. Free local calls. **Services:** ⨯🚙▲♻ Car-rental desk, babysitting. Secretarial services available. **Facilities:** 🏊⚖⨯🍽 🚼 1 restaurant, 1 bar (w/entertainment), games rm, lawn games, washer/dryer. **Rates:** Peak (Apr–Oct) $69–$79 S; $74–$84 D; $119 ste. Extra person $5. Children under age 18 stay free. Lower rates off-season. Parking: Outdoor, free. Golf packages avail. AE, CB, DC, DISC, JCB, MC, V.

≣≣≣ Ramada Hotel

1 Sheraton Dr, 16001; tel 814/946-1631 or toll free 800/272-6232; fax 814/946-0785. Plank Rd exit off US 220. Standard, clean, serviceable, and recently renovated. **Rooms:** 217 rms and stes. Executive level. CI 1pm/CO noon. Nonsmoking rms avail. Some rooms have mountain views. **Amenities:** 📺⚒💻 A/C, cable TV w/movies, dataport. Some units w/terraces, some w/whirlpools. **Services:** ⨯🚙▲♻ ♻ Babysitting. **Facilities:** 🏊⚖⨯🍽 🚼 2 restaurants, 2 bars (1 w/entertainment), games rm, whirlpool, washer/dryer. Five golf courses nearby. **Rates (CP):** Peak (Apr–Dec) $59–$72 S; $64–$77 D; $75–$135 ste. Extra person $5. Children under age 18 stay free. Lower rates off-season. AP and MAP rates avail. Parking: Outdoor, free. AE, CB, DC, DISC, EC, ER, JCB, MC, V.

RESTAURANTS 🍽

★ Allegro

3926 Broad Ave; tel 814/946-5216. At 40th St. **American/Italian.** A 20-year-old favorite with low lighting, trellises, and ivy in its three dining rooms. Portions are large and hearty, and—by popular demand—you can buy a jar of their Italian sauce at the counter to take home with you. **FYI:** Reservations recommended. Children's menu. Additional location: Seven-D Drive, Scotch Valley Country Club, Hollidaysburg (tel 695-6224). **Open:** Lunch Fri 11:30am–1pm; dinner Mon–Fri 4–9:30pm, Sat 4–10pm. **Prices:** Main courses $11–$24. AE, DC, DISC, MC, V. ❤🚼

★ The Dream

1500 Allegheny St, Hollidaysburg; tel 814/696-3384. At jct US 22. **American.** As befits its location in the historic area of town, the decor of this eatery is filled with antiques. For 40 years, this place has been packing in the locals for home-cooked meals, homemade soups, and desserts from the on-site bakery. There are four dining rooms, and two have fireplaces. **FYI:** Reservations not accepted. Children's menu. No liquor license. **Open:** Sun–Thurs 8am–9pm, Fri–Sat 8am–10pm. **Prices:** Main courses $5–$14. AE, DISC, MC, V. 📷🚼

★ Slick's Ivy Stone Restaurant

Bus US 220, Osterburg; tel 814/276-3131. From US 220 S, take Imler-Blue Knob exit, go S on old US 220 (3 mi); from US 220 N, take Osterburg exit, go N on old US 220 (3 mi). **American.** Servers in colonial dress and huge portions of good food make the trip here worthwhile. Fried chicken is a favorite, and the waffle dinner is also popular. **FYI:** Reservations accepted. Children's menu. Dress code. No liquor license. **Open:** Tues–Fri 11am–8:30pm, Sat 4–8:30pm, Sun 11am–8pm. Closed Dec 23–Mar. **Prices:** Main courses $6–$10. AE, MC, V. 📷🚼

US Hotel Restaurant & Tavern

401 S Juniata St, Hollidaysburg; tel 814/695-9924. At Wayne St. **New American.** Each of the three dining rooms here has its own 19th-century decor, but they all serve the same fare:

seafood, beef, chops, and homemade soups and desserts. The chef is experienced and the staff is friendly. **FYI:** Reservations accepted. Children's menu. **Open:** Lunch Mon–Fri 11am–2pm; dinner daily 4:30–10pm; brunch Sun 10am–2pm. **Prices:** Main courses $9–$20. DISC, MC, V. 🍴 ♿

ATTRACTIONS 📷

Baker Mansion Museum

3501 Oak Lane; tel 814/942-3916. Now the headquarters of the Blair County Historical Society, Baker Mansion was built circa 1845 for ironmaster Elias Baker. The Greek Revival house has walls made from limestone set in lead, and its remarkable interior features include Italian marble fireplaces and black-walnut woodwork. Among the large collection of furnishings is an entire hand-carved oak parlor suite imported from Belgium. Other exhibits deal with the Civil War and the iron industry. **Open:** Peak (Mem Day–Labor Day) Tues–Sun 1–4:30pm. **$**

Horseshoe Curve National Historic Landmark and Altoona Railroaders Memorial Museum

1300 9th Ave; tel 814/946-0834. In the mid-19th century, crossing the Allegheny Mountains was the key to the westward expansion of the railroads. The "Horseshoe Curve," a giant loop carved out of the mountains, was the engineering feat that made this possible. (Even today, more than 50 trains a day use the curve.) The on-site museum preserves the heritage of Altoona, which became the site of the largest railroad shops in the world. Some of the other attractions include the state's Official Steam Locomotive, a cable-car ride to the heights of the Curve and its panoramic views, and a large collection of railroad cars, including the private car of steel baron Charles Schwab. **Open:** Peak (May–Oct) daily 10am–6pm. Reduced hours off-season. **$$**

Fort Roberdeau Historic Site

Bellwood exit off US 220; tel 814/946-0048. Brigadier Daniel Roberdeau came to the Sinking Valley in search of lead in 1778, because American soldiers were running out of bullets. He built this fort to protect the militia sent to guard the miners. The reconstructed stockade and cabins are surrounded by 45 acres of fields and forests; there's also an archeology center, a 19th-century farmhouse, nature trails, and picnic facilities. **Open:** Mid-May–mid-Oct, Tues–Sat 11am–5pm, Sun 1–5pm. **$**

Bedford

Bedford's historic district includes "Old Bedford Village," a colonial area entered via a covered bridge. Fort Bedford Park is built on the site of a 1758 British fort. **Information:** Bedford County Tourism, 137 E Pitt St, Bedford, 15522 (tel 814/623-1771 or toll free 800/765-3331).

MOTEL 🏨

🏳🏳 Quality Inn

US 220, PO Box 171, 15522; tel 814/623-5188 or toll free 800/228-5151; fax 814/623-0814. Exit 11 off PA Tpk; PA Tpk exit off US 220. Standard but meticulously maintained accommodations for the discerning traveler. Near fishing, golfing, skiing, and historic Bedford. **Rooms:** 66 rms and stes. CI 3pm/CO 11am. Nonsmoking rms avail. **Amenities:** 🛏 A/C, cable TV. **Services:** 🛎 🧺 🍷 Babysitting. Coffee in lobby. **Facilities:** 🏊 🏋 🏊 ♿ 1 restaurant, 1 bar (w/entertainment). **Rates:** Peak (May–Oct) $57–$63 S; $63–$69 D; $80 ste. Extra person $6. Children under age 18 stay free. Lower rates off-season. Parking: Outdoor, free. AE, CB, DC, DISC, JCB, MC, V.

RESTAURANTS 🍽

★ Ed's Steak House

Bus US 220; tel 814/623-8894. At end of exit ramp of PA Tpk exit off US 220. **American.** The same family has operated this popular eatery since 1954, serving fresh-cut steaks plus seafood and Italian dishes. There are four dining rooms, a coffee shop, and a lounge; all have an attractive, simple decor. **FYI:** Reservations accepted. Children's menu. **Open:** Mon–Thurs 7am–9:30pm, Fri–Sat 7am–10pm, Sun 7am–9pm. **Prices:** Main courses $7–$11. AE, MC, V. 🍴 ♿

Jean Bonnet Tavern & Restaurant

US 30 and PA 31; tel 814/623-2250. 5 mi W of Bedford. **Continental.** This dining room has the feel of a historic roadhouse, with a huge fireplace and a beamed ceiling; the building itself is on the National Register of Historic Places. Three menu specials are offered daily (prime rib is a good choice on Thursday or Saturday) and the dessert menu is extensive. **FYI:** Reservations recommended. Children's menu. No smoking. **Open:** Mon–Thurs 11am–9pm, Fri–Sat 11am–10pm, Sun 8am–8pm. **Prices:** Main courses $7–$18. AE, DC, DISC, MC, V. 🍴 📷 ♿

ATTRACTION 📷

Old Bedford Village

US 220 N; tel 814/623-1156. A living history museum that recreates village life from the mid-18th to the mid-19th centuries. There are more than forty log buildings in the village, including homes, schoolhouses, craft shops, and a colonial farm. Costumed interpreters demonstrate cooking, blacksmithing, broom making, pottery, and other period crafts. The old log church is still in use, as is the Pendergass Tavern. **Open:** Peak (May–Aug) daily 9am–5pm. Reduced hours off-season. **$$$**

Bethlehem

Founded in 1741 by the Moravian Brethren. This has been an industrial area since the 18th century; today, steel of all types is manufactured here. Home of Lehigh University. **Information:** Bethlehem Area Chamber of Commerce, 509 Main St, Bethlehem, 18018 (tel 610/867-3788).

HOTELS 🏨

≣≣≣ Holiday Inn Hotel & Conference Center

US 22 and PA 512, 18017; tel 610/866-5800 or toll free 800/HOLIDAY; fax 610/867-9120. Exit 512 off US 22. This large, bright, clean hotel has an assortment of restaurants, bars, and meeting rooms. With lots of business travelers passing through, it's a very busy place. **Rooms:** 192 rms. CI 2pm/CO noon. Nonsmoking rms avail. **Amenities:** 🛁 🕭 📺 🍴 A/C, cable TV w/movies, refrig, voice mail. Some units w/terraces. **Services:** ✕ 🛎 ⬜ ⟲ **Facilities:** 🛋 🏌 ♨ 🖥 🛜 🏊 ⬧ 3 restaurants, 2 bars (1 w/entertainment), volleyball, lawn games. **Rates:** $69–$110 S; $69–$120 D. Extra person $10. Children under age 18 stay free. Min stay special events. Parking: Outdoor, free. AE, CB, DC, DISC, MC, V.

UNRATED Hotel Bethlehem

437 Main St, 18018; tel 610/867-3711 or toll free 800/545-5158; fax 610/867-0598. Center City exit off PA 378. Since 1921, this gracious, family-owned hotel has been offering charm and quality service to a loyal clientele. **Rooms:** 126 rms, stes, and effic. CI 2pm/CO 11am. Nonsmoking rms avail. **Amenities:** 🛁 🕭 🍴 A/C, cable TV, VCR, bathrobes. Some units w/whirlpools. Some rooms have refrigerators. **Services:** ✕ 🛎 ⬜ ⟲ ⬧ Twice-daily maid svce, car-rental desk, social director. Coffee in lobby. 24-hour security guards. **Facilities:** 🛋 1 restaurant, 1 bar (w/entertainment), beauty salon. **Rates (BB):** Peak (Apr–Aug/Nov 10–Dec 25) $58–$83 S; $68–$100 D; $108–$170 ste; $68–$100 effic. Extra person $10. Children under age 12 stay free. Lower rates off-season. Parking: Outdoor, free. AE, CB, DC, DISC, EC, MC, V.

MOTEL

≣≣ Comfort Inn

3191 Highfield Dr, 18017; tel 610/865-6300 or toll free 800/626-8401; fax 610/865-6300. I-78 to US 22, Nazareth Pike (PA 191) exit off US 22. Exceptional cleanliness and a friendly, accommodating staff set this otherwise standard business travelers' motel apart from others. **Rooms:** 116 rms and stes. CI 2pm/CO noon. Nonsmoking rms avail. Some rooms have outside entrances. Some have desks. **Amenities:** 🛁 🕭 A/C, cable TV w/movies, refrig, dataport, VCR. Some units w/whirlpools. **Services:** ✕ ⬜ ⟲ ⬧ Twice-daily maid svce, babysitting. Secretarial services available. **Facilities:** 🛋 🖥 1 restaurant (lunch and dinner only), 1 bar (w/entertainment), games rm. Adjoining restaurant/bar serves only light fare. **Rates (CP):** $53–$63 S; $59–$80 D; $70 ste. Extra person $6. Children under age 18 stay free. Parking: Outdoor, free. AE, CB, DC, DISC, EC, ER, JCB, MC, V.

ATTRACTIONS 📷

Historic Bethlehem-18th Century Industrial Area

52 W Broad St; tel 610/868-1513. Bethlehem's early industrial history is documented on this 10-acre site. Attractions include the Springhouse, a reconstruction of a building that sat along a Moravian spring. The Waterworks, Tannery, and Luckenbach Mill further document the Moravian way of life and the area's industrial development. The Goundie House, built in 1810 by a Moravian brewer, contains period furnishings and exhibits. Costumed interpreters offer tours of the district. **Open:** Daily 11am–2pm. $$$

Burnside Plantation

1461 Schoenersville Rd; tel 610/868-5044. The home of James Burnside, who settled here after three years as a Moravian missionary among the Native Americans. While other Moravians lived communally, Burnside's farm was the first private residence in the Bethlehem community when it was built in 1748. The main house is undergoing restoration to return it to its 1818 appearance. Other buildings in the grounds include the horsepower shed, in which a horse once trod in a circle to provide power for the threshing machine. **Open:** Mon–Fri 9am–4pm. **Free**

Bird-in-Hand

Pennsylvania Dutch village, featuring a noted farmer's market and one of the oldest operating hardware stores in the country. So named, according to one story, when two travelers debated whether to travel further or stay where they were for the night until one remarked, "A bird in the hand is worth two in the bush."

MOTEL 🏨

≣≣ Bird-in-Hand Family Inn

2740 Old Philadelphia Pike, PO Box 402, 17505; tel 717/768-8271 or toll free 800/537-2535; fax 717/768-1117. E of PA 896 on PA 340. This roadside motel consists of two buildings: the front section opens to the parking lot, while the quieter back section has enclosed hallways and indoor pool. **Rooms:** 100 rms, stes, and effic. CI 3pm/CO 11am. Nonsmoking rms avail. Average size and nicely furnished rooms. **Amenities:** 🛁 🕭 📺 A/C, cable TV, refrig, dataport. Some units w/whirlpools. VCRs and videos available. **Services:** ⟲ **Facilities:** 🛋 🖥 🛜 ⬧ 1 restaurant (see "Restaurants" below), basketball, volleyball, games rm, whirlpool, playground, washer/dryer. **Rates:** Peak (June–Aug) $75–$88 S or D; $100–$125 ste; $90–$100 effic. Extra person $8. Children under age 16 stay free. Lower rates off-season. Parking: Outdoor, free. AE, CB, DC, DISC, MC, V.

INN

▆▆ Village Inn of Bird-in-Hand

2695 Old Philadelphia Pike, PO Box 253, 17505; tel 717/ 293-8369 or toll free 800/914-2473. 1 mi E of PA 896 on PA 340. It was an inn in the 18th century, and it is an inn now. Guest registration takes place in the former barroom. Unsuitable for children under 12. **Rooms:** 11 rms. CI 3pm/CO noon. Nonsmoking rms avail. Some larger rooms have sofas and whirlpool tubs. **Amenities:** 🛏 ⚭ A/C, cable TV. Some units w/terraces, 1 w/fireplace, some w/whirlpools. **Services:** ⊋ Two-hour bus tour of the area is included in the rates. **Facilities:** Guest lounge. Swimming pool available nearby. **Rates (CP):** Peak (June 27–Oct 26) $85–$144 S or D. Lower rates off-season. Higher rates for special events/hols. Parking: Outdoor, free. Closed Dec 8–Dec 27/Jan 1–Jan 15. AE, DISC, MC, V.

RESTAURANTS 🍴

Bird-In-Hand Family Restaurant

2760 Old Philadelphia Pike; tel 717/768-8266. 2 mi E of PA 596 on PA 340. **Regional American/Pennsylvania Dutch.** A spacious dining room with Pennsylvania Dutch dioramas on the walls and a light-beige decor. The food is typical of regional fare—simple and hearty. Baked goods are available for takeout. **FYI:** Reservations accepted. Children's menu. Dress code. No liquor license. No smoking. **Open:** Peak (Apr–Oct) Mon–Sat 6am–9pm. **Prices:** Main courses $6–$10. MC, V. 👪 ⓖ

★ Plain & Fancy Farm

In Amish Farm Shops, 3121 Old Philadelphia Pike; tel 717/ 768-4400. On PA 340, 2 mi E of PA 896. **Regional American.** Part of a complex that includes shops and a theater, this large restaurant serves all-you-can-eat meals at long tables with checkered tablecloths. The set menu changes with the seasons, but always includes hearty family-style dishes like fried chicken, steak, mashed potatoes, and fruit pies. **FYI:** Reservations accepted. No liquor license. No smoking. **Open:** Mon–Sat 11:30am–8pm, Sun noon–7pm. **Prices:** Prix fixe $14. AE, DISC, MC, V. 👪 ⓖ

ATTRACTION 🏛

Amish Country Homestead

3121 Old Philadelphia Pike; tel 717/768-8400. The centerpiece here is a seven-room house furnished in the style of a typical 18th-century Amish home. The home and the other surrounding buildings—including a blacksmith shop, schoolhouse, and smokehouse—are furnished with period household items, pottery, children's toys, and other items. Guided tours offered. **Open:** Daily, call for schedule. **$**

Bloomsburg

Located along the Susquehanna River, Bloomsburg was laid out in 1802 at the foot of Spectator Bluff. Known for antique shops and covered bridges. Seat of Columbia County. **Information:** Columbia-Montour Tourist Promotion Agency, 121 Paper Mill Rd, Bloomsburg, 17815 (tel 717/784-8279).

MOTELS 🏨

▆▆ Econo Lodge at Bloomsburg

189 Columbia Mall Dr, 17815; tel 717/387-0490 or toll free 800/55-ECONO; fax 717/387-0893. Exit 34 off I-80. A cedar-paneled, lodgelike building in the parking lot of a shopping mall. The lobby is spacious, with high windows and a homelike decor. Excellent housekeeping and maintenance. **Rooms:** 80 rms, stes, and effic. CI 2pm/CO 11am. Nonsmoking rms avail. Some rooms have dataports. **Amenities:** 🛏 ⚭ A/C, satel TV w/movies. 1 unit w/terrace. Senior rooms have oversize door and sink handles, extra grabrails in bathrooms, large-button phones and adjustable shower heads. **Services:** ⊋ ⊲ Free coffee and tea in lobby (5am–11pm). Pet fee of $10. Friendly staff. **Facilities:** ⓖ Mall opens early to accommodate fitness walkers. **Rates:** Peak (Apr–Nov) $43–$47 S; $49–$54 D; $80 ste; $90 effic. Extra person $5. Children under age 18 stay free. Lower rates off-season. Parking: Outdoor, free. AE, CB, DC, DISC, ER, JCB, MC, V.

UNRATED Quality Inn Buckhorn

1 Buckhorn Rd, 17815; tel 717/784-5300 or toll free 800/ 228-5151; fax 717/387-0367. Exit 34 off I-80. An attractive, simple, modern motel near a large shopping mall. Also close to Kanoebeles Grove amusement resort and several state parks. **Rooms:** 120 rms. CI noon/CO noon. Nonsmoking rms avail. **Amenities:** 🛏 A/C, satel TV. Some units w/terraces. Executive rooms have speaker phones, fax machines, dataports, and voice mail. **Services:** ⊋ ⊲ Car-rental desk, babysitting. **Facilities:** ⓖ 1 restaurant, 1 bar. **Rates:** $50–$65 S; $55–$70 D. Extra person $5. Children under age 18 stay free. Min stay special events. Parking: Outdoor, free. AE, CB, DC, DISC, EC, ER, JCB, MC, V.

INN

▆▆▆ The Inn at Turkey Hill

991 Central Rd, 17815; tel 717/387-1500; fax 717/ 784-3718. Exit 35 off I-80, S on PA 487. This 1839 home has been enlarged several times, most recently when it became an inn in 1984. The property has been in the same family since 1942, and the management is friendly, helpful, and very competent. **Rooms:** 18 rms and stes. CI 2pm/CO noon. Nonsmoking rms avail. Large rooms furnished with high-quality antique reproductions. **Amenities:** 🛏 ⚭ 🍷 A/C, cable TV, dataport. Some units w/fireplaces, some w/whirlpools. **Services:** ✕ 🚗 🖼 ⊋ ⊲ Babysitting. **Facilities:** 🍽 1 restaurant (bkfst and dinner only; see "Restaurants" below), 1 bar, washer/dryer. **Rates (CP):** $85 S; $92 D; $145–$185 ste.

Extra person $15. Children under age 12 stay free. Higher rates for special events/hols. Parking: Outdoor, free. AE, DC, DISC, MC, V.

RESTAURANT 🍴

The Inn at Turkey Hill

991 Central Rd; tel 717/387-1500. Exit 35 off I-80, S on PA 487. **New American.** An original living room and dining room plus a glassed-in sun room comprise the dining areas. The surroundings are relaxed, the table settings are elegantly simple, and the food and service excellent. **FYI:** Reservations recommended. **Open:** Sun–Thurs 5–9pm, Fri–Sat 5–10pm. **Prices:** Main courses $15–$24. AE, DC, DISC, MC, V. 💟 ■

Boiling Springs

Small town founded in 1750 in the midst of Pennsylvania Dutch country.

RESORT 🏨

▧▧▧ Allenberry Inn

PA 174, 17007; tel 717/258-3211; fax 717/258-1464. 6 mi S of I-81 (exit 14 or exit 18). 57 acres. Noted for its long-running Playhouse, this large estate property has been operated by the same family for over half a century. **Rooms:** 61 rms; 1 cottage/villa. CI 3pm/CO noon. Nonsmoking rms avail. Stone Cottage units are individually furnished in period decor; Pine Ridge Cottage units are more modern and have larger baths; Meadow Lodge has standard hotel-style rooms. **Amenities:** 🗄 🅐 📠 🍴 A/C, TV. Some units w/whirlpools. **Services:** ✗ 🚗 🛎 🍽 Twice-daily maid svce, babysitting. **Facilities:** 🔥 🏊 🎿 🍽 🎱² 🎱 175 ⅍ 3 restaurants, 2 bars (1 w/entertainment), basketball, volleyball, lawn games, whirlpool, playground. Three award-winning restaurants, Olympic-size outdoor pool, four Har-Tru clay tennis courts. Fly fishing at Yellow Breeches, Broadway shows at Playhouse. **Rates:** Peak (Apr–Nov) $79 S; $98 D; $275 cottage/villa. Extra person $15. Children under age 17 stay free. Lower rates off-season. Parking: Outdoor, free. Fly-fishing school, murder-mystery weekend, and romantic packages avail. AE, CB, DC, DISC, MC, V.

RESTAURANT 🍴

⑤ Allenberry Inn Restaurants

PA 174 E; tel 717/258-3211. 6 mi S of I-81. **American.** There's a distinctive atmosphere in each of the three dining rooms at this large resort. The Carriage Room is settled deep among maples and rhododendrons with big windows to take in the scene, the German Lounge has light meals and weekend entertainment, and Fairfield Hall is a limestone dairy barn with high ceilings and mural walls. **FYI:** Reservations recommended. Guitar/singer. Children's menu. Dress code. No smoking. **Open:** Peak (Apr–Nov) breakfast daily 8– 10:30am; lunch daily 11am–2pm; dinner daily 5–10pm; brunch Sun 11:30am–2pm. **Prices:** Main courses $16–$24; prix fixe $19. AE, CB, DC, DISC, MC, V. 💟 ■ ▼ ⅍

Bradford

Just south of the New York state line in the Allegheny National Forest region, Bradford is a gateway for Allegheny Reservoir and Dam as well as the forest. **Information:** Bradford Area Chamber of Commerce, 10 Main St, Seneca Bldg, PO Box 135, Bradford, 16701 (tel 814/368-7115).

MOTEL 🏨

▧▧ Howard Johnson Motor Lodge

100 Davis St, 16701; tel 814/362-4501 or toll free 800/344-4656. Off I-219; Elm St exit from S, Forman St exit from N. Past its prime and unremarkable, this motel between the highway and the back of a strip mall is still serviceable as an overnight stop. **Rooms:** 120 rms. CI 3pm/CO noon. Non-smoking rms avail. **Amenities:** 🗄 🅐 📠 A/C, cable TV w/movies. Some units w/whirlpools. **Services:** 🛎 ↩ 🐕 Children's program, babysitting. **Facilities:** 🔥 250 1 restaurant, 1 bar. **Rates:** $56–$76 S or D. Extra person $10. Children under age 18 stay free. Parking: Outdoor, free. AE, CB, DC, DISC, JCB, MC, V.

LODGE

▧▧▧ Glendorn

1032 W Corydon St, 16701; tel 814/362-6511 or toll free 800/843-8568; fax 814/368-9923. 4 mi S of town. 1,280 acres. From the cast-iron gates to the redwood Big House to the four guest rooms and seven guest cabins, everything here is utterly luxurious. Once a private lodge, it reflects the oil wealth of the Dorn family, who built it. **Rooms:** 14 rms and stes; 7 cottages/villas. CI 2pm/CO 11am. **Amenities:** 🗄 🅐 🍴 CD/tape player, bathrobes. No A/C. Some units w/minibars, all w/terraces, all w/fireplaces. All cabins have full kitchens. **Services:** ✗ 🚗 🛎 Twice-daily maid svce. Lessons available for all the sports on premises. **Facilities:** 🔥 🚲 ⛺ 🏊 🎿 🎣 🎱³ ⛳ 30 Basketball, games rm, lawn games, washer/dryer. Skeet and trap shooting, archery, canoes, 60-foot pool. Beautiful creeks flow through the property. Fishing in four lakes. **Rates (AP):** $295 S or D; $295–$595 ste; $395–$895 cottage/villa. Extra person $100. Min stay wknds and special events. Parking: Outdoor, free. Rates vary with number of people in cabin. Closed Mar. No CC.

Breezewood

MOTEL

≣≣≣ Ramada Inn
Jct I-70/US 30, PO Box 307, 15533; tel 814/735-4005 or toll free 800/272-6232; fax 814/735-3228. Exit 12 off PA Tpk. Attractive motel with a vaulted ceiling in the lobby. This Ramada is away from the crowded Breezewood motel district, but close to restaurants. **Rooms:** 125 rms. CI 2pm/CO noon. Nonsmoking rms avail. Many rooms have nice mountain views. **Amenities:** A/C, satel TV w/movies. **Services:** ✕ Babysitting. VCRs and movies available for rent. **Facilities:** 1 restaurant, 1 bar, games rm, lawn games, sauna, whirlpool, playground. **Rates:** Peak (Mar–Oct) $49–$65 S; $57–$73 D. Extra person $8. Children under age 18 stay free. Lower rates off-season. Parking: Outdoor, free. AE, CB, DC, DISC, EC, JCB, MC, V.

Brookville

Named for the brooks flowing in and around town, Brookville is known for its Victorian-style downtown shopping district. **Information:** Magic Forests of West Central PA Tourism & Travel, RR 5, Box 47, Brookville, 15825 (tel 814/849-5197 or toll free 800/348-9393).

MOTELS

≣ Ramada Limited
235 Allegheny Blvd, 15825; tel 814/849-8381 or toll free 800/272-6232; fax 814/849-8386. Exit 13 off I-80. Clean and comfortable accommodations from Ramada's budget line. The staff is friendly, and historic Brookville's festivals and restaurants are nearby. **Rooms:** 69 rms. CI noon/CO noon. Nonsmoking rms avail. Furniture is a little worn, but rooms are spacious. **Amenities:** A/C, cable TV w/movies, dataport. Some units w/terraces. **Services:** Pets allowed for $5 fee. **Facilities:** 1 restaurant (lunch and dinner only), 1 bar (w/entertainment), washer/dryer. **Rates (CP):** Peak (May–Oct) $45–$65 S or D. Extra person $5. Children under age 18 stay free. Min stay special events. Lower rates off-season. Parking: Outdoor, free. AE, CB, DC, DISC, MC, V.

≣ Super 8 Motel
251 Allegheny Blvd, 15825; tel 814/849-8840 or toll free 800/800-8000. Exit 13 off I-80. Budget accommodations with basic services and meticulous housekeeping. **Rooms:** 57 rms and stes. CI 1pm/CO 11am. Nonsmoking rms avail. **Amenities:** A/C, cable TV w/movies. **Services:** **Facilities:** **Rates (CP):** Peak (Apr–Dec) $41–$46 S; $46–$51 D; $51–$61 ste. Extra person $5. Children under age 13 stay free. Lower rates off-season. Parking: Outdoor, free. Golf packages avail. AE, CB, DC, DISC, MC, V.

RESTAURANT

★ Meeting Place
209 Main St; tel 814/849-2557. Across from Courthouse. **American.** Original artifacts from this 1871 building are on display, and the high tin ceiling has been preserved. The menu ranges from quick bites to substantial dinners: homemade soups, fresh ground beef, slow-cooked corned beef, and homemade desserts. **FYI:** Reservations accepted. Blues/guitar/karaoke. Children's menu. **Open:** Peak (June–Aug) Mon–Thurs 8am–8:30pm, Fri 8am–9pm, Sat 9am–9pm, Sun 10am–7:30pm. **Prices:** Main courses $5–$11. AE, DISC, MC, V. ■

Bryn Athyn

A small town in Montgomery County, just NW of Philadelphia. Center of the Church of the New Jerusalem, based on the teachings of 18th-century philosopher Emmanuel Swedenborg.

ATTRACTIONS

Glencairn Museum
1001 Cathedral Rd; tel 215/938-2601. Glencairn was designed by Raymond Pitcairn (1885–1966), who also designed the Romanesque-Gothic Bryn Athyn Cathedral, as his personal home. The massive building now houses the Pitcairns' extensive collections of medieval art, Native American artifacts, and Greek, Roman, and Egyptian pieces. The building itself incorporates some of the objects they collected, and was built in true medieval fashion—not from architectural plans but from models, incorporating design decisions and the artisans' advice along the way. The Pitcairns left the building to the Academy of the New Church, part of the General Church of the New Jerusalem. **Open:** Mon–Fri 9am–5pm. $$

Bryn Athyn Cathedral
Cathedral Rd and Huntingdon Pike; tel 215/947-0266. Bryn Athyn Cathedral, begun in 1913, was designed by Raymond Pitcairn, son of the industrialist John Pitcairn. (It was the elder Pitcairn who established Bryn Athyn as a center of the Church of New Jerusalem.) Raymond Pitcairn sought to revive crafts that had not been practiced in centuries. The interior features work by old-world craftsmen, including stained glass, carved woodwork, and intricate metalwork, and the cathedral's design continued to evolve, in the medieval manner, throughout the long period of its construction. **Open:** Mon–Sun 1–4pm. **Free**

Bucks County

See Doylestown, Erwinna, Holicong, La Haska, Morrisville, New Hope, Newton, Warminster

Burnham

Once called Freedom Forge and Logan, Burnham was eventually renamed for an official of a local steel plant.

MOTEL 🛏

≣≣≣ Holiday Inn Lewistown

US 322 at Burnham exit, 17009; tel 717/248-4961 or toll free 800/HOLIDAY; fax 717/242-3013. This well-placed motel boasts a nice courtyard with pool, and a helpful staff. Popular with both business travelers and vacationers. **Rooms:** 120 rms. CI 2pm/CO noon. Nonsmoking rms avail. King rooms are slightly larger and have desks. **Amenities:** 🛏 🗲 A/C, cable TV w/movies, dataport. **Services:** ✕ 🛍 🖧 🛎 Car-rental desk. Coffee in lobby. **Facilities:** 🛋 [175] 🛟 1 restaurant, 1 bar (w/entertainment), washer/dryer. YMCA nearby. Tennis, miniature golf, walking trails, softball, and driving range within two miles. **Rates:** $59 S or D. Extra person $5. Children under age 18 stay free. MAP rates avail. Parking: Outdoor, free. Corporate, government, military, and AARP discounts avail. AE, CB, DC, DISC, JCB, MC, V.

Bushkill

See also Milford

Located in the Pocono Mountains region, east of Allentown. Gateway of the Delaware Water Gap National Recreation Area, a multi-use park surrounding 40 miles of the Delaware River.

ATTRACTIONS 🏛

Bushkill Falls

PA 209; tel 717/588-6682. Actually a series of eight falls, Bushkill has a total drop of over 300 feet. (The main falls drops 100 feet.) Nature trails, picnicking, fishing, and boating are all available in the area, as are exhibits on Native Americans and local wildlife. **Open:** Apr–Nov, daily 9am–sunset. $$$

Pocono Indian Museum

PA 209; tel 717/588-9338. Artifacts, weapons, and tools illustrate the lifestyle of the Delaware Indians, who once populated the Pocono Mountains. The exhibits trace the story of the Delaware's peaceful existence, from around 10,000 BC. There is an extensive library, and tribal artifacts are for sale. **Open:** Mon–Fri 10am–5:30pm, Sat 9:30am–6pm, Sun 9:30am–5pm. $$

Delaware Water Gap National Recreation Area

I-80; tel 717/588-2451. Named after the cut in the Appalachian Mountains through which the Delaware River flows, this park is located along a 40-mile stretch of the river on both the Pennsylvania and New Jersey sides. Mountains, valleys, and the river offer an abundance of outdoor activities in the park's 70,000 acres, including fishing, swimming, camping, canoeing, cross-country skiing, and skating. A 25-mile stretch of the Appalachian Trail runs through here, and there are miles of other, shorter hiking trails. Dingman's Campground is located north of Dingman's Ferry. **Open:** Daily sunrise–sunset. **Free**

Camp Hill

MOTEL 🛏

≣≣ Radisson Penn Harris Hotel

1150 Camp Hill Bypass, 17001; tel 717/763-7117 or toll free 800/333-3333; fax 717/763-4518. Exit 17 off PA Tpk, 6 mi N on PA 15. While the rooms were nicely renovated in 1994, the public areas of this large, suburban convention facility have somewhat dated, tired decor. **Rooms:** 250 rms and stes. Executive level. CI 3pm/CO noon. Nonsmoking rms avail. **Amenities:** 🛏 🗲 A/C, cable TV w/movies. 1 unit w/fireplace. **Services:** ✕ VP 🚐 🛍 🖧 🛎 Babysitting. Extra charge for pets. **Facilities:** 🛋 🏊 [1000] 🛟 2 restaurants, 1 bar (w/entertainment). **Rates:** Peak (mid-Apr–mid-Oct) $89–$119 S; $99–$129 D; $175–$375 ste. Extra person $10. Children under age 18 stay free. Min stay special events. Lower rates off-season. Parking: Outdoor, free. AE, CB, DC, DISC, JCB, MC, V.

Canadensis

Located in the Pocono Mountains region in Monroe County, SE of Scranton, with resorts and entertainment.

INN 🛏

≣≣≣ The Pine Knob Inn

PA 447, PO Box 295, 18325; tel 717/595-2532 or toll free 800/426-1460. ½ mi S of town. 6½ acres. The original building dates from about 1847, when bark from nearby hemlock trees (*Tsuga canadensis*) were used for tanning leather, giving the town both its first industry and its name. The property now includes cottages and a bungalow, and the trees are used only for shade. Unsuitable for children under 12. **Rooms:** 28 rms (9 w/shared bath); 1 cottage/villa. CI 2pm/CO 11am. Individually decorated rooms furnished with period antiques. Baths are old, but neat and attractive. **Amenities:** No A/C, phone, or TV. Some units w/fireplaces. Caswell-Massey toiletries. **Services:** Cheese, crackers, and candy in guest lounge. **Facilities:** 🛋 🏊 🎿 🛶 🎣 🐎1 [100] 1 restaurant (bkfst and dinner only), 1 bar, lawn games, guest lounge w/TV. Common room with fireplace and board games. Two gazebos on grounds; hiking trails nearby. **Rates (MAP):** $58 S w/shared bath, $76 S w/private bath; $125 D w/shared bath, $158–$190 D w/private bath; $190 cottage/villa. Extra person $30. Parking: Outdoor, free. AE, DISC, MC, V.

RESORT

≡≡≡ Hillside Lodge

PA 390, PO Box 268, 18325; tel 717/595-7551 or toll free 800/666-4455. 27 acres. Families on a budget come here during the summer, and couples enjoy ski weekends in the winter. **Rooms:** 27 rms and stes; 5 cottages/villas. CI 3pm/CO noon. Nonsmoking rms avail. Recently renovated rooms are large, with king bed, fireplace, and two-person hot tub. Many rooms have sofa beds. **Amenities:** 🛏 ⚲ A/C, cable TV, VCR. Some units w/terraces, some w/fireplaces, some w/whirlpools. **Services:** ⌂ Social director, babysitting. **Facilities:** 🛝 🖼 🎿 🛶 🎯 ⚓1 🏊60 1 restaurant (bkfst and dinner only), 1 bar (w/entertainment), basketball, volleyball, games rm, lawn games, playground. Activities range from summertime miniature golf, baseball, bocci, and shuffleboard, to wintertime sleigh rides. **Rates (MAP):** Peak (June 15–Labor Day) $138–$170 S or D; $180 ste; $180 cottage/villa. Extra person $51. Children under age 1 stay free. Min stay wknds. Lower rates off-season. Parking: Outdoor, free. Holiday weekend, ski, two-day, and murder-mystery packages avail. DISC, MC, V.

RESTAURANT 🍽

★ Pump House Inn

PA 390, Skytop Rd; tel 717/595-7501. **American.** Much of the original 1842 stagecoach stop remains, including the stone walls and hardwood floors. One dining room has a waterfall and plants and one is an enclosed porch. The menu changes seasonally, but the soup du jour and the nightly specials are always a good choice. **FYI:** Reservations recommended. No smoking. **Open:** Peak (June–Nov) Tues–Sat 5–9pm, Sun 2:30–8:30pm. **Prices:** Main courses $14–$25. DC, MC, V. ▰

Carbondale

RESTAURANT 🍽

Oliveri's Crystal Lake Hotel

PA 247; tel 717/222-3181. Exit 62 off I-81, PA 107 E for 3½ mi to PA 247 N for 8 mi. **American/Italian.** Food and drink are served in the hotel during the winter, then the restaurant moves to a lakeside building where there are lots of windows and decks for spring, summer, and fall. Pasta dishes are named after local "regulars"; veal is also a popular option. **FYI:** Reservations recommended. Piano. **Open:** Mon–Sat noon–midnight, Sun 4pm–midnight. **Prices:** Main courses $9–$25. AE, DISC, MC, V. ▰

Carlisle

A colonial town of tree-lined streets and buildings in the Pennsylvania Dutch region, offering unique shops and muse-

ums. Famous Revolutionary War fighter and nurse Molly Pitcher died and was buried here. Home of US Army War College.

MOTELS 🏨

≡≡ Appalachian Motor Inn

1825 Harrisburg Pike, 17013; tel 717/245-2242 or toll free 800/445-6715; fax 717/258-4881. On US 11, ½ mi N of exit 17 off I-81. Primarily for truck drivers, this two-story motel has neat rooms and efficient management. A convenient, clean place for a rest stop on the road. **Rooms:** 200 rms and stes. CI open/CO noon. Nonsmoking rms avail. Large, well-furnished rooms. **Amenities:** 🛏 A/C, cable TV w/movies. Some units w/whirlpools. **Services:** ⌂ **Facilities:** 🏊50 ⛥ 1 restaurant, 1 bar, games rm, washer/dryer. 24-hour restaurant has carry-out service. **Rates:** $45–$55 S or D; $125 ste. Extra person $5. Children under age 12 stay free. Parking: Outdoor, free. Higher rates on car show weekends. AE, CB, DC, DISC, MC, V.

≡≡≡ Embers Inn & Convention Center

1700 Harrisburg Pike, 17013; tel 717/243-1717 or toll free 800/692-7315; fax 717/243-6648. At jct US 11/I-81 near PA Tpk entrance. The rooms of this big convention center hotel surround a large building that contains all the facilities. The entrance resembles an imposing colonial manor house. **Rooms:** 274 rms, stes, and effic. CI 2pm/CO 11am. Nonsmoking rms avail. New wallpaper, rugs, and cherry-wood furniture in all rooms. **Amenities:** 🛏 ⚲ A/C, satel TV w/movies, dataport. Guests may request linen changes every other day (to save water and energy). **Services:** ✕ 🚗 🖼 ⌂ ⌂ Car-rental desk, babysitting. Staff skilled in handling large groups. **Facilities:** 🛝 ⚓2 🏊1500 ⛥ 1 restaurant, 1 bar (w/entertainment), volleyball, games rm, sauna, whirlpool. Putting green, softball diamond. **Rates:** Peak (Mar–Oct) $58–$68 S; $63–$73 D; $110–$190 ste; $110–$190 effic. Extra person $5. Children under age 18 stay free. Min stay special events. Lower rates off-season. Parking: Outdoor, free. AE, CB, DC, DISC, MC, V.

RESTAURANT 🍽

★ California Cafe

52 W Pomfret St; tel 717/249-2028. Just off Hanover St. **French.** French cuisine is served with a distinctive West Coast touch in the four intimate dining rooms of this popular place. The menu changes weekly, and two-course dinners are available for those with smaller appetites. **FYI:** Reservations recommended. No smoking. **Open:** Lunch Tues–Sat 11am–2pm; dinner Tues–Sat 5–9pm. Closed Dec 25–Jan 2. **Prices:** Main courses $15–$19. AE, CB, DC, DISC, MC, V. ♥ ▰ ⛥

Chambersburg

Established in 1764, Chambersburg later became an important trading center in the fertile Cumberland Valley area. Noted as the only Northern town destroyed by Confederate forces during the Civil War. **Information:** Cumberland Valley Visitors Council, 1235 Lincoln Way E, Chambersburg, 17201 (tel 717/261-1200).

MOTELS 🏨

≡ Days Inn

30 Falling Spring Rd, 17201; tel 717/263-1288 or toll free 800/329-7466; fax 717/263-6514. Exit 6 off I-81. A standard but nicely maintained property just off the interstate. **Rooms:** 107 rms. CI 2pm/CO 11am. Nonsmoking rms avail. All rooms have sofas. **Amenities:** 🔟 ⚕ A/C, cable TV w/movies, in-rm safe. Some rooms have refrigerators and dataports. VCRs and movies available. **Services:** 🖼 🍴 🚪 Car-rental desk, babysitting. **Facilities:** ⟦125⟧ ♿ **Rates (CP):** Peak (Apr–Oct) $48–$59 S; $54–$65 D. Extra person $7. Children under age 17 stay free. Lower rates off-season. Parking: Outdoor, free. AE, CB, DC, DISC, JCB, MC, V.

≡≡ Hampton Inn

955 Lesher Rd, 17201; tel 717/261-9185 or toll free 800/426-7866; fax 717/261-1984. Exit 5 off I-81. There's a brighter, softer feel about this property than one usually associates with chain motels. The lobby has a pale decor, polished floors, and piped-in classical music. **Rooms:** 124 rms. CI 2pm/CO noon. Nonsmoking rms avail. Bright, clean rooms. Angled, three-panel bath mirrors are a nice touch. **Amenities:** 🔟 ⚕ A/C, cable TV w/movies, refrig. VCRs and videos available. **Services:** 🖼 🍴 **Facilities:** 🏊 ⟦80⟧ ♿ **Rates (CP):** Peak (June–Aug) $54 S; $61 D. Children under age 18 stay free. Lower rates off-season. Parking: Outdoor, free. AE, CB, DC, DISC, MC, V.

≡≡ Howard Johnson Lodge

1123 Lincoln Way E, 17201; tel 717/263-9191 or toll free 800/446-4656; fax 717/263-4752. Exit 6 off I-81. A touch of the "grand" is in this appealing highway-side motel, with a large tiled lobby, a chandelier, and a comfortable sitting area. **Rooms:** 132 rms. CI noon/CO noon. Nonsmoking rms avail. **Amenities:** 🔟 ⚕ 📺 A/C, cable TV, refrig. Some units w/terraces. VCRs and movies available. **Services:** 🖼 🍴 **Facilities:** 🏊 ⟦125⟧ ♿ 1 restaurant, 1 bar, sauna. **Rates:** $44–$55 S; $54–$67 D. Extra person $7. Children under age 17 stay free. Parking: Outdoor, free. AE, CB, DC, DISC, MC, V.

≡ Travelodge

565 Lincoln Way E, 17201; tel 717/264-4187 or toll free 800/578-7878; fax 717/264-2446. Exit 6 off I-81. A downtown motel in a mixed residential/business area. **Rooms:** 52 rms. CI noon/CO noon. Nonsmoking rms avail. Some rooms have showers instead of tubs. **Amenities:** 🔟 ⚕ 📺 A/C, cable TV w/movies, refrig. Some units w/terraces. **Services:** 🍴 🚪 **Facilities:** ⟦110⟧ ♿ 1 restaurant, 1 bar. **Rates:** $51 S; $57 D.

Extra person $7. Children under age 16 stay free. Parking: Outdoor, free. Golf packages avail. AE, CB, DC, DISC, MC, V.

RESTAURANT 🍴

♣ Mercersburg Inn

405 S Main St, Mercersburg; tel 717/328-5231. Exit 3 off I-81, 10 mi on PA 16. **French/Seafood.** Housed in a Georgian mansion and surrounded by over six landscaped acres. The tables in the spacious first-floor dining room provide splendid views of the Tuscarora Mountains. Prix fixe dinner may include grilled beef tenderloin with port wine sauce or grilled salmon with saffron-Pernod butter and sun-dried tomato risotto. **FYI:** Reservations recommended. No smoking. **Open:** Fri–Sat 8–11pm. **Prices:** Prix fixe $45. DISC, MC, V. 🍴 🏔

Chester

See Philadelphia

Clarion

Nearby to Allegheny National Forest and named for the Clarion River.

MOTELS 🏨

≡≡ Comfort Inn

Dolby St, PO Box 385, 16214; tel 814/226-5230 or toll free 800/228-5150; fax 814/226-5231. Exit 9 off I-80. This bright and cheery property was built in 1996. The staff is friendly, and many rooms have views of a golf course across the street. **Rooms:** 81 rms and effic. CI 3pm/CO 11am. Nonsmoking rms avail. Thomasville furniture in each room. **Amenities:** 🔟 ⚕ A/C, cable TV w/movies, dataport, VCR. Some units w/whirlpools. VCRs available. Some rooms have refrigerators. **Services:** 🚐 🖼 🍴 Masseur. **Facilities:** ⟦35⟧ ♿ Playground, washer/dryer. Kitchen area in lobby. **Rates (CP):** Peak (May–Nov) $59–$79 S or D; $89–$99 effic. Extra person $5. Children under age 18 stay free. Min stay special events. Lower rates off-season. Parking: Outdoor, free. Golf packages avail. AE, CB, DC, DISC, JCB, MC, V.

UNRATED Holiday Inn

I-80 and PA 68, 16214; tel 814/226-8850 or toll free 800/596-1313; fax 814/226-9055. Exit 9 off I-80. Recently renovated motel featuring a Holidome atrium with indoor recreational facilities. Unrated due to ongoing major renovations. **Rooms:** 122 rms and stes. CI 2pm/CO noon. Nonsmoking rms avail. **Amenities:** 🔟 ⚕ A/C, cable TV w/movies, dataport, voice mail. Some units w/terraces. Complimentary morning newspaper and coffee. **Services:** ✗ 🚐 🖼 🍴 🚪 Fax service available. Free local calls. **Facilities:** 🏊 ⟦200⟧ ♿ 1 restaurant, 1 bar, games rm, sauna, playground, washer/

dryer. Free passes to nearby racquet and fitness center. **Rates (BB):** Peak (May–Sept) $79–$94 S or D; $100–$160 ste. Children under age 20 stay free. Min stay special events. Lower rates off-season. Parking: Outdoor, free. AE, CB, DC, DISC, JCB, MC, V.

RESTAURANT 🍴

★ Clarion Clipper

PA 68; tel 814/226-7950. 1 mi S of town. **American.** The riverboat decor of the exterior is not as apparent once you get inside. Menu specialties include certified Angus beef and roast chicken. **FYI:** Reservations accepted. Children's menu. **Open:** Daily 6:30am–10pm. **Prices:** Main courses $5–$13. AE, DC, DISC, MC, V. 👥 ♿

Clarks Summit

See Scranton

Coraopolis

Ten miles NW of Pittsburgh, Coraopolis was first settled in 1760, and named for the daughter of an influential citizen. The Monongahela River runs east of town.

HOTELS 🏨

⊨⊨ Courtyard by Marriott

450 Cherrington Pkwy, 15108; tel 412/264-5000 or toll free 800/321-2211; fax 412/264-7979. Located in an office park near the airport, this hotel caters to business travelers yet has limited services. **Rooms:** 148 rms and stes. CI 3pm/CO 1pm. Nonsmoking rms avail. Interior rooms face courtyard; others the parking lot. Suites and king rooms have sleep sofas. **Amenities:** 🖥 ♨ A/C, cable TV w/movies, dataport, voice mail. Some units w/terraces. **Services:** ✕ 🚐 🛍 🍴 Babysitting. Business services on request. Meal service is dinner only, Mon–Thurs. **Facilities:** 🛠 🏋 🏊40 ♿ 1 restaurant (bkfst and dinner only), 1 bar, whirlpool, washer/dryer. **Rates:** $49–$100 S or D; $120 ste. Children under age 18 stay free. MAP rates avail. Parking: Outdoor, free. AE, CB, DC, DISC, MC, V.

⊨⊨⊨ Embassy Suites

550 Cherrington Pkwy, 15108; tel 412/269-9070 or toll free 800/EMBASSY; fax 412/262-4119. A business hotel in an office park, with country-style architecture and a large, brick front porch with rocking chairs. Rooms are arranged around an attractive atrium with waterfalls and bridges. **Rooms:** 223 stes. CI 3pm/CO noon. Nonsmoking rms avail. Homelike decor. Some first-floor rooms pick up noise from the atrium restaurant. **Amenities:** 🖥 ♨ 📺 A/C, satel TV w/movies, refrig, dataport, VCR, voice mail. Microwaves. **Services:** ✕ 🚐 🛍 🍴 Social hour with free drinks and snacks. **Facilities:** 🛠 🏋 🏊650 ♿ 1 restaurant, 2 bars (1 w/entertain-

ment), games rm, sauna, whirlpool, washer/dryer. **Rates (BB):** Peak (Mar–Sept) $149 ste. Extra person $10. Children under age 12 stay free. Min stay special events. Lower rates off-season. Parking: Outdoor, free. AE, DC, DISC, MC, V.

⊨⊨⊨ Holiday Inn Pittsburgh Airport

1406 Beers School Rd, 15108; tel 412/262-3600 or toll free 800/333-4835; fax 412/262-6221. A standard airport hotel, with no surprises. **Rooms:** 257 rms and stes. Executive level. CI noon/CO noon. Nonsmoking rms avail. **Amenities:** 🖥 ♨ A/C, satel TV w/movies, dataport. Microwaves, VCRs, and refrigerators available. **Services:** ✕ 🚐 🛍 🍴 🐕 Car-rental desk, babysitting. Fax and copy services. **Facilities:** 🛠 🏊900 ♿ 1 restaurant, 1 bar, whirlpool, washer/dryer. Nearby fitness club. **Rates (BB):** $129 S or D; $150 ste. Extra person $10. Children under age 17 stay free. Min stay special events. MAP rates avail. Parking: Outdoor, free. Weekend rates avail. AE, CB, DC, DISC, MC, V.

⊨⊨⊨ Pittsburgh Airport Marriott

100 Aten Rd, 15108; tel 412/788-8800 or toll free 800/328-9297; fax 412/788-0743. This property caters to business travelers, with extensive meeting facilities and a spacious, elegant lobby with plenty of seating. **Rooms:** 314 rms and stes. Executive level. CI 3pm/CO noon. Nonsmoking rms avail. King rooms have sleep sofas. **Amenities:** 🖥 ♨ 🍽 A/C, satel TV w/movies, dataport, voice mail. **Services:** ✕ 🛎 🚐 🛍 🍴 🐕 Babysitting. Videos available. Laundry service weekdays only. Small pets only. **Facilities:** 🛠 🏋 🏊600 💻 ♿ 1 restaurant, 1 bar (w/entertainment), sauna, whirlpool. Nearby jogging trails. **Rates:** $99–$145 S; $99–$160 D; $164–$465 ste. Children under age 18 stay free. MAP rates avail. Parking: Outdoor, free. Weekend rates avail. AE, CB, DC, DISC, EC, ER, JCB, MC, V.

⊨⊨ Pittsburgh Plaza Hotel

1500 Beers School Rd, 15108; tel 412/264-7900 or toll free 800/542-8111; fax 412/262-3229. Standard airport facility built around a popular Eat 'n' Park chain restaurant. **Rooms:** 193 rms. CI 3pm/CO noon. Nonsmoking rms avail. **Amenities:** 🖥 ♨ A/C, cable TV. Some units w/terraces. **Services:** 🍴 🚐 🛍 🐕 Babysitting. Refundable $50 pet deposit. Complimentary happy hour with beer and wine from 5–7pm. **Facilities:** 🏋 🏊40 ♿ 1 restaurant, sauna. **Rates (CP):** $45–$60 S or D. Children under age 21 stay free. Parking: Outdoor, free. Park & Fly packages avail (includes one night lodging and parking). AE, DC, DISC, MC, V.

Cresco

In the heart of the Pocono Mountains and home to an award-winning country inn. Site of the first licensed trout hatchery in the state.

INN 🏨

≡≡≡ Crescent Lodge

Paradise Valley, 18326; tel 717/595-7486 or toll free 800/392-9400. PA 191 and PA 940. 28 acres. Rooms in the main lodge and the cottages of this attractive, family-run property are decorated in an elegant country style with lots of wood and wicker, well-coordinated floral prints, and quality detailing in artwork and brass. **Rooms:** 32 rms and effic; 6 cottages/villas. CI 2pm/CO 11am. Nonsmoking rms avail. **Amenities:** 🛏 ⚬ A/C, cable TV. Some units w/terraces, some w/fireplaces, some w/whirlpools. Some rooms have VCRs. Bathrobes provided in whirlpool rooms. **Services:** Complimentary country breakfast (served midweek only). **Facilities:** 🏄 🎿 🐎 ⚓1 [100] 1 restaurant (dinner only; *see* "Restaurants" below), 1 bar (w/entertainment), lawn games, guest lounge. Very attractive heated pool. Upscale gift shop. **Rates (BB):** Peak (June 15–Sept 15) $80–$150 D; $155–$195 effic; $120–$275 cottage/villa. Extra person $15. Min stay wknds and special events. Lower rates off-season. Parking: Outdoor, free. AE, CB, DC, DISC, MC, V.

RESTAURANT 🍽

Crescent Lodge

Paradise Valley; tel 717/595-7486. PA 191 and PA 940. **Continental.** The brick-and-ivory decor of the dining room of this large wood building is accented with outdoorsy prints, and fresh flowers are on the tables. Smoked Pennsylvania trout is a nice appetizer if you don't want Southern-style alligator; Pocono Mountain brook trout, beef Wellington, and grilled pork calvados are among the most popular main dishes. **FYI:** Reservations recommended. Piano. Children's menu. **Open:** Peak (July 4–Sept 7) Mon–Thurs 5:30–9pm, Fri–Sat 5:30–10pm, Sun 5:30–9pm. **Prices:** Main courses $17–$26. AE, CB, DC, DISC, MC, V.

Danville

Laid out in 1792 near the Susquehanna River on the North Branch of the Pennsylvania Canal, Danville features a historic district listed on the National Register. The discovery of iron ore here led to profitable iron foundries.

MOTEL 🏨

≡≡ The Pine Barn Inn

1 Pine Barn Place, 17821; tel 717/275-2071 or toll free 800/627-2276; fax 717/275-3248. Quaint, country-style property anchored by an old barn. **Rooms:** 65 rms. CI 2pm/CO 1pm. Nonsmoking rms avail. Rooms range from simple motel-style to rather elegant; four are in the original barn. **Amenities:** 🛏 A/C, cable TV. Some units w/whirlpools. **Services:** ✕ 🖥 🛎 🐕 Car-rental desk, masseur, babysitting. **Facilities:** [60] 1 restaurant, 1 bar. Large gift shop. Popular family restaurant

has good reputation and a cozy fireplace. **Rates:** $40–$60 S; $45–$75 D. Extra person $2. Children under age 16 stay free. Parking: Outdoor, free. AE, CB, DC, DISC, MC, V.

Denver

Small borough in the Pennsylvania Dutch region.

HOTEL 🏨

≡≡≡ Holiday Inn Lancaster County

PA 272, PO Box 129, 17517; tel 717/336-7541 or toll free 800/437-5711; fax 717/336-0515. Exit 21 off I-76, W ½ mi on PA 272. This newly redecorated, low-rise hotel blends nicely into the rural setting, yet is close to the Pennsylvania Turnpike. **Rooms:** 110 rms and stes. CI 2pm/CO noon. Nonsmoking rms avail. Large well-decorated rooms. **Amenities:** 🛏 ⚬ A/C, cable TV w/movies, dataport. King rooms have coffeemakers and hair dryers. **Services:** ✕ 🖥 🛎 **Facilities:** 🏄 [120] ⅙ 1 restaurant, 1 bar, washer/dryer. **Rates:** Peak (Apr–Nov) $79–$89 S or D; $79–$89 ste. Children under age 18 stay free. Min stay special events. Lower rates off-season. Parking: Outdoor, free. AARP discounts avail. AE, CB, DC, DISC, JCB, MC, V.

MOTEL

≡≡≡ Black Horse Lodge & Suites

2180 N Reading Rd, PO Box 343, 17517; tel 717/336-7563 or toll free 800/610-3805; fax 717/336-1110. 1 mi off I-76. This well-kept property on top of a hill is adjacent to a large antiques shop and close to the tourist attractions of northern Lancaster County. **Rooms:** 74 rms, stes, and effic. Executive level. CI open/CO noon. Nonsmoking rms avail. All rooms are large. Four luxury suites have marble tubs and TV in bathrooms. **Amenities:** 🛏 ⚬ 📺 🍴 A/C, cable TV w/movies, refrig. All units w/terraces, some w/whirlpools. Free in-room coffee and tea. **Services:** 🖥 🛎 🐕 Babysitting. Free local calls. **Facilities:** 🏄 ⅙ 1 restaurant, 1 bar, basketball, playground, washer/dryer. **Rates (CP):** Peak (Apr–Nov) $59–$99 S; $69–$129 D; $169–$229 ste; $69–$129 effic. Extra person $10. Children under age 13 stay free. Min stay special events. Lower rates off-season. Parking: Outdoor, free. Golf packages avail. AE, CB, DC, DISC, MC, V.

RESTAURANT 🍽

★ Zinn's Diner

PA 272 N; tel 717/336-1774. N of exit 21 off PA Tpk. **Regional American/Pennsylvania Dutch.** A large diner with booth seating, and works by local artists decorating the walls. The chicken pot pie and creamed chipped beef are popular, and the prices are reasonable. Expect to wait for a table during the busy season. **FYI:** Reservations not accepted. Children's menu. No liquor license. **Open:** Daily 6am–11pm. **Prices:** Main courses $6–$11. DISC, MC, V. 🖼 ⅙

Donegal

In the Laurel Highlands region of southwest Pennsylvania, Donegal is best known as the site of the Fallingwater house, one of Frank Lloyd Wright's most famous works.

MOTEL 🏨

⊨⊨ Days Inn at Donegal
PA 31, PO Box 184, 15628; tel 412/593-7536 or toll free 800/329-7466; fax 412/593-6165. Exit 9 off PA Tpk. A basic motel close to Hidden Valley and Seven Springs ski resorts. Fine if you're planning on spending most of your time on the slopes. **Rooms:** 34 rms. CI 2pm/CO 11am. Nonsmoking rms avail. Simple, clean rooms. **Amenities:** 🗝 🖐 A/C, cable TV. **Services:** 🖐 **Facilities:** 🗄 🖈 🏃 🏊 Volleyball, lawn games. **Rates (CP):** Peak (Dec 21–Mar) $68 S or D. Extra person $6. Children under age 13 stay free. Lower rates off-season. Parking: Outdoor, free. AE, MC, V.

RESORT

⊨⊨⊨ Hidden Valley Resort
1 Craighead Dr, Hidden Valley, 15502; tel 814/443-8000 or toll free 800/458-0175; fax 814/443-1907. Exit 9 off PA Tpk E, 8 mi on PA 31/exit 10 off PA Tpk W, US 219 S to W on PA 31 for 11 mi. 2,000 acres. An expansive, self-contained resort in the Laurel Highlands wilderness, with a homelike atmosphere and myriad recreation facilities for all seasons. **Rooms:** 87 effic; 128 cottages/villas. CI 4:30pm/CO noon. Nonsmoking rms avail. Units (many of which are privately owned) range from a large efficiency up to an entire four-bedroom home. **Amenities:** 🗝 🎿 Cable TV w/movies, refrig. No A/C. Some units w/terraces, some w/fireplaces, some w/whirlpools. **Services:** 🚗 🖐 🖐 Masseur, children's program, babysitting. Kids' camp. **Facilities:** 🗄 🚲 ⛰ 🏕 ▶18 🖈 🏃 🏊 🎱16 🎿4 🎽 📷300 ♨ 6 restaurants, 5 bars (2 w/entertainment), basketball, volleyball, games rm, racquetball, spa, sauna, whirlpool, beauty salon, playground, washer/dryer. Ski lodge. **Rates:** $85–$236 effic; $250–$700 cottage/villa. Extra person $23–$33. Children under age 14 stay free. Min stay peak and wknds. MAP rates avail. Parking: Outdoor, free. AE, CB, DC, DISC, MC, V.

ATTRACTION 🏛

Hidden Valley Ski Resort
4 Craighead Dr, Hidden Valley; tel 814/443-2600. This mountain, a particular favorite with beginners, has 17 trails (roughly split between easy, moderate, and difficult) with eight lifts and a vertical drop of 610 feet. Other features include cross-country trails, equipment rentals, and snow boarding. The ski school is especially renowned, and guests under 6 and over 69 ski for free. **Open:** Dec–Mar, daily. Call for schedule. **$$$$**

Doylestown

Seat of Bucks County. Settled in 1735, Doylestown was once an overnight stop for stage coach travelers between Philadelphia and Easton. Today, it offers a wealth of museums, architecture, shopping, and dining. **Information:** Bucks County Tourist Committee, 152 Swamp Rd, PO Box 912, Doylestown, 18901 (tel 215/345-4552 or toll free 800/836-2825).

INN 🏨

UNRATED Plumsteadville Inn
PA 611 and Stump Rd, Plumsteadville, 18949; tel 215/766-7500; fax 215/766-7123. US 20 N to PA 611 N. This charming inn, built in 1751, caters to couples looking for a romantic getaway. Common areas and guest rooms are filled with antiques. **Rooms:** 14 rms and stes. CI 2pm/CO noon. **Amenities:** 🗝 A/C. No TV. Continental breakfast on weekdays, full breakfast on weekends. **Facilities:** 🏃 📷120 1 restaurant, 1 bar (w/entertainment), guest lounge w/TV. **Rates (CP):** $79–$125 D; $79–$150 ste. Extra person $10. Parking: Outdoor, free. Weekday rates avail Sun–Thurs. AE, CB, DC, MC, V.

RESTAURANT 🍴

Cafe Arielle
In Doylestown Agriculture Works, 100 S Main St; tel 215/345-5930. S Main St off US 202. **French.** The atmosphere of this French country restaurant is romantic and elegant, yet relaxed. Local farmers provide fresh produce and seafood is delivered every other day. The kitchen is best known for rack of lamb, roast duckling, and fresh seafood. **FYI:** Reservations recommended. No smoking. **Open:** Lunch Wed–Fri noon–2:30pm; dinner Wed–Fri 6:30–9pm, Sat 6–9pm, Sun 5–8pm. **Prices:** Main courses $18–$24. AE, DC, MC, V. ❤ 👟

ATTRACTIONS 🏛

Mercer Museum
Pine and Ashland Sts; tel 215/345-0210. Housed in a building that looks like a castle, the Mercer Museum displays over 50,000 pieces of early American antiques, folk art, implements, and other Americana illustrating colonial life. The third floor of the museum houses the Spruance Library, a primary source for information on Bucks County history and genealogy. **Open:** Mon–Sat 10am–5pm, Sun noon–5pm. **$$**

Fonthill Museum
E Court St; tel 215/348-9461. This 44-room concrete castle was built by archeologist Henry Chapman Mercer in order to provide space to display his collections of decorative tiles, prints, and artifacts from around the world. Guided tours available. **Open:** Mon–Sat 10am–5pm, Sun noon–5pm. **$$**

James A Michener Art Museum
138 S Pine St; tel 215/340-9800. Located in the old Bucks County jail, built in 1884, the museum's collection of 20th-

century American art focuses on works by Bucks County artists. A permanent exhibit on Michener himself (author of *The Drifters* and many other best sellers) has such objects as the author's typewriter and an original manuscript. **Open:** Tues–Fri 10am–4:30pm, Sat–Sun 10am–5pm. **$$**

Pearl S Buck House
520 Dublin Rd, Hilltown; tel 215/249-0100. Buck lived in this stone farmhouse, which still contains some of her original furnishings. Buck was the daughter of missionaries and spent many years in China, and the museum contains artifacts she brought back with her. It also houses objects relating to her career as a writer, including her Pulitzer Prize for *The Good Earth,* and her writing desk. **Open:** Tues–Sat 10:30am–2:30pm, Sun 1:30–3pm. **$$**

Du Bois

In a narrow basin at the lowest pass in the Allegheny Mountains, this city is bisected by Sandy Lick Creek.

MOTELS

≡≡≡ Holiday Inn
Jct US 219/I-80, 15801; tel 814/371-5100 or toll free 800/465-4329; fax 814/375-0230. Exit 16 off I-80. This well-maintained, tidy motel is convenient to area eco-touring parks, Punxsutawney, and other hot spots. **Rooms:** 161 rms. CI 3pm/CO noon. Nonsmoking rms avail. **Amenities:** A/C, cable TV w/movies, dataport. Refrigerators and VCRs available. **Services:** ✗ 🚗 ⬛ ⏴ ⬩ **Facilities:** 🛋 🏌 400 & 1 restaurant, 1 bar (w/entertainment), washer/dryer. Free passes to local YMCA. Six golf courses within 10 miles. **Rates:** Peak (Apr–Sept) $66–$72 S or D. Extra person $6. Children under age 13 stay free. Lower rates off-season. Parking: Outdoor, free. AE, CB, DC, DISC, JCB, MC, V.

≡≡ Ramada Inn
Jct I-80/PA 255, 15801; tel 814/371-7070 or toll free 800/272-6232; fax 814/371-1055. At exit 17 off I-80. Set back from the interstate and sporting a large lobby with fireplace, this is a convenient base for exploring the area. **Rooms:** 94 rms. CI 1pm/CO noon. Nonsmoking rms avail. Mountain views from many rooms. **Amenities:** 🛋 A/C, cable TV. Some units w/terraces. VCRs available. **Services:** ✗ 🚗 ⬛ ⏴ ⬩ **Facilities:** 🛋 🏌 🛥 275 & 1 restaurant, 1 bar (w/entertainment), games rm, sauna, washer/dryer. Free passes to local YMCA. **Rates:** Peak (May–Sept) $59–$66 S; $69–$73 D. Extra person $10. Children under age 18 stay free. Lower rates off-season. Parking: Outdoor, free. AE, CB, DC, DISC, EC, JCB, MC, V.

Easton

Seat of Northampton County. Easton offers historic sites, vineyards, and the restored Lehigh Canal, with mule-drawn boats.

HOTEL

UNRATED Best Western Easton Inn
185 S 3rd St, 18042; tel 610/252-9131 or toll free 800/882-0113; fax 610/252-5145. At PA 611. A clean, bright hotel convenient to both business and vacation destinations, including Dorney Park and the Crayola Factory. **Rooms:** 85 rms. CI 3pm/CO noon. Nonsmoking rms avail. **Amenities:** 🛋 A/C, cable TV, refrig, dataport. 1 unit w/whirlpool. Microwaves. **Services:** ✗ ⏴ ⬩ **Facilities:** 🛋 🏌 250 & 1 restaurant (lunch and dinner only), 1 bar (w/entertainment). Delaware River State Park (across the street) has jogging and cross-country ski trails. Indoor pool open Apr–Dec only. **Rates (CP):** Peak (June 26–Sept 3) $49–$135 S or D. Extra person $10. Children under age 12 stay free. Min stay special events. Lower rates off-season. Parking: Outdoor, free. Family packages avail. AE, DC, DISC, JCB, MC, V.

ATTRACTIONS

National Canal Museum
PA 611; tel 610/250-6700. Displays on canals, coal mining, and industry illuminate the development of this region of Pennsylvania in the 19th century. Artifacts and models of old boats offer a glimpse of life on the water. Nearby, an authentic mule-driven canal boat staffed by costumed historical interpreters takes visitors on leisurely rides along the Lehigh Canal. **Open:** Mon–Sat 10am–4pm, Sun 1–5pm. **$$**

Crayola Factory
30 Centre Sq; tel 610/515-8000. Visitors can view interactive displays and exhibits that show the history of the crayon. The real visual treat is on the factory floor, where vats of brightly colored liquid are turned into the familiar Crayolas. There are also studios for other hands-on artistic experimenting, including computer graphics and printmaking. **Open:** Tues–Sat 9:30am–5pm, Sun noon–5pm. **$$$**

Edinboro

A year-round resort town on the shore of Edinboro Lake, and just 20 miles south of Lake Erie. Edinboro State College is located here.

HOTEL

≡≡ Edinboro Inn
US 6 N, 16412; tel 814/734-5650; fax 814/734-7532. A pseudo-castle on a pleasant hilltop near the business district. Adequate but not exceptional. **Rooms:** 105 rms and stes. CI 4pm/CO noon. Nonsmoking rms avail. **Amenities:** 🛋 A/C,

satel TV w/movies. Some units w/terraces. Coffeemakers, sofa beds in some rooms. **Services:** ✕ 🛎 **Facilities:** 🏋 🏊 ⟨300⟩ ⟨ 1 restaurant, 1 bar, games rm, sauna, washer/dryer. Surrounded by 18-hole public golf course with public outdoor pool. **Rates:** Peak (May–Oct) $75–$90 S or D; $90–$110 ste. Extra person $10. Children under age 18 stay free. Lower rates off-season. Parking: Outdoor, free. AE, DC, DISC, MC, V.

Ephrata

This historic Lancaster County borough was the site of Ephrata Cloister, an early communal society established by German Seventh-Day Adventists in 1735. Many artisans call Ephrata home today.

MOTEL 🏨

🛏 Dutchmaid Motel
222 N Reading Rd, 17522; tel 717/733-1720. On PA 272 N, ¼ mi N of US 322 W. Small, rural motel adequate for an overnight stop. **Rooms:** 20 rms. CI noon/CO 11am. Non-smoking rms avail. **Amenities:** 🛁 📞 A/C, cable TV. **Services:** 🛎 **Facilities:** 1 bar. **Rates:** Peak (Apr–Oct) $40–$48 S or D. Extra person $4. Children under age 5 stay free. Lower rates off-season. Parking: Outdoor, free. AE, MC, V.

RESTAURANTS 🍽

★ Akron Restaurant
333 S 7th St, Akron; tel 717/859-1181. On PA 272. **Regional American/Pennsylvania Dutch.** The rooms at this big, friendly eatery are tastefully decorated with print wallpaper and Pennsylvania Dutch artifacts and paintings. Menu highlights include baited chicken pie and fresh fruit pies. Bakery and gift shop on the premises. **FYI:** Reservations not accepted. Children's menu. No liquor license. **Open:** Peak (June–Sept) Mon–Thurs 6am–8pm, Fri–Sat 6am–9pm, Sun 11am–7pm. **Prices:** Main courses $6–$14. DISC, MC, V. 👪 💟

Nav Jiwan International Tea Room
In Self-Help International Craft Store, 240 N Reading Rd; tel 717/721-8400. On PA 272. **International.** The main room is decorated with a mixture of antique and wicker furnishings, and crafts from around the world. (One section has Indonesian-style seating with pillows and low brass tables.) The globetrotting menu features food of a different country each week, but there is always English high tea on the second and fourth Wednesdays of each month at 3pm. **FYI:** Reservations accepted. Children's menu. No liquor license. No smoking. **Open:** Peak (Nov 25–Dec 24) Mon–Thurs 10am–3pm, Fri 10am–8pm, Sat 10am–3pm. **Prices:** Main courses $8–$10. MC, V. 👪 ⟨

Restaurant at Doneckers
333 N State St; tel 717/738-9501. **American/French.** French cuisine with an American touch is served in two areas: the downstairs room with an open fireplace and casual decor, and the skylight-covered Country French room upstairs. (Prices rise with the elevation.) Menu specialties include Dover sole with strawberry sauce, as well as a variety of steaks. A dinner theater package is offered in summer. **FYI:** Reservations recommended. Children's menu. Dress code. No smoking. **Open:** Mon–Tues 11am–10pm, Thurs–Sat 11am–10pm. **Prices:** Main courses $10–$28. AE, CB, DC, DISC, MC, V. 💟 🏠 ⟨

ATTRACTION 🏛

Ephrata Cloister
632 W Main St; tel 717/733-6600. The Ephrata Cloister, an early radical religious community, was founded by the German Pietist Conrad Beissel in 1732. The community included male and female celibate orders, as well as a group of married householders; all pursued a rigorous spiritual existence emphasizing charity, self-discipline, and pursuit of non-material goals. The members excelled in such crafts as printing and bookmaking, and produced beautiful illuminated manuscripts which are still on view here in more than a dozen Medieval Germanic–style buildings. **Open:** Mon–Sat 9am–5pm, Sun noon–5pm. $$

Erie

The third-largest city in the state is on the shore of Lake Erie. Its bayfront is the backdrop for the US *Niagara*, a reconstruction of the ship used by Commodore Oliver Perry during the 1812 Battle of Lake Erie. Nearby Presque Isle, once Perry's headquarters, has been turned into a state park. **Information:** Tourist & Convention Bureau of Erie County, 1006 State St, Erie, 16501 (tel 814/454-7191).

HOTELS 🏨

🏨🏨🏨 Avalon Hotel
16 W 10th St, 16501 (Downtown); tel 814/459-2220 or toll free 800/822-5011; fax 814/459-2322. 10 blocks S of State St; exit off I-79 Bayfront Hwy. Extensively remodeled over the last several years, this period-furnished hotel is within walking distance of the Erie Playhouse and other downtown attractions. **Rooms:** 192 rms and stes. CI 2pm/CO 11am. Nonsmoking rms avail. Large rooms were recently refurbished in dark color scheme. Two floors of nonsmoking rooms. **Amenities:** 🛁 A/C, cable TV w/movies, voice mail. 1 unit w/terrace. Refrigerators in some rooms. **Services:** ✕ 🚐 🛎 🛎 **Facilities:** 🏋 ⟨1000⟩ ⟨ 1 restaurant, 1 bar. **Rates:** Peak (Mem Day–Labor Day) $64–$79 S or D; $74–$99 ste. Extra person $5. Children under age 16 stay free. Lower rates off-season. Parking: Indoor, free. AE, CB, DC, DISC, MC, V.

🏨🏨🏨 Bel Aire Hotel
2800 W 8th St, 16505; tel 814/833-1116 or toll free 800/888-8781; fax 814/838-3242. Exit 44B off I-79 W on 12th

St, N on PA 832, E on 8th St. A touch more luxurious than other hotels in the area, this well-maintained property is located near the entrance to Presque Isle State Park. **Rooms:** 151 rms and stes. CI 3pm/CO noon. Nonsmoking rms avail. Oldest rooms (dating from 1960 and 1983 and facing the parking lot) were renovated when a new batch of rooms were added in 1992. **Amenities:** 🛁 ⚙ 🖧 🍷 A/C, cable TV w/movies, dataport. Some units w/terraces. **Services:** ✕ 💷 🚐 🖼 ⤵ Babysitting. **Facilities:** 🛋 🏊 🍴 🍴 600 👤 2 restaurants (see ''Restaurants'' below), 1 bar (w/entertainment), sauna, whirlpool. Attractively landscaped pool has its own dining area. **Rates (CP):** Peak (May 15–Sept 15) $69–$109 S or D; $150–$200 ste. Extra person $10. Children under age 18 stay free. Min stay peak. Lower rates off-season. Parking: Outdoor, free. AE, CB, DC, DISC, MC, V.

🏨 Holiday Inn Downtown

18 W 18th St, 16501 (Downtown); tel 814/456-2961 or toll free 800/832-9101; fax 814/456-7067. 18 blocks S of State St exit off I-79 Bayfront Hwy. Despite a convenient downtown location, this motel suffers from a poor layout and a lack of maintenance. The outdoor balcony connecting all rooms has been enclosed, but the hallways can be cold. **Rooms:** 134 rms. CI 2pm/CO noon. Nonsmoking rms avail. Minimally furnished. **Amenities:** 🛁 ⚙ 🖧 A/C, cable TV w/movies, dataport. **Services:** ✕ 💷 🖼 ⤵ 🍽 Babysitting. **Facilities:** 🛋 🏊 200 👤 1 restaurant (bkfst and dinner only), 1 bar (w/entertainment), washer/dryer. **Rates (CP):** Peak (Mem Day–Labor Day) $80–$99 S or D. Extra person $4. Children under age 18 stay free. Min stay special events. Lower rates off-season. Parking: Outdoor, free. AE, CB, DC, DISC, MC, V.

MOTELS

🏨 Comfort Inn

8051 Peach St, 16509; tel 814/866-6666 or toll free 800/228-5150; fax 814/866-6666. Exit 6 off I-90. A well-tended property, convenient to I-90 and popular with interstate travelers. Comfortable lobby, with fireplace, is very welcoming. **Rooms:** 110 rms and stes. CI 3pm/CO noon. Nonsmoking rms avail. **Amenities:** 🛁 ⚙ A/C, satel TV w/movies, VCR. Some units w/terraces, some w/whirlpools. Some rooms have dataports. **Services:** 💷 🖼 ⤵ Videos available for rent. **Facilities:** 🛋 🏊 🍴 50 👤 Whirlpool. Guests may use indoor pool next door. **Rates (CP):** Peak (Apr 30–Nov 30) $90–$110 S or D; $110–$140 ste. Extra person $6. Children under age 18 stay free. Lower rates off-season. Parking: Outdoor, free. AE, CB, DC, DISC, ER, JCB, MC, V.

UNRATED Econo Lodge

8050 Peach St, 16509; tel 814/866-6666; fax 814/866-6666. Exit 6 off I-90 E. With a sculpture by a local artist in the lobby and an attractively landscaped pool area, this well-maintained motel was named 1995 Econo Lodge of the Year. **Rooms:** 97 rms. CI 3pm/CO noon. Nonsmoking rms avail. **Amenities:** 🛁 🍷 Cable TV w/movies. **Services:** ✕ 💷 ⤵ **Facilities:** 🛋 🚲

🍴 200 1 restaurant, sauna, whirlpool. Big-screen TV and bistro tables in lobby. **Rates (CP):** Peak (June–Oct) $70–$80 S; $90–$110 D. Extra person $6. Lower rates off-season. Parking: Indoor/outdoor, free. AE, CB, DC, DISC, JCB, MC, V.

🏨 Hampton Inn Erie

3041 W 12th St, 16505; tel 814/835-4200 or toll free 800/426-7866; fax 814/835-5212. 1½ mi W of exit 44B off I-79. Opened in late 1994, this fresh and cheery motel greets visitors with a neutral color scheme and Shaker-style furniture. **Rooms:** 100 rms. CI 3pm/CO noon. Nonsmoking rms avail. **Amenities:** 🛁 ⚙ A/C, cable TV w/movies, dataport. **Services:** 💷 🖼 ⤵ Coffee, tea, hot chocolate, and fresh fruit available 24 hours. Microwave in lobby. **Facilities:** 🛋 🏊 👤 **Rates (CP):** Peak (Mem Day–Labor Day) $89 S or D. Children under age 18 stay free. Min stay peak. Lower rates off-season. Parking: Outdoor, free. AE, CB, DC, DISC, MC, V.

🏨 Holiday Inn South

8040 Perry Hwy, 16509; tel 814/864-4911 or toll free 800/550-8040; fax 814/864-3743. Exit 7 off I-90. Three-building complex, convenient to I-90. **Rooms:** 216 rms. Executive level. CI 3pm/CO noon. Nonsmoking rms avail. **Amenities:** 🛁 ⚙ 🖧 A/C, satel TV w/movies, dataport. Some rooms have refrigerators. **Services:** ✕ 💷 🖼 ⤵ 🍽 Babysitting. Concierge in high season. **Facilities:** 🛋 🏊 300 👤 1 restaurant, 1 bar (w/entertainment), washer/dryer. Guests have privileges at nearby health club (not within walking distance). **Rates:** Peak (Mem Day–Labor Day) $89–$99 S or D. Extra person $6. Children under age 18 stay free. Lower rates off-season. Parking: Outdoor, free. AE, CB, DC, DISC, JCB, MC, V.

🏨 Howard Johnson Bed & Breakfast

7575 Peach St, 16509; tel 814/864-4811 or toll free 800/446-4656; fax 814/864-4811. Exit 6 off I-90. These four buildings have an awkward layout and dated exteriors—and the place needs some maintenance—but the rooms are surprisingly pleasant. **Rooms:** 110 rms. Executive level. CI 3pm/CO noon. Nonsmoking rms avail. Large rooms, with vaulted ceilings. **Amenities:** 🛁 A/C, satel TV. All units w/terraces. Refrigerators, coffeemakers, and alarm clocks in some rooms. **Services:** 💷 🖼 ⤵ 🍽 **Facilities:** 🛋 🏊 85 👤 Games rm, sauna, washer/dryer. Hallways are dark. **Rates (CP):** Peak (Mem Day–Labor Day) $79 S; $99 D. Extra person $10. Children under age 18 stay free. Lower rates off-season. Parking: Outdoor, free. AE, DC, DISC, MC, V.

🏨 Ramada Inn

6101 Wattsburg Rd, 16509; tel 814/825-3100 or toll free 800/374-1875; fax 814/825-0857. The dated exterior is decorated in shades of purple, pink, and green, but thankfully the rooms are tasteful and newly furnished. Sandwiched between the highway and a tractor-trailer sales yard. **Rooms:** 121 rms and stes. CI 3pm/CO noon. Nonsmoking rms avail. Privacy divider bisects large rooms. **Amenities:** ⚙ 🖧 A/C, cable TV w/movies, dataport. No phone. VCRs and refrigerators available. **Services:** ✗ 🚐 🛏 🛎 Babysitting. **Facilities:** 🏋 🏊 200 ♿ 1 restaurant, 1 bar (w/entertainment), basketball, volleyball, games rm, washer/dryer. **Rates:** Peak (June–Sept) $75 S; $85 D; $65–$100 ste. Extra person $8. Children under age 18 stay free. Lower rates off-season. Parking: Outdoor, free. AE, CB, DC, DISC, JCB, MC, V.

☰☰ Scott's Beachcomber Inn

2930 W 6th St, 16505; tel 814/838-1961. Shabby but proud, this conveniently located motel is awaiting renovation under its new owners. At entrance to Presque Isle State Park and within walking distance of Waldameer Park and Water World. **Rooms:** 58 rms, stes, and effic. CI noon/CO 11am. Nonsmoking rms avail. Outdated design, although wallpaper and art are recent. Small bathrooms. **Amenities:** 🛁 🛎 A/C, cable TV. Refrigerators and microwaves available. **Services:** 🛎 **Facilities:** 🏋 ♿ 1 beach (lake shore), lifeguard, lawn games, playground. Large play area. **Rates:** Peak (Mem Day–Labor Day) $90 S or D; $150 ste; $95 effic. Extra person $5. Children under age 12 stay free. Lower rates off-season. Parking: Outdoor, free. AE, DC, DISC, MC, V.

RESTAURANTS 🍽

Hoppers Brewpub

123 W 14th St (Downtown); tel 814/452-2787. 6 blocks S of State St exit off I-79 Bayfront Hwy. **Regional American/Pub.** Erie's refurbished art deco–style Union Station is still in use for trains, but it also contains this fun restaurant and microbrewery. A glass wall allows guests to watch the brewing process. Beer is used in all the recipes, like beer-batter cod, beer onion soup, beer bread, and beef on wick. **FYI:** Reservations accepted. Guitar. Children's menu. BYO. **Open:** Mon–Wed 11:30am–10pm, Thurs–Sat 11:30am–midnight, Sun 11am–8pm. **Prices:** Main courses $5–$16. AE, DISC, MC, V. 🍷 🍴 ♿

Marketplace Grill

319 State St (Downtown); tel 814/455-7272. 3 blocks S of State St exit off I-79 Bayfront Hwy. **American.** The dark brick and wood interior of this former 1890s tool and die factory is decorated with antique photos and oversized oil paintings. The extensive menu includes beef, chicken, seafood, pasta, salad and low-fat entrees; an all-you-can-eat pizza, pasta, and salad bar is offered at lunch time. **FYI:** Reservations accepted. Children's menu. **Open:** Mon–Thurs 11:30am–9:30pm, Fri–Sat 11:30am–11pm. **Prices:** Main courses $6–$16. AE, DC, DISC, MC, V. 🗹 ♿

Maxi's/Terrace Cafe

In Bel Aire Hotel, 2800 W 8th St; tel 814/838-9270. Exit 44-B off I-79, W on 12th St, N on PA 832, E on 8th St. **New American/Cafe.** Diners may choose from the bright umbrella-topped tables at the poolside terrace, an informal lounge, or a formal dining room. Sandwiches and salads are popular here, as well as hearty entrees like fresh tuna with fennel, sliced tenderloins of beef, roast pork loin with Dijon sauce, and tournedos of beef Rossini. **FYI:** Reservations accepted.

Guitar/jazz. Children's menu. **Open:** Daily 7am–midnight. **Prices:** Main courses $5–$31. AE, CB, DC, DISC, MC, V. ♥ 🍷 🗹 VP ♿

⑤ ✹ Plymouth Tavern Restaurant

1109 State St (Downtown); tel 814/453-6454. 11 blocks S of State St exit off I-79 Bayfront Hwy. **Pub.** The three buildings occupied by "The Plymouth" date to the late 19th century, and an interior of exposed brick and beams reflects their simple roots. Except for a few salads and one stir-fry dish, the menu consists entirely of sandwiches and burgers. **FYI:** Reservations accepted. **Open:** Mon–Sat 11am–2am, Sun 1pm–2am. **Prices:** Main courses $3–$5. No CC. 🍷 🍴 ♿

Pufferbelly

414 French St (Downtown); tel 814/454-1557. 4 blocks S of State St exit off I-79 Bayfront Hwy. **New American.** Eclectic and whimsical decor features a fire pole, knickknacks from several of Erie's grandest 19th-century homes, and a collection of firefighting equipment (including pumps, hooks, hoses, hats, and uniforms). The menu changes seasonally, but always features "hearty and healthy" cuisine, with a good selection of Southwestern and vegetarian dishes. **FYI:** Reservations accepted. Guitar/singer. Children's menu. **Open:** Mon–Thurs 11:30am–9:30pm, Fri 11:30am–10pm, Sat 11:30am–11pm, Sun 11am–8pm. **Prices:** Main courses $10–$16. AE, DISC, MC, V. 🖥 🍷 🍴 ♿

Smuggler's Wharf

3 State St; tel 814/459-4273. ¼ mi N of State St exit off I-79 Bayfront Hwy. **New American/Seafood.** Nautical-theme dining room (right on the bayfront at the city's public dock) includes three large fresh-water aquaria. New England clam chowder is a menu specialty. **FYI:** Reservations accepted. Piano/violin. Children's menu. **Open:** Peak (Mem Day–Labor Day) daily 11am–11pm. **Prices:** Main courses $7–$17. AE, MC, V. 🍷 🍴 🖼 🗹

Sweetwater Grill

2835 W 8th St; tel 814/835-7395. Exit 44B off I-79, W on 12th St. **American.** Large tables seat families or groups comfortably in this pleasant room near Presque Isle State Park. Brick-oven pizzas, fresh seafood, fresh pasta, and steaks are among the menu highlights. Selection of low-fat entrees also available. **FYI:** Reservations accepted. Children's menu. No smoking. **Open:** Mon–Fri 11:30am–10pm, Sat 5–10pm, Sun 11am–9pm. **Prices:** Main courses $6–$13. AE, DC, DISC, MC, V. 🗹

ATTRACTIONS 🏛

Erie Historical Museum and Planetarium

356 W 6th St; tel 814/871-5790. The museum occupies the Watston/Curtze Mansion, built by an Erie industrialist in 1889. The Richardsonian Romanesque building makes use of distinctive features such as mosaics, friezes, pre-milled decorative woodwork, and stained glass. The first floor contains period rooms and objects, including some of the original

furnishings. The other floors are given over to changing exhibitions on regional history and decorative arts and a rotating exhibit of works by Eugene Iverd, known for his cover illustrations for the *Saturday Evening Post*. The planetarium, open on Sundays (additional fee required), is housed in the former carriage house. **Open:** Peak (June–Aug) Tues–Fri 10am–5pm, Sat–Sun 1–5pm. Reduced hours off-season. **$**

Erie Art Museum
411 State St; tel 814/459-5477. Housed in the city's Old Custom House (circa 1839), this museum presents temporary exhibitions ranging from photography to lithography to installation art. The museum also has concerts, lectures, and workshops in everything from watercoloring to framemaking. **Open:** Tues–Sat 11am–5pm, Sun 1–5pm. **$**

Flagship *Niagara*
150 E Front St; tel 814/871-4596. A reconstruction of one of the brigs that took part in the Battle of Lake Erie in 1813, the *Niagara* actually contains a few of the original ship's timbers. (This was the battle of which Commodore Oliver Hazard Perry made his famous report, "We have met the enemy and they are ours.") The construction of Perry's fleet was a marvel in itself, requiring the importation of material and craftsmen from as far away as Pittsburgh and Philadelphia. The 198-foot vessel was rebuilt in 1913, 1933, and most recently in 1990. The ship will soon be the focus of a new nautical museum, and may be sailing in 1997. **Open:** Mon–Sat 9am–5pm, Sun 1–5pm. **$$**

Presque Isle State Park
PA 832; tel 814/871-4251. Presque Isle State Park, located on a seven-mile-long peninsula jutting into Lake Erie, is a 3,200-acre haven for outdoors enthusiasts. Many recreational opportunities are available, including boating, swimming, fishing (perch, walleye, and rainbow trout are especially plentiful), scuba diving, bird-watching, cross-country skiing, and duck hunting during the season. Miles of hiking trails traverse the peninsula. A visitor's center contains displays about the area's ecology, and educational programs are available. At the eastern end of the peninsula is the **Gull Point Natural Area,** an important habitat for nesting and migratory birds which is closed to the public except during the winter months. **Open:** Peak (Mem Day–Labor Day) daily 5am–11pm. Reduced hours off-season. **Free**

Penn Shore Winery and Vineyards
10225 East Lake Rd, North East; tel 814/725-8688. Tours of these caverns and vineyards, located in Concord grape territory, allow visitors to learn about the vintner's art. **Open:** Mon–Sat 9am–5:30pm, Sun 11am–5pm. **Free**

Erwinna

Bucks County town on the Delaware River north of Philadelphia. Home to noted winery.

RESTAURANT 🍴

Golden Pheasant Inn Restaurant
In Golden Pheasant Inn, 763 River Rd; tel 610/294-9595. **French.** The three dining rooms in this 1857 fieldstone house (situated between a canal and a river) enjoy lovely views. The interior has exposed beams, wood floors, and antique furnishings, and a deck and greenhouse are open in spring and summer. Menu specialties include rack of lamb and fresh seafood. **FYI:** Reservations recommended. No smoking. **Open:** Tues–Sun 5:30–9pm, Sun 11am–8pm. **Prices:** Main courses $16–$24. AE, CB, DC, DISC, MC, V. 🍷

Farmington

This township of just over 1,000 is the site of the state's largest cave as well as Fort Necessity National Battlefield, commemorating Washington's first battle and the start of the French and Indian War.

LODGE 🏨

≣≣ Summit Inn Resort
2 Skyline Dr, 15437; tel 412/438-8594 or toll free 800/433-8594. 1,200 acres. Thomas Edison, Henry Ford, and other notable guests have stayed in this 1907 inn. The two-story lobby still has its original mission-style furniture. **Rooms:** 94 rms and stes. CI 4pm/CO noon. Nonsmoking rms avail. Most rooms are spacious, but the decor is dated. **Amenities:** 🗄 ⚲ A/C, cable TV. **Services:** ✕ 🚗 ⏰ Social director, babysitting. **Facilities:** 🏌 ▸9 🏇 🏊 ⚽2 🎱 500 1 restaurant, 2 bars (1 w/entertainment), volleyball, games rm, lawn games, whirlpool. Olympic-size outdoor pool. **Rates:** $60–$85 S; $69–$95 D; $125 ste. Extra person $10. Children under age 13 stay free. Min stay wknds. MAP rates avail. Parking: Outdoor, free. Two-night minimum stay on weekends; three-night minimum stay on holiday weekends. Closed mid-Nov–mid-Apr. AE, DISC, MC, V.

RESORT

≣≣≣≣ Nemacolin Woodlands Resort
US 40, PO Box 188, 15437; tel 412/329-8555 or toll free 800/422-2736; fax 412/329-6153. 1,000 acres. An extremely attractive and well-run resort with elegant public spaces. Hundreds of pieces from the owner's $20 million art collection, including large Tiffany glass panels, works by Alexander Calder, and sculpture by Seward Johnson, are on display. The new 124-room luxury wing (scheduled to open in 1997) is patterned after the Ritz Hotel in Paris. **Rooms:** 98 rms and stes; 40 cottages/villas. CI 3pm/CO 11am. Nonsmoking rms avail. Decor varies from one room to another but all are nicely coordinated and cheerful. **Amenities:** 🗄 ⚲ 🍽 A/C, satel TV w/movies, dataport, voice mail, bathrobes. All units w/minibars, some w/terraces, some w/whirlpools. **Services:** 🍴 🔑 VP 🚗 🛳 ⏰ Twice-daily maid svce, social director,

masseur, children's program, babysitting. Daily tours of the art collection conducted by hotel staff. **Facilities:** 🔥 🚲 ⚓ ⛰ ▶36 🏊 🎿 🎣 🎿 🎱 📺4 🎮 📞 💻 ♿ 6 restaurants (*see* "Restaurants" below), 5 bars (2 w/entertainment), basketball, volleyball, games rm, lawn games, racquetball, spa, sauna, steam rm, whirlpool, beauty salon, playground. Small ski hill and chair lift with day lodge. Full-service spa features Frank Lloyd Wright reproduction furniture. Separate steam/sauna/whirlpool for men and women. **Rates:** Peak (Mem Day–Oct) $215–$225 S or D; $250–$395 ste; $185 cottage/villa. Extra person $20. Children under age 12 stay free. Min stay peak, wknds, and special events. Lower rates off-season. AP and MAP rates avail. Parking: Indoor, free. Spa, golf, and holiday packages avail. AE, CB, DC, MC, V.

RESTAURANTS 🍴

★ The Allures
In Nemacolin Woodlands Resort, US 40; tel 412/329-8555. **New American/Spa.** A casual eatery featuring creative, healthful fare like salmon fillet, and pan-seared turkey breast with potato-apple hash. Menu items from the resort's premier dining room are available during dinner hours. **FYI:** Reservations accepted. **Open:** Breakfast daily 7–11am; lunch daily 11am–5pm; dinner daily 6–10pm. **Prices:** Main courses $10–$18. AE, CB, DC, MC, V. 🅥🅟 ♿

Coal Baron
US 40 W, Uniontown; tel 412/439-0111. **Seafood/Steak.** The dining room is not snazzy, but the beef, seafood, veal and pasta specialties get a strong positive response from local reviewers. **FYI:** Reservations recommended. Children's menu. **Open:** Tues–Sat 4–11pm, Sun noon–8pm. **Prices:** Main courses $9–$48. AE, DC, DISC, MC, V. 🅥🅟

Fogelsville

Small Lehigh County town just west of Allentown.

INN 🏨

🏳🏳🏳🏳 Glasbern
2141 Pack House Rd, 18051; tel 610/285-4723; fax 610/285-2862. Exit 14B off I-78. 100 acres. A tranquil spot with extensive grounds. Flower, vegetable, and herb gardens sprinkle the landscape, and there are two trout ponds on the premises. The common room has a striking fireplace and the entire inn is furnished with fine antiques. **Rooms:** 24 rms and stes. CI 4pm/CO noon. Nonsmoking rms avail. **Amenities:** 🔥 ⚓ 🍴 A/C, cable TV w/movies, refrig, dataport, VCR, voice mail, bathrobes. Some units w/terraces, some w/fireplaces, some w/whirlpools. **Services:** ✕ 🛏 🍴 **Facilities:** 🔥 🎿 🍴20 ♿ 1 restaurant (bkfst and dinner only), 1 bar, whirlpool. **Rates (BB):** $95–$150 S; $110–$135 D; $145–$300 ste. Extra person $20. Min stay wknds and special events. Higher rates for special events/hols. Parking: Outdoor, free. MC, V.

Franklin

In the state's northwest region, Franklin was laid out in 1795 on a tract of 1,000 acres belonging to the state. Named for nearby Fort Franklin. **Information:** Venango County Area Tourist Promo Agency, 213 12th St, Franklin, 16323 (tel 814/432-8005).

HOTEL 🏨

🏳🏳🏳 The Inn at Franklin
1411 Liberty St, 16323; tel 814/437-3031 or toll free 800/437-3031; fax 814/437-7481. PA 8 to right on Liberty St. Bright, clean hotel decorated with old photographs of the area. **Rooms:** 83 rms. CI 2pm/CO 11am. Nonsmoking rms avail. Large and comfortable rooms. **Amenities:** 🔥 ⚓ 🍴 A/C, cable TV w/movies. 1 unit w/whirlpool. **Services:** ✕ 🚗 🛏 🍴 🍴 Complimentary passes to nearby YMCA. **Facilities:** 🎿 🍴 🍴400 💻 ♿ 1 restaurant, 1 bar (w/entertainment), beauty salon. **Rates (CP):** $60–$65 S or D. Extra person $5. Children under age 21 stay free. Parking: Outdoor, free. AE, CB, DC, DISC, MC, V.

Frazer

HOTEL 🏨

🏳🏳🏳 Sheraton Great Valley Hotel
707 Lancaster Ave, 19355; tel 610/524-5500 or toll free 800/325-3535; fax 610/524-1808. PA 30 and PA 202. This modern hotel is adjacent to a restaurant in an 18th-century house, and the historic theme of the region carries over to both. Antique furniture and fireplaces throughout. **Rooms:** 154 rms and stes. Executive level. CI 4pm/CO noon. Nonsmoking rms avail. Nicely furnished rooms. **Amenities:** 🔥 ⚓ 🍴 🍴 A/C, cable TV w/movies, dataport, voice mail. All units w/minibars, some w/whirlpools. **Services:** ✕ 🚗 🛏 🍴 Car-rental desk, babysitting. **Facilities:** 🔥 🍴 🍴200 ♿ 1 restaurant, 1 bar (w/entertainment), whirlpool, washer/dryer. Exceptionally attractive pool in sunroom. Guests have access to nearby fitness club. **Rates:** $145 S or D; $195–$395 ste. Extra person $15. Children under age 5 stay free. Parking: Outdoor, free. AE, DC, DISC, MC, V.

RESTAURANT 🍴

White Horse Restaurant
In Sheraton Great Valley Hotel, 707 Lancaster Ave; tel 610/524-5500. **Continental.** The building has been a public house since 1763, and colonial decor and candlelight dining preserve the mood in the intimate rooms. House specialties include filet mignon and assorted seafood and poultry dishes. **FYI:** Reservations recommended. Piano/singer. Dress code. **Open:** Breakfast Mon–Sat 6:30–11am, Sun 7:30–11am;

lunch daily 11:30am–noon; dinner daily 5:30–9:30pm. **Prices:** Main courses $12–$23. AE, DC, DISC, MC, V.

Gettysburg

Incorporated in 1806, this historic town near the Maryland border was the site of the decisive battle of the Civil War, which led to President Lincoln's famous Gettysburg Address. Both are commemorated at Gettysburg National Military Park Battlefield, the country's premiere battlefield shrine with 1,000 monuments and cannons along 35 scenic miles. **Information:** Gettysburg Travel Council, 35 Carlisle St, Gettysburg, 17325 (tel 717/334-6274).

HOTELS

Best Western Gettysburg Hotel 1797

1 Lincoln Sq, 17325; tel 717/337-2000 or toll free 800/528-1234; fax 717/337-2075. At jct US 30/Bus US 15. This six-story building in the center of town dates from 1797, but it was gutted by fire in 1980 and remained closed until 1990. Lots of history was made inside; it was the summer White House during Eisenhower's administration and is on the historical walking tour of the town. **Rooms:** 113 rms. CI 2pm/CO 11am. Nonsmoking rms avail. The largest rooms, facing the square, have sofas, hot tubs, and fireplaces. **Amenities:** A/C, cable TV. Some units w/fireplaces, some w/whirlpools. **Services:** Babysitting. Afternoon tea and cookies in the lobby. **Facilities:** 100 1 restaurant, 1 bar (w/entertainment). **Rates:** Peak (Apr–Oct) $95–$110 S; $105–$150 D. Extra person $10. Children under age 18 stay free. Lower rates off-season. Parking: Outdoor, free. AE, CB, DC, DISC, MC, V.

Holiday Inn Battlefield

516 Baltimore St, 17325; tel 717/334-6211 or toll free 800/HOLIDAY; fax 717/334-7183. At jct Bus US 15 S/PA 97 S. This five-story building is adjacent to the battlefield tours office and within walking distance of other museums. **Rooms:** 102 rms. CI 3pm/CO 11am. Nonsmoking rms avail. King rooms have sofa beds. **Amenities:** A/C, cable TV w/movies. **Services:** Babysitting. **Facilities:** 300 1 restaurant, 1 bar. **Rates:** Peak (Apr–Oct) $89–$105 S or D. Extra person $7. Children under age 19 stay free. Lower rates off-season. Parking: Outdoor, free. Corporate and AARP discounts avail. AE, CB, DC, DISC, JCB, MC, V.

MOTELS

Comfort Inn

871 York Rd, 17325; tel 717/337-2400 or toll free 800/228-5150; fax 717/337-2400. On US 30 E, 1½ mi W of jct US 15/US 30. Updated furnishings and security measures have made this an even more attractive place to stay. **Rooms:** 81 rms and stes. CI 2pm/CO 11am. Nonsmoking rms avail. **Amenities:** A/C, cable TV w/movies, dataport. Some units w/whirlpools. VCRs and hairdryers available upon request. **Services:** Battlefield tours leave from the motel. Complimentary 24-hour coffee. **Facilities:** 40 Whirlpool. Miniature golf, video arcade, and batting cage adjacent to motel. **Rates (CP):** Peak (June–Aug) $77–$82 S; $87–$90 D; $140 ste. Extra person $5. Children under age 17 stay free. Lower rates off-season. Parking: Outdoor, free. AE, CB, DC, DISC, JCB, MC, V.

Days Inn

865 York Rd, 17325; tel 717/337-0030 or toll free 800/DAYS-INN; fax 717/337-1002. On US 30 E, 1½ mi E of jct Bus US 15/US 30. Attractive motel with recently redecorated rooms. The lobby has an unusual and dramatic-looking sunken seating area, and area attractions are close by. **Rooms:** 113 rms. CI 2pm/CO noon. Nonsmoking rms avail. **Amenities:** A/C, cable TV w/movies, dataport. **Services:** Babysitting. Tours pick up at door. **Facilities:** 120 Games rm, washer/dryer. One block to game room and Family Fun Center with batting cages. Free passes to local YMCA with indoor pool. **Rates:** Peak (June–Oct) $62–$75 S; $80–$85 D. Extra person $5. Children under age 18 stay free. Lower rates off-season. Parking: Outdoor, free. Ski, shopping, and sightseeing packages avail. AE, CB, DC, DISC, MC, V.

Holiday Inn Express

869 York Rd, 17325; tel 717/337-1400 or toll free 800/HOLIDAY; fax 717/337-1400. On US 30 E, 1½ mi E of jct US 30/Bus US 15. Fresh accommodations in a historic atmosphere. Lobby is open and inviting. **Rooms:** 51 rms and stes. CI 2pm/CO 11am. Nonsmoking rms avail. **Amenities:** A/C, cable TV w/movies, dataport. **Services:** Battlefield tours available. **Facilities:** 15 Whirlpool. Indoor heated pool. Adjacent to family entertainment center. **Rates (CP):** Peak (Apr–Oct) $79–$89 S; $89–$99 D; $109–$129 ste. Extra person $10. Children under age 20 stay free. Min stay special events. Lower rates off-season. Parking: Outdoor, free. AE, CB, DC, DISC, MC, V.

Howard Johnson Lodge

301 Steinwehr Ave, 17325; tel 717/334-1188 or toll free 800/446-4656; fax 717/334-1188. On Bus US 15 S of town center. A small, well-maintained motel centered around a sizable pool. **Rooms:** 77 rms and effic. CI open/CO noon. Nonsmoking rms avail. Cabana rooms with king beds open directly to the pool area. **Amenities:** A/C, cable TV w/movies. All units w/terraces. **Services:** Babysitting. **Facilities:** 75 1 restaurant, 1 bar. **Rates:** Peak (Apr–Nov) $55–$99 S or D; $65–$109 effic. Children under age 18 stay free. Lower rates off-season. Parking: Outdoor, free. AE, CB, DC, DISC, JCB, MC, V.

≣≣≣ **Quality Inn Gettysburg Motor Lodge**
380 Steinwehr Ave, 17325; tel 717/334-1103 or toll free 800/228-5151; fax 717/334-1103. On Bus US 15 S, 1 mi from jct Bus US 15/US 30. Close to the battlefield and tour centers, this two-story motel was recently updated with a new indoor pool and luxury rooms. **Rooms:** 109 rms, stes, and effic. CI open/CO noon. Nonsmoking rms avail. **Amenities:** 🛢 🐾 🖪 A/C, cable TV. All units w/terraces, some w/whirlpools. Hairdryers on request. **Services:** 🛎 🕭 Babysitting. 24-hour coffee in lobby. **Facilities:** 🔚 🏌 🖻 🍴 🛗 1 bar, sauna, whirlpool, washer/dryer. Putting green. **Rates:** Peak (Apr–Oct) $67–$104 S or D; $92–$129 ste; $77–$114 effic. Children under age 18 stay free. Lower rates off-season. Parking: Outdoor, free. AE, CB, DC, DISC, MC, V.

≣≣≣ **Quality Inn Larson's**
401 Buford Ave, 17325; tel 717/334-3141 or toll free 800/228-5151; fax 717/334-1813. On US 30 W, 8 blks W of jct US 30 W/Bus US 15 S. Housed in a one-story, colonial style building next door to the old stone house that served as General Lee's headquarters. **Rooms:** 41 rms, stes, and effic. CI 3pm/CO noon. Nonsmoking rms avail. End rooms have two windows; one looks across the battlefield. **Amenities:** 🛢 🐾 A/C, cable TV. 1 unit w/terrace, 1 w/whirlpool. Complimentary coffee and tea. Some rooms have dataports, some have two phones. **Services:** 🖪 🕭 Babysitting. Battlefield tours available. **Facilities:** 🔚 🏌 🖻 🚹 1 restaurant, 1 bar, washer/dryer. **Rates:** Peak (Apr–Nov) $68–$80 S or D; $125–$165 ste; $125–$165 effic. Extra person $5. Children under age 18 stay free. Lower rates off-season. Parking: Outdoor, free. AE, CB, DC, DISC, JCB, MC, V.

INN

≣≣≣ **The Old Appleford Inn**
218 Carlisle St, 17325; tel 717/337-1711 or toll free 800/275-3373; fax 717/334-6228. On Bus US 15, 2 blks from jct US 30/Bus US 15. This large, brick Italianate mansion was built in 1867, and its rooms are named for Civil War figures. The parlor has a grand piano, and the sunroom is filled with plants. Unsuitable for children under 12. **Rooms:** 11 rms. CI 2pm/CO 11am. No smoking. Each room is individually decorated; two have canopy beds. **Amenities:** 🐾 A/C. No phone or TV. Some units w/fireplaces. **Services:** Babysitting, afternoon tea and wine/sherry served. Friendly staff. **Facilities:** Guest lounge. **Rates (BB):** Peak (Apr–Nov) $73–$93 S; $83–$113 D. Extra person $10. Lower rates off-season. Parking: Outdoor, free. AE, DISC, MC, V.

RESORT

≣≣≣≣ **Eisenhower Inn & Conference Center**
2634 Emmitsburg Rd, 17325; tel 717/334-8121 or toll free 800/776-8349; fax 717/334-6066. 5 mi S of town on Bus US 15. 75 acres. The sprawling, two-story main building encloses extensive meeting facilities and is surrounded by outdoor spaces ideal for picnicking. Some rooms open to the central atrium, others to a courtyard. **Rooms:** 203 rms and stes. CI 3pm/CO 11am. Nonsmoking rms avail. Larger-than-average rooms. **Amenities:** 🛢 🐾 A/C, cable TV w/movies, dataport. Some units w/terraces. King rooms have hairdryers. Refrigerators available. **Services:** ✕ 🖪 🕭 **Facilities:** 🔚 🎣 ▶₅ 🏊 🎿 🍴₂ 🎳 🖻 🚹 1 restaurant, 1 bar, basketball, volleyball, games rm, racquetball, sauna, whirlpool, washer/dryer. Picnic area with grills; fishing lake. Allstar Family Fun and Sports Complex with water ride, go-carts, and games. **Rates:** Peak (Apr–Oct) $87–$125 S or D; $175–$200 ste. Extra person $7. Children under age 19 stay free. Min stay special events. Lower rates off-season. Parking: Outdoor, free. Government and military discounts avail. AE, DISC, MC, V.

RESTAURANTS 🍽

Dobbin House Tavern
89 Steinwehr Ave; tel 717/334-2100. On US Bus 15 S near PA 975. **American.** Six rooms in this 1776 house are used for dining; full colonial and continental dinners are served upstairs and light fare downstairs in the Springhouse Tavern. Steaks and seafood anchor the menu. **FYI:** Reservations accepted. Jazz. Children's menu. **Open:** Peak (Apr–Nov) daily 5–9pm. **Prices:** Main courses $15–$30. AE, MC, V. ▪ 🍷 🚹

Farnsworth House
401 Baltimore St; tel 717/334-8838. 4 blks from Lincoln Sq on Bus US 15 S. **American.** More than a restaurant, this 1810 house holds a museum, a bookstore, an art gallery, and a tavern. Relics surround the rooms, and Civil War history is everywhere. The menu features authentic 19th-century recipes, including a fresh game pie stuffed with pheasant, duck, and turkey. **FYI:** Reservations recommended. Children's menu. No smoking. **Open:** Peak (Apr–Nov) daily 5–9:30pm. Closed Jan. **Prices:** Main courses $13–$18. AE, DISC, MC, V. ▪ 🍷 🖼

The Herr Tavern & Publick House
900 Chambersburg Rd; tel 717/334-4332. 1⅓ mi W of town on US 30. **American/Continental.** There are plenty of war relics in this 1816 tavern, as it is right on the battleground. The marble bar is impressive and the outdoor garden patio attractive. The cuisine goes beyond traditional American dishes, with an extensive wine list to back it up. **FYI:** Reservations recommended. Children's menu. **Open:** Mon–Sat 11am–9pm, Sun 5–9pm. **Prices:** Main courses $14–$20. AE, DISC, MC, V. ▪ 👥 🚹

ATTRACTIONS 🏛

Gettysburg National Military Park
Taneytown Rd; tel 717/334-1124. The Battle of Gettysburg, which took place here in July 1863, was the turning point of the Civil War. The battle put an end to Confederate incursions into the North, but the costs to both sides were astonishing. During the exhausting three-day battle, more shells were fired than in all the battles of the Napoleonic

wars, and there were a total of 51,000 casualties. President Lincoln returned to the battle site in November and gave his famous address. The battlefield includes the spot of "Pickett's Charge" and Seminary Ridge. (Guides are available but must be reserved in advance.) A cyclorama center offers a 356-foot painting of the battle, along with movies depicting the course of the fighting, and there is a 305-foot battlefield observation tower. Gettysburg National Cemetery is next to the park. **Open:** Daily 6am–10pm. **Free**

Eisenhower National Historic Site

97 Taneytown Rd; tel 717/334-1124. President Dwight Eisenhower and his wife Mamie bought the Allen Redding farm, next to Gettysburg National Military Park, as their retirement home. After leaving the White House in 1961, the Eisenhowers expanded the farm to a 230-acre estate and built the Georgian-style home, and experimented with farming and cattle breeding. Such global luminaries as Nikita Khruschev, Konrad Adenauer, and Charles de Gaulle visited the Eisenhowers during their years here. Access to the site is by shuttle bus only; tickets are available at the Gettyburg National Military Park visitors center. **Open:** Peak (Apr–Oct) daily 9am–4pm. Reduced hours off-season. **$$**

Greensburg

First settled in 1782, this residential town is located in the southern Alleghenies, a region of natural beauty and outdoor fun.

HOTELS 🏨

≣≣≣ Four Points Hotel Greensburg

100 Sheraton Dr (PA 30 E), 15601; tel 412/836-6060 or toll free 800/325-3535; fax 412/834-5640. Part of Sheraton's full-service, mid-scale chain, this property is undergoing a major renovation in 1996–1997. **Rooms:** 145 rms and stes. CI 3pm/CO noon. Nonsmoking rms avail. **Amenities:** 🛗 🍸 🖥 🍷 A/C, cable TV w/movies, dataport. Some units w/whirlpools. VCRs available. **Services:** 🍴 🚗 🖼 🛎 **Facilities:** 🏋 ▶9 🏊 🕭 1 restaurant, 1 bar (w/entertainment), volleyball, games rm, sauna. USGA-rated golf course. **Rates:** Peak (May–Dec) $84 S; $89 D; $140 ste. Extra person $5. Children under age 18 stay free. Lower rates off-season. MAP rates avail. Parking: Outdoor, free. AE, DC, DISC, MC, V.

≣≣≣ Mountain View Inn

101 Village Dr, 15601; tel 412/834-5300 or toll free 800/537-8709; fax 412/834-5304. Each of the three wings of this historic 1924 inn has a slightly different ambience. Public areas feature pine paneling, antiques, and fireplaces. **Rooms:** 56 rms and stes. Executive level. CI 3pm/CO noon. All have brass, canopied, or four-poster beds and coral wallpaper. Original section has the smallest rooms, Innkeeper's wing has the largest. **Amenities:** 🛗 🍸 🖥 A/C, satel TV, dataport.

Services: 🍴 🚗 🖼 🛎 Social director, babysitting. **Facilities:** 🏋 🏊 🖥 🕭 1 restaurant, 1 bar. The grounds have ponds and gazebos, and are popular for weddings. **Rates (CP):** $59–$95 S or D; $95–$120 ste. Extra person $8. Children under age 16 stay free. Parking: Outdoor, free. Weekday rates are lower. AE, DC, DISC, MC, V.

ATTRACTION 🎫

Bushy Run Battlefield

PA 993W, Jeanette; tel 412/527-5584. The site of Chief Pontiac's defeat by British forces in 1763. The battle marked the beginning of the decline of the Ottawa chief's rebellion, which had unified the Native American tribes against the colonists, and made possible the colonization of this part of Pennsylvania by European settlers. Guided tours available; the visitors center has exhibits relating to the era of the battle. **Open:** Wed–Sat 9am–5pm, Sun noon–5pm. **$**

Harrisburg

See also Carlisle, Hershey, Hummelstown, Mechanicsburg

The state capitol features a scenic and lively waterfront, numerous appealing parks, bathing beaches, cultural events, and historical sites. First laid out in 1785, Harrisburg was settled by representatives of several German religious sects and by Scotch-Irish immigrants. Today it remains a railway and industrial center. City Island, in the middle of the Susquehanna River, is a major recreational center. **Information:** Harrisburg-Hershey-Carlisle Tourism & Convention Bureau, 114 Walnut St, PO Box 969, Harrisburg, 17108 (tel 717/232-1377 or toll free 800/995-0969).

HOTELS 🏨

≣≣≣ Best Western Hotel Crown Park

765 Eisenhower Blvd, 17111; tel 717/558-9500 or toll free 800/253-0238; fax 717/558-8956. Exit 1 (PA 441) off I-283. This friendly, hilltop hotel caters to families visiting Hershey Park. **Rooms:** 167 rms and stes. CI 3pm/CO noon. Nonsmoking rms avail. Most rooms have sofa beds; some have irons, ironing boards, and hair dryers. **Amenities:** 🛗 🍸 🖥 A/C, cable TV w/movies, dataport, voice mail. **Services:** ✕ 🆅🅿 🚗 🖼 🛎 🛗 Twice-daily maid svce, babysitting. **Facilities:** 🏋 🍴 🏊 🕭 1 restaurant (bkfst only), 1 bar, sauna, whirlpool. Children under 12 eat free in restaurant. **Rates (BB):** Peak (Mem Day–Labor Day) $99–$109 S or D; $150 ste. Extra person $10. Children under age 12 stay free. Lower rates off-season. AP rates avail. Parking: Outdoor, free. Hershey Park package includes room, tickets, pizza, and gifts for children. AE, CB, DC, DISC, MC, V.

≣≣≣ Harrisburg Hilton & Towers

1 N 2nd St, 17101 (Downtown); tel 717/233-6000 or toll free 800/HILTONS; fax 717/233-6271. Capitol/2nd St exit off I-83 N ½ mi. Most locals consider this to be downtown

Harrisburg's best hotel. The stately yet modern building is near government offices, shopping, and the Museum of Scientific Discovery. **Rooms:** 341 rms and stes. Executive level. CI 3pm/CO noon. Nonsmoking rms avail. **Amenities:** A/C, cable TV w/movies, refrig, dataport. Some units w/terraces. Most rooms have fax machines. **Services:** X VP Car-rental desk, social director, children's program, babysitting. Vacation Station program for children in summer. **Facilities:** 2 restaurants, 2 bars (1 w/entertainment). **Rates:** Peak (Mar–June/Sept–Thanksgiving) $94–$144 S or D; $200–$500 ste. Extra person $10. Children under age 12 stay free. Lower rates off-season. Parking: Indoor, $2–$12/day. AE, CB, DC, DISC, JCB, MC, V.

Harrisburg Holiday Inn Hotel

I-33 & PA Tpk, New Cumberland, 17070; tel 717/774-2721 or toll free 800/HOLIDAY; fax 717/774-2485. Exit 18A off I-83. This upgraded property recently underwent a $2 million renovation. Convenient to major highways and the Harrisburg International Airport. **Rooms:** 196 rms and stes. Executive level. CI 3pm/CO 11am. Nonsmoking rms avail. King rooms have sleep sofas. **Amenities:** A/C, cable TV w/movies, dataport. Some units w/terraces. **Services:** X Car-rental desk, babysitting. Free airport transportation. **Facilities:** 1 restaurant, 2 bars (1 w/entertainment), games rm, whirlpool, washer/dryer. Heated indoor pool. **Rates:** $69–$99 S or D; $120–$160 ste. Extra person $10. Children under age 18 stay free. Min stay special events. Parking: Outdoor, free. AE, CB, DC, DISC, JCB, MC, V.

Ramada Inn on Market Square

23 S 2nd St, 17101; tel 717/234-5021 or toll free 800/2-RAMADA; fax 717/234-2347. The city bought this midrange downtown hotel and renovated it from top to bottom, then leased it to Ramada for operation. **Rooms:** 260 rms. CI 3pm/CO noon. Nonsmoking rms avail. **Amenities:** A/C, satel TV w/movies, dataport. Portable TDD devices for guests who are deaf or hard-of-hearing. **Services:** X Babysitting. **Facilities:** 1 restaurant, 1 bar, games rm, spa, washer/dryer. Sun deck. **Rates:** Peak (June–Sept) $99 S; $109 D. Extra person $10. Children under age 12 stay free. Lower rates off-season. Parking: Indoor, free. AE, DISC, MC, V.

MOTELS

Best Western Country Oven

300 N Mountain Rd, 17112; tel 717/652-7180 or toll free 800/528-1234; fax 717/541-8791. Exit 26 off I-81. An exceptionally clean establishment with a popular restaurant, this is a good choice for families on a trip to nearby Hershey. **Rooms:** 49 rms. CI 1pm/CO 11am. Nonsmoking rms avail. **Amenities:** A/C, cable TV, dataport. **Services:** X **Facilities:** 3 restaurants, 1 bar. **Rates (BB):** Peak (June–Oct) $47–$83 S; $55–$88 D. Extra person $3. Children

under age 12 stay free. Lower rates off-season. Parking: Outdoor, free. Breakfast and beverage vouchers included in room rate. AE, CB, DC, DISC, MC, V.

Holiday Inn East

4751 Lindle Rd, 17111; tel 717/939-7841 or toll free 800/637-4817; fax 717/939-9317. Exit 1 (PA 441) off I-283. This pleasant suburban motel sports a lobby with Oriental carpets, dark wood paneling, and a fountain. **Rooms:** 299 rms and stes. Executive level. CI 3pm/CO noon. Nonsmoking rms avail. **Amenities:** A/C, satel TV w/movies. Some units w/terraces, some w/whirlpools. **Services:** X Car-rental desk. **Facilities:** 1 restaurant, 2 bars (1 w/entertainment), basketball, volleyball, games rm, lawn games, whirlpool. Outdoor bar in summer. **Rates:** $89–$109 S; $89–$121 D; $114–$151 ste. Extra person $12. Children under age 19 stay free. Min stay special events. Parking: Outdoor, free. Higher rates during Hershey Antique Car Show in October. AE, CB, DC, DISC, JCB, MC, V.

Quality Inn Riverfront

525 S Front St, 17104; tel 717/233-1611 or toll free 800/4-CHOICE; fax 717/233-1611. Capitol/2nd St exit off I-83. This modern, stucco building is convenient to I-83 and adjacent to Shipoke National Historic District, the Susquehanna River, Riverfront Park, and a playground. Walk to downtown Harrisburg and the state capitol. **Rooms:** 117 rms. CI 3pm/CO noon. Nonsmoking rms avail. Some rooms have river views. **Amenities:** A/C, satel TV, dataport. **Services:** X Babysitting. **Facilities:** 1 restaurant (see "Restaurants" below), 1 bar. **Rates:** Peak (Apr–Oct) $39–$85 S; $49–$95 D. Extra person $7. Children under age 18 stay free. Lower rates off-season. Parking: Outdoor, free. AE, DC, DISC, ER, JCB, MC, V.

Residence Inn by Marriott

4480 Lewis Rd, 17111; tel 717/561-1900 or toll free 800/331-3131; fax 717/561-8617. Pelham Dr exit off PA 322. Styled like an apartment complex, this is a "home away from home" for long-term guests. **Rooms:** 80 effic. CI 3pm/CO noon. Nonsmoking rms avail. **Amenities:** A/C, satel TV, refrig, dataport, VCR. Some units w/fireplaces. Complimentary daily newspaper. **Services:** Children's program. Free grocery shopping. Light evening meal served Mon–Thurs. **Facilities:** Basketball, volleyball, washer/dryer. **Rates (CP):** $129–$159 effic. Children under age 18 stay free. Parking: Outdoor, free. AE, CB, DC, DISC, JCB, MC, V.

Sheraton Inn Harrisburg

800 E Park Dr, 17111; tel 717/561-2800 or toll free 800/325-3535; fax 717/561-8398. Exit 29 off I-83, E on Union Deposit, R on Park Dr. A dramatic lobby with skylight, trees, and a sunken lounge area set the Gaslight-era theme of this otherwise standard hotel for families and business travelers. **Rooms:** 178 rms and stes. CI 3pm/CO noon. Nonsmoking rms avail. **Amenities:** A/C, cable TV w/movies, voice

mail. Some units w/terraces. **Services:** ✗ 🚐 🖼 🛏 🛎 Babysitting. **Facilities:** 🖼 🛎 🅿️ ⅙ 1 restaurant, 2 bars (1 w/entertainment), spa, sauna, steam rm, whirlpool. **Rates:** Peak (May–Oct) $100–$105 S or D; $155–$175 ste. Extra person $10. Children under age 18 stay free. Min stay special events. Lower rates off-season. Parking: Outdoor, free. AE, CB, DC, DISC, MC, V.

RESTAURANTS 🍴

★ At Blue Mountain
2201 Fishing Creek Valley Rd; tel 717/599-5301. PA 443, 4 mi E of Susquehanna River. **American.** These facilities cover the spectrum. The Tavern has a *Cheers* atmosphere and family fare, the Garden Room tends toward New American style and cuisine, the Angino Garden hosts a family-style Sunday brunch, and the large Timber Trails picnic pavilion has space for groups of up to 500 people. **FYI:** Reservations recommended. Piano/singer. Children's menu. Dress code. No smoking. **Open:** Mon–Sat 4pm–midnight, Sun 11am–3pm. Closed Jan 1–15. **Prices:** Main courses $10–$33. AE, CB, DC, DISC, MC, V. ♥ 🖼 VP ⅙

Dutch Pantry Restaurant
5680 Allentown Blvd; tel 717/545-4789. Exit 26 off I-81N; exit 26A off I-81S. **Regional American.** Solid Pennsylvania Dutch favorites—meat loaf, pot pie, ham-and-bean soup—dominate the menu in this quiet family restaurant, which is part of a regional chain. **FYI:** Reservations accepted. Children's menu. **Open:** Daily 6am–10pm. **Prices:** Main courses $4–$11. AE, DISC, MC, V. 🖼 ⅙

Eat N' Park
4641 Lindle Rd; tel 717/986-9197. Exit 1 (PA 441) off I-283. **American.** The breakfast buffet is very popular, but everything on the menu is available 24 hours a day. Try the trademark "Smiley Face" cookies or another temptation from the in-house bakery. **FYI:** Reservations not accepted. Children's menu. No liquor license. **Open:** Daily 24 hrs. **Prices:** Main courses $5–$7. AE, DISC, MC, V. 🖼 🍴 ⅙

Pal-i-tesse
540 Race St; tel 717/236-2048. Capitol/2nd St exit off I-83, N on 2nd, left on Washington St, left on Front, veer right onto Race at light. **New American.** A small, intimate bistro adorned with the work of local artists. Popular choices include mushroom bisque, sausage with penne, and loin of venison with wild mushrooms. Three meatless entrees and nightly specials also available. **FYI:** Reservations recommended. **Open:** Lunch Tues–Fri 11am–2pm; dinner Tues–Sat 5–9pm. **Prices:** Main courses $14–$21. AE, CB, DC, DISC, MC, V. ♥

★ Passage to India
In Quality Inn Riverfront, 525 S Front St; tel 717/233-1202. Capitol/2nd St exit off I-83. **American/Indian.** Adjacent to the Shipoke National Historic District, this restaurant has introduced Indian cuisine to the area. Tandoori specialties

grilled in a clay oven are popular at dinner, and there is a lunch buffet. **FYI:** Reservations recommended. Children's menu. **Open:** Lunch Mon–Fri 11:30am–2:30pm, Sat–Sun noon–2:30pm; dinner Mon–Sat 5–10pm, Sun 5–9pm. **Prices:** Main courses $8–$19. AE, DC, DISC, MC, V. ♥ ⅙

ATTRACTIONS 🏛

Pennsylvania State Capitol
3rd and State Sts; tel 717/787-6810 or toll free 800/868-7672. Interactive exhibits provide information about 300 years of lawmaking, show the progress of a bill through the legislature, simulate a conversation with Benjamin Franklin, and let viewers send a personal message to their representatives. There is also a video presentation. Guided tours of the State Capitol building depart from the Welcome Center. **Open:** Mon–Fri 8:30am–4:30pm. **Free**

State Museum of Pennsylvania
3rd and North Sts; tel 717/787-4978. The state's official museum covers everything from the geological formation of what is now called Pennsylvania to the history of human settlement in the area. The museum's diverse science collection includes artifacts and a planetarium; historical exhibits cover archaeology, culture, technological and industrial development, and military history. **Open:** Tues–Sat 9am–5pm, Sun noon–5pm. **Free**

Fort Hunter Mansion and Park
5300 Front St; tel 717/599-5751. Fort Hunter was originally built during the French and Indian War, but was abandoned in 1763. Capt Archibald McAllister bought the property in 1787, and the site became a thriving frontier village. The captain's Federal-style mansion, built in stages between 1786 and 1870, overlooks the Susquehanna River; inside is a collection of furniture, toys, firearms, tools, and costumes dating mostly from the 19th century. Other buildings in the surrounding 35-acre park include an ice house, corncrib, stone arch bridge, and tavern. The 300-year-old buttonwood trees on the grounds date from the time of William Penn. **Open:** Peak (May–Nov) Tues–Sat 10am–4:30pm, Sun noon–4:30pm. Reduced hours off-season. **$$**

The Museum of Scientific Discovery
3rd and Walnut Sts, Strawberry Square; tel 717/233-7969. Visitors can climb aboard the vintage World War II Link Pilot trainer for a simulated flight, explore virtual reality in the Virtual Arena, and view a replica of a limestone cave complete with real stalactites and stalagmites. A new astronomy center features a planetarium (shows change seasonally). **Open:** Tues–Fri 9am–5pm, Sat 10am–5pm, Sun noon–5pm. **$$**

Hawley

In the Pocono Mountains region, this tiny borough offers attractions such as Upper Delaware National Scenic River,

Promised Land State Park, and several lakes. **Information:** Lake Wallenpaupack Association, PO Box 150, Hawley, 18428 (tel 717/226-2141).

MOTEL 🏨

≣≣ Gresham's Lakeview Motel
US 6 and PA 507, 18428; tel 717/226-4621. Vacationers who want to enjoy Lake Wallenpaupack and the Poconos without spending a lot of money will appreciate this clean and comfortable motel built in 1990. **Rooms:** 21 rms. CI 2pm/ CO 11am. Just the basics, but each room has a partial view of the lake. **Amenities:** 🛏 🕭 A/C, cable TV, dataport. All units w/terraces. **Services:** 🛎 **Facilities:** 🏃 🐟 Public beach across the road. **Rates:** Peak (July–Labor Day) $53–$73 S or D. Extra person $5. Children under age 5 stay free. Min stay wknds. Lower rates off-season. Parking: Outdoor, free. AE, DISC, MC, V.

INN

≣≣≣ The Settlers Inn at Bingham Park
4 Main Ave, 18428; tel 717/226-2993 or toll free 800/ 833-8527; fax 717/226-1874. US 6. 3 acres. This restored Tudor house is less than two miles from Lake Wallenpaupack, and its dining facilities are notable. An inviting lobby with a chessboard and comfortable chairs provide a homelike air. **Rooms:** 18 rms. CI 2pm/CO noon. No smoking. Individually decorated in a Victorian motif, with floral wallpaper and ivory or white bed coverlets. **Amenities:** 🕭 A/C. No phone or TV. Open linen closets so guests can help themselves to extra towels. Mineral water, mints, and bath salts in all rooms. **Services:** 🛎 Masseur, babysitting. Home-baked cookies, scones, and breads for sale. **Facilities:** 🏃 🐟 🟦 1 restaurant (*see* "Restaurants" below), 1 bar, guest lounge w/TV. **Rates (BB):** Peak (July–Oct) $85–$120 S or D. Extra person $15. Children under age 6 stay free. Min stay peak and wknds. Lower rates off-season. Parking: Outdoor, free. AE, DISC, MC, V.

RESORT

≣≣≣≣ Woodloch Pines
Rte 1, 18428; tel 717/685-7121 or toll free 800/572-6658; fax 717/685-1205. Off PA 590E. 250 acres. A relaxed country atmosphere, a wide range of activities, and personalized service draw families back to this resort year after year. Selected three times by *Better Homes and Gardens* as one of America's favorite vacation resorts. **Rooms:** 167 rms and stes. CI 4pm/CO 4pm. No smoking. **Amenities:** 🛏 🕭 🖵 A/C, cable TV, refrig. All units w/terraces. **Services:** 🚐 🛎 Social director, masseur, children's program, babysitting. Shuttle runs around the large property all day. **Facilities:** 🎣 🚲 ⛳ 🛶 ▶18 🏊 🏃 🐟 ⛳5 🛥 🟦 🕭 2 restaurants, 5 bars (1 w/entertainment), 1 beach (lake shore), lifeguard, basketball, volleyball, games rm, lawn games, racquetball, spa, sauna, steam rm, whirlpool, beauty salon, playground, washer/dryer.

Country store, deli, and bakery. Seasonal activities for kids include go-carting, snowmobiling, and ice skating. **Rates (AP):** Peak (June–Labor Day) $430–$505 S or D; $540 ste. Extra person $20. Children under age 2 stay free. Min stay. Lower rates off-season. MAP rates avail. Parking: Outdoor, free. AE, DISC, MC, V.

RESTAURANTS 🍴

Ehrhardt's Lakeside Restaurant
PA 507; tel 717/226-2124. US 6 to S on PA 507. **Burgers/ Seafood.** The view of Lake Wallenpaupack is splendid, especially from the outdoor decks, and the menu is varied. Photos of the lake from the 1920s decorate the walls, and the bar has a fun and friendly air. Most diners choose steak or seafood for dinner; croissant sandwiches and burgers are a good choice for lunch. **FYI:** Reservations recommended. Children's menu. **Open:** Peak (July–Aug) Mon–Thurs 11am– 10pm, Fri–Sat 11am–11pm, Sun 9am–10pm. **Prices:** Main courses $7–$20. AE, DISC, MC, V. 🏞 👨‍👩‍👧 🕭

The Settlers Inn
At Bingham Park, 4 Main Ave; tel 717/226-2993. On US 6 in town center. **Regional American/Eclectic.** The lobby is a favorite place to visit with friends before or after a meal in winter, while the wide front porch is the gathering spot in summer. Pheasant and trout are popular entree choices. The restaurant has its own smokehouse and herb garden, and all breads and rolls are homemade. Wine list features regional labels. **FYI:** Reservations recommended. Piano. Children's menu. No smoking. **Open:** Lunch daily 11:30am–2pm; dinner daily 5–9pm; brunch Sun 11:30am–2pm. **Prices:** Main courses $12–$20. AE, DISC, MC, V. ▮

Hershey

See also Hummelstown, Lebanon, Middletown

Known as "Chocolate Town USA" and site of the world's largest chocolate factory. Other attractions include amusement park and Hershey Gardens. **Information:** Harrisburg-Hershey-Carlisle Tourism & Convention Bureau, 114 Walnut St, PO Box 969, Harrisburg, 17108 (tel 717/232-1377 or toll free 800/995-0969).

HOTEL 🏨

≣≣≣ Holiday Inn Harrisburg/Hershey
604 Station Rd, Grantville, 17028; tel 717/469-0661 or toll free 800/HOLIDAY; fax 717/469-7755. Exit 28 off I-81. An attractive hotel convenient to Hershey and to Penn Down race track. The welcoming lobby is filled with attractive plants. **Rooms:** 195 rms and stes. Executive level. CI 3pm/ CO noon. Nonsmoking rms avail. Inside rooms are either poolside or pool view. **Amenities:** 🛏 🕭 A/C, cable TV w/movies, dataport. Some units w/terraces. **Services:** ✕ 🚐 🖼 🛎 ⬧ Car-rental desk. **Facilities:** 🎣 🟦 🟦 🕭 2

restaurants, 1 bar (w/entertainment), basketball, volleyball, games rm, spa, sauna, whirlpool, washer/dryer. **Rates:** Peak (June–Aug) $109–$119 S or D; $185 ste. Children under age 19 stay free. Lower rates off-season. Parking: Outdoor, free. Golf, Hershey Park, and B&B packages avail. AE, CB, DC, DISC, MC, V.

MOTELS

≣≣ Best Western Inn

US 422 at Sipe Ave, PO Box 364, 17033; tel 717/533-5665 or toll free 800/233-6338; fax 717/533-5675. 1 mi E of town on US 422. Thanks to two outdoor pools and a convenient location, this motel would make a good family choice for a Hershey vacation. **Rooms:** 124 rms and stes. CI 3pm/CO noon. Nonsmoking rms avail. **Amenities:** 📺 🍴 A/C, cable TV w/movies, dataport, voice mail. **Services:** 🖥 🍴 Babysitting. **Facilities:** 🏋 🚐 🚹 Games rm, washer/dryer. **Rates (CP):** Peak (July 5–Sept 1) $65–$129 S or D; $139–$199 ste. Extra person $5. Children under age 17 stay free. Min stay special events. Lower rates off-season. Parking: Outdoor, free. Hershey Park package includes two adult tickets. AE, CB, DC, DISC, ER, MC, V.

≣≣ Days Inn Hershey

350 W Chocolate Ave, 17033; tel 717/534-2162 or toll free 800/329-7466; fax 717/533-6409. US 422 exit off US 322. Attractive, basic motel within walking distance of Hershey Park. **Rooms:** 75 rms. Executive level. CI 3pm/CO 11am. Nonsmoking rms avail. **Amenities:** 📺 A/C, cable TV. **Services:** 🚐 🖥 🍴 **Facilities:** 🚹 **Rates (CP):** Peak (May–Sept) $59–$109 S; $69–$119 D. Extra person $5. Children under age 18 stay free. Lower rates off-season. Parking: Indoor/outdoor, free. AE, CB, DC, DISC, EC, JCB, MC, V.

≣≣≣ Hershey Lodge & Convention Center

W Chocolate Ave and University Dr, PO Box 446, 17033; tel 717/533-3311 or toll free 800/HERSHEY; fax 717/533-9642. On US 322. Long corridors lead through this large, sprawling convention motel. A bit tattered here and there. **Rooms:** 457 rms and stes. Executive level. CI 4pm/CO 11am. Nonsmoking rms avail. **Amenities:** 📺 🍴 🖥 A/C, cable TV. **Services:** 🖥 🚐 🖥 🍴 Social director, children's program, babysitting. **Facilities:** 🏋 🚴 🎿 🚹 🌊4 🎳 📍6000 🚹 3 restaurants, 2 bars (1 w/entertainment), volleyball, games rm, lawn games, sauna, whirlpool, playground, washer/dryer. Movie theater next door. **Rates:** Peak (Mem Day–Labor Day) $104–$136 S; $110–$142 D; $225–$650 ste. Extra person $10. Children under age 17 stay free. Lower rates off-season. MAP rates avail. Parking: Outdoor, free. AE, CB, DC, DISC, MC, V.

≣≣ White Rose Motel

1060 E Chocolate Ave, 17033; tel 717/533-9876; fax 717/533-6923. 1½ mi E of chocolate factory on US 422. Economical, clean choice for families on a Hershey Park visit. **Rooms:** 24 rms. CI 2pm/CO 11am. No smoking. **Amenities:** 📺 🍴 🖥 A/C, cable TV, refrig, dataport. All units w/terraces.

Services: 🖥 🍴 **Facilities:** 🏋 🚹 Playground. **Rates:** Peak (July 4–Sept 1) $39–$105 S; $44–$105 D. Extra person $5. Children under age 17 stay free. Lower rates off-season. Parking: Outdoor, free. DISC, MC, V.

RESORT

≣≣≣≣ The Hotel Hershey

Hotel Rd, PO Box 400, 17033; tel 717/533-2171 or toll free 800/HERSHEY; fax 717/533-8887. US 322 exit off I-83, then E to Hershey Park Dr. 226 acres. This grand hilltop hotel (modeled after one in Cairo) was built in 1933 by unemployed workers from Milton Hershey's chocolate factory, and has been a haunt of CEOs and celebrities for decades. Don't be put off by the austere check-in lobby; a much more ornate one is upstairs. **Rooms:** 241 rms and stes; 1 cottage/villa. CI 4pm/CO noon. Nonsmoking rms avail. Ask for one of the renovated rooms. **Amenities:** 🍴 🖥 A/C, satel TV w/movies, bathrobes. No phone. Some units w/terraces, 1 w/fireplace, some w/whirlpools. **Services:** 🍽 🖥 🎬 🚐 🖥 🍴 Twice-daily maid svce, social director, masseur, children's program, babysitting. Supervised child care in summer. **Facilities:** 🏋 🚴 📍9 🎿 🚹 🌊4 🎳 📍500 🖥 2 restaurants, 2 bars (1 w/entertainment), volleyball, games rm, lawn games, sauna, whirlpool. Bocci court. **Rates:** Peak (May 24–Sept 2) $120–$210 S; $130–$220 D; $170–$305 ste; $525 cottage/villa. Extra person $15. Children under age 18 stay free. Min stay special events. Lower rates off-season. MAP rates avail. Parking: Outdoor, free. AE, CB, DC, DISC, JCB, MC, V.

RESTAURANT 🍴

Friendly's Restaurant Hershey

1000 Reese Ave; tel 717/533-4190. US 422 at University Dr. **American.** Famous for ice cream, but the menu also boasts a long list of other comfort foods. **FYI:** Reservations not accepted. Children's menu. No liquor license. **Open:** Peak (Mem Day–Labor Day) Sun–Thurs 6am–midnight, Fri–Sat 6am–1am. **Prices:** Main courses $6–$8. AE, DISC, MC, V. 🖥 🚹

ATTRACTIONS 📷

Hersheypark

PA 743 and US 422; tel 717/534-4900. This sprawling, 100-acre complex features over 50 rides and attractions, including several water slides and roller coasters. (The new wooden Wildcat roller coaster is especially popular.) Theme areas, such as Rhine Land and Tudor Square, reflect the Pennsylvania German and Dutch heritage of the area, while an on-site arena hosts concerts and sporting events. **Open:** Peak (Mem Day–Labor Day) daily at 10am, closing times vary. **$$$$**

Indian Echo Caverns

US 322; tel 717/566-8131. Guided tours provide information about the history of these caverns and their discovery by local tribes. Visitors are allowed to pan for gemstones and view the stalactites, stalagmites, flowstones, and lakes. **Open:** Peak (Mem Day–Labor Day) daily 9am–6pm. Reduced hours off-season. $$$

Hidden Valley

See Donegal

Holicong

INN 🏨

≡≡≡ **Barley Sheaf Farm**
5281 York Rd (US 202), 18928; tel 215/794-5104; fax 215/794-5332. The only honking in this idyllic pastoral setting is that of geese paddling in the pond. The inn was built in 1740, and has a rustic brick-floored dining room and a sun porch overlooking grazing sheep in the meadows. Unsuitable for children under 8. **Rooms:** 12 rms. CI 2pm/CO 11am. No smoking. Stunning Victorian furnishings. **Amenities:** 🅟 A/C, dataport. No phone or TV. 1 unit w/terrace, some w/fireplaces. **Services:** Afternoon tea in the garden (when weather permits). Huge country breakfasts. **Facilities:** 🏋 🏊 🖥 🛗 Lawn games, washer/dryer, guest lounge w/TV. Business center located in a converted barn. **Rates (BB):** Peak (July–Oct) $115–$160 S; $130–$175 D; $175–$255 ste. Extra person $20. Children under age 3 stay free. Min stay wknds and special events. Lower rates off-season. Parking: Outdoor, free. AE, MC, V.

Hopwood

This small community southeast of Pittsburgh features 19th-century houses, many of them converted to restaurants and retail shops.

RESTAURANT 🍴

Sun Porch
US 40 E; tel 412/439-5734. **American.** Trellises on the walls simulate a garden look, and homestyle cooking makes this a good place to take the family. The lunch buffet has a large salad bar plus soups, six entrees, and dessert. **FYI:** Reservations accepted. Children's menu. BYO. **Open:** Tues–Fri 11am–8pm, Sat 4–9pm, Sun 11am–8pm. **Prices:** Main courses $7–$12. DISC, MC, V.

Hummelstown

Part of the greater Harrisburg area, this borough was founded in 1740 and was an important arms and munitions depot during the Revolutionary War.

MOTEL 🏨

≡≡ **Comfort Inn Hershey**
1200 Mae St, 17036; tel 717/566-2050 or toll free 800/355-2000; fax 717/566-8656. Hershey Park Dr exit off US 322, right at light. Nicely decorated public areas mark this motel, which stresses service to families. **Rooms:** 125 rms, stes, and effic. CI 4pm/CO 11am. Nonsmoking rms avail. **Amenities:** 🛗 🅟 A/C, cable TV. **Services:** 🚙 🏊 🍽 Discounted Hershey Park tickets available. **Facilities:** 🏋 🏊 🛗 Washer/dryer. **Rates (CP):** Peak (Mem Day–Labor Day) $69–$129 S; $79–$174 D; $99–$174 ste; $89–$159 effic. Extra person $10. Children under age 18 stay free. Lower rates off-season. Parking: Outdoor, free. AE, CB, DC, DISC, JCB, MC, V.

RESTAURANT 🍴

Hoss's Steak & Sea House
9009 Bridge Rd; tel 717/566-8799. 3 mi W of Hershey on US 322 E. **Seafood/Steak.** A regional steak and seafood chain, popular with families and senior citizens who go for the ground sirloin, fish, and salad bar. **FYI:** Reservations not accepted. Children's menu. No liquor license. **Open:** Sun–Thurs 10:30am–9:30pm, Fri–Sat 10:30am–10:30pm. **Prices:** Main courses $7–$39. AE, DISC, MC, V. 👪 ♨ 🛗

Huntingdon

An industrial borough on the Juniata River, first laid out in 1767. Huntingdon is home to Juniata College, and Raystown Lake State Park is close by.

MOTELS 🏨

≡≡ **Days Inn Raystown Lake**
US 22 and 4th St, 16652; tel 814/643-3934 or toll free 800/329-7466; fax 814/643-3005. A standard chain motel located in a business strip, with several restaurants nearby. **Rooms:** 76 rms. CI 1pm/CO 11am. Nonsmoking rms avail. Some rooms open to a breezeway, others face enclosed corridors. **Amenities:** 🛗 A/C, cable TV. VCRs available. **Services:** 🏊 🍽 🐾 Fee for pets. **Facilities:** 🏊 🛗 1 restaurant, 1 bar. Sports bar with wide-screen TV. **Rates:** Peak (Apr–Sept) $44 S; $56 D. Extra person $5. Children under age 13 stay free. Min stay special events. Lower rates off-season. Parking: Outdoor, free. AE, DC, DISC, MC, V.

≡≡ **Huntingdon Motor Inn**
US 22 and PA 26, 16652; tel 814/643-1133; fax 814/643-1331. There are fine views through the picture windows in most of the rooms of this quiet, clean, older motel. **Rooms:** 48 rms. CI 1pm/CO 11am. Nonsmoking rms avail. **Amenities:** 🛗 A/C, cable TV. Some units w/terraces. VCRs available. Complimentary coffee. **Services:** 🏊 🍽 🐾 Fee for pets. **Facilities:** 🛗 1 restaurant (lunch and dinner only), 1 bar.

Rates: $36–$40 S; $46–$55 D. Extra person $10. Children under age 13 stay free. Parking: Outdoor, free. AE, DC, DISC, MC, V.

ATTRACTION

Lincoln Caverns

US 22; tel 814/643-0268. Costumed interpreters explain the historical significance of this iron furnace, located on the "Path of Progress" in the southwestern region of the state. The furnace is especially complete and offers a glimpse of an important phase in the industrial development of the region. **Open:** Peak (Mem Day–Labor Day) daily 9am–7pm. Reduced hours off-season. **$$$**

Indiana

Chartered in 1805, this borough northeast of Pittsburgh first prospered from agriculture and timber, then from coal operations. A local museum pays tribute to native son Jimmy Stewart. Nearby Blue Spruce State Park offers boating, fishing, ice skating, and hiking. **Information:** Indiana County Tourist Bureau, 1019 Philadelphia St, Indiana, 15701 (tel 412/463-7505).

MOTELS

≡≡ Best Western University Inn

1545 Wayne Ave, 15701; tel 412/349-9620 or toll free 800/ 528-1234; fax 412/349-2620. Wayne Ave exit off US 119. Standard, comfortable accommodations with modern decor. **Rooms:** 107 rms and stes. CI 3pm/CO noon. Nonsmoking rms avail. Some rooms have dataports. **Amenities:** A/C, cable TV w/movies. 1 unit w/terrace. **Services:** "It's a Wonderful Life" tours during winter months. **Facilities:** 1 restaurant, 1 bar, games rm. Passes to local YMCA. **Rates:** $56 S; $61 D; $75 ste. Extra person $5. Children under age 13 stay free. Parking: Outdoor, free. AE, CB, DC, DISC, MC, V.

≡≡≡ Holiday Inn

1395 Wayne Ave, 15701; tel 412/463-3561 or toll free 800/ 477-3561; fax 412/463-8006. Wayne Ave exit off US 119. Recently renovated motel with attractive, spacious lobby and pleasant rooms. **Rooms:** 160 rms and stes. CI 3pm/CO noon. Nonsmoking rms avail. Rooms are somewhat small, but many have views of Holidome pool and recreation area. **Amenities:** A/C, cable TV w/movies, dataport. 1 unit w/whirlpool. Complimentary daily newspaper. **Services:** Free local calls. **Facilities:** 1 restaurant, 1 bar (w/entertainment), games rm, lawn games, sauna, whirlpool, washer/dryer. **Rates (BB):** $79 S or D; $79 ste. Extra person $6. Children under age 13 stay free. Min stay special events. AP and MAP rates avail. Parking: Outdoor, free. AE, CB, DC, DISC, JCB, MC, V.

Jenkintown

Named for Welsh pioneer William Jenkins, who settled here around 1697.

RESTAURANT

Stazi Milano

In Jenkintown Train Station, Township Lane 8 and Greenwood Ave; tel 215/885-9000. **Italian.** Four casually elegant dining rooms in the 1933 Jenkintown Train Station, each with a unique architectural style. Decor runs the gamut from old to new, and there's a remarkable collection of 20th-century art hanging on the walls. The bar's large windows provide a view of passing trains. The kitchen is best known for brick-oven bread, freshly prepared soups, and creative sauces. **FYI:** Reservations accepted. Jazz. Children's menu. No smoking. **Open:** Lunch Mon–Fri 11:30am–3pm; dinner Mon–Thurs 4–10:30pm, Fri–Sat 5pm–midnight, Sun 4–9pm. **Prices:** Main courses $7–$16. AE, DC, MC, V.

Jim Thorpe

This Pocono Mountains town was named for the famous Olympian athlete, who is buried here. Quaint Victorian Village features unique shops and boutiques, and hosts several festivals. Several local outfitters offer rafting trips down the Lehigh River.

INN

≡≡≡ The Inn at Jim Thorpe

24 Broadway, 18229; tel 717/325-2599 or toll free 800/ 329-2599; fax 717/325-9145. Exit 34 off PA Tpk, follow US 209 N 6 mi. The staff of this fine 1848 inn is friendly, helpful, and eager to tell guests about the sights of this historical town in the western Poconos. **Rooms:** 23 rms. CI 2pm/CO 11am. Nonsmoking rms avail. Decorated in shades of blue and violet, with quaint prints. Baths have pedestal sinks and marble floors. **Amenities:** A/C, cable TV w/movies, dataport. 1 unit w/fireplace, 1 w/whirlpool. **Services:** Babysitting. **Facilities:** 1 restaurant, 1 bar, guest lounge. Emerald Restaurant and Molly Maguire's Pub in the building. **Rates (CP):** $65–$250 D. Extra person $10. Children under age 5 stay free. Min stay wknds. Parking: Outdoor, free. Corporate rates avail. AE, DC, DISC, MC, V.

Johnstown

Once a prosperous steel-making center, Johnstown gained notoriety in 1889 when a dam burst on the Conemaugh River and the resulting flood destroyed the town, killing more than 2,000 residents. A flood museum chronicles the story. **Information:** Cambria County Tourist Council, 111 Market St, Johnstown, 15901 (tel 814/536-7993).

MOTELS 🏨

≣≣≣ Comfort Inn
455 Theatre Dr, 15904; tel 814/266-3678 or toll free 800/221-2222; fax 814/266-9783. Elton exit off US 219. Well-maintained motel with nice valley views. **Rooms:** 117 rms, stes, and effic. CI 2pm/CO noon. Nonsmoking rms avail. Most rooms are nonsmoking. **Amenities:** 🛁 A/C, cable TV, dataport, VCR. Some units w/whirlpools. **Services:** 🚐 ⊿ ⊅ ⊲ Babysitting. Video rentals available. Pet charge $6. **Facilities:** 🖼 🖳 💯 & Whirlpool, washer/dryer. Barbecue area. **Rates (CP):** Peak (May–Sept) $58 S; $64 D; $87–$97 ste; $97 effic. Extra person $6. Children under age 18 stay free. Lower rates off-season. Parking: Outdoor, free. AE, CB, DC, DISC, JCB, MC, V.

≣≣ Days Inn
1540 Scalp Ave, 15904; tel 814/269-3366 or toll free 800/325-2525; fax 814/269-3366. Scalp Ave exit off US 219. Adequate accommodations in a central location. **Rooms:** 144 rms and stes. CI noon/CO 11am. Nonsmoking rms avail. **Amenities:** 🛁 ⚬ A/C, cable TV. Some units w/whirlpools. **Services:** ⊿ ⊅ ⊲ Babysitting. Nominal fee for pets. **Facilities:** 🖼 🖳 350 & 1 restaurant (lunch and dinner only), 2 bars (w/entertainment), games rm, racquetball, spa, sauna. Pool in poor condition. **Rates (CP):** Peak (May–Sept) $47–$52 S; $49–$54 D; $80–$120 ste. Extra person $7. Children under age 19 stay free. Lower rates off-season. Parking: Outdoor, free. AE, CB, DC, DISC, MC, V.

ATTRACTIONS 📷

Johnstown Flood Museum
304 Washington St; tel 814/539-1889. The Johnstown Flood Museum, located in a former Carnegie Library building, documents one of the most horrific disasters in American history. In 1889, the breaking of the South Fork Dam caused a flood that killed 2,209 people. The museum displays artifacts and exhibits about the tragedy, and an Academy Award–winning film about the flood is regularly screened. Other exhibits deal with other aspects of Johnstown's history. **Open:** Daily 10am–5pm. $$

Johnstown Inclined Plane Railway
711 Edgehill Dr; tel 814/536-1816. Considered one of the steepest inclined railways in the world, the cable-driven Johnstown Inclined Plane hoists its 42-ton cars up an astonishing 71% grade. The observation deck at the top provides an expansive view of Johnstown, and a laser show is conducted on most evenings. **Open:** Daily 6:30am–10pm. $

Kennett Square

In the heart of the Brandywine Valley, Kennett Square is known as the "Mushroom Capital of the World," and is the site of the Phillips Mushroom Museum. Nearby Chadds Ford was Washington's headquarters during the Battle of Brandywine, in 1777.

HOTELS 🏨

≣≣ Brandywine River Hotel
US 1 and PA 100, Chadds Ford, 19317; tel 610/388-1200. A small hotel with quaint furnishings and a comfortable, country-style lobby and breakfast room. **Rooms:** 40 rms and stes. CI 2pm/CO 11am. Nonsmoking rms avail. Some rooms are quite romantic. **Amenities:** 🛁 ⚬ �🍴 A/C, cable TV w/movies. Some units w/fireplaces, some w/whirlpools. **Services:** ✕ ⊿ ⊅ ⊲ Twice-daily maid svce. **Facilities:** 🖳 & 1 restaurant (lunch and dinner only), 1 bar. **Rates (CP):** $125 S or D; $135–$169 ste. Extra person $10. Children under age 12 stay free. Parking: Outdoor, free. AARP discounts avail. AE, CB, DC, DISC, MC, V.

≣≣≣ Mendenhall Hotel and Conference Center
PA 52 (Kennett Pike), Mendenhall, 19357; tel 610/388-2100; fax 610/388-1184. Behind the modern exterior are a luxurious lobby paved with Italian green marble and rooms with homelike touches, furnished with country antique reproductions. **Rooms:** 70 rms and stes. CI 2pm/CO noon. Nonsmoking rms avail. All suites have high, four-poster beds. **Amenities:** 🛁 ⚬ 🍴 A/C, cable TV w/movies. All units w/minibars. **Services:** ✕ VP ⊿ ⊅ **Facilities:** 🖳 450 & 1 restaurant (lunch and dinner only), 1 bar. **Rates (CP):** $99 S; $109 D; $140–$190 ste. Extra person $20. Children under age 12 stay free. MAP rates avail. Parking: Outdoor, free. AARP discounts avail; romantic packages avail. AE, CB, DC, DISC, MC, V.

MOTEL

≣≣ Longwood Inn
815 E Baltimore Pike, 19348; tel 610/444-3515; fax 610/444-4285. A comfortable, traditionally furnished motor inn. **Rooms:** 28 rms. CI 1pm/CO noon. Nonsmoking rms avail. **Amenities:** 🛁 A/C, cable TV. All units w/terraces. **Services:** 🚐 ⊅ Car-rental desk. **Facilities:** 125 & 1 restaurant (bkfst and dinner only), 1 bar. **Rates (CP):** $69 S; $75 D. Extra person $6. Children under age 12 stay free. MAP rates avail. Parking: Outdoor, free. AE, DC, DISC, MC, V.

RESTAURANTS 🍴

Chadds Ford Inn
US 1 at PA 100, Chadds Ford; tel 610/388-7361. **Continental.** Intimate, candlelight dining in a restored 1736 tavern with lots of period atmosphere and prints by various members of the Wyeth family. The menu focuses on continental standards with a regional accent—fresh Pennsylvania mushrooms are added to many a dish. The cozy tavern has its own separate menu. **FYI:** Reservations recommended. Dress code.

No smoking. **Open:** Mon–Sat 11:30am–10pm, Sun 11am–9pm. **Prices:** Main courses $15–$25. AE, DC, DISC, MC, V. ▮

★ **Hank's Place**
US 1 at PA 100, Chadds Ford; tel 610/388-7061. **Diner.** A classic American roadside diner, with a clean, comfortable counter, lots of tables, homemade food, and breakfast served all day. The menu includes creamed chipped beef on toast, soups, pot pies, meat loaf, hot turkey sandwiches, and baked apples. **FYI:** Reservations not accepted. Children's menu. No liquor license. **Open:** Tues–Sat 5am–7pm, Sun 7am–3pm, Mon 5am–4pm. **Prices:** Main courses $3–$8. No CC. ▦

Kennett Square Inn
201 E State St; tel 610/444-5687. **Regional American.** The wainscotted rooms and beamed ceilings at this 1835 inn exude a cozy elegance, and the kitchen has long been acclaimed for using fresh local mushrooms to jazz up traditional meat and seafood dishes. **FYI:** Reservations recommended. Piano/rock. Children's menu. No smoking. **Open:** Mon–Tues 11:30am–9pm, Wed–Sat 11:30am–10pm, Sun 4–8pm. **Prices:** Main courses $11–$17. AE, CB, DC, MC, V. ▮

Mendenhall Inn
In Mendenhall Hotel and Conference Center, PA 52, Mendenhall; tel 610/388-1181. **Regional American.** The gracious surroundings include a fieldstone and wood-beam dining room, an oak-paneled tavern, and a crystal-bright garden room. The menu includes pheasant, quail, prime rib, and crab Imperial; many entrees incorporate local mushrooms. Center courtyard offers outdoor dining in warm weather. **FYI:** Reservations recommended. Harp/piano. Children's menu. Jacket required. **Open:** Lunch Mon–Sat 11:30am–2pm; dinner Mon–Sat 5–10pm, Sun 4–8pm; brunch Sun 10am–2pm. **Prices:** Main courses $20–$27. AE, DC, DISC, MC, V. ▮ ♿

The Terrace
In Longwood Gardens, Longwood Gardens; tel 610/388-6771. **Regional American.** High windows and a lovely garden patio make this the centerpiece of the famous DuPont horticultural gardens. The menu offers regional specialties including fresh mushrooms, seafood, and wines from local vineyards. Tour admission ($5) required. **FYI:** Reservations recommended. Children's menu. No smoking. **Open:** Peak (Mem Day–Oct) lunch Mon–Fri 11am–3pm, Sat–Sun 11am–4pm; dinner Tues–Sat 5–7:30pm. Closed Jan–Easter. **Prices:** Main courses $13–$18; prix fixe $18. AE, MC, V. ▦ ♿

ATTRACTIONS ▦

The Christian C Sanderson Museum
PA 100, Chadds Ford; tel 610/388-6545. Not a famous man himself, Sanderson knew the Wyeth family of artists, and collected some early Wyeth work. But he also accumulated offbeat objects like a piece of the raincoat worn by President Eisenhower at his second inauguration, and sawdust from the floor of a room in his home where the Rev Billy Sunday preached—all of which he carefully tagged and preserved. **Open:** Sat–Sun 1–4:30pm. **Free**

Brandywine Battlefield
PA 100, Chadds Ford; tel 601/459-3342. In September 1777, the Continental Army (under George Washington) met the British (under Gen Howe) at Brandywine Creek. Unfortunately, Washington failed to halt the British advance on Philadelphia, which was occupied two weeks later. The site includes the houses Washington and Lafayette used during the battle, which is re-enacted in September; the visitors center contains further exhibits. **Open:** Tues–Sat 9am–5pm, Sun noon–5pm. **$$**

Chaddsford Winery
PA 1, Chadds Ford; tel 610/388-6221. Visitors are introduced to the winemaking process as they are taken on tours of the winery and the cellars. Wine tastings offered. **Open:** Tues–Sat 10am–5:30pm, Sun noon–5pm. **$**

King of Prussia

Suburb of Philadelphia, known mostly for its shopping malls. Near to Valley Forge Historical National Park and Evansburg State Forest.

HOTELS ▦

≡≡ **Courtyard by Marriott**
1100 Drummers Lane, Wayne, 19087; tel 610/687-6700; fax 610/687-1149. Warner Rd exit off US 202. A bright, new facility with a very welcoming lobby (complete with TV, microwave, and fireplace) and a friendly staff. **Rooms:** 150 rms and stes. CI 3pm/CO 1pm. Nonsmoking rms avail. **Amenities:** ▦ ♨ ▦ A/C, cable TV w/movies, dataport, voice mail. All units w/terraces. Refrigerators in suites only. Hotwater dispensers and instant coffee in rooms. Microwaves on request. Free daily newspaper. **Services:** ▦ ▦ ▦ Complimentary coffee and cookies in lobby. **Facilities:** ▦ ▦ ▦ ♿ 1 restaurant (bkfst only), 1 bar, whirlpool, washer/dryer. Large, bright meeting rooms. Indoor pool is suitable for lap swimming. **Rates:** $59–$105 S or D; $119–$135 ste. Children under age 18 stay free. Min stay special events. Parking: Outdoor, free. AE, DC, DISC, MC, V.

≡≡≡ **The Park Ridge at Valley Forge**
480 N Gulph Rd, 19406; tel 610/337-1800; fax 610/337-4624. Recently renovated, this modern, full-service hotel is built around a center courtyard with a pool. **Rooms:** 265 rms and stes. Executive level. CI 3pm/CO 1pm. Nonsmoking rms avail. Luxury suites are bi-level. Interior rooms face the pool. **Amenities:** ▦ ♨ ▦ A/C, satel TV w/movies, dataport, voice mail. All units w/minibars, all w/terraces. **Services:** ▦ ▦ ▦ ▦ ▦ Social director. Complimentary shuttle to King of Prussia Mall. **Facilities:** ▦ ▦ ▦ ▦ ♿ 1 restaurant, 1 bar, basketball, washer/dryer. Golf course adjacent. Guest

privileges at local health club. **Rates:** $139 S or D; $225–$350 ste. Children under age 18 stay free. Parking: Outdoor, free. AE, CB, DC, DISC, MC, V.

≣ ≣ ≣ Sheraton Valley Forge/Plaza Suites Hotel

N Gulph Rd and 1st Ave, 19406; tel 610/265-1500 or toll free 800/325-3535; fax 610/768-3222. Multiple dining and entertainment venues keep this complex hopping, but the 30-year-old tower is showing its age. **Rooms:** 432 rms and stes. Executive level. CI 3pm/CO noon. Nonsmoking rms avail. Single and bi-level fantasy theme suites available. **Amenities:** 🛁 🗄 📺 A/C, cable TV w/movies, dataport, voice mail. Some units w/terraces, some w/fireplaces, some w/whirlpools. **Services:** ✗ ◑ VP 🚐 🖼 🖵 Car-rental desk, social director, masseur, babysitting. **Facilities:** 🛋 ⛳ 900 🖵 & 4 restaurants (*see* "Restaurants" below), 3 bars (1 w/entertainment), volleyball, racquetball, sauna, steam rm, whirlpool. Restaurants include Junior's Deli for sandwiches, Lily Langtry's for dinner theater. **Rates:** Peak (Feb–Mar/Nov–Dec) $140 S or D; $160 ste. Extra person $10. Children under age 12 stay free. Lower rates off-season. MAP rates avail. Parking: Outdoor, free. AE, CB, DC, DISC, MC, V.

≣ ≣ ≣ Valley Forge Hilton

251 W DeKalb Pike, 19406; tel 610/337-1200 or toll free 800/TRY-VSPA; fax 610/337-2224. Exit 24A off I-76. A handsome, recently renovated modern hotel that is usually alive with activity, but the guest rooms are discreetly removed from the action for complete privacy. **Rooms:** 340 rms and stes. Executive level. CI 2pm/CO noon. Nonsmoking rms avail. Junior suites, luxury suites, and concierge-level suites available. **Amenities:** 🛁 🗄 🍷 A/C, cable TV w/movies, dataport, voice mail. Some units w/minibars, some w/whirlpools. **Services:** ✗ ◑ 🚐 🖼 🖵 Babysitting. Free shuttle to King of Prussia Mall and area attractions. **Facilities:** 🛋 ⛳ 1000 & 2 restaurants, 2 bars (1 w/entertainment), games rm, spa, sauna, whirlpool, washer/dryer. Alexander's serves all meals, Kobe is a Japanese steak and seafood house. Complimentary health club membership for guests. **Rates:** $105–$125 S or D; $250–$450 ste. Extra person $10. Children under age 16 stay free. MAP rates avail. Parking: Outdoor, free. AE, CB, DC, DISC, MC, V.

≣ ≣ ≣ Valley Forge Marriott Suites

888 Chesterbrook Blvd, Wayne, 19087; tel 610/647-6700; fax 610/889-9420. At US 202. Spacious lobby with attractive flower arrangements and a friendly staff make this property a stand-out. **Rooms:** 229 stes. CI 3pm/CO noon. Nonsmoking rms avail. **Amenities:** 🛁 🗄 📺 🍷 A/C, satel TV w/movies, refrig, dataport, voice mail. All units w/minibars, some w/whirlpools. VCRs on request. **Services:** ✗ 🖼 🖵 **Facilities:** 🛋 ⛳ 150 & 1 restaurant, 1 bar, spa, sauna, whirlpool, washer/dryer. **Rates:** $139–$189 ste. Extra person $30. Children under age 12 stay free. Parking: Outdoor, free. Weekend packages (including breakfast) avail. AE, CB, DC, DISC, MC, V.

MOTELS

≣ ≣ Comfort Inn Valley Forge

550 W DeKalb Pike, 19406; tel 610/962-0700; fax 610/962-0218. A conventional chain motel, up-to-date and comfortably furnished. **Rooms:** 121 rms. CI 3pm/CO noon. Nonsmoking rms avail. **Amenities:** 🛁 🗄 A/C, cable TV w/movies, refrig. Some units w/minibars. Microwaves available. **Services:** 🚐 🖼 🖵 ◁ Car-rental desk, babysitting. **Facilities:** ⛳ 12 🖵 & Washer/dryer. **Rates (CP):** Peak (Mar–Oct) $99 S; $109 D. Extra person $10. Children under age 18 stay free. Min stay special events. Lower rates off-season. Parking: Outdoor, free. AE, CB, DC, DISC, JCB, MC, V.

≣ ≣ Courtyard by Marriott Devon

762 Lancaster Ave, Wayne, 19087; tel 610/687-6633 or toll free 800/321-2211; fax 610/687-1150. St Davids exit off I-476, 3 mi W on Lancaster Ave. Bright and new, with a lobby made particularly comfortable by a fireplace, TV, and complimentary fresh-brewed coffee. Aimed at business travelers. **Rooms:** 149 rms and stes. CI 3pm/CO 1pm. Nonsmoking rms avail. King rooms have sofa beds. All rooms have large desks. **Amenities:** 🛁 🗄 A/C, cable TV w/movies, voice mail. All units w/terraces. Microwaves and refrigerators available. Instant hot-water taps in rooms. **Services:** 🚐 🖼 🖵 Social director, masseur. **Facilities:** 🛋 ⛳ 30 & 1 restaurant (bkfst only), 1 bar, whirlpool, washer/dryer. **Rates:** Peak (May 7–June 2/Sept 21–Sept 30) $89–$99 S or D; $109–$119 ste. Children under age 12 stay free. Lower rates off-season. Parking: Outdoor, free. AE, CB, DC, DISC, MC, V.

≣ ≣ Hampton Inn

530 W DeKalb Pike, 19406; tel 610/962-8111 or toll free 800/HAMPTON; fax 610/962-5494. This modern, reasonably priced property is typical of the chain, with comfortable rooms and good fitness facilities. **Rooms:** 148 rms. CI 2pm/CO noon. Nonsmoking rms avail. **Amenities:** 🛁 🗄 A/C, cable TV w/movies, dataport. **Services:** 🚐 🖼 🖵 **Facilities:** ⛳ 32 & Sauna. **Rates (CP):** $74–$89 S or D. Children under age 18 stay free. Parking: Outdoor, free. AE, CB, DC, DISC, JCB, MC, V.

≣ ≣ ≣ Holiday Inn King of Prussia

260 Mall Blvd, 19406; tel 610/265-7500 or toll free 800/HOLIDAY; fax 610/265-4076. Busy, well-maintained motel adjacent to King of Prussia Mall. **Rooms:** 225 rms. CI 3pm/CO 11am. Nonsmoking rms avail. **Amenities:** 🛁 🗄 🍷 A/C, cable TV w/movies, dataport. **Services:** ✗ 🖼 🖵 **Facilities:** 🛋 ⛳ 1000 🖵 & 1 restaurant, 1 bar, racquetball, sauna, steam rm, whirlpool, beauty salon. Free use of on-site Bally's Fitness Center. **Rates:** $99–$109 S or D. Children under age 12 stay free. Lower rates off-season. Parking: Outdoor, free. Preferred Shoppers package (including mall discounts) avail. AE, CB, DC, DISC, MC, V.

INN

≣≣≣ The Wayne Hotel

139 E Lancaster Ave, Wayne, 19087; tel 610/687-5000 or toll free 800/962-5850; fax 610/687-8387. 1½ mi from exit 5 off I-476. This charming 1906 Victorian Inn, furnished in period style, is within walking distance of most of Wayne's shops and restaurants. **Rooms:** 37 rms, stes, and effic. CI 2pm/CO noon. Nonsmoking rms avail. **Amenities:** 🛏 🐕 📺 A/C, cable TV, refrig, dataport. 1 unit w/whirlpool. **Services:** ✕ ➡ 🚗 📠 🔔 Car-rental desk, afternoon tea served. Closed-captioned TV and phone available for deaf or hard-of-hearing guests. **Facilities:** 🏊 ⅖ 1 restaurant (*see* "Restaurants" below), 1 bar, guest lounge. Access to fitness room and pool (one mile away). **Rates (CP):** $110–$125 S or D; $150 ste; $150 effic. Children under age 12 stay free. Parking: Outdoor, free. AE, DC, MC, V.

RESTAURANTS 🍴

Lily Langtry's Victorian Theatre

In Sheraton Valley Forge Hotel, Gulph Rd and 1st Ave S; tel 610/337-2000. **American.** An elegant Victorian dining room, complete with flocked wallpaper and gas-lamp lighting, where the main attraction is the Las Vegas–style floor show that accompanies your meal. The menu lists mostly beef and seafood favorites. Show costs $15 per person, in addition to meal price. **FYI:** Reservations recommended. Dress code. **Open:** Lunch Tues–Thurs noon–2pm; dinner Tues–Thurs 6–8:30pm, Fri 6:30–9pm, Sat 5–9:30pm, Sun 4–8pm; brunch Sun 9am–1pm. **Prices:** Main courses $8–$30. AE, CB, DC, DISC, MC, V. ⅖

Restaurant Taquet

In The Wayne Hotel, 139 E Lancaster Ave, Wayne; tel 610/687-5005. St Davids exit off I-476, 1½ mi W on Lancaster Ave. **French.** A classic French brasserie with an elegant atmosphere and gourmet food to match: venison, smoked wild quail, striped bass. Wine cellar stocks more than 120 labels. **FYI:** Reservations recommended. Dress code. No smoking. **Open:** Tues–Thurs 11:30am–10pm, Fri–Sat 11:30am–10:30pm. **Prices:** Main courses $16–$24. AE, CB, DC, DISC, MC, V. ♥ ⅖

Valley Forge Brewing Company

In Gateway Shopping Center, 267 E Swedesford Rd, Wayne; tel 610/687-8700. **Pub.** There's a facade of a log cabin along the back wall and one of the dining areas is under a covered bridge in this gracious restaurant and brew pub. The menu includes pan-seared halibut and Irish lamb stew. All beers are English-style ales, brewed on the premises; BYO wine is allowed for a $5 corking fee. Pool tables in back. **FYI:** Reservations accepted. Children's menu. Beer only. **Open:** Sun–Wed 11am–10:30pm, Thurs–Sat 11am–11pm. **Prices:** Main courses $11–$16. AE, DISC, MC, V. ⅖

Kulpsville

Now a northern suburb north of Philadelphia, near to Evansburg State Forest and Nockamixon State Park and Lake.

MOTEL 🏨

≣≣ Days Inn

1735 Sumneytown Pike, PO Box 250, 19443; tel 215/368-5391 or toll free 800/329-7466; fax 215/368-7671. A corporate motel with few amenities; the small lobby has new furniture and a TV. **Rooms:** 53 rms. CI 1pm/CO 11am. Nonsmoking rms avail. **Amenities:** 🛏 🐕 A/C, cable TV w/movies, dataport. **Services:** 🚗 🔔 Car-rental desk. Morning coffee in lobby. VCRs available. **Facilities:** 🏊 **Rates:** Peak (Aug) $69 S; $79 D. Extra person $5. Children under age 12 stay free. Lower rates off-season. Parking: Outdoor, free. AE, CB, DC, DISC, MC, V.

La Haska

HOTEL 🏨

≣≣≣ Golden Plough Inn

US 202 and Street Rd, 18931; tel 215/794-4004; fax 215/794-4008. These six buildings offer Victorian-style accommodations in Peddler's Village, a busy tourist spot surrounded by serene countryside. **Rooms:** 60 rms and stes. CI 3pm/CO 11am. Nonsmoking rms avail. Large and sumptuously furnished. **Amenities:** 🛏 🐕 🍴 A/C, cable TV, refrig, dataport. All units w/minibars, some w/terraces, some w/fireplaces, some w/whirlpools. Welcome basket with snacks and champagne. Separate dining area with hot pot and instant coffee. **Services:** 📠 🔔 **Facilities:** 🏊 ⅖ 3 restaurants, 4 bars (1 w/entertainment). Golf privileges at local country club. **Rates (CP):** $95–$150 S or D; $175–$300 ste. Extra person $15. Children under age 5 stay free. MAP rates avail. Parking: Outdoor, free. AE, CB, DC, DISC, MC, V.

Lancaster

See also Mount Joy, Paradise

Lancaster, in the heart of Pennsylvania Dutch country, offers a renovated Old Town district with authentic period homes, courtyards, churches, Pennsylvania Dutch restaurants and craft shops, outlet stores, and family-fun attractions. Numerous Amish farms and noted wineries are nearby. **Information:** Pennsylvania Dutch Convention & Visitors Bureau, 501 Greenfield Rd, Lancaster, 17601 (tel 717/299-8901).

HOTELS

Best Western Eden Resort Inn

222 Eden Rd, 17601; tel 717/569-6444 or toll free 800/528-1234; fax 717/569-4208. At jct US 304/PA 272. Neat, well-maintained hotel made up of two buildings. The welcoming lobby is homelike, with living-room furniture and comfortable atmosphere. **Rooms:** 274 rms and stes. Executive level. CI 3pm/CO noon. Nonsmoking rms avail. Room suites face the indoor pool; club suites are in a separate building. Third floor has higher level of security. Rooms in the west wing are quieter. **Amenities:** A/C, satel TV w/movies, dataport. Some units w/terraces, some w/fireplaces, some w/whirlpools. **Services:** Babysitting. **Facilities:** 2 restaurants, 1 bar (w/entertainment), games rm, spa, sauna, whirlpool, playground, washer/dryer. **Rates:** Peak (June–Oct) $99–$129 S or D; $119–$179 ste. Extra person $10. Children under age 18 stay free. Lower rates off-season. Parking: Outdoor, free. AE, CB, DC, DISC, MC, V.

Brunswick Hotel

Queen and Chestnut Sts, PO Box 749, 17608 (Downtown); tel 717/397-4801 or toll free 800/233-0182; fax 717/397-4991. The many government buildings in this area draw guests to this full-sized hotel, which is within walking distance of many of the town's museums and restaurants. **Rooms:** 224 rms and stes. CI 2pm/CO noon. Nonsmoking rms avail. Rooms are larger than average. **Amenities:** A/C, cable TV w/movies. **Services:** **Facilities:** 1 restaurant, 1 bar (w/entertainment), washer/dryer. **Rates:** Peak (May–Oct) $62–$80 S; $70–$88 D; $85 ste. Extra person $6. Children under age 18 stay free. Lower rates off-season. Parking: Indoor, free. Group discounts avail. AE, CB, DC, DISC, MC, V.

Holiday Inn Lancaster Host Hotel

2300 Lincoln Hwy E, 17602; tel 717/299-5500 or toll free 800/233-0121; fax 717/295-5112. 1 mi from jct PA 462/US 30. Much of the original resort atmosphere remains at this 225-acre property, which now emphasizes its extensive conference facilities. **Rooms:** 330 rms and stes. Executive level. CI 4pm/CO noon. Nonsmoking rms avail. Rooms are spacious, looking out on the pool to one side and the golf course to the other. **Amenities:** A/C, cable TV w/movies. Some units w/terraces. **Services:** Social director, children's program, babysitting. **Facilities:** 27 2 restaurants, 2 bars (1 w/entertainment), basketball, volleyball, games rm, lawn games, whirlpool, playground, washer/dryer. **Rates:** Peak (July–Nov) $149–$159 S or D; $325–$500 ste. Extra person $10. Children under age 19 stay free. Lower rates off-season. Parking: Outdoor, free. AE, CB, DC, DISC, MC, V.

MOTELS

Hampton Inn

545 Greenfield Rd, 17601; tel 717/299-1200 or toll free 800/HAMPTON; fax 717/299-1155. Greenfield exit off US 30 E. A modern and well-kept chain motel. The lobby has the feel of a family living room, with several good spots to read and relax. **Rooms:** 129 rms and stes. CI 3pm/CO 11am. Nonsmoking rms avail. Although the furniture is dark wood, the size and pleasant decor make the rooms light and airy. **Amenities:** A/C, cable TV w/movies, dataport. Suites have microwaves, refrigerators, coffeemakers, and hair dryers. **Services:** Babysitting. Coffee available in lobby 24 hours. **Facilities:** 55 Whirlpool, washer/dryer. Well-equipped fitness center. **Rates (CP):** Peak (Apr–Nov) $84–$103 S or D; $103–$113 ste. Children under age 18 stay free. Lower rates off-season. Parking: Outdoor, free. AE, CB, DC, DISC, MC, V.

Holiday Inn East

521 Greenfield Rd, 17601; tel 717/299-2551 or toll free 800/HOLIDAY; fax 717/397-0220. Greenfield Rd exit off US 30. Although the landscaping in the front is minimal, the interior of this motel is very attractive and well maintained. **Rooms:** 189 rms. CI 3pm/CO noon. Nonsmoking rms avail. **Amenities:** A/C, cable TV w/movies, dataport. Refrigerators and hair dryers on request. **Services:** Children's program, babysitting. **Facilities:** 2 300 1 restaurant, 1 bar (w/entertainment), basketball, washer/dryer. **Rates:** Peak (Apr–Oct) $99 S or D. Children under age 17 stay free. Lower rates off-season. Parking: Outdoor, free. Rates are per room, not per person. AE, CB, DC, DISC, JCB, MC, V.

Lancaster Travelodge

2101 Columbia Ave, 17603; tel 717/397-4201 or toll free 800/578-7878; fax 717/397-7842. On PA 462. This two-story motel, surrounding a well-lighted parking area, is located near Franklin and Marshall College and St Joseph Medical Center. **Rooms:** 58 rms. CI 2pm/CO 11am. Nonsmoking rms avail. **Amenities:** A/C, cable TV. Some units w/terraces. **Services:** **Facilities:** 35 1 restaurant (lunch and dinner only), 2 bars (1 w/entertainment). **Rates:** Peak (Apr–Oct) $50–$66 S; $62–$78 D. Extra person $8. Children under age 18 stay free. Lower rates off-season. Parking: Outdoor, free. AE, CB, DC, DISC, MC, V.

Ramada Inn

2250 Lincoln Hwy E, 17602; tel 717/393-5499 or toll free 800/272-6232; fax 717/293-1014. On US 30, ½ mi E of jct PA 462/US 30. This popular family-friendly motel is adjacent to a 27-hole PGA golf course, across from a family theme park, and close to the Strasburg Railroad and Rockvale outlet stores. **Rooms:** 166 rms and stes. CI 3pm/CO 11am. Nonsmoking rms avail. The rooms are large, with good quality furnishings. **Amenities:** A/C, cable TV. Some units w/terraces. Most have refrigerators. **Services:**

Tours of Amish country can be arranged. **Facilities:** 1 bar, basketball, games rm, sauna, washer/dryer. **Rates (CP):** Peak (June–Oct) $79–$109 S or D; $129–$149 ste. Extra person $10. Children under age 18 stay free. Lower rates off-season. Parking: Outdoor, free. AE, CB, DC, DISC, MC, V.

Red Caboose Motel

312 Paradise Lane, PO Box 303, Strasburg, 17579; tel 717/687-5000. 1 mi E on PA 741 from jct PA 741/PA 896, then left on Paradise Lane. Sleep in a 25-ton N-5 caboose, dine in a Victorian rail car, and watch the Strasburg steam train pull into the station. This railroad fan's dream is near the National Toy Train museum and the Railroad Museum of Pennsylvania. **Rooms:** 39 rms, stes, and effic; 1 cottage/villa. CI 3pm/CO 11am. Couples Cabooses, Family Cabooses, Caboose Suites, and a Honeymoon Caboose make up the manifest of this train. **Amenities:** A/C, cable TV. No phone. 1 unit w/terrace, 1 w/whirlpool. TVs are mounted in old potbelly stoves. **Services:** **Facilities:** 1 restaurant (*see* "Restaurants" below), games rm, playground. Video game caboose. **Rates:** Peak (July–Aug) $60–$82 S or D; $90–$102 ste; $90 effic; $90 cottage/villa. Children under age 18 stay free. Min stay peak. Lower rates off-season. Parking: Outdoor, free. Weekday packages avail. DISC, MC, V.

RESORT

Willow Valley Resort

2416 Willow St Pike, 17602; tel 717/464-2711 or toll free 800/444-1714; fax 717/464-4784. 3 mi S of town on US 222. 100 acres. More like a small town than a resort, this development encompasses a golf course, shopping center, play areas, fitness facilities, restaurants, an Amish farm, condo units, and a retirement community. **Rooms:** 352 rms and stes. Executive level. CI 3pm/CO noon. Nonsmoking rms avail. Some rooms have pullout sofas. **Amenities:** A/C, cable TV, dataport. Some units w/terraces, some w/whirlpools. Free early-morning and late-night coffee. **Services:** Babysitting. **Facilities:** 2 restaurants (*see* "Restaurants" below), basketball, volleyball, games rm, sauna, whirlpool, playground, washer/dryer. Indoor and outdoor pools. **Rates:** Peak (June–Aug) $99–$129 S or D; $129 ste. Extra person $10. Children under age 6 stay free. Min stay wknds. Lower rates off-season. MAP rates avail. Parking: Outdoor, free. AE, DISC, MC, V.

RESTAURANTS

Avenues Restaurant & McFly's Pub

In Stevens House Condominium, 10 S Prince St; tel 717/299-3456. **American.** The main restaurant is supplemented by a pub in an enclosed, covered courtyard. Both dining areas offer a selection of 30 beers on tap, and an array of familiar American fare. **FYI:** Reservations accepted. Blues/jazz. Children's menu. **Open:** Sun–Mon 10am–2am, Tues–Sat 11:30am–2am. **Prices:** Main courses $9–$19. AE, CB, DC, DISC, MC, V.

★ Hoss's Steak & Sea House

1693 Oregon Pike; tel 717/393-9788. Oregon Pike exit off US 30 E. **Seafood/Steak.** One branch of a popular regional chain known for fast service and traditional steak and seafood choices, cooked to order. All entrees come with salad bar and dessert. **FYI:** Reservations not accepted. Children's menu. No liquor license. **Open:** Sun–Thurs 10:30am–9:30pm, Fri–Sat 10:30am–10:30pm. **Prices:** Main courses $8–$38. AE, DISC, MC, V.

★ Isaac's Restaurant & Deli

555 Greenfield Rd; tel 717/393-6067. Greenfield Rd exit off US 30 E. **Deli.** One member of a small, yet popular, local chain. The dining room is an open, airy space with lots of light. On the menu, expect to find a range of salads, soups, and deli sandwiches named after birds and plants. **FYI:** Reservations not accepted. Children's menu. No liquor license. **Open:** Mon–Thurs 10am–9pm, Fri–Sat 10am–10pm, Sun 11am–9pm. **Prices:** Main courses $4–$6. AE, DISC, MC, V.

★ Log Cabin Restaurant

11 Lehoy Forest Dr, Leola; tel 717/626-1181. 6 mi N of Lancaster on PA 272. **American.** Housed in a real log cabin, and former speakeasy, in the middle of Pennsylvania Dutch country. (You'll know you're on the right track when you pass through the covered bridge.) The menu offers a classy take on the family-style fare typically served in this region; charbroiled steak, fresh seafood, and homemade rolls and baked goods are particularly promising. **FYI:** Reservations recommended. Piano. Children's menu. Dress code. **Open:** Mon–Sat 5–10pm, Sun 4–9pm. **Prices:** Main courses $16–$35. AE, DC, MC, V.

$ Market Fare

In Arcade Building, 25 W King St; tel 717/299-7090. Grant and Market Sts. **New American.** A quiet, romantic place, where the menu offers a refreshing change from the traditional fare of this region. Light walls, dark wood, and plush upholstered chairs set the decor. **FYI:** Reservations accepted. Children's menu. **Open:** Lunch Mon–Sat 11am–2:30pm; dinner Sun–Mon 5–9pm, Tues–Sat 5–10pm; brunch Sun 11am–2pm. **Prices:** Main courses $10–$20. AE, CB, DC, DISC, MC, V.

$ ★ Miller's Smorgasbord

2811 Lincoln Hwy E, Ronks; tel 717/687-6621. On US 30 E, 2 mi E of PA 896. **Regional American.** Baked goods are made on the premises, and are available for carryout from the shop next door, along with local artwork and interesting souvenirs. Every meal is served as a smorgasbord here, even breakfast. **FYI:** Reservations recommended. No liquor license. No smoking. **Open:** Peak (June–Oct) daily 8am–9pm. **Prices:** Prix fixe $19. AE, DISC, MC, V.

Olde Greenfield Inn

595 Greenfield Rd; tel 717/393-0668. Greenfield exit off US 30 E. **Regional American/International.** Located in a restored 1820 farmhouse, this eatery is within walking distance of two hotels and the Lancaster visitor center. The atmosphere is upscale casual, with cozy seating in the wine cellar, in the green-walled main room or, during warm weather, outdoors. The wine list is long, and the menu ranges from Cajun to crepes to stir fry. **FYI:** Reservations recommended. Piano. Children's menu. **Open:** Breakfast Sat 8–11am, Sun 8am–2pm; lunch Tues–Sat 11am–2pm; dinner Mon–Sat 5–10pm; brunch Sun 11am–2pm. **Prices:** Main courses $13–$20. AE, CB, DC, DISC, MC, V. 🌳 ☎ &

The Pressroom

In The Steinman Hardware Building, 26-28 W King St; tel 717/399-5400. Next to Steinman Park. **American.** An old-time printing-press motif is carried out in the decor, and the sandwiches on the lunch menu carry names from the funny pages. But the polished wood tables are tastefully set with good china and stemware, and the dinner entrees are solid takes on traditional American dishes. **FYI:** Reservations recommended. Children's menu. **Open:** Lunch Mon–Sat 11:30am–3pm; dinner Mon–Thurs 5–9:30pm, Fri–Sat 5–10:30pm. **Prices:** Main courses $11–$17. AE, MC, V. ☎ &

⑤ The Red Caboose Restaurant

312 Paradise Lane, Strasburg; tel 717/687-5001. 1 mi E on PA 741 from jct PA 896. **Regional American/Pennsylvania Dutch.** These restored Pullman dining cars from the 1920s even simulate the sound and movement of a train; it's a fine way to show children how travel used to be. All dinners include appetizers, two vegetables, and an entree. **FYI:** Reservations accepted. Children's menu. No liquor license. No smoking. **Open:** Peak (June–Oct) daily 8am–8pm. **Prices:** Main courses $6–$10. AE, DISC, MC, V. 🖥 ⛰ 🎮

Stockyard Inn

1147 Lititz Pike; tel 717/394-7975. PA 501 and US 222. **American/Steak.** Each of the dining areas is decorated with a different mural, and polished wood gleams throughout. The menu focuses on beef and prime rib, although an appealing selection of seafood dishes is also available. **FYI:** Reservations recommended. Children's menu. **Open:** Tues–Sun 11:30am–9pm, Sat 4–9:30pm. **Prices:** Main courses $15–$30. AE, MC, V. 🖥

★ Willow Valley Resort Family Restaurant

In Willow Valley Resort, 2416 Willow St Pike; tel 717/464-2711. 3 mi S of Lancaster on US 222. **American/Pennsylvania Dutch.** It's your choice: Bring an appetite to this abundant smorgasbord or order smaller portions from the à la carte menu. The on-site bakery, with products available for takeout, has a excellent local reputation. **FYI:** Reservations not accepted. Children's menu. No liquor license. No smoking. **Open:** Mon–Sat 6am–9pm, Sun 8am–8pm. **Prices:** Main courses $5–$13. AE, DC, DISC, MC, V. ⛰ 🎮 &

ATTRACTIONS 📷

Landis Valley Museum

2451 Kissel Hill Rd; tel 717/569-0401. A living history museum that re-creates a rural Pennsylvania German town. The museum has 15 buildings, including a blacksmith's shop, farm buildings, a print and leatherworking shop, pottery shop, tavern, and the Landis Valley House Hotel. Exhibits illustrate what life would have been like for 19th-century residents. **Open:** Apr–Oct, Tues–Sat 9am–5pm, Sun noon–5pm. **$$$**

Amish Farm and House

2395 US 30 E; tel 717/394-6185. This 25-acre typical Amish farmstead (built in 1805) has a limekiln, blacksmith's shop, 70-foot-tall windmill, tobacco shed, and limestone quarry, all decorated with period Amish furnishings. The barnyard houses 23 different animals, including geese, horses, sheep, pigs, guinea fowl, cows, pheasants, and ducks. Guided tours explore the history, customs, and religion of the Amish. **Open:** Peak (June–Aug) daily 8:30am–6pm. Reduced hours off-season. **$$**

Hans Herr House and Museum

1849 Hans Herr Dr, Willow Street; tel 717/464-4438. Built in 1719, the Hans Herr house is said to be the oldest building in Lancaster County and the oldest surviving Mennonite meeting house in the country. The house and museum contain a blacksmith shop, farm tools, and objects relating to colonial life. Tours are given in the winter by appointment only, and special events are scheduled three times a year. **Open:** Mon–Sat 9am–4pm. **$$**

Historic Rock Ford

881 Rock Ford Rd; tel 717/392-7223. Rock Ford was the home of Gen Edward Hand, who served as Adjutant General to George Washington in the Revolutionary War. (After the war, he served in the US Congress and the State General Assembly.) His home is a four-story brick mansion in the Georgian style, and contains some of Hand's possessions among its furnishings. Also on view are archeological finds from the property. The **Kaufmann Museum** is housed on the site in a reconstructed 18th-century barn, and contains a variety of domestic handicrafts and decorative arts as well as furniture and firearms. **Open:** Tues–Fri 10am–4pm, Sat noon–4pm. **$$**

Dutch Wonderland Family Fun Park

2249 US 30 E; tel 717/291-1888. A 44-acre amusement park with more than 20 rides, a botanical garden, a wax museum, and live high-diving demonstrations. There's also an on-site campground, and a monorail to shuttle visitors around. **Open:** Peak (July–Labor Day) daily 10am–8pm. Reduced hours off-season. **$$$$**

Langhorne

Small suburb NE of Philadelphia, close to Delaware River Scenic Drive, Tyler State Park and Washington Crossing State Park.

ATTRACTION 📷

Sesame Place
US 1 and I-95; tel 215/752-7070. A hands-on family play park just 30 minutes from downtown Philadelphia. Kids can climb through three stories of sloping, swaying fun on the Nets and Climbs, or crawl through tubes and tunnels and splashing fountains at Mumford's Water Maze. All of the best-loved *Sesame Street* characters perform in stage revues at the Circle Theatre; indoors, the Computer Gallery offers puzzles, logic games, and more than 70 computer activities for kids 3 to 13. Bathing suits are recommended for the water rides. **Open:** Peak (mid-May–Aug) daily 9am–8pm. Reduced hours off-season. **$$$$**

Lebanon

Founded in the late 18th century, Lebanon is now a farming and manufacturing center. **Information:** Lebanon Valley Tourist & Visitors Bureau, 625 Quentin Rd, PO Box 329, Lebanon, 17042 (tel 717/272-8555).

HOTEL 🏨

🏨🏨 Quality Inn Lebanon Valley
625 Quentin Rd, 17042; tel 717/273-6771 or toll free 800/626-8242; fax 717/273-4882. On PA 72, ½ mi S of US 422. This bright, mid-rise motel is a good base for visiting the Hershey antique car shows. **Rooms:** 130 rms. CI 3pm/CO noon. Nonsmoking rms avail. Attractive cherry-wood furniture. **Amenities:** 🛏 ⚴ A/C, cable TV, dataport. Some units w/terraces. **Services:** ✗ ⊠ ⇦ **Facilities:** ⟨₁⟩ ⟨400⟩ ⟨₂⟩ 1 restaurant, 1 bar (w/entertainment), games rm, beauty salon. **Rates:** Peak (June–Aug/Oct) $80–$98 S; $90–$109 D. Extra person $7. Children under age 18 stay free. Lower rates off-season. Parking: Outdoor, free. Higher rates during car shows. AE, CB, DC, DISC, MC, V.

ATTRACTION 📷

Cornwall Iron Furnace
US 322, Cornwall; tel 717/272-9711. The well-preserved Cornwall Iron Furnace was in use from 1742 until 1883. Among the products cast here were cannon for the Continental Army during the Revolutionary War, as well as domestic tools. The furnace itself is surrounded by related facilities, such as an open-pit mine and a complete 19th-century miners' village. The visitors center, the former Charcoal House, houses exhibits about the ironmaking process. **Open:** Tues–Sat 9am–5pm, Sun noon–5pm. **$$**

Lewisburg

This borough on the west branch of the Susquehanna River was laid out in 1785; today, it is best known as the home of Bucknell University. **Information:** Susquehanna Valley Visitors Bureau, 219D Hafer Rd, Lewisburg, 17837 (tel 717/524-7234).

ATTRACTIONS 📷

Packwood House Museum
15 N Water St; tel 717/524-0323. By the time it stopped serving travelers in 1886, this house, which began as a log building in 1796, had metamorphosed into the 27-room structure visible today. Now a museum, the building contains period furniture, artifacts, decorative arts, and other objects related to Susquehanna Valley history. **Open:** Tues–Fri 10am–5pm, Sat 1–5pm, Sun 2–5pm. **$$**

Slifer House Museum
1 River Rd; tel 717/524-2271. This Victorian mansion was built in 1861 for Eli Slifer, the Pennsylvania Secretary of State. The restored building houses a collection of period furniture and objects, and there are gorgeous views of the Susquehanna River. Guided tours are available. **Open:** Peak (Apr–Dec) Tues–Sun 1–4pm. Reduced hours off-season. **$**

Ligonier

Home to 410-acre Idlewild Park, believed to be the oldest continuously operated amusement park in the country. **Information:** Laurel Highlands, Inc, 120 E Main St, Ligonier, 15658 (tel 412/238-5661).

MOTEL 🏨

UNRATED Ramada Inn Historic Ligonier
216 W Loyalhanna St, 15658; tel 412/238-9545 or toll free 800/272-6232; fax 412/238-9803. 1 block off US 30. The only sizable lodgings in the historic district of the town. **Rooms:** 66 rms and stes. CI 4pm/CO noon. No smoking. Nonsmoking rms avail. **Amenities:** 🛏 ⚴ A/C, satel TV. 1 unit w/whirlpool. **Services:** ✗ 🚗 ⇦ **Facilities:** ⟨₁⟩ ⟨250⟩ ⟨₂⟩ 1 restaurant, 1 bar. **Rates:** Peak (Mem Day–Labor Day) $69–$92 S or D; $150 ste. Extra person $6. Children under age 13 stay free. Min stay special events. Lower rates off-season. Parking: Outdoor, free. AE, MC, V.

ATTRACTION 📷

Idlewild Park
US 30; tel 412/238-3666. A family-oriented fun park offering 15 major rides as well as a pool and a miniature-golf course. Among the attractions are a trolley ride through Mister Rogers' Neighborhood (featuring the characters of Fred Rogers' popular childrens' television program), and

Story Book Forest, where nursery rhymes are brought to life. **Open:** June–Aug, Tues–Sun at 10am, closing times vary. **$$$$**

Manayunk

See Philadelphia

Mansfield

On the Tioga River, this scenic borough in the Allegheny Mountains is home to Army State University.

MOTEL 🏨

≣ ≣ ≣ Comfort Inn

300 Gateway Dr, 16933; tel 717/662-3000 or toll free 800/ 822-5470; fax 717/662-2551. US 15 at US 6. A bright, hilltop motel built in 1991. Floral, country decor in the lobby and spotless housekeeping throughout. **Rooms:** 100 rms. CI 2pm/CO noon. Nonsmoking rms avail. **Amenities:** 🛁 A/C, cable TV. Some units w/whirlpools. **Services:** 🖎 🖘 ✑ Car-rental desk. **Facilities:** 🐚 ♿ 1 restaurant (lunch and dinner only), 1 bar (w/entertainment), games rm. Two miles to 18-hole public golf course. **Rates (CP):** Peak (June–Oct) $49–$75 S; $59–$85 D. Extra person $6. Children under age 18 stay free. Lower rates off-season. MAP rates avail. Parking: Outdoor, free. AE, CB, DC, DISC, ER, JCB, MC, V.

Mechanicsburg

Named for the large number of its inhabitants who were mechanics in the foundries and machine shops of nearby Harrisburg.

MOTEL 🏨

≣ ≣ ≣ Holiday Inn Harrisburg West

5401 Carlisle Pike, 17055; tel 717/697-0321 or toll free 800/ 772-STAY; fax 717/697-5917. Jct I-81/US 11S. The coloni-al-style entrance leads to an open lobby. Outdoor facilities make this a suitable place for family reunions and corporate picnics. **Rooms:** 219 rms and stes. CI 3pm/CO noon. Non-smoking rms avail. **Amenities:** 🛁 ♨ 🖭 A/C, satel TV w/movies, dataport. Some units w/whirlpools. Refrigerators on request. **Services:** ✕ 🚐 🖎 🖘 ✑ Car-rental desk, babysitting. **Facilities:** 🐚 🐚 1000 ♿ 1 restaurant, 2 bars (w/entertainment), volleyball, playground, washer/dryer. Softball field, picnic area with barbecue pits, miniature-golf course. **Rates (CP):** Peak (June–Oct) $89 S or D; $125–$250 ste. Children under age 18 stay free. Min stay special events. Lower rates off-season. Parking: Outdoor, free. AE, CB, DC, DISC, MC, V.

Mercer

A small borough settled in 1795 on the Neshannock Creek north of Pittsburgh, Mercer is a farming and trade center for the region and close to Shenango Lake. Seat of Mercer County.

MOTEL 🏨

≣ ≣ ≣ Howard Johnson Lodge

835 Perry Hwy, 16137; tel 412/748-3030 or toll free 800/ 542-7674; fax 412/748-3484. Exit 2 off I-80. This well-maintained motel is a good stopover for families with chil-dren. **Rooms:** 102 rms and stes. Executive level. CI 3pm/CO noon. Nonsmoking rms avail. Rooms are comfortable but not cluttered. Refrigerators available on request. **Amenities:** 🛁 ♨ A/C, cable TV w/movies. Some units w/terraces. **Services:** ✕ 🚐 🖎 🖘 🖘 **Facilities:** 🐚 🐚 200 🖥 ♿ 1 restaurant, 1 bar, games rm, sauna, playground, washer/dryer. **Rates:** $67–$71 S; $68–$74 D; $108 ste. Extra person $6. Children under age 18 stay free. Parking: Outdoor, free. AE, CB, DC, DISC, JCB, MC, V.

RESTAURANT 🍴

★ Iron Bridge Inn

1438 Perry Hwy; tel 412/748-3626. 2½ mi S of exit 2 off I-80. **American/Steak.** Dine surrounded by a mounted moose, a polar bear, two boars, a carousel horse, and local rustic memorabilia. Two fireplaces make it cozy in winter. Steak and prime rib are specialties; Cajun-style seafood, sandwiches, and light entrees are also popular. **FYI:** Reserva-tions not accepted. Children's menu. **Open:** Mon–Thurs 11am–10pm, Fri–Sat 11am–11:30pm, Sun 10:30am–10pm. **Prices:** Main courses $8–$20. AE, DC, DISC, MC, V. 🍷 🍹 ♿

Middletown

On the Susquehanna River, this borough is named for its location halfway between Lancaster and Carlisle. The Middle-town and Hummelstown Railroad still offers 1920 vintage passenger cars for excursions into pastoral countryside.

HOTEL 🏨

≣ ≣ DoubleTree Club Hotel

815 Eisenhower Blvd, 17057; tel 717/939-1600 or toll free 800/222-TREE; fax 717/939-8763. Exit 19 off I-26; exit 2W (Highspire) off I-283. A comfortable and well-maintained family hotel, where a player piano welcomes arriving guests. **Rooms:** 176 rms, stes, and effic. CI 4pm/CO 11am. Non-smoking rms avail. Some rooms overlook cemetery. **Amenities:** 🛁 ♨ 🖭 A/C, satel TV, dataport. Suites have microwaves and refrigerators. **Services:** ✕ 🚐 🖎 🖘 24-hour complimentary coffee in lobby. **Facilities:** 🐚 🐚 500 ♿ 1

restaurant (dinner only), 1 bar, games rm, spa, sauna, washer/dryer. **Rates (CP):** Peak (June–Sept 3) $69–$89 S; $69–$109 D; $100–$130 ste; $100–$130 effic. Extra person $10. Children under age 18 stay free. Min stay special events. Lower rates off-season. Parking: Outdoor, free. Hershey Park package includes tickets and dinner. AE, CB, DC, DISC, JCB, MC.

RESTAURANT 🍴

Alfred's Victorian Restaurant
38 N Union St; tel 717/944-5373. From the Square go left onto Union, then go 1½ blocks. **Continental/Italian.** Waitresses in period costume move among Victorian antiques and elaborate stained-glass windows in this opulent house. What may be the tiniest bar in the state is upstairs, with snug seating for four. The kitchen specializes in Northern Italian cuisine. **FYI:** Reservations recommended. Dress code. **Open:** Lunch Mon–Fri 11:30am–2pm; dinner Mon–Sat 5–10pm, Sun 3–9pm. **Prices:** Main courses $15–$20. AE, CB, DC, DISC, MC, V. 💟 🍽

Milford

See also Bushkill

This small community in the Poconos is located inside Delaware Water Gap National Recreational Area.

MOTEL 🏨

🛏 Myer Motel
US 6 and PA 209, 18337; tel 717/296-7223 or toll free 800/764-MYER. Three generations of the same family have operated this country-style motel. Many guests return annually to hunt or fish; it's also handy for travelers along the interstate and for budget-conscious families looking for a rural retreat. **Rooms:** 19 rms. CI noon/CO 11am. Nonsmoking rms avail. Large rooms with extra seating and a good grade of furniture. **Amenities:** 🛁 🕎 🍽 A/C, cable TV, refrig. All units w/terraces. **Services:** 🛎 🧺 **Facilities:** Lawn games. **Rates:** Peak (June–Oct) $45–$75 S or D. Extra person $7. Children under age 12 stay free. Lower rates off-season. Parking: Outdoor, free. AE, DISC, MC, V.

INN

🛏🛏🛏 Cliff Park Inn & Golf Course
Cliff Park Rd, 18337; tel 717/296-6491 or toll free 800/225-6535; fax 717/296-3982. Exit 10 off I-84, US 6E for 2 mi, right on 7th St, go 1½ mi, entrance on left. 600 acres. This 1820 building has been in the Buchanan family for five generations. Flowers are all around, and a large porch with rocking chairs surrounds the inn. **Rooms:** 18 rms and stes. CI 2pm/CO noon. Nonsmoking rms avail. Some rooms have enclosed porches with wicker furniture. **Amenities:** 🛁 🕎 A/C, voice mail. No TV. Some units w/terraces, some w/fire-

places. **Services:** Cross-country skis, boots, and poles available. **Facilities:** 🎿 ⛷ 🎣 ♿ 1 restaurant, 1 bar, guest lounge w/TV. Golf course was built in 1913. **Rates (BB):** Peak (May 23–Oct) $140–$160 D; $160 ste. Extra person $20. Children under age 1 stay free. Min stay peak. Lower rates off-season. MAP rates avail. Parking: Outdoor, free. Golf and honeymoon packages avail. AE, CB, DC, DISC, MC, V.

RESTAURANT 🍴

Waterwheel Café & Bakery
In Upper Mill, 150 Water St; tel 717/296-2383. Exit 10 off I-84, right 2½ mi, right on 7th St to Water St. **Cafe/Eclectic.** Proximity to the Sawkill Stream was a necessity when this 18th-century mill was in operation; now it provides an excellent view through a wall of windows or an outdoor deck. Breakfast includes lots of fresh fruit, eight kinds of muffins, croissants, and danishes. Soups, breads, specialty sandwiches, and healthy-choice selections are available for lunch and dinner. **FYI:** Reservations recommended. BYO. **Open:** Mon–Thurs 8am–5pm, Fri–Sat 8am–9pm, Sun 8am–4:30pm. **Prices:** Main courses $13–$16. MC, V. 🏔

Morgantown

Just outside the greater Philadelphia area, this small community features lakes and historic sites.

RESTAURANT 🍴

Windmill Family Restaurant
Jct PA 10 and 23; tel 610/286-5980. Exit 22 off tpk. **Regional American/American.** Pennsylvania Dutch cooking prevails under the turning windmill blades of this local landmark where chicken-corn soup, Lancaster County ham with raisin sauce, and egg noodles in chicken broth are favorites. Desserts are homemade and baked goods are for sale at the counter. Senior discounts avail. **FYI:** Reservations not accepted. Children's menu. No liquor license. **Open:** Sun–Thurs 7am–10pm, Fri–Sat 7am–11pm. **Prices:** Main courses $3–$11. AE, DISC, MC, V. 👫 ♿

Morrisville

A suburb of Philadelphia on the Delaware River opposite Trenton, NJ. Robert Morris, an 18th-century banker often called the financier of the American Revolution, lived here.

ATTRACTIONS 🏛

Pennsbury Manor
400 Pennsbury Memorial Rd; tel 215/946-0400. In 1683, William Penn, founder of Pennsylvania, built his home on this site. (The current building is a reconstruction.) The 43 acres of the manor also have such essential buildings as a blacksmith shop, barn, icehouse, and smokehouse. Costumed

interpreters explain life in the 16th and 17th centuries, and various classes and special events are offered. **Open:** Tues–Sat 9am–5pm, Sun noon–5pm. **$$**

Barnes Foundation
300 N Latches Lane, Merion; tel 610/667-0290. Albert Barnes made his fortune selling patent medicine, and used it to create one of the most impressive art collections in the world. Among the 1,000 masterpieces Barnes accumulated (and which are only recently on public display) are 180 Renoirs and 80 Cézannes, as well as works by Tintoretto, Bosch, Seurat, Chardin, Delacroix, Corot, and Lorrain. Barnes also collected folk art, including works from the Amish country and the Southwest, and household objects of aesthetic value. **Open:** Thurs 12:30–5pm, Fri–Sun 9:30am–5pm. **$$**

Mount Joy

Located in a residential area just west of Lancaster.

INN
Cameron Estate Inn
1855 Mansion Lane, 17552; tel 717/653 1773; fax 717/653-9432. Rheems exit off PA 283E, then Colebrook Rd to right on Donegal Springs Rd. 15 acres. Wind through country roads to reach this rural property, originally a large estate and now an inn. Unsuitable for children under 12. **Rooms:** 17 rms and stes. CI 1pm/CO 10am. Nonsmoking rms avail. The spacious rooms are individually decorated. One unit is said to be haunted. **Amenities:** A/C. No phone or TV. Some units w/fireplaces. **Services:** Facilities: 1 restaurant (dinner only; see "Restaurants" below), lawn games, guest lounge w/TV. **Rates (CP):** Peak (Mar–Oct) $65–$115 S or D; $95–$115 ste. Extra person $10. Min stay wknds. Lower rates off-season. Parking: Outdoor, free. AE, CB, DC, DISC, MC, V.

RESTAURANTS
★ Bube's Brewery
In Central Hotel, 102 N Market St; tel 717/653-2160. 1 block off Main St. **Regional American.** A historic spot with three dining possibilities. The Bottling Works of the brewery once produced soft drinks and beer made from water drawn from limestone caverns below; lunch and dinner are served there now. Alois's serves a six-course dinner in the Victorian dining rooms of the old hotel, and The Catacombs, several stories below the street in the aging cellars, is open for dinner every night. **FYI:** Reservations recommended. Dress code. **Open:** Mon–Thurs 11am–midnight, Fri–Sat 11am–2am, Sun noon–midnight. **Prices:** Main courses $15–$29. DISC, MC, V.

Groff's Farm Restaurant
650 Pinkerton Rd; tel 717/653-2048. Pinkerton Rd off PA 772. **Regional American/German.** Authentic Pennsylvania Dutch fare, served either family style or à la carte. The 1756 farmhouse is filled with period antiques and wallpaper, and the hearty food is widely acclaimed. **FYI:** Reservations recommended. Children's menu. Dress code. **Open:** Lunch Tues–Sat 11:30am–1:30pm; dinner Tues–Fri 5–7:30pm, Sat 5–8pm. Closed weekdays in Jan. **Prices:** Main courses $14–$25; prix fixe $16–$25. AE, CB, DC, DISC, MC, V.

Restaurant
In Cameron Estate Inn, 1855 Mansion Lane; tel 717/653-1773. I-283 to 2nd Mount Joy exit. **American.** Winner of many awards, this restaurant features rustic cuisine from America and Europe. The lovely building dates from 1805, and was constructed by Dr John Watson, great-grandfather of President McKinley. **FYI:** Reservations recommended. Dress code. No smoking. **Open:** Mon–Thurs 6–8:30pm, Fri–Sat 5:30–9:30pm, Sun 10:30am–1:30pm. **Prices:** Main courses $13–$22. AE, CB, DC, DISC, MC, V.

Mount Pocono

A small borough between the Big Pocono and Toby Hanna State Parks. Nearby Lake Pocono offers many outdoor activities, including air tours of the area.

RESORTS
Caesar's Paradise Stream
PA 940, PO Box 99, 18344; tel 717/839-8881 or toll free 800/233-4141; fax 717/226-6982. Exit 8 off 380, PA 940 E for about 7 mi. 138 acres. A classic Poconos-style couples resort, with big-name entertainers and lots of indoor and outdoor activities. The decorating theme is neo-Roman, with columns, stone bridges, and tiled floors. Sybaritic or glitzy, depending on your attitude, but even detractors admit the place is well planned and beautifully maintained. **Rooms:** 164 rms and stes; 24 cottages/villas. CI 3pm/CO 11am. **Amenities:** A/C, cable TV, refrig, VCR. Some units w/terraces, all w/fireplaces, all w/whirlpools. Many units have pools and saunas. (Cleopatra suites have hot tubs shaped like huge champagne glasses!) Breakfast in bed available. Daily newspaper advises guests of activities. **Services:** Social director, masseur. **Facilities:** 2 restaurants, 2 bars (1 w/entertainment), basketball, volleyball, games rm, lawn games, racquetball, spa, whirlpool, washer/dryer. Free use of facilities at all four nearby Caesar's resorts. **Rates (MAP):** $500–$640 ste; $470 cottage/villa. Parking: Outdoor, free. Weekend (murder-mystery, country-and-western) and Valentine packages avail. AE, CB, DC, DISC, MC, V.

≡≡≡ Mount Airy Lodge

42 Woodland Rd, 18344; tel 717/839-8811 or toll free 800/441-4410. Exit 44 off I-80 to PA 611, follow signs. 2,500 acres. A vast resort property with a variety of indoor and outdoor activities. The service is solicitous and the grounds are well maintained, but years of heavy use are showing in the rooms. **Rooms:** 573 rms, stes, and effic. Executive level. CI 4pm/CO 11am. Nonsmoking rms avail. Decor dates from 1970s and needs revamping. **Amenities:** 🛏 A/C, cable TV, voice mail. Some units w/terraces, some w/fireplaces, some w/whirlpools. **Services:** ✗ ⊂⟩ ⇔ Social director, masseur, children's program, babysitting. Second-floor lobby hosts special events, including sketch artists and psychics. Service desk provides daily activity schedules, maps, and discount ski passes. **Facilities:** ⨍ ⚲ △ ⃟ ▶₁₈ ⊠ ⚓ 🏹 ◕₁ ⊌ ⬚₃₀₀₀ ⅋ 2 restaurants, 2 bars (1 w/entertainment), 1 beach (lake shore), lifeguard, basketball, volleyball, games rm, lawn games, racquetball, spa, sauna, steam rm. Small indoor ice rink. Snowmobiles and sleds available. Large gift shop. **Rates (MAP):** Peak (Mem Day–Labor Day) $150–$210 S or D; $240–$270 ste; $315 effic. Extra person $55. Children under age 4 stay free. Min stay peak, wknds, and special events. Lower rates off-season. Parking: Outdoor, free. AE, CB, DC, DISC, MC, V.

≡≡≡ Pocono Gardens Lodge

Paradise Valley, 18344; tel 717/839-8811 or toll free 800/441-4410. Exit 8 off I-380, PA 940 E for 8 mi on right. The main building needs renovation, but rooms are clean and have the basics plus some unique amenities. **Rooms:** 150 rms. Executive level. CI 4pm/CO 11am. **Amenities:** 🛏 A/C, cable TV, refrig, CD/tape player, voice mail. Some units w/terraces, some w/fireplaces, some w/whirlpools. Some rooms have pools, saunas, and heart-shaped whirlpool tubs. **Services:** ✗ Social director. Champagne and a seven-course meal served on Monday. **Facilities:** ⨍ △ ▶₁₈ ⊠ ⚓ 🏹 ◕₁ ⊌ 2 restaurants, 1 bar (w/entertainment), basketball, volleyball, games rm, lawn games, racquetball. Rowboats available to take out on the lake. Large gift shop. **Rates (MAP):** Peak (Mem Day–Labor Day) $150–$270 S or D. Extra person $55. Min stay peak, wknds, and special events. Lower rates off-season. Parking: Outdoor, free. Rates vary with accommodation, season, and length of stay. AE, CB, DC, DISC, MC, V.

≡≡ Strickland's Mountain Inn

Woodland Rd, 18344; tel 717/839-7155 or toll free 800/441-4410; fax 717/839-3814. Exit 44 off I-80 to PA 611 N, follow signs. 400 acres. This rustic couples-oriented resort on a hillside in the Poconos offers a range of activities. The facilities look old and well used, but the grounds are large. **Rooms:** 90 rms and stes; 33 cottages/villas. Executive level. CI 2pm/CO 11am. Decor is ready for an update. **Amenities:** 🛏 A/C, cable TV, CD/tape player, voice mail. Some units w/terraces, some w/fireplaces, some w/whirlpools. **Services:** ✗ ⊶ Social director, masseur. **Facilities:** ⨍ △ ▶₁₈ ⊠ ⚓ 🏹 ◕₁ ⊌ 1 restaurant, 4 bars (1 w/entertainment), basketball,

volleyball, games rm, lawn games, racquetball, sauna, whirlpool. Roller skating rink, shuffleboard, indoor and outdoor miniature golf, archery. Free use of facilities at Mount Airy Lodge and Pocono Gardens Lodge. **Rates (MAP):** Peak (Mem Day–Labor Day) $150–$230 S or D; $260–$275 ste; $260–$275 cottage/villa. Extra person $40–$50. Lower rates off-season. AP rates avail. Parking: Outdoor, free. Rates vary with room, season, and length of stay. Midweek rates lower. AE, CB, DC, DISC, MC, V.

RESTAURANTS 🍴

Bailey's Steakhouse

PA 611; tel 717/839-9678. Exit 8 off I-380 to PA 940 E to PA 611 N. **American/Steak.** This renovated manor home began as a convent for the Diocese of Scranton, and the interior shows lots of wood and stone, with ivory wallpaper and many prints and plants around the dining area. Ribs, fajitas, and steaks dominate the menu, and a patio is open in warm weather. **FYI:** Reservations recommended. Children's menu. **Open:** Mon–Thurs 11:30am–10pm, Fri–Sat 11:30am–11pm, Sun 11:30am–9pm. **Prices:** Main courses $9–$24. AE, DISC, MC, V. 🍽 👪 ♥ ⅋

Damenti's

PA 309, Mountaintop; tel 717/788-2004. Exit 39 off I-80/Exit 42 off I-81. **Italian/Steak.** A popular dining spot for nearly 50 years, this Italian steak house is in an old home in the mountains that creates an elegant, yet rustic air. Steaks and crab meat are popular, and there are always four daily specials and homemade desserts. **FYI:** Reservations recommended. **Open:** Tues–Sat 5–10pm, Sun 4–9pm. **Prices:** Main courses $12–$36. AE, MC, V. ⅋

Myerstown

West of Harrisburg, this small borough laid out in 1768 offer dozens of 18th-and 19th-century structures. Light manufacturing and tourism drive the local economy.

MOTEL 🏨

≡≡≡ Lantern Lodge Motor Inn

411 N College St, 17067; tel 717/866-6536 or toll free 800/262-5564; fax 717/866-6536. On PA 501, 1 block N of US 422. A modern motel with a distinctly European feel. **Rooms:** 77 rms and stes; 2 cottages/villas. CI 2pm/CO 11am. Nonsmoking rms avail. Rooms feature attractive hardwood Pennsylvania House furniture and heated bathroom floors. Cottages have three bedrooms, living room, kitchen, dining room, and two baths. **Amenities:** 🛏 ⚟ ⊡ A/C, cable TV. All units w/terraces, some w/fireplaces, 1 w/whirlpool. **Services:** ✗ ⊠ ⊂⟩ Car-rental desk, masseur, babysitting. **Facilities:** ⬚₁₀₀ ⅋ 1 restaurant, 2 bars (1 w/entertainment), beauty salon, playground. Free public pool two blocks away. **Rates:** Peak (Apr–Nov) $60–$90 S; $80–$95 D; $110–$225 ste; $150–

$175 cottage/villa. Extra person $10. Children under age 12 stay free. Lower rates off-season. Parking: Outdoor, free. AE, CB, DC, DISC, MC, V.

New Hope

Artists and craftspeople favor this scenic river town just north of Philadelphia. Unique shopping and dining, and proximity to the Delaware Canal and Washington Crossing Historical Park, draw many visitors.

MOTEL

UNRATED Best Western New Hope Inn

6426 Lower York Rd, 18938; tel 215/862-5221 or toll free 800/467-3202; fax 215/862-5847. US 202, 2 mi W of Historic New Hope. A basic hotel catering to the corporate traveler. The small lobby is clean and bright. **Rooms:** 152 rms. CI 3pm/CO 11am. Nonsmoking rms avail. All rooms were refurbished in 1995. **Amenities:** A/C, cable TV, dataport. **Services:** **Facilities:** 1 restaurant (bkfst and dinner only), 1 bar (w/entertainment), washer/dryer. **Rates:** Peak (Apr–Dec) $85–$149 S or D. Children under age 18 stay free. Min stay special events. Lower rates off-season. Parking: Outdoor, free. AE, CB, DC, DISC, MC, V.

INNS

Black Bass Hotel

3774 River Rd, Lumberville, 18933; tel 215/297-5770; fax 215/297-0262. US 202 to PA 32 N. 5 acres. British royal memorabilia and Victorian antiques make this property an Anglophile's dream. Splendid views of the Delaware River. Has been operating as an inn since the 1740s. No children permitted. Unsuitable for children under 18. **Rooms:** 9 rms and stes (7 w/shared bath). CI 2pm/CO 11am. Nonsmoking rms avail. Fine woodwork and hardwood floors. **Amenities:** A/C. No phone or TV. Some units w/terraces. **Services:** Twice-daily maid svce. **Facilities:** 1 restaurant (see "Restaurants" below), 2 bars (1 w/entertainment), guest lounge. **Rates (CP):** $125–$175 ste. Min stay wknds. Parking: Outdoor, free. AE, CB, DC, DISC, ER, MC, V.

UNRATED Hacienda Inn

36 W Mechanic St, 18938; tel 215/862-2078 or toll free 800/272-2078; fax 215/862-9119. Exit 32S off US 202; after ½ mi turn right on W Mechanic St. Features a more relaxed atmosphere than that of most inns in this area. This is the place to stay if you don't care about (or don't want) a room furnished with antiques. **Rooms:** 33 rms and stes. CI 2pm/CO noon. No smoking. **Amenities:** A/C, cable TV, refrig. Some units w/terraces, some w/fireplaces, some w/whirlpools. **Services:** **Facilities:** 1 restaurant (dinner only), 1 bar (w/entertainment), washer/dryer,

guest lounge. Guests can use nearby tennis courts. **Rates (CP):** $55–$100 D; $95–$160 ste. Extra person $25. Min stay wknds. Parking: Outdoor, free. AE, MC, V.

Holly Hedge Bed & Breakfast

6897 Upper York Rd, 18938; tel 215/862-3136 or toll free 800/378-4496; fax 215/862-0960. Exit 32N off US 202, then 263W. 25 acres. Built in 1740, this building has had previous lives as a residence and a school. Today's inn is surrounded by beautiful scenery (including several ponds) and is loaded with country charm and ambience. **Rooms:** 14 rms; 3 cottages/villas. CI 2pm/CO 11am. No smoking. Large rooms, furnished with Victorian antiques. **Amenities:** A/C. No TV. Some units w/terraces, some w/fireplaces. **Facilities:** Washer/dryer, guest lounge w/TV. Library. **Rates (BB):** Peak (May–Dec) $95–$150 D; $95–$150 cottage/villa. Extra person $18. Children under age 1 stay free. Lower rates off-season. Parking: Outdoor, free. AE, CB, DC, DISC, MC, V.

Hotel du Village

2535 North River Rd, 18938; tel 215/862-5164; fax 215/862-9788. This country estate—a popular romantic getaway—has lots of rustic charm. Built in 1895 as a country residence and later used as a young ladies' finishing school, it has been an inn since 1977. No children under 12 on weekends. **Rooms:** 19 rms. CI 2pm/CO 11am. Nonsmoking rms avail. **Amenities:** A/C. No phone or TV. 1 unit w/whirlpool. **Services:** Twice-daily maid svce. **Facilities:** 1 restaurant (dinner only), 1 bar, playground, guest lounge. **Rates (CP):** $85–$100 D. Extra person $5. Children under age 12 stay free. Min stay peak and wknds. Parking: Outdoor, free. AE, DC.

Logan Inn

10 W Ferry St, 18938; tel 215/862-2300. Exit 32S off US 202, go 2 mi to right on W Ferry St. Built circa 1722, this building has housed an inn since 1727. With so much history, you'd expect a few ghosts (in fact, one of the rooms is supposedly haunted), though there's also lots of hustle and bustle from the tavern downstairs. **Rooms:** 16 rms and stes. CI 3pm/CO noon. Nonsmoking rms avail. Colonial period furnishings and fresh flowers in rooms. **Amenities:** A/C, cable TV. **Services:** **Facilities:** 1 restaurant, 1 bar. Cozy Terry Tavern has fireplace and fine woodwork. Alfresco dining in summer. **Rates (BB):** $75–$150 D; $95–$150 ste. Extra person $15. Min stay wknds. Parking: Outdoor, free. Corporate rates avail. AE, CB, DC, MC, V.

Wedgwood Collection of Historic Inns

11 W Bridge St, 18938; tel 215/862-2520. Three 19th-century homes on over two acres of carefully landscaped grounds in the historic district. Interiors are filled with lots of Wedgwood pottery and original artwork, and there's a fireplace in the cozy main parlor. **Rooms:** 18 rms and stes. CI 3pm/CO 11am. No smoking. Ceiling fans, fresh flowers, and

Victorian furniture; many rooms have four-poster canopy beds. **Amenities:** ☎ ⚴ A/C, cable TV, bathrobes. Some units w/terraces, some w/fireplaces. Refrigerators available. **Services:** ⊙— ⊠ ⎘ ⊲⊳ Twice-daily maid svce, car-rental desk, social director, babysitting, wine/sherry served. Extensive country breakfast served on a sunny enclosed porch; afternoon tea and pastries. **Facilities:** ⬚ ⫞ ⊠ ⎗²⁴ ⚹ Lawn games, sauna, steam rm, whirlpool, playground, guest lounge w/TV. Privileges at local swim and tennis club. **Rates (BB):** $100–$170 D w/shared bath; $180–$205 ste. Extra person $30. Min stay wknds. Parking: Outdoor, free. Midweek discounts avail. AE, MC, V.

RESTAURANTS 🍴

♥ Centre Bridge Inn Restaurant
In Centre Bridge Inn, 2998 N River Rd; tel 215/862-9139. Exit 32N off PA 202. **French.** Housed in a 1705 building alongside the Delaware River. The main dining room is old and romantic, with open beams, wooden pillars, white walls, and a huge, open hearth. The kitchen has a reputation for serving up generous portions of country French cuisine. **FYI:** Reservations recommended. **Open:** Dinner Mon–Thurs 5:30–9:30pm, Fri–Sat 5:30–10pm, Sun 3:30–8pm; brunch Sun 11:30am–2:30pm. **Prices:** Main courses $17–$29. AE, MC, V. ♥ ▤ ♔ 🖼 ⛰ VP

Hotel Du Village Restaurant
In Hotel Du Village, 2535 N River Rd; tel 215/862-9911. **French.** French cuisine prepared with garden-fresh ingredients draws diners to this rich, mahogany-paneled dining room on a large country estate. Fireplaces at either end of the room add to the warm yet rustic charm. **FYI:** Reservations recommended. Children's menu. Dress code. **Open:** Wed–Thurs 5:30–10pm, Fri–Sat 5:30–11:30pm, Sun 3–9pm. Closed two wks in Jan. **Prices:** Main courses $14–$19. AE, DC. ♥ 🖼 ⚹

Jenny's
In Peddler's Village, Jct US 202/Street Rd; tel 215/794-4021. **Continental.** The dining room at this upscale family eatery is decorated in Victorian and country furnishings, with beautiful stained-glass windows. The food is country French, and the Sunday brunch features Dixieland jazz. Prix fixe $11 dinner special available Tue–Fri, 4–6pm. **FYI:** Reservations recommended. Jazz. **Open:** Lunch Tues–Sat 11am–3pm; dinner Sun 4:30–8pm, Tues–Thurs 4–9pm, Fri 4–10pm, Sat 5–10pm; brunch Sun 11am–3pm. **Prices:** Main courses $18–$25. AE, CB, DC, DISC, MC, V. ♥

Restaurant
In Black Bass Hotel, 3774 River Rd, Lumberville; tel 215/297-5770. 6 mi from exit 32N off US 202. **New American.** The original owners of this inn were loyal to England in 1776, and the present management has retained an Anglophilic flavor in the current decor. Antique selling tables and butcher blocks rest on hardwood floors beneath exposed beams in the five dining rooms, and views of the Delaware River and canal are dramatic. Fresh fish and wild game are the stars of the menu. **FYI:** Reservations recommended. Piano/violin. No smoking. **Open:** Mon–Sat noon–10pm, Sun 11am–10pm. **Prices:** Main courses $18–$27. AE, CB, DC, DISC, MC, V. ♥ ▤ ⛰ ⚹

ATTRACTION 📷

Parry Mansion
45 S Main St; tel 215/862-5148. The home of lumberman Benjamin Parry, a wealthy New Hope resident, is now a museum. Parry built the home in 1784, and it remained in his family until 1966. The museum's collection of furniture and objects from several different periods documents the evolution of the house and of the town. **Open:** May–Dec, Fri–Sun 1–5pm. $$

New Stanton

Just SE of Pittsburgh, this borough of some 2,000 is in the heart of the Laurel Highlands resort area.

MOTELS 🏨

≝≝ Days Inn
127 W Byers Ave, 15672; tel 412/925-3591 or toll free 800/DAYS-INN; fax 412/925-9859. A standard, well-maintained motel, convenient to both I-70 and the Pennsylvania Turnpike. **Rooms:** 140 rms. CI 2pm/CO 11am. Nonsmoking rms avail. **Amenities:** ☎ 🖥 A/C, satel TV w/movies. Some units w/terraces. Single rooms have microwaves, refrigerators, and dataports. **Services:** ✕ 🚗 ⊠ ⎘ **Facilities:** ⬚ ⫞ ⊠ ⎙ ⎗³⁰⁰ ⚹ 1 restaurant (bkfst and dinner only), 1 bar (w/entertainment), washer/dryer. Three ski slopes nearby. **Rates:** Peak (Apr–Oct) $49 S; $54–$58 D. Extra person $5. Children under age 18 stay free. Lower rates off-season. Parking: Outdoor, free. Ski packages avail. AE, DISC, MC, V.

≝≝ Howard Johnson Lodge
112 W Byers Ave, 15672; tel 412/925-3511 or toll free 800/446-4656. An extremely clean, family-operated motel, with a large, grassy courtyard. **Rooms:** 87 rms. CI 1pm/CO noon. Nonsmoking rms avail. **Amenities:** ☎ ⚴ A/C, cable TV w/movies. All units w/terraces. Refrigerators on request. **Services:** 🚗 ⊠ ⎘ ⊲⊳ VCRs and videos available for rent. Pets in smoking rooms only; credit card deposit required. **Facilities:** ⬚ ⫞ ⊠ ⚹ 1 restaurant, playground. **Rates (CP):** Peak (June–Sept) $61–$73 S or D. Extra person $5. Children under age 18 stay free. Lower rates off-season. Parking: Outdoor, free. Ski packages avail. AE, DC, DISC, MC, V.

Newton

ATTRACTION 📷

Buckingham Valley Vineyard and Winery
1521 PA 413, Buckingham; tel 215/794-7188. Located 4 mi
N of Newton, Buckingham Valley Vineyards produces estate-
bottled vintage varietal wines. A family business founded in
1966, the farm vineyard uses both traditional methods and
high technology. (While some wines are aged in small oak
casks, other vintages are produced in sterile stainless steel
tanks.) The vineyards and wine cellars can be toured, and the
wines sampled for free. Wine is also sold by the bottle or the
case. **Open:** Peak (Mar–Dec) Tues–Sat 11am–6pm, Sun
noon–4pm. **Free**

Newtown

The Langhorne Players, a popular contemporary theater
company, and a noted winery bring distinction to this small
borough just north of Philadelphia.

RESTAURANT 🍽

Jean Pierre's
101 S State St; tel 215/968-6201. 3 mi from Newtown exit
(PA 332 W) off I-95. **French.** Chef Jean Pierre Tardy
consistently gets high praise for the food and service in his
charming Country French–style eatery. The building dates
from 1743 and its decor features antique furniture, paintings
of Paris, fresh flowers, and polished hardwood floors. **FYI:**
Reservations accepted. Dress code. No smoking. **Open:**
Lunch Tues–Fri 11am–2pm; dinner Tues–Sat 5:30–9pm,
Sun 4–8pm. **Prices:** Main courses $22–$29. AE, CB, DC,
DISC, MC, V. ♜

Norristown

A Philadelphia suburb, laid out in 1704 on the Schuylkill
River.

RESTAURANT 🍽

Trolley Stop
PA 73; tel 610/584-4849. **New American/Continental.** A
turn-of-the-century trolley car provides a unique setting in
which to enjoy steak, seafood, and pasta entrees. The cozy bar
curves around an open-fire brazier, adding to the charm.
FYI: Reservations recommended. Piano/singer. Children's
menu. **Open:** Mon–Thurs 11:30am–11pm, Fri–Sat
11:30am–midnight, Sun 11am–9pm. **Prices:** Main courses
$10–$30. AE, CB, DC, DISC, MC, V. 💟 ⚜

Oil City

An important oil and petroleum center during the 19th
century, Oil City is still a major energy-producing area.

HOTEL 🏨

≡≡≡ Holiday Inn
1 Seneca St, 16301 (Downtown); tel 814/677-1221 or toll
free 800/HOLIDAY; fax 814/677-0492. PA 8 to right on
Seneca St. This new-looking building is actually 30 years old,
but it is in excellent condition. Business travelers to this
industrial area make up most of the clientele, supplemented
in summer by vacationers who come to ride the nearby scenic
railroad and take in the region's history. **Rooms:** 106 rms and
stes. Executive level. CI 3pm/CO noon. Nonsmoking rms
avail. **Amenities:** �ⓩ A/C, cable TV w/movies, dataport,
in-rm safe. Some units w/whirlpools. **Services:** ✕ 🚐 ⚐
🛎 **Facilities:** 🏋 250 ⚜ 1 restaurant, 1 bar (w/entertain-
ment), washer/dryer. **Rates:** Peak (June–Aug) $69 S; $79 D;
$116 ste. Extra person $10. Children under age 12 stay free.
Lower rates off-season. MAP rates avail. Parking: Outdoor,
free. AE, CB, DC, DISC, MC, V.

Paoli

RESTAURANT 🍽

Willistown Grille
4 Manor Rd; tel 610/695-8990. Manor Rd at Lancaster Ave.
Continental. A cozy and clubby dining room with dark green
decor and paintings of Philadelphia's old-money Main Line
society on the walls. The menu is focused on the continental
classics, although the chef will try to honor any special
requests. **FYI:** Reservations recommended. **Open:** Mon–Fri
11:30am–10pm, Sat 5am–10pm. **Prices:** Main courses $12–
$20. AE, DC, DISC, MC, V. VP ⚜

Paradise

Township in Pennsylvania Dutch country, just NE of Lancaster, on the Pequea Creek.

RESTAURANT 🍽

★ Historic Revere Tavern
3063 Lincoln Hwy; tel 717/687-8601. On US 30 about 5 mi
E of PA 896. **Seafood/Steak.** Stone walls and a fireplace
dominate the main dining room in this warm and romantic
spot. Beef and seafood are the chief offerings on the dinner
menu; a lighter lunch menu is served in the adjoining carriage
house. Service is friendly throughout. **FYI:** Reservations
recommended. Children's menu. Dress code. **Open:** Lunch

Mon–Sat 11am–3pm; dinner Mon–Sat 5–10pm, Sun 4–9pm. **Prices:** Main courses $10–$29. AE, CB, DC, DISC, MC, V. 🍷 📷 🖼 ♿

Philadelphia

See also Bryn Athyn, King of Prussia, Langhorne, Morrisville, New Hope, Newtown, Norristown, Willow Grove

The state's largest city, Philadelphia was first laid out in 1682, chartered in 1701, and was the colonial capital during most of the Revolutionary War. It became the birthplace of the Declaration of Independence, the Constitution, and the Bill of Rights, and was the new nation's capital until 1800. Today's Philadelphia is known for its historic attractions, colorful neighborhoods, world-class restaurants, and educational institutions, including the University of Pennsylvania and Temple University. **Information:** Philadelphia Convention & Visitors Bureau, 1515 Market St #2020, Philadelphia, 19102 (tel 215/636-3300).

PUBLIC TRANSPORTATION

SEPTA (Southeastern Pennsylvania Transportation Authority) operates an extensive network of trolleys, buses, commuter trains, and subways in and around Philadelphia. Fares for any SEPTA route are $1.50, transfers cost 40¢. For more information, call SEPTA (tel 215/580-7800) between 6am and midnight daily.

HOTELS 🏨

≡≡≡≡ Adam's Mark Philadelphia

City Ave and Monument Rd, 19131; tel 215/581-5000 or toll free 800/444-ADAM; fax 215/581-5069. City Ave exit off US 76 W. The building itself looks a bit like an airport control tower, but inside, the service and amenities really shine. **Rooms:** 515 rms and stes. Executive level. CI 3pm/CO noon. Nonsmoking rms avail. All rooms have two armchairs, round wood table, and wall-length drapes. **Amenities:** 📞 🛁 🍴 A/C, cable TV w/movies, dataport, voice mail. Some units w/whirlpools. **Services:** ✕ 🔑 📹 🚐 🛄 🍽 Twice-daily maid svce, car-rental desk, masseur, babysitting. **Facilities:** 🏋 🏊 🏊 🖥 2 restaurants, 2 bars (w/entertainment), racquetball, spa, sauna, whirlpool, beauty salon, washer/dryer. Extensive health and sports facilities include Nautilus and stairstepper machines. **Rates:** $95–$157 S or D; $185–$310 ste. Children under age 12 stay free. Parking: Indoor, free. AE, CB, DC, DISC, MC, V.

≡≡≡≡ The Bellevue Hotel

1415 Chancellor Court, 19102 (Downtown); tel 215/893-1776 or toll free 800/221-0833. Known until recently as Atop The Bellevue (due to its location on the 19th floor of an office tower), now under new management and known as just The Bellevue. Unfortunately, the office lobby is much more imposing than the hotel's unimpressive lobby/lounge. **Rooms:** 290 rms and stes. Executive level. CI 3pm/CO noon.

Nonsmoking rms avail. Rooms are undistinguished, except for elaborate drapes and tie-backs. Windows can be opened only with key from maintenance department and only after guests signs legal waiver; soundproofing is less than dependable. **Amenities:** 📞 🛁 🍴 A/C, cable TV, dataport, bathrobes. All units w/minibars, 1 w/whirlpool. Turndown service on request; large, well-stocked minibar; two-line speaker phones. **Services:** 🍽 🔑 📹 🚐 🛄 🍽 Twice-daily maid svce, masseur, children's program, babysitting. Well-intentioned but inconsistent staff; luggage can take a long time getting from street level entrance to 18th-floor rooms. Cookies and milk for kids at bedtime. **Facilities:** 🍴 1700 🖥 ♿ 3 restaurants (see "Restaurants" below), 2 bars (1 w/entertainment), sauna. The 19th-floor public rooms include the blue-and-white Ethel Barrymore Room, for afternoon tea and Sunday brunch; the grand, wood-paneled bar and lounge/library (now disfigured with a TV set); and the rotunda-like restaurant, known as The Founders' Room for its statues of the nation's Founding Fathers. Guest privileges at The Sporting Club at The Bellevue (next door, above the parking garage), an extraordinary 93,000-square-foot, multilevel arena with NBA-size basketball court (popular with visiting celebrities) and 100-station fitness center. **Rates:** $205–$850 S or D; $950–$1,250 ste. Extra person $15. Children under age 12 stay free. Parking: Indoor, $22/day. Rates are slightly less than those of its nearby competitors but, except for the Sporting Club, the Bellevue also offers much less in the way of service and amenities. AE, CB, DC, DISC, ER, JCB, MC, V.

≡≡ Best Western Center City

501 N 22nd St, 19130 (Center City); tel 215/568-8300; fax 215/559-9448. 1 block N of Ben Franklin Pkwy. Perched on a small hill behind the Auguste Rodin Museum, and close to the Museum of Art, restaurants, and shops. **Rooms:** 183 rms and stes. CI 3pm/CO noon. Nonsmoking rms avail. Rooms on south side have views of skyline and the Benjamin Franklin Pkwy, known as "the Champs Elysée of Philadelphia." **Amenities:** 📞 A/C, cable TV. **Services:** 🛄 🍽 Children's program, babysitting. **Facilities:** 🍴 🏊 60 ♿ **Rates:** $69–$89 S; $79–$99 D; $159 ste. Extra person $10. Children under age 16 stay free. Parking: Outdoor, free. AE, CB, DC, DISC, MC, V.

≡≡ Best Western Independence Park Inn

235 Chestnut St, 19106; tel 215/922-4443 or toll free 800/624-2988; fax 215/922-4487. An inviting lobby with comfortable seating, a fireplace, and historic ambience distinguish this hotel located across from the Visitors Center. **Rooms:** 36 rms. CI 3pm/CO noon. Nonsmoking rms avail. Brightest rooms overlook atrium. Some others have views of Independence Park. **Amenities:** 📞 🛁 🍴 A/C, cable TV w/movies, dataport. King rooms have two telephones. **Services:** 🛄 🍽 Babysitting. Coffee and tea in lobby. Video rentals. Continental breakfast served on lovely china by waiters in atrium dining room. **Facilities:** 40 ♿ **Rates (CP):**

$125–$145 S; $135–$155 D. Extra person $10. Children under age 18 stay free. Corporate, group, and weekend package rates avail. AE, DC, DISC, JCB, MC, V.

≣≣≣ Clarion Suites Convention Center
1010 Race St, 19107; tel 215/922-1730 or toll free 800/CLARION; fax 215/922-6258. A mid-rise, all-suites hotel with a bright and attractive lobby and large rooms. It is not obvious that this was once the Bentwood Furniture factory. **Rooms:** 96 effic. CI 3pm/CO 11am. Nonsmoking rms avail. Units resemble apartments, with high ceilings and full kitchens. Two top-floor suites have spiral staircases to roof deck. **Amenities:** 🛅 ⚲ 🎦 🍴 A/C, cable TV w/movies, refrig, dataport. **Services:** ✗ ⌨ 🚐 🛅 ↵ ⬗ Babysitting. Copy and fax services. Coffee all day in lobby. **Facilities:** 🛖 [250] ⚐ 1 restaurant (lunch and dinner only), 1 bar. **Rates (CP):** $130–$160 effic. Extra person $10. Children under age 18 stay free. Parking: Indoor, $8/day. Group and seasonal (Dec–Jan) discounts avail. AE, DC, DISC, MC, V.

≣≣ Comfort Inn at Penn's Landing
100 N Columbus Blvd, 19106; tel 215/627-7900 or toll free 800/228-5158; fax 215/238-0809. Exit 16 off I-95, left on Delaware Ave, 1½ mi on left. A modest yet pleasant chain hotel, close to major routes and overlooking the Delaware River and the Philadelphia skyline. **Rooms:** 185 rms and stes. CI 3pm/CO noon. Nonsmoking rms avail. Thick soundproofing reduces the highway sounds somewhat. **Amenities:** 🛅 ⚲ 🎦 A/C, cable TV w/movies, dataport, voice mail. Safe-deposit boxes, refrigerators, hair dryers, dataports available. **Services:** 🚐 🛅 ↵ Babysitting. Courtesy van to historic attractions and shopping. **Facilities:** [45] ⚐ 1 bar. **Rates (CP):** Peak (Apr–Oct) $99–$109 S; $109–$119 D; $109–$119 ste. Extra person $10. Children under age 18 stay free. Lower rates off-season. Parking: Outdoor, $6–$10/day. Senior discounts avail. AE, DC, DISC, MC, V.

≣≣≣ DoubleTree Guest Suites
4101 Island Ave, 19153; tel 215/365-6600 or toll free 800/222-TREE; fax 215/492-9858. Island Ave exit off I-95. An enclosed square with a covered lobby area, located in a light industrial zone near the airport and I-95. Geared to business travelers. **Rooms:** 251 rms and stes. CI 3pm/CO noon. Nonsmoking rms avail. Some rooms have conference tables. **Amenities:** 🛅 ⚲ 🎦 🍴 A/C, cable TV w/movies, refrig, dataport. All units w/minibars, 1 w/whirlpool. **Services:** ✗ 🚐 🛅 ↵ Car-rental desk, babysitting. **Facilities:** 🛖 🏋 🍴 [325] ⚐ ⚐ 1 restaurant, 1 bar (w/entertainment), basketball, volleyball, spa, sauna, whirlpool. Guests can use facilities at Days Inn next door. **Rates:** Peak (Mar–June/Sept–Nov) $99–$165 S or D; $99–$165 ste. Extra person $15. Children under age 18 stay free. Lower rates off-season. Parking: Outdoor, free. AE, CB, DC, DISC, MC, V.

≣≣≣ DoubleTree Hotel Philadelphia
Broad St at Locust St, 19107 (Center City); tel 215/893-1600 or toll free 800/222-TREE; fax 215/893-1663. 3 blocks S of Market St, near City Hall. Located in the heart of the business and cultural district of the city, this hotel is within walking distance of a variety of theaters and restaurants. The atmosphere is urban, the lobby is bright and pleasant, and the staff emphasizes service. **Rooms:** 427 rms and stes. Executive level. CI 3pm/CO noon. Nonsmoking rms avail. **Amenities:** 🛅 ⚲ 🍴 A/C, cable TV w/movies, dataport. "Towers Level" rooms include continental breakfast, afternoon tea, coffeemakers, and bathrobes. All rooms have ironing boards and irons; refrigerators on request. **Services:** ✗ ⌨ ⓥ🅿 🚐 🛅 ↵ Social director, babysitting. Chocolate chip cookies at check-in. **Facilities:** 🛖 🏋 🍴 [650] ⚐ ⚐ 2 restaurants, 1 bar, racquetball, spa, sauna, steam rm, whirlpool. Noteworthy health club has three outdoor deck areas, attractive whirlpool, tanning salon, outdoor jogging track. **Rates:** Peak (Mar–Nov) $125–$199 S or D; $199–$300 ste. Extra person $15. Children under age 18 stay free. Lower rates off-season. Parking: Indoor, $13/day. AE, CB, DC, DISC, MC, V.

≣≣≣ Embassy Suites Center City
1776 Benjamin Franklin Pkwy, 19103 (Center City); tel 215/561-1776 or toll free 800/EMBASSY; fax 215/963-0122. This all-suites, 28-story hotel is close to the Franklin Institute Science Museum and the Please Touch Museum, so it's especially popular with families. **Rooms:** 288 stes. CI 4pm/CO noon. Nonsmoking rms avail. Many rooms have good city views; all have high-quality, modern furniture. **Amenities:** 🛅 ⚲ 🎦 🍴 A/C, cable TV w/movies, dataport, voice mail. All units w/terraces. **Services:** ✗ ⌨ ⓥ🅿 🚐 🛅 ↵ ⬗ Babysitting. Complimentary cocktails daily 5–7pm. **Facilities:** 🍴 [200] ⚐ 1 restaurant, 1 bar, sauna, washer/dryer. Access to Wyndham Hotel health club for small daily fee. **Rates (BB):** $169–$219 ste. Extra person $15. Children under age 14 stay free. Parking: Indoor, $16/day. AE, DC, DISC, EC, ER, JCB, MC, V.

≣≣≣≣≣ Four Seasons Hotel Philadelphia
One Logan Sq, 19103-6933 (Center City); tel 215/963-1500 or toll free 800/332-3442; fax 215/963-9506. The location—across from the St Peter and St Paul Cathedral, facing Logan Square's famed Calder Fountain, and close to several of the city's famed museums—appeals to both business and vacation travelers. A curve of driveway leads to an elegant marble foyer; the inner courtyard hosts light lunches and drinks in summer. Now 12 years old and scheduled for serious renovation, although most guests will hardly notice the wear and tear. **Rooms:** 371 rms and stes. CI 3pm/CO 1pm. Nonsmoking rms avail. Custom-made reproductions of Philadelphia Federal furniture, soft earth-tone colors, and American Primitive paintings create a comfortable and soothing atmosphere. Extra large bathrooms with marble vanities. **Amenities:** 🛅 ⚲ 🍴 A/C, cable TV w/movies, dataport, voice mail, in-rm safe, bathrobes. All units w/minibars, some w/terraces. All rooms come with two-line speaker phones; extra details like door chimes, liqueur glasses in the minibar. **Services:** 🍽 ⌨ ⓥ🅿 🚐 🛅 ↵ ⬗ Twice-daily maid svce,

masseur, children's program, babysitting. Sharp, cordial service; round-the-clock concierge; overnight or four-hour laundry service available for a fee. **Facilities:** ⛳ 🏊 🛎 💻 ♿ 3 restaurants (*see* "Restaurants" below), 1 bar (w/entertainment), sauna, whirlpool, beauty salon. Restaurants include the swank Fountain Restaurant and the more intimate Swann Cafe; spacious lounge for afternoon tea and soft jazz combo in the evening. Pet amenities include dog biscuits served on a tray, just like regular room service. Children's perks include games, books, playpens, cookies, popcorn, and kid-sized bathrobes. Airy, flower-decked pool and 13-station fitness center with well-appointed, wood-paneled dressing rooms; swimwear and exercise gear for rent. **Rates:** $250–$280 S; $280–$310 D; $300–$1,290 ste. Extra person $30. Children under age 18 stay free. Parking: Indoor, $18/day. AE, CB, DC, DISC, EC, ER, JCB, MC, V.

Holiday Inn Independence Mall
4th and Arch Sts, 19106 (Center City); tel 215/923-8660 or toll free 800/THE-BELL; fax 215/923-4633. 1 block N of Market St; historic area exit off I-95 to 4th St, S on 4th St. Families fill this place in summer because it is in the heart of the historic area near the Liberty Bell and Independence Park. **Rooms:** 364 rms and stes. CI 4pm/CO 11am. Nonsmoking rms avail. Rooms have Colonial decor. **Amenities:** 🛏 🏊 A/C, satel TV w/movies, dataport. Refrigerators and hair dryers on request. **Services:** ✕ 🔑 🚐 🛎 🍽 Manager's reception poolside every Wednesday in summer. **Facilities:** ⛳ 🏊 💻 ♿ 2 restaurants, 1 bar, washer/dryer. Outdoor pool open in summer. Sports bar in lobby has 13 TVs. **Rates:** Peak (May–Oct) $89–$158 S; $99–$168 D; $275 ste. Extra person $10. Children under age 12 stay free. Lower rates off-season. Parking: Outdoor, $10/day. Family discounts avail. AE, CB, DC, DISC, MC, V.

Holiday Inn Select Center City
18th and Market Sts, 19103 (Center City); tel 215/561-7500 or toll free 800/HOLIDAY; fax 215/561-4484. A modern skyscraper in the heart of downtown, renovated in 1994 and offering a high level of service to business travelers. **Rooms:** 445 rms and stes. Executive level. CI 3pm/CO noon. Nonsmoking rms avail. Large rooms; most have views of downtown. **Amenities:** 🛏 🏊 🛎 🍽 A/C, cable TV w/movies, dataport, voice mail. Some units w/whirlpools. **Services:** ✕ 🚐 🛎 🍽 Babysitting. **Facilities:** ⛳ 🏊 🍽 💻 ♿ 1 restaurant, 1 bar, washer/dryer. **Rates:** Peak (Mar–Nov) $175–$195 S; $195–$215 D; $500 ste. Extra person $10. Children under age 18 stay free. Lower rates off-season. Parking: Indoor, $17/day. AE, CB, DC, DISC, JCB, MC, V.

Howard Johnson Executive Hotel
1300 Providence Ave, Chester, 19013; tel 610/876-7211. Exit 6 off I-95. Convenient to the International Airport and catering to business travelers, this hotel is ready for some maintenance. **Rooms:** 100 rms. CI 1pm/CO noon. Nonsmoking rms avail. **Amenities:** 🛏 🏊 A/C, cable TV w/movies, voice mail. **Services:** ✕ 🚐 🍽 🍽 **Facilities:** ⛳ 🏊 🍽 1 restau-

rant, sauna, washer/dryer. **Rates:** $53–$63 S; $58–$68 D. Extra person $6. Children under age 18 stay free. MAP rates avail. Parking: Outdoor, free. AE, CB, DC, DISC, EC, ER, JCB, MC, V.

Korman Suites Hotel & Conference Center
2001 Hamilton St, 19130; tel 215/569-7000; fax 215/569-1422. 2 blocks N of Ben Franklin Pkwy. An abstract neon sculpture tops one of the two high-rise buildings. Close to the Museum of Art and the public library, it has short-term rooms plus long-term corporate apartments. Elegant lobby. **Rooms:** 99 rms, stes, and effic. CI 3pm/CO 11am. Nonsmoking rms avail. North- and south-facing rooms have fine views. **Amenities:** 🛏 🏊 🛎 A/C, cable TV w/movies, refrig, dataport. **Services:** ✕ 🔑 🛎 Social director, masseur, babysitting. Free shuttle service to downtown departs every half hour. **Facilities:** ⛳ 🏊 🍽 ♿ 1 restaurant, 1 bar (w/entertainment), racquetball, spa, whirlpool, beauty salon, washer/dryer. **Rates:** $99–$159 S or D; $139–$249 ste; $99–$159 effic. Extra person $10. Children under age 18 stay free. Parking: Indoor, free. AE, CB, DC, MC, V.

The Latham
135 S 17th St, 19103 (Center City); tel 215/563-7474 or toll free 800/LATHAM-1; fax 215/568-0110. At Walnut St in Rittenhouse Square area. A warm, intimate hotel with a focus on charm, congeniality, and small attentions. The lobby is more like a living room, with mahogany furniture, Oriental rugs, and flowers. The building itself is a historic landmark. **Rooms:** 138 rms and stes. Executive level. CI 3pm/CO 1pm. Nonsmoking rms avail. Most rooms have traditional decor; corner rooms are larger and have bay windows. **Amenities:** 🛏 🏊 🛎 🍽 A/C, cable TV w/movies, voice mail, in-rm safe, bathrobes. Some units w/minibars. Sixth-floor executive suites have dataports, VCRs, three phones, and ergonomic desk chairs. **Services:** ✕ 🔑 🆅🅿 🚐 🛎 🍽 Twice-daily maid svce, car-rental desk, babysitting. Complimentary shoe shine. Turndown service with Godiva chocolates. **Facilities:** 🍽 💻 ♿ 2 restaurants (*see* "Restaurants" below), 2 bars. Guests receive use of nearby health club with Olympic-size pool. **Rates:** $165–$220 S; $185–$240 D; $325–$425 ste. Extra person $20. Children under age 18 stay free. Parking: Indoor, $14/day. Weekend packages avail. AE, CB, DC, DISC, JCB, MC, V.

Omni Hotel at Independence Park
4th and Chestnut Sts, 19106 (Center City); tel 215/925-0000 or toll free 800/THE-OMNI; fax 215/925-1263. In historic district. An award-winning, upscale hotel with chandeliers, marble floors and tables, and lots of glass. Most tourist attractions are within easy walking distance. **Rooms:** 150 rms and stes. CI 3pm/CO noon. Nonsmoking rms avail. Marble accents in bathrooms and understated shades of beige and blue in the rooms give a contemporary look. All rooms have park views. **Amenities:** 🛏 🏊 🛎 🍽 A/C, cable TV w/movies, dataport, voice mail. All units w/minibars, 1 w/whirlpool. All rooms have fax machine, iron and ironing board. VCRs

available. Complimentary daily newspaper. **Services:** 〇 ☞ 〔VP〕 🚐 🖼 ⤴ Twice-daily maid svce, babysitting. Complimentary morning coffee in lobby. **Facilities:** 🔥 📺 〔125〕 🖥 ⅋ 1 restaurant (*see* "Restaurants" below), 1 bar, spa, sauna, whirlpool. Lap pool with attendant. Masseur available on request. **Rates:** Peak (Apr–June/Sept–Nov) $159–$229 S or D; $325–$550 ste. Extra person $20. Children under age 21 stay free. Lower rates off-season. Parking: Indoor, $14–$20/day. Holiday rates and off-season packages avail. AE, CB, DC, DISC, EC, ER, JCB, MC, V.

≣≣≣ Penn's View Inn

Front and Market Sts, 19106 (Center City); tel 215/922-7600 or toll free 800/331-7634; fax 215/922-7642. Penn's Landing exit off I-95 (exit 15 off I-95 S/exit 16 off I-95 N); 1 block N of Market St, near Delaware River. This small, European-style inn is in a historic building in the most quaint part of town. The emphasis here is on personalized service. **Rooms:** 38 rms and stes. CI 3pm/CO noon. Nonsmoking rms avail. Rooms have marble baths. **Amenities:** 🛏 ⅋ A/C, cable TV, dataport. Some units w/terraces, some w/fireplaces, some w/whirlpools. Four rooms facing river have fireplaces, whirlpools, bathrobes, and hair dryers. Refrigerators on request. **Services:** ✕ ☞ 🚐 🖼 ⤴ Car-rental desk, babysitting. Masseur available. **Facilities:** 〔200〕 ⅋ 1 restaurant (*see* "Restaurants" below), 1 bar (w/entertainment). Nominal fee for health club one mile away. **Rates (CP):** $99–$132 S or D; $150–$175 ste. Children under age 12 stay free. Parking: Outdoor, $6/day. AE, CB, DC, EC, ER, JCB, MC, V.

≣≣≣ Penn Tower Hotel

Civic Center Blvd at 34th St, 19104; tel 215/387-8333 or toll free 800/356-PENN. The University of Pennsylvania owns this high-rise hotel, and it is convenient to both the school and the hospital. **Rooms:** 175 rms and stes. Executive level. CI 3pm/CO 11am. Nonsmoking rms avail. North-facing rooms have views of northwest Philadelphia and the archaeology museum. **Amenities:** 🛏 ⅋ A/C, cable TV w/movies, dataport. Some units w/minibars. **Services:** ✕ ☞ 🚐 🖼 ⤴ Twice-daily maid svce, car-rental desk, social director, babysitting. **Facilities:** 〔500〕 🖥 ⅋ 1 restaurant, 1 bar (w/entertainment). Guests may use university sports facilities. **Rates:** Peak (Sept–May) $124–$144 S or D; $275–$475 ste. Extra person $10. Children under age 13 stay free. Lower rates off-season. MAP rates avail. Parking: Indoor, $9/day. AE, DC, DISC, MC, V.

≣≣≣ Philadelphia Airport Marriott Hotel

4509 Island Ave, 19153; tel 215/492-9000 or toll free 800/228-9290; fax 215/492-6799. Airport exit off I-95. The closest hotel to the airport; guests can walk directly to Terminal B on an enclosed bridge. Direct access to Center City via high speed rail line. Service-oriented staff. **Rooms:** 419 rms and stes. Executive level. CI 4pm/CO noon. Nonsmoking rms avail. Well-equipped, modern rooms. Many have writing desks. **Amenities:** 🛏 ⅋ 🍴 A/C, cable TV w/movies, dataport, voice mail. **Services:** ✕ 🚐 🖼 ⤴ 🧺 Car-rental

desk, social director, masseur, babysitting. **Facilities:** 🔥 📺 〔1000〕 🖥 ⅋ 1 restaurant, 1 bar, spa, whirlpool, washer/dryer. **Rates:** Peak (Apr–May/Sept–Oct) $79–$149 S or D; $150–$400 ste. Lower rates off-season. Parking: Indoor, $7/day. AE, CB, DC, DISC, EC, ER, JCB, MC, V.

≣≣≣≣ Philadelphia Marriott

1201 Market St, 19107 (Center City); tel 215/972-6700 or toll free 800/228-9290; fax 215/625-6000. Between 12th and 13th Sts. A 23-story, ultra-modern hotel opened in 1994. An indoor skyway leads to the Convention Center across the street, and other attractions are nearby. The lobby is the size of a city block and has nice seating areas and much greenery. **Rooms:** 1,200 rms and stes. Executive level. CI 4pm/CO noon. Nonsmoking rms avail. Rooms on floors 6 through 23 have views of the city. **Amenities:** 🛏 ⅋ 🍴 A/C, cable TV w/movies, dataport, voice mail. Some units w/whirlpools. All rooms have irons and ironing boards. Executive-level rooms (on the top two floors) have office amenities and workstations. **Services:** 〇 ☞ 〔VP〕 🚐 🖼 ⤴ 🧺 Twice-daily maid svce, car-rental desk, social director, babysitting. Masseur on call. **Facilities:** 🔥 📺 〔5000〕 🖥 ⅋ 4 restaurants, 3 bars, games rm, spa, sauna, steam rm, whirlpool, beauty salon, washer/dryer. Starbucks coffee bar located in lobby. Sports bar has game room, pool table, and big-screen TVs. Direct internal connection to SEPTA subways and airport train. **Rates:** Peak (Mar–Nov) $139–$159 S; $159–$179 D; $375–$1,000 ste. Children under age 7 stay free. Lower rates off-season. Parking: Indoor, $20/day. Convention and weekend packages avail. AE, CB, DC, DISC, MC, V.

≣≣≣ Philadelphia Marriott West

111 Crawford Ave, West Conshohocken, 19428; tel 610/941-5600 or toll free 800/228-9290; fax 610/941-4425. Conshohocken exit off I-476 or I-76. Since opening in 1991, this attractive hotel has become popular among locals who come to the restaurant and bar for evening entertainment. Accommodating staff. **Rooms:** 288 rms and stes. Executive level. CI 3pm/CO noon. Nonsmoking rms avail. **Amenities:** 🛏 ⅋ 🍴 A/C, cable TV w/movies, dataport, voice mail. Complimentary newspaper. Refrigerators and CD/tape players available on request. **Services:** ✕ ☞ 🚐 🖼 ⤴ Car-rental desk, masseur, babysitting. **Facilities:** 🔥 📺 〔500〕 ⅋ 1 restaurant (*see* "Restaurants" below), 2 bars (w/entertainment), sauna, steam rm, whirlpool. Beautiful, glass-enclosed pool has fine views, but is too small for lap swimming. Extensive fitness center. Easy access to 11.5-mile Schuylkill Trail (for biking or jogging). **Rates:** $93–$164 S; $93–$194 D; $295 ste. Extra person $30. Children under age 18 stay free. Parking: Indoor/outdoor, free. Weekend rates avail. AE, CB, DC, DISC, MC, V.

≣≣≣ Radisson Hotel Philadelphia Airport

500 Stevens Dr, 19113; tel 610/521-5900 or toll free 800/333-3333; fax 610/521-4362. Exit 9A (Essington) off I-95. Far enough from the airport to be quieter than other area hotels. **Rooms:** 350 rms and stes. CI 3pm/CO noon. Non-

smoking rms avail. **Amenities:** A/C, cable TV w/movies, dataport. Some units w/terraces. **Services:** X Car-rental desk, babysitting. **Facilities:** 1 restaurant, 2 bars, games rm, whirlpool. Attractive pool landscaping. **Rates:** $125–$145 S; $135–$155 D; $250–$500 ste. Extra person $10. Children under age 18 stay free. Parking: Outdoor, free. AE, CB, DC, DISC, JCB, MC, V.

≡≡≡ Radnor Hotel

591 E Lancaster Ave, St David's, 19087; tel 610/688-5800 or toll free 800/537-3000; fax 610/341-3299. Exit 5 off I-476. This corporate travelers' hotel has the quaint atmosphere of an inn. **Rooms:** 167 rms. Executive level. CI 3pm/CO noon. Nonsmoking rms avail. Some rooms have safes and refrigerators. **Amenities:** A/C, satel TV w/movies, dataport, voice mail. Some suites have three phones. **Services:** Car-rental desk. Weekend entertainment in bar. **Facilities:** 2 restaurants, 1 bar (w/entertainment), games rm. **Rates:** $120–$180 S or D. Children under age 18 stay free. MAP rates avail. Parking: Outdoor, free. AE, DC, DISC, MC, V.

≡≡≡≡ Rittenhouse Hotel

210 W Rittenhouse Sq, 19103; tel 215/546-9000 or toll free 800/635-1042; fax 215/732-3364. This world-class hotel is popular with celebrities and visiting foreign dignitaries. In an upscale residential and commercial area, it is within easy walking distance of stores, cultural events, and museums. An outdoor terrace with fountains and shops adjoins the lovely lobby. **Rooms:** 121 rms and stes. CI 3pm/CO 1pm. Nonsmoking rms avail. All rooms have views of the park or the city. Suites have decor by Ralph Lauren or Laura Ashley. **Amenities:** A/C, cable TV, dataport, VCR, in-rm safe, bathrobes. All units w/minibars, some w/whirlpools. Fax machines and two-line phones in every room. Scales and TVs in bathrooms. **Services:** Twice-daily maid svce, car-rental desk, social director, masseur, babysitting. Courtesy Town Car. Dog walking available. Foreign newspapers, time-zone clocks, posted exchange rates in lobby. **Facilities:** 2 restaurants, 2 bars, spa, sauna, steam rm, beauty salon. Spa facilities are $10 per day on weekdays, free on weekends. **Rates:** $240–$260 S; $265–$285 D; $400–$450 ste. Extra person $25. Children under age 16 stay free. Parking: Indoor, $21/day. Weekend packages avail. AE, CB, DC, DISC, MC, V.

≡≡≡≡ The Ritz-Carlton Philadelphia

17th St and Chestnut St, 19103 (Center City); tel 215/563-1600 or toll free 800/241-3333; fax 215/567-2822. In the Liberty Place complex. Traditional Ritz-Carlton elegance and comforts fill the 6th through 12th floors of this centrally located office tower. **Rooms:** 170 rms and stes. CI 3pm/CO noon. Nonsmoking rms avail. Rooms feature elegant period furniture, armoires with TV and minibars, spotless bathrooms of white-and-gray marble. (Windows do not open, however.) **Amenities:** A/C, cable TV w/movies, dataport, VCR, CD/tape player, bathrobes. All units w/mini-

bars, some w/terraces. **Services:** Masseur, babysitting. Complimentary town-car service. Afternoon tea, accompanied by a pianist, virtually takes over the entire lobby lounge from 2pm to 5pm; Champagne Brunch on Sunday. **Facilities:** 1 restaurant, 2 bars (1 w/entertainment). Two-story, 70-shop mall (Shops at Liberty Place) is downstairs. **Rates:** $265–$295 S; $285–$325 D; $375–$575 ste. Extra person $20. Children under age 18 stay free. Min stay special events. Parking: Indoor, $13–$19/day. Uncommonly interesting packages—Bed & Breakfast Getaway, The Club Package, A Special Occasion, A Weekend All Your Own, Art Lovers' Weekend—all with valet parking. AE, CB, DC, DISC, JCB, MC, V.

≡≡≡ Sheraton Society Hill

1 Dock St, 19106; tel 215/238-6000 or toll free 800/325-3535. An attractive, pleasantly landscaped building on a cobblestone street, with a spacious atrium lobby where a pianist plays daily. **Rooms:** 365 rms and stes. Executive level. CI 3pm/CO noon. Nonsmoking rms avail. **Amenities:** A/C, satel TV w/movies, voice mail. Some units w/mini-bars, some w/terraces, 1 w/whirlpool. Club-level rooms have dataports and a larger desk area. Starbucks coffee in rooms. **Services:** Car-rental desk, masseur, babysitting. Nintendo and video rentals. **Facilities:** 2 restaurants, 2 bars (1 w/entertainment), sauna, whirlpool. **Rates:** $125–$195 S; $145–$215 D; $350–$550 ste. Extra person $20. Children under age 17 stay free. MAP rates avail. Parking: Indoor, $12.50–$18.50/day. AE, CB, DC, DISC, EC, ER, JCB, MC, V.

≡≡≡ Sheraton University City

36th and Chestnut Sts, 19104; tel 215/387-8000 or toll free 800/325-3535; fax 215/387-5939. Exit 39 off US 76 W. Standard high-rise chain hotel, near the University of Pennsylvania, shops, and ethnic restaurants. **Rooms:** 375 rms and stes. Executive level. CI 3pm/CO 1pm. Nonsmoking rms avail. Some rooms have attractive views of campus. **Amenities:** A/C, cable TV w/movies, dataport, voice mail. **Services:** X Twice-daily maid svce, car-rental desk, babysitting. Food service at pool during summer. **Facilities:** 2 restaurants, 1 bar (w/entertainment), games rm. **Rates:** Peak (Mar–May/Sept–Oct) $69–$145 S or D; $195–$295 ste. Extra person $10. Children under age 17 stay free. Lower rates off-season. MAP rates avail. Parking: Indoor, $10/day. AE, CB, DC, DISC, MC, V.

≡≡≡ The Warwick

17th and Locust Sts, 19103 (Center City); tel 215/735-6000 or toll free 800/523-4210; fax 215/790-7766. 2½ blocks S of Market St, between Walnut and Spruce Sts. A historic old apartment building, renovated in 1994. The bright, welcoming lobby of this European-style boutique hotel has a spacious, comfortable feel. **Rooms:** 156 rms and stes. CI 2pm/CO noon. Nonsmoking rms avail. All rooms have city views. Suites are large, with separate parlors. **Amenities:** A/C, cable TV w/movies, dataport. **Services:** X

Masseur, babysitting. Attentive service. **Facilities:** [500] & 3 restaurants, 2 bars (1 w/entertainment), beauty salon. Free passes to nearby health club. **Rates:** Peak (Apr–June/Sept–Nov) $135–$175 S; $145–$180 D; $180–$290 ste. Extra person $15. Children under age 18 stay free. Lower rates off-season. Parking: Indoor, $14.75/day. Packages related to local events (flower shows, art exhibits) avail. AE, CB, DC, MC, V.

≡≡≡≡ Wyndham Franklin Plaza Hotel
17th and Race Sts, 19103 (Center City); tel 215/448-2000 or toll free 800/822-4200; fax 215/448-2864. Broad St exit off US 676. A modern high-rise hotel with a full range of services, two blocks from the foot of the Benjamin Franklin Parkway. City Hall and the Franklin Institute museum are within walking distance. **Rooms:** 758 rms and stes. Executive level. CI 3pm/CO noon. Nonsmoking rms avail. Most rooms have spectacular views of downtown. **Amenities:** 🛏 🔥 📺 🍷 A/C, cable TV w/movies, dataport, voice mail. **Services:** ✕ ⊶ VP 🖼 ⊐ Car-rental desk, social director, masseur. **Facilities:** 🏋 🌊1 🏓 🏊2200 💻 & 2 restaurants, 1 bar, basketball, racquetball, squash, spa, sauna, steam rm, whirlpool, beauty salon. Guests have access to private health club with saunas, tennis, racquetball, and swimming. **Rates:** $150–$170 S; $170–$190 D; $300–$2,000 ste. Extra person $20. Parking: Indoor, $13/day. AE, CB, DC, DISC, MC, V.

INNS

≡≡ Gables
4520 Chester Ave, 19104 (University City); tel 215/662-1918. An 1889 brick Victorian house in a quiet section of University City. The public areas are tastefully decorated with antiques, and the owners live on the premises in their own separate area. **Rooms:** 10 rms (5 w/shared bath). CI 3pm/CO 11am. No smoking. Nicely restored and individually decorated with antiques. **Amenities:** 🔥 A/C, TV. No phone. 1 unit w/terrace, some w/fireplaces. **Services:** 🚗 ⊐ Afternoon tea and wine/sherry served. Breakfast usually includes muffins, fresh fruit, quiche or casseroles. **Facilities:** [15] Guest lounge. Off-street parking. **Rates (BB):** $60 S w/shared bath, $70 S w/private bath; $70 D w/shared bath, $80 D w/private bath. Extra person $10. Parking: Outdoor, free. AE, MC, V.

≡≡ Thomas Bond House
129 S 2nd St, 19106; tel 215/923-8523 or toll free 800/845-BOND; fax 215/923-8504. A nicely appointed, four-story colonial house that once belonged to a prominent Philadelphia doctor, with elegant, comfortable public rooms and individually decorated bedrooms. **Rooms:** 12 rms. CI 3pm/CO noon. Nonsmoking rms avail. Suites are L-shaped, with electric fireplaces, whirlpools in bathrooms, four-poster beds. **Amenities:** 🛏 🔥 🍷 A/C, satel TV. Some units w/fireplaces, some w/whirlpools. **Services:** Free local calls. Complimentary wine and cheese at daily social hour. **Facilities:**

Checkers, chess, books, and daily newspapers in lobby. Guest privileges at nearby health club (with pool) for small fee. $90–$160 D. Extra person $15. AE, DC, DISC, MC, V.

RESTAURANTS 🍴

Aglio
937 E Passyunk Ave (South Philadelphia); tel 215/336-8008. **Italian.** An old-fashioned trattoria tucked into a block of row houses in heavily Italian South Philly. The contemporary, northern Italian menu ranges from pasta and seafood to chops and venison. Roasted cloves of garlic (*aglio* is the Italian word for garlic) are spread on fresh, hot bread before it is brought to the table. The waiters take pride in their cappuccino, and there's an extensive wine list. **FYI:** Reservations recommended. **Open:** Sun–Mon 5:30–9pm, Tues–Thurs 5:30–10pm, Fri–Sat 5:30–11pm. Closed last wk of Aug. **Prices:** Main courses $10–$26. AE, DC, MC, V. [VP]

Azalea
In The Omni Hotel, 4th and Chestnut Sts (Center City); tel 215/925-0000. Overlooking Independence Park, 1 block S of Market St. **Regional American.** An elegant, opulent eatery with dramatic views of Independence Park. Chef Aliza Green has created imaginative treatments of American regional dishes like cold roast chicken with quince mayonnaise, and sirloin with mustard seed and fresh herbs. The homemade fettuccine is also notable. **FYI:** Reservations recommended. Children's menu. **Open:** Mon–Thurs 6:30am–9pm, Fri 6:30am–9:30pm, Sat 7am–10pm, Sun 7am–9pm. **Prices:** Main courses $17–$29; prix fixe $32. AE, DISC, MC, V. 💙 [VP] &

★ Bookbinder's 15th Street
215 S 15th St; tel 215/545-1137. **Seafood.** The fourth generation of the Bookbinders, an old Philadelphia family, runs this offshoot of the legendary Old Original Bookbinder's (*see below*). Fresh seafood includes baskets of clams, buckets of Chincoteague oysters, whole Maine lobster, snapper soup laced with sherry, and Bookbinder's classic mussels in red sauce. Discount parking in the lot across the street. **FYI:** Reservations recommended. Children's menu. **Open:** Mon–Fri 11:30am–10pm, Sat 4–11pm, Sun 3–10pm. **Prices:** Main courses $16–$22. AE, DC, DISC, MC, V. &

Cafe Preeya
2651 Huntingdon Pike, Huntingdon Valley; tel 215/947-6195. On PA 232. **International/Thai.** Bamboo shades and lots of greenery set the mood at this Thai-inspired eatery. Food is beautifully presented, and can be adjusted to the diner's preferred level of spiciness. **FYI:** Reservations accepted. BYO. No smoking. **Open:** Mon–Thurs 4–10pm, Fri–Sat 4–11pm, Sun 4–9pm. **Prices:** Main courses $13–$22. MC, V. 💙

Charlie's Water Wheel
1526 Sansom St (Center City); tel 215/563-4155. 2 blocks S of City Hall. **Deli/Middle Eastern.** Lunchtime crowds pack

into this basement dining room, where huge quantities of pickles, fried mushrooms, meatballs, and other freebies are brought to the table along with your order. The food is a wacky combination of Glatt Kosher and Middle Eastern: try a shwarma turkey hoagie or a grilled chicken breast hoagie with the fresh Moroccan salad. **FYI:** Reservations accepted. No liquor license. No smoking. **Open:** Mon–Tues 8:30am–4pm, Wed 8:30am–8pm, Fri 8:30am–sunset, Sun 4–8pm. **Prices:** Main courses $6–$7. AE, MC, V. ▮

Ciboulette

In The Bellevue Hotel, 200 S Broad St; tel 215/790-1210. **French.** In an elegant, 19th-century French baroque dining room, Chef Bruce Lim serves French Provençal cuisine, prepared from all-organic meat, poultry, vegetables, and herbs. Appetizer portions are available for those with smaller appetites, or those who would prefer to sample a variety of dishes. Entrees might include sea bass steamed in olive oil, or seared slices of duck; desserts include crème brûlée and lemon galette. Wine tastings on the first Sunday of each month. **FYI:** Reservations recommended. Jacket required. **Open:** Mon–Thurs 5:30–9pm, Fri–Sat 5:30–10:30pm. **Prices:** Main courses $6–$15. AE, MC, V. ♥ VP &

Circa

1518 Walnut St; tel 215/545-6800. **Californian.** In this former bank building, you can dine in the security of a vault surrounded by safe deposit boxes, or have a drink at the bank's balcony, now a bar. Flavorful menu choices might include duck ravioli with goat cheese and sun-dried cherries, or roast shrimp with spinach and pine nuts. Clubgoers invade at 10:30pm Thurs–Sat for dancing. **FYI:** Reservations recommended. Dancing. Dress code. **Open:** Lunch Tues–Fri 11:30am–2:30pm; dinner Sun–Wed 4:30–10pm, Thurs–Sat 4:30–11pm. **Prices:** Main courses $15–$17. AE, DC, MC, V. ▮ VP &

City Tavern

138 S 2nd St at Walnut (Center City); tel 215/413-1443. **American.** This spacious, rebuilt 1773 landmark pub was a center of economic, social, and political life in pre-Revolutionary Philadelphia. It still oozes history, with an authentically costumed staff, spare furnishings, and historically accurate recipes. (No canned, frozen, or preserved foods here!) Menu choices straight out of the 18th century include lobster pie, rack of lamb, and venison. **FYI:** Reservations recommended. Harpsichord. Children's menu. **Open:** Peak (May–Oct) Mon–Thurs 11:30am–10pm, Fri–Sat 11:30am–11pm, Sun 11:30am–8pm. **Prices:** Main courses $18–$26. AE, CB, DC, DISC, MC, V. ▮ ♥ &

★ Cobblefish

443 Shurs Lane, Manayunk; tel 215/483-5478. Exit 31 off I-76. **Seafood.** A real seafood joint with bright fish murals on the walls and a fun, relaxed atmosphere. Frequented by families, couples, and locals. **FYI:** Reservations recommend-

ed. Children's menu. BYO. No smoking. **Open:** Mon–Thurs 5:30–10pm, Fri–Sat 5:30–11pm, Sun 4–8:30pm. Closed Aug 1–7. **Prices:** Main courses $13–$16. AE, MC, V. VP &

Cutler's Grand Cafe & Bar

In Commerce Center Office Buildings Complex, Market St at 20th St (Center City); tel 215/851-6262. **American.** Set back from the street and overlooking an attractive outdoor plaza with trees and fountains, this spacious eatery is especially popular with the after-work singles crowd. Mesquite-grilled fresh salmon is a real treat, as are the homemade soups. Pastas range from yakisoba noodles to fettuccine; pizzas, lamb chops, game, and steaks fill out the extensive menu. **FYI:** Reservations recommended. Children's menu. **Open:** Mon–Thurs 11:30am–10pm, Fri 11:30am–11pm, Sat 5–11pm, Sun 5–9pm. **Prices:** Main courses $11–$17. AE, CB, DC, DISC, MC, V. ♥ &

Dilullo

1407 Locust St (Center City); tel 215/546-2000. **Italian.** This opulent but romantic space includes a huge copper antipasto cart, oversized impressionist and expressionist prints, booths separated by etched glass, and wrought-iron armchairs. The antipasto course features choices like sautéed buffalo-milk mozzarella and marinated pepperoni, while typical entrees include thin-sliced monkfish in lemon sauce. For dessert, there's strong, rich espresso and Dilullo's own homemade gelato. The adjoining bar/cafe is open for lunch. **FYI:** Reservations recommended. Piano. Dress code. **Open:** Peak (Sept–May) lunch Mon–Fri 11:45am–2pm; dinner Sat 5–11pm. Closed last 10 days of Aug. **Prices:** Main courses $17–$20; prix fixe $23. AE, DC, MC, V. ♥ ♥ &

DiNardo's Famous Crabs

312 Race St (Center City); tel 215/925-5115. Exit 17 off I-676, 2 blocks N of Market St. **Seafood.** The building was an inn for Tory soldiers in 1776, and later it served as a prison for Confederate soldiers. Today, the well-lighted chambers have subtly striped wallpaper, huge crab specimens, various net buoys, and simple Formica tables. Prime live catches from Texas and Louisiana are flown up north daily, and experienced hands from the original DiNardo's in Wilmington dredge the crabs with house seasoning made up of 24 secret spices. Oyster crackers with horseradish are a popular accompaniment. Nightly specials also include steaks, chicken, burgers, salads, and sandwiches. **FYI:** Reservations recommended. Children's menu. **Open:** Mon–Thurs 11am–10pm, Fri–Sat 11am–11pm, Sun 9am–3pm. **Prices:** Main courses $13–$22. AE, CB, DC, MC, V. ▮ ▦ ♥ &

Diner on the Square

1839 Spruce St (Center City); tel 215/735-5787. 1 block S of Rittenhouse Square. **American/Diner.** Even if there's a weekend line at this cheerful 1950s diner, the fast service will keep it moving. A landmark for burgers, fries, soup-and-salad, apple pie, and homemade milk shakes, the Diner offers seating at the counter or in red-vinyl booths. **FYI:** Reservations not accepted. No liquor license. **Open:** Daily 24 hrs. **Prices:** Main courses $5–$8. No CC. 📳

The Dining Room
In The Ritz-Carlton Philadelphia, 17th and Chestnut Sts at Liberty Place (Center City); tel 215/563-1600. **New American.** This bright, elegant, formal room on the second floor of the hotel is open only for breakfast and lunch. The menu features new twists on the classics, like Maine lobster tail with coconut risotto and pickled ginger crackling. The wine list is the same as in the Grill Room (see below). **FYI:** Reservations recommended. Piano. Children's menu. Jacket required. **Open:** Breakfast Mon–Sat 7:30–11am; lunch Tues–Sat 11:30am–2:30pm; brunch Sun 10:30am–2pm. **Prices:** Lunch main courses $11–$21. AE, CB, DC, DISC, MC, V. 💙 VP ♿

D'Lucce's
72-74 Poplar Ave, Conshohocken; tel 610/834-8124. Conshocken exit off I-76. **Italian/Seafood.** A cozy, homey restaurant known more for its food than its ambience. Favorites include homemade pasta, filet mignon, and clams and mussels prepared Italian style. Luscious desserts. **FYI:** Reservations accepted. Children's menu. No smoking. **Open:** Mon–Sat 11am–10pm. **Prices:** Main courses $9–$19. MC, V.

Dock Street Brewery & Restaurant
In Two Logan Sq, 18th and Cherry Sts (Center City); tel 215/496-0413. 3 blocks E of City Hall. **Eclectic/Brasserie.** This art deco brasserie on the ground floor of a large office building is a busy place at lunch time. The menu varies from eclectic appetizers to sandwiches and burgers to duck cassoulet, but the real feature is the beer. The brewery creates 66 styles throughout the year, ranging from Thomas Jefferson's Ale to German lagers and Belgian fruit beers, and six samples are always available. **FYI:** Reservations accepted. Blues/jazz. Children's menu. Beer only. **Open:** Mon–Thurs 11:30am–11:30pm, Fri 11:30am–1:30am, Sat noon–1:30am, Sun noon–10:30pm. **Prices:** Main courses $12–$16. AE, CB, DC, DISC, MC, V. 💙 ♿

✿ Founders Atop the Bellevue
In Bellevue Hotel, Broad and Walnut Sts (Center City); tel 215/893-1776. 2 blocks S of City Hall. **Continental/Eclectic.** Only the highest high-rises have a better view of the city than does this 19th-floor dining room, where domed ceilings, plaster rococo ornamentation, and statues of Philadelphia luminaries add to the grandeur. (The book-filled bar is a cozy contrast.) Fish, steaks, and chops make up the bulk of the menu, although more adventurous choices (like shrimp and scallops with lemongrass essence and braised bok choy) are there for those who want them. Large wine list. **FYI:** Reservations recommended. Dancing. **Open:** Breakfast Mon–Sat 7–10am, Sun 7–9:30am; lunch Mon–Sat 11:30am–2:30pm; dinner daily 5:30–10pm; brunch Sun 10:30am–2:30pm. **Prices:** Main courses $28–$35. AE, DISC, MC, V. 🏔 VP ♿

The Fountain
In The Four Seasons Hotel Philadelphia, One Logan Sq (Center City); tel 215/963-1500. At foot of Benjamin Franklin Pkwy. **Continental.** Starched tablecloths and silver candlesticks set the tone at this very formal dining room with great street-level views of Logan Square. Chef LaCroix's dinner menu changes daily, with entrees like pan-roasted Virginia squab or braised red snapper with asparagus tips and shiitake mushrooms scented with tarragon water. The popular foie gras is American, not a canned import. **FYI:** Reservations recommended. Children's menu. Jacket required. **Open:** Breakfast daily 6:30–11am; lunch Mon–Sat 11:30am–2:15pm; dinner daily 5:30–10pm; brunch Sun 11am–2:30pm. **Prices:** Main courses $29–$36; prix fixe $67. AE, CB, DC, DISC, MC, V. 💙 💙 VP ♿

Friday Saturday Sunday
261 S 21st St; tel 215/546-4232. **Regional American/Continental.** A casual eatery located in a tiny and whimsically decorated row house. The menu is surprisingly sophisticated, with American classics such as crab cakes as well as continental mainstays like filet mignon with béarnaise and roast duck with cherries and port sauce. The house specialty is cream of mushroom soup made from local mushrooms. **FYI:** Reservations recommended. **Open:** Lunch Mon–Fri 11:30am–2:30pm; dinner Mon–Sat 5:30–10:30pm, Sun 5–10pm. **Prices:** Main courses $13–$20. AE, DC, MC, V. 💙

✿ The Garden
1617 Spruce St (Center City); tel 215/546-4455. 3 blocks S of Market St between 16th and 17th Sts. **Continental.** Charm and elegance in a high-ceilinged townhouse plus a large garden for dining in fine weather. Known for steaks, fresh seafood (including a total of 20 oyster appetizers), and wild game. Delightfully rich desserts finish the meal. **FYI:** Reservations recommended. **Open:** Lunch Mon–Fri 11:30am–1:30pm; dinner Mon–Fri 5:30–9pm, Sat 5:30–9:30pm. **Prices:** Main courses $16–$25. AE, CB, DC, MC, V. 💙 🍴 🍽 💙 VP

Grill Room
In The Ritz-Carlton Philadelphia, 17th and Chestnut Sts at Liberty Place (Center City); tel 215/563-1600. **American.** The room itself is stunning, with large crystal chandeliers, royal-blue carpets, dark cabinets, and handblown cobalt-blue goblets, and the service is impeccable. (If you have reason to leave your seat, you'll find that your napkin is refolded when you return.) Entrees include a variety of grilled meats—including filet mignon, salmon, and sea bass—and the freshest local produce. The wine list is large, and international in scope. **FYI:** Reservations recommended. Children's menu. Jacket required. **Open:** Breakfast Sun 6:30–11:30am; lunch Mon–Fri 11:30am–2:30pm; dinner daily 5:30–10:30pm. **Prices:** Main courses $16–$29. AE, CB, DC, DISC, MC, V. 💙 VP ♿

Harmony Vegetarian Restaurant
135 N 9th St (Chinatown); tel 215/627-4520. 2 blocks N of Market St. **Chinese/Vegetarian.** Family-owned and -operated eatery with an appropriately soothing New Age atmosphere. The adventurous, wide-ranging menu uses soybeans, tofu, and homemade wheat gluten as healthy alternatives to the usual meat, fish, and poultry. No eggs or dairy products are used. **FYI:** Reservations accepted. BYO. No smoking. **Open:** Mon–Thurs 11am–10pm, Fri–Sat 11am–11:30pm, Sun 11am–10pm. **Prices:** Main courses $6–$13. AE, DISC, MC, V. &

♣ Hikaru
4348 Main St, Manayunk; tel 215/487-3500. Exit 31 off I-76. **Japanese.** The downstairs room features teppan specialties (prepared right at the table), while a sushi bar and Japanese-style seating are upstairs. Tempura and sukiyaki also available. **FYI:** Reservations recommended. No smoking. Additional locations: 607 S 2nd St, Philadelphia (tel 627-7110); 108 S 18th St, Philadelphia (tel 496-9950). **Open:** Lunch Wed 11:45am–2:30pm, Thurs–Fri 11am–2:30pm, Sat–Sun noon–3pm; dinner Mon–Thurs 5–10pm, Fri 5–11pm, Sat 4:30–11pm, Sun 3–9:30pm. **Prices:** Main courses $12–$30. AE, CB, DC, DISC, MC, V. ♥ &

Imperial Inn
142 N 10th St (Chinatown); tel 215/627-5588. 2 blocks N of Market St. **Chinese.** A reliable, locally-favored place housed in a spacious and elegant room with traditional Chinese appointments. The kitchen specializes in Szechuan cuisine, but there are a few Mandarin and Cantonese dishes as well. **FYI:** Reservations accepted. **Open:** Mon–Thurs 11am–12:30am, Fri–Sat 11am–2am, Sun 11am–midnight. **Prices:** Main courses $6–$14. AE, CB, DC, MC, V. &

Jack's Firehouse
2130 Fairmount Ave; tel 215/232-9000. Across from Eastern Penitentiary Museum. **Regional American.** Engine Company #1, the first firehouse in the city, is now a dark-paneled restaurant serving regional cuisine. Many of the choices have organic and local ingredients, the menu changes daily, and the chef will accommodate special orders for children. An unusual variety of game (gopher, bear, bison, even beaver tail) is listed in season. The long wine list changes constantly, and tastings are offered. Free 12-acre parking lot across the street. **FYI:** Reservations recommended. Country music/jazz. Children's menu. No smoking. **Open:** Lunch daily 11:30am–2:30pm; dinner daily 4:30–10:30pm. **Prices:** Main courses $14–$22. AE, DC, MC, V. ▪ &

Jake's
4365 Main St, Manayunk; tel 215/483-0444. Exit 31 off I-76. **New American/Eclectic.** California-style menu specialties, served in elegant surroundings. Extensive wine list. **FYI:** Reservations recommended. No smoking. **Open:** Lunch Mon–Sat 11:30am–2:30pm; dinner Mon–Thurs 5:30–

9:30pm, Fri 5:30–10:30pm, Sat 5–10:30pm, Sun 5–9pm; brunch Sun 10:30am–2:30pm. **Prices:** Main courses $20–$25. AE, DC, MC, V. ♥ VP

★ Jim's Steaks
400 South St (Center City); tel 215/928-1911. At 4th St. **Regional American.** Follow your nose (and the crowds) to this modest haunt to get top-rated cheesesteak sandwiches and hoagies. **FYI:** Reservations not accepted. Beer only. **Open:** Mon–Thurs 10am–1am, Fri–Sat 10am–2am, Sun noon–10pm. **Prices:** Main courses $4–$6. No CC. &

Judy's Cafe
3rd and Bainbridge Sts (Center City); tel 215/928-1968. 1 block S of South St. **American/Eclectic.** Popular with the over-60 crowd and local gays, this modest and intimate dining room is accented with terra-cotta walls, photo-realist paintings, and a strip of neon over the well-stocked bar. Home-cooked flair and fresh ingredients go into the eclectic menu, where meat loaf, pasta, trout, and salmon are the most popular entree options. **FYI:** Reservations accepted. **Open:** Mon–Thurs 5:30pm–midnight, Fri–Sat 5:30pm–1am, Sun 10:30am–10pm. **Prices:** Main courses $9–$16. AE, CB, DC, MC, V.

★ Kansas City Prime
4417 Main St, Manayunk; tel 215/482-3700. Exit 31 off I-76. **Seafood/Steak.** The food and the chef of this elegant, casual restaurant have been featured in several gourmet magazines. The bar is a late night hotspot for area professionals. **FYI:** Reservations recommended. **Open:** Sun–Thurs 5:30–11pm, Fri–Sat 5:30pm–midnight. **Prices:** Main courses $20–$28. AE, CB, DC, DISC, MC, V. ♥ VP

La Famiglia
8 S Front St; tel 215/922-2803. **Italian.** A private, warm setting of hand-hammered Venetian chandeliers and majolica tiles. Most pastas are made on site, and meats are carved at tableside. Nightly specials might include artichoke and shrimp, or fresh truffles (in season) with homemade ravioli. If you take a trip downstairs to the rest rooms, be sure to check out the huge wine cellar and the circa-1680 foundation of the building. **FYI:** Reservations recommended. **Open:** Lunch Tues–Fri noon–2pm; dinner Tues–Fri 5:30–9pm, Sat 5:30–10pm, Sun 5–8:30pm. Closed last week in Aug. **Prices:** Main courses $22–$65. AE, DC, MC, V. ♥ VP

La Grolla Bar & Trattoria
782 S 2nd St (Center City); tel 215/627-7701. 3 blocks S of South St, between Fitzwater and Catherine Sts. **Italian.** The name of this charmingly old-world trattoria is Italian for "cup of friendship," and the service is indeed very warm and friendly. The menu focuses on co-owner Mamma Massaglia's pasta, game, and wild mushroom dishes. On Sundays, a special, eight-course Game Dinner is served (reservations required). **FYI:** Reservations recommended. **Open:** Mon–Thurs 5–10pm, Fri–Sat 5–11pm. **Prices:** Main courses $10–$19. AE, CB, DC, MC, V. ♥ ♥

La Tazza
110 Cotton St, Manayunk; tel 215/487-6522. Exit 31 off I-76. **Coffeehouse/Italian.** Local artists and intellectuals flock to this funky hangout for its pastries, sandwiches, and gourmet coffee. Unusual artwork decorates the walls and a variety of entertainment—from blues to comedy to jazz to poetry reading—is available. **FYI:** Reservations not accepted. No liquor license. **Open:** Mon 8am–7pm, Tues–Thurs 8am–11pm, Fri–Sat 8am–midnight, Sun 9am–10pm. **Prices:** Main courses $4–$5. No CC.

♣ Le Bec-Fin
1523 Walnut St; tel 215/567-1000. **French.** By any measure, this is a world-class restaurant. Chef Georges Perrier and his classical French haute cuisine are always drawing praise, cholesterol be damned. The only dinner choice is the $102 prix fixe meal (hors d'oeuvres, fish course, main course, salad, cheese, and coffee) with all the desserts you can eat. The menu changes seasonally, but usually includes some rarities (pheasant, venison, pigeon) and some mainstays (lobster, venison, escargots), all served in rich yet creative sauces—butter sauce infused with black truffles, or perhaps garlic butter with chartreuse and hazelnuts. Lunch is also prix fixe, and a relative steal at $36; wines start at around $40 per bottle. Surroundings are 19th century, with fine fabrics and intricate pink and salmon wallpaper. Needless to say, reservations are essential. **FYI:** Reservations recommended. Guitar. Jacket required. **Open:** Lunch Mon–Thurs 11:30am–1:30pm, Fri 11:30am–2pm; dinner Mon–Thurs 6–9pm, Fri–Sat 6–9:30pm. **Prices:** Prix fixe $102. AE, DC, DISC, MC, V. ♥ VP ♿

Le Bus
3402 Sansom St (University City); tel 215/387-3800. **Cafe/Bakery.** This small local chain began life as a real bus, which delivered fresh-baked bread to other eateries in the Philly area. The bus is now parked for good, and the menu has expanded to include a wide range of dishes from gourmet sandwiches to crab cakes. Specials may include jerk chicken with rice, or moussaka. Pastries and breads are also available. **FYI:** Reservations not accepted. Beer only. Additional location: 4266 Main St, Manayunk (tel 487-2663). **Open:** Peak (Sept–June) Mon–Fri 7:30am–10:30pm, Sat 9am–10:30pm, Sun 10am–10:30pm. **Prices:** Main courses $6–$8. No CC.

★ Le Bus
4266 Main St, Manayunk; tel 215/487-2663. Exit 31 off I-76. **New American.** This child-friendly spot offers hearty, American-style food made with fresh ingredients. Le Bus is best known for its breads, which it sells at more than 100 locations throughout the Philadelphia area. **FYI:** Reservations accepted. Children's menu. Additional location: 3402 Sansom St, Philadelphia (tel 387-3800). **Open:** Mon–Fri 11am–10pm, Sat–Sun 9:30am–10pm. **Prices:** Main courses $7–$13. MC, V.

★ Litto's Bakery/Caffee
910 Christian St; tel 215/627-7037. ½ block from 9th St Italian Market. **Continental/Italian.** The third generation of the Litto family recently took the helm of this family business near the Italian Market. The front room still has family pictures on the walls, and the biscotti case is still filled regularly, but lunch and dinner are now served in a back room. Service is informal and friendly. **FYI:** Reservations accepted. BYO. **Open:** Tues–Thurs 11am–10pm, Fri–Sat 11am–11pm, Sun 10am–2:30pm. Closed 2 weeks in July/August. **Prices:** Main courses $8–$17. AE, CB, DC, DISC, MC, V.

Marabella's
1420 Locust St; tel 215/545-1845. **Italian.** A small, casual bistro with soft, terra-cotta colors and a lively clientele. All meals are preceded by a basket of bread served with roasted peppers and garlic; appetizers range from classic Philadelphia mussels in red sauce to an unusual shellfish platter. For the main course, there are pastas (from spaghetti and meatballs to tortellini with goat cheese), pizza, and grilled seafood. Gelati and ricotta cheesecake are the most popular desserts. **FYI:** Reservations accepted. Jazz. Children's menu. Additional location: 17th St and Ben Franklin Pkwy (tel 981-5555). **Open:** Peak (Sept–May) Mon–Thurs 11:30am–10pm, Fri–Sat 11:30am–11pm, Sun 4:30–10pm. **Prices:** Main courses $6–$18; prix fixe $17–$21. AE, CB, DC, DISC, MC, V.

Marra's
1734 E Passyunk Ave (South Philadelphia); tel 215/463-9249. Between 12th and 13th Sts. **Italian/Pizza.** Four dining rooms offer a genuine taste of old-time Italian Philadelphia: dark-wood paneling, vinyl-covered booths, and a jukebox loaded with records by Frank Sinatra, Jerry Vale, Mario Lanza, and Dion and the Belmonts. The pizza pies are baked in an enormous brick oven, which has been in use since the place first opened in 1927. **FYI:** Reservations recommended. Children's menu. **Open:** Tues–Thurs 11:30am–11pm, Fri–Sat 11:30am–midnight, Sun 2–11pm. **Prices:** Main courses $5–$13. No CC.

Meiji-En
In Pier 19, Delaware Ave at Callowhill St; tel 215/592-7100. **New American/Japanese.** Two sides of the large dining area offer views of the Delaware River. Chefs prepare food tableside in a teppanyaki room, a sushi bar is in operation, and other dining areas are available. Seafood predominates, but there are also hot pot stews and organic salads. American-style brunch on Sundays. **FYI:** Reservations recommended. Jazz. Children's menu. **Open:** Lunch Mon–Fri 11:30am–2:30pm; dinner Sun–Thurs 5–9:30pm, Fri–Sat 5–11pm; brunch Sun 10:30am–2:30pm. **Prices:** Main courses $15–$37. AE, CB, DC, DISC, MC, V. VP ♿

★ Melrose Diner
15th St and Snyder Ave (South Philadelphia); tel 215/467-6644. 1 block W of Broad St exit off I-95. **American/Diner.** Scrapple and eggs, creamed chipped beef, and the like

are dished out at this classic (some would say kitschy) diner 10 blocks north of the sporting stadiums in South Philly. Homemade desserts are the attractions, and everything is available for takeout. The employees here are extraordinarily loyal: four have worked here for 50 years, and several others have passed the 20-year mark. **FYI:** Reservations not accepted. No liquor license. **Open:** Daily 24 hrs. **Prices:** Main courses $5–$12. No CC. ▊ ▦ 🕑

Michel's

In The Latham, 135 S 17th St (Center City); tel 215/563-9444. At Walnut St, 2 blocks S of Market St on Rittenhouse Sq. **French.** Writer/chef Michel Richard opened this restaurant in 1993, and current chef Tom Power continues the tradition of "home cooking with a French accent." It is a modern, small, stylish place with windows that look out on busy Walnut St. Peppered tuna with potato-shallot cakes is a popular entree choice. **FYI:** Reservations recommended. No smoking. **Open:** Breakfast Mon–Fri 6:30–10:30am, Sat–Sun 7:30–10:30am; lunch daily 11:30am–2:30pm; dinner daily 5:30–10:30pm. **Prices:** Main courses $15–$24. AE, DC, DISC, MC, V. ▢ ⚬

Morton's of Chicago

One Logan Square (Center City); tel 215/557-0724. 19th St at Cherry St. **Seafood/Steak.** A typical example of this high-end chain, which excels in steak and seafood and is known for its 24-ounce porterhouse. The dining room is decorated in an old/new mixture of red brick, stucco, and glass, and has booths as well as a mezzanine dining area. The wine list emphasizes American labels. **FYI:** Reservations recommended. Jacket required. **Open:** Lunch Mon–Fri 11:30am–2:30pm; dinner Mon–Sat 5:30–11pm, Sun 5–10pm. **Prices:** Main courses $17–$30. AE, CB, DC, MC, V. ● VP

New Delhi

4004 Chestnut St; tel 215/386-1941. **Indian.** Soothing sitar music wafts through this large dining room, providing an excellent accompaniment to the Northern Indian cuisine. There's a buffet at lunch and dinner; specialties include chicken tikka masala (chicken breast in tomato sauce with onions and bell peppers) and vegetable malai kofta (vegetable balls served in a creamy and mild curry sauce). **FYI:** Reservations accepted. Beer and wine only. **Open:** Lunch Mon–Fri noon–3pm, Sat noon–4pm, Sun noon–4pm; dinner Mon–Thurs 4:30–10:30pm, Fri 4:30–11:30pm, Sat 4–11:30pm, Sun 4–10:30pm. **Prices:** Main courses $6–$12. AE, DISC, MC, V.

New Mexico Grille

50 S 2nd St; tel 215/922-7061. **Tex-Mex.** Look for the cactus in the windows of this Southwestern spot, formerly known as "Los Amigos." The same owner continues to serve up hearty chili, burritos, and nachos in addition to grilled meats and seafood; free-range chicken and fresh mussels are especially popular. There's a wide range of peppers, and entrees can be made as spicy as you like. **FYI:** Reservations recommended.

Children's menu. **Open:** Peak (June–Aug) Mon–Thurs 11:30am–11pm, Fri–Sat 11:30am–1am. **Prices:** Main courses $9–$15. AE, CB, DC, MC, V. VP

Old Original Bookbinders

125 Walnut St; tel 215/925-7027. **American/Seafood.** Not to be confused with Bookbinder's on 15th St, this local landmark founded in 1865 has a clubbier atmosphere: lots of brass and wood, photos of famous patrons lining the walls. Seafood is the primary focus of the menu (fresh Maine lobster, crab Imperial) but there are also steaks and chops. Adjacent gift shop sells city souvenirs, pies, and cans of the most popular soups served in the restaurant—snapper with sherry, New England clam chowder, and Manhattan clam chowder. **FYI:** Reservations recommended. Children's menu. Dress code. **Open:** Mon–Fri 11:45am–10pm, Sat 4:30–10pm, Sun 3–9pm. **Prices:** Main courses $22–$25. AE, CB, DC, DISC, MC, V. VP ⚬

★ Pat's King of Steaks

1237 E Passyunk Ave (South Philadelphia); tel 215/468-1546. Washington Ave exit off I-95. **Regional American.** Legend says this is where the classic Philly cheesesteak sandwich was invented. The cooks here are lightning fast, which is a good thing considering the crowds of locals, tourists, and political types who come here at all hours. Just a word of advice: Read the instructions before you speak, or you'll risk a scolding from the order taker. **FYI:** Reservations not accepted. No liquor license. **Open:** Daily 24 hrs. **Prices:** Main courses $5. No CC. 🕑

Philadelphia Fish & Company

207 Chestnut St; tel 215/625-8605. At 2nd St, across from US Customs House. **Eclectic/Seafood.** Modern and bright, with light wood chairs and tables, but the large windows overlook the historic area of Independence Park. Innovative seafood dishes inspired by the Pacific Rim include seared Asian-Cajun tuna, lobster ravioli, and grilled Mahi with Japanese eggplant. Notable for good service, and with many specials. **FYI:** Reservations recommended. **Open:** Mon–Thurs 11:30am–10pm, Fri–Sat 11:30am–midnight, Sun 3–10pm. **Prices:** Main courses $15–$20. AE, DC, MC, V. ▲

The Regatta

In Philadelphia Marriott West, 111 Crawford Ave, West Conshohocken; tel 610/941-5600. Conshohocken exit off I-476 or I-76. **American/Italian.** A local hotspot for Philadelphia professionals, where pictures of the Schuylkill River and an antique boat hanging from the ceiling set a nautical theme. Bountiful, inexpensive luncheon buffet. **FYI:** Reservations recommended. Piano. **Open:** Mon–Thurs 6am–11pm, Fri–Sun 7am–11pm. **Prices:** Main courses $14–$22. AE, CB, DC, DISC, MC, V. ⚬

Ristorante Panorama

In Penn's View Inn, Front and Market Sts (Center City); tel 215/922-7800. **Italian.** Statuary, murals, greenery, and marble floors lend an luxurious ambience to this trattoria, where northern Italian cuisine is the specialty. The fish entree changes daily, and there's homemade pasta along with veal and chicken dishes. The owner claims to have the largest wine bar in America, with 120 wines available by the glass. **FYI:** Reservations recommended. No smoking. **Open:** Lunch Mon–Fri noon–2:30pm; dinner daily 5:30–11pm. **Prices:** Main courses $9–$21. AE, CB, DC, ER, MC, V. ♥ �

Ruth's Chris Steak House
260 Broad St (Center City); tel 215/790-1515. 2 blocks S of City Hall. **American/Steak.** The former headquarters of the Atlantic Richfield Company houses this location of the national chain. Dark wood appointments, antiques, and a large wooden bar evoke an earlier time of Philadelphia elegance. Steaks are the specialty, but other meats and fish are served; the barbecue shrimp appetizer is a favorite. Long wine list. **FYI:** Reservations recommended. **Open:** Lunch Fri noon–2pm; dinner Mon–Sat 5–11:30pm, Sun 5–10:30pm. **Prices:** Main courses $17–$29. AE, CB, DC, DISC, MC, V. ♥ VP ♿

★ The Saloon
750 S 7th St (South Philadelphia); tel 215/627-1811. Washington Ave exit off I-75. **Italian/Steak.** One of South Philadelphia's most elegant restaurants is in these two converted row houses, decorated with dark wood and antiques. The menu is filled with Italian standards like clams casino, crabmeat salad, and lightly breaded veal with sweet peppers, although more adventurous choices (such as sautéed radicchio with shiitake mushrooms) are also available. The wine list emphasizes Italian labels. **FYI:** Reservations recommended. Piano. **Open:** Lunch Tues–Fri 11:30am–2pm; dinner Mon–Sat 5–10:30pm. Closed week of July 4th. **Prices:** Main courses $12–$27. AE. ♥

★ Samuel Adams Brew House
1516 Sansom St (Center City); tel 215/563-2326. Two blocks S of City Hall. **American/Pub.** Live music, a collegiate setting, and boutique beer attract a young crowd to this spot, the first brew pub in the city. The food is standard pub grub—sandwiches, burgers, fries—but the brewery is the star. (If you want a more substantial meal, the Sansom Street Oyster House is right downstairs.) Only beer made on the premises is sold (the aroma of hops and other ingredients wafts through constantly), and four or five varieties generally are available. Cover charge on weekends. **FYI:** Reservations accepted. Blues/guitar/rock. Children's menu. Beer only. **Open:** Mon–Sat 11am–2am. **Prices:** Main courses $10–$12. AE, DC, DISC, MC, V. ■

Sansom Street Oyster House
1516 Sansom St (Center City); tel 215/567-7683. 2 blocks S of City Hall. **Regional American/Seafood.** With high-back booths and goblets of oyster crackers sitting on each table, this restaurant looks as authentic as it is; the Mink family has sold seafood since 1947. Oysters, clams, and mussels are the specialties, and there are Belgian ales, Samuel Adams draft from the brew pub upstairs, and Pennsylvania wines to wash it

all down. **FYI:** Reservations accepted. **Open:** Mon–Sat 11am–10pm. **Prices:** Main courses $12–$24. AE, DC, DISC, MC, V. ■ ♿

Society Hill Hotel
301 Chestnut St; tel 215/925-1919. Across from Visitors Center. **American/Eclectic.** The popular outdoor area of this small, mellow bar/cafe is opposite Independence National Historical Park, making it a great spot for people-watching. The light menu features burgers, club sandwiches, omelettes, and salads. Bigger appetites go for the football-sized cheesesteaks. Extensive weekend brunch. **FYI:** Reservations not accepted. Piano. **Open:** Mon–Sat 11am–2am, Sun 11am–midnight. **Prices:** Main courses $5–$8. AE, MC, V. ■ ♨

★ Sonoma's
4411 Main St, Manayunk; tel 215/483-9400. Exit 31 off I-76. **Californian/Italian.** Casual, yet upscale restaurant where the "beautiful people" go to be seen, especially in the two popular bars. Award-winning cuisine. **FYI:** Reservations accepted. Children's menu. Dress code. **Open:** Sun–Thurs 11am–11pm, Fri–Sat 11am–midnight. **Prices:** Main courses $10–$15. AE, CB, DC, DISC, MC, V. ◨ VP ♿

♣ Striped Bass
1500 Walnut St; tel 215/732-4444. **Seafood.** Superstar chef Alison Barshak hangs her toque in this upscale eatery housed in a former bank building. Dining is in an open, high-ceilinged space, where a 16-foot steel sculpture of a leaping bass watches over the exhibition kitchen. Entrees include striped bass with goat cheese tamale cake, pasilla pepper reduction, and blood orange–jicama salad. Wine list is extensive and mostly domestic. **FYI:** Reservations recommended. Jacket required. No smoking. **Open:** Lunch Mon–Fri 11:30am–2:30pm; dinner Mon–Thurs 5–11pm, Fri–Sat 5–11:30pm, Sun 5–10pm; brunch Sat–Sun 11am–2:30pm. **Prices:** Main courses $33. AE, CB, DC, MC, V. VP ♿

♣ Susanna Foo
1512 Walnut St (Center City); tel 215/545-2666. 1 block W of Broad St. **Chinese/Eclectic.** Owned and operated by Philly's star Chinese chef. The food is an eclectic blend of modern Asian and classic Chinese, ranging from sautéed Mandarin sea scallops with almond, lemon zest, and white beans to sautéed filet mignon with leeks and coriander in Szechuan peppercorn sauce. Imaginative dim sum (pork-stuffed jalapeños, lamb wantons, tiny spring rolls) available at lunch and dinner. **FYI:** Reservations recommended. Dress code. No smoking. **Open:** Lunch Mon–Fri 11:30am–2:30pm; dinner Mon–Thurs 5:30–10pm, Fri–Sat 5:30–11pm. **Prices:** Main courses $15–$26; prix fixe $42–$55. AE, DC, MC, V. ♥

Thai Palace
117 South St; tel 215/925-2764. **Thai.** An airy yet intimate room in soft shades of pink, with comfortable seating. The food is only moderately spicy but can be spiced up on request. Selections include chicken *ka prow* (chicken with

fried hot pepper) served with basil-lemongrass sauce. Vegetarian menu available. **FYI:** Reservations accepted. No liquor license. **Open:** Mon–Thurs 5–10pm, Fri–Sat 5–11pm, Sun 4–10pm. **Prices:** Main courses $8–$15. AE, DISC, MC, V.

Tree Tops

In Rittenhouse Hotel, 210 W Rittenhouse Sq (Center City); tel 215/546-9000. Between Walnut St and Locust Sts. **Regional American.** A very open, light-filled eatery with two dining rooms, both of which overlook lovely Rittenhouse Square. The decor and color scheme are understated, and there's comfortable seating at tables with chairs as well as banquettes. The menu includes fish, veal, and beef entrees with interesting garnishes; light fare is available in the adjoining bar. **FYI:** Reservations recommended. Children's menu. **Open:** Mon–Thurs 6:30–10pm, Fri–Sat 6:30–11pm, Sun 6:30–10pm. **Prices:** Main courses $14–$25. AE, DC, DISC, MC, V. VP &

★ The Triangle Tavern

Passyunk Ave at 10th and Reed Sts (South Philadelphia); tel 215/467-8683. Washington Ave exit off I-95. **Italian.** A corner bar and old-style eatery serving up generous portions of homestyle Italian food. (The dining room is in the back of the bar.) Chicken cacciatore, gnocchi, spaghetti in white clam sauce, and mussels in red sauce are good enough to make anyone say "Mamma Mia!" Every Friday and Saturday night for 40 years, the same band has belted out everything from Sinatra to contemporary pop tunes, and the dishwashers often come out of the kitchen to sing along. **FYI:** Reservations accepted. Jazz/rock. **Open:** Sun–Thurs 11am–11pm, Fri–Sat 11am–1am. **Prices:** Main courses $7–$14. No CC.

The Victor Cafe

1303 Dickinson St (South Philadelphia); tel 215/468-3040. **Italian.** This favorite haunt of musicians has been in the DiStefano family since 1918, when it began as an RCA Victor record shop that happened to serve dessert; legend has it that Mario Lanza developed his love of opera here. All the waiters are professional singers, and the walls are covered with decades of memorabilia. Add that to the library of 45,000 recordings, and entertainment is rarely lacking. The food is classic Italian, and the wine list is long. **FYI:** Reservations recommended. Singer. Dress code. No smoking. **Open:** Mon–Fri 5–10pm, Sat–Sun 4:30–10pm. **Prices:** Main courses $13–$22. AE, CB, DC, MC, V.

★ Walt's King of the Crabs

804-806 S 2nd St (Center City); tel 215/339-9124. 4 blocks S of South St. **Seafood.** Operated by the same family for several generations, Walt's has a reputation for reasonably priced seafood, steaks, chicken, and pasta. All platters come with cole slaw and french fries. Weekend lines can be outrageously long, but they generally move fast. **FYI:** Reservations recommended. **Open:** Mon–Thurs 11am–11pm, Fri–Sat 11am–midnight, Sun 1–11pm. **Prices:** Main courses $3–$14. CB, MC, V.

White Dog Cafe

3420 Sansom St; tel 215/386-9224. **Regional American.** The 19th-century mystic and theosophist Madame Blavatsky once lived in this row house; today, the restaurant housed here attracts academics from the nearby University of Pennsylvania as well as the city's power brokers. Locally produced duck, pork, lamb, and produce are the basis of the menu, and everything is accompanied by homemade rolls and muffins. Wines are mostly American and there are microbrews on tap. **FYI:** Reservations recommended. Jazz/piano. Children's menu. No smoking. **Open:** Mon–Fri 11:30am–midnight, Sat–Sun 11am–midnight. **Prices:** Main courses $12–$21. AE, CB, DC, DISC, MC, V. ▣ &

Zanzibar Blue

305 S 11th St (Center City); tel 215/829-0300. Between Spruce and Pine Sts. **New American/International.** Jazz floats over into the dining room at this restaurant, nestled into a quiet block south of Spruce Street. The menu ranges from regional American dishes like pan-fried catfish to stir fry to pollo pando (West Indian chicken in coconut-curry sauce). **FYI:** Reservations recommended. Jazz. Jacket required. No smoking. **Open:** Dinner Sun–Thurs 5:30pm–midnight, Fri–Sat 5:30pm–1am; brunch Sun 11am–2pm. **Prices:** Main courses $15–$21. AE, CB, DC, DISC, MC, V. ● VP

Zocalo

36th and Lancaster Ave; tel 215/895-0139. **South American/Southwestern.** This brightly painted, upbeat dining room provides the perfect atmosphere in which to eat Mexican classics such as enchiladas and tostadas. For the more adventurous diner, Zocalo also offers seafood tacos, butterflied Cornish game hen, and Yucatan-style grilled chicken breast. **FYI:** Reservations recommended. Children's menu. No smoking. **Open:** Lunch Mon–Fri noon–2:30pm; dinner Mon–Thurs 5:30–10pm, Fri–Sat 5:30–11pm, Sun 5–9:30pm. **Prices:** Main courses $12–$17; prix fixe $14–$15. AE, CB, DC, DISC, MC, V.

REFRESHMENT STOPS ▽

Passero's Gourmet Coffee & Espresso Bar

In 230 South Broad Street Building, 1401 Locust St at Broad St (Center City); tel 215/546-2515. **Coffeehouse.** The city's first chain of espresso vendors prides itself on expertise in coffee, especially in making espresso and cappuccino. This microcafe is a cute nook in a large neo-Gothic building, with light green faux-finished walls, a small wooden bar, and a handful of bar stools. Pastries and gourmet sandwiches are also available. Additional locations: 1800 John F Kennedy Blvd (tel 587-1333); 1601 John F Kennedy Blvd (tel 567-3410). **Open:** Mon–Fri 7am–5pm. No CC.

Torreo Coffee & Tea Company

130 S 17th St (Center City); tel 215/988-0061. 2 blocks S of Market St, between Chestnut and Walnut Sts. **Coffeehouse/Desserts.** This modern, bright, family-owned spot is a good place for a light repast of sandwiches, muffins, pastries,

bagels, or biscotti. The selection of 30 fresh-roasted coffees and dozens of varieties of tea make a nice meal accompaniment or finisher. **Open:** Mon–Sat 6:30am–6pm. DISC, MC, V.

ATTRACTIONS

HISTORIC BUILDINGS AND MONUMENTS

Independence National Historical Park

(Center City); tel 215/597-8974 or TDD 215/597-1785. Independence National Historic Park is made up of 26 sites, including 20 buildings that are open to the public. At the center of the park is Independence Hall, the former home of the Liberty Bell. The building, designed by Alexander Hamilton and built between 1732 and 1756, was the site of many historic events, including the adoption of the Declaration of Independence and the writing of the Constitution. The Liberty Bell, now in its own pavilion, was cast in 1751 but only received its name in the 19th century, when it was adopted as a symbol of freedom by abolitionists.

In addition to Independence Hall, there are many lesser-known sights, like Franklin Court (where Benjamin Franklin's house stood until it was torn down in the early 19th century) and Mikveh Israel Cemetery (the oldest Jewish cemetery in Philadelphia). Other important "firsts" in the park include Library Hall, the oldest subscription library in the United States, and St George's Church, the oldest Methodist Church in the country.

Several of the buildings were the homes of prominent figures of the colonial period, like the Todd House, where Dolley Todd lived until she married her second husband and became Dolley Madison. The Deshler Morris House (located in Germantown), built shortly before the American Revolution, belonged to a local merchant, and was later used as headquarters by British general Sir William Howe, and in 1793 by President George Washington. The Thaddeus Kosciuszko National Memorial pays tribute to the Polish American revolutionary and engineer who lived here in 1797–98. Other buildings include Congress Hall, where the Congress met from 1790 to 1800, and the reconstructed City Tavern, where visitors can dine where the first Congress members and leading Philadelphians once argued over dinner. The park has a wealth of antiques, paintings (by American masters like Peale, West, Sully, and Pine), and important objects in the 54 historic room reconstructions and 45 exhibit areas scattered throughout the sites.

The main visitors center, a block away from Independence Hall, can provide maps and brochures (in 13 different languages), and other information about the park. **Open:** Daily 9am–5pm. **Free**

Edgar Allan Poe National Historic Site

532 N 7th St; tel 215/597-8780. During his six years in Philadelphia, Poe published such works as "The Fall of the House of Usher" and "The Tell-Tale Heart," although much of his life here is as mysterious as his stories. Poe, his wife Virginia, and his mother-in-law moved here sometime between the fall of 1842 and June 1843; they left in April 1844, and their possessions vanished as well. The house is now unfurnished because of a lack of information about the original contents. There are two other buildings on the grounds, offering a slide show and information on the author's tragic life. **Open:** Daily 9am–5pm. **Free**

Declaration House (Graff House)

7th and Market Sts; tel 215/597-2505. In the summer of 1776, bricklayer Jacob Graff Jr rented two rooms of his house to a young Virginian named Thomas Jefferson. A delegate to the Continental Congress, Jefferson drafted the Declaration of Independence in Graff's house. The building was reconstructed in 1975, and contains exhibits on the Declaration (including a film), period furnishings, and reproductions of the chair and desk Jefferson used during his stay. **Open:** Daily 9am–5pm. **Free**

Betsy Ross House

239 Arch St; tel 215/627-5343. It is unknown whether Quaker seamstress Betsy Ross actually made the first American flag of thirteen stars and stripes, but she did ship's flags for the American fleet. The small house is separated from the street by Atwater Kent Park, where Ross and her husband are buried. The period parlor, tiny bedrooms, and work areas contain colonial-era artifacts and household tools. **Open:** Peak (June–Aug) daily 9am–6pm. Reduced hours off-season. **$**

Carpenters' Hall

320 Chestnut St; tel 215/925-0167. Originally the guildhall of the city's carpenters, this was the site of many key events in the American Revolution. Built in 1773, the building was used by the first Continental Congress as a meeting site in 1774. The following year, secret meetings at the hall between American representatives (including Benjamin Franklin and John Jay) and a French agent ensured French support for the revolution. The hall today is mostly empty, except for an exhibit of colonial building methods, portraits, and the chairs that the first Congress used. Part of Independence National Historic Park. **Open:** Tues–Sun 10am–4pm. **Free**

Elfreth's Alley

126 Elfreth's Alley; tel 215/574-0560. The oldest residential street in the United States and a registered National Historic Landmark. Established between 1702 and 1704, this cobblestoned alley is lined with 30 small homes which display diverse architectural styles of the 18th and early 19th centuries. At its inception, the alley was home to artisans connected with the shipping trades. Later, immigrants made it a miniature melting pot. Almost torn down in 1937, the homes are now preserved by the residents and the Elfreth's Alley Association. The Mantua Maker's Museum House at #126 offers walking tours and special programs, such as the Fete

Days' Open House in June and the Holiday Candlelight House Tour in December. **Open:** Peak (Mar–Nov) Tues–Sat 10am–4pm. Reduced hours off-season. **$**

MUSEUMS

Philadelphia Museum of Art
26th St and Ben Franklin Pkwy; tel 215/763-8100 or 684-7500. The third-largest art museum in the country, the Philadelphia Museum of Art houses many impressive masterpieces, with a focus on the 19th and 20th centuries. The most famous works here include Cézanne's monumental *Bathers* and Marcel Duchamp's radical *Nude Descending a Staircase*, which so outraged the public in 1913 that one derisive critic said it should be called "explosion in a shingle factory." Works by later innovators like Jasper Johns and Jackson Pollock can be found in the modern galleries. The museum has many works by Philadelphian Thomas Eakins, whose paintings evoke the city of the last century, and fine collections of Colonial, Amish, Shaker, and Pennsylvania German objects. **Open:** Tues and Thurs–Sun 10am–5pm, Wed 10am–8:45pm. **$$$**

Pennsylvania Academy of Fine Arts
118 N Broad St at Cherry St; tel 215/972-7600. The heyday of the Pennsylvania Academy, the first art school in the country, was the mid-19th century, when the city was still the center of American artistic activity. The current building is itself a Victorian masterpiece, designed by Frank Furness and built in 1876. The academy's **Museum of American Art** includes work by such masters as Thomas Eakins, Benjamin West, the Peales, and Mary Cassatt. Other galleries show work by the current students and teachers at the school. **Open:** Tues–Sat 10am–5pm, Sun 11am–5pm. **$$**

The Rodin Museum
Benjamin Franklin Pkwy, between 21st and 22nd Sts; tel 215/763-8100. Apart from its kindred museum in Paris, Philadelphia's Rodin Museum has the largest collection of the sculptor's work in the world. The permanent collection includes 129 sculptures, 72 drawings, and several sketchbooks. Among the works on display are *The Thinker*, *The Gates of Hell*, and *The Burghers of Calais*. Donation suggested. **Open:** Tues–Sun 10am–5pm.

Curtis Center Museum of Norman Rockwell Art
6th and Sansom Sts; tel 215/922-4345. A complete collection of Norman Rockwell's *Saturday Evening Post* covers is now housed in this museum, which occupies the original Curtis Publishing Building. In addition, there are Rockwell lithographs, collotypes, prints, and sketches, produced during the artist's 60-year career. (Admission is free if visitors mention *Frommer's America on Wheels.*) **Open:** Mon–Sat 10am–4pm, Sun 11am–4pm. **$**

Athenaeum of Philadelphia
219 S 6th St; tel 215/925-2688. Founded in 1814 and beautifully restored in 1975, the Athenaeum contains almost 1 million items related to architecture in its library. The former 19th-century private subscription library also hosts changing exhibits about architecture and design, while a first-floor gallery exhibits rare books, drawings, and photographs. **Open:** Mon–Fri 9am–5pm. **Free**

The Official Museum of Philadelphia History/ Arwater Kent Museum
15 S 7th St; tel 215/922-3031. Founded in 1938 as Philadelphia's official history museum, the Atwater Kent contains an incredible variety of items reflecting everyday life in Philadelphia from 1680 to 1880: dolls, dioramas, cigar-store Indians, period toy shops, and train tickets are among the 75,000 pieces in the permanent collection. The museum also sponsors a concert series and a variety of educational programs. **Open:** Wed–Mon 10am–4pm. **$**

Afro-American Historical and Cultural Museum
7th and Arch Sts; tel 215/574-0380. The museum has been called the only building in the country specifically designed to display the African American heritage. The structure of the five-story building is modeled after African mud houses. Ascending through five levels of exhibitions, the visitor follows the path from African roots to the role blacks have played in the development of the United States. The exhibits on slavery are the most dramatic and informative, emphasizing that the slave trade was not restricted to North America. The three upper levels deal with black history and culture after emancipation, including the roles of black cowboys, inventors, athletes, politicians, and organizations. **Open:** Tues–Sat 10am–5pm. **$$**

National Museum of American Jewish History
55 N 5th St (Independence Mall); tel 215/923-3811. The museum's permanent exhibition, "The American Jewish Experience: From 1654 to the Present," uses portraits, documents, letters, books, religious articles, and other artifacts to illustrate Jewish involvement in American society, culture, religion, economy, and politics. Smaller rotating exhibits supplement the main presentation and special events (readings, storytelling, films, concerts) are offered. A new exhibition will open in 1997. **Open:** Mon–Thurs 10am–5pm, Fri 10am–3pm, Sun noon–5pm. **$$**

Mummers Museum
1100 S 2nd St; tel 215/336-3050. The Mummers, long a fixture in the Philadelphia New Year's Day Parade, are famous for their brightly colored, feathered costumes and lively string music. The tradition stretches back to colonial times, influenced both by English country fairs and enhanced by African American culture and music of the 19th century. The museum has prize-winning costumes on view, and visitors can learn to do the "Mummer's strut." **Open:** Tues–Sat 9:30am–5pm, Sun noon–5pm. **$**

The Franklin Institute
222 N 20th St; tel 215/448-1200. Occupying an entire city block, the Franklin Institute contains exhibits on astronomy, biotechnology, communications, earth science, mechanics,

and transportation. The institute was a pioneer in interactive displays, and the approach is distinctly hands-on: visitors can ride a 350-ton locomotive, sit in a modern jet or in the Wright brothers' biplane, or walk through a giant recreation of a heart. The Mandell Futures Center contains computerized exhibits and interactive video, including driving simulators and a "jamming" room with musical synthesizers. The Tuttleman Omniverse Theater presents science-oriented programs on a 180° screen; there is also a planetarium. Part of the museum contains the Franklin Memorial and a display of objects belonging to Benjamin Franklin. **Open:** Science Museum: Mon–Sat 9:30am–5pm, Sun 9:30am–6pm. Mandell Center: Mon–Wed 9:30am–5pm, Thurs–Sat 9:30am–9pm, Sun 9:30am–6pm. **$$$**

The Academy of Natural Sciences
1900 Benjamin Franklin Pkwy; tel 215/299-1000. The academy has a variety of dioramas and displays, but is perhaps best known for its dinosaurs. There are more than a dozen specimens, including a *Tyrannosaurus rex*. In one interactive exhibit, children don goggles and dig for dinosaur bones and fossils. "What on Earth!" is an interactive exhibit on geology. The diorama halls include displays on North American, Asian, and African flora and fauna. Special events, lectures, and animal-handling demonstrations take place periodically. **Open:** Mon–Fri 10am–4pm, Sat–Sun 10am–5pm. **$$$**

University of Pennsylvania Museum of Archaeology and Anthropology
33rd and Spruce Sts; tel 215/898-4000. With over thirty galleries and more than a million objects, the University of Pennsylvania Museum of Archaeology and Anthropology is like a tour of world civilizations from the Maori to the Maya. Founded in 1887, the museum has conducted over 300 expeditions, which have provided the larger part of its holdings. Exhibits include a 12-ton granite Sphinx of Ramses II, a lead sarcophagus from Tyre, colossal architectural remains from Memphis, and the famous treasure trove of the Royal Tombs of Ur. The exhibit on the art and science of Egyptian mummification is particularly popular. **Open:** Tues–Sat 10am–4:30pm, Sun 1–5pm. **$$**

Please Touch Museum
210 N 21st St; tel 215/963-0667. Designed specifically for children under age seven, the museum is housed in former factory buildings and has a wide range of hands-on activities. "Growing Up" is designed for both parents and children to learn about human development; "Studio PTM" is a replica of a TV studio in which children can play all the parts in front of and behind the scenes. Educational programs and crafts are also available. **Open:** Daily 9am–4:30pm. **$$$**

CHURCHES

Arch Street Meeting House
320 Arch St (Olde City); tel 215/627-2667. The original brick Meeting House was built in 1804 on a site donated to the Religious Society of Friends (better known as the Quakers) by William Penn in 1693. The building was expanded in 1811 and 1968, and is still used each year for the national Yearly Meeting of the society. In addition to the meeting room, there are displays of Bibles, Quaker objects, and a history of the life and religion of William Penn. **Open:** Mon–Sat 10am–4pm. **Free**

Christ Church in Philadelphia
2nd St above Market (Olde City); tel 215/922-1695. The current structure on the site was built in 1754, but the site was used as a burial ground even before then. The churchyard contains the remains of seven signers of the Declaration of Independence and several signers of the Constitution, including Benjamin Franklin. Other people buried here include the captain of the USS *Constitution*, the printer who made the first broadside of the Declaration of Independence, and the captain who brought the Liberty Bell to the United States. Christ Church is a functioning Episcopal church to this day, with a collection of historic objects, paintings, and furniture. Inside the church, guides are always available. **Open:** Mon–Fri 9am–5pm, Sun 1–5pm. **Free**

Gloria Dei
916 Swanson St; tel 215/389-1513. Considered the oldest church in the state, the Gloria Dei, or Old Swedes' Church, was built in 1700. The congregation was founded in 1646, when Swedes first settled the area (predating English settlement). The church became part of the Episcopal Church in 1845, and is still in use today. There is also a churchyard, a rectory, a miniature parish hall, and a one-room museum. The church contains many historical artifacts, including ship models hung from the ceiling. **Open:** Apr–Oct, daily 9am–5pm. **Free**

PARKS AND GARDENS

Penn's Landing
Columbus Blvd, between Market and Lombard Sts. In recent years, this long-neglected reminder of Philadelphia's maritime past has made a comeback. A number of historic vessels are tied up here, including one of Admiral Halsey's World War II submarines and the dreadnought **USS Olympia** (tel 215/922-1848), Admiral Dewey's flagship during the Spanish American War. Museums include the **Port of History Museum** (tel 215/925-3804) and the Philadelphia Maritime Museum, while the Great Plaza, a festive, multitiered amphitheater, hosts many summer festivals. Restaurants and retail shops round out the picture. Tour boats and water taxis depart from the docks.

Philadelphia Zoological Gardens
34th St and Girard Ave; tel 215/243-1100. When it opened in 1874, the Philadelphia Zoo was the nation's first. Its collection of 1,500 animals features many endangered species, including a pride of six white lions plus gorillas, orangutans, and ring-tailed lemurs. The $6 million Carnivore Kingdom houses snow leopards and jaguars, and newly designed habitats like the World of Primates and the African

Plains present the animals in more natural environments. The very popular Camel Rides start next to the Treehouse, while a children's zoo lets kids pet and feed baby zoo and farm animals. A monorail takes visitors who are pressed for time on a 20-minute "safari" around the 42-acre complex. **Open:** Mon–Fri 9:30am–5pm, Sat–Sun 9:30am–6pm. **$$$**

Historic Bartram's Garden
54th St and Lindbergh Blvd (Southwest Philadelphia); tel 215/729-5281. Considered the country's oldest botanical garden, Bartram's Garden was started in 1731 by Quaker farmer John Bartram. Despite his lack of education, Bartram and his son William identified and cultivated over 200 American plants. John Bartram rose to become Royal Botanist under George III and received tributes from such eminent scientists as Linnaeus. Among the plants growing here are the *Franklinia altamaha,* which Bartram saved from extinction and named for his friend Benjamin Franklin, and what is believed to be the last of the three original ginkgo trees imported to America. **Open:** Grounds: daily sunrise–sunset. House Tours: Peak (May–Oct) Wed–Sun noon–4pm. Reduced hours off-season. **$**

OTHER ATTRACTIONS

Philadelphia Visitors Center
16th St and John F Kennedy Blvd; tel 215/636-1666 or toll free, 800/537-7676. The Philadelphia Visitors Center is staffed by volunteers ready to answer visitors' questions and calls. They also distribute the city's "Official Visitor's Guide," with maps, up-to-date info about events and restaurants, and tips for shopping, transportation, lodging, and entertainment. **Open:** Daily 9am–5pm. **Free**

Reading Terminal Market
12th and Arch Sts; tel 215/922-2317. In 1693, the first urban market in the colonies opened in Philadelphia. Today, the Reading Terminal Market continues the tradition of the farmer's market, with 80 merchants selling everything from free-range chickens and goose eggs to cannolis and espresso. A market has been located under the tracks of the terminal since the turn of the century. Now, in addition to farm products sold by the Amish, there are foods from around the world, as well as local specialties like Philadelphia cheesesteaks and scrapple. **Open:** Mon–Sat 8am–6pm. **Free**

University of Pennsylvania
34th and Walnut Sts; tel 215/898-5000. This private, now coeducational, Ivy League institution was founded by Benjamin Franklin and others in 1740. Since then, Penn has grown to 22,000 students, 4 undergraduate and 12 graduate schools, and over 100 academic departments. The university boasts the first medicine (1760), law (1790), and business (1881) schools in the country. Its 260-acre campus houses important museums (the University Museum of Archaeology and Anthropology, the Institute for Contemporary Art) and the Annenberg Center for the Performing Arts.

US Mint
5th and Arch Sts; tel 215/597-7350. This US Mint building was the first authorized by the government during President George Washington's first term in office. Today, the modern machinery inside turns out 1,500,000 coins per hour. A tour shows visitors how money is made—from the red-hot slabs of metal to the stamping and counting of the finished coins. **Open:** Peak (July–Aug) daily 9am–4:30pm. Reduced hours off-season. **Free**

PROFESSIONAL SPORTS

CoreStates Spectrum
Broad and Pattison Sts; tel 215/336-3600. Primarily used as a sports arena, the Spectrum is home court for the Philadelphia 76ers NBA basketball team as well as ice hockey's Philadelphia Flyers. It also hosts specialty events such as the US Pro Indoor Tennis Championships, and is one of the city's main venues for rock concerts. **Open:** Call for schedule. **$$$$**

Veterans Stadium
Broad St and Pattison Aves; tel 215/686-1776. A graceful bowl-shaped stadium seating from 58,000 to 68,000 people. The Philadelphia Phillies of baseball's National League and the Eagles of the NFL play home games here. **Open:** Call for schedule. **$$$$**

Pine Forge

RESTAURANT ⑪

Gracie's
Manatawny Rd; tel 610/323-4004. 3 mi from PA 100. **Eclectic.** The unassuming building holds an out-of-this-world interior, with decor ranging from Caribbean to New Age. The menu is equally innovative, with healthful entrees such as St Lucian shrimp barbarde, Tuscan salmon, French country pork chop, and grill-seared tofu marinara. **FYI:** Reservations recommended. Jazz. Dress code. **Open:** Wed–Sat 5–10pm. **Prices:** Main courses $20–$32. AE, DC, MC, V. &

Pittsburgh

See also Coraopolis, Hopwood, Mercer, New Stanton

Pittsburgh's location at the junction of east-west transportation arteries and its proximity to immense reserves of raw materials led to its role as an industrial center for the nation. It is still a world-class center for manufacturing of steel, pig iron, and coke; computer services and health care also contribute to the economy. Cultural attractions include the Frick Art Museum, the Heinz Hall Performance Center, and the Andy Warhol Museum; educational institutions include Carnegie Mellon University and the University of Pittsburgh. The Pittsburgh Steelers and the Pittsburgh Pirates play at Three Rivers Stadium, so named because it sits at the point where the Monongahela and Allegheny Rivers unite to form the Ohio River. **Information:** Greater Pittsburgh Convention & Visitors Bureau, Four Gateway Center #514, Pittsburgh, 15222 (tel 412/281-7711).

PUBLIC TRANSPORTATION

The **Port Authority of Allegheny County** (tel 412/442-2000) operates city buses (fare is $1.25), the Monongahela trolley to Mount Washington ($1), and a limited subway system (free downtown, 75¢ elsewhere).

HOTELS 🏨

▤▤▤▤ DoubleTree Hotel Pittsburgh

1000 Penn Ave, 15222 (Downtown); tel 412/281-3700 or toll free 800/367-8478; fax 412/227-4500. A business-oriented hotel right across the street from the city's convention center. The atrium lobby has fresh floral arrangements, comfortable seating, and a pleasant air. **Rooms:** 616 rms, stes, and effic. Executive level. CI 3pm/CO noon. Nonsmoking rms avail. Well-appointed rooms have armoires and nicely coordinated fabrics. **Amenities:** 🛅 🛋 📺 ✎ A/C, cable TV w/movies, voice mail. All units w/minibars, 1 w/whirlpool. **Services:** ⦿ 🗝 VP 🚐 🖂 ↩ ✑ Masseur, babysitting. **Facilities:** 🏋 🏊 1000 🖳 ও 2 restaurants, 2 bars, spa, sauna, steam rm, whirlpool. Large workout room available for extra fee. Indoor lap pool has city views and is free to guests. **Rates:** Peak (mid-March–Sept 3) $160 S; $180 D; $250–$1,500 ste; $460–$620 effic. Children under age 19 stay free. Lower rates off-season. Parking: Indoor, $13/day. AE, CB, DC, DISC, EC, JCB, MC, V.

▤▤▤ Harley Hotel Pittsburgh

699 Rodi Rd, 15235; tel 412/244-1600 or toll free 800/321-2323; fax 412/829-2334. This corporate hotel in a suburb east of the city is perched on a hill in the woods. **Rooms:** 152 rms. CI 3pm/CO 11am. Nonsmoking rms avail. Attractive room furnishings, with upholstered headboards and granite-topped dresser and desk. Queen rooms have sofa beds. **Amenities:** 🛅 🛋 A/C, cable TV w/movies, dataport. Some units w/terraces. Refrigerators available. **Services:** ✕ 🚐 🖂 ↩ Free van transportation to points within five-mile radius. **Facilities:** 🏋 🏊 2 300 ও 1 restaurant (see "Restaurants" below), 1 bar (w/entertainment), sauna, whirlpool, washer/dryer. Olympic-size indoor pool with spacious lounge area. Outdoor pool adjacent to woods. Free use of nearby Bally's Health Club. **Rates:** Peak (Sept–Mar) $106–$116 S or D. Extra person $10. Children under age 18 stay free. Lower rates off-season. MAP rates avail. Parking: Outdoor, free. Weekend packages avail. AE, DC, DISC, MC, V.

UNRATED Holiday Inn Allegheny Valley

180 Gamma Dr, 15238; tel 412/963-0600 or toll free 800/HOLIDAY; fax 412/963-7852. Exit 10 off PA 28 (RIDC Rd). Located in an industrial park ten miles north of downtown, the weekday business here is primarily businesspeople. **Rooms:** 223 rms, stes, and effic. CI 2pm/CO noon. Nonsmoking rms avail. Mini-suites have two queen beds.

Amenities: 🛅 🛋 A/C, cable TV. Some units w/terraces. Some units have microwaves and refrigerators. Crown suites have full cooking facilities. **Services:** ✕ 🖂 ↩ **Facilities:** 🏋 🏊 100 ও 1 restaurant, 1 bar, games rm, washer/dryer. **Rates:** $90 S or D; $95 ste; $125–$135 effic. Extra person $9. Parking: Outdoor, free. AE, CB, DC, DISC, JCB, MC, V.

▤▤▤ Holiday Inn McKnight

4859 McKnight Rd, 15237; tel 412/366-5200 or toll free 800/HOLIDAY; fax 412/366-5682. Exit 18 (US 19) off I-279. Located on a quiet hill overlooking Pittsburgh's North Hills area. Rooms are well-kept and the staff is attentive. **Rooms:** 147 rms and stes. Executive level. CI 2pm/CO noon. Nonsmoking rms avail. **Amenities:** 🛅 🛋 📺 ✎ A/C, satel TV w/movies, dataport. Special phones for deaf and hard of hearing guests. **Services:** ✕ 🖂 ↩ ✑ **Facilities:** 🏋 300 ও 1 restaurant (see "Restaurants" below), 1 bar (w/entertainment), washer/dryer. Use of nearby health club for nominal fee. **Rates:** Peak (May–Sept) $105–$125 S or D; $109–$150 ste. Extra person $10. Children under age 19 stay free. Min stay special events. Lower rates off-season. Parking: Outdoor, free. Best Breaks packages avail. AE, CB, DC, DISC, JCB, MC, V.

▤▤▤ Holiday Inn Select

100 Lytton Ave, 15213; tel 412/682-6200 or toll free 800/864-8287; fax 412/682-5745. This business travelers' hotel has amenities not found in most other Holiday Inns. Located in the heart of the university district. **Rooms:** 251 rms and stes. Executive level. CI 3pm/CO noon. Nonsmoking rms avail. **Amenities:** 🛅 📺 ✎ A/C, cable TV w/movies, voice mail. Some units w/minibars. **Services:** ✕ 🗝 🚐 🖂 ↩ ✑ Twice-daily maid svce, car-rental desk, social director. Free local calls. Free van transportation within five-mile radius. **Facilities:** 🏋 🏊 400 🖳 ও 1 restaurant, 1 bar (w/entertainment), spa, sauna, washer/dryer. Jazz in bar on weekends. **Rates:** $135 S or D; $144–$154 ste. Children under age 18 stay free. Parking: Indoor/outdoor, $12/day. Weekend rates avail. AE, DC, DISC, MC, V.

UNRATED The Pittsburgh Hilton & Towers

600 Commonwealth Dr, 15222 (Downtown); tel 412/391-4600 or toll free 800/HILTONS; fax 412/594-5161. Gateway Center. A downtown hotel overlooking Point State Park. **Rooms:** 712 rms and stes. Executive level. CI 3pm/CO noon. Nonsmoking rms avail. Tower rooms have VCRs with free movies, fax machines, bathrobes, private check-in and check-out. **Amenities:** 🛅 🛋 A/C, satel TV w/movies, dataport, voice mail. All units w/minibars. **Services:** ✕ 🗝 VP 🚐 🖂 ↩ ✑ Masseur, babysitting. **Facilities:** 🏊 2200 🖳 ও 2 restaurants, 1 bar, beauty salon, playground. Cappuccino bar in lobby. **Rates:** $148–$198 S; $173–$223 D; $345 ste. Extra person $25. Children under age 18 stay free. Min stay special events. MAP rates avail. Parking: Indoor, $14–$20/day. Weekend rates avail. AE, CB, DC, DISC, JCB, MC, V.

UNRATED **Ramada Hotel**

1 Bigelow Sq, 15219; tel 412/281-5800 or toll free 800/225-5858; fax 412/281-8467. This downtown, all-suites property was formerly an apartment building, so there are cooking facilities in all its spacious rooms. **Rooms:** 311 stes. CI 3pm/CO noon. Nonsmoking rms avail. One-bedroom and junior suites. **Amenities:** 🛗 🐧 🖥 🦤 A/C, cable TV w/movies, dataport, voice mail. All units w/minibars. **Services:** ✗ VP 🚐 🖎 🌛 Masseur, babysitting. Valet parking only; vehicles over 6'2" high will not fit in garage. **Facilities:** 🔥 💪 🏊 600 🖎 1 restaurant, 1 bar, sauna, steam rm, beauty salon, washer/dryer. Full-service, private health club on third floor is free to guests; large pool in a glassed-in room with city views adjoins health club. **Rates (CP):** Peak (May–June/Sept–Oct) $135–$155 ste. Extra person $10. Children under age 18 stay free. Lower rates off-season. Parking: Indoor, $5/day. Weekend packages avail. AE, CB, DC, DISC, MC, V.

🏁🏁🏁🏁 **The Westin William Penn**

530 William Penn Way, 15219 (Downtown); tel 412/281-7100 or toll free 800/228-3000; fax 412/553-5252. A beautifully renovated hotel, built in 1916. The impressive lobby boasts crystal chandeliers, ornate moldings, and a grand piano. **Rooms:** 595 rms and stes. Executive level. CI 3pm/CO 1pm. Nonsmoking rms avail. Mahogany furniture and tastefully coordinated fabrics grace the rooms. Mirrors are gold framed, and the baths are marble. **Amenities:** 🛗 🐧 🦤 A/C, cable TV w/movies, dataport, voice mail. Some units w/minibars, 1 w/whirlpool. **Services:** 🍴 VP 🚐 🖎 🌛 🐕 Babysitting. **Facilities:** 💪 1200 🖥 💪 2 restaurants, 2 bars (1 w/entertainment), beauty salon, day-care ctr. Upscale restaurant, clubby pub, and cafe all on premises. **Rates:** Peak (Mar–mid-Nov) $160–$200 S or D; $335–$1,700 ste. Extra person $20. Children under age 19 stay free. Lower rates off-season. Parking: Indoor, $10.25/day. Weekend B&B packages avail. AE, CB, DC, DISC, ER, JCB, MC, V.

🏁🏁🏁 **Wyndham Garden Hotel**

1 Wyndham Circle, 15275 (Pittsburgh Airport); tel 412/695-0002 or toll free 800/WYNDHAM. This corporate hotel in the RIDC office park is a busy place on weekdays. A recent $4 million renovation has made it as good as new. **Rooms:** 140 rms and stes. CI 4pm/CO noon. Nonsmoking rms avail. **Amenities:** 🛗 🐧 🖥 🦤 A/C, satel TV w/movies, dataport, voice mail. Recliners in all rooms. **Services:** ✗ 🚐 🖎 🌛 **Facilities:** 🔥 💪 300 💪 1 restaurant, 1 bar. **Rates (CP):** $94 S or D; $94 ste. Extra person $10. Children under age 12 stay free. Parking: Outdoor, free. Weekend rates and "Park & Fly" packages avail. AE, DC, DISC, MC, V.

MOTELS

🏁🏁 **Hampton Inn**

3315 Hamlet St, 15213; tel 412/681-1000 or toll free 800/HAMPTON. Neat and pleasant, with limited amenities but adjacent to area universities. **Rooms:** 133 rms. CI 2pm/CO noon. Nonsmoking rms avail. Even-numbered rooms have good views of downtown. **Amenities:** 🛗 🐧 🦤 A/C, cable TV w/movies, dataport. **Services:** 🚐 🖎 🌛 🐕 Car-rental desk. Transportation from airport is free, but there's a fee for trips to the airport. Free shuttles to downtown and nearby neighborhoods. **Facilities:** 💪 **Rates (CP):** $84–$95 S; $95–$99 D. Children under age 18 stay free. Parking: Outdoor, free. Discounts to guests on university or hospital business. AE, DC, DISC, EC, ER, MC, V.

🏁🏁 **Howard Johnson Inn South**

5300 Clairton Blvd, 15236; tel 412/884-6000 or toll free 800/I-GO-HOJO; fax 412/884-6009. This standard motel in an area southeast of downtown does mostly corporate business. **Rooms:** 95 rms. CI 3pm/CO noon. Nonsmoking rms avail. Doubles are spacious, with two sinks. Much of the furniture is new. **Amenities:** 🛗 🐧 A/C, cable TV w/movies. All units w/terraces. Refrigerators on request. **Services:** 🖎 🌛 🐕 Full breakfast on weekends only. (Continental breakfast on weekdays.) **Facilities:** 🔥 120 💪 **Rates (BB):** $69–$79 S; $79–$89 D. Extra person $10. Children under age 18 stay free. Parking: Outdoor, free. AE, DC, DISC, EC, ER, JCB, MC, V.

INN

🏁🏁🏁 **The Priory**

614 Pressley St, 15212; tel 412/231-3338; fax 412/231-4838. Exit 13 off I-279. The current owners saved this 1888 priory from demolition and converted it to a lovely inn. **Rooms:** 24 rms and stes. CI 3pm/CO noon. Each room is individually decorated with antiques or faithful reproductions. **Amenities:** 🛗 🐧 A/C, cable TV. **Services:** 🖎 🌛 Babysitting, wine/sherry served. Honor bar in public sitting room. **Facilities:** 550 🖥 Guest lounge. **Rates (CP):** $97–$137 S; $107–$157 D; $105–$155 ste. Extra person $10. Children under age 7 stay free. Higher rates for special events/hols. Parking: Outdoor, free. Weekend rates avail. AE, DC, DISC, MC, V.

RESTAURANTS 🍴

The Balcony

5520 Walnut St (Shadyside); tel 412/687-0110. **Californian.** A popular local hangout on the second floor of a former movie theater, overlooking residential Shadyside's commercial hub. The wide-ranging menu includes gourmet pizzas, pasta, and seafood. Music six nights per week. **FYI:** Reservations accepted. Jazz. Children's menu. **Open:** Mon–Thurs 11:30am–midnight, Fri–Sat 11:30am–1am, Sun 10:30am–pm. **Prices:** Main courses $11–$17. AE, DC, DISC, MC, V.

Blarney Stone Restaurant

30 Grant Ave; tel 412/781-1666. Etna exit off PA 26 (Butler St becomes Grant Ave). **American/Irish.** This popular place serves Irish favorites, alongside traditional American fare, in a spacious facility that seats up to 800. On weekends, the lively pub features a folk singer and the restaurant is transformed into a dinner theater. **FYI:** Reservations recommend-

ed. Dinner theater/singer. Children's menu. No smoking. **Open:** Tues–Thurs 11am–10pm, Fri–Sat 11am–1am, Sun 10:30am–9pm. **Prices:** Main courses $13–$20. AE, CB, DC, DISC, MC, V. [VP] &

British Bicycle Club
923 Penn Ave (Downtown); tel 412/391-9623. Near Convention Center. **American.** Victorian-era British motifs set the tone of this casual restaurant near the convention center. A bar in the front leads to a small dining room and balcony in the rear, where guests chow down on burgers, steaks, salads, and other pub grub. **FYI:** Reservations accepted. **Open:** Mon–Fri 10am–10pm. Closed 1st week of July. **Prices:** Main courses $9–$17. AE, CB, DC, DISC, MC, V. &

Cafe Victoria
946 Western Ave (North Side); tel 412/323-8881. At Allegheny Ave. **New American/International.** The 1875 house has been restored to authentic Victorian decor: two gas fireplaces warm the dining rooms, Oriental rugs cover the floors, and lace accents the tables. An additional candlelit private dining room serves two to four people for special occasions. The menu changes seasonally. **FYI:** Reservations recommended. **Open:** Lunch Tues–Sat 11:30am–3pm; dinner Tues–Sat 5:30–9pm; brunch Sun 10:30am–2pm. **Prices:** Main courses $15–$33. AE, CB, DC, DISC, MC, V. ♥ ▦ [▣]

The Carlton
In One Mellon Bank Center, 500 Grant St (Downtown); tel 412/391-4099. At 5th Ave. **New American/American.** Dark wood paneling, subdued lighting, and recessed booth seating set a cozy mood. The menu changes daily, but is likely to list veal saltimbocca and 14-oz prime rib steaks, along with unique appetizers like wild mushroom ravioli and lobster quesadillas. **FYI:** Reservations recommended. Children's menu. **Open:** Lunch Mon–Fri 11:30am–2:30pm; dinner Mon–Thurs 5–10pm, Fri–Sat 5–11pm. **Prices:** Main courses $17–$29. AE, CB, DC, DISC, MC, V. &

★ The Common Plea
310 Ross St (Downtown); tel 412/281-5140. 3rd Ave at Ross St. **Italian.** A favorite among the city's judicial set, this intimate dining room is near the court buildings and has a menu that looks like legal papers. Entrees (pasta, seafood, beef) come with an antipasto bar, salad, a side of pasta, fresh fruit, and Cenci cookies. **FYI:** Reservations recommended. Children's menu. **Open:** Lunch Mon–Fri 11:30am–2:30pm; dinner Mon–Sat 5–10pm. **Prices:** Main courses $20–$38; prix fixe $25. AE, DC, MC, V. [▼] [VP]

The Grand Concourse
In Station Square, 1 Station Square; tel 412/261-1717. On Monongahela River just across Smithfield Bridge. **Seafood.** A unique and nostalgic eatery located in the splendid 1901 Pittsburgh & Lake Erie Railroad terminal on the Monongahela River. The main dining hall rises several stories and is covered by an arched, stained-glass ceiling. Seafood is the specialty, including Maine lobster, Maryland crab cakes, and

salmon in parchment. **FYI:** Reservations recommended. Piano. Children's menu. **Open:** Lunch Mon–Fri 11:30am–2pm; dinner Mon–Thurs 4:30–10pm, Fri–Sat 4:30–11pm, Sun 4:30–9pm; brunch Sun 10am–2:30pm. **Prices:** Main courses $10–$39. AE, CB, DC, DISC, MC, V. ▦ [▼] &

India Garden
328 Atwood St; tel 412/682-3000. Off Forbes Ave. **Indian.** A pleasantly decorated eatery on a residential street near the universities. The menu includes traditional Indian favorites like tandoori chicken, fish curry, and lamb vindaloo, along with a good selection of vegetarian dishes. **FYI:** Reservations accepted. BYO. No smoking. Additional location: 3813 William Penn Hwy, Monroeville (tel 372-0400). **Open:** Lunch Tues–Sun 11:30am–2:30pm; dinner Tues–Sun 5–10pm. **Prices:** Main courses $7–$14. AE, DISC, MC, V.

Jimmy Tsang's
5700 Center Ave; tel 412/661-4226. 3 blocks N of 5th Ave. **Chinese.** This cavernous eatery offers traditional Chinese decor and serves familiar favorites plus more exotic options like Peking duck and Mongolian beef. Wine list includes Chinese and Japanese labels. **FYI:** Reservations accepted. **Open:** Mon–Thurs 11:30am–10pm, Fri–Sat 11:30am–11pm, Sun 4–10pm. **Prices:** Main courses $6–$17. AE, CB, DC, MC, V. &

Le Mont Restaurant
1114 Grandview Ave (Mount Washington); tel 412/431-3100. Off McArdle Roadway. **Continental.** With regional and national awards for fine dining and romantic atmosphere, this long-time Pittsburgh favorite has splendid views of the city from its perch atop Mount Washington. Menu specialties include rack of lamb Persille and fresh wild game. **FYI:** Reservations recommended. Piano. Children's menu. Dress code. **Open:** Mon–Sat 5–11pm, Sun 4–10pm. **Prices:** Main courses $19–$53. AE, CB, DC, DISC, MC, V. [▲] [▼] [VP] &

Longnecker's
In Holiday Inn McKnight, 4859 McKnight Rd; tel 412/366-5200. Exit 18 off I-279. **Seafood/Steak.** The menu here ranges from pasta and gourmet pizzas to an extensive array of steak and seafood. The Friday night seafood buffet (accompanied by a live jazz combo) is popular with the locals. All main courses include salad bar. **FYI:** Reservations accepted. Jazz. Children's menu. Additional location: Greentree Holiday Inn, 401 Holiday Dr (tel 922-8100). **Open:** Breakfast daily 6:30am–2pm; dinner daily 5–10pm; brunch Sun 10am–2pm. **Prices:** Main courses $7–$22. AE, CB, DC, DISC, MC, V. &

Louis Tambellini's
860 Saw Mill Run Blvd; tel 412/481-1118. **Italian/Seafood.** This cavernous family-run restaurant seats 750 diners in several large rooms, both at tables and in booths. A huge rectangular bar in the center of one room seats an additional 60 patrons. An extensive menu includes many fish and pasta entrees, with daily lunch and dinner specials available. **FYI:**

Reservations accepted. Children's menu. Dress code. **Open:** Mon–Sat 11:30am–10pm. **Prices:** Main courses $13–$30. AE, MC, V. 🅅🅿 ♿

★ **Mallorca**
228 E Carson St (Southside); tel 412/488-1818. At 23rd St. **Continental/Spanish.** A pretty and popular room in an older Southside building with painted pillars, large windows, and lots of greenery, this Spanish restaurant specializes in paella, baby goat, and three-pound T-bone steaks. There's a long list of seafood dishes, too. **FYI:** Reservations recommended. **Open:** Mon–Thurs 11:30am–10:30pm, Fri–Sat 11:30am–11:30pm, Sun noon–10pm. **Prices:** Main courses $11–$24. AE, DC, DISC, MC, V. ♿

1902 Landmark Tavern
24 Market Sq (Market Square); tel 412/471-1902. **American.** Built in 1896 and converted to a restaurant in 1902, this brick building is decorated in brass, stained glass, and lots of dark wood. The menu is equally traditional, with mostly beef, chicken and fish standards, plus a smattering of shellfish appetizers. **FYI:** Reservations recommended. **Open:** Mon–Sat 11:30am–11pm. **Prices:** Main courses $13–$24. AE, CB, DC, DISC, MC, V. 🅅🅿 ♿

Old Country Buffet
In North Hills Village Shopping Center, 4801 McKnight Rd; tel 412/366-5200. Exit 18 off I-279 onto McKnight Rd (US 19). **American.** Diners at this huge-and-bustling eatery may fill up at the salad bar, choose a meat, scoop up some vegetables and breads, and stop off at the dessert stations—all for a single price. Children from 2 to 10 pay 50 cents for each year of their age. **FYI:** Reservations not accepted. No liquor license. No smoking. Additional locations: 591 Clairton Blvd, Pleasant Hills (tel 653-0732); Great Southern Shopping Center, Bridgeville (tel 257-8640). **Open:** Mon–Thurs 11am–8:30pm, Fri–Sat 11am–9:30pm, Sun 10:30am–8pm. **Prices:** Main courses $7. MC, V. ♿

★ **Pasta Piato**
726 Bellefonte (Shadyside); tel 412/621-5547. **Italian.** This intimate spot in the shopping district of residential Shadyside serves northern Italian cuisine with a focus on pasta: gnocchi Rossi, argilla pentola, and fazzoletti are all popular. **FYI:** Reservations not accepted. Children's menu. **Open:** Lunch Mon–Sat 11:30am–3pm; dinner Mon–Thurs 4:30–10pm, Fri–Sat 4:30–11pm, Sun 4–9pm. **Prices:** Main courses $10–$22. AE, MC, V.

Poli
2607 Murray Ave (Squirrel Hill); tel 412/521-6400. Exit 8 off I-376. **Italian/Seafood.** This elegant, wood-paneled restaurant has several modern-styled dining rooms, all with brocade upholstered chairs and dim lighting. Seafood, veal, and pasta are all excellent, and the long wine list has won a *Wine Spectator* Award of Excellence. **FYI:** Reservations not

accepted. Dress code. **Open:** Tues–Sat 11:30am–11pm, Sun 11am–9:30pm. **Prices:** Main courses $10–$25. AE, CB, DC, MC, V. 🅥 🆅 🅅🅿 ♿

Red Bull Inn
5202 Campbells Run Rd; tel 412/787-2855. Campbells Run or Moon Run exit off I-279. **Seafood/Steak.** A home-like steak house, with large booths, family-size tables, and floral decor. Prime rib or lobster dinner specials for two are a popular choice. **FYI:** Reservations accepted. Piano. Children's menu. **Open:** Mon–Thurs 11am–11pm, Fri 11am–midnight, Sat 4pm–midnight, Sun 4–9pm. **Prices:** Main courses $11–$24. AE, CB, DC, DISC, MC, V. 🖼 🆅

Ruth's Chris Steak House
In PPG Place, 6 PPG Place; tel 412/391-4800. **Steak.** Part of a popular steak house chain, this particular branch has an elegant, clubby atmosphere with wood paneling and beveled-glass inserts. The menu is primarily beef, but fish and chicken also are served. Free evening parking in garage. **FYI:** Reservations recommended. Dress code. **Open:** Lunch Mon–Fri 11:30am–3pm; dinner Mon–Thurs 5–10pm, Fri–Sat 5–10:30pm, Sun 5–8:30pm. **Prices:** Main courses $40–$45. AE, DC, MC, V. ♿

Samurai
In Virginia Mansion Condo Complex, 2100 Greentree Rd; tel 412/276-2100. Exit 4 off I-279, S on PA 121 (Greentree Rd) about 5 mi. **Japanese.** Chefs cook on a grill in the center of a large dining table at this traditional Teppan Yushoku steak house. Meals include choice of appetizer, rice, and vegetables; vegetarian dishes are also available. **FYI:** Reservations recommended. Children's menu. **Open:** Lunch Mon–Fri 11:30am–2pm; dinner Mon–Thurs 5:30–10pm, Fri 5:30–11pm, Sat 5–11:30pm, Sun 4:30–9pm. **Prices:** Main courses $11–$40. AE, CB, DC, DISC, MC, V.

Scoglio
In Fifth Avenue Place, 120 Fifth Avenue Place (Downtown); tel 412/391-1226. **Italian.** This innovative kitchen updates Italian cuisine with combinations like banana peppers stuffed with sweet sausage and herbs, porcini mushroom pasta, and chargrilled swordfish with roasted-garlic sauce. **FYI:** Reservations recommended. Additional location: 429 4th Ave (tel 263-0545). **Open:** Mon–Fri 11:30am–9pm, Sat 5–9pm. **Prices:** Main courses $11–$27. AE, CB, DC, DISC, MC, V. ♿

Thai Garden
346 Atwood St; tel 412/687-8424. Off Forbes Ave. **Thai.** Traditional (and not-so-traditional) Asian specialties, including General Tso chicken, pad thai, and fried mango ice cream. **FYI:** Reservations accepted. BYO. **Open:** Lunch Mon–Sat 11:30am–2:30pm; dinner Mon–Sat 5–10pm. **Prices:** Main courses $7–$13. AE, DISC, MC, V.

Top of the Triangle
In USX Tower, 600 Grant St (Downtown); tel 412/471-4100. At 6th Ave. **American/French.** The views of downtown are spectacular from this dining room on the 62nd floor of

Pittsburgh's tallest building. The menu features veal, seafood, and beef entrees, with nightly specials and an extensive wine list. Complimentary limousine service to area theaters is included with dinner reservations. **FYI:** Reservations recommended. Piano. Children's menu. Dress code. **Open:** Lunch Mon–Fri 11:30am–3pm, Sat noon–3pm; dinner Mon–Thurs 5:30–10pm, Fri–Sat 5:30–11pm, Sun 4–9pm. **Prices:** Main courses $16–$30. AE, DC, DISC, MC, V. 💗 🏞 💟 ♿

ATTRACTIONS 🏛

MUSEUMS

Andy Warhol Museum
117 Sandusky St; tel 412/237-8300. Pittsburgh native Andrew Warhola grew up to become one of the most influential 20th-century American artists. Warhol broke down the barriers between popular and "high" art, and left a diverse body of work, including his celebrity portraits and famous images of soup cans, electric chairs, and car crashes. The museum that celebrates his accomplishments is housed in an eight-story former warehouse and is part of the Carnegie Institute. It contains more than 500 of Warhol's works. In addition to paintings, there is a film and video collection, collaborative works, and family photographs. Exhibitions of work by other artists are also mounted. **Open:** Thurs–Sat 11am–8pm, Wed and Sun 11am–6pm. $$

The Carnegie Museums of Art and Natural History
4400 Forbes Ave (Oakland); tel 412/622-3131. The art museum was founded by industrial magnate Andrew Carnegie in 1895 as a progressive, forward-thinking museum that would collect not only old masters but "the old masters of tomorrow." Expanded many times, the museum recently added the Heinz Architectural Center, and has extensive collections in Asian art, African art, film, and video, in addition to the recently reinstalled pre-1945 American and European fine and decorative arts collections. Works by van Gogh, Cézanne, and Monet are among the highlights. The Carnegie Museum of Natural History, located in the same complex, is best known for its hall of dinosaurs, but it also has fine displays of minerals, precious stones, and zoology. **Open:** Tues–Sat 10am–5pm, Sun 1–5pm. $$

Carnegie Science Center
1 Allegheny Ave; tel 412/237-3300. This learning and entertainment complex has a wide array of hands-on science and technology exhibits, including an exhibit on food processing technology, a foundry, and a miniature railroad. There is also a planetarium and an Omnimax theater with a four-story-high screen, as well as the USS *Requin*, a World War II submarine. Special children's programs are available. **Open:** Mon–Thurs 10am–5pm, Fri–Sun 10am–6pm. $$

Frick Art Museum
7227 Reynolds Ave; tel 412/371-0600. This Renaissance mansion was once the home of steel baron Henry Clay Frick, and the art inside was collected by his daughter, Helen Clay Frick. Artists with works on display include Old Masters such as Rubens, Fragonard, and Tintoretto. There is also a collection of furniture that belonged to Marie Antoinette, as well as Chinese porcelains, Flemish furniture, and early Renaissance tapestries. **Open:** Tues–Sat 10am–5:30pm, Sun noon–6pm. **Free**

Pittsburgh Children's Museum
1 Landmark Square, Old Post Office Building; tel 412/322-5058. Various hand-on exhibits teach children about anatomy and technology via a do-it-yourself silkscreening studio, puppet shows, and other displays. **Open:** Peak (mid-June–Labor Day) Mon–Sat 10am–5pm, Sun noon–5pm. Reduced hours off-season. $$

PARKS AND GARDENS

National Aviary
Ridge and Arch Sts; tel 412/323-7235. The only independent (outside of a zoo) indoor bird facility in North America. The aviary houses almost 500 colorful and exotic birds representing six continents. Among the residents are the thumb-size ruby-throated hummingbird, the enormous Andean condor (with its 10-foot wing span), and two American bald eagles. Many of the species in these windowless habitats are endangered and rarely seen except in the wild. **Open:** Daily 9am–4:30pm. $$

Phipps Conservatory
Schenley Park Dr; tel 412/622-6915. The Phipps Conservatory, located inside Schenley Park, has a remarkable and constantly changing variety of flowers. Themed areas include a tropical garden and an exceptional collection of orchids. **Open:** Tues–Sun 9am–5pm. $

Rodef Shalom Biblical Botanical Garden
4905 5th Ave; tel 412/621-6566. This unusual garden contains plants of ancient Israel, as well as plants with Biblical names. There are over 100 species, including wheat, barley, millet, pomegranate, tamarisk, ancient herbs, lotus, waterlilies, and papyrus. Special exhibitions shed light on the ancient use of these plants and the role they have played in history. **Open:** June–mid-Sept, Sun–Thurs 10am–2pm, Sat noon–1pm. **Free**

Pittsburgh Zoo
Highland Ave; tel 412/665-3640. This 65-acre zoo houses over 4,000 animals, some of them endangered. The animals live in habitats that mimic natural settings, including reproductions of the rain forest and the African savannah. There is also an extensive aquarium with coral reefs, sharks, and penguins; and a reptile house. Merry-go-round; train rides. **Open:** Peak (Mem Day–Labor Day) daily 10am–6pm. Reduced hours off-season. $$$

UNIVERSITY OF PITTSBURGH

Cathedral of Learning
5th Ave and Bigelow Blvd; tel 412/624-6000. This huge Gothic tower is 42 stories tall. Inside, classrooms created and

decorated by craftspeople from 23 different countries represent Pittsburgh's multicultural spectrum; there's also a colonial-style Early American Room. Guided tours available. **Open:** Mon–Sat 9:30am–3pm, Sun 11am–3pm. **$**

Heinz Memorial Chapel

5th and S Bellefield Aves; tel 412/624-4157. This modern, French Gothic–style structure features stained-glass windows that are 73 feet high. Guided tours available; concerts and other programs occasionally offered. **Open:** Mon–Fri 9am–4pm, Sun 1–5pm. **Free**

Stephen Foster Memorial

Forbes Ave at Bigelow Blvd; tel 412/624-4100. A memorial devoted to the life and work of America's first professional songwriter. In addition to examples of Foster's music and possessions of the Foster family, the memorial contains over 30,000 manuscripts, musical instruments, portraits, recordings, scores, and other objects for the study of American music. Holdings include what is thought to be the only portrait of Foster painted during his lifetime, and his copybook from 1851–1860, which contains manuscript versions of such songs as "Old Folks at Home" ("Swanee River"). **Open:** Mon–Fri 9am–4pm. **Free**

OTHER ATTRACTIONS

Hartwood

215 Saxonburg Blvd; tel 412/767-9200. This re-creation of a 16th-century Tudor mansion was actually built in 1929, and is now operated by Allegheny County as a museum. The house itself is furnished with English and American antiques, and is open to visitors. The surrounding 629 acres of rolling countryside offer a variety of outdoor activities including hayrides; trails for hiking, horseback riding, and cross-country skiing; and summer theatrical, dance, and musical productions. **Open:** Apr–Dec, Wed–Sat 10am–3pm, Sun noon–4pm. **$**

The Duquesne Incline

1220 Grandview Ave; tel 412/381-1665. This incline was built in the 19th century to service the otherwise inaccessible communities at the top of Pittsburgh's Mount Washington. (The cars carried horses and wagons in addition to pedestrian passengers.) There were once as many as 17 inclines serving the hills around the city, but the Duquesne Incline is one of only two remaining. The brightly colored cars, and their cherry, oak, and maple interiors, have been restored to their original appearance. At the upper station, a new observation deck offers a panoramic view of the city. **Open:** Mon–Sat 5:30am–12:45am, Sun 7am–12:45am. **$**

Sandcastle

Exit 8 off I-376; tel 412/462-6666. Sandcastle has over a dozen water slides, as well as other water activities like hot tubs and swimming pools. Go-carts, miniature golf, and other amusements are available for those who would rather not get wet. **Open:** Mem Day–Labor Day, daily 11am–7pm. **$$$$**

Kennywood

4800 Kennywood Blvd, West Mifflin; tel 412/461-0500. Begun in 1898 as a trolley park by the Monongahela Street Railway Company, Kennywood has since been turned into a traditional amusement park. There are 32 major rides, including three wooden roller coasters, a water coaster, and the new 80-mph Steel Phantom roller coaster. Two of the trolley park's original buildings, a carousel pavilion and a restaurant, are still in use. **Open:** Mid-May–Labor Day, daily 11am–10pm. **$$$$**

PERFORMING ARTS

Civic Arena

600 Stadium Circle; tel 412/333-7328. This technological marvel boasts a huge retractable stainless steel roof, commonly said to be three times the size of the dome of St Peter's Basilica in Rome. The arena can hold 20,000 people and is used for hockey games and other sporting events, as well as concerts and performances. **Open:** Call for schedule. **$$$$**

Benedum Center

719 Liberty Ave; tel 412/263-2560. Formerly the Stanley Theater, the current incarnation of the Benedum Center was christened in 1987. The magnificently restored theater is the home to opera, ballet, and dance companies, as well as the Pittsburgh Symphony. There are over 200 performances at the center each year, including Broadway productions. **Open:** Call for schedule. **$$$$**

PROFESSIONAL SPORTS

Three Rivers Stadium

300 Stadium Circle; tel 412/321-0650. This stadium, named for the confluence of the Allegheny, Monongahela, and Ohio Rivers in Pittsburgh, is home to the Pittsburgh Pirates (of baseball's National League) and the Pittsburgh Steelers of the NFL. **Open:** Call for schedule. **$$$$**

Pocono Mountains

For lodgings, dining, and attractions, see Bushkill, Canadensis, Cresco, Hawley, Jim Thorpe, Milford, Mount Pocono, Stroudsburg, Tannersville, Union Dale

This year-round resort area in northeastern Pennsylvania encompasses more than 2,000 square miles of lush forest, 150 lakes (including Lake Wallenpaupack, one of the largest man-made lakes in the state), hundreds of streams, and some of the loveliest waterfalls in the eastern United States.

Seven state parks (including **Hickory Run** and **Lehigh Gorge** in White Haven, **Big Pocono** in Henryville, and **Promised Land** in Greentown) and the **Delaware Water Gap National Recreation Area** provide ample opportunities for summertime hiking, camping, mountain biking, and boating, while plentiful supplies of black bass, trout, and walleye will keep anglers busy. Autumn brings hayrides, antiques fairs, and a blaze of colorful foliage; in winter, seasonal resorts open for skiing, snow boarding, ice fishing, and snowmobiling. Accommodations in the region range from lush all-inclusive resorts to romantic "couples-only" inns to rustic lodges.

Information: Pocono Mountains Vacation Bureau, 1004 Main St, Stroudsburg, 18360 (tel 717/424-6050 or toll free 800/POCONOS).

Pottstown

A manufacturing borough at the junction of the Manatawny Creek and the Schuylkill River. Laid out in 1754 and named for John Potts, colonial ironmaster and town founder.

MOTELS 🏨

≣≣ Comfort Inn

99 Robinson St, 19464; tel 610/326-5000 or toll free 800/879-2477; fax 610/970-7230. PA 100, 1 mi N of US 422. A handsome, brick-faced building with spacious rooms, English Revival furniture, and a cheerful staff. **Rooms:** 121 rms. CI 2pm/CO noon. Nonsmoking rms avail. **Amenities:** 🛁 🍴 A/C, cable TV w/movies, voice mail. VCRs, Nintendo, dataports, microwaves, refrigerators available. **Services:** ✗ 🚗 🖼 🧺 🐾 Fax services avail. **Facilities:** 🎱 🖾 🔟 🚶 Washer/dryer. **Rates (CP):** $62–$89 S or D. Extra person $7. Children under age 18 stay free. Min stay special events. Parking: Outdoor, free. AE, DC, DISC, MC, V.

≣≣ Holiday Inn Express

1600 Industrial Hwy, 19464; tel 610/327-3300 or toll free 800/HOLIDAY; fax 610/327-9447. At US 422 and Armand Hammer Blvd. Although the motel is well maintained, the limited amenities make it most suitable for short stays. **Rooms:** 120 rms and stes. CI 3pm/CO noon. Nonsmoking rms avail. Modern furnishings in a comfortable setting. **Amenities:** 🛁 🍴 A/C, cable TV w/movies, dataport. **Services:** 🖼 🧺 🐾 Car-rental desk. **Facilities:** 🎱 🔟 🚶 Games rm. Discount on meals at adjacent Express Kitchen. **Rates:** $69 S or D; $125 ste. Extra person $5. Children under age 19 stay free. Parking: Outdoor, free. AE, DC, DISC, JCB, MC, V.

RESTAURANT 🍴

Coventry Forge Inn

3360 Coventryville Rd; tel 610/469-6222. **French.** Each room of this 18th-century farmhouse provides a unique setting for classic French cuisine; most have fireplaces or a view of the countryside. Lamb and veal are among the most popular entrees, and all baked goods are made on site. Candlelight and pewter plates add to the atmosphere. **FYI:** Reservations recommended. Jacket required. **Open:** Tues–Fri 5:30–9pm, Sat 5–10pm. Closed 2 wks in Feb. **Prices:** Main courses $17–$25. AE, DC, MC, V. ♥ 📷 🏞

Reading

Incorporated in 1783 on the Schuykill River, Reading is one of the most important commercial and industrial centers in the state. Diverse industries include large railroad shops and textile manufacturing. Reading was one of the first places in the country to manufacture iron products and the town supplied cannons during in the Revolution. Over 300 outlet stores draw visitors to the area today. **Information:** Reading & Berks County Visitors Bureau, PO Box 6677, Reading, 19610 (tel 610/375-4085 or toll free 800/443-6610).

HOTELS 🏨

≣≣≣ Inn at Reading

1040 Park Rd, Wyomissing, 19610; tel 610/372-7811 or toll free 800/383-9713; fax 610/372-4545. On US 422 W; exit 21 off PA Tpk. A large property with lots of long, dark hallways. **Rooms:** 248 rms and stes. Executive level. CI 3pm/CO 11am. Nonsmoking rms avail. **Amenities:** 🛁 🍴 A/C, cable TV w/movies, dataport, voice mail. Some units w/minibars. **Services:** ✗ 🚗 🖼 🧺 🐾 Babysitting. **Facilities:** 🎱 🖾 🔟 🚶 1 restaurant, 2 bars (1 w/entertainment), games rm, playground. Sports bar. **Rates:** Peak (Sept–Thanksgiving) $79–$109 S; $89–$119 D; $89–$129 ste. Extra person $7. Children under age 18 stay free. Lower rates off-season. Parking: Outdoor, free. Higher rates during Keystone Nationals auto race in September. AE, CB, DC, DISC, ER, MC, V.

≣≣≣ Sheraton Berkshire Hotel

US 422 W, Wyomissing, 19610; tel 610/376-3811 or toll free 800/892-6887; fax 610/375-7562. Papermill Rd exit off US 422. This complex consists of two separate units; the luxury rooms are in a five-story tower section. **Rooms:** 255 rms and stes. Executive level. CI 4pm/CO noon. Nonsmoking rms avail. Large, attractively furnished rooms; some luxury rooms have fireplace and whirlpool. **Amenities:** 🛁 🍴 A/C, cable TV w/movies. Some units w/terraces. **Services:** ✗ 🚗 🖼 🧺 🐾 Children's program, babysitting. **Facilities:** 🎱 🖾 🔟 🚶 2 restaurants, 1 bar (w/entertainment), volleyball, games rm, lawn games, sauna, whirlpool. Putting green, attractive indoor pool, well-equipped fitness center. Bistro and coffee shop on premises. **Rates:** Peak (Apr–Nov) $108–$140 S; $118–$150 D; $159–$195 ste. Extra person $10. Children under age 18 stay free. Lower rates off-season. Parking: Outdoor, free. Weekend packages avail. AE, CB, DC, DISC, JCB, MC, V.

MOTELS

≣≣ Comfort Inn

2200 Stacey Dr, 19605; tel 610/371-0500 or toll free 800/228-5150; fax 610/478-9421. Off US 222 N. This plain white building is grouped with two other motels near the industrial section of Reading, off the Warren Street Bypass. The lobby is clean and modern, and the furniture looks new. **Rooms:** 60

rms and stes. CI 2pm/CO 11am. Nonsmoking rms avail. Large and attractive rooms. **Amenities:** 🗄️🉐📺 🍴A/C, cable TV w/movies, dataport, voice mail. Some units w/whirlpools. **Services:** 📠🛏️ **Facilities:** 🍽️ 45 💻 ♿ **Rates (CP):** Peak (Mar 31–Dec 10) $55–$115 S; $65–$125 D; $65–$125 ste. Extra person $5. Children under age 18 stay free. Lower rates off-season. Parking: Outdoor, free. AE, CB, DC, DISC, JCB, MC, V.

≣ Wellesley Inn
910 Woodland Ave, Wyomissing, 19610; tel 610/374-1500 or toll free 800/444-8888. Paper Mill Rd exit off US 422. This boxy, four-story stucco building is located in a developing part of town. The lobby is small but the rooms are fine for a short stay. **Rooms:** 105 rms. Executive level. CI 2pm/CO 11am. Nonsmoking rms avail. **Amenities:** 🗄️🉐📺 A/C, cable TV w/movies. **Services:** 📠🛏️🍴 **Facilities:** ♿ **Rates (CP):** Peak (Aug–Nov) $35–$105 S or D. Extra person $5. Children under age 18 stay free. Lower rates off-season. Parking: Outdoor, free. AE, DC, DISC, MC, V.

RESTAURANTS 🍴

Alpenhof Bavarian
903 Morgantown Rd; tel 610/373-1624. Lancaster Avenue exit off US 222. **American/German.** It's a winding drive along back roads to this chalet-style restaurant, where the large tables are covered with checkered tablecloths and beer steins adorn the walls. Meat specialties come from a local German butcher, including Wiener schnitzel made of fresh veal. Shish-kabobs and sauerbraten with dumplings and red cabbage are also reliable choices. **FYI:** Reservations recommended. Children's menu. **Open:** Lunch Mon–Fri 11:30am–2pm; dinner Tues–Fri 5–8:30pm, Sat 5–9pm, Sun 11:30am–7pm. **Prices:** Main courses $9–$17. AE, MC, V. 🍽️ 📷

♣ Green Hills Inn
2444 Morgantown Rd; tel 610/777-9611. Green Hills exit off I-176 S, left on PA 10 (Morgantown Rd). **New American/French.** Opened in 1805 as the Sorrel Horse Tavern. The three dining rooms are decorated with antiques and botanical prints, and fine china and silver make the tables shine. The kitchen blends classic cooking and nouvelle cuisine: grilled duck breast with merlot and fig puree, and lobster with shiitake mushrooms and fresh pasta are among the popular entrees. **FYI:** Reservations recommended. **Open:** Lunch Tues–Fri 11:30am–1:30pm; dinner Mon–Fri 5:30–9pm, Sat 5:30–9:30pm. **Prices:** Main courses $17–$24. AE, CB, DC, DISC, MC, V. 🍽️♿

Joe's Bistro 614
614 Penn Ave, West Reading; tel 610/371-9966. Penn Ave exit off US 422, go W. **New American.** A low-key offshoot of the popular Joe's Restaurant (*see below*). The bright, peach-and-yellow dining room looks out onto a busy shopping street, making this a great spot for people-watching. Poached oysters (served Mexican or Polish style) and portobello pizza are popular. **FYI:** Reservations recommended. BYO. No

smoking. **Open:** Lunch Tues–Sat 11:30am–2:30pm; dinner Tues–Sat 5–9pm. Closed Christmas–Jan 1. **Prices:** Main courses $12–$20. AE, CB, DC, DISC, MC, V. 🌑♿

♣ Joe's Restaurant
450 S 7th St; tel 610/373-6794. Penn St exit off US 422, go E. **New American/Game.** Fine silver, china, and linen set a romantic mood, and even the menu is perfect for a meal *à deux*. Entrees include Cervena venison tenderloin with tamarind and black chanterelles, spring casserole of goose breast, and ostrich. Huge wine list. **FYI:** Reservations recommended. No smoking. **Open:** Tues–Sat 5:30–9pm. Closed last 2 weeks in Feb. **Prices:** Main courses $28–$37; prix fixe $28–$33. AE, CB, DC, DISC, MC, V. 🌑 VP

Moselem Springs Inn
Jct US 222/662, Fleetwood; tel 610/944-8213. Between Reading and Allentown. **Regional American/American.** Conestoga wagons filled the parking lot when this brick inn began serving travelers back in 1852. Pennsylvania Dutch fare and traditional steaks and seafood make up the menu, and the $11 prix fixe light dinner is popular. All the meats are smoked on the premises. **FYI:** Reservations recommended. Children's menu. **Open:** Mon–Sat 11:30am–9pm, Sun 11:30am–8pm. **Prices:** Main courses $10–$18; prix fixe $11. AE, CB, DC, MC, V. 🍽️♿

ATTRACTIONS 🏛️

Hopewell Furnace National Historic Site
2 Mark Bird Lane, Elverson; tel 610/582-8773. One of the finest examples of a rural American 19th-century iron plantation. Ironmaster Mark Bird built the first charcoal-fueled furnace on this site in 1771, which was chosen for its proximity to settlements and to raw materials. During the American Revolution, Hopewell Furnace made cannon, shot, and shells for the American army; later, the furnace produced iron pots, stoves, and doors for the state penitentiary before shutting down for good in 1883. In addition to tours of the restored furnace, waterwheel, ironmaster's mansion, and other buildings, visitors can participate in such programs as "moulder for a day" and learn molding and casting skills. (Advance reservations for hands-on programs required.) An audiovisual orientation is available in the visitors center. **Open:** Daily 9am–5pm. $

Daniel Boone Homestead
US 422 to Daniel Boone Rd, Birdsboro; tel 610/582-4900. Located 9 mi E of Reading. The frontier hero was born here in 1734, and lived in the house until 1750, when he moved to North Carolina. The house, which contains authentic 18th-century furnishings, sits on almost 600 acres; other buildings on the grounds include a blacksmith shop and barn, and there are hiking trails in the surrounding woods. **Open:** Tues–Sat 9am–5pm, Sun noon–5pm. $$

Crystal Cave Park
PA 143, Kutztown; tel 610/683-6765. Crystal Cave, located halfway between Allentown and Reading, has been operating as an attraction since it was discovered in 1871. Highlights include the Cathedral Chamber, the Totem Pole, and the Giant's Tooth, all made up of frozen folds of rock. Above ground, there's a rock and mineral shop, a nature trail, and a picnic area. Amish buggy rides also available. **Open:** Mar–Nov, daily 9am–5pm. $$$

Scranton

See also Tunkhannock, Union Dale

A large manufacturing city in the Pocono Mountains. Chief local products include iron ore and high-quality coal. Cultural attractions include the Steamtown National Historic Museum.

HOTELS

The Inn at Nichols Village
1101 Northern Blvd, Clarks Summit, 18411; tel 717/587-1135 or toll free 800/642-2215; fax 717/586-7140. US 6 and 11. Four well-maintained buildings, including two good restaurants, comprise this easily accessible hotel. **Rooms:** 134 rms and stes. Executive level. CI 2pm/CO noon. Nonsmoking rms avail. **Amenities:** A/C, cable TV w/movies, dataport. Some units w/terraces, some w/whirlpools. **Services:** Masseur, babysitting. Complimentary morning coffee in lobby, along with choice of four daily newspapers. **Facilities:** 2 restaurants (see "Restaurants" below), 1 bar, games rm, spa, sauna. Well-equipped business center. Beautifully landscaped indoor pool. **Rates:** Peak (July–Aug) $116 S; $126 D; $179 ste. Extra person $10. Children under age 18 stay free. Lower rates off-season. Parking: Outdoor, free. Ski packages avail. AE, DC, DISC, MC, V.

Radisson Lackawanna Station Hotel
700 Lackawanna Ave, 18503 (Downtown); tel 717/342-8300 or toll free 800/347-6888; fax 717/342-0380. Exit 53 off I-81, follow Central Scranton Expwy to Lackawanna Ave. A unique hotel housed in a renovated 1908 train station (listed on the National Register of Historic Places), with a stately Italian marble lobby and a stained-glass atrium ceiling. **Rooms:** 145 rms and stes. CI 3pm/CO noon. Nonsmoking rms avail. Simple, well-coordinated decor in large, elegant rooms. **Amenities:** A/C, cable TV w/movies, dataport, voice mail. Some units w/whirlpools. Upscale toiletries and makeup/shaving mirrors in bathrooms. **Services:** **Facilities:** 2 restaurants (see "Restaurants" below), 2 bars (w/entertainment), games rm, spa, sauna, whirlpool. One casual and one formal restaurant on premises. **Rates (CP):** Peak (Sept–mid-Nov) $99 S; $109–

$139 D; $189 ste. Extra person $10. Children under age 18 stay free. Lower rates off-season. Parking: Indoor/outdoor, free. AE, DC, DISC, MC, V.

Ramada Plaza Hotel
820 Northern Blvd, Clarks Summit, 18411; tel 717/586-2730 or toll free 800/272-6232; fax 717/587-0740. US 6 and US 11. Attractive chain hotel popular with businesspeople. **Rooms:** 104 rms and stes. CI 1pm/CO noon. Nonsmoking rms avail. **Amenities:** A/C, cable TV. Refrigerators on request. **Services:** **Facilities:** 1 restaurant, 1 bar (w/entertainment). **Rates:** Peak (Jan–Apr) $75–$85 S or D; $95 ste. Extra person $7. Children under age 18 stay free. Lower rates off-season. Parking: Outdoor, free. Ski packages avail. AE, DC, DISC, MC, V.

Victoria Inns
Rte 315, Pittston Township, 18640; tel 717/655-1234 or toll free 800/937-INNS; fax 717/655-2267. Exit 48B off I-81 S; exit 48 off I-81 N; exit 37 off PA Tpk. Between Scranton and Wilkes-Barre, but outside the urban rush. Rooms are clean and rates are reasonable for this area. **Rooms:** 100 rms and stes. CI 2pm/CO 11am. Nonsmoking rms avail. Sparsely decorated, with a few prints on the walls and basic furniture. **Amenities:** A/C, cable TV w/movies. Some units w/whirlpools. Rooms stocked with bottled water and plentiful towels. **Services:** **Facilities:** 2 restaurants (see "Restaurants" below), 1 bar (w/entertainment), washer/dryer. One casual and one fine-dining restaurant. **Rates:** Peak (May–Oct) $60–$73 S or D; $99–$169 ste. Extra person $6. Children under age 12 stay free. Lower rates off-season. Parking: Outdoor, free. AE, CB, DC, DISC, MC, V.

MOTELS

Hampton Inn at Montage
Montage Mountain Rd and Davis St, 18507; tel 717/342-7002 or toll free 800/HAMPTON; fax 717/342-7012. Exit 51 off I-81. Built in 1994, this chain motel is 2½ miles from Montage Mountain ski area. The lobby is large and welcoming, and the rooms are well decorated. **Rooms:** 129 rms and stes. CI 3pm/CO noon. Nonsmoking rms avail. Rooms have mountain views, silk floral arrangements, and pleasant wall decor. **Amenities:** A/C, satel TV w/movies. Some units w/fireplaces, some w/whirlpools. **Services:** **Facilities:** Whirlpool. Free ski racks in hallway. **Rates (CP):** $65–$75 S; $70–$80 D; $90–$150 ste. Children under age 18 stay free. Parking: Outdoor, free. Ski packages avail. AE, CB, DC, DISC, MC, V.

Holiday Inn Scranton East
200 Tigue St, Dunmore, 18512; tel 717/343-4771 or toll free 800/HOLIDAY; fax 717/343-5171. Exit 1 off I-38W. Families and active travelers will appreciate this comfortable and well-kept motel with a spacious lobby. **Rooms:** 139 rms. Executive level. CI 3pm/CO noon. Nonsmoking rms avail. Most rooms are nonsmoking. **Amenities:** A/C, satel TV.

Some units w/whirlpools. **Services:** ✕ 🚐 🖼 🛏 🐕 Friendly, eager staff. **Facilities:** 🔒 🏊 🔟 🔢 🔒 1 restaurant, 1 bar, games rm, whirlpool. **Rates:** Peak (May 25–Sept 7) $79–$129 S or D. Children under age 12 stay free. Lower rates off-season. Parking: Outdoor, free. Ski packages avail. AE, CB, DC, DISC, JCB, MC, V.

INN

▆▆▆ The Beaumont Inn

PA 309, PO Box 207, Dallas, 18612; tel 717/675-7100. Between Tunkhannock and Dallas. A pretty inn with beautifully decorated rooms, a charming entry, and a well-regarded dining room. **Rooms:** 10 rms. CI 2pm/CO 11am. Quality linens and appointments. **Amenities:** 📺 🔑 🍴 A/C, cable TV. Live plants decorate each room. **Services:** ✕ 🐕 **Facilities:** 🔟 1 restaurant (*see* "Restaurants" below), 1 bar (w/entertainment). **Rates (CP):** $59–$89 D. Extra person $10. Children under age 10 stay free. Parking: Outdoor, free. AE, DC, MC, V.

RESTAURANTS 🍴

♣ Amici

1300 Morgan Hwy, Clarks Summit; tel 717/586-3000. PA 307. **New American/Italian.** The four friendly partners who run this place turn out notable homemade pastas, seafood dishes, and desserts. The brick building overlooks the woods, and plenty of windows take in the view. **FYI:** Reservations recommended. Piano. Children's menu. **Open:** Tues–Sat 5–10pm, Sun 4–9pm. Closed week of July 4. **Prices:** Main courses $12–$24. AE, MC, V. 🍷 🔒

♣ The Beaumont Inn

PA 309, Dallas; tel 717/675-7100. **Continental/Eclectic.** Dark wood trim with Victorian artwork sets the room decor, and the stencilled ceiling is echoed in patterns on the curtains and china. Tuna niçoise, lobster ravioli, and escargots are popular, and the attractive food presentation matches the elegant understatement of the room. **FYI:** Reservations recommended. **Open:** Lunch Mon–Sat 11am–2:30pm; dinner Mon–Thurs 5–9pm, Fri–Sat 5–10pm, Sun 3–8pm; brunch Sun 9am–2pm. **Prices:** Main courses $13–$22. AE, DC, MC, V. 🍷

★ Bianco's Cafe

87 Wyoming Ave, Wyoming; tel 717/693-3110. At Fourth St. **Italian/Pizza.** A family-run restaurant in a renovated house. Pasta, seafood, and pizza are always served fresh and hot. **FYI:** Reservations recommended. **Open:** Tues–Sat 5–11pm, Sun 2–11pm. **Prices:** Main courses $7–$21. DC, DISC, MC, V.

Billy's Seafood & Steakhouse

Rear 618 S Blakely St, Dunmore; tel 717/961-1130. Exit 55 B off I-81, follow Blakely St. **Seafood/Steak.** The carpet and wallpaper are a bit worn, but the food and service at this old-fashioned Italian restaurant have an excellent reputation. For more than 50 years, Billy's has been serving steak and seafood with Italian (and even a bit of German) flair. Shrimp scampi and honeycomb tripe over pasta are specialties. **FYI:** Reservations recommended. Children's menu. **Open:** Mon–Fri 11am–10pm, Sat 4–11pm, Sun 10am–9pm. **Prices:** Main courses $8–$24. AE, CB, DC, DISC, MC, V. ▼

$ Breakers

In Victoria Inns, PA 315, Pittston Township; tel 717/655-1234. Exit 48 off I-81; exit 37 off PA Tpk. **American/Cafe.** Music and menu options change with the season at this bright, light, airy dining room. Expect large portions at reasonable prices, along with an attractive presentation. **FYI:** Reservations accepted. **Open:** Mon–Sat 6:30am–10pm, Sun 7am–10pm. **Prices:** Main courses $5–$11. AE, CB, DC, DISC, MC, V. 🔒

Carmen's

In Radisson Lackawanna Station Hotel, 700 Lackawanna Ave (Downtown); tel 717/342-8300. Exit 53 off I-81, follow Central Scranton Expwy to Lackawanna Ave. **Continental/Italian.** An attractive Italian restaurant in the Grand Lobby of a classic train station. Caesar salad (prepared tableside) and the complimentary antipasto are a good meal starter, followed up by any of the pastas and veal dishes. Ladies will be treated to a rose. **FYI:** Reservations recommended. Piano. **Open:** Breakfast Mon–Fri 6:30–11am, Sat 7–11am; lunch Mon–Sat 11am–2:30pm; dinner daily 5–10pm; brunch Sun 10am–2pm. **Prices:** Main courses $10–$19. AE, CB, DC, DISC, MC, V. 🍷 ▬ ▼ 🆅🅿 🔒

★ Cooper's

701 N Washington Ave (Downtown); tel 717/346-6883. **Seafood/Steak.** A huge variety of seafood and an award-winning kitchen attract diners to this shiplike restaurant, where the pub and three dining rooms all carry out a nautical theme with nets, lanterns, and sailing memorabilia. Filet mignon and seafood Newburg are notable entree choices. **FYI:** Reservations not accepted. Guitar/piano/singer. Children's menu. Additional location: 304 Kennedy Blvd, Pittston (tel 654-6883). **Open:** Mon–Fri 11am–11pm, Sat 11am–midnight, Sun noon–11pm. **Prices:** Main courses $8–$30. DISC, MC, V. 📷

Farley's

Adams Ave and Linden St (Center City); tel 717/346-3000. Near courthouse. **American/Pub.** This is *the* Irish pub in town, attracting an after-work crowd and university students with its friendly, fun atmosphere. The beef is certified Angus, and steaks and burgers are popular choices. **FYI:** Reservations recommended. Piano/singer. **Open:** Daily 11am–2am. **Prices:** Main courses $8–$24. DISC, MC, V. 🔒

★ Grotto Pizza

PA 415, Harveys Lake; tel 717/639-1264. **Italian/Pizza.** Something in the sauce, or perhaps the reasonable prices or consistent attention to quality, has turned this 1953 pizza place into a sizable regional chain. The big Grand Slam

Sports Bar is a local gathering place. **FYI:** Reservations not accepted. Children's menu. Additional location: Wyoming Valley Mall, Wilkes-Barre (tel 822-6600). **Open:** Peak (May–Oct) daily 11am–2am. **Prices:** Main courses $5–$13. MC, V.

Marvelous Muggs

26 Montage Mountain Rd, Moosic; tel 717/961-1551. Exit 51 from I-81. **American/Eclectic.** Old favorites such as burgers, sandwiches, salads, steaks, and chicken are supplemented by low-fat selections and sweet potato fries. Walls are decorated with "Mugg Shots," pictures of customers taken in the photography studio on the premises. **FYI:** Reservations not accepted. Children's menu. **Open:** Sun–Thurs 11am–11pm, Fri–Sat 11am–midnight. **Prices:** Main courses $6–$15. AE, DC, DISC, MC, V.

ReRuns

In Abington Shopping Center, 1000 State St, Clarks Summit; tel 717/586-5566. US 6 and 11. **American/Burgers.** Movie classics are the theme here, with famous faces on the walls and TV sets showing old flicks. A basic menu of appetizers, salads, burgers, and sandwiches make it a "thumbs up" with kids. **FYI:** Reservations recommended. Blues/karaoke/rock. Children's menu. **Open:** Mon–Sat 11am–2am, Sun 9am–midnight. **Prices:** Main courses $9–$17. DC, DISC, MC, V.

Robata of Tokyo

244 Adams Ave (Center City); tel 717/961-3675. Central Scranton Expwy to right on Adams Ave. **Japanese.** Hibachi dinners cooked tableside and served with soup, salad, shrimp, appetizer, fresh vegetables, fried rice, and tea. There is also a sushi bar. **FYI:** Reservations recommended. **Open:** Lunch Mon–Fri 11:30am–2:30pm; dinner Mon–Sun 5–10:30pm. **Prices:** Main courses $8–$23. AE, MC, V.

★ The Ryah House

In The Inn at Nichols Village, 1101 Northern Blvd, Clarks Summit; tel 717/587-4124. US 6 and 11. **Continental/Eclectic.** The brick-walled dining room is open to the cooking area, and the bar/lounge has a central fireplace surrounded by small tables for sharing the popular cheese fondue. Salmon in Chambord sauce and tournedos au poivre are favorites on the dinner menu, and the wine list was named the finest in northeast Pennsylvania by *Wine Spectator*. **FYI:** Reservations recommended. Jazz/piano/singer. **Open:** Mon–Thurs 5–10pm, Fri–Sat 5–11pm. **Prices:** Main courses $16–$23. AE, CB, DC, DISC, MC, V.

Sibio's

1240 Quincy Ave, Dunmore; tel 717/346-3172. Blakely St exit off I-81, bear right at fork, then right on Grove St. **Italian/Seafood.** An elegantly decorated place with solicitous service and romantic surroundings. Salmon, veal, and chicken caesar salad keep the regulars coming back. **FYI:** Reserva-

tions recommended. **Open:** Lunch Mon–Fri 11am–2:30pm; dinner Mon–Fri 4:30–10pm, Sat 4:30–11pm. **Prices:** Main courses $8–$19. AE, DC, MC, V.

ATTRACTIONS

Steamtown National Historic Site

Lackawanna Ave and Cliff St; tel 717/340-5200. Located on the site of the Delaware, Lackawanna and Western Railroad yard in Scranton, Steamtown pays tribute to the steam railroads that enabled the settling of the West and brought immigrants to communities like Scranton. Steamtown has a large collection of locomotives, freight cars, passenger cars, and maintenance equipment. There is a 90-foot-diameter turntable used for turning engines toward the roundhouse, where the collection is still maintained and repaired. A variety of tours and excursions are offered. **Open:** Daily 9am–5pm. $$$

Catlin House

232 Monroe Ave; tel 717/344-3841. Built in 1912, Catlin House is the home of the Lackawanna Historical Society. In addition to furnishings dating from the 18th through the 20th centuries, the building houses exhibits on the cultural, social, and economic history of the region, as well as a research library. **Open:** Tues–Fri 9am–5pm. **Free**

Lackawanna Coal Mine

Exit 38 off PA Turnpike, exits 57B or 51 off I-81; tel 717/963-MINE or toll free 800/238-7245. Located in 200-acre McDade Park, the Lackawanna Coal Mine offers a glimpse into the era when Scranton was the anthracite capital of the world. Tours descend 300 feet into an actual mine, where a miner explains what it was like to work on hands and knees collecting coal. Above ground, the park offers recreational facilities and a summer theater. **Open:** Apr–Nov, daily 10am–4:30pm. $$$

Scranton Iron Furnaces

159 Cedar Ave; tel 717/963-3208. The iron industry was a vital part of Scranton's economy until the turn of the century. These furnaces date from 1841–1857, and were built by the Lackawanna Iron and Coal Company. The four monumental stone towers of the blast furnaces give an idea of the early industry of the area. **Open:** Daily 8am–sunset. $$

Montage Mountain Ski Resort

Exit 51 off I-81; tel 717/969-SNOW or toll free 800/GOT-SNOW. Montage Mountain's 1,000-foot vertical drop is served by seven lifts. The mountain has 20 trails, and ski instruction, equipment rentals, and entertainment are available. In the off-season, Montage Mountain switches over to summertime activities such as water slides and mountain biking. **Open:** Dec–Mar, daily, call for schedule. $$$$

Jack Frost Mountain

I-80, Blakeslee; tel 717/443-8425. This Poconos ski resort offers 21 alpine trails (40% expert, 40% intermediate, and 20% novice) served by seven lifts; the vertical drop is 600 feet.

Cross-country trails (50 km groomed, 30 km ungroomed), equipment rental, snowboarding, and ski lessons are also available. **Open:** Dec–Mar, daily, call for schedule. **$$$$**

Shamokin Dam

Small northern Pennsylvania town near the Susquehanna River and the Allegheny National Forest. Site of the world's largest inflatable dam, which is pumped up each spring to create a lake.

MOTEL

≣≣≣ **Days Inn Sunbury-Selinsgrove**
US 11/15, PO Box 487, 17876; tel 717/743-1111 or toll free 800/DAYS-INN; fax 717/743-1190. 3 mi N of Selinsgrove. A well-run motel near all area attractions. **Rooms:** 220 rms. CI 1pm/CO noon. Nonsmoking rms avail. Rooms open either to pool courtyard or to parking lot. **Amenities:** A/C, cable TV w/movies, dataport. **Services:** X ⟋ ⟍ ⟍ **Facilities:** ⟍ ⟍ 1 restaurant (bkfst and dinner only), 1 bar, washer/dryer. Lake offers boating and fishing in summer. **Rates:** Peak (May–Sept) $48–$58 S; $53–$63 D. Extra person $5. Children under age 18 stay free. Lower rates off-season. Parking: Outdoor, free. AE, CB, DC, DISC, MC, V.

Sharon

This city on the Ohio border claims to be the home of the world's largest shoe store and the world's largest off-price fashion store. **Information:** Mercer County Tourist Agency, One W State St, Sharon, 16146 (tel 412/981-5880).

MOTELS

≣≣≣ **Radisson Hotel Sharon**
I-80 and PA 18, PO Box 596, West Middlesex, 16159; tel 412/528-2501 or toll free 800/333-3333; fax 412/528-2306. Exit 1N off I-80. The lobby displays antique carved furnishings with pearl inlays from a palace in Thailand, and the exceptional atrium and pool areas continue the Asian theme with sculptures of birds and fish. **Rooms:** 153 rms and stes. CI 3pm/CO noon. Nonsmoking rms avail. **Amenities:** A/C, cable TV w/movies. Some units w/minibars, some w/terraces, some w/whirlpools. All room doors equipped with the "Club" security device. Nintendo games. **Services:** X ⟋ ⟍ ⟍ Masseur. **Facilities:** ⟍ ⟍ ⟍ 2 restaurants, 1 bar (w/entertainment), games rm, spa, sauna, whirlpool, washer/dryer. **Rates:** $80–$88 S; $90–$98 D; $150–$200 ste. Extra person $8. Children under age 17 stay free. Parking: Outdoor, free. AE, CB, DC, DISC, JCB, MC, V.

≣≣≣ **Shenango Valley Comfort Inn**
PA 18 and Wilson Rd, West Middlesex, 16159; tel 412/342-7200 or toll free 800/221-2222; fax 412/342-7213. Exit 1N off I-80. A convenient location is the principal advantage of this unremarkable (but very clean) motel. **Rooms:** 61 rms and stes. Executive level. CI 1:30pm/CO 11am. Nonsmoking rms avail. **Amenities:** A/C, satel TV. Some units w/whirlpools. **Services:** ⟋ ⟍ ⟍ **Facilities:** ⟍ ⟍ ⟍ Games rm, steam rm, whirlpool. **Rates (CP):** Peak (June–Sept) $75 S or D; $85–$115 ste. Extra person $5. Children under age 16 stay free. Lower rates off-season. Parking: Outdoor, free. AE, CB, DC, DISC, MC, V.

RESTAURANTS

Hot Rod Cafe
101 Chestnut St; tel 412/981-3123. Off PA 18, 4½ mi N of exit 1N off I-80. **Pizza.** Upon entering this whimsical theme eatery, diners follow "Route 66" from the Capone family's 1929 Ford beer truck to the bulletproof GMC Suburban used in *Rambo III* to reach the dining room, where more motoring nostalgia awaits. The menu lists a variety of pizza, sandwiches, pasta, and seafood entrees, all bearing auto-related names. **FYI:** Reservations not accepted. Blues/country music/rock. Children's menu. **Open:** Peak (Mem Day–Sept) Tues–Fri 4pm–2am, Sat–Sun noon–2am. **Prices:** Main courses $5–$15. AE, DISC, MC, V.

★ **Quaker Steak & Lube**
101 Chestnut St; tel 412/981-WING. Off PA 18, 4½ mi N of exit 1N off I-80. **Burgers.** This converted gas station—with cars ranging from a 1915 Austro Omega to a 1946 Sunbeam Talbot to a 1977 Corvette hanging from the ceiling—now "pumps out" 18 million chicken wings a year. The light-hearted menu also has sandwiches, burgers, kabobs, and finger foods. Race fans can dine in the Thunder Alley room. **FYI:** Reservations not accepted. Children's menu. **Open:** Daily 11am–2am. **Prices:** Main courses $4–$14. AE, DISC, MC, V.

Tully's Pub & Grille
110 Connelly Blvd; tel 412/981-3123. Off PA 18, 4½ mi N of exit 1N off I-80. **Steak.** A former Penn Central Railroad station, built in 1886 to serve the New York–Chicago line. Piled-high reuben sandwiches and grilled-to-perfection steaks are specialties. Chicken, salads, and seafood also available. **FYI:** Reservations accepted. Dancing. Children's menu. **Open:** Mon–Sat 4pm–2am, Sun noon–2am. **Prices:** Main courses $5–$16. AE, DISC, MC, V.

Smoketown

RESTAURANT

Good N' Plenty
PA 896; tel 717/394-7111. **Regional American/Pennsylvania Dutch.** All dinners at this family-style eatery include at least three meat choices, plus vegetables, dessert, and choice of coffee, tea, or lemonade. Long tables seat 14 to 18 people, and you are introduced to your tablemates before you dine.

FYI: Reservations not accepted. No liquor license. No smoking. **Open:** Mon–Sat 11:30am–8pm. Closed Jan. **Prices:** Prix fixe $13. MC, V. ⬛ ⚕

Somerset

Located in the state's Laurel Highlands region, Somerset was first laid out in 1795. Today, it is home to the Somerset Historical Center and a noted winery.

MOTELS ⊞

⬛⬛ Holiday Inn

202 Shaffer St, PO Box 191, 15501; tel 814/445-9611 or toll free 800/354-7405; fax 814/445-5815. Exit 10 off PA Tpk. A clean, comfortable motel with a friendly staff. Close to skiing, hiking, biking, fishing, hunting, boating, golf, rafting, the Somerset Historic Center, and a variety of restaurants. **Rooms:** 102 rms. CI 2pm/CO noon. Nonsmoking rms avail. **Amenities:** ⊞ ⚲ A/C, cable TV, dataport. Some rooms have coffeemakers. **Services:** ✕ ⬛ ⬛ ⬛ Babysitting. VCRs and movies available. **Facilities:** ⬛ ⬛ ⬛ ⚕ 1 restaurant, 1 bar (w/entertainment). **Rates:** Peak (Dec–Mar) $89 S; $99 D. Extra person $10. Children under age 18 stay free. Lower rates off-season. Parking: Outdoor, free. AE, CB, DC, DISC, JCB, MC, V.

⬛⬛ Ramada Inn

PA Tpk exit 10, PO Box 511, 15501; tel 814/443-4646 or toll free 800/272-6232; fax 814/445-7539. Exit 10 off PA Tpk. Lots of recreational possibilities, including outlet shopping, are near this business/family travelers' motel with a fireplace in its large lobby. **Rooms:** 152 rms and stes. CI 2pm/CO noon. Nonsmoking rms avail. **Amenities:** ⊞ ⚲ A/C, cable TV w/movies. **Services:** ✕ ⬛ ⬛ ⬛ Babysitting. VCR and movie rentals. **Facilities:** ⬛ ⬛ ⬛ ⚕ 1 restaurant, 1 bar (w/entertainment), games rm, sauna, whirlpool. **Rates:** Peak (Jan–Feb) $78 S; $88 D; $125 ste. Extra person $10. Children under age 18 stay free. Lower rates off-season. Parking: Outdoor, free. AE, CB, DC, DISC, MC, V.

State College

Settled in 1859, State College sits between the Bald Eagle Ridge and the Seven Mountains in the Nittany Valley. Today, it is best known as the site of Pennsylvania State University. **Information:** Center County Lion Country Visitors & Convention Bureau, 1402 S Atherton St, State College, PA 16801 (tel 814/231-1400).

HOTELS ⊞

⬛⬛⬛ Atherton Hotel

125 S Atherton St, 16801; tel 814/231-2100 or toll free 800/832-0132; fax 814/237-1130. Between College and Beaver Aves. Nicely appointed hotel in a convenient downtown location, with a friendly, service-oriented staff. **Rooms:** 150 rms and stes. Executive level. CI 3pm/CO noon. Nonsmoking rms avail. Suites can accommodate up to five guests. **Amenities:** ⊞ ⚲ ⬛ A/C, cable TV w/movies, dataport, bathrobes. Some units w/whirlpools. **Services:** ✕ ⬛ ⬛ ⬛ ⬛ Babysitting. Full-time guest services staff member. **Facilities:** ⬛ ⬛ ⬛ ⚕ 1 restaurant, 1 bar. Nearby athletic center free to guests. **Rates (BB):** Peak (Aug–Oct) $89 S; $99 D; $160 ste. Extra person $10. Children under age 16 stay free. Min stay special events. Lower rates off-season. Parking: Indoor, free. AE, DC, DISC, MC, V.

⬛⬛⬛ Days Inn Penn State

240 S Pugh St, 16801; tel 814/238-8454 or toll free 800/329-7466; fax 814/234-3377. 2 blocks S of College Ave. The large lobby has an atrium and a fountain, and the public areas are emphasized in this centrally located property, close to restaurants, shopping, and the Penn State campus. **Rooms:** 184 rms and stes. CI 3pm/CO noon. Nonsmoking rms avail. **Amenities:** ⊞ ⚲ A/C, cable TV w/movies, voice mail. **Services:** ✕ ⬛ ⬛ ⬛ ⬛ Car-rental desk. Continental breakfast not served on weekends. **Facilities:** ⬛ ⬛ ⬛ ⬛ ⬛ ⬛ ⚕ 2 restaurants, 1 bar (w/entertainment), games rm, sauna. **Rates (CP):** $50–$95 S; $60 $100 D; $150–$200 ste. Extra person $7. Children under age 18 stay free. Min stay special events. AP and MAP rates avail. Parking: Indoor/outdoor, free. AE, CB, DC, DISC, JCB, MC, V.

⬛⬛⬛ Nittany Lion Inn

200 W Park Ave, 16803; tel 814/231-7500 or toll free 800/233-7505; fax 814/231-7510. At N Atherton St. This large, nicely appointed hotel is on the campus of Penn State and is operated by the university. The attractive, colonial-styled buildings are decorated throughout with high-quality period furnishings. **Rooms:** 237 rms and stes. CI 3pm/CO noon. Nonsmoking rms avail. **Amenities:** ⊞ ⚲ ⬛ A/C, cable TV. Some units w/terraces, some w/whirlpools. Many rooms have dataports. Refrigerators available on request. **Services:** ✕ ⬛ ⬛ ⬛ Babysitting. Excellent security. **Facilities:** ⬛ ⬛ ⬛ ⬛ ⬛ ⚕ 2 restaurants, 1 bar, spa, whirlpool. Use of campus facilities. **Rates:** $85 S; $95 D; $105–$115 ste. Extra person $10. Children under age 13 stay free. AP and MAP rates avail. Parking: Indoor/outdoor, free. Multi-night stays have priority during special events. AE, CB, DC, DISC, MC, V.

⬛⬛⬛⬛ Penn State Scanticon Conference Center

215 Innovation Blvd, 16803; tel 814/863-5000 or toll free 800/893-4602; fax 814/863-5001. Penn State Research Park exit off US 322. Located in the 180-acre PSU Research Park, this ultra-modern hotel (built in 1994) has state-of-the-art meeting facilities and a friendly staff. Sleek Scandinavian design. **Rooms:** 150 rms and stes. CI 3pm/CO noon. Nonsmoking rms avail. Most units have sweeping views of Nittany Valley. **Amenities:** ⊞ ⚲ A/C, cable TV w/movies, dataport, voice mail. All units w/minibars. **Services:** ✕ ⬛ ⬛ ⬛ ⬛ Car-rental desk, masseur, babysitting. **Facilities:** ⬛ ⬛ ⬛ ⬛

🖥 [1300] 💻 & 2 restaurants, 1 bar (w/entertainment), spa, sauna, whirlpool, washer/dryer. **Rates:** Peak (Mar–Oct) $105–$165 S; $110–$175 D; $145–$215 ste. Extra person $10. Children under age 13 stay free. Min stay special events. Lower rates off-season. AP and MAP rates avail. Parking: Outdoor, free. AE, CB, DC, DISC, MC, V.

MOTELS

≣≣ Best Western State College Inn

1663 S Atherton St, 16801; tel 814/237-8005 or toll free 800/635-1177; fax 814/238-8805. At Branch Rd. Just a mile from the Penn State campus, but set back from the street, this is a quiet and convenient place. There's also pretty landscaping and a windowed elevator. **Rooms:** 141 rms and stes. CI 3pm/CO noon. Nonsmoking rms avail. Good-quality furnishings. **Amenities:** 🔟 & A/C, cable TV w/movies, dataport. Some units w/whirlpools. Complimentary morning newspaper and coffee. Coffeemakers available on request. **Services:** 🚗 🖼 🍴 Free local calls. **Facilities:** 🏃 🦞 🖥 [150] & 1 bar, games rm, sauna, whirlpool. **Rates (CP):** $56 S; $64 D; $85 ste. Children under age 19 stay free. Min stay special events. Parking: Outdoor, free. Special winter rates avail. AE, CB, DC, DISC, MC, V.

≣≣ Holiday Inn Penn State

1450 S Atherton St, 16801; tel 814/238-3001 or toll free 800/465-4329; fax 814/237-1345. Exit 24 off I-80, then PA 26 to Bus US 322. The largest hotel in town and only 1½ miles from Penn State University. Very popular with visiting parents. **Rooms:** 288 rms. CI 2pm/CO noon. Nonsmoking rms avail. Many units face the courtyard and pool. **Amenities:** 🔟 & A/C, cable TV w/movies, dataport. **Services:** ✕ 🚗 🖼 🍴 Car-rental desk, babysitting. **Facilities:** 🖼 🏃 🦞 🖳 🖥 [240] & 1 restaurant, 1 bar, games rm, washer/dryer. Access to nearby health club for small fee. Public playground across the street. **Rates:** Peak (Mar–Nov) $49–$69 S; $49–$76 D. Extra person $7. Children under age 19 stay free. Min stay special events. Lower rates off-season. Parking: Outdoor, free. AE, CB, DC, DISC, JCB, MC, V.

RESORT

≣≣≣≣ Toftrees Hotel, Resort & Center

1 Country Club Lane, 16803; tel 814/234-8000 or toll free 800/458-3602; fax 814/238-4404. Toftrees exit off US 322. 1,500 acres. This upscale, wooded resort caters to business travelers and golfers, but is comfortable and convenient for all who might be visiting the town or the university. **Rooms:** 131 rms and stes. CI 3pm/CO noon. Nonsmoking rms avail. Some condos on golf course available. Many rooms have nice views of Nittany Valley. **Amenities:** 🔟 & 🖭 A/C, cable TV w/movies. Some units w/terraces, some w/whirlpools. **Services:** ✕ 🔑 🚗 🖼 🍴 Friendly and efficient staff. **Facilities:** 🖼 ▶ [18] 🏌 🦞 🖳 🖥 [300] & 2 restaurants, 2 bars (1 w/entertainment), volleyball. Championship PGA golf course rated best in state by *Golf Digest*. **Rates:** Peak (Apr–Nov) $95

S; $110 D; $135–$150 ste. Extra person $15. Children under age 13 stay free. Min stay special events. Lower rates off-season. Parking: Outdoor, free. AE, DC, DISC, MC, V.

ATTRACTIONS 🏛

Pennsylvania State University

US 322, University Park; tel 814/865-4700. Penn State (established in 1855) sits on a beautiful campus in the Nittany Mountains—hence the name Nittany Lions, applied to the school's successful sports teams. The 5,000-acre campus features a number of interesting museums, including the Frost Entomological Museum, the Palmer Museum of Art, and the Earth and Mineral Sciences Museum (*see below*).

Earth and Mineral Sciences Museum and Gallery

122 Steidle Building, University Park; tel 814/865-6427. Located at Pennsylvania State University, this museum contains more than 22,000 specimens of rocks, minerals, and fossils, as well as glass, ceramics, metals, plastics and other synthetic materials, and scientific and mining equipment. Extensive exhibits reveal the physical properties of these minerals, many of which played an important role in the state's history. **Open:** Mon–Fri 9am–5pm, Sat–Sun 1–5pm. **Free**

Centre Furnace Mansion

1001 E College Ave; tel 814/234-4779. Ironmaster Moses Thompson, whose family lived in the Centre Furnace Mansion from 1842 to 1891, donated a neighboring 200-acre plot to a new school—later to become Pennsylvania State University. The mansion has recently been restored to its 19th-century appearance, and today it contains a growing collection of antique furniture, including original Thompson family furnishings donated by their descendants. **Open:** Sun–Mon, Wed, and Fri 1–4pm. **Free**

Stroudsburg

Borough of some 5,000 residents, located in the Pocono Mountains foothills. Nearby Delaware Water Gap National Recreational Area draws visitors interested in outdoor activities. **Information:** Carbon County Tourist Promo Agency, 1004 Main St, Stroudsburg, 18360 (tel 717/325-3673).

MOTEL 🏨

≣≣ Shannon Inn

Rte 5, PO Box 5202, East Stroudsburg, 18301; tel 717/424-1951 or toll free 800/424-8052; fax 717/424-7782. Exit 52 off I-80. In an area of elaborate resorts, this is a simple motel with lower rates than most properties in the Poconos. **Rooms:** 120 rms. CI 3pm/CO 11am. Nonsmoking rms avail. Very basic rooms and small baths. **Amenities:** 🔟 A/C, cable TV, dataport. **Services:** ✕ 🖼 Security patrol. **Facilities:** 🖼 🏃 🦞 [50] 1 restaurant (lunch and dinner only), 1 bar (w/entertainment), washer/dryer. **Rates (CP):** Peak (May 15–Sept 15)

$60–$90 S; $65–$95 D. Extra person $5–$10. Children under age 18 stay free. Min stay special events. Lower rates off-season. Parking: Outdoor, free. Ski, golf, and holiday weekend packages avail. AE, DC, DISC, MC, V.

RESTAURANT 🍽

Peppe's Ristorante
In Eagle Valley Mall, PA 209 N, East Stroudsburg; tel 717/421-4460. Exit 52 off I-80, left onto PA 447 N, then right onto PA 209 N. **Italian.** A friendly, efficient staff serves large portions of well-made Italian food in this pleasant dining room with brick archways. Caesar salad, prepared tableside, is a meal in itself, while veal and seafood are popular for heartier appetites. Daily lunch special includes soup, salad, entree, and coffee or tea. **FYI:** Reservations recommended. Children's menu. **Open:** Lunch Mon–Fri 11:30am–2:30pm; dinner Mon–Fri 5:30–10pm, Sat 4–11pm, Sun 3–9pm. **Prices:** Main courses $10–$23. AE, DC, DISC, MC, V. &

ATTRACTION 📷

Quiet Valley Living Historical Farm
1000 Turkey Hill Rd; tel 717/992-6161. At this living history museum, role players and costumed guides demonstrate daily farm activities of the colonial era: spinning, weaving, meat smoking, gardening, handcrafts, cooking, and tending animals. Special programs focus on such topics as "tramp art," tinsmithing, and herb lore. A variety of hands-on activities, educational workshops, and seasonal events take place throughout the year. **Open:** Mid-June–Labor Day, Mon–Sat 9:30am–5:30pm, Sun 1–5:30pm. $$$

Tannersville

Small community located in the Pocono State Forest and near to the Delaware Water Gap National Recreation Area.

RESORT 🏨

≣≣≣ The Summit Resort
PA 715 S, PO Box 130, 18372; tel 717/629-0203 or toll free 800/233-8250; fax 717/629-9003. Exit 45 off I-80, turn left; 500 yards on left. 100 acres. It's couples only at this rustic, château-like resort offering plenty of sports facilities and amenities. The welcoming lobby is filled with plants and a waterfall. **Rooms:** 284 rms and stes; 60 cottages/villas. CI 3:30pm/CO 11:30am. Sparsely decorated rooms. **Amenities:** 🛁 🍷 A/C, cable TV, VCR. Some units w/terraces, all w/fireplaces, some w/whirlpools. **Services:** Social director. Breakfast in bed available. Movies available for rent. **Facilities:** 🖼 🚴 ⛷ 📷 🏃 🎿 ⚽2 🎱2 🎳 1 restaurant, 2 bars (1 w/entertainment), basketball, volleyball, lawn games, racquetball, sauna, steam rm, whirlpool. Snack bar, large gift shop. Snowmobiling, miniature golf, archery, rifle range, ice/roller skating rink. Golf nearby at discounted rates. **Rates**

(AP): $140–$220 D; $299–$445 ste; $375 cottage/villa. Min stay peak and special events. Parking: Outdoor, free. Holiday and theme weekend packages avail. AE, DISC, MC, V.

ATTRACTION 📷

Camelback Ski Resort
Camelback Rd; tel 717/629-1661 or 233-8100 (ski conditions). Located in Big Pocono State Park, Camelback has spent more than $7 million on development over the past three years, and now has 32 trails and 12 lifts (including 2 high-speed quads) as well as extensive snowmaking. Snowboarding is also available. There are four lodges, two rental shops, a retail shop, daycare facilities, and a PSIA ski school. Camelback offers various bargain packages, including midweek rates, "value days," season passes, group rates, and a "frequent skier" program. The area also has a full round of summer activities, including hiking, swimming, water slide, alpine slide, and batting cages. **Open:** Peak (Dec–Mar), Mon-Fri 8:30am–5pm, Sat–Sun 7:30am–5pm. Reduced hours off-season. $$$$

Titusville

America's first oil well was drilled at this small town near Oil Creek in 1859. The event is commemorated at Drake Well Museum, and the town's historic district includes luxurious homes from the oil-boom days.

RESORT 🏨

≣≣≣ Cross Creek Resort
15867 Oil City–Titusville Rd, PO Box 432, 16354; tel 814/827-9611; fax 814/827-2062. On PA 8, 4 mi S of Titusville. 485 acres. An upscale yet casual resort with subdued green decor, dark-wood and wicker furniture, and vistas of the golf course. **Rooms:** 94 rms. CI 4pm/CO 2pm. Nonsmoking rms avail. Twenty rooms are in the main building; the others are in motel-style buildings along the parking lot. **Amenities:** 🛁 🍷 A/C, cable TV. Some units w/terraces. **Services:** 🚐 📷 🐕 Car-rental desk, babysitting. Staff is friendly and helpful. **Facilities:** 🖼 🏌27 🎱2 🏊400 🍷 1 restaurant, 1 bar (w/entertainment), volleyball, games rm. Gift shop and pro shop on premises. **Rates:** Peak (Apr 15–Oct 15) $95–$115 S or D. Children under age 12 stay free. Min stay wknds. Lower rates off-season. MAP rates avail. Parking: Outdoor, free. Golf packages predominate in high season, so there are a limited number of rooms available for walk-ins. AE, CB, DC, DISC, MC, V.

ATTRACTION 📷

Drake Well Museum
PA 8; tel 814/827-2797. The Drake Well harks back to a time when this area was the focus of America's first oil boom. The 239-acre park contains a full-size replica of the world's first

oil well, drilled by Edwin L Drake in 1859, as well as dioramas and working models depicting the birth of the oil industry. **Open:** Peak (May–Oct) Mon–Sat 9am–5pm, Sun noon–5pm. Reduced hours off-season. **$$**

Tunkhannock

Small town on the Susquehanna, NW of Scranton.

RESORT 🏨

☰☰☰ Shadowbrook Inn & Resort

US 6, 18657; tel 717/836-2151 or toll free 800/955-0295. 2 mi E of town. 458 acres. The motel portion is convenient for interstate travelers, while the resort portion attracts families and golfers. **Rooms:** 55 rms and effic. CI 2pm/CO noon. Nonsmoking rms avail. Rooms are large, clean, and comfortable. **Amenities:** 🛎 🔥 🍴 A/C, cable TV w/movies, refrig, dataport. Some units w/terraces, some w/whirlpools. **Services:** ✕ 🛎 Social director. **Facilities:** 🏕 🚣 🏊₁₈ 🏋 🏐 🎱₄₀₀ 2 restaurants, 1 bar (w/entertainment), volleyball, games rm, lawn games, racquetball, sauna. Miniature-golf course, bowling alley. **Rates (CP):** $48–$80 S; $58–$90 D; $75–$85 effic. Extra person $12. Children under age 12 stay free. Parking: Outdoor, free. Senior discounts avail; golf packages avail. AE, CB, DC, DISC, MC, V.

RESTAURANTS 🍽

The Fireplace

US 6; tel 717/836-9662. Outskirts of Tunkhannock. **Seafood/Steak.** The waiters hardly expect diners to finish the huge steaks and burgers at this rustic restaurant, where take-home containers are the norm. Crisp, fresh salads served in seashell bowls are available for lighter appetites. **FYI:** Reservations not accepted. Children's menu. **Open:** Sun–Thurs 11am–10pm, Fri–Sat 11am–11pm. **Prices:** Main courses $6–$20. AE, DC, DISC, MC, V. 🎦 📺

★ Remington's

203 E Tioga St; tel 717/836-2401. US 6. **Continental/Eclectic.** Six rooms of this fine old Victorian home are used for dining, and there's a player piano in the foyer. The lunch menu is a bargain, featuring fresh soups and salads; the Weiner schnitzel is a local dinner favorite. **FYI:** Reservations recommended. Children's menu. BYO. No smoking. **Open:** Tues–Thurs 11am–9pm, Fri–Sat 11am–10pm, Sun 5–8pm. **Prices:** Main courses $7–$16. AE, DISC, MC, V. ❤

Union Dale

Resort area in the Poconos, NE of Scranton.

INNS 🏨

☰☰ The Carousel

Rte 3, 18470; tel 717/679-2600. Exit 63 off I-81 to PA 374 E, follow signs to Elk Mountain, left at stop sign, 1 mi on right. 7 acres. A chalet with a carousel motif, this B&B is just two miles from Elk Mountain and the guest rooms have excellent views. **Rooms:** 8 rms. CI 2pm/CO 11am. No smoking. **Amenities:** No A/C, phone, or TV. **Services:** 🛎 Babysitting. Après-ski coffee, tea, hot chocolate, and snacks. Discount lift tickets available. **Facilities:** 🏊 ⅄ Sauna, whirlpool, guest lounge w/TV. Sauna and hot tub on first floor. Guest lounge with TV, fireplace, and lots of couches and magazines. **Rates (BB):** Peak (Dec–Mar) $85 D. Extra person $15. Children under age 4 stay free. Min stay peak and wknds. Lower rates off-season. Parking: Outdoor, free. AE, MC, V.

☰☰☰ Stone Bridge Inn & Restaurant

Rte 3, 18470; tel 717/679-9200; fax 717/679-9201. Exit 63 off I-81 N, PA 374 E past Elk Mountain, go 1 mi right at stop sign, 1 mi on right. 162 acres. Two miles from Elk Mountain, this attractive inn emphasizes its natural surroundings with beautiful landscaping and trails. The rooms have homey touches like cross-stitch hangings and dried flower arrangements. **Rooms:** 12 rms, stes, and effic. CI 3pm/CO noon. No smoking. High ceilings; many rooms have loft areas accessible by ladder. **Amenities:** A/C, TV. No phone. 1 unit w/terrace, some w/fireplaces. **Services:** Babysitting. **Facilities:** 🏊 1 restaurant (dinner only; *see* "Restaurants" below), 1 bar (w/entertainment), guest lounge. Golf nearby. **Rates (CP):** Peak (Dec–Apr) $75–$115 D; $85–$110 ste; $110–$145 effic. Extra person $5–$15. Children under age 1 stay free. Min stay peak and wknds. Lower rates off-season. Parking: Outdoor, free. Rates vary by season, type of room, and number of occupants. AE, MC, V.

☰☰☰ Wiffy Bog Farm Bed and Breakfast

West Clifford, 18470; tel 717/222-9865. Exit 63 off I-81 N to PA 374 E for 3½ mi. 80 acres. Well-suited to families with children, this inn is decorated in country style with some antique touches. There's a large country kitchen, a comfortable living room with a TV/VCR and wood-burning stove, a game room, and a music room with harp and piano. Proximity to Elk Mountain makes it perfect for skiers. **Rooms:** 12 rms, stes, and effic (4 w/shared bath). CI 2pm/CO 11am. No smoking. Interesting, individual decor. Suites have separate living room and full kitchen. **Amenities:** 🔥 A/C. No phone or TV. Some units w/terraces. Caswell-Massey toiletries. Lots of books and magazines on night tables. **Services:** 🛎 🛎 Masseur, babysitting, afternoon tea served. Popcorn, tea, and hot chocolate served to returning skiers each afternoon. **Facilities:** 🏔 🚣 🏊 🏊 Games rm, whirlpool, guest lounge w/TV. Outdoor hot tub on a large wooden deck, and plenty of towels at the door. Pond on the farm for swimming and fishing. **Rates (BB):** Peak (Jan–Feb) $50–$85 S w/shared bath, $50–$85 S w/private bath; $60–$100 D w/shared bath; $65–$105 D w/private bath; $85–$120 ste; $85–$120 effic. Extra person $25–$40. Children under age 3 stay free. Min stay peak and wknds. Lower rates off-season. Parking: Outdoor, free. AE, CB, DC, DISC, MC, V.

RESORT

≣≣≣≣ Caesar's Pocono Palace

PA 209, PO Box 1400, Marshalls Creek, 18335; tel 717/588-6692 or toll free 800/233-4141; fax 717/588-0754. Exit 52 off I-80, follow PA 209 N 4 mi to light; turn right, follow signs. 350 acres. Waterfalls and Roman statuary are the hallmarks of this secluded property in the woods. Popular entertainers perform regularly, and some sort of planned activity for couples is always underway. Maintenance is constant and the grounds are spotless. **Rooms:** 189 rms and stes. CI 3pm/CO 11am. **Amenities:** 🛏 🖨 A/C, cable TV w/movies, refrig. Some units w/terraces, some w/fireplaces, all w/whirlpools. VCRs in some rooms. Rooms in the more expensive Tower section have champagne glass–shaped whirlpool tubs, steam showers for two, and glass-enclosed rooms with pool, sauna, and massage table. **Services:** ✗ Social director, masseur. **Facilities:** 🏠 ⛷ ⛰ ▶🏌🏊🚤⛵🏀² ⛸ 🛶 400 ⛷ 2 restaurants, 2 bars (1 w/entertainment), 1 beach (lake shore), lifeguard, basketball, volleyball, games rm, lawn games, racquetball, spa, sauna, steam rm, whirlpool. Free access to facilities at the three other Caesar's Pocono resorts. Snowmobiles, rowboats, ice skating on pond. Sports center has modern fitness equipment, tanning beds, pro shop, boxing ring, pool tables, games. Beach volleyball, driving range. **Rates (MAP):** $390–$500 S or D; $550–$720 ste. Parking: Outdoor, free. Multi-night stays only. Rates vary with unit and length of stay; most include some meals. AE, CB, DC, DISC, MC, V.

RESTAURANT 🍽

Stone Bridge Inn & Restaurant

Rte 3; tel 717/679-9500. Exit 63 off I-81 N, PA 374 E past Elk Mountain, right at stop sign, 1 mi on right. **American/Pub.** A rustic post-and-beam building in the woods near Elk Mountain, where diners can enjoy specialties like salmon with dill, roast pork tenderloin, and veal. There's pub grub in the tavern and outdoor service on the patio in spring and summer. **FYI:** Reservations recommended. Blues/folk. Children's menu. **Open:** Wed–Thurs 5–9pm, Fri–Sat 5–10pm, Sun 4–9pm. Closed last two weeks of Apr. **Prices:** Main courses $8–$20. AE, MC, V. 🍴

Valley Forge

See also King of Prussia

Site of the famed winter 1777–78 encampment of George Washington and the Continental Army, as commemorated at Valley Forge National Historical Park.

ATTRACTION 🏛

Valley Forge National Historical Park

PA 23 and N Gulph Rd; tel 610/783-1077. George Washington and the Continental Army spent a brutal winter in Valley Forge in 1777–78. The 12,000 troops were plagued by shortages of supplies, bad weather, and disease, and 2,000 of them died. The army did not decamp until June. The 3,500-acre park includes fortifications used during the battle and the headquarters used by Washington; furnishings and displays include archeological objects and associated field records, a collection of revolutionary arms and accouterments, and military manuscripts. A variety of monuments and markers, and re-creations of log buildings and cannon, are scattered throughout the park. **Open:** Daily 9am–5pm. **Free**

Warminster

RESTAURANT 🍽

Pronto! Italian Restaurant & Bar

544 York Rd; tel 215/672-3300. Off PA 263. **Italian.** The interior of this pretty 1767 building is decorated with antique signs and furniture as well as booths made from old-time buggies; modern sculpture adds a counterpoint in the five dining rooms. As you might guess, pastas dominate the menu. **FYI:** Reservations accepted. Children's menu. **Open:** Mon–Tues 11:30am–9pm, Wed–Thurs 11:30am–10pm, Fri 11:30am–11pm, Sat 4–11pm, Sun 4–9pm. **Prices:** Main courses $5–$16. AE, CB, DC, DISC, MC, V. 🍴 💟 ⛷

Warren

On the Allegheny River in northwestern Pennsylvania, Warren was settled around 1795 and is now a borough of some 12,000. Seat of Warren County. **Information:** Travel Northern Alleghenies, 315 2nd Ave, PO Box 804, Warren, 16365 (tel 814/726-1222).

MOTEL 🏨

≣≣≣ Holiday Inn Warren

210 Ludlow St, 16365; tel 814/726-3000 or toll free 800/446-6814; fax 814/726-3720. At jct US 6/US 62. A bright, clean, and up to date hotel with an exceptionally pleasant staff. **Rooms:** 112 rms and stes. CI 3pm/CO noon. Nonsmoking rms avail. All rooms have been renovated within the last two years. **Amenities:** 🛏 🖨 📺 A/C, cable TV. Some units

w/terraces. **Services:** X ⌷ ⌷ ⌷ **Facilities:** ⌷ ⌷ ⌷ ⌷ 2 restaurants (*see* "Restaurants" below), 1 bar (w/entertainment), games rm, sauna. **Rates:** Peak (June–Oct 20) $63 S; $69 D; $111 ste. Extra person $5. Children under age 18 stay free. Min stay special events. Lower rates off-season. Parking: Outdoor, free. AE, DC, DISC, MC, V.

RESTAURANT

Tootsie's
In Holiday Inn Warren, 210 Ludlow St; tel 814/726-3000. At jct US 6/US 62. **American.** Breakfast and lunch are served poolside under an atrium, while dinner is in the formal dining room. Each dinner begins with linguini in clam sauce, followed by a salad, rolls, sherbet, and finally, the main course. "Platters for two" include a seafood or surf-and-turf meal served with fruit, vegetables, choice of potato, and a split of champagne. **FYI:** Reservations accepted. Children's menu. **Open:** Breakfast Mon–Fri 6:30–11am, Sat 7:30am–1pm, Sun 8am–1pm; lunch daily 11am–2pm; dinner Mon–Thurs 5–9pm, Fri–Sat 5–10pm, Sun 5–8pm. **Prices:** Main courses $6–$18. AE, DC, DISC, MC, V. &

ATTRACTION

Allegheny National Forest
Forest Supervisor's Office, 222 Liberty St; tel 814/726-2710 or TTD 814/726-2710. With half a million acres of forest land, this national park has a variety of scenic terrain, including lakes, rivers, and wetland areas. Outdoor activities include hiking, backpacking, camping, cross-country skiing, bird-watching, snowmobiling, horse and llama riding, ice fishing, tobogganing and sledding, canoeing, and boating, and there are more than 500 miles of streams for fishing enthusiasts. The many different public campsites have a range of facilities; in addition, there are privately operated cabins and motels in the area. At the other end of the spectrum is the Hickory Creek Wilderness, where there are no facilities at all (but great solitude). Special attractions within the forest include the Kinzua Dam and the nearby fish hatcheries and huge carp; Heart's Content National Scenic Area, where there are stands of 300–400 year-old pines, hemlocks, and beeches; and one of only two wild elk herds east of the Mississippi River. The Allegheny Reservoir Scenic Drive, Longhouse National Scenic Byway, and Clarion River Driving Tour have many scenic overlooks. Self-guided tour maps are available at the visitors center in Warren. **Open:** Office: Mon–Fri 7:30am–4:30pm. **Free**

Washington

Originally a Delaware Indian village known as Catfish Camp, the area was settled by Europeans in 1781. David Bradford, leader of the Whiskey Rebellion, lived here.

HOTEL

Holiday Inn Meadow Lands
340 Race Track Rd, 15301; tel 412/222-6200 or toll free 800/HOLIDAY; fax 412/228-1977. Exit 8B off I-79. The race track is right next door to this attractive, well-maintained hotel, whose spacious, bright lobby has terra cotta tile, a large fireplace, and lots of seating. **Rooms:** 138 rms and stes. Executive level. CI 2pm/CO noon. Nonsmoking rms avail. Rooms facing the road get traffic noise. **Amenities:** ⌷ ⌷ ⌷ ⌷ A/C, satel TV w/movies, dataport. 1 unit w/whirlpool. **Services:** X ⌷ ⌷ ⌷ ⌷ **Facilities:** ⌷ ⌷ ⌷ ⌷ 1 restaurant, 2 bars (w/entertainment), games rm, spa, sauna, steam rm, whirlpool, playground. Large swimming pool and playground. **Rates:** $89–$109 S or D; $250 ste. Children under age 13 stay free. Parking: Outdoor, free. AE, CB, DC, DISC, MC, V.

MOTEL

Ramada Inn
1170 W Chestnut St, 15301; tel 412/228-9750 or toll free 800/2-RAMADA; fax 412/223-2912. Exit 4 off I-70. This older, neatly kept lodging is in a quiet location atop a hill overlooking Washington. **Rooms:** 93 rms. CI 2pm/CO noon. Nonsmoking rms avail. Standard motel rooms, but very clean. **Amenities:** ⌷ ⌷ A/C, cable TV. Refrigerators on request. **Services:** X ⌷ ⌷ **Facilities:** ⌷ ⌷ 1 restaurant, 1 bar, playground. Large swimming pool surrounded by lawn. **Rates (CP):** $56–$66 S; $62–$72 D. Extra person $6. Children under age 18 stay free. Parking: Outdoor, free. AE, CB, DC, MC, V.

Washington Crossing

This is the site where George Washington and his troops crossed the Delaware River on Christmas night in 1776. Delaware River Scenic Drive passes through town.

ATTRACTION

Washington Crossing Historic Park
PA 32; tel 215/493-4076. Gen George Washington's crossing of the Delaware on Christmas night of 1776, and his dawn assault on Trenton, have passed into national legend. This 500-acre park seeks to capture the importance of Washington's bravery via a collection of 13 historic buildings. There is also a wildflower preserve and a 100-foot-high tower from which the entire area can be viewed. A yearly re-enactment of the crossing takes place at Christmas. **Open:** Daily 9am–5pm. **Free**

Wellsboro

This small borough, founded in 1806, is reminiscent of the New England towns from which its early settlers arrived.

Wide, tree-lined boulevards with gaslights set a quaint tone. **Information:** Tioga County Tourist Promo Agency, 114 Main St, Wellsboro, 16901 (tel 717/724-0635).

MOTELS 🏨

≣≣ Canyon Motel
18 East Ave, 16901; tel 717/724-1681 or toll free 800/255-2718; fax 717/724-5202. On US 6, in town center. A simple, attractive motel in its second generation of family ownership. High standards of maintenance and cleanliness. **Rooms:** 28 rms and stes. CI 1pm/CO 11am. Nonsmoking rms avail. Nicely decorated rooms open onto parking lot. **Amenities:** 🛏 ⬙ 🍴 A/C, cable TV w/movies, refrig, dataport. 1 unit w/fireplace, 1 w/whirlpool. Microwaves in all rooms. **Services:** 🛎 🍴 🛎 Car-rental desk, babysitting. Hospitable staff. **Facilities:** 🏠 ⚓ ⬙ Volleyball, playground. **Rates (CP):** Peak (Apr 15–Nov 1) $28–$35 S; $40–$49 D; $55 ste. Extra person $5. Children under age 12 stay free. Lower rates off-season. MAP rates avail. Parking: Outdoor, free. AE, CB, DC, DISC, MC, V.

≣≣≣ The Penn Wells Hotel & Lodge
4 Main St, PO Box 158, 16901; tel 717/724-2155 or toll free 800/545-2446; fax 717/724-2270. On US 6/PA 287. The "lodge" part of this property has motel-type units. In summer, 73 additional rooms are available in the historic hotel a block away. **Rooms:** 55 rms. CI 3pm/CO noon. Nonsmoking rms avail. Rooms are attractively decorated and carefully kept. **Amenities:** 🛏 ⬙ A/C, cable TV, dataport. Some units w/terraces. **Services:** 🍴 **Facilities:** 🏠 ⚓ 🛎 🛎 ⬙ 1 restaurant (*see* "Restaurants" below), 1 bar, spa, sauna, whirlpool, playground. Excellent indoor pool and fitness facilities. **Rates:** Peak (May–Nov) $55–$61 S; $59–$69 D. Extra person $5. Children under age 18 stay free. Min stay special events. Lower rates off-season. MAP rates avail. Parking: Outdoor, free. Golf packages avail. AE, DC, DISC, MC, V.

RESTAURANT 🍴

Ⓢ ★ The Mary Wells Dining Room
In The Penn Wells Hotel & Lodge, 62 Main St; tel 717/724-2111. On PA 660. **American.** In a historic 1926 hotel with a dark wood and beige plaster interior, this handsome restaurant serves classy food at very attractive prices. The sauces are a pleasant surprise, and the servers are attentive. Notice the big flag on the lobby wall, made of 1,438 Christmas tree ornaments from a local glass factory. **FYI:** Reservations recommended. Piano. Children's menu. Dress code. **Open:** Peak (May–Nov) breakfast daily 7–11am; lunch daily 11:30am–2pm; dinner Sun–Thurs 5–9pm, Fri–Sat 5–10pm; brunch Sun 9am–2pm. **Prices:** Main courses $7–$17. AE, DC, DISC, MC, V. ∎

West Chester

Just west of Philadelphia, West Chester was incorporated in 1799 and is close to the Brandywine Battlefield and Marsh Creek State Park. Seat of Chester County. **Information:** Chester County Tourist Bureau, 601 Westown Rd #170, West Chester, 19382 (tel 610/344-6365).

HOTEL 🏨

UNRATED Holiday Inn West Chester
943 S High St, 19382; tel 610/692-1900 or toll free 800/HOLIDAY; fax 610/436-0159. Jct US 202/322 at Business US 322. This recently renovated motel offers an unusual amount of privacy due to its sprawling grounds. **Rooms:** 145 stes and effic. CI 3pm/CO noon. Nonsmoking rms avail. Country furnishings and pleasant decor. **Amenities:** 🛏 ⬙ 🛎 A/C, cable TV w/movies, dataport, voice mail. All units w/minibars. **Services:** ✕ 🔑 🚗 🛎 🍴 🛎 Babysitting. **Facilities:** 🏠 🛎 ⬙600⬙ ⬙ 1 restaurant, 1 bar, basketball, volleyball, games rm, lawn games, washer/dryer. **Rates:** $82 S or D; $105 ste; $115 effic. Children under age 6 stay free. Parking: Outdoor, free. AE, CB, DC, DISC, MC, V.

RESTAURANTS 🍴

The Chancery Restaurant & Pub
15 S High St; tel 610/344-0530. West Chester Univ exit off US 202. **Pub.** A re-created Victorian English setting complete with flocked wallpaper, frosted glass doors, and walnut wainscoting. The restaurant's menu offers pasta, seafood, and steaks while the snug, dark, and very British pub has snacks, soups, and sandwiches. **FYI:** Reservations recommended. Blues. Children's menu. Dress code. No smoking. **Open:** Peak (Sept–June) Tues–Thurs 11:30am–9pm, Fri 11:30am–10pm, Sat–Sun 5–10pm. **Prices:** Main courses $13–$22. AE, DISC, MC, V. ∎ ⬙

Dilworthtown Inn
Old Wilmington Pike, 19382 tel 610/399-1390. **American.** This historic inn has had a colorful history, including considerable damage inflicted by British soldiers in 1777. Today, the candlelight and gas lamps aim to re-create the charm of the past. The menu features an elaborate array of seafood, game, and choice cuts of meat; the wine list has over 800 labels. The 15 interior dining rooms are supplemented by outdoor dining in the stable courtyard. **FYI:** Reservations recommended. Jacket required. **Open:** Mon–Fri 5:30–10pm, Sat 5–10pm, Sun 3–8pm. **Prices:** Main courses $18–$26. AE, CB, DC, DISC, MC, V. ∎ ⬙ ⬙ ⬙

Magnolia Grille
In West Goshen Center, 971 Paoli Pike; tel 610/696-1661. **Regional American/Cajun.** A northern version of a New Orleans cafe, complete with wrought-iron accents, black-and-white tiles, and a menu featuring jambalaya, shrimp gumbo, and blackened catfish. The popular breakfast is available any time. The restaurant shares space and atmosphere with the

Chester County Book Company. **FYI:** Reservations accepted. Children's menu. BYO. **Open:** Mon–Thurs 9am–9pm, Fri–Sat 9am–9:30pm, Sun 9am–4pm. **Prices:** Main courses $6–$11. AE, CB, DC, DISC, MC, V. &

The Restaurant and The Bar

18-22 W Gay St; tel 610/431-0770. West Chester Univ exit off US 202. **Regional American.** The Restaurant features art deco designs and quiet dining, while The Bar is a classic, turn-of-the-century barroom, with a tin ceiling, long walnut bar, and cozy padded booths. Each menu features grilled fish, stir-fry dishes, and pasta. Sidewalk and patio dining are available in warm weather. **FYI:** Reservations recommended. Piano/rock. **Open:** Mon–Fri 11:30am–10pm, Sat 11:30am–11pm. **Prices:** Main courses $7–$15. AE, MC, V. 🍴 &

West Conshohocken

See Philadelphia

Wilkes-Barre

In the Pocono Mountains region on the Susquehanna River, Wilkes-Barre was settled around 1772 and is now a mining and manufacturing center with 50,000 residents.

HOTELS 🏨

🎗🎗🎗 Best Western East Mountain Inn

2400 East End Blvd, 18702; tel 717/822-1011 or toll free 800/528-1234; fax 717/822-6072. Exit 47A from I-81 to PA 115. The hilltop location cuts traffic noise, and the two restaurants plus a great pool and fitness center make this a good choice for business and family travelers. **Rooms:** 156 rms and stes. CI 3pm/CO 11am. Nonsmoking rms avail. **Amenities:** 🛏 🕸 🍷 A/C, cable TV w/movies, dataport, VCR. Some units w/terraces. Microwaves and refrigerators available. **Services:** ✕ 🚐 🛅 🕰 Complimentary morning coffee in lobby. **Facilities:** 🛠 🏋 🐾 💪 ⎿235⏌ & 2 restaurants, 1 bar, games rm, sauna, whirlpool, playground, washer/dryer. Glass-enclosed pool. **Rates:** $87–$102 S or D; $115–$120 ste. Extra person $5. Children under age 18 stay free. AP and MAP rates avail. Parking: Outdoor, free. AE, CB, DC, DISC, MC, V.

🎗🎗🎗 Ramada Hotel on the Square

20 Public Sq, 18701 (Downtown); tel 717/824-7100 or toll free 800/2-RAMADA; fax 717/823-5599. Exit 47B off I-81, PA 309 N to exit 2, left on Wilkes-Barre Blvd to Market St. Businesspeople appreciate the downtown location, while skiers make this a base for schussing the slopes outside the city. **Rooms:** 177 rms and stes. Executive level. CI 3pm/CO 11am. Nonsmoking rms avail. **Amenities:** 🛏 🕸 A/C, cable TV w/movies, voice mail. Some units w/whirlpools. Complimentary morning newspaper. Free continental breakfast served

weekdays only. **Services:** ✕ 🚐 🛅 🕰 Babysitting. **Facilities:** 🐾 💪 ⎿500⏌ 💻 & 2 restaurants (*see* "Restaurants" below), 1 bar (w/entertainment), washer/dryer. Pool and fitness center at nearby YMCA. One casual restaurant, one for fine dining on premises. **Rates (CP):** Peak (May–Oct) $67 S; $72 D; $125–$225 ste. Extra person $5. Children under age 18 stay free. Lower rates off-season. Parking: Indoor/outdoor, free. Ski packages to Montage Mountain avail; group and corporate rates avail. AE, CB, DC, DISC, MC, V.

MOTEL

🎗🎗 Holiday Inn

800 Kidder St, 18702; tel 717/824-8901 or toll free 800/HOLIDAY; fax 717/824-9310. Exit 47B off I-81, take PA 309 N to exit 1. A well-maintained motel close to the highway and downtown. **Rooms:** 120 rms. Executive level. CI 2pm/CO 11am. Nonsmoking rms avail. **Amenities:** 🛏 🕸 🍷 A/C, cable TV w/movies, dataport. **Services:** ✕ 🛅 🕰 👜 **Facilities:** 🛠 ⎿150⏌ 1 restaurant, 1 bar, washer/dryer. Free passes to fitness center five minutes away. **Rates:** Peak (Mar–Oct) $69 D. Extra person $10. Children under age 16 stay free. Lower rates off-season. Parking: Outdoor, free. AE, CB, DC, DISC, JCB, MC, V.

INN

🎗🎗🎗🎗 Bischwind

PA 115 S, PO Box 7, Bear Creek, 18602; tel 717/472-3820. Exit 47A off I-81. 8 acres. This elegant English manor house hosted Theodore Roosevelt and William Howard Taft when they were presidents of the United States. Unsuitable for children under 12. **Rooms:** 5 rms and stes. CI 2pm/CO noon. No smoking. Flowers and antiques everywhere, including some four-poster canopy beds swathed in lace and covered with down comforters. Three-bedroom wing with kitchen, dining room, and living room also available. **Amenities:** No A/C, phone, or TV. Some units w/fireplaces, 1 w/whirlpool. Bubble bath at the tubs. **Services:** Afternoon tea served. Complimentary fruit and cheese upon arrival. Five-course breakfast served in the dining room. **Facilities:** Guest lounge. **Rates (BB):** $150–$200 D; $235 ste. Parking: Outdoor, free. Rates vary according to room. DISC, MC, V.

RESORT

🎗🎗🎗 The Woodlands

1073 PA 315, 18702; tel 717/824-9831 or toll free 800/556-2222, 800/762-2222 in PA; fax 717/824-8865. Exit 47B off I-81 or exit 76 off PA Tpk. 60 acres. Rustic looks and an open, airy feeling from the multitude of windows and abundance of light wood pervade this attractive complex. **Rooms:** 179 rms, stes, and effic; 26 cottages/villas. CI 3pm/CO noon. Nonsmoking rms avail. More expensive streamside rooms have lovely terraces overlooking the creek. **Amenities:** 🛏 🕸 A/C, satel TV w/movies, dataport, voice mail. Some units w/terraces, 1 w/whirlpool. **Services:** ✕ 🆅🅿 🚐 🛅 🕰 👜

Twice-daily maid svce, masseur, babysitting. **Facilities:** 🛋️ 🏖️ 🐎 📷 🍽️ 1025 1 restaurant, 4 bars (3 w/entertainment), basketball, volleyball, games rm, lawn games, spa, sauna, steam rm, whirlpool, beauty salon. Complete fitness center and health spa with massage therapy and tanning beds. The 17,000-gallon whirlpool is billed as the largest on the East Coast. **Rates (BB):** Peak (June–Oct) $69–$125 S or D; $125–$175 ste; $300–$450 effic; $300–$450 cottage/villa. Extra person $10. Children under age 12 stay free. Lower rates off-season. Parking: Outdoor, free. Ski packages avail. AE, CB, DC, DISC, MC, V.

RESTAURANTS 🍴

The Bear Creek Inne
PA 115, Bear Creek; tel 717/472-9045. **Seafood/Steak.** Deer snack in the fields surrounding this old home atop a hill. Steaks, seafood, and veal are favorites, and salad and dessert bars are included with all dinners. **FYI:** Reservations recommended. Children's menu. **Open:** Mon–Sat 4–10pm, Sun noon–8pm. **Prices:** Main courses $9–$25. AE, CB, DC, DISC, MC, V. 🍽️ 🚭

★ The Beer Deli Restaurant
175 Welles St, Forty Fort; tel 717/288-8141. Exit 4 off PA 309 N. **Burgers/Deli.** Homemade soups and chili, angel-hair pasta with broccoli, Philly cheesesteaks, and pizzas are the specialties at this plant-filled, renovated warehouse. Servers bring a complimentary dessert at the end of the meal. **FYI:** Reservations not accepted. Beer only. **Open:** Sun–Thurs 10am–9:30pm, Fri–Sat 10am–10pm. **Prices:** Lunch main courses $2–$5. DISC, MC, V. 👪 🚗

Casey's
533 Scott St (East End); tel 717/824-4008. Exit 48 off I-81. **Burgers/Pub.** A bar/pub feeling prevails at this local hangout. The burgers are thick and the fries are home cut; wings and pizza are also on the menu. There are 150 beers, and service is friendly and quick. **FYI:** Reservations accepted. Local bands. Children's menu. **Open:** Mon–Sat 11am–2am, Sun 11am–10pm. **Prices:** Main courses $5–$13. AE, DC, DISC, MC, V. ⚹

Keenans Irish Pub
In The Ramada Hotel on the Square, 20 Public Sq (Downtown); tel 717/824-7100. **Burgers/Pub.** An "everybody knows your name" sort of place with a loyal local following and a horseshoe-shaped bar. The menu is standard pub grub: burgers, club sandwiches, and other munchies. **FYI:** Reservations accepted. Jazz/piano/singer. Children's menu. **Open:** Daily 11am–11pm. **Prices:** Main courses $4–$11. AE, CB, DC, MC, V. ⚹

♣ The Saber Room
84 Butler St; tel 717/829-5743. Exit 2 from 309N, take Wilkes-Barre Blvd to Butler St, turn right, go 1½ blocks. **French/Italian.** Chandeliers, green-textured wallpaper with gold borders, and waiters in black tuxedos create a formal atmosphere, and the copper-and-brass bar is billed as the oldest in the city. Top menu choices include tournedos Amaretto, cold lobster tail, veal in basil-lemon beurre blanc sauce, and rack of lamb. The wine list is impressive. **FYI:** Reservations recommended. **Open:** Lunch Mon–Fri 11am–2:30pm; dinner Mon–Sat 5–11pm. **Prices:** Main courses $11–$36. AE, MC, V. ♥

Williamsport

Once known as the lumber capital of the world, Williamsport features a historic district with eight blocks of mansions and old churches. Birthplace of Little League baseball, as commemorated at the Little League Museum. **Information:** Lycoming County Tourist Promo Agency, 454 Pine St, Williamsport, 17701 (tel 717/326-1971).

MOTEL 🏨

⧉⧉⧉ Quality Inn
234 Montgomery Pike, 17701; tel 717/323-9801 or toll free 800/221-2222; fax 717/322-5231. US 15, 1 mi S of Williamsport. Business travelers are the primary users of this well-kept property, but families enjoy it in summer. **Rooms:** 118 rms and stes. CI 3pm/CO noon. Nonsmoking rms avail. The furnishings are of good quality, and some rooms have pleasant views of the mountains and Williamsport. **Amenities:** 🛏️ ☎ A/C, cable TV w/movies. Executive rooms, refurbished in 1996, have extra amenities. **Services:** ✕ 🚗 📠 🛎️ Babysitting. **Facilities:** 🛋️ 🍽️ 350 ⚹ 1 restaurant (bkfst and dinner only), 1 bar (w/entertainment), games rm, washer/dryer. **Rates:** $54 S; $60 D; $120 ste. Extra person $6. Children under age 18 stay free. Parking: Outdoor, free. AE, CB, DC, DISC, EC, ER, JCB, MC, V.

ATTRACTIONS 🏛️

Hiawatha Paddlewheeler
Reach Rd exit off I-180; tel 717/321-1205 or toll free 800/358-9900. The *Hiawatha*, a replica of a 19th-century riverboat, departs from Susquehanna State Park (*see below*). The hour-long cruises include lectures on the history of the river's communities and life in the days when paddlewheelers like the *Hiawatha* plied their trade along its shores. Theme cruises are also conducted throughout the year. **Open:** Peak (June–Aug) Tues–Sat, hours vary. Reduced hours off-season. $$$

Susquehanna State Park
Reach Rd exit off PA 220; tel toll free 800/358-9900. Located on the banks of the Susquehanna River, this park preserves some of the natural habitat of this once-bustling lumbering center. Visitors can picnic, walk, or take a ride on a replica of a river boat. **Open:** Daily sunrise–sunset. $

Willow Grove

A small suburb of Philadelphia, convenient to attractions of the capital city and greater Philadelphia area, including Delaware Scenic Drive and Tyler State Park.

HOTEL 🏨

≣≣ Courtyard by Marriott

2350 Easton Rd, 19090; tel 215/830-0550 or toll free 800/321-2211; fax 215/830-0572. Exit 27 off PA Tpk. The lobby is bright, with a fireplace, TV, and fresh-brewed coffee, and the staff is cheery. **Rooms:** 149 rms and stes. CI 4pm/CO noon. Nonsmoking rms avail. **Amenities:** 🛏 🐕 A/C, cable TV w/movies, dataport, voice mail. All units w/terraces. Hot-water dispensers and instant coffee. Hairdryers and refrigerators in suites. Children's toys and games available. **Services:** 🚗 🛎 🍽 Car-rental desk, babysitting. **Facilities:** 🏋 🍴 🏊40 🦽 1 restaurant (bkfst only), 1 bar, whirlpool, day-care ctr, washer/dryer. **Rates:** $89–$114 S or D; $140 ste. Children under age 21 stay free. Parking: Outdoor, free. Weekend rates and Sesame Place packages avail. AE, DC, DISC, MC, V.

MOTELS

≣≣ Days Inn Horsham

245 Easton Rd, 19044; tel 215/674-2500 or toll free 800/DAYS-INN; fax 215/674-0145. Exit 27 off PA Tpk. The lobby is a little plain, but the personnel are friendly and security is good. **Rooms:** 171 rms. CI 3pm/CO noon. Nonsmoking rms avail. Rooms for guests with disabilities are spacious and better than average. **Amenities:** 🛏 🐕 A/C, cable TV w/movies, dataport. Some units w/whirlpools. Refrigerators available. **Services:** 🚗 🛎 🍽 Car-rental desk. **Facilities:** 🍴 🏊130 🦽 Spa, whirlpool, washer/dryer. Restaurant next door will bill to room. **Rates (CP):** $82–$88 S; $88–$115 D. Extra person $8. Children under age 18 stay free. Parking: Outdoor, free. Sesame Place packages avail. AE, DC, DISC, MC, V.

UNRATED Hampton Inn

1500 Easton Rd, 19090; tel 215/659-3535 or toll free 800/846-8346; fax 215/659-4040. Exit 27 off PA Tpk, then ½ mi S on PA 611. Simple, clean accommodations for business travelers. The comfortable lobby offers a TV area and freshly brewed coffee. **Rooms:** 150 rms. CI 3pm/CO noon. Nonsmoking rms avail. **Amenities:** 🛏 🐕 A/C, cable TV w/movies, dataport. Some units have refrigerators and microwaves. **Services:** 🚗 🛎 🍽 Free local calls. **Facilities:** 🍴 🏊125 🦽 Sauna. Free passes to Bally's Health Spa. **Rates (CP):** Peak (June–Oct) $80–$94 S or D. Children under age 18 stay free. Lower rates off-season. Parking: Outdoor, free. AE, CB, DC, DISC, MC, V.

ATTRACTION 🏛

Graeme Park

859 County Line Rd, Horsham; tel 215/343-0965. Graeme Park was built in 1722 as the residence of Sir William Keith, Provincial Governor of Pennsylvania. Known at that time as "Fountain Low" because of the abundance of natural springs in the area, it was later purchased by Dr Thomas Graeme. Graeme remodeled the interior of the house, but the exterior has changed little in two centuries. Today the stone house contains few furnishings, and its many original architectural features are visible. "Living History" days take place throughout the year. **Open:** Thurs–Sat 10am–4pm, Sun noon–4pm. $$

York

York was settled, in the rolling farmland of Pennsylvania Dutch Country, around 1741. It served as the nation's first capital and it was here the Continental Congress met to sign the Articles of Confederation. Today it is a manufacturing center and is perhaps best known as the headquarters of Harley-Davidson Motorcycles. **Information:** York County Convention & Visitors Bureau, One Market Way E, PO Box 1229, York, 17405 (tel 717/848-4000 or toll free 800/673-2429).

HOTELS 🏨

≣≣≣ Holiday Inn Holidome & Conference Center

2000 Loucks Rd, 17404; tel 717/846-9500 or toll free 800/HOLIDAY; fax 717/764-5038. Off PA 74 just N of US 30. Snazzy Holidome has miniature golf, a whirlpool, a pool, and a fitness center. Popular with businesspeople and families alike. **Rooms:** 181 rms. CI 3pm/CO noon. Nonsmoking rms avail. King rooms have sofa beds. **Amenities:** 🛏 A/C, cable TV w/movies, dataport, voice mail. Some units w/terraces. Free morning newspapers delivered to rooms. **Services:** ✗ 🛎 🍽 🐕 **Facilities:** 🏋 🍴 🏊600 💻 🦽 1 restaurant, 1 bar (w/entertainment), sauna, whirlpool, playground. Free access to health club one block away. **Rates:** $89 S or D. Children under age 12 stay free. Parking: Outdoor, free. AARP discounts avail. AE, CB, DC, DISC, MC, V.

≣≣≣ The Yorktowne Hotel

48 E Market St, 17405; tel 717/848-1111 or toll free 800/233-9324; fax 717/854-7678. Exit 9 off I-83 (Bus I-83 S) to PA 462. The large lobby of this National Historic Landmark hotel has a wrought-iron and wood decor, with paintings and draperies evoking turn-of-the-century elegance. **Rooms:** 152 rms, stes, and effic. Executive level. CI 3pm/CO noon. Nonsmoking rms avail. Separate seating areas with sofa, chair, and coffee table. **Amenities:** 🛏 🐕 📺 🍽 A/C, cable TV, dataport. **Services:** ✗ 📼 🚗 🛎 🍽 **Facilities:** 🍴 🏊450 🦽 2 restaurants, 2 bars, beauty salon. Shops and restaurant off

the lobby. **Rates:** $52–$89 S; $57–$96 D; $90–$250 ste; $89–$96 effic. Extra person $7. Children under age 18 stay free. Parking: Outdoor, free. AE, DC, DISC, MC, V.

MOTELS

🏨🏨 Hampton Inn
1550 Mount Zion Rd, 17402 (Galleria Mall); tel 717/840-1500 or toll free 800/HAMPTON; fax 717/840-1567. Upscale example of the Hampton chain, with an attractively furnished lobby. **Rooms:** 144 rms, stes, and effic. CI 3pm/CO 11am. Nonsmoking rms avail. Armoires used as closets. **Amenities:** 🛎 🔥 A/C, cable TV, dataport, voice mail. Refrigerators and microwaves on request. **Services:** 🖼 🔄 🕭 Babysitting. 24-hour coffee in lobby. **Facilities:** 🃏 🔦 🔲 50 🔥 Whirlpool, washer/dryer. **Rates (CP):** $71–$75 S; $79–$83 D; $87–$95 ste; $87–$95 effic. Children under age 18 stay free. Parking: Outdoor, free. AE, CB, DC, DISC, MC, V.

🏨🏨🏨 Holiday Inn Arsenal Road
334 Arsenal Rd, 17402; tel 717/845-5671 or toll free 800/HOLIDAY; fax 717/845-1898. I-83 at US 30. Landscaping is minimal, but rooms are spacious. Fine for a quick stop. **Rooms:** 100 rms and effic. CI 3pm/CO noon. Nonsmoking rms avail. **Amenities:** 🛎 🔥 A/C, satel TV w/movies, dataport. **Services:** ✕ 🖼 🔄 Children's program, babysitting. **Facilities:** 🃏 300 🔥 1 restaurant, 1 bar, volleyball, washer/dryer. Free admission to local health club. **Rates:** $75 S or D; $75 effic. Children under age 12 stay free. Parking: Outdoor, free. AE, CB, DC, DISC, JCB, MC, V.

🏨🏨🏨 Holiday Inn Market Street
2600 E Market St, 17402; tel 717/755-1966 or toll free 800/HOLIDAY; fax 717/755-6936. Exit 8 off I-83, go 1 mi on PA 462 E. Well-kept, older motel. **Rooms:** 120 rms and stes. CI 3pm/CO noon. Nonsmoking rms avail. King rooms have sofas. **Amenities:** 🛎 🔥 🖳 A/C, satel TV w/movies, dataport. Refrigerators and microwaves available. **Services:** ✕ 🚐 🖼 🔄 🕭 Babysitting. **Facilities:** 🃏 300 🔥 1 restaurant, 1 bar, beauty salon, washer/dryer. **Rates:** $75–$89 S or D; $150–$225 ste. Children under age 19 stay free. Parking: Outdoor, free. Rates are by the room, not by the number of occupants. AE, CB, DC, DISC, JCB, MC, V.

🏨 York Travelodge
132-140 N George St, 17401; tel 717/843-8974 or toll free 800/578-7878; fax 717/852-0682. Exit 9W off I-83; go left on N George St. Minimal facilities and amenities, but the rooms are in good condition. Fine for a quick stay. **Rooms:** 57 rms. CI 2pm/CO 11am. Nonsmoking rms avail. Rooms are simple, clean, and neat. **Amenities:** 🛎 🖳 A/C, cable TV. **Services:** 🔄 🕭 **Rates:** Peak (Apr–Nov) $40–$45 S; $45–$50 D. Children under age 12 stay free. Lower rates off-season. Parking: Outdoor, free. AE, CB, DC, DISC, MC, V.

RESTAURANT 🍽

★ San Carlo's
333 Arsenal Rd; tel 717/854-2028. Exit 9 off I-83, US 30 E to left at first light. **American.** The original fieldstone walls and wood beams of this 175-year-old dairy barn are hung with wagon wheels and lanterns, and the bar entrance is through the front of an old car. The menu is much more basic, with prime rib and seafood being the most popular entrees. **FYI:** Reservations accepted. Karaoke. Children's menu. **Open:** Daily 4–10pm. **Prices:** Main courses $10–$15. AE, DC, DISC, MC, V. 🍽 📷 🔥

VIRGINIA

A State of Love

They knew what they were doing back in 1969 when they decided that "Virginia is for lovers." Long ocean beaches beckon for hand-in-hand strolls. Mountain vistas entice arms to be slipped softly around shoulders. Fireplaces in comfortable resorts invite cuddling on cold winter nights.

For nature lovers, Virginia is a beauty—from the Eastern Shore, where wild ponies live on Assateague Island and where peregrine falcons, snow geese, snowy egrets, and great blue herons have all been spotted, to the Blue Ridge Mountains and the Shenandoah Valley, dappled with wildflowers, dogwood, and azaleas in spring, fiery with foliage in fall. The Skyline Drive and the Blue Ridge Parkway are two of the most scenic drives in America.

But those whose love is most rewarded in Virginia are lovers of American history. The country was born here when the first permanent English settlement in the New World took root on the banks of the James River in 1607. And the colonial past lives on in 18th-century Williamsburg, a gem of restoration and reconstruction where wigs are still powdered, the minuet is still taught, and the militia still drilled. The American Revolution was won at Yorktown, and 7 of the first 12 presidents were born and lived in Virginia. Some of their homes—such as Mount Vernon and Monticello—provide a crash course in 18th- and 19th-century art, architecture, agriculture, domestic economics, and political thought. Preserved here, too, are the battlefields where tens of thousands of men died during the bloody Civil War. And African American history has markers embedded in Virginia's soil. Slaves' quarters are still visible at numerous plantations, such as Carter's Grove near Williamsburg, in this state where slavery first took hold. The Booker T Washington National Monument preserves the plantation cabin—dirt floor, glassless windows—that was this great American's boyhood home.

Virginia has much more to offer besides history—a spa resort in the town of Hot

Springs that has hosted presidents from Jefferson through Reagan, horse farms in green rolling Hunt Country, and a growing wine industry. But when it comes to the number, significance, and evocative power of its historical treasures, no state in the Union can rival the Old Dominion.

A Brief History

Jamestown When the *Susan Constant, Godspeed,* and *Discovery* dropped anchor off Cape Charles on April 26, 1607, it was the end of a long and cramped voyage for 105 colonists who had left England seeking gold and fortune in the New World. The difficult journey was only a prelude to things to come, beginning with an attack by Native Americans on that first day. Abandoning Cape Charles, the colonists explored the wide rivers on the western shore of the Chesapeake Bay before settling on a small island 60 miles upstream. They named the river James, for their King James I, and their new home Jamestown.

Nearly half their lot died the first year, victims of starvation, Native American raids, and typhoid fever. Only the heroics of a mercenary braggart named Captain John Smith held the colony together. Smith is remembered, however, for having been saved from execution by Pocahontas, daughter of the powerful chief Powhatan.

The colonists never found gold, but in 1613 John Rolfe, who later married Pocahontas, introduced a mild version of tobacco, which quickly found favor in most of Europe. Profits and more colonists flowed into Jamestown and other new settlements along the rivers. In 1619, the settlers chose the members of America's first legislative body, the House of Burgesses. That same year, a Dutch ship unloaded 20 Africans to work as indentured servants. For the English colonists, it was the first step down a long road to freedom. For African Americans, it was the beginning of slavery.

Fun Facts

- The world's largest office building, the Pentagon contains more than 6.5 million square feet of space and almost 18 miles of corridors.
- Memorial Day, which originated in Petersburg, VA, is actually of Confederate origin. National observance of the holiday began after the Civil War, when Petersburg schoolgirls decorated the graves of soldiers who died fighting for the Confederacy.
- In Richmond, adventurers can take a white-water rafting trip through the center of the metropolis.
- The College of William and Mary, in Williamsburg, is the second-oldest college in the United States (only Harvard University is older). It opened its doors in 1694.
- Norfolk's innovative recycling program created "Mount Trashmore," a mountain of trash that has been reborn as a children's playground.
- Virginia has more miles of trout streams than roads.
- Virginia's Natural Bridge, which spans Cedar Creek, stands 215 feet tall and is one of the Seven Natural Wonders of the World.

Williamsburg In 1699, the colonists moved their capital from cramped Jamestown to nearby Williamsburg, which soon became a center of agitation for an independent America. While the Burgesses debated, English settlers were advancing westward into the hills of central Virginia joined by Scotch-Irish and German settlers moving in from Pennsylvania. Out on the frontier, the pioneers ran into both hostile Native Americans and the French, who were encroaching onto British-claimed land from the west. When the French and Indian War broke out in the 1750s, the colonial government turned to a young surveyor to lead the Virginia militia: George Washington.

The British won that war, but when King George III increased colonial taxes to pay for it, protests against "taxation without representation" erupted up and down the Atlantic seaboard. In Williamsburg, the infamous Stamp Act of 1765 caused the House of Burgesses to pass the Virginia Resolves, calling for colonial rights based on a constitution. The Stamp Act was repealed in 1766, but a hated tax on tea remained. After the Boston Tea Party in 1773, Richard Henry Lee led the House of Burgesses in creating a standing committee to communicate with the other colonies to discuss grievances against Britain. In turn, that led to the first Continental Congress, which met in Philadelphia the following year.

Liberty or Death In 1775, fiery orator Patrick Henry delivered one of the most famous speeches in American history. Urging that the Virginia militia be armed, he stood in Richmond's St John's Church and shouted: "Is life so dear or peace so sweet as to be purchased at the price of chains and slavery? Forbid it, Almighty God! I know not what course others may take, but as for me, give me liberty, or give me death!"

Hostilities already had broken out at Lexington and Concord by the time the Second Continental Congress met in 1775 and declared war on Great

Britain. To lead its Continental Army, the Congress chose George Washington.

At this point the colonists were fighting to defend their rights as British subjects. However, meeting in Williamsburg during June 1776, the Virginia Convention urged its congressional delegates to vote for independence, and it passed a Bill of Rights drafted by George Mason. A month later in Philadelphia, 33-year-old Virginian Thomas Jefferson based the Declaration of Independence on Mason's bill. Issued on July 4, 1776, Jefferson's document turned the 13 colonies into a new nation.

Yorktown The American Revolution raged for five more years. Virginia saw little fighting until 1781, when a British army under Lord Cornwallis was encamped at Yorktown. Washington quickly marched his army south from New York and trapped Cornwallis between his forces and the French navy offshore. Cornwallis's surrender on October 19, 1781, led directly to American independence.

Birthplace of Presidents The new nation relied heavily on Virginians in its early years, giving the Old Dominion a new nickname, "Birthplace of Presidents."

After the Articles of Confederation, which had set up a loose league of 13 states in 1781, proved unworkable, a Constitutional Convention met in Philadelphia in 1787 to devise a new national government. Jefferson was in France, but the delegates chose Washington as their president. Another Virginian, James Madison, fought for a Bill of Rights and crafted the bicameral Virginia Compromise, under which members of the House of Representatives are elected proportionally by population, while each state has two Senators.

Taking office in 1789 as the first president, Washington selected Jefferson as his secretary of state and carved the District of Columbia out of Maryland and Virginia, including all of what is now Arlington and most of Alexandria (they were later returned to Virginia).

As the third president, Jefferson almost doubled the size of the United States by adding the Louisiana Purchase. Madison followed Jefferson to the White House in 1809 and led the nation into the War of 1812, during which he and wife Dolley narrowly escaped before the British burned the Capitol and White House. The fifth president, Virginian James Monroe, author of the Monroe Doctrine, continued the nation's westward push.

In all, Virginia provided 7 of America's first 12 presidents. The others were Charles City County neighbors William Henry Harrison and John Tyler, and Zachary Taylor. Woodrow Wilson was born in Staunton, although he was living in New Jersey when he was elected in 1912.

The Civil War While its native sons were busy governing on the Potomac, Virginia reverted to its agricultural ways. The quiet times were short-lived, however, for slavery soon became the cause of much national tension. In 1859, abolitionist John Brown staged a raid on Harper's Ferry, a federal arsenal now in West Virginia but then in Virginia. When abolitionist Abraham Lincoln was elected president in 1860, the cotton-growing states of the Deep South seceded from the Union and formed the Confederacy. When they fired on Fort Sumter in South Carolina in April 1861, the war had begun. Virginia quickly seceded, Richmond became the capital of the Confederacy, and within a year a Virginian named Robert E Lee became commander of its Army of Northern Virginia.

Virginia was the main battleground of six major Union campaigns to capture Richmond. The first was stopped in July of 1861 at the First Battle of Manassas. The second campaign advanced up the peninsula between the York and James Rivers in 1862 but bogged down just nine miles from Richmond. Lee stopped the third campaign at the Second Battle of Manassas later that same year. The fourth came through Fredericksburg in December 1862 and nearly reached Richmond before Lee turned it back. The fifth, early in 1863, was stopped at Chancellorsville, where Lee suffered the loss of General Stonewall Jackson, accidentally shot by his own men.

Tired of indecisive generals, Lincoln in 1864 picked the unrelenting Ulysses S Grant to head all Union armies. Grant soon launched a sixth and final campaign against the Confederate capital. His first battle with Lee came during the Wilderness Campaign west of Fredericksburg. Lee technically won, but instead of retreating as his predecessors had, Grant skirted Lee's forces until June 1864, when he laid siege to Petersburg, a key railroad junction 23 miles south of Richmond. The ensuing nine-month standoff took its toll on the rebels, and on April 1, 1865, Grant's forces broke through the Confederate line.

With Richmond lost, Lee retreated westward

toward Danville, last capital of the Confederacy. He got as far as Appomattox Court House, where Grant's forces blocked his way. On April 8, 1865, the two great generals met in the living room of Wilbur McLean's farmhouse. Lee's surrender that day ended Virginia's four-year ordeal.

Recovery   Like the rest of the South, Virginia lay devastated. Its farms were ruined, one-seventh of its white men were either dead or disabled, its slaves were free but unemployed, its few industries lay in shambles, and one-third of its land was now named West Virginia. But the survivors slowly began to recover. Eastern plantation owners turned to sharecropping to make their large holdings productive. New railroads opened up coal mining in the west and turned Hampton Roads into a major port. And thanks to its popularity during the Civil War, tobacco became even more lucrative.

Prosperity didn't come to all, however, for the sharecropping system effectively replaced slavery, and so-called Jim Crow laws at the turn of the century legalized segregation, making second-class citizens of all Virginians of African descent. Then the Great Depression aggravated the poverty that was still prevalent in many parts of the state. Things finally turned upward for good during World War II, when federal military spending brought prosperity to northern Virginia, Hampton Roads, and the coal fields of the west.

Modern Virginia   Once the domain of large plantations, today's Virginia is a mix of farms and factories, small towns, and cities, its economy dependent on agriculture, manufacturing, service industries, tourism, and government. A prosperous commercial crescent has developed along an urban corridor that begins in northern Virginia and follows I-95 south to Richmond and I-64 east to Hampton Roads.

A Closer Look
GEOGRAPHY

Shaped like a triangle, Virginia stretches more than 400 miles from the beaches and marshes along the Atlantic Ocean westward to the ridges and peaks of the Allegheny Mountains.

Tidewater is what Virginians call the eastern quarter of their state, a flat coastal plain flanking the mighty Chesapeake Bay and split into three long peninsulas (or "necks" in local parlance) by the Potomac, Rappahannock, York, and James Rivers. Antebellum plantations still occupy the heavily wooded banks of these broad rivers. However, the towns where tobacco and cotton were once kings (Norfolk, Portsmouth, Newport News, Hampton, and Virginia Beach) have grown to form a sprawling metropolis on the shores of Hampton Roads, the world's largest natural harbor and home to America's biggest naval base. Just to the south of these vibrant cities lies the forbidding wilderness of the Great Dismal Swamp, a national wildlife refuge.

The **Eastern Shore,** Virginia's share of the Delmarva Peninsula, is barely visible across Hampton Roads. The southern tip of the peninsula, it is tied to the mainland by the thin thread of the 17.6-mile Chesapeake Bay Bridge-Tunnel, which reaches from Norfolk to Cape Charles and is the longest such structure in the world. Countless waterways and islands slice through the ocean and bay coasts of this sparsely populated rural area, whose

---

DRIVING DISTANCES

Charlottesville

64 mi NE of Lynchburg
69 mi NW of Richmond
115 mi NE of Roanoke
120 mi SW of Washington, DC
163 mi NW of Norfolk
242 mi SE of Charleston, WV

Lynchburg

51 mi NE of Roanoke
64 mi SW of Charlottesville
113 mi SW of Richmond
184 mi SW of Washington, DC
207 mi NW of Norfolk
233 mi SE of Charleston, WV

Norfolk

94 mi SE of Richmond
163 mi SE of Charlottesville
200 mi SE of Washington, DC
207 mi SE of Lynchburg
259 mi SE of Roanoke
405 mi SE of Charleston, WV

Richmond

69 mi SE of Charlottesville
94 mi NW of Norfolk
109 mi SW of Washington, DC
113 mi NE of Lynchburg
164 mi NE of Roanoke
311 mi SE of Charleston, WV

Roanoke

51 mi SW of Lynchburg
115 mi SW of Charlottesville
164 mi SW of Richmond
182 mi SE of Charleston, WV
223 mi SE of Washington, DC
259 mi NW of Norfolk

economic mainstays are farming and raising millions of chickens. Chincoteague National Wildlife Refuge and Assateague Island National Seashore, both near the quaint village of Chincoteague, are havens for wild ponies and birds. Out in the Chesapeake, residents of remote Tangier Island still speak with the Elizabethan lilt of their ancestors.

Central Virginia lies to the west of the coastal plain, its rolling hill country often called the Piedmont, the state's industrial and intellectual heartland. Here are such exciting small cities as Richmond, Virginia's vibrant capital; Charlottesville, home of Thomas Jefferson's Monticello and the University of Virginia; Petersburg, whose fall meant the end of the Confederacy; and Lynchburg, proud of historic homes that tobacco built.

Northern Virginia, at the top of the Piedmont, is now the wealthiest part of the Old Dominion. Once no more than Washington, DC's sleepy suburbs, Arlington, Alexandria, Falls Church, and Fairfax County have exploded with high-tech firms and now have the state's largest and most diverse urban population, highest per-capita income, and worst traffic jams. But history lives, with Old Town Alexandria, the Arlington National Cemetery, and George Washington's Mount Vernon attracting millions of visitors every year. To the south are historic Fredericksburg and its Civil War battlefields. To the west are the undulating hills, fashionable small towns, manicured estates, and well-groomed horses of the Virginia Hunt Country.

Moving westward across the state, the Piedmont rises until it meets the **Blue Ridge,** first of the seemingly endless ridges that form the Appalachian Mountains. Along its spine run the breathtaking Skyline Drive and, continuing where it leaves off, the Blue Ridge Parkway, two of America's most scenic roadways.

The **Shenandoah Valley,** beyond the Blue Ridge, was the breadbasket of the Confederacy and saw its share of Civil War battles. Here are picturesque, historic towns such as Winchester, New Market, Harrisonburg, Staunton, and Lexington. Here, too, is Mother Nature's work—above ground at Natural

Bridge and Hot Springs and underneath at Luray Caverns.

The **Southwest Blue Ridge Highlands** to the south of the Shenandoah grow ever higher and more spectacular as you drive into Virginia's western tail from busy Roanoke. This mountainous region sports Mount Rogers, Virginia's highest peak and home of its own national recreation area; quaint towns such as Abingdon and Big Stone Gap; the 850-foot Natural Tunnel; the largest canyon east of the Mississippi at Breaks Interstate Park; and Cumberland Gap, Daniel Boone's doorway to Kentucky.

AVG MONTHLY TEMPS (°F) & RAINFALL (IN)		
	Richmond	Hot Springs
Jan	36/3.2	29/3.0
Feb	39/3.2	32/2.9
Mar	48/3.6	41/3.7
Apr	56/3.3	50/3.4
May	66/3.8	60/4.2
June	74/3.6	67/3.4
July	78/5.0	71/4.5
Aug	77/4.8	70/3.7
Sept	70/3.3	63/3.4
Oct	59/3.5	53/3.8
Nov	50/3.2	43/3.5
Dec	40/3.3	33/2.8

CLIMATE

Of Virginia's four temperate seasons, the warm days and cool evenings of spring and autumn are unquestionably the best times to sightsee, especially when the leaves change color in early autumn. Summers can be uncomfortably hot and humid. Winters can range unpredictably from bitterly cold to relatively moderate. Wintertime snow is common in the mountains, less so in northern and central Virginia, and infrequent on the Eastern Shore and in Tidewater.

During most of the year, rain tends to fall in cloudy, damp periods, with a wet day or two followed by brilliant sunshine. Summer features intense thunderstorms, which are usually brief but should be taken seriously; seek shelter.

WHAT TO PACK

Outdoor summer activities demand shorts and lightweight shirts, blouses, and dresses—but remember that air conditioning can make restaurants, shops, and indoor attractions seem like Alaska. Spring and autumn evenings—and even summer ones in the mountains—can be nippy enough for a jacket or wrap. Winter requires moderately heavy coats, hats, boots, and gloves. Some restaurants require men to wear jackets and ties, but smart casual attire usually will fit in.

A few items will be useful anytime, including comfortable walking shoes, a hat, sunglasses, and a folding umbrella. Bring sunscreen and insect repellent during the summer months.

TOURIST INFORMATION

The **Virginia Division of Tourism,** 901 E Byrd St, Richmond, VA 23219 (tel 804/786-2051, fax 804/786-1919), provides free copies of its annual *Virginia Travel Guide,* which is full of information about attractions, activities, accommodations, and special events throughout the state. The Division also maintains a World Wide Web page (http://www.Virginia.org) with a searchable database.

If you're in Richmond, the central **Welcome Center** is in the Bell Tower, Capitol Square (tel 804/786-4484).

DRIVING RULES AND REGULATIONS

The speed limit is 65 mph on rural interstate highways, 55 mph in built-up areas and on state highways. In-town speed limits vary. Driver and all front-seat passengers must wear seat belts, and children under age 4 or less than 40 pounds must ride in an approved safety seat. Drunk-driving laws are strictly enforced, and the penalties are severe. Carrying open containers of alcohol in vehicles is unlawful.

RENTING A CAR

Traveling by car is the best way to see the Old Dominion, and rentals are widely available in the metropolitan areas. Some shopping around is in order, since promotional deals, weekend rates, age requirements, and group discounts can vary. Your travel agent can provide advice.

Here are the major companies with offices in Virginia, along with their toll-free numbers:

- **Alamo** (tel toll free 800/327-9633)
- **Avis** (tel 800/831-2847)
- **Budget** (tel 800/527-0700)
- **Dollar Rent-A-Car** (tel 800/800-4000)
- **Hertz** (tel 800/654-3131)
- **National** (tel 800/227-7368)
- **Thrifty** (tel 800/367-2277)

ESSENTIALS

Area Code: The area code for northeastern Virginia (including Alexandria, Fairfax, and most of the DC suburbs) is **703.** The area from Leesburg south through the Shenandoah Valley and the southwestern Blue Ridge High-lands is in the **540** area code. Central Virginia (including Lynchburg, Richmond, and Charlottesville) is in **804,** while southeastern Virginia (including Norfolk, Williamsburg, and the Eastern Shore) is in **757.**

Emergencies: Call **911** for police, the fire department, or an ambulance from anywhere within Virginia.

Liquor Laws: Many grocery and convenience stores sell beer and wine. A few localities now have privately owned "package stores," but in most places other types of liquor can be purchased only from government-operated Alcohol Beverage Control (ABC) stores. Licensed restaurants and bars can dispense alcoholic beverages by the glass (known as "liquor by the drink" in Virginia). The statewide legal drinking age is 21, and proof of age including a photo may be required.

Taxes: The sales tax is 4½% in most of Virginia. Some localities add another half a percent to this statewide levy, and many jurisdictions also impose additional taxes on hotel rooms.

Time Zone: All of Virginia is in the Eastern time zone. Daylight saving time is observed from the first Sunday in April until the last Sunday in October.

Best of the State

Below is a general overview of some of the top sights and attractions in Virginia. To find out more detailed information, look under "Attractions" under individual cities in the listings portion of this book.

WHAT TO SEE AND DO

Battlefields Virginians are justly proud of their role in winning the American Revolution and, although it was in a lost cause, of the blood their young men spilled during the Civil War. That pride shows in numerous preserved battlefields such as **Yorktown,** where Cornwallis' surrender ended the Revolutionary War; **Manassas National Battlefield Park,** scene of two early Confederate successes; and the **Fredericksburg and Spotsylvania National Mil-**

itary Park, which also embraces sites related to the battles of Chancellorsville and the Wilderness. Richmond National Battlefield Park includes the bloody Cold Harbor battlefield, where 7,000 Union troops were killed or wounded in a mere 30 minutes in 1864; and Petersburg National Battlefield was the scene of the nine-month siege that clinched the final Union victory. The farmhouse where Lee surrendered is today the Appomattox Court House National Historic Park.

Beaches   Sand and sun reign supreme along Virginia's Atlantic coast: The 27 miles of Virginia Beach constitute the world's longest resort beach. Those who object to hotels and cottages will find the 45 totally undeveloped miles of Assateague Island National Seashore a more congenial paradise.

Cuisine   Like their Maryland neighbors to the north, Virginians enjoy the bounty of the Chesapeake Bay, which means seafood lovers can get their fill from one end of the state to the other. Another local delicacy is strong Virginia country ham from the smokehouses of Smithfield. And in the fall, don't miss those wonderfully fresh Shenandoah Valley apples and the sweet cider made from them.

Family Favorites   Two major theme parks attract local families and visitors alike. Kids of any age enjoy the wild rides, water park, ice show, and *Star Trek* characters at Paramount's King's Dominion, 20 miles north of Richmond. At Busch Gardens Williamsburg, they learn about the Old World at nine re-created 17th-century European villages, then get their thrills on rides like the Loch Ness Monster. For an equally interesting and more educational outing, the entire family can take a history lesson at Colonial Williamsburg, then detour several miles southwest to Jamestown or northeast to Yorktown. All three are now part of the Colonial National Historical Park.

Museums   Beyond the multitude of fine institutions dedicated to preserving its illustrious past, Virginia has museums for those interested in everything from outer space to the briny deep. Two particularly renowned finearts museums are the Chrysler Museum of Art, in Norfolk, especially noted for its 8,000-piece glass collection, including much Tiffany glass, and Richmond's Virginia Museum of Fine Arts, noted not only for paintings but also for the largest collection of Fabergé objets d'art outside Russia.

Historic Buildings & Sites   For visitors, Virginians' reverence for the past means well-preserved historic sites in almost every nook and cranny of the state, beginning with Colonial Williamsburg, the granddaddy of all restored towns, where 88 buildings surviving from the 18th century have been supplemented with some 500 buildings reconstructed on their original sites. Nearby are Jamestown, remnant of the first permanent English settlement in the New World, and Yorktown, a Revolutionary War battlefield and old colonial town.

Other key sights include George Washington's Mount Vernon, one of the most-loved and most-visited sites in America, and George Mason's nearby Gunston Hall. In the Charlottesville area is the hilltop Monticello that Thomas Jefferson designed for himself in 16th-century Italian style; the homes of the fourth and fifth presidents, James Madison's Montpelier and James Monroe's Ash Lawn-Highland, are nearby. In Richmond is the Virginia State Capitol, also designed by Thomas Jefferson. Other estates belonging to the nation's forefathers, their relatives, and contemporaries include Scotchtown, near Richmond, Patrick Henry's plantation home; Kenmore, in Fredericksburg, built for George Washington's sister, Betty; and several 18th-century tobacco planters' plantations on the James River.

Natural Wonders   From the uninhabited Atlantic barrier islands and the Great Dismal Swamp to the impressive limestone formation known as the Natural Bridge, at Lexington, and the limestone caves of the Shenandoah Valley—Virginia boasts many natural attractions worth a visit. Some have been turned into commercial enterprises, but most are in their God-given state. The Blue Ridge Mountains are themselves a natural wonder.

Parks   Virginia literally is dotted with national and state parks, wildlife reserves, and recreation areas, beginning with Shenandoah National Park. Sandwiched between the Alleghenies and the Blue Ridge Mountains, it extends from Front Royal, 90 miles west of Washington, DC, to Rockfish Gap, about 90 miles west of Richmond. In addition, many of the mountain ridges flanking the Shenandoah Valley are managed as national forests, offering a wide range of outdoor activities, from picnicking to rock climbing.

Scenic Drives   Many of Virginia's major highways —I-81, which runs north-south in the western part of the state, and I-64, which cuts east-west across the center, for example—are scenic drives in their own right, but it's difficult to top the glorious views from the **Skyline Drive** and **Blue Ridge Parkway.** Actually one road, these two drives snake northward along the Blue Ridge some 400 miles from North Carolina's Great Smoky Mountains to Front Royal. Other scenic roads include the **Colonial Parkway** through Jamestown, Williamsburg, and Yorktown; the **George Washington Memorial Parkway** along the Potomac River from Arlington to Mount Vernon; and the **Chesapeake Bridge-Tunnel** across the mouth of Chesapeake Bay.

Wineries Wine has been made in Virginia since Jamestown days, and the Piedmont—especially around **Charlottesville** and **Middleburg**—is now home to about 40 commercial wineries. Many are open to the public and offer tastes of their produce.

EVENTS AND FESTIVALS

STATEWIDE

- **Historic Garden Week.** Gardens and grounds of more than 200 landmarks are open only during the last week in April. Contact Garden Club of Virginia, 112 E Franklin St, Richmond, VA 23219 (tel 804/644-7776).

TIDEWATER

- **International Azalea Festival,** Norfolk. Parades, ceremonies, crowning of queen, military displays in honor of NATO. Second and third weeks in April. Call 757/622-2312.
- **Seafood Festival,** Chincoteague. All-you-can-eat feast at Tom's Cove. First weekend in May. Advance tickets necessary from Eastern Shore Chamber of Commerce, Drawer R, Melfa, VA 23410 (tel 757/336-6161).
- **Harborfest,** Norfolk. Boat races, tall ships, military demonstrations, fireworks, partying at Town Point Park. First weekend in June. Call 757/627-5329.
- **Pony Swim and Auction,** Chincoteague. Famous roundup when local cowpokes herd wild ponies across Assateague Channel to Memorial Park. Last Wednesday in July. Call 757/336-6161.
- **Yorktown Day,** Yorktown. Celebrates Cornwallis' surrender in 1781, at Yorktown Battlefield. October 19. Call 757/898-3400.

NORTHERN VIRGINIA

- **Robert E Lee Birthday Celebration,** Alexandria and Arlington. Music, food, open houses at Lee's Boyhood Home, Alexandria, and at Arlington House, Arlington National Cemetery. January 19. Call 703/557-0613.
- **George Washington's Birthday,** Alexandria. Three days of Old Town parades, open house at Mount Vernon, banquet and costume ball at Gadsby's Tavern. Weekend preceding the third Monday in February. Call 703/838-4200. Other celebrations in Fredericksburg (tel 540/373-1776); George Washington's Birthplace National Monument (tel 804/224-1732); Mary Washington House (tel 540/373-1569); and Winchester (tel 540/662-6550).
- **Vintage Virginia Wine Festival,** Great Meadow Steeplechase Course, The Plains. Chance to taste the state's best vintages. First weekend in May. Call toll free 800/277-CORK.
- **Virginia Hunt Country Stable Tour,** Upperville. One of the few times private estates and horse farms are open to the public. Memorial Day weekend. Call 540/592-3711.
- **Memorial Day Service,** Arlington. The President lays a wreath on the Tomb of the Unknowns, Arlington National Cemetery. Last Monday in May. Call 202/475-0856.
- **Virginia Scottish Games,** Alexandria. Bagpipes and fiddles, Highland dancing and games, Scottish foods. Late July. Call 703/838-5005.

CENTRAL VIRGINIA

- **James Madison's Birthday,** Montpelier, Orange County. Ceremony and reception at Madison's home. March 16. Call 540/672-2728.
- **Patrick Henry Speech Reenactment,** Richmond. Hear "Give me liberty or give me death" at St John's Church, site of the Second Virginia Convention (1775). Sunday closest to March 23. Call 804/648-5015.
- **Thomas Jefferson's Birthday,** Charlottesville. Wreath laying, fife-and-drum corps, speeches at Monticello. April 13. Call 804/984-9822.
- **Dogwood Festival,** Charlottesville. Parade, queen's coronation, fireworks, fashion show, other events while the dogwoods bloom. Mid-April. Call 804/295-3141.
- **James River Bateau Festival,** Lynchburg to Richmond. A moving eight-day festival follows a boat race down the James River. Mid-June. Call 804/847-1811.
- **Ashlawn-Highland Summer Festival,** Charlottesville. President James Monroe's home hosts

opera, concerts, traditional bonfire. Late June to mid-August. Tickets at box office (tel 804/293-4500).

- **Virginia State Fair,** State Fairgrounds, Richmond. Agriculture exhibits and judging, carnival rides. Last week in September. Call 804/228-3200.

SHENANDOAH VALLEY

- **Highland Maple Festival,** Monterey. Celebrates rising of the sap with demonstrations, crafts, antique sale. Second and third weekends in March. Call 540/468-2550.
- **Virginia Horse Festival,** Lexington. Equestrian events, competitions, auctions, and art shows. Mid-April. Call 540/463-4300.
- **Shenandoah Apple Blossom Festival,** Winchester. Five days of celebrations kick off the valley's number one crop. Parade, beauty pageant, marathon, arts and craft shows. First week in May. Call 540/662-3863.
- **Shenandoah Valley Music Festival,** Orkney Springs. Jazz under the stars. Saturdays in July and August, Labor Day weekend. Call 540/459-3396.

SOUTHWEST BLUE RIDGE HIGHLANDS

- **Chautauqua Festival in the Park,** Wytheville. A week's worth of antiques, arts and crafts shows, music, and ballet. Mid-June. Call 540/223-3365.
- **Virginia Highlands Festival,** Abingdon. Appalachian Mountain culture on display, featuring musicians, artists, antiques, handcrafts. Late July. Call 540/676-2282 or toll free 800/435-3440.
- **Old Time Fiddlers' Convention,** Galax. Oldest and largest annual gathering of country musicians. Mid-August. Call 540/236-0668.

SPECTATOR SPORTS

Auto Racing   Stock-car and drag racing are big-time sports in Virginia, which has more than 25 race tracks and speedways. **Richmond International Raceway** (tel 804/345-7223) and **Martinsville Speedway** (tel 540/956-3151) host Winston Cup and Busch Grand National Series races. Hampton's **Langley Raceway** (tel 757/865-1992) holds NASCAR or Winston Cup races. **Bristol International Raceway** (tel 423/764-1161), on the Tennessee side of Bristol, has the world's fastest half-mile NASCAR track.

Baseball   Virginia doesn't have major league baseball, but two Class AAA teams vie for fans' affections: the **Norfolk Tides** (tel 757/622-2222) and the **Richmond Braves** (tel 804/359-4444 or toll free 800/849-4627). Three teams avidly compete in Class A: the **Salem Buccaneers** (tel 540/389-3333), the **Lynchburg Red Sox** (tel 804/528-1144), and the **Prince William Cannons,** who play near Woodbridge (tel 703/590-2311).

College Athletics   Several universities play intercollegiate football, basketball, and baseball schedules during the respective seasons. Leaders of the pack are the **University of Virginia Cavaliers** (or "Wahoos") in Charlottesville (for schedules and ticket information, call 804/924-8821 or toll free 800/542-8821 from within Virginia), and the **Virginia Tech Hokies** in Blacksburg (tel 540/231-6731 or toll free 800/828-3244).

Horse Racing   Steeplechase racing is the sport of kings in the Old Dominion. The biggest of these is the **Virginia Gold Cup,** at The Plains in early May (tel 540/347-2612 or toll free 800/69-RACES). Not far behind are the **Strawberry Hill Races,** at Richmond's Strawberry Hill Exposition & Convention Center in mid-April (tel 804/228-3200).

Ice Hockey   The minor league **Hampton Roads Admirals** play from October through March at the Norfolk Scope (tel 757/640-1212).

ACTIVITIES A TO Z

Bicycling   Scenic roads beckon bicyclists throughout Virginia, including all 214 miles of the **Blue Ridge Parkway** from Waynesboro south to the North Carolina line. The beautiful **Mount Vernon Trail,** 17 miles along the Potomac River from Arlington to the first president's home, is connected to the 184-mile towpath trail of the C&O Canal National Historical Park in Maryland and Washington, DC. The Boston-to-Florida East Coast Bicycle Trail continues another 253 miles south to the John H Kerr Reservoir on the North Carolina line. Other favorites are the 13-mile Colonial Parkway between Yorktown and Jamestown, 16 miles in Chincoteague National Wildlife Refuge, and the 57 miles in New River Trail State Park between Galax and Pulaski. Most main towns along the routes have bike rental shops.

Birdwatching   Both the Eastern Shore and Blue Ridge Mountains are major flyways for migratory birds. Hundreds of resident species can be found in several national parks and wildlife refuges, including the world-class Chincoteague National Wildlife Refuge.

Boating   The Atlantic Ocean, Chesapeake Bay, 15 major lakes, and rivers galore make boating a major activity. Marinas are numerous and hundreds of boat launching sites are available. For information about boating laws and regulations, contact the **Virginia Department of Game and Inland Fisheries,** 4010 W Broad St, Richmond, VA 23230 (tel 804/367-0939).

Camping   Campgrounds abound in Virginia's 21 national and 35 state parks, and the state has more than 150 private campgrounds and RV parks. For a list of state parks, contact the **Virginia Department of Conservation and Recreation,** 203 Governor St, Suite 302, Richmond, VA 23219 (tel 804/786-1712). For information about private facilities, write or call the **Virginia Campground Association,** 2101 Libbie Ave, Richmond, VA 23230 (tel 804/288-3065).

Canoeing   Rivers like the **Shenandoah, James, Maury,** and **New** offer slow-moving waters as well as Class IV mountain rapids. Several outfitters rent canoes (and inner tubes) and provide guides in Bentonville, Luray, Front Royal, and other towns along the South Fork of the Shenandoah. Other popular put-in spots are at Lexington and Scottsville on the James, and in Pembroke on the gorgeous New River, which cuts its way through the famous New River Gorge into West Virginia.

Cruising   Visitors can see Virginia from the water by taking a sightseeing cruise of Norfolk and Hampton harbors; by cruising down the Potomac from Alexandria to Mount Vernon; or down the James River from Richmond and Hopewell to the plantations lining the riverbank. Full-day cruises to unique Tangier Island leave from Reedville on the mainland side of the Chesapeake and from Onancock on the Eastern Shore.

Fishing   The state has rich saltwater fishing grounds, more than 250 species of freshwater fish, and 185 streams stocked with 850,000 trout annually. Licenses are required for both saltwater and freshwater fishing. For details contact the **Virginia Department of Game and Inland Fisheries,** 4010 W Broad St, Richmond, VA 23230 (tel 804/367-9369).

Golf   Duffers will find more than 130 golf courses, including courses that are considered among the best in America at four resorts—Williamsburg Inn and Kingsmill in Williamsburg, The Homestead in Hot Springs, and Wintergreen. For information about private courses, call the Golf Line of the **Virginia Resorts Association** (tel toll free 800/932-2259).

Hiking   Virginia has hundreds of miles of trails through its thousands of acres of parks, national forests, and recreation areas. Leading the list are the state's 450-plus miles of the winding, 2,100-mile-long **Appalachian Trail,** which follows the scenic ridges above the Blue Ridge Parkway and Skyline Drive. Entry points are at every road crossing.

SELECTED PARKS & RECREATION AREAS

- **Shenandoah National Park,** Rte 4, Box 348, Luray, VA 22835-9051 (tel 540/999-3500)
- **Assateague Island National Seashore,** Rte 175, Chincoteague, VA (tel 757/336-6161)
- **George Washington National Forest,** 101 N Main St, PO Box 233, Harrisonburg, VA 22801 (tel 540/564-8300)
- **Jefferson National Forest,** 5162 Valleypointe Pkwy, Roanoke, VA 24019 (tel toll free 800/446-9670)
- **Chincoteague National Wildlife Refuge,** 8259 Beach Rd, PO Box 62, Chincoteague, VA 23336 (tel 757/336-6122)
- **Great Dismal Swamp National Wildlife Refuge,** 3100 Desert Rd, PO Box 349, Suffolk, VA 23439 (tel 757/986-3705)
- **Bear Creek Lake State Park,** Rte 629, Cumberland, VA (tel 804/492-4410)
- **Douthat State Park,** Rte 1, Box 212, Millboro, VA 24460 (tel 703/862-7200)
- **Goshen Pass Natural Park,** Rte 39, Lexington, VA (tel 540/862-7200)
- **Grayson Highlands State Park,** Rte 2, Box 141, Mouth of Wilson, VA 24363 (tel 540/579-7092)
- **Lake Anna State Park,** Rte 601, Fredericksburg, VA (tel 540/854-5503)
- **Natural Tunnel State Park,** Rte 871, Weber City, VA (tel 540/940-2674)
- **Prince William Forest Park,** PO Box 209, Rte 619, Triangle, VA 22172 (tel 703/221-4706)
- **Seashore State Park and Natural Area,** 2500 Shore Dr, Virginia Beach, VA 23451 (tel 757/481-2131)
- **Westmoreland State Park,** Rte 1, Box 600, Montross, VA 22520 (tel 804/493-8821)

Horseback Riding Stables are especially numerous around Leesburg and Middleburg in the Hunt Country west of Washington, DC, and up and down the Shenandoah Valley, where Lexington's **Virginia Horse Center** (tel 540/463-4300) hosts horse-related functions all year. Riding is easily arranged throughout these areas.

Hunting Wild game includes squirrel, grouse, bear, deer, bobcat, fox, duck, goose, rabbit, pheasant, and quail. For information about licenses, seasons, and bag limits, contact the **Virginia Department of Game and Inland Fisheries,** 4010 W Broad St, Richmond, VA 23230 (tel 804/367-9369).

Shopping As would be expected in a state so deeply rooted in American history, almost every town and village in the Old Dominion has boutiques filled with colonial and Victorian-era antiques. Local handicrafts can be found in the Shenandoah Valley and in the southwest highlands, especially exquisite pottery. Discount shoppers will find a number of outlet centers throughout Virginia, all of them dwarfed by the 240 stores in Woodbridge's **Potomac Mills Mall** (tel 703/490-5948), the world's largest outlet center.

Skiing Virginia has four downhill skiing resorts: **Bryce Mountain** (tel 540/856-2122) in Bayse, **The Homestead** (tel 540/839-5500), **Massanutten** (tel 540/289-9441) near Harrisonburg, and **Wintergreen** (tel 804/325-2200).

Tennis Many hotels and resorts have courts for their guests' use, and most cities and towns maintain courts open to the public.

Water Sports Virginia Beach offers a wide range of water sports, from jet skiing and powerboat racing to snorkeling and scuba diving. Most resorts and hotels can help make arrangements.

Driving the State

Start	Winchester
Finish	Natural Bridge
Distance	175 miles
Time	2–4 days
Highlights	Rolling hills dotted with farms and apple orchards; magnificent underground caverns and a 215-foot-high natural bridge; historic small towns; Civil War battlefields and museums; graves of Robert E Lee and Stonewall Jackson; birthplace of Woodrow Wilson

Following the route of I-81 (one of America's most scenic interstate highways) and US 11 (the historic Valley Pike), this tour takes you the length of Virginia's lovely Shenandoah Valley, whose Shawnee name means "Daughter of the Stars." The two highways go up and down over hill and dale through some of the region's most beautiful countryside. As a backdrop, the gentle folds of the Blue Ridge Mountains rise to the east of the Valley; to the west begin the rugged Allegheny Mountains. At the end of the tour, US 11 actually crosses the awesome Natural Bridge, where George Washington carved his initials. In addition to this wonder, you'll visit several underground caverns, and detour into the primordial woodlands of Shenandoah National Park and the George Washington National Forest. As the "Breadbasket of the Confederacy," the Valley was fought over throughout the Civil War, and several battlefields and museums still remind the traveler of that bloody conflict.

Atop the Blue Ridge Mountains to the east run two of America's premier scenic roads: The **Skyline Drive** and the **Blue Ridge Parkway.** A multitude of sharp curves and a strictly enforced 45-mph speed limit translate into slow-going traffic, but the mountain vistas make a detour on either road worth the extra time.

For additional information on accommodations, restaurants, and attractions in the region covered by the tour, look under specific cities in the listings portion of this book.

I-81, US 11, US 50, US 340, US 522, and VA 7 all give easy access to the first stop:

1. **Winchester,** the Valley's oldest town and its unofficial "Apple Capital." Settled in 1732 by Quakers and Germans, Winchester was twice George Washington's headquarters, first when he surveyed the area and later when he commanded Virginia's militia during the French and Indian Wars. You'll want to visit the small stone building where Washington had his office, at W Cork and S Braddock Sts (tel 540/662-4412). Winchester changed hands 70 times during the Civil War. When Confederate Gen Thomas J "Stonewall" Jackson was in town, he made his headquarters 5 blocks north of Washington's at 415 N Braddock St (tel 540/667-3242).

Begin your tour of these and other historic attractions by taking exit 313 off I-81 and following the signs to the **Winchester-Frederick County Visitor Center,** 1360 S Pleasant Valley Rd (tel 540/662-4135). It's on the grounds of **Abram's Delight,** Winchester's oldest home, built of native limestone in 1754 on an attractive site by a lake. Or you can go straight to the **Old Town Welcome Center,** N Cameron and Boscawen Sts (tel 540/722-6367), in the heart of the historic district. Both centers have walking-tour brochures and are open daily 9am–5pm. (One walking tour visits youthful haunts of country music legend Patsy Cline, a Winchester native whose grave is south of town on VA 644 just west of US 522.)

From Winchester, both I-81 and US 11 go 12 miles "up" the Valley (that is, south) to:

2. **Middletown,** a small roadside village noted for its antique shops; the **Wayside Theater,** Main St (tel 540/869-1776), which presents excellent theatrical productions from the end of May to mid-October; and **Belle Grove Plantation** (tel 540/869-2028), a late 18th-century graystone manor house 2 miles south of town off US 11. Now a National Trust museum, Belle Grove was built between 1794 and 1797 by Major Issac Hite, who relied on his brother-in-law, Thomas Jefferson, for architectural advice. The building has Palladian-style front win-

Take a Break

You can sample more Colonial charm at the **Wayside Inn** (tel 540/869-1797), on US 11 in the heart of Middletown. Travelers have been taking meals and renting rooms at this establishment since 1797. Today, the beautifully restored dining room serves fine traditional Virginian cuisine, some from recipes handed down since Jeffersonian times. Lunch entrees cost $6–$11; dinner main courses cost $14–$23.

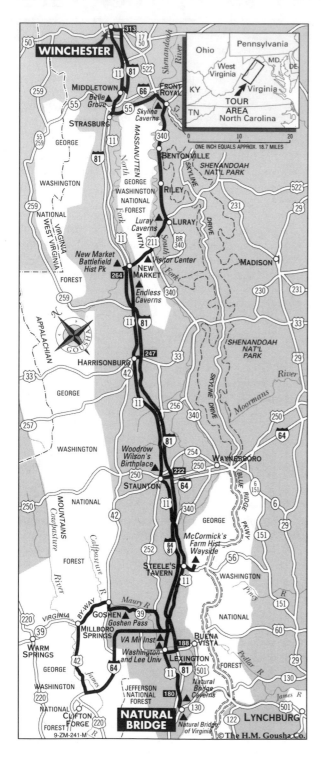

During the Civil War, Union Gen Philip Sheridan's troops were camped on the open fields around the house when Confederate forces under General Jubal Early staged a surprise attack. The Rebels initially won the Battle of Cedar Creek, but Sheridan rallied his troops and turned defeat into victory. There's a small battlefield visitors center on the road to the plantation.

From Belle Grove, drive 3 miles south on US 11 until you reach:

3. **Strasburg,** where children will enjoy the hands-on Civil War museum at **Hupps Hill Battlefield Park** (tel 540/465-5884), at the north end of town. The number of antique shops around Strasburg's stoplight demonstrate why this little town is known as the "Antique Capital of Virginia." Turn left at the light and drive a block east on VA 55 to the **Strasburg Museum** (tel 540/465-3175) in the old railroad station, where Stonewall Jackson brought his stolen Union locomotives after the Great Train Raid on Martinsburg, West Virginia.

Head east from Strasburg on VA 55. Ahead of you looms **Massanutten Mountain,** a long ridge which cuts the Shenandoah Valley into two parts. I-81 and US 11 run down the west side. You'll drive around the north end for 11 miles to US 340. Turn right here and drive south along a commercial strip full of restaurants into:

4. **Front Royal,** where the notorious Confederate spy Belle Boyd pried secrets from her Union lovers. Turn left on Main St at the **Warren County Court House** and drive 3 blocks east to the local **Visitors Center** (tel 540/635-3185) in the old railroad station. Get a walking-tour map here and explore the **Belle Boyd Cottage,** 101 Chester St (tel 540/636-1446). Other attractions include the **Warren Rifles Confederate Museum,** 95 Chester St (tel 540/636-6982), featuring memorabilia from the War Between the States. Trolley tours operate from the visitors center during warm weather.

The northern entrance to the Skyline Drive and **Shenandoah National Park** is on US 340, just south of town. One mile beyond the entrance are **Skyline Caverns** (tel 540/635-4545 or toll free 800/296-4545), where an underground waterfall plummets 37 feet into a trout stream. The cave also is noted for rare, flower-like anthodite formations.

From the caverns, drive south on US 340 (Stonewall Jackson Memorial Hwy), which parallels the winding South Fork of the Shenandoah River and runs through the villages of **Bentonville, Compton,** and **Riley.** Private companies in each of these villages rent canoes and inner tubes for river excursions. Follow this scenic road 24 miles south to:

dows and columns, and the interior is furnished with period antiques.

5. **Luray,** best known for **Luray Caverns** (tel 540/743-6551), Virginia's largest underground wonderland. Tourists have been visiting the caverns since they were discovered in 1878, making Luray one of the state's most popular attractions. Paved walkways lead down to such cavernous wonders as the **Great Stalactite Pipe Organ,** which can actually play music. Outside the cavern stands a carillon and the **Car and Carriage Caravan,** a fine collection of antique automobiles and carriages.

The caverns are 2 miles west of Luray on the US 211 Bypass, upon which you'll continue up and over Massanutten Mountain for 15 miles. This is the most scenic part of the tour, so stop at the overlooks for views back across the Valley. At the top of New Market Pass sits the **visitors center** (tel 540/564-8300) of **George Washington National Forest.** From here, proceed on down the mountain's west side to:

6. **New Market,** where the entire student body of Virginia Military Institute (VMI) marched up from Lexington to help defeat a larger Union force on May 15, 1864. Turn right just west of I-81 and drive to the end of the service road to the **New Market Battlefield Historical Park** (tel 540/740-3101). Maintained by VMI, the battlefield and its Hall of Valor Civil War Museum are dedicated to the Civil War students and all other young men who have served their country. (On the way to the park, you'll pass a cavalry museum and the New Market Battlefield Military Museum; neither is part of the VMI operation.) The Shenandoah Valley Travel Association has a **tourist information office** (tel 540/740-3132) opposite the Battlefield Park turnoff; it has a free reservations phone, in case you decide to stay overnight in the area.

Take a Break

New Market has the usual collection of fast food restaurants at its I-81 interchange, but for good home cooking, visit the **Southern Kitchen** (tel 540/740-3514), on US 11 less than ½ mile south of the stoplight. Since 1955, Ruby Newland and family have been serving lightly breaded fried chicken and other local fare. Her establishment has a 1950s small-town ambience, including a soda fountain in one dining room. Main courses cost $6–$12.

For another look underground, proceed 3 miles south on US 11 to **Endless Caverns** (tel 540/740-3993, or 800/544-CAVE). As far as anyone knows, this cave really is endless; you'll see stalactites, stalagmites, giant columns, and limestone pendants. From here, keep driving 18 miles south on either I-81 or US 11 to **Harrisonburg,** an agricultural center, home of James Madison University, and a good stopping place for a meal or an overnight stay. If you choose not to rest here, push on south another 25 miles to:

7. **Staunton,** pronounced "STAN-ton" by the locals, where President Woodrow Wilson was born in 1856 in the Presbyterian Manse. His minister-father soon moved to a church in Georgia, but Staunton still claims the World War I leader as its own. **Woodrow Wilson's Birthplace,** Coalter and Frederick Sts (tel 540/885-0897), a handsome Greek Revival building, is now a national shrine and the local welcome center. A next-door museum has exhibits on Wilson's life.

Across the street is **Mary Baldwin College,** a noted "finishing" school for girls. Walking-tour maps for Staunton's Victorian downtown are available at Wilson's Birthplace and at the **Staunton/Augusta County Travel Information Office** (tel 540/332-3972), near exit 222 off I-81 (follow US 250 west and the tourist information signs).

Also worth a visit is the nearby **Museum of American Frontier Culture,** also off US 250 west of exit 222 (tel 540/332-7850). This living museum contains working 19th-century farms, one local and one each from England, Northern Ireland, and Germany. Staff members in period costumes plant fields and tend livestock.

Staunton offers a good place for an overnight rest. The town has good chain motels near exit 222 off I-81 (near the tourist information office and the Museum of American Frontier Culture). Two properties in town have their own special ambiance: The **Belle Grae Inn** (515 W Frederick St), with rooms in a well-restored Victorian house; and the European-style **Frederick House** at 28 N New St.

From Staunton, continue south on I-81 or US 11 for 16 miles to Steele's Tavern. Turn left there on VA 606 and drive a mile east to:

8. **McCormick's Farm Historic Wayside** (tel 540/377-2255), where Cyrus McCormick revolutionized farming by building the first effective grain reaper in 1831. The farm's log blacksmith shop and grist mill are now a museum where you can see one of Cyrus' first machines. The farm is open daily April–December, 9am–5pm; January–March, Monday–Friday 9am–5pm.

Return to US 11 or I-81 and head south 16 miles to:

9. **Lexington,** among the most historic and photogenic towns in the Valley, with a lovingly restored downtown, Washington and Lee (W&L) University, and the Virginia Military Institute (VMI). You'll have much to see in this resting place of generals Stonewall Jackson, Robert E Lee, and George C Marshall—and Jackson's and Lee's horses. Begin at the **Lexington Visitors Center,** 102 E Washington St (tel 540/463-3777), which provides an excellent brochure with walking and driving tour maps. Be sure to visit the **Stonewall Jackson House,** 8 E Washington St (tel 540/463-2552), where the Confederate hero lived while teaching philosophy at VMI. The home features many of his possessions and has photographs and a slide show about Jackson's residency here. The **Virginia Military Institute Museum** in Jackson Memorial Hall, VMI Campus (tel 540/464-7232), facing VMI's fabled Parade Ground, contains Jackson's stuffed horse and the bullet-pierced raincoat he was wearing the night his own men accidentally shot him at Chancellorsville. The VMI campus also is home to the **George C Marshall Museum and Library** (tel 540/463-2552), named in honor of the 1906 alumnus who became the Army's Chief of Staff during World War II and who, as Secretary of State, won the Nobel Peace Prize for creating the Marshall Plan.

From the end of the Civil War until his death in 1870, General Robert E Lee served as president of Washington and Lee University, which adjoins VMI (the brick sidewalks belong to VMI; the concrete ones to Washington and Lee). Lee designed the president's house on campus and supervised the building of the Victorian-Gothic **Lee Chapel** (tel 540/463-8768), his burial place and shrine. The chapel, which today is used for concerts and other events, contains both Edward Valentine's white marble statue of Lee and Charles Wilson Peale's portrait of George Washington. Lee's office in the lower level of the building has been preserved as a museum, and his famous horse Traveller is buried in a plot outside.

From Lexington, a gorgeous 60-mile side trip follows the Virginia By-Way (VA 39) northwest from Lexington through the Goshen Pass, where the Maury River cuts an 1,800-foot-deep gorge through the Allegheny Mountains. Return via VA 42 and I-64, certainly one of the most beautiful interstate highways anywhere.

From Lexington, drive 12 miles south on US 11, where the highway actually crosses:

10. **Natural Bridge** (tel 540/291-2121 or toll free 800/533-1410), a 215-foot-tall limestone arch over Cedar Creek. Some people consider this 90-foot-long structure to be one of the world's greatest natural wonders. George Washington surveyed the property in the mid-1700s and carved his initials on the arch, and Thomas Jefferson bought it in 1774. Even though the bridge is a major commercial tourist attraction today, it is still fascinating to walk along the creek under the soaring bridge and see Washington's initials.

Also here are the **Natural Bridge Zoo** and the **Natural Bridge Wax Museum,** which has more than 100 life-size figures of leading characters in the area's history and folklore. And you can make a final foray underground into **Natural Bridge Caverns.** The Natural Bridge area has a restaurant and lodging facilities on the premises.

From Natural Bridge, both I-81 and US 11 go 39 miles south to Roanoke, the largest city in western Virginia and the gateway to the state's ruggedly beautiful Southwest Highlands. Or you can backtrack to Lexington and take I-64 east to Charlottesville and Richmond, or west to Beckley and the beginning of the driving tour "New River Gorge to the Highlands" (see the West Virginia chapter).

Driving the State

Start	Richmond
Finish	Yorktown
Distance	100 miles
Time	1–5 days
Highlights	Civil War battlefields; antebellum plantations along the scenic James River; tributes to early American history at Jamestown, Williamsburg, and Yorktown; amusement parks

Following the so-called Plantation Route (VA 5) and the aptly named Colonial Parkway, this tour explores the peninsula between the James and York Rivers where the history of English-speaking America began (at Jamestown) and later flourished (in Williamsburg). Wealthy colonial landowners used their tobacco profits to build grand manor houses on the James River. George Washington won the American Revolution by trapping Lord Cornwallis at Yorktown in 1781. And during the Civil War, Union General George McClellan led a bloody but unsuccessful campaign up this peninsula.

The major plantations between Richmond and Jamestown can be seen in one day. Some plantations and farms have small bed-and-breakfast operations, but most travelers stay in Richmond or Williamsburg, each of which demands at least a day's visit.

For additional information on accommodations, restaurants, and attractions in the region covered by the tour, look under specific cities in the listings portion of this book.

I-95, I-64, US 1, and US 301 all converge at:

1. **Richmond,** Virginia's state capital since 1780, capital of the Confederacy from 1861-1865, and today a blend of historic neighborhoods, modern downtown high-rises, and sprawling suburban industrial complexes. Begin your visit at the **Metro Richmond Visitors Center,** 1710 Robin Hood Rd (tel 804/782-2777), in an old railway station opposite The Diamond baseball stadium (near exit 78 off I-95). Children can climb aboard a steam engine and red caboose while adults gather a wealth of information about the city.

   From the visitors center, proceed to such sights as the **State Capitol,** 9th and Grace Sts (tel 804/358-4901), designed in the Classical Revival style by Thomas Jefferson; the 1741 **St John's Church,** 2401 E Broad St (tel 804/648-5015); **John Marshall House,** 818 E Marshall St (tel 804/648-7998), the restored home of a notable American patriot

and US chief justice from 1801–1835; the **Museum of the Confederacy,** 1201 E Clay St (tel 804/649-1861), with the largest Confederate collection in the country, most of it contributed by veterans; the lovely **Monument Avenue** and its median-strip statues to Civil War heroes; the **Edgar Allen Poe Museum,** 1914–1916 E Main St (tel 804/648-5523), which documents the poet's life; and the **Virginia Museum of Fine Arts,** The Boulevard and Grove Ave (tel 804/367-0844), with impressive collections of art nouveau, art deco, 19th- and 20th-century French paintings, contemporary American art, and works from India, Tibet, and Nepal.

Begin your driving tour at **Chimborazo Park,** 3315 E Broad St, in the historic Church Hill residential neighborhood. During the Civil War, the now-vacant fields in the park were the site of a hospital that treated some 76,000 Confederate wounded. The red brick building is the visitors center for the **Richmond Battlefield National Park** (tel 804/226-1981). Inside you'll find displays dealing with the Civil War fighting that raged around Richmond, and maps plotting a 60-mile driving tour through the scattered battlefields on the eastern side of the city.

From the visitors center, turn left on Broad St and proceed west to 25th St, observing on the corner **St John's Church,** the white clapboard structure where Patrick Henry gave his "Liberty or Death" speech. Turn left on 25th St, go 3 blocks south, and turn left (east) on Main St (VA 5). Keep going east on VA 5, bearing right at the fork leading under the railroad trestle (this Y-intersection is not well marked). You may be surprised at how quickly this heavily industrial part of town ends and beautiful rural countryside begins.

Continue east 6 miles to Battlefield Park Rd. If you aren't a Civil War buff, keep going straight on VA 5 to the third stop. But if you are, turn right into:

2. **Fort Harrison,** the largest single section of the Richmond Battlefield National Park. The crape myrtle–fringed road runs 6½ miles past the remains of Forts Gilmer, Gregg, Johnson, Harrison, and Hoke—earthwork structures that were built as part of the city's Confederate defense. Union forces captured Fort Harrison in September 1864, but the armies then settled down into trench warfare until the war ended six months later. Fort Harrison has its own small visitors center, which is open daily

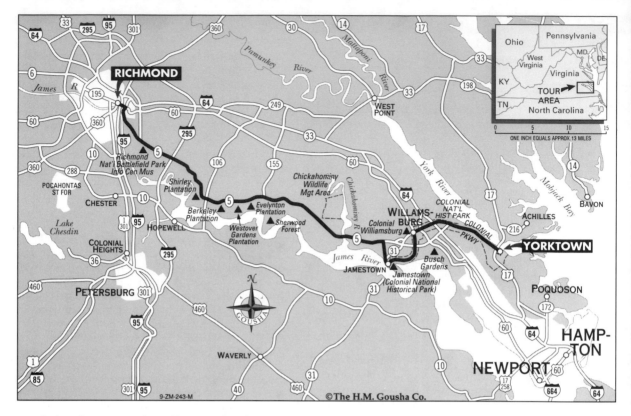

during the summer 9am–5pm, weekends only during spring and fall. From here, continue south to Fort Hoke, where Hoke-Brady Rd forks to the left and ends at Union-built Fort Brady overlooking the James River.

From Fort Brady, backtrack 1 mile and turn right on Kingsland Rd (ignoring the signs for VA 5 and Richmond) and drive 5 miles east through forests and fields until it dead-ends at VA 5, known here as New Market Rd. There is no road sign, but turn right and head east 8½ miles to VA 608. Turn right there and follow the signs to:

3. Shirley Plantation, Charles City (tel 804/829-5121), founded in 1613 as Virginia's first plantation and home of the Carter-Lee family since its square brick manor house was built on a riverside knoll in 1724. Noted for its hanging staircase, the mansion is where Anne Hill Carter married Revolutionary War hero Henry "Lighthorse Harry" Lee. (As a youth, their son Robert E Lee used to play here while visiting his grandfather.) Open daily, except Christmas, from 9am–5pm.

From Shirley, backtrack to VA 5, turn right, and drive 3 miles east to the signs for:

4. Berkeley Plantation, Charles City (tel 804/829-6018), where a small party of settlers came ashore

in 1619 and promptly gave thanks for their safe journey from England. Despite the Pilgrims of Massachusetts getting all the credit, this group actually celebrated the first Thanksgiving in America, and the event is duly commemorated annually on the first Sunday in November. The Harrison family bought the Berkeley land in 1691 and in 1726 built the Georgian-style mansion, which belonged to Benjamin Harrison V, who signed the Declaration of Independence and whose son and grandson, William Henry Harrison and Benjamin Harrison, both served as president of the United States. Benedict Arnold's British troops sacked the plantation during the American Revolution, and General George McClellan made it one of his headquarters during the Peninsula Campaign of 1862. Open daily, except Christmas Day, 8am–5pm.

After you leave Berkeley, turn right on the narrow dirt road and drive 2 miles south to **Westover Plantation** (tel 804/829-2882), whose Georgian manor house was built in the 1730s by William Byrd II. His many descendants have gone on to make names for themselves as governors, senators, and explorers. Of all the James River plantations, Westover makes best use of its waterfront location and enjoys a great river view. The house is open only during Historic Garden Week in late April, but you can tour the classical gardens daily, except Christmas, 9am–6pm. Leave your $2 admission in an honor box by the brick gate next to the river.

Take a Break

Westover's owners have turned one of their outbuildings into the **Coach House Tavern** (tel 804/829-6003), a Colonial-style eatery with panel windows looking out to the manor house gardens. In keeping with tradition, the menu offers such Virginia fare as pork barbecue, country ham, and crab cakes. Lunch main courses cost $5–$11. Open daily for lunch only, except Christmas, 11:30am–3pm.

Now drive back to VA 5, turn right and continue east 1½ miles to **Westover Church,** where Captain William Perry, who died in 1637, is buried within the riverside grounds. His tombstone is America's third-oldest grave marker. The church itself was constructed in the 1730s. Another ½ mile east on VA 5 brings us to:

5. **Evelynton Plantation** (tel 804/829-5075), which William Byrd II gave as a dowry for his daughter Evelyn, who is believed to have died of a broken heart when he refused permission for her to marry the man she loved. She is buried at Westover Church, but some say her ghost still roams this adjacent property. The plantation was bought in 1847 by Edward Ruffin Jr, son of the man who fired the first shot on Fort Sumter, SC, to begin the Civil War. The original mansion was burned during a Civil War skirmish. The present Colonial Revival structure dates back to 1935, but it looks as if it were built two centuries earlier. The house and boxwood gardens are open daily (except Christmas, Thanksgiving, and New Year's Day), 9am–5pm.

Take a Break

Other than the Coach House Tavern at Berkeley Plantation, your best bet for a meal in these parts is the pleasant **Indian Fields Tavern** (tel 804/ 829-5004), in a restored Victorian-era farmhouse 2½ miles east of Evelynton on VA 5. Emphasis is on local ham, pork sausage, and crab cakes, with scrumptious sandwiches offered at lunch. Lunch entrees cost $6–$12; dinner main courses, $15–$22.

From Indian Fields Tavern, drive 5½ miles east on VA 5 to the last of our plantation stops:

6. **Sherwood Forest** (tel 804/829-5377), home of President John Tyler, the nation's 10th vice-president who succeeded to the White House in 1841 upon the death of his neighbor, President William Henry Harrison. The original part of this long, clapboard house was built in 1660, but it was expanded over the years until reaching the length of a football field. Although not on the water, it is the only James River plantation with its own ballroom, and it contains a remarkable collection of Tyler family memorabilia. The grounds are open daily 9am–5pm; house tours are by appointment only.

From Sherwood Forest, continue 14½ miles east on VA 5, crossing the Chickahominy River to VA 614 (Grennsprings Rd). Turn right and make your way south 2 miles to a traffic light at VA 31. Go straight through the light into the major tourist attraction of:

7. **Jamestown,** which today consists of two historical parks commemorating North America's first permanent English-speaking settlement, established here in 1607. The first park is **Jamestown Settlement** (tel 757/253-4838), where you will see recreations of **Powhatan Indian Village,** with many exhibits dealing with Native American culture and technology in 17th-century coastal Virginia; **James Fort,** built by Captain John Smith and his colonists in 1607; and the three cramped ships that transported the colonists from England. A pavilion contains actual artifacts from that era. Costumed staff members provide information about the village, fort, and ships. The settlement is open daily, except Christmas and New Year's Day, 9am–5pm.

The other place to visit here is the Jamestown portion of **Colonial National Historical Park** (tel 757/229-1773). This national park is on the actual 17th-century "James Cittie" settlement location. Although little is left other than some excavated foundations and part of a brick church tower, there is a 1907 reconstruction of **Memorial Church,** site of America's first elected assembly, the House of Burgesses. Don't miss the **Glasshouse,** where costumed staff members make glass just as the colonists did. Walking trails wander through the old settlement site, and a 5-mile drive loops through the pitch and tar swamp whose mosquitoes made life miserable for the colonists. The park is open daily during the summer 8:30am–5:30pm; during spring and fall, until 5pm; and during the winter; until 4:30pm. Admission is $8 per vehicle, $2 per biker or pedestrian.

From Jamestown, take the Colonial Pkwy for 9 miles, first along the James River's scenic banks and then north until you go through a tunnel. On the north side, take a left around the traffic circle to the visitors center of:

8. **Colonial Williamsburg,** the beautifully restored old capital with 88 original buildings and more than 500 structures that have been painstakingly rebuilt on their 18th-century foundations. Here you can visit the **Capitol** building, the **Governor's Palace,** taverns, houses, a hospital, and galleries. A number of 18th-century craft demonstrations are offered in the historic area, including cabinetmaking, silversmithing, printing, wigmaking, and candlemaking. Staff members in period costumes actually reenact life as it was during the 1700s, and they even speak the English of that day. Cars aren't allowed in the historic area, but shuttle buses leave every few minutes from the **visitor center** (tel 757/220-7645), where you can get booklets and maps, watch an introductory film, and buy tickets to see the historic area.

A few attractions near Williamsburg are worth a visit, starting with **Busch Gardens,** off US 60 about 3 miles east of the historic district (tel 757/253-3350). This 360-acre amusement park has rides and shows amid reproductions of 17th-century hamlets. **Water Country USA,** off VA 199 northeast of town (tel 757/229-9300), is a water-oriented theme park with 40 acres of man-made attractions such as a wave pool, rapids, and an Olympic-size swimming pool. And if you're "born to shop," you can head for **Williamsburg Pottery Factory** (tel 757/564-3326) or the huge collection of outlet shops 5 miles west of town on Richmond Rd (US 60).

When you've had a thorough look around Williamsburg, get back on the Colonial Pkwy and drive 11½ miles north to:

9. **Yorktown,** where George Washington defeated Lord Cornwallis in 1781 and for all practical purposes won the American Revolution. Follow the signs to the **Yorktown Victory Center** (tel 757/887-1776), where you can learn about the siege that led to Cornwallis's surrender. An excellent 28-minute film follows the American and French armies' routes to Yorktown, and costumed guides explain what 18th-century life was like on a farm and in the Continental Army camp outside. Open daily, except Christmas and New Year's Day, 9am–5pm.

From the Victory Center, turn right and drive downhill along Water St, enjoying the view of the York River. Turn right on Read St and drive uphill to a left on Ballard St, then a left at the sign for the National Park. That will take you to the National Park Service's **visitor center** (tel 757/898-3400), the starting point for touring the battlefields, which is open daily 8:30am–sunset. A museum displays Washington's actual sleeping tent and many other artifacts from the time of his victory. Get a visitor's guide with maps and set out on the 7-mile Battlefield Route and the 10-mile Encampment Route. Be prepared to stop along these gorgeous drives to explore particular points of interest, such as the **Grand French Battery,** the early 18th-century **Moore House,** and **Surrender Field.**

Other sights may be viewed in town, including several historic homes; the restored **Swan Tavern,** Main and Ballard Sts (tel 757/898-3033), with an antiques shop; and the 98-foot marble **Victory Monument,** authorized by Congress in 1781 but not actually built until a century later.

From Yorktown, US 17 leads south to Newport News, where it intersects with I-64. Go east to Norfolk and Virginia Beach, or west to return to Richmond.

Virginia Listings

Abingdon

Historic town settled in the 1760s in southwest Blue Ridge Highlands. Seat of Washington County. **Information:** Washington County Chamber of Commerce, 179 E Main St, Abingdon, 24210 (tel 540/628-8141).

HOTEL 🏨

▆▆▆▆ Camberley's Martha Washington Inn
150 W Main St, 24210; tel 540/628-3160 or toll free 800/555-8000; fax 540/628-7652. Exit 17 off I-81. A mid-1980s restoration turned this 1832 mansion and former college into a magnificent hotel with elegant antique furnishings. Many parlors on the lobby floor, which opens to verandas with rocking chairs. Each floor also has a veranda. **Rooms:** 61 rms and stes. Executive level. CI 3pm/CO 11am. Nonsmoking rms avail. Individually furnished units. **Amenities:** 🛏 ⚱ A/C, cable TV. Some units w/fireplaces, some w/whirlpools. Free sparkling water in rooms. **Services:** ✕ ☞ VP ⌆ ⌇ Twice-daily maid svce, babysitting. Southern hospitality prevails. Bellhop brings complimentary afternoon tea to rooms. **Facilities:** ⅙ 2 restaurants (lunch and dinner only), 1 bar. Reduced rates at nearby fitness center. **Rates (CP):** $135–$270 S or D; $170–$425 ste. Extra person $10. Children under age 12 stay free. Min stay special events. MAP rates avail. Parking: Outdoor, free. AE, CB, DC, DISC, MC, V.

MOTELS

▆▆ Alpine Motel
882 E Main St, PO Box 615, 24210; tel 540/628-3178; fax 540/628-4247. Exit 19 off I-81. Large, well-kept grounds on a hill with views of the highlands combine with numerous nearby restaurants and a short two-mile drive to the Barter Theater to make this a desirable spot. **Rooms:** 19 rms. CI noon/CO 11am. Nonsmoking rms avail. **Amenities:** 🛏 ⚱ A/C, cable TV, dataport. Local calls free. **Services:** ⌇ Copy, fax, notary services available. **Facilities:** ⅙ Playground. Hiking and biking nearby (within three miles). **Rates:** Peak (Apr–Nov) $36–$47 S or D. Extra person $4. Children under age 12 stay free. Min stay special events. Lower rates off-season. Parking: Outdoor, free. Senior discounts avail, golf packages avail. AE, DISC, MC, V.

▆▆ Comfort Inn Abingdon
170 Jonasboro Rd, PO Box 2223, 24210; tel 540/676-2222 or toll free 800/228-5150; fax 540/676-2222 ext 307. Exit 14 off I-81. A modern, well-furnished chain motel just five minutes from Abingdon's historic district. **Rooms:** 80 rms. CI 2pm/CO noon. Nonsmoking rms avail. Traditional decor is well suited to this historic area. **Amenities:** 🛏 ⚱ A/C, cable TV w/movies. **Services:** ⌆ ⌇ **Facilities:** 🏊 ⅙ **Rates (CP):** Peak (Apr–Oct) $45–$70 S; $50–$80 D. Extra person $10. Children under age 18 stay free. Min stay special events. Lower rates off-season. Parking: Outdoor, free. AE, DC, DISC, JCB, MC, V.

▆▆ Holiday Inn Express
940 E Main St, 24210; tel 540/676-2829 or toll free 800/465-4329; fax 540/676-2605. Exit 19 off I-81. One of the top representatives of its chain, this modern facility is close to historic district and numerous restaurants. Large lobby has TV and comfortable seating. **Rooms:** 80 rms and stes. Executive level. CI 2pm/CO 11am. Nonsmoking rms avail. Exceptionally well-kept rooms are done in soothing pastels. **Amenities:** 🛏 ⚱ 📺 A/C, cable TV w/movies. Some units w/whirlpools. Some have refrigerators. **Services:** ⌆ ⌇ **Facilities:** 🏊 🍴 ⅙ Washer/dryer. **Rates (CP):** Peak (Apr–Nov) $49–$54 S; $54–$59 D; $80–$85 ste. Extra person $5. Children under age 19 stay free. Lower rates off-season. Parking: Outdoor, free. AE, CB, DC, DISC, JCB, MC, V.

RESTAURANTS 🍴

★ Starving Artist Cafe
In Depot Sq, 134 Wall St; tel 540/628-8445. Exit 17 off I-81. Turn left on Main St, then left onto Wall St. **Eclectic.** As befits the name, rotating art exhibits adorn the walls of this informal cafe. Traditional fare includes house-specialty Maryland-style crab cakes, plus Cajun prime rib and vegetarian entrees. Lunch features sandwiches named for artists and authors. **FYI:** Reservations not accepted. Children's menu. Beer and wine only. **Open:** Lunch Mon 11am–2pm, Tues–Sat 11am–3pm; dinner Tues–Sat 5–9pm. Closed 1st week in September. **Prices:** Main courses $15–$18. AE, MC, V. 🍴

$ The Tavern
222 E Main St; tel 540/628-1118. Exit 17 off I-81. Turn right at Main St. **International/Vegetarian.** Built in 1779, this faithfully restored tavern with exposed beams, wooden tables, and plank floors provides an intimate ambience as well as a sense of community. Patio and second-floor porch have outside seating overlooking gardens. Chef prepares many traditional meals in untraditional manner and is willing to depart from menu on request. Aroma of smoking meat lures Saturday lunch clientele back for dinner. After-dinner drinks sipped by fire. Reservations taken in two-hour slots. **FYI:** Reservations recommended. Children's menu. **Open:** Daily 11am–10pm. **Prices:** Main courses $12–$20. AE, DISC, MC, V. 🍴🏛🖼♿

Alexandria

See also Mount Vernon, Springfield

Just south of Washington, DC, on the Potomac River. Settled in the early 18th century, the city maintains its historic flavor with an abundance of restored sites, many associated with George Washington. **Information:** Alexandria Convention and Visitors Bureau, 221 King St, Alexandria, 22314 (tel 703/838-4683)

HOTELS 🏨

☰☰☰ Best Western Old Colony
625 1st St, at N Washington St, 22314 (Old Town); tel 703/548-6300 or toll free 800/528-1234; fax 703/684-7782. Exit 1 off I-95. Follow US 1 north. Formerly part of a larger property, this older hotel has been remodeled and is quite attractive and pleasant. **Rooms:** 171 rms and stes. CI 3pm/CO noon. No smoking. Rooms are larger than average, but baths are cramped. Some rooms are in adjacent Conference Center. **Amenities:** 📺❄🗄 A/C, cable TV w/movies. Some units w/terraces, some w/whirlpools. Refrigerators available for a fee. Some rooms have dataports. **Services:** ✕🚐🖼🛎 Complimentary hors d'oeuvres in lounge Monday to Friday 5–7pm. **Facilities:** 📷🏋🏊♿ 1 restaurant, 1 bar (w/entertainment), games rm, spa, sauna, whirlpool. Nicely appointed, dark-wood bar and restaurant off lobby. Gazebo on rooftop available for meetings or lounging. Shares many facilitites with the Holiday Inn next door. **Rates:** Peak (Mar–Apr/Sept–Oct) $129 S; $139 D; $159–$179 ste. Extra person $10. Children under age 17 stay free. Lower rates off-season. Parking: Indoor/outdoor, free. Weekend packages avail. AE, DC, DISC, MC, V.

☰☰ Comfort Inn Landmark
6254 Duke St, 22312; tel 703/642-3422 or toll free 800/435-6868; fax 703/642-3422. Exit 3B off I-395. This well-maintained hotel is located near several large shopping centers. **Rooms:** 148 rms. CI 2pm/CO noon. No smoking. Some king-bed rooms have easy chairs. **Amenities:** 📺🗄 A/C,

cable TV w/movies. Some units w/whirlpools. **Services:** 🖼🛎 Car-rental desk. Free van to Van Dorn Metro station. **Facilities:** 📷🏊♿ 1 restaurant, 1 bar. Restaurant serves breakfast and dinner Monday to Saturday, breakfast only Sunday. **Rates (CP):** Peak (Apr–June) $60 S; $66 D. Extra person $6. Children under age 12 stay free. Lower rates off-season. Parking: Outdoor, free. AE, CB, DC, DISC, MC, V.

☰☰☰ Courtyard by Marriott
2700 Eisenhower Ave, 22314; tel 703/329-2323 or toll free 800/428-1105; fax 703/329-2323. Exit 2 off I-95. The courtyard is missing at this mid-rise hotel, but clubby public rooms with bright wood paneling lend a nice ambience. Essentially a business travelers' establishment. Located near a Metro station in a commercial office park. **Rooms:** 176 rms and stes. CI 3pm/CO 1pm. Nonsmoking rms avail. Bright, attractively decorated rooms have large desks. **Amenities:** 📺❄🗄 A/C, satel TV w/movies. Some units w/terraces, 1 w/whirlpool. **Services:** ✕🖼🛎 Free shuttle to Eisenhower Ave Metro station. **Facilities:** 🏋🏊♿ 1 restaurant, 1 bar, whirlpool. Lobby restaurant serves breakfast buffet, express lunch, and à la carte dinners. **Rates:** Peak (mid-Feb to June/Sept–Nov) $112–$122 S; $122–$125 D. Extra person $10. Children under age 12 stay free. Lower rates off-season. Parking: Indoor/outdoor, free. AE, CB, DC, DISC, MC, V.

☰☰ DoubleTree Guest Suites
100 S Reynolds St, 22304; tel 703/370-9600 or toll free 800/424-2900; fax 703/370-0467. At Duke St. Families will find comfortable temporary homes at this converted apartment building with spacious, well-equipped studios and one- and two-bedroom apartments. Within walking distance of restaurants and shops. **Rooms:** 225 effic. CI 3pm/CO noon. Nonsmoking rms avail. Nicely furnished and decorated in earth tones, all units have sleep sofas, full kitchens, and dining areas. **Amenities:** 📺❄🗄🍴 A/C, cable TV w/movies, refrig. Some units w/terraces. All apartments except junior models are equipped with dishwashers and two TVs. **Services:** ✕🖼🛎🐾 Free shuttle to Van Dorn Metro station. **Facilities:** 📷🏋🏊♿ 1 restaurant (bkfst and dinner only), 1 bar, washer/dryer. **Rates (CP):** Peak (Apr–Oct) $150–$225 effic. Extra person $20. Children under age 18 stay free. Lower rates off-season. Parking: Outdoor, free. AE, DC, DISC, MC, V.

☰☰☰ Embassy Suites
1900 Diagonal Rd, 22314; tel 703/684-5900 or toll free 800/EMBASSY; fax 703/684-1403. Exit 1 off I-95. Between Duke and King Sts. This all-suite hotel with a stunning, garden-like atrium enjoys a convenient location opposite King Street Metro and Alexandria Amtrak stations. Shops and restaurants adjacent. **Rooms:** 268 stes. CI 3pm/CO noon. Nonsmoking rms avail. All units except Presidential suites have sleep sofas. Homey, richly furnished living rooms have round tables, while large armoires conceal closet space, TVs, and desks. **Amenities:** 📺❄🗄🍴 A/C, cable TV w/movies, refrig, voice mail. Some units w/terraces. Wet bars, microwaves, and

two TVs in each unit. **Services:** ✕ ▨ Complimentary evening cocktails served in atrium. Free shuttle to heart of Old Town. **Facilities:** ⌂ ⛐ 🚐 💻 ♿ 1 restaurant (lunch and dinner only), 2 bars (1 w/entertainment), games rm, sauna, whirlpool, washer/dryer. Indoor pool opens to sun deck. **Rates (CP):** Peak (Apr–May/Sept–Oct) $99–$500 ste. Extra person $15. Children under age 12 stay free. Lower rates off-season. Parking: Indoor, $5–$10/day. Weekend rates by suite type, not number of occupants. AE, CB, DC, DISC, JCB, MC, V.

⬛⬛ Executive Club Suites

610 Bashford Lane at N Washington St, 22314 (Old Town); tel 703/739-2582 or toll free 800/535-2582; fax 703/548-0266. Exit 1 off I-95. Formerly an apartment building, this comfortable all-suites hotel is conveniently located on the northern end of Old Town Alexandria, near National Airport. Ideal for stays of a week or longer. **Rooms:** 78 stes. CI 3pm/CO noon. Nonsmoking rms avail. All units are attractively decorated with dark wood furniture and are equipped with kitchens and sleep sofas. Floor plans vary. **Amenities:** 🛁 ☕ 📺 A/C, cable TV w/movies, refrig, dataport, voice mail. Rooms have irons and ironing boards, and two TVs. **Services:** 🚐 ▨ 🍴 🛎 Babysitting. Dinner provided once a week, outside in good weather. Complimentary wine, beer, and soda at evening sessions. Free shuttle to Metro station. **Facilities:** ⌂ ⛐ 🚐 💻 ♿ Sauna, washer/dryer. **Rates (CP):** Peak (Mar–Oct) $139 ste. Children under age 18 stay free. Lower rates off-season. Parking: Outdoor, free. AE, CB, DC, DISC, MC, V.

UNRATED Holiday Inn Hotel & Suites

625 1st St, 22314 (Old Town); tel 703/548-6300; fax 703/548-8032. The newer section of a larger property that was split; it contains most of the facilities. **Rooms:** 170 rms and stes. CI 3pm/CO noon. Nonsmoking rms avail. Rooms are large, comfortable, and well decorated. **Amenities:** 🛁 ☕ A/C, cable TV w/movies, dataport. Some units w/terraces, some w/whirlpools. Executive suites have whirlpools. **Services:** ✕ 🚐 🍴 🛎 Free shuttle to airport or Metro. **Facilities:** ⌂ 🚲 ⛐ 🚐 💻 1 restaurant, 1 bar (w/entertainment), sauna, whirlpool, washer/dryer. Very complete fitness center. Rooftop gazebo. **Rates:** $119–$130 S; $129–$140 D; $150–$190 ste. Extra person $10. Children under age 17 stay free. Parking: Indoor/outdoor, free. Weekend packages avail. AE, CB, DC, DISC, MC, V.

⬛⬛⬛ Holiday Inn Select Old Town

480 King St, 22314 (Old Town); tel 703/549-6080 or toll free 800/368-5047. Exit 1 off I-95, at Pitt St. Few Holiday Inns can match the charm of this Federal-style brick structure, built around a courtyard. Period reproductions abound, in both the elegant lobby and the rooms. **Rooms:** 227 rms and stes. Executive level. CI 3pm/CO noon. Nonsmoking rms avail. Relatively spacious rooms. King-bed units have sleep sofas and tables rather than desks. **Amenities:** 🛁 ☕ 📺 🍴 A/C, satel TV w/movies, dataport, voice mail, in-rm safe. All units w/minibars, some w/terraces. Suites have balconies overlook-

ing the courtyard. **Services:** ✕ 🗝 🚐 ▨ 🍴 🛎 Twice-daily maid svce, babysitting. Free shuttle to Metro station. Morning coffee and danish, afternoon coffee and cookies, evening snacks in lobby. Manager's reception every Wednesday. **Facilities:** ⌂ ⛐ 🚐 💻 ♿ 2 restaurants, 1 bar, games rm, spa, sauna, beauty salon. **Rates:** Peak (Mar–June/Sept–Nov) $144 S or D; $195 ste. Extra person $20. Children under age 19 stay free. Min stay special events. Lower rates off-season. Parking: Indoor, $6/day. Weekend packages avail. AE, CB, DC, DISC, JCB, MC, V.

⬛⬛⬛ Sheraton Suites

801 N St Asaph St at N Madison St, 22314 (Old Town); tel 703/836-4700 or toll free 800/235-3535; fax 703/548-4514. Exit 1 off I-95. Near the northern end of Old Town, this brick building contains comfortable suites plus many amenities offered by full-service hotels. **Rooms:** 249 stes. Executive level. CI 3pm/CO 1pm. Nonsmoking rms avail. Most units are identical except for bed arrangement. About half have sleep sofas. **Amenities:** 🛁 ☕ 📺 🍴 A/C, cable TV w/movies, refrig, dataport, voice mail. Some units w/terraces. All units are equipped with wet bars, irons, and ironing boards. Microwaves. **Services:** ✕ 🚐 ▨ 🍴 🛎 Car-rental desk. **Facilities:** ⌂ ⛐ 🚐 💻 ♿ 1 restaurant, 1 bar (w/entertainment), whirlpool, washer/dryer. **Rates:** Peak (Mar–June/Sept–Nov) $170–$200 ste. Extra person $15. Children under age 17 stay free. Lower rates off-season. Parking: Indoor, $7/day. Weekend packages avail. AE, CB, DC, DISC, EC, ER, JCB, MC, V.

MOTELS

⬛ Econo Lodge Old Town

700 N Washington St at Wythe St, 22314 (Old Town); tel 703/836-5100 or toll free 800/237-2243; fax 703/519-7015. Exit 1 off I-95, N on US 1. A very basic but clean motel convenient to Old Town sights, shops, and restaurants. **Rooms:** 39 rms. CI 1pm/CO 11am. Nonsmoking rms avail. Spacious rooms have bright wood-grained furniture, large dressing areas outside bath. Upstairs rooms have entries off interior corridors; downstairs units open to parking lot or balcony walkway. **Amenities:** 🛁 ☕ A/C, cable TV. Some units w/terraces. **Services:** 🚐 🍴 🛎 Pet deposit required. **Facilities:** ♿ **Rates:** Peak (Mem Day–Labor Day) $55–$65 S; $65–$95 D. Extra person $5. Children under age 18 stay free. Lower rates off-season. Parking: Outdoor, free. AARP, over-50 discounts avail. AE, DC, DISC, MC, V.

⬛⬛ Hampton Inn

4800 Leesburg Pike, 22302; tel 703/671-4800 or toll free 800/HAMPTON; fax 703/671-2442. 1 mi W on VA 7. A modern, well-managed motel with a lovely atrium lobby. Numerous restaurants, shopping centers, and discount clothing stores are within walking distance. **Rooms:** 130 rms. CI 3pm/CO noon. Nonsmoking rms avail. Rooms with king-size beds have work areas. **Amenities:** 🛁 ☕ 🍴 A/C, cable TV w/movies. **Services:** ▨ 🍴 Babysitting. Free local calls.

Facilities: 🏕️ 🛥️ 🛗 ⚒️ Pool is surrounded by concrete deck without landscaping. **Rates (CP):** $82–$89 S or D. Children under age 18 stay free. Parking: Outdoor, free. Weekend rates avail. AE, DC, DISC, MC, V.

INN

▤ ▤ ▤ Morrison House
116 S Alfred St, 22314 (Old Town); tel 703/838-8000 or toll free 800/367-0800; fax 703/684-6283. Although built in 1985, this comfortable, federal-style brick inn has the feel of 18th-century Alexandria, with period reproductions throughout its elegant lounge (with working fireplace), library, and dining room. **Rooms:** 45 rms and stes. CI 3pm/CO noon. Nonsmoking rms avail. All rooms have large mahogany armoires containing closet space and TVs. Two deluxe units have canopy beds. **Amenities:** 📺 🅰️ 🍷 A/C, cable TV w/movies, bathrobes. **Services:** 🍽️ 🛎️ 🅅🅿️ 📧 ✂️ Car-rental desk, babysitting. Big chocolate chip cookies as welcoming gifts. Complimentary morning coffee and afternoon high tea. **Facilities:** 🍴 ⚒️ 2 restaurants, 1 bar (w/entertainment), guest lounge. Health-club facilities available nearby. **Rates:** Peak (Mar–June/Sept–Nov) $185–$205 S or D; $295 ste. Children under age 18 stay free. Min stay special events. Lower rates off-season. Parking: Outdoor, $6/day. AE, CB, DC, MC, V.

RESTAURANTS 🍴

★ Bilbo Baggins Wine Café and Restaurant
208 Queen St (Old Town); tel 703/683-0300. Between Lee and Fairfax Sts. **New American/Italian.** A huge oak wine chest graces one of the five dining rooms in this cozy establishment noted for its cellar. Varnished wood, some exposed brick, and varying ceiling heights in these old residences add informal charm. Creative pasta dishes are the specialty, along with grilled beef, veal, and seafood served with unusual sauces. Daily specials can include grilled salmon topped with a purée of Maine fiddlehead greens. Salads and sandwiches offered at all meals. Breads and desserts made on premises, and there are 10 microbrews on tap. **FYI:** Reservations accepted. **Open:** Lunch Mon–Sat 11:30am–2:30pm; dinner Mon–Sat 5:30–10:30pm, Sun 4:30–9:30pm; brunch Sun 11:30am–2:30pm. **Prices:** Main courses $10–$16. AE, CB, DC, DISC, MC, V. 💟 ⚒️

The Chart House
1 Cameron St (Old Town); tel 703/684-5080. **Seafood/Steak.** This tropical-style restaurant under a high peaked roof furnishes fine river views through its window-paneled walls. Potted plants, cane furniture, and staff dressed in Hawaiian-print shirts set a relaxed, islandy tone. Steaks, seafood, and pasta are the highlights of a limited menu augmented by daily specials featuring catches from far-off places like Hawaii and Nova Scotia. Large salad bar, included with main courses. **FYI:** Reservations recommended. Children's menu. Dress code. **Open:** Dinner Mon–Thurs 5–10pm, Fri–Sat 5–11pm, Sun 4–10pm; brunch Sun 11am–2:30pm. **Prices:** Main courses $13–$30. AE, CB, DC, DISC, MC, V. 🚤 🏔️ ⚒️

East Wind
809 King St (Old Town); tel 703/836-1515. Between Columbus and Alfred Sts. **Vietnamese.** Rose carpets, tablecloths, and wall panels balance nicely with knotty pine room dividers supporting rows of tropical plants. This upscale eatery is known for consistently fine cuisine, especially seafood and pork dishes. **FYI:** Reservations recommended. Dress code. Additional location: 2635 Connecticut Ave, Washington DC (tel 202/265-1360). **Open:** Lunch Mon–Fri 11:30am–2:30pm; dinner daily 5:30–10pm. **Prices:** Main courses $8–$16. AE, DC, DISC, MC, V.

★ Fish Market
105 King St at Union St (Old Town); tel 703/836-5676. **Seafood.** Large, pub-like establishment with several dining rooms and bars on two levels. Traditional Chesapeake-style seafood main courses and salads are offered, plus burgers and sandwiches for both lunch and dinner. **FYI:** Reservations accepted. Guitar/piano/singer. Dress code. **Open:** Mon–Sat 11:15am–2am, Sun 11:15am–midnight. **Prices:** Main courses $6–$15. AE, CB, DC, MC, V. ⚒️

★ Gadsby's Tavern
138 N Royal St, at Cameron St (Old Town); tel 703/548-1288. **American.** The 18th-century costumes of the staff complement the period furniture and decor of what were the dining rooms of the City Hotel (1792), a registered national landmark. (The original tavern is now a museum next door.) The menu offers contemporary regional favorites as well as dishes from Alexandria's pre-Revolutionary days. During summer, steamed blue crabs are served in the rear courtyard, where a full bar is set up. **FYI:** Reservations recommended. Children's menu. Dress code. No smoking. **Open:** Lunch Mon–Sat 11:30am–3pm; dinner Sun–Sat 5:30–10pm; brunch Sun 11am–3pm. **Prices:** Main courses $14–$23. CB, DC, DISC, ER, MC, V. ◾ ⚒️

Geranio
722 King St (Old Town); tel 703/548-0088. Between Washington and Columbus Sts. **Italian.** Archways join the two dining rooms of this building, which dates to the 1860s. Whitewashed brick walls and flowers brighten this place, a local favorite since 1976. Northern Italian seafood is featured, along with predominantly homemade pastas. Lobster with light tomato sauce over linguine is served all year. **FYI:** Reservations recommended. Dress code. **Open:** Lunch Mon–Fri 11:30am–2:30pm; dinner Mon–Sat 6–10:30pm, Sun 5:30–9:30pm. **Prices:** Main courses $11–$16. AE, DC, MC, V. 🖼️ ⚒️

★ Hard Times Café
1404 King St (Old Town); tel 703/683-5340. Between West and Peyton Sts. **Pub/Southwestern.** A bar at the rear lends a pub-like atmosphere to this small establishment. Oak booths

are designed to resemble a Texas-style cafe. Texas- and Cincinnati style chilies are served plain or with spaghetti or beans. **FYI:** Reservations not accepted. Children's menu. Beer and wine only. Additional location: 3028 Wilson Blvd, Arlington (tel 528-2233). **Open:** Sun–Wed 11am–10pm, Thurs–Sat 11am–11pm. **Prices:** Main courses $5–$7. AE, MC, V.

La Bergerie Restaurant Français
In The Shops at Crilleg, second floor, 218 N Lee St (Old Town); tel 703/683-1007. Between Cameron and Queen Sts. **French.** Exposed antique brick and individually lit paintings lend elegant charm to this fine French restaurant, where round booths provide privacy and a romantic atmosphere. Owner/chef adds his own Basque specialties to a traditional French menu. **FYI:** Reservations recommended. Jacket required. **Open:** Lunch Mon–Sat 11:30am–2:30pm; dinner Mon–Sat 6–10:30pm. **Prices:** Main courses $15–$24. AE, CB, DC, DISC, MC, V.

Landini Brothers
115 King St (Old Town); tel 703/836-8404. Between Lee and Union Sts. **Northern Italian.** Stone walls and rough-hewn beams from this building's days as a colonial warehouse give this eatery lots of rustic but romantic charm. Daily Tuscan-style specials stand out. **FYI:** Reservations recommended. Dress code. **Open:** Mon–Sat 11:30am–11pm, Sun 3–10pm. **Prices:** Main courses $12–$21. AE, CB, DC, DISC, MC, V.

⑤ ★ Le Gaulois Café Restaurant
1106 King St (Old Town); tel 703/739-9494. Between Henry and Fayette Sts. **French.** This comfortable spot is decorated like a country French living room, with working fireplace, grandfather clock, china cupboard, memento plates, and paintings. Seasonal menus feature excellent home-style fare, emphasizing seafood in traditional sauces. **FYI:** Reservations recommended. Dress code. **Open:** Lunch Mon–Sat 11:30am–5pm; dinner Mon–Thurs 5:30–10:30pm, Fri–Sat 5:30–11pm; brunch. **Prices:** Main courses $7–$16. AE, CB, DC, DISC, MC, V.

Le Refuge
127 N Washington St (Old Town); tel 703/548-4661. Between King and Cameron Sts. **French.** Exposed wooden beams and walls adorned with paintings and knickknacks from France set an appropriate ambience at this small establishment specializing in country-style French cuisine, including homemade pâtés. **FYI:** Reservations recommended. Dress code. **Open:** Lunch Mon–Sat 11:30am–2:30pm; dinner Mon–Sat 5:30–10pm. **Prices:** Main courses $14–$20. AE, CB, DC, MC, V.

★ Murphy's
713 King St (Old Town); tel 703/548-1717. Between Washington and Columbus Sts. **Cajun/Irish/Pub.** A long bar dominates this typical dark-wood Irish pub. Stew from the old country and corned beef and cabbage are complemented by charbroiled and Cajun-style main courses and pub-style burgers and sandwiches. Irish bands entertain from 9pm daily. **FYI:** Reservations accepted. Children's menu. Additional location: 2609 24th St NW, Washington DC (tel 202/462-7171). **Open:** Mon–Thurs 11am–midnight, Fri–Sat 11am–1:30am, Sun 10am–midnight. **Prices:** Main courses $6–$11. AE, CB, DC, MC, V.

⑤ Radio Free Italy
In Torpedo Factory Food Pavillion, 5 Cameron St at the Potomac River (Old Town); tel 703/683-0361. **Italian.** Pasta and wood-fired pizzas are the chief offerings, along with Italian-style meat and chicken dishes. Order carryout items downstairs or à la carte on the mezzanine. Take-out items can be carried to brick patio overlooking the river. **FYI:** Reservations accepted. Children's menu. **Open:** Daily 11:30am–11pm. **Prices:** Main courses $7–$14. AE, DC, DISC, MC, V.

★ RT's Restaurant
3804 Mount Vernon Ave; tel 703/684-6010. Near Commonwealth Ave. **Cajun/Seafood.** Among the three-dimensional modern art lining the walls of this varnished-oak pub/eatery is a work containing the unwashed plate used by President Clinton, who with Vice President Gore and their wives came to partake of spicy Cajun-style seafood and such regional favorites as Maryland fried oysters. **FYI:** Reservations recommended. Children's menu. **Open:** Mon–Thurs 11am–10:30pm, Fri–Sat 11am–11pm, Sun 4–9pm. **Prices:** Main courses $12–$19. AE, CB, DC, DISC, MC, V.

Santa Fe East
110 S Pitt St (Old Town); tel 703/548-6900. Between King and Prince Sts. **Southwestern.** Several cozy dining rooms run the gamut from formal to outdoor. There are two working fireplaces. A limited menu features Southwestern-influenced cuisine, such as blue-corn tortillas layered with smoked chicken and cheese. **FYI:** Reservations recommended. Guitar. Dress code. **Open:** Mon–Thurs 11:30am–10pm, Fri–Sat 11:30am–11pm, Sun 11am–10pm. **Prices:** Main courses $10–$19. AE, MC, V.

★ Taverna Cretekou
818 King St (Old Town); tel 703/548-8688. Between Columbus and N Alfred Sts. **Greek.** Arches and white stucco create a Mediterranean island atmosphere, appropriate for one of the most popular Greek restaurants in the region. A cross-section of traditional dishes is offered, five of which can be sampled as part of the house special. Live Greek entertainment Tuesday, Wednesday, and Thursday evenings. A lamb roasts in the courtyard dining area in fine weather. **FYI:** Reservations recommended. Big band. Dress code. **Open:** Lunch Tues–Fri 11:30am–2:30pm, Sat noon–4pm, Sun 11am–3pm; dinner Tues–Fri 5–10:30pm, Sat 4–11pm, Sun 5–9:30pm. **Prices:** Main courses $11–$16. AE, MC, V.

The Tea Cosy
119 S Royal St (Old Town); tel 703/836-8181. Between King and Prince Sts. **British.** Framed antique advertisements grace this bright, cheerful tearoom. Authentic Cornish pasty, shepherd's pie, and sausage rolls lead the list of offerings. Adjacent shop sells British goods. **FYI:** Reservations not accepted. Dress code. Beer and wine only. No smoking. **Open:** Sat–Thurs 10am–6pm, Fri 10am–7pm. **Prices:** Main courses $3–$10. DISC, MC, V.

★ **Tempo**
4231 Duke St; tel 703/370-7900. Exit 3A off I-395, at N Gordon St. **Californian/French/Italian.** Bright white walls hung with large seascapes have completely transformed this former service station into a pleasant small dining room, whose steel rafters and ventilator tubes now add to the charm. A blend of Italian, French, and California cuisines include some creative pasta offerings and reflect the origins of the proprietors, a French-born chef and his California-bred wife. Off the beaten path in a predominantly suburban residential area, this find is a local favorite for quality and value. **FYI:** Reservations recommended. **Open:** Lunch Sun–Fri 11:30am–2:30pm; dinner Mon–Sat 5:30–10pm, Sun 5:30–9pm. **Prices:** Main courses $9–$17. AE, CB, DC, DISC, MC, V.

Two Nineteen Restaurant
219 King St (Old Town); tel 703/549-1141. Between Fairfax and Lee Sts. **Creole.** The main dining rooms are elegant recreations of Victorian-era New Orleans mansions, while the bars and outdoor dining area are casual and relaxed. French-accented Creole cuisine is the chef's specialty, along with grilled meats and traditional Chesapeake seafood. **FYI:** Reservations recommended. Jazz. Dress code. **Open:** Mon–Thurs 11am–10:30pm, Fri–Sat 11am–1am, Sun 10am–10pm. **Prices:** Main courses $14–$24. AE, CB, DC, DISC, MC, V. ◉ ⊜

Union Street Public House
121 S Union St (Old Town); tel 703/548-1785. Between King and Prince Sts. **New American/Seafood.** Exposed brick, dark wood, and tin ceilings give this lively pub/restaurant a charming ambience. In addition to salads and pub-style sandwiches, the menu offers grilled beef, chicken, and seafood plus a selection of pasta dishes. Raw bar serves up oysters and clams on the half shell. **FYI:** Reservations accepted. Children's menu. **Open:** Mon–Sat 11:30am–1:15am, Sun 11am–1:15am. **Prices:** Main courses $9–$17. AE, CB, DC, DISC, MC, V. ▮ ▦

The Warehouse Bar and Grill
214 King St (Old Town); tel 703/683-6868. Between Fairfax and Lee Sts. **Seafood/Steak.** Cartoons of numerous local and national celebrities line the walls of this pleasantly decorated steak and seafood emporium. Upstairs, the other dining room sits under a skylight. Meat and fish served with a variety of sauces are the chief offerings, though a limited sandwich menu is available. **FYI:** Reservations recommended. Chil-

dren's menu. Dress code. **Open:** Breakfast Sat 8:30am–10:30pm; lunch Mon–Sat 11am–4pm; dinner Mon–Thurs 5–10:30pm, Fri–Sat 4–11pm, Sun 4–9:30pm; brunch Sun 9:30am–4pm. **Prices:** Main courses $13–$19. AE, CB, DC, DISC, MC, V. ♿

REFRESHMENT STOP ☕

★ **The Deli on the Strand**
211 the Strand (Old Town); tel 703/548-7222. Entrance on S Union St, between Duke and Prince Sts. **Deli.** An attractive wood interior brightens this modern deli, a favorite with locals and bicyclists passing through Old Town. The only seating is outside on a narrow deck. Sandwiches and salads are made fresh daily behind the display case. **Open:** Daily 8am–8pm. AE, MC, V.

ATTRACTIONS 📷

Christ Church
118 N Washington St; tel 703/549-1450. This sturdy Georgian-style red-brick church would be an important national landmark even without its two most distinguished members, George Washington and Robert E Lee. It has been in continuous use since 1773. Traditionally, the president of the United States attends a service here on a Sunday close to Washington's birthday and sits in his pew. The bell tower, galleries, and organ were added in the early 1800s, the "wineglass" pulpit in 1891; however, much of the church has been restored to its original appearance. The Parish Hall contains an exhibit on the history of the church. The church yard was Alexandria's first and only burial ground until 1805; the remains of 36 Confederate soldiers are interred here. **Open:** Mon–Sat 9am–4pm. **Free**

The Lyceum
201 S Washington St; tel 703/838-4994. This Greek Revival building houses exhibits focusing on Alexandria's history from colonial times through the 20th century. Built in 1839, the Lyceum served as a lecture, meeting, and concert hall, a hospital during the Civil War, and a private residence. Tourist information about Alexandria and all of Virginia is also available here. **Open:** Mon–Sat 10am–5pm, Sun 1–5pm. **Free**

Fort Ward Museum and Park
4301 W Braddock Rd; tel 703/838-4848. A 45-acre museum, park, and historic site, the area centers on an actual Union fort, erected in the early 1860s as part of a system of forts designed to protect Washington, DC. Self-guided tours begin at the Fort Ward ceremonial gate; visitors can explore the replica of an officer's hut and the restored Northwest Bastion. The museum has Civil War weaponry and other artifacts, and also features changing exhibits. Concerts are given on selected evenings in summer; living history programs on certain weekends (call for details). Picnic areas with grills are near the fort. **Open:** Daily 9am–sunset. **Free**

Gadsby's Tavern Museum

134 N Royal St; tel 703/838-4242. Alexandria was at the crossroads of colonial America, and Alexandria's center was Gadsby's Tavern. It consists of two buildings (one Georgian, one federal) dating from 1770 and 1792, respectively. The rooms have been restored to their 18th-century appearance using colonial inventories that include such minutiae as lemon squeezers.

Guided tours (30 minutes) offered throughout the day illustrate the important role of taverns in 18th-century American social life; special living history tours are offered the last Sunday of every month. A colonial-style restaurant occupies three restored tavern rooms. **Open:** Peak (Apr–Sept) Tues–Sat 10am–5pm, Sun 1–5pm. Reduced hours off-season. **$**

Alexandria Black History Resource Center

638 N Alfred St; tel 703/838-4356. Housed in a 1940s building that originally housed the black community's first public library, the center exhibits historical objects, photographs, documents, and memorabilia relating to African Americans in Alexandria from the 18th century forward. The permanent collection is supplemented by twice-yearly rotating exhibits, and walking tours and other activities are offered. **Open:** Tues–Sat 10am–4pm. **Free**

Boyhood Home of Robert E Lee

607 Oronoco St; tel 703/548-8454. Revolutionary War cavalry hero Henry "Light Horse Harry" Lee brought his wife, Ann Hill Carter, and their five children to this early federal-style mansion in 1812, when Robert E Lee was five years old. A tour of the house, which was built in 1795, provides a glimpse into the gracious lifestyle of Alexandria's gentry. The tour covers the entire house, including the nursery, Mrs Lee's room, the parlor, the winter and summer kitchens, and the back garden, which features a boxwood garden and a magnolia tree planted in 1812. **Open:** Feb–mid-Dec, Mon–Fri 10am–3:30pm, Sat 10am–3:30pm, Sun 1–3:30pm. **$**

Ramsay House

221 King St; tel 703/838-4200 or 838-5005 (24-hr events recording). Built in the mid-1720s, Ramsay House is one of the oldest remaining structures in Alexandria. Today it serves as a visitor information center and houses the Convention and Visitors Bureau. Here visitors can pick up a self-guided walking tour map and brochures about the area, find out about special events that might be taking place, and purchase discounted tickets for five historic Alexandria properties. A 13-minute video gives an overview of Alexandria's rich past. Guided walking tours depart from the house. **Open:** Daily 9am–5pm. **Free**

Lee-Fendall House

614 Oronoco St; tel 703/548-1789. Frequent visitor "Light Horse Harry" Lee never actually lived here, but he did sell the land to Philip Richard Fendall (himself a Lee on his mother's side), who built the house in 1785. Thirty-seven Lees occupied the house over the next 118 years. Guided tours of the house provide insight into family life in the 1850s

and include the colonial garden, with its magnolia and chestnut trees, roses, and boxwood-lined paths. A permanent collection of doll houses and miniature architecture is supplemented by changing special exhibits. Tours last about 30 minutes and depart continually throughout the day. **Open:** Tues–Sat 10am–4pm, Sun noon–4pm. **$**

Carlyle House

121 N Fairfax St; tel 703/549-2997. Built in 1753, Carlyle House was an important social and political center in colonial Alexandria. Maj Gen Edward Braddock, commander-in-chief of British forces in North America, made the house his headquarters during the French and Indian Wars. Tours of the house last 40 minutes, and include the parlor and study where Braddock met with five colonial governors to ask them to raise taxes to finance his campaign. Rooms are furnished in period style; one room contains an exhibit explaining 18th-century construction methods. **Open:** Tues–Sat 10am–4:30pm, Sun noon–4:30pm. **$**

Friendship Firehouse

107 S Alfred St; tel 703/838-3891. The Friendship Fire Company was Alexandria's first firefighting organization, established in 1774. Local tradition names George Washington as one of the founding members. In 1855 the original building burned down and the fashionable Italianate structure that stands today was erected on the same spot. It houses a museum with exhibits on the history of firefighting and the Friendship Company. **Open:** Fri–Sat 10am–4pm, Sun 1–4pm. **Free**

Stabler-Leadbeater Apothecary

105 S Fairfax St; tel 703/836-3713. This landmark drugstore originally opened in 1792; when it fell prey to the Depression in 1933, its doors were simply locked, with most of the herbs, potions, and patent medicines remaining in their drawers. The apothecary today looks much as it did when it was in operation, its shelves lined with antique hand-blown medicinal bottles and patent medicines, mortars and pestles, pill rollers, and scales stamped with the royal crown. The shop's comprehensive records include an 1802 order for castor oil from Martha Washington at Mount Vernon. **Open:** Mon–Sat 10am–4pm, Sun 1–5pm. **$**

Old Presbyterian Meeting House

321 S Fairfax St; tel 703/549-6670. This brick church was built by Scottish pioneers in 1775. Though it wasn't George Washington's church, the Meeting House bell tolled continuously for four days after his death in December 1799, and memorial services were preached from the pulpit here by Presbyterian, Episcopalian, and Methodist ministers. The original Meeting House was gutted by a lightning fire in 1835, but it was restored around the old walls in the style of the day a few years later. In 1949 the building was reopened by the Presbyterian Church (USA) and looks today much as it

did in the mid-18th century. Interred in the church graveyard are many notable Alexandrians. **Open:** Tues–Fri 9am–3pm; Sun services at 8:30 and 11am. **Free**

Schooner *Alexandria*
Jones Point Park; tel 703/549-7078. A Baltic trader vessel built in 1929, this Swedish three-masted, gaff-rigged topsail schooner was remodeled for passenger use in the 1970s. Tours of the ship explore above and below deck, and visit one stateroom (the others are used by the crew) and the rather elegant Main Salon downstairs. **Open:** Sat–Sun noon–5pm. **Free**

Appomattox

Famous as the site of Confederate Gen Robert E Lee's surrender. Nearby to Buckingham-Appomattox State Forest and Holiday Lake State Park. **Information:** Appomattox County Chamber of Commerce, PO Box 704, Appomattox, 24522 (tel 804/352-2621).

ATTRACTIONS 🏛

Appomattox Court House National Historic Park
Tel 804/352-8987. Located approximately 20 mi E of Appomattox on VA 24. Here, on April 9, 1865, in the parlor of Wilmer McLean's house, Robert E Lee's surrender of the Army of Northern Virginia to Ulysses S Grant signaled the end of a bitter conflict. The 27 houses, stores, courthouse, and tavern that comprised the little village called Appomattox Court House have been restored, and visitors today can walk the country lanes in rural stillness where these events took place. Maps of the park are available at the Visitors Center, which also features slide presentations and exhibits. Several buildings are open to the public. **Surrender Triangle,** where the Confederates laid down their arms, is outside Kelly House. **Open:** Sept–May, daily 8:30am–5pm; June–Aug, daily 9am–5:30pm. **$**

Holliday Lake State Park
Tel 804/248-6308. Holliday Lake is a 250-acre state park located 8 miles from Appomattox Court House National Historical Park (see above). The lake is a popular swimming site Memorial Day–Labor Day; guided canoe trips are offered during the summer season. In addition, Holliday Lake offers superior fishing all year round (a Virginia state fishing license is required). Boat rentals are also available.

Other park activities and facilities include camping, hiking, a horseshoe pit, and beach volleyball. **Open:** Daily sunrise–sunset. **$**

Arlington
See also Washington, DC

Across the Potomac River from Washington, DC, with government and business buildings, residential neighborhoods, and famous sites such as Arlington National Cemetery. **Information:** Arlington Chamber of Commerce, 2009 N 14th St #111, Arlington, 22201 (tel 703/525-2400).

HOTELS 🛏

≣≣ Best Western Arlington Inn and Tower
2480 S Glebe Rd, 22206 (South Arlington); tel 703/979-4400 or toll free 800/426-6886; fax 703/685-0051. Exit 7B off I-395. Some rooms in this clean hotel are in the original two-story motel block, which dates from the 1960s, while others are in a modern eight-story tower built in the 1980s. **Rooms:** 325 rms. CI 3pm/CO noon. Nonsmoking rms avail. Opening directly to parking lot, old-wing rooms are slightly larger whereas tower rooms are somewhat better equipped. All have two vanities, and some have sofas. **Amenities:** 🛏 ⚲ A/C, satel TV w/movies. **Services:** 🚗�'🖂🖴 Car-rental desk. Free shuttle to Metro stations. **Facilities:** ⚲ 🍽 [200] ⚿ 1 restaurant, 1 bar, games rm, washer/dryer. **Rates:** Peak (Mar 15–Labor Day/Oct) $69–$120 S; $79–$120 D. Extra person $10. Children under age 18 stay free. Lower rates off-season. Parking: Outdoor, free. Weekend packages avail. AE, CB, DC, DISC, MC, V.

≣≣≣ Comfort Inn Enterprise Square
1211 N Glebe Rd at Washington Blvd, 22201 (Ballston); tel 703/247-3399 or toll free 800/228-5150; fax 703/524-8739. Exit 71 off I-66. A clean and comfortable chain hotel occupying part of a modern office building with a brick facade. Within walking distance of Ballston Commons shopping mall, several restaurants, and Metro station. **Rooms:** 126 rms and stes. CI noon/CO 11am. Nonsmoking rms avail. In addition to a standard hotel room, junior suites have a separate sitting room and can be joined with a third room to make a large suite. **Amenities:** 🛏 A/C, cable TV w/movies. **Services:** ✗🖂🖴 Twice-daily maid svce. **Facilities:** [30] ⚿ 1 restaurant, 1 bar, playground. Guests have access to nearby health club with pool for a fee. Coffee shop–style restaurant with separate bar. **Rates (CP):** Peak (Mar–Nov 15) $106 S or D. Extra person $5. Children under age 18 stay free. Lower rates off-season. Parking: Indoor, free. Weekend rates avail. AE, DC, DISC, MC, V.

≣≣≣ Courtyard by Marriott Crystal City
2899 Jefferson Davis Hwy, 22202; tel 703/549-3434 or toll free 800/847-4775; fax 703/549-0320. Exit 9 off I-395. Take US 1 to 27th St S; head east. Unlike most of this chain, this high-rise hotel lacks a courtyard, but makes up for it in services and amenities. Large mahogany-paneled lounge and dining area have a clublike elegance. **Rooms:** 272 rms and stes. CI 3pm/CO 1pm. Nonsmoking rms avail. King rooms

have love seats, some convertible. **Amenities:** 🔒🕐📺 📶A/C, cable TV w/movies, dataport, voice mail. 1 unit w/terrace. All rooms have irons and ironing boards. **Services:** ✗🚗🖼️🛎️ **Facilities:** 🏋️‍♂️🍴🚐 ⚓ 1 restaurant (bkfst and dinner only), 1 bar, spa, whirlpool, washer/dryer. **Rates:** Peak (Mar–June/Sept–Nov) $99–$144 S; $109–$159 D; $200–$300 ste. Extra person $15. Children under age 12 stay free. Lower rates off-season. Parking: Indoor, $10/day. Weekend packages avail. AE, CB, DC, DISC, MC, V.

≣≣≣ Crystal Gateway Marriott

1700 Jefferson Davis Hwy, 22202 (Crystal City); tel 703/920-3230 or toll free 800/228-9290; fax 703/271-5212. Exit 9 off I-95; entrance on S Eads St. An attractive, full-service high-rise hotel catering to groups. Underground passage leads to Crystal City shopping mall and Metro station. Some public areas are under an angled skylight, creating an open and airy feeling. **Rooms:** 694 rms and stes. Executive level. CI 4pm/CO noon. Nonsmoking rms avail. Rooms are tastefully decorated with dark wood furniture and elegant armoires, which hold TVs. **Amenities:** 🔒🕐 A/C, cable TV w/movies, dataport, voice mail. **Services:** ✗🗝️ 🚗🖼️🛎️⚓ Babysitting. **Facilities:** 🏋️‍♂️🍴🚐 💻⚓ 3 restaurants, 2 bars (1 w/entertainment), spa, sauna, whirlpool, washer/dryer. **Rates:** Peak (Feb–Mar/July–Aug) $139–$182 S; $159–$202 D; $169 ste. Children under age 18 stay free. Lower rates off-season. Parking: Indoor, $10/day. Weekend rates avail. AE, CB, DC, DISC, JCB, MC, V.

≣≣≣ DoubleTree Hotel National Airport

300 Army-Navy Dr, 22202; tel 703/416-4100 or toll free 800/222-TREE; fax 703/416-4126. Exit 9 off I-395. This hotel sports two towers with a skylighted lobby in between. **Rooms:** 632 rms and stes. Executive level. CI 3pm/CO noon. Nonsmoking rms avail. Standard hotel rooms, some with fine views over the Potomac River, are in the older north tower. Best views are from odd-numbered rooms. The newer tower has executive rooms, with sofas, and suites, which have a sitting parlor with couch. **Amenities:** 🔒🕐 A/C, cable TV w/movies, dataport, voice mail. Some units w/terraces, some w/whirlpools. **Services:** ✗🚗🖼️🛎️⚓ Car-rental desk, masseur, babysitting. Free shuttle to Pentagon, Pentagon City mall, and Metro station. **Facilities:** 🏋️‍♂️🏊🚐🍴 ⚓ 2 restaurants, 2 bars (1 w/entertainment), racquetball, spa, sauna, whirlpool. On the top floor, the Penthouse Restaurant and revolving Skydome Lounge take advantage of the views. Pleasant, garden-like cafe at lobby level. **Rates:** Peak (Mar 15–June 15/Sept–Nov 15) $105–$175 S or D; $250 ste. Extra person $20. Children under age 18 stay free. Lower rates off-season. Parking: Indoor/outdoor, $10/day. AE, CB, DC, DISC, JCB, MC, V.

≣≣ The Executive Club

108 S Courthouse Rd, 22204 (Fort Myer); tel 703/522-2582 or toll free 800/535-2582; fax 703/486-2694. 2nd St S exit off VA 27 N. This converted brick apartment complex consists of two-story buildings around an attractive courtyard

with pool and a patio with umbrella tables. Convenient to Fort Myer. Excellent for long-term stays. **Rooms:** 74 stes. CI noon/CO noon. All units are fully equipped apartments with either a bedroom or a bedroom with den. Comfortably furnished with color-coordinated decor. **Amenities:** 🔒🕐📺 A/C, cable TV w/movies, refrig, voice mail. **Services:** 🚗🖼️ 🛎️⚓ Babysitting. Evening happy hour daily. **Facilities:** 🏋️‍♂️🚐💻 Spa, sauna, whirlpool, washer/dryer. **Rates (CP):** $139 ste. Parking: Outdoor, free. Long-term rates avail. AE, CB, DC, DISC, MC, V.

≣≣≣ Howard Johnson National Airport Hotel

2650 Jefferson Davis Hwy, 22202 (Crystal City); tel 703/684-7200 or toll free 800/278-2243; fax 703/684-3217. Exit 9 off I-395. A well-maintained high-rise hotel on southern end of Crystal City. Convenient to National Airport. **Rooms:** 279 rms and stes. Executive level. CI 4pm/CO noon. Nonsmoking rms avail. All rooms tastefully decorated, though standard units are small. Executive-level rooms are larger, equipped with two vanities and love seats. **Amenities:** 🔒🕐📺 A/C, satel TV w/movies, dataport, voice mail. All units w/terraces. **Services:** ✗🗝️🚗🖼️🛎️⚓ Car-rental desk, babysitting. Free shuttle to airport, Metro, and local restaurants. **Facilities:** 🏋️‍♂️🚐🍴 ⚓ 1 restaurant, 1 bar, washer/dryer. Moderately priced chain restaurant on premises. **Rates:** Peak (Mar–June/Sept–Oct) $119–$139 S; $129–$149 D; $250 ste. Extra person $10. Children under age 18 stay free. Lower rates off-season. Parking: Indoor, $7/day. Weekend packages avail. AE, CB, DC, DISC, MC, V.

≣≣≣ Hyatt Arlington at Key Bridge

1325 Wilson Blvd, 22209 (Rosslyn); tel 703/525-1234 or toll free 800/233-1234; fax 703/875-3393. At N Nash St. A concrete-and-glass structure amid surrounding high-rise office buildings. Convenient to shops, restaurants, Rosslyn Metro station. Recent renovations spiffed up rooms. **Rooms:** 302 rms and stes. Executive level. CI 3pm/CO noon. Nonsmoking rms avail. Business Plan rooms have large desks. **Amenities:** 🔒🕐📺 📶A/C, cable TV w/movies, voice mail. All units have irons and ironing boards. **Services:** ✗🗝️📼🖼️🛎️ Children's program. **Facilities:** 🚐🍴💻⚓ 2 restaurants, 2 bars, washer/dryer. **Rates:** $79–$179 S; $79–$204 D; $225–$450 ste. Extra person $7. Children under age 18 stay free. Parking: Indoor, $6/day. Weekend rates include free parking. AE, CB, DC, DISC, JCB, MC, V.

≣≣≣ Hyatt Regency Crystal City

2799 Jefferson Davis Hwy (US 1), 22202; tel 703/418-1234 or toll free 800/233-1234; fax 703/418-1289. Exit 9 off I-395; left at 28th St. At this V-shaped high-rise hotel, glass-enclosed elevators ascend from a skylighted, three-story atrium with bar, lounge, and trees. Caters to groups and business travelers. **Rooms:** 685 rms and stes. Executive level. CI 3pm/CO noon. Nonsmoking rms avail. Rooms with king-size beds have love seats; those with two beds do not. **Amenities:** 🔒🕐📺 📶A/C, satel TV w/movies, dataport, voice mail. Some units w/minibars, some w/terraces, 1 w/whirlpool. Business Plan rooms have fax machines. Suites have wet bars. **Services:** ✕ 🗝 VP 🚐 🛄 🛎 Babysitting. Complimentary morning newspaper delivered to room weekdays. Concierge arranges discounts for tennis and golf at local clubs. Free shuttle to and from Metro station, shops, and restaurants. **Facilities:** 🔢 📞 [1800] 💻 ⚹ 2 restaurants, 2 bars, sauna, steam rm, whirlpool. Rooftop restaurant. Rather small outdoor pool on second floor. **Rates:** Peak (Mar 15–June 15/Sept–Nov) $170–$195 S or D; $225–$750 ste. Extra person $25. Children under age 18 stay free. Lower rates off-season. Parking: Indoor, $10/day. AE, CB, DC, DISC, MC, V.

≣≣≣ Key Bridge Marriott Hotel

1401 Lee Hwy (US 29), at Fort Myer Dr, 22209 (Rosslyn); tel 703/524-6400 or toll free 800/327-9789; fax 703/243-3280. Exit 73 off I-66. Recent renovation has brought rooms in this second-oldest Marriott property up to same level as elegant dark-wood lobby and excellent location. Within walking distance of Georgetown (across Key Bridge) and within blocks of Rosslyn Metro station. **Rooms:** 584 rms and stes. Executive level. CI 3pm/CO 1pm. Nonsmoking rms avail. Rooms from fifth floor up have great views. Those in front look to Washington, DC; those in rear to Georgetown and Potomac River. Dark wood furniture has rich appearance. **Amenities:** 🕋 ⚱ A/C, cable TV w/movies, voice mail. Some units w/terraces. All units have irons and ironing boards. Windows can be opened in about half the rooms. **Services:** ✕ 🗝 🛄 🛎 ⟲ Car-rental desk, babysitting. Free shuttle to Metro station. **Facilities:** 🔢 📞 [700] 💻 ⚹ 2 restaurants, 2 bars (1 w/entertainment), spa, sauna, whirlpool, beauty salon, washer/dryer. Top-floor restaurant enjoys views of Washington, DC. Adjacent bar is popular spot for weekend dancing. Attractive indoor-outdoor pool area. **Rates:** $89–$169 S or D; $235–$500 ste. Extra person $20. Children under age 18 stay free. AP rates avail. Parking: Indoor/outdoor, $6/day. Weekend packages include free parking. AE, CB, DC, DISC, MC, V.

≣≣ Quality Hotel Arlington

1200 N Courthouse Rd at Arlington Blvd, 22201; tel 703/524-4000 or toll free 800/228-5151; fax 703/524-1046. Exit 8 off I-395. A once-small motel, this well-managed and constantly improving property has expanded to include two former apartment buildings and a large meeting facility. Hosts groups and small conventions. **Rooms:** 400 rms and effic. Executive level. CI 3pm/CO noon. Nonsmoking rms avail. Units are of various sizes and shapes. A few still have kitchens. Club Royale rooms and Quality Suites have sleeper sofas. Comfort Tower has standard rooms with one queen or double bed. Original motel rooms are equipped with two beds. **Amenities:** 🕋 A/C, cable TV w/movies, refrig. Some units w/terraces, some w/whirlpools. Club Royale rooms and Quality Suites have wet bars, hair dryers, coffeemakers. **Services:** ✕ 🛄 🛎 Those staying in Club Royale–level rooms receive continental breakfast and evening cordials in attend-

ed lounge. **Facilities:** 🔢 📞 [275] ⚹ 1 restaurant, 1 bar, spa, sauna, washer/dryer. Resort-size pool surrounded by extensive concrete deck, largest in Arlington County. Restaurant has pleasant dining room with picture windows on three sides. **Rates:** Peak (Mar 20–Sept 10) $75–$82 S; $82–$87 D; $110 effic. Extra person $6–14. Children under age 18 stay free. Lower rates off-season. Parking: Outdoor, free. Weekend rates avail. AE, DC, DISC, MC, V.

≣≣≣ Renaissance Arlington Hotel

950 N Stafford St, 22203 (Ballston); tel 703/528-6000 or toll free 800/228-9898; fax 703/528-4386. Exit 71 off I-66. With excellent location above Ballston metro station, this comfortable hotel occupies lower seven levels of high-rise condominium building. Elevated walkways lead from lobby to shopping mall. Easily the best hotel in the Ballston area. **Rooms:** 209 rms and stes. Executive level. CI 3pm/CO noon. Nonsmoking rms avail. Nicely appointed rooms have colonial-style furniture. **Amenities:** 🕋 ⚱ 🖥 ⚹ A/C, satel TV w/movies, refrig, voice mail. Some units w/minibars. **Services:** ✕ 🛄 🛎 ⟲ Club Level has daily newspapers and complimentary breakfast. **Facilities:** 🔢 📞 [400] 💻 ⚹ 1 restaurant, 1 bar (w/entertainment), spa, sauna, whirlpool, washer/dryer. Deli and cafe on premises. **Rates:** Peak (Jan 15–July 1/Sept–Dec 15) $135–$175 S; $150–$190 D; $195 ste. Extra person $15. Children under age 16 stay free. Lower rates off-season. Parking: Indoor, free. Weekend rates avail. AE, CB, DC, DISC, JCB, MC, V.

≣≣≣≣ The Ritz-Carlton Pentagon City

1250 S Hayes St, 22202; tel 703/415-5000 or toll free 800/241-3333; fax 703/415-5061. Exit 9B off I-395. Rich wood paneling, Oriental rugs, and European tapestries adorn the elegant public areas of this full-service, luxury hotel. Adjoins the Fashion Center shopping mall and Pentagon City Metro station. **Rooms:** 345 rms and stes. Executive level. CI 3pm/CO noon. Nonsmoking rms avail. All rooms are plushly appointed with cherrywood furniture, fabric wallpaper, paintings, and comfortable easy chairs. The Ritz-Carlton suite has two bedrooms and a full kitchen. Club-level units enjoy partial view of Washington. **Amenities:** 🕋 ⚱ ⚹ A/C, cable TV w/movies, dataport, voice mail, in-rm safe, bathrobes. All units w/minibars. Fax machines in all rooms. **Services:** 🍽 🗝 VP 🚐 🛄 🛎 Twice-daily maid svce, car-rental desk, masseur, babysitting. **Facilities:** 🔢 📞 [450] 💻 ⚹ 1 restaurant, 1 bar (w/entertainment), spa, sauna, steam rm, whirlpool, beauty salon. Lobby Lounge serves continental breakfast, buffet lunch, afternoon tea, and light evening fare. Lap pool in fitness center. **Rates:** Peak (Mar–May/Sept–Oct) $189–$229 S; $209–$249 D; $289–$500 ste. Extra person $20. Children under age 18 stay free. Lower rates off-season. Parking: Indoor, $22/day. Weekend packages avail. AE, CB, DC, DISC, JCB, MC, V.

≣≣≣ Sheraton National Hotel

900 S Orme St, 22204 (Navy Annex); tel 703/521-1900 or toll free 800/468-9090; fax 703/521-0332. Exit 8 off I-395.

Follow Washington Blvd W to Columbia Pike. Convenient to the Pentagon and Navy Annex, this comfortable high-rise hotel has great views over Washington, DC, and surrounding area. Youth tour groups are segregated in lower-level wing. **Rooms:** 424 rms and stes. Executive level. CI 3pm/CO 1pm. Nonsmoking rms avail. Front rooms have best views. All units have two vanities. King rooms have sofa beds and easy chair. **Amenities:** 🛅 🕭 📠 A/C, cable TV w/movies. Some units w/minibars. **Services:** ✕ 🚐 🖎 🛜 Free shuttle to Metro, shopping mall. **Facilities:** 🗔 🍴 2000 🖵 🕭 2 restaurants, 2 bars, spa, sauna, washer/dryer. Lobby-level Café Brasserie has tropical ambience. On the top level, formal Stars Restaurant and indoor pool with sun deck share the views. **Rates:** $120 S or D; $140 ste. Extra person $15. Children under age 16 stay free. Parking: Indoor, $3/day. Weekend packages avail. AE, DC, DISC, MC, V.

MOTELS

📧📧 The Americana Hotel
1400 Jefferson Davis Hwy, 22202 (Crystal City); tel 703/979-3772 or toll free 800/548-6261; fax 703/979-0547. Exit 9 off I-395. The last family-owned and -operated motel near National Airport, this exceptionally clean and well-maintained establishment is now dwarfed by the surrounding high-rise towers of Crystal City. Early 1960s-era building and attentive owners create an atmosphere that harkens back to a less-hurried time. **Rooms:** 100 rms. CI noon/CO 11am. Nonsmoking rms avail. Rooms in front subject to highway noise. Decor is tasteful; dark wood furniture adds touch of class. **Amenities:** 🛅 A/C, cable TV, refrig. Some units w/terraces. **Services:** 🚐 🖎 🛜 **Facilities:** Washer/dryer. **Rates (CP):** Peak (Mar–Oct) $60–$65 S or D. Extra person $5. Children under age 18 stay free. Lower rates off-season. Parking: Outdoor, free. AE, CB, DC, DISC, MC, V.

📧📧 Arlington Cherry Blossom Travelodge
3030 Columbia Pike, 22204 (South Arlington); tel 703/521-5570 or toll free 800/578-7878; fax 703/271-0081. Exit 7B off I-395. A clean, well-maintained older motel. Pentagon City Mall and Metro station less than two miles away. **Rooms:** 76 rms and effic. CI 2pm/CO noon. Nonsmoking rms avail. Efficiency units have dining tables. **Amenities:** 🛅 🕭 📠 A/C, cable TV w/movies, refrig. **Services:** ✕ 🖎 🛜 Car-rental desk, babysitting. Free local calls. **Facilities:** 🍴 20 🕭 1 restaurant (lunch and dinner only), 1 bar, washer/dryer. Guests have free access to pool two blocks away. **Rates (CP):** Peak (Mar 15–Nov 10) $64–$76 S or D; $76 effic. Extra person $7. Children under age 18 stay free. Lower rates off-season. Parking: Outdoor, free. AARP discounts avail. AE, CB, DC, DISC, JCB, MC, V.

📧📧 Days Inn Arlington
2201 Arlington Blvd (US 50), 22201 (Fort Myer); tel 703/525-0300 or toll free 800/329-7466; fax 703/525-5671. At Pershing Dr. This clean but dated 1960s motel has been reasonably well maintained; two-story U-shaped structures are built around parking lot and small pool. Walking distance to Fort Myer, shops. **Rooms:** 128 rms. CI 2pm/CO noon. Nonsmoking rms avail. Bright modern furniture and spreads make rooms attractive. Some units on ends of buildings are larger than most others. **Amenities:** 🛅 🕭 A/C, cable TV w/movies. **Services:** 🖎 🛜 Car-rental desk, babysitting. Free van to Metro station. **Facilities:** 🗔 125 1 restaurant, 1 bar. Family-style restaurant off lobby. **Rates:** Peak (Apr–Sept) $58–$85 S or D. Extra person $7. Children under age 17 stay free. Lower rates off-season. Parking: Outdoor, free. AE, CB, DC, DISC, JCB, MC, V.

RESTAURANTS 🍴

Atami
3155 Wilson Blvd (Clarendon); tel 703/522-4787. **Japanese.** Very large traditional Japanese prints and paper lanterns lend an appropriate air to this cozy establishment noted for sushi and sashimi, which are prepared at a bar at the rear of the dining room. (All-you-can-eat sushi for $25.) Cooked meals such as teriyaki, tempura, and yosenabe also available. **FYI:** Reservations recommended. **Open:** Mon–Thurs 11am–10pm, Fri–Sat 11am–10:30pm, Sun 5–10pm. **Prices:** Main courses $9–$15. MC, V.

Bangkok Gourmet
523 S 23rd St at S Eads St (Crystal City); tel 703/521-1305. **Thai.** Mirrors along one wall and bright white paint elsewhere make this narrow storefront establishment seem bigger than it is. Linen and flowers add elegance. Young chef prepares variety of gourmet Thai selections; menu changes quarterly. Small sidewalk dining area is enclosed during cool months. **FYI:** Reservations accepted. No smoking. **Open:** Lunch Mon–Fri 11am–2:30pm; dinner daily 5:30–10pm. **Prices:** Main courses $9–$16; prix fixe $21–$27. CB, DC, DISC, MC, V. 🍽

Ⓢ Cafe Dalat
3143 Wilson Blvd (Clarendon); tel 703/276-0935. **Vietnamese.** Behind a plain storefront is one of the better bargains in Little Saigon (the area around Clarendon Metro station), if not one of its most elegant restaurants. It has small dark wood tables, stucco walls adorned with maps and paintings of Vietnam, and the original pressed-tin ceiling of the building's mercantile days. A wide range of family-style Vietnamese dishes, with emphasis on grilled seafood and crepes stuffed with shrimp, chicken, and vegetables. **FYI:** Reservations not accepted. No smoking. **Open:** Sun–Thurs 11am–9:30pm, Fri–Sat 11am–10:30pm. **Prices:** Main courses $6–$9. MC, V.

Carlyle Grand Café
In Shirlington Village, 4000 S 28th St, at I-395; tel 703/931-0777. **New American/Californian.** Black-and-white tile floors, lots of plants, and art deco touches highlight this large, two-story establishment. Downstairs is pub-like, while upstairs dining room under a huge skylight is somewhat more formal. Wicker and rattan chairs lend a California air. Menu

offers a mix of Cajun, West Coast, and other regional selections, most light and healthful. Call ahead for priority on waiting list. **FYI:** Reservations not accepted. No smoking. **Open:** Mon–Tues 11:30am–11pm, Wed–Thurs 11:30am–midnight, Fri–Sat 11:30am–1am, Sun 10am–11pm. **Prices:** Main courses $11–$17. AE, MC, V. 🍰 ☑ &

⑤ Chez Froggy

509 S 23rd St, at S Eads St (Crystal City); tel 703/979-7676. US 1 exit off I-395. **French.** A narrow storefront establishment with a row of tables down each side and walls hung with French impressionist reproductions. Known for frogs' legs sautéed in butter and garlic, plus fish prepared with traditional French sauces. Daily specials depend on availability of produce. A neighborhood favorite. **FYI:** Reservations accepted. Dress code. **Open:** Lunch Mon–Fri 11am–2pm; dinner Mon–Sat 5:30–10pm. Closed 2 weeks in Aug. **Prices:** Main courses $11–$20. CB, DC, DISC, MC, V. 🍰

Delhi Dhaba Indian Café and Carry Out

2424 Wilson Blvd; tel 703/524-0008. **Indian.** Guests order cafeteria-style in the front of this very clean establishment and take their meals, on Styrofoam trays and plates, to a simple but attractive dining room at the rear. TVs playing Indian music videos provide ethnic atmosphere. Local young professionals and families who have emigrated from India flock here for authentic but inexpensive northern Indian cuisine, such as chicken and lamb kabobs prepared in tandoori ovens, plus spicy meat, seafood, and vegetable curries. Located 2 blocks west of Courthouse Metro. **FYI:** Reservations not accepted. Beer and wine only. No smoking. **Open:** Sun–Thurs 11am–10pm, Fri–Sat 11am–11pm. **Prices:** Main courses $4–$6. AE, CB, DC, DISC, MC, V. 🚗 &

Food Factory

4221 N Fairfax Dr (Ballston); tel 703/527-2279. **Indian/Middle Eastern/Afghan.** Arches and plastic flowers add a slight bit of charm to this carryout restaurant with cafeteria-style display case and Formica tables arranged in long rows. Char-grilled beef, lamb, and chicken kabobs, wrapped in large pieces of fresh Afghan-style bread, are the specialty. Meat and vegetable curries served too. All meat slaughtered by Islamic ritual. Very popular among local South Asian immigrants and as a good-value lunch spot for nearby office workers. Entrance is from parking lot at rear of building. **FYI:** Reservations not accepted. No liquor license. **Open:** Mon–Fri 11am–10pm, Sat–Sun noon–10pm. **Prices:** Main courses $7–$10. No CC.

★ Hard Times Café

3028 Wilson Blvd (Clarendon); tel 703/528-2233. **Regional American.** Subdued lighting from lamps hung over wooden booths, state flags, and historical photos give this chili parlor a pub-like atmosphere. Larger of two dining rooms looks like small-town eatery with bar in one corner. Specialties are spicy vegetarian and Texas- and Cincinnati-style chilies served with

beans or spaghetti, plus pub-style chicken wings, burgers, and sandwiches. Popular with young professionals. **FYI:** Reservations not accepted. Children's menu. Additional location: 1404 King St, Old Town Alexandria (tel 683-5340). **Open:** Mon–Thurs 11:30am–10pm, Fri–Sat 11:30am–11pm, Sun noon–10pm. **Prices:** Main courses $4–$6. AE, MC, V. &

Hunan Number 1

3033 Wilson Blvd at N Garfield St (Clarendon); tel 703/528-1177. **Chinese.** Bas-relief scenes on walls and porcelain statues transmit elegance at one of the more upscale Chinese restaurants in Arlington. Chef specializes in live Maine lobsters, kept in dining room tank, as well as shrimp, scallops, and whole fish in spicy Hunan-style sauces. Entrance on N Garfield St. **FYI:** Reservations recommended. **Open:** Daily 11am–2am. **Prices:** Main courses $10–$15. AE, DISC, MC, V. 🖼 &

⑤ La Cantinita's Havana Café

3100 Clarendon Blvd (Clarendon); tel 703/524-3611. **Cuban.** Coral and lagoon colors evoke Miami's South Beach at this family-owned, Cuban-style cafe with widely spaced tables. Picture windows and recessed photo of tropical beach give feeling of even more space. Such Havana favorites as shredded beef, marinated roast pork, and pressed sandwiches at lunchtime. **FYI:** Reservations not accepted. **Open:** Mon–Fri 11am–11pm, Sat 4–11pm, Sun 4–10pm. **Prices:** Main courses $8–$15. DISC, MC, V. 🍰 🖼 &

Little Viet Garden

3012 Wilson Blvd (Clarendon); tel 703/522-9686. **Vietnamese.** A small but pleasing bistro-style establishment whose lush garden-like decor sets it off from other Little Saigon restaurants. Outdoor dining at umbrella tables in fine weather. House specialties are crispy Vietnamese spring rolls and such main courses as grilled beef wrapped in vine leaves. Dinner specials daily. Jazz plays on speakers, and live jazz bands perform outdoors in July. **FYI:** Reservations not accepted. **Open:** Lunch Mon–Fri 11am–2:30pm, Sat–Sun 11am–5pm; dinner daily 5–10pm. **Prices:** Main courses $6–$11. AE, CB, DC, DISC, MC, V. 🍰

⑤ ★ Matuba

2915 Columbia Pike, at Walter Reed Dr (South Arlington); tel 703/521-2811. **Japanese.** Dining room a bit cramped but pleasantly trimmed and furnished with bright varnished wood. Sushi is prepared at a bar in the rear, but cooked Japanese meals are also available. **FYI:** Reservations recommended. Beer and wine only. **Open:** Lunch Mon–Fri 11:30am–2pm; dinner Sun–Thurs 5:30–10pm, Fri–Sat 5:30–10:30pm. **Prices:** Main courses $7–$12; prix fixe $9. AE, MC, V.

Nam Viet

1127 N Hudson St (Clarendon); tel 703/522-7110. At Wilson Blvd. **Vietnamese.** Subdued lighting, blood-red chairs, and pink tablecloths give this narrow restaurant a touch of class. Walls are adorned with smoked mirror panels and paintings of Vietnamese landscapes. Chef specializes in marinated chicken, beef, pork, and shrimp char-grilled on skewers and served over noodles and vegetables. **FYI:** Reservations recommended. **Open:** Sun–Thurs 10am–10pm, Fri–Sat 10am–11pm. **Prices:** Main courses $7–$13; prix fixe $15–$25. AE, MC, V. 🍴

Pho Cali/The Quality Seafood Place

1621 S Walter Reed Dr, at S Glebe Rd (South Arlington); tel 703/920-9500. **Vietnamese.** A rose-and-pink color scheme accented with potted plants, hanging baskets, and year-round strips of holly belie the storefront appearance of this pleasant establishment known for its Vietnamese-style Dungeness crabs and Chesapeake Bay renditions of spiced blue crabs. Northern Vietnam hot pots are a specialty. **FYI:** Reservations recommended. **Open:** Sun–Thurs 10am–10pm, Fri–Sat 10am–11pm. **Prices:** Main courses $5–$16; prix fixe $20. AE, CB, DC, DISC, MC, V. 🍴 ♿

⑤ Pho 75

In Colonial Village Shopping Center, 1711 Wilson Blvd (Rosslyn); tel 703/525-7355. At N Quinn St. **Vietnamese.** A very plain and simple establishment with Formica-top tables in long rows and a few Vietnamese photos to lend a bit of atmosphere. Noted not for decor but for budget prices for the only item offered: excellent noodle soups with a variety of meats and vegetable toppings. **FYI:** Reservations not accepted. No liquor license. Additional location: 3103 Graham Rd, Falls Church (tel 204-1490). **Open:** Daily 9am–8pm. **Prices:** Main courses $5–$7. No CC.

⑤ ★ Queen Bee Restaurant

3181 Wilson Blvd (Clarendon); tel 703/527-3444. **Vietnamese.** Prepare to wait for a table on weekends at this place, long a favorite with locals. Mirrored panels along one wall give a feeling of space while reflecting large Vietnamese photos and paintings on the other. Lighting is subdued. Vietnamese dishes are very well prepared, making this one of the area's best bargains. **FYI:** Reservations not accepted. Beer and wine only. **Open:** Daily 11am–10pm. **Prices:** Main courses $6–$9. AE, MC, V.

★ Red Hot & Blue

1600 Wilson Blvd (Rosslyn); tel 703/276-7427. At N Pierce St. **Barbecue.** Photos of famous politicians and blues musicians create a pub-like aura at this Memphis-style barbecue house, one of whose founding partners was the late Lee Atwater, advisor to President George Bush and an amateur blues guitarist. Smoked pork ribs, either "dry" or "wet" in the Memphis tradition, are the main offering, plus barbecued chicken, burgers, and sandwiches. Occasional live entertainment when blues artists are in town. Carryout available. **FYI:** Reservations not accepted. Children's menu. Additional location: 3014 Wilson Blvd, Clarendon (tel 243-1510). **Open:** Mon–Thurs 11am–10pm, Fri–Sat 11am–11pm, Sun 11am–10pm. **Prices:** Main courses $5–$10. AE, MC, V. ♿

★ Ristorante Portofino

526 S 23rd St (Crystal City); tel 703/929-8200. At S Eads St. **Italian.** What was once the living room of a private home is now an elegant dining room with nonworking fireplace and drawn shutters. A second eating area is like an enclosed garden with multitude of tropical plants and white cafe tables and chairs. Northern Italian–style chicken, veal, and fish dishes predominate on the menu. **FYI:** Reservations recommended. Dress code. **Open:** Lunch Mon–Fri 11am–2pm; dinner daily 5–10pm. **Prices:** Main courses $14–$19. AE, CB, DC, MC, V. ♥

Tom Sarris' Orleans House

1213 Wilson Blvd, at N Lynn St (Rosslyn); tel 703/524-2929. **New American.** The main dining room is designed like a New Orleans courtyard; dining is on the main level and on balconies set off by wrought-iron railings. Famous for reasonably priced cuts of prime rib. Also offers steaks and seafood items. Popular with tourists and meat-and-potato locals. **FYI:** Reservations not accepted. Children's menu. **Open:** Mon–Fri 11am–11pm, Sat 4–11pm, Sun 4–10pm. **Prices:** Main courses $6–$15. AE, DISC, MC, V.

Ashland

North of Richmond in central Virginia, Ashland was named for the Kentucky home of statesman Henry Clay. **Information:** Ashland/Hanover Chamber of Commerce, 112 N Railroad Ave, Ashland, 23005 (tel 804/798-1722).

MOTELS 🏨

≡≡ Best Western Hanover House

10296 Sliding Hill Rd, PO Box 1215, 23005; tel 804/550-2805 or toll free 800/528-1234; fax 804/550-3843. Exit 86 off I-95. A clean and comfortable if not overly attractive motel. **Rooms:** 93 rms. CI 3pm/CO noon. Nonsmoking rms avail. **Amenities:** 🛁 🍷 A/C, satel TV w/movies. **Services:** 🧺 Twice-daily maid svce. **Facilities:** 🏊 👨‍🍳 200 1 restaurant, washer/dryer. **Rates:** Peak (May–Sept) $32–$65 S; $38–$75 D. Extra person $5. Children under age 12 stay free. Lower rates off-season. Parking: Outdoor, free. AE, CB, DC, DISC, MC, V.

≡≡ Days Inn

I-95 and VA 207, PO Box 70, Carmel Church, 22546; tel 804/448-2011 or toll free 800/329-7466. Exit 104 off I-95. A clean, comfortable, and well-landscaped facility convenient to Paramount's Kings Dominion amusement park. **Rooms:** 122 rms. CI 2pm/CO noon. Nonsmoking rms avail. **Amenities:** 🛁 A/C, cable TV, in-rm safe. **Services:** 🧺 🛎️ **Facilities:** 🏊 ♿ 1 restaurant (bkfst only), games rm, playground. **Rates:** Peak (Mar–Sept) $70–$75 S or D. Extra person $5. Children under age 12 stay free. Lower rates off-season. Parking: Outdoor, free. AE, CB, DC, DISC, JCB, MC, V.

≣≣≣ **Holiday Inn Ashland/Richmond**
810 England St (VA 54 at I-95), 23005; tel 804/798-4231 or toll free 800/922-4231; fax 804/798-9074. Exit 92 off I-95. Convenient to Paramount's Kings Dominion amusement park, this comfortable motel has well-landscaped grounds. On a strip with fast-food restaurants, service stations. **Rooms:** 167 rms and stes. CI 3pm/CO 11am. Nonsmoking rms avail. **Amenities:** 🛏 🅰 🖵 A/C, cable TV w/movies. Some units w/terraces. **Services:** ✕ 🚗 🖼 🕻 Complimentary coffee and newspapers. Nintendo games. **Facilities:** 🏊 🖵 🖵175 🚹 1 restaurant, 1 bar (w/entertainment), day-care ctr, washer/dryer. Fender's Lounge has entertainment Friday and Saturday evenings. **Rates:** Peak (June–Sept) $66–$96 S or D; $76 ste. Children under age 16 stay free. Lower rates off-season. Parking: Outdoor, free. AE, CB, DC, DISC, MC, V.

≣≣ **Holiday Inn Express**
24011 Ruther Glen Rd, Ruther Glen, 22546; tel 804/448-2608 or toll free 800/HOLIDAY; fax 804/448-0084. Exit 104 off I-95. Brand new in 1996, this highway motel offers surprisingly elegant accommodations. Friendly, helpful staff. **Rooms:** 62 rms. CI open/CO 11am. Nonsmoking rms avail. Large rooms, good furnishings. **Amenities:** 🛏 A/C, cable TV w/movies. **Services:** 🕻 🕻 **Facilities:** 🏊 🖵12 🚹 Electronic key automatically reprogrammed for each guest. **Rates (CP):** Peak (May–Sept) $80–$89 S or D. Children under age 13 stay free. Lower rates off-season. Parking: Outdoor, free. AE, CB, DC, DISC, JCB, MC, V.

≣≣ **Howard Johnson**
23786 Rodgers Clark Blvd, Ruther Glen, 22546; tel 804/448-2499 or toll free 800/654-2000; fax 804/448-2499. Exit 104 (VA 207) off I-95. A brand new motel with a small lobby and no frills, but with large, nicely decorated rooms and all the essentials for an overnight stop along the highway. Rates are competitive for the area. **Rooms:** 42 rms and stes. Executive level. CI 2pm/CO noon. Nonsmoking rms avail. Two suites have whirlpool tubs. **Amenities:** 🛏 A/C, cable TV. Some units w/whirlpools. **Services:** 🕻 🕻 Pet charge varies from $5 to $15, depending on size. **Facilities:** 🚹 **Rates (CP):** Peak (Mar–Sept) $65–$68 S or D; $85–$88 ste. Extra person $5. Children under age 12 stay free. Lower rates off-season. Parking: Outdoor, free. AE, MC, V.

≣≣ **Ramada Inn Ashland**
806 England St, 23005; tel 804/798-4262; fax 804/798-7009. Exit 92 off I-95. A clean, comfortable chain motel on a strip with fast-food restaurants, service stations. **Rooms:** 88 rms. CI 2pm/CO noon. Nonsmoking rms avail. **Amenities:** 🛏 A/C, cable TV w/movies. Free coffee and newspapers. **Services:** 🕻 **Facilities:** 🏊 🖵12 🚹 1 restaurant. **Rates:** Peak (May 30–Sept 7) $64–$69 D. Extra person $5. Children under age 18 stay free. Lower rates off-season. Parking: Outdoor, free. AE, CB, DC, DISC, MC, V.

INN

≣≣≣ **The Henry Clay Inn**
114 N Railroad Ave, PO Box 135, 23005; tel 804/798-3100 or toll free 800/343-4565; fax 804/752-7555. 15 mi N of Richmond, exit 92 off I-95. The perfect place for those who prefer the comfort, hospitality, and charm of a country inn. Beautifully and elegantly furnished. Front porch is lined with rocking chairs. Large parlor has fireplace. The second-floor balcony adds to appeal. **Rooms:** 15 rms and stes. CI 2pm/CO 11am. Each room individually decorated, yet all provide high-quality accommodations and simple luxury. **Amenities:** 🛏 🅰 A/C, cable TV. Some units w/whirlpools. **Services:** ✕ 🕻 Homemade breads and muffins served at breakfast. **Facilities:** 🖵40 🚹 1 restaurant, guest lounge. Small restaurant, art gallery, gift shop. **Rates (CP):** $65–$80 S or D; $125–$145 ste. Extra person $15. Children under age 12 stay free. Parking: Outdoor, free. AE, MC, V.

RESTAURANTS 🍴

Homemades by Suzanne
102 N Railroad Ave; tel 804/798-8331. Exit 92 off I-95. Follow England St west to Railroad Ave, turn right. **Deli.** Wonderful aromas come from goodies baking in this restaurant near Ashland's historic railroad. Emphasis is on fresh, homemade edibles rather than decor: a hodgepodge of bare wood tables, baskets, wall murals, and prints. Best are sandwiches, salads, and desserts. **FYI:** Reservations not accepted. No liquor license. No smoking. Additional location: 10 S 6th St, Richmond (tel 775-2116). **Open:** Mon–Fri 9am–6pm, Sat 10am–3pm. **Prices:** Main courses $5–$14. AE, CB, DC, DISC, MC, V. ▬

The Smokey Pig
US 1; tel 804/798-4590. Exit 92B off I-95. **Barbecue/Burgers.** This Southern-style barbecue house is festooned with ceiling fans, Tiffany lamps, checked tablecloths under glass tops, plants, and lots of pig prints, collectibles, and crafts. Specialty is pit-cooked pork, including ribs, although menu also offers a variety of beef and seafood dishes. **FYI:** Reservations accepted. **Open:** Tues–Sat 11am–9pm, Sun noon–9pm. **Prices:** Main courses $3–$19. MC, V. 🚹

ATTRACTIONS 🏛

Scotchtown
Beaverdam; tel 804/227-3500. Follow VA 671 to VA 685 north to Scotchtown. One of Virginia's oldest plantation houses, Scotchtown is a charming white clapboard home built by Charles Chiswell of Williamsburg, probably around 1719. Patrick Henry bought the house in 1770, and a year later came to live here with his wife and six children. The house has been beautifully restored and furnished with 18th-century antiques, some of them associated with the Henry family. In the study, Henry's mahogany desk-table remains, and bookshelves still hold his law books. Special events include

the Scottish Festival Games in late May and Christmas Candlelight Tours the first weekend in December. **Open:** Peak (May–Oct) Tues–Sat 10am–4:30pm, Sun 1:30–4:30pm. Reduced hours off-season. Closed Nov–Mar. **$$**

Paramount's Kings Dominion
Exit 98 off I-95, Doswell; tel 804/876-5000. This 400-acre family amusement park offers 44 rides and attractions and 10 live shows throughout the day. The park's star attraction is **Sky Pilot,** a flight trainer–style ride that simulates aerobatic flight maneuvers. **Wild Water Canyon** is a wet-and-wild ride simulating white-water rafting with all the thrills and excitement, but without the danger. Other favorites include **The Outer Limits: Flight of Fear** (an indoor roller coaster that catapults rider through four inversions), **Nickelodeon Splat City,** and the **Days of Thunder** racing simulator. **Open:** Peak (June–Labor Day) daily 10:30am–10pm. Reduced hours off-season. Closed Oct–Mar. **$$$$**

Basye

In the Shenandoah Valley, northwest of New Market, with lots of outdoor recreation and mountain views.

LODGE 🏨

≣ ≣ **Sky Chalet Mountain Lodge**
VA 263 W, PO Box 300, 22810; tel 540/856-2147; fax 540/856-2436. Exit 273 off I-81. 12 mi W on VA 263. Quaint mountaintop lodges have spectacular views. Orkney Springs, home of Shenandoah Music Festival in summer, is three miles away. Skiing, golf, hiking, swimming, fishing, and canoeing are minutes away. **Rooms:** 5 rms, stes, and effic; 5 cottages/villas. CI 3pm/CO 11am. Cozy cabins are rustic and simple but clean and heated. **Amenities:** No A/C, phone, or TV. Some units w/terraces, some w/fireplaces. Rocking chairs and hammocks. **Services:** 🚗 🍴 🥤 **Facilities:** 🍽 🏊15 2 restaurants (dinner only; *see* "Restaurants" below), 1 bar. **Rates (CP):** Peak (May–Nov) $29–$54 S; $34–$59 D; $39–$79 ste; $69–$99 effic; $99–$200 cottage/villa. Extra person $10. Children under age 5 stay free. Min stay special events. Lower rates off-season. Parking: Outdoor, free. DC, DISC, MC, V.

RESTAURANT 🍴

★ **Sky Chalet Country Restaurant**
In Sky Chalet Mountain Lodge, VA 263 W; tel 540/856-2625. Exit 273 off I-81. **American/Continental.** Great views and a genuinely rustic mountain atmosphere, thanks to wooden chairs and tables, large stone fireplace, and a stuffed moose head. Relaxed and casual but fine dining. Although regular menu is traditional, weekends see European specials. Veranda overlooks valley. **FYI:** Reservations recommended. Children's menu. **Open:** Peak (May–Sept) Fri–Sun 5–9pm. **Prices:** Main courses $10–$20. MC, V. 🍷 🏔

Bedford

See also Hardy

South-central Virginia town close to both the Blue Ridge Parkway and the Appalachian Trail. **Information:** Bedford Area Chamber of Commerce, 305 E Main St, Bedford, 24523 (tel 540/586-9401).

INN 🏨

≣ ≣ ≣ ≣ **The Manor at Taylor's Store**
Rte 1 Box 533, Wirtz, 24184; tel 540/721-3951 or toll free 800/248-6267; fax 540/721-5243. Off VA 122 N. 120 acres. Set in a beautiful section of the Blue Ridge foothills, this manor house dates to 1820. The Southern hospitality includes gift baskets for special occasions and close attention to special requests—they'll even stock guests' favorite wines, with advance notice. **Rooms:** 9 rms and stes (2 w/shared bath); 1 cottage/villa. CI 6pm/CO 11am. No smoking. Individually decorated with fine period antiques. **Amenities:** 🛁 🍴 A/C, bathrobes. No TV. Some units w/terraces, some w/fireplaces, some w/whirlpools. **Services:** 🚗 Twice-daily maid svce, masseur, babysitting, afternoon tea served. Hot air balloon rides available. European dinner baskets, including wine, on request. **Facilities:** 🔺 🏊 🚣 🛶 30 Games rm, lawn games, whirlpool, guest lounge w/TV. Guest kitchen has coffee, tea, and snacks. Lounge with wide screen TV and video library, formal parlor with grand piano. Six spring-fed ponds on site, for swimming, canoeing, and fishing. **Rates (BB):** $95 S or D w/shared bath; $80–$170 S or D w/private bath; $80–$170 ste; $90–$190 cottage/villa. Extra person $20. MAP rates avail. Parking: Outdoor, free. MC, V.

LODGE 🏨

≣ ≣ ≣ **Peaks of Otter Lodge**
MM 86 Blue Ridge Pkwy, PO Box 489, 24523; tel 540/586-1081; fax 540/586-4420. Located on the Blue Ridge Pkwy at the base of Sharp Top Mountain, this lodge is very popular at leaf-changing time, when it provides spectacular views of an array of colors. **Rooms:** 63 rms and stes. CI 3pm/CO noon. Nonsmoking rms avail. Rooms furnished in pale-blue country rustic style. Glass walls, which open to individual patios, provide lake and mountain views. **Amenities:** 🛁 🍴 A/C. No TV. Some units w/terraces. Ranger station across road gives interpretive nature talks. Restored pioneer farm within short hike. **Services:** 🥤 **Facilities:** 🏊 🚣 60 👍 2 restaurants, 1 bar. **Rates:** Peak (Oct) $68–$73 S or D; $90–$105 ste. Extra person $7. Children under age 16 stay free. Lower rates off-season. MAP rates avail. Parking: Outdoor, free. MC, V.

Big Stone Gap

Noted for its mountain scenery, and named for the gap in the mountains through which the Powell River emerges.

MOTEL ▥

☰ Country Inn

627 Gilley Ave, PO Box 142, 24219; tel 540/523-0374; fax 540/523-5043. Hidden in the highlands close to the Kentucky border, this rural motel offers a night's sleep and little more. Apparent dinginess comes from age, not lack of cleanliness. Saving grace is proximity to the *Lonesome Pine* outdoor drama. **Rooms:** 44 rms. CI noon/CO noon. Nonsmoking rms avail. Clean rooms are sparse and basic, with old furniture. **Amenities:** ☎ ⟁ A/C, cable TV w/movies. **Services:** ⟲ **Facilities:** RV park is adjacent to motel. **Rates:** $30–$32 S; $35 D. Extra person $3. Parking: Outdoor, free. AE, CB, DC, DISC, MC, V.

ATTRACTIONS ▣

Southwest Virginia Museum

10 W 1st St; tel 540/523-1322. This four-story Victorian mansion contains exhibits detailing the human history of this region. Topics include Native Americans, settlers, and workers in the coal industry, which prospered here around the turn of the century. Two of the second-floor galleries chronicle the life and times of prominent local citizens, including eight-term US Congressman C Bascom Slemp. The museum shop features ornate reproduction jewelry, books, toys, and porcelain dolls. **Open:** Peak (Mem Day–Labor Day) Mon–Thurs 10am–4pm, Fri 9am–4pm, Sat 10am–5pm, Sun 1–5pm. Reduced hours off-season. Closed Jan–Feb. **$**

June Tolliver House

Jerome St at Clinton Ave; tel 540/523-4707 or 523-1235. The heroine of John Fox Jr's turn-of-the-century bestseller *The Trail of the Lonesome Pine* lived here while attending school. The novel tells the story of a romance between a beautiful young mountain woman and a handsome mining engineer from the Northeast against the backdrop of the great coal and iron boom that brought so many drastic changes to the mountain people's way of life. Free guided tours include 19th-century parlor furnishings, June Tolliver's bedroom, and the John Fox Jr Memorial Room.

In the adjoining **June Tolliver Playhouse,** a 2½-hour musical stage adaptation of *The Trail of the Lonesome Pine* by Earl Hobson Smith is performed June through Labor Day. Visitors may call toll free 800/362-0149 to make reservations for the show. **Open:** Mid-May–mid-Dec, Tues–Wed 10am–5pm, Thurs–Sat 10am–9pm, Sun 2–6pm. **$$$**

John Fox Jr House and Museum

117 Shawnee Ave; tel 540/523-2747 or 523-1235. This National and Virginia Historic Landmark serves both as a museum and a memorial to the Fox family. Built in 1888, the house is filled with beautiful furnishings and mementos of John Fox and his family. While living here, Fox wrote *The Trail of the Lonesome Pine, The Little Shepherd of Kingdom Come,* and other full-length novels in addition to more than 500 short stories. **Open:** Mem Day–Labor Day, Tues–Sun 2–5pm. **$**

Blacksburg

This Allegheny Mountain town is home to Virginia Polytechnic Institute and State University, the largest university in Virginia. **Information:** Blacksburg–Montgomery County Visitors Center, 141 Jackson St, Blacksburg, 24060 (tel 540/552-4061).

HOTEL ▥

☰☰☰ Blacksburg Marriott

900 Prices Fork Rd, 24060; tel 540/552-7001 or toll free 800/228-9290; fax 540/552-0827. Exit 118 of I-81. A large stone fireplace, balcony, and tall ceilings in the public areas provide a warm welcome to this hotel just minutes from Virginia Tech and shopping centers. **Rooms:** 148 rms and stes. Executive level. CI 3pm/CO noon. Nonsmoking rms avail. Very spacious rooms are elegantly appointed with dark furniture and floral decor. **Amenities:** ☎ ⟁ ☏ A/C, cable TV w/movies, dataport. Some units w/terraces. **Services:** ✕ 🚐 ⊿ ⟲ 🖫 Complimentary coffee in lobby. **Facilities:** ⛳ 🎾 450 ⟁ 2 restaurants, 1 bar, games rm, whirlpool, playground. Patios with tables and chairs face an interior courtyard with swimming pool. **Rates:** $89–$99 S or D; $150–$160 ste. Extra person $10. Children under age 18 stay free. Min stay special events. Parking: Outdoor, free. Weekend packages avail. AE, JCB.

MOTELS

☰☰☰ Best Western Red Lion Inn

900 Plantation Rd, 24060; tel 540/552-7770; fax 540/552-6346. Exit 118 off I-81. Follow US 460 W for 10 miles, to Prices Fork Rd. Attractive English tudor-style inn is located on 13 acres, making the nearby highway seem far away. Stone walls and fireplace in lobby are inviting; outside gazebo is romantic. Near Virginia Tech, Radford University, and good fishing. **Rooms:** 104 rms and stes. Executive level. CI noon/CO 11am. Nonsmoking rms avail. **Amenities:** ☎ ⟁ A/C, cable TV w/movies. **Services:** ✕ ⊿ ⟲ 🖫 Small pets only. Complimentary daily newspaper. **Facilities:** ⛳ 🎾3 400 ⟁ 1 restaurant, 1 bar, playground. Restaurant serves on patio, weather permitting. **Rates:** Peak (Mar–May/Aug–Nov) $49–$56 S; $57–$69 D; $130 ste. Extra person $6. Children under age 17 stay free. Min stay special events. Lower rates off-season. Parking: Outdoor, free. AE, CB, DC, DISC, MC, V.

≡≡ Comfort Inn
3705 S Main St, 24060; tel 540/951-1500 or toll free 800/228-5150; fax 540/951-1530. Exit 118 off I-81. Convenient to the center of town, this modern facility is favored by those attending Virginia Tech functions. **Rooms:** 80 rms and stes. CI 3pm/CO 11am. Nonsmoking rms avail. Rooms are exceptionally well furnished with dark woods and subdued floral upholstery. **Amenities:** 🛁 🍷 A/C, cable TV w/movies, dataport. Complimentary daily newspaper. **Services:** 🖼 🖐 🦺 **Facilities:** 🛗 🔟 🏊 Pool enjoys a spectacular panoramic view of the Blue Ridge Mountains. **Rates (CP):** $53–$61 S or D; $85 ste. Extra person $5. Children under age 18 stay free. Min stay special events. Parking: Outdoor, free. AE, CB, DC, DISC, ER, JCB, MC, V.

≡≡ Holiday Inn Blacksburg
3503 Holiday Lane, 24060; tel 540/951-1330 or toll free 800/465-4329; fax 540/951-4847. Exit 118 off I-81. Close to Virginia Tech, downtown Blacksburg, and recreational areas. **Rooms:** 98 rms and stes. Executive level. CI 3pm/CO noon. Nonsmoking rms avail. Some rooms have recliners. **Amenities:** 🛁 🍷 A/C, cable TV w/movies, dataport. 1 unit w/whirlpool. Some units have coffeemakers, refrigerators. **Services:** ✕ 🖼 🖐 🦺 **Facilities:** 🛗 🔲 1 restaurant, 1 bar (w/entertainment), washer/dryer. **Rates:** $54 S or D; $125 ste. Extra person $5. Children under age 19 stay free. Min stay special events. Parking: Outdoor, free. AE, CB, DC, DISC, MC, V.

Breaks Interstate Park

Established by a joint action of the Kentucky and Virginia legislatures in 1954, Breaks Interstate Park covers more than 4,500 acres of woodland and striking mountain scenery that span the border between the two states. Within the park, the Russell Fork River has carved the largest canyon east of the Mississippi. More than 5 miles long and 1,600 feet deep, the canyon surrounds the river with sheer vertical walls throughout most of the park. The river winds around the **Towers,** an imposing pyramid of rocks over ½-mile long and ⅓-mile wide. Overlooks along the way provide spectacular views.

The park has 13 hiking trails, ranging from easy to extremely steep. Wooded areas are ideal for birdwatching. Other facilities include a swimming pool, boat dock and rentals, lake and pond fishing, horseback riding, and camping. The **visitor center** (tel 540/865-4413 or 865-4414), located 7 miles north of Haysi off VA 80, features natural and historical exhibits, as well as an exhibit on the local coal industry. For more information, contact Breaks Interstate Park, PO Box 100, Breaks, VA 24607.

Bristol

Established in 1850 as the town of Goodson, but renamed Bristol in 1890 for the contiguous town in Tennessee of the same name. Today, the two towns share the same main street. **Information:** Bristol Chamber of Commerce, 20 Volunteer Pkwy, PO Box 519, Bristol, TN 24201 (tel 615/989-4850).

MOTELS 🏨

≡≡ Comfort Inn
2368 Lee Hwy, 24201; tel 540/466-3881 or toll free 800/4-CHOICE; fax 540/466-6544. Exit 5 off I-81. A quiet, small motel tucked into a hillside yet offering convenient access to the interstate. Proximity to Bristol International Raceway makes this a popular spot for NASCAR fans. **Rooms:** 60 rms and stes. CI noon/CO 11am. Nonsmoking rms avail. **Amenities:** 🛁 🍷 A/C, cable TV w/movies. Some units w/whirlpools. **Services:** 🖼 🖐 **Facilities:** 🛗 🔟 🏊 **Rates (CP):** Peak (May–Oct) $55–$175 S; $65–$195 D; $125–$225 ste. Extra person $7. Children under age 18 stay free. Min stay special events. Lower rates off-season. Parking: Outdoor, free. AE, CB, DC, DISC, ER, JCB, MC, V.

≡≡ Ramada Inn
2221 Euclid Ave, 24201; tel 540/669-7171 or toll free 800/465-4329; fax 540/669-8694. Exit 3 off I-81. This large and sprawling property is in the city, yet the units face a large hillside, giving a woodsy feel. **Rooms:** 123 rms. CI noon/CO noon. Nonsmoking rms avail. **Amenities:** 🛁 🍷 A/C, cable TV w/movies. Some units w/terraces. **Services:** ✕ 🖼 🖐 🦺 Security officer patrols this spread-out establishment at night. **Facilities:** 🛗 🔲 🏊 1 restaurant (bkfst and dinner only), 1 bar. **Rates:** $55–$60 S; $60–$65 D. Children under age 18 stay free. Min stay special events. Parking: Outdoor, free. AE, CB, DC, DISC, MC, V.

Brookneal

Central Virginia town near the Falling River. The last home and burial site of Patrick Henry is nearby. **Information:** Brookneal Area Chamber of Commerce, PO Box 387, Brookneal, 24528 (tel 804/376-2795).

ATTRACTION 🏛

Red Hill–Patrick Henry National Memorial
Tel 804/376-2044. Located at VA 40 and County Rtes 600 and 619; follow signs. The fiery orator's last home, Red Hill is a modest frame farmhouse, authentically reconstructed on the original foundation after fire destroyed it in 1919. The overseer's cottage that Patrick Henry used as a law office is an original structure. Henry retired to Red Hill in 1794 after serving five terms as governor of Virginia. Failing health forced him to refuse numerous posts, including those of chief justice of the Supreme Court and secretary of state.

The Visitors Center presents a 15-minute video on Henry's life at Red Hill and exhibits a large collection of Henry memorabilia, including Peter Rothermel's painting depicting Patrick Henry's famous speech before the Virginia House of Burgesses ("If this be treason, make the most of it"). The site's most striking feature, the osage orange tree, standing 64 feet tall and spanning 96 feet, is listed in the American Forestry Hall of Fame. **Open:** Peak (Apr–Oct) daily 9am–5pm. Reduced hours off-season. **$**

Carmel Church

See Ashland

Chantilly

See Dulles Int'l Airport

Charles City

On the James River, west of Williamsburg, and noted as the birthplace of two US presidents: William Henry Harrison and John Tyler. Settlers celebrated the first Thanksgiving Day here in 1619, and during the Civil War the familiar tune "Taps" was written here.

RESTAURANT 🍴

★ **David's White House Restaurant**
3560 N Courthouse Rd, Providence Forge; tel 804/966-9700. Exit 214 off I-64; go 4 mi on VA 155. **Regional American/American.** Housed in a turn of the century structure, the dining room here manages to be both elegant (white tablecloths, linen napkins) and relaxed. Traditional Tidewater dishes include backfin crab cakes, baked Virginia ham garnished with bourbon-glazed apples, and grilled duck breast with fried grits. **FYI:** Reservations recommended. Guitar/singer. Children's menu. **Open:** Tues–Sat 6:30am–10pm, Sun 11am–10pm. **Prices:** Main courses $13–$22. AE, MC, V. 🛄&

ATTRACTIONS 📷

Berkeley
12602 Harrison Landing Rd; tel 804/829-6018. In 1691 Berkeley was acquired by the Harrison family, members in good standing of Virginia's aristocratic ruling class. Following a 10-minute slide presentation, 20-minute guided tours of the house are given by guides in colonial dress. Allow at least another half hour to explore the magnificent grounds and gardens. **Open:** Daily 9am–5pm. **$$$**

Shirley Plantation
501 Shirley Plantation Rd; tel 804/829-5121. Another historic James River plantation, Shirley was founded in 1613 and

has been in the same family since 1660. The present mansion dates from 1723. The house survived the Revolution, the Civil War, and Reconstruction, as did the dependencies, which include an 18th-century laundry (later used as a schoolhouse, where Robert E Lee had lessons as a boy). Several 35-minute tours are given throughout the day. **Open:** Daily 9am–5pm. **$$$**

Charlottesville

Noted as site of Thomas Jefferson's home, Monticello, and the University of Virginia, this Central Virginia city was incorporated in 1802. Located in fertile Piedmont farm region, noted for its apples and textile mills. Birthplace of explorers Lewis and Clark and site of James Monroe's home, Ash Lawn. Keep in mind that many local hotels take reservations one year in advance for U of Virginia graduation week. **Information:** Charlottesville–Albemarle County Chamber of Commerce, 5th and E Market Sts, PO Box 1564, Charlottesville, 22902 (tel 804/295-3141).

HOTELS 🏨

≡≡≡ Courtyard by Marriott
638 Hillsdale Dr, 22901; tel 804/973-7100 or toll free 800/321-2211; fax 804/973-7128. Exit 124 off I-64. Take US 29 N 2 miles. Very attractive hotel close to the highway and a major shopping mall but far enough removed to be quiet. Immaculate grounds have well-tended flowers and shrubs. University of Virginia and historic sights are three miles away. **Rooms:** 150 rms and stes. CI 3pm/CO noon. No smoking. Attractive and clean. Convenient for business travelers, rooms have desk, ample seating on sofa. **Amenities:** 🛁 🅰 A/C, cable TV w/movies, refrig. Some units w/minibars, some w/terraces. Instant coffee and hot-water tap. **Services:** ✕ 🚐 🖼 💬 Complimentary coffee and tea in lobby. **Facilities:** 🏋 🏊 ⛳ & 1 restaurant, 1 bar, whirlpool, washer/dryer. Lobby lounge with TV. Well-equipped exercise room. Guests can use health club 1½ miles away. **Rates:** $54–$85 S or D; $72 ste. Children under age 18 stay free. Min stay special events. Parking: Outdoor, free. AE, CB, DC, DISC, MC, V.

≡≡ English Inn of Charlottesville
2000 Morton Dr, 22903; tel 804/971-9900 or toll free 800/786-5400; fax 804/977-8008. Well-kept grounds surround this Tudor-style hotel with an attractive lobby. Friendly and helpful staff. **Rooms:** 88 rms and stes. CI 2pm/CO noon. No smoking. Recent major renovation. **Amenities:** 🛁 🅰 A/C, cable TV. Some units w/minibars. VCRs and movies can be rented. **Services:** 🚐 🖼 💬 Babysitting. Complimentary tea and coffee available 24 hours in conservatory. **Facilities:** 🏋 🏊 & Sauna. Copy machine in lobby. **Rates (CP):** $65 S; $70 D; $70–$75 ste. Extra person $7. Children under age 18 stay free. Parking: Outdoor, free. AE, CB, DC, DISC, MC, V.

Holiday Inn Monticello

1200 Fifth St, 22901; tel 804/977-5100 or toll free 800/465-4329; fax 804/293-5228. Exit 120 off I-64. This typical Holiday Inn is well maintained and has small but neatly landscaped and attractive grounds. Easy to find and convenient to interstate and university. **Rooms:** 135 rms and stes. Executive level. CI 2pm/CO noon. No smoking. New beds, carpet, wallpaper, and bedspreads were added in 1995. **Amenities:** A/C, cable TV w/movies. **Services:** Facilities: 1 restaurant, 1 bar, washer/dryer. **Rates:** $66–$76 S or D; $110 ste. Children under age 18 stay free. Min stay special events. Parking: Outdoor, free. AE, CB, DC, DISC, MC, V.

MOTELS

Econo Lodge South

400 Emmet Street (US 29), 22903; tel 804/296-2104 or toll free 800/424-4777; fax 804/296-2104. Exit 118B off I-64. A very basic but clean facility directly across a major highway from the University of Virginia athletic center. Reservations are necessary due to close proximity to university. **Rooms:** 60 rms. CI 1pm/CO 11am. No smoking. Recently upgraded, with new carpet, curtains, and bedspreads. **Amenities:** A/C, cable TV. Several rooms have small refrigerators and microwaves. **Services:** Free morning coffee. **Facilities:** Restaurant next door. **Rates:** Peak (May–Oct) $41–$51 S; $45–$55 D. Extra person $5. Children under age 18 stay free. Lower rates off-season. Parking: Outdoor, free. AE, DC, DISC, MC, V.

Hampton Inn

2035 India Rd, 22906; tel 804/978-7888 or toll free 800/426-7866; fax 804/973-0436. A basic, functional, and clean hotel devoid of most extras. Located in an attractive shopping center, easily seen from US 29. **Rooms:** 130 rms and stes. Executive level. CI 2pm/CO noon. No smoking. Small, clean, adequate rooms with no frills. **Amenities:** A/C, cable TV w/movies. **Services:** Babysitting. Complimentary morning newspapers. All-day coffee. **Facilities:** Front door locked 11pm–6am. **Rates (CP):** $56–$66 S; $58–$64 D; $100 ste. Children under age 18 stay free. Min stay special events. Lower rates off-season. Parking: Outdoor, free. AE, CB, DC, DISC, MC, V.

RESORT

Boar's Head Inn and Sports Club

US 250 W, PO Box 5307, 22903; tel 804/296-2181 or toll free 800/476-1988; fax 804/977-1306. Exit 118B off I-64. Follow US 250 W for 1½ miles. 53 acres. An attractive resort from the outside, with well-groomed grounds containing trees, benches, flowers, and a lake with tame geese for guests to feed. Lobby a bit dark and worn. **Rooms:** 173 rms, stes, and effic. Executive level. CI 4pm/CO noon. No smoking. Rooms are light and airy. **Amenities:** A/C, cable TV w/movies. Some units w/minibars, some w/terraces, some w/fireplaces. **Services:** Social director, masseur, children's program, babysitting. **Facilities:** 3 restaurants, 1 bar (w/entertainment), racquetball, squash, sauna, playground. **Rates:** $129–$275 S; $139–$285 D; $210 ste; $210 effic. Extra person $10. Children under age 16 stay free. Min stay special events. Parking: Outdoor, free. AE, DC, DISC, MC, V.

RESTAURANTS

C&O Restaurant

515 E Water St; tel 804/971-7044. **Regional American/French.** Brick walls and exposed beams hint at history and romance at this small restaurant in an early-20th-century house in historic downtown area. Though jackets are required in the formal upstairs dining room, downstairs bistro is more casual. Menu features international styles of seafood and meat dishes. Reservations recommended upstairs, not accepted in bistro. **FYI:** Dress code. **Open:** Lunch Mon–Fri 11:30am–3:00pm; dinner Sun–Thurs 5:30–10:00pm, Fri–Sat 5:30–11:00pm. Closed Jan 1–14. **Prices:** Main courses $8–$17. AE, MC, V.

The Coffee Exchange

In the Downtown Mall, 120 E Main St; tel 804/295-0975. **Coffeehouse.** A small but clean and attractive coffeehouse full of aromas from roasted beans and fresh-baked muffins, breads, and desserts. Sandwiches, salads, and light, inexpensive meals also featured. Coffees can be ordered by mail. A favorite of downtown workers. **FYI:** Reservations not accepted. Beer and wine only. No smoking. **Open:** Mon–Sat 7:30am–5pm, Sun 9am–5pm. **Prices:** Main courses $4–$6. DISC, MC, V.

Eastern Standard

In the Downtown Mall, 102 Old Preston Ave; tel 804/295-8668. **New American/Californian.** Small restaurant in an older building at the end of the Downtown Mall. Not a place for a special meal or fancy night out, but a pleasant-enough place to grab a quick bite while shopping or sightseeing. Healthful sandwiches include a vegetarian broccoli burger. **FYI:** Reservations accepted. Blues/guitar/jazz. **Open:** Dinner Tues–Thurs 5–10pm, Fri–Sat 5–11pm. **Prices:** Main courses $12–$18. AE, DISC, MC, V.

The Hardware Store Restaurant

In the Downtown Mall, 316 E Main St; tel 804/977-1518. **Eclectic.** An old brick-walled commercial building converted to an eatery that caters to the college crowd. Subdued lighting softens the noisy, crowded yet fun place to eat. Circular stairs lead to upstairs area. A wide variety of items includes sandwich combinations, delicious desserts, old-fashioned sodas. **FYI:** Reservations recommended. **Open:** Mon–Thurs 11am–9pm, Fri–Sat 11am–10pm. **Prices:** Main courses $5–$12. AE, CB, DC, DISC, MC, V.

Miller's
In the Downtown Mall, 109 W Main St; tel 804/971-8511. **American.** This small bar/restaurant in a historic building has a long bar backed by a huge mirror. Small, close tables and stage at one end hint at evening entertainment aimed at college students. In daylight, cleanliness leaves much to be desired. Pub-style sandwiches and grilled steak, chicken, and fish. **FYI:** Reservations not accepted. Blues/jazz. **Open:** Mon–Fri 11:30am–1:30am, Sat 5pm–1:30am. **Prices:** Main courses $6–$10. AE, MC, V.

ATTRACTIONS

Monticello
VA 53; tel 804/984-9822 or 984-9800. Monticello was the home of Thomas Jefferson, who designed the house and oversaw its construction. The estate, considered an architectural masterpiece, was the first Virginia plantation to sit atop a mountain (great houses were usually built close to rivers). The house was originally Palladian in design, but Jefferson later incorporated features of Parisian architecture, having been inspired by the homes of French noblemen during his tenure as minister to France. Construction first began in 1769, but over a 40-year period Jefferson continued to expand, remodel, and rebuild parts of his home.

The house is restored as closely as possible to its appearance during Jefferson's retirement years. Nearly all of the furniture and household items were owned by Jefferson or his family. The garden has been extended to its original 1,000-foot length, and the Mulberry Row dependencies—including the smokehouse, blacksmith shop, nailery, servants' quarters—have been excavated. (The name comes from the mulberries Jefferson had planted there.) Guided tours of the gardens and grounds, and specialized tours of the plantation community, are available daily during spring, summer, and fall as part of general admission.

In the entrance hall, which was a museum in Jefferson's day, is a seven-day calendar clock, one of Jefferson's inventions, which still works. Just off the entrance hall are Jefferson's high-ceilinged bedroom, where he died in 1826 at age 83, and the library, which contained 6,000 books that Jefferson later gave to the Library of Congress. The tour also includes Jefferson's study, which contains one of his telescopes; the parlor, a semi-octagonal room with a Jefferson-designed parquet cherry floor; the dining room; and the orchard and gardens.

Jefferson's grave in the family burial ground (still in use) is inscribed with his own words: "Here was buried Thomas Jefferson / Author of the Declaration of American Independence / of the Statute of Virginia for Religious Freedom / and Father of the University of Virginia." After visiting the graveyard, visitors may take a shuttle bus back to the parking area or follow a path through the woods. **Open:** Peak (Mar–Oct) daily 8am–5pm. Reduced hours off-season. **$$$**

Ash Lawn–Highland
James Monroe Pkwy (County Rd 795); tel 804/293-9539. Located 2½ miles past Monticello (see above) on County Rd 795. James Monroe's influence on early American history goes beyond his accomplishments as the nation's fifth president. Monroe fought in the Revolution, was wounded at Trenton, recovered, and went on to hold more offices than any other president, including several foreign ministries.

In 1793 he purchased 1,000 acres adjacent to Monticello, where he built an estate he called Highland (the name Ash Lawn dates to 1838). Monroe served as ambassador to Britain and Spain; was four times governor of Virginia; served as Jefferson's ambassador to France, where he negotiated the Louisiana Purchase; held various cabinet posts; and was elected president in 1816. When Monroe retired from office in 1825, he was deeply in debt and was forced to sell the beloved farm where he'd hoped to spend his last days.

Today the 535-acre estate is owned and maintained as a working farm by the College of William and Mary (Monroe's alma mater). Guided tours include the five remaining original rooms, along with the basement kitchen, the overseer's cottage, restored slave quarters, and the smokehouse. Some of the Monroes' furnishings and other belongings are still here. Livestock, vegetable and herb gardens, and colonial craft demonstrations recall elements of daily life on the Monroe's plantation. Horses, cattle, and sheep graze in the fields and peacocks roam the boxwood gardens. Many special events throughout the year (phone ahead). **Open:** Peak (Mar–Oct) daily 9am–6pm. Reduced hours off-season. **$$$**

Virginia Discovery Museum
Tel 804/977-1025. Located at the east end of the Downtown Mall, this facility offers numerous hands-on exhibits and programs for young people. The Colonial Log House, an authentic structure that once stood on a site in New Bedford, Virginia, is outfitted with 19th-century furnishings. A series of exhibits deals with the senses and the Fun and Games exhibit has an array of games, including bowling and giant checkers. Changing exhibits, arts and crafts studio. Free admission first Sunday of every month. **Open:** Tues–Sat 10am–5pm, Sun 1–5pm. **$$**

Historic Michie Tavern
VA 53; tel 804/977-1234. Built in 1784 by William Michie to capitalize on the well-traveled stagecoach route that ran through his property. The Michies also farmed and operated a general store, and their descendants owned the property until 1910. It was moved to its present location near Monticello (see above) and painstakingly restored. Behind the tavern are reproductions of the old log kitchen, dairy, smokehouse, ice house, and root cellar. The general store has been re-created, along with a crafts shop; the Virginia Wine Museum is also on the premises. Behind the store is a gristmill that has operated continuously since 1797.

The tavern still plays host to travelers in much the same style as it did two centuries ago. In the "Ordinary," a converted log cabin with original hand-hewn walls and beamed ceilings, Southern cuisine is served on pewter plates at rustic oak tavern tables (daily 11:30am–3pm). **Open:** Daily 9am–5pm. **$$$**

University of Virginia

University Ave; tel 804/924-7969. Jefferson's "academical village," the University of Virginia is graced with spacious lawns, serpentine-walled gardens, colonnaded pavilions, and a classical rotunda inspired by the Pantheon in Rome. Rightly called the father of this institution, Jefferson conceived it, wrote the charter, raised the money for its construction, selected the site, drew the plans, laid the cornerstone in 1817, supervised construction, served as the first rector, selected the faculty, and created the curriculum.

The focal point of the university and starting point of tours is the **Rotunda** (at Rugby Road), restored according to Jefferson's original design. The tour includes the oval chemistry room; the Rotunda bell, once used to wake students at dawn; classrooms; the library; and the magnificent colonnaded **Dome Room**. The room occupied by Edgar Allan Poe when he was a student here is furnished as it would have been in 1826 and is open to visitors.

The Alexander Galt statue of Jefferson on the second floor of the Rotunda (originally the main entry level) is said to be an excellent likeness; another statue, by Sir Moses Ezekiel, is on the esplanade north of the Rotunda. **Free**

McGuffey Art Center

201 2nd St NW; tel 804/295-7973. Downtown facility where local artists and craftspeople have studio exhibits and sell their creations. The **Second Street Gallery,** showing contemporary art from all over the United States, is also located here. **Open:** Tues–Sat 10am–5pm, Sun noon–5pm. **Free**

Oakencroft Vineyard

Barracks Rd; tel 804/296-4188. There have been vineyards here since the 18th century, and Thomas Jefferson hoped one day to produce quality wines in Virginia. This vineyard, set on 17 acres of rolling farmland, has a tasting room housed in a red barn, and offers rustic tables for picnicking. A self-guided tour takes about 20 minutes. **Open:** Peak (Apr–Nov) daily 11am–5pm. Reduced hours off-season. Closed Jan–Feb. **Free**

Chesapeake

Formed in 1963 by merger of Norfolk County and the town of South Norfolk, this city at the mouth of the James River is a major shipping center. **Information:** Hampton Roads Chamber of Commerce–Chesapeake, 400 Volvo Pkwy, PO Box 1776, Chesapeake, 23320 (tel 757/547-2118).

MOTELS 🏨

▤▤ Comfort Suites

1550 Crossways Blvd, 23320; tel 757/420-1600 or toll free 800/428-0562; fax 757/420-0099. Exit 289B off I-64. Follow Greenbrier Pkwy S to Crossways Center; go north on Crossways Blvd. This modern motel close to industrial parks has amenities to appeal to business travelers. Nice lobby has high-quality furnishings; adjacent area with TV, comfortable seating. Lots of nearby shopping, including a major mall. **Rooms:** 124 stes. CI 2pm/CO 11am. Nonsmoking rms avail. All units are large suites, very well furnished and appointed. Brass lamps, sofa beds, arched walls give a homey feel. **Amenities:** 🛏 ⚲ A/C, cable TV w/movies, refrig. Some units w/terraces. Microwaves. **Services:** ▣ 🍴 **Facilities:** 🛗 🛝 ▣ ♿ Spa, sauna, steam rm, whirlpool, washer/dryer. Nice pool area. Whirlpool is within a wooden gazebo. **Rates (CP):** Peak (May 15–Sept 15) $75–$100 ste. Extra person $7. Children under age 18 stay free. Lower rates off-season. Parking: Outdoor, free. Government rates avail. AE, DC, DISC, MC, V.

▤▤ Days Inn

1433 N Battlefield Blvd, 23320; tel 757/547-9262 or toll free 800/258-5353; fax 757/547-4334. Exit 290B off I-64. This budget motel is close to shopping, hospital, and office parks. **Rooms:** 88 rms and effic. CI 2pm/CO noon. Nonsmoking rms avail. **Amenities:** 🛏 A/C, cable TV w/movies, refrig. Some units w/terraces. **Services:** ▣ 🍴 **Facilities:** 🛗 ▣ ♿ Washer/dryer. Peak (Mem Day–Labor Day) $75–$95 S or D; $75–$95 effic. Extra person $5. Children under age 18 stay free. Lower rates off-season. Parking: Outdoor, free. AE, DISC, MC, V.

▤▤ Hampton Inn

701A Woodlake Dr, 23320; tel 757/420-1550 or toll free 800/HAMPTON; fax 757/424-7414. Exit 289A off I-64. Go north on Greebrier Pkwy ⅛ mile; turn right on Woodlake Dr. Located in light industrial park, this clean chain motel is popular with business travelers. Lobby has microwave, TV, and ample seating. **Rooms:** 119 rms. CI 2pm/CO noon. Nonsmoking rms avail. **Amenities:** 🛏 ⚲ A/C, cable TV w/movies. **Services:** ▣ 🍴 Twice-daily maid svce. **Facilities:** 🛗 ▣ ♿ **Rates (CP):** Peak (May 1–Sept 5) $55–$70 S or D. Children under age 18 stay free. Min stay special events. Lower rates off-season. Parking: Outdoor, free. AE, DC, DISC, MC, V.

▤▤▤ Holiday Inn Chesapeake

725 Woodlake Dr, 23320; tel 757/523-1500 or toll free 800/HOLIDAY; fax 757/523-0683. Exit 289A off I-64. Go north on Greenbrier Pkwy for ⅛ mile; turn right on Woodlake Dr. This comfortable chain motel is popular with business travelers. **Rooms:** 230 rms and stes. CI 2pm/CO noon. Nonsmoking rms avail. Attractively decorated rooms. **Amenities:** 🛏 ⚲ ▣ 🍴 A/C, cable TV w/movies. Some units w/minibars. Spacious suites have wet bars, microwaves, and refrigerators.

Services: ✗ 🚐 🖼 🍽 Twice-daily maid svce. **Facilities:** 🛠 🖥 🖳 ⅙ 1 restaurant (*see* "Restaurants" below), 1 bar, spa, whirlpool. Attractive indoor pool area has vaulted ceiling, skylight. **Rates:** $76–$80 S; $84–$88 D; $98–$106 ste. Extra person $8. Children under age 18 stay free. Min stay special events. Parking: Outdoor, free. Sweetheart packages avail. AE, CB, DC, DISC, JCB, MC, V.

RESTAURANTS 🍴

Key West
In Holiday Inn Chesapeake, 725 Woodlake Dr; tel 757/523-1500. Exit 289A off I-64. Follow Greenbrier Pkwy N to Woodlake Dr, turn right. **Regional American/Seafood/ Steak.** Walls of windows with view of outdoor fountains give this motel restaurant a light and cheerful ambience. Value-priced nightly specials ($9–$11) include such offerings as pork tenderloin with orange pecan sauce and backfin crab cake, and come with vegetables, salad, rolls, dessert. Regular menu has seafood, steak, chicken, pork selections. **FYI:** Reservations accepted. Children's menu. **Open:** Peak (Mar–Nov) daily 6:30am–10pm. **Prices:** Main courses $9–$17. AE, DISC, MC, V. 🍷 ⅙

The Locks Pointe at Great Bridge
136 Battlefield Blvd N; tel 757/547-9618. Exit 290B off I-64, 4½ mi S on VA 168. **Seafood/Steak.** White tablecloths with green toppers set a dressy but casual atmosphere for this popular restaurant overlooking the Intracoastal Waterway. Solarium room used for Sunday brunch. Fresh seafood imaginatively prepared with spices and sauces is the highlight. Soft-shell crab seasonally; chicken, filet mignon round out the menu. Hodad's bar has patio seating, indoor dining area, and menu that includes raw bar, sandwiches, pasta. Live entertainment on summer weekends. Hodad's open daily 4pm–2am. **FYI:** Reservations recommended. Children's menu. **Open:** Lunch Tues–Fri 11am–3pm; dinner Tues–Sat 5–10pm, Sun 3–9pm; brunch Sun 11am–3pm. **Prices:** Main courses $11–$18. AE, MC, V. 🛥 🏞 ⅙

Chincoteague

See also Tangier Island

Named after a Native American term meaning "beautiful land across the water," the main village on Chincoteague Island is home to Chincoteague National Wildlife Refuge. Nearby Assateague Island National Seashore contains over 200 species of birds, and wild ponies that have roamed free for centuries. **Information:** Chincoteague Chamber of Commerce, PO Box 258, Chincoteague, 23336 (tel 757/336-6161).

MOTELS 🏨

Assateague Inn
6570 Chicken City Rd, 23336; tel 757/336-3738; fax 757/336-1179. VA 175 E exit off US 13. This condominium complex enjoys a quiet spot among pine trees at the edge of an attractive marsh. **Rooms:** 26 rms and effic. CI 3pm/CO 11am. **Amenities:** 🛁 🖥 A/C, cable TV w/movies, refrig. All units w/terraces. Efficiencies have microwaves and cook-tops. **Services:** 🍽 Babysitting. **Facilities:** 🛠 🎱 🖳 Lawn games, spa, whirlpool, playground. Picnic tables and grills. Pier into creek for crabbing. Restaurant nearby. **Rates:** Peak (July–Aug) $4062–$62 S or D; $5692–$96 effic. Extra person $5. Children under age 13 stay free. Min stay wknds. Lower rates off-season. Parking: Outdoor, free. AE, CB, DC, DISC, MC, V.

Beach Road Motel
6151 Maddox Blvd, 23336; tel 757/336-6562. VA 175 E exit off US 13. Although this very simple motel has few amenities, it's absolutely clean and neat and is maintained to a high standard. Nicely landscaped grounds. **Rooms:** 20 rms and effic; 2 cottages/villas. CI 2pm/CO 11am. Nonsmoking rms avail. **Amenities:** 🛁 🖥 A/C, cable TV, refrig. 1 unit w/terrace. **Services:** 🍽 **Facilities:** 🛠 Picnic tables and outdoor grills. **Rates:** Peak (June 17–Sept 4) $43–$63 S; $53–$74 D; $63–$85 effic; $63–$85 cottage/villa. Extra person $5. Children under age 10 stay free. Min stay peak. Lower rates off-season. Parking: Outdoor, free. AE, DISC, MC, V.

Birchwood Motel
3650 Main St, 23336; tel 757/336-6133 or toll free 800/411-5147; fax 757/336-6535. Exit US 13 at VA 175 E; turn right at light, then go ½ mi. This older motel is in exceptionally fine condition. Large lawn. **Rooms:** 41 rms and effic; 2 cottages/villas. CI 2pm/CO 11am. Nonsmoking rms avail. Standard motel-style rooms except for two large, family-size units. **Amenities:** 🛁 🖥 A/C, cable TV, refrig. **Services:** 🍽 **Facilities:** 🛠 🚲 Lawn games, playground. Shuffleboard. **Rates:** Peak (June 17–Sept 5) $67 S; $72–$82 D; $87–$110 effic. Extra person $5. Min stay special events. Lower rates off-season. Parking: Outdoor, free. Cottages rent by week only (from $475/wk). Closed Dec–Mar. AE, DISC, MC, V.

Comfort Inn
25297 Lankford Hwy, PO Box 205, Onley, 23418; tel 757/787-7787 or toll free 800/228-5150; fax 757/787-4641. This new, well-kept, hospitable establishment is a good place to stop between the Chesapeake Bay Bridge Tunnel and the turnoff to Chincoteague. In a rural area with few motels. Onancock and the Tangier Island ferry are 1½ miles away. **Rooms:** 80 rms and stes. CI 3pm/CO 11am. Nonsmoking rms avail. All rooms have very attractive furnishings. **Amenities:** 🛁 🖥 A/C, cable TV, refrig. Deluxe models have microwaves and VCRs. **Services:** 🍽 **Facilities:** 🛠 🖳 ⅙ **Rates (CP):** Peak (June 1–Sept 18) $50–$56 S; $56–$62 D; $64–

$79 ste. Extra person $5. Children under age 18 stay free. Lower rates off-season. Parking: Outdoor, free. AE, CB, DC, DISC, EC, ER, JCB, MC, V.

▤▤ Driftwood Motor Lodge
7105 Maddox Blvd, PO Box 575, 23336; tel 757/336-6557 or toll free 800/553-6117; fax 757/336-6558. VA 175 exit off US 13, left at light, right on Maddox Blvd. The closest motel to the national wildlife refuge, this is an attractive, well-kept, and comfortable base for exploration and trips to the beach. **Rooms:** 52 rms. CI 3pm/CO 11am. Nonsmoking rms avail. All rooms are spacious and attractive. Some have views across street to the marshlands. **Amenities:** 🛏 A/C, cable TV w/movies, refrig. All units w/terraces. **Services:** ⊂Ɔ Babysitting. **Facilities:** 🔋 **Rates:** Peak (July 1–Sept 7) $45–$82 S or D. Extra person $6. Children under age 12 stay free. Min stay wknds. Lower rates off-season. Parking: Outdoor, free. Closed Dec 23–Dec 30. AE, DC, DISC, MC, V.

▤▤▤ Island Motor Inn
4391 N Main St, 23336; tel 757/336-3141; fax 757/336-1483. VA 175 E exit off US 13, turn left at last bridge and go 3 blocks. This very pretty motel enjoys a spectacular waterfront setting on the Intracoastal Waterway. **Rooms:** 60 rms. CI 3pm/CO 11am. Nonsmoking rms avail. All rooms have views of Chincoteague Bay. **Amenities:** 🛏 A/C, cable TV w/movies, refrig. All units w/terraces. **Services:** ⊂Ɔ Babysitting. Very accommodating staff. **Facilities:** 🔋 1 restaurant (bkfst only), spa, whirlpool, washer/dryer. Coffee shop/bakery. **Rates:** Peak (June 10–Sept 6) $88–$150 S or D. Extra person $10. Children under age 15 stay free. Min stay peak. Lower rates off-season. Parking: Outdoor, free. AE, DC, DISC, MC, V.

▤ Lighthouse Motel
4218 N Main St, 23336; tel 757/336-5091. VA 175 E exit off US 13. This neat, clean, and simple older motel is on the main street of town. Owners continually upgrade the facility. **Rooms:** 25 rms and effic. CI 2pm/CO 11am. Nonsmoking rms avail. Basic but clean rooms are of various sizes in three separate buildings. **Amenities:** 🛏 A/C, cable TV, refrig. 1 unit w/terrace. **Services:** ⊂Ɔ **Facilities:** 🔋 Whirlpool. Screened pavilion for picnics. **Rates:** Peak (June 18–Sept 17) $45–$55 D; $55–$65 ste. Extra person $5. Min stay peak and wknds. Lower rates off-season. Parking: Outdoor, free. Closed Dec–Mar. CB, DC, DISC, MC, V.

▤▤▤ The Refuge Motor Inn
7058 Maddox Blvd, PO Box 378, 23336; tel 757/336-5511 or toll free 800/544-8469; fax 757/336-6134. VA 175 E exit off US 13. Built of gray wood and appearing more like a residential condominium complex than a motel, this attractive establishment is well situated near the national wildlife refuge. Horses on property are for viewing, not riding. **Rooms:** 72 rms and effic. CI 3pm/CO 11am. No smoking. All units are attractive. Suites are lovely and large and have skylights and full kitchens. **Amenities:** 🛏 A/C, cable TV,

refrig. All units w/terraces, some w/whirlpools. **Services:** ⊂Ɔ Masseur, babysitting. Narrated boat cruises on Chincoteague Channel are of particular interest to bird-watchers. **Facilities:** 🔋 Lawn games, sauna, whirlpool, playground, washer/dryer. Excellent year-round pool area. **Rates:** Peak (June 10–Sept 4) $80–$95 S or D; $160 effic. Extra person $8. Children under age 12 stay free. Min stay wknds. Lower rates off-season. Parking: Outdoor, free. AE, DC, DISC, MC, V.

▤ Sea Hawk Motel
6250 Maddox Blvd, 23336; tel 757/336-6527. VA 175 E exit off US 13. Although the decor is dated, this roadside motel is clean and well maintained. **Rooms:** 28 rms and effic; 3 cottages/villas. CI 2pm/CO 11am. Basic motel units and very large efficiencies are decorated in 1960s earth tones and adorned with bright paintings and prints. **Amenities:** 🛏 A/C, satel TV, refrig. **Services:** ⊂Ɔ Babysitting. **Facilities:** 🔋 Playground. **Rates:** Peak (June 10–Sept 8) $60 S or D; $62 effic. Extra person $5. Min stay wknds and special events. Lower rates off-season. Parking: Outdoor, free. Cottages/villas rent by week only ($475/wk). Closed Dec–Jan. AE, DISC, MC, V.

▤▤ Sea Shell Motel
3720 Willow St, 23336; tel 757/336-6589. VA 175 E exit off US 13. Although older, this is a comfortable, neat, and clean motel. **Rooms:** 40 rms and effic; 6 cottages/villas. CI 1pm/CO 11am. Nonsmoking rms avail. Units were recently redecorated. Efficiencies are home-like and spacious, with large eat-in kitchens. **Amenities:** 🛏 A/C, cable TV, refrig. **Services:** ⊂Ɔ Babysitting. **Facilities:** 🔋 Picnic tables sit on a deck under trees. **Rates:** Peak (June 17–Sept 6) $60–$66 S or D. Extra person $4. Min stay wknds and special events. Lower rates off-season. Parking: Outdoor, free. Cottages/villas and efficiencies rent by week only (from $450–$500/wk). Closed Mar 15–Oct 31. AE, DC, DISC, MC, V.

▤▤ Sunrise Motor Inn
4491 Chicken City Rd, PO Box 185, 23336; tel 757/336-6671; fax 757/336-1226. Exit US 13 at VA 175 E. This simple, attractive motel is exceptionally clean and neat. **Rooms:** 24 rms and effic. CI 2pm/CO 11am. **Amenities:** 🛏 A/C, cable TV, refrig. **Services:** ⊂Ɔ **Facilities:** 🔋 Pool has a slide for kids. Screened pavilion, grills, and picnic tables on the lawn. **Rates:** Peak (June 12–Sept 8) $62 S or D. Extra person $6. Children under age 12 stay free. Min stay wknds. Lower rates off-season. Parking: Outdoor, free. Efficiencies rent by week only (from $500/wk). AE, DC, DISC, MC, V.

▤▤▤ Waterside Motor Inn
3761 S Main St, PO Box 347, 23336; tel 757/336-3434; fax 757/336-1878. VA 175 E exit off US 13. Located on the Intracoastal Waterway. **Rooms:** 45 rms and effic. CI 2:30pm/CO 11am. Nonsmoking rms avail. All rooms have nice views of boats and sunsets; the higher the floor, the better the view. **Amenities:** 🛏 A/C, cable TV w/movies, refrig. All units

w/terraces. Deluxe rooms have VCRs. **Services:** 🛎 Babysitting. **Facilities:** 🏊 🅿 ⛴ 🍽 🛗 ⚕ Spa, whirlpool. Pool located beside the Waterway. Pier with boat slips available for boating and windsurfing. Very pretty solarium with whirlpool and exercise equipment has water view. Picnic tables by the water. **Rates:** Peak (June 7–Sept 15) $90–$145 S or D. Extra person $5. Children under age 12 stay free. Min stay peak. Lower rates off-season. Parking: Outdoor, free. Efficiencies rent by week only (from $500/wk). AE, CB, DC, DISC, MC, V.

INN

🏨🏨🏨 Channel Bass Inn

6228 Church St, 23336; tel 757/336-6148 or toll free 800/249-0818. This Victorian house has been carefully restored inside, with beautiful public areas. Unsuitable for children under 10. **Rooms:** 5 rms and stes. CI 2pm/CO 11am. No smoking. Very attractive rooms have high-quality furnishings and period decor. **Amenities:** ⚕ A/C, bathrobes. No phone or TV. **Services:** ✗ Afternoon tea served. **Facilities:** Guest lounge. **Rates:** Peak (May–Sept) $89–$145 S; $99–$155 D; $135–$165 ste. Min stay wknds and special events. Lower rates off-season. MAP rates avail. Parking: Outdoor, free. MC, V.

RESTAURANTS 🍴

⑤ Etta's Family Restaurant

East Side Dr; tel 757/336-5644. At Assateague Channel. **American/Seafood.** A friendly staff and pretty view of passing boats make this simple, bright waterfront room a nice family dining choice. Traditional dishes, plus small-appetite selections for children and adults 60 and over. **FYI:** Reservations accepted. Children's menu. No liquor license. **Open:** Peak (July–Aug) lunch daily 11am–5pm; dinner daily 5–9pm; brunch Sun 11am–2pm. Closed Columbus Day–Mar. **Prices:** Main courses $9–$16. DISC, MC, V. 🍴 🖼 👪 💟 ⚕

Landmark Crab House

In Landmark Plaza, N Main St; tel 757/336-5552. Exit US 13 at VA 175 E. **Seafood/Steak.** Hatch-cover tables and red accents adorn this room with large windows overlooking the bay. Outdoor deck perfect for great sunsets. Seafood, especially crab, shrimp, and clams, are the big deals here, with a few beef and chicken selections. Beef is said to be of very good quality. Large salad bar. Breads are baked on premises. Adjacent Shucking House Cafe serves breakfast and lunch in an attractive pierside setting. **FYI:** Reservations recommended. Piano. Children's menu. Dress code. **Open:** Peak (May–Sept) breakfast daily 8–11:30am; lunch daily 11:30am–3pm; dinner daily 5–10pm. Closed Nov–Mar. **Prices:** Main courses $12–$20. AE, DISC, MC, V. 🍴 🖼 👪 💟 ⚕

The Village Restaurant

6576 Maddox Blvd; tel 757/336-5120. Exit US 13 at VA 175 E. **American/Seafood.** Light, attractive, simple decor and traditional American entrees, with an emphasis on fresh seafood. **FYI:** Reservations accepted. Children's menu. **Open:** Daily 5–10pm. **Prices:** Main courses $12–$20. AE, DC, DISC, MC, V. ⚕

ATTRACTIONS 📷

Oyster and Maritime Museum

7125 Maddox Rd; tel 757/336-6117. On display here is a large collection of fossils, exhibits, and dioramas documenting the history of Chincoteague and the surrounding region. Also live marine specimens, films; research library. **Open:** Peak (May–Labor Day) Mon–Sat 10am–5pm, Sun noon–4pm. Reduced hours off-season. **$**

Chincoteague National Wildlife Refuge

Assateague Island; tel 757/336-6122. **Chincoteague National Wildlife Refuge** is owned and managed by the US Fish and Wildlife Service. In spring or fall, when visitors are few, the refuge offers miles of undisturbed marsh, lake, and ocean vistas with shorebirds, ponies, and other wildlife. The refuge visitor center is open all year, but hours vary seasonally. Another visitor center, at Toms Cove, is managed by the National Park Service (tel 757/336-6577).

Marguerite Henry's children's book, and later, the film, *Misty of Chincoteague,* aroused wide interest in the annual **Pony Penning and Swim.** Every July, Chincoteague's wild ponies (actually stunted horses) are rounded up on the island and swim the inlet to the mainland. Foals are sold at auction, and the rest swim back to the island.

Birdwatchers know Assateague Island as a prime Atlantic Flyway habitat known for sightings of peregrine falcons, snow geese, great blue herons, and snowy egrets. The annual Waterfowl Week is generally held around Thanksgiving.

Outdoor activities on Assateague also include shell collecting (most productive at the tip of Toms Cove), and hiking and biking. Also on Assateague Island is the **Assateague Island National Seashore.** For more information contact Refuge Manager, Chincoteague Wildlife Refuge, PO Box 62, Chincoteague, VA 23336 (tel 757/336-5593). **Open:** Daily, year-round. Call for hours. **$$**

Clifton

See also Manassas

Picturesque village east of Manassas outside Washington, DC. Once frequented by US presidents and other notables who came for its warm mineral springs. **Information:** Fairfax County Chamber of Commerce, 8391 Old Courthouse #300, Vienna, 22182 (tel 703/749-0400).

RESTAURANT 🍴

The Hermitage Inn

7134 Main St; tel 703/266-1623. Exit 53 off I-66. **Californian/French/Mediterranean.** The two-story clapboard building dates from the mid-19th century, when this small picturesque village was frequented by US presidents and other notables. Like the quaint village, the restaurant retains lots of historical ambience. Flagstone patio provides al fresco dining in fine weather. **FYI:** Reservations recommended. Dress code. **Open:** Lunch Tues–Sat 11:30am–2:30pm; dinner Tues–Sat 6–10pm, Sun 5–9pm; brunch Sun 11:30am–3pm. **Prices:** Main courses $14–$27. AE, CB, DC, DISC, MC, V. 🍴 ⚓🖼

Clifton Forge

See also Covington

Located in George Washington National Forest, on the banks of the James River. This old railroad town (named after James Clifton's iron furnace) is home to the Historical Society Archives of C&O and CSX railroads. **Information:** Allegheny Highlands Chamber of Commerce, 203 Commercial Ave, Clifton Forge, 24422 (tel 540/862-4969).

RESTAURANT 🍴

⑤✹ Michel Café and French Restaurant

424 E Ridgeway St; tel 540/862-4119. Exit 24 off I-64. **French.** Hidden away in the Virginia highlands, this authentic country French cafe is outfitted with wood paneling, stucco walls, a collection of French artifacts, and window boxes full of flowers. Regular menu features backfin crab cakes, pepper steak, and Allegheny Mountains trout, but daily specials depend on fresh seasonal ingredients. Well worth a very short side trip off I-64. **FYI:** Reservations accepted. **Open:** Mon–Sat 5–9pm. **Prices:** Main courses $11–$22. AE, CB, DC, DISC, MC, V.

ATTRACTION 🏛

Douthat State Park
Rte 1, Millsboro; tel 540/862-7200. Located 8 mi N of Clifton Forge. Some of Virginia's most outstanding mountain scenery can be found in this park. A 50-acre lake, stocked with trout, has a sandy swimming beach, camping, cabins, and picnic areas. A restaurant overlooks the lake. **Open:** Daily 8am–10pm. $

Covington

See also Clifton Forge

Site of the nation's only curved-span covered bridge, Covington is noted for outdoor recreation and mountain scenery. Seat of Allegheny County. **Information:** Allegheny Highlands Chamber of Commerce, 241 W Main St, Covington, 24426 (tel 540/962-2178).

MOTELS 🏨

▬▬▬ Comfort Inn

203 Interstate Dr, 24426; tel 540/962-2141 or toll free 800/221-2222; fax 540/965-0964. Exit 16 off I-64. Near the George Washington National Forest and Douthat State Park, both with fishing, hunting, hiking, and camping. **Rooms:** 99 rms and stes. Executive level. CI 3pm/CO 11am. Nonsmoking rms avail. Standard rooms are in a traditional motel building. Suites in newer Executive Annex have sitting rooms. **Amenities:** 🛁 📺 🍷 A/C, cable TV w/movies, VCR. Suites have 2 TVs. **Services:** 🛎 🍴 ⟨⟩ **Facilities:** 🏊 🚗120 ⚓ 2 restaurants, 1 bar (w/entertainment), whirlpool. **Rates (CP):** $62 S; $71 D; $70–$79 ste. Extra person $8. Children under age 18 stay free. Parking: Outdoor, free. AE, CB, DC, DISC, EC, ER, JCB, MC, V.

▬▬▬ Holiday Inn Covington

820 E Madison St, PO Box 920, 24426; tel 540/962-4951 or toll free 800/465-4329; fax 540/965-5714. Exit 16 off I-64. On a hillside above the interstate with a nice view of surrounding mountains. Proximity to restaurants and shopping center. **Rooms:** 79 rms. CI 2pm/CO 11am. Nonsmoking rms avail. **Amenities:** 🛁 ⚓ 📺 A/C, cable TV w/movies. **Services:** ✕ 🛎 🍴 ⟨⟩ **Facilities:** 🏊 🚗225 ⚓ 1 restaurant, 1 bar. **Rates:** $66 S; $75 D. Extra person $8. Children under age 18 stay free. Min stay special events. Parking: Outdoor, free. AE, CB, DC, DISC, JCB, MC, V.

Culpeper

Located in northern Virginia, this town (founded in 1759) was a major crossroads during westward expansion. The largest cavalry battle of the Civil War took place here. Seat of Culpeper County. **Information:** Culpeper County Chamber of Commerce, 133 W Davis St, Culpeper, 22701 (tel 540/825-8628).

MOTELS 🏨

▬▬ Culpeper Comfort Inn

890 Willis Lane, 22701; tel 540/825-4900; fax 540/825-4900. Intersection of US 29 and US 29 Business. An exceptionally clean and neat motel with very attractive grounds sporting pretty flowers. **Rooms:** 49 rms. CI 2pm/CO 11am. No smoking. **Amenities:** 🛁 ⚓ 📺 A/C, cable TV w/movies. **Services:** 🛎 🍴 ⟨⟩ Children's program. $15 pet fee. Continental breakfast more elaborate than most. **Facilities:** 🏊 ⚓ Small pool is nicely landscaped. **Rates (CP):** $58 S; $66 D. Extra person $8. Parking: Outdoor, free. AARP discounts avail; government and corporate rates avail. AE, DC, DISC, MC, V.

▬▬ Holiday Inn

US 29 S at US 29 Bypass, PO Box 1206, 22701; tel 540/825-1253 or toll free 800/HOLIDAY; fax 540/825-7134. An older but clean and well-managed motel convenient to highway. Attractive for families on the road. Convenient to Commonwealth Park, historic Culpeper, Civil War battlefields. **Rooms:** 159 rms and stes. CI noon/CO noon. No smoking. Clean, adequate-size rooms. **Amenities:** 🛁 ⚹ A/C, satel TV w/movies. **Services:** ✕ 🖳 🗗 🕭 Babysitting. Visual smoke detectors available. **Facilities:** 🛗 [300] 🕭 1 restaurant, 1 bar (w/entertainment), washer/dryer. **Rates:** Peak (June–Oct) $49–$59 S; $53–$60 D. Extra person $4. Children under age 18 stay free. Lower rates off-season. Parking: Outdoor, free. AE, CB, DC, DISC, JCB, MC, V.

Danville

Last capitol of the Confederacy during the Civil War, Danville is now a textile and industrial center. **Information:** Danville Area Chamber of Commerce, 635 Main St, PO Box 1538, Danville, 24543 (tel 804/793-5422).

MOTELS 🏨

▤▤ Best Western of Danville
2121 Riverside Dr, 24541; tel 804/793-4000 or toll free 800/528-1234; fax 804/799-5516. Built on the river, close to a major city route with restaurants, shopping malls. **Rooms:** 99 rms. Executive level. CI noon/CO noon. Nonsmoking rms avail. Some rooms have river views. Dark mahogany furnishings give air of solidity and repose. **Amenities:** 🛁 ⚹ A/C, cable TV w/movies. Some units w/whirlpools. **Services:** 🗗 **Facilities:** 🛗 [65] 🕭 Free golf at local club. Picnic tables and a small dock on river for guests' use. **Rates (CP):** $69–$79 S or D. Extra person $5. Children under age 16 stay free. Parking: Outdoor, free. AE, CB, DC, DISC, MC, V.

▤▤▤ Howard Johnson Hotel
100 Tower Dr, 24540; tel 804/793-2000 or toll free 800/654-2000; fax 804/792-4621. Exit 58W off US 29. Only five minutes from downtown and adjacent to a large shopping mall, motel sits high atop a hill overlooking highway. **Rooms:** 118 rms. Executive level. CI 2pm/CO noon. Nonsmoking rms avail. Well-furnished and spacious rooms. **Amenities:** 🛁 ⚹ A/C, cable TV w/movies. Some units w/terraces. **Services:** 🖳 🗗 **Facilities:** 🛗 [150] 🕭 1 restaurant, 1 bar, washer/dryer. **Rates:** $62–$64 S; $70–$72 D. Extra person $8. Children under age 18 stay free. Min stay special events. Parking: Outdoor, free. AE, CB, DC, DISC, ER, JCB, MC, V.

▤▤ Stratford Inn
2500 Riverside Dr, 24540; tel 804/793-2500 or toll free 800/326-8455; fax 804/793-6960. This older motel in the city boasts an excellent restaurant and easy access to downtown. **Rooms:** 160 rms and stes. CI noon/CO noon. Nonsmoking rms avail. **Amenities:** 🛁 📻 🕾 A/C, cable TV. Some units w/whirlpools. **Services:** ✕ 🖳 🗗 🕭 Car windshields cleaned gratis each morning, weather permitting. **Facilities:** 🛗 🛝 [140] 🕭 1 restaurant, 1 bar (w/entertainment), whirlpool, washer/dryer. Attractive area with heated pool. Passes

available to local health club. **Rates (BB):** $55 S or D; $88 ste. Extra person $5. Children under age 19 stay free. Min stay special events. Parking: Outdoor, free. AE, CB, DC, DISC, EC, ER, JCB, MC, V.

RESTAURANT 🍽

★ Bogies
927 S Main St; tel 804/793-4571. On US 86S, 1½ mi S of jct US 29/58. **American/Steak.** Bogart movies provide the theme, and dark furnishings and judicious use of reds and lighting lend an intimate cafe atmosphere. Steaks featured at dinner, lighter fare at lunch. **FYI:** Reservations accepted. Piano. Children's menu. **Open:** Mon–Thurs 11am–10pm, Fri 11am–11:30pm, Sat 5–11:30pm, Sun 5–10pm. **Prices:** Main courses $10–$15. AE, MC, V. 🍸🕭

ATTRACTION 📷

Danville Museum of Fine Arts and History (Last Capitol of the Confederacy)
975 Main St; tel 804/793-5644. Notified that General Lee's forces would be unable to prevent the fall of Richmond, President Davis and the Confederate government fled to Danville. For a few weeks in the spring of 1865 this restored Victorian mansion (1857), home of Maj W T Sutherlin, served as the Confederate capitol. Part of the mansion, including the library, parlor, and the bedroom used by Davis, has been restored. The remainder of the house serves as a historical and fine arts museum, with a permanent collection that includes furniture, decorative arts, silver, textiles, and historical costumes. **Open:** Tues–Fri 10am–5pm, Sat–Sun 2–5pm. **Free**

Duffield

Located in the southwest Blue Ridge Highlands, this small town (population 54) in the Jefferson National Forest is the home of Natural Tunnel State Park, which is noted for spectacular scenery.

ATTRACTION 📷

Natural Tunnel State Park
Tel 540/940-2674. Follow signs along US 23 and VA 871E. Named for an 850-foot-long tunnel, 100 feet in diameter, that was cut through a limestone ridge by Stock Creek. The tunnel itself is accessible to the public; other scenic features include a wide chasm between steep stone walls, surrounded by several pinnacles or "chimneys." Facilities include a visitor center, campsite, picnic grounds, an amphitheater, swimming pool, and chairlift. **Open:** Daily sunrise–sunset. **$**

Dulles Int'l Airport

See also Reston, Sterling

HOTELS 🏨

⊨⊨ Comfort Inn Dulles Int'l Airport

4050 Westfax Dr, Chantilly, 22021; tel 703/818-8200 or toll free 800/325-7760; fax 703/968-6871. 7 mi S of Airport; exit 53 off I-66, follow VA 28 N to US 50 W. This modern, seven-story brick hotel in a near-rural setting has a friendly staff and more amenities than usual for members of this motel chain. **Rooms:** 140 rms. CI 3pm/CO noon. Nonsmoking rms avail. All rooms are clean and comfortable. L-shaped king units. **Amenities:** 🛁 🕹 ☎ A/C, cable TV w/movies. Refrigerators and microwaves available. King units have dataports. **Services:** 🚐 ⌷ 🍴 ☞ **Facilities:** 🏋 🏌 📼 ⚒ Games rm, whirlpool, washer/dryer. Indoor pool opens to fenced patio for sunning. Pool open weekday mornings and evenings, all day Saturday and Sunday. **Rates (CP):** Peak (Apr–May/Sept–Oct) $65–$75 S; $70–$75 D. Extra person $10. Children under age 18 stay free. Lower rates off-season. Parking: Outdoor, free. Weekend and long-term rates avail. AE, CB, DC, DISC, ER, JCB, MC, V.

⊨⊨ Comfort Inn Herndon

200 Elden St, Herndon, 22070; tel 703/437-7555 or toll free 800/221-2222; fax 703/437-7572. 4 mi E of Dulles Airport, exit 10 off Dulles Toll Rd. A comfortable chain hotel with attractive lobby. Convenient to Dulles Airport, shops, restaurants. **Rooms:** 103 rms and stes. CI 2pm/CO noon. Nonsmoking rms avail. "Suites" are large standard rooms with a living room area and sofa. **Amenities:** 🛁 ☎ A/C, cable TV w/movies, refrig. Suites have microwaves. **Services:** 🚐 ⌷ 🍴 **Facilities:** 📼 ⚒ Guests get discounts at nearby restaurants. **Rates (CP):** $72 S; $78 D; $89 ste. Children under age 18 stay free. Parking: Outdoor, free. Weekend rates avail. AE, CB, DC, DISC, JCB, MC, V.

⊨⊨⊨ Courtyard by Marriott Herndon

533 Herndon Pkwy, Herndon, 22070; tel 703/478-9400 or toll free 800/321-2211. Exit 11 off Dulles Toll Rd. A typical example of this comfortable chain. Attractive lobby with fireplace and walls of windows looking out to landscaped courtyard. Convenient to shops, restaurants. **Rooms:** 146 rms and stes. CI 3pm/CO noon. Nonsmoking rms avail. King rooms have sofas. **Amenities:** 🛁 🕹 A/C, satel TV w/movies, dataport, voice mail. Some units w/terraces. Suites have refrigerators, two TVs. All have hot-water tap for coffee/tea. **Services:** ✗ 🚐 ⌷ 🍴 **Facilities:** 🏋 📼 ⚒ 1 restaurant (bkfst only), 1 bar, whirlpool, washer/dryer. **Rates:** $97 S; $107 D; $115 ste. Extra person $10. Children under age 12 stay free. Parking: Outdoor, free. Weekend rates avail. AE, CB, DC, DISC, MC, V.

⊨⊨⊨ Hyatt Dulles

2300 Dulles Corner Blvd, Herndon, 22071; tel 703/713-1234 or toll free 800/233-1234; fax 703/713-3410. Exit 10 off Dulles Toll Rd, follow VA 285 to Frying Pan Rd. Attractive, lush lobby with skylights and fountain distinguishes this modern hotel in an office-park setting. **Rooms:** 317 rms and stes. Executive level. CI 3pm/CO noon. Nonsmoking rms avail. Counters divide living and sleeping areas. **Amenities:** 🛁 🕹 ☎ A/C, cable TV w/movies, dataport, voice mail. Some units w/minibars. TVs on counter swivel between living and sleeping areas. Rooms have irons and ironing boards. Refrigerators available. **Services:** ✗ 🚐 ⌷ 🍴 ☞ Babysitting. Will arrange tennis and golf. **Facilities:** 🏋 🏊 📼 💻 ⚒ 1 restaurant, 1 bar (w/entertainment), spa, sauna, whirlpool. Pool opens to attractive courtyard, has weekday morning and evening hours only. Restaurant and bar partially share lobby skylights. **Rates:** $149 S; $174 D; $250–$650 ste. Extra person $25. Children under age 18 stay free. Parking: Outdoor, free. Weekend packages avail. AE, DC, DISC, MC, V.

⊨⊨⊨ Washington Dulles Airport Hilton

13869 Park Center Rd, Herndon, 22071; tel 703/478-2900 or toll free 800/909-8124; fax 703/478-9286. Exit 9A off Dulles Access Rd. Follow VA 28 S to McLearen Rd; turn left, then left into hotel. A comfortable hotel housed in a modern semicircular building connected to an office complex with shops and restaurants. Attractive lobby. **Rooms:** 301 rms and stes. Executive level. CI 3pm/CO noon. Nonsmoking rms avail. Spacious rooms have bright modern furniture and light drapes and spreads. Baths have separate dressing areas. **Amenities:** 🛁 🕹 ☎ A/C, cable TV w/movies, dataport, voice mail. **Services:** 🍴 🚐 ⌷ 🍴 ☞ Car-rental desk, masseur. **Facilities:** 🏋 🏊 📼 💻 ⚒ 1 restaurant, 2 bars, racquetball, spa, sauna, steam rm, whirlpool, beauty salon. Indoor-outdoor pool is part of state-of-the-art health club. Zodiac lounge has sports bar ambience. **Rates:** $79–$180 S; $79–$190 D; $120–$190 ste. Extra person $10. Children under age 18 stay free. Parking: Indoor/outdoor, free. AE, CB, DC, DISC, MC, V.

⊨⊨⊨ Washington Dulles Airport Marriott

333 W Service Rd, Chantilly, 22021; tel 703/471-9500 or toll free 800/228-9290; fax 703/661-6785. In Dulles Airport complex; follow Service Rd west to hotel. The only hotel actually on the Dulles Airport grounds, this sprawling 1972 building underwent a complete renovation in 1994, which brought it back to Marriott standards of cleanliness and comfort. Sits on 22 acres beside a man-made lake. **Rooms:** 370 rms and stes. Executive level. CI 4pm/CO noon. Nonsmoking rms avail. Spacious rooms furnished with dark, colonial-style furniture and bright spreads and drapes. Lots of light from floor-to-ceiling windows. **Amenities:** 🛁 🕹 ☎ A/C, satel TV w/movies, voice mail. Some units w/terraces. **Services:** ✗ 🚐 ⌷ 🍴 Car-rental desk, babysitting. **Facilities:** 🏋 🏊 📼 💻 ⚒ 1 restaurant, 1 bar, lawn

games, spa, sauna, whirlpool, washer/dryer. Large picnic area with basketball and volleyball courts, horseshoe and softball areas. Indoor pool opens to outdoor pool in landscaped courtyard with extensive, resort-like area for sunning. **Rates:** Peak (Labor Day–July 4) $70–$145 S or D; $105–$265 ste. Extra person $15. Children under age 18 stay free. Lower rates off-season. Parking: Outdoor, free. AE, CB, DC, DISC, MC, V.

☰☰☰ Washington Dulles Marriott Suites

13101 Worldgate Dr, Herndon, 22070; tel 703/709-0400 or toll free 800/228-9290; fax 703/709-0426. Exit 10 off Dulles Toll Rd. This attractive all-suites hotel at end of modern shopping center with restaurants, movie theaters, copy center with computer rentals. **Rooms:** 253 stes. CI 3pm/CO 1pm. Nonsmoking rms avail. French doors separate sitting area from bedroom. Large baths have doors to both sleeping and sitting areas. All units have king beds; some have sofas. **Amenities:** 🛏 ⓐ ▣ ➔ A/C, cable TV w/movies, refrig, dataport. All units have wet bars, irons and ironing boards, two TVs. Phones have call-waiting. **Services:** ✗ 🖥 ⌧ ⇄ Twice-daily maid svce. Morning coffee in lobby. **Facilities:** 🗗 ➡ 🔟 ⅙ 1 restaurant, 1 bar, sauna, washer/dryer. Attractive indoor-outdoor pool area has large sun deck off third floor. Guests have free use of adjoining health club. **Rates:** Peak (Mar–Jun/Sept–Dec) $140 ste. Extra person $15. Children under age 16 stay free. Lower rates off-season. Parking: Indoor/outdoor, free. Weekend packages avail. AE, DC, DISC, MC, V.

MOTEL

☰☰ Marriott Residence Inn

315 Elden St, at Herndon Pkwy, Herndon, 22070; tel 703/435-0044 or toll free 800/331-3131; fax 703/437-4007. 4 mi E of Dulles Airport, exit 10 off Dulles Toll Rd. Essentially an apartment complex built around a central courtyard with outdoor pool. Attractive lobby has fireplace, coffeepot, tables and chairs for meals and guest get-togethers. Most guests stay weeks or more. **Rooms:** 168 effic. CI 3pm/CO noon. Nonsmoking rms avail. Attractive and comfortably furnished units vary from studios to two-bedroom apartments. All have full kitchens. **Amenities:** 🛏 ⓐ ▣ A/C, cable TV w/movies, refrig, dataport, voice mail. Some units w/terraces, some w/fireplaces, some w/whirlpools. All units have ironing boards; irons, VCRs, videos, and hair dryers are available. **Services:** ⌧ ⇄ ⇆ Breakfast served in lobby, as are full dinner on Wednesday and light snacks Monday, Tuesday, Thursday. **Facilities:** 🗗 ◗1 🔟 ⅙ Playground, washer/dryer. All-purpose sports court for tennis, volleyball, basketball. Guests have free use of nearby health club. **Rates (CP):** Peak (Apr–Nov 15) $79–$145 effic. Children under age 21 stay free. Lower rates off-season. Parking: Outdoor, free. Weekend packages avail. AE, CB, DC, DISC, JCB, MC, V.

RESTAURANT 🍽

★ The Ice House Café and Oyster Bar

760 Elden St, Herndon; tel 703/471-4256. Exit 2 off Dulles Toll Rd, 4 mi E of Airport. **Regional American/Continental/Thai.** Mounted moose, walrus, and deer heads give hunting-lodge charm to this storefront eatery. The varnished tongue-in-groove pine walls are adorned with turn-of-the-century photos of Herndon, then a small rural town. Limited menu offers a mix of American, continental, and Thai cuisines. Live jazz Friday and Saturday nights. Park next door in former service station lot. **FYI:** Reservations recommended. Jazz. Dress code. **Open:** Lunch Mon–Fri 11:30am–2:30pm; dinner Mon–Thurs 5:30–10pm, Fri–Sat 5:30–10:30pm, Sun 5:30–8:30pm. **Prices:** Main courses $12–$19. AE, DC, MC, V. ■

ATTRACTION 🎫

Sully Plantation

3701 Pender Dr, Chantilly; tel 703/437-1794. Built in 1794, Sully was the home of Richard Bland Lee—Northern Virginia's first Congressman and an uncle of Robert E Lee. The 1,500-acre estate consisted of an elegant manor house, separate kitchen/laundry, dairy, smokehouse, and slave quarters. Visitors can tour the house, furnished with Federal-period antiques, and stroll through the gardens and outbuildings. **Open:** Peak (Mar–Dec) Wed–Mon 11am–4pm. Reduced hours off-season. **$$**

Emporia

Small central Virginia farming community on the Meherrim River. It provides lodging to 400,000 people yearly, due mainly to its location halfway between Florida and New York. Seat of Greensville County. **Information:** Emporia/Greensville Chamber of Commerce, 425-I S Main St, Emporia, 23847 (tel 804/348-0722).

MOTELS 🏨

☰☰ Hampton Inn

1207 W Atlantic St, 23847; tel 804/634-9200 or toll free 800/HAMPTON; fax 804/634-9200 ext 100. Exit 11B off I-95. Follow US 58 W for ½ mile. A clean, modern chain motel just off I-95. **Rooms:** 115 rms and effic. CI 2pm/CO 11am. Nonsmoking rms avail. **Amenities:** 🛏 A/C, cable TV w/movies. **Services:** ⇄ ⇆ **Facilities:** 🗗 ⅙ Restaurant adjacent. **Rates (CP):** Peak (June–Sept) $65–$70 S or D; $75 effic. Children under age 18 stay free. Min stay wknds. Lower rates off-season. Parking: Outdoor, free. AE, DISC, MC, V.

☰☰☰ Holiday Inn

311 Florida Ave, 23847; tel 804/634-4191 or toll free 800/HOLIDAY; fax 804/634-4191. Exit 11A off I-95; jct US 58 E. A well-kept chain motel just off I-95. **Rooms:** 144 rms. CI 2pm/CO noon. Nonsmoking rms avail. Nicely appointed.

Amenities: 🏠 ⚸ A/C, cable TV w/movies. Some units w/terraces. **Services:** ✗ 🖼 ↵ ⬗ Babysitting. **Facilities:** 🏋 [75] ⚼ 1 restaurant, 1 bar, playground, washer/dryer. Spacious pool area. Picnic under shade trees on grounds. **Rates (BB):** $47–$59 S or D. Extra person $6. Children under age 19 stay free. Parking: Outdoor, free. AE, CB, DC, DISC, MC, V.

Fairfax

Established in 1805 and named for Lord Fairfax, one of its early landowners. Now a sprawling Washington suburb noted for historic attractions, including the Courthouse that holds the wills of George and Martha Washington. Seat of Fairfax County. **Information:** Central Fairfax Chamber of Commerce, 3975 University Dr #350, Fairfax, 22030 (tel 703/591-2450).

HOTELS 🏨

🛏🛏 Comfort Inn University Center
11180 Main St, at Jermantown Rd, 22030 (Fair Oaks); tel 703/591-5900 or toll free 800/221-2222; fax 703/591-5900. Exit 57A off I-66. Go 1 mile on US 50 E to Jermantown Rd. Convenient to Fair Oaks Mall and the Patriot Center, this clean, well-managed chain motel has more than the usual facilities for such establishments. **Rooms:** 212 rms and effic. CI 3pm/CO 11am. Nonsmoking rms avail. Majority of units have full kitchens hidden by louvered walls. **Amenities:** 🏠 🖥 ⚶ A/C, cable TV w/movies, refrig. Some units w/whirlpools. Some units have whirlpools in bedroom area, with sliding glass window to bath. **Services:** ✗ 🖼 ↵ ⬗ Car-rental desk, masseur, babysitting. **Facilities:** 🏋 ⬛ [500] 💻 ⚼ 1 restaurant (lunch and dinner only), 1 bar, games rm, beauty salon, playground, washer/dryer. Chinese restaurant on premises. Public park with tennis courts next door. **Rates (CP):** Peak (Mar 15–Nov 1) $79–$95 S or D; $105 effic. Extra person $10. Children under age 18 stay free. Lower rates off-season. Parking: Outdoor, free. Weekend packages avail. AE, DC, DISC, MC, V.

🛏🛏 Courtyard by Marriott Fair Oaks
11220 Lee Jackson Hwy (US 50), at Jermantown Rd, 22030 (Fair Oaks); tel 703/273-6161 or toll free 800/321-2211; fax 703/273-3505. At Fair Oaks Corporate Center. Convenient to Fair Oaks Mall and the Patriot Center, this comfortable motor hotel is built around a landscaped courtyard. Attractive lobby area has fireplace. **Rooms:** 144 rms and stes. CI 3pm/CO 1pm. Nonsmoking rms avail. Designed with business travelers in mind, rooms have large desks. **Amenities:** 🏠 ⚸ 🖥 A/C, satel TV w/movies. Some units w/terraces. Long phone cords and hot-water dispensers for coffee and tea. **Services:** 🖼 ↵ **Facilities:** 🏋 ⬛ [90] ⚼ 1 restaurant (bkfst only), 1 bar, whirlpool, washer/dryer. Lobby restaurant serves breakfast only. **Rates:** $66–$89 S; $67–$94 D; $79–$102 ste. Children under age 18 stay free. Parking: Outdoor, free. Weekend packages avail. AE, DC, DISC, MC, V.

🛏🛏 Hampton Inn
10860 Lee Hwy, at Fairchester Dr, 22030; tel 703/385-2600 or toll free 800/HAMPTON; fax 703/385-2742. Exit 60 off I-66. This modern motor hotel, near Fair Oaks Mall and the Patriot Center, is within walking distance of shops and restaurants. **Rooms:** 86 rms. CI 3pm/CO noon. Nonsmoking rms avail. All units are pleasantly decorated with blond wood furniture and bright fabrics. **Amenities:** 🏠 ⚸ 🖥 A/C, satel TV w/movies. **Services:** 🖼 ↵ **Facilities:** ⬛ [30] ⚼ **Rates (CP):** $69–$79 S or D. Children under age 18 stay free. Parking: Outdoor, free. Weekend packages avail. AE, DC, DISC, MC, V.

🛏🛏🛏 Hyatt Fair Lakes
12777 Fair Lakes Circle, 22033; tel 703/818-1234 or toll free 800/233-1234; fax 703/818-3140. Exit 55 off I-66. Close to Fair Oaks Mall and county government offices, this attractive modern high-rise sits in a 620-acre office park. A spacious lobby under skylights has an outdoor ambience. **Rooms:** 316 rms and stes. Executive level. CI 3pm/CO noon. Nonsmoking rms avail. All rooms are suite-size, with dividers between sitting and sleeping areas. End units are semicircular and have floor-to-ceiling windows. All rooms have separate vanities outside shower/toilet. **Amenities:** 🏠 ⚸ 🖥 A/C, satel TV w/movies. 1 unit w/whirlpool. Business Plan units have business center. **Services:** ✗ 🚐 🖼 ↵ ⬗ Twice-daily maid svce, children's program, babysitting. Complimentary shuttle to Fair Oaks Mall, Dulles Int'l Airport, and Vienna Metro station. **Facilities:** 🏋 ⚽ ⬛ [450] 💻 ⚼ 1 restaurant, 1 bar, spa, sauna, whirlpool. Restaurant and bars are off the lobby. Golf arranged at local courses. **Rates:** $129–$139 S; $144–$154 D; $375 ste. Extra person $25. Children under age 18 stay free. Parking: Outdoor, free. AE, CB, DC, DISC, ER, JCB, MC, V.

🛏 Wellesley Inn
10327 Lee Hwy, 22030 (Fairfax City); tel 703/359-2888 or toll free 800/444-8888; fax 703/385-9186. Exit 60 off I-66. An attractive, antique-brick building adjacent to shops and restaurants, this basic chain hotel offers clean rooms but few other facilities or services. **Rooms:** 83 rms and stes. CI 2pm/CO 11am. Nonsmoking rms avail. Pleasantly decorated with light-tone fabrics, rooms have separate vanities. All have dinette tables with two chairs. **Amenities:** 🏠 ⚸ 🖥 A/C, cable TV w/movies. **Services:** ✗ 🖼 ↵ ⬗ Babysitting. **Facilities:** ⚼ Adjacent Red Lobster restaurant provides limited room service. **Rates (CP):** Peak (Mar–Nov 1) $55–$70 S or D; $85 ste. Children under age 12 stay free. Lower rates off-season. Parking: Outdoor, free. Weekend rates avail. AE, CB, DC, DISC, MC, V.

MOTEL

🛏🛏 Holiday Inn Fairfax City
3535 Chain Bridge Rd, 22030 (Fairfax City); tel 703/591-5500 or toll free 800/HOLIDAY; fax 703/591-7483. Exit 60 off I-66. Built in 1967, this brick-and-stone motel

enjoys a park-like setting among shade trees and landscaped grounds. Attractive public areas with large picture windows were recently refurbished. **Rooms:** 127 rms and stes. CI 3pm/CO noon. Nonsmoking rms avail. King-bed rooms have full-size sofa beds. **Amenities:** 🛏 🕸 A/C, cable TV w/movies. **Services:** ✗ 🖼 🛏 🛎 Complimentary morning coffee and newspapers in lobby. Guests get discount at nearby gym. **Facilities:** 🛁 🏊 ⅙ 1 restaurant (bkfst and dinner only), washer/dryer. Beautifully landscaped pool area is the highlight here. **Rates:** $89–$99 S or D; $99–$109 ste. Extra person $6. Children under age 12 stay free. Parking: Outdoor, free. Weekend packages avail. AE, CB, DC, DISC, JCB, MC, V.

RESTAURANT 🍴

Artie's

In Fairfax Circle Center, 3260 Old Lee Hwy (Fairfax City); tel 703/273-7600. Exit 62 off I-66, S to US 29, W to Fairfax Circle. **New American/Pub.** Lots of bright brass, varnished oak, and a pressed-tin ceiling make for Victorian charm, while tropical plants growing under skylights add a California touch to this neighborhood pub/restaurant. Specialties are light pasta dishes, but pub fare and grilled items also are offered. **FYI:** Reservations not accepted. Dress code. No smoking. **Open:** Sun 10:30am–10pm, Mon–Thurs 11:30am–11pm, Fri–Sat 11:30am–midnight. **Prices:** Main courses $10–$15. AE, MC, V. 📧 ⅙

Falls Church

This noted business center also offers historic attractions from the Revolutionary and Civil Wars. Located in northern Virginia, west of Washington, DC. **Information:** Greater Falls Church Chamber of Commerce, 417 W Broad St #207, PO Box 491, Falls Church, 22040 (tel 703/532-1050).

HOTEL 🏨

≣≣≣ Fairview Park Marriott

3111 Fairview Park Dr, 22042; tel 703/849-9400. Exit 8 off I-495. Follow US 50 E to Fairview Park Dr S. This relatively new hotel, set on attractive grounds in an office park near the Capital Beltway, has impressive public areas that combine traditional furnishings with modern architectural touches. Building wraps around a multi-tiered courtyard with fountain pools. **Rooms:** 430 rms and stes. Executive level. CI 4pm/CO noon. Nonsmoking rms avail. Comfortably furnished with business travelers in mind; each unit has large desks and comfortable easy chairs. **Amenities:** 🛏 🕸 A/C, satel TV w/movies, voice mail. Some units w/minibars, some w/terraces. **Services:** ✗ 🔑 VP 🚗 🖼 🛏 🛎 Babysitting. Free shuttle to Dunn Loring Metro station. Concierge-level units on two floors enjoy attended lounge, complimentary breakfast, evening snacks. **Facilities:** 🛁 🏋 🏊 ⅙ 1 restaurant, 2 bars (1 w/entertainment), games rm, spa, sauna, whirlpool,

washer/dryer. **Rates:** $130 S; $155 D; $275 ste. Min stay wknds. Parking: Indoor, free. Weekend packages avail. AE, CB, DC, DISC, MC, V.

MOTEL

≣≣ Best Western Falls Church Inn

6633 Arlington Blvd, at Annandale Rd, 22042; tel 703/532-9000 or toll free 800/336-3723; fax 703/237-0730. Exit 8 off I-495. An older but well maintained motel convenient to downtown Falls Church and to discount stores at Seven Corners Shopping Center. Other shops and restaurants are within walking distance. Popular with groups. **Rooms:** 106 rms and effic. CI 1pm/CO noon. Nonsmoking rms avail. King rooms in front of building are spacious by motel standards. All units have two vanities. **Amenities:** 🛏 🕸 📺 A/C, cable TV w/movies. **Services:** ✗ 🖼 🛏 Babysitting. **Facilities:** 🛁 🏊 1 restaurant, 1 bar. **Rates (CP):** Peak (Mar 15–Sept) $65–$76 S; $71–$82 D; $76 effic. Extra person $5. Children under age 18 stay free. Lower rates off-season. Parking: Outdoor, free. AE, DC, DISC, MC, V.

RESTAURANTS 🍴

Duangrat's Thai Restaurant

5878 Leesburg Pike (Bailey's Cross Roads); tel 703/820-5775. W of jct VA 7/244. **Thai.** Storefront location on a busy highway belies the quiet elegance of this fine ethnic eatery offering near-gourmet cuisine at affordable prices. Specialties are whole crispy fish, delicately sweet ginger chicken, and Panang beef prepared with coconut milk. Lunch sampler plates, offered Monday to Thursday 11:30am–2:30pm, are excellent value. **FYI:** Reservations recommended. Dress code. No smoking. **Open:** Lunch Mon–Fri 11:30am–2:30pm, Sat–Sun 11:30am–5pm; dinner Sun–Thurs 5–10:30pm, Fri–Sat 5–11pm. **Prices:** Main courses $9–$21. AE, DC, MC, V.

Fortune Chinese Seafood Restaurant

In Greenforest Shopping Center, 5900 Leesburg Pike (Bailey's Cross Roads); tel 703/998-8888. W of jct VA 7/VA 244. **Chinese.** A storefront restaurant with large dining room attractively decorated with Chinese paintings and furniture. Tanks hold live lobsters and crabs for seafood specialties; dim sum served from a cart daily 11am–3pm. Often hosts large groups, such as wedding parties. **FYI:** Reservations not accepted. Dress code. **Open:** Sun–Thurs 11am–10pm, Fri–Sat 11am–11:30pm. **Prices:** Main courses $9–$36. AE, MC, V. ⅙

Haandi

In Falls Plaza Shopping Center, 1222 W Broad St (West Falls Church); tel 703/533-3501. Exit 66 off I-66; go ½ mile on VA 7 S. **Indian.** Recessed stylized landscapes create impression of looking out onto the subcontinent's passing scene, while chandeliers add elegance. Booths line each wall, with well-spaced tables down the middle. Specialties are chicken and lamb kabobs. Curries are delicate and well seasoned, in the northern Indian style. Reservations accepted Sunday to Thursday only. Smoking allowed at lunch only. **FYI:** Reservations not accepted. Dress code. **Open:** Lunch daily 11:30am–2:30pm; dinner Sun–Thurs 5–10pm, Fri–Sat 5–10:30pm. **Prices:** Main courses $8–$14. AE, CB, DC, MC, V.

Lan's Vietnamese Restaurant

7236 Arlington Blvd; tel 703/204-2882. At Graham Rd. **Vietnamese.** A small, cozy family-owned restaurant with booths on one side and a long row of tables on the other. Mirrors make narrow space seem larger. Home-style specialties include crispy noodles and seafood, grilled pork vermicelli, and low-fat chicken grilled with lemon sauce. **FYI:** Reservations recommended. **Open:** Sun–Thurs 11am–10pm, Fri–Sat 11am–11pm. **Prices:** Main courses $5–$8. AE, MC, V.

Mountain Jack's

127 E Broad St; tel 703/532-6500. **Seafood/Steak.** Lots of dark paneling gives a cozy feeling to this popular steak house. Booths in one of the three dining areas are spacious but can be subject to noise coming from nearby bar. Regular tables are spaced closer together but are in quieter areas. Best known for prime rib and char-grilled steaks and seafood, either plain or with a variety of French-accented sauces. **FYI:** Reservations recommended. Comedy/country music/guitar. Dress code. **Open:** Lunch Mon–Fri 11:30am–2pm; dinner Mon–Thurs 5–10pm, Fri–Sat 5–11pm, Sun noon–9pm. **Prices:** Main courses $13–$19. AE, CB, DC, MC, V. &

Panjshir

924 W Broad St; tel 703/536-4566. 1 mi off VA 7 S. **Afghan.** Subdued lighting, dark paneling, booths, and widely spaced tables set the mood at this small but pleasant restaurant. Very popular with local residents for its excellently prepared selections, including several kabobs and mint-accented dumplings with meat and yogurt sauce. **FYI:** Reservations not accepted. Additional location: 224 W Maple Ave, Vienna (tel 281-4183). **Open:** Lunch Mon–Sat 11am–2pm; dinner daily 5–10pm. **Prices:** Main courses $13–$16. AE, DISC, MC, V.

♥ ★ Peking Gourmet Inn

In Culmore Shopping Center, 6029 Leesburg Pike (Bailey's Cross Roads); tel 703/671-8088. ½ mi W of jct VA 7/244. **Chinese.** Photos of famous politicians, media personalities, and entertainers overwhelm the Chinese lanterns and paintings at one of the area's most popular Asian restaurants. Attracted by gourmet-quality Peking duck and other northern Chinese specialties, President Bush dined here several times while in the White House. The establishment is easily overlooked in the nondescript Culmore Shopping Center. **FYI:** Reservations recommended. Dress code. **Open:** Sun–Thurs 11am–10:30pm, Fri–Sat 11am–midnight. **Prices:** Main courses $7–$30; prix fixe $21–$30. AE, MC, V.

ATTRACTION 📷

The Falls Church

115 E Fairfax St; tel 703/532-7600. This church was reconstructed in 1959 according to the original plans of the 1732 church building. The original building was used as a recruiting center during the Revolution and as a hospital during the Civil War. **Open:** Sun–Fri; call for hours. **Free**

Farmville

Located in central Virginia SW of Richmond, this small town sits on the Appomattox River and is nearby to Twin Lakes State Park. Seat of Prince Edward County. **Information:** Farmville Chamber of Commerce, 116 N Main St, PO Box 361, Farmville, 23901 (tel 804/392-3939).

MOTEL 🏨

📧📧 Days Inn

US 15 and US 460 Bypass, 23901; tel 804/392-6611 or toll free 800/DAYS-INN; fax 804/392-9774. Built of brick in 1990, this clean, efficiently run motel is convenient to Longwood College and within walking distance of restaurants and shops. **Rooms:** 60 rms. CI 2pm/CO 11am. Nonsmoking rms avail. Standard motel rooms. **Amenities:** 🐟 💧 A/C, cable TV w/movies. **Services:** 🖼 🛎 **Facilities:** 🔓 🎱 ‎12 ‎& **Rates (CP):** $51 S; $59 D. Extra person $5. Children under age 18 stay free. Parking: Outdoor, free. AE, CB, DC, DISC, MC, V.

Fredericksburg

Historic city halfway between Washington, DC and Richmond, VA on the Rappahannock River. **Information:** Fredericksburg-Stafford-Spotsylvania Chamber of Commerce, 4201 Plank Rd, PO Box 7476, Fredericksburg, 22404 (tel 540/786-7080).

MOTELS 🏨

📧📧 Best Western Johnny Appleseed Inn

543 Warrenton Rd (US 17 N), 22406; tel 540/373-0000 or toll free 800/633-6443; fax 540/373-5676. Exit 133B off I-95. Although area around motel is paved, property has 15 acres and backs on woods. Convenient to historic district and adjacent to restaurant. Lobby is uninspired but clean. **Rooms:** 88 rms. CI 2pm/CO noon. Nonsmoking rms avail. Clean, with motel-style furniture. **Amenities:** 🐟 A/C, cable TV. **Services:** 🛎 🍴 Coffee and tea in lobby. **Facilities:** 🔓 ‎200‎ 1 restaurant, 1 bar, basketball, playground, washer/dryer. Tent for gatherings. **Rates:** Peak (May–Sept) $44–$50 S; $52–$58 D. Extra person $6. Children under age 18 stay free. Lower rates off-season. Parking: Outdoor, free. AARP discount avail. AE, CB, DC, DISC, MC, V.

≣≣ Comfort Inn Southpoint

5422 Jefferson Davis Hwy, 22407; tel 540/898-5550 or toll free 800/221-2222; fax 540/891-2861. Exit 126 off I-95 S, or exit 126B off I-95 N. A modern motel in the Massaponax Outlet Shopping Center. **Rooms:** 125 rms. Executive level. CI 2pm/CO noon. Nonsmoking rms avail. Rooms have light, attractive walls and carpets, coordinated spreads and drapes. Colonial-style furniture and pictures of historic local buildings add atmosphere. **Amenities:** 🛏 🕭 A/C, cable TV w/movies, dataport. Some units w/whirlpools. **Services:** ⌂ ⌂ Guests receive discounts at outlet shops. **Facilities:** 🛣 📶 📋 ᶜ Spa, sauna, whirlpool. **Rates (CP):** Peak (June–Aug) $63 S or D. Extra person $6. Children under age 18 stay free. Lower rates off-season. Parking: Outdoor, free. AE, DC, DISC, ER, JCB, MC, V.

≣≣ Econo Lodge

Jct I-95/VA 3 W, 22404; tel 540/786-8374 or toll free 800/424-4777; fax 540/786-8811. Exit 130B off I-95. A small, inexpensive, and friendly motel with old and new buildings. Quiet location away from the highway, which can be difficult to find. Other restaurants and large mall with movie theater are nearby. **Rooms:** 96 rms. CI open/CO 11am. Nonsmoking rms avail. Recently painted and refurnished. **Amenities:** 🛏 A/C, cable TV. **Services:** ⌂ **Facilities:** ᶜ Rates (CP): Peak (June 14–Aug) $33–$40 S; $38–$45 D. Extra person $5. Children under age 18 stay free. Lower rates off-season. Parking: Outdoor, free. AE, DISC, MC, V.

≣≣ Hampton Inn

2310 William St, 22401; tel 540/371-0330 or toll free 800/426-7866; fax 540/371-1753. Exit 130A off I-95. Located in commercial area with many nearby shops, restaurants, beauty salon. Convenient to historic district and large mall. Central courtyard has minimal shrubs and other plants. **Rooms:** 166 rms. CI 3pm/CO noon. Nonsmoking rms avail. Clean, with soft color schemes. **Amenities:** 🛏 🕭 A/C, cable TV w/movies, dataport. Some units w/whirlpools. **Services:** ⌂ ⌂ **Facilities:** 🛣 📶 ᶜ Washer/dryer. Fenced, well-landscaped pool area. **Rates (CP):** Peak (May–Oct) $54–$59 S; $59–$68 D. Children under age 18 stay free. Lower rates off-season. Parking: Outdoor, free. AE, CB, DC, DISC, MC, V.

≣≣≣ Holiday Inn North

564 Warrenton Rd (US 17 N), 22405; tel 540/371-5550 or toll free 800/HOLIDAY; fax 540/373-3641. Exit 133B off I-95 N, or exit 133 off I-95 S. Attractive, well-maintained motel surrounded by extensive plantings. Lobby furnished with colonial reproductions. Convenient to historic district. **Rooms:** 148 rms. CI 2pm/CO noon. Nonsmoking rms avail. Clean, fresh rooms have pleasingly soft color scheme. **Amenities:** 🛏 🕭 A/C, cable TV w/movies, dataport. Some units w/terraces, some w/whirlpools. Refrigerators and microwaves available. **Services:** ✗ 📺 ⌂ ⌂ ⌂ Babysitting. Will help arrange airport transfers. **Facilities:** 🛣 📶 ᶜ 1 restaurant, 1 bar (w/entertainment), playground, washer/dryer. Attractive pool area surrounded by motel units. Bar can be noisy. **Rates:** Peak (Apr–Oct) $47–$52 S; $52–$65 D. Extra person $7. Children under age 18 stay free. Lower rates off-season. Parking: Outdoor, free. AE, CB, DC, DISC, JCB, MC, V.

≣≣ Holiday Inn South

5324 Jefferson Davis Hwy, 22408; tel 540/898-1102 or toll free 800/465-4239; fax 540/898-2017. Exit 126 off I-95. Flower beds help brighten entrance to this motel near Massaponax Outlet Shopping Center. Convenient to historic district, Mary Washington College, and nearby restaurants and shops. **Rooms:** 195 rms. CI 3pm/CO noon. Nonsmoking rms avail. Although somewhat dark, rooms are fairly well decorated. **Amenities:** 🛏 🕭 A/C, cable TV w/movies, dataport. **Services:** ✗ ⌂ ⌂ ⌂ **Facilities:** 🛣 📶 ᶜ 1 restaurant (see "Restaurants" below), 1 bar, games rm, sauna, whirlpool, washer/dryer. **Rates:** Peak (Apr–Aug) $59–$65 S or D. Extra person $6. Children under age 18 stay free. Lower rates off-season. Parking: Outdoor, free. AE, CB, DC, DISC, JCB, MC, V.

INNS

≣≣ Fredericksburg Colonial Inn

1707 Princess Anne St, 22401; tel 540/371-5666. 3 acres. White picket fence and blue awning and shutters give this curved, two-story white structure, a Civil War–era appearance. The mood continues inside, where there are mid-19th-century furnishings and a wide staircase that leads from the lobby to a landing with two grandfather clocks and then on to the second floor. **Rooms:** 30 rms and stes. CI 2pm/CO 11am. Each unit is differently decorated: mostly Victorian furniture among some Empire and Early American. Civil War pictures adorn walls. **Amenities:** 🛏 🕭 A/C, cable TV, refrig. **Services:** ⌂ Babysitting. **Facilities:** 📶 ᶜ Guest lounge w/TV. **Rates (CP):** $55 S or D; $65 ste. Extra person $6. Children under age 13 stay free. Parking: Outdoor, free. AE, MC, V.

≣≣≣ Kenmore Inn

1200 Princess Anne St, 22401 (Old Town); tel 540/371-7622 or toll free 800/437-7622; fax 540/371-5480. Exit 130B off I-95, at Lewis St. Local residents like to relax on white wicker furniture on the long front porch of this 1796 house, located on a tree-lined street in the historic district. **Rooms:** 13 rms and stes. CI 2pm/CO noon. All rooms are large, and each is individually decorated in colonial style. Cozy corner sitting area has table with two glasses and decanter of sherry. **Amenities:** 🛏 🕭 A/C, voice mail. No TV. 1 unit w/fireplace. **Services:** 🍴 📺 📺 📶 ⌂ Car-rental desk, social director, babysitting, wine/sherry served. Masseur on call. Staff makes extra effort to meet special needs. **Facilities:** 📶 ᶜ 2 restaurants, 2 bars (1 w/entertainment), guest lounge w/TV. **Rates (CP):** $85 S; $95 D; $150 ste. Extra person $10. Children under age 8 stay free. AP and MAP rates avail. Parking: Outdoor, free. AE, DC, MC, V.

≣≣≣≣ **Richard Johnston Inn**
711 Caroline St, 22401 (Old Town); tel 540/899-7606. Exit 130B off I-95. This antique-laden 18th-century house is a convenient place to stay for those in search of a quiet, restful retreat. The Old Town trolley stops in front and can take you to historical buildings, antique and other shops, and interesting restaurants. Unsuitable for children under 12. **Rooms:** 9 rms and stes. CI 2pm/CO 11am. No smoking. Clean, comfortable rooms furnished with period furniture, including upholstered chairs and sofas, lovely canopy beds; two suites on lower level open to terrace. **Amenities:** 🛁 A/C, cable TV, refrig. No phone. **Services:** 🔑 Afternoon tea served. Breakfast served in beautiful dining room. **Facilities:** 🔟 Guest lounge. **Rates (CP):** $90–$115 S or D; $130 ste. Extra person $10. Parking: Outdoor, free. AE, MC, V.

RESORT

≣≣≣ **Sheraton Inn Fredericksburg**
2801 Plank Rd, PO Box 618, 22404; tel 540/786-8321 or toll free 800/682-1049; fax 540/786-3957. Exit 133B off I-95, W on VA 3 to first light. 310 acres. Extensive plantings throughout the grounds are a pleasing touch at this resort convenient to historic district, Mary Washington College. **Rooms:** 193 rms and stes. CI 3pm/CO noon. Nonsmoking rms avail. Nicely appointed, well-coordinated rooms have colonial-style furniture. **Amenities:** 🛁 🗄 A/C, cable TV w/movies, refrig, dataport. All units w/terraces, 1 w/whirlpool. **Services:** ✕ 🍴 🖼 🛎 Babysitting. Rental cars delivered to site. Food can be ordered from pool area. **Facilities:** 🏊 🏋️ 🎾 🛶 🍴 Ⓜ 1 restaurant, 1 bar (w/entertainment), basketball, volleyball, lawn games. Restaurant has large informal patio for outdoor dining in good weather. **Rates (CP):** Peak (Mar 15–Nov 3) $119 S or D; $225–$275 ste. Extra person $10. Children under age 18 stay free. Min stay special events. Lower rates off-season. MAP rates avail. Parking: Outdoor, free. AE, CB, DC, DISC, MC, V.

RESTAURANTS 🍴

★ **La Petite Auberge**
311 William St (VA 3); tel 540/371-2727. Exit 130B off I-95. Between Charles and Princess Anne Sts. **French/European.** An attractive garden-like setting with cushioned metal chairs, brick walls, and many oil paintings, including some by local artists. Chef is very innovative. Curried chicken salad is especially good. Crabmeat selections and smoked trout with local sweet-red-pepper jelly lead dinner list. **FYI:** Reservations recommended. **Open:** Lunch Mon–Sat 11:30am–2:30pm; dinner Mon–Sat 5:30–10pm. **Prices:** Main courses $8–$20. AE, DC, MC, V. 🟢 🔽

♣ **Le Lafayette**
623 Caroline St; tel 540/373-6895. Exit 130B off I-95. Follow VA 3 (William St) east into downtown. **Regional American/French.** Lovely old house with colonial touches, including wide moldings, chair rails, Windsor-style chairs, large windows, plank floors, and period colors and wallpaper. Limited menu of traditional French fare is augmented by daily specials. **FYI:** Reservations recommended. Dress code. **Open:** Lunch Tues–Sun 11:30am–3pm; dinner Tues–Sun 5:30–10:30pm; brunch Sun 11:30am–3pm. **Prices:** Main courses $12–$22; prix fixe $13. AE, CB, DC, DISC, MC, V. 🟢 🖥

★ **Sammy T's**
801 Caroline St at Hanover St; tel 540/371-2008. Exit 130B off I-95. Follow VA 3 (William St) east into downtown. **American/Middle Eastern/Vegetarian.** Tavern decor prevails, with mirror-backed bar running the length of wall. Seating is all high wooden booths. Wood walls painted white sport travel posters. Ceiling is old-fashioned metal. Soups, sandwiches, salads, and other light food, plus some entrees. A friendly neighborhood-style pub with regular local clientele. **FYI:** Reservations not accepted. Dress code. Beer and wine only. **Open:** Mon–Sat 7:30am–midnight, Sun 7:30am–9pm. **Prices:** Main courses $5–$8. AE, DISC, MC, V. 📷 &

Santa Fe Grill and Saloon
216 William St; tel 540/371-0500. Exit 130B off I-95. Follow VA 3 (William St) east into downtown. **Southwestern/Tex-Mex.** An eye-catching, red-and-black storefront establishment with western decor suits its southwestern and Tex-Mex entrees, all prepared fresh on premises. Good choice for families or anyone young at heart. **FYI:** Reservations accepted. Dress code. **Open:** Peak (Easter–Thanksgiving) Mon–Thurs 11:30am–10pm, Fri–Sat 11:30am–11pm, Sun noon–8pm. **Prices:** Main courses $7–$16. AE, DISC, MC, V. 🍴 📷

Shoney's Family Restaurant
2203 Plank Rd (VA 3); tel 540/371-5400. Exit 130A off I-95. Follow VA 3 W. **American.** Real and plastic plants and a tan-brown-green color scheme are the decor at this chain restaurant, featuring a well-lit buffet area. Large selection of items aimed at satisfying a family's tastes. **FYI:** Reservations not accepted. Children's menu. No liquor license. **Open:** Daily 6am–midnight. **Prices:** Main courses $6–$8. AE, DISC, MC, V. 📷 &

Ⓢ ★ **The Smythe's Cottage and Tavern**
303 Fauquier St; tel 540/373-1645. Exit 130B off I-95. Follow VA 3 (William St) east into downtown. **Regional American/Continental/Southern Colonial.** A white picket fence surrounds this small white cottage with blue trim, which sits under large trees. Colonial decor inside is accompanied by traditional southern-style fare, such as fresh crab cakes, biscuits served with country ham. Friendly staff adds to warm tavern-like feeling. **FYI:** Reservations recommended. Children's menu. **Open:** Mon–Thurs 11am–9pm, Fri–Sat 11am–10pm, Sun noon–9pm. **Prices:** Main courses $11–$18. MC, V. 🟢 🍴 🖼 🖼

Sophia Street Station
503 Sophia St; tel 540/371-3355. **Continental.** Lots of railroad memorabilia in one small dining area and lounge of

this old riverfront station. Trains are etched into mirror over bar. A club car room hosts more formal dining, while main dining room, with dark flowered vinyl tablecloths and plastic floral arrangements, has less ambience. House special is prime rib, but menu contains range of entrees, burgers, sandwiches, and salads. **FYI:** Reservations recommended. Guitar. Children's menu. Dress code. **Open:** Daily 11:30am–10pm. **Prices:** Main courses $8–$20. AE, DISC, MC, V. 👥 ✓ &

ATTRACTIONS 📷

Fredericksburg Area Museum and Cultural Center
907 Princess Anne St; tel 540/371-5668. The museum occupies the 1816 Town Hall, located in Market Square. The first floor houses temporary exhibits relating to regional and cultural history; permanent exhibits on the second floor cover Native American history all the way through the modern era, along with audiovisual presentations and crafts demonstrations. Symposia are also held. On the third floor, the hall's 19th-century council chamber is another area used for changing exhibits. **Open:** Peak (Mar–Nov) Mon–Sat 9am–5pm, Sun 1–5 pm. Reduced hours off-season. $

James Monroe Museum and Memorial Library
908 Charles St; tel 540/654-1043. James Monroe came to Fredericksburg in 1786 to practice law and went on to hold a number of public offices before becoming the fifth president of the United States. His shingle hangs outside this low brick building, which is furnished with pieces from the Monroes' White House years or their retirement home.

The museum contains two Rembrandt Peale portraits of Monroe and such personal items as the formal attire he wore as US ambassador to the court of Napoleon, his dueling pistols, and his wife's wedding slippers. Monroe was the only US president besides Washington who fought in the Revolution, and he shared the grim winter at Valley Forge. Among the items on display are the gun and canteen he carried into battle. The library of some 10,000 books is a reconstruction of Monroe's own personal collection. Guided tours available. **Open:** Peak (Mar–Nov) daily 9am–5pm. Reduced hours off-season. $

Hugh Mercer Apothecary Shop
1020 Caroline St; tel 540/373-3362. Dr Hugh Mercer practiced medicine and operated this shop from 1761 to 1776, before giving his life as a Revolutionary War brigadier general. Presented in a living history format, tours are conducted by Mercer's "house wench," a guide in period costume, who discusses colonial medicinal practices and surgical techniques. Medical implements of the era are introduced, which include bleeding devices, a tooth key, and amputation instruments. The downstairs apothecary displays medicinal herbs and other potions commonly dispensed in the 18th century. The herbs are grown on site in the physic

garden, which is open to the public; signs describe the plants and explain their uses. **Open:** Peak (Mar–Nov) daily 9am–5pm. Reduced hours off-season. $

Rising Sun Tavern
1304 Caroline St; tel 540/371-1494. This was originally a residence, built in 1760 by Charles Washington, George's youngest brother. From the 1790s it served as a tavern for 30 years. The building has been restored, not reconstructed, although the 17th-and 18th-century furnishings are not all originals. The 30-minute tour provides many insights into colonial life, and includes the Great Room, the ladies' retiring room, the taproom, and the bedrooms, including a room where Lafayette once stayed. The tavern's original license is displayed in the downstairs hall. **Open:** Peak (Mar–Nov) daily 9am–5pm. Reduced hours off-season. $

St George's Episcopal Church
905 Princess Anne St; tel 540/373-4133. Martha Washington's father and John Paul Jones's brother are buried in the graveyard of this church. Members of the first parish congregation included Mary Washington and Revolutionary War generals Hugh Mercer and George Weedon. The original church was built in 1732; the current Romanesque structure (which boasts three signed Tiffany windows) was completed in 1849. During the Battle of Fredericksburg the church was hit at least 25 times, and in 1863 it was used by General Lee's troops for religious revival meetings. In 1864, when wounded Union soldiers filled every available building in town, it was used as a hospital. **Open:** Mon–Sat 9am–5pm; Sun services at 8 and 10:30am. **Free**

The Presbyterian Church
810 Princess Anne St; tel 540/373-7057. This Presbyterian church dates to the early 1800s, though the present Greek revival building was completed in 1855. Like St George's, it served as a hospital during the Civil War. Cannonballs in the front left pillar and scars on the walls of the loft and belfry remain to this day. The present church bell replaced one that was given to the Confederacy to be melted down for making cannons. **Open:** Mon–Sat 8:30am–4pm, Sun service at 11am (summer, 10am). **Free**

Masonic Lodge Number 4
Princess Anne and Hanover Sts; tel 540/373-5885. Not only is this the mother lodge of the father of our country, it's also one of the oldest Masonic lodges in America, established, it is believed, around 1735. Although the original building was down the street, the Masons have been meeting at this address since 1812. On display are a silver punchbowl used to serve Lafayette, a Gilbert Stuart portrait of Washington in its original gilt federalist frame, and the 1668 Bible on which Washington took his Masonic obligation (oath). Tours are given throughout the day. **Open:** Mon–Sat 9am–4pm, Sun 1–4pm. $

Fredericksburg and Spotsylvania National Military Park

120 Chatham Lane; tel 540/371-0802. This national park preserves the memory of four major Civil War battles that took place in the area between 1862 and 1864, including the battle that claimed the life of Gen "Stonewall" Jackson (the Battle of Chancellorsville) and the first-ever meeting of Gen Robert E Lee and Gen Ulysses S Grant (the Battle of the Wilderness).

A self-guided driving tour of the park begins at the **Fredericksburg Battlefield Visitor Center** and takes in 16 major sites relating to the battles. The center offers tour brochures, museum displays, and a 12-minute slide show orientation. Tapes and tape players are available for rent that give audio tours describing each battle in detail. **Open:** Daily 9am–sunset. **Free**

The Courthouse

Princess Anne and George Sts; tel 540/372-1066. Fans of architecture will appreciate a short visit to this building. Designed by James Renwick, who also designed New York's St Patrick's Cathedral as well as the Renwick Gallery and the original Smithsonian "Castle" in Washington, DC, this Gothic Revival courthouse was built 1853 and is still used for that purpose. **Open:** Mon–Fri 9am–4pm. **Free**

Mary Washington House

1200 Charles St; tel 540/373-1569. George Washington purchased this house for his mother, Mary Ball Washington, in 1772. She was 62 years old and had been living at nearby Ferry Farm since 1739. Lafayette paid his respects to Mary Washington here during the Revolution. In 1789 Washington received his mother's blessing before going to New York to be inaugurated as president. He did not see her again; she died later that year. Hostesses in colonial garb give 30-minute tours throughout the day. **Open:** Peak (Mar–Nov) daily 9am–5pm. Reduced hours off-season. **$**

Belmont

224 Washington St; tel 540/654-1015. Situated on 27 hillside acres overlooking the falls of the Rappahannock River, Belmont began as an 18th-century farmhouse (the central 6 rooms of the house date to the 1790s) and was enlarged to a 22-room mansion by a later owner. The house is furnished with art treasures, family heirlooms, and European antiques of American artist Gari Melchers, who lived here from 1916 until his death in 1932. There are many wonderful paintings in the house, including works by Brueghel, Rodin, and Melchers himself. Guided tours available. **Open:** Peak (Mar–Nov) Mon–Sat 10am–5pm, Sun 1–5pm. Reduced hours off-season. **$**

Chatham

120 Chatham Lane; tel 540/373-4461. This pre-Revolutionary mansion, built between 1768 and 1771 by wealthy planter William Fitzhugh, has figured prominently in American history. During the Civil War, the house, then belonging to J Horace Lacy, served as headquarters for Federal commanders and as a Union field hospital. Lincoln visited the house and Walt Whitman and Clara Barton cared for the wounded here. Self-guided tours include five rooms of the house. **Open:** Daily 9am–5pm. **Free**

Kenmore

1201 Washington Ave; tel 540/373-3381. This mid-18th-century Georgian mansion was built for Betty Washington (George's sister) by her husband, Fielding Lewis, one of the wealthiest planters in Fredericksburg. The original plantation covered nearly 1,300 acres and produced tobacco, grains, and flax. Today the house is meticulously restored to its colonial appearance. All of the woodwork and paneling are original, as are the molded plaster ceilings and cornices. The authentic period furnishings include several Lewis family pieces. The tour winds up in the kitchen, where spiced tea and gingerbread (Mary Washington's recipe, the same she served to Lafayette in 1784) are served. **Open:** Peak (Mar–Nov) daily 9am–5pm. Reduced hours off-season. **$$**

Caledon Natural Area

11617 Caledon Rd, King George; tel 540/663-3861. Caledon, while overseen by the Virginia Division of State Parks, is actually a natural area, not a park. Only 800 of its 2,579 acres are available for public use, and only for passive recreational use such as picnicking, hiking, and bird-watching. No overnight camping facilities are available.

Four miles of hiking trails travel through Caledon's hardwood forest, one of the few remaining hardwood forest preserves in this region, and another three-mile trail leads to the banks of the Potomac. The rest of the natural area is restricted to provide a protected habitat for American bald eagles. In the summer, Caledon shelters one of the largest concentrations of bald eagles in this part of the country, as well as more than 200 other species of birds. The area is one of the most popular bird-watching spots in Virginia. **Open:** Daily 8am–sunset; visitors center, Mem Day–Labor Day, call for hours. **Free**

Lake Anna State Park

6800 Lawyers Rd, Spotsylvania; tel 540/854-5503. A 2,000-acre park bordering a 13,000-acre man-made lake, Lake Anna State Park is adjacent to VA 601 off VA 208. The lake was created in 1971 to provide coolant water for a Virginia Power nuclear plant. The state park was officially opened in 1983. The visitor center is a modern facility housing exhibits of local wildlife and history, as well as interpretive displays on gold mining. (The Goodwin Gold Mine was established nearby in the 1830s; gold mining in this area reached its peak in the 1840s.)

Boating and fishing on the lake are the most popular activities here, but the park also offers eight nature trails, lakefront picnic areas, and a new swimming complex. Interpretive programs on nature and history are offered during the summer, which include children's programs, gold panning, and pontoon boat tours of the lake. **Open:** Daily 8am–sunset. **$**

Stratford Hall Plantation

VA 214, Stratford; tel 540/493-8038. This house, magnificently set on 1,600 acres above the Potomac, is renowned not only for its distinctive architectural style but for the illustrious family who lived here. Thomas Lee (1690-1750), who served as governor of the Virginia colony, built Stratford in the late 1730s. The Lees of Virginia played major roles in the formation of the United States: Richard Henry Lee, the delegate who made the motion for independence in the Continental Congress; his brother, Francis Lightfoot Lee, a signer of the Declaration of Independence; Henry "Light Horse Harry" Lee, a hero of the Revolutionary War; and his son, General Robert E Lee, the legendary Confederate military leader.

Guided tours of the restored house include the paneled Great Hall, which runs the depth of the house; the winter kitchen and estate offices; and the nursery, which contains Robert E Lee's crib. After the tour, guests can stroll the meadows and gardens of the 1,600-acre estate, which is still operated as a working farm. **Open:** Daily 9am-4:30pm. **$$$**

Front Royal

Named for the royal oak that stood in the town square during the Revolutionary War, this small town in the Shenandoah Valley is near the Shenandoah River and George Washington National Forest. Seat of Warren County. **Information:** Front Royal-Warren County Chamber of Commerce, 414 E Main St, PO Box 568, Front Royal, 22630 (tel 540/635-3185 or toll free 800/338-2576).

HOTEL

≡≡≡ Quality Inn Skyline Drive

10 Commerce Ave, 22630; tel 540/635-3161. Exit 6 off I-66 W, or exit 13 off I-66 E. A nicely turned-out hotel with interesting decorating touches in rooms and efficient and inviting facilities, from the gift shop to the bar. **Rooms:** 107 rms. CI 1pm/CO 11am. Nonsmoking rms avail. All king rooms have pull-out sofas. Some rooms have wood trim, a half-timbered look, and mahogany furnishings. **Amenities:** A/C, cable TV w/movies. Microwaves and refrigerators in 25% of rooms. **Services:** X Turndown service on request. **Facilities:** 1 restaurant, 1 bar (w/entertainment). Nice restaurant. **Rates (CP):** Peak (Sept-Oct) $65-$89 S or D. Extra person $9. Children under age 18 stay free. Lower rates off-season. Parking: Outdoor, free. Special golf and ski packages avail. AE, DISC, MC, V.

MOTELS

≡ Scottish Inn

533 S Royal Ave, 22630; tel 540/636-6168 or toll free 800/251-1962; fax 540/636-3120. Exit 13 off I-66. A basic, clean, no-frills facility offering a modest rate. Reserve early during October. **Rooms:** 20 rms. CI open/CO 11am. Nonsmoking rms avail. **Amenities:** A/C, cable TV w/movies. Irons available at desk. Roll-away beds for $4. **Services:** **Facilities:** Copy machine in lobby. **Rates:** Peak (July-Oct) $46-$50 S or D. Extra person $4. Children under age 12 stay free. Lower rates off-season. Parking: Outdoor, free. Weekly rates avail, except in high season. MC, V.

≡≡ Twin Rivers Motel

1801 Shenandoah Ave, 22630; tel 540/635-4101. 1¾ mi S of I-66. This modest facility is well kept and, mindful of families, has some helpful facilities. Located at northern entrance to Skyline Dr. **Rooms:** 20 rms. CI noon/CO 11am. Nonsmoking rms avail. Basic clean rooms. 1 room with king-size bed. **Amenities:** A/C, cable TV w/movies. **Services:** Roll-aways available. Pets are sometimes allowed with a deposit. **Facilities:** Outdoor grill area, swing set. **Rates:** Peak (Apr-Oct) $39 S; $44 D. Extra person $5. Lower rates off-season. Parking: Outdoor, free. AE, MC, V.

ATTRACTIONS

Sky Meadows State Park

11012 Edmonds Lane, Delaplane; tel 540/592-3556. Rich in history, this peaceful 1,800-acre park on the eastern side of the Blue Ridge Mountains has rolling pastures, woodlands, and scenic vistas. The park offers only primitive hike-in campsites; hiking trails include access to the Appalachian Trail. Visitor center, nature and history programs spring-fall. **Open:** Daily 8am-sunset. **$**

Warren Rifles Confederate Museum

95 Chester St; tel 540/636-6982. Preserved here are numerous pieces of Confederate memorabilia from the Civil War. Included are battle flags, weapons, uniforms, letters, diaries, and other personal effects. **Open:** Mid-Apr-Oct, Mon-Sat 9am-4pm, Sun noon-4pm. **$**

Belle Boyd Cottage

101 Chester St; tel 540/636-1446. Moved in 1982 from its original location, this restored cottage was the home of Confederate spy Belle Boyd. For two years Boyd supplied the Confederacy with valuable intelligence obtained by her close contact with Union forces occupying Front Royal, information that resulted in a decisive victory for the South at the Battle of Front Royal (May 21, 1862). Guided tours; an 1862 formal garden surrounds the house. A reenactment of the Battle of Front Royal is staged the second weekend in May. **Open:** Apr-Oct, Mon-Fri 11am-4pm, Sat-Sun by appointment. **$**

Galax

See also Hillsville

In the southwest Blue Ridge highlands, SW of Roanoke, and named for a mountain evergreen plant abundant in the area. **Information:** Galax-Carroll-Grayson Chamber of Commerce, 405 N Main St, Galax, 24333 (tel 540/236-2184).

ATTRACTION 📷

New River Trail State Park
Austinville; tel 540/699-6778. Still under development, New River Trail is a 57-mile-long state park that follows an abandoned railroad right-of-way from Galax northeast to Pulaski. Much of the area fronts the historic and scenic New River. The trail includes two tunnels and three major bridges, with nearly 30 smaller bridges and trestles. The park is ideal for hiking, bicycling, and horseback riding, and it also serves as a link to numerous other outdoor recreation areas, including Mount Rogers National Recreation Area.

    Shot Tower Historical State Park, the headquarters area for New River Trail State Park, is located roughly at the midpoint of the trail, about 27 miles northeast of Galax (just off US 52, near where the highway crosses the New River). Built around 1807, the Shot Tower stands 75 feet high and is 20 feet square at its base; its stone walls are 2½ feet thick, possibly to maintain a constant temperature for the cooling shot. **Open:** Daily sunrise–sunset. **$**

George Washington Birthplace National Monument

Located 40 mi E of Fredericksburg, off VA 3 and VA 204. Encompassing some 500 acres along Pope's Creek (a tributary of the Potomac), this park contains a charming re-creation of Washington's first home. He was born here on February 22, 1732, the first child of Augustine and Mary Ball Washington. When George was 3½ the family moved to the Mount Vernon estate.

    The original house burned to the ground in 1779, and there were no records to indicate what it looked like. The present house, known as **Memorial House,** is representative of a typical plantation house of the 1700s, and has been furnished with pieces appropriate to the period.

    The **visitor center** (open daily 9am–5pm) screens a 14-minute film. Tours include the house, the herb garden, and a separate building that contains the kitchen and a weaving room. Graves of some Washington family members, including George's father, are in a small burial ground on the property. Children will particularly enjoy the small-scale farm, with horses, chickens, and cows. For more information, contact Superintendent, George Washington Birthplace National Monument, RR 1, Box 717, Washington's Birthplace, VA 22443 (tel 804/224-1732).

Great Falls

A suburban community NW of Washington, DC at the fall line of the Potomac River.

RESTAURANTS 🍴

Falls Landing Restaurant
In Village Center, 774 Walker Rd; tel 703/759-4650. At Georgetown Pike. **Eclectic/Seafood.** Dark beams, colonial-style furniture, and exposed brick set an elegant and romantic tone. Continental preparation of fresh lobster (always on the menu), fish, and local seasonal items such as soft-shell crab are the main attractions. Salads and vegetables included in price of main courses. **FYI:** Reservations recommended. Children's menu. Dress code. **Open:** Lunch Mon–Fri 11:30am–2:30pm; dinner Mon–Thurs 5:30–10pm, Fri–Sat 5:30–10:30pm, Sun 4–9pm. **Prices:** Main courses $16–$22. AE, CB, DC, DISC, MC, V. ♥ 🕭

🏆 ★ L'Auberge Chez François
332 Springvale Rd at Beach Mill Rd; tel 703/759-3800. From Georgetown Pike, follow Springvale Rd north to Beach Mill Rd. **French.** A well-dressed but relaxed crowd usually packs this charming country French chalet in a near-rural setting. It's long been one of this area's most popular spots to celebrate such special occasions as birthdays, anniversaries, and marriage proposals—so popular, in fact, that reservations are taken up to four months in advance. Classical French cooking is on order, with some country-style selections mixed with creative dishes that have inspired a cookbook by the chef/owner. **FYI:** Reservations recommended. Children's menu. Dress code. **Open:** Tues–Sat 5:30–9:30pm, Sun 1:30–8pm. **Prices:** Main courses $30–$40. AE, DC, DISC, MC, V. 🕭

★ Serbian Crown Restaurant
In Old Mill Market Sq, 1141 Walker Rd at Colvin Mill Rd; tel 703/759-4150. **French/Russian/Serbian.** Dark, intimate dining rooms and a section with picture windows and flower baskets are hung with large paintings of Eastern European personages and landscapes. Chicken Kiev, Serbian stuffed cabbage, and Dover sole meunière can be found on this ethnically diverse menu. An excellent value at $22, the early-bird four-course dinner is popular prior to shows at nearby Wolftrap Farm Park for the Performing Arts. Nightly entertainment by pianist or Gypsy musicians. **FYI:** Reservations recommended. Piano. Dress code. **Open:** Lunch Mon–Thurs 11:30am–2:20pm; dinner Mon–Fri 5:30–10pm, Sat–Sun 4–9pm. **Prices:** Main courses $16–$26. AE, MC, V. ♥ 💟 🕭

Hampton

At the mouth of the James River in the Tidewater area of Virginia, Hampton was first settled around 1610. Home of Fort Monroe, America's only active-duty moat-encircled fort, and the US Air Force's Langley Field. **Information:** Virginia Peninsula Chamber of Commerce, Six Manhattan Sq #100, PO Box 7269, Hampton, 23666 (tel 757/766-2000).

MOTELS

Fairfield Inn

1905 Coliseum Dr, 23666; tel 757/827-7400 or toll free 800/228-2800; fax 757/827-7400. Exit 263B off I-64. A budget, no-frills motel within walking distance of Hampton Coliseum. **Rooms:** 134 rms. CI 3pm/CO noon. Nonsmoking rms avail. Some rooms overlook pool. Card-key security system. **Amenities:** A/C, satel TV w/movies. Security patrol on weekends and during special events. **Services:** Facilities: Lobby has microwave. **Rates (CP):** Peak (June–Sept) $55–$60 S; $60–$64 D. Extra person $4. Children under age 12 stay free. Lower rates off-season. Parking: Outdoor, free. Military rates avail. AE, DC, DISC, MC, V.

Hampton Inn

1813 W Mercury Blvd, 23666; tel 757/838-8484 or toll free 800/HAMPTON; fax 757/826-0725. Exit 263B off I-64. A budget chain motel close to Hampton Coliseum, shopping, restaurants, and movie theaters. Attracts business travelers. **Rooms:** 132 rms. CI 3pm/CO noon. Nonsmoking rms avail. Wardrobes instead of closets. **Amenities:** A/C, cable TV w/movies. **Services:** X Adjacent Holiday Inn provides room service during restaurant hours. **Facilities:** Guests may use pool, fitness center, game room at adjacent Holiday Inn. **Rates (CP):** Peak (May 24–Dec 31) $69 S or D. Extra person $6. Children under age 18 stay free. Min stay special events. Lower rates off-season. Parking: Outdoor, free. AE, DC, DISC, ER, MC, V.

Holiday Inn Hampton Coliseum Hotel

1815 W Mercury Blvd, 23666; tel 757/838-0200 or toll free 800/842-9370; fax 757/838-4964. Exit 263B off I-64. A large motel close to Hampton Coliseum. Spacious, airy public areas includes atrium with restaurant, bar, pool, fitness center, game room. **Rooms:** 321 rms and stes. Executive level. CI 3pm/CO noon. Nonsmoking rms avail. Newer rooms have indoor corridors; some overlook atrium. Mauve accents, dark-finished art deco–style furniture. **Amenities:** A/C, cable TV w/movies, voice mail. Some units w/terraces, some w/whirlpools. Free daily newspaper. Refrigerators on request. **Services:** X Babysitting. Free shuttle to Norfolk or Williamsburg airports. **Facilities:** 1 restaurant, 1 bar, games rm, sauna, whirlpool, washer/dryer. Fitness trail begins on premises, ends at Hampton Coliseum. **Rates:** Peak (May–Sept) $89–$96 S or D; $132–$180 ste. Extra person $7. Children under age 18

stay free. Min stay special events. Lower rates off-season. AP and MAP rates avail. Parking: Outdoor, free. AE, DC, DISC, MC, V.

RESTAURANTS

♥ Captain George's Seafood Restaurant

2710 W Mercury Blvd; tel 757/826-1435. Exit 263A off I-64. **Seafood/Steak.** Resin-coated tables with recessed rope and seashells, ceiling fans, and stained-glass murals with sea scenes set nautical tone. Separate, larger room has wooden tables, captain-style chairs, white cloth napkins. Seafood buffet with wide selection or traditional seafood dishes à la carte. **FYI:** Reservations not accepted. Children's menu. Additional locations: 1956 Laskin Rd, Virginia Beach (tel 804/428-3494); 2272 Old Pungo Ferry Rd, Virginia Beach (tel 804/721-3463). **Open:** Daily 4:30–10pm. **Prices:** Main courses $16–$31; prix fixe $22. AE, MC, V.

♥ Fisherman's Wharf Seafood Restaurant

14 Ivy Home Rd; tel 757/723-3113. Exit 265A off I-64. Follow LaSalle Ave south to Kecoughtan Rd (US 60) east; turn right on Ivy Home Rd. **Seafood.** Many windows offer an expansive water view of Hampton Roads harbor, while nautical decor includes padded captain's chairs; brass ship lanterns. Huge wooden ship's hull supports grand seafood buffet, with more than 75 items. Popular choices include baked shrimp stuffed with backfin crab meat and Australian rock-lobster tail. **FYI:** Reservations recommended. Children's menu. Additional location: 1571 Bayville St, Norfolk (tel 804/480-3133). **Open:** Mon–Fri 5–10pm, Sat 4–10:30pm, Sun 12–10pm. **Prices:** Main courses $14–$30; prix fixe $22. AE, CB, DC, DISC, MC, V.

ATTRACTIONS

Virginia Air and Space Center/Hampton Roads History Center

600 Settlers Landing Rd; tel 757/727-0900. The official visitor center for NASA Langley Research Center, this museum is located in downtown Hampton. Interactive exhibits let visitors launch a rocket, visit the planet Mars, or view themselves as an astronaut working in space. Ten air and space craft are suspended from the center's 94-foot ceiling, including the *Apollo 12* command module. Large-screen IMAX films are shown daily (additional fee charged).

The **Hampton Roads History Center** tells the 400-year history of Hampton, one of the oldest towns in the United States. Exhibits include an 18th-century custom house and tavern. **Open:** Peak (May–Aug) Mon–Wed 10am–5pm, Thurs–Sun 10am–7pm. Reduced hours off-season. **$$$**

Casemate Museum

Exit 268 off I-64; tel 757/727-3391. Located on the active army base of Fort Monroe, where Jefferson Davis was imprisoned in 1865 after the Civil War. Visitors can view displays of military memorabilia and enter the sparsely furnished room where Davis was held prisoner. **Open:** Daily 10:30am–4:30pm. **Free**

Hampton University Museum
Hampton University; tel 757/727-5308. Hampton University was founded in 1868 to provide an education for newly freed African Americans. The museum is housed in the Academy Building, an 1881 landmark on the waterfront in the historic section of the campus. Notable holdings include an African collection comprising more than 2,700 art objects and artifacts representing 887 ethnic groups and cultures; also works by Harlem Renaissance artists and extensive Oceanic, Asian, and Native American collections. **Open:** Mon–Fri 8am–5pm, Sat–Sun noon–4pm. **Free**

Hardy

See also Bedford

Located SE of Roanoke, Hardy was the boyhood home of Booker T Washington.

ATTRACTION

Booker T Washington National Monument
VA 122 S; tel 540/721-2094. Although Booker T Washington called his boyhood home a plantation, the Burroughs farm was small—207 acres—with never more than 11 slaves. The cabin where Washington was born was also the plantation kitchen. He and his brother and sister slept on a dirt floor and there was no glass in the windows. Overcoming the obstacles of poverty and prejudice, he achieved national prominence as an author, educator, founder of the Tuskegee Institute in Alabama, and adviser to presidents.

Several farm buildings have been reconstructed and programs are given on plantation life, slavery, and Washington's illustrious career. The visitor center offers a slide show and distributes a self-guided plantation tour map of the original Burroughs property. **Open:** Daily 9am–5pm. **Free**

Harrisonburg

See also Monterey

HOTEL

Sheraton Four Points Hotel
1400 E Market St, 22801; tel 540/433-2521 or toll free 800/325-3535; fax 540/434-0253. Exit 247A off I-81. A modern hotel boasting a large lobby fireplace. Close to ski area and tours of Civil War battlefields. **Rooms:** 138 rms and stes. Executive level. CI 3pm/CO noon. Nonsmoking rms avail. **Amenities:** A/C, cable TV w/movies. Some units w/terraces. **Services:** Facilities: 1 restaurant, 1 bar (w/entertainment), sauna, whirlpool. Cafe.

Exceptionally large indoor pool area surrounded by patio tables. Guests have free use of nearby fitness club. **Rates:** Peak (Sept 29–Oct 31) $91–$105 S; $103–$117 D. Extra person $12. Min stay special events. Lower rates off-season. Parking: Outdoor, free. AE, CB, DC, DISC, EC, ER, JCB, MC, V.

MOTELS

Comfort Inn
1440 E Market St, 22801; tel 540/433-6066 or toll free 800/221-2222; fax 540/433-0793. Exit 247A off I-81. A city motel near restaurants, malls, and James Madison University. Massanutten ski resort is 10 miles away. **Rooms:** 60 rms. CI 3pm/CO noon. Nonsmoking rms avail. Light and airy rooms decorated in soft pastels. **Amenities:** A/C, cable TV w/movies. **Services:** Facilities: **Rates (CP):** Peak (May–Oct) $65–$85 S or D. Extra person $5. Children under age 18 stay free. Lower rates off-season. Parking: Outdoor, free. AE, CB, DC, DISC, ER, JCB, MC, V.

Econo Lodge
1703 E Market St, PO Box 1311, 22802; tel 540/433-2576 or toll free 800/424-4777; fax 540/433-2576 ext 198. Exit 247 off I-81, ½ mile E on US 33. In the heart of the Shenandoah Valley, this chain motel is near James Madison University, Skyline Dr, Civil War battlefields, museums, and outdoor activities. **Rooms:** 88 rms and stes. Executive level. CI 2pm/CO 11am. Nonsmoking rms avail. All units recently refurbished. **Amenities:** A/C, cable TV w/movies. Some units w/whirlpools. **Services:** Facilities: Pretty view from pool area. **Rates (CP):** Peak (Apr–Dec) $36–$66 S; $42–$66 D; $70–$90 ste. Extra person $5. Children under age 18 stay free. Min stay special events. Lower rates off-season. Parking: Outdoor, free. AE, DC, DISC, JCB, MC, V.

HoJo Inn
605 Port Republic Rd, PO Box 68, 22801 (James Madison University); tel 540/434-6771 or toll free 800/446-4656. Exit 245 off I-81. A well-maintained older property directly opposite James Madison University. **Rooms:** 134 rms. CI 2pm/CO noon. Nonsmoking rms avail. Rooms are extremely large by today's motel standards. **Amenities:** A/C, cable TV. All units w/terraces. **Services:** Facilities: 1 restaurant. **Rates:** $40–$50 S; $50–$60 D. Extra person $5. Children under age 18 stay free. Min stay special events. Parking: Outdoor, free. AE, CB, DC, DISC, ER, JCB, MC, V.

Ramada Inn
1 Pleasant Valley Rd, 22801; tel 540/434-9981 or toll free 800/434-7456; fax 540/434-7088. Exit 243 off I-81. A quiet location with wonderful view of the surrounding hills. **Rooms:** 130 rms. CI 2pm/CO noon. Nonsmoking rms avail. Basic motel-style rooms. **Amenities:** A/C, cable TV w/movies. **Services:** Facilities: 1 restaurant (bkfst and dinner only), 1 bar. Tennis and golf nearby. **Rates:**

Peak (July–Oct) $51 S; $56 D. Extra person $6. Children under age 18 stay free. Lower rates off-season. Parking: Outdoor, free. AE, DC, DISC, MC, V.

RESTAURANT 🍽

★ Texas Steakhouse and Saloon

1688 E Market St; tel 540/433-3650. Exit 247 off I-81. **Steak.** Large fireplace, stuffed animals, and western flair make this an all-around favorite with college students, families, and businesspeople. Mesquite-grilled steaks are the main attraction, but menu also offers ribs, "Texas pheasant" (chicken), and sandwiches. **FYI:** Reservations not accepted. Children's menu. **Open:** Mon–Thurs 11am–10pm, Fri–Sat 11am–11pm, Sun 11am–10pm. **Prices:** Main courses $8–$18. AE, DISC, MC, V. 🎸 🎠 ⚹

ATTRACTION 📷

George Washington National Forest

I-81; tel 540/564-8300. Deerfield Ranger District accessible 10 miles west on US 250. The George Washington National Forest covers more than a million acres of mountains and valleys in northwestern Virginia and West Virginia. Steeped in American tradition, it has served as a westward passage for Native Americans and pioneers and as a battleground in the Revolutionary and Civil Wars. In addition to a wide variety of wildflowers and other flora, there is abundant wildlife. Species include bear, deer, turkey, grouse, and 160 species of songbird.

Numerous old woods roads and hiking trails offer the best access to the various areas of the forest, including part of the famous **Appalachian Trail**. Among the other activities enjoyed in the forest are picnicking, camping, sightseeing, hunting, fishing, swimming, and boating. For detailed information contact the Forest Supervisor, George Washington National Forest, Harrison Plaza, Harrisonburg, VA 22801. **Open:** Daily sunrise–sunset. **Free**

Herndon

See Dulles Int'l Airport

Hillsville

MOTEL 🏨

⬛⬛ Knob Hill Motor Lodge

305 E Stuart Dr, 24343; tel 540/728-2131. Exit 14 off I-77. About 3 mi E on US 221/58. Convenient to the interstate and the Blue Ridge Pkwy, this homey older establishment is popular with those attending the annual Galax Fiddler's Convention. **Rooms:** 19 rms. CI 2pm/CO 11am. Nonsmoking rms avail. **Amenities:** 🛎 🍷 A/C, cable TV w/movies.

Services: 🆅🅿 ⬜ 🍴 Babysitting. **Rates:** Peak (Mar–Oct) $37–$40 S; $40–$46 D. Extra person $5. Lower rates off-season. Parking: Outdoor, free. AE, MC, V.

Hopewell

MOTEL 🏨

⬛⬛ Days Inn

4911 Oaklawn Blvd, 23860; tel 804/458-1500 or toll free 800/458-3297; fax 804/458-9159. Exit 4 off I-95. An attractive brick structure with tile roof and pretty courtyard pool. Convenient to restaurants, some offering discounts to guests. Good location for touring James River Plantations. **Rooms:** 115 rms. CI noon/CO 11am. Nonsmoking rms avail. Pleasant and comfortable. **Amenities:** 🛎 A/C, cable TV, refrig. Some units w/whirlpools. **Services:** 🍴 Shuttle to nearby locations. Coffee in lobby. Complimentary barbecue on Wednesday. **Facilities:** 🎱 🏓 ⚹ Games rm, washer/dryer. **Rates (CP):** $65 S; $75 D. Children under age 12 stay free. Parking: Outdoor, free. AE, DC, DISC, MC, V.

Hot Springs

Located in the Allegheny Mountains and noted for its mineral springs and outdoor activities. **Information:** Bath County Chamber of Commerce, PO Box 718, Hot Springs, 24445 (tel 540/839-5409).

MOTEL 🏨

⬛⬛ Roseloe Motel

US 220 N, PO Box 590, 24445; tel 540/839-5373. A small, quiet motel just minutes from the Homestead resort and such activities as skiing, golfing, canoeing, horseback riding, and soaking in mineral springs. **Rooms:** 14 rms and effic. CI 3pm/CO noon. No smoking. Units with kitchens ideal for families. **Amenities:** 🛎 A/C, cable TV w/movies. **Services:** ⬜ 🍴 🚐 **Facilities:** 🧗 🎾 **Rates:** $36–$46 S or D; $50–$53 effic. Extra person $4. Parking: Outdoor, free. DISC, MC, V.

RESORT

⬛⬛⬛⬛ The Homestead

US 220 N, PO Box 2000, 24445; tel 540/839-5500 or toll free 800/336-5771; fax 540/839-7782. Exit 151B off I-18. Follow US 220 N to Hot Springs. 15,000 acres. Combining rich historical ambience with present-day elegance, this deluxe resort is nestled in the Allegheny Mountains. Travelers have come for rejuvenating benefits of natural hot springs since the 18th century. **Rooms:** 521 rms and stes. Executive level. CI 4pm/CO noon. No smoking. Recently renovated, choice west wing rooms have paintings and photographs reflecting history of area and resort's construction. **Amenities:** 🛎 🍷 📺 🍷 A/C, cable TV w/movies, refrig, bathrobes. Some units w/minibars, some w/terraces, some w/fireplaces. **Services:** ✗ 🖦 VP 🚗 🖼 ↺ Twice-daily maid svce, social director, masseur, children's program, babysitting. Attentive staff fulfills most guest requests. Instruction in skiing, ice skating, golf, and fly fishing. **Facilities:** 🎲 🚴 ▣ ▶54 ⛵ 🎣 🍴11 🛎 1500 💻 ♿ 7 restaurants, 2 bars (1 w/entertainment), games rm, lawn games, spa, sauna, steam rm, whirlpool, beauty salon, playground. Olympic-size ice-skating rink, bowling lanes, carriage rides, shooting club, cinema. **Rates:** Peak (Mid-Apr–mid-Nov) $157–$194 S; $314–$388 D; $538 ste. Extra person $25. Min stay special events. Lower rates off-season. AP and MAP rates avail. Parking: Outdoor, $7/day. Children 5–12 stay for $29 each; children 13–18 for $50 each. AE, DISC, MC, V.

Irvington

In Virginia's Tidewater area at the mouth of the Rappahannock River, Irvington is noted for its beaches and water sports.

RESORTS 🏨

≣≣≣ The Tides Inn

King Carter Dr, PO Box 480, 22480 (Carter's Creek); tel 804/438-5000 or toll free 800/843-3746; fax 804/438-5222. Exit 130B off I-95. 500 acres. Venerable riverside retreat enjoys beautiful water and forest views. Lovely, well-kept buildings and grounds plus friendly staff create relaxed, well-mannered atmosphere. Attractive public areas with plentiful seating. **Rooms:** 110 rms and stes. CI 3:30pm/CO 2pm. Nonsmoking rms avail. Superb waterview units are homey, with well-coordinated drapes, spreads, and wallpaper. Bathrobes furnished on request. Baseboards and crown molding give a historic air. **Amenities:** 🗄 🛁 ▣ ♦ A/C, cable TV. Some units w/terraces, 1 w/whirlpool. **Services:** ✗ 🖦 VP 🚗 🖼 ↺ ◁ Twice-daily maid svce, car-rental desk, social director, children's program, babysitting. **Facilities:** 🎲 🚴 △ ▣ ▶27 🎣 ⛵4 🍴 200 ♿ 3 restaurants, 2 bars (1 w/entertainment), 1 beach (cove/inlet), lifeguard, basketball, volleyball, games rm, lawn games, playground, washer/dryer. The 9-hole, par-3 golf course is free to guests. Lovely restaurants. Guests use local fitness center for small fee. Yacht available for river rides. **Rates (MAP):** Peak (Apr 5–Nov 9) $184–$363 S; $258–$408 D; $375–$699 ste. Extra person $55. Children under age 10 stay free. Min stay peak, wknds, and special events. Lower rates off-season. AP rates avail. Parking: Outdoor, free. Closed Jan–Feb. AE, DC, MC, V.

≣≣≣≣ The Tides Lodge

1 St Andrews Lane, PO Box 309, 22480 (Carter's Creek); tel 804/438-6000 or toll free 800/248-4337; fax 804/438-5950. Exit 130B off I-95. 175 acres. Well-kept grounds leading to this rustic-looking lodge are part of golf course shared with Tides Inn. Very attractive Scottish motif to large lobby with long reception desk. **Rooms:** 58 rms; 1 cottage/villa. Execu-

tive level. CI 3:30pm/CO 1pm. Nonsmoking rms avail. Attractive rooms have pictures of hunting scenes and carry on Scottish motif of public areas. Good-quality furniture with comfortable seating arrangements. **Amenities:** 🗄 🛁 ▣ ♦ A/C, cable TV, refrig, bathrobes. All units w/minibars, all w/terraces, 1 w/fireplace. **Services:** ✗ VP 🚗 🖼 ↺ ◁ Twice-daily maid svce, car-rental desk, social director, children's program, babysitting. Golf clinics, yacht cruises, morning newspapers. Will arrange car rental, appointments at beauty salon in town. Van or gondola rides to Tides Inn. **Facilities:** 🎲 🚴 △ ▣ ▶45 🎣 ⛵2 🍴 🛎 120 ♿ 2 restaurants, 1 bar (w/entertainment), volleyball, lawn games, sauna, playground, washer/dryer. Fitness center nearby. **Rates:** Peak (Sept–Oct) $120–$144 S; $160–$208 D; $275–$299 cottage/villa. Extra person $30. Children under age 18 stay free. Min stay peak, wknds, and special events. Lower rates off-season. AP and MAP rates avail. Parking: Outdoor, free. Closed Jan–Mar. DISC, MC, V.

ATTRACTION 🏛

Historic Christ Church

VA 3; tel 804/438-6855. Elegant in its simplicity and virtually unchanged since it was completed in 1735, Christ Church was a gift to the community from one man, Robert "King" Carter. Among Carter's descendants are eight governors of Virginia, two US presidents, Gen Robert E Lee, and Chief Justice of the US Supreme Court Edward D White.

Inside the church, the pulpit and all 26 original pews remain. Heating and lighting systems were never added, so the church is now only used for services during the summer. Robert Carter's tomb and the graves of several relatives are on the grounds. **Open:** Daily 9am–5pm. **Free**

Jamestown

For lodgings and dining, see Williamsburg

This island between the James and York Rivers was the site of the first English settlement in America. Founded in 1607 by Capt John Smith and still rich in historic ambience, it is also the site of a 1,500-acre wilderness area.

ATTRACTIONS 🏛

Jamestown Settlement

VA 31 S, Yorktown; tel 757/253-4838. The story of the first English settlement in the New World is documented here in museum exhibits and living-history demonstrations. The exploits of Capt John Smith, leader of the colony; his legendary rescue from execution by the Powhatan princess Pocahontas; and a vivid picture of life in 17th-century Virginia are all re-created near the original site of the first colony.

The **indoor/outdoor museum,** operated by the Commonwealth of Virginia, is open all year. After purchasing tickets, visit the changing exhibit gallery just off the lobby and then the orientation theater to view a 20-minute film that provides an introduction to Jamestown. Beyond the theater, three permanent galleries feature artifacts, documents, decorative objects, dioramas, and graphics relating to the Jamestown period. The English Gallery focuses on Jamestown's beginnings in the Old World. The Powhatan Indian Gallery explores the origins and culture of the Native Americans who lived near Jamestown. The Jamestown Gallery deals with the history of the colony during its first century of existence.

Leaving the museum complex, visitors come directly into the **Powhatan Indian Village,** representing the culture and technology of a highly organized chiefdom of 32 tribes that inhabited coastal Virginia in the early 17th century. There are several mat-covered longhouses as well as a garden and a ceremonial dance circle. Historical interpreters tend gardens, tan animal hides, and make bone and antler tools, flint-knap projectile points, and pottery.

Triangular **James Fort** is a re-creation of the one constructed by the Jamestown colonists on their arrival in the spring of 1607. Inside are 18 primitive wattle-and-daub structures representing Jamestown's earliest buildings. Interpreters are engaged in activities typical of early 17th-century life.

A short walk from James Fort are reproductions of the three ships that transported the 104 colonists to Virginia. Visitors can board and explore the largest ship, the 110-foot *Susan Constant,* and talk with an interpreter about the 4½-month voyage from England. The *Godspeed* retraced the 1607 voyage from England to Virginia in 1985. The smallest ship, *Discovery,* is often open to visitors in the summer and is used for demonstrations of 17th-century sailing techniques.

Open: Daily 9am–5pm. **$$$**

Jamestown, the Original Site

VA 31 S, Yorktown; tel 757/229-1733. Exploration of the actual site of the first permanent English settlement in America begins at the **Visitor Center,** where a 12-minute orientation film is shown every 30 minutes.

Exhibits at the center document the 92 years when Jamestown was the capital of Virginia. From the visitor center, a footpath leads to the actual site of **"James Cittie,"** where reconstructed brick foundations of 17th-century homes, taverns, shops, and the statehouse are enhanced by artists' renderings and recorded narratives. Spring through fall there are frequent half-hour guided tours of the site, and in summer there are living-history programs. Directly behind the remains of the tower of one of Virginia's first brick churches (1639) is the **Memorial Church,** a 1907 gift of the Colonial Dames of America. It houses remnants of early Jamestown churches.

The footpath continues to the seawall, believed to be the site of the original James Fort and the May 13, 1607 landing site. There are many monuments and memorials throughout James Cittie; a memorial cross marks some 300 shallow graves of colonists who died during the "Starving Time," the winter of 1609–10.

A fascinating five-mile loop drive begins at the Visitor Center parking lot and winds through 1,500 acres of woodland and marsh that have been allowed to return to a natural state. Markers and large paintings interpret aspects of the daily activities of the colonists—tobacco growing, lumbering, silk production, pottery making, farming, etc. Audio tours for rent in the bookstore.

Open: Daily 9am–5pm. **$$$**

Keswick

RESORT 🏨

≣ ≣ ≣ ≣ **Keswick Inn**
701 Country Club Dr, 22947; tel 804/979-3440 or toll free 800/274-5391; fax 804/979-3457. Exit I-64 at Shadwell (US 250). 600 acres. An elegant English country house with beautifully landscaped grounds overlooking a golf course and lake. Very quiet. Everything is designed for guests' comfort. The resort, decorated in Laura Ashley fabrics and wall coverings, is owned by the late designer's former husband. **Rooms:** 48 rms and stes. CI noon/CO noon. No smoking. Beautiful rooms are individually decorated in luxurious styles. **Amenities:** 🛏 🕭 🍹 A/C, cable TV w/movies, bathrobes. Some units w/terraces. **Services:** 🍽 🛎 🚗 🖼 🏌 Twice-daily maid svce, social director, masseur, babysitting. Guests enjoy full country breakfast, traditional English afternoon tea, and gourmet five-course dinners. **Facilities:** 🛗 🚴 🎣 ▶18 🎾 🏊6 🐴 🛥 🖥 ⛑ 2 restaurants, 1 bar, games rm, lawn games, spa, sauna, steam rm, whirlpool, beauty salon. **Rates (MAP):** $195–$645 S or D; $645 ste. Extra person $25. Min stay special events. Parking: Outdoor, free. AE, DC, MC, V.

Keysville

This small college town and farming community was named after John Keys, first settler and tavern owner.

MOTEL 🏨

≣ **Sheldons Motel**
VA 2, PO Box 189, 23947; tel 804/736-8434; fax 804/736-9402. ¼ mi S of jct US 15/360. An older motel with an attractive colonial style. Rough-hewn exterior of adjacent restaurant helps compensate for the plain rooms fronting the parking lot. **Rooms:** 39 rms. CI noon/CO noon. Nonsmoking rms avail. Surprisingly clean, comfortable, and spacious rooms. Some have pleasing view of rolling hills of dairy farm across road. **Amenities:** 🛏 🕭 A/C, cable TV w/movies, refrig. **Services:** 🏌 🖼 **Facilities:** 🖥 ⛑ 1 restaurant. Adjacent

restaurant is a local favorite, specializing in fresh pork dishes and other country fare. **Rates:** Peak (Mem Day–Labor Day) $32–$48 S; $34–$48 D. Extra person $6. Children under age 11 stay free. Lower rates off-season. Parking: Outdoor, free. Rates highest on weekends. AE, DISC, MC, V.

Leesburg

Founded in 1758 and later named for Francis "Lightfoot" Lee, a signer of the Constitution, this northern Virginia city is set in the rolling hills of Loudoun County's hunt and horse country. **Information:** Loudoun County Chamber of Commerce, 5 Loudoun St SW, #A, Leesburg, 22075 (tel 703/777-2176).

HOTEL 🏨

🏚🏚 Ramada Inn at Carradoc Hall
1500 E Market St, 22075; tel 703/771-9200 or toll free 800/552-6702; fax 703/771-1575. 2 mi E of jct US 15/VA 7. Perched atop a green knoll on eight scenic acres, this 1773 mansion (now supplemented by a low-slung, red plank building with a white porch railing) has been converted to a unique hotel. A bit worn in areas, but an interesting property with an air of history about it. **Rooms:** 126 rms and stes. CI open/CO noon. Nonsmoking rms avail. All rooms redone recently. Interesting old furniture, including two-poster beds, but some furnishings are chipped. **Amenities:** 🏚🗄 A/C, satel TV w/movies, dataport. Microwaves, refrigerators, and hair dryers available. **Services:** ✕ 🛏 🗄 🛎 **Facilities:** 🏋 🍽350 2 restaurants, 1 bar (w/entertainment). Working brick fireplace and cozy sitting area. Free golfing across the highway. **Rates (CP):** $65 S; $69 D; $105 ste. Extra person $7. Children under age 12 stay free. Parking: Outdoor, free. AE, CB, DC, DISC, MC, V.

INN

🏚🏚🏚 The Leesburg Colonial Inn
19 S King St, 22075; tel 703/777-5000 or toll free 800/392-1332; fax 703/777-7000. The second floor of this 1758 house contains the inn; two highly praised restaurants are below. Inn decor is 18th century, with French wallpaper, Persian rugs, and original oak floors. **Rooms:** 10 rms and stes. CI 2pm/CO noon. Nonsmoking rms avail. Modern touches, such as wet bars or whirlpools in some rooms, do not detract from the ambience. Queen-size poster beds. **Amenities:** 🏚🗄 A/C, cable TV w/movies. Some units w/minibars, some w/fireplaces, some w/whirlpools. Fresh flowers and chocolates. **Services:** ✕ 🛏 🗄 🛎 Afternoon tea and wine/sherry served. **Facilities:** 🍽15 2 restaurants, 1 bar (w/entertainment), washer/dryer, guest lounge. **Rates (BB):** $58–$150 S; $78–$150 ste. Children under age 10 stay free. Higher rates for special events/hols. Parking: Outdoor, free. AE, CB, DC, DISC, MC, V.

RESORT

🏚🏚🏚 Lansdowne Conference Resort
44050 Woodridge Pkwy, 22075; tel 703/729-8400 or toll free 800/541-4801; fax 703/729-4096. Landsdowne Blvd exit off VA 7. 20.5 acres. An elegant hostelry set apart from the world on rolling green hills, but only a short distance from highway. Emphasis here is on staff professionalism, tasteful decor, and first-rate facilities. **Rooms:** 305 rms and stes. CI 4pm/CO noon. Nonsmoking rms avail. Half of the rooms have king beds, the other half double beds. **Amenities:** 🏚🗄🍸 A/C, cable TV w/movies, dataport, voice mail. Some units w/terraces, 1 w/whirlpool. VCRs and refrigerators available. Irons and ironing boards in every room. **Services:** ✕ 🔑 📹 🚗 🗄 🛎 Car-rental desk, masseur, children's program, babysitting. In-room dining. Two concierges: one for business groups, one for individual travelers. TV message centers throughout the lobby. **Facilities:** 🏋 ⛳ ▶18 🏊 🎾🏖 5 🛶 🍽500 🖥 🚻 3 restaurants (see "Restaurants" below), 2 bars, volleyball, games rm, racquetball, spa, sauna, steam rm, whirlpool, beauty salon. Fully supervised playroom for children 3–12. Stonewall's tavern offers darts, billiards, shuffleboard. A 5,000-square-foot health club includes combination locks on wood lockers, towels, trainer, shop. Spa offers full complement of services, including facials, massages. Cafe adjoining pool. Fishing and recreation field ¼ mile away at Potomac River. **Rates:** $129–$169 S or D; $250–$850 ste. Children under age 12 stay free. Parking: Outdoor, free. AE, DC, DISC, MC, V.

RESTAURANTS 🍴

⑤ The Green Tree
15 S King St; tel 703/777-7246. **American/Old English.** The 18th-century heritage of this building is reflected in the restaurant's decor (Williamsburg stemware, ladder-back chairs) and even in its cuisine, which includes recipes supposedly used by Thomas Jefferson. Two working fireplaces and servers in period costume add to the ambience. Special period dinners are served throughout the day on Thanksgiving and Christmas. All-you-can-eat Sunday brunch is especially popular. **FYI:** Reservations recommended. Singer. Children's menu. **Open:** Peak (June–Sept) daily 11am–10pm. **Prices:** Main courses $11–$17; prix fixe $13. AE, CB, DC, DISC, MC, V. 🍖 📷 💟

The Potomac Grill
In Lansdowne Resort, 44050 Woodridge Pkwy; tel 703/729-4106. Landsdowne Blvd exit off VA 7. **Regional American/Steak.** Large windows look onto open land and mountains surrounding this intimate dining room, while inside mahogany tables and sturdy chairs make for a clubby atmosphere. The simple decor, with understated elegance, matches the hearty menu. Specialty is rib-eye steaks. **FYI:**

Reservations recommended. Piano/singer. **Open:** Lunch daily 11am–3pm; dinner Tues–Sat 5:30–10pm. **Prices:** Main courses $18–$26. AE, DC, DISC, MC, V. 🖼️ ⑁

★ **Tuscarora Mill Restaurant**
In Market Station Complex, 203 Harrison St SE; tel 703/771-9300. 1 block S of VA 7. **New American/Cafe.** This 1899 mill, with massive timber construction and original grain bins, is artfully utilized as a restaurant. Known for its wine list—one of the most extensive in the area—Tuscarora Mill has been written up in wine magazines and offers a wine tasting every two months. Specialty is fresh seafood. Offers selected "small plate" entrees. The cafe/bar in front is a rustic setting for lighter fare. A spacious rear area with fireplace is also available for groups. **FYI:** Reservations recommended. **Open:** Lunch Mon–Fri 11:30am–2:30pm, Sat 11:30am–3pm, Sun noon–3pm; dinner Mon–Thurs 5:30–9:30pm, Fri–Sat 5:30–10pm, Sun 5–9pm. **Prices:** Main courses $14–$19. AE, MC, V. ♥ 🖳 ⑁

ATTRACTIONS 🖼️

Loudoun Museum
14–16 Loudoun St SW; tel 703/777-7427. Chronicles the history of Loudoun County from the colonial era to the present. Exhibits feature Native American artifacts, Civil War memorabilia, audiovisual presentations, and more. Some hands-on and changing exhibits; lectures and workshops; gift shop. The museum also presents tours of historic homes and gardens of Leesburg (by reservation). **Open:** Mon–Sat 10am–5pm, Sun 1–5pm. **Free**

Ball's Bluff Battlefield
Fairfax Station; tel 703/352-5900 or 729-0596. Located just off US 15, north of the VA 7 junction. Ball's Bluff Battlefield was the site of the third major engagement of the Civil War (Oct 21, 1861). A total of 3,400 troops were involved, with Union forces under the command of Edward Dickinson Baker, US senator from Oregon. Surrounded by Confederate forces, fully half of Baker's force was either killed, wounded, or captured. Baker himself was killed, the only senator ever killed in battle. His death brought about the first major congressional investigation into war conduct. At this battle, Oliver Wendell Holmes Jr, later to become Chief Justice of the Supreme Court, was wounded.

A ¾-mile walking trail circles the 170-acre battlefield; guided tours may be arranged in advance. A living history re-enactment takes place on the weekend day nearest the October 21 anniversary of the battle. **Open:** Daily sunrise–sunset. **Free**

Waterford Village
Country Rd 662 off VA 9, Waterford; tel 540/882-3018. The enchanting hamlet of Waterford, with numerous 18th- and 19th-century buildings, is a National Historic Landmark. A Quaker from Pennsylvania named Amos Janney built a mill here in the 1740s. Other Quakers followed, and by 1840 most of the buildings now on Main Street were in place. In 1870 the railroad bypassed Waterford, slowing the pace of change so that much of the town remains preserved today. **Free**

Leon

RESTAURANT 🍴

Prince Michel Restaurant
In Prince Michel de Virginia Winery, US 29 S, Box 77; tel 703/547-9720. Between Culpepper and Madison, Va. **French.** Fresh flowers, pastel colors, and floor-to-ceiling trompe l'oeil murals make this restaurant on the lower level of the winery seem like a small European cafe. Patio facing display vineyard and Blue Ridge Mountains offers pleasant outdoor dining when weather permits. Well-known chef cooks in French style using fresh herbs, fruit, and vegetables. Menu changes daily. **FYI:** Reservations recommended. Jazz. Jacket required. **Open:** Lunch Thurs–Sat noon–2pm, Sun 11:30am–2:30pm; dinner Thurs–Sat 6–9pm. **Prices:** Prix fixe $50. AE, MC, V. 🍴 🖼️ VP ⑁

Lexington

See also Natural Bridge

Site of Virginia Military Institute (VMI), sometimes called the West Point of the South, and the home of Confederate War heroes Robert E Lee and Thomas J "Stonewall" Jackson. Washington and Lee University is also here. To the south is the famous Natural Bridge, one of the seven natural wonders of the world. **Information:** Lexington–Rockbridge County Chamber of Commerce, 10 E Washington St, Davidson Tucker House #1, Lexington, 24450 (tel 540/463-5375).

MOTELS 🖼️

🛏️🛏️ Buena Vista Motel
447 E 29th St (US 60), Buena Vista, 24416; tel 540/261-2138; fax 540/261-4430. Exit 188A off I-81, 3 mi E on US 60. An older motel close to town, conveniently located minutes from historic Lexington, Blue Ridge Pkwy, Virginia Horse Center. **Rooms:** 19 rms. CI 11am/CO 11am. Nonsmoking rms avail. Exceptionally spacious rooms. **Amenities:** 🔒 A/C, cable TV. **Services:** ✗ ⇦ ⇨ **Facilities:** 🔲 1 restaurant. **Rates:** Peak (July–Oct) $32–$36 S; $40–$52 D. Extra person $4. Lower rates off-season. Parking: Outdoor, free. AE, DISC, MC, V.

🛏️🛏️ Comfort Inn
US 11 S, PO Box 905, 24450; tel 540/463-7311 or toll free 800/628-1956; fax 540/463-4590. Exit 188B off I-81; exit 55 off I-64. Although it's close to the city, large grounds give a country-like feeling. **Rooms:** 80 rms. CI 2pm/CO 11am. Nonsmoking rms avail. Exceptionally clean. **Amenities:** 🔒 ⑁ 🔲 A/C, cable TV w/movies. **Services:** ✗ 🖼️ ⇦ ⇨ Lobby

offers 24-hour coffee, decks of cards, and board games, adding touch of hospitality. **Facilities:** ⚄ ⚄ Heated indoor pool is especially appreciated in winter. **Rates:** Peak (June–Aug) $72–$77 S; $77–$79 D. Extra person $5. Children under age 18 stay free. Lower rates off-season. Parking: Outdoor, free. AE, CB, DC, DISC, MC, V.

≣≣≣ Holiday Inn Express

US 11 at I-64, PO Box 11088, 24450; tel 540/463-7351 or toll free 800/480-3043. Exit 55 off I-64; or exit 188B off I-81, then 3 mi on US 11N. Extensive grounds give a country flavor to this motel. Usually is booked heavily on special college weekends. **Rooms:** 72 rms. CI 3pm/CO 11am. Nonsmoking rms avail. Recent recarpeting gives bright and fresh look. **Amenities:** ⚄ ⚄ A/C, cable TV w/movies. **Services:** ✕ ⚄ ⚄ Babysitting. **Facilities:** ⚄ ⚄ **Rates:** Peak (May–Sept) $71–$79 S; $75–$84 D. Extra person $5. Children under age 13 stay free. Lower rates off-season. Parking: Outdoor, free. AE, CB, DC, DISC, MC, V.

INN

≣≣≣ Alexander-Witherow House and McCampbell Inn

11 N Main St, 24450; tel 540/463-2044; fax 540/463-7262. These circa-1790 city inns are across Main St from each other in the heart of Lexington's historic district and minutes from Virginia Military Institute. **Rooms:** 23 rms. CI 2pm/CO noon. Nonsmoking rms avail. Faithfully restored rooms are furnished with antiques. Each unit has its own ambience, but all are spacious. **Amenities:** ⚄ ⚄ ⚄ A/C, cable TV w/movies, refrig. Some units w/minibars. **Services:** ⚄ ⚄ Babysitting, wine/sherry served. **Facilities:** ⚄ 1 restaurant (bkfst and dinner only). Pool and tennis courts at nearby Maple Hall available to guests. **Rates:** Peak (Apr–June/Sept–Oct) $80–$120 S; $95–$135 D. Extra person $15. Lower rates off-season. Parking: Outdoor, free. MC, V.

RESTAURANTS 🍽

★ Harbs'

19 W Washington St; tel 540/464-1900. Exit 188B off I-81 Follow US 60 (Nelson St) west; turn right at Jefferson St, and right onto Washington St. **Cafe/Vegetarian.** Lively cafe and outdoor patio in historic downtown, with art exhibitions monthly. Candlelight dinners. Freshly baked breakfast and sandwich breads, pasta, salads, and gourmet soups are regular features. Dinner menu varies weekly but always includes a vegetarian pasta. Picnic baskets prepared for theater outings. **FYI:** Reservations accepted. Children's menu. **Open:** Sun 9am–3pm, Mon 8am–3pm, Tues–Thurs 8am–9pm, Fri–Sat 8am–10pm. **Prices:** Main courses $7–$13. MC, V. ⚄

★ The Palms

101 W Nelson St; tel 540/463-7911. Exit 188B off I-81. **American/Cafe/Eclectic.** Wooden tables and chairs combine with bright green booths to make this a favorite with local residents and the college crowd, who come for an eclectic mix of freshly prepared foods. Good eats, friendly people, and the energy of a college town together with historic ambience. **FYI:** Reservations not accepted. Children's menu. **Open:** Mon–Fri 11:30am–2am, Sat 10am–2am, Sun 10am–11pm. **Prices:** Main courses $7–$14. DISC, MC, V. ⚄

The Willson-Walker House Restaurant

30 N Main St; tel 540/463-3020. Exit 188B off I-81 N; exit 181 off I-81 S. **New American.** An 1820s classical revival home decorated with period antiques, located in Lexington's downtown historic district. Gourmet American cuisine, especially seafood. **FYI:** Reservations recommended. Children's menu. Dress code. No smoking. **Open:** Peak (Apr–Dec) lunch Tues–Sat 11:30am–2:30pm; dinner Tues–Sat 5:30–9pm. **Prices:** Main courses $10–$19. AE, MC, V. ⚄ ⚄ ⚄

ATTRACTIONS 📷

Lee Chapel and Museum

Washington and Lee University; tel 540/463-8768. Robert E Lee served as president of Washington College from 1865 until his death in 1870. Soon thereafter, the school's name was changed to Washington and Lee University. The magnificent Victorian-Gothic brick and native limestone chapel was built in 1867 at Lee's request. A white marble sculpture of Lee by Edward Valentine portrays the general recumbent. Lee's remains are in a crypt below the chapel along with those of other family members. Among the museum's most important holdings are Charles Wilson Peale's portrait of George Washington wearing the uniform of a colonel in the British army and the painting of General Lee in Confederate uniform by Theodore Pine. The portraits hang in the chapel auditorium. **Open:** Peak (mid-Apr–mid-Oct) Mon–Sat 9am–5pm, Sun 2–5pm. Reduced hours off-season. **Free**

Stonewall Jackson House

8 E Washington St; tel 540/463-2552. Maj Thomas Jackson came to Lexington in 1851 to take a post as teacher of physics and artillery tactics at VMI. In 1858 Jackson purchased this house, five blocks from campus. He lived here with his wife until 1861, when he left to answer Gen Lee's summons. Two years later, "Stonewall" Jackson's body was returned to Lexington for burial at the Presbyterian church cemetery on South Main Street.

The house has been restored and contains many of Jackson's personal possessions. Appropriate period furnishings duplicate items on the inventory of Jackson's estate made shortly after his death at Chancellorsville in 1863. Photographs, text, and a slide show tell the story of the Jacksons' stay here. **Open:** Peak (June–Aug) Mon–Sat 9am–6pm, Sun 1–6pm. Reduced hours off-season. **$$**

Virginia Military Institute Museum

Jackson Memorial Hall; tel 540/464-7232. Sometimes called the West Point of the South, VMI opened in 1839. The most dramatic episode in the school's history took place during the Civil War Battle of New Market (May 15, 1864). More than

200 teenage VMI cadets, called upon to reinforce Confederate defenses, played a major role in blocking a Union advance. A month later, Union Gen David Hunter retaliated, burning VMI to the ground. The VMI Museum displays uniforms, weapons, and memorabilia from cadets who attended the college and fought in numerous wars. Of special note are the VMI coatee (tunic) that belonged to Gen George S Patton Jr (VMI, 1907), and Stonewall Jackson's VMI uniform coat and the bullet-pierced raincoat he wore at the Battle of Chancellorsville. **Open:** Mon–Sat 9am–5pm, Sun 2–5pm. **Free**

George C Marshall Museum

VMI Campus; tel 540/463-7103. This impressive white building houses the archives and research library of Gen of the Army George Catlett Marshall, a 1901 graduate of VMI. Marshall's illustrious military career included service in World War I as Gen Pershing's aide-de-camp, and in World War II, as army chief of staff and secretary of defense under President Truman. But he is probably best known for the Marshall Plan, which fostered the postwar economic recovery of Europe. He became the first career soldier to receive the Nobel Prize for Peace (1953). Marshall's Nobel medallion is among the personal items on display at the museum. **Open:** Peak (Mar–Oct) daily 9am–5pm. Reduced hours off-season. **$**

Virginia Horse Center

Tel 540/463-7060. Located on VA 39W, near the intersection of I-64 and I-81. Sprawling across nearly 400 acres just outside Lexington, the center offers horse shows, seminars, and sales of fine horses. Annual events include an Arabian Horse Show, US Ponies of America Association events, American Saddlebred Horse Association shows, Miniature Horse Classic, and qualifying competitions for the Pan American Games. Also on the schedule are English and Western riding demonstrations, equine art and photography shows, wagon rides, fox-hunting demonstrations, and tack equipment displays. For a full program of events and associated fees, contact the center at PO Box 1051, Lexington, VA 24450. **Open:** Call for schedule.

Lorton

Northern Virginia town, founded in the 18th century between the Occoquan and Potomac Rivers.

ATTRACTIONS 🧳

Gunston Hall

10709 Gunston Rd; tel 703/550-9220. This was the magnificent estate of George Mason (1725–92), the statesman and political thinker who drafted the Virginia Declaration of Rights (after which the US Bill of Rights was modeled) and whose ideas formed the basis of the Declaration of Independence. A member of the committee that drafted the US Constitution, Mason refused to sign the ratified version because it didn't abolish slavery or, initially, contain a Bill of Rights.

An 11-minute film introduces visitors to the estate, and there is a small museum of Mason family memorabilia. In Mason's library and study is the writing table on which he penned the Virginia Declaration of Rights. The tour also includes several outbuildings, including the kitchen, dairy, laundry, and schoolhouse. Also on the grounds is the family graveyard where Mason himself is buried. **Open:** Daily 9:30am–5pm. **$$**

Pohick Church

9301 Richmond Hwy; tel 703/339-6572. Built in the 1770s from plans drawn up by George Washington, this church has been restored to its original appearance and has an active Episcopal congregation. The interior was designed by George Mason, owner of Gunston Hall, with box pews like those common in England at the time. During the Civil War Union troops stabled their horses in the church and stripped the interior—the east wall was used for target practice. **Open:** Daily 9am–4:30pm. **Free**

Pohick Bay Regional Park

6501 Pohick Bay Dr; tel 703/339-6104. Located near Gunston Hall (see above) on VA 242, this is a 1,000-acre park occupyies a spectacular bayside setting on the historic Mason Neck peninsula. It has one of the largest swimming pools on the East Coast, and offers boat access to the Potomac (sailboat and paddleboat rentals are available), 150 campsites, a 4-mile bridle path, scenic nature trails, and 18-hole golf course and pro shop, miniature golf, and sheltered picnic areas with grills. **Open:** Daily 8am–sunset. **$$**

Mason Neck State Park

7301 High Point Rd; tel 703/550-0960. An 1,800-acre area of marsh and uplands, this park is a primary nesting site for the American bald eagle. Weekend guided canoe trips (Apr–Oct; reservation necessary) offer the best chance of viewing bald eagles in their natural habitat, but some are occasionally spotted closer to developed areas. Best viewing in winter, and in the morning and evening. Visitor center with exhibits, information (summer only); hiking, picnicking. **Open:** Daily 8am–sunset. **$**

Luray

See also New Market, Stanley

Named for Luray Caverns, a 400 million-year-old series of limestone caves hidden beneath the Blue Ridge Mountains. **Information:** Luray–Page County Chamber of Commerce, 46 E Main St, Luray, 22835 (tel 540/743-3915).

MOTELS 🏨

⊨ Intown Motel

410 W Main St, 22835; tel 540/743-6511; fax 540/743-6511. Convenient to downtown and the caverns, this motel is basic but clean. It's owned and operated by a family, who all work to help guests. **Rooms:** 40 rms. CI open/CO noon. Nonsmoking rms avail. Rooms have nicely integrated decor. Honeymoon room is larger and has better furnishings. **Amenities:** 🛏 A/C, cable TV w/movies. **Services:** ✕ ⤺ ⤻ **Facilities:** ⌂ 1 restaurant, lawn games, playground. **Rates:** Peak (Apr–Nov) $33–$85 S; $38–$85 D. Extra person $5. Children under age 18 stay free. Lower rates off-season. Parking: Outdoor, free. AE, CB, DC, DISC, EC, MC, V.

⊨⊨ Luray Caverns Motel East

US 211, PO Box 748, 22835; tel 540/743-4531. Across from the entrance to Luray Caverns, with view in back of mountain greenery. **Rooms:** 24 rms; 18 cottages/villas. CI 11am/CO 11am. Larger-than-average rooms with pleasant decor. Cottages, some with two rooms, are not as bright but are good for families. Mattresses could be better. **Amenities:** 🛏 A/C, cable TV. Some units w/terraces. **Services:** ⤺ ⤻ **Facilities:** ⌂ 🔥 **Rates:** $55–$70 S or D; $55–$70 cottage/villa. Children under age 16 stay free. Parking: Outdoor, free. Golf packages avail. AE, DISC, MC, V.

⊨⊨ Luray Caverns Motel West

US 211, PO Box 748, 22835; tel 540/743-4536. This white colonial-style motel located opposite Luray Caverns has a beautiful view and sparkling-clean accommodations. While modest in decor, it's a change from larger motels. **Rooms:** 18 rms. CI 11am/CO 11am. All are ground-level rooms, all have view of mountains; one apartment with screened-in porch available. **Amenities:** 🛏 A/C, cable TV. Some units w/terraces. **Services:** ⤺ ⤻ **Facilities:** ⌂ **Rates:** $55–$70 S or D. Extra person $7. Children under age 16 stay free. Parking: Outdoor, free. Golf packages avail. AE, DISC, MC, V.

⊨⊨⊨ Ramada Inn

US 211 E Bypass, PO Box 389, 22835; tel 540/743-4521 or toll free 800/2-RAMADA; fax 540/743-6863. Set at the base of the Blue Ridge Mountains, this hotel offers acres of green space, a lobby with antique furnishings, and a museum of presidential memorabilia including items from John Adams's desk. **Rooms:** 101 rms. CI 3pm/CO noon. Nonsmoking rms avail. Stunning "Antique Luxury" rooms, with period furnishings and wallpaper. **Amenities:** 🛏 🍴 A/C, cable TV w/movies. Some units w/whirlpools. VCRs, microwaves, and refrigerators free upon request. Computer/fax jack at front desk. **Services:** ✕ ⤺ Turndown service available upon request. **Facilities:** ⌂ 🏓 [150] 🖥 🔥 1 restaurant, 1 bar, lawn games, playground, washer/dryer. Bakery and gift shop. Bar with super TV, miniature golf. **Rates:** Peak (June–Nov) $55–$96 S or D. Extra person $7. Children under age 18 stay free. Lower rates off-season. Parking: Outdoor, free. Special ski and golf packages avail. AE, CB, DC, DISC, ER, JCB, MC, V.

LODGES

⊨⊨⊨ Big Meadows Lodge

Skyline Drive MM 51.2, PO Box 727, 22835; tel 540/999-2221 or toll free 800/999-4714; fax 540/743-7883. A rustic lodge offering many nature activities and splendid mountain views from main lounge and dining room. National Park Service visitor center and interpretive area nearby. **Rooms:** 83 rms and stes; 10 cottages/villas. CI 3pm/CO noon. Nonsmoking rms avail. Rustic rooms have chestnut wall paneling. **Amenities:** No A/C, phone, or TV. Some units w/terraces, some w/fireplaces. **Services:** ⤺ Car-rental desk. **Facilities:** 🏃 🔥 1 restaurant, 1 bar (w/entertainment), playground. Horseback riding available nearby. Many nature and hiking trails. **Rates:** $77–$85 S or D; $90–$96 ste; $65–$67 cottage/villa. Extra person $5. Children under age 16 stay free. MAP rates avail. Parking: Outdoor, free. Closed mid-Nov–mid-Mar. AE, DC, DISC, MC, V.

⊨⊨⊨ Skyland Lodge

Skyline Drive MM 41.8, PO Box 727, 22835; tel 540/999-2211 or toll free 800/999-4714; fax 540/743-7883. Exit 264 off I-81. Set high in the mountains on Skyline Dr in Shenandoah National Park, this lodge has spectacular views of the valley below. **Rooms:** 177 rms and stes; 19 cottages/villas. CI 2pm/CO noon. Nonsmoking rms avail. A mix of accommodations, from quaint rustic cabins to spacious new suites. **Amenities:** Cable TV. No A/C or phone. All units w/terraces, some w/fireplaces. **Services:** ⤺ Children's program. **Facilities:** [30] 🔥 1 restaurant, 1 bar, playground. Hiking trails, horseback and pony riding nearby. **Rates:** $72–$95 S or D; $115 ste; $46–$77 cottage/villa. Extra person $5. Children under age 16 stay free. MAP rates avail. Parking: Outdoor, free. Closed mid-Nov–mid-Mar. AE, DC, DISC, MC, V.

RESTAURANTS 🍽

★ Brookside Restaurant

US 211 E; tel 540/743-5698. **American.** There's nothing fancy here, but this basic family-owned restaurant is a favorite with locals. The old stone structure with wagon-wheel lights and fans spinning overhead is filled with knickknacks and framed country scenes. The decor matches the country cooking, featuring an all-you-can-eat buffet. Lighter, healthier fare also offered. The specialties here are the desserts, especially the peach cobbler. **FYI:** Reservations accepted. Children's menu. Beer and wine only. **Open:** Peak (June–Oct) daily 7am–9pm. Closed mid-Dec–mid-Jan. **Prices:** Main courses $6–$14. AE, CB, DC, DISC, MC, V. 🏔 👥

Parkhurst Restaurant

US 211; tel 540/743-6009. 2 mi W of Luray Caverns. **International.** This onetime country inn set high above the highway offers elegant dining in a front dining area with a chandelier and dark wood and in two larger, modern rooms. The large paneled bar area also has tables. Restaurant is one of 300 *Wine Spectator* Award winners in the country. The specialty is colonial-style steak. **FYI:** Reservations recommended. Children's menu. **Open:** Sun–Thurs 4–10pm, Fri–Sat 4–11pm. **Prices:** Main courses $11–$24. AE, CB, DC, DISC, MC, V. ❤ ⛰

ATTRACTION 🏛

Luray Caverns

US 211; tel 540/743-6551. The formation of these caverns, an extensive series of limestone caves and streams, began over 400 million years ago, as water from the surface penetrated the limestone through cracks resulting from shifting of the earth's crust. As water filled the gaps, it dissolved more and more rock, gradually carving out the underground labyrinth of rooms and passageways. Stalactites, formed by water dripping from the ceilings, and stalagmites, formed from the ground up, meet and form columns. In an active case such as Luray, these formations "grow" 1 cubic inch every 120 years.

The caverns are noted for the beautiful cascades of natural colors found on interior walls. Also of note is the "stalacpipe" organ, which combines the work of man and nature. It produces music when stalactites are tapped by rubber-tipped plungers triggered by an electronic keyboard. Guided one-hour tours depart every 20 minutes. **Open:** Peak (mid-June–Labor Day) daily 9am–7pm. Reduced hours off-season. **$$$$**

Lynchburg

Founded in the 18th century by a group of Quakers. Nearby Forest is the site of Thomas Jefferson's "other home," a 4,800-acre plantation. **Information:** Lynchburg Chamber Visitors Center, 216 12th St, Lynchburg, 24504 (tel 804/847-1811).

HOTELS 🏨

☰☰☰ Holiday Inn

US 29 and Odd Fellows Rd, PO Box 10729, 24506; tel 804/847-4424 or toll free 800/465-4329; fax 804/846-4965. 2 mi S of downtown. Detached units surround a large grassy lawn with pool, creating a safe area for children. **Rooms:** 256 rms and stes. Executive level. CI 3pm/CO noon. Nonsmoking rms avail. **Amenities:** 🔐 ⓞ A/C, cable TV w/movies. **Services:** ✗ �'🚐' ☒ ⌨ Babysitting. **Facilities:** 🗂 ⌨150 ⅙ 1 restaurant, 1 bar, washer/dryer. **Rates:** $60–$70 S or D; $96–$100 ste. Parking: Outdoor, free. AE, DC, DISC, MC, V.

☰☰☰ Holiday Inn Select

601 Main St, 24504 (Downtown); tel 804/528-2500 or toll free 800/HOLIDAY; fax 804/528-0062. Exit US 29 at Main St. A nicely appointed, very clean hotel in the heart of Lynchburg. **Rooms:** 255 rms. Executive level. CI 3pm/CO noon. Nonsmoking rms avail. **Amenities:** 🔐 ⓞ 🖭 ⌨ A/C,

cable TV w/movies. Some units w/minibars, some w/whirlpools. **Services:** ✗ 🅅🄿 🚐 ☒ ⌨ Babysitting. **Facilities:** 🗂 🚽 ⌨900 ⅙ 1 restaurant, 1 bar, whirlpool. **Rates:** Peak (May–Nov) $72–$92 S; $82–$102 D. Extra person $10. Children under age 18 stay free. Lower rates off-season. Parking: Indoor/outdoor, free. AE, DC, DISC, MC, V.

☰☰ Howard Johnson Lodge

US 29 N, PO Box 10729, 24506; tel 804/845-7041 or toll free 800/446-4656; fax 804/845-0222. 2 mi N of downtown. Located opposite a shopping mall. **Rooms:** 70 rms. CI 2pm/CO noon. No smoking. The front rooms enjoy views of the Blue Ridge Mountains from their private patios. **Amenities:** 🔐 A/C, cable TV w/movies. All units w/terraces. **Services:** ✗ ☒ ⌨ 🍴 **Facilities:** 🗂 ⅙ 1 restaurant, washer/dryer. **Rates:** Peak (May–Oct) $62–$69 S; $69–$75 D. Extra person $7. Children under age 18 stay free. Lower rates off-season. Parking: Outdoor, free. AE, CB, DC, DISC, JCB, MC, V.

☰☰ Lynchburg Comfort Inn

US 29 and Odd Fellows Rd, PO Box 10729, 24506; tel 804/847-9041 or toll free 800/221-2222; fax 804/847-8513. 2 mi S of downtown. Attractively set in a semiwooded area, yet close to the city. The pool is good for children since it is well protected from roads. **Rooms:** 123 rms. Executive level. CI 3pm/CO noon. Nonsmoking rms avail. **Amenities:** 🔐 A/C, cable TV w/movies. Some units w/terraces. **Services:** ✗ 🔑 🚐 ☒ ⌨ 🍴 **Facilities:** 🗂 ⌨250 ⅙ **Rates (CP):** $64–$98 S or D. Extra person $5. Children under age 18 stay free. Parking: Outdoor, free. AE, DC, DISC, MC, V.

☰☰☰ Lynchburg Hilton

2900 Candlers Mountain Rd, 24502; tel 804/237-6333 or toll free 800/445-8667; fax 804/237-4277. 3½ mi S of downtown. Take exit 128W off US 29; or exit US 460 at Candlers Mountain Rd. Exceptional decor accents this fine hotel. Great attention paid to lighting in rooms and lobby. **Rooms:** 167 rms and stes. Executive level. CI 2pm/CO 11am. Nonsmoking rms avail. **Amenities:** 🔐 ⓞ 🖭 A/C, cable TV w/movies. Rooms for guests with disabilities equipped with visual signal for telephone rings. **Services:** ✗ 🚐 ☒ ⌨ Babysitting. **Facilities:** 🗂 🚽 ⌨450 🖳 ⅙ 1 restaurant, 1 bar (w/entertainment), spa, whirlpool, beauty salon, washer/dryer. **Rates:** $95 S; $115 D; $446 ste. Extra person $20. Children under age 18 stay free. Parking: Outdoor, free. AE, MC, V.

MOTELS

☰☰ Best Western Lynchburg

2815 Candlers Mountain Rd, 24502; tel 804/237-2986 or toll free 800/528-1234; fax 804/237-2987. 3½ mi S of downtown. Exit Candlers Mountain Rd N off US 460; or exit 128W off US 29. A very clean motel with a friendly, efficient staff. Located near shopping mall and restaurants. **Rooms:** 87 rms. Executive level. CI 2pm/CO 11am. Nonsmoking rms avail. **Amenities:** 🔐 A/C, cable TV. **Services:** ☒ ⌨

Facilities: 🏠 ⬜20 ⬧ Rates (CP): Peak (Apr–Oct) $65 S; $70 D. Extra person $4. Lower rates off-season. Parking: Outdoor, free. AE, DC, DISC, MC, V.

≣≣≣ Days Inn Lynchburg
3220 Candlers Mountain Rd, 24502; tel 804/847-8655 or toll free 800/787-DAYS; fax 804/846-DAYS. Exit 8B off US 29; Candlers Mountain Rd exit off US 460. An exceptionally attractive and well-managed chain motel with congenial staff. Conveniently located near shopping mall and restaurants. **Rooms:** 131 rms. Executive level. CI 2pm/CO noon. Nonsmoking rms avail. **Amenities:** 🔒 ⬧ A/C, cable TV w/movies. All units w/terraces. **Services:** ✕ 🚐 ⬧ ⬧ **Facilities:** 🏠 ⬜40 ⬧ 1 restaurant, playground. Guests bowl free at neighboring lanes. **Rates (BB):** Peak (May–Oct) $59–$125 S; $64–$125 D. Extra person $8. Children under age 18 stay free. Lower rates off-season. Parking: Outdoor, free. AE, CB, DC, DISC, JCB, MC, V.

≣ Timberlake Motel
11222 Timberlake Rd, 24502; tel 804/525-2160; fax 804/525-5104. On US 460, 2 mi W of US 29. A small, basic roadside motel operated by a family. Close to many restaurants, easy access to Lynchburg attractions. **Rooms:** 41 rms. CI 2pm/CO 11am. Nonsmoking rms avail. Comfortable rooms are clean, quiet. **Amenities:** 🔒 ⬧ A/C, cable TV w/movies, refrig. 1 unit w/whirlpool. **Services:** ⬧ ⬧ **Facilities:** 🏠 Whirlpool, washer/dryer. **Rates:** $43–$57 S or D. Extra person $3. Children under age 12 stay free. Parking: Outdoor, free. Weekly rates avail. AE, DC, DISC, MC, V.

RESTAURANTS 🍴

Café France
In Forest Plaza West Shopping Center, 3225 Old Forest Rd; tel 804/385-8989. US 501 N exit off US 29. **New American/Continental/Eclectic.** A tasteful and quiet eatery with a pastel color scheme featuring prints of flowers and posters. Many daily specials prepared with fresh seafood, veal, lamb, and vegetables. Carryout available; small gourmet shop has wide selection of wines. "Cigar friendly" after 9:45 pm. **FYI:** Reservations recommended. Children's menu. **Open:** Lunch Tues–Sat 11:30am–3pm; dinner Tues–Sat 5:30–10pm. **Prices:** Main courses $6–$24. AE, MC, V. ⬧

★ Crown Sterling
6120 Fort Ave; tel 804/239-7744. Exit US 501 S at Fort Ave. **Seafood/Steak.** Wood panels, two fireplaces, and candles give an understated elegance to this steak house, which has served a loyal local following for more than 20 years. **FYI:** Reservations accepted. Children's menu. **Open:** Mon–Sat 5–10pm. **Prices:** Main courses $12–$23. AE, CB, DC, DISC, MC, V. ● 📷 ⬧

The Farm Basket
2008 Langhorne Rd; tel 804/528-1107. Exit US 460 or US 29 at US 501 Business N. **Regional American.** Part of a small, delightful complex featuring a fresh-fruit-and-vegeta-ble stand, gourmet food and kitchen shop, and a crafts gallery, this lunchtime eatery has country-style decor and spacious windows overlooking a large deck and creek. Light lunches feature freshly made seasonal specialties. **FYI:** Reservations accepted. No liquor license. No smoking. **Open:** Mon–Sat 10am–5pm. **Prices:** Lunch main courses $4–$7; prix fixe $6. MC, V. 🔺

ATTRACTIONS 📷

Thomas Jefferson's Poplar Forest
Country Rd 661, Forest; tel 804/525-1806. Located 5 mi SW of Lynchburg. The home Jefferson designed and used as his personal retreat from 1806 to 1823, Poplar Forest was at one time the seat of a 4,800-acre plantation that was a main source of Jefferson's income. In 1806, while he was president, Jefferson assisted the masons in laying the foundation for the dwelling. Tours of the octagon-shaped, unfurnished building allow visitors an up-close perspective on the state-of-the-art restoration currently taking place. A variety of public celebrations are held throughout the year, including an Independence Day celebration. **Open:** Apr–Nov, Wed–Sun 10am–4pm. **$$**

South River Meeting House
5810 Fort Ave; tel 804/239-2548. Pioneer Quakers settled in this area in the middle of the 18th century. They established the South River Meeting House in 1754, and completed the present stone building in 1798. Due to economic hardship, their opposition to slavery, and the expectation of civil unrest, the Quakers had left the area by the 1830s; most went to Ohio and other free states.

In 1899 the Presbyterians purchased the ruins of the abandoned Meeting House, restored the building as a church, and held their first service in 1901. The restored church was named the Quaker Memorial Presbyterian Church in honor of its heritage.

Several early Quaker leaders are buried in the adjacent cemetery, and today the church is a Virginia Historic Landmark, listed on the National Register of Historic Places. Guided tours of the site can be arranged. **Open:** Peak (Sept–May) Mon–Fri 9am–3pm. Reduced hours off-season. **Free**

Manassas

Established in 1851, this Northern Virginia town derived its name from its location at the junction of the Orange and Alexandria Railroad, and the Manassas Gap Railroad. Site of the first major battle of the Civil War, commemorated at Manassas National Battlefield Park. Seat of Prince William County. **Information:** Prince William County–Greater Manassas Chamber of Commerce, 8963 Center St, PO Box 495, Manassas, 22110 (tel 703/368-6600).

HOTELS

Best Western

8640 Mathis Ave, 22110; tel 703/368-7070 or toll free 800/258-7177; fax 703/368-7292. Exit 53 off I-66. An acceptable facility with clean appearance and decor, spacious lobby, cordial staff. Closer to downtown Manassas than to battlefield and interstate area, making it a bit quieter than those busy places. **Rooms:** 60 rms. CI 3pm/CO 11am. Nonsmoking rms avail. Appearance is pleasing, though some furniture is scarred. **Amenities:** A/C, cable TV w/movies. Some units w/whirlpools. Refrigerators and microwaves available. Coffeemakers in some rooms. **Services:** Babysitting. **Facilities:** 1 restaurant, 1 bar, sauna, steam rm, whirlpool, washer/dryer. Small area for exercise has stationary bike, sauna, whirlpool. **Rates:** $56–$60 S; $54–$75 D. Extra person $5. Children under age 12 stay free. Min stay special events. Parking: Outdoor, free. AE, DC, DISC, MC, V.

Courtyard by Marriott

10701 Battleview Pkwy, 22110; tel 703/335-1300 or toll free 800/321-2211; fax 703/335-9442. Exit 47B off I-66. A touch of elegance and luxury, from the nicely decorated sitting areas in the lobby to the landscaped courtyard. **Rooms:** 149 rms and stes. CI 3pm/CO 1pm. Nonsmoking rms avail. **Amenities:** A/C, cable TV w/movies, refrig. All units w/terraces. Shower massage. Instant hot-water tap for coffee/tea in each bathroom. King suites include refrigerator, TV in bedroom and parlor. **Services:** **Facilities:** 1 restaurant, 1 bar, whirlpool, washer/dryer. **Rates:** Peak (Mar–Oct) $66–$84 S; $71–$84 D; $79–$84 ste. Extra person $5. Children under age 18 stay free. Lower rates off-season. Parking: Outdoor, free. Weekend packages avail. Rates based on room, not occupancy. Discounts for seven consecutive nights. AE, CB, DC, DISC, MC, V.

Hampton Inn

7295 Williamson Blvd, 22110; tel 703/369-1100 or toll free 800/HAMPTON; fax 703/369-1100 ext 101. Exit I-66 at VA 234; inn ahead at 2nd light. An inviting facility with cordial staff, pleasant decor, and lobby seating area with tables and hanging plants. Near Manassas battlefield. **Rooms:** 125 rms and stes. CI 3pm/CO 11am. Nonsmoking rms avail. Five suites have king-size bed and sitting room. **Amenities:** A/C, cable TV w/movies. Some units w/whirlpools. Refrigerators available free. Hair dryers available at desk. Suites have two phones. **Services:** Coffee is available in lobby seating area. Roll-away beds available free. **Facilities:** Washer/dryer. Guest laundry on premises. **Rates (CP):** $56–$58 S; $63–$65 D; $125 ste. Children under age 18 stay free. Min stay special events. Parking: Outdoor, free. AE, DC, DISC, MC, V.

Holiday Inn Manassas Battlefield

10800 Vandor Lane, 22110; tel 703/335-0000 or toll free 800/HOLIDAY; fax 703/361-8440. Exit 47B off I-66. A chain motel that underwent total renovation in 1994. **Rooms:** 159 rms. CI 2pm/CO noon. Nonsmoking rms avail. Rooms have blended decor, pleasant sitting areas. **Amenities:** A/C, cable TV w/movies. Some units w/terraces. VCRs available. **Services:** Children's program. **Facilities:** 1 restaurant (bkfst and dinner only), 1 bar (w/entertainment), washer/dryer. **Rates:** Peak (Apr–Oct) $64–$69 S; $69–$75 D. Extra person $6. Children under age 18 stay free. Lower rates off-season. Parking: Outdoor, free. AE, CB, DC, DISC, JCB, MC, V.

MOTEL

Days Inn

10653 Balls Ford Rd, 22110; tel 703/368-2800 or toll free 800/DAYS-INN; fax 703/368-0083. Exit 47B off I-66. No frills but all the basics, plus a pleasant decor. Convenient to interstate, battlefield, restaurant. **Rooms:** 120 rms. CI 2pm/CO 11am. Nonsmoking rms avail. Rooms are clean, but some small upkeep problems (need for new carpet, upholstery) were noted in one room. **Amenities:** A/C, cable TV w/movies, VCR. **Services:** **Facilities:** Washer/dryer. **Rates:** Peak (Apr–Aug) $58 S or D. Extra person $6. Children under age 18 stay free. Lower rates off-season. Parking: Outdoor, free. Battlefield Package includes room and admission to battlefield. AE, CB, DC, DISC, MC, V.

RESTAURANTS

★ Mike's Diner

8401 Digges Rd; tel 703/361-5248. **American.** With its huge windows and wall panels sporting impressionist murals, Mike's is a bright and fun place for travelers looking for large servings, solid American fare, and old-fashioned booths. This local favorite with a friendly staff provides seating up front if you have to wait for the good food. Specials include "ribs night" and a basic meat-and-veggies plate. Breakfast available 24 hours a day. **FYI:** Reservations not accepted. Blues/jazz. Children's menu. **Open:** Daily 24 hrs. **Prices:** Main courses $6–$11. AE, MC, V.

Pargo's

10651 Balls Ford Rd; tel 703/369-5800. Exit 47 off I-66. **Regional American.** This trendy restaurant filled with hanging plants creates a colorful atmosphere with picture windows, balloons, multilevel floors, brick walls, and chrome-framed pop art. Salads and pastas are favorites, and food is served with flair. Some booths and some tables with lamps or candles offer more intimate dining. **FYI:** Reservations not accepted. Children's menu. **Open:** Mon–Thurs 11am–midnight, Fri–Sat 11am–1am, Sun 11am–11pm. **Prices:** Main courses $8–$18. AE, DC, DISC, MC, V.

ATTRACTIONS

Manassas Museum

9101 Prince William St; tel 703/368-1873. Established in 1974, the Manassas Museum interprets the history and culture of the northern Virginia Piedmont region. The museum's collection includes prehistoric tools, Civil War weapons and uniforms, Victorian costumes, quilts, and many other items from the past. There is an extensive collection of photographs, and two video programs describe the settlement of the area and the legacy of the Civil War. The museum also provides architectural and walking/driving tour brochures covering the Old Town district. **Open:** Tues–Sun 10am–5pm. **$**

Manassas National Battlefield Park

6511 Sudley Rd (VA 234); tel 703/361-1339. The first massive clash of the Civil War took place here on July 21, 1861, when a force of 35,000 well-equipped but poorly trained Union troops commanded by Gen Irvin McDowell were met by Gen P G T Beauregard's Confederate army, which was deployed along a stream known as Bull Run. The 10 hours of heavy fighting that ensued shocked both sides and shattered hopes for a quick end to the war. It was here that Col (later Gen) Thomas Jackson earned the nickname "Stonewall."

North and South met again on the fields of Manassas in August 1862. The second Battle of Manassas secured Gen Robert E Lee's place in history—his 55,000 men soundly defeated the Union army under Gen John Pope.

The two battles are commemorated at the 5,000-acre battlefield park. The visitors center has a museum, a 13-minute slide show, and a battle map program that tell the story of the battles. There are a number of self-guided walking tours that highlight Henry Hill, Stone Bridge, and the other critical areas of the First Manassas battlefield. A 12-mile driving tour covers the sites of Second Manassas, which raged over a much larger area. **Open:** Peak (May–Aug) daily 8:30am–6pm. Reduced hours off-season. **$**

Marion

This town of approximately 6,000 residents in the southwest Blue Ridge Highlands abounds with outdoor activities, offering the Holston River, the Appalachian Trail, Hungry Mother State Park, and other outdoor attractions. **Information:** Chamber of Commerce of Smyth County, 124 W Main St, PO Box 924, Marion, 24354 (tel 540/783-3161).

MOTEL 🏨

🚬🚬 Best Western Marion

1424 N Main St, 24354; tel 540/783-3193 or toll free 800/528-1234; fax 540/783-3193 ext 1184. Exit 47 off I-81. This older city motel offers easy access to Hungry Mother State Park and Mount Rogers National Recreation Area. **Rooms:** 119 rms. CI 1pm/CO noon. Nonsmoking rms avail. Rooms are exceptionally large by today's standards. **Amenities:** 📺 ♨ A/C, cable TV w/movies, dataport. Refrigerators, coffeemakers, and microwaves on request. **Services:** ✕ 🖼 🛏 🛎 **Facilities:** 🛗 🛗 ⑤ 1 restaurant (lunch and dinner only), 1

bar (w/entertainment). Complimentary golf privileges at local course. **Rates (CP):** $60–$65 S or D. Extra person $5. Children under age 18 stay free. Min stay special events. Parking: Outdoor, free. AE, DC, DISC, MC, V.

ATTRACTIONS 🏛

Grayson Highlands State Park

Tel 540/579-7092 or 579-7142 (visitor center). This 5,000-acre park is located near Virginia's highest point, Mount Rogers. Grayson Highlands State Park offers nine scenic hiking trails, one leading to the 5,729-ft summit of Mount Rogers. Bordering the park on the north, the Mount Rogers National Recreation Area (see below) includes a section of the Appalachian Trail that also leads to the summit. In addition to day-use hours, the park offers overnight camping at 73 sites; reservations are suggested on weekends and holidays. There are also three picnic areas, bridle paths and stables for visiting horses, and a special camping area for visitors bringing horses and trailers.

The visitor center houses a craft shop, a bookstore, and a museum of local history. In one of the picnic areas is a model homestead, with authentically reconstructed pioneer log cabins and a barn. An array of special events held at the park include weekend entertainment programs for campers, planned hikes throughout the summer, and the Grayson Highlands Fall Festival, an annual event offered in late September. **Open:** Daily 8am–10pm. **$**

Hungry Mother State Park

Tel 540/783-3422. Located 4 mi N of Marion on VA 16. Comprising beautiful woodlands and a 108-acre lake in the heart of the mountains, Hungry Mother has long been a regional favorite. The park features a sandy beach and bathhouse, boat launch, hiking trails, and a handicapped-accessible fishing pier. Campsites and cabins are available. Restaurant, visitor center. **Open:** Daily sunrise–sunset. **$**

Mount Rogers National Recreation Area

VA 16; tel 540/783-5196. Encompassing some 117,000 acres in the central Appalachians, Mount Rogers National Recreation Area includes some of the most varied topography in the eastern United States, from dense forests to large, open grasslands. The highest point in the state, Mount Rogers (5,729 feet) is located here. Hiking is extremely popular; 60 miles of the Appalachian Trail run through the area, along with numerous other trails.

Campgrounds with improved facilities are located throughout the area. The two largest, Beartree and Grindstone, feature hard-surfaced campsites, drinking water, and bathhouses with flush toilets and warm showers. In addition, Beartree Campground, 7 mi E of Damascus on VA 58, has a sandy swimming beach and a stocked 14-acre lake for fishing. Grindstone Campground, on VA 603 between Konnarock and Troutdale, offers easy access to hiking trails and to several challenging mountain bike trails.

For further information, write to Area Ranger, Mount Rogers National Recreation Area, Rte 1, Box 303, Marion, VA 24354. **Open:** Peak (Mem Day–Labor Day) daily 8am–4:30pm. Reduced hours off-season. **Free**

Martinsville

In southern Virginia 32 miles W of Danville, this Henry County seat was founded in 1791. Antique dealers abound. **Information:** Martinsville–Henry County Chamber of Commerce, 115 Broad St, PO Box 709, Martinsville, 24114 (tel 540/632-6401).

MOTELS 🏨

⊨⊨ Best Western Inn

US 220 Business N, PO Box 1183, 24114; tel 540/632-5611 or toll free 800/388-3934; fax 540/632-1168. A city motel adjacent to a shopping center. Center of town is less than five minutes away. **Rooms:** 97 rms. CI 3pm/CO noon. Nonsmoking rms avail. **Amenities:** 🎬 ⚗ 📶 A/C, cable TV w/movies. **Services:** ✕ ⛽ 🐕 **Facilities:** 🛗 📶 [300] 🕭 1 restaurant, 1 bar (w/entertainment), washer/dryer. Pool backs to a wooded hill, giving sense of seclusion. **Rates:** $43–$53 S; $49–$59 D. Extra person $8. Children under age 11 stay free. Min stay special events. Parking: Outdoor, free. AE, CB, DC, DISC, EC, ER, MC, V.

⊨⊨⊨ Dutch Inn

633 Virginia Ave, Collinsville, 24078; tel 540/647-3721; fax 540/647-4857. Exit US 220 Business at Martinsville. A towering windmill stands at entrance to this motel. Close to a NASCAR speedway and the Blue Ridge Mountains, this is a popular location. Shopping nearby. **Rooms:** 150 rms and stes. Executive level. CI 3pm/CO noon. Nonsmoking rms avail. Rooms are spacious and well kept. **Amenities:** 🎬 🍴 A/C, cable TV w/movies, bathrobes. Some rooms have refrigerators. **Services:** ✕ 🖨 ⛽ 🐕 Babysitting. 24-hour coffee in lobby. **Facilities:** 🛗 📶 [30] 🕭 1 restaurant, 1 bar, sauna, whirlpool. Restaurant is a local favorite. Pool surrounded by trees. **Rates:** $50–$60 S; $60–$70 D; $90 ste. Extra person $8. Children under age 16 stay free. Min stay. Parking: Outdoor, free. AE, CB, DC, DISC, MC, V.

McLean

See also Tysons Corner

Northern Virginia suburb and site of the headquarters of the Central Intelligence Agency. Patowmack Canal and Great Falls Park are some 20 miles away. **Information:** Fairfax County Chamber of Commerce, 8391 Old Courthouse #300, Vienna, 22182 (tel 703/749-0400).

RESTAURANTS 🍴

Café Taj

In Marketplace Shops, 1379 Beverly Rd at Old Dominion Dr (Downtown); tel 703/827-0444. **Indian.** Marble floors and a small fountain make this small, cafe-style dining room furnished with stark ebony tables and chairs feel a bit like the Taj Mahal. Chicken, beef, and lamb from the tandoori oven are specialties, with a few vegetarian curries too. **FYI:** Reservations not accepted. **Open:** Lunch daily 11:30am–2:30pm; dinner Sun–Thurs 5:30–10pm, Fri–Sat 5:30–10:30pm. **Prices:** Main courses $8–$13. AE, DC, DISC, MC, V. 🕭

★ Evans Farm Inn

1696 Chain Bridge Rd; tel 703/356-8000. N on VA 123 to Dolly Madison Blvd. **American.** This farmhouse is on a 28-acre estate complete with barnyard animals and vegetable garden supplying fresh produce. Colonial America is the theme, including serving staff attired in period costume. Exposed beams, 18th-century furniture, and five working fireplaces add to the charm. Traditional American fare predominates, including Virginia country ham. Breads, cakes, and pies are baked on premises. Romantic Sitting Duck Pub on lower level serves lunch and dinner daily, brunch Sunday 11am–2pm. **FYI:** Reservations recommended. Piano. Children's menu. Dress code. **Open:** Lunch Mon–Fri 11:30am–2:30pm, Sat 11:30am–3pm; dinner Mon–Sat 5–11pm, Sun noon–9pm; brunch Sun 11am–2pm. **Prices:** Main courses $14–$24. AE, CB, DC, DISC, MC, V. 💗 🍴 🖼 🕭

⑤ J R's Stockyards Inn

8130 Watson St; tel 703/893-3390. Exit I-495 at International Dr. **Seafood/Steak.** Built to resemble an Old West ranch house, this award-winning steak house, with rough-hewn walls and exposed beams, seems almost barn-like. Smoky aroma of thick steaks over a wood fire fills the place. Also prime rib and some seafood selections. **FYI:** Reservations recommended. Dress code. Additional location: 9401 Lee Highway, Fairfax (tel 591-8448). **Open:** Lunch Mon–Fri 11:30am–2:30pm; dinner Mon–Thurs 5:30–10pm, Fri–Sat 5:30–11pm, Sun 5–9:30pm. **Prices:** Main courses $11–$26. DC, DISC, MC, V. 💗

Kazan Restaurant

In McLean Shopping Center, 6813 Redmond Dr; tel 703/734-1960. At old Chain Bridge Rd off VA 123. **Middle Eastern/Turkish.** A Turkish motif reigns in this relatively small dining room with tent-like drapes hanging from its ceiling. Deep-blue wall tiles and brass pitchers from the old country add to the romance. Authentic Turkish cuisine includes kabobs and several meat and seafood dishes with exotic spices. A few continental dishes placate the less adventurous. **FYI:** Reservations recommended. Children's menu. Dress code. No smoking. **Open:** Lunch Mon–Fri 11am–3pm; dinner Mon–Thurs 5–10pm, Fri–Sat 5–11pm. **Prices:** Main courses $12–$17. AE, CB, DC, DISC, MC, V. 💗 🕭

⭐ La Mirabelle

In McLean Square Shopping Center, 6645 Old Dominion Dr; tel 703/893-8484. Exit 11 off I-495. **French.** European country ambience prevails in this heavy-beamed dining room with a fireplace in one corner and tufted booths along walls hung with mirrored panels and Impressionist paintings. Ceiling spotlights set off the tables. Traditional French menu is about equally divided between meat and seafood. Popular piano bar sits in front, away from dining room. **FYI:** Reservations recommended. Piano. Dress code. **Open:** Lunch Mon–Fri 11:30am–2pm; dinner Mon–Sat 5–9pm, Sun 5–8pm. **Prices:** Main courses $14–$24; prix fixe $20. AE, CB, DC, DISC, MC, V. 💚 🖼

Meadows of Dan

RESTAURANTS 🍴

Le Chien Noir

In Château Morrisette Winery, Winery Rd, PO Box 766; tel 540/593-2865. Near MM 172 of the Blue Ridge Pkwy, at jct US 221/58. **Eclectic/International.** Unpretentious French country decor amid exposed beams, stucco walls, fireplaces, and hardwood floors. Several dining rooms, each with its own character. An outdoor patio overlooks the vineyard. Seasonal menus contain freshly prepared lamb and fish. Calling ahead is strongly recommended since hours may change and inclement weather can close Blue Ridge Parkway. Jazz concert and festival second Saturday of each month June to October. Winery open daily. **FYI:** Reservations recommended. Jazz. Beer and wine only. No smoking. **Open:** Lunch Wed–Sat 11am–2pm, Sun 11am–3pm; dinner Fri–Sat 6–9pm. Closed Christmas week. **Prices:** Main courses $12–$19. AE, MC, V. 💚 🍽 🖼 🏞 ♿

Mabry Mill

MM 176, Blue Ridge Pkwy; tel 540/952-2947. Between US 58 and US 221. **Regional American.** Casual dining in a rustic, home-like atmosphere at the site of a gristmill, sawmill, and blacksmith shop on the Blue Ridge Parkway. A self-guided tour of the premises illustrates these pioneer industries. Specialties are cornmeal and buckwheat pancakes made from grains stone-ground in the adjacent gristmill. Hiking, camping, and picnicking nearby. **FYI:** Reservations not accepted. Children's menu. No liquor license. No smoking. **Open:** Peak (June–Aug) daily 8am–7pm. Closed Nov–May. **Prices:** Lunch main courses $2–$6. AE, CB, DC, DISC, MC, V. 🍺 📷 ♿

Middleburg

One hour west of Washington, DC, this charming historic village in Virginia Hunt Country has only 500 permanent residents. Upscale homes, shops, and nearby estates and vineyards add to sense of country gentility.

INN 🏨

🏳🏳🏳🏳 Red Fox Inn

2 E Washington St, 20117; tel 540/687-6301 or toll free 800/223-1728; fax 540/687-6053. Dating back to 1728, this impressive and elegant inn consists of five historic structures within a city block. It captures the flavor of colonial living while at the same time providing modern touches. Hospitable innkeepers. Fresh flowers throughout. **Rooms:** 24 rms and stes. CI 3pm/CO noon. Individually decorated rooms and suites have antiques or reproductions. Some suites large enough for grand piano, with view of backyard. **Amenities:** 🗝 🛎 A/C, cable TV, CD/tape player, bathrobes. Some units w/terraces, some w/fireplaces. Some rooms have two phones, refrigerators. Fireplaces are electric. **Services:** ✗ 🍴 Petit fours and the morning paper in each room add to the sense of pampering. Can make arrangements for area activities, such as horseback riding and balloon rides. Business services at desk. Night watchman on duty. **Facilities:** 🛎 30 ♟ restaurants, 2 bars (1 w/entertainment). Noted restaurants on premises. **Rates (CP):** Peak (Mar–June/Sept–Dec) $135–$145 S or D; $145–$245 ste. Extra person $25. Lower rates off-season. Parking: Outdoor, free. Romantic weekend getaway packages avail. AE, CB, DC, DISC, JCB, MC, V.

RESTAURANTS 🍴

⭐ Coach Stop Restaurant

9 E Washington St (US 50); tel 540/687-5515. Exit 57B off I-66 W. **American.** This cozy restaurant captures the flavor of its community with hunt-country photos and paintings and a dark-paneled bar the length of a wall. Winner of the *Wine Spectator* Award. A local favorite, the family-run facility offers such specialties as homemade onion rings, fresh seafood, and calf's liver. **FYI:** Reservations recommended. Children's menu. **Open:** Mon–Sat 7am–9:30pm, Sun 8am–9pm. **Prices:** Main courses $11–$17. AE, CB, DC, DISC, MC, V. 📷

⭐ Red Fox Inn and Mosby's Tavern

2 E Washington St (US 50); tel 540/687-6301. Exit 57B off I-66 W. **Regional American/Continental.** Old pine floors, Windsor chairs, pewter mugs, and low-beamed ceiling transport you back to 1728, when the inn first opened. Fine dining by a fireplace or in Mosby's Tavern, an oak-paneled pub, also with a fireplace, where more casual fare is served. The focus is on continental and regional cuisine, including Old Virginia classics such as peanut soup and crab cakes. **FYI:** Reservations recommended. **Open:** Breakfast Sat–Sun 8–10am; lunch Mon–Fri 11am–5pm, Sat 11am–4pm; dinner Mon–Fri

5–9pm, Sat 5–9:30pm, Sun 4–8pm; brunch Sat 11am–4pm, Sun noon–4pm. **Prices:** Main courses $19–$23; prix fixe $37–$45. AE, CB, DC, DISC, MC, V. ♥ ■ ▣

Middletown

Founded in 1796, this small town was named for its location between Winchester and Woodstock. The Virginia State Arboretum is nearby.

ATTRACTION

Belle Grove Plantation
US 11; tel 540/869-2028. One of the finest homes in the Shenandoah Valley, this beautiful stone mansion was built in the late 1700s by Maj Isaac Hite, whose grandfather, Joist Hite, first settled in the valley in 1732. Thomas Jefferson was actively involved in Belle Grove's design; the Palladian-style front windows and columns are an example of his influence. The interior is furnished with period antiques.

During the Civil War the house suffered considerable damage during the Battle of Cedar Creek. Union Gen Philip Sheridan's army, which occupied the plantation, was attacked by Confederate forces led by Gen Jubal Early on October 19, 1864. The result was a decisive victory for the Confederacy, but Sheridan was still able to sweep through the valley, laying waste to the rich farmlands that were the breadbasket of the South. **Open:** Apr–Oct, Mon–Sat 10:15am–3:15pm, Sun 1:15–4:15pm. $$

Midlothian

MOTEL

≡≡≡ Days Inn Chesterfield
1301 Huguenot Rd, at US 60 and VA 147, 23113; tel 804/794-4999 or toll free 800/325-2525; fax 804/794-1022. 6 mi W of Richmond. Adjacent to Chesterfield Towne Center Mall. This property makes you feel very comfortable, almost pampered, as compared with other chain motels. Shopping mall and numerous restaurants, shops, and activities are nearby. **Rooms:** 120 rms and stes. CI 3pm/CO noon. Decor is simple and tasteful. Each spacious unit has a desk. **Amenities:** ⊓ ⬙ ▤ A/C, cable TV. **Services:** ⟲ **Facilities:** ⌂ ⬙ 1 restaurant, washer/dryer. **Rates (CP):** $55 S; $60 D. Children under age 18 stay free. Parking: Outdoor, free. AE, DISC, MC, V.

Monterey

Surrounded by George Washington National Forest in the Shenandoah Valley. Seat of Highland County. **Information:** Highland County Chamber of Commerce, PO Box 223, Monterey, 24465 (tel 540/468-2550).

INN

≡≡≡ Highland Inn
450 Main St, PO Box 40, 24465; tel 540/468-2143. On the National Register of Historic Places, this large, quaint country home built in 1904 has not been gentrified by innkeepers. George Washington National Forest surrounds property. Excellent choice during Highland Maple Festival in March. **Rooms:** 17 rms and stes. CI 2pm/CO 11am. Mix of nicely kept furniture and antiques. **Amenities:** ⬙ Cable TV. No A/C or phone. Ceiling fans. **Services:** ⬚ ⟲ **Facilities:** 1 bar, guest lounge. Tavern open during dining room hours (Wed–Sat 6–8pm, Sun 11am–2pm). **Rates (CP):** $49–$69 D; $75–$79 ste. Parking: Outdoor, free. MC, V.

Mountain Lake

Located in the southwest Blue Ridge Highlands and site of one of only two natural freshwater lakes in the state.

RESORT

≡≡≡ Mountain Lake
VA 700, 24136; tel 540/626-7121 or toll free 800/346-3334; fax 540/626-7172. Exit US 460 at VA 700N, or take exit 118 off I-81. Beautiful mountaintop resort hotel, 50 miles southwest of Roanoke, overlooks one of only two natural freshwater lakes in Virginia. Some 2,500 acres protected by Mountain Lake Wilderness Conservancy. Hotel open to individual guests only on weekends from November 1 through April 30. **Rooms:** 66 rms and stes; 15 cottages/villas. Executive level. CI 5pm/CO 11am. No smoking. **Amenities:** ⬚ No A/C or TV. Some units w/terraces, some w/fireplaces, some w/whirlpools. Window and ceiling fans make up for lack of air conditioning. **Services:** ✕ ⒱Ⓟ ⬛ ⟲ Social director, masseur, children's program, babysitting. **Facilities:** ⬮⬯ ⬙ ⬚ ⬚ ⬙ ▤¹ ▤ ▣ 1 restaurant, 1 bar, 1 beach (lake shore), lifeguard, games rm, lawn games, sauna, whirlpool, playground, washer/dryer. Hiking trails. Indoor recreational facility with billiards, table tennis, shuffleboard, and ice skating. Fishing tours, wine-and-cheese lake cruises, horse-drawn carriage and sleigh rides. Two TV lounges with VCRs. **Rates (MAP):** Peak (May–Oct) $95–$200 S; $145–$245 D; $110 ste; $85 cottage/villa. Extra person $25. Children under age 4 stay free. Min stay special events. Lower rates off-season. AP rates avail. Parking: Outdoor, free. AE, DC, DISC, MC, V.

Mount Vernon

For lodgings and dining, see Alexandria, Fairfax, Springfield

Famous as the home and burial site of George and Martha Washington. Their gracious home on the banks of the Potomac is America's most-visited estate.

ATTRACTIONS 🏛

Mount Vernon

Tel 703/780-2000. Access via George Washington Memorial Parkway (VA 400), which ends at Mount Vernon. The Mount Vernon estate was purchased in 1858 by the Mount Vernon Ladies' Association from John Augustine Washington, great-grandnephew of the first president.

There is no formal guided tour, but attendants stationed throughout the house and grounds answer questions and a map is provided. The house is an outstanding example of colonial architecture. Many of the furnishings are original pieces acquired by Washington, and the rooms have been repainted in the original colors favored by George and Martha. There are a number of family portraits, and the rooms are appointed as if actually in day-to-day use. A four-acre exhibit called "George Washington, Pioneer Farmer" includes a replica of Washington's 16-sided barn and fields of crops he grew. A museum on the property contains memorabilia and explains details of the restoration project. "Slave Life" and "Garden and Landscape" guided tours take place seasonally. **Open:** Peak (Apr–Aug) daily 8am–5pm. Reduced hours off-season. **$$$**

Woodlawn Plantation

Tel 703/780-4000. Located 3 miles west of Mount Vernon on US 1, Woodlawn was originally a 2,000-acre section of Washington's Mount Vernon estate (today some 130 acres remain). He gave it as a wedding gift to his adopted daughter (and Martha's actual granddaughter) Eleanor Parke Custis and her fiancé, Maj Lawrence Lewis (who was Washington's nephew). The restored mansion and formal gardens reflect many periods of its history. Tours, given on the half hour, last 30 minutes.

Also on the grounds are **Grand View,** a house built 100 yards from the mansion in 1858 (not open to the public); and Frank Lloyd Wright's **Pope–Leighy House,** built in Falls Church in 1940 and moved here in 1964 after it was slated for demolition. It was a prototype of Wright's "Usonian" style of architecture, which aspired to make well-designed housing accessible to middle-income people. **Open:** Peak (Feb–Dec) daily 9:30am–4:30pm. Reduced hours off-season. **$$**

George Washington's Grist Mill Historic State Park

5514 Mount Vernon Memorial Hwy; tel 703/550-0960 or 780-3383 (weekends). Located 3 mi W of Mount Vernon on VA 225. The Woodlawn part of Mount Vernon contained a gristmill that neighboring farmers used for grinding corn and wheat. In 1932 the Virginia Conservation Commission purchased part of the property known as Dogue Run Farm, on which the mill and other buildings had been located. The site was excavated, and part of the original wheel, part of the trundlehead (complete with wheel buckets), and other articles were found. Guided tours of the mill (45 min) are given throughout the day. Picnicking. **Open:** Mem Day–Labor Day, Sat–Sun 10am–6pm. **$**

Natural Bridge

Named for a huge natural stone bridge worshipped by Native Americans, surveyed by George Washington, and later purchased by Thomas Jefferson. An extensive series of caverns lie 34 floors below the bridge.

RESORT 🏨

≣≣≣ Natural Bridge of Virginia Resort

US 11, PO Box 57, 24578; tel 540/291-2121 or toll free 800/533-1410; fax 540/291-1896. Exit 175 off I-81. 1,600 acres. A full-service resort nestled in the Shenandoah Valley and surrounded by mountains and streams. **Rooms:** 180 rms and stes. CI 3pm/CO noon. Nonsmoking rms avail. **Amenities:** 🛏 A/C, cable TV w/movies. Some units w/terraces. **Services:** ✕ 🛎 🐕 Babysitting. Pets allowed in older part of hotel. **Facilities:** 🎿 ⛄ 🏊 🏌 💪² 🎱 🎳 💻 3 restaurants, 1 bar (w/entertainment), games rm, playground. Indoor miniature golf. **Rates:** Peak (Apr–Oct) $69–$89 S or D; $125 ste. Children under age 18 stay free. Lower rates off-season. MAP rates avail. Parking: Outdoor, free. AE, DC, DISC, MC, V.

ATTRACTION 🏛

Natural Bridge of Virginia

Exits 175 and 180 off I-81; tel 540/291-2121 or toll free 800/533-1410. Thomas Jefferson called this bridge of limestone "the most sublime of nature's works . . . so beautiful an arch, so elevated, so light and springing, as it were, up to heaven." The bridge was part of a 157-acre estate Jefferson acquired in 1774 from King George III. It was included in the survey of western Virginia carried out by George Washington, who carved his initials into the face of the stone. The bridge rises 215 feet above Cedar Creek; its span is 90 feet long and spreads at its widest to 150 feet. It is believed that the Monocan tribes used the bridge as a passageway and fortress, and it was worshipped by them as "the bridge of God."

A 45-minute sound-and-light show, *The Drama of Creation,* is conducted nightly beneath the bridge. Across the parking lot from the upper bridge entrance is the Natural Bridge Wax Museum. **Open:** Daily 8am–sunset. **$$$**

New Market

This Shenandoah Valley town lies over several series of caverns, and was the site of a major Civil War battle.

Information: New Market Area Chamber of Commerce, E Lee Hwy, PO Box 57, New Market, 22844 (tel 540/740-3212).

HOTEL

≝≝ Quality Inn Shenandoah Valley

I-81 and VA 211, 22844; tel 540/740-3141 or toll free 800/221-2222. Despite its highway location, this property offers a lovely view of mountains. **Rooms:** 101 rms. CI noon/CO 2pm. Nonsmoking rms avail. Rooms feature two-poster beds and nice fixtures. Bridal suite and conference suite available. **Amenities:** A/C, cable TV w/movies. VCRs and videos available for rent. **Services:** Room service available from restaurant (separate from hotel, but within the facility). Safe deposit boxes available at desk. **Facilities:** 1 restaurant, games rm, playground, washer/dryer. Miniature golf. **Rates:** Peak (May–Sept) $56–$62 S; $62–$72 D. Extra person $6. Children under age 18 stay free. Lower rates off-season. Parking: Outdoor, free. AE, DISC, MC, V.

MOTEL

≝≝ The Shenvalee

9660 Fairway Dr, 22844; tel 540/740-3181; fax 540/740-8931. Off Congress St. This 1920s brick mansion with white columns, built on a knoll above its golf course, has separate motel unit adjoining. **Rooms:** 42 rms. CI 3pm/CO 1pm. Nonsmoking rms avail. All rooms afford a view of either mountains or golf course. **Amenities:** A/C, cable TV, refrig. Some units w/terraces. **Services:** Turn-down service on request. Accommodating staff. Fax machine available in office. **Facilities:** 1 restaurant, 1 bar, beauty salon. Outside snack bar area near pool and golf course. **Rates:** Peak (Apr–Nov) $36–$55 S; $44–$65 D. Extra person $10. Children under age 13 stay free. Lower rates off-season. Parking: Outdoor, free. Golf packages avail. AE, CB, DC, MC, V.

ATTRACTION

New Market Battlefield State Historical Park

Tel 540/740-3101. From I-81 exit 67 take US 211W, then an immediate right onto County Rd 305 (George Collins Pkwy); the battlefield is 1¾ miles away, at the end of the road.

The park commemorates the heroism of 250 cadets from the Virginia Military Institute, who participated in a Civil War battle on May 15, 1864. Faced with an attack by superior numbers, Gen John C Breckenridge was forced to call upon VMI for reinforcements. The cadets joined the battle, which resulted in the defeat of the Union force commanded by Maj Gen Franz Sigel.

The **Hall of Valor Civil War Museum** presents a film about the battle, and another about Stonewall Jackson's Shenandoah campaign. The final Confederate assault on the Union line is covered in a self-guided tour of the grassy field.

In the center of the line of battle was the **Bushong Farmhouse,** today a museum of 19th-century Valley life. **Open:** Daily 9am–7pm. **$$$**

Newport News

Located at the confluence of four rivers (James, York, Elizabeth, and Nansemond) as they empty into Chesapeake Bay at Hampton Roads harbor, Newport News is a major player in the shipbuilding, defense, and import/export industries. **Information:** Virginia Peninsula Chamber of Commerce, Six Manhattan Sq #100, PO Box 7269, Hampton, 23666 (tel 757/766-2000).

HOTELS

≝≝≝ The Inn at Kiln Creek

1003 Brick Kiln Blvd, 23602; tel 757/874-2600; fax 757/988-3237. Exit 255B off I-64. Lodging on beautiful grounds of a country club, so naturally it feels more like a golf club than a hotel. Excellent facilities. **Rooms:** 16 rms. CI 3pm/CO noon. Nonsmoking rms avail. Tasteful furnishings. Sliding glass doors open to patio overlooking golf course. **Amenities:** A/C, cable TV w/movies, refrig, in-rm safe. All units w/terraces. **Services:** Twice-daily maid svce, social director. **Facilities:** 2 restaurants, 2 bars, lawn games, spa, sauna, steam rm, whirlpool. Indoor/outdoor pools. **Rates:** $80 S; $100 D. Children under age 12 stay free. AP and MAP rates avail. Parking: Outdoor, free. Corporate and member rates avail. AE, MC, V.

≝≝≝ Omni Newport News

1000 Omni Way Blvd, 23606; tel 757/873-6664 or toll free 800/THE-OMNI; fax 757/873-1732. Exit 258A off I-64, then S on US 17 for ¼ mi. The best digs in Newport News, this upscale property in wooded office park caters to business travelers and conferences. Great attention to detail in public areas. Modern-style lobby overlooking pool has vaulted ceilings, beautiful lighting fixtures, fireplace. **Rooms:** 183 rms and stes. CI 3pm/CO noon. Nonsmoking rms avail. Mauve color scheme, including pleated shades. Parlor rooms have two full sofas, dining tables for six, wet bars with brass stools. Motion detectors activate climate-control system when guests enter units. **Amenities:** A/C, cable TV w/movies, dataport. Some units w/fireplaces, some w/whirlpools. **Services:** Twice-daily maid svce, masseur, babysitting. **Facilities:** 1 restaurant, 2 bars (w/entertainment), volleyball, lawn games, spa, sauna, steam rm, whirlpool, washer/dryer. Indoor pool with adjacent fitness room. Golf nearby. **Rates:** $99–$109 S; $109–$129 D; $295–$395 ste. Extra person $10. Children under age 17 stay free. Min stay special events. MAP rates avail. Parking: Outdoor, free. AE, CB, DC, DISC, JCB, MC, V.

MOTEL

≣≣≣ Ramada Inn and Conference Center

950 J Clyde Morris Blvd (VA 17 N), 23601; tel 757/599-4460 or toll free 800/841-1112; fax 757/599-4336. Exit 258B off I-64. Newly renovated motel has a range of accommodations to appeal to both families and business travelers. **Rooms:** 220 rms and stes. Executive level. CI 2pm/CO noon. No smoking. Cheerful, tasteful decor. Suites have dark-finished Queen Anne furniture, beige accents. **Amenities:** 🛏 🅰 A/C, cable TV w/movies. Some units w/whirlpools. Suites available with coffeemakers, refrigerators. **Services:** ✕ 🚐 ⊠ 🛎 ⬲ Morning coffee available in lobby. Ramada Business Club members have access to business services, complimentary newspaper, drink coupon. **Facilities:** 🛠 🖼 🖥 700 🖥 ⬧ 1 restaurant, 1 bar, games rm. **Rates:** Peak (Mem Day–Labor Day) $65–$75 S or D; $50–$175 ste. Extra person $5. Children under age 18 stay free. Min stay special events. Lower rates off-season. Parking: Outdoor, free. AE, CB, DC, DISC, MC, V.

ATTRACTION 🏛

Mariners' Museum

100 Museum Dr; tel 757/596-2222. In a pleasant, 550-acre park setting, with a lake, picnic areas, and walking trails, the Mariners' Museum is dedicated to preserving the culture of the sea and its tributaries. Handcrafted ship models, scrimshaw, maritime paintings, decorative arts, working steam engines, and more are displayed in spacious galleries. An 18-minute film tells about worldwide maritime activity. Occasional demonstrations by costumed historical interpreters. **Open:** Daily 10am–5pm. $$$

Norfolk

See also Chesapeake, Hampton, Newport News, Portsmouth, Virginia Beach

Located on the Elizabeth River, on the south side of Hampton Roads harbor, Norfolk is blessed with one of the best natural harbors in the world. Millions of tons of cargo move through this port every year. Norfolk boasts a 50-mile waterfront and is the location of extensive US Navy installations, including the world's largest naval base. **Information:** Norfolk Convention and Visitors Bureau, 236 E Plume St, Norfolk, 23510 (tel 757/441-5266).

PUBLIC TRANSPORTATION

The **Tidewater Regional Transit System (TRT)** (tel 804/640-6300) bus system serves Norfolk, Virginia Beach, Portsmouth, and Chesapeake. Fare is $1.50 anywhere and exact change is required.

HOTELS 🏨

≣≣≣ Howard Johnson Hotel

700 Monticello Ave, 23510; tel 757/627-5555 or toll free 800/682-7678; fax 757/533-9651. In downtown Norfolk on US 460, 1 block S of jct US 58. Large chain hotel adjacent to Norfolk Scope and Chrysler Hall complex, six blocks from Waterside Festival Marketplace and Nauticus National Maritime Center. **Rooms:** 344 rms. CI 3pm/CO noon. Nonsmoking rms avail. Attractively furnished. One unit is very large and has a kitchen equipped with full-size appliances. **Amenities:** 🛏 A/C, cable TV w/movies. Some units w/minibars. **Services:** ✕ 🚐 ⊠ 🛎 ⬲ Complimentary shuttle to downtown attractions. **Facilities:** 🛠 🖥 800 ⬧ 1 restaurant, 1 bar (w/entertainment), games rm, washer/dryer. Large swimming pool. Comedy club on premises operates Thursday to Saturday evenings. **Rates:** Peak (Mem Day–Labor Day) $80–$150 S or D. Extra person $10. Children under age 12 stay free. Min stay special events. Lower rates off-season. Parking: Outdoor, free. AE, DC, DISC, MC, V.

≣≣≣ Norfolk Airport Hilton

1500 N Military Hwy, 23502 (Norfolk Int'l Airport); tel 757/466-8000 or toll free 800/422-7474; fax 757/466-8000. Exit 281 off I-64. Follow signs to Military Hwy, turn left, go ¾ mile to hotel. Location is central to naval bases and downtown Norfolk. **Rooms:** 250 rms and stes. CI 3pm/CO 1pm. Nonsmoking rms avail. **Amenities:** 🛏 🅰 🖥 🍴 A/C, cable TV w/movies, refrig, bathrobes. Some units w/minibars, 1 w/terrace. **Services:** ✕ ⬛ VP 🚐 ⊠ 🛎 Complimentary snacks and entertainment in lounge Monday to Friday. **Facilities:** 🛠 🖥 750 🖥 ⬧ 3 restaurants, 1 bar (w/entertainment), spa, sauna, steam rm, whirlpool. Pool has patio and seating area. **Rates:** Peak (May–Aug) $109–$139 S; $119–$149 D; $225–$300 ste. Extra person $10. Children under age 12 stay free. Lower rates off-season. Parking: Outdoor, free. AE, CB, DC, DISC, MC, V.

≣≣≣≣ Norfolk Waterside Marriott

235 Main St, 23510 (Downtown); tel 757/627-4200 or toll free 800/228-9290; fax 757/628-6452. Opened in 1991 just one block from the waterfront, Norfolk's best digs have an elegant lobby with crystal lamps, vases, chandeliers, antiques, marble floors, and overstuffed furniture. **Rooms:** 404 rms and stes. Executive level. CI 4pm/CO noon. No smoking. Spacious rooms are very well appointed and decorated. **Amenities:** 🛏 🅰 A/C, cable TV w/movies, voice mail. Some units w/minibars, 1 w/fireplace, 1 w/whirlpool. **Services:** ✕ ⬛ VP 🚐 ⊠ 🛎 ⬲ Babysitting. **Facilities:** 🛠 🖥 1400 🖥 ⬧ 2 restaurants, 2 bars (w/entertainment), games rm, spa, sauna, whirlpool, washer/dryer. Indoor pool opens to outdoor sunning area. **Rates:** Peak (May 26–Sept 9) $80–$119 S or D; $250 ste. Children under age 17 stay free. Lower rates off-season. Parking: Indoor, $8–$10/day. AE, CB, DC, DISC, ER, JCB, MC, V.

≣≣≣≣ Omni International Hotel

777 Waterside Dr, 23510 (Downtown); tel 757/622-6664 or toll free 800/THE-OMNI; fax 757/625-8271. Conveniently located on the waterfront adjacent to the Waterside shops, this modern hotel has a large marble entrance and lobby with excellent furnishings and seating. **Rooms:** 442 rms and stes.

Executive level. CI 3pm/CO noon. No smoking. Well-appointed rooms range from standard to large suites. **Amenities:** 📺 🅰 🍷 A/C, cable TV w/movies, voice mail. Some units w/terraces, 1 w/whirlpool. Wet bars in suites. **Services:** ✗ 🖛 ⓥⓟ 🚗 📇 🛎 🖐 Car-rental desk, babysitting. No pets over 25 lbs. **Facilities:** 🏋 🏌 💻 🖐 1 restaurant, 1 bar (w/entertainment). Jogging path nearby. **Rates:** $108–$145 S or D; $175 ste. Extra person $15. Children under age 17 stay free. Min stay special events. Parking: Indoor/outdoor, $3–$8/day. AE, CB, DC, DISC, JCB, MC, V.

≣≣ Ramada Norfolk
345 Granby St, 23510; tel 757/622-6682 or toll free 800/2-RAMADA; fax 757/623-5949. Exit I-64 at I-264. Dating to 1906, this downtown hotel is within walking distance of Waterside Festival Marketplace and Nauticus National Maritime Center. Old-style lobby has lots of wooden columns. **Rooms:** 124 rms. Executive level. CI 3pm/CO noon. Nonsmoking rms avail. Tasteful, traditionally furnished rooms have two small baths. **Amenities:** 📺 🅰 A/C, cable TV w/movies. Some units w/minibars. Refrigerators and microwaves available. **Services:** ✗ 📇 🛎 🖐 Golf arranged. **Facilities:** 🏌 🖐 1 restaurant, 1 bar (w/entertainment). Guests have use of Downtown Athletic Club and YMCA for fee. **Rates:** Peak (Mem Day–Labor Day) $65–$89 S or D. Extra person $10. Children under age 18 stay free. Min stay special events. Lower rates off-season. Parking: Indoor/outdoor, free. AE, DISC, MC, V.

MOTELS

≣≣≣ Best Western Center Inn
1 Best Sq, 23502; tel 757/461-6600 or toll free 800/237-5517; fax 757/466-9093. Exit 284A off I-64. Almost hidden behind the Best Products store, this gray wooden structure surrounds a central area with clubhouse and indoor and outdoor pools, offering a relaxed atmosphere. **Rooms:** 152 rms and stes. CI 3pm/CO noon. Nonsmoking rms avail. **Amenities:** 📺 A/C, cable TV w/movies, refrig, voice mail. **Services:** ✗ 🚗 📇 🛎 Babysitting. **Facilities:** 🏌 🏋 🖐 1 restaurant, 1 bar, sauna, whirlpool, washer/dryer. **Rates (CP):** Peak (May 15–Sept 15) $59–$71 S or D; $125–$135 ste. Extra person $6. Children under age 12 stay free. Min stay special events. Lower rates off-season. Parking: Outdoor, free. AE, DISC, MC, V.

≣≣ Econo Lodge Ocean View Beach–West
9601 4th View St at US 60, 23503; tel 804/480-9611 or toll free 800/768-5425; fax 804/480-1307. Exit 273 off I-64. A clean and modern chain motel across street from Ocean View Beach. **Rooms:** 71 rms, stes, and effic. CI 2pm/CO 11am. No smoking. Small room for guests with disabilities lacks adequate turn space. **Amenities:** 📺 🅰 A/C, cable TV w/movies, refrig. 1 unit w/terrace. Efficiencies have sink, stove, small refrigerator, dining table for two. VCRs, coffeemakers available. **Services:** 🛎 🖐 Pet deposit $50. **Facilities:** 🏊 🖐 Spa, sauna, whirlpool, washer/dryer. Hot tub. Fishing pier across

street. **Rates (CP):** Peak (May 20–Sept 10) $51–$63 S; $56–$64 D; $79 ste; $69 effic. Extra person $5. Children under age 18 stay free. Min stay special events. Lower rates off-season. Parking: Outdoor, free. AE, CB, DC, DISC, JCB, MC, V.

≣≣ Hampton Inn Norfolk Naval Base
8501 Hampton Blvd, 23505; tel 757/489-1000 or toll free 800/HAMPTON; fax 757/489-4509. I-564 exit off I-64; 2½ mi E on Terminal Blvd; ½ mi N on Hampton Blvd. Clean, modern chain motel adjacent to Norfolk Naval Base and many fast-food restaurants. **Rooms:** 119 rms and effic. CI 2pm/CO 11am. Nonsmoking rms avail. Bright and clean. **Amenities:** 📺 A/C, cable TV w/movies. Some units w/whirlpools. **Services:** 📇 🛎 Babysitting. Children's program, from Memorial Day to Labor Day, consists of videos shown in lobby. **Facilities:** 🏌 🖐 Whirlpool. **Rates (CP):** $64–$70 S; $70 D; $70–$78 effic. Children under age 18 stay free. Parking: Outdoor, free. AE, DC, DISC, MC, V.

≣≣ Norfolk Hampton Inn Airport
1450 Military Hwy, 23502 (Norfolk Int'l Airport); tel 757/466-7474 or toll free 800/426-7866; fax 757/466-7474 ext 309. Exit 281 off I-64. Basic chain motel offering no surprises. **Rooms:** 130 rms. CI 3pm/CO noon. Nonsmoking rms avail. **Amenities:** 📺 🅰 A/C, cable TV w/movies. **Services:** 🚗 📇 🛎 Accommodating staff renders high-quality service for such an establishment. Free local calls. **Facilities:** 🏌 🍴 🖐 Guests have free use of local health club. **Rates (CP):** Peak (Mem Day–Labor Day) $61 S or D. Children under age 18 stay free. Lower rates off-season. Parking: Outdoor, free. AE, DC, DISC, MC, V.

RESTAURANTS 🍴

Doumar's
1900 Monticello Ave; tel 757/627-4163. Exit I-264 at City Hall Ave; turn right on St Paul's Blvd, go 1 mile to Monticello Ave. **Barbecue/Burgers.** Interesting today for the historical perspective if not the culinary experience, this was Virginia's first drive-in and the state's first restaurant to have a soda fountain. In fact, service still comes right to your car. Inside seating is old-fashioned booths and counter. Other than ice cream, only sandwiches are offered, with barbecue the house specialty. Cones have been homemade here since 1904 (original machine is on display). **FYI:** Reservations not accepted. No liquor license. **Open:** Mon–Thurs 8am–11pm, Fri–Sat 8am–midnight. **Prices:** Main courses $1–$3. No CC. 🍺

★ Elliot's
1421 Colley Ave; tel 757/625-0259. **Regional American/Burgers.** Walls lined with old signs and memorabilia going back to the 1930s adorn this casual local favorite. Children's menu is a coloring book, and kids have used crayons to cover an entire wall with their creations. Favorites are chicken Alexander, seafood dishes, and burgers. **FYI:** Reservations

accepted. Children's menu. Dress code. **Open:** Sun–Thurs 11am–10pm, Fri–Sat 11am–midnight. **Prices:** Main courses $9–$15. AE, CB, DC, DISC, MC, V. ♨ 👥 ♿

Fisherman's Wharf Seafood Restaurant
In Willoughby Bay Marina, 1571 Bayville St; tel 757/480-3113. Exit 272 off I-64 E. **Seafood/Steak.** Overlooking Willoughby Bay, the open, airy dining room is accented with brass railings, nautical pictures, tables with inlaid shells, hanging plants, Tiffany-style lamps, and oak columns. Seafood buffet offers wide variety of seafood and fresh vegetables. **FYI:** Reservations accepted. Comedy. Children's menu. **Open:** Daily 11am–10pm. **Prices:** Main courses $14–$28; prix fixe $19. AE, DC, MC, V. ⛰ 👥 ♿

Il Porto Ristorante
In Waterside, 333 Waterside Dr; tel 757/627-4400. **Italian.** Hand-painted walls surround spotlit tables in the dining room, and a candlelit bar with a grand piano is off to one side. Excellent view of Norfolk harbor from dining room and outside eating area. A variety of traditional veal, seafood, poultry, and pasta dishes from the old country. **FYI:** Reservations accepted. Piano. Children's menu. Dress code. **Open:** Daily 11am–11:30pm. **Prices:** Main courses $9–$15. AE, DC, MC, V. ♨ ⛰ ♿

Magnolia Steak
749 W Princess Anne Rd (Ghent); tel 757/625-0400. At Colley Ave. **Seafood/Steak.** Lighted sailing pictures adorn the walls of this family-oriented restaurant with adjacent games room with billiard tables and sports on TV. Burgundy color scheme and overstuffed upholstered chairs at mahogany tables. An outside area seating 30 is used most of the year. Certified Angus beef is popular. Seafood dishes, pastas, and chicken also offered. Vegetables are fresh; desserts, homemade. **FYI:** Reservations accepted. **Open:** Mon–Fri 11:30am–1:30am, Sat–Sun 4pm–1:30am. **Prices:** Main courses $8–$23. AE, DISC, MC, V. ♨ 👥 ♿

Phillips Seafood Restaurant
In Waterside, 333 Waterside Dr; tel 757/627-6600. **Seafood.** Excellent view of the downtown waterfront from booths raised a step above floor level in this seafood emporium, part of a regional chain. Checked tablecloths and wrought-iron tables. Menu features traditional Chesapeake Bay seafood, with specials changing daily to reflect fresh catch. Outdoor dining and drinking area in good weather. Band plays in bar Friday and Saturday evenings. **FYI:** Reservations accepted. Piano. Children's menu. Dress code. **Open:** Daily 11am–10pm. **Prices:** Main courses $14–$22. AE, DC, DISC, MC, V. ♨ ⛰ ♿

★ Ship's Cabin Seafood Restaurant
4110 E Ocean View Ave; tel 757/362-4659. Exit 278 off I-64. **New American/Seafood.** Sporting great views from perch on the Chesapeake Bay, and with a nautical theme augmented by large plants under high cathedral ceilings, this popular restaurant is top-notch. Low brick walls with mahog-

any caps divide dining room into sections. Attractive fireplace in bar is open to all sides. Daily specials feature fresh, mostly local seafood. Also known for seafood kabobs and lamb shank. Sauces as well as desserts, ice creams, and sorbets made on premises. **FYI:** Reservations recommended. Dress code. No smoking. **Open:** Peak (Mem Day–Labor Day) Mon–Thurs 5:30–9:30pm, Fri–Sat 5:30–10:30pm, Sun 5–9:30pm. **Prices:** Main courses $14–$25. AE, DC, MC, V. ♥ 🖼 ⛰ ♿

★ Surf Rider West
723 Newtown Rd; tel 757/461-6488. Exit 284B off I-64, 2 blocks beyond Virginia Beach Blvd. **Seafood.** Wooden booths and tables and local beach decor lend a casual family atmosphere to this member of a small seafood restaurant chain. All seafood is fresh daily, including all–lump meat crab cakes. **FYI:** Reservations not accepted. Dress code. **Open:** Mon–Sat 11am–10pm. **Prices:** Main courses $9–$16. AE, DISC, MC, V. 👥

★ Uncle Louie's
In Wards Corner Shopping Center, 132 E Little Creek Rd; tel 757/480-1225. Exit 276 off I-64. Turn left at 2nd light. **Regional American/Seafood/Steak.** A storefront deli is only part of this fine, multifaceted establishment. Behind the deli, wall hangings, murals, and a coordinated color scheme create an upbeat, casual atmosphere in a nicely decorated restaurant divided into sections by waist-high walls adorned with brass and glass fixtures. Etched-glass doors lead to bar and grill sections. Coffee shop specializes in freshly ground coffees and serves tea daily 2–5pm. Fresh seafood and Angus beef steaks are specialties. Bakery on premises provides fresh bread and desserts. **FYI:** Reservations recommended. Jazz. Children's menu. **Open:** Daily 8am–2am. **Prices:** Main courses $11–$17. AE, DC, DISC, MC, V. 👥 🚗 ♿

ATTRACTIONS 🏛

Nauticus, the National Maritime Center
1 Waterside Dr (Downtown); tel 757/664-1000 or toll free 800/664-1080. A high-tech, interactive museum combining educational content with entertainment. The 160,000-square-foot facility features nautical themes including shipbuilding, the US Navy, maritime commerce, and the marine environment.

Major exhibits include **Virtual Adventure,** a simulated submarine ride where participants must cooperate in order to complete their assigned mission; **Aegis Theater,** a multimedia naval battle simulation; the **Nauticus Theater,** with a screen that rolls back to reveal a huge picture window overlooking one of America's largest and busiest natural harbors; the **Maritime Theater,** with a video presentation on the past and future of the shipbuilding industry; and the **Marine Exploratorium,** a roomful of large, colorful interactives for children, including a real ship's bridge, periscopes, and a giant wave tank.

A large area is devoted to marine biology and environmental science, where visitors can study all kinds of sea creatures and observe scientists working in marine biology and oceanographic labs right on the exhibit floor. Exhibits in this area include Touchpool, Shark Encounter, Underwater Archeology, Charting, and Earth Monitoring.

The second level of the facility houses the **Hampton Roads Naval Museum.** The collection is especially strong in naval artwork, ship models, and underwater artifacts. Guided tours are given by staff volunteers, many of whom are retired US Navy personnel.

Nauticus also includes a 600-foot pier where US Navy, foreign, and commercial vessels are available for tours. The pier is also the location for spectacular laser shows with music and fireworks (nightly in summer). Restaurant; gift shop. **Open:** Peak (Mem Day–Labor Day) daily 10am–7pm. Reduced hours off-season. **$$$$**

Norfolk Naval Base Tour

9079 Hampton Blvd; tel 757/444-7955. Norfolk has the world's largest naval installation, and visitors can take a guided bus tour of the base, enhanced by informed commentary by Navy personnel. Sights include aircraft and aircraft carriers, submarines, and training centers. The bus passes Admiral's Row, a strip of Colonial Revival houses built at the turn of the century for the Jamestown Exposition. On weekends from 1 to 4:30pm there may be visits to selected ships in port (admission free). Tickets may be purchased at the TRT kiosk at Waterside, Nauticus (see above), or at the Naval Tour Office on Hampton Blvd. **Open:** Apr–Oct, daily 9am–2:30pm. **$$**

Chrysler Museum of Art

245 W Olney Rd; tel 757/664-6200. Walter P Chrysler Jr began to collect art at the age of 13, with the purchase of a small landscape by Renoir. Today, his magnificent collection spans artistic periods from ancient Egypt to the present. A 3,500-print photography collection includes works by Ansel Adams, W Eugene Smith, and others. The 10,000-piece glass collection, one of the finest and most comprehensive in the world, includes 200 Tiffany pieces. Adjoining is an outstanding collection of art nouveau furniture. Other first-floor galleries exhibit ancient Indian, Islamic, Oriental, African, and pre-Columbian art. Most second-floor galleries are devoted to European and American painting and sculpture. **Open:** Tues–Sat 10am–4pm, Sun 1–5pm. **$**

Douglas MacArthur Memorial

MacArthur Sq; tel 757/441-2965. Located on MacArthur Square, between City Hall Ave and Plume St, at Bank St. The memorial is housed in Norfolk's recently renovated old city hall, an imposing domed structure with a columned front portico. Visitors view a film that uses news footage to document the major events of MacArthur's life. Eleven galleries are filled with memorabilia ranging from historic World War II surrender documents to the general's famous corncob pipe. **Open:** Mon–Sat 10am–5pm, Sun 11am–5pm. **Free**

Hunter House Victorian Museum

240 W Freemason St; tel 757/623-9814. Built in 1894 in the Richardsonian Romanesque style, this was the home of prominent Norfolk merchant and banker James Wilson Hunter and his family. Rich in architectural details, the house displays an extensive collection of Victorian furnishings and decorative art, including a Renaissance Revival bedchamber suite, a period children's nursery, and several stained-glass windows. An exhibit of early 20th-century medical equipment, including an electrocardiograph machine, belonged to the late Dr James Wilson Hunter Jr. Guided tours offered every half-hour. **Open:** Apr–Dec, Wed–Sat 10am–3:30 pm, Sun noon–3:30pm. **$**

Moses Myers House

331 Bank St; tel 757/664-6200. This handsome, early Federal brick town house set in a pretty garden was home to five generations of the Myerses from 1792 to 1930. The furnishings, most of them original, provide a unique glimpse into the lives of Jewish immigrants in 18th-century America. **Open:** Apr–Dec, Tues–Sat 10am–5pm, Sun noon–5pm. **$**

Norfolk Botanical Gardens

Azalea Garden Rd; tel 757/441-5830. Immediately adjacent to Norfolk International Airport, this botanical garden encompasses 155 acres and features 12 miles of pathways. From early April to mid-June the grounds are brilliantly abloom with azaleas, roses, rhododendrons, and wildflowers. The Statuary Vista is a beautiful setting for Moses Ezekiel's heroic-size statues (originally intended for the Corcoran Gallery in Washington) of great painters and sculptors— Rembrandt, Reubens, Dürer, and da Vinci, among others. Notable, too, are the medicinal-herb garden and Italian Renaissance Garden. Guided trackless train and boat tours are available during the summer (additional fee charged). Educational programs, gift shop, cafe. **Open:** Peak (mid-Apr–mid-Oct) daily 9am–7pm. Reduced hours off-season. **$**

Carrie B

The Waterside; tel 757/393-4735. The *Carrie B,* a reproduction of a 19th-century Mississippi riverboat, offers daytime and sunset cruises of Norfolk's harbor from the Waterside. Depending on the tour, visitors can see the shipyard, with nuclear subs and aircraft carriers, the naval base, or the site of the Civil War battle between the *Monitor* and the *Merrimac.* A 2½-hour sunset cruise is offered in the summer. **Open:** Call for schedule. **$$$$**

Orange

Northern Virginia city on the Robinson River. Site of James Madison's home, Montpelier. Seat of Orange County. **Information:** Orange County Chamber of Commerce, 13323 James Madison Hwy, PO Box 146, Orange, 22960 (tel 540/ 672-5216).

INN 🏨

≣≣ The Hidden Inn

249 Caroline St at jct US 15/VA 20, 22960; tel 540/672-3625 or toll free 800/841-1253; fax 540/672-5029. 7 acres. This attractive restored Victorian home surrounded by huge trees is now a bed-and-breakfast. Close to a major intersection for easy accessibility, and a short drive to restaurants and historic sites. Children are not encouraged in the main house, but an adjacent building accommodates families. Unsuitable for children under 12. **Rooms:** 10 rms. CI 3pm/CO noon. Each room individually decorated. Some have old-fashioned wardrobes in lieu of closets. Separate honeymoon cottage with whirlpool. **Amenities:** 🛁 A/C, cable TV. No phone. Some units w/terraces, some w/fireplaces, some w/whirlpools. **Services:** Afternoon tea served. Full country breakfast. Candlelight picnic for two served in room on a large outside porch. **Facilities:** Guest lounge w/TV. **Rates (BB):** $59 S; $99–$159 D. Extra person $20. Min stay wknds. Parking: Outdoor, free. Closed Dec 24–25. AE, MC, V.

ATTRACTIONS 🏛

Montpelier

VA 20, Montpelier Station; tel 540/672-2728. Located 4 mi SW of Orange on VA 20 S. From 1723 to 1844, the 2,700-acre estate overlooking the Blue Ridge Mountains was home to three generations of the Madison family.

Born in 1751, James Madison rose to prominence early in life. At the 1776 Constitutional Convention in Williamsburg, he made sure that the guarantee of religious freedom was included in the Virginia Declaration of Rights. Later, as a member of the federal Constitutional Convention, he worked for passage of the Bill of Rights and for the creation of the executive departments, efforts that earned him the title "Father of the Constitution." After four terms in Congress, Madison became secretary of state under Jefferson and in 1809 succeeded Jefferson as president, leading the new nation during the War of 1812. Madison's final years were taken up with the University of Virginia, where he served as rector.

The estate changed hands many times between 1844 and 1901, when it was acquired by William du Pont Sr. His daughter added the steeplechase course and initiated the **Montpelier Hunt Races,** which are still held here every November. The National Trust acquired the property after her death in 1984 and the home was opened to the public in 1987.

Restoration efforts seek to compromise between the Madison and du Pont eras; the Madison rooms will be presented as they were in the 18th century, while the du Pont rooms will reflect their 20th-century appearance. As work progresses on the sparsely furnished 55-room house, exhibits document its transformation. While it is already an interesting tour, much more research and restoration work will be needed before Montpelier takes its place alongside similar Virginia attractions. **Open:** Daily 10am–4pm. **$$$**

James Madison Museum

129 Caroline St; tel 540/672-1776. Dedicated to the fourth president of the United States, this museum contains exhibits dealing with Madison's life and times. Madison artifacts in the main exhibit include presidential correspondence, fashions associated with his wife, Dolley, books from his personal library, and other personal items. Special exhibits are presented on a regular basis. Tours may be arranged by calling in advance. **Open:** Peak (Mar–Nov) Mon–Fri 9am–4pm, Sat–Sun 1–4pm. Reduced hours off-season. **$$**

Petersburg

See also Hopewell, South Hill

Founded as a trading post in 1645, Petersburg soon became a strategic center of commerce, trade, and transportation. Today, it is a popular tourist destination, with a quaint Old Towne commercial district. **Information:** Hopewell Area–Prince George County Chamber of Commerce, 108 N Main St, PO Drawer 1297, Hopewell, 23860 (tel 804/458-5536).

HOTEL 🏨

≣≣≣ Petersburg Ramada

380 E Washington St, 23803; tel 804/733-0000 or toll free 800/473-0005; fax 804/733-3927. Exit 50D off I-95 N; exit 52 off I-95 S. Conscientiously staffed hotel with nicely decorated lobby. Convenient to attractions, sights, golf course. **Rooms:** 200 rms and stes. Executive level. CI 3pm/CO noon. Nonsmoking rms avail. Although simple and not new, rooms are clean and comfortable. Doors secured with access cards instead of keys. **Amenities:** 🛁 A/C, satel TV w/movies, refrig. Not all rooms have remote-controlled TVs. **Services:** ✕ 🚐 ⏁ ⏁ **Facilities:** 🏊 500 ♿ 1 restaurant, 1 bar (w/entertainment), washer/dryer. Outdoor pool is on second floor. Lounge has dancing on weekends. Small kitchen off lobby equipped with microwave, dining tables, refreshments. **Rates (CP):** $49–$90 S or D; $75–$95 ste. Extra person $5. Children under age 18 stay free. Parking: Indoor/outdoor, free. AE, CB, DC, DISC, MC, V.

MOTELS

≣≣≣ Best Western Petersburg

405 E Washington St, 23803; tel 804/733-1776 or toll free 800/528-1234; fax 804/861-6339. Exit 50D off I-95 N; exit 52 off I-95 S. A clean, comfortable motel near historic attractions. **Rooms:** 124 rms. CI 2pm/CO noon. Nonsmoking rms avail. **Amenities:** 🛁 A/C, cable TV w/movies, refrig. Some units w/whirlpools. **Services:** ✕ 🚐 ⏁ ⏁ Complimentary coffee. **Facilities:** 🏊 200 ♿ 1 restaurant, games rm,

washer/dryer. Guests can use YMCA. **Rates (CP):** $40–$55 S or D. Extra person $5. Children under age 12 stay free. Parking: Outdoor, free. AE, DC, DISC, ER, JCB, MC, V.

≣≣ Days Inn

12208 S Crater Rd, 23805; tel 804/733-4400 or toll free 800/325-2525; fax 804/861-9559. Exit 45 off I-95. A comfortable motel conveniently located near historic sites, plantations. **Rooms:** 154 rms. CI 2pm/CO 11am. Nonsmoking rms avail. Attractive and comfortable rooms. **Amenities:** 🛎 ⚲ A/C, cable TV, refrig. **Services:** ⬑ ⬸ Complimentary coffee in lobby. Free transportation to Fort Lee. **Facilities:** 🖼 ৳⌇ 🔲 ৬ 1 restaurant, whirlpool, playground, washer/dryer. Pleasantly landscaped and well-maintained pool area. **Rates:** Peak (June–Sept) $45–$50 S; $49–$55 D; $65–$75 effic. Children under age 18 stay free. Lower rates off-season. Parking: Outdoor, free. AE, CB, DC, DISC, EC, JCB, MC, V.

RESTAURANT 🍴

King's on Washington

3221 W Washington Rd; tel 804/732-5861. **Barbecue/Seafood.** A traditional southern-style barbecue house, this simply decorated establishment with booths and tables is widely known in these parts for its big brick fireplace in which pork and beef constantly smoke to perfection over hickory coals. Carvers stand at end of long counter and wield cleavers to slice or mince the barbecue to patrons' desires. Crispy fried chicken and homemade apple pie are other pleasers. A local favorite since 1946. Carryout available. **FYI:** Reservations accepted. Children's menu. No liquor license. **Open:** Tues–Sun 7am–9pm. **Prices:** Main courses $5–$14. MC, V.

ATTRACTIONS 💼

OLD TOWNE PETERSBURG

Petersburg Visitor's Center

425 Cockade Alley (at Old St); tel 804/733-2400 or toll free 800/368-3595. Petersburg has played an important role as a strategic center of commerce, trade, and transportation since before the Revolution. Residents—including one of the largest free black populations of any American city—enjoyed a comfortable lifestyle here typical of any industrialized city in the South. After a devastating fire destroyed the old town in the summer of 1815, a brick commercial district rose in its place. It quickly became a major crossroads for boats trading ships on the Appomattox River, and a major railroad center.

Explorations of Old Towne should begin at the **Visitors Center (McIlwaine House),** built in 1815 by Mayor George Jones. Tour guides are on hand to provide information, help plan itineraries, and secure reservations. A "Petersburg Pass" is available here that provides admission to the Siege Museum, Old Blandford Church, the Farmers Bank, Trapezium House, and Centre Hill Mansion (see below). **Open:** Daily 9am–5pm.

Old Blandford Church

321 S Crater Rd; tel 804/733-2396. Built in 1735, this church has become a memorial to Southern soldiers who perished in the Civil War. There are 15 magnificent stained-glass windows designed by Louis Comfort Tiffany, each contributed by a southern state. About 30,000 Confederate soldiers are buried in Blandford Cemetery, where the first Memorial Day was observed in June 1866. **Open:** Daily 10am–5pm. $

Farmers Bank

Tel 804/733-2400. Tours of this building begin at the Visitors Center (see above). Built in 1817, the Petersburg Branch of the Farmers Bank of Virginia included living space on the upper floors for the cashier and his family. The original safe and vault are still here, and there is an authentic printing press of the type used when Confederate banks were allowed to print their own currency. $$

Siege Museum

15 W Bank St; tel 804/733-2404. The story of how the citizens of Petersburg endured the 10-month siege of their town is preserved in this museum. Lavish lifestyles in the years preceding the Civil War gave way to a bitter struggle for survival in the last days of the Confederacy. The museum is located in the Exchange Building, built in 1839 as a commodities market. **Open:** Daily 10am–5pm. $

Trapezium House

244 N Market St; tel 804/733-2402. Tours begin at the Siege Museum (see above). Built by Charles O'Hara in 1817, this house was built without parallel walls or right angles because, as legend has it, O'Hara's West Indian slave told him that such a house could not harbor evil spirits. **Open:** Apr–Oct, daily. Call for hours. $

Centre Hill Mansion

Center Hill Court; tel 804/733-2401. A showcase of Southern living and style, Centre Hill Mansion was built in 1823 in the federal style by the prominent Bolling family. The interior was later remodeled in the Greek Revival style of the 1840s. Ornate woodwork and plaster motifs accent a collection of period furnishings, including an 1886 rosewood Knabe Art grand piano. **Open:** Daily 10am–5pm. $

OTHER ATTRACTIONS

Petersburg National Battlefield Park

VA 36; tel 804/732-3531. The last major campaign of the Civil War in Virginia took place around this quiet town along the Appomattox River. The visitor center offers a museum as well as a map presentation relating the story of the siege of Petersburg, which lasted from June 1864 to April 1865.

The park encompasses some 2,700 acres. The main four-mile battlefield driving tour has wayside exhibits and audio stations; some stops have short walking tours. Most fascinating is the site of the Crater, a huge man-made depression in the ground. It was formed when a group of Pennsylvania militia, including many miners, dug a passage beneath Confederate lines and exploded 4 tons of powder, creating the 170-by-60-foot crater. An extended driving tour follows the entire 16-mile siege line.

Grant relentlessly kept up his attempts to capture the city, although the cost in men was brutal. Finally, on April 2, 1865, Grant's all-out assault smashed through Lee's right flank, and that night Lee evacuated Petersburg. One week later came the surrender at Appomattox Court House. The **Five Forks Unit,** located about six miles southwest, preserves the site where Union forces finally broke the Confederate line. **Open:** Daily 8am–sunset. **$$**

Portsmouth

Located on the Elizabeth River opposite Norfolk, Portsmouth is an important commercial and industrial center. Its historic 17th-century downtown area draws visitors. **Information:** Hampton Roads Chamber of Commerce–Portsmouth, 524 Middle St, PO Box 70, Portsmouth, 23705 (tel 757/397-3453).

MOTEL 🏨

≣≣≣ Holiday Inn Olde Towne Waterfront
8 Crawford Pkwy, at Green St, 23704; tel 757/393-2573 or toll free 800/HOLIDAY; fax 757/399-1248. 1 mi from downtown Norfolk. Located on the Elizabeth River, motel is popular with military and tour guests. **Rooms:** 232 rms and stes. CI 4pm/CO noon. Nonsmoking rms avail. Rooms with water views face either the adjacent marina or the river, which bustles with tugboats, military vessels, yachts. **Amenities:** 🛁 📺 A/C, cable TV w/movies. Water-view rooms have refrigerators. **Services:** ✕ 🖼 🧺 🛎 Public fax in lobby. **Facilities:** 🏋 🚵 🏊 ⬜ Ᏸ 1 restaurant, 1 bar (w/entertainment), washer/dryer. Guests can use tennis courts at adjacent apartment complex. **Rates:** $82–$86 S; $86–$89 D; $175 ste. Extra person $6. Children under age 19 stay free. Min stay special events. Parking: Indoor/outdoor, free. Discounts for patrons of adjacent marina. AE, CB, DC, DISC, MC, V.

RESTAURANT 🍽

The Max
425 Water St; tel 757/397-0176. **New American/Seafood/Steak.** On the downtown Portsmouth waterfront, this large restaurant looks across harbor to Norfolk. Open and cheerful atmosphere created by colorful vinyl tablecloths, pastel napkins, deep-rose woodwork, and contemporary gray chairs. A favorite: chunks of shrimp and scallops in lobster sauce served over rice. Fresh daily catch can be ordered several ways. Beef and pasta dishes also available. **FYI:** Reservations recommended. Children's menu. Dress code. **Open:** Mon–Thurs 11:30am–10pm, Fri 11:30am–11pm, Sat 5–10pm, Sun noon–9pm. **Prices:** Main courses $8–$17. AE, DISC, MC, V. 🏔 Ᏸ

ATTRACTIONS 🏛

THE PORTSMOUTH MUSEUMS

Naval Shipyard Museum
2 High St; tel 757/393-8591. Established in 1949, this museum contains many artifacts, ship models, and other items relating to the seafaring history of this area from the time of its first settlement. Highlights include scale models of the Confederate ironclad CSS *Virginia* and other historic vessels associated with the port at Hampton Roads. **Open:** Tues–Sat 10am–5pm, Sun 1–5pm. **$**

Lightship Museum
London Slip; tel 757/393-8591 or 393-8741. Lighted beacons that helped mariners avoid dangerous shoals and enter safely into harbors at night were not all atop lighthouses. Years ago, lights were fixed to the tall masts of ships that anchored for months at a time in strategic locations off the coastline. Commissioned in 1916, *Lightship 101,* after 48 years of service in the Coast Guard, was donated to the city of Portsmouth in 1964 and permanently moored at the foot of Loudon Blvd. Now restored to its original condition, the ship serves as a floating museum illustrating the living and working conditions of those who served aboard the lightships during their many months at sea. **Open:** Tues–Sat 10am–5pm, Sun 1–5pm. **$**

1846 Courthouse
420 High St; tel 757/393-8983. Home of three local arts organizations. The **Fine Arts Gallery,** which houses changing art exhibitions, is undergoing an expansion that will involve all three levels of the building. The **Children's Museum,** formerly on the first floor, is being moved to a new building ½ block away in the Middle Street Mall. The adjoining **Community Arts Center** houses classrooms and laboratories, as well as galleries with permanent and changing exhibits. **Open:** Tues–Sat 10am–5pm, Sun 1–5pm. **$**

Children's Museum
421 High St; tel 757/393-8983. Recently reopened in a new dedicated museum space, this hands-on museum especially for children features 14 exhibit galleries and a planetarium. **Open:** Tues–Fri 10am–5pm, Sat 10am–9pm, Sun 1–5pm. **$$**

OTHER ATTRACTIONS

Hill House
221 North St; tel 757/393-0241. Built in the early 1800s, this four-story dwelling now serves as the headquarters of the Portsmouth Historical Association. The house contains the original furnishings collected by generations of the Hill family over 150 years. It remains in original condition after only limited renovation over the years. **Open:** Wed 12:30–5pm, Sat–Sun 1–5pm. **$**

Radford

Located on the New River, in the Blue Ridge Highlands. Site of Radford University and Claytor Lake State Park. **Information:** Radford Chamber of Commerce, 1126 Norwood St, Radford, 24141 (tel 540/639-2202).

MOTELS 🏨

≡≡≡ Best Western Radford Inn
1501 Tyler Ave, PO Box 1008, 24141; tel 540/639-3000 or toll free 800/628-1955; fax 540/639-3000. Exit 109 off I-81. This large property in Williamsburg is in a rural setting. Large stone fireplace in lobby. Close to the university and downtown. **Rooms:** 72 rms. CI 3pm/CO noon. Nonsmoking rms avail. Very clean and spacious rooms, many with a view of pool and countryside. **Amenities:** 🛏 🥤 A/C, cable TV w/movies. **Services:** ✕ 🖼 ⇪ ⬦ **Facilities:** 🛗 ⬛ ⛐ 1 restaurant, 1 bar (w/entertainment), games rm, sauna, whirlpool. **Rates:** $67–$72 S or D. Extra person $6. Children under age 12 stay free. Min stay special events. Parking: Outdoor, free. AE, CB, DC, DISC, MC, V.

≡≡ Comfort Inn
1501 Tyler Ave, PO Box 1008, 24141; tel 540/639-4800 or toll free 800/221-2222. Exit 109 off I-81. Although in town, this property sits well enough back on rural land to give a country feel. **Rooms:** 32 rms and stes. CI 3pm/CO noon. No smoking. Exceptionally well-furnished rooms. **Amenities:** 🛏 🔲 🥤 A/C, cable TV w/movies. 1 unit w/whirlpool. **Services:** ✕ 🖼 ⇪ ⬦ **Facilities:** ⛐ Games rm. Guests have pool privileges at Best Western Radford Inn next door. **Rates:** $62–$64 S; $67–$69 D; $135 ste. Extra person $5. Children under age 18 stay free. Min stay special events. Parking: Outdoor, free. AE, DC, DISC, MC, V.

≡≡ Dogwood Lodge
7073 Lee Hwy, 24141; tel 540/639-9338. Exit 98 off I-81 N; exit 109 off I-81 S. Quiet, grassy setting high on a hill, back from the highway, and almost out of town. **Rooms:** 15 rms. CI noon/CO 11am. Each unit is individually decorated. **Amenities:** 🛏 A/C, cable TV. All units w/terraces. **Services:** 🖼 ⇪ ⬦ **Facilities:** Picnic tables on lawn. **Rates:** $25 S; $32–$34 D. Extra person $5. Children under age 12 stay free. Min stay special events. Parking: Outdoor, free. DISC, MC, V.

ATTRACTION 🏛

Claytor Lake State Park
Richmond; tel 540/674-5492. Located on VA 660, just off I-81 exit 101. Wooded hills and a 4,500-acre lake provide the setting for fishing, swimming, boating, camping, and hiking. Sport fishing is especially popular. The historic Howe House features exhibits on the life of early settlers in the region. **Open:** Daily, call for hours. **$**

Reedville

The small village of Reedville, located on Cockrell's Creek, an inlet of Chesapeake Bay, provides a living image of the past with its Victorian mansions and seafaring atmosphere.

ATTRACTION 🏛

Fisherman's Museum
Main St; tel 804/453-6529. The museum consists of two buildings: the Walker House (circa 1875) is a restored fisherman's home, while the Covington Building contains two galleries of fishing artifacts and artwork. **Open:** Peak (May–Oct) daily 10:30am–4:30pm. Reduced hours off-season. **Free**

Reston

See also Dulles Int'l Airport

HOTELS 🏨

≡≡≡≡ Hyatt Regency Reston
1800 Presidents St, 22090; tel 703/709-1234 or toll free 800/233-1234; fax 703/709-2291. Exit 12 to Reston Pkwy off Dulles Access Rd. Reminiscent of the grand hotels of another era, this Hyatt offers luxurious seclusion from the bustle of the town center. Guests enter through a massive lobby of marble and polished wood. A subdued parlor and a bright atrium are just off the main lobby. **Rooms:** 514 rms and stes. Executive level. CI 3pm/CO noon. Nonsmoking rms avail. Well-integrated, restful decor with paintings and homey, traditional furnishings. Some have two bathrooms, large plants, and unique lighting fixtures. Suites have conference tables and kitchen areas. **Amenities:** 🛏 🔲 🥤 A/C, cable TV w/movies, dataport, voice mail. Some units w/whirlpools. Refrigerators and VCRs available. **Services:** ✕ 🔑 🅥🅟 🚗 🖼 ⇪ Car-rental desk, masseur, babysitting. **Facilities:** 🛗 🎾 ⬛ 🖥 ⛐ 2 restaurants, 2 bars (1 w/entertainment), spa, sauna, whirlpool. State-of-the-art health club equipment. Atrium has a small but inviting indoor pool and a large whirlpool. Biking, hiking, and tennis nearby. **Rates:** $179 S; $204 D; $350–$500 ste. Extra person $25. Parking: Indoor/outdoor, free. Weekend packages avail. AE, CB, DC, DISC, EC, ER, JCB, MC, V.

≡≡≡ Sheraton Reston Hotel
11810 Sunrise Valley Dr, 22091; tel 703/620-9000 or toll free 800/392-7666; fax 703/860-1594. Exit 3 off Dulles Toll Rd. Follow Reston Pkwy (VA 602) south to Sunrise Valley Dr, turn left. Situated in an attractive office-park setting on the outskirts of the planned community of Reston, this modern hotel wraps around a landscaped, resort-like courtyard with kidney-shaped swimming pool and large sun deck. **Rooms:** 302 rms and stes. Executive level. CI 3pm/CO 1pm. No smoking. Comfortable rooms are decorated in light color schemes. Some are in a tower, others in low-rise building

forming semicircle around courtyard. **Amenities:** 🛅 👗 🖵 A/C, cable TV w/movies, refrig. Some units w/minibars. VCRs available. **Services:** 🍽 🚐 ⚟ ⌇ Children's program, babysitting. Free shuttle to shopping and restaurants. **Facilities:** ⛳ 🏌 🎾 🖵 👗 1 restaurant, 1 bar (w/entertainment), spa, sauna, whirlpool, playground. Reston Golf Course across the street. **Rates (CP):** Peak (Mar–June/Sept–Nov) $99–$102 S; $109–$112 D; $175 ste. Extra person $10. Children under age 18 stay free. Lower rates off-season. Parking: Outdoor, free. Weekend packages avail. AE, CB, DC, DISC, MC, V.

Richmond

See also Ashland, Midlothian

In the heart of central Virginia at the head of the James River is Virginia's capital and largest city, once the capital of the short-lived Confederate States of America. The area abounds with antebellum homes and estates and is a mecca for commerce, trade, and cultural activities. **Information:** Metro Richmond Convention and Visitors Bureau, 550 E Marshall, Box C250, Richmond, 23219 (tel 804/782-2777).

PUBLIC TRANSPORTATION

The **Greater Richmond Transit Company** (tel 804/358-GRTC) operates a system of public buses. Base fare is $1.25, and most routes are in service from 5am to midnight.

HOTELS 🛏

📭📭📭 The Berkeley Hotel

1200 E Cary St, 23219 (Shockoe Slip); tel 804/780-1300; fax 804/343-1885. Exit 74A off I-95 N, or exit 79 off I-95 S. In the historic Shockoe Slip district and surrounded by restaurants, shops, and attractions, this fine hotel boasts superior-quality furnishings and an inviting and elegant ambience. Most guests are repeat business travelers. **Rooms:** 55 rms. CI 2pm/CO noon. Nonsmoking rms avail. Standard rooms have two double beds. Executive units have king bed. **Amenities:** 🛅 👗 🖵 A/C, cable TV. Some units w/terraces, 1 w/whirlpool. Executive units equipped with bottled water. **Services:** ✕ 🗝 🚐 ⚟ ⌇ Twice-daily maid svce, masseur. Downtown shuttle van. European-style turndown service. **Facilities:** 🍸 🖵 👗 1 restaurant. Restaurant is acclaimed. Free use of major private health club nearby. **Rates:** $135–$175 S or D. Extra person $15. Children under age 16 stay free. Parking: Indoor, free. AE, CB, DC, DISC, MC, V.

📭📭📭📭 Commonwealth Park Suites Hotel

9th and Bank Sts, PO Box 455, 23203; tel 804/343-7300; fax 804/343-1025. A European-style luxury hotel across from the state capitol and within walking distance of downtown shops and restaurants. **Rooms:** 59 stes. CI 3pm/CO noon. Nonsmoking rms avail. Luxurious suites with dark wood furniture, lovely sitting rooms, marble baths. Some have two bedrooms. **Amenities:** 🛅 👗 A/C, TV w/movies, refrig. All

units w/minibars. **Services:** 🍽 🚐 ⚟ ⌇ ⌇ Twice-daily maid svce, masseur, babysitting. Emphasis on high-quality service. **Facilities:** 🍸 👗 2 restaurants, spa, sauna, whirlpool. Restaurants consist of casual breakfast/lunch facility and formal dining room serving dinner. **Rates:** Peak (Sept–May) $125–$145 ste. Children under age 18 stay free. Lower rates off-season. Parking: Indoor, $10/day. Weekend rates avail. AE, CB, DC, DISC, MC, V.

📭📭 Courtyard by Marriott

6400 W Broad St, 23229; tel 804/282-1881 or toll free 800/321-2211; fax 804/288-2934. Exit 183B off I-64. Follow Broad St for ¼ mi. A beige complex built around a landscaped courtyard with outdoor swimming pool. Primarily caters to businesspeople, but perfectly adequate for families and other travelers. **Rooms:** 145 rms and stes. CI 4pm/CO noon. Nonsmoking rms avail. Rooms have pluses for business travelers, such as desks. **Amenities:** 🛅 👗 A/C, satel TV, refrig, voice mail. Some units w/terraces. Long phone cords, hot-water taps for tea and coffee. Irons and ironing boards. **Services:** ⌇ Dinner delivery from nearby restaurants. **Facilities:** 🍸 🏊 👗 1 restaurant (bkfst only), whirlpool, washer/dryer. Honor bar in lobby during evenings. **Rates:** $84–$99 S or D; $84–$99 ste. Parking: Outdoor, free. AE, CB, DC, DISC, JCB, MC, V.

📭📭📭📭 The Jefferson Hotel

Franklin and Adams Sts, 23220 (Downtown); tel 804/788-8000 or toll free 800/424-8014; fax 804/344-5162. Exit 76B off I-95. Go south on US 1/301 to Franklin St, turn left. Originally built in 1895 and completely renovated during the 1980s at a cost of $34 million, the Jefferson is Richmond's premier hotel. A downtown landmark, the beaux arts brick building is a stunning blend of Renaissance and other architectural styles popular at the turn of the century. Inside, a statue of Thomas Jefferson stands under the Palm Court's circular, 70-foot-wide skylight. The colonnaded lobby sports a magnificent polished marble staircase strongly reminiscent of the one Rhett Butler carried Scarlett O'Hara up in *Gone with the Wind*. **Rooms:** 275 rms and stes. CI 3pm/CO noon. Nonsmoking rms avail. Rooms are decorated in 57 different luxurious styles. **Amenities:** 🛅 👗 🍵 A/C, cable TV w/movies, voice mail, bathrobes. All units w/minibars, some w/terraces, some w/whirlpools. **Services:** 🍽 🗝 ⚟ 🚐 ⚟ ⌇ Twice-daily maid svce, masseur. **Facilities:** 🏊 🎉 2 restaurants, 1 bar, spa, beauty salon. Lemaire, a full-service gourmet restaurant, is named for Jefferson's White House maitre d'hôtel. TJ's Restaurant and Bar offers casual dining. The private library has a solid African mahogany fireplace and some of the hotel's original book collection. Free use of YMCA across the street. **Rates:** Peak (Mar–June/Sept–Nov 15) $145–$185 S; $165–$205 D; $245 ste. Extra person $15. Children under age 16 stay free. Lower rates off-season. Parking: Outdoor, $10–$11/day. Romance and other packages avail. AE, DC, DISC, MC, V.

🛏🛏🛏 **Omni Richmond Hotel**

100 S 12th St, at Cary St, 23219 (Shockoe Slip); tel 804/344-7000 or toll free 800/THE-OMNI; fax 804/648-1029. Exit 75A off I-95. Although showing some wear and tear, this busy hotel enjoys a convenient downtown location. **Rooms:** 363 rms and stes. Executive level. CI 3pm/CO 1pm. Nonsmoking rms avail. **Amenities:** 🕾 ⚲ 🍷 A/C, cable TV w/movies, CD/tape player, voice mail, bathrobes. All units w/minibars. **Services:** ✗ 🗝 VP 🖼 ↺ Twice-daily maid svce, car-rental desk, babysitting. **Facilities:** 🔂 800 💻 2 restaurants (*see* "Restaurants" below), 2 bars, day-care ctr. **Rates:** $125–$165 S; $139–$175 D; $210 ste. Extra person $15. Children under age 18 stay free. Parking: Indoor, $8/day. AE, CB, DC, DISC, MC, V.

🛏🛏🛏 **Richmond Marriott**

500 E Broad St, 23219 (Downtown); tel 804/643-3400 or toll free 800/228-9290; fax 804/788-1230. Exit 74C off I-95. Go straight 9½ blocks on Broad St to hotel. One of Richmond's largest hotels, with many facilities and amenities. Popular with families and conventioneers. **Rooms:** 401 rms and stes. Executive level. CI 4pm/CO noon. Nonsmoking rms avail. **Amenities:** 🕾 ⚲ A/C, cable TV w/movies, voice mail. Executive suites have bathrobes. Phones in club-level rooms have view screens. Irons and ironing boards. **Services:** ✗ 🗝 VP 🚐 ↺ Twice-daily maid svce. Club level has well-appointed concierge lounge. **Facilities:** 🔂 🛢 1700 💻 ⅃ 1 restaurant, 1 bar, games rm, spa, sauna, steam rm, whirlpool, washer/dryer. Pool is small but extremely well kept. **Rates:** $109–$119 S or D; $200–$500 ste. Children under age 15 stay free. Parking: Indoor/outdoor, $7/day. AE, CB, DC, DISC, MC, V.

MOTELS

🛏🛏🛏 **Best Western Governor's Inn**

9826 Midlothian Tpk, 23235; tel 804/323-0007 or toll free 800/528-1234; fax 804/272-0759. Exit I-95 at Midlothian Tpk W. Resembling a palace or castle, this motel is adjacent to shopping, restaurants, businesses. **Rooms:** 83 rms and stes. Executive level. CI 3pm/CO noon. Nonsmoking rms avail. Spacious rooms. **Amenities:** 🕾 ⚲ A/C, cable TV, in-rm safe. Some units w/whirlpools. 25-inch TVs. **Services:** ✗ ↺ **Facilities:** ⅃ 1 restaurant (dinner only), 1 bar. **Rates (CP):** Peak (June–Sept) $44–$61 S; $49–$66 D; $65–$110 ste. Extra person $5. Children under age 16 stay free. Lower rates off-season. Parking: Outdoor, free. AE, CB, DC, DISC, MC, V.

🛏🛏 **Comfort Inn Executive Center**

7201 W Broad St, 23294; tel 804/672-1108 or toll free 800/228-5150; fax 804/755-1625. Exit 183C off I-64. Just outside downtown Richmond, this establishment consists of three buildings with elegant, warmly decorated lobby. **Rooms:** 123 rms. CI 2pm/CO 11am. Nonsmoking rms avail. Furnishings are attractive, of better quality than at some Comfort Inns. **Amenities:** 🕾 A/C, cable TV. **Services:** 🖼 ↺ Complimentary newspaper. Deluxe continental breakfast and refreshments, including fresh fruits, in lobby. **Facilities:** 🔂 20 ⅃ Sauna, whirlpool, washer/dryer. **Rates (CP):** $72 S or D. Extra person $6. Children under age 18 stay free. Parking: Outdoor, free. AE, DC, DISC, MC, V.

🛏🛏 **Comfort Inn Midtown Conference Center**

3200 W Broad St, 23230; tel 804/359-4061 or toll free 800/228-5150; fax 804/359-3189. Exit 78 off I-95. Recent renovation spiffed up this comfortable hotel west of downtown Richmond, convenient to sights and attractions. **Rooms:** 190 rms and stes. CI 2pm/CO noon. Nonsmoking rms avail. Attractively furnished. **Amenities:** 🕾 A/C, cable TV w/movies. Some units w/minibars. Suites have microwaves, wet bars, refrigerators. **Services:** ↺ ↻ Twice-daily maid svce. Complimentary newspapers. Free local calls. **Facilities:** 🔂 450 💻 ⅃ Washer/dryer. **Rates (CP):** $54–$59 S or D; $125 ste. Extra person $5. Children under age 18 stay free. Parking: Indoor, free. AE, CB, DC, DISC, JCB, MC, V.

🛏🛏 **Days Inn North**

1600 Robin Hood Rd, 23220 (Northside); tel 804/353-1287 or toll free 800/325-2525; fax 804/355-2659. Exit 78 off I-95. Conveniently located near the tourist information office and the Diamond baseball stadium. **Rooms:** 99 rms. CI 3pm/CO noon. Nonsmoking rms avail. Units are not impressively decorated. **Amenities:** 🕾 A/C, cable TV, in-rm safe. **Services:** ↺ ↻ **Facilities:** 🔂 100 1 restaurant. **Rates:** $51 S; $55 D. Extra person $5. Children under age 14 stay free. Parking: Outdoor, free. AE, DC, DISC, MC, V.

🛏🛏🛏 **Holiday Inn Koger Center South**

1021 Koger Center Blvd, 23235; tel 804/379-3800 or toll free 800/465-4329; fax 804/379-2763. Exit I-95 at Midlothian Turnpike; drive west 2 miles, turn right. Surrounded by businesses, shops, restaurants. Attractive lobby has marble floors, fountains, landscaped atrium. **Rooms:** 200 rms and stes. CI 3pm/CO 11am. Nonsmoking rms avail. Spacious rooms and baths. **Amenities:** 🕾 🖵 A/C, cable TV. Some units w/minibars, 1 w/whirlpool. **Services:** ✗ 🚐 🖼 ↺ Children's program. Outstanding staff. **Facilities:** 🔂 🛢 750 ⅃ 1 restaurant, 1 bar (w/entertainment), washer/dryer. Mystery Cafe dinner theater on premises. Large pool and pretty restaurant. **Rates:** $84 S or D; $225 ste. Extra person $7. Children under age 18 stay free. Parking: Outdoor, free. AE, DC, DISC, MC, V.

🛏🛏 **Motel 6**

5704 Williamsburg Rd, Sandston, 23150 (Richmond Int'l Airport); tel 804/222-7600; fax 804/222-4153. Exit 197A off I-64. A basic motel across street from Virginia Aviation Museum, near Richmond International Raceway. **Rooms:** 120 rms. CI noon/CO noon. Nonsmoking rms avail. Rooms are clean and comfortable. **Amenities:** 🕾 A/C, cable TV. **Services:** ↺ ↻ Free coffee in lobby. **Facilities:** 🔂 ⅃ Several nearby restaurants offer discounts to guests. **Rates:** Peak

(May–Nov) $28–$34 S or D. Extra person $6. Children under age 17 stay free. Lower rates off-season. Parking: Outdoor, free. AE, DC, DISC, MC, V.

INN

☰☰☰☰ Linden Row Inn

101 N 1st St, 23219 (The Fan); tel 804/783-7000 or toll free 800/348-7424; fax 804/648-7504. Built in 1847, this inn has charm and character in abundance, plus a location convenient to historic landmarks, museums, and other attractions. The brick-walled garden is said to have been Edgar Allen Poe's inspiration for his "Enchanted Garden." **Rooms:** 71 rms and stes. CI 3pm/CO noon. Nonsmoking rms avail. Each room has authentic Victorian furnishings. Those facing the garden have more of a country flair than other units. **Amenities:** 🛏 ♨ A/C, cable TV. Some units w/fireplaces. **Services:** ⧄ 🆅🅿 🚗 ⬡ 🎵 Twice-daily maid svce, wine/sherry served. Free downtown transportation. Complimentary evening wine-and-cheese reception. Free use of nearby YMCA health club. **Facilities:** 🔲 🖥 ♿ 1 restaurant, 1 bar, guest lounge w/TV. **Rates (CP):** $84–$144 D; $114–$144 ste. Extra person $10. Children under age 18 stay free. Higher rates for special events/hols. Parking: Indoor, $3/day. AE, CB, DC, DISC, MC, V.

RESTAURANTS 🍴

Bill's Barbecue

3100 North Blvd; tel 804/358-8634. Exit 78 off I-95. **Barbecue.** Very plain, simple decor with a few live plants in this popular barbecue house with booths and cafe-style counter with stools. Minced smoked pork is the house specialty. Drive-through window serves carryout orders. Good place for country-style breakfasts. **FYI:** Reservations not accepted. No liquor license. **Open:** Peak (Apr–Nov) Mon–Sat 7am–11pm, Sun 10am–11pm. **Prices:** Main courses $5–$7. No CC. ♿

Coppola's Delicatessen

2900 W Cary St, at Colonial St (Carytown); tel 804/359-NYNY. **Deli/Italian.** Decor includes mirrors, Italian food products, prints, and maps of regions of Italy. Spaghetti's the specialty on an extensive menu of Italian deli fare: cheeses, sausages, olives, pickles, and antipasti. **FYI:** Reservations not accepted. Beer and wine only. No smoking. **Open:** Mon–Wed 10am–8pm, Thurs–Sat 10am–9pm. **Prices:** Main courses $5–$7. MC, V. ⬟

Gallego

In Omni Richmond Hotel, 100 S 12th St (Shockoe Slip); tel 804/344-7000. Exit 75A off I-95. **Seafood/Steak.** Atmosphere of old-fashioned men's club prevails at this premium steak house, thanks to lots of dark wood and overstuffed chairs. Dim lighting adds a romantic touch. New York strips and porterhouses head the list, plus veal, lamb, pork chops, grilled chicken, salmon, and swordfish. **FYI:** Reservations

accepted. Dress code. **Open:** Tues–Thurs 5–10pm, Fri–Sat 5–10:30pm. **Prices:** Main courses $19–$26. AE, DC, DISC, MC, V. ⬤ 🆅🅿 ♿

Grace Place Natural Food Restaurant and Store

826 W Grace St (The Fan); tel 804/353-3680. Between Schaeffer and Laurel Sts. **Vegetarian.** Decor is simple yet appealing and comfortable: antique wood tables, framed prints, wildflowers as table decorations. Vegetarian fare is the focus, including a variety of salads, homemade soups, and freshly baked desserts. Outdoor dining is encouraged when weather permits. **FYI:** Reservations accepted. Beer and wine only. No smoking. **Open:** Tues–Sat 11am–9pm. **Prices:** Main courses $9–$10. MC, V. ⬟

James River Wine Bistro

1520 W Main St, at Lombardy St (The Fan); tel 804/358-4562. **Californian/International.** Ceiling fans, paintings, statues, fountains, sideboards, plants, and mirrors create simple elegance throughout the three dining rooms, bar, and outdoor patio. Listed on National Register of Historic Places, building was built soon after the Civil War and was used as a high school from 1870 to 1970. Menu offers a mix of cuisines, from Italian to Thai to southwestern, with accent on items from the mesquite grill. **FYI:** Reservations recommended. **Open:** Tues–Sun 11:30am–12:30am. **Prices:** Main courses $3–$19. AE, DISC, MC, V. ⬤ ■ ⬟

★ Joe's Inn

205 N Shields Ave (The Fan); tel 804/355-2282. Between Grove and Hanover Sts. **Diner.** Casual hangout, with pictures of Miami Dolphins (owner's favorite NFL team) on walls, jukebox, wooden booths, ceiling fans. Famous for huge portions of pasta served with a variety of sauces. A local institution since 1952. **FYI:** Reservations accepted. Children's menu. **Open:** Mon–Thurs 9am–midnight, Fri–Sat 8am–2am. **Prices:** Main courses $4–$10. AE, MC, V. ⬚ ♿

Peking Pavillion

1302 E Cary St (Shockoe Slip); tel 304/649-8888. **Chinese.** Ornate wood dividers provide privacy in one of the few Shockoe Slip restaurants in existence for more than 10 years, making it a Richmond staple. Traditional, expertly prepared Peking duck. Champagne brunch is very popular. **FYI:** Reservations accepted. Dress code. **Open:** Lunch Mon–Fri 11:30am–2:15pm; dinner Sun–Thurs 5–9:30pm, Sat 5–10:30pm; brunch Sun 11:30am–2pm. **Prices:** Main courses $7–$14; prix fixe $12–$30. AE, MC, V.

Sam Miller's Warehouse

1210 E Cary St (Shockoe Slip); tel 804/644-5465. Exit 74A off I-95. **New American/Seafood/Steak.** Large, open dining area conveys the feel of the area when it was a market and warehouse district. Whole Maine lobster, an unusual find on Richmond menus, is a favorite; prime rib's another. An easygoing, fun place. **FYI:** Reservations recommended.

Blues/guitar/jazz/karaoke. Children's menu. **Open:** Peak (Sept–Dec/Apr–May) Mon–Sat 11am–2am, Sun 10am–2am. **Prices:** Main courses $15–$25. AE, DC, MC, V. ⦿ 🔳 📷 ♿

★ Strawberry Street Café
421 N Strawberry St (The Fan); tel 804/353-6860. Between Park and Stuart Aves. **New American/Cafe.** Stained-glass windows and an art-deco flair highlight this neighborhood hangout. An antique bathtub serves as a well-stocked salad bar. Homemade chicken pot pie, gourmet burgers, chicken quesadillas, eggs Benedict with lump crabmeat, and fantastic crab-artichoke dip lead the menu. Located near Strawberry Street Vineyard, restaurant sports extensive wine list. Sunday brunch is very popular. **FYI:** Reservations accepted. **Open:** Lunch Mon–Fri 11:30am–2:30pm; dinner Sun–Thurs 5–10:30pm, Fri–Sat 4:30pm–midnight; brunch Sat 11am–4:30pm, Sun 10am–4:30pm. **Prices:** Main courses $5–$16. AE, MC, V. ♿

Texas-Wisconsin Border Café
1501 W Main St, at Plum St (The Fan); tel 804/355-2907. **Tex-Mex/Eastern European.** A small cafe casually adorned with ceiling fans, prints, license plates from the Southwest, mirrors, and hunting trophies. As name implies, menu offers an unusual mix from Texas (chili is well regarded) and Wisconsin (bratwurst, potato pancakes, kielbasa, and other German and Polish selections). **FYI:** Reservations not accepted. **Open:** Daily 11am–2am. **Prices:** Main courses $4–$8. MC, V. ♿

★ The Tobacco Company Restaurant
12th and Cary Sts (Shockoe Slip); tel 804/782-9431. Exit 74A off I-95. **Seafood/Steak.** Downtown professionals are attracted to this restaurant in an 1860s-vintage tobacco warehouse next to the Omni Richmond Hotel. Enormous brass-fixture bar, lots of well-groomed plants, overstuffed Victorian sofas, and Tiffany lamps. Skylights make it light and airy in daytime. Exposed antique elevator overlooks large atrium while accessing various levels with two dining rooms, bar, nightclub. Extensive selection of salads; otherwise, mostly beef and seafood. Bar open 11:30am–2am daily. **FYI:** Reservations accepted. Big band/piano. Dress code. **Open:** Lunch Mon–Sat 11:30am–2:30pm; dinner Mon–Fri 5:30–10:30pm, Sat 5–11pm, Sun 5:30–10pm; brunch Sun 11am–2:30pm. **Prices:** Main courses $14–$30. AE, MC, V. ♿

ATTRACTIONS 🖼

Pocahontas State Park
10301 State Park Rd, Chesterfield; tel 804/796-4255. Comprising more than 7,000 acres, this park offers fishing and boating on Beaver Lake, as well as hiking, biking, and picnicking. Many facilities are accessible to people with disabilities, including the swimming pool. Individual and group campsites; interpretive programs in summer. **Open:** Daily sunrise–sunset. $

Virginia State Capitol
9th and Grace Sts; tel 804/786-4344. Designed by Thomas Jefferson while he was serving as minister to France, the Virginia State Capitol closely resembles a Roman temple built in Nîmes during the 1st century AD. It is the second-oldest working capitol in the United States, in continuous use since 1788.

The capitol's **rotunda** has a domed skylight ornamented in renaissance style. The room's dramatic focal point is Houdon's life-size statue of George Washington, said to be a perfect likeness. Busts of the seven other US presidents from Virginia—Jefferson, Madison, Monroe, William Henry Harrison, Tyler, Taylor, and Wilson—are also in the rotunda.

The old **Hall of the House of Delegates** is now a museum. The former senate chamber, still used for occasional committee meetings, is where Stonewall Jackson's body lay in state after his death in 1863.

Free 30-minute tours of the capitol are given throughout the day. On the capitol grounds are the **Executive Mansion,** official residence of governors of Virginia since 1813; and the old **Bell Tower,** built in 1824, which houses the official Virginia Division of Tourism's Welcome Center. **Open:** Peak (Apr–Nov) daily 9am–5pm. Reduced hours off-season. **Free**

Governor's Mansion
Capitol Square; tel 804/371-2642. The oldest governor's residence in continuous use in the United States, this two-story federal-style landmark was completed in 1813 and has been the official residence of Virginia's chief executives ever since. Guided tours visit the first floor of the mansion, as well as the gardens. **Open:** By appointment only. **Free**

Museum and White House of the Confederacy
1201 E Clay St; tel 804/649-1861. The Museum of the Confederacy houses the largest and most comprehensive collection of Confederate Civil War memorabilia in the country, much of it contributed by veterans, who often served as guides in the early days. Many of the war's major events and campaigns are documented, and exhibits include a replica of Lee's headquarters, period clothing, uniforms, weapons, memorabilia, and art. Research library (open by appointment only); gift shop. Living history programs scheduled in summer.

Next door to the museum is the mansion known as the **White House of the Confederacy.** This classical revival house was the official residence of Confederate President Jefferson Davis from 1861 to 1865, when Richmond served as the capital of the Confederacy. There are 11 period rooms of original furnishings, all decorated in the high Victorian style. Guided tours begin with a short history of the mansion, and take in two floors of the house. **Open:** Mon–Sat 10am–5pm, Sun noon–5pm. **$$$**

Science Museum of Virginia/Ethyl UNIVERSE Theater
2500 W Broad St; tel 804/367-6552 or toll free 800/659-1727. There are few "do not touch" signs in this

museum's galleries, which house more than 250 exhibits on crystals, electricity, aerospace, chemistry, and physics. The museum also features a Foucault pendulum and one of the world's largest analemmic sundials. Not to be missed are the shows at the 300-seat Ethyl UNIVERSE Planetarium/Space Theater, which include Omnimax films as well as sophisticated multimedia shows. The Science Museum is housed in the former Broad Street Station, designed in 1919 by John Russell Pope.

The museum also operates the **Virginia Aviation Museum** (tel 804/236-3622) located near the Richmond International Airport. A "shrine to the golden age of aviation," this facility (open daily 9:30am–5pm) boasts an extensive collection of vintage flying machines. **Open:** Peak (Mem Day–Labor Day) Mon–Thurs 9:30am–5pm, Fri–Sat 9:30am–7pm, Sun 11:30am–5pm. Reduced hours off-season. $$$

Virginia Museum of Fine Arts
Boulevard and Grove Ave; tel 804/367-0844. Impressive collections housed here include art nouveau, art deco, 19th- and 20th-century French paintings, contemporary American art, and art from India, Nepal, and Tibet. The largest public Fabergé collection outside Russia—more than 300 objets d'art created for Czars Alexander III and Nicholas II—is also on display here. Other highlights include the Goya portrait *General Nicholas Guye,* a rare life-size marble statue of the Roman emperor Caligula, and Monet's *Iris by the Pond.*

The **West Wing** houses the Mellon Collection of 20th-century British, French, and American paintings, drawings, prints, and sculpture; also the Sydney and Frances Lewis Collection of contemporary American painting and sculpture. A decorative art collection includes works by Tiffany and furnishings by Frank Lloyd Wright.

Open: Tues–Wed and Fri–Sun 11am–5pm, Thurs 11am–8pm. $$

Richmond Children's Museum
740 Navy Hill Dr; tel 804/643-5436. This unusual museum seeks to introduce children to the arts, nature, and the world around them with participatory exhibits, classes, and workshops. Amateur spelunkers can investigate stalagmites and stalactites in the Cave. Playworks invites children to dress up and see what it feels like to be a police officer, a banker, or a shopkeeper. **Open:** Mon–Fri 9am–5pm, Sat 10am–5pm, Sun 1–5pm. $$

Valentine Museum
1015 E Clay St; tel 804/649-0711. Located in the elegant federal-style Wickham-Valentine House, built in 1812 by attorney John Wickham. Highlights of the house include spectacular decorative wall paintings, perhaps the rarest and most complete set in the nation; the Oval Parlor; and the circular Palette Staircase. Exhibits cover social and urban history, decorative and fine arts, textiles, architecture, and more. Guided house tours, included in the price of admission

to the museum, are given hourly. On-site cafe serves breakfast and lunch. **Open:** Mon–Sat 10am–5pm, Sun noon–5pm. $$

Richmond National Battlefield Park
3215 E Broad St; tel 804/226-1981. A prime military objective throughout the Civil War, Richmond experienced seven major Union assaults in the course of the conflict; in April 1865, when the city finally fell into federal hands, its fall heralded the end of the Confederacy.

A 60-mile tour of battlefields begins at the **Chimborazo Visitor Center** at the park headquarters on E Broad Street. A 12-minute slide show about the Civil War is shown throughout the day, along with *Richmond Remembers,* a 25-minute film documenting the impact of the Civil War on the Confederate capital. A three-hour auto-tape tour can be rented that describes the Seven Days Campaign of 1862. Park rangers are on hand to answer questions.

There are smaller visitor centers at **Fort Harrison,** about 8 miles southeast, and at **Cold Harbor,** about 10 miles northeast. The latter was the scene of a particularly bloody 1864 engagement in which 7,000 of Gen U S Grant's men were killed or injured in just 30 minutes. Living military history reenactments take place during the summer; inquire at Chimborazo. The Cold Harbor center is staffed year-round, there are brochures, a bulletin board, electric map, and interpretive exhibits. Fort Harrison is staffed spring through fall. **Open:** Daily 9am–5pm. **Free**

Maggie L Walker National Historic Site
110½ E Leigh St; tel 804/780-1380. Daughter of a former slave, Maggie L Walker was an especially gifted woman who achieved success in the world of finance and business and rose to become the first woman bank president in the country. She also became owner and editor of a newspaper. The bank she headed continues today as the Consolidated Bank and Trust, the oldest African American–operated bank in the United States.

This red-brick house was Walker's residence from 1904 until her death in 1934, and remained in the Walker family until 1979. It has been restored to its 1930s appearance. **Open:** Wed–Sun 9am–5pm. **Free**

St Paul's Episcopal Church
815 E Grace St; tel 804/643-3589. Consecrated in November 1845, St Paul's was designed in Greek Revival style by Philadelphia architect Thomas S Stewart. The steeple was originally surmounted by an 11-foot octagonal spire, which was removed (as were other church spires in town) following a hurricane in 1900. The striking plaster work of the ceiling interweaves Greek, Hebrew, and Christian motifs radiating from the symbol of the Trinity. Stained-glass windows were added, beginning in 1890. They include eight windows from the Tiffany studios and two windows designed as memorials to Robert E Lee. The partition behind the altar, a mosaic

rendering of da Vinci's *The Last Supper,* is also by Tiffany. Sunday services are at 7:45, 9, and 11am. **Open:** Daily 10am–4pm. **Free**

St John's Episcopal Church

2401 E Broad St; tel 804/648-5015. Originally known as the "church on Richmond Hill," St John's dates back to 1741. Edgar Allan Poe's mother and signer of the Declaration of Independence George Wythe are buried in the graveyard. The congregation actually predates the church; it was established in 1611, and Alexander Whitaker, the first rector, ministered to the local tribes, instructed Pocahontas in Christianity, and baptized her.

The Second Virginia Convention met here in 1775 to discuss the rights of American subjects of the English king. In attendance were Thomas Jefferson, George Washington, and Patrick Henry, who gave his now-famous "liberty or death" speech here.

The 20-minute tour includes the original 1741 entrance and pulpit, the exquisite stained-glass windows, and the pew where Patrick Henry sat during the convention. From the last Sunday in May through the first Sunday in September, a living history program is staged, re-creating the convention, complete with actors in period garb and a reading of Patrick Henry's speech. **Open:** Mon–Sat 10am–3:30pm, Sun 1–3:30pm. **$**

Agecroft Hall

4305 Sulgrave Rd; tel 804/353-4241. This Tudor manor house was originally built in the north of England, in the late 15th century. In the 1920s, when the house was threatened with destruction, Mr and Mrs T C Williams Jr bought it, had it carefully taken down (every beam and stone numbered), and shipped it to Richmond for reconstruction in an elegant neighborhood overlooking the James River.

Inside the house is a collection of tapestries, armor, pewter, paintings, and furnishings from the Tudor and Stuart periods. Guided tours (40 min) begin with a 12-minute slide presentation. Outside are a formal sunken English garden and three re-created 17th-century gardens (separate admission available). **Open:** Tues–Sat 10am–4pm, Sun 12:30–5pm. **$$**

Edgar Allan Poe Museum

1914–1916 E Main St; tel 804/648-5523. This complex consists of four buildings (enclosing an "Enchanted Garden") wherein the poet's life is documented. The Old Stone House (ca 1736) contains a shop and is where a video presentation initiates guided tours of the museum. The other three buildings were added to house the growing collection of Poe artifacts and publications, now the largest in existence.

Among the items on display are photographs, portraits, documents, and other personal memorabilia. The Raven Room includes artist James Carling's evocative illustrations of "The Raven"; there is also an exhibition gallery featuring rotating exhibits. Tours are given throughout the day. **Open:** Tues–Sat 10am–4pm, Sun–Mon 1–4pm. **$$**

John Marshall House

818 E Marshall St; tel 804/648-7998. From 1801 to 1835, John Marshall served as Chief Justice of the Supreme Court, where he helped establish the American system of constitutional law and judicial review. The house was completed in 1790 and is still largely intact. Original furnishings and personal items have been supplemented by period antiques and reproductions. The gracious dining room features a period mahogany banquet table, set with porcelain, silver, glassware, and a Waterford crystal épergne. Guided tours take about 30 minutes; there's also a 10-minute film orientation. **Open:** Peak (Apr–Sept) Tues–Sat 10am–5pm. Reduced hours off-season. Closed Jan–Mar. **$**

Wilton House

215 S Wilton Rd; tel 804/282-5936. Originally built about 14 miles down the James River in 1753, this stately Georgian mansion was painstakingly disassembled and moved to its present site in 1933. Most of the original floors, mantels, brass fixtures, and paneling were preserved; fine period furnishings have been added. **Open:** Mar–Jan, Tues–Sat 10am–4:30pm, Sun 1:30–4:30pm. **$$**

Hollywood Cemetery

412 S Cherry St; tel 804/648-8501. Established in 1847, this is the burial place of two presidents of the United States (Monroe and Tyler), six Virginia governors, Confederate President Jefferson Davis, and Confederate generals J E B Stuart and George Pickett. Pickett's grave is alongside those of his men who fell at the Battle of Gettysburg. Maps are for sale in the office on weekdays only. **Open:** Daily 8am–5pm. **Free**

Lewis Ginter Botanical Garden

1800 Lakeside Ave; tel 804/262-9887. In the 1880s, self-made Richmond millionaire, philanthropist, and amateur horticulturist Lewis Ginter built the Lakeside Wheel Club as a summer playground for the city's elite. His niece, Grace Arents, converted the property into a hospice for sick children and initiated extensive horticultural projects. Rare trees and shrubs were imported and planted in large beds on the front lawn, greenhouses were constructed, and a white gazebo and trellised seating areas were covered in rambling roses and clematis.

Today, the garden offers extensive collections and ever-changing displays of flowers, grasses, trees, and shrubs. The Botanical Garden includes the Henry M Flagler Perennial Garden, Grace Arents Garden, Madeline Livesay Friendship Garden, The Children's Garden, Cottage Garden, and the Martha and Reed West Island Garden. **Open:** Daily 9:30am–4:30pm. **$**

Maymont House and Park

1700 Hampton St; tel 804/358-7166. Located just north of the James River, between the Boulevard (VA 161) and Meadow St. In 1886, Maj James Henry Dooley purchased a 100-acre dairy farm in Richmond, on which he built an opulent, 33-room mansion surrounded by beautifully landscaped grounds, including extensive Italian and Japanese gardens. The hay barn is today the **Mary Parsons Nature Center,** with outdoor habitats for bison, elk, and bears. At the **Children's Farm,** youngsters can feed chickens, piglets, goats, cows, and sheep. A collection of horse-drawn carriages is on display at the **Carriage House,** and carriage rides are offered on weekends (Apr–mid-Dec). A tram operates on the grounds daily Apr–Oct. Guided tours of the house are available Tues–Sun. **Open:** Peak (Apr–Oct) daily 10am–7pm. Reduced hours off-season. **Free**

Meadow Farm Museum

Mountain Rd, Glen Allen; tel 804/672-5520. Located 12 mi N of Richmond. Dr John Mosby Sheppard raised his family, practiced medicine, and ran a farm here in the mid-19th century. Tour guides dressed in period clothing interpret rural middle-class life as Dr Sheppard knew it. Exhibits trace the family through several generations, and include a barn, a farrier's shop, and a facsimile of Dr Sheppard's medical office. **Open:** Peak (mid-Mar–mid-Dec) Tues–Sun noon–4pm. Reduced hours off-season. **Free**

6th Street Marketplace

Tel 804/648-6600. Located along 6th St across Marshall, Broad, and Grace Sts. Part of a major urban-renewal effort in downtown Richmond, the Marketplace is concentrated on a glass-enclosed, elevated pedestrian bridge spanning Broad Street. It houses about 35 retail stores, a food court (in the historic Blues Armory, used to house Confederate troops during the Civil War), and several restaurants. Every Friday from May through September there's a street party with live bands and refreshments between 5 and 9pm. **Open:** Mon–Sat 10am–6pm, Sun 12:30–5:30pm. **Free**

Roanoke

See also Bedford, Hardy

Nestled between the Blue Ridge and Allegheny Mountains in the Shenandoah Valley, this city of 100,000 residents is a cultural, medical, industrial, and commercial center. Within minutes of Jefferson and George Washington National Forests and the Appalachian Trail. Nearby Salem (the Roanoke County seat) was founded in 1802; it borders Roanoke to the west. **Information:** Roanoke Valley Convention and Visitors Bureau, 114 Market St, Roanoke, 24011-1402 (tel 540/342-6025).

HOTELS 🏨

🏛🏛🏛 Holiday Inn Tanglewood

4468 Starkey Rd SW, 24014; tel 540/774-4400 or toll free 800/465-4329; fax 540/774-1195. Exit US 220 or I-581 at Va 419 N; turn right onto Starkey Rd. Located in southwest Roanoke and close to most attractions, this is a surprisingly quiet yet fun place to stay. **Rooms:** 196 rms and stes. Executive level. CI 3pm/CO noon. Nonsmoking rms avail. All

are in one area away from meeting rooms, restaurant, and lounge. **Amenities:** 🛏 🐾 A/C, cable TV w/movies. **Services:** ✕ 🍳 🚐 📨 🍽 🍷 Car-rental desk. Staff is energetic and helpful. Shoe shines available. **Facilities:** 🛋 [900] 🔥 1 restaurant, 1 bar (w/entertainment). Very lively Elephant Walk lounge is a local favorite, with disc jockey and dance floor. Guests pay $5 to use Roanoke Athletic Club, which has tennis, pool, racquetball, full fitness center. **Rates:** $98 S or D; $138 ste. Children under age 17 stay free. Parking: Outdoor, free. AE, DC, DISC, MC, V.

🏛🏛🏛🏛 Hotel Roanoke & Conference Center

110 Shenandoah Ave, 24016 (Downtown); tel 540/985-5900 or toll free 800/222-8733; fax 540/345-2890. Exit 143 off I-81 to Wells Ave. There has been a Hotel Roanoke on this spot since 1887, when the town was called Big Lick. The grand old lady has been restored over a period of years, and now has high-tech conveniences along with its Florentine marble floors, frescoes, and vaulted ceilings. Even if you don't stay here it's worth a walk uphill just to see the rich, black walnut–paneled lobby with its Oriental rugs and leather lounge furniture. **Rooms:** 332 rms and stes. CI 3pm/CO noon. Nonsmoking rms avail. Rooms were completely rebuilt during the restoration, and feature elegant appointments and regional art. Views of downtown and the mountains. **Amenities:** 🐾 A/C, cable TV w/movies, dataport, voice mail. No phone. 1 unit w/terrace, some w/fireplaces. Many rooms have two, dual-line telephones. Nintendo in all. **Services:** 🍽 🔑 [VP] 🚐 📨 🍷 Babysitting. Experienced, accommodating staff. **Facilities:** 🛋 🍴 [2441] 🔥 1 restaurant (see "Restaurants" below), 1 bar (w/entertainment), sauna. Enclosed pedestrian walkway to Market Square. **Rates:** $119–$139 S; $129–$149 D; $195–$450 ste. Extra person $10. Children under age 18 stay free. Min stay special events. Parking: Outdoor, $3–$5/day. AE, CB, DC, DISC, MC, V.

🏛🏛🏛 Radisson Patrick Henry Hotel

617 S Jefferson St, 24011 (Downtown); tel 540/345-8811 or toll free 800/833-4567; fax 540/342-9908. Exit 143 off I-81. This 1925 Virginia historic landmark is on the National Register of Historic Places. Beautifully decorated large lobby invites guests to play chess, chat, write letters, or read. **Rooms:** 125 stes and effic. Executive level. CI 3pm/CO noon. Nonsmoking rms avail. Nicely furnished with four-poster beds, wallpaper, hunting and flower prints, cabinet-held TVs, large closet space. **Amenities:** 🛏 🐾 📺 🍷 A/C, cable TV w/movies, refrig, dataport. Some units w/minibars. **Services:** ✕ 🍳 [VP] 🚐 📨 🍷 **Facilities:** [800] 1 restaurant (dinner only), 1 bar, games rm, beauty salon, washer/dryer. Guest passes to YMCA and YWCA nearby. **Rates:** $150 ste; $109–$119 effic. Extra person $10. Children under age 17 stay free. Min stay special events. Parking: Indoor/outdoor, $3/day. AE, DC, DISC, JCB, MC, V.

🏛🏛🏛 Roanoke Airport Marriott

2801 Hershberger Rd NW, 24017 (Roanoke Regional Airport); tel 540/563-9300 or toll free 800/228-9290; fax 540/

563-9300 ext 7910. Exit 3 W off I-581. Although located in a commercial area, this is a quiet hotel with enough property and landscaping to feel insulated. The first floor is spacious, with many sitting areas in addition to the lobby, restaurants, and lounges. Close to a large enclosed shopping mall featuring life-size dinosaurs modeled after the ones in *Jurassic Park*. **Rooms:** 320 rms and stes. Executive level. CI 3pm/CO noon. Nonsmoking rms avail. **Amenities:** 🔔 🅰 🍽 A/C, cable TV w/movies. Some units w/terraces. Some rooms have dataports. **Services:** 🍽 🔑 VP 🚐 🛍 ⟲ ⟳ Coffee and newspapers in lobby during morning. **Facilities:** 🎱 🏊 ⛳ 🏌 🎿 ⛷ 2 restaurants (*see* "Restaurants" below), 2 bars (1 w/entertainment), sauna, whirlpool. Indoor and outdoor pools. **Rates:** $109–$129 S; $119–$139 D; $209 ste. Extra person $10. Children under age 18 stay free. Min stay special events. Parking: Outdoor, free. AE, CB, DC, DISC, JCB, MC, V.

MOTELS

🛏 Budget Host Blue Jay Motel

5399 W Main St, Salem, 24153; tel 540/380-2080 or toll free 800/283-4678. Exit 132 off I-81. Older, homey motel nestled in the mountains. Owners live on premises. **Rooms:** 14 rms and effic. CI 2pm/CO 2pm. Nonsmoking rms avail. **Amenities:** 🔔 🅰 A/C, cable TV. **Services:** 🚐 ⟳ **Facilities:** 🎿 Washer/dryer. **Rates:** Peak (May–Oct) $34–$42 S; $38–$45 D; $39–$50 effic. Extra person $5. Children under age 18 stay free. Lower rates off-season. Parking: Outdoor, free. AE, DISC, MC, V.

🛏🛏 Days Inn Civic Center

535 Orange Ave, 24016; tel 540/342-4551 or toll free 800/329-7466; fax 540/343-3547. Exit 4E off I-581 S. A chain motel favored by families and business travelers because of its close proximity to downtown Roanoke and the historic City Market. **Rooms:** 257 rms. CI 2pm/CO 11am. Nonsmoking rms avail. **Amenities:** 🔔 A/C, cable TV w/movies. **Services:** 🛍 ⟳ ⟲ Babysitting. **Facilities:** 🎿 🏊 **Rates:** Peak (June–July) $52 S; $57 D. Extra person $6. Children under age 18 stay free. Lower rates off-season. Parking: Outdoor, free. AE, CB, DC, DISC, MC, V.

🛏🛏 Days Inn Interstate

8118 Plantation Rd, 24019 (Hollins); tel 540/366-0341 or toll free 800/952-4200; fax 540/366-3935. Exit 146 off I-81. Near Hollins College and less than a 10-minute drive to downtown Roanoke, this chain motel has plenty of parking for RVs and trucks. An old N&W railroad car lends historic interest to the grounds. **Rooms:** 123 rms and stes. CI noon/CO noon. Nonsmoking rms avail. Some units are open to interior corridors, others to outside of building. Those close to I-81 can be noisy. **Amenities:** 🔔 🅰 A/C, cable TV w/movies, dataport. 1 unit w/minibar. Morning newspaper delivered to room. **Services:** 🚐 🛍 ⟳ VCRs for rent. **Facilities:** 🎿 🏊⁣₁₅₀ 🅰 1 restaurant (bkfst and dinner only), 1

bar, basketball, playground. **Rates:** $42–$50 S; $52–$60 D; $80 ste. Extra person $6. Children under age 12 stay free. Parking: Outdoor, free. AE, CB, DISC, MC, V.

🛏🛏🛏 Holiday Inn Airport

6626 Thirlane Rd, 24019; tel 540/366-8861 or toll free 800/HOLIDAY; fax 540/366-8861. Exit 143 off I-81. Conveniently located minutes from downtown Roanoke and Salem, regional airport, and Valley View Mall, the largest shopping complex in the area. **Rooms:** 163 rms. Executive level. CI 3pm/CO noon. Nonsmoking rms avail. Eight family rooms have two double beds, couch, and two bathrooms. **Amenities:** 🔔 🅰 📺 A/C, satel TV w/movies. **Services:** ✕ 🚐 🛍 ⟳ **Facilities:** 🎿 🏊⁣₆₀₀ 🅰 1 restaurant, 1 bar. Free use of nearby fitness club and discounted passes to two nearby golf courses. **Rates:** $55–$80 S or D. Extra person $4. Children under age 19 stay free. Parking: Outdoor, free. AE, CB, DC, DISC, JCB, MC, V.

🛏🛏 Holiday Inn Civic Center

501 Orange Ave, 24016; tel 540/342-8961 or toll free 800/HOLIDAY. Exit 4E off I-581 S. A convenient motel to downtown Roanoke and the Civic Center, both an easy five minutes away. **Rooms:** 152 rms and stes. CI 3pm/CO noon. Nonsmoking rms avail. **Amenities:** 🔔 🅰 A/C, satel TV w/movies. **Services:** ✕ 🛍 ⟳ ⟲ **Facilities:** 🎿 🏊⁣₁₀₀ 🖥 1 restaurant, 1 bar. Restaurant is a local favorite for Sunday brunch. **Rates:** $60–$68 S; $64–$72 D; $110–$150 ste. Extra person $4. Children under age 12 stay free. Parking: Outdoor, free. AE, CB, DC, DISC, JCB, MC, V.

🛏 Knights Inn

301 Wildwood Rd, Salem, 24153; tel 540/389-0280 or toll free 800/843-5644; fax 540/387-1553. Exit 137 off I-81. A good location within walking distance of many restaurants and minutes' drive to Dixie Caverns, Roanoke College, downtown Salem, and shopping mall. **Rooms:** 66 rms and effic. CI 3pm/CO 11am. Nonsmoking rms avail. Simple but very clean rooms. Some have refrigerators. **Amenities:** 🔔 🅰 A/C, cable TV w/movies. **Services:** 🛍 ⟳ **Facilities:** 🅰 **Rates:** Peak (Mar–Sept) $33–$39 S; $39–$46 D; $41–$55 effic. Extra person $4. Children under age 18 stay free. Lower rates off-season. Parking: Outdoor, free. No discounts during special events. AE, DISC, MC, V.

🛏🛏🛏 Quality Inn Roanoke/Salem

179 Sheraton Dr, PO Box 460, Salem, 24153; tel 540/562-1912 or toll free 800/228-5151; fax 540/562-0507. Exit 141 off I-81. Extremely quiet, nicely decorated motel with beautiful mountain views. **Rooms:** 120 rms and stes. CI 3pm/CO 11am. Nonsmoking rms avail. **Amenities:** 🔔 🅰 A/C, cable TV w/movies. Some units w/terraces. Refrigerators, hair dryers, and dataports provided upon request. **Services:** ✕ 🚐 🛍 ⟳ ⟲ **Facilities:** 🎿 ⛳ 🏊⁣₂₀₀ 🅰 1 restaurant (dinner only), 1 bar, volleyball, playground, washer/dryer. Putting green, badminton court, picnic tables, barbecue. Bus and truck parking. **Rates (CP):** Peak (May–Oct) $51–$57 S; $55–$61 D;

$102–$114 ste. Extra person $6. Children under age 18 stay free. Lower rates off-season. Parking: Outdoor, free. AE, CB, DC, DISC, EC, ER, JCB, MC, V.

≣≣≣ Ramada Inn Roanoke

1927 Franklin Rd SW, 24014; tel 540/343-0121 or toll free 800/272-6232 in the US, 800/854-7854 in Canada; fax 540/343-0121 ext 599. Exit I-581 at Wonju St; turn left at Franklin Rd, go 3 blocks. A stream winds through this motel's grounds, across the street from a beautiful park. **Rooms:** 125 rms. CI 3pm/CO noon. Nonsmoking rms avail. Newly furnished, rooms have paintings with rural themes in pastels. **Amenities:** 🛏 ♨ A/C, cable TV w/movies. Dataports available on request. Suites have refrigerators. **Services:** ✗ ◿ 🖐 🐕 Babysitting. **Facilities:** 🔥 🚹250 🔥 1 restaurant (lunch and dinner only), 1 bar (w/entertainment), washer/dryer. Free use of nearby Gold's Gym. Tennis courts in park across street. **Rates:** Peak (Apr–Oct) $52–$99 S or D. Extra person $7. Children under age 18 stay free. Lower rates off-season. Parking: Outdoor, free. AE, DC, DISC, MC, V.

RESTAURANTS 🍴

✹ Buck Mountain Grille

US 220 S at Blue Ridge Pkwy; tel 540/776-1830. 2 mi S of Roanoke. **New American/Vegetarian.** Slip off the Blue Ridge Parkway or out of Roanoke to this restaurant with pleasing white walls accented with plants and monthly art shows. Booth and table seating. Eclectic and varied menu offers something for everyone, from pasta with crab and pesto to filet mignon. Unpretentious but professional service. **FYI:** Reservations accepted. Children's menu. **Open:** Lunch Tues–Sun 11am–3pm; dinner Tues–Thurs 5–9pm, Fri–Sat 5–10pm, Sun 5–9pm. **Prices:** Main courses $7–$19. AE, CB, DC, DISC, MC, V. 🔥

La Maison

5732 Airport Rd; tel 540/366-2444. Exit 2N off I-581. **Continental/Seafood.** Each room of this 1929 Georgian-style mansion is decorated with an abundance of Impressionist art, antiques, and paintings. Even the closets are part of the decor. Known for Virginia seafood sausage appetizer (their own recipe) and baked Alaska. Prime rib specials, Friday night seafood buffet, Sunday brunch. One small room available for intimate dinners. **FYI:** Reservations recommended. Piano. Children's menu. **Open:** Tues–Thurs 5–9pm, Fri–Sat 5–10pm, Sun 11:30am–2pm. **Prices:** Main courses $10–$19. AE, CB, MC, V. ♥ ◼ ⬆ 🔥 🔥

♟ The Library

In Piccadilly Square, 3117 Franklin Rd SW; tel 540/985-0811. Exit I-581 at Wonju St; turn right at Franklin St (US 220 business S), go ½ mile. **Continental/French.** Roanoke's longtime favorite for special occasions, this elegant, quiet establishment is appointed with gold-framed paintings, shelves of books, and a huge brass espresso/cappuccino machine. Traditional French dishes, rack of lamb, Dover sole, and tableside preparation of cherries jubilee. Great attention to all details, from food preparation and service to exquisite table settings featuring Italian china. **FYI:** Reservations recommended. Jacket required. No smoking. **Open:** Mon–Sat 6–10pm. **Prices:** Main courses $13–$25. AE, CB, DC, MC, V. ♥ 🚗

Macado's

120 Church St (Downtown); tel 540/342-7231. Off I-581. **Deli/Eclectic.** This fun establishment makes guests of all ages feel comfortable in its many informal dining areas. The eclectic, funky decor includes old bicycles and auto parts which hang from the ceiling. A sandwich-lover's delight, menu also offers quiches, pastas, and many sweets. Mesquite-grilled chicken and turkey are popular. Front of restaurant has deli, wine and cheese shop. **FYI:** Reservations not accepted. Children's menu. Additional location: 4237 Electric Rd (tel 776-9884). **Open:** Mon–Thurs 10am–midnight, Fri–Sat 10am–1:30am, Sun 10am–10pm. **Prices:** Main courses $5–$7. AE, MC, V. 🔥 🔥

♟ The Regency Room

In The Hotel Roanoke and Conference Center, 110 Shenandoah Ave (Downtown); tel 540/985-5900. From I-81 exit 143 (I-581) to exit 5. **Regional American/Continental.** A natural environment for Friday afternoon high tea or full dining. The high ceilings, fine window dressings, trees, and cut flowers at the tables create an exciting atmosphere. The peanut soup is locally famous, and has been served here for over 50 years. Other favorites are the spoonbread, steak Diane, and the Hunter's Duet with mesquite-grilled venison. **FYI:** Reservations recommended. Dancing/Trio. Children's menu. Dress code. **Open:** Breakfast Mon–Fri 6:30–10:30am, Sat–Sun 7am–10:30pm; lunch daily 11:30am–2pm; dinner Mon–Sat 5–10pm, Sun 5–9pm. **Prices:** Main courses $15–$30. AE, CB, DC, DISC, MC, V. ♥ ◼ ⬆ 🆅🅿 🔥

Remington's

In Roanoke Airport Marriott, 2801 Hershberger Rd NW (Roanoke Regional Airport); tel 540/563-9300. 6 mi N of downtown Roanoke; exit 3W off I-581. **Regional American.** Decoratively folded napkins, tasteful table settings, old pieces of china, hunting prints, and low-hanging lights lend intimacy to this hotel restaurant. Menu changes several times a year to accommodate seasonal items. **FYI:** Reservations recommended. **Open:** Mon–Sat 6–10pm. **Prices:** Main courses $17–$24. AE, DC, DISC, MC, V. 🔥

ATTRACTIONS 🏛

CENTER IN THE SQUARE

Science Museum of Western Virginia and Hopkins Planetarium

Tel 540/342-5710. Five floors of interactive exhibits exploring energy, weather, and health; Chesapeake Bay Touch Tank, animal area. **Hopkins Planetarium** presents a variety of star shows (phone for schedule). **Open:** Mon–Sat 10am–5pm, Sun 1–5pm. **$$**

Art Museum of Western Virginia

One Market Square; tel 540/342-5760. Levels 1 and 2. On display here are works that range from tribal African to contemporary American. Features ArtVenture, an interactive children's art center with hands-on materials, texture wall, and rotating exhibits. **Open:** Tues–Sat 10am–5pm, Sun 1–5pm. **Free**

Roanoke Valley History Museum

One Market Square, Level 3; tel 540/342-5770. Contains documents, tools, costumes, and weapons that tell the story of Roanoke from pioneer days to the 1990s. Rotating exhibits. **Open:** Tues–Fri 10am–4pm, Sat 10am–5pm, Sun 1–5pm. **$**

Mill Mountain Theater

One Market Square SE; tel 540/342-5740. Box office located on Level 1. This theater company offers dramas, musicals, comedies, children's productions, and lunchtime readings, and year-round matinee and evening performances. Phone for schedule and ticket information. **$$$$**

OTHER ATTRACTIONS

Mill Mountain Star

Erected in 1949, this red neon sculpture stands 88 feet tall and uses 2,000 feet of neon tubing. It is visible from many parts of the city, but to see it up close (and for a panoramic view of the city), take Walnut Ave to the Mill Mountain Parkway Spur Road.

Ruther Glen

See Ashland

Salem

See Roanoke

Shenandoah National Park

Encompassing over 190,000 acres of mountains and forest, Shenandoah National Park was developed to rescue the slowly disappearing forest and declining animal population of the Shenandoah Valley. The Civilian Conservation Corps (CCC) built recreational facilities in the 1930s, and, in 1939, the Skyline Drive was completed. Today over two-fifths of the park is considered wilderness, with more than 100 species of trees. Animals have returned, and sightings of smaller animals are frequent. Many of the park's natural wonders are visible from 75 designated overlooks along the **Skyline Drive**. The 105.4-mile drive runs the length of the park; access is sometimes limited November–March.

In spring, the green of leafing trees moves up the ridge at the rate of about 100 feet per day. Wildflowers begin to bloom in late April; by late May the azaleas are in bloom, and the dogwood is at its height. Rhododendrons are in bloom in early June. Fall foliage, usually at its peak between October 10 and 25, attracts the most visitors to the park.

The northern park entrance is near the junction of I-81 and I-66, a mile south of Front Royal. The southern entrance is at Rockfish Gap, near the junction of US 250 and I-64, 18 miles east of Staunton. Park headquarters is 4 miles west of Thornton Gap and 4 miles east of Luray on US 211. There are two visitor centers in the park that provide information, interpretive exhibits, films, slide shows, and nature walks. Dickey Ridge Visitor Center (MP 4.6) is open April–November. Byrd Visitor Center (MP 51) at Big Meadows is usually open daily, April–November. For more information contact the Superintendent, Shenandoah National Park, Rte 4, Box 348, Luray, VA 22835 (tel 540/999-3500).

South Hill

Located in south central Virginia, southwest of Petersburg. A tobacco farming area, nearby to the Meherrin River and Lake Gaston. **Information:** South Hill Chamber of Commerce, 201 S Mecklenberg Ave, South Hill, 23970 (tel 804/447-4547).

MOTEL 🏨

📧 Comfort Inn

US 58 at I-85, 23970; tel 804/447-2600 or toll free 800/221-2222; fax 804/447-2590. Exit 12 off I-85. Go west on US 58; make a U-turn at second light. A basic but clean motel located among a bevy of restaurants, shops, and discount stores. Convenient to Lake Gaston. **Rooms:** 50 rms. CI 11am/CO 11am. Nonsmoking rms avail. **Amenities:** 🏨 🍽 A/C, cable TV w/movies. Most units have refrigerators and microwaves. **Services:** 🛏 🛎 **Facilities:** ৬ Whirlpool. Guests can use facilities at nearby health club. **Rates (CP):** Peak (Mem Day–Labor Day) $45–$67 S or D. Extra person $6. Children under age 12 stay free. Lower rates off-season. Parking: Outdoor, free. Highest rates on weekends. AE, DISC, MC, V.

Springfield

In northern Virginia at the Capital Beltway, close to Old Town Alexandria as well as all Washington, DC, attractions. **Information:** Springfield Chamber of Commerce, PO Box 823, Springfield, 22150 (tel 703/912-4988).

HOTEL 🏨

☰☰☰ Springfield Hilton

6650 Loisdale Rd, 22150; tel 703/971-8900 or toll free 800/ HILTONS; fax 703/971-8527. Exit 169A off I-95, follow VA 644 E to Loisdale Rd, turn right. Located opposite a large shopping mall, this comfortable establishment offers the best accommodations in the Springfield area, highlighted by an attractive greenhouse lounge and indoor pool area. **Rooms:** 245 rms and stes. Executive level. CI 3pm/CO 1pm. Non-smoking rms avail. Kings have sleep sofas. Parlor suites have one or two interconnecting bedrooms and are outfitted with reproduction antiques. **Amenities:** 🛁 🕹 A/C, satel TV w/movies. **Services:** ✗ 🖨 🛎 **Facilities:** 🏊 600 🏌 1 restaurant, 1 bar (w/entertainment). Guests have free use of nearby health club. **Rates:** $109–$119 S; $119–$129 D; $270–$360 ste. Extra person $10. Children under age 16 stay free. Parking: Outdoor, free. AE, CB, DC, DISC, MC, V.

Stanley

INN 🏠

☰☰☰ Jordan Hollow Farm Inn

VA 2, 22851; tel 540/778-2285; fax 540/778-1759. Off US 340. 144 acres. This colonial horse farm in a secluded hollow offers homey but elegant country lodging and a 1790 farmhouse for dining. Views at the inn are of the duck pond, grazing horses and goats, porch-sleeping cats, and rolling hills, meadows, and forests beyond. **Rooms:** 20 rms. CI 3pm/ CO noon. No smoking. The vine-covered lodge building, Arbor View, is surrounded by a sun deck, and houses 16 individually decorated units with private bath and handmade furniture; each suitable for up to four people. In Mare Meadow, a hand-hewn log lodge, are four rooms, some with porches, nice for couples but not suitable for young children. All rooms open to outside. **Amenities:** 🛁 🕹 A/C, TV. All units w/terraces, some w/fireplaces, some w/whirlpools. Cable TV in nine rooms. **Services:** 🚗 🖨 🛎 Dinner can be brought to room. Fax machine, computer, and roll-aways available. Many services, such as bellhop, on request. Daily newspaper. **Facilities:** 🚲 ⛳ 🎿 32 1 restaurant (bkfst and dinner only; see "Restaurants" below), 2 bars, games rm, lawn games, washer/dryer, guest lounge. Small gift shop. Stable with horses, for beginners or advanced riders, provides trail rides, some riding instruction, and picnic rides and carriage drives by prior arrangement. Guests can use public pool and recreation area across road for a small fee. Golf and tennis nearby. **Rates (MAP):** Peak (June–Oct) $115–$155 S; $140–$180 D. Extra person $35. Children under age 16 stay free. Lower rates off-season. Parking: Outdoor, free. Service charge of 10% but no gratuities. Children 5–16 pay only for food. AE, CB, DC, DISC, MC, V.

RESTAURANT 🍽

Jordan Hollow Farm Inn

VA 2; tel 540/778-2285. **American/Continental/French.** This 1790 farmhouse contains 200-year-old log cabin rooms and 100-year-old rooms with fox-country and West African decor. Fireplaces, antique furnishings, country curtains, and wallpaper add to sense of place. Front-yard tables sit under shade trees. Cuisine is "country continental with a French touch"; quail, pasta, and home-baked bread are favorites. **FYI:** Reservations recommended. Children's menu. No smoking. **Open:** Peak (Apr–Nov) breakfast daily 8:30–10:30am; dinner daily 6–8pm. **Prices:** Prix fixe $22. AE, DISC, MC, V. ♥ 🍽 🚪 🏨

Staunton

This Shenandoah Valley city has a wealth of historical and architectural attractions. Birthplace of Woodrow Wilson. **Information:** Augusta-Staunton-Waynesboro Visitors Bureau, 116 W Beverly St, PO Box 58, Staunton, 24402 (tel 540/332-2869).

HOTEL 🏨

☰☰ Comfort Inn

1302 Richmond Ave, at jct US 250/I-81, 24401; tel 540/886-5000 or toll free 800/221-2222; fax 540/886-6643. Exit 222 off I-81. Adjacent to the Museum of American Frontier Culture and numerous restaurants, including a 24-hour waffle house, this highway hotel also is convenient to the Blue Ridge Mountains. **Rooms:** 97 rms and stes. Executive level. CI 3pm/CO 11am. No smoking. **Amenities:** 🛁 🕹 📺 A/C, cable TV w/movies. Some units w/whirlpools. **Services:** 🖨 🛎 Complimentary newspaper daily. **Facilities:** 🏊 🏌 **Rates (CP):** $57–$66 S or D; $64 ste. Extra person $8. Children under age 18 stay free. Parking: Outdoor, free. Senior discounts avail. AE, CB, DC, DISC, ER, JCB, MC, V.

MOTELS

☰☰☰ Holiday Inn Staunton

I-81 and Woodrow Wilson Pkwy, PO Box 3209, 24402; tel 540/248-6020 or toll free 800/932-9061; fax 540/248-2902. Exit 225 off I-81. Conveniently located near American Museum of Frontier Culture, Woodrow Wilson Birthplace, wineries, and other attractions. **Rooms:** 112 rms. CI 3pm/ CO noon. No smoking. **Amenities:** 🛁 🕹 A/C, cable TV w/movies. Some units w/terraces. **Services:** ✗ 🚗 🖨 🛎 Babysitting. **Facilities:** 🏊 350 🏌 1 restaurant, 1 bar. Guests have golf, tennis, and health club privileges at adjacent Country Club of Staunton. Health club includes indoor tennis, racquetball, and junior Olympic-size pool. **Rates:** $78 S or D; $95 ste. Extra person $6. Children under age 18 stay free. Parking: Outdoor, free. AE, CB, DC, DISC, JCB, MC, V.

☰☰☰ Innkeeper

I-81 and Woodrow Wilson Pkwy, PO Box 2526, 24402; tel 540/248-5111 or toll free 800/822-9899; fax 540/248-5111. Exit 225 off I-81. A former Sheraton, this motel enjoys a quiet location with pastoral views yet is just minutes from historic downtown Staunton. Central courtyard is spacious and well landscaped. **Rooms:** 100 rms. CI 3pm/CO 11am. No smoking. Many rooms have a view of the countryside. **Amenities:** 🗃 🖢 A/C, cable TV. Some rooms have dataports. Complimentary daily newspaper. **Services:** ✕ 🖎 🖵 🖏 **Facilities:** 🖼 🖳150 🖦 Washer/dryer. **Rates (CP):** Peak (May–Oct) $56–$65 S or D. Extra person $5. Children under age 16 stay free. Lower rates off-season. Parking: Outdoor, free. AE, DC, DISC, MC, V.

INNS

☰☰☰☰ Belle Grae Inn

515 W Frederick St, 24401; tel 540/886-5151; fax 540/886-6641. This city inn boasts a number of separate houses as well as the historic main house. Azaleas bloom in lovely grounds. Very close to a number of restored Victorian historic sites. Unsuitable for children under 6. **Rooms:** 14 rms and stes; 7 cottages/villas. CI 3pm/CO 11am. Extremely private rooms with varied antiques and reproductions. **Amenities:** 🗃 🖬 A/C, cable TV, bathrobes. Some units w/terraces, some w/fireplaces. **Services:** Afternoon tea and wine/sherry served. Truly gracious hospitality. Guests greeted with tea and cookies. Pre-dinner drinks served during parlor conversation. Ice brought to rooms. **Facilities:** 🖳70 🖦 1 restaurant (see "Restaurants" below), guest lounge. Live entertainment in the Bistro. **Rates (BB):** $85–$145 D; $180–$300 cottage/villa. Extra person $35. Min stay peak. MAP rates avail. Parking: Outdoor, free. AE, MC, V.

☰☰☰ Frederick House

28 N New St, at Frederick St, PO Box 1387, 24401; tel 540/885-4220 or toll free 800/334-5575. A European-style hotel in the center of town, with many fine old buildings and restaurants nearby. It comprises five connected town houses and has a pleasant herb and flower garden in rear. Furnishings are antiques or reproductions, and atmosphere is very homey. Smoking is not permitted on premises. **Rooms:** 14 rms and stes. CI 3pm/CO 11am. Rooms vary in decor and size. **Amenities:** 🗃 A/C, cable TV w/movies, bathrobes. Some units w/terraces, some w/fireplaces. **Services:** 🖎 Babysitting, afternoon tea served. **Facilities:** 🖳20 1 restaurant, guest lounge w/TV. Guests can use health club next door. **Rates (AP):** Extra person $20. Parking: Outdoor, free. AE, CB, DC, DISC, MC, V.

RESORT

☰☰☰ Ingleside Resort

1410 Commerce Rd, PO Box 1018, 24402; tel 540/248-1201 or toll free 800/251-1962; fax 540/248-1003. Exit 225 off I-81. Go west on Woodrow Wilson Parkway 1 mile; turn right at US 11 N. 80 acres. A three-year renovation began in 1995 for this older resort. High points include spectacular views of the Blue Ridge Mountains and the private 18-hole golf course. **Rooms:** 210 rms and stes. CI 3pm/CO noon. No smoking. Rooms are newly decorated and spacious, with tasteful yet comfortable furniture. **Amenities:** 🗃 🖢 A/C, satel TV, refrig. Some units w/terraces. Some rooms have coffeemakers. **Services:** ✕ 🖎 🖵 Babysitting. **Facilities:** 🖼 🏌18 🎾2 🖳600 🖦 3 restaurants, 3 bars, lawn games, playground. **Rates:** Peak (Mar–Oct) $42–$50 S; $50–$60 D; $100 ste. Extra person $12.50. Children under age 12 stay free. Min stay special events. Lower rates off-season. AP and MAP rates avail. Parking: Outdoor, free. Rates are exceptionally reasonable for a resort of this size and scope. AE, CB, DC, MC, V.

RESTAURANTS 🍴

♥ The Belle Grae Inn and Bistro

In the Belle Grae Inn, 515 W Frederick St; tel 540/886-5150. Exit 222 off I-81. Follow US 250 to Coalter St, turn right on Frederick St. **American.** The inn's dining room is furnished in Victorian fashion, with dark wooden tables and chairs and starched white tablecloths, a fitting place to enjoy superbly prepared and presented meals. The Bistro, in another building, offers lighter food. A favorite of both locals and visitors. **FYI:** Reservations recommended. Piano. No smoking. **Open:** Dinner daily 6–9pm; brunch Sun 7:30am–2pm. **Prices:** Main courses $14–$20. AE, MC, V. ♥ 🍴 🖦

★ The Beverly Restaurant

12 E Beverley St; tel 540/886-4317. Exit 222 off I-81. Follow US 250 W to Frederick, turn left, left at Central, and left at Beverley St. **Diner.** The small diner/restaurant in the center of historic Staunton has country-style decor and friendly, casual atmosphere. Sandwiches and lighter meals provide alternative to fast-food restaurants. Known for teatime Wednesday and Friday afternoons. **FYI:** Reservations not accepted. No liquor license. **Open:** Mon–Fri 6:30am–7pm, Sat 6:30am–4pm. **Prices:** Main courses $4–$7. MC, V.

The Depot Grille

In Staunton Station, 42 Middlebrook Ave; tel 540/885-7332. Exit 222 off I-81. Follow US 250 into Staunton; turn left on Greenville Rd, then left at Augusta St. **Seafood/Steak.** Railroad memorabilia is appropriate decor in this casual restaurant in an old rail depot, now an Amtrak station. Long wooden bar was built in 1856. Steaks and seafood with a good variety of lighter fare. **FYI:** Reservations accepted. Children's menu. No smoking. **Open:** Sun–Thurs 11am–10:30pm, Fri–Sat 11am–11:30pm. **Prices:** Main courses $8–$20. AE, DISC, MC, V. 🍴 🖦

ATTRACTIONS 🏛

Woodrow Wilson Birthplace and Museum

24 N Coalter St; tel 540/885-0897. This handsome Greek Revival building, built in 1846 by a Presbyterian congregation as a manse for their ministers, stands next to an excellent

museum detailing Wilson's life. The home portrays life in 1856, the year of Wilson's birth. (Although the family left Virginia before his first birthday, Wilson always referred to himself as a Virginian.)

The museum's galleries trace Wilson's career from Princeton University to his two terms as President (1913–21). In the carriage house is Wilson's presidential limousine, a Pierce-Arrow. **Open:** Peak (Mar–Nov) daily 9am–5pm. Reduced hours off-season. **$$$**

Museum of American Frontier Culture

Tel 540/332-7850. Located west of I-81 near exit 2221, the living history museum consists of four European and American farmsteads from the 17th, 18th, and 19th centuries. Staff members in period costume plant fields, tend livestock, and do domestic chores. **Open:** Peak (mid-Mar–Nov) daily 9am–5pm. Reduced hours off-season. **$$$**

Sterling

HOTEL 🏨

≣≣≣ Holiday Inn Dulles

1000 Sully Rd (VA 28) at Holiday Dr, 20166; tel 703/471-7411 or toll free 800/HOLIDAY; fax 703/471-7411 ext 515. 1½ mi N of Dulles Airport. exit 2 off Dulles Toll Rd. Go north on Sully Rd to Holiday Dr. Pleasant hotel with full facilities near Dulles Airport. Extensive 1994 renovation spiffed up everything from lobby to rooms. **Rooms:** 300 rms. Executive level. CI 3pm/CO noon. No smoking. Dark wood furniture adds elegance to rooms, which have desks and other features attractive to business travelers. King-bed units have reclining easy chairs. **Amenities:** 🛅 🔥 🍽 A/C, cable TV w/movies, voice mail. Long telephone cords. Some rooms have coffeemakers and microwaves. **Services:** ✕ 🚐 🛆 🗇 ⟨⟩ Car-rental desk, babysitting. Free shuttle to nearby malls. **Facilities:** 🔂 ⛳ 🏊 🖥 ♿ 1 restaurant, 1 bar (w/entertainment), games rm, sauna, whirlpool, washer/dryer. Guests on executive level have use of lounge with library. Attractive indoor pool area. Lively Scrooples Bar is popular local hangout, with billiard room, Friday-night barbecues, DJ spinning dance tunes every evening. **Rates:** Peak (Mar–June) $125–$140 S or D. Children under age 18 stay free. Lower rates off-season. Parking: Outdoor, free. Rates include up to four people per room. Seniors discounts, weekend rates avail. AE, CB, DC, DISC, MC, V.

MOTEL

≣≣ Hampton Inn Dulles

45440 Holiday Dr, 22170; tel 703/471-8300 or toll free 800/HAMPTON; fax 703/471-8300 ext 408. 1½ mi N of Dulles Airport. Exit 2 off Dulles Toll Rd. Follow Sully Rd (VA 28) to Holiday Dr, turn right. A comfortable motel convenient to Washington's Dulles International Airport. **Rooms:** 126 rms. CI noon/CO noon. No smoking. Standard king-bed rooms

have recliners and desks. Armoire-like cabinets serve as closets. **Amenities:** 🛅 🔥 🍽 A/C, satel TV w/movies. Some rooms have refrigerators. **Services:** 🚐 🛆 🗇 ⟨⟩ Children's program. Coffee available all day in lobby. Free morning newspapers. Free local calls. **Facilities:** ♿ Washer/dryer. Picnic area. Guests may use facilities at adjacent Holiday Inn (including exercise room, pool, restaurant, popular bar). **Rates (CP):** Peak (Apr–June/Sept–Oct) $70–$75 S; $75–$80 D. Children under age 18 stay free. Lower rates off-season. Parking: Outdoor, free. AE, CB, DC, DISC, MC, V.

Strasburg

Founded in 1761, this small Shenandoah Valley town retains its historic ambience. Dairy production and farming are the chief industries. **Information:** Strasburg Chamber of Commerce, PO Box 42, Strasburg, 22657 (tel 540/465-3187).

HOTEL 🏨

≣≣≣ Hotel Strasburg

213 Holliday St, 22657; tel 540/465-9191 or toll free 800/348-8327; fax 540/465-4788. Exit 298 off I-81. This three-story Victorian was converted from a hospital to an inn in 1915 and offers an eclectic mix of old furnishings and modern touches. The friendly staff adds a sense of down-home hospitality. Furnishings are on consignment from local antique dealers, so patrons can shop without leaving the inn. **Rooms:** 29 rms and stes. CI 2pm/CO 11am. Nonsmoking rms avail. All units are unique, and some offer separate sitting area. **Amenities:** 🛅 🔥 A/C, cable TV. Some units w/terraces, some w/whirlpools. **Services:** 🗇 ⟨⟩ Twice-daily maid svce, masseur, babysitting. Continental breakfast Monday to Friday. **Facilities:** 🍽 1 restaurant (*see* "Restaurants" below), 1 bar, 1 beach (cove/inlet). Small beach a mile away. **Rates (CP):** $74 S or D; $89–$165 ste. Extra person $15. Children under age 16 stay free. Parking: Outdoor, free. AE, DC, DISC, MC, V.

RESTAURANT 🍴

★ Hotel Strasburg Restaurant

In Hotel Strasburg, 213 Holliday St; tel 540/465-9191. Exit 298 off I-81. **Regional American/Continental.** Country dining amid Victorian-age elegance. Period antiques and lace-curtained windows complement southern hospitality, service, and food. Choices range from light salads to filets, and favorites are chicken Shenandoah, pot pies, and pecan pie. Depot Lounge, with railroad memorabilia, offers lighter fare. **FYI:** Reservations recommended. Children's menu. Dress code. No smoking. **Open:** Lunch daily 11:30am–2:30pm; dinner Mon–Thurs 5–9pm, Fri–Sat 5–10pm, Sun 3–9pm; brunch Sun 11:30am–2:30pm. **Prices:** Main courses $9–$19. AE, CB, DC, DISC, MC, V. 🏛

ATTRACTION 🖼

Strasburg Museum
E King St (VA 55); tel 540/465-3175. Housed in a 100-year-old landmark building that was originally an earthenware and pottery factory, this museum displays exhibits of local history. Artifacts from Native American, colonial, and Civil War eras are included. **Open:** May–Oct, daily 10am–4pm. **$**

Tangier Island

For lodgings and dining, see Chincoteague

This tiny island, cut off from the Virginia mainland by Chesapeake Bay, was discovered by Captain John Smith in 1608. There are no cars allowed anywhere on the island—mostly because the narrow 17th-century streets are too narrow to accommodate them—and entertainment consists mainly of walking around the island and enjoying the fresh sea air. The locals, who speak in a distinctive accent said to be a holdover from Elizabethan times, earn their living by oystering, crabbing, and clamming.

Cruises depart from the Hopkins General Store, near the town wharf in Onancock (tel 757/787-8220). The ferry leaves at 10am, Monday–Saturday, from June through September.

Tappahannock

This town's name is derived from a native American term meaning "waters moving back and forth from the tides." Seat of Essex County. **Information:** Tappahannock–Essex County Chamber of Commerce, PO Box 481, Tappahannock, 22560 (tel 804/443-5241).

MOTEL 🖼

≣≣ Days Inn
US 17 S, PO Box 1356, 22560; tel 804/443-9200 or toll free 800/325-2525; fax 804/443-2663. Located S of Tappahannock Center. A fairly attractive, two-story red-brick building with a few shrubs in front. **Rooms:** 60 rms. CI 2pm/CO 11am. Nonsmoking rms avail. Plain but clean rooms. **Amenities:** 📺 A/C, cable TV. **Services:** 🍽 **Facilities:** ♟ **Rates (CP):** $39–$45 S; $45–$57 D. Extra person $6. Children under age 12 stay free. Parking: Outdoor, free. AARP discounts avail. AE, DC, DISC, MC, V.

Troutville

This small community NE of Roanoke is within minutes of Blue Ridge Parkway and Appalachian Trail.

MOTELS 🖼

≣≣ Comfort Inn Troutville
2654 Lee Hwy S, 24175; tel 540/992-5600 or toll free 800/628-1957; fax 540/992-5600. Exit 150A off I-81. Just minutes from Hollins College and the Blue Ridge Pkwy, surrounded by many restaurants, and close to a full-service truck stop. **Rooms:** 72 rms. CI 2pm/CO 11am. Nonsmoking rms avail. **Amenities:** 📺 A/C, cable TV, dataport. **Services:** 🛎 **Facilities:** ♟ **Rates (CP):** Peak (Apr–Nov) $59–$65 S or D. Children under age 18 stay free. Lower rates off-season. Parking: Outdoor, free. AE, CB, DC, DISC, ER, MC, V.

≣≣ Howard Johnson Motor Lodge
US 220, PO Box 100, 24175; tel 540/992-3000 or toll free 800/446-4656; fax 540/992-4000. Exit 150B off I-81. A very quiet motel located in a wooded area. Numerous restaurants and services nearby. **Rooms:** 70 rms. Executive level. CI 1pm/CO noon. Nonsmoking rms avail. Exceptional attention paid to rooms. **Amenities:** 📺 A/C, satel TV w/movies, in-rm safe. All units w/terraces. **Services:** 🛎 **Facilities:** ♟ 1 restaurant, playground. **Rates:** Peak (Apr–Oct) $48–$70 S; $54–$70 D. Extra person $6. Children under age 18 stay free. Min stay special events. Lower rates off-season. Parking: Outdoor, free. AE, CB, DC, DISC, ER, JCB, MC, V.

Tysons Corner

See also McLean

Bustling business and commercial area outside of Washington, DC. Home to the East Coast's largest shopping mall. Nearby Vienna is site of Wolf Trap Foundation for the Performing Arts. **Information:** Fairfax County Chamber of Commerce, 8391 Old Courthouse #300, Vienna, 22182 (tel 703/749-0400).

HOTELS 🖼

≣≣≣ Best Western Tysons Westpark
8401 Westpark Dr, McLean, 22102; tel 703/734-2800 or toll free 800/533-3301; fax 703/821-8872. Exit 10 off I-495. This unpretentious full-service hotel offers comfortable rooms and facilities attractive to families. **Rooms:** 301 rms and stes. Executive level. CI 3pm/CO noon. Nonsmoking rms avail. Attractively decorated units have dark wood furniture and double vanities. **Amenities:** 📺 A/C, cable TV w/movies, dataport, voice mail. Refrigerators available. **Services:** ✖ 🛎 **Facilities:** ♟ 1 restaurant, 1 bar (w/entertainment), games rm, spa, sauna, whirlpool, washer/dryer. Although indoors, restaurant has patio-like ambience with exposed-brick walls, wrought-iron railing, lots of plants. **Rates:** Peak (Mar–Oct) $95–$105 S or D; $125 ste. Children under age 12 stay free. Lower rates off-

season. Parking: Outdoor, free. Extra-person rates apply only when cot required. Weekend packages avail. AE, CB, DC, DISC, JCB, MC, V.

☰☰☰ Embassy Suites Tysons Corner

8517 Leesburg Pike, Vienna, 22182; tel 703/883-0707 or toll free 800/EMBASSY; fax 703/883-0694. Exit 10B off I-495. Follow VA 7 W for 1½ miles. Glass elevators and all corridors overlook an attractive atrium at this comfortable, all-suites hotel. **Rooms:** 232 stes. CI 3pm/CO noon. Nonsmoking rms avail. Suites have separate parlor with sleep sofa and a king-size bed (no doubles or twins). "Evergreen" units (for those with allergies) and two-bedroom suites available. **Amenities:** 🛅 🖨 ❄ A/C, cable TV w/movies, refrig, dataport, voice mail. All units have wet bars and two TVs. Microwaves on request. **Services:** ✗ 🍴 🖨 ↺ Car-rental desk. Full breakfast, included in rates, served in atrium. Manager's reception each evening with complimentary cocktails. **Facilities:** 🏊 🛎 60 ፟ 1 restaurant, 1 bar, games rm, sauna, whirlpool, washer/dryer. Deli-style restaurant opens to atrium at lobby level. Lavender-and-green lounge bar in center of atrium is accented with brass rails. **Rates (BB):** Peak (Apr–May/Oct) $159 ste. Extra person $10. Children under age 12 stay free. Lower rates off-season. Parking: Outdoor, free. AE, DC, DISC, JCB, MC, V.

☰☰☰ Holiday Inn Tysons Corner

1960 Chain Bridge Rd, McLean, 22102; tel 703/893-2100 or toll free 800/HOLIDAY; fax 703/356-8281. Exit 11B off I-495. The buildings of this mid-rise hotel wrap around a lovely landscaped courtyard. Both Tysons Corner malls are within walking distance. **Rooms:** 316 rms. Executive level. CI 3pm/CO 1pm. Nonsmoking rms avail. King-bed rooms have recliners with reading lamp. Dark colonial-style furniture adds class. **Amenities:** 🛅 🖨 ❄ A/C, cable TV w/movies, dataport, voice mail, in-rm safe. **Services:** ✗ 🖨 ↺ Free van transfers to nearby office buildings. **Facilities:** 🏊 🛎 500 ፟ 1 restaurant, 1 bar, whirlpool, washer/dryer. Restaurant has attractive garden-like setting. Junior Olympic-size indoor pool opens to courtyard. **Rates:** Peak (Mar–Jun/Sept–Nov) $119–$134 S or D. Extra person $15. Children under age 18 stay free. Lower rates off-season. Parking: Indoor/outdoor, free. Weekend rates avail. AE, CB, DC, DISC, EC, ER, JCB, MC, V.

☰☰☰☰ McLean Hilton at Tysons Corner

7920 Jones Branch Dr, McLean, 22102; tel 703/847-5000 or toll free 800/HILTONS; fax 703/761-5207. Exit 10B off I-495, off Westpark Dr. Full-service hotel housed in a stunning triangular building. Fountains lend a cool, relaxing ambience to atrium bar and lounge. Manicured office-park setting is near Tysons Corner shopping malls; entertainers appearing at nearby Wolf Trap Farm often stay here. **Rooms:** 458 rms and stes. Executive level. CI 3pm/CO noon. Nonsmoking rms avail. Entry to most units is off atrium walkways. Bright, modern furniture and coordinated color schemes. Door numbers in braille. **Amenities:** 🛅 🖨 ❄ A/C, cable TV

w/movies, dataport, voice mail. All units w/minibars. Deluxe rooms have irons and ironing boards. Club-level rooms have VCRs, robes, makeup mirrors, valet stands. **Services:** ✗ 🖨 🖨 ↺ Twice-daily maid svce, social director, babysitting. **Facilities:** 🏊 🚲 🏋 🛎 1000 💻 ፟ 1 restaurant, 2 bars (1 w/entertainment), games rm, spa, sauna, washer/dryer. Pool has doors opening to sun deck. Restaurant is off atrium. Flamingo's has sports bar/nightclub atmosphere. **Rates:** $120–$195 S; $140–$215 D; $275–$1,000 ste. Children under age 18 stay free. Parking: Outdoor, free. AE, CB, DC, DISC, JCB, MC, V.

☰☰☰☰ The Ritz-Carlton Tysons Corner

1700 Tysons Blvd, McLean, 22102; tel 703/506-4300 or toll free 800/241-3333; fax 703/506-4305. Exit 11B off I-495, follow VA 123 S. Rich wood paneling, paintings hung on fabric walls, and Oriental rugs on marble floors complete the elegant scene at this luxury hotel attached to the upscale Galleria at Tysons II shopping mall. Arrival lobby is at street level, whereas main lobby, along with mall entrance, is an elevator ride up on fourth floor. **Rooms:** 399 rms and stes. Executive level. CI 3pm/CO noon. Nonsmoking rms avail. Dark woods, fabric wall coverings, and marble baths grace every room. The two-bed rooms contain oversize twins instead of doubles. Spacious executive suites have french doors separating parlor from bedroom. **Amenities:** 🛅 🖨 ❄ A/C, cable TV w/movies, dataport, voice mail, in-rm safe, bathrobes. All units w/minibars, some w/fireplaces, some w/whirlpools. Luxury-level rooms have VCRs and fax machines. **Services:** 🍴 🖨 VP 🖨 ↺ Twice-daily maid svce, masseur, babysitting. Those on luxury level can take advantage of concierge lounge with five food presentations daily. Front desk converts foreign currency. Complimentary shoe shines. **Facilities:** 🏊 🛎 1200 💻 ፟ 1 restaurant (*see* "Restaurants" below), 1 bar (w/entertainment), spa, sauna, steam rm, whirlpool, beauty salon. Tennis and golf arranged at local clubs. **Rates:** $159–$189 S or D; $375–$1,200 ste. Children under age 21 stay free. Parking: Indoor/outdoor, free. AE, CB, DC, DISC, JCB, MC, V.

☰☰☰☰ Sheraton Premiere at Tysons Corner

8661 Leesburg Pike, Vienna, 22182; tel 703/448-1234 or toll free 800/572-ROOM; fax 703/893-8193. Exit 10B off I-495. A stunning high-rise tower whose surrounding public areas have lots of marble, columns, and skylights to create an outdoorsy yet elegant mood. **Rooms:** 455 rms and stes. Executive level. CI 4pm/CO noon. Nonsmoking rms avail. King rooms have angled windows and views from tower. **Amenities:** 🛅 🖨 ❄ A/C, cable TV w/movies, dataport. Some units w/whirlpools. **Services:** 🍴 VP 🚐 🖨 ↺ Masseur, babysitting. Free local calls on club level. **Facilities:** 🏊 🏋 🛎 1200 💻 ፟ 3 restaurants, 2 bars (1 w/entertainment), racquetball, spa, sauna, whirlpool, beauty salon. Extensive meeting areas, including grand ballroom, are well designed and attractive. Indoor pool with "waterfall." **Rates:** $155 S; $170 D; $325–$450 ste. Parking: Indoor/outdoor, free. Weekend packages avail. AE, CB, DC, DISC, JCB, MC, V.

≣≣≣ Tysons Corner Marriott

8028 Leesburg Pike, at Towers Crescent Dr, Vienna, 22182; tel 703/734-3200 or toll free 800/228-9290; fax 703/734-5763. Exit 10 of I-495, follow VA 7 W. This high-rise hotel enjoys a convenient location immediately adjacent to Tysons Corner Center shopping mall. **Rooms:** 390 rms and stes. Executive level. CI 4pm/CO noon. Nonsmoking rms avail. All rooms have rich wood furniture and earth-tone decor. King-bed rooms have easy chairs. **Amenities:** 🛎 🦯 A/C, cable TV w/movies, dataport, voice mail. **Services:** ✗ 🕎 🛍 ↩ Free shuttle to Dunn Loring Metro station. **Facilities:** 🔥 🚲 🏊 ⓹ ⚓ 1 restaurant, 2 bars (1 w/entertainment), sauna, whirlpool, washer/dryer. Attractive indoor pool under skylights on second floor. Popular Studebaker's bar and disco is on ground level. **Rates:** Peak (Mar–Nov) $129–$139 S; $149–$159 D; $250 ste. Extra person $10. Children under age 12 stay free. Lower rates off-season. Parking: Indoor/outdoor, free. Weekend packages avail. AE, CB, DC, DISC, JCB, MC, V.

MOTELS

≣≣ Comfort Inn Tysons Corner

1587 Spring Hill Rd, Vienna, 22182; tel 703/448-8020 or toll free 800/4-CHOICE, 800/4-CHOICE, 800/828-3297 in VA; fax 703/448-0343. Exit 10 off I-495. An exceptional value for the Tysons Corner area. Three motel blocks with standard rooms flank a central courtyard. Separate reception and restaurant buildings. **Rooms:** 250 rms and stes. CI 3pm/CO noon. Nonsmoking rms avail. King-bed rooms have easy chairs; otherwise, all units are identical except for bed arrangements. Vanities are outside toilet/shower. **Amenities:** 🛎 🦯 📺 🍴 A/C, cable TV w/movies, dataport. Some units w/terraces. Phones have call-waiting. **Services:** 🚐 🕎 ↩ Twice-daily maid svce, car-rental desk, babysitting. Free van to Dunn Loring Metro station and shops in Tysons area. Free local calls. **Facilities:** 🔥 🏊 ⚓ 1 restaurant (lunch and dinner only), washer/dryer. Fuddrucker's restaurant on premises. Guests get discount at nearby health club. **Rates:** Peak (Apr–Oct) $75–$95 S or D; $105 ste. Extra person $5. Children under age 16 stay free. Lower rates off-season. Parking: Outdoor, free. AE, CB, DC, DISC, JCB, MC, V.

≣≣≣ Marriott Residence Inn Tysons Corner

8616 Westwood Center Dr, Vienna, 22182; tel 703/893-0120 or toll free 800/331-3131; fax 703/790-8896. Exit 10 of I-495. Modern, California-style complex offering fully equipped apartments of varying sizes built around a landscaped pool area. **Rooms:** 96 effic. CI 3pm/CO noon. Nonsmoking rms avail. All units have fully equipped kitchens. Penthouse models have sleeping lofts overlooking spacious living area. **Amenities:** 🛎 🦯 📺 A/C, cable TV, refrig, dataport, VCR. Some units w/terraces, some w/fireplaces.

VCRs, tape library available. **Services:** ✗ 🕎 ↩ ↩ Babysitting. Grocery shopping. Evening cookouts or group meals provided for a fee. Maid service and linen changed every two days during long-term stays. Nonrefundable $85 fee required for pets. **Facilities:** 🔥 🚲 🏊 📺 ⚓ Basketball, volleyball, whirlpool, washer/dryer. Modern lobby lounge has TV and fireplace and serves breakfast and weeknight manager's specials. **Rates (CP):** $139–$189 effic. Extra person $10. Children under age 18 stay free. Parking: Outdoor, free. AE, CB, DC, DISC, JCB, MC, V.

RESTAURANTS 🍴

★ Clyde's of Tysons Corner

8332 Leesburg Pike at Chain Bridge Rd, Vienna; tel 703/734-1901. Exit 10B off I-495 to VA 7 W. **Pub.** One of the largest restaurants in northern Virginia, this version of the Clyde's chain is noted for its Palm Terrace, which has a soaring skylight and wall-size murals with frolicking satyrs. (Noted artists and artisans have contributed to decor). Pub-style sandwiches and burgers are augmented by regional seafood selections and grilled steaks. DJ spins tunes for dancing Friday and Saturday evenings. One of the area's most popular spots, it's often packed on weekends. **FYI:** Reservations recommended. Children's menu. **Open:** Mon–Sat 11am–2am, Sun 10am–2am. **Prices:** Main courses $9–$15. AE, CB, DC, DISC, MC, V. ❤ 🖼 👥 📺 💳 ⚓

★ Da Domenico's

1992 Chain Bridge Rd, McLean; tel 703/790-9000. At Leesburg Pike (VA 7). **Italian.** This unusual dining room is designed like a Victorian Virginia home. Fretwork sets off a fake front porch, and smaller dining areas inside are furnished to evoke that era. Emphasis is on traditional Italian pasta, veal, beef, and seafood, plus daily specials determined by availability of local produce. Friendly host sometimes sings opera at tableside. **FYI:** Reservations recommended. Dress code. No smoking. **Open:** Mon–Fri 11:30am–11pm, Sat 5–11pm. **Prices:** Main courses $10–$23. AE, CB, DC, DISC, MC, V.

★ Fedora Café

8521 Leesburg Pike, Vienna; tel 703/556-0100. Exit I-495 at VA 7 W. **New American.** Wall coverings to match a rose marble bar set the theme at this spacious cafe with open kitchen and deli case at the entrance. Tiffany lighting and dark woods add to upscale ambience. Many char-grilled items are complemented by unusual offerings, such as pheasant ravioli. **FYI:** Reservations recommended. Jazz/piano. No smoking. **Open:** Lunch Mon–Fri 11:30am–3pm, Sat noon–3pm; dinner Mon–Thurs 4:30–10:30pm, Fri–Sat 4:30–11pm, Sun 4:30–9:30pm; brunch Sun 10:30am–2:30pm. **Prices:** Main courses $9–$19. AE, CB, DC, DISC, MC, V. ❤ 👥 ⚓

Hunan Lion II

In the Galleria at Tysons II, 2001 International Dr, McLean; tel 703/883-1938. Exit 11 off I-495. **Chinese.** There is no

Chinese decor here, but bright wood chairs go nicely with beige walls to create a modern, cheerful atmosphere. Menu offers a wide variety of Cantonese dishes, highlighted by daily specials derived from fresh local produce. **FYI:** Reservations not accepted. **Open:** Mon–Sat 11:30am–10pm, Sun 11:30am–9pm. **Prices:** Main courses $6–$17. AE, DC, MC, V. &

★ Marco Polo Restaurant
245 W Maple Ave at Pleasant St, Vienna; tel 703/281-3922. Exit 62 off I-66. Go north on Nutley St to W Maple Ave; head east. **Italian.** A number of small nooks with subdued lighting and dark-wood trim add a feeling of intimacy to this otherwise large restaurant. Northern Italian seafood and pasta dishes have been the specialties since 1973. Italian buffet offered Thursday evenings. Luncheon buffet Tuesday to Friday. **FYI:** Reservations recommended. Children's menu. Dress code. **Open:** Mon–Thurs 11am–10pm, Fri–Sat 11am–11pm. **Prices:** Main courses $11–$18. AE, CB, DC, MC, V. ▾ &

♥ Morton's of Chicago
In Fairfax Square, 8075 Leesburg Pike at Aline Ave, Vienna; tel 703/883-0800. Exit 10 off I-495 to VA 7 W. **Steak.** A lively but elegant dining room trimmed in rich mahogany, a wall full of photos of regulars and celebrities, and various displays of fresh food highlight this member of the Chicago steak house chain noted for top-quality steaks, veal, lamb, and fish, all displayed as a "living menu," which allows guests to choose their own cuts. **FYI:** Reservations recommended. Dress code. **Open:** Lunch Mon–Fri 11:30am–2:30pm. **Prices:** Main courses $18–$30. AE, CB, DC, MC, V. ● VP &

Nizam's Restaurant
In Village Green Shopping Center, 523 W Maple Ave at Nutley St, Vienna; tel 703/938-8948. Exit 62 off I-66. Go north on Nutley St. **Middle Eastern/Turkish.** Various plates and Turkish knickknacks give this blond-wood dining room an ethnic flavor to match the thinly sliced doner kabobs and other traditional Turkish specialties. A popular local eatery since 1977. **FYI:** Reservations recommended. Dress code. No smoking. **Open:** Lunch Tues–Fri 11am–3pm; dinner Tues–Thurs 5–10pm, Fri–Sat 5–11pm, Sun 4–10pm. **Prices:** Main courses $13–$18. AE, DC, DISC, MC, V. ● &

★ Phillips Seafood Grill
8300 Boone Blvd, Vienna; tel 703/442-0400. Exit 10 off I-495 to VA 7 at Gallows Rd. **Italian/Seafood.** Dark wood, brass rails, and discreet lighting lend casual elegance to this upscale spot sandwiched between two high-rise office buildings. Dining rooms are divided to include space for some private tables; one room is under a lovely stained-glass dome. Specialties are char-grilled fish and lobster, plus traditional Chesapeake-style crab cakes and spiced shrimp. **FYI:** Reservations accepted. Children's menu. No smoking. **Open:** Lunch

Mon–Fri 11:30am–2:30pm; dinner Mon–Fri 5–10pm, Sat 5–10:30pm, Sun 5–9pm. **Prices:** Main courses $8–$18. AE, CB, DC, DISC, MC, V. ● ⚓ ▦ ▾ &

Primi Piatti
In Fairfax Square, 8045 Leesburg Pike, at Aline Ave, Vienna; tel 703/893-0300. Exit 10 off I-495 to VA 7 W. **Italian.** Potted tropical plants divide this open, cafe-style dining room accented by varnished wood chairs and moldings. Each table boasts a basket of fresh bread sticks. A wide variety of pastas, pizzas, and meat dishes are offered, all prepared in traditional styles from throughout Italy. **FYI:** Reservations recommended. **Open:** Lunch Mon–Fri 11:30am–2:30pm; dinner Mon–Thurs 5:30–10pm, Fri–Sat 5:30–10:30pm. **Prices:** Main courses $11–$18. AE, CB, DC, DISC, MC, V. ● ▦ VP &

♥ The Restaurant
In the Ritz-Carlton Tysons Corner, 1700 Tysons Blvd, McLean; tel 703/506-4300. Exit 11 B off I-495. **Regional American.** Plushly upholstered chairs and antique furnishings highlight the elegant, continental-style dining room of this luxury hotel. A limited dinner menu comprises gourmet American and continental cuisine, with an emphasis on healthful ingredients. Dinners are either two, three, or four courses only. Luncheon buffets are popular. **FYI:** Reservations recommended. Blues/cabaret/jazz/piano. Children's menu. Dress code. **Open:** Daily 6:30–10pm. **Prices:** Main courses $12–$25; prix fixe $34–$45. AE, CB, DC, DISC, ER, MC, V. ● VP &

Ristorante Bonaroti
In Wolftrap Shops, 428 E Maple Ave, Vienna; tel 703/281-7550. Exit 62 off I-66. Go north on Nutley St to W Maple Ave; go east 1 mile. **Italian.** Reproductions of the Italian masters, including Michelangelo, set an appropriate theme in this pleasant, living room–like restaurant noted for northern Italian cuisine. Homemade pastas. Extensive wine list. **FYI:** Reservations recommended. Children's menu. Dress code. **Open:** Lunch Mon–Fri 11:30am–3pm; dinner Mon–Sat 5–10:30pm. **Prices:** Main courses $12–$20. AE, CB, DC, MC, V.

Vienna

See Tysons Corner

Virginia Beach

Noted oceanside resort at the mouth of Chesapeake Bay east of Norfolk, featuring year-round family attractions. **Information:** Virginia Beach Convention and Visitors Bureau, 2101 Parks Ave #500, Virginia Beach, 23451 (tel 757/437-4700).

HOTELS 🏨

≣≣≣ The Atrium Resort Hotel

21st St and Artic Ave, 23451; tel 757/491-1400 or toll free 800/967-8483; fax 757/491-7901. Exit I-64 at Virginia Beach; two blocks from oceanfront. Attractive six-story atrium lobby outshines some units at this time-share operation two blocks from the beach. **Rooms:** 96 stes. CI 3pm/CO 10AM. No smoking. All units are two-room suites with two double beds, full kitchens. **Amenities:** 🛅 🐶 A/C, cable TV w/movies, refrig. **Services:** 🛌 🐶 Babysitting. Masseur and other services available at nearby Ocean Key Hotel. **Facilities:** 🏋 🍸 🕭 Spa, whirlpool, washer/dryer. **Rates:** Peak (Mem Day–Labor Day) $109 ste. Extra person $10. Children under age 18 stay free. Lower rates off-season. Parking: Indoor/outdoor, free. Weekly rates and discounts avail. AE, CB, DC, DISC, MC, V.

≣≣≣ Barclay Towers Resort Hotel

809 Atlantic Ave, 23451 (Oceanfront); tel 757/491-2700 or toll free 800/344-4473; fax 757/428-3790. Between 8th and 9th Sts. This hotel offers fabulous views from its oceanfront, boardwalk location. **Rooms:** 84 stes. CI 3pm/CO 11am. No smoking. All units are two-bedroom suites equipped with kitchens, sleep sofas. Time-share units sometimes available at same rates. **Amenities:** 🛅 🎛 A/C, cable TV w/movies, refrig. All units w/terraces. Irons and ironing boards. Complimentary daily newspaper. **Services:** ✗ 🅅🅟 🛌 🐶 Babysitting. **Facilities:** 🏋 🍸 🔟 🕭 1 restaurant, 1 bar, 1 beach (ocean), lifeguard, games rm, spa, sauna, steam rm, whirlpool, washer/dryer. Restaurant, bar, and nightclub face ocean. **Rates:** Peak (June 17–Sept 4) $169–$179 ste. Extra person $10. Children under age 18 stay free. Lower rates off-season. Parking: Outdoor, free. Weekly rates avail. AE, CB, DC, DISC, MC, V.

≣≣≣ Best Western Oceanfront

1101 Atlantic Ave, 23451; tel 757/422-5000 or toll free 800/631-5000; fax 757/422-5000. Between 11th and 12th Sts. This hotel right on the oceanfront and boardwalk offers great views from all rooms and pool. **Rooms:** 110 rms and stes. CI 3pm/CO 11am. No smoking. King-bed suites have sleep sofas. Honeymoon suite has waterbed. **Amenities:** 🛅 🐶 🎛 A/C, cable TV w/movies. All units w/terraces, 1 w/whirlpool. Suites have wet bars, refrigerators, and microwaves. **Services:** ✗ 🖭 🛌 🐶 Babysitting. Services for guests with disabilities include a "suitcase" with special items. **Facilities:** 🏋 🚲 🕭 1 restaurant, 1 bar (w/entertainment), 1 beach (ocean), lifeguard, games rm, washer/dryer. Nightly entertainment and dancing on premises. **Rates:** Peak (June 15–Sept 15) $100–$135 S or D; $225 ste. Extra person $10. Children under age 12 stay free. Min stay wknds. Lower rates off-season. Parking: Outdoor, free. Weekly rates avail. AE, CB, DC, DISC, MC, V.

≣≣≣ The Breakers Resort Inn

16th St at the Oceanfront, 23451; tel 757/428-1821 or toll free 800/237-7532; fax 757/422-9602. A grassy lawn separates this eight-story building from the ocean beach in heart of resort area. **Rooms:** 56 rms and stes. CI 3pm/CO noon. Murphy beds in living room of king suites. **Amenities:** 🛅 🎛 A/C, cable TV w/movies, refrig. All units w/terraces, some w/whirlpools. King suites have whirlpools in bedroom. **Services:** 🐶 Babysitting. **Facilities:** 🏋 🚲 🕭 1 restaurant, 1 beach (ocean), lifeguard, washer/dryer. Free bicycles. Coffee shop with poolside dining serves morning breakfast, evening wine. **Rates:** Peak (June 24–Labor Day) $110–$120 S or D; $150 ste. Extra person $8. Children under age 12 stay free. Min stay peak. Lower rates off-season. Parking: Indoor/outdoor, free. Golf, honeymoon, anniversary packages avail. AE, DC, DISC, MC, V.

≣≣≣≣ The Cavalier

42nd St and Oceanfront, 23451; tel 757/425-8555 or toll free 800/980-5555; fax 757/428-7957. Actually two hotels operated as one, the landmark Cavalier on the Hill was built in 1927 and still is a very traditional and elegant beach resort. Beautifully landscaped, partially treed grounds; Cavalier is spelled out in sculptured bushes on a bed of white rocks. Furnished with antiques, public areas are steeped in historic ambience. Ceiling fans cool large sitting rooms. Original 3 wings are being completely renovated. Opened in 1987, the high-rise Cavalier on the Ocean presents modern elegance while upholding the property's reputation for luxury and service. **Rooms:** 400 rms and stes. Executive level. CI 3pm/CO 11am. No smoking. Rooms in the older building are large, traditionally and exceptionally outfitted with antiques, crown molding, mahogany wardrobe closets with beveled glass to hide TVs, large baths with black and white tile and separate sinks. Units in newer oceanfront building are equally spacious and elegantly appointed, have modern baths. **Amenities:** 🛅 A/C, cable TV w/movies, refrig, voice mail. Some units w/terraces, some w/whirlpools. Some bathrooms have bidets. **Services:** ✗ 🖭 🅅🅟 🛌 🐶 Social director, children's program, babysitting. Shuttle between the buildings. Extensive children's program includes feeding the kids. **Facilities:** 🏋 🚲 🏌 🏊2 🏊2 🍸 🔟 💻 🕭 3 restaurants, 3 bars (1 w/entertainment), 1 beach (ocean), lifeguard, board surfing, games rm, lawn games, sauna, playground. Putting green. **Rates:** Peak (Mem Day–Labor Day) $99–$185 S or D; $209–$700 ste. Extra person $20. Children under age 18 stay free. Min stay special events. Lower rates off-season. Parking: Indoor/outdoor, $5/day. AE, CB, DC, DISC, MC, V.

≣≣≣ Clarion Resort and Conference Center

501 Atlantic Ave, 23451 (Oceanfront); tel 757/422-3186 or toll free 800/345-3186; fax 757/491-3379. Between 5th and 6th Sts. Located on the oceanfront and boardwalk. **Rooms:** 168 rms, stes, and effic. CI 3pm/CO 11am. No smoking. Suites have small kitchens. Time-share units account for 94 of the rooms; these may be available at higher rates. **Amenities:** 🛅 🐶 🎛 A/C, cable TV w/movies, refrig, VCR. All units w/terraces, some w/whirlpools. Suites have TVs in both

sitting and sleeping rooms. Complimentary daily newspaper. **Services:** X ⚿ VP 🖼 🛎 Masseur, children's program, babysitting. Full-time social director supervises activities from daily aerobic classes to board games. **Facilities:** 🏋 🚲 🍴1 🛥 📠250 ⚿ 1 restaurant, 2 bars (1 w/entertainment), 1 beach (ocean), lifeguard, games rm, spa, sauna, steam rm, whirlpool, washer/dryer. The pool here is on the rooftop, with view of the ocean. Award-winning restaurant. Coin-operated laundry. Tanning salon. **Rates:** Peak (June 20–Aug 20) $150 S or D; $220 ste; $200 effic. Extra person $10. Children under age 12 stay free. Min stay peak and wknds. Lower rates off-season. Parking: Indoor, free. Weekly rates and special golf, fishing, tennis packages avail. AE, DC, DISC, MC, V.

≡≡ Comfort Inn
2800 Pacific Ave, at 28th St, 23451; tel 757/428-2203 or toll free 800/441-0684; fax 757/422-6043. A nice, clean place to stay, one block from the oceanfront in the resort area. **Rooms:** 135 rms. CI 2pm/CO 11am. No smoking. Efficiency with small kitchen available. **Amenities:** 🏋 A/C, cable TV w/movies. **Services:** 🖼 🛎 Babysitting. Free local calls. Complimentary daily newspaper. **Facilities:** 🏋 🚲 🛥 📠25 ⚿ Games rm, whirlpool, washer/dryer. **Rates (CP):** Peak (July–Aug) $99–$149 S or D. Extra person $8. Children under age 18 stay free. Min stay peak and special events. Lower rates off-season. Parking: Outdoor, free. Family and golf packages avail. AE, CB, DC, DISC, ER, JCB, MC, V.

≡≡ Comfort Inn Oceanfront
2015 Atlantic Ave, 23451; tel 757/425-8200 or toll free 800/443-4733; fax 757/425-6521. Between 20th and 21st Sts. An all-suites hotel right on the ocean and overlooking the boardwalk in the heart of the resort district. Attractive lobby with large plants and flowers, good seating with view of ocean. **Rooms:** 83 stes. CI 3pm/CO 11am. No smoking. All units have sleep sofas and kitchenettes. **Amenities:** 🏋 A/C, cable TV w/movies, refrig. All units w/terraces, 1 w/whirlpool. Complimentary daily newspaper. **Services:** ⚿ 🖼 🛎 Babysitting. **Facilities:** 🏋 🚲 🛥 📠15 💻 ⚿ 1 beach (ocean), lifeguard. Indoor pool overlooks ocean. Covered high-rise parking on same level as some rooms. **Rates (CP):** Peak (June 11–Labor Day) $149–$195 ste. Extra person $10. Children under age 12 stay free. Min stay peak. Lower rates off-season. Parking: Indoor/outdoor, free. Weekly rates, AARP discounts avail. AE, DC, DISC, MC, V.

≡≡≡ Courtyard by Marriott
5700 Greenwich Rd, 23462; tel 757/490-2002 or toll free 800/321-2211; fax 757/490-0169. Exit 284B off I-64. Like most others of this chain, which is oriented toward business travelers, this hotel with tastefully decorated lobby is built around a central, landscaped courtyard. Quiet location. **Rooms:** 146 rms and stes. CI 3pm/CO noon. Nonsmoking rms avail. **Amenities:** 🏋 A/C, satel TV w/movies. Some units w/minibars, some w/terraces. Hot-water dispenser for coffee and tea in all units. Suites have refrigerators. **Services:** 🖼 🛎 Babysitting. Coffee in lobby. **Facilities:** 🏋 🛥 📠60 ⚿ 1

restaurant (bkfst only), 1 bar, whirlpool, washer/dryer. **Rates:** Peak (Mem Day–Sept) $75–$85 S or D; $95 ste. Children under age 18 stay free. Min stay peak. Lower rates off-season. Parking: Outdoor, free. AE, DC, DISC, MC, V.

≡≡ The Dolphin Inn
1705 Atlantic Ave, 23451 (Oceanfront); tel 804/491-1420 or toll free 800/365-3467; fax 804/425-8390. Between 17th and 18th Sts. An all-suites hotel on the oceanfront and boardwalk, providing great views. Undergoing much-needed renovation in 1996. **Rooms:** 54 stes. CI 3pm/CO 11am. No smoking. All units have sleep sofas. **Amenities:** 🏋 🛎 🖼 A/C, cable TV w/movies, refrig. All units w/terraces, all w/whirlpools. King suite has VCR, 2 TVs, 2 balconies, whirlpool in each room. Mirror permits ocean views from whirlpool. **Services:** 🖼 🛎 Babysitting. **Facilities:** 🏋 🚲 ⚿ 1 beach (ocean), lifeguard, washer/dryer. Rooftop deck and heated pool house, but pool is in poor condition. **Rates:** Peak (Mem Day–Labor Day) $179 ste. Extra person $10. Children under age 12 stay free. Min stay wknds. Lower rates off-season. Parking: Indoor, free. Weekly rates, AARP discounts avail. AE, DC, DISC, MC, V.

≡≡≡≡ Founders Inn & Conference Center
5641 Indian River Rd, 23464; tel 757/424-5511 or toll free 800/926-4466; fax 757/366-0613. Exit 286B off I-64. Go east on Indian River Rd for ¼ mile. A high-quality, no-smoking, no-alcohol facility operated by and adjacent to the Christian Broadcasting Network. Spacious grounds include pond with waterfowl. Beautiful public areas have colonial-style appointments and architecture. **Rooms:** 248 rms and stes. Executive level. CI 4pm/CO noon. Very tasteful furnishings range from formal mahogany to country-style light woods and plaid bedspreads. **Amenities:** 🏋 🛎 A/C, cable TV w/movies, voice mail, bathrobes. 1 unit w/terrace, some w/fireplaces. **Services:** X ⚿ VP 📞 🖼 🛎 Social director, children's program, babysitting. Camp Founders Club has children's camp, whose activities include organized sports, storytelling. VCR rentals available. **Facilities:** 🏋 🚲 🏃 🛥4 🛥 📠1500 ⚿ 2 restaurants (see "Restaurants" below), lawn games, racquetball, spa, sauna, playground, washer/dryer. 120-seat dinner theater. Guests can watch taping of *The 700 Club* cable TV show. Bookstore. Excellent fitness center with instructors. Guests can play at two nearby golf courses. **Rates (CP):** Peak (Mid-Mar–mid-Nov) $79–$94 S or D; $250 ste. Extra person $15. Children under age 17 stay free. Lower rates off-season. Parking: Outdoor, free. Many packages available featuring trips to Virginia Beach, Colonial Williamsburg. AE, CB, DC, DISC, MC, V.

≡≡≡ Four Sails Resort
3301 Atlantic Ave, 23451 (Oceanfront); tel 757/491-8100 or toll free 800/227-4213; fax 757/491-0573. Between 33rd and 34th Sts. On the ocean and boardwalk, this 13-story time-share building is family oriented. **Rooms:** 57 stes. CI 3pm/CO 11am. Units are one- and two-bedroom apartments, all with ocean views, full kitchens, queen-size sleep sofas.

Amenities: 🛏 🛗 📺 A/C, cable TV w/movies, refrig, VCR, CD/tape player. All units w/terraces, all w/whirlpools. TVs in sitting and sleeping areas, microwaves. Video rentals at front desk. **Services:** ✗ 🏖 🍽 Children's program, babysitting. **Facilities:** 🏋 🚴 🛎 ♿ 1 restaurant, 1 bar, 1 beach (ocean), lifeguard, spa, sauna, washer/dryer. **Rates:** Peak (May 30–Oct 15) $160–$180 ste. Extra person $5. Children under age 17 stay free. Min stay wknds. Lower rates off-season. Parking: Indoor/outdoor, free. Weekly rates avail. AE, DC, DISC, MC, V.

≡≡ New Castle Motel

Oceanfront at 12th St, 23451; tel 757/428-3981 or toll free 800/346-3176; fax 757/491-4394. On the beach and boardwalk. **Rooms:** 83 rms, stes, and effic. CI 2pm/CO 11am. All rooms have ocean views. **Amenities:** 🛏 📺 A/C, cable TV w/movies, refrig. Some units w/minibars, all w/terraces, some w/fireplaces, some w/whirlpools. Bedroom whirlpools, brass bath fixtures in all units. Microwaves. **Services:** ✗ 🍽 Babysitting. **Facilities:** 🏋 🚴 🏊40 ♿ 1 restaurant, 1 beach (ocean), lifeguard, whirlpool, washer/dryer. Sun deck on fifth floor has hot tub. Free use of bicycles. Snack shop on premises. Some parking in a high-rise deck on same floors as rooms. **Rates:** Peak (June 24–Aug) $125–$135 S or D; $175 ste; $135–$148 effic. Extra person $8. Children under age 17 stay free. Min stay special events. Lower rates off-season. Parking: Indoor/outdoor, free. AE, CB, DC, DISC, MC, V.

≡≡ Princess Anne Inn

25th St at Oceanfront, 23451; tel 757/428-5611 or toll free 800/468-1111; fax 757/425-5815. Enjoys excellent views from location in middle of Virginia Beach oceanfront. **Rooms:** 60 rms. CI 3pm/CO 11am. No smoking. Large rooms all have ocean views, but many are in need of maintenance. **Amenities:** 🛏 A/C, cable TV w/movies, refrig. All units w/terraces, some w/whirlpools. Microwaves. **Services:** ✗ 🍽 🐾 Pets under 20 lbs. **Facilities:** 🏋 🚴 🏊100 ♿ 1 beach (ocean), lifeguard, sauna, whirlpool. Pool area has tanning booth. **Rates:** Peak (July–Aug) $120–$135 S or D. Extra person $5. Children under age 12 stay free. Min stay wknds. Lower rates off-season. Parking: Outdoor, free. AARP discounts avail. AE, DC, DISC, MC, V.

≡≡≡ Station One Hotel

2321 Atlantic Ave, 23451 (Oceanfront); tel 757/491-2400 or toll free 800/435-2424; fax 757/491-8204. Between 23rd and 24th Sts. Located on the boardwalk next to the Life Saving Museum and an outdoor stage with daily entertainment during summer. **Rooms:** 104 stes. CI 3pm/CO 11am. No smoking. **Amenities:** 🛏 📺 A/C, cable TV w/movies, refrig. All units w/terraces. **Services:** ✗ 🏖 🍽 Babysitting. **Facilities:** 🏋 🚴 🛎 🏊100 ♿ 1 restaurant, 1 bar, 1 beach (ocean), lifeguard, sauna, whirlpool, washer/dryer. Restaurant on fourth floor has ocean view. Pool area has hot tub, extensive sun deck. Parking in adjacent high-rise garage at room levels. **Rates:** Peak (Mem Day–Labor Day) $139–$159 ste. Extra person $7. Children under age 17 stay free. Min stay peak and wknds. Lower rates off-season. Parking: Indoor, free. Weekly rates and AARP discounts avail. AE, CB, DC, MC, V.

≡≡≡≡ Virginia Beach Resort Hotel

2800 Shore Drive (US 60), at Great Neck Rd, 23451; tel 757/481-9000 or toll free 800/468-2722, 800/422-4747 in VA; fax 757/496-7429. Enjoys a great location on Chesapeake Bay with private beach and beautiful sunsets. **Rooms:** 295 stes. Executive level. CI 4pm/CO 11am. No smoking. All units are suites with bay views, separate sleeping and sitting areas. **Amenities:** 🛏 A/C, cable TV w/movies, refrig. All units w/terraces, some w/whirlpools. Microwaves, wet bars. **Services:** ✗ 🚐 🏖 🍽 Car-rental desk, masseur, children's program, babysitting. **Facilities:** 🏋 🚴 🏕 🛎 🛎 🏊500 ♿ 2 restaurants (see "Restaurants" below), 1 bar (w/entertainment), 1 beach (bay), spa, sauna, whirlpool, washer/dryer. Overlooking bay, large sun deck surrounds outdoor portion of pool. Water sports equipment rental on premises. Guests can play at nearby Virginia Beach Tennis Club (transportation provided). **Rates:** Peak (Mem Day–Labor Day) $155–$165 ste. Extra person $10. Children under age 18 stay free. Min stay special events. Lower rates off-season. Parking: Indoor/outdoor, free. AE, CB, DC, DISC, MC, V.

MOTELS

≡≡ Days Inn Airport

5708 Northampton Blvd, 23455 (Norfolk Int'l Airport); tel 757/460-2205 or toll free 800/325-2525; fax 757/363-8089. Exit 282 off I-64. This chain motel is close to Chesapeake Bay Bridge-Tunnel, naval bases. **Rooms:** 148 rms and stes. CI 3pm/CO noon. Nonsmoking rms avail. **Amenities:** 🛏 📺 A/C, cable TV w/movies, refrig. **Services:** 🚐 🏖 🍽 **Facilities:** 🏋 🛎 🏊250 ♿ Sauna. **Rates:** Peak (Apr–Sept) $55–$65 S; $65–$75 D; $95–$125 ste. Extra person $5. Children under age 12 stay free. Lower rates off-season. Parking: Outdoor, free. AE, CB, DC, DISC, EC, ER, JCB, MC, V.

≡≡ Econo Lodge Chesapeake Beach

2968 Shore Dr (US 60), 23451; tel 757/481-0666 or toll free 800/424-4777; fax 757/481-4756. Chain motel one block from Chesapeake Bay beaches. **Rooms:** 41 rms and stes. CI 3pm/CO 11am. No smoking. **Amenities:** 🛏 A/C, cable TV, refrig. Microwaves. **Services:** 🍽 **Facilities:** 🏋 ♿ **Rates:** Peak (Mem Day–Labor Day) $78–$93 S; $83–$98 D; $93–$109 ste. Children under age 12 stay free. Lower rates off-season. Parking: Outdoor, free. Military discounts avail. AE, CB, DC, DISC, MC, V.

≡≡ The Executive Inn

717 S Military Hwy, 23464; tel 757/420-2120 or toll free 800/678-3466; fax 757/523-2516. Located ¼ mi N of Indian River Rd. Older, independent motel close to shopping and restaurants. **Rooms:** 101 rms. CI 4pm/CO 11am. Nonsmoking rms avail. Rooms show some wear and tear but are clean. **Amenities:** 🛏 A/C, cable TV w/movies. Some rooms have refrigerators. **Services:** ✗ 🏖 🍽 🐾 **Facilities:** 🏋 🏊150 ♿

Games rm, washer/dryer. **Rates:** Peak (Mem Day–Labor Day) $69–$75 S or D. Extra person $5. Children under age 12 stay free. Lower rates off-season. Parking: Outdoor, free. AE, CB, DC, DISC, MC, V.

⊨⊨ Fairfield Inn by Marriott
4760 Euclid Rd, 23462; tel 757/499-1935 or toll free 800/228-2800; fax 757/499-1935. VA 44 exit off I-64, take exit 3B (Independence/Pembroke), left on Euclid Rd. Adjacent to a wooded area off the Virginia Beach Expressway, this L-shaped motel flanking a pool is centrally located to shopping, the beach, Oceana Naval Air Station, and Little Creek Amphibious Base. **Rooms:** 134 rms. CI 3pm/CO noon. Nonsmoking rms avail. All rooms are essentially the same except for bed configuration. **Amenities:** 🛏 🗗 A/C, cable TV w/movies. **Services:** 🖎 🗗 **Facilities:** 🗗 🔢 👐 Free guest use of Gold's Gym, 4 miles away. **Rates:** Peak (May–Labor Day) $54–$71 S; $59–$76 D. Children under age 18 stay free. Lower rates off-season. Parking: Outdoor, free. AE, DC, DISC, MC, V.

RESORT

⊨⊨⊨ Ramada Plaza Resort Ocean Front
57th and Atlantic Ave, PO Box 7630, 23457-7630; tel 757/428-7025 or toll free 800/685-5105; fax 757/428-2921. Pacific or Atlantic Ave to 57th St. At the quieter north end of the beach, this high-rise hotel has a wide range of facilities, including a splendid indoor/outdoor pool and a concierge level. **Rooms:** 215 rms. Executive level. CI 3pm/CO 11am. Nonsmoking rms avail. Rooms have either ocean or pool views. **Amenities:** 🛏 🗗 🍽 A/C, cable TV w/movies, refrig, dataport, bathrobes. All units w/terraces. **Services:** ✕ 🖦 🚗 🖎 🗗 Children's program, babysitting. Whale watching programs. **Facilities:** 🗗 🚲 🍽 🔢 🖥 👐 1 restaurant (see "Restaurants" below), 2 bars, 1 beach (ocean), volleyball, sauna, whirlpool. Golf nearby. **Rates (CP):** Peak (Mem Day–Labor Day) $150–$195 S or D. Extra person $10. Children under age 18 stay free. Min stay wknds and special events. Lower rates off-season. MAP rates avail. Parking: Outdoor, free. AE, DC, DISC, MC, V.

RESTAURANTS 🍴

★ Alexander's on the Bay
4536 Ocean View Ave; tel 757/464-4999. At Fentress Rd. **Continental/Seafood.** Great view over Chesapeake Bay, along with the requisite nautical theme. Menu offers creative options like tuna Norfolk (sautéed yellowfin tuna capped with artichoke hearts, backfin crabmeat, and hollandaise sauce). Outside dining area near bar has limited menu. **FYI:** Reservations recommended. Dress code. **Open:** Mon–Thurs 5:30–10pm, Fri–Sat 5–10:30pm, Sun 5–9pm. **Prices:** Main courses $16–$30. AE, CB, DC, DISC, MC, V. 🌐 🖳 🖼 VP

★ Blue Pete's
1400 N Muddy Creek Rd; tel 757/426-2005. **Seafood/Steak/Pasta.** Lovely natural setting makes this well worth the drive to Tabernacle Creek in Back Bay National Wildlife Refuge. Dine inside or on creekside decks nearly surrounding building. Trees in creek are lighted at night. Inside are old furniture, plants, and great views. Menus feature original watercolor paintings of the restaurant, and among the best items are prime rib, broiled seafood. Vegetables are fresh, and desserts are homemade. Casual attire appropriate. Capt Dave Kelly's 45-minute wildlife refuge cruises depart restaurant's dock. **FYI:** Reservations accepted. Children's menu. Dress code. **Open:** Daily 6–10pm. Closed Nov–Feb. **Prices:** Main courses $17–$30. AE, DC, MC, V. 🖳 🖼 🖵 👐

Captain George's Seafood Restaurant
1956 Laskin Rd; tel 757/428-3494. **Seafood.** Famous for its all-you-can-eat seafood buffet, this restaurant looks like the bow of an old ship, while inside sports nautical decor. Crowds seem smaller because main dining room is divided into sections. **FYI:** Reservations not accepted. Children's menu. Dress code. Additional location: 2272 Old Pungo Ferry Rd (tel 804/721-3463). **Open:** Peak (summer) Mon–Thurs 4:30–10:30pm, Fri–Sun 4–10:30pm. **Prices:** Main courses $17–$31; prix fixe $23. AE, MC, V. 🖼 👐

★ Gus' Mariner Restaurant
In Ramada Plaza Resort Ocean Front, 57th St and Oceanfront; tel 757/425-5699. **Burgers/Seafood.** A well-appointed, casual hotel eatery with some of the area's best ocean views from giant windows right on the boardwalk. Excellent seafood makes this a favorite with locals as well as visitors. **FYI:** Reservations accepted. Children's menu. Dress code. **Open:** Breakfast daily 7–10am; lunch daily 11:30am–3pm; dinner daily 3–10pm. **Prices:** Main courses $15–$27. AE, CB, DC, DISC, MC, V. 🖳 🖼 🔢 🖵 👐

★ Henry's at Lynnhaven Inlet
3319 Shore Dr; tel 757/481-7300. Located 5 miles from oceanfront, just before Lynnhaven Bridge. **Seafood/Steak.** Families are attracted to this open, airy seafood restaurant. Regional seafood dishes include crab soup and soft-shell crabs. Outside porch extends over Lynnhaven Inlet, giving close views of passing pleasure craft. **FYI:** Reservations not accepted. Children's menu. Dress code. **Open:** Peak (Apr–Sept) Mon–Sat 11am–11pm, Sun 10am–11pm. **Prices:** Main courses $9–$15. AE, DC, DISC, MC, V. 🖼 🔢 VP 👐

Le Chambord
324 N Great Neck Rd; tel 757/498-1234. At Laskin Rd. **Continental/French.** One of the area's class acts, this elegant establishment with cobblestone, gas-lit entrance has overstuffed, semicircular booths and monogrammed china. Fine French cuisine and a few chef's creations like poached Carolina shrimp and sautéed chicken served over lemon pasta. Even the marble bathrooms are classy. **FYI:** Reservations recommended. Piano. Children's menu. Dress code. **Open:** Lunch daily 11:30am–3pm; dinner daily 6–11pm. **Prices:** Main courses $16–$19. AE, CB, DC, DISC, ER, MC, V. 🌐 🖀 🚗 👐

Ⓢ The Lighthouse

1st St and Atlantic Ave, at Rudee Inlet; tel 757/428-7974. **Seafood/Steak.** Situated on both the ocean beach and Rudee Inlet, this seafood emporium enjoys incredible water views from all dining areas, including a covered one outside. Fresh local seafood dishes are the specialty, with a buffet during summer. Chef's nightly specials are less expensive than items from regular menu. Early birds and seniors get 10% discount. **FYI:** Reservations recommended. Children's menu. Dress code. **Open:** Peak (Mem Day–Labor Day) Mon–Fri noon–11pm, Sat–Sun 10:30am–11pm. **Prices:** Main courses $13–$26; prix fixe $18. AE, CB, DC, DISC, MC, V. 🍴 🏞 ✅ ♿

Lynnhaven Fish House Restaurant

22350 Starfish Rd; tel 757/481-0003. On Shore Dr, approximately 4 miles from the oceanfront, next to Lynnhaven Fishing Pier. **Seafood/Steak.** Bay and beach decor accents this seafood restaurant right on the Chesapeake Bay. Menu offers a wide range of regional seafood favorites and more-diverse items, such as scallops Lynnhaven and casserole Prince, a medley of seafood baked in a special sauce. **FYI:** Reservations not accepted. Children's menu. Dress code. **Open:** Daily 11:30am–10:30pm. **Prices:** Main courses $11–$19. AE, CB, DC, DISC, MC, V. 🏞 ♿

Morrison's Cafeteria

In Hilltop North Shopping Center, 981 Laskin Rd; tel 757/422-4755. **American/Home Cooking.** Like its sibling cafeterias found in shopping centers throughout the region, families and seniors come here for simple meat selections and southern-style vegetables at reasonable prices. Nothing fancy here, although the wait staff will bus your table. **FYI:** Reservations not accepted. Children's menu. Dress code. No liquor license. **Open:** Peak (Mem Day–Labor Day) daily 11am–9pm. **Prices:** Main courses $5–$10. AE, DISC, MC, V. 👪 ♿

Ⓢ Piccadilly Cafeteria

In Lynnhaven Mall, 701 Lynnhaven Pkwy; tel 757/340-8788. Exit 284A off I-64. **Cafeteria.** There's nothing fancy about the Piccadilly Cafeterias, but there is something very fresh, as in everything being made from scratch, with no frozen or canned meats or vegetables. Even the mashed potatoes are real. For cafeterias, it's home-style cooking at its best. **FYI:** Reservations not accepted. Children's menu. No liquor license. **Open:** Daily 11am–8:30pm. **Prices:** Main courses $3–$8. AE, DC, DISC, MC, V. 👪 ♿

★ Steinhilber's Thalia Acres Inn

653 Thalia Rd; tel 757/340-1156. Exit 284A off I-64; follow VA 44 to exit 3B, turn right at Virginia Beach Blvd, left at Thalia Rd. **Seafood/Steak.** This restaurant has been a local favorite since 1939. Shrimp fried in a special sauce are famous. Other original sauces add flavors to various seafood entrees. **FYI:** Reservations not accepted. Dress code. **Open:** Mon–Sat 5–10pm. **Prices:** Main courses $15–$39. MC, V. 💛 🍴

Surf Rider

In Haygood Shopping Center, 928 Diamond Springs Rd; tel 757/497-3534. Exit 284A off I-64. Take VA 44 to exit 3B; follow Independence Blvd to Haygood Rd. **Burgers/Seafood.** Padded booths, wooden tables, and a nautical theme mark this family-oriented establishment known for its flounder, soft-shell crabs, scallops, and other seafood. Desserts are homemade. **FYI:** Reservations not accepted. Dress code. **Open:** Mon–Tues 11:30am–10pm, Wed–Thurs 11:30am–midnight, Fri–Sat 11:30am–1am. **Prices:** Main courses $8–$15. MC, V. 👪 ♿

Swan Terrace

In Founders Inn and Conference Center, 5641 Indian River Rd; tel 757/366-5777. Exit 286B off I-64. Follow Indian River Rd east for ¼ mile. **American.** A very large and open floor plan, light-colored wood accents, and cream walls make this a very airy hotel dining room. Tasteful, traditional-style furnishings, a brass candelabra, fireplace, and plants add to pleasant environment. American heritage cuisine features filet mignon Jamestown, Kansas City rib eye, and Maryland crab cakes. Buffet at lunch. **FYI:** Reservations recommended. Harp/piano. Children's menu. No liquor license. No smoking. **Open:** Peak (Apr–Dec) breakfast daily 7–10am; lunch daily 11am–2pm; dinner daily 5–9pm. **Prices:** Main courses $13–$20. AE, DISC, MC, V. 🍴 📷 ✅ ♿

★ Tandom's Pine Tree Inn

2932 Virginia Beach Blvd (Lynnhaven); tel 757/340-3661. **Regional American/Continental/Seafood.** Opened as the Pine Tree Inn in 1927, this extremely well-appointed restaurant with chair rails, wallpaper, lanterns, a chandelier, and candlelight exudes a comfortable feeling. Fresh fish, shellfish, beef, veal, and chicken selections served with continental sauces, all complemented by an excellent salad bar graced with fresh oysters and clams. Friendly and efficient staff adds a casual feeling. **FYI:** Reservations recommended. Piano. Children's menu. **Open:** Lunch Mon–Sat 11:30am–2:30pm; dinner Mon–Sat noon–9pm, Sun 10:30am–9pm. **Prices:** Main courses $15–$20. AE, CB, DC, DISC, MC, V. 💛 🚗 ✅ ♿

Tradewinds

In Virginia Beach Resort and Conference Center, 2800 Shore Dr at Great Neck Rd; tel 757/481-9000. Exit 284A off I-64. Turn left at end of VA 44 (Virginia Beach Expwy), go north on 83rd St (turns into Shore Dr). **Continental/Seafood.** Right on the Chesapeake Bay, this place has great views (especially at sunset) and appropriate nautical decor. Center island has shrimp and oyster bar. Specialties are seafood, steaks, and Italian dishes. Fish du jour is freshly caught. Outside area near bar offers drinks and light dining from shrimp and oyster bar. **FYI:** Reservations recommended. Piano. Children's menu. Dress code. **Open:** Peak (Apr–Oct) breakfast Mon–Sat 7–11am, Sun 7–10am; lunch Mon–Sat

11am–3pm; dinner daily 5–10pm; brunch Sun 10am–3pm. **Prices:** Main courses $17–$24. AE, CB, DC, DISC, MC, V. ♥ 🏖 🏔 &

ATTRACTIONS 🏛

Virginia Marine Science Museum
717 General Booth Blvd; tel 757/425-FISH. This entertaining and educational museum, located across Rudee Inlet just south of the resort area, focuses on Virginia's marine environment. Many of the exhibits are interactive, and visitors can view live sea animals in their natural living conditions. There is even a boardwalk that makes the marsh, its waterfowl, and other animals part of the experience. A summer 1996 expansion tripled the museum's size, adding a 300,000-gallon open ocean aquarium housing sharks and other ocean dwellers, a 70,000-gallon sea turtle aquarium, an outdoor aviary, and an IMAX theater. Guided tours available. **Open:** Peak (Mem Day–Labor Day) daily 9am–sunset. Reduced hours off-season. $$

Ocean Breeze Park
849 General Booth Blvd; tel 757/425-1241 (recorded info) or 800/678-WILD. An amusement park with attractions for all ages, Ocean Breeze offers Wildwater Rapids, a water park with flumes, slides, tube rides, and activity pools; Shipwreck Golf, a 36-hole miniature golf course with a nautical theme; Motorwork go-cart racing for all ages; and Strike Zone batting cage area. Pay-per-play charges apply at all except Wildwater Rapids. **Open:** Mem Day–Labor Day, daily. Call for hours. $$$$

First Landing/Seashore State Park and Natural Area
2500 Shore Dr; tel 757/481-2131. Located 5 mi N on US 60, at Cape Henry. One of Virginia's most popular parks, First Landing/Seashore offers recreational activities along with an opportunity to explore a unique habitat featuring lagoons, large cypress trees, and rare plants. The visitor center has exhibits explaining this coastal environment. Recreational facilities include boat ramps, hiking and bicycle trails, campsites and cabins, and picnicking. **Open:** Daily 8am–sunset. $

Warm Springs

Small Shenandoah Valley town famous for its natural springs, which are 96°F year-round. Seat of Bath County.

INN 🏛

≡≡≡≡ Inn at Gristmill Square
VA 645, 24484; tel 757/839-2231. A beautiful country inn composed of four buildings plus a restaurant/pub is located in a rural area within walking distance of historic Warm Springs pools. Many outdoor activities in area. **Rooms:** 16 rms and effic. CI 2pm/CO noon. Large, comfortable rooms are individually decorated with antiques and reproductions.

Amenities: 🛏 ⓩ 🖥 A/C, cable TV, refrig. Some units w/terraces, some w/fireplaces, 1 w/whirlpool. **Services:** ⌑ Babysitting. **Facilities:** 🔲 🍽 🎱3 🏊40 1 restaurant (see "Restaurants" below), 1 bar, sauna, playground, guest lounge. Two golf courses within 20-minute drive. **Rates:** $65–$75 S; $85–$95 D. Extra person $10. Children under age 12 stay free. MAP rates avail. Parking: Outdoor, free. DC, JCB, MC.

RESTAURANT 🍽

♥ Waterwheel Restaurant
In the Inn at Gristmill Square, VA 645; tel 757/839-2231. **American/Continental.** In a rural highlands retreat, much of the old gristmill remains (grain sometimes seeps from the hoppers), creating a charmingly rustic yet peaceful, intimate atmosphere for fine dining. Fresh trout and daily pastas are the specialties. Wine cellar open for guests to make own selections. **FYI:** Reservations accepted. No smoking. **Open:** Sun–Thurs 6–9pm, Fri–Sat 6–10pm. **Prices:** Main courses $18–$22. DISC, MC, V. ♥ 🖥

Warrenton

In the heart of a rich farmland area in northern Virginia, this city of 5,000 is also the site of several wineries and horse farms. Seat of Fauquier County. **Information:** Warrenton–Fauquier County Visitor Center, 183A Keith St, PO Box 127, Warrenton, 22186 (tel 540/347-4414).

MOTELS 🏨

≡≡ Hampton Inn
501 Blackwell Rd, 20186; tel 540/349-4200 or toll free 800/426-7866; fax 540/349-4200. Exit 52 off US 29 S. Set back from the road in a peaceful country setting, surrounded by the sound of singing birds. Lobby area with antiques is a pleasant place to read. **Rooms:** 100 rms and stes. CI 2pm/CO noon. No smoking. Old wardrobes rather than closets give otherwise standard rooms a bit of personality. **Amenities:** 🛏 ⓩ A/C, cable TV w/movies. Hair dryers available. 1 suite with refrigerator and microwave. **Services:** ⌂ ⌑ 24-hour fax. Turndown service on request. Full breakfast buffet in lobby area. **Facilities:** 🔲 🏋 🏊18 & Washer/dryer. Picnic area under trees, with tables and barbecue. **Rates (CP):** Peak (Mar 31–Oct) $59–$69 S or D; $90 ste. Children under age 18 stay free. Lower rates off-season. Parking: Outdoor, free. Special rates for 7-day stay. AE, CB, DC, DISC, MC, V.

≡ HoJo Inn
6 Broadview Ave, 22186; tel 540/347-4141 or toll free 800/IGO-HOJO; fax 540/347-5632. Exit US 17 or US 211 at Broadview Ave. Perky little place with average furnishings and decor but some nice touches, such as sitting area with tables overlooking the pool. **Rooms:** 79 rms. CI 11am/CO 11am. No smoking. King-bedded units are spacious. Furniture a bit tired, but rooms are clean. **Amenities:** 🛏 A/C,

cable TV w/movies. All units w/terraces. Some rooms have refrigerators. **Services:** 🛏 🛎 Free coffee in lobby. Turn-down service available on request. **Facilities:** 🛋 ⟨30⟩ ⟨ **Rates:** $35–$46 S or D. Extra person $5. Children under age 18 stay free. Parking: Outdoor, free. AE, CB, DC, DISC, MC, V.

RESTAURANT ⍾

Napoleon's

67 Waterloo St; tel 540/347-1200. **American/Cafe.** Located in an 1830s-era house, this restaurant offers seating in the original section, on the terrace, or in the newer addition. All provide a nice atmosphere in which to eat such specialties as fettuccine and filet mignon. **FYI:** Reservations recommended. Singer. **Open:** Peak (Mar–Oct) Sun–Thurs 11am–midnight, Fri–Sat 11am–1am. **Prices:** Main courses $10–$15. DISC, MC, V. ▮

Washington

This quaint town of around 200 residents was established by George Washington in 1749. Within minutes of Skyline Drive and the Shenandoah National Forest. Seat of Rappahannock County.

INN 🏚

🕎 The Inn at Little Washington

Middle and Main Sts, PO Box 300, 22747; tel 540/675-3800; fax 540/675-3100. Turn-of-the-century house with double verandas, deftly restored and enlarged around a garden courtyard. Unsuitable for children under 10. **Rooms:** 12 rms and stes. CI 3pm/CO noon. Rooms furnished with antiques and lots of whimsy (like reproduction 1940s-style radios), but lots of comforts too (heated towel racks, half canopies above the beds, reading lamps beside beds and armchairs). **Amenities:** 🛏 🖳 🖓 A/C, bathrobes. No TV. Some units w/terraces, some w/whirlpools. Complimentary mineral water; fresh flowers. **Services:** ✕ ⓋⓅ 🖼 🛏 Twice-daily maid svce, babysitting, afternoon tea served. Complimentary afternoon tea with cookies. Cordial and efficient staff. **Facilities:** 🚲 ⟨20⟩ 1 restaurant (dinner only; *see* "Restaurants" below), 1 bar, guest lounge. Small lounge/library on second floor. **Rates (CP):** $250–$390 S or D; $410–$525 ste. Extra person $40. Higher rates for special events/hols. Parking: Outdoor, free. Rates vary by day of week, month, and holidays. Guests are strongly advised to make reservations for room and restaurant at same time, as far ahead as possible. MC, V.

RESTAURANT ⍾

♣ The Inn at Little Washington

Middle and Main Sts; tel 540/675-3800. Off US 211. **American/French.** Vaguely Victorian decor, with tasseled lamps hanging low over the tables, and peach-and-cream drapes; there's also a tented pavilion. The chef emphasizes local produce in the imaginative, meticulously prepared and presented dishes, which may include rabbit sausage with sauerkraut braised in Virginia Riesling; grilled poussin (young chicken) marinated in blackberry vinegar; native rockfish roasted with forest mushrooms, pinenuts, and ruby grapes; and warm rhubarb pizza with ginger ice cream. The outstanding wine list features three pages of half-bottles ($15–$95) and a page of Virginia wines ($21–$45 per bottle). Reservations should be made weeks in advance. **FYI:** Reservations recommended. No smoking. **Open:** Dinner Wed–Fri 6–9:30pm, Sat 5:30–9:30pm, Sun 4–8:30pm. **Prices:** Prix fixe $78–$98. MC, V. ♥

Waynesboro

Located in the Shenandoah Valley west of Charlottesville at the foot of the Blue Ridge Mountains. Within minutes of Skyline Drive and the Blue Ridge Parkway. **Information:** Waynesboro–East Augusta Chamber of Commerce, 301 W Main St, Waynesboro, 22980 (tel 540/949-8203).

MOTELS 🏨

⧉⧉⧉ Comfort Inn

640 W Broad St, 22980; tel 540/942-1171 or toll free 800/221-2222. Exit 96 off I-64. Close to downtown and within minutes of Skyline Dr and Blue Ridge Pkwy, motel sits on a hill. **Rooms:** 75 rms. CI noon/CO noon. No smoking. Very attractive. **Amenities:** 🛏 A/C, cable TV. Some units w/terraces. Some rooms with microwaves and refrigerators. Complimentary daily newspaper. **Services:** 🖼 🛏 🛎 Babysitting. **Facilities:** 🛋 ⟨ Very nice pool area and patio with tables and chairs. Guests have free use of YMCA health club. Fax and copier available. **Rates (CP):** Peak (May–Oct) $45–$55 S; $55–$65 D. Extra person $5. Children under age 18 stay free. Lower rates off-season. Parking: Outdoor, free. AE, CB, DC, DISC, ER, JCB, MC, V.

⧉⧉⧉ Inn at Afton

Jct I-64, US 250, Skyline Dr, and Blue Ridge Pkwy, PO Box 849, 22980; tel 540/942-5201 or toll free 800/465-4329; fax 540/943-8746. Exit 99 off I-64. Scenic is the operative word at this motel high atop Afton Mountain at the entrance to both Skyline Dr and Blue Ridge Pkwy. Convenient location and great views make it popular in season. **Rooms:** 118 rms. Executive level. CI 3pm/CO noon. No smoking. All rooms are spacious; some have mountain views. **Amenities:** 🛏 A/C, satel TV. **Services:** ✕ 🖼 🛏 🛎 **Facilities:** 🛋 ⟨200⟩ ⟨ 1 restaurant, 1 bar (w/entertainment), washer/dryer. Restaurant and lounge overlook mountains and valleys. **Rates:** Peak (Aug–Oct) $57–$75 S or D. Children under age 18 stay free. Lower rates off-season. Parking: Outdoor, free. AE, CB, DC, DISC, JCB, MC, V.

Williamsburg

See also Jamestown, Yorktown

This historic city between the James and York Rivers offers nationally acclaimed attractions, including Busch Gardens and Colonial Williamsburg. Seat of James City County. **Information:** Williamsburg Area Convention and Visitors Bureau, 201 Penniman Rd, PO Box 3585, Williamsburg, 23187 (tel 757/253-0192).

HOTELS 🏨

≣≣≣ Fort Magruder Inn

US 60 E, PO Box KE, 23187; tel 757/220-2250 or toll free 800/582-1010; fax 757/220-3215. Exit 242A off I-64. Built on a Civil War battle site, this hotel is popular for conventions; its many amenities make it an enjoyable place to stay. **Rooms:** 303 rms and stes. Executive level. CI 3pm/CO noon. Nonsmoking rms avail. Tastefully decorated and appointed. Spacious suites have exquisite furnishings. **Amenities:** 🛜 🉐 🖭 🍷 A/C, cable TV. Some units w/minibars, some w/terraces. Several suites have wet bars, refrigerators. **Services:** ✕ 🗝 🚗 🛎 🍽 Twice-daily maid svce, babysitting. This hotel prides itself on service and hospitality. Free shuttle to Merchants Square in historic area. **Facilities:** 🛟 🚲 🏊 🎾 🚤 ⛳ 1 restaurant, 1 bar (w/entertainment), games rm, spa, sauna, whirlpool, washer/dryer. Indoor and outdoor pools, exercise room. Golfing arranged at Kingsmill Resort. **Rates:** Peak (May–Labor Day) $108–$128 S or D; $175–$200 ste. Children under age 18 stay free. Lower rates off-season. Parking: Outdoor, free. Package available including tickets to Busch Gardens or Colonial Williamsburg. AE, CB, DC, DISC, MC, V.

≣≣≣ The Williamsburg Hospitality House

415 Richmond Rd, 23185; tel 757/229-4020 or toll free 800/932-9192; fax 757/220-1560. Exit 238 off I-64. Across the street from the College of William and Mary, this hotel has large, beautiful, traditionally decorated public areas. Pleasant flagstone courtyard has umbrella tables, flowering trees, and fountain. **Rooms:** 296 rms and stes. CI 3pm/CO noon. Nonsmoking rms avail. Rooms are tastefully furnished with 18th-century reproductions. Suites are individually decorated in styles ranging from colonial to art deco. **Amenities:** 🛜 🍷 A/C, cable TV w/movies. **Services:** ✕ 🗝 🛎 🍽 Social director, babysitting. Business services include notary and 24-hour fax. Concierge arranges golf at five area courses. **Facilities:** 🛟 🚤 ⛳ 2 restaurants, 1 bar. **Rates:** Peak (Mar 15–Dec 15) $123–$133 S or D; $300–$500 ste. Extra person $10. Children under age 18 stay free. Min stay special events. Lower rates off-season. Parking: Indoor/outdoor, free. AE, CB, DC, DISC, MC, V.

MOTELS

≣≣ Best Western Colonial Capitol Inn

111 Penniman Rd, PO Box FA, 23187; tel 757/253-1222 or toll free 800/446-9228; fax 757/229-9264. Exit 238 off I-64. This family-oriented motel is two blocks from the historic area and five minutes from Busch Gardens. **Rooms:** 86 rms. CI 2pm/CO noon. Nonsmoking rms avail. **Amenities:** 🛜 🉐 A/C, cable TV. **Services:** 🍽 🛎 **Facilities:** 🛟 ⛳ Playground. Grassy area. **Rates:** Peak (June 17–Sept 4) $79–$95 S or D. Extra person $5. Children under age 12 stay free. Min stay special events. Lower rates off-season. Parking: Outdoor, free. Colonial Capital package covers two nights and ticket to either Colonial Williamsburg or Busch Gardens. AE, DC, DISC, MC, V.

≣≣ Capitol Motel

924 Capitol Landing Rd, 23185; tel 757/229-5215 or toll free 800/368-8383; fax 757/220-3810. Exit 238 off I-64, follow VA 143 E to Capital Landing Rd. This pleasant, family-oriented, older budget motel is under new management. Large trees on and around premises. **Rooms:** 58 rms and stes. CI noon/CO 11am. Nonsmoking rms avail. Recent update of room furnishings. Some units have renovated bathrooms with pretty blue accents. New bedspreads and door locks throughout. Suites are roomy, with vanity area outside bathroom. **Amenities:** 🛜 A/C, cable TV. Some units w/terraces. **Services:** 🍽 Twice-daily maid svce. **Facilities:** 🛟 ⛳ Pleasant pool area with four matching gazebos, good-quality lounge chairs. **Rates:** Peak (June 10–Sept 4) $50–$60 S or D; $70 ste. Extra person $5. Children under age 12 stay free. Lower rates off-season. Parking: Outdoor, free. AARP discount avail. AE, CB, DC, DISC, JCB, MC, V.

≣≣ Captain John Smith Motor Lodge

2225 Richmond Rd, 23185; tel 757/220-0710 or toll free 800/933-6788. Exit 234 off I-64. Take VA 646 S to US 60 E, go 3 mi. Clean, budget-priced motel, close to Williamsburg Pottery. **Rooms:** 67 rms. CI 3pm/CO 11am. Nonsmoking rms avail. All rooms are decorated with mint-green and beige accents. **Amenities:** 🛜 🖭 A/C, cable TV w/movies. Some rooms have microwaves and refrigerators. **Services:** 🍽 **Facilities:** 🛟 Games rm. **Rates:** Peak (June–Sept) $60–$62 S; $64–$69 D. Extra person $5. Children under age 11 stay free. Lower rates off-season. Parking: Outdoor, free. Senior discounts avail. AE, DC, DISC, MC, V.

≣≣ Comfort Inn Historic Area

120 Bypass Rd, 23185; tel 757/229-2000 or toll free 800/544-7774; fax 757/220-2826. Exit 238 off I-64. VA 143 E to VA 132 S to US 60 W. Budget motel a mile from historic area. Attractive lobby has decorative tile floor, large fireplace. **Rooms:** 152 rms. CI 3pm/CO 11am. Nonsmoking rms avail. Room furnishings are being updated. Some units have Queen Anne furniture, framed prints by local artist. **Amenities:** 🛜 A/C, cable TV. Some units w/terraces. **Services:** 🗝 🛎 🍽 🛎 **Facilities:** 🛟 ⛳ Games rm, washer/

dryer. Pool with wood deck and four matching gazebos is popular with families. **Rates (CP):** Peak (Mid-June–Labor Day) $79–$99 S or D. Extra person $5. Children under age 18 stay free. Min stay special events. Lower rates off-season. Parking: Outdoor, free. Senior discount by advance reservation, depending on availability. AE, CB, DC, DISC, ER, JCB, MC, V.

≣≣≣ Courtyard by Marriott
470 McLaws Circle, 23185; tel 757/221-0700 or toll free 800/321-2211; fax 757/221-0741. Exit 242A off I-64. Like all Marriott Courtyards, this motel is geared to business travelers, but it's close to Busch Gardens, making it attractive to families as well. **Rooms:** 151 rms and stes. CI 4pm/CO noon. Nonsmoking rms avail. Comfortable rooms have large desks. Some open to courtyard, including some poolside units. **Amenities:** 🛎 ⏰ A/C, cable TV w/movies. Some units w/terraces. Long phone cords, hot-water dispenser for coffee and tea. Refrigerators available. **Services:** 🔑 🛄 🍽 Social director. **Facilities:** 🛗 🛠 🏊 ♿ 1 restaurant (bkfst and dinner only), 1 bar, games rm, whirlpool, washer/dryer. Indoor/outdoor pool. **Rates:** Peak (June–mid-Sept) $109–$119 S or D; $149–$169 ste. Children under age 18 stay free. Lower rates off-season. Parking: Outdoor, free. Government and military rates avail. AE, DC, DISC, MC, V.

≣≣≣ Days Inn Busch Gardens Area
90 Old York Rd, 23185; tel 757/253-6444 or toll free 800/635-5366; fax 757/253-0986. Exit 242B off I-64. This new facility in a wooded area is directly across from Water Country USA. **Rooms:** 210 rms. CI 3pm/CO 11am. Nonsmoking rms avail. **Amenities:** 🛎 A/C, cable TV w/movies, in-rm safe. Refrigerators and microwaves available on request. **Services:** 🛄 🍽 **Facilities:** 🛗 🏊 ♿ 1 restaurant, 1 bar, games rm, washer/dryer. Bar operates during high season only, when motel is popular with construction workers. Pool table in winter. **Rates:** Peak (Mem Day–Labor Day) $89–$99 S or D. Extra person $5. Children under age 18 stay free. Min stay special events. Lower rates off-season. Parking: Outdoor, free. AE, DC, DISC, MC, V.

≣≣≣ Econo Lodge Historic Area
1402 Richmond Rd, 23185; tel 757/220-2367 or toll free 800/999-ECON; fax 757/220-3527. Exit 238 off I-64. This family-oriented motel is located midway between the Williamsburg Pottery and the historic area. **Rooms:** 149 rms. CI 3pm/CO 11am. Nonsmoking rms avail. **Amenities:** 🛎 A/C, satel TV w/movies. Some units w/terraces. Coffee in lobby. **Services:** 🛄 🍽 **Facilities:** 🛗 ♿ 1 restaurant (dinner only), 1 bar (w/entertainment), games rm, sauna, whirlpool, playground. Attractive indoor pool in solarium with whirlpool and sauna. Outdoor pool is shared with adjacent motel. **Rates:** Peak (Mar–Oct) $79–$89 S or D. Extra person $10. Children under age 16 stay free. Min stay wknds and special events. Lower rates off-season. Parking: Outdoor, free. AE, DC, DISC, MC, V.

≣≣≣ The George Washington Inn
500 Merrimac Trail, 23185; tel 757/220-1410 or toll free 800/666-8888; fax 757/220-4662. Exit 238 off I-64. A large, comfortable independent motel midway between Busch Gardens and the historic area. Amenities appeal to commercial guests and tourists alike. **Rooms:** 250 rms and stes. CI 2pm/CO 11am. Nonsmoking rms avail. Renovated in 1993, units feature blue-and-burgundy color scheme. All have two vanities, two sinks. Many of the tastefully appointed suites have dining table for four, sleep sofa. **Amenities:** 🛎 A/C, cable TV w/movies. Many suites have refrigerators; some have microwaves. **Services:** 🛄 🍽 🍷 Babysitting. **Facilities:** 🛗 🛠 🍴 ♿ 1 restaurant (dinner only), 1 bar (w/entertainment), games rm, spa, sauna, whirlpool. Olympic-size pool, enclosed in solarium with sliding doors, is largest indoor pool in area. Separate dry saunas for men and women. Meeting facilities are third-largest in Williamsburg. Restaurant is famous for its smorgasbord. **Rates:** Peak (May–Sept) $89–$99 S or D; $179–$200 ste. Extra person $10. Children under age 17 stay free. Lower rates off-season. MAP rates avail. Parking: Outdoor, free. AE, DC, DISC, MC, V.

≣≣ Governor's Inn
506 N Henry St, 23187; tel 757/229-1000 or toll free 800/HISTORY; fax 757/220-7019. Exit 238 off I-64. Located just outside the historic area, this budget-priced, family-oriented motel is part of the Colonial Williamsburg Hotels Group. **Rooms:** 200 rms. CI 3pm/CO noon. Nonsmoking rms avail. Newly renovated, all rooms have attractive blue and beige colors. **Amenities:** 🛎 ⏰ A/C, cable TV w/movies, voice mail. **Services:** 🛄 🍽 🍷 Children's program, babysitting. Shuttle to Williamsburg Woodlands for continental breakfast, and to historic area. 24-hour security. Free coffee in lobby. **Facilities:** 🛗 🚲 ♿ Games rm. Williamsburg Woodlands facilities (some for fee) available to guests include two pools, tennis, table tennis, shuffleboard, miniature golf, and bikes. Guests also have free use of indoor pool and fitness center discount at Williamsburg Lodge. **Rates:** Peak (Apr 5–May/Oct–Dec) $45–$100 S or D. Extra person $8. Min stay peak. Lower rates off-season. Parking: Outdoor, free. Rates include up to four people per room. Closed Jan–Mar 15. AE, DISC, MC, V.

≣≣ Hampton Inn Williamsburg Center
201 Bypass Rd, 23185; tel 757/220-0880 or toll free 800/289-0880; fax 757/229-7175. Exit 238 off I-64. Go ¼ mi E on VA 143 to VA 132, follow VA 132 S to US 60 E (Bypass Rd). A mile from the historic area, this modern, clean motel has many facilities uncommon for this chain. **Rooms:** 122 rms. CI 3pm/CO 11am. Nonsmoking rms avail. **Amenities:** 🛎 A/C, cable TV w/movies. 1 unit w/minibar, some w/whirlpools. **Services:** 🛄 🍽 **Facilities:** 🛗 🍴 ♿ Games rm, sauna, whirlpool. **Rates (CP):** Peak (May 29–Sept 5) $89–$99 S or D. Children under age 18 stay free. Min stay special events. Lower rates off-season. Parking: Outdoor, free. Rates cover up to five people per room. AE, DC, DISC, MC, V.

Heritage Inn

1324 Richmond Rd, 23185; tel 757/229-6220 or toll free 800/782-3800; fax 757/229-2774. Exit 238 off I-64. VA 143 E to VA 132 S to US 60 E to Richmond Rd. This small, charming motel is within walking distance of the College of William and Mary, adjacent to shops and cinema. Williamsburg-style Christmas decorations during the season. An Easter egg hunt is held annually. **Rooms:** 54 rms. CI 3pm/CO noon. Nonsmoking rms avail. Traditional furnishings include four-poster beds and armoires for TVs. Signed historical prints adorn the walls. **Amenities:** 🛅 A/C, cable TV. **Services:** 🏃 Deluxe continental breakfast ($4 per person) features homemade items daily. **Facilities:** 🛆 Beautiful domed dining room is available for plantation-style dinners on a group basis. Roomy pool area. **Rates:** Peak (June 15–Labor Day) $36–$72 S or D. Extra person $6. Children under age 18 stay free. Lower rates off-season. Parking: Outdoor, free. AE, CB, DC, DISC, MC, V.

Holiday Inn Downtown

814 Capitol Landing Rd, 23185; tel 757/229-0200 or toll free 800/368-0200; fax 757/220-1642. Exit 238 off I-64. Tastefully decorated in the colonial style, this comfortable and modern motel is a mile from the historic area. **Rooms:** 137 rms and stes. CI 3pm/CO noon. Nonsmoking rms avail. Bright and cheerful rooms contain good-quality furnishings. **Amenities:** 🛅 A/C, cable TV. **Services:** ✕ 🏃 Social director. **Facilities:** 🛆 🎾 350 🛆 1 restaurant, 1 bar, spa, sauna, whirlpool, washer/dryer. Large and airy Holidome contains pool, whirlpool, shuffleboard, putting green, and waterfall cascading from restaurant area. Exercise room and sauna are adjacent. **Rates:** Peak (Jun 15–Aug) $54–$99 S or D; $89–$265 ste. Extra person $7. Children under age 18 stay free. Min stay peak. Lower rates off-season. Parking: Outdoor, free. AE, CB, DC, DISC, ER, JCB, MC, V.

Motel 6

3030 Richmond Rd, 23185; tel 757/565-3433; fax 757/565-1013. Exit 234 off I-64. Set back from the highway in a partially treed area, this budget motel has attractive grounds. Located three miles from Williamsburg Pottery and four miles from the historic area. **Rooms:** 169 rms. CI 3pm/CO 11am. Nonsmoking rms avail. Clean and modern rooms. **Amenities:** 🛅 A/C, satel TV. **Services:** 🏃 **Facilities:** 🛆 Washer/dryer. **Rates:** Peak (May–Sept) $46 S or D. Extra person $4. Children under age 18 stay free. Lower rates off-season. Parking: Outdoor, free. AE, DC, DISC, MC, V.

Quality Inn Colony

309 Page St, PO Box FF, 23187; tel 757/229-1855 or toll free 800/443-1232; fax 757/229-3470. Exit 238 off I-64. This homey, colonial-style motel was recently renovated while keeping its existing charm. Pleasant exterior walkways feature a zig-zag brick pattern, white columns, and mint-colored tongue-in-groove paneling. **Rooms:** 59 rms. CI 2pm/CO 11am. Nonsmoking rms avail. Each room has an outer louvered door, which is nice for privacy and fresh air. **Amenities:** 🛅 A/C, cable TV w/movies, VCR. Some units w/whirlpools. Outdoor chairs. **Services:** 🏃 Car-rental desk, babysitting. **Facilities:** 🛆 Washer/dryer. Restaurant is adjacent. **Rates (CP):** Peak (June 15–Oct) $99–$115 S or D. Extra person $8. Children under age 16 stay free. Min stay peak, wknds, and special events. Lower rates off-season. Parking: Outdoor, free. Limit of two children per room. Closed Jan–Feb. AE, CB, DC, DISC, MC, V.

Williamsburg Woodlands

VA 132 off US 60 (Bypass Rd), PO Box B, 23187; tel 757/229-1000 or toll free 800/HISTORY; fax 757/221-8942. Exit 238 off I-64. A renovated motel operated by Colonial Williamsburg, it has a wonderful woodsy setting especially appealing to families. Genuine, natural feeling. Enough diversions on grounds to make guests forget about other attractions. **Rooms:** 315 rms and stes. CI 3pm/CO noon. Nonsmoking rms avail. Updated rooms have authentic Amish-crafted pine poster beds, chests of drawers, armoires. Earth tones. Beautiful forest-green bedspreads, botanical-type prints by local artist featuring the trees found on property. **Amenities:** 🛅 A/C, cable TV w/movies. Some units w/minibars. **Services:** 🏃 Social director, children's program, babysitting. Available mid-June to Labor Day, Young Colonials children's program keep kids busy while parents get away for lunch or dinner. **Facilities:** 🛆 700 🛆 2 restaurants (see "Restaurants" below), 1 bar, games rm, sauna, day-care ctr, playground. A pool for diving, another for swimming. Badminton, miniature golf, shuffleboard, horseshoes, volleyball, table tennis. Nature trail with water cascade. Guests may use facilities at Williamsburg Lodge, including fitness center, golf. **Rates:** Peak (Apr–May/Oct/Dec) $99–$105 S or D; $105 ste. Children under age 18 stay free. Min stay special events. Lower rates off-season. MAP rates avail. Parking: Outdoor, free. AE, DC, DISC, MC, V.

RESORTS

Kingsmill Resort

1010 Kingsmill Rd, 23185; tel 757/253-1703 or toll free 800/832-5665; fax 757/253-8246. Exit 242A off I-64. 2,900 acres. Peaceful and secluded gated community, by the edge of the James River. Only 15–20 minutes from the area's prime attractions. Owned by Anheuser-Busch. **Rooms:** 407 rms and stes. CI 4pm/CO noon. Suites bright and airy, some rooms small and cramped. Pantries in some rooms. Best bets are newer rooms and suites overlooking the river or pond. **Amenities:** 🛅 A/C, cable TV w/movies, refrig, voice mail, bathrobes. All units w/terraces, some w/fireplaces. **Services:** ✕ 🏃 Twice-daily maid svce, car-rental desk, social director, masseur, children's program, babysitting. Complimentary shuttle around resort; discounted tickets for Busch Gardens and Colonial Williamsburg. Sometimes amateurish staff; lax housekeeping. **Facilities:** 🛆 54 🛆 13 🛆

📺 🛏 ♿ 3 restaurants (*see* "Restaurants" below), 4 bars (2 w/entertainment), 1 beach (bay), games rm, lawn games, racquetball, spa, sauna, steam rm, whirlpool, day-care ctr, playground, washer/dryer. First-rate golf and tennis facilities, though resort guests vie with several hundred club members for tee times and court time. Complimentary use of par-3 course. Indoor and outdoor pools. **Rates:** Peak (Apr–Oct) $170–$215 S or D; $230 ste. Extra person $20. Children under age 18 stay free. Lower rates off-season. Parking: Outdoor, free. Special packages for families and tennis players are good buys. AE, CB, DC, DISC, MC, V.

≣≣≣≣ The Williamsburg Inn

Francis St at S England St, PO Box 1776, 23187 (Colonial Williamsburg); tel 757/229-1000 or toll free 800/447-8679; fax 757/220-7096. Exit 238 off I-64. A unique confluence of comfort and refinement, history and pleasure. Luxury inn features colonial restorations and exquisite gardens and lawns, ponds, and 45 holes of championship golf. **Rooms:** 138 rms and stes; 84 cottages/villas. CI 3pm/CO noon. Nonsmoking rms avail. Three types of accommodations: the spacious, Regency-style rooms (with period armoires for TVs) in the inn itself; less expensive rooms in the contemporary garden annex, Providence Hall (ideal for families); and rooms, suites, and cottages (the last of which are particularly good bargains) in authentically restored buildings nearby, in the historic area. **Amenities:** 📞 🗄 A/C, cable TV w/movies, dataport, voice mail, bathrobes. Some units w/terraces, some w/fireplaces. **Services:** 🍽 🗝 VP 🚗 🖼 🛎 Twice-daily maid svce, car-rental desk, social director, masseur, children's program, babysitting. Complimentary afternoon tea featuring harp music in the East Lounge. Some sharp service, some sloppy service. Concierge issues tickets for Colonial Williamsburg attractions and makes reservations for the taverns and shows. Full hotel services, including room service, for guests in Providence Hall and cottages. **Facilities:** 🏌 🚴 ▶45 🖼 🎣8 📺 🍴65 🖥 ♿ 1 restaurant (*see* "Restaurants" below), 1 bar (w/entertainment), lawn games, sauna, steam rm, whirlpool, beauty salon, day-care ctr. One of the pools is spring-fed, for adults only. Two 18-hole golf courses and one 9-hole executive course. Tazewell Fitness Center with spa and indoor pool in affiliated hotel, Williamsburg Lodge, across the street. Lounges with woodburning fireplaces. **Rates:** Peak (Mar–Dec) $245–$325 S or D; $375–$575 ste; $169–$220 cottage/villa. Extra person $12. Min stay special events. Lower rates off-season. Parking: Outdoor, free. AE, CB, DC, DISC, MC, V.

≣≣≣ Williamsburg Lodge

310 S England St, PO Box 1776, 23187 (Colonial Williamsburg); tel 757/229-1000 or toll free 800/HISTORY; fax 757/220-7799. Exit 238 off I-64, ¼ mi E on VA 143, S on VA 132, left on Francis St, right on S England St. 3 acres. Bordering the historic area and renowned Golden Horseshoe golf course, this lodge offers a casual, relaxed atmosphere enhanced by beautiful grounds, fountain, resident ducks, covered brick walkways lined with wooden rocking chairs. **Rooms:** 315 rms and stes. CI 3pm/CO noon. Nonsmoking rms avail. Early American decor, spacious, thoughtfully appointed. Tazewell Wing has folk-art motif, with many handmade quilts decorating the hallways. **Amenities:** 📞 A/C, cable TV w/movies, voice mail. Some units w/terraces, some w/fireplaces, some w/whirlpools. Some units have beautifully landscaped patios with rocking chairs. **Services:** ✕ 🗝 VP 🖼 🛎 Social director, masseur, children's program, babysitting. **Facilities:** 🏌 🚴 ▶45 🖼 🎣6 📺 🍴950 🖥 ♿ 2 restaurants, 3 bars (1 w/entertainment), lawn games, spa, sauna, steam rm, whirlpool, beauty salon, day-care ctr, washer/dryer. Championship golf course is ranked among best in country. Impressive Tazewell Fitness Center has spa services, aerobic classes, and indoor lap pool equipped with underwater stereo. **Rates:** Peak (Apr–May/Sept–Oct/Dec) $185–$235 S or D; $475–$685 ste. Extra person $12. Children under age 12 stay free. Lower rates off-season. MAP rates avail. Parking: Indoor/outdoor, free. Popular Williamsburg Plan includes admission to historic area, meals in a colonial tavern or on premises, and admission to fitness club. Golf Plan includes meals from a variety of restaurants, golf cart for 18 holes a day. AE, DC, DISC, MC, V.

RESTAURANTS 🍴

Aberdeen Barn

1601 Richmond Rd; tel 757/229-6661. Exit 238 off I-64. **Seafood/Steak.** Lots of wood, beamed ceilings with wagon-wheel lights, rich red carpet, and wooden tables make for cozy, intimate air at this steak house. Claim to fame is corn-fed beef: prime rib, barbecued baby-back ribs. Fresh catches too. **FYI:** Reservations recommended. Children's menu. **Open:** Sun–Thurs 5–9:30pm, Fri–Sat 5–10pm. Closed Jan 1–Jan 15. **Prices:** Main courses $14–$29. AE, DISC, MC, V. 🖼 ♿

A Good Place to Eat

In Merchants Sq, 410 Duke of Gloucester St; tel 757/229-4370. Exit 238 off I-64. **Fast food.** Several dining areas (some with tables, others with booths) give a little class to this fast-food restaurant in the historic area. Patio has wire chairs and tables with big umbrellas. Pancakes, biscuits, muffins for breakfast; burgers, sandwiches, salads for lunch and dinner. Yogurt, ice cream sundaes are desserts. **FYI:** Reservations not accepted. Dress code. No liquor license. **Open:** Peak (June–Aug) daily 8am–10pm. **Prices:** Main courses $4–$8. MC, V. 🍴 🖼

Berret's Seafood Restaurant

In Merchants Sq, 199 S Boundary St; tel 757/253-1847. Exit 238 off I-64. **Seafood/Steak.** Transformation from old Esso station to seafood restaurant makes for a unique setting, with many eating spaces of unusual shapes and sizes, large windows, tile or original brick floors, wooden tables and chairs, white tablecloths. Modern brass fireplace and white canvas ceiling baffles give a contemporary look. Original local artwork displayed. Good sampling of Virginia seafood includes traditional and creative items, such as peanut-crusted soft-shell crab (in season). Outdoor pavilion open in warm weather. **FYI:** Reservations recommended. Children's menu. **Open:** Peak (Mem Day–Oct) daily 11:30am–10pm. **Prices:** Main courses $15–$19. AE, MC, V. ▨ ▨▨ ♿

The Bray Dining Room
In the Kingsmill Resort, 1010 Kingsmill Rd; tel 757/253-3900. Exit 242A off I-64. Follow VA 199 W to US 60 E. **Regional American/Continental.** James River view, tasteful furnishings, floral upholstered chairs, large wood columns, and wood trim adorn this resort's fine dining room. Outdoor dining on balcony with river view, weather permitting. Service erratic. Basic cuisine is continental, but summer and winter menus add such regional choices as roast rack of Virginia spring lamb and Virginia fallow deer chops. Friday seafood nights are popular. Buffets at lunch. **FYI:** Reservations recommended. Piano. Dress code. No smoking. **Open:** Peak (Apr–Dec) breakfast Mon–Fri 6:45–9:30am; lunch Mon–Fri 11:30am–1:30pm; dinner daily 6–9pm; brunch Sun 9:30am–2:30pm. **Prices:** Main courses $18–$24. AE, DC, DISC, MC, V. ▨ ▨ ▨ ♿

Cascades
In Williamsburg Woodlands, VA 132, off US 60 bypass; tel 757/229-1000. Exit 238 off I-64. **Regional American.** This restaurant features dark paneled ceilings and a woodsy view. Green wooden chairs and dark-finished butcher-block tables contribute to a relaxed, casual atmosphere attractive to families. Separate dining room has circular tables, cane chairs, domed-motif ceiling. Traditional Virginia favorites highlighted by southern sampler and regional seafood. Virginia wines also featured. **FYI:** Reservations recommended. Children's menu. **Open:** Peak (Apr–May/Oct/Dec) breakfast Mon–Sat 7:30–10am; lunch Mon–Sat 11:30am–2pm; dinner Sun–Mon 5:30–9pm; brunch–Sun 8am–2pm. Closed 1 week in Jan. **Prices:** Main courses $8–$19; prix fixe $17–$20. AE, DC, DISC, MC, V. ▨ ▨ ♿

Chowning's Tavern
Duke of Gloucester St; tel 757/229-2141. Exit 238 off I-64, VA 143 E to VA 132 S. **Regional American.** Part of Colonial Williamsburg, this reconstructed 18th-century tavern is heavy with historic ambience. Rustic wooden tables, eclectic wooden chairs, a heavily traveled plank floor, beamed ceilings, and fireplaces give patrons an idea of what dining was like back then. Traditional meats from the region are offered; Brunswick stew's a favorite. Happy hour, known as Gambols, features period games and beverages such as grog and julep. Lively music. **FYI:** Reservations recommended. Guitar/singer. Children's menu. No smoking. **Open:** Peak (Mem Day–Labor Day) daily 11am–1am. Closed Jan. **Prices:** Main courses $16–$23. AE, DISC, MC, V. ▨ ▨

Christina Campbell's Tavern
Waller and Lafayette Sts; tel 757/229-2141. Exit 238 off I-64. **Regional American/Seafood/Steak.** Another reconstructed 18th-century tavern featuring wooden furniture and floors of that period. Started by a widow, the colonial original was a favorite of George Washington and other notables. Intimate basement room has brick floors and walls, high-backed booths. Seafood offerings include Chesapeake Bay jambalaya with scallops and country ham. **FYI:** Reservations recommended. Guitar/singer. Children's menu. No smoking. **Open:** Peak (Mar–Oct/Dec) lunch Tues–Sat 11:30am–3:30pm; dinner Tues–Sat 5–9pm. Closed Jan–mid-Feb. **Prices:** Main courses $17–$24. AE, DISC, MC, V. ▨

Dynasty Chinese Restaurant
1621 Richmond Rd; tel 757/220-8888. Exit 238 off I-64; VA 143 E to VA 132 S to US 60 W. **American/Chinese/Vegetarian.** Tasteful, out-of-the-ordinary decor includes goldfish pond with orchids and other plants, large urns, rich blue upholstered chairs, white tablecloths with blue toppers, and wooden arches. Spicy western Chinese cuisine is good enough to warrant owners teaching cooking classes. **FYI:** Reservations accepted. Children's menu. **Open:** Daily noon–midnight. **Prices:** Main courses $7–$20; prix fixe $6–$11. AE, CB, DC, DISC, MC, V. ▨▨ ▨ ♿

Fireside Steak House and Seafood
1995 Richmond Rd; tel 757/229-3310. Exit 238 off I-64, VA 143 E to VA 132 S to US 60 W. **Seafood/Steak.** Under same ownership for two decades, this unpretentious steak and seafood restaurant dishes up quality and consistency year after year. A warm, rich look is enhanced by stylish, dark-colored wood chairs, red tablecloths, and corner fireplace. Black leather booth seats available. Prime rib is house specialty, but fresh catch, chicken kabobs, and ham steaks with glazed pineapple ring also served daily. **FYI:** Reservations accepted. Children's menu. **Open:** Mon–Sat 4:30–11pm, Sun noon–10pm. **Prices:** Main courses $9–$17. AE, MC, V. ▨▨ ▨

The Jefferson Inn
1453 Richmond Rd; tel 757/229-2296. VA 143 E to VA 132 S to US 60 W. **Regional American/Seafood/Steak.** Melon-colored tablecloths are set off by solid black plates, giving a casual yet dressy look to this restaurant operated by the same family since 1956. Folk-art-motif draperies, nicely framed prints, waitresses in colonial-style uniforms add historic atmosphere. Southern-style specialties include fried chicken, Virginia ham, grain-fed catfish, cornbread stuffing, Surry sausages. Peanut soup is a delight. **FYI:** Reservations recommended. Children's menu. No smoking. **Open:** Daily 4–10pm. **Prices:** Main courses $9–$32. AE, DISC, MC, V. ▨ ♿

Kings Arms Tavern
Duke of Gloucester St; tel 757/229-2141. Exit 238 off I-64. **American.** Another of Colonial Williamsburg's reconstructed 18th-century taverns, this one has 11 dining rooms, all with rustic wooden floors and furniture from the era. Specialties are from old recipes, including Virginia peanut soup, Smith-

field ham with grape sauce, filet mignon stuffed with oysters. **FYI:** Reservations recommended. Guitar/singer. Children's menu. Dress code. No smoking. **Open:** Lunch daily 11:30am–2:30pm; dinner daily 5–9:30pm. Closed Feb 11–Mar 8. **Prices:** Main courses $19–$26. AE, DC, DISC, MC, V. ▇▮ ♥

Le Yaca
In Village Shops at Kingsmill, US 60 E; tel 757/220-3616. Exit 242 off I-64, VA 199 W to US 60 E. **French.** Six separate dining areas, each with different furnishings, range from wicker to cafe-style at this elegant yet homey establishment widely celebrated in the area. Patrons are greeted by rustic, arched fireplace, where legs of lamb roast in cooler months. French country cuisine runs from poached salmon with hollandaise to roast duckling with black-currant sauce. Most dinners include four courses. **FYI:** Reservations recommended. **Open:** Lunch Mon–Sat 11:30am–2pm; dinner Mon–Sat 6–9:30pm. Closed Jan 1–Jan 15. **Prices:** Main courses $21–$42. AE, CB, DC, MC, V. ♥ 🖼 &

Old Chickahominy House
1211 Jamestown Rd; tel 757/229-4689. Jct VA 199/31 S. **Regional American.** Ladder-back chairs, semi-rustic wooden tables and flooring, a fireplace, grandfather clock, ornately framed pictures, large table with candelabra give historic flair to this cozy, cottage-like house. Homemade Virginia specialties offered, including ham biscuits, Brunswick stew. Filling plantation-style breakfast is good value. **FYI:** Reservations not accepted. Beer and wine only. No smoking. **Open:** Breakfast daily 8:30–10:15am; lunch daily 11:30am–2:15pm. Closed 2 weeks in Jan. **Prices:** Lunch main courses $2–$6. MC, V. ▇

⭐ Pierce's Pitt Bar-B-Que
447 Rochambeau Dr; tel 757/565-2955. Exit 234A off I-64, E on Rochambeau Dr. **Barbecue/Fast food.** Bright orange-and-yellow booths and tables accent this regionally famous barbecue and fast-food restaurant. Consistently good pork barbecue is cooked for eight hours daily in four hardwood-fired grills and served with Pierce's patented sauce. Chicken, ham, and burgers round out the menu. **FYI:** Reservations not accepted. No liquor license. **Open:** Peak (Mar–Nov) Sun–Thurs 7am–9pm, Fri–Sat 7am–10pm. **Prices:** Main courses $3–$6. MC, V. 📷

♥ The Regency Dining Room
In the Williamsburg Inn, Francis St at South England St (Colonial Williamsburg); tel 757/229-1000. Exit 238 off I-64. **Regional American/French.** Has a nice old-fashioned gentility, with courteous, attentive service. Elegant regency decor, tall windows overlooking lawns and gardens, crystal chandeliers, and candle-lit tables. Main dining room is spacious enough to offer ballroom dancing on weekends. Menu offerings focus on classic American cuisine. **FYI:** Reservations recommended. Dancing/guitar/harp/jazz/piano. Children's menu. Jacket required. **Open:** Breakfast daily 7:30–10am;

lunch Mon–Sat noon–2pm; dinner daily 6–9pm; brunch Sun noon–2pm. **Prices:** Main courses $22–$32. AE, CB, DC, DISC, MC, V. ♥ VP &

♥ Shields Tavern
Duke of Gloucester St; tel 757/229-2141. Exit 238 off I-64. **New American/Seafood/Steak.** Another of Colonial Williamsburg's reconstructed 18th-century eateries, with 11 dining rooms outfitted in the colonial style. The Shields' Sampler appetizer comprises a variety of tastes from the 1700s. For entrees there are traditional favorites, such as Virginia ham, crab cakes, seafood, and spoon bread. **FYI:** Reservations recommended. Guitar/singer. Children's menu. No smoking. **Open:** Breakfast daily 8:30–10am; lunch daily 11:30am–3pm; dinner daily 5:15–9:30pm. Closed Feb–Mar. **Prices:** Main courses $15–$25. AE, DC, DISC, MC, V. ▇ &

⭐ Trellis Cafe, Restaurant & Grill
In Merchants Sq, Duke of Gloucester St; tel 757/229-8610. Exit 238 off I-64. **Regional American.** A bustling atmosphere reigns during dinner hours at this casual but upscale eatery, whose different dining areas include a recessed cafe and outdoor patio. Menus change seasonally. The hallmark is creativity and freshness, with seafood and produce delivered daily. Hardly any canned or frozen ingredients are used. Even the ice cream is homemade. Legendary for desserts, owner/chef Marcel Desaulniers is author of *Death by Chocolate* (named for seven-layer extravaganza) and hosts nationwide cable TV cooking program. **FYI:** Reservations recommended. Guitar. Children's menu. **Open:** Lunch Mon–Sat 11am–2:30pm; dinner daily 5–9:30pm; brunch Sun 11am–2:30pm. **Prices:** Main courses $14–$24; prix fixe $20. AE, MC, V. ▇ 🍽 ♥ &

ATTRACTIONS 🏛

COLONIAL WILLIAMSBURG ATTRACTIONS

Colonial Williamsburg
In 1699 the Virginia Colony abandoned the mosquito-infested swamp that was Jamestown for a planned colonial city six miles inland. They named it Williamsburg for the reigning English monarch, King William of Orange.

Royal Governor Francis Nicholson laid out the new capital. His plan alotted every house on the main street a half-acre of land and included public greens. The governor's residence was completed in 1720. The town prospered and soon became the major political and cultural center of Virginia. Many of the turbulent events leading up to the Declaration of Independence occurred here.

The **Colonial Williamsburg Visitor Center** is located off US 60 Bypass, just east of VA 132 (tel 757/229-1000). Block tickets are on sale here—with prices ranging from $25 to $33 for adults, $15 to $19 for children—to the dozens of attractions that make up Colonial Williamsburg. (Most attractions are open daily 9am–6pm during the peak summer months.) In addition, the center offers shopping opportunities, maps, guidebooks, lodging and dining information, and evening activities, as well as two reservation services (one for hotel reservations and one for reservations at the four colonial taverns run by the Colonial Williamsburg Foundation). A 35-minute orientation film, *Williamsburg—The Story of a Patriot,* is shown continuously throughout the day.

Governor's Palace
A complete reconstruction of the stately Georgian mansion used as the official headquarters of seven royal governors and Virginia's first two state governors. Today, the interior is meticulously furnished with authentic colonial pieces. Tours, given continuously throughout the day, wind up in the gardens, where visitors can explore the elaborate geometric parterres, topiary work, bowling green, and a holly maze patterned after the one at Hampton Court.

The Capitol
Virginia legislators met in the H-shaped capitol at the eastern end of Duke of Gloucester St throughout most of the 18th century. The original capitol was built in 1704, burned down in 1747, rebuilt in 1753, and burned down again in 1832. The reconstruction is of the first 1704 building, complete with Queen Anne's coat-of-arms adorning the tower and the Great Union flag flying overhead. Tours are given throughout the day.

Raleigh Tavern
Reconstructed on its original site in 1932, using data from inventories of past proprietors and information gleaned from archeological excavations, the tavern occupies a central location on the north side of Duke of Gloucester St. After the Governor's Palace, this was the social and political hub of the town. Named for Sir Walter Raleigh, the original tavern, which burned down in 1859, included two dining rooms, the famed Apollo Room (scene of elegant entertainments), a club room, a billiards room, and a bar where ale and hot rum punch were the favored drinks. Present-day visitors can still buy such 18th-century confections as gingerbread and Shrewsbury cake, and cider to wash it down, at the Raleigh Tavern bakery in the rear.

Wetherburn's Tavern
Though less important than the Raleigh Tavern (see above), Wetherburn's also played an important role in colonial Williamsburg. Henry Wetherburn ran a tavern here from 1738 until his death in 1760. It was subsequently used as a school for young ladies, a boardinghouse, and a store. The heart of yellow pine floors are original, so guests can actually walk in the footsteps of George Washington, who was an occasional patron.

George Wythe House
On the west side of the Palace Green is the elegant restored brick home of George Wythe (pronounced "With")—foremost classics scholar in 18th-century Virginia, noted lawyer and teacher (his students included Thomas Jefferson, Henry Clay, and John Marshall), and member of the House of Burgesses. He was the first Virginia signer of the Declaration of Independence. The house served as Washington's headquarters prior to the siege of Yorktown and Rochambeau's after the surrender of Cornwallis.

Domestic crafts typical of the time are demonstrated by artisans in the outbuildings. The 18th-century crafts practiced on the grounds of Wythe House are among numerous similar exhibits throughout the Historic Area; a total of more than 100 master craftspeople are part of an effort to present an accurate picture of colonial society.

Publick Gaol
The jail opened in 1704; debtors' cells were added in 1711 and keeper's quarters were added in 1722. The thick-walled red-brick building served as the Williamsburg city jail through 1910. The building today is restored to its 1720s appearance.

Peyton Randolph House
The Randolph family was one of the most prominent—and wealthy—in colonial Virginia, and Peyton Randolph was one of its most distinguished members. Known as the "great mediator," he was unanimously elected president of the First Continental Congress in Philadelphia in 1774 and, although he was a believer in nonviolence and hoped the colonies could amicably settle their differences with England, was a firm patriot.

The house (actually two connected houses) dates to 1715. It is today restored to the period of about 1770, and is open to the public for self-guided tours with period-costumed interpreters in selected rooms. The windmill, in back of the house, is a post mill of a type popular in the 18th century.

Brush–Everard House
One of the oldest buildings in Williamsburg, the Brush–Everard House was occupied without interruption from 1717 through 1946. It was built by armorer and gunsmith John Brush, although its most distinguished owner was Thomas Everard, two-time mayor of Williamsburg. Though not as wealthy as Wythe or Randolph, Everard was a part of their elite circle. He enlarged the house, adding the two wings that give it a "U" shape. Today the home is restored and furnished to its appearance during Everard's residence. The smokehouse and kitchen out back are original.

James Geddy House & Foundry
This two-story, L-shaped 1762 building was the home of James Geddy Sr, an accomplished gunsmith and brass founder. Visitors to this house will see how a comfortably situated middle-class family lived in the 18th century. Unlike the fancier abodes, the Geddy House has no wallpaper or oil paintings; a mirror and spinet from England, however, indicate relative affluence.

The Magazine and Guardhouse
The magazine is a sturdy octagonal brick building constructed in 1715 to house ammunition and arms for the defense of the British colony. It has survived intact to the present day. Today the building is once again stocked with 18th-century

equipment—British-made flintlock muskets, cannons and cannonballs, barrels of powder, bayonets, and drums, the latter for communication purposes.

Horse-drawn carriage rides around the historic district leave from the hitching post in front of the Magazine. Reservations are required, and can be made at the Greenow Lumber House.

Carter's Grove

A magnificent plantation home that has been continuously occupied since 1755. The estate is reached via a scenic, one-way, seven-mile wilderness road traversing streams, meadows, woodlands, and ravines. The road (take South England St and follow the signs) is open 8:30am–4pm; you must return to Williamsburg via VA 60.

Robert "King" Carter, Virginia's wealthiest planter, purchased the 1,400-acre property for his daughter, Elizabeth. Today 700 acres remain. Between 1751 and 1754, Elizabeth's son, Carter Burwell, built the beautiful, 2½-story, 200-foot-long mansion, which is considered "the final phase in the evolution of the Georgian mansion." The West Drawing Room is often called the "Refusal Room"; legend has it that Southern belle Mary Cary refused George Washington's proposal of marriage in the room, and Rebecca Burwell said "no" there to Thomas Jefferson.

On the grounds of the mansion are a partially reconstructed 1619 village, **Wolstenholme Town,** slave quarters of the 1700s, and the **Winthrop Rockefeller Archeology Museum.** At the reception center, housed in a red cedar building, visitors can view a 14-minute slide presentation and examine displays of historic photographs and documents. **Open:** Peak (mid-Mar–Dec) Tues–Sun 10am–6pm. Reduced hours off-season. $$$

Bassett Hall

Tel 757/229-1000, ext 4119. Though colonial in origin, Bassett Hall was the mid-1930s residence of Mr and Mrs John D Rockefeller Jr, and it is restored and furnished to reflect their era. The mansion's name, however, derives from Burwell Bassett, a nephew of Martha Washington. Bassett lived here from 1800 to 1839.

The Rockefellers purchased the 585-acre property in the late 1920s and moved into the restored dwelling in 1936. In spite of the changes they made, much of the interior is original. The furniture is 18th- and 19th-century American in Chippendale, federal, and empire styles. Hundreds of examples of ceramics and china are on display, as are collections of 18th- and 19th-century American and English glass, Canton enamelware, and folk art.

Forty-minute tours of the house are given between 9am and 4:45pm daily (except Wednesdays) by reservation only. Tours conclude in the garden, which can be explored at leisure.

Abby Aldrich Rockefeller Folk Art Center

The works of folk art displayed at Bassett Hall (above) are just a small sampling of enthusiast Abby Aldrich Rockefeller's extensive collection. This museum contains more than 4,000 folk-art paintings, sculptures, and art objects. The collection includes household ornaments and useful wares (hand-stenciled bed covers, butter molds, pottery, utensils, painted furniture), mourning pictures (embroideries honoring departed relatives or national heroes), family and individual portraits, shop signs, carvings, whittled toys, calligraphic drawings, weavings, quilts, and paintings of scenes from everyday life.

Public Hospital

Opened in 1773, the "Public Hospital for Persons of Insane and Disordered Minds" was America's first mental institution. Before its advent, the mentally ill were often thrown in jail or confined to the poorhouse. The self-guided tour includes a 1773 cell, with its filthy straw-filled mattress on the floor, ragged blanket, and manacles; and an 1845 cell, which shows the vast improvement in patient care that resulted from new attitudes toward the mentally ill during what is known as the "Moral Management Period." The Public Hospital is open daily.

DeWitt Wallace Decorative Arts Gallery

Adjoining the Public Hospital is a 62,000-square-foot museum housing some 10,000 17th- to 19th-century English and American decorative art objects. In its galleries are period furnishings, ceramics, textiles, paintings, prints, silver, pewter, clocks, scientific instruments, mechanical devices, and weapons. The Lila Acheson Wallace Garden, on the upper level, centers on a pond with two fountains, a trellis-shaded seating area at one end, and a six-foot gilded bronze statue of Diana by Augustus Saint-Gaudens at the other.

OTHER ATTRACTIONS

Busch Gardens Williamsburg

1 Busch Gardens Blvd; tel 757/253-3350. This 360-acre family amusement park consists of several re-created 17th-century villages. More than 30 rides and a variety of themed shows, restaurants, and shops are offered. Among the most popular rides is the Big Bad Wolf (a suspended roller coaster that culminates in an 80-foot plunge into the "Rhine River") and the Loch Ness Monster (a steel coaster with two 360° loops and a 130-foot drop). A monorail line runs to the Anheuser-Busch Hospitality Center, which offers brewery tours. **Open:** Peak (mid-May–Aug) Sun–Fri 10am–10pm, Sat 10am–midnight. Reduced hours off-season. Closed Nov–Mar. $$$$

Water Country USA

176 Water Country Pkwy; tel 757/229-9300. Located near the intersection of I-64 and VA 199. The region's largest water theme park features more than 30 water rides and slides, live entertainment, shopping, and restaurants—all set to a 1950s "surfer" theme. "Big Daddy Falls" takes guests on a river-rafting adventure through a series of flumes, tunnels, and water "explosions"; Surfer's Bay wave pool produces a

perfect 3½-foot wave every 4 seconds; and the Jet Stream water slide propels riders at up to 25 mph into a splashdown pool. **Open:** May–mid-Sept. Call for hours. **$$$$**

York River State Park
5526 Riverview Rd; tel 757/566-3036. Located 8 mi NW of Williamsburg. This park is known for its rare and delicate estuarine environment, where fresh and salt water meet to create a habitat rich in marine and plant life. One of four estuaries designated as a part of the Chesapeake Bay National Estuarine Research Reserve is located within the park. Visitor center with exhibits focusing on the history, use, and preservation of the York River and its marshes. Activities include hiking, boating, fishing, and picnicking. **Open:** Daily 8am–sunset. **$**

Winchester

North of Shenandoah National Park in northern Virginia, this is the oldest colonial city west of the Blue Ridge Mountains. Seat of Frederick County. **Information:** Winchester–Frederick County Visitor Center, 1360 S Pleasant Valley Rd, Winchester, 22601 (tel 540/662-4118).

HOTELS

Hampton Inn
1655 Apple Blossom Dr, 22601; tel 540/667-8011 or toll free 800/HAMPTON; fax 540/667-8033. Exit 313 off I-81. Go west on US 50. A sparkling-clean, tasteful facility with inviting lobby area with tables and chairs. **Rooms:** 103 rms and stes. CI 2pm/CO noon. Nonsmoking rms avail. Comfortable, eye-pleasing rooms. Some offer pull-out sofa, reclining chairs; one suite has wet bar, fridge, Murphy bed, and queen-size bed; can double as a meeting room. **Amenities:** A/C, cable TV w/movies. Dataports available. **Services:** Microwave in lobby. **Facilities:** 20 **Rates (CP):** $45–$50 S; $50–$56 D; $65 ste. Children under age 18 stay free. Parking: Outdoor, free. AE, CB, DC, DISC, MC, V.

Travelodge
160 Front Royal Pike, 22602; tel 540/665-0685 or toll free 800/578-7878; fax 540/665-0689. Exit 313 off I-81. A delightful facility with friendly, dedicated staff. Lobby has a genteel mood courtesy of mahogany furniture as well as a separate coffee area with TV and tables with soda-fountain chairs. **Rooms:** 149 rms and stes. CI noon/CO 11am. Nonsmoking rms avail. Mahogany furnishings and white brick walls give sparkling rooms a distinctive personality. Some suites have two extra-large rooms, oversize baths, kitchenette, and dining area. **Amenities:** A/C, cable TV w/movies. Some units w/whirlpools. **Services:** Car-rental desk. **Facilities:** 300 Washer/dryer. Discounts at nearby Nautilus Club. **Rates (CP):** Peak (July–Oct) $55–$60 S or D; $100 ste. Extra person $5. Children under age 17 stay free. Lower rates off-season. Parking: Outdoor, free. AE, CB, DC, DISC, ER, JCB, MC, V.

MOTELS

Best Western Lee-Jackson Motor Inn
711 Millwood Ave, 22601; tel 540/662-4154 or toll free 800/528-1234; fax 540/662-2618. At jct US 50/522, off I-81. Comfortable rooms and friendly staff here, plus some nice touches like flowers blooming in wooden tubs around the parking lot. **Rooms:** 140 rms, stes, and effic. CI 3pm/CO noon. Nonsmoking rms avail. Rooms have a king bed or two double beds. **Amenities:** A/C, cable TV. Some units w/whirlpools. Many rooms have microwaves and refrigerators. Many deluxe suites have large-screen TVs. **Services:** Car-rental desk. **Facilities:** 500 2 restaurants, 1 bar, washer/dryer. Grassy pool area is pleasant. Special arrangements for guests at nearby Nautilus Club. **Rates:** Peak (Apr–Oct) $42–$54 S or D; $65 ste; $42–$54 effic. Extra person $5. Children under age 12 stay free. Min stay special events. Lower rates off-season. Parking: Outdoor, free. AE, CB, DC, DISC, MC, V.

Holiday Inn
I-81 and US 50 E, 22601; tel 540/667-3000 or toll free 800/HOLIDAY; fax 540/722-2730. Exit 313 off I-81. Well-maintained facility with nicely appointed lobby containing sitting area, chandelier, and mahogany furniture. **Rooms:** 175 rms and stes. Executive level. CI 3pm/CO noon. Nonsmoking rms avail. Pleasant, clean rooms in good condition. Some open onto courtyard pool area. **Amenities:** A/C, cable TV w/movies. Coffeemakers available in some rooms. VCRs for rent. Queen-bed suites have microwaves and refrigerators. **Services:** Fax available. **Facilities:** 2 150 1 restaurant, 1 bar. Nautilus club arrangement. Inviting pool area with deck, umbrella tables. Nearby golf club offers reduced rate to guests. **Rates:** $49–$79 S or D; $75 ste. Children under age 18 stay free. Min stay special events. Parking: Outdoor, free. Some packages include continental breakfast. Golf packages avail. AE, DC, DISC, MC, V.

RESTAURANT

China Gourmet Restaurant
210 Millwood Ave; tel 540/722-3333. Exit 313 off I-81. Near jct US 50/522. **Chinese.** Padded red booths and pink tablecloths, soft music, and Chinese wall decorations are the backdrop at this small, quiet Chinese restaurant. House specialties are Peking duck and seafood. Staff is friendly and eager. **FYI:** Reservations recommended. **Open:** Mon–Thurs 11am–10pm, Fri–Sat 11am–10:30pm, Sun 11:30am–9:30pm. **Prices:** Main courses $6–$19. AE, DC, DISC, MC, V.

ATTRACTIONS

Abram's Delight
1340 S Pleasant Valley Rd; tel 540/662-6519. Adjoining the Winchester Visitors Center is a native limestone residence built in 1754 by Quaker Isaac Hollingsworth. The house is fully restored and furnished with simple 18th-century pieces. Guided tours last 40 minutes. **Open:** Apr–Oct, Mon–Sat 10am–4pm, Sun noon–4pm. **$$**

Stonewall Jackson's Headquarters
415 N Braddock St; tel 540/667-3242. This Victorian cottage, used by Stonewall Jackson during the winter of 1861–62, is filled with maps, photos, and memorabilia. A must for Civil War buffs. **Open:** Apr–Oct, Mon–Sat 10am–4pm, Sun noon–4pm. **$$**

Handley Library
100 W Piccadilly St; tel 540/662-9041. Begun in 1907, from an endowment by Judge John Handley, this beaux arts–style library was opened to the public in 1912. The building, as designed by New York architects Stewart Barney and Otis Chapman, was meant to represent a book—the rotunda being the spine and the two wings the open pages. The rotunda is crowned by a copper-covered dome with glass inside. A modern wing (completed in 1979) contains a children's room and a local-history archive room. **Open:** Mon–Wed 10am–9pm, Thurs–Sat 10am–5pm. **Free**

Wintergreen

This small town in the George Washington National Forest is within minutes of an 11,000-acre resort offering a multitude of year-round recreational opportunities.

RESORT

Wintergreen Resort
PO Box 706, 22958; tel 804/325-2200 or toll free 800/325-2200; fax 804/325-6760. Follow US 250 to VA 151 S for 14¼ mi to VA 664. 11,000 acres. A high-quality mountaintop resort with well-tended grounds and immaculate facilities. A relaxed, home-like atmosphere prevails. Wide range of activities. **Rooms:** 340 cottages/villas. CI 4pm/CO noon. Only condominiums and rental homes available, and each is decorated by its owner, so styles vary. **Amenities:** A/C, cable TV w/movies, refrig, voice mail. All units w/terraces, some w/fireplaces, some w/whirlpools. **Services:** Car-rental desk, social director, masseur, children's program, babysitting. Ski and snow-boarding equipment rental and lessons available. **Facilities:** 36 23 5 restaurants, 2 bars (1 w/entertainment), basketball, volleyball, games rm, lawn games, spa, sauna, whirlpool, daycare ctr, playground, washer/dryer. Bars have seasonal entertainment. **Rates:** Peak (Dec 20–Mar 20) $85 cottage/villa.

Children under age 18 stay free. Min stay peak and special events. Lower rates off-season. AP and MAP rates avail. Parking: Outdoor, free. AE, DISC, MC, V.

Woodstock

In the Shenandoah Valley near the north fork of the Shenandoah River. Seat of Shenandoah County. **Information:** Woodstock Chamber of Commerce, PO Box 605, N Main St, Woodstock, 22664 (tel 540/459-2542).

HOTEL

Ramada Inn
1130 Motel Dr, 22664; tel 540/459-5000 or toll free 800/2-RAMADA; fax 540/459-8219. Exit 281 off I-81. A comfortable facility set back from highway. A double fireplace in lobby and antique pieces in the hallway that are appropriate for the country setting. **Rooms:** 126 rms. CI 3pm/CO 11am. Nonsmoking rms avail. Integrated decor. **Amenities:** A/C, cable TV w/movies. **Services:** **Facilities:** 1 restaurant (bkfst and dinner only), 1 bar. Restaurant offers daily specials, Sunday brunch. **Rates:** Peak (June–Oct) $54–$58 S; $62–$67 D. Extra person $8. Children under age 18 stay free. Lower rates off-season. Parking: Outdoor, free. Ski packages avail in season. AE, DC, DISC, MC, V.

INN

Inn at Narrow Passage
US 11 S, 22664; tel 540/459-8000; fax 540/459-8001. 5 acres. This early American log inn was once Stonewall Jackson's headquarters and is impeccably restored with antiques, hand-crafted colonial reproductions, and fireplaces, all in a rustic atmosphere. Rustic log-cabin lobby with comfy sitting area, games, and refrigerator; porches; and chairs under shade trees add to peaceful setting. **Rooms:** 12 rms. CI 2pm/CO 11am. Beautifully presented, spotless, and country-fresh, each room is different. A country flavor is created by four-poster canopy beds and pine furnishings. **Amenities:** A/C. No TV. Some units w/terraces, some w/fireplaces. **Services:** Ice delivered to rooms. Lemonade or hot cider served on the back porch in season. Fly fishing on the Shenandoah River. **Facilities:** 1 restaurant (bkfst only). Cozy dining area for guests only. **Rates (BB):** $75–$95 S; $90–$110 D. Extra person $8. Parking: Outdoor, free. MC, V.

Wytheville

Amid two sections of the Jefferson National Forest in the southwest Blue Ridge highlands, Wytheville is also the site of Stony Fork Recreation Area, Big Walker Mountain Tunnel, and Wytheville Community College. **Information:** Wytheville-Wythe-Bland Chamber of Commerce, 150 E Monroe St, PO Box 563, Wytheville, 24382 (tel 540/223-3365).

MOTELS

≣≣ Best Western Wytheville Inn
355 Nye Rd, 24382; tel 540/228-7300 or toll free 800/528-1234; fax 540/228-4223. Exit 41 off I-77 or exit 72 off I-81. A homey atmosphere prevails at this motel, whose exceptionally quiet, well-landscaped grounds afford fine views of the Blue Ridge. **Rooms:** 100 rms and stes. CI 2pm/CO noon. No smoking. **Amenities:** A/C, cable TV w/movies. **Services:** **Facilities:** Rates (CP): $38–$48 S; $45–$54 D; $85 ste. Extra person $6. Children under age 18 stay free. Parking: Outdoor, free. AE, CB, DC, DISC, MC, V.

≣≣ Days Inn
150 Malin Dr, 24382; tel 540/228-5500 or toll free 800/325-2525; fax 540/228-6301. Exit 73 off I-81 and I-77. Location near two major interstates makes this a popular spot. **Rooms:** 118 rms. Executive level. CI 3pm/CO noon. No smoking. Recently renovated, rooms offer views of the surrounding mountains. **Amenities:** A/C, cable TV w/movies. **Services:** Complimentary morning coffee and doughnuts. **Facilities:** Games rm. Two restaurants, including a local favorite, are just steps away. **Rates:** Peak (Mar–Nov 15) $42–$48 S; $44–$50 D. Extra person $5. Children under age 18 stay free. Lower rates off-season. Parking: Outdoor, free. AE, CB, DC, DISC, MC, V.

≣≣≣ Ramada Inn
955 Pepper's Ferry Rd, 24382; tel 540/228-6000 or toll free 800/272-6232 in the US, 800/854-7854 in Canada; fax 540/228-6000 ext 151. Exit 41 off I-77 or exit 72 off I-81. Although just minutes from a highway and a popular outlet mall, this motel enjoys a rural location with refreshing views of pastures and mountains. **Rooms:** 154 rms. CI 2pm/CO noon. No smoking. Units are exceptionally secure and well soundproofed. **Amenities:** A/C, cable TV w/movies. Refrigerators available on request. **Services:** X Babysitting. **Facilities:** 1 restaurant, 1 bar, washer/dryer. Lounge and adjoining bar are quiet and soothing. **Rates:** Peak (May 15–Nov) $52–$65 S; $69 D. Extra person $5. Children under age 19 stay free. Min stay special events. Lower rates off-season. Parking: Outdoor, free. AE, CB, DC, DISC, EC, ER, JCB, MC, V.

≣≣ Shenandoah Inn
120 Lithia Rd, at I-77 and I-81, 24382; tel 540/228-3188 or toll free 800/446-4656; fax 540/228-6458. Exit 73 off I-81. Extremely scenic location with excellent views of surrounding mountains is also convenient to two major interstates, many restaurants. **Rooms:** 100 rms. CI 2pm/CO noon. No smoking. **Amenities:** A/C, cable TV w/movies. All units w/terraces. Breezy patios with tables and chairs face the mountain panorama. **Services:** **Facilities:** **Rates:** Peak (Apr–Sept) $47–$75 S or D. Extra person $6. Children under age 18 stay free. Lower rates off-season. Parking: Outdoor, free. AE, CB, DC, DISC, MC, V.

RESTAURANT

★ Scrooge's
In Scrooge's Village, Holston Rd; tel 540/228-6622. Exit 70 off I-81. **American/Continental.** Wood-paneled, English-style interior with soft lighting and brass and burgundy accents. This popular, casual diner has moderate prices and comfortable, understated elegance. Spaciousness adds to relaxed dining. Steaks, seafood, and lighter fare. **FYI:** Reservations recommended. Children's menu. **Open:** Mon–Fri 5–10pm, Sat–Sun 5–11pm. **Prices:** Main courses $7–$17. AE, DISC, MC, V.

Yorktown

Settled in 1631, Yorktown was the setting of the last major battle in the American Revolution. Today, it offers numerous historic sites and national parks. Seat of York County. **Information:** Virginia Peninsula Chamber of Commerce, Six Manhattan Sq #100, PO Box 7269, Hampton, 23666 (tel 757/766-2000).

MOTEL

≣≣ Duke of York Motor Inn
508 Water St, PO Box E, 23690; tel 757/898-3232; fax 757/898-5922. On the Yorktown waterfront, at Ballard St. This independently owned motel is on the York River waterfront, in historic Yorktown. The view takes in the Coleman Bridge and Coleman Point. **Rooms:** 57 rms. Executive level. CI 2pm/CO noon. Nonsmoking rms avail. The property slopes, so some units have better views than others. **Amenities:** A/C, cable TV. Some units w/terraces. **Services:** **Facilities:** 1 restaurant (bkfst and lunch only), 1 beach (cove/inlet), lifeguard. Beach across street has lifeguards. **Rates:** Peak (May–Sept) $41–$69 S; $49–$69 D. Extra person $8. Children under age 12 stay free. Lower rates off-season. Parking: Outdoor, free. AE, DC, DISC, MC, V.

RESTAURANT

★ Nick's Seafood Pavilion
Water St at Buckner St; tel 757/887-5269. On the Yorktown waterfront. **Greek/Seafood/Steak.** Pink tablecloths and napkins, bright-aqua domed ceiling, old chandeliers and ornately framed mirrors, wait staff dressed in bolero vests and small round hats all create festive ambience. Seafood kabobs—including lobster, shrimp, and scallops—are a favorite. **FYI:** Reservations not accepted. Children's menu. **Open:** Daily 11am–10pm. **Prices:** Main courses $6–$35. AE, CB, DC, MC, V.

ATTRACTIONS 🖼

COLONIAL NATIONAL HISTORICAL PARK

Yorktown Battlefield

Located 14 miles NE of Williamsburg on Colonial Pkwy. Yorktown was the setting for the last major battle of the American Revolution. The siege of Yorktown began on September 28, 1781, when American and French troops under Washington occupied a line encircling the town within a mile of the army led by Cornwallis. When Cornwallis evacuated almost all of his forward positions in order to concentrate his forces closer to town, Washington was able to move his men to within 1,000 yards of British lines. On October 16, following a last-ditch and fruitless attempt to launch an attack, Cornwallis tried to escape with his troops across the York River to Gloucester Point, but a violent storm scattered his ships. The next day, the British signaled their desire to discuss terms for surrender.

The **Yorktown Battlefield Visitor Center** (tel 757/898-3400) screens a 16-minute documentary, *Siege at Yorktown*. Museum displays include Washington's actual headquarters tent, exhibits on Cornwallis's surrender and the events leading up to it, and dioramas detailing the siege. One exhibit gives an "on-the-scene" account of the battle from the viewpoint of a 13-year-old soldier in the Continental Army. Auto tours following the seven-mile Red Route and the nine-mile Yellow Route begin at the center.

For more information on the National Historical Park, contact Superintendent, Colonial National Historical Park, PO Box 210, Yorktown, VA 23690. **Open:** Daily 8:30am–5pm. **Free**

Cornwallis Cave

According to legend, Gen Cornwallis lived here in two tiny "rooms" during the final days of the Yorktown siege. The two rooms were carved out by various occupants of the cave—which tradition says included the pirate Blackbeard. Confederate soldiers later enlarged the shelter and added a roof. A taped narrative at the entrance tells the story. The cave is at the foot of Great Valley, right on the river.

Dudley Digges House

This restored 18th-century white weatherboard house, located at Main and Smith Sts, is a private residence and may only be viewed from the outside. Its dormer windows set in the roofline and other features, as well as the surrounding outbuildings, are typical of Virginia architecture in the mid-1700s. Owner Dudley Digges was a Revolutionary patriot who served with Patrick Henry, Benjamin Harrison, and Thomas Jefferson on the Committee of Correspondence.

Grand French Battery

From this area, in the French section of Washington's first siege line, French soldiers manning cannons, mortars, and howitzers fired on British and German mercenary troops.

Moore House

When Lord Cornwallis realized the inevitability of his defeat, he sent a message to Gen Washington: "Sir, I propose a cessation of hostilities for 24 hours, and that two officers may be appointed by each side, to meet at Mr Moore's house to settle terms for the surrender of the posts of Yorktown and Gloucester." Washington granted Cornwallis just two hours to submit general terms. Representatives from both armies met in this house on the afternoon of October 18, 1781.

The house was pretty much abandoned (even used as a cow barn) until John D Rockefeller Jr purchased it in 1931 and the National Park Service restored it to its colonial appearance. It is today furnished with period pieces, some of which are believed to have been in the house during the surrender negotiations. **Open:** Peak (June–Aug) daily 10am–4:30pm. Reduced hours off-season. **Free**

Nelson House

Nelson and Main Sts. Scottish merchant Thomas ("Scotch Tom") Nelson was a prosperous planter, landowner, and owner of the Swan Tavern (see below) by the time he died in 1745. He left a vast estate, which his descendants—including several prominent Revolutionary leaders, one of them a signer of the Declaration of Independence—further enlarged. In 1814, when fire struck the town, church services were temporarily held in the house. During the gala event of Lafayette's visit to Yorktown, the general lodged here.

Though damaged, the house survived the Battle of Yorktown and was even seized by Cornwallis. Nelson's descendants continued to occupy the house until 1907. The National Park Service acquired the house in 1968 and restored it to its original appearance. Ranger-guided tours take 30 to 45 minutes. **Open:** Peak (May–Aug) daily 10am–4:30pm. Reduced hours off-season. **Free**

Surrender Field

Here the imagination can evoke the images of the British march out of Yorktown. From here, the Yellow Route leads to the sites of Washington's and Rochambeau's headquarters, a French cemetery and artillery park, and allied encampment sites.

Swan Tavern

Tel 757/898-3033. For over a century the Swan Tavern, at the corner of Main and Ballard Sts, was Yorktown's leading hostelry. Originally owned by Thomas Nelson, it was in operation 20 years before Williamsburg's famous Raleigh. The Swan was demolished in 1863 by an ammunition explosion at the courthouse across the street, rebuilt, and destroyed again by fire in 1915. Today it is reconstructed as per historical research, and the premises house an antique shop. **Open:** Call for hours.

OTHER ATTRACTIONS

Grace Episcopal Church

Church St; tel 757/898-3261. Located on Church St near the river, Grace Church dates back to 1697 and has been an active house of worship since then. Gunpowder and ammunition were stored here during the siege of Yorktown. During the Civil War, the church served as a hospital. The original communion silver, made in England in 1649, is still in use. Thomas Nelson Jr, a signer of the Declaration of Independence, is buried in the adjacent graveyard. **Open:** Daily 9am–5pm. **Free**

Sessions House

Just across from the Nelson House, this is the oldest house in Yorktown, built in 1692 by Thomas Sessions. At least five US presidents have visited the house. It is a private residence and not open to the public.

Yorktown Victory Center

Tel 757/887-1776. Located 1 mi S of Yorktown, via Old VA 238. Set on 21 acres overlooking part of the battlefield of 1781, the center offers an excellent orientation to Yorktown attractions. Upon arrival, visitors follow a timeline walkway, "Road to Revolution," to the main building. Exhibits located in pavilions along the way illustrate the relationship between the colonies and Britain beginning in 1750. The timeline ends inside the main building with an exhibit on the first battles of the war and a 12-foot-tall copy of the Declaration of Independence.

In the outdoor **Continental Army Camp,** costumed interpreters re-create the lives of men and women who took part in the Revolution. Another outdoor exhibit, the **Farmsite,** provides an insight into what life was like for a small planter starting over after the Revolution.

A Time of Revolution, an evocative 18-minute film, transports visitors to a Continental Army encampment on the eve of the siege, as soldiers reflect on the War that has brought them together. **Open:** Daily 9am–5pm. **$$**

The Customhouse

Tel 757/898-4788. Dating to 1721, this sturdy brick building at the corner of Main and Read was originally the private warehouse of Richard Ambler, collector of ports. It became Gen J B Magruder's headquarters during the Civil War. Today it is maintained by the Daughters of the American Revolution as a museum. **Open:** Sat–Sun. Call for hours.

COLONIAL NATIONAL HISTORICAL PARK

Victory Monument

Main St. News of the victory at Yorktown reached Philadelphia on October 24, 1781. On October 29 the Continental Congress resolved "that the United States . . . will cause to be erected at York, in Virginia, a marble column, adorned with emblems of the alliance between the United States and his Most Christian Majesty; and inscribed with a succinct narrative of the surrender of Earl Cornwallis to his excellency General Washington, Commander in Chief of the combined forces of America and France . . . "

The highly symbolic 98-foot marble shaft overlooking the York River was completed in 1884. The podium is adorned with 13 female figures hand in hand in a solemn dance to denote the unity of the 13 colonies; beneath their feet is the inscription ONE COUNTRY, ONE CONSTITUTION, ONE DESTINY. Its stars represent the "constellation" of states in the Union in 1881. Atop the shaft is the figure of Liberty.

WEST VIRGINIA

The Mountain State

In West Virginia it's possible to find some elements of the plantation south, the agricultural midwest, and the industrial northeast. And yet the state is singularly its own. Its most characteristic feature is the mountains that give it its nickname.

Part of the ancient Appalachian chain, the mountains roll from one end of the state to the other, covered with forests and sliced through with rivers and streams.

Over the course of its history, people have been drawn to West Virginia because of the natural riches both above and below its surface. Fortunes have been made extracting coal and natural gas from below ground and hauling lumber from the hills. Still, about three-quarters of the state remains forested, with a million or so acres set aside in national and state forests, parks, and recreation areas.

Combine all that natural endowment with a continuing effort to preserve it in its unspoiled state and the result is a scenic grandeur that is not only wonderful to behold, but also a challenge to the sports minded. West Virginia has the best white-water rafting in the eastern United States and the best skiing south of New England. It has a host of trails that hikers, bikers, and horseback riders can follow along rivers, over old covered bridges, and through old railroad tunnels deep into the heart of the wilderness.

The state also has more urbane attractions. If restored towns, historic homes, and period rooms are your cup of tea, there are plenty of relics from the colonial era, Civil War days, and the early 20th century. The state has gracious inns and luxury resort spas as well as ubiquitous campgrounds. It also has a busy calendar of events to keep its rich heritage alive and acquaint visitors with its people and their crafts and customs. You can come back from your trip with a suitcase stuffed with handmade quilts, art glass, and apple butter and a head full of lingering country tunes.

West Virginia remains a mostly rural state, a place where the stunning beauty of nature can be enjoyed for its own sake or put to practical use in a host of outdoor recreation pursuits. It's also a state where you'll find the colorful history of a proud people carefully preserved in ways in which even the jaded traveler can rejoice. You'll see for yourself when you get there.

A Brief History

Ancient Times For Native American hunters who roamed the Ohio and Kanawha Valleys as early as 15,000 years ago, the region's wealth was in its teaming game and fish. Hundreds of Native American burial mounds have survived, dating back to about 100 BC.

Just as West Virginia served as a vast hunting ground for them, it did as well for English explorers in the 1600s. European settlement was delayed until the early 18th century, however, because of the rugged mountains and Native American hostility.

Early Settlers In 1731, a man named Morgan Morgan arrived in Berkeley County and became the first European to build a permanent home in the area which was then part of Virginia. The next year, German families from Pennsylvania founded the town of New Mecklenberg, now Shepherdstown. Other colonists soon began settling farther south and west.

Pioneer Life Products from the east could not easily reach this mountainous remote area, so those early settlers were self-reliant. By 1800, however, some small industries had begun, and soon Ohio River steamboats and the opening of the National Pike brought boom times and turned Wheeling into a manufacturing center.

A State Is Born Settlers in the western part of the state, unhappy with the eastern planters who con-

trolled the far-away state government and paid little heed to their needs out on the frontier, had talked of separating from Virginia as early as 1820.

When Virginia seceded from the Union in 1861, its 26 western counties declared the secession void, adopted a plan to abolish slavery, and applied to Congress for admission to the Union as a separate state. President Abraham Lincoln signed the statehood bill on June 20, 1863. (After the Civil War, Virginia tried to get West Virginia back, but the response of the state whose official motto is *Montani semper liberi*—Mountaineers are always free—was, more or less, "Nothing doing.")

West Virginia was not a major battlefield during the Civil War, but because its border land was prized by both sides, it saw its share of skirmishes. The engagement at Phillippi in June 1861 began campaigns that gave Union forces control of northwestern Virginia, while the Eastern Gateway and Greenbrier Valley continued to be held by the Confederates.

Into the Present Completion of the Baltimore and Ohio Railroad to Wheeling in 1853 had laid the groundwork for West Virginia to prosper after the war. Coal mines were opened and other natural resources were discovered. Towns along the Ohio soon doubled in size. By the 1890s, railroads covered the state, and job-seeking immigrants had arrived to mine the coal upon which both the state and its economy rested. In the 1920s, there were bitter, often violent struggles for workers' right to organize themselves into unions.

The still-thriving chemical industry of the Kanawha Valley began during World War I. During World War II, Charleston was one of the single greatest centers of wartime production in the United States. Although the coal industry declined after the war, other industries—such as glass—grew. Today, mining has again become viable, but tourism—in a state with abundant parkland—is increasing in importance.

Fun Facts

• West Virginia was conceived when Union loyalists in the western counties of Virginia, angered by Virginia's secession, convened in Wheeling in 1861 and signed a "Declaration of Independence" from Virginia. Statehood was granted on June 20, 1863.

• Pearl S Buck, the only American woman to win both the Pulitzer and the Nobel Prizes for Literature, was born in Hillsboro in 1892.

• The legendary Greenbrier resort in White Sulphur Springs, one of America's oldest existing grand hotels, has been a vacation spot for 33 US presidents since its establishment in the early 19th century.

• West Virginia is home to the largest conical earthen mound in North America. The Adena Indian burial mound, 69 feet high and 900 feet in circumference at its base, was constructed in stages from 250 to 150 BC.

• The first Mother's Day service was held at Andrews Methodist Church in Grafton on May 10, 1908.

A Closer Look

GEOGRAPHY

Vast forests, deep gorges, pristine wildernesses, roiling white water, and wooded trails combine to give the "Mountain State" a wild and free natural beauty, its scenic wonders still largely unspoiled by economic development.

The **Eastern Gateway** sticks out like a panhandle between Maryland and the Potomac River to the north and Virginia and the Shenandoah River to the south, affording easy access to the Appalachian Trail, the Chesapeake and Ohio Canal National Historical Park, warm mineral springs, and white-water rafting.

The town of Harpers Ferry, only 60 miles from Washington, DC, draws an increasing number of urbanites seeking a bit of country on the weekend or a home away from the bustle of the city.

Southwest of this gateway, the **Potomac Highlands,** up in the Allegheny Mountains, is a booming outdoor recreation area year-round. The Monongahela National Forest stretches over most of the area, and the Allegheny Trail and the powerful Cheat River both wind through it. The wild Gauley River begins here, and the Greenbrier, the longest free-flowing river in the East, runs the length of Pocahontas County. Thousands of musicians and dancers come to **Elkins,** the largest town in the highlands, for its celebrated music workshops and festivals.

In the central **Mountain Lakes** region, you'll have more luck shopping for bait and locally made glass than you will finding a neon sign proclaiming a nightspot. What you will find are seven lakes, two state parks, and five impressive trout streams.

DRIVING DISTANCES

Charleston

56 mi E of Huntington
112 mi NW of Bluefield
164 mi SW of Wheeling
221 mi SW of Pittsburgh, PA
331 mi NW of Richmond, VA
339 mi NW of Charlotte, NC
380 mi SW of Washington, DC

Wheeling

60 mi SW of Pittsburgh, PA
164 mi NE of Charleston
193 mi NE of Huntington
229 mi NE of Beckley
292 mi NW of Washington, DC
347 mi NW of Richmond, VA
504 mi N of Charlotte, NC

Bluefield

112 mi SE of Charleston
197 mi SE of Huntington
261 mi NW of Charlotte, NC
262 mi SW of Richmond, VA
310 mi SW of Washington, DC
341 mi SW of Pittsburgh, PA

Huntington

56 mi W of Charleston
112 mi NW of Beckley
193 mi SW of Wheeling
197 mi NW of Bluefield
277 mi SW of Pittsburgh, PA
436 mi SW of Washington, DC

Mountaineer Country in the north has both old-time coal commerce and agrarian charm, and the state university at Morgantown. **Fairmont** has coal, and the Monongahela River to transport it. Tradition runs deep in the **Clarksburg-Bridgeport** area, with a year-round calendar of living-history programs.

The narrow **Northern Panhandle,** wedged between Pennsylvania and Ohio, is bordered on the west by the Ohio River, whose scenic waterfront ensures that cities like **Wheeling** remain hubs of activity. The West Virginia Border Islands, a series of Ohio River islands, some only a few yards from towns and cities, comprise the state's first national wildlife refuge.

The **Mid-Ohio** region, with its hills rising from the state's western border, the Ohio River, eastward toward the heartland of the state, drew adventurers and pioneers in its early days. Their tradition of self-sufficiency survives in a wealth of crafts shops, centers, and fairs throughout the region's seven counties. **Parkersburg** is here, a riverfront hub of commercial and cultural activity.

Major cities like the university town of Huntington and the riverfront capital city of **Charleston** dominate the far southwestern **Metro Valley.** The greater Charleston area includes many small towns and communities in the Kanawha Valley. Farther south is "Coal Country" and the town of **Matewan,** site of an infamous anti-union massacre during West Virginia's "Mine Wars" early in the century.

Rivers, mountains, coal, and railroads are the key to the southern **New River–Greenbrier Valley.** The New River takes on the Greenbrier River here before plunging into the famous boulder-strewn New River Gorge, one of the most popular white-water rafting destinations in the eastern United States. And the healing waters of White Sulphur Springs bubble up from the earth here. The coal industry operates along the southernmost border—the view at Bluefield is likely to be of railroad cars carrying black rock.

CLIMATE

The state's climate is generally humid, with hot summers and cool-to-cold winters. Temperatures rarely top 90°F in the mountains, and winters are seldom bitterly cold except at the highest elevations.

Rainfall is moderate throughout the state. Annual snowfall can be 10 feet to 15 feet in some higher areas.

AVG MONTHLY TEMPS (°F) & RAINFALL (IN)		
	Romney	Charleston
Jan	28/2.2	32/2.9
Feb	32/2.1	35/3.0
Mar	41/2.9	46/3.6
Apr	51/2.0	55/3.3
May	61/3.4	63/3.9
June	69/3.2	71/3.6
July	73/3.7	75/4.9
Aug	72/3.2	74/4.0
Sept	65/3.0	68/3.2
Oct	54/2.8	56/2.9
Nov	44/2.8	47/3.6
Dec	34/2.2	37/3.4

WHAT TO PACK

The seasons won't fool you in West Virginia. Bring shorts for summer, mittens for winter, sweaters for fall, and rainwear for spring. In the mountains and forests you'll appreciate long pants and jackets even in summer. It's a casual state that emphasizes outdoor recreation, so pack accordingly. Unless you're heading for a ritzy resort or a metropolitan area, you won't need a dressy outfit. Other handy things to pack are a folding umbrella, travel alarm, good walking shoes or boots, sunglasses, and, in summer, insect repellent.

TOURIST INFORMATION

Contact the **West Virginia Division of Tourism and Parks,** State Capitol, Charleston, WV 25305 (tel toll free 800-CALL WVA) for the free *West Virginia: It's You* magazine-format travel guide; booklets on state parks, lodging, and activities ranging from golf to white-water rafting; and guides to the larger counties. Each of the state's eight regions has its own visitors bureau listed in the state guide.

West Virginia Online maintains a World Wide Web page (http://wvweb.com) with general information about the state and its attractions.

DRIVING RULES AND REGULATIONS

The Interstate speed limit is 65 mph unless otherwise posted. The driver and front-seat passengers must wear seat belts. Children from three to nine years old must wear seat belts whether in the back or front seat; children under three must ride in an approved child safety seat. Approved safety helmets for both motorcycle driver and passenger are required.

RENTING A CAR

Major car-rental companies are represented in the larger cities; your travel agent can help you find the best deal. Here are their toll-free numbers:

- **Avis** (tel toll free 800/831-2847)
- **Budget** (tel 800/527-0700)
- **Enterprise** (tel 800/325-8007)
- **Hertz** (tel 800/654-3131)
- **National** (tel 800/227-7368)
- **Thrifty** (tel 800/367-2277)

ESSENTIALS

Area Code: The area code for the entire state is **304.**

Emergencies: Call **911** in most counties; for highway questions or emergencies, call 304/558-3028.

Liquor Laws: The drinking age is 21; alcohol is sold at licensed private stores and at some convenience stores.

Taxes:	The West Virginia sales tax is 6%. In addition, some municipalities may impose lodging taxes up to 3%.
Time Zone:	All of West Virginia is in the Eastern time zone. Daylight saving time (one hour earlier than EST) is in effect from the first Sunday of April until the last Sunday in October.

Best of the State

Below is a general overview of some of the top sights and attractions in West Virginia. To find out more detailed information, look under "Attractions" in the listings portion of this book.

WHAT TO SEE AND DO

The Great Outdoors   Three-fourths of this state is forest, much of it showcased in state parks and forests and the **Monongahela National Forest.** In this land, mountains burst with wildflowers and migratory birds in the spring, and hiking trails wind above swift rivers. Visit the windswept moor of **Dolly Sods Wilderness,** travel the **Greenbrier River Trail** (by bike or foot) and view the 60-foot falls at **Blackwater Falls State Park.** With 2,000 miles of mountain streams alone, West Virginia offers water pleasures in abundance. The beauty of the New River is unmatched, as can be ascertained by standing atop the New River Gorge Bridge, the largest single-arch span bridge in the world.

Historic Buildings & Sites   The largest conical Indian burial mound in North America, about 2,000 years old, is at **Grave Creek Mound State Park,** a national historic landmark in the northern panhandle. **Harpers Ferry,** where abolitionist John Brown raided a federal arsenal in 1859 in order to arm a slave rebellion, is now a national historical park. A peaceful town of restored homes and shops, it is the state's most visited attraction.

Numerous towns—**Shepherdstown, Bethany, Wellsburg, Charleston**—have historic districts of more than passing architectural interest. In addition, Charleston has the **State Capitol,** a magnificent structure designed by Cass Gilbert in 1932 and topped by a 293-foot gold dome. The 18th- and 19th-century buildings of **Lewisburg** are a national historic district; nearby, at White Sulphur Springs, is **The Greenbrier Resort,** also a national historic landmark. The springs, discovered in 1778, still provide healing waters. West Virginia also has the nation's first spa, established in 1776 as the town of Bath but now known as **Berkeley Springs.**

Wheeling has a generous supply of Victorian-era residential and commercial buildings, as well as the **Wheeling Suspension Bridge,** the longest suspension bridge in the world when it was built in 1849. The state also has a wealth of old covered bridges, from the 24-foot **Laurel Creek Covered Bridge** (1910) to the 148-foot **Barrackville Covered Bridge** (1853).

Family Favorites   In addition to family excursions in white-water rafts, children will love cruising on the old sternwheelers that ply the Ohio between Wheeling and Huntington. The **Cass Historic District** is a turn-of-the-century lumber town, and in summer, you can ride from the town up to Bald Knob, the state's second-highest peak, aboard the **Cass Scenic Railroad,** which preserves the steam locomotives and logging cars that used to haul lumber to the mill. Another vintage train, the **Potomac Eagle,** operates on wilderness trips along the South Branch of the Potomac, from Romney to Petersburg; spotting eagles en route is part of the fun. Kids also enjoy Wheeling's 65-acre **Oglebay Park Zoo,** including the planetarium.

Mountain State Folklore   The state's folk culture thrives in a multitude of arts and crafts shows and festivals. From mid-July to mid-August in Elkins, you can study quilt-making or old-time fiddling at the **Augusta Heritage Arts Workshops,** weeklong classes in traditional Appalachian music, dance, and crafts taught by master musicians and artisans. You can also revel in the state's rich heritage at Charleston's **Vandalia Gathering** over Memorial Day weekend—music, dance, storytelling, a quilt show, even a liar's contest are part of this event. Or sing along with country-music greats at Wheeling's **Capitol Music Hall,** or tune into *Jamboree USA,* America's oldest live country music program, broadcast over WWVA in Wheeling. In July, *Jamboree USA* presents an outdoor **Jamboree in the Hills,** the "Super Bowl" of country music.

EVENTS AND FESTIVALS

- **Mountain State 25K Cross-Country Ski Marathon,** Davis. Race through Monongahela National Forest to Blackwater Falls State Park. Late January. Call 304/866-4114.
- **Rendezvous on the River,** Parkersburg. Muzzleloaders and mountain men set up a primitive encampment at Blennerhassett Island. First weekend in May. Call 304/428-3000.
- **Greenbrier Trail Bike Trek,** Cass to Ronceverte. Sponsored by the American Lung Association of West Virginia. Mid-May. Call toll free 800/LUNG USA.
- **Webster County Woodchopping Festival,** Webster Springs. Week prior to Memorial Day. Call 304/847-7666.
- **Vandalia Gathering,** Charleston. Music, dancing, craft shows, and other events celebrate the state's multiple heritages. Memorial Day weekend. Call 304/558-0220.
- **National Pike Festival,** Wheeling. Wagons retrace the trek along the National Road from Pennsylvania to the Ohio River. Memorial Day weekend. Call toll free 800/828-3097.

- **Dandelion Festival,** White Sulphur Springs. Dandelion wine, arts and crafts. Memorial Day weekend. Call toll free 800/284-9440.
- **Mountain State Arts and Crafts Fair,** Ripley. Late June through early July. Call 304/372-7866.
- **Jamboree in the Hills,** Wheeling. Country stars from *Jamboree USA* perform outdoors. Mid-July. Call toll free 800/624-5456.
- **Gauley Bridge Anniversary and Civil War Days,** Gauley Bridge. Battle reenactment and pageantry. Early August. Call 304/632-2504.
- **Augusta Heritage Festival,** Elkins. Concerts with folk musicians, jam sessions, crafts exhibits, winding up the Augusta Heritage Arts Workshops. Mid-August. Call 304/636-1903.
- **Appalachian Arts and Crafts Festival,** Beckley. Juried art show, southern West Virginia's largest quilt show. Last full weekend in August. Call 304/252-7328.
- **Sternwheel Regatta Festival,** Charleston. Top entertainment, sternwheel paddleboat races, parades. Late August through early September. Call 304/348-6419.
- **Stonewall Jackson Heritage Arts and Crafts Jubilee,** Weston. Civil War battle reenactments and other events. Labor Day weekend. Call 304/269-1863.
- **Mason-Dixon Festival,** Morgantown. River regatta, events along the Monongahela. September. Call 304/599-1104.
- **Apple Butter Festival,** Berkeley Springs. Crafts, music, home cooking, and apple butter made in the streets. Columbus Day weekend in October. Call 304/258-3738.
- **Bridge Day,** Fayetteville. Jumpers parachute from New River Gorge Bridge. Crafts and music. Third Saturday in October. Call 304/465-5617.
- **Old Tyme Christmas,** Harpers Ferry. Period decorations, festivities. First two weekends in December. Call 304/725-8019, or toll free 800/848-TOUR.

SPECTATOR SPORTS

Auto Racing Summit Point Raceway, outside Charles Town (tel 304/725-8444), is an important location on the SCC-MARRs circuit, offering Grand Prix–style racing. The **West Virginia Motor Speedway,** south of Parkersburg (tel 304/489-1889), is considered one of the best dirt tracks in the nation.

Baseball While there are no big-league professional teams in the state, the Cincinnati Reds Class A farm team, the **Charleston Wheelers** (tel 304/9250-8222), can be seen at Watt-Powell Baseball Park. The **Bluefield Orioles** (tel 304/327-2448), farm team for the Baltimore Orioles, play at Bowen Field in Bluefield.

College Football In Morgantown, West Virginia University's nationally ranked football team, the **Mountaineers,** plays at Mountaineer Field. Call toll free 800/352-2512 for schedules and tickets.

Dog Racing Wheeling Downs (tel 304/232-5050 or toll free 800/445-9475) offers year-round greyhound racing and a clubhouse restaurant at the southern tip of Wheeling Island in the Ohio River. **Tri-State Greyhound Park,** at Cross Lanes near Charleston (tel 304/776-1000 or toll free 800/999-7172), also offers year-round racing.

Horse Racing The **Charles Town Racetrack** (tel 304/725-7001 or toll free 800/725-7001) is the home of year-round thoroughbred racing and, in September, of the West Virginia Breeder's Classic, the state's richest race. **Mountaineer Racetrack and Resort** (tel 304/387-2400), midway between Weirton and Chester, offers year-round thoroughbred racing as well as the extensive lodging, dining, and sports facilities of a resort.

Ice Hockey West Virginia is home to two East Coast League teams: the **Huntington Blizzard** (tel 304/697-PUCK), who skate at the Huntington Civic Center, and the **Wheeling Thunderbirds,** who face off at the Wheeling Civic Center. The season runs October through April.

ACTIVITIES A TO Z

Biking & Hiking West Virginia offers extensive trail systems, including a number of old railroad beds converted to trails for hikers, bikers, and horseback riders. In particular, mountain bikers at all levels can find some of the best terrain in the East here—marked trails, old logging roads, and single tracks. The **Allegheny Trail** is a 220-mile footpath that runs from northern West Virginia south to the Greenbrier Valley, connecting state parks and forests along the way. It includes the 75-mile Greenbrier River Rail Trail, an old Chesapeake and Ohio Railroad grade that follows the river south from Cass to Caldwell. Another former railroad bed, the North

Bend Rail Trail, runs in an east-west direction across the northern part of the state, cutting through tunnels and across bridges from east of Parkersburg to west of Clarksburg. Used by hikers, bikers, and horseback riders, it forms part of the 5,500-mile American Discovery Trail.

For more information call toll free 800/CALL WVA, or contact the **West Virginia Scenic Trails Association,** PO Box 4042, Charleston, WV 25304; the **Rails-to-Trails Council** (tel 304/722-6558); or the **Monongahela National Forest Supervisor** (tel 304/636-1800).

Camping   Opportunities for camping range from "roughing it" to hooking up the RV; the season usually runs from late April through October. Campgrounds, from primitive to deluxe, are available in state parks, forests, and wildlife management areas; in many, rustic cabins and cottages are a further option. The George Washington National Forest and the Monongahela National Forest also provide campsites. For more information contact the **West Virginia Division of Tourism and Parks,** State Capitol Complex, 2109 Washington St E, PO Box 50312, Charleston, WV 25305-0312 (tel toll free 800/CALL WVA).

Cruising   Authentic 19th-century sternwheelers cruise the Ohio, Kahawha, and Little Kanawha Rivers, operating from the riverfront in Wheeling, Huntington, Parkersburg, Charleston, and other towns. Excursions range from breakfast, lunch, and dinner cruises to daylong sightseeing trips. Cruises to Blennerhasset Island are available out of Parkersburg. For information, call toll free 800/CALL WVA.

Fishing & Hunting   Dense wildlife areas, deep lakes, and churning rivers lure sportsmen. Hunting and fishing licenses are required throughout the state. Licenses for nonresidents, including short-term licenses for state recreational areas, are available from nearly 800 license agents. Regulations are available from the **West Virginia Division of Natural Resources** in Charleston. Call 304/558-2771. License application forms may be obtained by calling 304/558-2758. For information on wildlife management areas, call 304/558-2754.

Golf   West Virginia has 31 18-hole public golf courses in addition to courses at private resorts. **Cacapon State Park** (tel 304/258-1022) boasts a Robert Trent Jones championship course, and at the base of **Snowshoe Mountain** is a Gary Player–designed golf course featuring canyons and cliffs. Call toll free 800/CALL WVA for more information.

Horseback Riding   A number of state parks offer horseback riding, and private outfits offer adventures on horseback by the hour, the day, or longer, including tours of Blackwater Falls State Park and overnight pack trips in Canaan Valley. Call toll free 800/CALL WVA.

Rock Climbing   Considered by many to be the best climb in the East, **Seneca Rocks** is for beginners or expert climbers. (For information, call 304/567-2827 or 304/257-4488). The **New River Gorge** offers more than 20 miles of cliffs with 700 completed routes and more being explored. Call toll free 800/CALL WVA.

White-Water Rafting & Canoeing   West Virginia is justifiably known as the white-water capital of the

---

SELECTED PARKS & RECREATION AREAS

- **Appalachian National Scenic Trail,** PO Box 807, Harpers Ferry, WV 25425 (tel 304/535-6331)
- **Gauley River National Recreation Area,** 104 Main St, PO Box 246, Glen Jean, WV 25846 (tel 304/465-0508)
- **Ohio River Islands National Wildlife Refuge,** PO Box 1811, Parkersburg, WV 26102 (tel 304/422-0752)
- **Babcock State Park and Glade Creek Grist Mill,** HC 35, Box 150, Clifftop, WV 25831 (tel 304/438-3004)
- **Blackwater Falls State Park,** Drawer 490, Davis, WV 26260 (tel 304/259-5216)
- **Camp Creek State Park,** PO Box 119, Camp Creek, WV 25820 (tel 304/425-9481)
- **Greenbrier River Trail State Park,** PO Box 275, Marlinton, WV 24954 (tel toll free 800/336-7009)
- **Hawks Nest State Park,** PO Box 857, Ansted, WV 25812 (tel 304/658-5212)
- **Little Beaver State Park,** Rte 9, Box 179, Beaver, WV 25813 (tel 304/763-2494)
- **North Bend State Park,** off WV 31, Cairo, WV 26337 (tel 304/643-2931)
- **Tygart Lake State Park,** Rte 1, Box 260, Grafton, WV 26354 (tel 304/265-3383)
- **Valley Falls State Park,** Rte 6, Box 244, Fairmont, WV 26555 (tel 304/363-3319)
- **Watoga State Park,** 2101 Washington St East, PO Box 50312, Charleston, WV 25303 (tel 304/799-4087)

East. The New River winds 53 miles through a deep gorge past some of the state's most gorgeous scenery. The **Gauley River,** a 26-mile stretch of white water, is rated the number two river in North America, and number seven in the world.

Whitewater rapids are classed from I to VI for difficulty. Novices can usually run I to II stretches without guides. Segments classed from III to V require paddling skills or qualified leadership, provided by professional outfitters. Class VI water demands the utmost skill.

For information, contact the West Virginia Professional River Outfitters (tel 304/346-4660), or call toll free 800/CALL WVA.

Skiing West Virginia's Potomac highlands area offers the best skiing in the Mid-Atlantic, both downhill and cross-country, from Thanksgiving weekend to mid-April. **Timberline** is ranked third in the southeast by *Snow Country* report. At the **White Grass Ski Touring,** groomed trails lead nordic skiers to the Dolly Sods Wilderness area. For the booklet *Skiing West Virginia,* call toll free 800/CALL WVA.

NEW RIVER GORGE TO THE HIGHLANDS

Start	Beckley
Finish	Canaan Valley
Distance	280 miles
Time	3–6 days
Highlights	Gorgeous mountain scenery; the awesome New River Gorge; vast national forests and wilderness areas; outdoor theater; visits inside natural caverns and a coal mine; historic towns; a Civil War battlefield; Pearl S Buck's birthplace; a train ride up a steep mountain

Beginning in southern West Virginia at the dramatic, 53-mile-long New River Gorge, this tour takes you northward through the rugged Allegheny Mountains. Much of the drive travels through the Monongahela National Forest, whose nearly 1 million acres contain some of the largest wilderness areas east of the Mississippi. You'll stop at old-fashioned country stores rather than 7-11s, and eat fried chicken instead of filet mignon, for this is a sparsely populated area where deserted roads climb steep mountains and tiny villages are tucked away in lovely valleys. It's a long drive, but West Virginia's great natural beauty will make every mile worth it.

Because the route takes you along very steep and winding mountain roads, be sure your vehicle is in top condition. The mountains get heavy snow during winter, so make this drive only between April and October. The best time for this trip is late September and the first two weeks of October, when the mountains are ablaze with autumn colors.

For additional information on accommodations, restaurants, and attractions in the region covered by the tour, look under specific cities in the listings portion of this book.

I-77 and I-64 converge at the first stop:

1. **Beckley,** the coal-mining town that is the transportation and accommodation hub of southern West Virginia. Take exit 44 to Harper Rd east then turn left on Ewart Ave and follow the signs to the **Beckley Exhibition Coal Mine,** located in New River Park (tel 304/256-1747), one of America's most unusual museums. Veteran miners tell stories and explain how coal is extracted during 45-minute tours via a "man trip" train through 1,500 feet of tunnels under Beckley. Drop in the **visitor center** of the Southern West Virginia Convention & Visitor Bureau, 418 Neville St (tel 304/252-7328), next to the museum's gift shop, where you can get your bearings and obtain maps and information about the region, including white-water rafting on the New River.

The New River Gorge National River runs its 53-mile course north of Beckley, and although we will soon see this awesome canyon, take the time to drive 25 miles north of Beckley on US 19 to the New River Gorge Bridge. The world's longest single-steel-arch bridge, this structure spans the gorge 876 feet above the river. The **Canyon Rim Visitor Center,** WV 19 in Lansing (tel 304/574-2115), has spectacular views of the gorge at its north end and complete information about this national treasure.

From Beckley, follow I-64 east 13 miles to exit 129B, then turn left and drive 5 miles north on WV 9 to:

2. **Grandview Park,** which sits 1,440 feet above the deepest part of the New River Gorge. From mid-June to mid-August, the park is home to **Theater West Virginia,** an outdoor repertory company famous for *Hatfields & McCoys* and *Honey in the Rock,* two original plays based on West Virginia lore. The park **visitor center,** exit 129B off I-64 (tel 304/256-6800 or toll free 800/666-9142), is open from Memorial Day to Labor Day.

Backtrack to I-64 and head east for 13 miles down into the New River Gorge. Take exit 139 on the north side of the bridge, turn left on WV 20, and head south up the canyon's side for 3 miles, where an overlook provides a view of Sandstone Falls. From there, descend 7 miles south to:

3. **Hinton,** an old railroad town at the confluence of the New and Greenbrier Rivers. The New River Gorge begins its northwestward journey at Hinton. The **Summers County Visitor Center** on 206 Temple St (turn left at the stoplight) (tel 304/466-5332), shares quarters with a railroad museum and consignment crafts shop; all three are worth a visit. The visitors center provides a walking tour map of the brick streets in Hinton's historic district and directions to **Bluestone Dam,** which harnesses the New River to create lovely **Bluestone Lake,** one of the region's most popular recreation spots. The National Park Service has a summertime **visitor center** on WV 3 (cross the bridge and bear left) (tel 304/466-2805), which is open Memorial Day–Labor Day, Wednesday–Sunday 8am–7:30pm, and

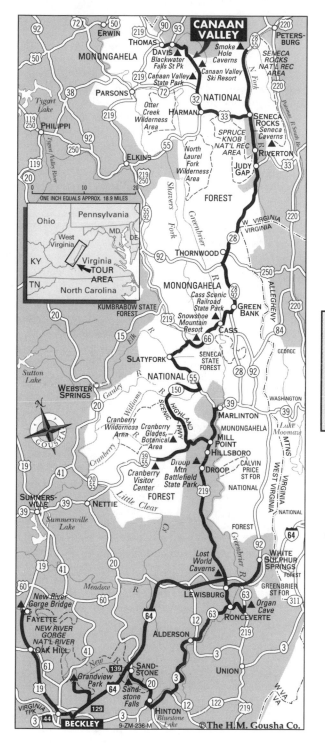

Monday–Tuesday 8am–4pm. For refreshment, national chain fast-food outlets are along the river on WV 107 (go straight at the stoplight).

The fast way to the next stop is to backtrack 10 miles north on WV 20 and head east on I-64 for another 31 miles, but you'll want to take the shorter but slower route by driving 39 miles, beginning with WV 3 east along the banks of the gentle Greenbrier River. After 5 miles, you'll climb over Big Bend Tunnel, dug between 1870 and 1872 as a railroad shortcut. At the top sits a statue of John Henry, the legendary digger who died after a race with a new-fangled steel drill. At 10 miles, you'll pass the **Graham House,** built of logs in 1772. At 12 miles look for the **Pence Springs Hotel,** off WV 3 (tel 304/445-2606), a popular 1920s retreat, then a women's prison, and now a country inn. At 21 miles, you'll reach Alderson, a pretty town where you can walk across the old bridge over the Greenbrier.

Take a Break

For inexpensive pizza, sandwiches, burgers, and home-cooked meals, stop at the **Big Wheel Family Restaurant** (tel 301/445-7832), on WV 3 just before Alderson. The same family has operated this small-town eatery since the late 1950s; it's plain and simple with standard American fare.

From Alderson, take WV 12 north, then WV 63 east 12 miles to Ronceverte (French for Greenbrier). Turn left on US 219 and proceed north 2 miles through a commercial strip and the state fairgrounds to:

4. **Lewisburg,** where surveyor Andrew Lewis found a spring in 1751 and, as a general, built **Fort Savannah** during the French and Indian Wars. Part of the fort and a host of other old buildings make this beautiful town worth a walking tour. Turn left on Washington St at the traffic signal, go 2 blocks west and turn left on Church St to the **Lewisburg Visitors Center,** 105 Church St (tel 304/645-1000), opposite the **Old Stone Presbyterian Church,** the oldest place of worship west of the Alleghenies. The center has an excellent walking tour booklet of the town and maps for nearby driving tours (which include covered bridges). Two underground excursions highlighting the natural wonders of stalactites and stalagmites are near Lewisburg: **Lost World Caverns,** 3 miles north of town via Court St (tel 304/645-6677); and **Organ Cave,** east of Ronceverte via WV 63 (tel 304/647-5551). **The Greenbrier Trail,** a hiking and biking

path along an old railroad bed, starts at Caldwell (3 miles east of Lewisburg on US 60) and ends 80 miles north at Cass.

Located on I-64, Lewisburg has good chain motels and **The General Lewis Inn,** a charming, antique-filled hostelry built in 1834. The inn also is the best place in Lewisburg to dine. Or you can drive 6 miles east on I-64 or US 60 and stay at the luxurious **Greenbrier** or one of the motels in White Sulphur Springs.

From Lewisburg, take US 219 north for 26 miles across a rolling valley and then up onto flat-top Droop Mountain and:

5. **Droop Mountain Battlefield State Park** (tel 304/653-4254), where Union forces attacked a Confederate stronghold in 1863 and drove the Rebels out of the new state of West Virginia for the last time. A loop road, which goes past a small Civil War museum featuring a contemporary *New York Times* report of the battle, passes an overlook with a fine view before rejoining US 219. The park has picnic facilities and outhouse-style toilets.

From the park, it's 4 miles down the mountain and across the lovely "Lower Levels" valley to:

6. **Hillsboro,** where author Pearl S Buck was born in her mother's ancestral home. Although the only American woman ever to win both the Pulitzer and Nobel Prizes spent only one summer here when she was 9 years old, the **Pearl S Buck Birthplace** (tel 304/653-4430), ¼ mile north of town on US 219, looks very much like it did when she was born on June 26, 1892. Open May–October, Monday–Saturday 9am–5pm; Sunday 1–5pm. Admission is $4 adults, $1 children 18 and under.

Take a Break

For an ice cream cone, a soft drink out of an old-fashioned Pepsi-Cola vending machine, or some fresh cookies, stop in the **Hillsboro General Store** (tel 304/653-4414), a throwback to the 1890s on US 219 as you drive into town.

From Hillsboro, continue north on US 219 for 2 miles to Mill Point. You can go straight north there for 9 miles to Marlinton for a look at the **Pocahontas County Historical Museum,** at WV 39 (tel 304/799-4973), which has displays on regional history, and rejoin the tour north of town on US 219 atop Lick Mountain. Otherwise, turn left on WV 39 west and climb uphill 6 miles to:

7. **Cranberry Mountain Visitor Center** (tel 304/653-4826 or 846-2695), a key entry to the many recreational activities in the huge Monongahela National Forest. Stop at the center for information about the nearby **Cranberry Glades Botanical Area,** where swampy bogs sit in a bowl at a 3,400-foot altitude; here you can observe rare plants and wildlife usually found in the tundra of Canada. A paved road ½ mile beyond the visitor center drops into the glades, where boardwalks go through the bogs.

From the visitors center, go straight on WV 150 (part of the Highland Scenic Hwy) for a lovely 23-mile drive along the crest of 4,600-foot-tall Cranberry Mountain. There are overlooks along the way, including one of Cranberry Glades. At the road's end on Lick Mountain, turn left on US 219 north, which drops precipitously into the narrow and extraordinarily beautiful Pleasant Valley. (Have your camera ready, especially if you want photos of an old barn with a Mail Pouch chewing tobacco sign still on its side.) After 10 miles you reach Slatyfork, which consists of the century-old:

8. **Sharp's County Store,** where you can look at stuffed animals, old farming tools, and Civil War relics in its museum-like front windows. You can also fill the tank, use the restrooms, and snack on a deli sandwich and a cold soda. Sharp's is open during the warm months, Monday–Saturday 7am–8pm, Sunday 8am–6pm.

From Sharp's, continue north on US 219 for 4 miles to WV 66. Turn right here and drive 1 mile east to:

9. **Snowshoe Mountain Resort,** on US 219 (tel 304/572-5252), one of the Mid-Atlantic's largest wintertime ski areas. During the summer, activities here include mountain biking, tennis, golf at the Gary Player–designed Hawthorne Valley course, a chili cook-off in July, and the Snowshoe Symphony Weekend in August.

The resort has the only large, up-to-date accommodations between Lewisburg and Canaan Valley, so it's the logical place to spend a night. **The Inn at Snowshoe,** on WV 66 just east of the US 219 intersection, is another modern hotel in the valley below the resort.

From Snowshoe, drive east on WV 66 across Little Mountain to the:

10. **Cass Scenic Railroad State Park** (tel 304/456-4300), where a powerful steam locomotive pulls a train to a lookout atop 4,842-foot-tall Bald Knob, just as it did when this timber line was built in 1911. Excursions run daily from Memorial Day to Labor Day, weekends in September, daily the 1st 2 full weeks in October, and weekends again for the rest of October. Dinner trains operate on Saturday during July and August and on Labor Day weekend.

For information on schedules and fares, call 800/ CALL WVA.

Train ticket holders can also visit nearby historical and wildlife museums, and the **Cass General Store** is full of souvenirs. The **Last Run Restaurant** is open Sunday–Wednesday 8:30am–6pm, Thursday–Saturday 8:30am–8pm, when the train is running.

At Cass, you'll cross the Greenbrier River for the last time and drive 5 miles east on WV 66, then left onto WV 28. From there, go north 3 miles to:

11. **Green Bank,** where the huge radio telescopes of the **National Radio Astronomy Observatory,** WV 28/ 92 (tel 304/456-2011), probe the depths of outer space. Free observatory tours providing a wealth of facts about space and radio waves take place daily, mid-June through August, 9am–4pm.

From Green Bank, continue 34 miles north on WV 28, climbing up and over the Allegheny Front, a mighty mountain which is the eastern continental divide (water on the west side flows into the Ohio and Mississippi Rivers; on the east, into the Potomac and Chesapeake Bay). A gravel road at the top of the pass leads to the summit of 4,861-foot Spruce Knob, the highest point in West Virginia. The mountain and its adjacent lake are part of **Spruce Knob-Seneca Rocks National Recreation Area** (tel 304/257-4442).

From the Front, you'll descend on WV 28 along the North Fork River through Judy Gap and Riverton to WV 55. Turn right there and drive a few hundred yards east to the **visitor center** of:

12. **Seneca Rocks,** whose 900-foot, quartzite formation may make you feel like you're in Wyoming, not West Virginia. These Tuscarora sandstone towers are among the most popular rock climbing venues in the eastern states, but you can also fish, hike, picnic, and camp on the site. The visitors center has information about the surrounding national recrea-

tion area. Other nearby attractions include **Seneca Caverns** (tel 304/567-2691) at Riverton, the largest commercial cavern in the state, and **Smoke Hole** Cavern (tel 304/257-4442), which has the nation's 2nd highest underground ceiling, is 13 miles north on WV 28.

Take a Break

South of Seneca Rocks on WV 28 and US 33 stands **Hedrick's 4-U Restaurant** (tel 304/567-2111), a clean, unpretentious establishment serving sandwiches, salads, steaks, country ham, fried chicken, seafood, and home-baked bread.

From the rocks, take US 33 west back up over the Allegheny Front for 12 miles to **Harman.** Turn right there on WV 32 and climb 9 miles north into:

13. **Canaan Valley** (pronounced *Ca-nain,* rhymes with main), a high plateau whose 3,200-foot altitude and surrounding mountains have made it a year-round resort, with skiing from Thanksgiving to April and golf, tennis, hiking, hunting, mountain biking, white-water rafting, and other activities the rest of the year. The valley includes **Canaan Valley State Park** (tel 304/866-4121), **Blackwater Falls State Park** (tel 304/259-5216), and the towns of **Davis** and **Thomas.**

The easiest way out of the mountains is via US 219 north from Thomas to I-64 at Keyers Ridge, Maryland, 51 miles away. Once in Maryland (15 miles from Thomas), you can make good time on US 219, which is wide and well-graded all the way to the Interstate. You will pass through Deep Creek Lake, the end of the driving tour "Western Maryland" (see the Maryland chapter). If you're heading east, you can do that trip in reverse.

West Virginia Listings

Ansted

Located 50 miles SE of Charleston, on the New River Gorge. Nearby to the Kanawha River and to Hawks Nest State Park, with splendid mountain views. Hico, a few miles east of Ansted, offers white-water excursions on both the New River and the Gauley River.

ATTRACTIONS

Hawks Nest State Park
WV 60; tel 304/658-5212. This park offers incredible views of the area and access to the New River. A lodge and restaurant are perched on the edge of the gorge, and tramway service (daily Memorial Day–Labor Day, reduced hours off-season) provides visitors with a scenic ride to the lake below. Also overlooking the canyon is a small rustic museum displaying artifacts of the Native Americans and the early pioneers who inhabited the area. Recreational opportunities near the park include whitewater rafting on the river, swimming in an outdoor pool, hiking, and picnicking. **Open:** Daily 6am–10pm. **Free**

Mountain River Tours
Sunday Rd, Hico; tel toll free 800/822-1386. These river specialists are in their 20th season of conducting white-water trips on the Gauley and New Rivers. All excursions use self-bailing boats. The price of a trip includes a continental breakfast. Campgrounds, hot showers, dining area. **Open:** Apr–Oct, daily 7am–10pm. **$$$$**

Barboursville

East of Huntington, this small town, settled in 1813, is near to Beech Fork State Park.

MOTELS

Comfort Inn Barboursville
3441 US 60 E, 25504; tel 304/736-9772 or toll free 800/221-2222; fax 304/736-4386. Exit 20 off I-64. E ½ mi on US 60. Good location just off interstate. **Rooms:** 131 rms. Executive level. CI 1pm/CO noon. Nonsmoking rms avail. Basic motel rooms are neat and clean. **Amenities:** A/C, cable TV. **Services:** **Facilities:** **Rates (CP):** $50 S or D. Extra person $4. Children under age 18 stay free. Parking: Outdoor, free. AE, DC, DISC, MC, V.

Holiday Inn Gateway
6007 US 60 E, 25504; tel 304/736-8974 or toll free 800/248-2426; fax 304/736-8974. Exit 20 off I-64. Nice grounds cover 15 acres, with buildings around a central courtyard. **Rooms:** 208 rms and stes. CI 2pm/CO noon. Nonsmoking rms avail. Pleasant rooms recently refurbished. **Amenities:** A/C, satel TV w/movies. **Services:** Babysitting. **Facilities:** 1 restaurant, 2 bars (1 w/entertainment), games rm, lawn games, spa, sauna, beauty salon, playground, washer/dryer. Heated indoor pool, volleyball courts. **Rates:** $70 S or D; $210 ste. Extra person $6. Children under age 19 stay free. Min stay special events. Parking: Outdoor, free. AE, CB, DC, DISC, MC, V.

RESTAURANT

★ **Gateway Restaurant**
In the Holiday Inn Gateway, 6007 US 60 E; tel 304/736-8974. 9 mi E of Huntington, exit 20 off I-64 W 3 mi on US 60. **American.** Nicer decor than usual for motel restaurants. Specializes in prime rib, country ham, turkey, and ribs. Reasonably priced buffets are a regular feature. Children under 12 eat free when dining with parents who are motel guests. **FYI:** Reservations accepted. Children's menu. **Open:** Daily 6am–10pm. **Prices:** Main courses $7–$17. AE, DC, DISC, MC, V.

ATTRACTION

Beech Fork State Park
5601 Long Branch Rd; tel 304/522-0303. This year-round vacation park is situated on 2,100 acres surrounding Beech Fork Lake. The 760-acre artificial lake offers fishing and boating; other facilities at the park include basketball courts and camping sites. **Open:** Daily 6am–10pm. **Free**

Beckley

See also Daniels

A coal-mining city located in the Greenbrier Valley. Nearby New River Gorge National River, despite its name, is one of the world's oldest waterways. Seat of Raleigh County. Lansing, to the north of Beckely, is home to the oldest white-water outfitter in the state. **Information:** Southern WV Convention and Visitors Bureau, PO Box 1799, Beckley, 25802-1799 (tel 304/252-2244).

HOTEL

≣ ≣ ≣ Beckley Hotel & Conference Center

1940 Harper Rd, 25801; tel 304/252-8661 or toll free 800/274-6010; fax 304/253-4496. Exit 44 off I-77. Highlights at this vast complex include a center court, a giant lobby with a fireplace, and Williamsburg Square, a village-like indoor shopping mall. **Rooms:** 191 rms and stes. CI 3pm/CO noon. Nonsmoking rms avail. **Amenities:** A/C, cable TV w/movies. 1 unit w/whirlpool. **Services:** Driving range has PGA pro instructor; there are five golf courses nearby. Exceptionally large heated pool has water-polo facilities. **Facilities:** 2 restaurants, 1 bar, games rm, whirlpool, washer/dryer. **Rates:** Peak (May–Nov) $65–$80 S; $70–$90 D; $100–$360 ste. Extra person $5. Children under age 18 stay free. Min stay special events. Lower rates off-season. Parking: Outdoor, free. AE, CB, DC, DISC, MC, V.

RESTAURANT

★ The Char

100 Char Dr; tel 304/253-1760. Exit 44 off I-77. Follow WV 3 W, go right at fork. **Italian/Seafood/Steak.** Done up in an upscale country style, this restaurant and bar offer casual dining in a rural setting. Huge picture windows overlook a lily pond. Outdoor benches. Steaks, chops, seafood, and pasta are most popular. **FYI:** Reservations not accepted. Dress code. **Open:** Mon–Fri 6–10pm, Sat 6–11pm. Closed Jan. **Prices:** Main courses $9–$34. AE, CB, DISC, MC, V. &

ATTRACTIONS

Beckley Exhibition Coal Mine

Ewart Ave, New River Park; tel 304/256-1747. Experienced coal miners lead tours 1,500 feet underground into what was once a working coal mine. The 45-minute trip highlights the process of low-seam coal mining from its earliest manual stages to modern mechanized operation. Mine temperature is a constant 58°F. **Open:** Apr–Oct, daily 10am–5:30pm. $$$

Wildwood House Museum

S Kanawha St; tel 304/252-8614. This historic home (circa 1836) was the residence of Gen Alfred Beckley, founder of Raleigh County and the city of Beckley. Listed on the National Register of Historic Places, the building is furnished with original period pieces. Authentic rooms include a Victorian parlor with handcrafted cherry furniture and a frontier kitchen with a "dry sink." **Open:** May–Oct, Sat 10am–4pm, Sunday 2–4pm. $

Babcock State Park

WV 41; tel 304/438-3004. Start a visit at the administration building at the park entrance. In addition to providing information about the area, the rustic sandstone building houses a restaurant and commissary. Across from the center is the Glade Creek Grist Mill, a fully operable grain mill that is a monument to the over 500 mills that once thrived in West Virginia. Visitors may purchase freshly ground whole-wheat, cornmeal, or buckwheat flour. The park itself is situated on 4,127 acres and features a trout stream, Boley Lake, and 20 miles of hiking trails. Paddleboats and rowboats are available for rent, and swimmers can use an outdoor pool. Camping, stables, tennis courts, playgrounds, picnic areas. **Open:** Daily sunrise–sunset. **Free**

Wildwater Rafting

US 19 and Milroy Grose Rd, Lansing; tel toll free 800/WVA-RAFT. The oldest white-water outfitter in West Virginia, Wildwater offers 12 different raft trips at all levels on the Gauley and New Rivers. **Open:** Mar–Oct, daily. Call for hours. $$$$

Berkeley Springs

This tiny town at the base of the Cacapon Mountains has long been noted for its warm mineral springs. (George Washington and his family often visited, and they purchased many of the original lots.) The original village green is now the site of Berkeley Springs State Park. **Information:** Berkeley Springs–Morgan County Chamber of Commerce, 304 Fairfax St, Berkeley Springs, 25411 (tel 304/258-3738).

HOTEL

≣ ≣ ≣ Country Inn

207 S Washington St, 25411; tel 304/258-2210 or toll free 800/822-6630; fax 304/258-3986. Exit 1B off I-70. This gracious, all-brick colonial country inn has homey touches like old-fashioned porches. Adjoins Berkeley Springs' village green and state-owned spa, featuring mineral water baths where George Washington soaked. Sitting-room art gallery for reading, piano playing, or games. **Rooms:** 68 rms and stes. CI 3pm/CO noon. Nonsmoking rms avail. Each room individually decorated with charming country fabrics. All have private baths. Honeymoon suite. Computer/fax jack in lobby. **Amenities:** A/C, cable TV. Suites have refrigerators. **Services:** Masseur, babysitting. **Facilities:** 1 restaurant, 1 bar (w/entertainment), spa, whirlpool, beauty salon. VCRs, movies for rent. Renaissance Spa has whirlpool baths, plush salon, European facials, body massage. Spacious

dining room has Saturday night dancing. **Rates:** $37–$85 S or D; $105–$145 ste. Extra person $10. Children under age 16 stay free. Min stay wknds. Parking: Outdoor, free. AE, DC, DISC, MC, V.

LODGES

≣≣≣ Cacapon Lodge

Cacapon State Park, WV 1, PO Box 304, 25411; tel 304/258-1022 or toll free 800/CALL-WVA; fax 304/258-5323. WV 522, 10 mi S of Berkeley Springs. 6,000 acres. Set amid mountain woodlands, this 6,000-acre, state-run resort park offers a 50-room lodge as well as 30 cabins and an 11-room inn. Huge, wood-paneled room off lobby, with fireplace, offers view of grounds, and plain but pleasant dining room looks out on Cacapon Mountain. **Rooms:** 61 rms; 30 cottages/villas. CI 4pm/CO noon. Most rooms have queen-size beds. Old inn rooms with hand-hewn log beams are more rustic than other units, and most share a bath. **Amenities:** 🛏 A/C, cable TV. Some units w/fireplaces. Neither cabins nor inn rooms have TVs. **Services:** ✕ ⋓ Social director, children's program. Naturalist program offered, for adults and children. Weekend activities scheduled. **Facilities:** △ ⋺ ▶18 ♠ ⋈ ⋐2 ⌷150⌷ 1 restaurant, 1 beach (lake shore), lifeguard, volleyball, games rm, playground. Horseback and hiking trails; six-acre lake for fishing, swimming, and boating. Robert Trent Jones Jr golf course, with golf pro on duty. **Rates:** Peak (May–Oct) $34–$50 S; $36–$57 D; $65–$105 cottage/villa. Extra person $6. Children under age 12 stay free. Min stay wknds. Lower rates off-season. Parking: Outdoor, free. Golf package offered, with rate by season. Dinner theater package in winter. AE, MC, V.

≣≣≣ Coolfont Resort & Conference Center

1777 Cold Run Valley Rd, 25411; tel 304/258-4500 or toll free 800/888-8768; fax 304/258-5499. Follow WV 9 from Berkeley Springs. 1,350 acres. Peaceful and rustic resort set on 1,350 wooded acres between Cacapon Mountain and Warm Springs Ridge. Family-owned and -operated, with a variety of special programs and activities. Emphasis on relaxation and recreation. **Rooms:** 250 rms, stes, and effic; 45 cottages/villas. CI 4pm/CO noon. Nonsmoking rms avail. Lodge rooms, chalets, mountaineer homes, log cabins, and hillside hideaways; most have stoves (with wood provided). Rooms are individually decorated with country touches like rocking chairs and quilted hangings. **Amenities:** 🛏 ⋔ A/C, dataport, voice mail. No TV. Some units w/terraces, some w/fireplaces, some w/whirlpools. Most chalets have double-size whirlpool tubs. **Services:** ⋓ Social director, masseur, children's program, babysitting. Entertainment on weekends. Recreational, cultural, and health activities offered, ranging from seminar with Pulitzer Prize–winning poet to daily exercise classes. **Facilities:** ⛗ ⋞ △ ⋺ ♠ ⋇ ⋈ ⋐3 ⌷⌷ ⌷250⌷ 1 restaurant, 1 bar (w/entertainment), 1 beach (lake shore), basketball, volleyball, games rm, lawn games, spa, sauna, whirlpool, beauty salon, playground, washer/dryer. Separate 9,000-square-foot swim and fitness center with 60-foot pool, exercise equipment, etc. Hiking trails. Lake for swimming and fishing. Cooperative arrangement for golf at nearby Cacapon Lodge. Camping. **Rates (MAP):** Peak (Apr–Oct) $77–$124 S or D; $77–$124 ste; $425–$750 effic; $77–$124 cottage/villa. Children under age 6 stay free. Min stay wknds. Lower rates off-season. Parking: Outdoor, free. Special packages avail. AE, DC, DISC, MC, V.

ATTRACTIONS 🏛

Berkeley Castle

WV 9; tel 304/258-3274. Built in 1885 by Col Samuel Taylor Suite, this Victorian mansion features a stone-walled ballroom, a pine-paneled library, a wide carved staircase, a tower room, and period furnishings. **Open:** Peak (June–Oct) daily 8am–8pm. Reduced hours off-season. **Free**

Berkeley Springs State Park

121 S Washington State Park; tel 304/258-2711. Mineral waters flowing from the springs in this park maintain a constant temperature of 74°F and have long been thought to possess medicinal powers. Popular with both Native Americans and the colonial elite, the spa was also frequented by George Washington. Among the services offered are mineral baths, massage therapy, and heat treatments. **Open:** Daily 10am–6pm. **Free**

Cacapon Resort State Park

WV 1; tel 304/258-1022. This 6,000-acre retreat at the foot of Cacapon Mountain offers swimming, fishing, and boating on Cacapon Lake; golfing on an 18-hole golf course; and hiking and horseback riding on 27 miles of trails. **Open:** Daily sunrise–sunset. **Free**

Bluefield

In the state's Greenbrier Valley, this city was named for a blue flower that flourishes throughout the area. **Information:** Bluestone Convention and Visitors Bureau, 500 Bland St, PO Box 4099, Bluefield, 24701 (tel 304/325-8438).

MOTELS 🏨

≣≣≣ Holiday Inn

US 460, 24701; tel 304/325-6170 or toll free 800/465-4329; fax 304/325-6170 ext 324. Exit 1 off I-77. Well-landscaped property sits on a hill above the highway and has pleasant views of the surrounding mountains. Restaurants and shops nearby. Popular for regional conventions. **Rooms:** 118 rms and stes. CI 2pm/CO noon. Nonsmoking rms avail. **Amenities:** 🛏 ⋔ A/C, cable TV, dataport. Refrigerators and VCRs available on request. **Services:** ✕ ⊿ ⋓ ⋓ Babysitting. **Facilities:** ⛗ ⌷325⌷ ⋐ 2 restaurants, 1 bar (w/entertainment), sauna. **Rates:** $65–$91 S or D; $135–$170 ste. Extra person $7. Children under age 18 stay free. Parking: Outdoor, free. BB rates avail. AE, CB, DC, DISC, JCB, MC, V.

☰☰☰ Ramada East River Mountain

3175 E Cumberland Rd, 24701; tel 304/325-5421 or toll free 800/272-6232; fax 304/325-6045. Exit 1 off I-77 Follow US 52 N to US 460. Nestled on the side of a mountain, this motel has a great view. **Rooms:** 98 rms and stes. Executive level. CI 2pm/CO noon. Nonsmoking rms avail. **Amenities:** 🛁 🐾 A/C, cable TV w/movies. Coffeemakers in some rooms. **Services:** ✕ 🖎 🖙 🖘 Pets under 25 pounds only. **Facilities:** 🖼 🏋 🔲 🔲 ⅃ restaurant, 1 bar (w/entertainment), games rm, sauna, steam rm, whirlpool. Large restaurant features stone wall and fireplace. Large indoor area with pool and sports. TV lounge. **Rates:** Peak (Mar–Aug) $55–$67 S or D; $105 ste. Extra person $5. Children under age 18 stay free. Lower rates off-season. Parking: Outdoor, free. AE, CB, DC, DISC, EC, JCB, MC, V.

Bridgeport

Founded in 1764, as a trading post. Just outside of town is a covered bridge, known as one of the "kissing bridges." **Information:** Bridgeport/Clarksburg Convention and Visitors Bureau, 158 Thompson Dr, Bridgeport, 26330 (tel 304/842-7272 or toll free 800/368-4324).

MOTELS 🏨

☰☰ Days Inn

112 Tolley St, 26330; tel 304/842-7371 or toll free 800/329-7466; fax 304/842-3904. Exit 119 off I-79. A planned renovation will make over this older motel and add new units and business center. **Rooms:** 62 rms. CI 2pm/CO 11am. Nonsmoking rms avail. **Amenities:** 🛁 A/C, cable TV. Some units w/whirlpools. **Services:** ✕ 🖎 🖙 Babysitting. **Facilities:** 🖼 🔲 🔲 Games rm, whirlpool. Indoor-outdoor heated pool. Nightclub on premises. **Rates (BB):** $58 S; $67 D. Extra person $8. Children under age 12 stay free. Parking: Outdoor, free. AE, DC, DISC, MC, V.

☰☰ Holiday Inn

100 Lodgeville Rd, 26330; tel 304/842-5411 or toll free 800/HOLIDAY; fax 304/842-7258. Exit 119 off I-79. Although the front is not particularly pleasing, the recently refurbished interior is appealing. **Rooms:** 160 rms and stes. Executive level. CI 2pm/CO noon. Nonsmoking rms avail. Average-quality rooms for this chain. **Amenities:** 🛁 🐾 🖳 A/C, cable TV w/movies, in-rm safe. **Services:** ✕ 🚗 🖎 🖙 🖘 Children's program, babysitting. **Facilities:** 🖼 🔲 🔲 ⅃ restaurant, 1 bar, washer/dryer. Pool and children's pool are attractive. **Rates:** Peak (Apr–Oct) $65–$80 S; $70–$85 D; $85–$100 ste. Extra person $5. Children under age 19 stay free. Min stay special events. Lower rates off-season. Parking: Outdoor, free. AE, CB, DC, DISC, MC, V.

Buckhannon

Home of Wesleyan College and near the noted West Virginia State Wildlife Center, a modern zoo and wildlife "orphanage." Seat of Upshur County. **Information:** Buckhannon/Upshur Convention and Visitors Bureau, 16 S Kanawha St, PO Box 431, Buckhannon, 26201 (tel 304/472-1722).

ATTRACTIONS 🏛

West Virginia State Wildlife Center

WV 20; tel 304/924-6211. This zoo displays animals in their natural habitats and features wildlife indigenous to West Virginia, such as black bears, river otters, elk, bison, mountain lions, and timber wolves. **Open:** Daily 9am–sunset. **$**

Audra State Park

Audra Park Rd; tel 304/457-1162. Located along the Middle Fork River, the park offers swimming as well as riverside camping and picnicking. Hikers can choose from a variety of trails that traverse natural rock formations. **Open:** Daily 7am–10pm. **Free**

Cairo

Quaint village of some 300 people, located in the mid-Ohio Valley Region. Named for Cairo, Egypt, because of its fertile river land.

ATTRACTION 🏛

North Bend State Park

WV 31; tel 304/643-2931. Fishing streams and abundant wildlife make this park a popular year-round destination. Activities and facilities include horseshoes, basketball, softball, bicycle rentals, horseback riding, and a paved hiking trail. Campgrounds, miniature golf, tennis courts. **Open:** Daily sunrise–sunset. **Free**

Cass

Small town on the Greenbrier River in the Monongahela National Forest. Home of Cass Scenic Railroad State Park; nearby Snowshoe Mountain Ski Resort also draws visitors.

ATTRACTION 🏛

Cass Scenic Railroad State Park

WV 66; tel 304/456-4300. Operating on the same line built in 1902 to haul logs to the mill town of Cass, the Cass Scenic Railroad now brings passengers to Bald Knob, the second-highest peak in the state. Original Shay steam locomotives and refurbished logging flatcars transport visitors on the scenic tour past some of the most breathtaking views of mountain scenery in West Virginia. Fall foliage tours, summer dinner trips. **Open:** May–Oct, call for schedule. **$$$$**

Charleston

See also Crosslanes

First settled in 1794, Charleston's location in a fertile valley surrounded by important natural resources (such as coal, oil, and two major rivers) assured its growth. The state capitol is also a trading center, a manufacturing center, and a city rich with urban delights and history. Its riverfront skyline displays the contrasts the city holds, from commercial towers to classic old structures, and visitors can enjoy everything from bustling nightlife to authentic stern-wheeler cruises. Seat of Kanawha County. **Information:** Charleston Convention and Visitors Bureau, 200 Civic Center Dr, Ste 002, Charleston, 25301 (tel 304/344-5075).

HOTELS 🏨

📼📼📼 Charleston Marriott Town Center
200 Lee St E, 25301; tel 304/345-6500 or toll free 800/228-9290; fax 304/353-3722. Exit 58C off I-64. Beautiful, tasteful lobby and public areas highlight this downtown hotel. **Rooms:** 352 rms and stes. Executive level. CI 4pm/CO noon. Nonsmoking rms avail. Modern rooms with upscale furniture. **Amenities:** 🛁 🧊 A/C, cable TV w/movies. All units w/terraces. Radios in bedside cabinets. **Services:** ✗ 🔑 🖼 🔃 Car-rental desk, masseur. Helpful, courteous staff. **Facilities:** 🗂 ●1 🏋️ 🛏️1000 🚻 2 restaurants (see "Restaurants" below), 1 bar, games rm, spa, sauna, steam rm, whirlpool, washer/dryer. Indoor pool with whirlpool opens to rooftop deck. **Rates:** $119–$139 S or D; $250–$300 ste. Children under age 18 stay free. Parking: Indoor, $3.50/day. Rates cover up to five people per room. AE, CB, DC, DISC, ER, JCB, MC, V.

📼 Knights Inn
6401 MacCorkle Ave SE, 25304; tel 304/925-0451 or toll free 800/843-5644; fax 304/925-4703. Exit 95 off I-64. A basic no-frills motel. **Rooms:** 130 rms. CI 4pm/CO noon. Nonsmoking rms avail. Rooms show their age but are clean. **Amenities:** 🛁 A/C, cable TV. **Services:** 🔃 🔃 Complimentary coffee all day. **Facilities:** 🗂 🏊10 🚻 **Rates:** $39–$44 S; $45–$50 D. Extra person $6. Children under age 18 stay free. Parking: Outdoor, free. AE, DC, DISC, MC, V.

MOTELS

📼📼📼 Ramada Plaza Hotel and Inn Charleston
2nd Ave and B St, 25303 (South Charleston); tel 304/744-4641 or toll free 800/2-RAMADA; fax 304/744-4525. Exit 56 off I-64. Although located in an industrial area this quite pleasant hotel has large lobby with beautiful antiques. **Rooms:** 245 rms, stes, and effic. CI 2pm/CO noon. Nonsmoking rms avail. Nicely furnished rooms. **Amenities:** 🛁 🧊 A/C, cable TV, voice mail. Some units w/terraces. Phones in bathrooms. **Services:** ✗ 🚐 🖼 🔃 🔃 Car-rental desk. **Facilities:** 🗂 🏊 🏋️ 🛏️400 🚻 1 restaurant, 3 bars (1 w/entertainment), games rm, whirlpool. Large bars feature DJs.

Rates: $60–$100 S; $65–$110 D; $150–$175 ste; $60–$80 effic. Extra person $5. Children under age 18 stay free. Parking: Outdoor, free. AE, CB, DC, DISC, EC, ER, JCB, MC, V.

📼📼 Red Roof Inn
4006 MacCorkle Ave SW, 25309 (South Charleston); tel 304/744-1500 or toll free 800/THE-ROOF; fax 304/744-8268. Exit 54 off I-64. In a suburban area yet just minutes away from downtown Charleston. One of the better members of Red Roof chain. **Rooms:** 137 rms. CI noon/CO noon. Nonsmoking rms avail. Rooms are very clean. **Amenities:** 🛁 A/C, cable TV. Units for guests with disabilities especially well equipped, including accessible thermostats. **Services:** 🔃 🔃 Complimentary morning coffee in lobby. **Facilities:** 🏋️ 🚻 Spa. Guests have free use of health club across street. **Rates:** Peak (Apr 30–Nov 1) $45–$55 D. Extra person $5. Children under age 18 stay free. Lower rates off-season. Parking: Outdoor, free. AE, CB, DC, DISC, MC, V.

RESTAURANTS 🍽️

★ 5th Quarter Steak House
201 Clendenin St; tel 304/345-2726. Exit 58B off I-64. Follow Virginia St to Clendenin St, turn left. **Burgers/Seafood/Steak.** Large brick fireplace reaches to ceiling at one end of this popular local eatery. Old-fashioned mood is enhanced by round globe lights and railroad lanterns. Large burgers, steaks, seafood are augmented by extensive salad bar. **FYI:** Reservations accepted. Blues/country music/jazz. Children's menu. **Open:** Lunch Mon–Fri 11am–2:30pm, Sat–Sun 11am–4pm; dinner Mon–Thurs 5–10pm, Fri 5–11pm, Sat 4–11pm, Sun 4–9pm. **Prices:** Main courses $10–$20. AE, CB, DC, DISC, MC, V. 🖼️ 🚻 🔽 🚻

💲★ Harper's
In Charleston Marriott Town Center, 200 Lee St E; tel 304/345-6500. Exit 58C off I-64. **Burgers/Seafood/Steak.** Pleasantly light, airy atmosphere enhanced by wood tables, cloth-upholstered chairs, many plants. Attractively presented buffets offered for breakfast, lunch, and dinner. Sandwiches and pizza also available. **FYI:** Reservations not accepted. Children's menu. **Open:** Daily 6:30am–10pm. **Prices:** Main courses $8–$20. AE, DC, DISC, MC, V. 🚻 🚗 🚻

🍷 Tarragon
In Charleston Marriott Town Center, 200 Lee St E; tel 304/345-6500. Exit 58C off I-64. **Seafood/Steak.** Not a typical hotel dining room, this upscale restaurant has very sedate surroundings. Visiting chefs prepare special menus during their 10-day stays. Regular menu is well divided between traditional seafood and meat. Incredible wine list includes fine vintages and champagnes, some available by the glass. **FYI:** Reservations recommended. Jacket required. **Open:** Mon–Sat 5:30–11pm. **Prices:** Main courses $15–$22. AE, CB, DC, DISC, MC, V. 💟 🚗 🚻

ATTRACTIONS 🏛

State Capitol
Kanawha Blvd; tel 304/348-3809. Designed by Cass Gilbert, the architect of the US Treasury and the US Supreme Court building, the capitol is constructed of buff limestone over a steel frame and features a 293-foot-high gilded dome. A two-ton crystal chandelier hangs 180 feet above the rotunda floor. Tours (available Mon–Fri 9am–3:15pm, Sat 1–5pm) begin at the rotunda information desk.

Within the capitol complex is the **Cultural Center,** featuring a craft shop, reference and archive libraries, and a theater. On the lower level is the **West Virginia State Museum,** tracing the history of the state from Native American migration to the early 20th century, with diplays highlighting a settler's cabin, the Civil War, and a general store. **Open:** Mon–Fri 9am–5pm, Sat–Sun 1–5pm. **Free**

Sunrise Museum and Science Hall
746 Myrtle Rd; tel 304/344-8035. The Sunrise Mansion was once the home of William A MacCorkle, governor of West Virginia from 1893 to 1897. Today it houses a science center that contains over 30 hands-on art and science exhibits as well as a planetarium. A companion mansion, Torquilstone, was built by MacCorkle for his son in 1928 and now houses the Sunrise Art Museum. Sunrise is situated on 16 acres of wooded grounds and offers a nature trail and gardens. **Open:** Wed–Sat 11am–5pm, Sun noon–5pm. **$$**

Kanawha State Forest
WV 2; tel 304/558-3500. This 9,250-acre forest is noted among naturalists for its diverse wildflower and bird population. There are 25 miles of hiking trails, including the Spotted Salamander Trail designed for blind and wheelchair-bound visitors. Swimming pool, stables, fully equipped campgrounds, playground. **Open:** Daily 6am–10pm. **Free**

Charles Town

In the Eastern Gateway region, northwest of Washington, DC. Site of the famous trial of abolitionist John Brown at the Jefferson County Courthouse and his subsequent hanging. The area is also known for horse breeding and racing. Seat of Jefferson County. **Information:** Jefferson County Chamber of Commerce, 200 E Washington St, PO Box 426, Charles Town, 25414 (tel 304/725-2055).

MOTEL 🛏

▤ Towne House Motor Lodge
549 E Washington St, 25414; tel 304/725-8441 or toll free 800/227-2339; fax 304/725-5484. ½ mi E of downtown. Clean, no-frills facility within walking distance of downtown. Thoroughbred racing is just across the highway. Cordial staff. **Rooms:** 115 rms, stes, and effic. CI 2pm/CO 11am. Nonsmoking rms avail. Tidy, clean rooms; a variety of suites and cottage-style efficiencies available. Quieter accommodations are in the back. **Amenities:** 🎛 A/C, satel TV, refrig. Six efficiencies have stove; all rooms have small refrigerators. **Services:** 🛎 Early check-in available. **Facilities:** 🛋 ▭50▭ 1 restaurant, basketball, volleyball. **Rates:** Peak (Apr 15–Nov 15) $30 S; $35 D; $90 ste; $40 effic. Extra person $4. Children under age 12 stay free. Lower rates off-season. Parking: Outdoor, free. On weekends and holidays, doubles rate only. AE, CB, DC, MC, V.

RESTAURANTS 🍴

♟ Charles Washington Inn
210 W Liberty St; tel 304/725-4020. 1½ blocks NW of intersection of VA 9 and US 340. **New American/Seafood.** This 1787 house, named for George Washington's brother, is nestled between two towering sycamore trees. The three interior dining rooms and pub (all with authentic colonial furnishings) are supplemented by an extensive outdoor dining area with a garden. Menu specialties include original-recipe broiled crab cakes and Cajun seafood étoufée. **FYI:** Reservations recommended. Children's menu. **Open:** Mon–Thurs 11:30am–9pm, Fri–Sat 11:30am–10pm, Sun 4–9pm. **Prices:** Main courses $9–$18. AE, DISC, MC, V. 🍷 🖼

♟ Iron Rail Inn & Quinn Cellar Pub
124 E Washington St; tel 304/725-0052. At Samuel St. **American/International.** The decor of this 1795 house reflects two eras in the structure's life, with dining in a Victorian west wing or a Colonial east wing. English antiques are throughout, with some eclectic country modern touches. Veal marsala and steak au poivre are specialties; the stone-and-brick pub downstairs serves both the dinner menu and lighter fare. Hours may vary during winter months. **FYI:** Reservations recommended. Children's menu. **Open:** Lunch Tues–Fri 11:30am–2pm; dinner Tues–Sat 5–9:30pm. **Prices:** Main courses $16–$20. AE, DC, DISC, MC, V. 🍷 🖼

ATTRACTIONS 🏛

Jefferson County Courthouse
N George St; tel 304/725-9761. This 1836 Greek Revival–style building was the site of the famous 1859 treason trial of John Brown. Partially destroyed during the Civil War, it has been extensively renovated, and visitors can tour the building, which is still in use today. **Open:** Mon–Thurs 9am–5pm, Fri 9am–7pm. **Free**

Jefferson County Museum
200 E Washington St; tel 304/725-8628. The small museum documents the history of the county, with special emphasis on the Civil War. Among the items on display are a Confederate flag from Stewart's Horse Artillery and personal items belonging to abolitionist John Brown. **Open:** Apr–Nov, Mon–Sat 10am–4pm. **Free**

Site of the John Brown Gallows
S Samuel St. The site where John Brown was hung for treason is marked by a pyramid of stones said to have been taken from

his cell in the Charles Town Jail. Witnesses of the 1859 execution included Gen Stonewall Jackson and Virginia militiaman John Wilkes Booth. **Open:** Daily sunrise–sunset. **Free**

Clarksburg

Founded in 1785, and named for George Rogers Clark of the Lewis and Clark expeditions. The discovery of oil in the late 19th century led to its development as a factory town, and local companies still turn out products ranging from building blocks to toy marbles. Seat of Harrison County. Nutter Fort, just south of Clarksburg, is convenient to Watter Smith State Park and the West Fork River. The town of Salem (once called Fort New Salem) was settled in 1788 and is still known for its fine 18th-century buildings. **Information:** Bridgeport/ Clarksburg Convention and Visitors Bureau, 158 Thompson Dr, Bridgeport, 26330 (tel 304/842-7272 or toll free 800/ 368-4324).

MOTEL 🏨

≣≣ Comfort Inn
250 Emily Dr, 26301; tel 304/623-2600 or toll free 800/ 221-2222; fax 304/622-5240. Exit 119 off I-79. Good location as part of shopping mall. **Rooms:** 112 rms, stes, and effic. CI noon/CO noon. Nonsmoking rms avail. Room for guests with disabilities has only wide door, no other special facilities. **Amenities:** 🛏 A/C, satel TV, refrig. **Services:** 🛎 🍽 **Facilities:** 🏊 ₺ **Rates (CP):** Peak (Apr–Oct) $48–$52 S; $52 ste; $52 effic. Extra person $5. Children under age 18 stay free. Lower rates off-season. Parking: Outdoor, free. AE, CB, DC, DISC, MC, V.

ATTRACTION 🏛

Fort New Salem
US 50, Salem; tel 304/782-5245. Located near the campus of Salem-Teikyo University, this collection of relocated log structures re-creates a 19th-century frontier settlement. Mountain artisans practice crafts and trades of the 19th century in the 17 cabins. There are also seasonal events, such as the Spirit of Christmas in the Mountains held in early December. **Open:** Peak (May–Oct) Wed–Fri 10am–5pm, Sat–Sun 1–5pm. Reduced hours off-season. Closed Jan–Apr. **$**

Crosslanes

This city of some 11,000 is mostly a bedroom community for the Charleston area. **Information:** Charleston Convention and Visitors Bureau, 200 Civic Center Dr, Ste 002, Charleston, 25301 (tel 304/344-5075).

MOTEL 🏨

≣≣ Comfort Inn
102 Racer Dr, 25313; tel 304/776-8070 or toll free 800/ 798-7886; fax 304/776-6460. Exit 47 off I-64. Convenient location minutes from Charleston. **Rooms:** 112 rms and stes. CI 2pm/CO noon. Nonsmoking rms avail. Standard motel-style rooms are pleasant. **Amenities:** 🛏 ₺ 🖥 A/C, cable TV, refrig, CD/tape player. **Services:** ✕ 🍽 **Facilities:** 🏊 🍳 ₺ 1 bar, whirlpool. **Rates (CP):** Peak (Apr–Oct) $52 S or D; $65 ste. Extra person $5. Children under age 18 stay free. Lower rates off-season. Parking: Outdoor, free. AE, CB, DC, DISC, MC, V.

Daniels

Located in the Greenbrier Valley SE of Beckley, Daniels is home to Glade Springs Resort, a 3,500-acre resort close to the New River and Little Beaver State Park.

RESORT 🏨

≣≣≣ Glade Springs Resort
3000 Lake Dr at US 19, 25832; tel 304/763-2000 or toll free 800/634-5233; fax 304/763-3398. Exit 125 off I-64, or exit 28 off I-77. 3,500 acres. Convenient to two interstate highways and just 12 minutes from downtown Beckley, this 3,500-acre resort nestled in the mountains offers space, quiet, outdoor and indoor sports, and other activities. **Rooms:** 69 stes; 6 cottages/villas. Executive level. CI 3pm/CO noon. Nonsmoking rms avail. **Amenities:** 🛏 ₺ 🖥 A/C, cable TV, refrig. Some units w/terraces, some w/fireplaces, some w/whirlpools. Units have oversize whirlpools and two TVs. Some units with VCRs, hair dryers. **Services:** 🛎 🍽 🛍 Children's program, babysitting. Security guards at entrance around the clock plus roving security guards. **Facilities:** 🏊 🚲 🎾 ▶18 ⛷ 🏃 🎿 ⛳2 🏊3 🏓 🍳 ₺ 1 restaurant, 1 bar (w/entertainment), basketball, volleyball, games rm, racquetball, squash, sauna, whirlpool, playground, washer/dryer. Highly rated golf course, two fishing lakes. Heliport. **Rates:** Peak (Apr–Oct) $78–$92 ste; $275–$325 cottage/villa. Extra person $10. Children under age 12 stay free. Lower rates off-season. Parking: Outdoor, free. Golf packages avail. AE, MC, V.

Davis

Resort community in the Monongahela National Forest. **Information:** Potomac Highlands Convention and Visitors Bureau, Executive Office Plaza, Ste 113, Elkins, 26241 (tel 304/636-8400).

LODGE 🏨

≡≡≡ Blackwater Lodge
In Blackwater Falls State Park, PO Box 490, 26260; tel 304/259-5216 or toll free 800/225-5982; fax 304/259-5881. Exit I-68 at US 219 S. Situated in a beautiful park with friendly deer. Comfortable lobby has sofas, chairs, piano. **Rooms:** 55 rms; 25 cottages/villas. CI 3pm/CO noon. Nonsmoking rms avail. Units aren't fancy but are clean and neat and have incredible mountain views. Lodge rooms are on second floor, with no elevator access. **Amenities:** 🔒 A/C, cable TV. Some units w/terraces, some w/fireplaces. **Services:** ✕ 🖛 🛎 Masseur, children's program, babysitting. A naturalist plans events and gives talks. **Facilities:** ⚠ 🏠 ⛵ 🏖 🚣 🎿 ⚲2 🏊 ⛵ 1 restaurant, 1 beach (lake shore), lifeguard, games rm, lawn games, playground. **Rates:** Peak (Mem Day–Labor Day/Dec 16–Feb 28) $69 D; $468 cottage/villa. Extra person $6. Children under age 12 stay free. Min stay wknds and special events. Lower rates off-season. Parking: Outdoor, free. AE, MC, V.

RESORTS

≡≡≡ Black Bear Resort
Rte 1, Box 55, 26260; tel 304/866-4391 or toll free 800/553-BEAR. 40 mi S of Keyser's Ridge. A well-maintained, remote, wonderfully peaceful and quiet resort with lots of outdoors space. Convenient to ski lodges, boat rentals, horseback riding. **Rooms:** 10 stes; 50 cottages/villas. CI 4pm/CO 11am. Nonsmoking rms avail. Both suites and pedestal units (small ground floor, larger upstairs) are large, with full kitchens. **Amenities:** 🔒 ⛲ 🖬 Cable TV, refrig. No A/C. All units w/terraces, all w/fireplaces, some w/whirlpools. Pedestal units have washers and dryers. **Services:** 🛎 **Facilities:** 🏋 🏠 🏖 🚣 🎿 ⚲1 🏊 ⛵ 1 restaurant (dinner only), 1 bar, games rm, lawn games, playground, washer/dryer. Heated indoor pool with large outdoor deck. **Rates:** Peak (Dec 15–Mar 15) $110 ste; $140–$160 cottage/villa. Min stay. Lower rates off-season. Parking: Outdoor, free. DISC, MC, V.

≡≡≡ Canaan Valley Resort & Conference Center
HC 70, Box 330, 26260; tel 304/866-4121 or toll free 800/622-4121; fax 304/866-2172. 35 mi NE of Elkins. 6,000 acres. Panoramic view of Allegheny Mountains from all angles of this two-story multiservice resort in Canaan Valley Resort State Park. **Rooms:** 250 rms and stes; 23 cottages/villas. CI 4pm/CO noon. Nonsmoking rms avail. All rooms similarly decorated with integrated decor of eye-pleasing fabrics. They face out in motor-lodge style. **Amenities:** 🔒 🖬 🍴 A/C, cable TV w/movies. Shower massage. **Services:** 🛎 Children's program, babysitting. Tennis and golf lessons available. Park naturalist and nature programs. Secretarial service. **Facilities:** 🏋 🚴 🏠 ⛳18 🚣 🎿 🏊6 🥾 ⛵ 🏌 2 restaurants, 2 bars (1 w/entertainment), games rm, spa, sauna, whirlpool, playground, washer/dryer. 18 miles of hiking trails. 34 campsites. Scenic chair lift. Miniature golf.

Golf pro shop, driving range; ice skating; 33 slopes for downhill skiing, and many trails for cross-country skiing. Cafe, coffee shop. **Rates:** Peak (May 20–Oct 23) $49–$73 S; $55–$79 D; $119 ste; $125–$194 effic. Extra person $6. Children under age 12 stay free. Min stay peak. Lower rates off-season. Parking: Outdoor, free. Many packages avail midweek only. Some cabins have seven-night minimum during high season. AE, CB, DC, DISC, MC, V.

ATTRACTIONS 🏛

White Grass Ski Touring Center
Freeland Rd; tel 304/866-4114. Located ½ mile north of Canaan Valley Resort State Park. Specialists in cross-country skiing, White Grass offers backcountry and machine-groomed trails, as well as lessons, guides, and ski schools. A rustic lodge provides specialized equipment sales and a natural foods cafe. **Open:** Dec–Mar, daily 8am–8pm. $$$

Blackwater Falls State Park
WV 32; tel 304/259-5216. This park is most noted for its amber-colored waters, dyed by tannic acids from fallen hemlock and red spruce needles, that converge in a five-story plunge known as Blackwater Falls. In summer visitors can swim and boat in Pendleton Lake and enjoy the tennis courts, volleyball courts, and riding stables. Some of West Virginia's heaviest snowfalls occur in the Blackwater Falls region in winter, and the park offers cross-country skiing on over 20 miles of trails. The **Blackwater Nordic Center** offers cross-country ski instruction, equipment rentals, and backcountry guides. **Open:** Daily sunrise–sunset. **Free**

Canaan Valley Resort State Park
WV 32; tel 304/866-4121. This park, set in a valley 3,200 feet above sea level and surrounded by mountain peaks, is a major winter sports area. The 240-acre ski facility offers downhill skiing, chairlifts, cross-country trails, and ice skating. Also located on the 6,015-acre resort are an 18-hole golf course, an indoor/outdoor pool, hiking trails, and tennis courts. **Open:** Daily 10am–8pm. $

Timberline Four Seasons Resort
WV 32; tel 304/866-4801. Located in an Alpine valley high in the Allegheny Mountains, Timberline is known for its abundant natural snowfall. Over 150 inches of natural snow falls on the mountain each season, while consistently wintry temperatures provide great snow making weather from November through March. Five lifts (one triple, one double, and three surface) shuttle skiers up the 4,268-foot peak, while 25 trails (about half of them black-diamond, or difficult) bring them back down. Night skiing is offered on Thursday through Sunday until 9pm during the season.

Snowboarders are welcome on all trails and snowboard lessons and rentals are available daily. (Timberline's 200-foot half-pipe is a popular venue for boarding competitions.) A 17-km back-country trail system is mapped and marked for adventurers, and a one ride lift ticket is offered for back country skiers heading out from the mountain's summit. Rental shop, ski school, restaurant **$$$$**

Elkins

Located in the Potomac Highlands, this city of some 8,000 was settled in 1889 and is adjacent to the Monongahela National Forest. Nearby Riverton is close to 4,800-foot Spruce Knob, the highest point in the state. Seat of Randolph County. **Information:** Potomac Highlands Convention and Visitors Bureau, Executive Office Plaza, Ste 113, Elkins, 26241 (tel 304/636-8400).

ATTRACTIONS 📷

Monongahela National Forest
Jct US 219/250/33; tel 304/636-1800. A variety of trees can be found in the 908,000 acres of national forest stretching along the eastern coast of West Virginia, including cherry, maple, oak, yellow poplar, cedar, and even cactus. Rivers and streams support a coldwater fishery that features native and stocked trout. Other popular activities include bird watching, rock climbing, hiking, rafting, canoeing, and both primitive and developed camping. **Open:** Daily sunrise–sunset. **Free**

Seneca Caverns
I-33, Riverton; tel 304/567-2691. Guided tours of the state's largest caverns highlight **Mirror Lake,** an underground waterpool that reflects formations overhead, and the **Grand Ballroom,** 60 feet long, 30 feet wide, and as high as 70 feet, with a natural balcony on its back wall. Stalagmite and stalactite formations in the caves include Niagara Falls Frozen Over, Fairyland, Candy Mountain, and the Upside Down Well. **Open:** Mem Day–Labor Day, daily 8am–7pm. **$$$**

Fairmont

Built in 1820 on a series of steep hills, the city is divided by the Monongahela River. Seat of Marion County. **Information:** Marion County Convention and Visitors Bureau, 316 Monroe St, PO Box 1258, Fairmont, 26555 (tel 304/363-7037).

MOTELS 🏨

🚉🚉 Days Inn
1185 Airport Rd, 26554; tel 304/367-1370 or toll free 800/329-7466; fax 304/367-1800. Although just off I-79, this motel is tucked away in an extremely quiet, peaceful area. **Rooms:** 98 rms. CI 2pm/CO noon. Nonsmoking rms avail. Rooms are quite pleasant, with coordinated decor. Fairly upscale for a Days Inn. **Amenities:** 🛏 A/C, cable TV. **Services:** 🛎 🖨 **Facilities:** 🏋 🕭 Games rm. **Rates (CP):** $47 S

or D. Extra person $5. Children under age 18 stay free. Min stay special events. Parking: Outdoor, free. AE, DC, DISC, MC, V.

🚉🚉 Holiday Inn
I-79 and Old Grafton Rd, 26554; tel 304/366-5500 or toll free 800/HOLIDAY; fax 304/363-3975. Exit 137 off I-79. A chain motel with incredible views of the surrounding countryside. **Rooms:** 106 rms. Executive level. CI 1pm/CO noon. Nonsmoking rms avail. Pleasant units are kept neat and clean. **Amenities:** 🛏 🕭 📞 A/C, cable TV w/movies, refrig, in-rm safe. Some units have microwaves. VCRs available for fee. **Services:** ✕ 🖨 🖨 🕭 Babysitting. Special kids program in summer. **Facilities:** 🏊 🎱 🕭 1 restaurant, 1 bar. **Rates:** Peak (Mar–Oct) $69 S or D. Extra person $5. Children under age 19 stay free. Lower rates off-season. Parking: Outdoor, free. AE, DC, DISC, MC, V.

🚉 Red Roof Inn
Rte 1, PO Box 602, 26554; tel 304/366-6800 or toll free 800/THE-ROOF; fax 304/366-6812. Exit 132 off I-79. Convenient location near Middletown Mall. **Rooms:** 109 rms. CI noon/CO noon. Nonsmoking rms avail. New owners took over in 1994. **Amenities:** 🛏 A/C, cable TV. **Services:** 🖨 🕭 **Facilities:** 🎱 🕭 **Rates:** $48 S or D. Extra person $3. Children under age 16 stay free. Parking: Outdoor, free. Senior discounts avail. AE, CB, DC, DISC, MC, V.

RESTAURANT 🍽

⑤ ★ Muriale's Restaurant
1742 Fairmont Ave Ext; tel 304/363-3190. Exit 132 off I-79. Follow WV 250 N for approximately 1½ miles. **American/ Italian/Seafood.** This large, nothing-fancy but pleasant restaurant has wood tables and wood-backed chairs. Walls are lined with copper pots and old pictures. Extensive menu is heavy on Italian and seafood. Freshly baked basil bread is complimentary at each table. Excellent dessert tray. **FYI:** Reservations recommended. Children's menu. No smoking. **Open:** Sun–Thurs 10am–9pm, Fri–Sat 11am–10pm. **Prices:** Main courses $8–$16. AE, DC, DISC, MC, V. 🍴 🕭

ATTRACTION 📷

Prickett's Fort State Park
Exit 139 off I-79; tel 304/363-3030. Located on the site of an early frontier stronghold, this park features a reconstruction of a 1774 fort. Demonstrations of pioneer crafts are held within the compound, which features 16 cabins, a meeting hall, and a storehouse. The park also offers picnic grounds, an amphitheater, and access to the Monongahela River. An 18th-century Christmas market is held weekends from Thanksgiving through Christmas. **Open:** Apr–Dec, Mon–Sat 10am–5pm, Sun noon–5pm. **$$**

Fayetteville

This small Greenbrier Valley town is convenient to the New River and Babcock State Park. Seat of Fayette County.

ATTRACTION 🛍

Rivers Resort Complex

US 19; tel toll free 800/879-7483. Located on the New River Gorge, Rivers offers white-water trips on the New, Cheat, and Gauley Rivers. Daily white-water excursions include a continental breakfast, equipment, transportation to the river, and a buffet lunch on the riverbank. Facilities at the resort complex include camping grounds, volleyball courts, horseshoe pits, and the Red Dog River Saloon. **Open:** Peak (May–Oct) daily 8am–7pm. Reduced hours off-season. **$$$$**

Grafton

Located in a cup-shaped valley surrounded by steep hills, Grafton is known as a railroad center and trading center for farmers and miners. Native citizen Anna Jarvis brought distinction to the city when she organized the first Mothers Day celebration here in 1908. Seat of Taylor County. **Information:** Grafton–Taylor County Convention and Visitors Bureau, 214 W Main St, Rm 205, Grafton, 26354 (tel 304/265-3938).

MOTEL 🛏

≋ Crislip Motor Lodge

300 Moritz Ave, 26354; tel 304/265-2100. Exit 119 off I-79; E on US 50. A nice, well-kept motel from the 1950s in a pretty, peaceful setting away from town. Good place to relax. **Rooms:** 40 rms. CI 3pm/CO 11am. Rooms and baths are spacious. **Amenities:** 🛏 📺 A/C, cable TV. **Services:** ✕ 🆅🅿 🛎 🍴 **Facilities:** 🛗 ♿ **Rates:** $34 S; $43 D. Extra person $4–$5. Children under age 12 stay free. Parking: Outdoor, free. AE, CB, DC, DISC, MC, V.

LODGE

≋≋≋ Tygart Lake State Park Lodge

Rte 1, PO Box 258, 26354; tel 304/265-2320 or toll free 800/CALL-WVA. Take US 119 S into Grafton; follow signs to state park and lodge. A true case of "almost heaven" at this comfortable, state-owned lodge surrounded by gorgeous countryside. View of lake is magnificent. **Rooms:** 20 rms; 10 cottages/villas. CI 3pm/CO noon. Nonsmoking rms avail. Although average, rooms are clean and comfortable. Some face outside, others face indoor corridors. **Amenities:** 🛏 A/C, cable TV. **Services:** 🛎 Children's program. Park ranger plans nature outings and events. **Facilities:** ⚠ 🅿 🏊 ⛷ 🚤 100 ♿ 1 restaurant, 1 beach (lake shore), lifeguard, playground. Dining room overlooks lake. Section of lake surrounded by "concrete" beach and adjacent grassy area. **Rates:** Peak (May

24–Sept 4) $42–$58 S; $49–$64 D; $424–$460 cottage/villa. Extra person $6. Children under age 12 stay free. Lower rates off-season. Parking: Outdoor, free. Cabins rent by week only (from $385/wk). Closed Nov–mid-Apr. AE, MC, V.

ATTRACTIONS 🛍

West Virginia National Cemetery

431 Walnut St; tel 304/265-2044. One of two national cemeteries in the state, this contains the grave of the first Union soldier killed by Confederate forces: T Bailey Brown. **Open:** Daily 24 hours. **Free**

Tygart Lake State Park

Off WV 92; tel 304/265-3383. The highlight is the lake created by the US Army Corps of Engineers in the 1930s. Popular activities on its 11 square miles of water include swimming, scuba diving, boating, fishing, and waterskiing. Cabins, lodge, marina, camping. **Open:** Daily 6am–10pm. **Free**

Green Bank

Located in the Potomac Highlands, in the eastern part of the state. Site of the National Radio Astronomy Observatory, featuring some of the world's largest radio telescopes. **Information:** Potomac Highlands Convention and Visitors Bureau, Executive Office Plaza, Ste 113, Elkins, 26241 (tel 304/636-8400).

ATTRACTION 🛍

National Radio Astronomy Observatory

Jct WV 28/92; tel 304/456-2011. This is the location of the state-of-the art Green Bank Telescope. Other large radio telescopes at this location investigate quasars, pulsars, galaxies, stars, planets, and Milky Way gas clouds. **Open:** Peak (mid-June–Labor Day) daily 9am–4pm. Reduced hours off-season. Closed Nov–mid-June. **Free**

Harpers Ferry

A tiny town amid the Blue Ridge Mountains at the confluence of the Shenandoah and Potomac Rivers with a view Thomas Jefferson once described as "worth a trip across the Atlantic." Famous as site of abolitionist John Brown's 1859 raid on the US Armory. The National Park Service has headquarters here and maintains part of the town as a National Monument. The Appalachian Trail crosses into the region at Harpers Ferry and it is home to Appalachian Trail Conference headquarters.

HOTEL 🛏

≋≋ Hilltop House Hotel

Ridge St, PO Box 930, 25425; tel 304/535-2132 or toll free 800/338-8319; fax 304/535-6322. Exit 340 at Union St, then R on Washington St. This historic hostelry dates from 1888, and has hosted Mark Twain, Alexander Graham Bell, Carl Sandburg, Pearl S Buck, and Woodrow Wilson. The place lacks some modern amenities, but some think that the authentic air of faded glory makes up for it. **Rooms:** 62 rms and stes. CI 2pm/CO 11am. Unique, individually decorated rooms; most with river views. Reproduction iron bedsteads, white curtains, flowered comforters, and large old dressers. **Amenities:** 🛁 A/C, cable TV. Some units w/terraces, some w/whirlpools. **Services:** 🛎 🗑 Ice, hair dryers, irons available at front desk. Transportation to/from airport (for a fee) or local train stations (for free). **Facilities:** 🎿 ⚓ [105] 1 restaurant, 1 bar. Sun porch above river available for dinner meetings. Table tennis. **Rates:** $65–$150 S or D; $95 ste. Extra person $7. Children under age 2 stay free. Min stay peak. Parking: Outdoor, free. Murder mystery weekend packages avail. AE, DC, DISC, MC, V.

MOTEL

☰☰☰ Cliffside Inn & Conference Center

US 340, PO Box 786, 25425; tel 304/535-6302 or toll free 800/STAY-HERE; fax 304/535-6313. Set atop a hill a mile from Harpers Ferry National Historical Park, this property affords a commanding view of the surrounding mountains. Large, half-timbered lobby provides a charming welcome. **Rooms:** 100 rms and stes. CI 3pm/CO 11am. Nonsmoking rms avail. Modest but spacious rooms. One suite available with queen-size brass bed; eight poolside rooms. All units have either mountain or valley view. **Amenities:** 🛁 A/C, satel TV w/movies. Some units w/terraces. Suite has refrigerator, 25-inch color TV. **Services:** ✗ 🛎 🖼 🗑 🍽 **Facilities:** 🎱 🎿 ⚓ ⚲2 [500] ⚿ 2 restaurants, 1 bar (w/entertainment), basketball, volleyball, games rm, lawn games. The bar/lounge also serves food, and the restaurant, which features a buffet, enjoys a nice view. Dataports in conference rooms. Gift shop offers local crafts and country wares. **Rates:** Peak (Apr–Oct) $44–$58 S; $50–$58 D; $95 ste. Extra person $6. Children under age 12 stay free. Lower rates off-season. Parking: Outdoor, free. Getaway packages include meals and beverages. AE, CB, DC, DISC, MC, V.

RESTAURANT 🍽

★ The Anvil Restaurant

1270 Washington St; tel 304/535-2582. Exit US 340 at Harpers Ferry. **Regional American/Seafood.** Comfy and convivial, with brick entryway, fireplaces in both bar and dining room, sturdy oak furniture, and some booths in bar area. Seafood is a draw; lighter fare available in bar section. Each evening brings a special: one night a week, it's all-you-can-eat shrimp; another is Mexican night. In a side dining room, mementos from *The Anvil*, a play about John Brown's trial, adorn the walls. **FYI:** Reservations accepted. Children's

menu. No smoking. **Open:** Sun 11am–9pm, Tues–Thurs 11am–9pm, Fri–Sat 11am–10pm. **Prices:** Main courses $10–$18. AE, DC, DISC, MC, V. ♥ 🍽 🖼 ♿

ATTRACTIONS 📷

Harpers Ferry National Historical Park

US 340; tel 304/535-6298. This beautiful spot at the confluence of the Shenandoah and Potomac Rivers—where Maryland, West Virginia, and Virginia meet—was the scene of a violent confrontation between abolitionists led by John Brown and US Marines under the command of Col Robert E Lee.

Today visitors can tour preserved streets, shops, houses, and public buildings that appear much as they did when this town flourished and prospered in the mid-19th century. Begin exploring at the **visitor center,** where there are maps for self-guided tours as well as shuttle buses to Lower Town. Ranger-led tours also initiate here three or four times a day. Some of the highlights of the area include Lower Town, featuring media presentations, restored buildings, and exhibits about the original town; Bolivar Heights, for the opportunity to walk in the footsteps of Abraham Lincoln and Stonewall Jackson; Camp Hill, the location of Harper Cemetery; and the Virginius Island area, once home to a thriving 19th-century industrial town. At Loudoun Heights, hikers can ascend the Blue Ridge Mountains via the historic and scenic Appalachian Trail. **Open:** Daily 8am–5pm. **Free**

John Brown Wax Museum

High St; tel 304/535-6342. Re-creates the career of the famed abolitionist through life-size exhibits featuring electronic lighting, sound, and animation. **Open:** Peak (Apr–Dec) daily 9am–5pm. Reduced hours off-season. Closed Jan. **$**

Hillsboro

A small village of some 200 at the southern end of the Monongahela National Forest. Birthplace of author Pearl S Buck (*The Good Earth*).

ATTRACTIONS 📷

Pearl S Buck House

US 219; tel 304/653-4430. This columned white frame house was the home of the only American woman to win both the Pulitzer and the Nobel Prizes for literature. Displayed in the home are period furnishings and memorabilia from Buck's literary accomplishments. **Open:** May–Nov, Mon–Sat 9am–5pm, Sun 1–5pm. **$$**

Watoga State Park

Jct US 219/WV 39; tel 304/799-4087. Located in the Appalachian highlands on the Virginia border, West Virginia's largest state park encompasses 10,100 acres. Recreational opportunities (most available Mem Day–Labor Day only) include swimming and trout fishing in the Greenbrier River, rowboat and paddleboat rentals, cross-country skiing and hiking trails, picnicking, and tennis. Restaurant, campgrounds (open Apr–Nov), cabins. **Open:** Daily 6am–10pm. **Free**

Droop Mountain Battlefield State Park
US 219; tel 304/653-4254. The oldest state park in West Virginia, this was the site of the Battle of Droop Mountain, fought on November 6, 1863, in which the Union army thwarted serious efforts by the Confederacy to control West Virginia. Hiking trails throughout the park point out highlights of the battle. Picnic area, ski trails, museum. **Open:** Daily 6am–10pm. **Free**

Hinton

See also Princeton

Located in the Greenbrier Valley, close to Bluestone Lake and Pipestem Resort State Park. Seat of Summers County. **Information:** Summers County Convention and Visitors Bureau, 206 Temple St, Hinton, 25951 (tel 304/466-5420).

ATTRACTIONS

Hinton Historic District
206 Temple St; tel 304/466-5420. In 1872, Hinton became the center of a major C&O terminal yard and a building boom swept the area. Today there are over 20 National Historical Sites here, including the Parker Opera House, built in 1885; the colonial revival–style Second Baptist Church, the oldest African American church in the area; and the C&O passenger depot, still an active train station after more than 100 years. The Summers County Visitors Center, located at the address above, provides self-guided tour maps of the town and its historical buildings. **Open:** Daily 9am–5pm. **Free**

New River Scenic Whitewater Tours
Hinton Bypass off WV 20; tel toll free 800/292-0880. The Gauley River has long been a popular spot with white-water enthusiasts for its pristine water and world-class white water. This company specializes in tours down the river geared to all skill levels. Half-day, full-day, and multi-day excursions. Meals included on most trips. **Open:** Mar–Oct, daily 8am–6pm. **$$$$**

Bluestone Dam
WV 20; tel 304/466-1234. Closing a 2,048-foot gap between mountains, this concrete gravity dam rises 165 feet above the stream bed. The dam holds back an average 2,040 surface acres of water; the tail waters below offer fishing and canoeing. A visitors center is located at the top of the structure. Tours are offered by the US Army Corps of Engineers June through August on Tues and Wed at 1:30pm and Fri and Sat at 2pm. **Free**

Pipestem Resort State Park
WV 20; tel 304/466-1800. Situated near the Bluestone Dam recreation area, this park features an 18-hole golf course, a pool, tennis and basketball courts, miniature golf, a nature center, and stables. Long Branch Lake and Bluestone River afford a variety of fishing and boating opportunities. A unique feature of the park is the Pipestem Aerial Tramway that transports visitors from the Canyon Rim Center to the rugged floor of Bluestone Canyon. **Open:** Daily 6am–10pm. **Free**

Bluestone State Park
WV 20; tel 304/466-2805. This heavily wooded park lies adjacent to Bluestone Lake, making it a popular destination in the southern section of the state. Boating, fishing, hiking trails, a pool, boat-launching facilities, and a marina are some of the attractions here. Camping, cabins. **Open:** Daily sunrise–sunset. **Free**

Huntington

Along the banks of the Ohio River, this railroad town and bustling manufacturing center is world-famous for its hand-blown glass. It's also a comfortable university town offering riverfront concerts, museums, wide avenues, and landscaped parks. Seat of Cabell County. **Information:** Cabell/Huntington Convention and Visitors Bureau, #2 Civic Center Plaza, PO Box 347, Huntington, 25708 (tel 304/525-7333).

HOTEL

Radisson Hotel Huntington
1001 3rd Ave, 25701; tel 304/525-1001 or toll free 800/333-3333; fax 304/525-1001 ext 2041. Exit 11 off I-64. Attractive atrium—with trees, sitting areas, tables beside pool—makes this hotel seem removed from its downtown location a block from Ohio River. **Rooms:** 200 rms and stes. Executive level. CI 3pm/CO noon. Nonsmoking rms avail. Warm and comfortable rooms, with upscale furnishings. **Amenities:** A/C, cable TV w/movies. 1 unit w/whirlpool. VCRs and refrigerators can be rented at front desk. **Services:** Masseur, babysitting. **Facilities:** 1 restaurant, 1 bar, spa, sauna, steam rm. Lively restaurant with bar and entertainment. **Rates:** $88–$110 S or D; $160–$377 ste. Extra person $10. Children under age 16 stay free. Min stay special events. Parking: Indoor, free. AE, DC, DISC, MC, V.

MOTELS

Holiday Inn Downtown/University Area
1415 4th Ave, 25701; tel 304/525-7741 or toll free 800/828-9016; fax 304/525-3508. Exit 11 off I-64. One of only two in-town motels convenient to commercial center, Marshall University. **Rooms:** 137 rms and stes. CI 4pm/CO noon. Nonsmoking rms avail. Pleasant rooms recently refurbished. Three economy suites have Murphy beds. **Amenities:**

A/C, satel TV w/movies. **Services:** ✕ 🚐 🖼 🕳 🦽 Masseur. Guests who ask are provided breakfast. **Facilities:** 🏊 🍽 �‍250 ₺ 1 restaurant, 1 bar. **Rates:** $70–$76 S; $76 D; $90–$100 ste. Extra person $5. Children under age 18 stay free. Parking: Outdoor, free. AE, CB, DC, DISC, JCB, MC, V.

🏨 Ramada Inn

5600 US 60 E, 25705; tel 304/736-3451 or toll free 800/ 228-2828; fax 304/736-3451. Exit 20 off I-64. A three-story brick motel, convenient to malls, restaurants, downtown. **Rooms:** 120 rms. CI 2pm/CO noon. Nonsmoking rms avail. Comfortable units all recently refurbished. **Amenities:** 🛏 A/C, satel TV. All units w/terraces. **Services:** 🚐 🖼 🕳 🦽 Babysitting. **Facilities:** 🏊 🍽 �‍75 ₺ 1 restaurant, 1 bar. **Rates:** $55 S; $60 D. Extra person $5. Children under age 18 stay free. Parking: Outdoor, free. AE, CB, DC, DISC, EC, ER, JCB, MC, V.

RESTAURANT 🍴

♥ ★ Rebels and Redcoats Tavern

412 7th Ave W; tel 304/523-8829. Exit 8 off I-64. Follow US 52 N to 7th Ave, turn left. **American/Seafood/Steak.** Consistently rated one of West Virginia's top restaurants, this place has the aura of a men's club, with dark wood-paneled walls, moldings, candles on walls, leaded-glass windows. Prime rib is the focus, either regular or Cajun-style. Also seafood, rack of lamb, chops. **FYI:** Reservations recommended. **Open:** Lunch Mon–Sat 11:30am–2:30pm; dinner Mon–Thurs 5:30–10pm, Fri–Sat 5:30–11pm. **Prices:** Main courses $7–$42. AE, DC, DISC, MC, V. ♥ 🍴 🚗

ATTRACTIONS 🖼

Central City Historic District

Exit 6 off I-64; tel toll free 800/635-6329. Between 1893 and 1909 this was a flourishing manufacturing town known as St Cloud. The well-preserved Victorian frame houses, brick streets, and cast-iron fences here reflect residential fashions of the times and turn-of-the-century tastes. Visitors can tour the town and view the historic homes, including the Parsons-Abott-Mosser house, a High Victorian frame residence built in 1870 for Capt H Chester Parsons, a leading figure in the settlement of Huntington. **Open:** Daily 9am–4:30pm. **Free**

Huntington Museum of Art

2033 McCoy Rd; tel 304/529-2701. This indoor/outdoor complex features gallery space, nature trails, an observatory with a Celestron-14 telescope, a junior art museum, a sculpture garden, and an amphitheater. Permanent collections include Appalachian folk art, American and European paintings, Georgian Silver, pre-Columbian art, and hand-blown glass. **Open:** Tues–Sat 10am–5pm, Sun noon–5pm. **Free**

Camden Park

Exit 6 off I-64; tel 304/429-4321. A family tradition since 1902, this amusement park features 28 rides including a new looping roller coaster and a log flume. In addition, this is the location of the *C P Huntington* sternwheel excursion boat offering 45-minute narrated rides along the Ohio River. **Open:** Peak (May–Aug) daily 10am–10pm. Reduced hours off-season. Closed Oct–Mar. **$$$**

Hamon Glass

102 Hamon Dr; tel 304/757-9067. Specialists in blown glass and glass sculpture, the design team of Robert and Veronnica Hamon give demonstrations of the glass-sculpting process and present exhibitions of their glasswork. **Open:** Mon–Fri 9am–4pm. **Free**

Blenko Glass

Exit 28 off I-64, Milton; tel 304/743-9081. Located 16 mi E of Huntington, Blenko is best known as a stained-glass producer. Creations from the factory can be seen in such locations as New York City's St Patrick's Cathedral and Grant's Tomb, and the Rose Window in the Washington Cathedral. In addition to a small museum with examples of blown glass, the Blenko visitors center has a special observation deck where visitors can watch molten glass take its final form. Tours are available Mon–Fri 8am–3pm. **Open:** Mon–Sat 8am–4pm, Sun noon–4pm. **Free**

Pilgrim Glass

Exit 1 off I-64, Ceredo; tel 304/453-3553. Located 5 mi W of Huntington. Pilgrim is most noted for its cameo glass, a process where several colors of molten glass are cast in layers and, when cool, carved into designs. Visitors can see this unique process as well as traditional glass blowing at the visitor observation platform. **Open:** Mon–Sat 9am–5pm, Sun 1–5pm. **Free**

Lewisburg

The discovery of a spring in 1751 at the intersection of two Native American trails led to growth of "Lewis's Spring," later known as Lewisburg. Minutes from White Sulphur Springs, and nearby to Greenbrier River and Lost World Caverns. Seat of Greenbrier County. **Information:** Lewisburg Convention and Visitors Bureau, 105 Church St, Lewisburg, 24901 (tel 304/645-1000 or toll free 800/833-2068).

MOTELS 🏨

🏨 Briar Inn Motel and Convention Center

540 N Jefferson St, 24986; tel 304/645-7722; fax 304/ 645-7865. Exit 169 off I-64. Proximity to I-64, center of town, many restaurants, and golfing at The Greenbrier in White Sulphur Springs is a plus for this motel. **Rooms:** 164 rms, stes, and effic. CI 2pm/CO 11am. Nonsmoking rms avail. **Amenities:** 🛏 🕭 A/C, satel TV. Some units w/whirlpools. **Services:** ✕ 🚐 🖼 🕳 🦽 Staff arranges tours of local attractions. Pets allowed for $10 charge. **Facilities:** 🏊 🍽 �‍500 ₺ 1 restaurant, 1 bar (w/entertainment), games rm.

Rates: $42–$47 S or D; $70–$75 ste; $62–$67 effic. Extra person $5. Children under age 12 stay free. Parking: Outdoor, free. AE, DC, DISC, JCB, MC, V.

≋ ≋ Budget Host Fort Savannah

204 N Jefferson St, 24901; tel 304/645-3055 or toll free 800/678-3055. Exit 169 off I-64; go south on US 219 for 1½ miles. Located next to the remains of a late-18th-century fort and well and across from a park, this is a comfortable place for families. Within walking distance of downtown historic district. **Rooms:** 65 rms. CI 2pm/CO noon. Nonsmoking rms avail. **Amenities:** 📺 🗄 A/C, cable TV. Dataports in some rooms. **Services:** ✗ 🖼 🕼 🖦 **Facilities:** 🖫 ⬛60 1 restaurant, 1 bar (w/entertainment), games rm, whirlpool, washer/dryer. **Rates:** Peak (Apr–Oct) $50–$60 S or D. Extra person $5. Children under age 18 stay free. Lower rates off-season. Parking: Outdoor, free. AE, DISC, MC, V.

≋ ≋ Days Inn

635 N Jefferson St, 24901; tel 304/645-2345 or toll free 800/329-7466. Exit 169 off I-64; go north on US 219 for ¼ mile. Sitting atop a hill, this motel is close to restaurants, a country club golf course, medical colleges, The Greenbrier, and the West Virginia Fairgrounds. **Rooms:** 26 rms. CI noon/CO 11am. Nonsmoking rms avail. Simple yet immaculately clean rooms. **Amenities:** 📺 🗄 A/C, cable TV. Rollaway bed available for extra fee. **Services:** 🖦 **Rates (CP):** $40–$75 S; $45–$85 D. Extra person $5. Children under age 12 stay free. Min stay special events. Parking: Outdoor, free. AE, JCB, MC, V.

INN

≋ ≋ ≋ The General Lewis Inn

301 E Washington St, 24901; tel 304/645-2600 or toll free 800/628-4454; fax 304/645-2600. 1 acre. Relaxing in rocking chairs on the veranda or patio and looking out over grounds with a goldfish pond and an old stagecoach evokes memories of days gone by. So too does a plethora of antiques in this comfortable inn, part of which is a circa-1834 home. Conveniently located in historic Lewisburg, near museums and Revolutionary and Civil War sites. **Rooms:** 25 rms and stes. CI 3pm/CO 11am. No smoking. Of varying sizes, rooms are decorated with antiques handed down by the area's early settlers. **Amenities:** 📺 🗄 A/C, cable TV. **Services:** 🖦 🕼 Ice placed in rooms each afternoon. Extra fees for pets, cribs. **Facilities:** 🖫 1 restaurant (see "Restaurants" below), guest lounge. **Rates:** $54–$82 S; $64–$92 D; $82–$92 ste. Extra person $10. Children under age 3 stay free. Min stay special events. Higher rates for special events/hols. Parking: Outdoor, free. AE, MC, V.

RESTAURANT 🍴

The General Lewis Inn Dining Room

301 E Washington St; tel 304/645-2600. Exit 169 off I-64. Follow US 219 south, turn left at 1st traffic light, go 2 blocks. **Regional American.** Dining room in this original 1834 home is filled with antiques, adding to down-home ambience. Cocktails sipped in living room or on patio. Old-fashioned meals of mountain trout, country ham, and homemade soups, breads, and desserts. **FYI:** Reservations accepted. Children's menu. Dress code. No smoking. **Open:** Breakfast Mon–Sat 7–11am, Sun 7:30–11am; lunch Mon–Sat 11:30am–2pm; dinner Mon–Sat 6–9pm, Sun noon–9pm. **Prices:** Main courses $10–$18. AE, MC, V. ■ 🖼 &

ATTRACTION 🏛

Lewisburg Historic District

105 Church St; tel 304/645-1000. Set amid the Allegheny Mountains, the area appears much the way it did 200 years ago. A steeple clock tolls the hour, antebellum homes have often been occupied by the same families for generations, gaslamps light the streets, and there are no overhead power lines. Start a walking tour at the visitors center to obtain self-guided tour maps. Special locations include the **Old Stone Presbyterian Church**, 200 Church St; built in 1796, it is the oldest church in continuous use west of the Alleghenies. **North House**, 101 Church St, was originally a tavern when it was built in 1820. Distinguished by its heavily carved ornate woodwork; it now serves as the museum of the Greenbrier Historical Society. **Open:** Mon–Sat 9am–5pm, Sun 1–5pm. **Free**

Logan

In the heart of coal country and nearby to Chief Logan State Park, a 3,300-acre forest popular for hiking and camping. Seat of Logan County. **Information:** Logan County Chamber of Commerce, PO Box 218, Logan, 25601 (tel 304/752-1324).

ATTRACTIONS 🏛

Chief Logan State Park

WV 119; tel 304/792-7125. Set on 3,300 acres in the heart of coal country, this park is a popular camping and hiking location. Pool, physical-fitness trail, tennis courts, miniature golf. **Open:** Daily 6am–10pm. **Free**

Watters Smith Memorial State Park

Exit 110 off I-79; tel 304/745-3081. This historical park features a late-1700s farm; the original Smith family home (circa 1876); and a museum that houses many early farm artifacts. There's also swimming, picnicking, and hiking. **Open:** Mem Day–Labor Day, daily 11am–7pm. **Free**

Madison

Located SW of Charleston on the Pond Fork River. Close to the Big Ugly and Fork Creek Public Hunting Area, as well as the Coal River. Seat of Boone County.

ATTRACTION 🖼

Water Ways
WV 119; tel 304/369-1235. A water park featuring water slides, a pool, an 18-hole miniature-golf course, and picnic grounds. **Open:** Mem Day–Labor Day, daily 11am–8pm. **$$$**

Martinsburg

One of the state's oldest towns, it was originally laid out in 1775 as a colonial village and later became a busy mill town. Today it is one of the fastest growing cities in the state. Site of historic homes and buildings, and outlet stores that draw shoppers from as far away as Baltimore and Washington, DC. Seat of Berkeley County. Hedgesville, located between Martinsburg and Berkeley Springs, is nearby to the Potomac River, Back Creek, and Sleepy Creek Public Hunting and Fishing Area. **Information:** Martinsburg–Berkeley County Chamber of Commerce, 208 S Queen St, Martinsburg, 25401 (tel 304/267-4841).

HOTELS 🏨

🗎🗎 Comfort Inn
2800 Aikens Center, 25401; tel 304/263-6200 or toll free 800/622-3416; fax 304/263-6200 ext 113. Exit 16 E off I-81. Nicely decorated facility, though not fancy. Large lobby features super-size TV, tables, fresh apples, 24-hr coffee, comfy sofa, large easy chairs. **Rooms:** 109 rms and stes. CI 3pm/CO noon. Nonsmoking rms avail. **Amenities:** 🛁 ◎ A/C, cable TV w/movies, dataport. Some units w/whirlpools. **Services:** △ ⅃ Very professional staff. Fax machine available. **Facilities:** 🛱 ➊ ⌗300 ⅃ ⅃ Games rm. **Rates (CP):** Peak (Aug–Oct) $65–$85 S or D; $90 ste. Extra person $6. Children under age 18 stay free. Lower rates off-season. Parking: Outdoor, free. AE, DC, DISC, EC, MC, V.

🗎🗎🗎 Holiday Inn
301 Foxcroft Ave, 25401; tel 304/267-5500 or toll free 800/HOLIDAY, 800/325-3535 in the US, 800/268-9393 in Canada; fax 304/267-3899. Exit 13 off US 81. Set in a shopping plaza just off interstate, but distant enough from other facilities to be quiet and restful. Adjacent to residential neighborhood. Spacious lobby with elegant furnishings, carpeting. **Rooms:** 120 rms and stes. CI 3pm/CO noon. Nonsmoking rms avail. **Amenities:** 🛁 ◎ A/C, satel TV w/movies, dataport. **Services:** ✗ △ ⅃ ⅃ **Facilities:** 🛱 ▦4 ➊ ⌗400 ⅃ 1 restaurant, 1 bar, volleyball, sauna, whirlpool, washer/dryer. Indoor heated pool and adjoining spa/health club are nicely designed and maintained. **Rates:** $79 S or D; $135–$185 ste. Children under age 12 stay free. Parking: Outdoor, free. AE, CB, DC, DISC, EC, ER, JCB, MC, V.

MOTELS

🗎🗎 Comfort Suites
WV 9 E, PO Box 2599, 25401; tel 304/263-8888 or toll free 800/263-0170; fax 304/263-1540. Exit 12 off I 81 to WV 9 E; go 5.1 mi toward Charles Town. This sparkling, new property emphasizes hospitality. High-ceilinged lobby is inviting and classy. **Rooms:** 76 rms and stes. CI 4pm/CO noon. Nonsmoking rms avail. Standard but appealing rooms with nice touches like armoires and pull-out sofas. King rooms are larger and have whirlpools. **Amenities:** 🛁 ◎ A/C, cable TV w/movies, refrig, dataport, voice mail. Some units w/whirlpools. Complimentary daily newspaper. Microwaves available. **Services:** △ ⅃ Coffee, microwavable meals, and snacks available 24 hours. **Facilities:** 🛱 ➊ ⌗125 ⅃ Whirlpool, washer/dryer. **Rates:** Peak (May–Oct) $51–$66 S; $57–$72 D; $60–$76 ste. Extra person $5. Children under age 18 stay free. Lower rates off-season. Parking: Outdoor, free. Golf packages avail. AE, CB, DC, DISC, JCB, MC, V.

🗎 Days Inn Shenandoah
209 Viking Way, 25401; tel 304/263-1800 or toll free 800/329-7466. Exit 13 off US 81. Clean and comfortable facility, conveniently located in a shopping plaza. **Rooms:** 64 rms and stes. CI 3pm/CO noon. Nonsmoking rms avail. **Amenities:** 🛁 A/C, satel TV. **Services:** △ ⅃ ⅃ Coffee in lobby. Fax service available. **Facilities:** ⅃ Washer/dryer. Shopping plaza has chain restaurants. **Rates (CP):** Peak (Apr–Nov) $54–$59 S or D; $70 ste. Extra person $6. Children under age 18 stay free. Lower rates off-season. Parking: Outdoor, free. AE, DC, DISC, MC, V.

🗎 Knights Inn
1599 Edwin Miller Blvd, 25401; tel 304/267-2211 or toll free 800/843-5644; fax 304/267-9606. Exit 16 E off US 81. Clean and hospitable. Stone pillars a nice architectural touch, setting this apart from usual chain motel. **Rooms:** 59 rms and effic. CI noon/CO noon. Nonsmoking rms avail. Basic rooms have good color coordination and are impressively clean. **Amenities:** 🛁 A/C, cable TV w/movies. Six kitchenettes available with microwave, refrigerator. VCRs for rent. **Services:** ⅃ ⅃ Free coffee in lobby. **Facilities:** ⌗12 **Rates:** Peak (June–Aug) $40 S; $47 D; $51 effic. Extra person $5. Children under age 17 stay free. Lower rates off-season. Parking: Outdoor, free. AE, DC, DISC, MC, V.

RESORT

🗎🗎🗎 The Woods Resort & Conference Center
Mountain Lake Rd, PO Box 5, Hedgesville, 25427; tel 304/754-7977 or toll free 800/248-2222; fax 304/754-8146. Exit 16W off I-81 to WV 9W. 12 mi W of Martinsburg. 1,800 acres. A woodsy resort offering rustic but comfortably sophisticated accommodations and facilities for the harried city-dweller. **Rooms:** 60 rms and stes; 12 cottages/villas. CI 4pm/CO noon. Nonsmoking rms avail. The Walden Lodge rooms, overlooking pond and pool, contain pine furniture and king-

size beds. Evergreen Lodge rooms are oversize and have open ceilings. The two-bedroom cabins have shower-only baths, kitchens. **Amenities:** ☎ A/C, cable TV w/movies, refrig. Some units w/terraces, some w/fireplaces, all w/whirlpools. **Services:** ⌨ Masseur, babysitting. Business services available in conference room. **Facilities:** ⌗ ▶27 🛝 ⛳3 🎾2 🍴 🍷 50 ⛷ 1 restaurant, 1 bar (w/entertainment), basketball, volleyball, lawn games, racquetball, spa, sauna, whirlpool, playground, washer/dryer. Fitness center features weight room and massages. Inside pool is heated. Snack bar. Entertainment in bar/restaurant Saturday evenings. **Rates (MAP):** Peak (Oct) $85–$125 S or D; $135 ste; $140 cottage/villa. Extra person $10. Children under age 6 stay free. Min stay wknds. Lower rates off-season. Parking: Outdoor, free. Golf packages avail. AE, DC, MC, V.

ATTRACTIONS 🏛

General Adam Stephen House
309 E John St; tel 304/267-4434. Constructed between 1774 and 1789, this was the home of Gen Adam Stephen, a contemporary of George Washington and Patrick Henry. The house is decorated with period furnishings, and the adjacent Triple Brick Museum contains items of local historical significance. **Open:** May–Oct, Sat–Sun 2–5pm or by appointment. **Free**

Boarman Arts Center
208 S Queen St; tel 304/263-0224. This gallery represents West Virginian artists through year-round juried exhibits that are open to the public. Recent showings have focused on Black History Month; youth art; American etchings in black and white; and a retrospective of Cubert L Smith, a popular local artist. **Open:** Mon–Fri 10am–5pm. **Free**

Mill Point

In the Monongahela National Forest in the state's Potomac Highlands region, this small community is nearby to Cranberry Glades, Watoga State Park, Highland Scenic Highway, Greenbrier River, and the 75-mile Greenbrier River Trail. **Information:** Potomac Highlands Convention and Visitors Bureau, Executive Office Plaza, Ste 113, Elkins, 26241 (tel 304/636-8400).

ATTRACTION 🏛

Cranberry Glades Botanical Area
Jct WV 39/150; tel 304/653-4826 or 846-2695. Part of the Monongahela National Forest, the botanical area was created to preserve the natural ecosystem and protect native plant life for future generations. The Cranberry Glades Visitor Center houses interpretive displays about the plants and trees on the 750 acres of the preserve. A half-mile boardwalk traverses two of the areas, providing visitors with an opportunity to view cranberries on the vine, wild orchids blooming in July,

and black bears feasting on skunk cabbage. The first two weeks of October the glades are open daily for fall foliage tours. Visitors are restricted to the boardwalk area; however, tours of the area are available if reservations are made in advance. On summer weekends naturalist guides lead hour-long tours beginning at 2pm. **Open:** Peak (Mem Day–Labor Day) daily 9am–5pm. Reduced hours off-season. **Free**

Mineral Wells

Located minutes south of Parkersburg, this town of some 1,800 lies between the Ohio and the Little Kanawha Rivers. **Information:** Parkersburg Convention and Visitors Bureau, 350 7th St, Parkersburg, 26101 (tel 304/428-1130).

MOTEL 🏨

≣≣ Comfort Suites
I-77 and WV 14 S, PO Box 108, 26150; tel 304/489-9600 or toll free 800/228-5150; fax 304/489-1896. Exit 170 off I-77. A pleasant drive leads to this all-suites motel with massive stone fireplace in lobby. **Rooms:** 116 rms, stes, and effic. CI 4pm/CO noon. Nonsmoking rms avail. Spacious, wonderfully furnished units have large bathrooms. **Amenities:** ☎ A/C, cable TV, refrig, VCR, voice mail. Some units w/whirlpools. Microwaves. **Services:** ✗ 🚐 📠 ⌨ Babysitting. Full complimentary breakfast Tuesday through Friday, continental other mornings. Apple cider served in lobby during winter. Full business services. **Facilities:** ⌗ 🍷 130 ⛷ 1 bar (w/entertainment), games rm, spa, sauna, whirlpool, washer/dryer. Attractive indoor-outdoor pool. **Rates (BB):** $71–$96 S; $76–$96 D; $146 ste; $76–$82 effic. Extra person $6. Children under age 18 stay free. Parking: Outdoor, free. AE, CB, DC, DISC, MC, V.

Morgantown

Spread over a narrow valley where Deckers Creek joins the Monongahela River, and surrounded by coal fields. This mixture of abundant water and coal makes it an ideal location for glass blowing. Dents Run Bridge, a covered bridge dating from the 19th century, is nearby. Seat of Monongahela County. **Information:** Northern WV Convention and Visitors Bureau, 709 Beechurst Ave, Seneca Center, 26505 (tel 304/292-5081).

HOTELS 🏨

≣≣≣ Euro-Suites Hotel
501 Chestnut Ridge Rd, 26505; tel 304/598-1000 or toll free 800/678-4837; fax 304/599-2736. Exit 7 off I-68. Wonderful lobby with baby grand piano invites sitting and relaxing in comfortable sofas and chairs. A relatively new hotel with friendly, helpful staff. **Rooms:** 74 stes. CI 3pm/CO 1pm. Nonsmoking rms avail. Rooms are tastefully decorated, from

wallpaper to artwork. **Amenities:** ⌘ ⚷ ▣ A/C, cable TV, refrig, dataport, voice mail. Suites have microwaves. **Services:** ▤ 🚗 ⬛ 🍴 Masseur, babysitting. **Facilities:** 🏕 ▣110 ⚷ 1 bar. Guests can use extensive recreational facilities at Lakeview Resort. **Rates (CP):** $90–$151 ste. Extra person $10. Children under age 19 stay free. Min stay special events. Parking: Outdoor, free. AE, CB, DC, DISC, MC, V.

🗲 Hotel Morgan

127 High St, 26505; tel 304/292-8401; fax 304/292-4601. Take I-68 or I-79 to downtown. Although Morgantown's former premier hotel has seen better days, its lobby and grand ballroom retain vestiges of its former glory. New owners promise to refurbish. **Rooms:** 92 rms and stes. CI noon/CO 11am. Most rooms are rather small, although some are combined into larger units. Comfortable but dated furniture in older rooms, while renovated units are better equipped. **Amenities:** ⌘ Cable TV. No A/C. **Services:** Validated parking a treat in downtown. **Facilities:** Bakery located just off the lobby. **Rates:** $40 S or D; $75–$150 ste. Extra person $10. Children under age 19 stay free. Min stay special events. Parking: Outdoor, free. AE, DISC, MC, V.

MOTELS

🗲🗲 Comfort Inn

WV 9, PO Box 225, 26505; tel 304/296-9364 or toll free 800/221-2222; fax 304/296-0469. Exit 1 off I-68. Follow US 119 to WV 9. A comfortable, clean, modern motel. **Rooms:** 80 rms. CI 3pm/CO noon. Nonsmoking rms avail. Rooms are spacious and well maintained. **Amenities:** ⌘ ⚷ A/C, cable TV, dataport, in-rm safe. Some units w/whirlpools. **Services:** ⬛ 🍴 **Facilities:** 🏕 🏕 ▣20 ⚷ Whirlpool. Lovely pool in rear. Restaurant on premises but not in the building. **Rates (CP):** $60–$115 S; $65–$115 D. Extra person $7. Children under age 19 stay free. Min stay special events. Parking: Outdoor, free. AE, DC, DISC, EC, MC, V.

🗲🗲 Hampton Inn

1053 Van Voorhis Rd, 26505; tel 304/599-1200 or toll free 800/426-7866; fax 304/599-1200 ext 133. Exit 155 off I-79. A basic, clean, and well-maintained motel. **Rooms:** 107 rms and stes. CI 2pm/CO noon. Nonsmoking rms avail. Quite pleasant rooms have three large mirrors placed to give full view. **Amenities:** ⌘ ⚷ A/C, cable TV, dataport, voice mail. **Services:** ⬛ 🍴 Morning coffee and doughnuts in office. **Facilities:** ▣25 ⚷ **Rates (CP):** Peak (Feb–Nov) $68 S or D; $100 ste. Children under age 19 stay free. Min stay special events. Lower rates off-season. Parking: Outdoor, free. AE, DC, DISC, MC, V.

🗲🗲 Holiday Inn

1400 Saratoga Ave, 26505 (Star City); tel 304/599-1680 or toll free 800/465-4329; fax 304/598-0989. Exit 155 off I-79. A typical Holiday Inn built in the 1970s. **Rooms:** 147 rms. CI 2pm/CO noon. Nonsmoking rms avail. Rooms are a bit tired, but clean. **Amenities:** ⌘ ⚷ A/C, satel TV w/movies, in-rm safe. **Services:** ✕ ⬛ 🍴 🍽 **Facilities:** 🏕 ▣500 ⚷ 1 restaurant,

1 bar. **Rates:** $68 S or D. Children under age 19 stay free. Min stay special events. Parking: Outdoor, free. AE, CB, DC, DISC, MC, V.

🗲🗲🗲 Ramada Inn

US 119, at jct I-68/I-79, PO Box 1242, 26505; tel 304/296-3431 or toll free 800/272-6232, 800/272-6232, 800/834-9766 in WV; fax 304/296-3431 ext 441. This motel enjoys a commanding view of the surrounding mountains. Lovely lobby contains fountain and lots of greenery. **Rooms:** 159 rms and stes. Executive level. CI 2pm/CO noon. Nonsmoking rms avail. **Amenities:** ⌘ ⚷ ▣ 🍴 A/C, satel TV, dataport, voice mail. Some units w/whirlpools. **Services:** ✕ 🚗 ⬛ 🍴 🍽 **Facilities:** 🏕 🏕 🏕 ▣500 ⚷ 1 restaurant, 1 bar (w/entertainment), basketball, volleyball, games rm. Outdoor heated pool. **Rates:** $60 S or D; $125–$185 ste. Extra person $5. Children under age 19 stay free. Min stay special events. Parking: Outdoor, free. AE, CB, DC, DISC, EC, JCB, MC, V.

RESORT

🗲🗲🗲 Lakeview Resort and Conference Center

WV 6, PO Box 88A, 26505; tel 304/594-1111 or toll free 800/624-8300; fax 304/594-9472. Exit 10 off I-68. 6 acres. Lovely drive through two golf courses leads to this resort, whose public areas are quite charming. Lobby invites long sits. **Rooms:** 187 rms and stes; 52 cottages/villas. CI 4pm/CO 2pm. Nonsmoking rms avail. Rooms were refurbished in 1995. **Amenities:** ⌘ ⚷ A/C, cable TV w/movies, dataport. Some units w/terraces, some w/fireplaces. **Services:** ✕ 🚗 ⬛ 🍴 Masseur, babysitting. **Facilities:** 🏕 🏕 ▶36 🏕 🏕 🏕 🏕 ▣850 ⚷ 2 restaurants (see "Restaurants" below), 1 bar (w/entertainment), volleyball, games rm, racquetball, spa, sauna, steam rm, whirlpool, day-care ctr, playground. Beautifully maintained golf courses. Pontoon boats holding up to 15 people available on the lake. **Rates:** Peak (Apr 8–Nov 15) $135 S; $145 D; $215–$395 ste; $280 cottage/villa. Extra person $10. Children under age 19 stay free. Min stay special events. Lower rates off-season. AP and MAP rates avail. Parking: Outdoor, free. AE, CB, DC, DISC, MC, V.

RESTAURANTS 🍴

The Glasshouse Grille

In Seneca Center, 709 Beechurst Ave; tel 304/296-8460. Exit I-79 at Star City; follow US 119 S. **Continental/Eclectic/Seafood.** Occupying part of an old glass factory, this restaurant exudes historic charm. Leaded windows and beautiful glass chandeliers are everywhere. Famous lump-meat crab cakes headline an eclectic menu, including fettuccine and filet mignon. Desserts are homemade and herbs are grown in onsite garden. **FYI:** Reservations recommended. Children's menu. **Open:** Lunch Mon–Sat 11am–2pm; dinner Mon–Thurs 5–9pm, Fri–Sat 5–9:30pm. **Prices:** Main courses $10–$18. AE, DISC, MC, V. 🔲 ⚷

Reflections on the Lake

In Lakeview Resort and Conference Center, WV 6, Box 88A; tel 304/594-1111. Exit 10 off I-68. **Seafood/Steak.** A hushed atmosphere prevails in this lovely, club-like restaurant with widely spaced tables. Such well-prepared selections as chicken stir-fry, herbed duck breast, and veal piccata. **FYI:** Reservations recommended. Comedy/dancing. Children's menu. Dress code. **Open:** Dinner Sun–Thurs 6–10pm, Fri–Sat 6–10:30pm; brunch Sun 11am–2pm. **Prices:** Main courses $16–$22. AE, CB, DC, DISC, MC, V. 💚 🏞 ♿

ATTRACTIONS 🏛

Cook-Hayman Pharmacy Museum

1124 Health Sciences N; tel 304/293-5101. This replica of a 19th-century pharmacy contains such artifacts as an antique pill cutter, a mill to grind barks and roots, and the glass percolator used to steep ground herbs to extract their medicinal qualities. Demonstrations of 18th-century implements are conducted for visitors with advance notice. **Open:** Peak (Sept–May) Mon–Fri 9am–5pm. Open by appointment in off-season. **Free**

Personal Rapid Transit System

99 8th St; tel 304/293-5011. Connecting West Virginia University's two campuses with downtown Morgantown, this is the world's first totally automated transportation system. The entire system is controlled through computers that determine routes and destinations. In addition to providing transportation for the over 26,000 students and employees of WVU, the PRTS serves as a national transportation research laboratory for Boeing Aerospace and the Urban Mass Transit Administration of the US Department of Transportation. **Open:** Peak (Sept–May) Mon–Fri 6:30am–10:15pm, Sat 9:30am–5pm. Reduced hours off-season. **$**

West Virginia University Core Arboretum

Monongahela Blvd; tel 304/293-5201. A variety of diverse habitats can be seen from the eight hiking trails that traverse the 50 acres of this arboretum. The north-flowing river that runs through the grounds makes this an excellent site to observe migratory birds. **Open:** Daily sunrise–sunset. **Free**

Nitro

Northwest of Charleston on the Kanawha River. Nitro was born as a "boom" town during World War I, when it was the site of a major government explosives plant.

MOTEL 🏨

≡ Best Western Motor Inn

4115 1st Ave, 25143; tel 304/755-8341 or toll free 800/528-1234; fax 304/755-2933. Exit 45 off I-64. Basic but clean motel, convenient to I-64 but far enough away to enjoy quiet location. **Rooms:** 28 rms. CI noon/CO 11am. Nonsmoking rms avail. New furnishings make rooms pleasant. **Amenities:** 🛁 A/C, cable TV. **Services:** ⌚ **Rates:** $40 S; $44 D. Extra person $5. Children under age 12 stay free. Parking: Outdoor, free. AE, CB, DC, DISC, MC, V.

ATTRACTION 🏛

Waves of Fun

1 Valley Park Dr; tel 304/562-0518. West Virginia's largest water park features waterslides, a white-water tube run, and a giant wave pool. Artificial beach, picnic area, changing rooms. **Open:** Mem Day–Labor Day, Mon–Sat 11am–7pm, Sun noon–7pm. **$$$**

Nutter Fort

RESTAURANT 🍴

♥ ✦ Jim Reid's Restaurant and Lounge

1422 Buckhannon Pike; tel 304/623-4909. 1 mi S of Clarksburg, exit 119 off I-79 Drive toward Clarksburg on US 50; head south on Joyce Ave. **American/Seafood/Steak.** Candle-lit for dinner and decorated like a club room, this restaurant feels like a comfortable English pub. Fresh seafood ranges from shrimp scampi to swordfish with almonds. Steak and some other meat dishes offered. Large servings. **FYI:** Reservations recommended. Children's menu. Dress code. **Open:** Lunch Wed–Fri 11am–2pm; dinner Tues–Sat 5–10pm, Sun noon–8pm. **Prices:** Main courses $10–$25; prix fixe $14–$18. MC, V. 💚 🚗

Parkersburg

A commercial, cultural, and historic center located at the juncture of the Ohio and Little Kanawha Rivers. Rich supplies of oil, coal, and gas have kept Parkersburg factories busy making products ranging from furniture to porcelain. Old stern-wheelers leave from Point Park for the short trip to Blennerhassett Island, once an 1811 "Eden on the River" for Irish aristocrats. **Information:** Parkersburg Convention and Visitors Bureau, 350 7th St, Parkersburg, 26101 (tel 304/428-1130).

HOTEL 🏨

≡≡≡ The Blennerhassett Clarion Hotel

320 Market St, 26101 (Downtown); tel 304/422-3131 or toll free 800/262-2536; fax 304/485-0267. Exit 176 off I-77. Follow US 50 W to Market St. This lovely, turreted Victorian-era (1889) brick hotel is a friendly place to stay. **Rooms:** 104 rms and stes. CI 2pm/CO noon. Nonsmoking rms avail. **Amenities:** 🛁 ❄ 🗄 A/C, cable TV w/movies. Some rooms have hair dryers. **Services:** ✕ 🖃 VP 🚗 🖼 ⌚ Car-rental desk. **Facilities:** 🔲 ♿ 2 restaurants, 1 bar. Guests have free use of pool, sauna, steam room, whirlpool, fitness facilities at local YMCA. **Rates:** Peak (May–Oct) $69–$74 S or D; $95–

$105 ste. Extra person $6. Children under age 18 stay free. Min stay special events. Lower rates off-season. Parking: Outdoor, free. AE, DC, DISC, MC, V.

MOTELS

≣≣ Best Western Inn
I-77 and US 50 E, 26101; tel 304/485-6551 or toll free 800/528-1234; fax 304/485-0679. Exit 176 off I-77. Clean, neat, older motel enjoys choice location. **Rooms:** 67 rms. CI noon/CO 11am. Nonsmoking rms avail. All bedding and furniture recently updated. **Amenities:** 🕿 ⏻ 🍽 A/C, cable TV. Suites have full-length mirrors and small refrigerators. **Services:** 🛍 🍴 🍷 **Facilities:** 🏊 💯 ♿ Attractive heated pool. **Rates:** Peak (Apr–Nov 1) $48–$55 S or D. Extra person $4. Children under age 18 stay free. Lower rates off-season. Parking: Outdoor, free. AE, CB, DC, DISC, MC, V.

≣≣ Red Roof Inn
3714 E 7th St, 26101; tel 304/485-1741 or toll free 800/THE-ROOF; fax 304/485-1746. Exit 176 off I-77. Follow US 50 W for ½ mile. One of the better members of the Red Roof chain. **Rooms:** 107 rms. CI 1pm/CO noon. Nonsmoking rms avail. **Amenities:** 🕿 A/C, cable TV. **Services:** ✕ 🛍 🍴 🍷 Shoney's Restaurant, just off the property, provides some room service. **Facilities:** 📋 ♿ **Rates:** Peak (Apr–Sept) $40–$50 S; $48–$58 D. Extra person $3. Children under age 18 stay free. Min stay special events. Lower rates off-season. Parking: Outdoor, free. AE, CB, DC, DISC, MC, V.

RESTAURANTS 🍴

♥★ Point of View
Star Ave and River Hill Rd; tel 304/863-3366. Exit 176 off I-77; US 50 W to VA 68 S to Star Ave. **Seafood/Steak.** Large windows render views of the Ohio River from a perch high on a hill overlooking Blennerhassett Island. Caring staff roasts chicken and ribs over an interior spit. Other options range from shrimp over fettuccine to filet mignon. Coffee bar offers 20 choices of fresh beans. Very popular. Reservations essential on Saturday. **FYI:** Reservations recommended. Children's menu. Dress code. **Open:** Lunch Mon–Fri 11:30am–2pm; dinner Mon–Thurs 5:30–9:00pm, Fri–Sat 5:30–10:00pm; brunch Sun 11:30am–2:30pm. **Prices:** Main courses $10–$17. AE, CB, DC, DISC, MC, V. ♥ 🏔 👪 🍷

★ Sebastian's
3420 Murdoch Ave; tel 304/485-8800. Exit 176 off I-77. Follow US 50 W to WV 14 N. **American/Burgers/Seafood.** Stained-glass wall panels handmade by a local artist are interesting. Prime rib is the most popular, but other selections include lobster, steaks, and pasta. Good choice for both families and business travelers. **FYI:** Reservations recommended. Children's menu. **Open:** Mon–Thurs 11am–10pm, Fri–Sat 11am–11pm, Sun 11am–9pm. **Prices:** Main courses $7–$16. AE, DC, DISC, MC, V. 👪 🚗 ♿

ATTRACTIONS 🏛

Henry Cooper Log Cabin Museum
City Park; tel 304/422-7841. Considered to be a classic example of American logwork, this cabin combines hand hewing with chinking between the logs to create a gabled roof and rectangle design. The Daughters of the American Pioneers maintain the museum and conduct tours of the grounds. **Open:** Mem Day–Labor Day, Sun 1:30–4:30pm. **$**

Blennerhassett Island Historical State Park
Point Park; tel 304/428-3000. The park is actually an island that must be reached by sternwheelers departing from Point Park in downtown Parkersburg. Blennerhassett Island is the location of a mansion built by Harman Blennerhassett in 1800, destroyed by fire in 1811, and reconstructed in 1975. Bicycle rentals, picnicking, guided mansion tours, horse-drawn wagon rides, and a crafts village with demonstrations are featured on the island. **Open:** May–Oct, Tues–Sun noon–5:30pm. **$$**

Fenton Art Glass Company
Williamstown exit off I-77, Williamstown; tel 304/375-7772. Located 12 mi N of Parkersburg. Fenton is highly regarded for its 91 years of producing quality handmade glassware using innovative techniques. Visitors interested in seeing the glassmaking process firsthand can take a free tour of the factory. Each piece of glass is individually blown or pressed by hand utilizing centuries-old techniques and tools. A museum and theater features a 24-minute movie on the glassmaking process and a display of early blown glass and unique pieces from the Fenton collection. Gift shop and factory outlet. **Open:** Peak (April–Dec) Mon–Fri 8am–8pm, Sat 8am–5pm, Sun 12:15–5pm. Reduced hours off-season. **Free**

Petersburg

On the South Branch of the Potomac River and nearby to Smoke Hole Recreational Area, Lost River State Park, and moor-like landscape of Dolly Sods National Recreational Area. Seat of Grant County.

HOTEL 🏨

≣≣ Hermitage Motor Inn
203 Virginia Ave, PO Box 1077, 26847; tel 304/257-1711; fax 304/257-4330. Circa 1840 inn on National Register of Historic Places has been used as a hostelry since 1881. Original three-story main building plus new addition and an adjacent motor lodge. **Rooms:** 39 rms and effic. CI 2pm/CO noon. Nonsmoking rms avail. New rooms are spacious, with integrated decor and framed photos of scenic West Virginia. There are six older rooms, not as fresh, in original inn. **Amenities:** 🕿 A/C, cable TV w/movies. Some rooms have microwaves and refrigerators. **Services:** 🍷 **Facilities:** 🏊 ♿ 1 restaurant (lunch and dinner only; see "Restaurants" below), 1 bar, whirlpool. Attractive pool with wooded sitting area.

Driving range just off premises. **Rates:** $39–$41 S; $44–$49 D; $210 effic. Extra person $6. Children under age 12 stay free. Parking: Outdoor, free. AE, CB, DC, DISC, MC, V.

MOTEL

🗏🗏 Homestead Inn and Motel

Rte 3, PO Box 146, 26847; tel 304/257-1049. Rock gardens and plentiful flowers add to country flavor of this sparkling-clean facility with a view of the mountains and large farm adjoining its six-acre setting. **Rooms:** 12 rms. CI 1pm/CO 11am. Nonsmoking rms avail. All rooms individually decorated with a country-wildlife mural on one wall and coordinated knickknacks. Country reproduction furnishings. **Amenities:** 🛅 🕭 A/C, cable TV w/movies, refrig. All rooms have old wooden icebox-design refrigerators. **Services:** ✕ 🚐 ⏚ **Facilities:** 👌 Courtesy room for continental breakfast contains microwave, ice machine, tables, coffeepot, toaster. Adjoining gift shop sells local handicrafts. Picnic tables in rear and benches around the property for enjoying the mountain views. **Rates (CP):** Peak (Apr–Oct) $45–$55 S or D. Extra person $5. Children under age 6 stay free. Lower rates off-season. Parking: Outdoor, free. AE, CB, DC, DISC, MC, V.

RESTAURANT 🍴

★ Brooke's Landing

In the Hermitage Motor Inn, 203 Virginia Ave (WV 55); tel 304/257-2355. **Seafood/Steak/Pasta.** Located in a 19th-century hotel listed on the National Register of Historic Places, the multiroom dining area is home to casual dining at oak tables and chairs. Lounge has fireplace, and one dining area sports both old wooden floor and fireplace. The sun room has a wall of lace-paneled windows and Victorian lamps. Buffet and daily specials available. **FYI:** Reservations accepted. **Open:** Mon–Sat 11am–9pm, Sun 11am–3pm. **Prices:** Main courses $10–$17. AE, DISC, MC, V. 🍲 🖾

Point Pleasant

Located at the confluence of the Ohio and Kanawha Rivers. Point Pleasant Battle Monument State Park commemorates one of the first skirmishes of the Revolutionary War. **Information:** Mason County Area Chamber of Commerce, 305 Main St, Point Pleasant, 25550 (tel 304/675-1050).

ATTRACTIONS 🎒

West Virginia State Farm Museum

WV 1; tel 304/675-5737. Dedicated to preserving the farm heritage of West Virginia, this museum complex functions as a window to the past. There are over 31 reconstructed buildings, including a one-room schoolhouse, a Lutheran church, and a country store. A blacksmith and other traditional craftspeople use authentic tools to create their finished wares. Antique farm equipment, such as threshing machines, cultivators, and tractors, are also on display. **Open:** Tues–Sat 9am–5pm, Sun 1–5pm. **Free**

Point Pleasant Battle Monument State Park

Main St; tel 304/675-0869. This 85-foot monument commemorates what some consider to be the first battle of the Revolutionary War. It was here that frontiersmen, led by Col Andrew Lewis, fought British-supported Chief Hokolesqua ("Cornstalk") and his Shawnee tribe. The **Mansion House Museum**, operated by the Daughters of the American Revolution, contains artifacts of the early settlers of the area, as well as war memorabilia. **Open:** Park, daily 9am–9pm; museum, May–Nov, daily 9am–4:30pm. **Free**

Princeton

See also Hinton

In the southern Greenbrier Valley, this city of some 7,000 is close to two state parks—Pipestem Resort and Camp Creek—as well as the Bluestone River. Seat of Mercer County. **Information:** Princeton–Mercer County Chamber of Commerce, 910 Oakvale Rd, Princeton, 24740 (tel 304/487-1502).

MOTELS 🏨

🗏🗏 Comfort Inn

US 460 and Ambrose Lane, PO Box 222, 24740; tel 304/487-6101 or toll free 800/228-5150; fax 304/425-7002. Exit 9 off I-77, US 460 W. An exceptionally well-landscaped property, this motel is near Pipestem State Park, colleges, a shopping mall, and restaurants. **Rooms:** 51 rms and stes. CI 1/CO noon. Nonsmoking rms avail. Clean and fresh rooms are decorated in soothing pastel colors. **Amenities:** 🛅 🕭 A/C, cable TV w/movies. Some units w/whirlpools. **Services:** 🛆 ⏚ Apple cider served in the evening. **Facilities:** 👌 Whirlpool. Outdoor hot tub. **Rates (CP):** Peak (May–Oct) $65–$79 S or D; $85–$99 ste. Extra person $6. Children under age 18 stay free. Min stay special events. Lower rates off-season. Parking: Outdoor, free. AE, CB, DISC, JCB, MC, V.

🗏🗏 Days Inn

I-77 and US 460, PO Box 830, 24720; tel 304/425-8100 or toll free 800/329-7466; fax 304/425-8100. Exit 9 off I-77. Drive west on US 460 for ½ mile, turn left at light. Close to state parks and two ski areas, this older property recently changed hands. New owners have made renovations and expect to make more. **Rooms:** 122 rms and effic. CI 3pm/CO 11am. Nonsmoking rms avail. Some rooms have dataports. **Amenities:** 🛅 🕭 A/C, cable TV. Some units w/whirlpools. **Services:** 🛆 ⏚ 🖔 Pets allowed for $5 fee. **Facilities:** 🗏 🐾 🖾 👌 Whirlpool. Pleasant outdoor area with picnic tables, benches, and barbecue grills. Large indoor heated pool.

Rates (CP): $59–$62 S or D; $71 effic. Extra person $5. Children under age 16 stay free. Parking: Outdoor, free. AE, CB, DC, DISC, JCB, MC, V.

RESTAURANT 🍴

Johnston's Inn and Restaurant

Worrell St; tel 304/425-7591. Exit 9 off I-77. **American/Italian.** This country-style restaurant attached to a motel near I-77, shopping centers, and services is a popular spot for casual dining. Wooden tables and booths and a local reputation for good food, mostly steaks and Italian cuisine. **FYI:** Reservations accepted. Children's menu. **Open:** Mon–Sat 6:30am–10:30pm, Sun 6:30am–10pm. **Prices:** Main courses $10–$30. AE, CB, DC, DISC, MC, V.

Romney

The second-oldest town in the state, located near the South Branch of the Potomac River. US 50, which runs through town, offers beautiful mountain views. Several outfitters in town offer eagle watching treks. **Information:** Hampshire County Chamber of Commerce, HC 74, Box 2000, Sunrise Professional Bldg, Romney, 26757 (tel 304/822-7221).

ATTRACTION 📷

Potomac Eagle

WV 28; tel 304/822-7464. This three-hour narrated excursion begins at Wappocomo Station, where passengers board vintage 1920s railroad cars for their trip through the south branch of the Potomac River, known as the Trough. Pristine waters, pastureland, and farms dating from the 1700s are a few of the scenic highlights, but the big draw for wildlife enthusiasts is the frequent sightings of bald eagles. This valley is the eastern home of the American bald eagle, and the train often passes both the adult bird and nests of eaglets. Special excursions include Civil War reenactments, dinner trips, and fall foliage tours. **Open:** May–Nov, call for schedule. **$$$$**

Seneca Rocks

Famous among rock climbers as the home of Seneca Rocks National Recreation Area.

ATTRACTIONS 📷

Seneca Rocks National Recreation Area

Jct WV 28/US 33; tel 304/257-4442. A popular hiking and climbing destination, this quartzite formation rises 900 feet above North Fork Valley. At the foot of the rocks is a visitors center with exhibits and displays that explain the area's geology and history. Although the 375 climbing routes are the main draw here, fishing, picnicking, and camping are also available. **Open:** Peak (Apr–Oct) daily 9am–5:30pm. Reduced hours off-season. **Free**

Smoke Hole Caverns

Jct WV 28/WV 55; tel 304/257-4442. Unique aspects of this cavern include a crystal-clear coral pool filled with golden and rainbow trout, the world's longest ribbon stalactite, and cave ceilings reaching a towering 274 feet. Temperatures in the cave remain a constant 56°F. **Open:** Peak (Mem Day–Labor Day) daily 8am–9pm. Reduced hours off-season. **$$$**

Shepherdstown

Founded in 1727, Shepherdstown is the state's oldest continuously settled community. It was originally called New Mecklenburg by its German settlers, but renamed Shepherdtown in 1798 by Thomas Shepherd. George Washington considered locating the nation's capital at this pretty town on the Potomac River. Today, the town offers an interesting mix of historic homes, trendy shops, and country living.

INN 🛏

🏨🏨🏨🏨 Bavarian Inn and Lodge

WV 480, PO Box 30, 25433; tel 304/876-2551; fax 304/876-9355. Exit 16 E off I-81; take VA 45 to Shepherdstown. 11 acres. Appealing gray-stone mansion with acres of rolling lawn. Some Bavarian-style chalets overlook the Potomac River. **Rooms:** 73 rms and stes. CI 3pm/CO noon. Nonsmoking rms avail. Individually decorated rooms, many with canopied four-poster beds, large baths, sitting areas. **Amenities:** 🛁 ⚏ ☎ A/C, cable TV w/movies, dataport. Some units w/terraces, some w/fireplaces, some w/whirlpools. **Services:** ⌂ Social director. Gracious, accommodating staff enjoy providing extras to guests. **Facilities:** 🏊 🚴 ▶ 18 🏢 🎾 🏐 ⚓ 1 restaurant (see "Restaurants" below), 1 bar (w/entertainment). Restaurant noted for its cuisine. Rathskeller on lower level offers casual dining and weekend entertainment. Affiliated with adjoining private golf club. **Rates:** Peak (Sept) $85–$135 S or D; $115–$165 ste. Extra person $10. Children under age 12 stay free. Min stay special events. Lower rates off-season. Parking: Outdoor, free. AE, CB, DC, DISC, MC, V.

RESTAURANTS 🍴

Ⓢ Bavarian Inn Restaurant

WV 480; tel 304/876-2551. Exit 16 E off I-81; then WV 45 to Shepherdstown. **Continental/German/Seafood.** With its dark wood entryway and framed photos of famous guests, the restaurant affords a touch of elegance in a country setting. Decorations include hand-painted bud vases with a pink carnation, books, crystal sconces, and a display of china, while the spacious main dining room enjoys views of either the Potomac River or manicured lawns. Quite reasonably priced for the superior service, well-presented food, and serene dining atmosphere. Specialties are sauerbraten and wild game (boar, venison, or pheasant, depending on the season). **FYI:** Reservations recommended. Piano/singer. Children's menu. Dress code. **Open:** Breakfast daily 7:30–10:30am; lunch Mon–Sat 11:30–2:30am; dinner Mon–Sat 5–10pm, Sun noon–9pm. **Prices:** Main courses $14–$20. AE, CB, DC, DISC, MC, V. 💟 🖼 🏞 ♿

✦ Yellow Brick Bank Restaurant

Princess and W German Sts; tel 304/876-2208. **New American/Italian.** A popular bistro housed in a 1906 bank building on Shepherdstown's main street. The art-deco decor is refreshing and sophisticated in this largely historic area. The food is fresh American and northern Italian: grilled meats, seafood, and unique appetizers such as grilled portobello mushrooms with lemon butter. Lighter fare is offered in the Wicker Room. **FYI:** Reservations recommended. Dress code. **Open:** Mon–Sat 11:30am–10pm, Sun 11am–10pm. **Prices:** Main courses $9–$22. DC, MC, V. 🍺

ATTRACTION 🧳

Historic Shepherdstown Museum

German and Princess Sts; tel 304/876-0910. The oldest town in West Virginia is celebrated in this museum featuring a collection of artifacts, furnishings, and documents that trace the history and commerce of the area. **Open:** Apr–Oct, Sat 11am–5pm, Sun 1–4pm. **Free**

Snowshoe

Located in the heart of ski country: Snowshoe Mountain Ski Resort, the Elk River Cross County Ski Center and the Silver Creek Ski Resort are all nearby.

HOTEL 🧳

🛏🛏🛏 The Inn at Snowshoe

WV 66 at US 219, PO Box 10, 26209; tel 304/572-5252; fax 304/572-3218. Turn east off US 219 to hotel. Modern, very comfortable hotel situated in a valley six miles below Snowshoe Mountain Resort, which manages the property. Cass Scenic Railroad is 11 miles away. **Rooms:** 150 rms. CI 5pm/ CO 11am. No smoking. **Amenities:** 📺 ☕ A/C, cable TV. **Services:** ✗ 🍽 **Facilities:** 📷 🚲 🎣 🏊 🏀 🎿 ♿ 1 restaurant, 1 bar, games rm, sauna, whirlpool, washer/dryer. Golf, tennis, skiing, mountain biking, and other sports available nearby. Guests have access to facilities at Snowshoe Mountain Resort. **Rates:** Peak (mid-Nov–mid-Apr) $76–$109 S or D. Lower rates off-season. Parking: Outdoor, free. Off-season rates are approximately half those in winter. AE, MC, V.

ATTRACTION 🧳

Snowshoe Mountain Resort

Snowshoe Dr; tel 304/572-1000. During the November-to-April ski season, schlussers flock here to enjoy the 53 slopes and trails, with a vertical drop of 1,500 feet. A total of eight triple chair lifts, two quad chair lifts, and one double chair lift can handle over 18,100 skiers per hour. The trails offer challenges for skiers of all levels of expertise (with 41% easy runs, 41% more difficult runs, and 18% most difficult runs) and there are 100 ski and snowboard instructors on staff for those who would like to improve their technique. The mountaintop lodge village offers six restaurants, nine nightclubs, and three rental shops.

Snowshoe' extensive trail system is turned over to mountain bikers in the summer. Over 100 miles of terrain range from beginner to expert, with quiet, forested areas along old railgrades and kamikaze downhill runs. Two Mountain Biking Centers (one located at the base of the mountain and one at the Silver Creek Lodge) offer guided tours, trail advice, and bicycle rentals and service. Other warm-weather options include horseback riding, hayrides, hiking, swimming, and guided nature programs. $$$$

Summersville

In the state's central section. Summersville Lake, the largest in West Virginia, is close by. **Information:** Summersville Area Chamber of Commerce, 801 W Webster Rd, Ste 1, Box 567, Summersville, 26651 (tel 304/872-1588).

ATTRACTIONS 🧳

Summersville Lake

WV 129; tel 304/872-3412. Created by the Army Corps of Engineers in the 1960s, this scenic lake boasts 60 miles of shoreline and its 2,280-ft dam is the second-largest east of the Mississippi. Clear waters make the lake a popular destination for scuba divers, anglers, boaters, and sightseers. Public beach. **Open:** Office, daily 7:15am–4pm. **Free**

Carnifex Ferry Battlefield State Park

WV 129; tel 304/872-0825. The site of a major Civil War battle that eventually led to this area's participation in the statehood movement. The **Patterson House** (open weekends, Mem Day–Labor Day) was situated between Union and Confederate lines; today, it houses relics of the battle. The park also offers hiking, picnicking, and playgrounds. **Open:** Daily sunrise–sunset. **Free**

Weston

Founded in 1818, this picturesque town is noted for its ornate Victorian architecture. Jackson's Mill, the boyhood home of Stonewall Jackson, is nearby. **Information:** Lewis County Convention and Visitors Bureau, PO Box 379, Weston, 26452 (tel 304/269-7328).

MOTEL 🧳

🛏🛏 Comfort Inn

I-79 and US 33 E, PO Box 666, 26452; tel 304/269-7000 or toll free 800/228-5150; fax 304/269-7000. Exit 99 off I-79.

Surrounded by beautiful scenery. **Rooms:** 60 rms. CI 3pm/ CO noon. Nonsmoking rms avail. Although of average size, rooms are quite pleasing. **Amenities:** 🛍 A/C, cable TV. **Services:** VP 🐾 **Facilities:** 🛋 ⅃ 1 restaurant, 1 bar. **Rates (CP):** Peak (Mem Day–Oct) $55–$60 S or D. Extra person $6. Children under age 18 stay free. Lower rates off-season. Parking: Outdoor, free. AE, DC, DISC, MC, V.

ATTRACTIONS 🏛

Jackson's Mill
US 19; tel 304/269-5100. Now a state 4-H camp, this historic area was the boyhood home of Thomas "Stonewall" Jackson. The grounds include an operating gristmill; the Old Mill Museum, which depicts the 19th-century culture of the area; and the Jackson family graveyard. **Open:** Mem Day–Labor Day, Tues–Sun noon–5pm. **$**

Stonewall Jackson Lake State Park
US 19; tel 304/269-0523. The highlight of this park is the 2,650-acre lake, the result of the damming of the West Fork River in the 1980s. The lake has some of the best fishing in the state, in addition to water sports; however, no swimming is allowed. Hunting, camping, and hiking are other popular activities. **Open:** Daily 6am–10pm. **$**

Wheeling

In the Northern Panhandle on the Ohio River, this riverfront city was settled in 1769 and given a building boost when the National Road was built through town. Once the state capitol and current seat of Ohio County, today it remains an important commercial and manufacturing center, with steel mills, iron works, and metal factories. A newly developed riverfront area offers a landscaped riverside trail and scenic waterway cruises on authentic stern-wheelers. Nearby Triadelphia was founded in 1824, and is a popular stop for visitors to Castle Run Lake, Burches Run Lake, and Bears Rock Lake. **Information:** Wheeling Convention and Visitors Bureau, 1310 Market St, Wheeling, 26003 (tel 304/ 233-7709).

HOTEL 🏨

≣≣ Hampton Inn
795 National Rd, 26003; tel 304/233-0440 or toll free 800/ HAMPTON; fax 304/233-2198. Exit 2A off I-70. A pleasant hotel that is clean, neat, and orderly. Convenient to restaurants and shops. **Rooms:** 104 rms. CI 3pm/CO noon. Nonsmoking rms avail. Although basic, rooms are clean and well kept. **Amenities:** 🛍 🖋 A/C, cable TV, voice mail. VCRs available. **Services:** 🖂 ⅃ Free local calls. **Facilities:** 🖾 🖼 ℉ 🚹 🛋 **Rates (CP):** $53–$59 S; $58–$64 D. Children under age 19 stay free. Parking: Outdoor, free. AE, CB, DC, DISC, MC, V.

MOTELS

≣≣ Best Western Wheeling Inn
949 Main St, at 10th St, 26003; tel 304/233-8500 or toll free 800/528-1234; fax 304/233-8500 ext 345. Exit 1A off I-70. An older, well-maintained motel in the heart of Wheeling, with great views of the Ohio River. **Rooms:** 80 rms and stes. CI 2pm/CO noon. Nonsmoking rms avail. Average older rooms have small baths, large sink area. **Amenities:** 🛍 🖋 A/C, cable TV. Some units w/whirlpools. **Services:** ✗ VP 🖂 ⅃ Masseur. Free morning newspapers. **Facilities:** 🖼 💯 1 restaurant (lunch and dinner only), 1 bar, spa, sauna, steam rm, whirlpool. Riverside restaurant has glass-enclosed deck for year-round use. Free use of nearby health spa. **Rates (CP):** $39–$58 S; $44–$63 D; $108 ste. Extra person $10. Children under age 12 stay free. Parking: Outdoor, free. AE, DC, DISC, MC, V.

≣≣ Days Inn
I-70 and Dallas Pike, Triadelphia, 26059; tel 304/547-0610 or toll free 800/329-7466; fax 304/547-9029. Exit 11 off I-70. The highlight of this comfortable motel is the unusual entry to the bar—a converted truck cab. **Rooms:** 106 rms. CI noon/CO 11am. Nonsmoking rms avail. **Amenities:** 🛍 🖋 A/C, satel TV w/movies. Some units w/whirlpools. VCRs and refrigerators available on request. Accessories for guests with disabilities, including close-captioned TV, alarms for door and phone, available upon request. Five rooms have heart-shaped whirlpools. **Services:** ✗ ⅃ 🐾 **Facilities:** 🖾 🚹 🖼 💯 🛋 1 restaurant (bkfst and dinner only), 1 bar. **Rates (CP):** $44 S; $47 D. Extra person $6. Children under age 19 stay free. Parking: Outdoor, free. AE, CB, DC, DISC, MC, V.

RESORT

≣≣≣ Oglebay Resort & Conference Center
Wilson Lodge WV 88 N, 26003; tel 304/243-4000 or toll free 800/624-6988; fax 304/243-4070. 1,500 acres. The lodge and cabins are part of Oglebay Park, the former farm of a wealthy industrialist who left the property to the city of Wheeling. **Rooms:** 204 rms and stes; 50 cottages/villas. CI 3pm/CO noon. Nonsmoking rms avail. Pine paneling contributes to the retro feel of the motel-style rooms. **Amenities:** 🛍 🖋 📺 A/C, cable TV, dataport. Some units w/terraces, some w/fireplaces. **Services:** 🚗 🖂 ⅃ Children's program, babysitting. **Facilities:** 🖾 ⛰ 🏹 ℉ 36 🏌 🎿 🚹 🍵 5 🖼 6 💯 🛋 1 restaurant, 1 bar, basketball, games rm, spa, whirlpool, playground, washer/dryer. **Rates:** Peak (June 15–Aug 15) $132 S; $142 D; $145 ste; $750–$1,425 cottage/villa. Children under age 19 stay free. Min stay wknds. Lower rates off-season. MAP rates avail. Parking: Outdoor, free. Cottages rented by the week only during high season. AE, CB, DC, DISC, MC, V.

RESTAURANTS 🍴

Christopher's Cafeteria

10 Elmgrove Crossing Mall; tel 304/242-4100. Exit 5 off I-70. **American/Cafeteria.** A colonial atmosphere reigns at this very good American-style cafeteria, where waitresses continually clear the tables. Cafeteria line has roast beef, potatoes, and vegetables. Breads and desserts baked on premises. **FYI:** Reservations accepted. Children's menu. No liquor license. **Open:** Mon–Sat 11:30am–8pm, Sun 11am–8pm. **Prices:** Main courses $3–$6. No CC. 🖼 &

Stratford Springs Lodge

355 Oglebay Dr; tel 304/233-5100. Exit 2A off I-70 Follow WV 88 N. **American.** Pink tablecloths and napkins, pink-and-green drapes, and lovely china grace the dining room at the now-defunct Wheeling Country Club. Golf course and gracious grounds surround the building. The menu consists primarily of meat and chicken dishes, with some seafood. **FYI:** Reservations recommended. Children's menu. Dress code. **Open:** Mon–Sat 7am–10pm, Sun 9am–9pm. **Prices:** Main courses $6–$35. AE, MC, V. 🍴 &

ATTRACTIONS 🏛

Oglebay Park

Exit 2A off I-79; tel tel 304/243-4000 or toll free 800/624-6988. This 1,500-acre resort began as Waddington Farms, the home of Col Earl W Oglebay, who willed his estate to the city of Wheeling for public use. On the grounds are Schenk Lake, stables, tennis courts, an outdoor pool, jogging trails, and an 18-hole golf course. Among the highlights of Oglebay are the Good Children's Zoo, a 65-acre natural habitat for North American animals; Waddington Gardens, with turn-of-the-century flower gardens; and the Oglebay Institute Museum, featuring the Sweeney Punch Bowl, the largest hand-blown glass piece in existence. **Open:** Daily sunrise–sunset. **Free**

The Point

Grandview St; tel 304/639-1093. From the observation deck 465 feet above the Ohio River, visitors can see the entire Victorian cityscape of Wheeling as well as two states, three counties, 11 churches, and 11 bridges. Inside is a small pictorial museum housing a compilation of photos that recreate the town's history. **Open:** Call for schedule. $

Capitol Music Hall

1015 Main St; tel toll free 800/624-5456. The oldest, and one of the largest, theaters in West Virginia, this is the stage for **Jamboree USA**, one of the oldest live country music programs in the country. Every Saturday night since its 1933 premiere, the stars of country music have performed on its stage. Recent entertainers have included Kathy Mattea, Tammy Wynette, and Little Texas. Every summer Jamboree USA moves outdoors for **Jamboree in the Hills,** an outdoor concert billed as the "Super Bowl of Country Music." **Open:** Call for schedule. $$$$

Centre Market

Exit 1A off I-70; tel 304/234-3878. Built in 1853, the Upper Market House is the only cast iron–columned market in the country. Lower Market House, built in 1890, is a Romanesque brick structure. These market houses have been in continuous operation since the mid-19th century and provide many of the same services now as they did then. The interior is a good place to sample homemade food specialties, and there are many small shops with an array of handcrafts and antiques. **Open:** Mon–Sat 10am–6pm. **Free**

Grave Creek Mound State Park

WV 2; tel 304/843-1410. This Adena Indian burial site is the largest conical earthen mound of its kind. Adjacent to the burial ground is the Delf Norona Museum and Cultural Center, which houses a collection of artifacts from the Adena period (1000 BC to AD 1), as well as exhibits about the cultural life of this prehistoric people. **Open:** Mon–Sat 10am–4:30pm, Sun 1–5pm. $

White Sulphur Springs

See also Lewisburg

In the Greenbrier Valley near the Virginia border, this 19-century health-resort town has long drawn visitors from all walks of life. Greenbrier State Forest is also nearby. Ronceverte, SW of town on the Greenbrier River, offers white-water rafting. **Information:** White Sulphur Springs Chamber of Commerce, PO Box 11, White Sulphur Springs, 24986 (tel 304/536-2500).

MOTEL 🏨

▤▤ Old White Motel

865 E Main St (US 60 E), PO Box 58, 24986; tel 304/536-2441 or toll free 800/867-2441. Exit 181 off I-64. Go ½ mile west on US 60. An older but well-maintained motel on large lawn with views of the West Virginia highlands. Convenient to The Greenbrier and other golf courses. **Rooms:** 26 rms. CI noon/CO 11am. Nonsmoking rms avail. **Amenities:** 📺 & A/C, cable TV. Rollaway beds available. **Services:** 🛎 🚗 **Facilities:** 🍴 Restaurant next door will deliver to room. **Rates:** $30–$46 S or D. Extra person $5. Children under age 12 stay free. Parking: Outdoor, free. AE, CB, DC, DISC, MC, V.

RESORT

⊕ The Greenbrier

Off I-64, 24986; tel 304/536-1110 or toll free 800/624-6070; fax 304/536-7854. Exit 181 off I-64 W, or exit 175 off I-64 E. 6,500 acres. As grand as they come, this imposing white palace of old-world elegance nestled in the Allegheny Mountains has grounds so vast there are 10 acres for every guest room. A throwback to yesteryears of civility and social norms; a place where gentlemen must still wear a jacket and tie for dinner. Predictably popular for business conferences. **Rooms:** 556 rms and stes; 69 cottages/villas. CI 3pm/CO noon. Nonsmoking rms avail. Some are spacious, some snug, and every room is different from its neighbor—some have decor that is almost giddy, with bold greens and flashy reds. **Amenities:** 🔟 ⚷ 🍴 A/C, dataport, voice mail, bathrobes. All units w/minibars, some w/terraces, some w/fireplaces. Fireplaces in the lounges, complimentary afternoon tea with classical duo. Historical tours of the hotel, horticultural tours of the grounds. **Services:** 🍽 VP 🚐 🗺 🔑 Twice-daily maid svce, social director, masseur, children's program, babysitting. Enormous breakfasts. Experienced, dedicated staff. **Facilities:** 🛗 🚲 🐟 ▶54 ⚓ 🎿 🎣 ⛳15 📷 5 🛝 🏊1000 🖥 ♿ 5 restaurants, 4 bars (2 w/entertainment), volleyball, games rm, lawn games, spa, sauna, steam rm, whirlpool, beauty salon, day-care ctr, playground. 24 shops, 2 putting greens, 2 heated platform tennis courts, indoor tennis, lane bowling, trap and skeet shooting, falconry, horse-drawn carriage rides. Ice skating and horse-drawn sleigh rides in winter. **Rates (MAP):** Peak (Apr–Oct) $250–$572 S; $366–$602 D; $650 ste; $602 cottage/villa. Extra person $125. Children under age 18 stay free. Min stay special events. Lower rates off-season. Parking: Indoor/outdoor, free. Automatic additions to bills include $14.25 per person per day for maids and waiters. For such an august "Hotel of the Presidents," with so many extras, the resort is not at all overpriced. AE, DC, MC, V.

RESTAURANT 🍴

Blake's Restaurant and Lounge

705 E Main St; tel 304/536-1221. Exit 181 off I-64, go ½ mi W on US 60. **Continental.** This unassuming building next to the Old White Motel has a casual cafe as well as a more formal dining room. The menu is surprisingly diverse: the chef takes pride in his German specials, and there are vegetarian, light fare, and deli selections, too. A favorite with skiers. **FYI:** Reservations accepted. Children's menu. **Open:** Peak (May–Dec) Mon–Sat 7:30am–9pm, Sun 7:30am–8pm. **Prices:** Main courses $7–$20. DC, MC, V.

ATTRACTIONS 📷

Organ Cave

US 219, Ronceverte; tel 304/647-5551. During the Civil War, Gen Robert E Lee's troops used this cave as both a safe haven and an important source of saltpeter, an essential ingredient in gunpowder. Today visitors can tour the over 40 miles of mapped passageways in the cave to see limestone and calcite formations, including one that resembles a giant church organ. **Open:** Peak (Apr–Oct) daily 9am–7pm. Reduced hours off-season. **$$$**

Greenbrier State Forest

I-64; tel 304/536-1944. Located 3 mi S of White Sulphur Springs. Popular activities at this 9,302-acre forest include trout fishing in Anthony Creek and fishing in the Greenbrier River. A swimming pool is open during the summer. Facilities including restrooms, a gift shop, and a visitors center are open from the second week of April to the last week of October. Hiking and fitness trails, shooting range, playground area, and picnic sites are open year-round. Camping, cabins. **Open:** Daily 6am–10pm. **Free**

Index

Listings are arranged alphabetically, followed by a code indicating the type of establishment, and then by city, state, and page number. The codes for type of establishment are defined as follows: (H) = Hotel, (M) = Motel, (I) = Inn, (L) = Lodge, (RE) = Resort, (R) = Restaurant, (RS) = Refreshment Stop, (A) = Attraction.

Z

Terms and Conditions

- Offer includes 10% discount off all time and mileage charges on Cruise America or Cruise Canada vehicles only.

- Offer not available in conjunction with other discount offers or promotional rates.

- Excludes rental charges, deposits, sales tax, amd fuels.

- Normal rental conditions and customer qualification procedures apply.

- Members must reserve through Central Reservations only, at least one week in advance of pick up and mention membership affiliation at time of reservation.

  For reservations, call: 1-800-327-7799 US and Canada

- By acceptance and use of this offer, member agrees to the above conditions.

- Offer expires December 31, 1997.

Save 10%   **Save 10%**

Offer expires December 31, 1997.

**Savings are subject to certain restrictions and availability.
Valid for flights on most airlines.**

Minimum Ticket Price	Save
$200.00	$25.00
$250.00	$50.00
$350.00	$75.00
$450.00	$100.00

Terms and Conditions

1. Advance reservations required.
2. Coupon must be presented at check-in.
3. Coupon cannot be combined with any other special offers, discounted rates.
4. Subject to availability.
5. Valid through December 31, 1997.
6. No photo copies allowed.

Travelodge

For reservations, call 1-800-578-7878 or your travel agent and ask for the 5CPN discount.

All reservations must be made by calling our toll free reservation system, Superline. Any reservation requiring a guarantee must be guaranteed with the corporate V.I.P. identification number and the individual traveler's major credit card. If a guaranteed reservation is made and subsequently neither used nor cancelled, the corporate traveler will be billed for the one night's room charge plus tax.

expires December 31, 1997

Redeemable at participating Dollar® locations only.

This coupon entitles you to a one class upgrade from a compact or economy car to the next higher car group at no extra charge. Simply make a reservation for a compact or economy class car, then present this coupon to any Dollar rental agent when you arrive. You'll receive an upgrade to the next car class at no additional charge. Upgrade subject to vehicle availability. Renter must meet Dollar age, driver and credit requirements. This coupon must be surrendered at time of rental and may not be used in conjunction with any other offer and has no cash value. **EXPIRES 12/15/97.**

For worldwide reservations, call your travel agent or **800-800-4000**

DOLLAR.
RENT A CAR
DOLLAR MAKES SENSE.

Mention code "afbg2" when you place your first order and receive 15% OFF

Offer expires December 31, 1997

PO Box 5485-AF2, Santa Barbara, CA 93150

Magellan's

10% OFF

- Available at participating properties.
- This coupon cannot be combined with any other special discount offer.
- Limit one coupon per room, per stay. Expires December 31, 1997.
- Not valid during blackout periods or special events.
- Void where prohibited.
- No reproductions accepted.

1-800-DAYS INN

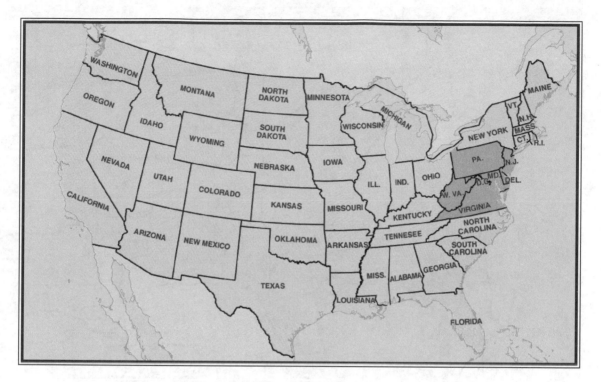

CONTENTS

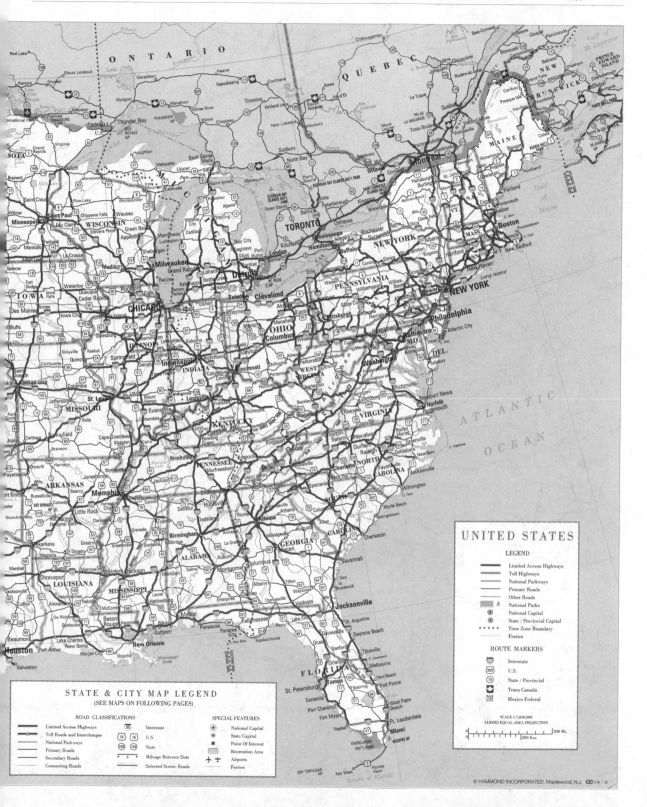

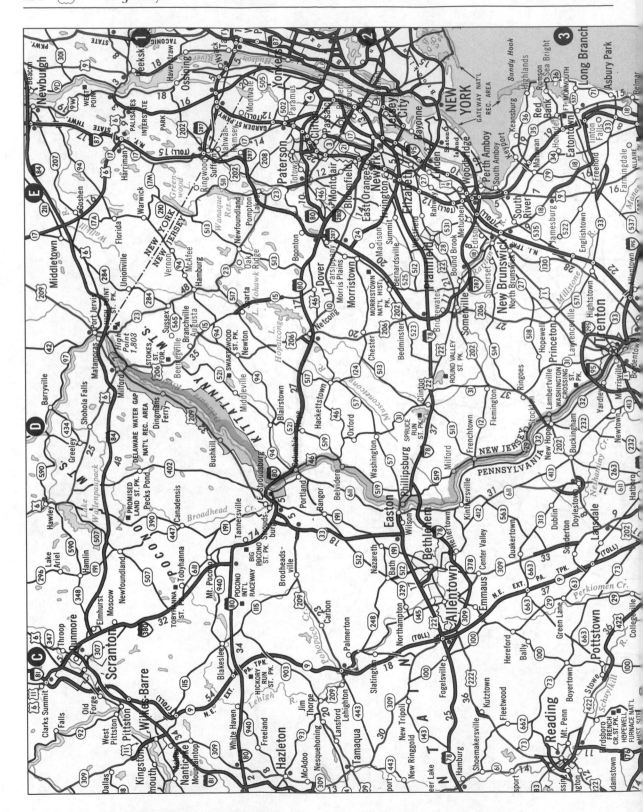

4

5

6

Index

Asbury Park	E 3
Atlantic City	E 5
Audubon	B 2
Augusta	D 2
Avalon	D 6
Barnegat Light	E 4
Bay Head	E 4
Bayonne	E 2
Beach Haven	E 5
Beemerville	D 2
Belvidere	D 2
Bernardsville	E 2
Bloomfield	E 2
Bordentown	D 3
Bound Brook	E 3
Bridgeport	D 4
Bridgeton	D 5
Bridgewater	E 2
Brigantine	E 3
Burlington	D 4
Camden	D 4,B 2
Cape May	D 6
Cape May Point	D 6
Clifton	E 2
Collingswood	B 2
Dover	E 2
East Orange	D 2
East Rutherford	D 2
Eatontown	E 3
Edison	E 4
Elizabeth	E 2
Farmingdale	E 3
Flemington	D 3
Fort Lee	D 5
Freehold	E 2
Frenchtown	D 3
Glassboro	D 4
Gloucester City	B 2
Hackettstown	D 2
Haddonfield	B 2
Hammonton	D 4
Highlands	E 2
Hightstown	E 3
Hoboken	E 2
Holmdel	E 2
Hope	D 2
Irvington	E 2
Jackson	E 4
Jamesburg	E 3
Jersey City	E 2
Lakewood	E 3
Lambertville	D 3
Lawrenceville	D 3
Linden	E 2
Long Branch	E 3
Madison	E 2
Mahwah	E 2
Margate City	E 5
McAfee	D 2
Medford	D 4
Metuchen	E 3
Middleville	E 2
Milford	D 2
Millville	D 5
Montclair	E 2
Montvale	E 4
Morristown	E 2
Mount Holly	D 4
Netcong	E 2
New Brunswick	E 3
Newark	E 2
Newfoundland	E 2
Oak Ridge	D 5
Ocean City	C 5
Oxford	D 2
Paramus	E 2
Parsippany	E 2
Passaic	E 2
Paterson	E 2
Pennsauken	D 3
Perth Amboy	E 2
Philipsburg	E 2
Plainfield	E 2
Pleasantville	D 4
Point Pleasant	E 3
Princeton	D 3
Rahway	E 2
Ramsey	E 3
Red Bank	E 3
Ringwood	E 2
Rumson	E 2
Salem	E 5
Sea Bright	E 5
Seaside Heights	E 4
Secaucus	E 2
Somerset	E 2
Somers Point	E 3
Somerville	D 3
South River	E 3
Spring Lake	E 3
Stockton	D 3
Stone Harbor	D 6
Summit	E 2
Sussex	D 1
Tinton Falls	E 3
Toms River	E 4
Totowa	E 2
Trenton	D 3
Vernon	D 2
Vineland	D 5
Westfield	E 2
Wildwood	D 6
Wildwood Crest	D 6
Willingboro	D 4
Woodbridge	E 3
Woodbury	B 2

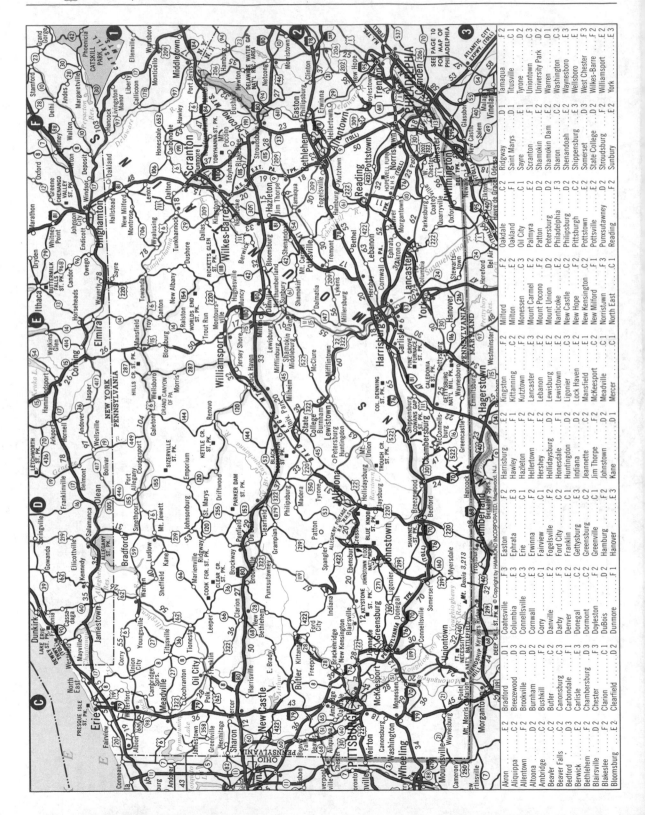

Akron	E 2	Bradford	D 1	Coatesville	F 3	Easton	F 2	Harrisburg	E 2	Kingston	E 1	Milford	F 1	Ridgway	C 2	Tamaqua	D 1
Aliquippa	C 2	Breezewood	D 3	Columbia	E 2	Ephrata	E 3	Hawley	F 1	Kittanning	C 2	Milton	D 2	Saint Marys	C 1	Titusville	C 1
Allentown	F 2	Brookville	C 2	Connellsville	C 3	Erie	C 1	Hazleton	E 2	Kutztown	F 2	Monessen	C 3	Sayre	E 1	Tyrone	D 2
Altoona	D 2	Burnham	D 2	Cornwall	E 2	Erwinna	C 1	Hellertown	F 2	Lancaster	E 2	Mount Carmel	E 2	Scranton	F 1	Uniontown	C 3
Ambridge	C 2	Bushkill	F 2	Corry	C 1	Fairview	C 1	Hershey	E 2	Lebanon	E 2	Mount Pocono	F 2	Shamokin	E 2	University Park	D 2
Beaver	C 2	Butler	C 2	Danville	D 2	Fogelsville	F 2	Hollidaysburg	D 2	Lewisburg	D 2	Mount Union	D 2	Shamokin Dam	E 2	Warren	D 1
Beaver Falls	C 2	Canonsburg	C 3	Darby	F 3	Ford City	C 2	Honesdale	F 1	Lewistown	D 2	Nanticoke	E 2	Sharon	B 2	Washington	C 3
Bedford	D 3	Carbondale	F 1	Denver	E 2	Franklin	C 1	Huntingdon	D 2	Ligonier	C 3	New Castle	C 2	Shenandoah	E 2	Waynesboro	D 3
Berwick	E 2	Carlisle	E 2	Donegal	C 3	Gettysburg	D 3	Indiana	C 2	Lock Haven	D 2	New Hope	F 2	Shippensburg	D 3	Wellsboro	E 1
Bethlehem	F 2	Chambersburg	D 3	Dormont	D 3	Greensburg	C 2	Jeannette	C 2	Mansfield	E 1	New Kensington	C 2	Somerset	C 3	West Chester	F 3
Blairsville	C 2	Chester	F 3	Doylestown	F 2	Greenville	C 1	Johnstown	C 2	McKeesport	C 2	New Milford	F 1	State College	D 2	Wilkes-Barre	E 2
Blakeslee	F 2	Clarion	C 1	DuBois	C 1	Hamburg	D 2	Kane	C 1	Meadville	C 1	Norristown	F 2	Stroudsburg	F 2	Williamsport	E 2
Bloomsburg	E 2	Clearfield	D 2	Dunmore	D 2	Hanover	E 3			Mercer	C 1	North East	C 1	Sunbury	E 2	York	E 3

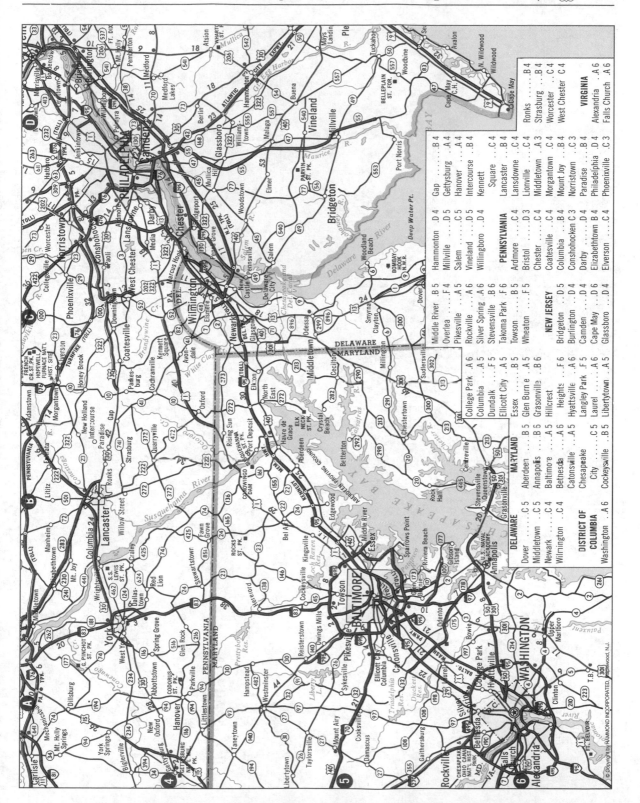

Gap	D 4	Gettysburg	D 5		
		Hanover	C 5		
		Intercourse	D 5	**VIRGINIA**	
		Kennett Square	B 4	Ronks	B 4
		Lancaster	B 4	Strasburg	B 4
		Lansdowne	C 4	Worcester	C 4
		Lionville	C 4	West Chester	C 4
PENNSYLVANIA		Middletown	A 3	Alexandria	A 6
Ardmore	C 4	Morgantown	C 4	Falls Church	A 6
Bristol	D 3	Mount Joy	B 4		
Chester	C 4	Norristown	C 3		
Coatesville	B 4	Paradise	D 4		
Columbia	B 4	Philadelphia	D 4		
Conshohocken	C 3	Phoenixville	C 3		
Darby	D 4				
Elizabethtown	B 4				
Everson	D 4				

Hammonton	D 4		
Millville	D 5		
Salem	C 5		
Vineland	D 5		
Willingboro	D 4		

Middle River	B 5		
Overlea	F 4		
Pikesville	A 5		
Rockville	A 6		
Silver Spring	A 6		
Stevensville	B 6		
Takoma Park	F 6		
Towson	B 5		
Wheaton	F 5		
NEW JERSEY			
Bridgeton	D 5		
Burlington	D 4		
Camden	D 4		
Cape May	D 6		
Glassboro	D 4		

College Park	A 6		
Columbia	A 5		
Dundalk	F 5		
Ellicott City	A 5		
Essex	B 5		
Glen Burne	A 5		
Grasonville	B 6		
Heights	F 6		
Hyattsville	A 6		
Langley Park	F 5		
Laurel	C 5		
Libertytown	B 5		

Aberdeen	B 5		
Annapolis	B 5		
Baltimore	A 5		
Bethesda	A 6		
Catonsville	A 5		
Chesapeake City	C 5		
Cockeysville	B 5		

MARYLAND			

DELAWARE			
Dover	C 5		
Middletown	C 5		
Newark	C 4		
Wilmington	C 4		

DISTRICT OF COLUMBIA			
Washington	A 6		

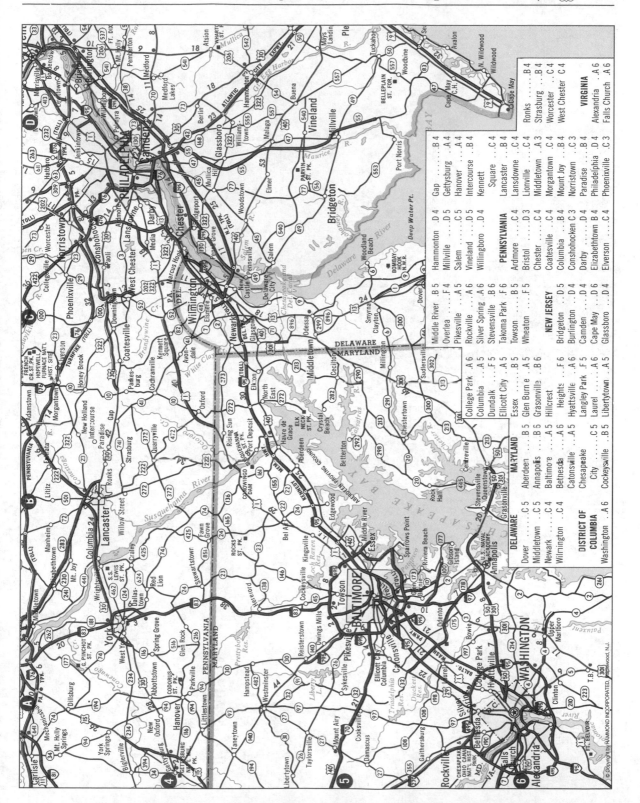

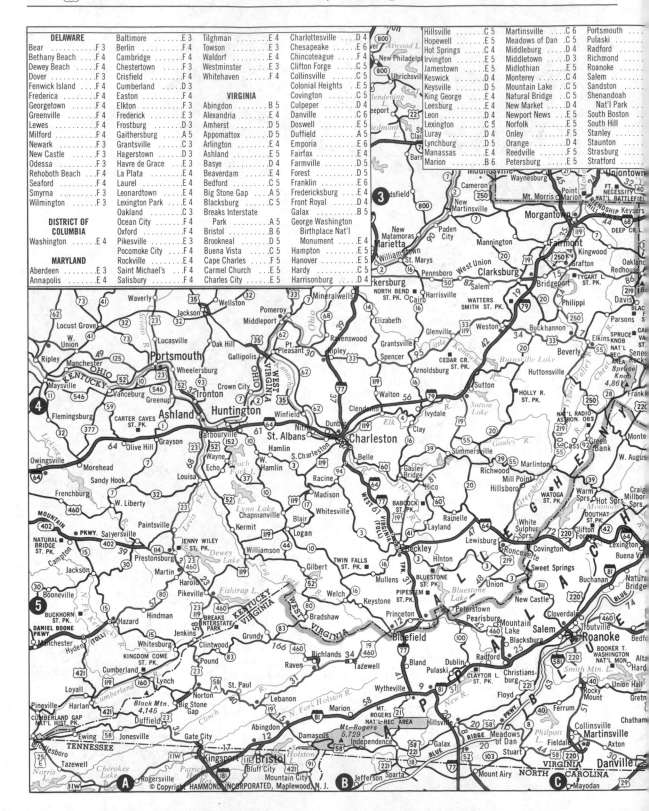

Suffolk ...... E 6	**WEST VIRGINIA**	Elkins .... C 4	Mill Point .....C 4	Saint Albans ....B 4
Tangier Island ...F 5	Barbourville .....A 4	Fairmont ......C 3	Martinsburg ...D 3	Salem ....C 3
Tappahannock ...E 5	Berkeley Springs .B 3	Grafton ....C 3	Mineralwells ...B 3	Seneca Rocks ...C 4
Troutville .....C 5	Beckley ....B 5	Green Bank .....C 4	Morgantown ...C 3	South Charleston B 4
Virginia Beach ...F 6	Beverly ....C 4	Harpers Ferry ...D 3	Moundsville ...B 3	Summersville ...B 4
Warm Springs ...C 4	Bluefield ....B 5	Hedgesville .....D 3	Nitro ....B 4	Triadelphia .....C 3
Warrenton .....D 4	Bridgeport ......C 3	Hico ....B 4	New Martinsville .B 3	Weirton ....B 2
Washington .....D 4	Buckhannon ....C 3	Hillsboro ....C 4	Nutter Fort .....C 3	Welch ....B 5
Waynesboro .....D 4	Cairo ....B 3	Hinton ....B 5	Parkersburg ....B 3	Weston ....C 4
Williamsburg ...E 5	Cass ....C 4	Huntington .....A 4	Petersburg .....D 4	Wheeling ....C 3
Winchester .....D 3	Charleston ......B 4	Keyser ....C 3	Point Pleasant ..A 4	White Sulphur
Wintergreen .....D 4	Charles Town ...C 3	Lansing ....B 4	Princeton ......B 5	Springs ....C 5
Woodstock .....D 4	Clarksburg ......C 3	Lewisburg ......C 5	Richwood ......C 4	Williamson ......B 5
Wytheville .....B 5	Davis ....C 4	Logan ....B 5	Romney ....C 3	Williamstown ...B 3
Yorktown ....E 5	Dunbar ....B 4	Madison ....B 4	Ronceverte .....C 5	Winfield ....B 4

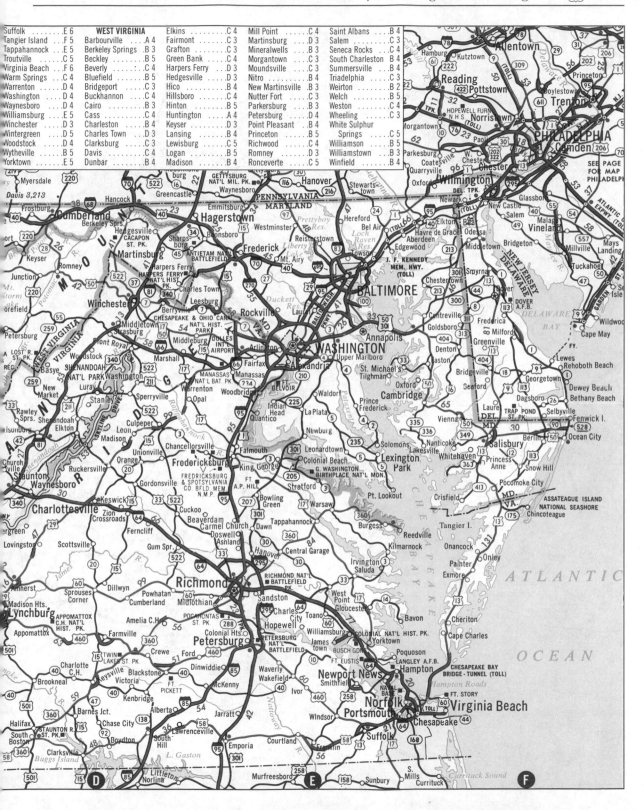

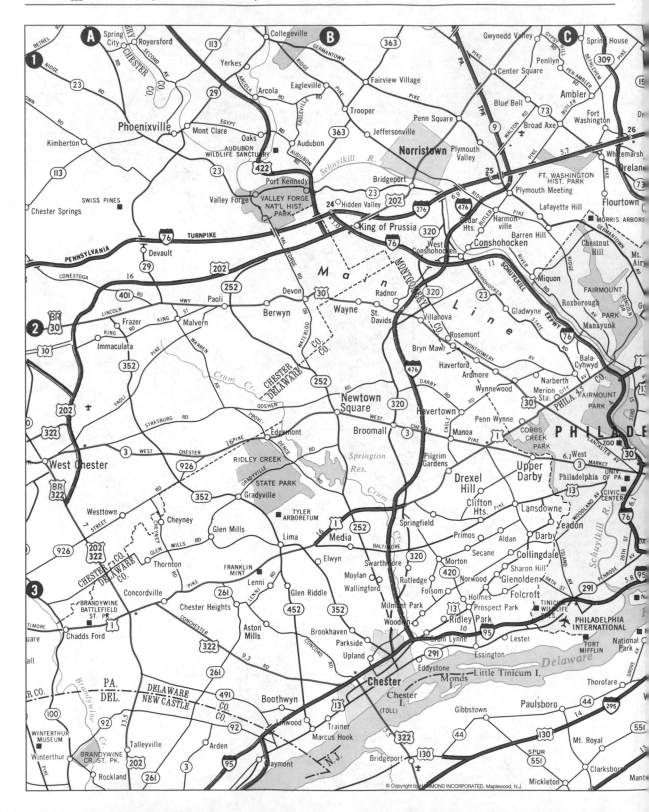

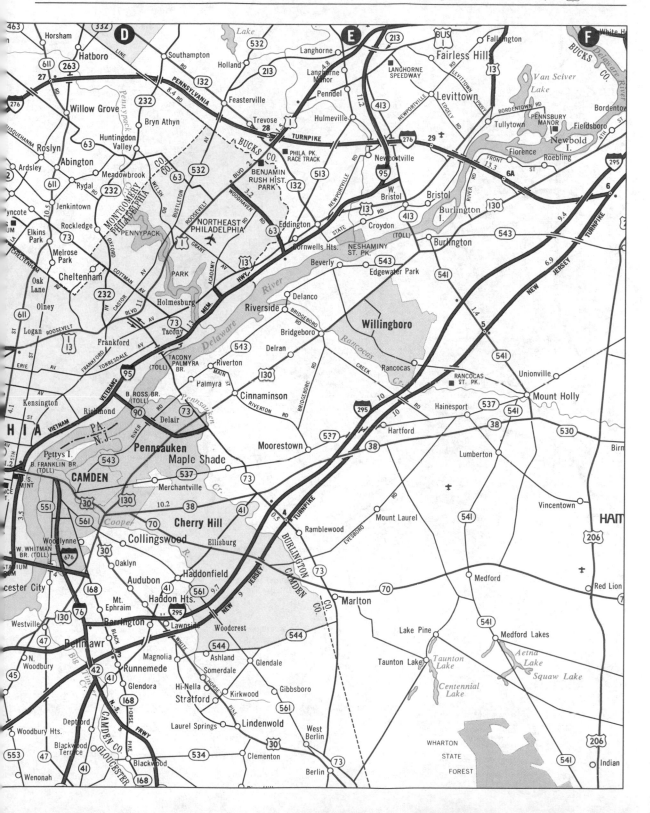

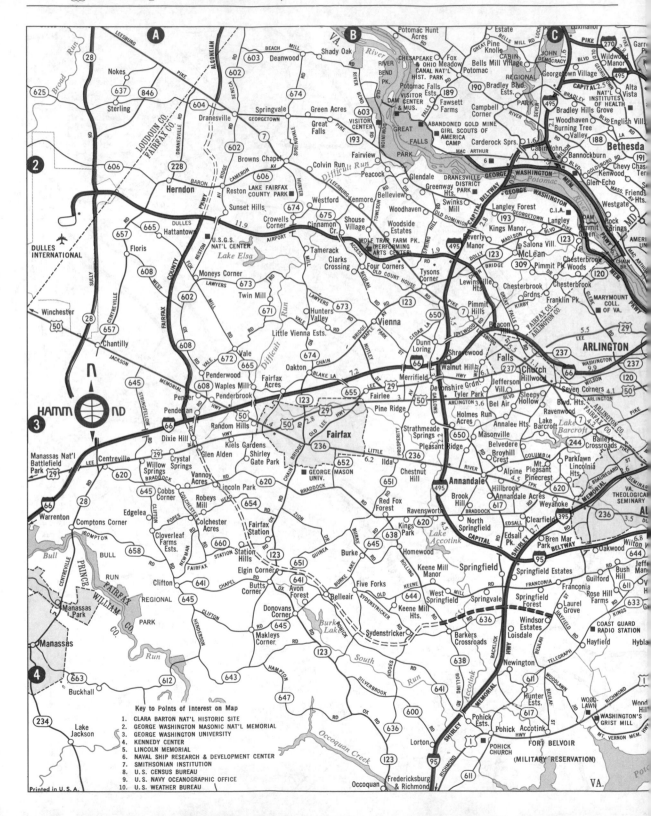

Key to Points of Interest on Map
1. CLARA BARTON NAT'L HISTORIC SITE
2. GEORGE WASHINGTON MASONIC NAT'L MEMORIAL
3. GEORGE WASHINGTON UNIVERSITY
4. KENNEDY CENTER
5. LINCOLN MEMORIAL
6. NAVAL SHIP RESEARCH & DEVELOPMENT CENTER
7. SMITHSONIAN INSTITUTION
8. U.S. CENSUS BUREAU
9. U.S. NAVY OCEANOGRAPHIC OFFICE
10. U.S. WEATHER BUREAU

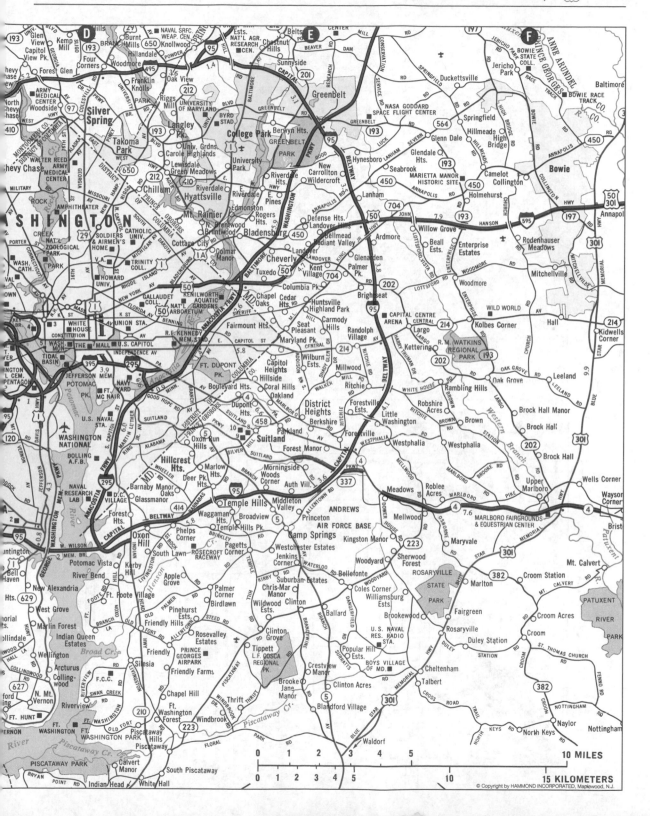

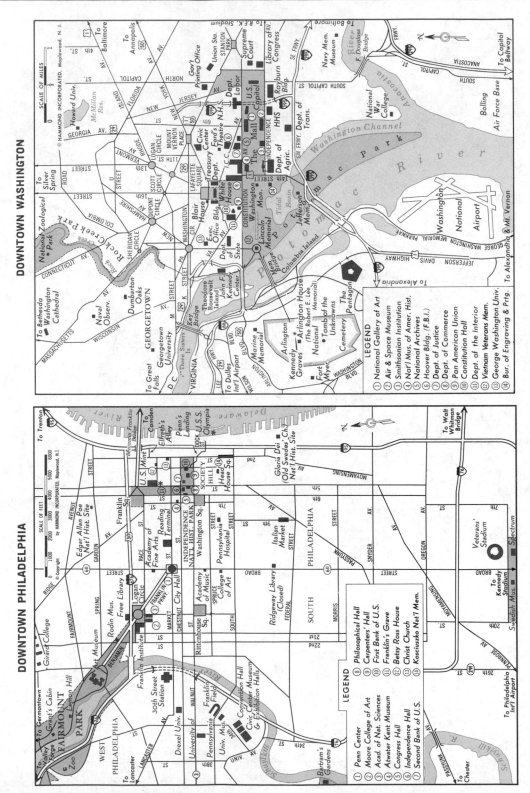

DOWNTOWN WASHINGTON

LEGEND
1. National Gallery of Art
2. Air & Space Museum
3. Smithsonian Institution
4. Nat'l Mus. of Amer. Hist.
5. National Archives
6. Hoover Bldg. (F.B.I.)
7. Dept. of Justice
8. Dept. of Commerce
9. Pan American Union
10. Constitution Hall
11. Dept. of the Interior
12. Vietnam Veterans Mem.
13. George Washington Univ.
14. Bur. of Engraving & Prtg.

DOWNTOWN PHILADELPHIA

LEGEND
1. Penn Center
2. Moore College of Art
3. Acad. of Nat. Sciences
4. Atwater Kent Museum
5. Congress Hall
6. Independence Hall
7. Second Bank of U.S.
8. Philosophical Hall
9. Carpenters' Hall
10. First Bank of U.S.
11. Franklin's Grave
12. Betsy Ross House
13. Christ Church
14. Kosciuszko Nat'l Mem.

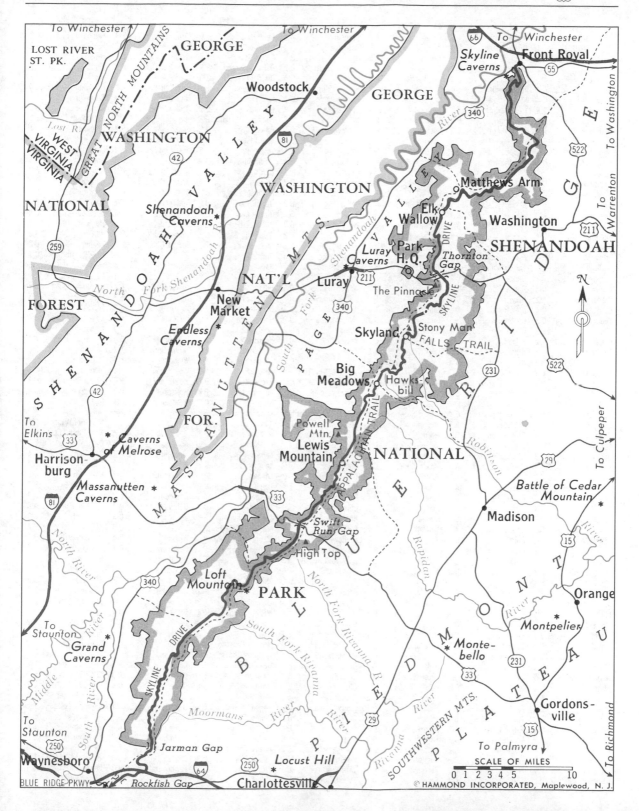

To Winchester

LOST RIVER
ST. PK.

GEORGE

To Winchester

66

To Winchester

Skyline
Caverns

Front Royal

55

GREAT NORTH MOUNTAINS

Woodstock

GEORGE

340

WEST
VIRGINIA
VIRGINIA

Lost R.

WASHINGTON

81

42

To Washington

522

SHENANDOAH VALLEY

WASHINGTON

Matthews Arm

Elk
Wallow

Washington

211

To Warrenton

NATIONAL

259

Shenandoah
Caverns

Park
H.Q.

Thornton
Gap

SHENANDOAH

SKYLINE DRIVE

Shenandoah R.

NAT'L

Luray
Caverns

211

N

MASSANUTTEN MTS.

FOREST

North Fork Shenandoah R.

New
Market

Luray

340

The Pinnacle

Skyland

Stony Man

FALLS TRAIL

231

R
I
D
G
E

522

42

South Fork

PAGE

Big
Meadows

Hawks-
bill

To
Elkins

33

Caverns
of Melrose

FOR.

Powell
Mtn.

Lewis
Mountain

NATIONAL

Robinson

79

To Culpeper

Harrison-
burg

81

Massanutten
Caverns

APPALACHIAN TRAIL

Battle of Cedar
Mountain

33

Madison

15

North River

Swift
Run Gap

High Top

B
L
U
E

North Fork Rivanna R.

Rapidan R.

Orange

To
Staunton

340

Loft
Mountain

PARK

Montpelier

River

Grand
Caverns

SKYLINE DRIVE

Middle River

South River

B

South Fork Rivanna R.

Rivanna R.

Monte-
bello

P
I
E
D
M
O
N
T

231

33

Gordons-
ville

To
Staunton

Moormans River

River

P

River

SOUTHWESTERN MTS.

29

Ritanna R.

P
L
A
T
E
A
U

15

To Richmond

Jarman Gap

Locust Hill

To Palmyra

SCALE OF MILES

0 1 2 3 4 5   10

Waynesboro

250

64

Rockfish Gap

250

Charlottesville

BLUE RIDGE PKWY.

© HAMMOND INCORPORATED, Maplewood, N. J.

PHILADELPHIA AND VICINITY
(See map on p. 10)

DELAWARE

Arden .... A 4
Claymont ...... B 4
Rockland ...... A 4
Talleyville ..... A 4
Winterthur ..... A 4

NEW JERSEY

Ashland .... D 3
Audubon ...... D 3
Barrington ..... D 3
Bellmawr ...... D 3
Berlin .... E 4
Beverly .... E 2
Blackwood ..... D 4
Blackwood Ter. .. D 4
Bridgeboro ..... E 2
Bridgeport ..... B 4
Burlington ..... E 2
Camden .... D 3
Cherry Hill ..... D 3
Cinnaminson ... E 2
Clarksboro ..... C 4
Collingswood ... D 3
Delanco .... E 2
Delran .... E 2
Deptford ...... D 3
Edgewater Park . E 2
Fieldsboro ..... F 1
Florence ...... F 1
Gibbsboro ..... E 3
Gibbstown ..... C 3
Glendale ...... E 3
Glendora ...... D 3
Gloucester City . D 3
Haddonfield ... D 3
Haddon Heights . D 3
Hainesport .... E 2
Hartford ...... E 2
Hi-Nella ...... D 3
Kirkwood ...... D 3
Laurel Springs .. D 3
Lawnside ...... D 3
Lindenwold .... E 3
Magnolia ...... D 3
Mansfield ..... F 2
Mantua .... C 4
Maple Shade ... D 3
Marlton .... E 3
Medford ...... F 3
Merchantville .. D 3
Mickleton ..... C 4
Moorestown ... E 2
Mount Ephraim . D 3
Mount Holly ... F 2
Mount Laurel .. E 3
Mount Royal ... C 4
National Park .. C 3
North Woodbury D 3
Oaklyn .... D 3
Palmyra ...... D 2
Paulsboro ..... C 3
Pennsauken ... D 2
Rancocas ..... E 2
Ramblewood ... E 3
Red Lion ...... F 3
Riverside ..... E 2
Riverton ...... D 2

Roebling ...... F 1
Runnymeade ... D 3
Somerdale ..... D 3
Stratford ...... D 3
Thorofare ..... C 3
Turnersville ... D 4
Vincentown .... F 3
West Berlin .... E 4
Westville ...... D 3
Willingboro .... E 2
Woodbury ..... C 3
Woodbury Heights D 4
Woodlynne .... D 3

PENNSYLVANIA

Abington ...... D 1
Aldan .... C 3
Ambler .... C 1
Arcola .... B 1
Ardsley .... D 1
Ardmore ...... C 2
Aston Mills .... B 3
Audubon ...... B 1
Bala-Cynwyd ... C 2
Barren Hill .... C 2
Berwyn .... B 2
Blue Bell ...... C 1
Boothwyn ..... B 3
Bridgeport .... B 1
Bristol .... E 2
Broad Axe ..... C 1
Brookhaven ... B 3
Broomall ...... B 2
Bryn Athyn .... D 1
Bryn Mawr .... B 2
Cedar Heights .. C 2
Center Square .. C 1
Chadds Ford ... A 3
Cheltenham ... D 2
Chester .... B 3
Chester Heights . A 3
Chester Springs . A 2
Chestnut Hill .. C 2
Cheyney ...... A 3
Clifton Heights . C 3
Collegeville ... B 1
Collingdale .... C 3
Concordville ... A 3
Conshohocken . C 2
Cornwells Heights E 2
Croydon ...... E 2
Crum Lynne ... B 3
Darby .... C 3
Devault ...... A 2
Devon .... B 2
Dresher ...... B 3
Drexel Hill .... C 3
Eagleville ..... B 1
Eddystone .... B 3
Edgemont ..... A 3
Elkins Park .... D 2
Elwyn .... B 3
Essington ..... C 3
Exton .... A 2
Fairless Hills .. E 1
Fairview Village . B 1
Fallsington .... F 1
Feasterville ... D 1
Flourtown ..... C 2
Folcroft ...... C 3
Folsom .... B 3
Fort Washington . C 1

Frazer .... A 2
Germantown ... C 2
Gladwyne ..... C 2
Glenolden ..... C 3
Glen Riddle ... B 3
Glenside ...... C 2
Gradyville .... B 3
Gwynedd Valley . C 1
Harmonville ... C 2
Hatboro ...... D 1
Haverford .... C 2
Havertown .... B 2
Hidden Valley .. B 2
Holland .... D 1
Holmes .... C 3
Hulmeville .... E 1
Huntingdon Valley .D 1
Immaculata ... A 2
Jeffersonville .. B 1
Jenkintown ... D 2
Kensington ... D 2
Kimberton .... A 1
King of Prussia . B 2
Kulpsville .... B 1
Lafayette Hill .. C 2
Langhorne .... E 1
Langhorne Manor . E 1
Lansdowne .... C 3
Lenni .... B 3
Lester .... C 3
Levittown ..... E 1
Lima .... B 3
Linwood ...... B 3
Malvern ...... A 2
Manoa .... C 2
Maple Glen ... C 1
Marcus Hook .. B 4
Meadowbrook . D 1
Media .... B 3
Melrose Park .. D 2
Mendenhall ... A 3
Merion Station .. C 2
Milmont Park .. B 3
Miquon ...... C 2
Mont Clare ... A 1
Morton .... B 3
Moylan .... B 3
Narberth ..... C 2
Newportville .. E 1
Newtown Square .B 2
Norristown ... B 1
Norwood ..... C 3
Oaks .... B 1
Oreland ...... C 1
Paoli .... B 2
Parkside ...... B 3
Penllyn ...... C 1
Penndel ...... E 1
Penn Square .. B 1
Penn Wynne .. C 2
Philadelphia ... C 2
Phoenixville ... A 1
Pilgrim Gardens . B 3
Plymouth Meeting C 1
Port Kennedy .. B 1
Primos .... C 3
Prospect Park .. C 3
Radnor .... B 2
Ridley Park ... C 3
Rockledge .... D 2
Rosemont ..... C 2
Roslyn .... D 1

Royersford .... A 1
Rutledge ...... B 3
Rydal .... D 1
St. Davids ..... B 2
Secane .... C 3
Sharon Hill ... C 3
Southampton .. D 1
Springfield .... B 3
Swarthmore ... B 3
Thornton ..... A 3
Trainer .... B 3
Trevose ...... E 1
Trooper ...... B 1
Tullytown ..... F 1
Upland .... B 3
Upper Darby ... C 3
Valley Forge ... B 2
Villanova ..... B 2
Wallingford ... B 3
Wayne .... B 2
West Bristol ... E 2
West Chester .. A 3
W. Conshohocken B 2
Westtown ..... A 3
Whitemarsh ... C 1
Willow Grove .. D 1
Woodlyn ..... B 3
Wyncote ...... C 2
Wynnewood ... C 2
Yeadon .... C 3
Yerkes .... B 1

WASHINGTON AND VICINITY
(See map on p. 12)

DIST. OF COLUMBIA

Washington .... D 2

MARYLAND

Alta Vista ..... C 2
Ardmore ...... E 2
Bannockburn ... C 2
Bellefonte .... E 4
Bellmead ..... E 2
Berkshire ..... E 3
Berwyn Heights . E 2
Bethesda ..... C 2
Birdlawn ...... E 4
Bladensburg ... E 2
Boulevard Heights .E 3
Bowie .... F 2
Brentwood .... D 2
Brock Hall .... F 3
Brown .... F 3
Cabin John .... C 2
Campbell Corner C 2
Camp Springs .. E 3
Capitol Heights . E 3
Carmody Hills .. E 3
Cedar Heights .. E 3
Chapel Hill ... D 4
Chapel Oaks ... E 3
Cheverly ..... E 2
Chevy Chase .. D 2
Chillum ...... D 2
Clinton .... E 4
Clinton Grove .. E 4
College Park ... E 2
Collington ..... F 2
Colmar Manor . E 2
Columbia Park . E 2

Coral Hills .... E 3
Cottage City ... D 2
Croom Station . F 4
Defense Heights . E 2
District Heights . E 3
Duckettsville .. F 2
East Pines .... E 2
Edmonston ... D 2
Fairmount Heights E 3
Forest Glen ... D 2
Forest Heights . D 3
Forestville .... E 3
Ft. Washington Pk. D 4
Four Corners .. D 2
Friendly ...... D 4
Friendship Heights C 2
Garrett Park ... C 2
Glassmanor ... D 3
Glenarden .... E 2
Glen Echo .... C 2
Glenn Dale ... F 2
Greenbelt ..... E 2
Hall .... F 3
High Bridge ... F 2
Hillandale .... D 2
Hillcrest Heights . D 3
Hillside ...... E 3
Holmehurst ... F 2
Huntsville .... E 3
Hyattsville .... D 2
Hynesboro ... E 2
Jenkins Corner . E 4
Jericho Park ... E 2
Kensington ... D 2
Kent Village ... E 2
Kenwood ..... C 2
Kettering ..... F 3
Knollwood .... D 2
Kolbes Corner . F 3
Landover ..... E 2
Landover Hills . E 2
Langley Park .. D 2
Lanham ...... E 2
Largo .... E 3
Leeland ...... F 3
Lewisdale .... D 2
Little Washington E 3
Marlow Heights . E 3
Marlton .... F 4
Maryvale ..... F 4
Meadows ..... E 3
Mellwood .... F 3
Millwood ..... E 3
Mitchellville ... F 2
Morningside .. E 3
Mount Calvert . F 4
Mount Rainier . D 2
New Carrollton . E 2
North Brentwood E 2
N. Chevy Chase . D 2
Oak Grove .... F 3
Oakland ...... E 3
Oak View .... D 2
Oxon Hill .... D 3
Pagetts Corner . E 4
Palmer Corner . E 4
Palmer Park ... E 2
Parkland ..... E 2
Phelps Corner . D 3
Pine Knolls ... C 2
Piscataway ... D 4
Potomac ..... C 2

Princeton ..... E 3
Riggs Mill .... D 2
Ritchie .... E 3
River Bend .... D 4
Riverdale ..... E 2
Riverdale Heights E 2
Riverview .... D 4
Rock Springs .. C 2
Rogers Heights . E 2
Seabrook ..... E 2
Seat Pleasant .. E 3
Sherwood Forest . E 4
Silesia .... D 4
Silver Spring .. D 2
Somerset ..... C 2
South Lawn ... E 3
Springfield .... F 2
Suitland ...... E 3
Sunnyside .... E 2
Takoma Park .. D 2
Temple Hills .. E 3
Thrift .... E 4
Tippett .... E 4
Tuxedo .... E 2
University Park . E 2
Upper Marlboro . F 3
Westgate ..... C 2
Westphalia ... F 3
White Hall .... D 4
Wildercroft ... E 2
Willow Grove .. F 2
Windbrook ... E 4
Woodhaven ... C 2
Woodmoor ... F 2
Woodmore ... D 2
Woodside .... D 2
Woodyard .... E 4

VIRGINIA

Accotink ..... C 4
Alexandria .... C 3
Alpine .... C 3
Annandale .... C 3
Arcturus ..... D 4
Arlington ..... C 3
Baileys Crossroads C 3
Beacon Hill ... C 3
Bel Air .... C 3
Belleair ...... B 4
Belleview ..... B 2
Bell Haven .... D 4
Belvedere .... C 3
Bren Mar ..... C 3
Brook Hill .... C 3
Buckhall ..... A 4
Burke .... B 4
Centreville ... A 3
Chantilly ..... A 3
Chesterbrook . C 2
Clearfield ..... C 3
Clifton .... A 4
Cobbs Corner . A 3
Collingwood .. D 4
Colvin Run .... B 2
Deanwood .... B 2
Dixie Hill .... A 3
Dranesville ... A 2
Dunn Loring .. B 3
Edgelea ...... C 3
Fairfax .... B 3
Fairfax Station . B 3
Fairhaven .... C 4

Fairlee .... B 3
Fairview ...... B 2
Falls Church .. C 3
Floris .... A 2
Four Corners .. B 2
Franconia .... C 4
Glen Alden ... A 3
Glendale ..... B 2
Great Falls ... B 2
Groveton ..... C 4
Guilford ...... C 4
Hattantown ... A 2
Hayfield ...... C 4
Herndon ..... A 2
Hillbrook ..... C 3
Hillwood ..... C 4
Hollindale .... C 4
Homewood ... B 4
Huntington ... D 4
Ilda .... B 3
Kenmore ..... B 2
Lake Barcroft .. C 3
Langley ...... C 2
Laurel Grove .. C 4
Lincolnia Heights C 3
Lincoln Park .. A 3
Loisdale ...... C 4
Lorton .... B 4
Manassas .... A 4
Manassas Park . A 4
Masonville ... C 3
McLean ...... C 2
Merrifield .... B 3
Mount Pleasant . C 3
Mount Vernon . D 4
Newington ... C 4
Nokes .... A 2
N. Mount Vernon . D 4
North Springfield . C 3
Oakton ...... B 3
Oakwood ..... C 4
Occoquan .... B 4
Parklawn ..... C 3
Peacock ...... B 2
Pender .... A 3
Penderbrook .. A 3
Pinecrest ..... C 3
Pohick .... C 4
Ravensworth .. B 3
Ravenwood ... C 3
Reston .... A 2
Seven Corners . C 3
Shady Oak .... B 3
Shrevewood .. B 3
Sleepy Hollow . C 3
Springfield .... C 4
Springvale .... B 2
Springvale .... C 4
Sterling ...... A 2
Sunset Hills .. A 2
Sydenstricker . B 4
Tamerack .... B 2
Twin Mill ..... B 3
Tysons Corner . B 2
Vale .... A 3
Vienna .... B 3
Wellington ... D 4
Westford ..... C 3
West Grove ... D 4
W. Springfield . B 4
Weyanoke .... C 3
Woodhaven ... B 2